CONTENTS

DISCOVERING AUVERGNE RH

Aigueperse 106
Ambert 109
Annonay 117
Gorges de l'Ardèce 122
Ardes-sur-Couze 130
Arlempdes 133
Aubenas 134
Aurillac 142
Auzon 152
Lac d'Aydat 154
Château de la
    Bastie-d'Urfé 156
Beaujolais. 157
Besse-en-Chandesse . . 171
Billom 178
Bort-les-Orgues 183
Bourbon-
    l'Archambault 187
La Bourboule 191
Brioude 196
Monts du Cantal 205
Monts du Cézallier 213
La Chaise-Dieu 216
Le Chambon-
    sur-Lignon. 221
Charroux. 223
Châtelguyon 226
Châtillon-sur-
    Chalaronne 228
Chaudes-Aigues. 230
Chazelles-sur-Lyon 232
Clermont-Ferrand 233
Condat 256
La Côte-St-André 259
Courpière 261
Crémieu 263
Crest. 268
La Dombes. 271
Monts Dôme 275
Château D'Effiat 284
Vallée de l'Eyrieux 286
Feurs 291
Monts du Forez 292
Gannat 298
Plateau de Gergovie . . . 299
Hauterives 301

Hérisson 303
Lac d'Issarlès 304
Issoire 309
Lalouvesc 317
Lamastre 318
Lapalisse 320
Lavaudieu 324
Lezoux 326
Le Lioran. 327
Gorges de la Loire 329
Lyon 336
Monts du Lyonnais . . . 386
Massiac 390
Mauriac. 392
Le Monastier-
    sur-Gazeille. 397
Monistrol-sur-Loire. . . . 399
Montbrison 401
Le Mont-Dore 405
Le Mont-d'Or Lyonnais 409
Montélimar 411
Montluçon 416
Morestel 421
Moulins 423
Murat. 432
Château de Murol 434
Orcival. 437
Aven d'Orgnac 438
Lac de Paladru 441
Pérouges 444
Le Pilat 449
Privas. 455
Le Puy-en-Velay 459
Riom 473
Riom-ès-Montagnes . . 479
Roanne 483
Romans-sur-Isère 492
Royat 496
Ruynes-en-Margeride . 500
Saint-Agrève 503
St-Antoine-l'Abbaye . . . 504
Saint-Cernin 507
St-Étienne 509
St-Flour 520
St-Germain-Laval 525

St-Nectaire. 527
St-Pourçain-sur-Sioule. 531
St-Saturnin. 534
Ste-Croix-en-Jarez. 536
Salers. 538
Massif du Sancy 541
Saugues 548
Serrières 551
Gorges de la Sioule 553
Souvigny 557
Massif du Tanargue. . . . 560
Tauves 562
Thiers. 563
Tournemire 573
Tournon-sur-Rhône . . . 574
Trévoux 577
Le Tricastin. 579
Forêt de Tronçais 582
Gorges de la Truyère. . . 587
Valence 591
Vals-les-Bains 599
Les Vans 602
Vichy 607
Vic-le-Comte. 617
Vic-sur-Cère 621
Vienne. 626
Villars-les-Dombes 640
Villefranche-sur-Saône 641
Viviers 644
Parc naturel régional des .
    Volcans d'Auvergne 649
Volvic. 650
Parc Européen du
    Volcanisme Vulcania. 655
Yssingeaux. 656

Index. 658
Maps and Plans . 674
Legend. 676

HOW TO USE THIS GUIDE

Orientation

To help you grasp the "lay of the land" quickly and easily, so you'll feel confident and comfortable finding your way around the region, we offer the following tools in this guide:

- Detailed table of contents for an overview of what you'll find in the guide, and how it is organized.
- Map of the region at the front to the guide, with the Principal Sights highlighted for easy reference.
- Detailed maps for major cities and villages, including driving tour maps and larger-scale maps for walking tours.
- Map of 11 Regional Driving Tours, each one numbered and color coded.

Practicalities

At the front of the guide, you'll see a section called "Planning Your Trip" that contains information about planning your trip, the best time to go, different ways of getting to the region and getting around, basic facts and tips for making the most of your visit. You'll find driving and themed tours, and suggestions for outdoor fun. There's also a calendar of popular annual events for the area. Information on shopping, sightseeing, kids' activities and sports and recreational opportunities is also included.

LODGINGS

We've made a selection of hotels and arranged them within the cities, categorized by price to fit all budgets (see the Legend at the back of the guide for an explanation of the price categories). For the most part, we selected accommodations based on their unique regional quality, their regional feel, as it were. So, unless the individual hotel embodies local ambience, it's rare that we include chain properties, which typically have their own imprint. If you want a more comprehensive selection of Auvergne Rhône Valley accommodations, see the red-cover *Michelin Guide France*.

RESTAURANTS

We thought you'd like to know the popular eating spots in the area. So we selected restaurants that capture the Auvergne and even Lyonnais experience—those that have a unique regional flavor and local atmosphere. We're not rating the quality of the food per se. As we did with the hotels, we selected restaurants for many towns and villages, categorized by price to appeal to all wallets. If you want a more comprehensive selection of dining recommendations in the region, see the red-cover *Michelin Guide France*.

AUVERGNE
RHÔNE VALLEY

J. Damase/MICHELIN

Executive Editorial Director   David Brabis
Chief Editor   Cynthia Clayton Ochterbeck

THE GREEN GUIDE AUVERGNE RHÔNE VALLEY

Editor	Gwen Cannon
Principal Writer	Terry Marsh
Production Coordinator	Allison M. Simpson
Cartography	Alain Baldet, Michelle Cana, Peter Wrenn
Photo Editor	Cecile Koroleff, Lydia Strong
Proofreader	Gaven R. Watkins
Layout & Design	Nicole Jordan
Cover Design	Laurent Muller, Ute Weber

Contact Us:

The Green Guide
Michelin Maps and Guides
One Parkway South
Greenville, SC 29615
USA
☎ 1-800-423-0485
www.michelintravel.com
michelin.guides@us.michelin.com

Michelin Maps and Guides
Hannay House
39 Clarendon Road
Watford, Herts WD17 1JA
UK
☎ (01923) 205 240
travelpubsales@uk.michelin.com

Special Sales:

For information regarding bulk sales,
customized editions and premium sales,
please contact our Customer Service
Departments:
USA   1-800-423-0485
UK   (01923) 205 240
Canada 1-800-361-8236

Note to the reader

One Team …
A Commitment to Quality

There's just one reason our team is dedicated to producing quality travel publications—you, our reader. We want you to get the maximum benefit from your trip—and from your money. In today's multiple-choice world of travel, the options are many, perhaps overwhelming.

In our guidebooks, we try to minimize the guesswork involved with travel. We scout out the attractions, prioritize them with star ratings, and describe what you'll discover when you visit them.

To help you orient yourself, we provide colorful and detailed, but easy-to-follow maps. Floor plans of some of the cathedrals and museums help you plan your tour.

Throughout the guides, we offer practical information, touring tips and suggestions for finding the best views, good places for a break and the most interesting shops.

Lodging and dining are always a big part of travel, so we compile a selection of hotels and restaurants that we think convey the feel of the destination, and organize them by geographic area and price. We also highlight shopping, recreational and entertainment venues, especially the popular spots.

If you're short on time, driving tours are included so you can hit the highlights and quickly absorb the best of the region.

For those who love to experience a destination on foot, we add walking tours, often with a map. And we list other companies who offer boat, bus or guided walking tours of the area, some with culinary, historical or other themes.

In short, we test and retest, check and recheck to make sure that our guidebooks are truly just that: a personalized guide to help you make the most of your visit. After all, we want you to enjoy traveling as much as we do.

The Michelin Green Guide Team

PLANNING YOUR TRIP

WHEN AND WHERE TO GO   16

Driving Tours. 16
Themed Tours. 19
Eco-Tourism. 23
When to Go 24

KNOW BEFORE YOU GO   26

Useful Web Sites 26
Tourist Offices. 26
International Visitors 28
Accessibility. 29

GETTING THERE   30

By Air 30
By Sea 30
By Rail 30
By Coach/ Bus. 31
Getting Around 32
Driving in France 32

WHERE TO STAY AND EAT   34

Where to Stay 34
Where to Eat 35

WHAT TO DO AND SEE   39

Outdoor Fun 39
Activities for Children. 44
Spas 44
Calendar of Events. 44
Shopping 46
Discounts 47

USEFUL WORDS & PHRASES 48

BASIC INFORMATION   50

INTRODUCTION TO AUVERGNE RHÔNE VALLEY

NATURE   58

Rhône Valley 58
Auvergne 62
Flora and Fauna 67

HISTORY   70

Time Line 70
Famous Local Figures. 76

ART AND CULTURE   80

Architecture and Art. 80
Traditional Rural Housing 94
Traditions in the Auvergne 96
Literary Life 97

THE REGION TODAY   99

Economy. 99
Food and Drink 101

SYMBOLS

- 🐾 **Tips to help improve your experience**
- 👤 **Details to consider**
- 💶 **Entry Fees**
- 🚶 **Walking tours**
- 🔒 **Closed to the public**
- 🕐 **Hours of operation**
- 🕐 **Periods of closure**

Attractions

Principal Sights are arranged alphabetically. Within each Principal Sight, attractions for each town, village, or geographical area are divided into local Sights or Walking Tours, nearby Excursions to sights outside the town, or detailed Driving Tours—suggested itineraries for seeing several attractions around a major town. Contact information, admission charges and hours of operation are given for the majority of attractions. Unless otherwise noted, admission prices shown are for a single adult only. Discounts for seniors, students, teachers, etc. may be available; be sure to ask. If no admission charge is shown, entrance to the attraction is free.

If you're pressed for time, we recommend you visit the three- and two-star sights first: the stars are your guide.

STAR RATINGS

Michelin has used stars as a rating tool for more than 100 years:

★★★	Highly recommended
★★	Recommended
★	Interesting

SYMBOLS IN THE TEXT

Besides the stars, other symbols in the text indicate tourist information 🛈; wheelchair access ♿; on-site eating facilities ✗; camping facilities △; on-site parking 🅿; sights of interest to children Kids; and beaches ⚓.

See the box appearing on the Contents page for other symbols used in the text.

See the Maps explanation below for symbols appearing on the maps.

Throughout the guide you will find peach-coloured text boxes or sidebars containing anecdotal or background information. Green-coloured boxes contain information to help you save time or money.

Maps

All maps in this guide are oriented north, unless otherwise indicated by a directional arrow. See the map Legend at the back of the guide for an explanation of other map symbols. A complete list of the maps found in the guide appears at the back of this book.

Addresses, phone numbers, opening hours and prices published in this guide are accurate at press time. We welcome corrections and suggestions that may assist us in preparing the next edition. Please send your comments to:

Michelin Maps and Guides
Hannay House
39 Clarendon Road
Watford, Herts WD17 1JA
UK
travelpubsales@uk.michelin.com
www.michelin.co.uk

Michelin Maps and Guides
Editorial Department
P.O. Box 19001
Greenville, SC 29602-9001
USA
michelin.guides@us.michelin.com
www.michelintravel.com

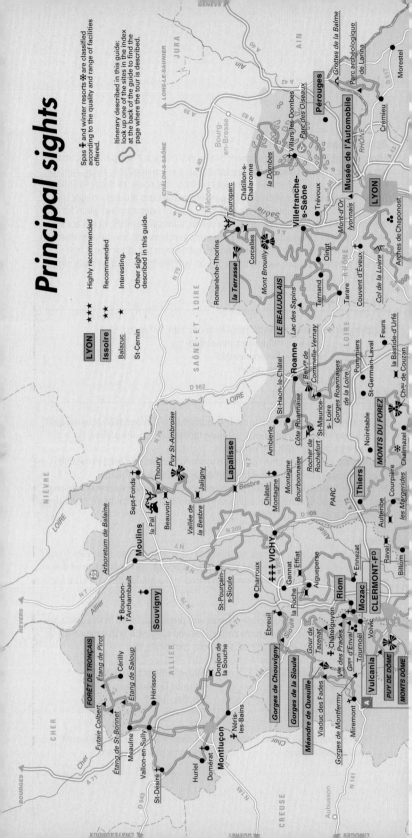

Driving tours

For descriptions of these tours,
turn to the Planning Your Trip section following.

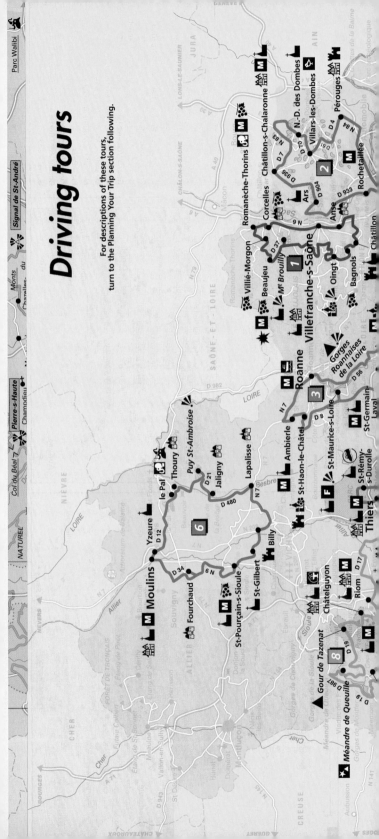

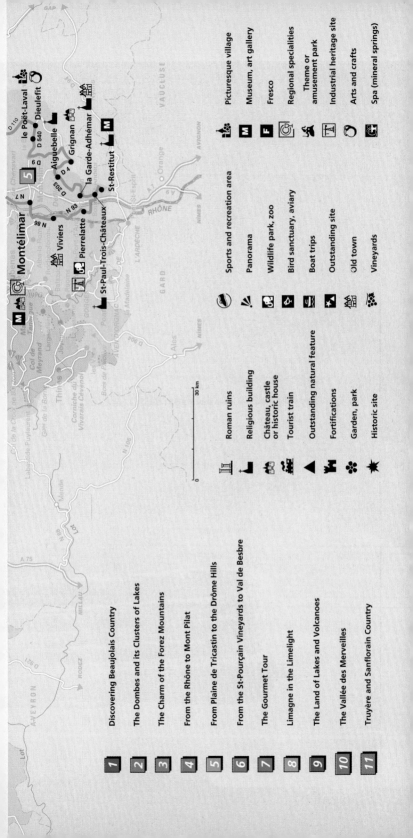

Chaude-Aigues mineral spring
J. Damase/MICHELIN

WHEN AND WHERE TO GO

Driving Tours

♿ *See the Driving Tours map on pp 11–13.*

1 BEAUJOLAIS COUNTRY

Round tour of 129km/80mi leaving from Villefranche-sur-Saône

This pretty tour of the sun-drenched slopes of Beaujolais naturally starts from Villefranche-sur-Saône, seen by many as the capital of the famous Beaujolais *appellation*. The former walled city of Belleville is now an important winemaking centre but it has kept many vestiges of its 12C church, notably an interesting series of capitals. Corcelles Château boasts a fine 17C vat whose aromas will make your head spin! The "Hameau du Vin" and its "station" set up in Romanèche-Thorins form a small museum that pays tribute to the noble traditions that have governed the art of wine making throughout the centuries, and the adjoining safari park will delight young children. In Beaujolais each vineyard has developed its own peculiarities: the Fleurie grapes yield a young, lively wine, whereas the Villié-Morgon bottles are usually for laying down. A great many *crus* can be found in Beaujeu, a town wholly devoted to the commerce of wine. After pausing to admire the stunning panorama stretching from Mont Brouilly to the Saône plain, pay a visit to the Salles-Arbuissonnas-en-Beaujolais Priory, dating back to the 10C. The two châteaux of Montmelas-St-Sorlin and Jarnioux are your next stop, leading to the quaint village of Oingt, perched on a hillside and crowned by a tower. Driving through the Bagnols vineyards, you reach Châtillon and its 12C stronghold. In St-Jean-des-Vignes, the Museum of Geology explains the origins of the topography which characterises the Beaujolais region and which has produced its unique *terroir*. The tour ends with the village of Chazay-d'Azergues, from where you can return to Villefranche via Anse.

2 THE DOMBES AND ITS CLUSTERS OF LAKES

Round tour of 155km/96.5mi leaving from Lyon

Leaving from Lyon, a city that has successfully taken up the challenges of modern life while preserving its historical legacy, this tour is a charming nature trail dotted with ancient monuments. Stop to admire the medieval towers of Rochetaillée Château and then press on to Ars, famous for its bishop who was canonised in 1925 and who is the patron saint of all parish bishops. After visiting Ambérieux-en-Dombes, another town with religious associations awaits you: Châtillon-sur-Chalaronne, where St Vincent de Paul founded the first brotherhood of charity and where you can visit the Apothicairerie. The tour then takes you to the Romanesque church in St-Paul-de-Varax and the 19C Notre-Dame-des-Domes Abbey, which was instrumental in draining the surrounding plains. The bird sanctuary in Villars-les-Dombes is the perfect spot for a family outing, and the brick castle in Le Montellier is an impressive sight indeed. The hilltop village of Pérouges, circled by ancient ramparts and crossed by winding

The village of Oingt

streets, is often used as a backdrop for historical films. Finally, after a halt in Montluel, you can return to the city of Lyon and its many attractions.

③ THE CHARM OF THE FOREZ MOUNTAINS

Round tour of 200km/124mi leaving from Roanne
The region generally referred to as Forez comprises a range of mountains, a series of plains, a natural park and a web of meandering roads. This tour begins in Roanne, a Roman city today known for its textile and food-processing industries. After a short drive through vineyards producing a lively rosé wine, you will reach pretty Ambierle with its old Cluniac priory, Flamboyant Gothic church and museum devoted to traditional costumes and lore. The fortified village of St-Haon-le-Châtel features some interesting Renaissance houses and the nearby Tache Dam, which dominates the local vineyards, is the starting-point for charming country walks across the Monts de la Madeleine. Driving down the Gorges Roannaises de la Loire, you come to St-Maurice-sur-Loire, where the church apse boasts remarkable 13C frescoes and the keep commands a fine panorama of the gorges. Also steeped in history are the two towns of St-Germain-Laval and Pommiers and their intricate network of cobbled alleys. After visiting the Château de la Vigne et du Vin in Boën, drop by the fortress in Sail-sous-Couzan and feast your eyes on the Forez plain. Château de la Bastie-d'Urfé was once the residence of the famed writer Honoré d'Urfé, whose romantic novel *L'Astrée* set a new literary trend in early-17C France. A more austere atmosphere permeates the 14C church in Champdieu and the old convent of Montbrison, dominated by its 18C dome and circled by stone ramparts. Although the living quarters within the castle was destroyed by a fire in the 18C, Montrond-les-Bains is a pleasant fortified city whose spa is ideal for treating diabetes and other disorders. After a breath of fresh air, strolling through

the bird sanctuary at the Écopôle du Forez, resume your history lesson by exploring the ancient city of Feurs and visiting its Gallo-Roman Museum of Archaeology. The delightful medieval hamlet of Villerest has a curious museum retracing the history of fire and its domestic uses through the ages. The Loire gorges cutting across the rocky plains leads you back to Roanne, where the tour can be nicely concluded with a boat ride.

④ FROM THE RHÔNE TO MONT PILAT

Round tour of 170km/105.6mi leaving from St-Étienne
The tour begins in St-Étienne, a city with deep-rooted traditions that has kept abreast of the times, and houses an admirable Museum of Modern Art. Your voyage then takes you to St-Chamond, the site of a factory producing armoured vehicles, Rive-de-Gier and St-Genis-Laval. You approach Lyon via the antique city of Oullins. As for the modern metropolis, frequently dubbed France's second capital, it offers a host of museums, cafés, restaurants and historical monuments. Further on, you reach Vienne, yet another Roman city, whose Jazz Festival enjoys a prestigious reputation. At your next stop, Condrieu, take a seat on the sunny quays and sip a glass of *viognier*, the local white wine, as you watch boats gliding into port. After visiting Pélussin and its museum, do not miss the stunning vista afforded by the Crêt de l'Œillon, extending over the Rhône Valley and Crêt de la Perdrix. For a sweeping panorama, try the viewing table on the Pics du Mézenc. If weather conditions are favourable, why not tackle one of the skiing slopes at Le Bessat or venture down the formidable gully appropriately named "Chasm of Hell"? Round off the tour with a pleasant drive back to St-Étienne and a visit to the famous confectioner Weiss, whose chocolates will literally melt in your mouth...

5 FROM PLAINE DE TRICASTIN TO THE DRÔME HILLS

Round tour of 210km/130mi leaving from Montélimar

The starting-point of this tour is Montélimar, world famous for its delicious nougat topped with chopped hazelnuts and almonds! But the city is also a popular tourist destination, and has many attractions, including the Miniature Museum. The former episcopal town of Viviers leads to the Plaine du Tricastin, where Pierrelatte, encircled by three mountainous ranges, is home to a nuclear power plant, not to mention a crocodile farm... In St-Paul-Trois-Châteaux, make a point of visiting the cathedral and the Maison de la Truffe. For a change of scene, after admiring the church in St-Restitut, take time to check out the wine cellars at Le Cellier des Dauphins. History lovers will appreciate the White Penitents' Chapel in La Garde-Adhémar and the abbey church at Notre-Dame-d'Aiguebelle. You drive through a series of charming villages, including La Bégude-de-Mézenc, Le Poët-Laval, a medieval gem housing a former commandery, and Dieulefit, a bustling city dedicated to local arts and crafts. After leaving Soyons, you head for the Saoû Forest nestling at the foot of a sheer cliff face and offering pleasantly shaded walks. Or you may prefer to seek refuge in the keep at Crest. Finally, your drive back to nougat country introduces you to the pretty towns of Marsanne and Mirmande.

6 FROM THE ST-POURÇAIN VINEYARDS TO VAL DE BESBRE

Round tour of 160km/99.5mi leaving from St-Pourçain

The vineyards around St-Pourçain yield a lively, fragrant white wine stored in local cellars which it is your duty to taste...in moderation! The more academic visitors will enjoy studying the numerous medieval frescoes that enliven the tiny churches dotted around St-Pourçain; the murals at Le Saulcet deserve special mention.

After your exertions at the sports and leisure park in Le Pal, follow the course of the River Besbre, which guides you to Thoury and its pink-sandstone castle, to Jaligny and its Renaissance château, and finally to Lapalisse, a popular place among anglers because of its silvery waters teeming with trout and carp.

7 THE GOURMET TOUR

Round tour of 250km/155mi leaving from Ambert

This tour pays tribute to Fourme d'Ambert, a deliciously smooth blue cheese made with cow's milk that is typical of the region. Made around Ambert and on the Forez heights, this delicacy is presented in the shape of a large circular slab speckled with blue and is lesser known but more subtle than the traditional Roquefort cheese. The nearby town of Thiers is the country's leading knife manufacturer and you will be ideally equipped to carve a generous slice of Fourme d'Ambert and savour it along the banks of the River Dore.

8 LIMAGNE IN THE LIMELIGHT

Round tour of 250km/155mi leaving from Clermont-Ferrand

After leaving Clermont-Ferrand, the bustling yet discreet capital of the Auvergne, you will encounter the curious lava flows of Volvic stone where the famous mineral water has its source. Your next stop is Billom, where a pleasant climate combines with a fine morning mist and a soft light reminiscent of the great Impressionist works. This stunning landscape is enhanced by the golden sunflower fields contrasting with the brown earthy plains, overshadowed by the volcanic range looming above the horizon.

9 THE LAND OF LAKES AND VOLCANOES

Round tour of 415km/258mi leaving from Le Mont-Dore

Whatever your reasons for visiting the Auvergne, you can but succumb to the charm of Puy de Sancy, the highest peak towering above central France. The Dore mountain range and Pays des Couzes form a natural setting of outstanding beauty, enclosing a cluster of deep blue lakes with shimmering waters (Guéry, Servière, Aydat, Godivelle, Chambon). The surrounding villages too are worthy of note: Montpeyroux and its colony of artists and craftsmen; St-Nectaire, where the local cow's milk cheese is matured on a bed of rye; Besse and its Alpine skiing resort; lastly Orcival, graced with a fine Romanesque basilica.

1 0 THE VALLÉE DES MERVEILLES

Round tour of 335km/208mi leaving from Brioude
Before setting out on this tour, pay a visit to the Basilique St-Julien in Brioude and admire the intricate carvings adorning the Romanesque east end. Following the peaceful, lazy meanderings of the Sénouire, you discover the abbeys of Lavaudieu and La Chaise-Dieu, where the chancel houses early splendid 16C tapestries from Brussels and Arras. The Allier, on the other hand, is an impetuous river whose waters swell between Monistrol and Lavoûte-Chilhac. While the more adventurous tourists engage in

a spot of canoeing or rafting, ramblers and cyclists can pause to admire the Romanesque church of Chanteuges and the flower-decked streets in St-Arcons. The pretty painted churches dotted around the Haut-Allier region have earned it the name of "Vallée des Merveilles" (Valley of Wonders). As you continue on the tour, you come upon the Puy-en-Velay, one of the most extraordinary and unforgettable sites in France, sitting like a crown on the landscape it dominates.

1 1 TRUYÈRE AND SANFLORAIN COUNTRY

Round tour of 270km/168mi leaving from St-Flour
St-Flour, the starting-point of the tour, is perched on a basaltic plateau that faces south. You will be charmed by the landscapes around Les Margerides and by the chaotic course of the Truyère, which has carved sharp chasms between the Cantal and Aveyron. After reaching Pierrefort and tucking into a tasty *aligot* consisting of mashed potatoes seasoned with garlic and Cantal cheese, you can pay a visit to the spa resort of Chaudes-Aigues. From the fine medieval castle of Pesteils, perched on its rocky outcrop, drive up to Plomb du Cantal, the highest summit of the range, where you will be greeted by a calm, soothing atmosphere and a sweeping expanse of lush countryside.

Themed Tours

HISTORY

Routes historiques are signposted local itineraries following an architectural and historical theme, accompanied by an explanatory booklet, available from local tourist offices.
The **Route historique des châteaux d'Auvergne** takes in a selection of the best castles in the region: imposing ruined fortresses as well as elegant manor houses; some of these house exhibitions, organise concerts and sports events; others offer bed-and-

Lavaudieu

S. Sauvignier/MICHELIN

breakfast accommodation or are open late in the evening to enable visitors to appreciate their fascinating atmosphere. There are six itineraries: Bourbonnais, Limagnes, Volcans, Livradois-Forez, Montagnes cantaliennes and Haute-Loire. For more information, apply to Route historique des châteaux d'Auvergne, 17 rue des Minimes, 63000 Clermont-Ferrand, ☎ 04 73 19 12 16; www.route-chateaux-auvergne.org.

On the way to Santiago de Compostela – Pilgrims on their way to pay homage to the relics of St James the Great have been going through the Auvergne since the Middle Ages. Two itineraries converge on Le Puy-en-Velay: one from Lyon via St-Ferréol and Monistrol-sur-Loire, the other from Cluny via Pommiers and Montbrison. Beyond Le Puy, the via podiensis (GR 65) leads to Roncevaux and the Spanish border (28 days on foot).

ARCHITECTURAL HERITAGE

Viaducts – The introduction of railways in this mountainous region meant the construction of several impressive viaducts spanning the Truyère, the Sioule, the Allier and the Besbre rivers. Six of these are now listed among the region's historic monuments: Garabit and Barajol (Cantal), La Récoumène (Haute-Loire), Les Fades (Puy-de-Dôme), Neuvial and Rouzat (Allier). An itinerary linking them is available from tourist offices.

TRADITIONS AND NATURE

The **Route des jardins du Massif Central** links 27 botanical gardens dedicated to the preservation and promotion of the Massif Central's vegetation. Information from Le Jardin pour la Terre, 63220 Arlanc, ☎ 04 73 65 00 71; www.jardinsmassifcentral.com. The **Route des métiers en Livradois-Forez** winds its way across the Parc naturel regional du Livradois-Forez, linking authentic workshops where ancient crafts are perpetuated: Maison des Couteliers (cutlers' workshop)

in Thiers, Maison du Verre (glass workshop) in Puy-Guillaume, Moulin Richard-de-Bas (traditional mill) and Musée de la Fourme (cheese museum) in Ambert. Information from the Parc naturel regional du Livradois-Forez, Masion du Parc, 63880 Saint-Gervais-sous-Meymont, ☎ 04 73 95 57 57; www.parc-livradois-forez.org; Route des Metiers, ☎ 06 30 95 07 28; Email: route.des.metiers@wanadoo.fr; www.routedesmetiers.com.

The **Route des Villes d'Eaux** links the region's numerous spas. Information from La Route des Villes d'Eaux, 8 avenue Anatole-France, 63130 Royat, ☎ 04 73 34 72 80; www.villesdeaux.com.

The **Route des Fromages** is a gourmet tour of the main farming areas producing the best cheeses the Auvergne has to offer: Saint-Nectaire, Fourme d'Ambert, Bleu d'Auvergne, Cantal and Salers; a map is available from tourist offices or from the Association des fromages d'Auvergne, 52 avenue des Pupilles-de-la-Nation, 15000 Aurillac, ☎ 04 71 48 66 15; www.fromages-aoc-auvergne.com.

WINE-TASTING

Côtes d'Auvergne (Puy-de-Dôme) – Some 1 240ha/3 064 acres produce five different wines: Madargue, Châteaugay and Chanturgue north of Clermont-Ferrand, Corent and Boudes south of Clermont- Ferrand. The Fédération viticole du Puy-de-Dôme, place de la Mairie, 63340 Boudes, ☎ 04 73 96 49 00, proposes a Route des Vins divided into three itineraries exploring the Riomois, Clermontois and Lembronnais areas.

Saint-Pourçain (Allier) – This is one of the oldest wine-growing areas in France; destroyed by phylloxera at the end of the 19C, the vines have been gradually replanted and the vineyards now cover 600ha/1 483 acres. Information from the Office de Tourisme en Pays Saint-Pourcinois, 29 Rue Marcelin Berthelot, 03500 Saint-Pourcain, ☎ 04 70 45 32 73; www.tourismesaintpourcinois.com (map with itinerary and addresses of recommended cellars). The following centres provide information about wine-growing in the Rhône Valley:

Beaujolais – Le Pays Beaujolais (bookings of tours and accommodation, guides/interpreters), contact the Maison du tourisme, 96 rue de la Sous-Préfecture, 69400 Villefranche-sur-Saône, ☎ 04 74 07 27 50; www.beaujolais.com.

Côtes-du-Rhône – You can browse at www.vins-rhone.com or contact the Maison des vins de Tournon (16 avenue du Maréchal-Foch, 07300 Tournon, ☎ 04 75 07 91 50) and the Maison des vins d'Avignon (6 rue des Trois-Faucons, 84024 Avignon Cedex, ☎ 04 90 27 24 00) to obtain a list of cellars, wine-tour itineraries etc.

Another Point of View

Visitors who are not pressed for time may enjoy the countryside from an unusual or different perspective, allowing the best possible appreciation of local art and architecture, country life and wildlife.

TOURIST TRAINS

These offer the opportunity of discovering some spectacular scenery, removed from busy modern communications routes. Contacts include:

Chemin de Fer du Vivarais, Avenue de la gare - 07300 Tournon-sur-Rhone-Ardeche ☎ 04 78 28 83 34; www.ardeche-train.com. Three viaducts, two tunnels and spectacular views.

Chemin de Fer du Haut-Rhône, Office du tourisme, 1 rue du Rhone, 38390 Montalieu Vercieu, ☎ 04 74 88 48 56; www.paysdelapierre.org. 50min steam-train journey between Montalieu and the Pont de Sault-Brenaz.

Chemin de Fer Touristique du Velay, Office de Tourisme de Tence, ☎ 04 71 59 81 99. Several daily trips between Tence and Ste-Agrève along the Lignon Valley (mid-July to end of August).

Chemin de Fer Touristique d'Anse, Association Voie de 38cm, 8 avenue de la Libération, 69480 Anse, ☎ 04 74 60 26 01; runs from Easter to the last Sunday in October on Sundays, holidays (also Saturdays from June to September) in the afternoon.

Train touristique des Monts du Lyonnais, RN 89, La Giraudière, 69690 Brussieu, ☎ 04 74 70 90 64 (reservations); www.monts-du-lyonnais.org. Exhibition of railway stock in Ste-Foy-l'Argentière station (end of the line). In addition, a steam train (Hobby 69) runs on Sundays from June to September.

Train touristique de l'Ardèche méridionale, Viaduc 07, Gare de Vogué, 07200 Vogué, ☎ 04 75 37 03 52. Picturesque 14km/8.7mi journey from Vogüé to St-Jean-le-Centenier.

Train de la découverte du Livradois-Forez, Several possibilities along the Dore Valley between Courpière and La Chaise-Dieu via Ambert. AGRIVAP "train touristique", La Gare, 63600 Ambert, ☎ 04 73 82 43 88.

Train touristique des Gorges de l'Allier, Magnificent unspoilt landscapes unfold on this journey between Langeac and Langogne. The train runs through 53 tunnels and negotiates steep slopes and tricky bends. Office du tourisme des Gorges de l'Allier, Place Aristide Briand 43300 Langeac, ☎ 04 71 77 05 41.

Le Train touristique Garabit, Guided tour from Aurillac via Le Lioran, Murat and the Garabit viaduct where the train stops for a while. Office de Tourisme du Pays de Saint-Flour : 17 bis pl Armes 15100 Saint Flour, ☎ 04 71 60 22 50.

Autorail touristique Gentiane Express, A fine journey through the summer pastures of the famous Salers cattle, from Bort-les-Orgues to Lugarde via Riom-ès-Montagne and the Barajol viaduct. Daily in July and August, Sundays and holidays from mid-April to September (3 to 6hr there and back); information and bookings, Office du tourisme de Bort-les-Orgues ☎ 05 55 96 02 49, or Office du tourisme du Pays Gentiane (Riom-ès-Montagnes), ☎ 04 71 78 07 37.

FROM ABOVE

For a bird's-eye view of the region either as passenger or pilot, try one of the following.

Hot-air balloons
Contact local tourist offices, or:

France Montgolfière,
24, rue Nationale, 41400 Montrichard, ☎ 02 54 32 20 48; www.franceballoons.com.

Objectif Montgolfière,
14, rue de Bellevue, Le Mas, 63970 Aydat, ☎ 04 73 60 11 90; www.objectif-montgolfiere.com.

Quatre Vents,
Aéronaute Montrodeix 63870 Orcines. ☎ 04 73 62 29 30; flight

over the Chaîne des Puys or the Sancy mountain range.

Montgolfière club du Velay,
Pouzols, 43200 St-Jeures,
☎ 04 71 65 47 89.

Les Montgolfières d'Annonay,
BP 111, 07102 Annonay Cedex,
☎ 04 75 67 57 56; www.ima7.com.

Centre aérostatique de l'Ardèche,
RN 82, 07430 St Clair.
☎ 04 75 33 71 30.

L'Association des Montgolfières en Velay, 55 avenue des Champs-Élysées, Chadrac, 43770 le Puy-en-Velay, ☎ 04 71 02 73 18.

Light aircraft and gliders

Aéro-club d'Auvergne,
Avenue Youri Gagarine, 63000 Clermont-Ferrand.
Email: aeroclub.auvergne@tele2.fr,
☎ 04 73 92 00 56.

Aéro-club Pierre-Herbaud,
Aérodrome d'Issoire, BP 33, 63501 Issoire Cedex, ☎ 04 73 89 16 62; http://perso.orange.fr/acph/.

Aéro-club du Livradois,
Le Poyet, 63600 Ambert,
☎ 04 73 82 01 64.

Helicopters

Héli Volcan, Aérodrome d'Issoire, 63500 Issoire, ☎ 04 73 55 03 60; www.helivolcan.com.

Aéroport de Clermont-Ferrand-Aulnat, 63510 Aulnat,
☎ 04 73 62 70 67;
www.clermont-fd.cci.fr.

Microlights

Aéro-club Combrailles,
École de pilotage ULP Multi-axes, 63640 St-Priest-des-Champs,
☎ 04 73 86 84 52.

Up, up and away

J. Damase/MICHELIN

Auvergne ULM,
   Prouilbat, 63310 Riom,
   ☎ 04 73 68 69 22.

Air libre, vallée verte, place de l'Office
   de tourisme, 63710 St-Nectaire,
   ☎ 04 73 88 57 95; flights over the
   Massif du Sancy.

Eco-Tourism

RIVER AND CANAL CRUISING

Self-skippered holidays
Boats can be hired in Port-sur-Saône,
Gray, St-Jean-de-Losne and Roanne to
explore the Saône and the Rhône from
Corre to Port-St-Louis-du-Rhône. The
main harbours on the way are Lyon,
Les Roches-de-Condrieu and Valence
l'Éperviève; a basic service is available
in St-Germain-au-Mont-d'Or, Tournon-
sur-Rhône, Viviers and Avignon. In the
Lyon region, a series of mooring places
along the Saône enables visitors to
enjoy the surrounding area: Caluire,
Albigny, Collonges-au-Mont-d'Or,
Rochetaillée, Neuville-sur-Saône and
Lyon. More information is available
from **Bureau de la Plaisance,** 2 rue
de la Quarantaine, 69321 Lyon Cedex
05, ☎ 04 72 56 59 28.
The stretch of canal between Roanne
and Briennon offers a pleasant journey
with several locks along the way;
contact **Marins d'Eau Douce,** Port de
Plaisance de Briennon 42720, ☎ 04 77
69 92 92.

Cruises
Several companies organise boat trips
of variable length along the Rhône,
the Isère and canals in the Loire
region.

Aquaviva organise one-week cruises
from March to November between
Châlon-sur-Saône and Avignon. Information and bookings, ☎ 01 45 75 52
60 (Paris number).

Naviginter offer cruises and boat
trips (with or without meals) along the
Rhône and Saône rivers; information

and bookings, 13 bis quai Rambaud,
69002 Lyon, ☎ 04 78 42 96 81.

Royan-Vercors propose cruises along
the River Isère (departures from La
Sône and St-Nazaire-en-Royans);
information and bookings, Site des
Tufières, 38840 La Sône, ☎ 04 76 64
43 42.

NATURE PARKS AND RESERVES

Parks
The region described in this guide
includes four regional nature parks:

**Parc naturel régional des Vol-
   cans d'Auvergne** (👜 see Parc
   naturel régional des VOLCANS
   D'AUVERGNE). Château Montlosier
   63970 Aydat - ☎ 04 73 65 64 00;
   Parc.volcans@wanadoo.fr,
   www.parc-volcans-auvergne.com.

**Parc naturel régional Livradois-
   Forez** (👜 see Monts du FOREZ).
   For information, contact the
   Maison du Parc, BP 17, 63880 St-
   Gervais-sous-Meymont,
   ☎ 04 73 95 57 57;
   www.parc-livradois-forez.org.

Parc naturel regional du Pilat
   (👜 see Le PILAT). For information,
   contact the Maison du Parc, Moulin de Virieu, 42410 Pélussin,
   ☎ 04 74 87 52 00;
   www.parc-naturel-pilat.fr.

**Parc naturel régional des Monts
   d'Ardèche** (👜 see AUBENAS). This
   is the most recently created of the
   four parks; for information, apply
   to PNR des Monts d'Ardèche, La
   Prade, BP3, 07560 Montpezat-
   sous-Bauzon, ☎ 04 75 94 35 20;
   www.parc-monts-ardeche.fr.

Nature reserves and nature-
discovery centres
The following organise activities on
the theme of nature:

Vallée de Chaudefour, Maison de la
   Réserve naturelle de la Vallée de
   Chaudefour, Parc naturel regional

des Volcans d'Auvergne, 63790 Chambon-sur-Lac, ☎ 04 73 88 68 80; www.grandevallee.com/parc/chaudefour - guided tours (dogs are not allowed, even on a leash).

Sagnes de la Godivelle,
63850 La Godivelle, ☎ 04 73 65 64 00 or 04 73 71 78 12 (July-August, last two weekends in June and first two weekends in September: 2-6pm).

Val d'Allier, Outings are organised by the Ligue pour la Protection des Oiseaux. For information, contact the Espace Nature du Val d'Allier, 8-12 boulevard de Nomazy, 03000 Moulins, ☎ 04 70 44 46 29.

Centre permanent d'initiatives pour l'Environnement,
avenue Nicolas-Rambourg, Tronçais, 03360 St-Bonnet-Tronçais, ☎ 04 70 06 14 69.

Office national des Forêts,
Les Portes d'Avermes, 03000 Avermes, ☎ 04 70 46 82 00; www.onf.fr. Rambles through Tronçais Forest.

Espace Nature du Val d'Allier,
🐾 *see address above.*

DONKEYS AND HORSE-DRAWN CARAVANS

In Stevenson's footsteps – How about a walk with a donkey for company and to amuse the children? Contact the **Fédération Nationale Ânes et Randonnées** (FNAR), Le Pré du Meinge, 26560 Eourres, ☎ 04 92 65 09 07; www.ane-et-rando.com or the **Comité Départemental du Tourisme** in Privas at ☎ 04 75 64 04 66, for the list of places where donkeys may be hired.

Equine adventures – Horse-drawn caravans, complete with bunk-beds and basic kitchen facilities, may be hired in some areas to follow a planned itinerary; contact the Parc

Lac Chambon

J. Damase/MICHELIN

naturel régional du Pilat, ☎ 04 74 87 52 00 or local tourist offices.

SNOWSHOEING AND SLEDGING

Nature lovers will appreciate **snowshoeing tours** across the Sancy and Cantal mountains (beginners are advised to go on guided tours); binoculars are essential to spot leaping moufflons! Information is available from tourist offices.

Sledging also offers a fascinating experience across the snow-covered Auvergne mountains. Contact Association Les P'tits Loups de la Banne, route Banne-d'Ordanche, 63150 Murat-le-Quaire, ☎ 04 73 81 09 39; www.neige.planetepuydedome.com.

When to Go

The region covered by this guide presents a great variety of climatic conditions in all seasons. Spring weather is unpredictable: there may be heavy snowfall at higher altitudes while at the same time the valleys are fragrant with the blossoms of fruit trees. In late spring, the Auvergne region can be spectacularly beautiful, as the melting snow swells the rivers and cascades. The summer months are generally sunny and warm. The Ardèche Gorges are especially popular in July and August, when there are so many small craft on the water that it looks a bit like the motorway! Along the River Rhône, the weather in autumn is usually mild, but in other regions (such as the Cévennes) heavy rains are likely to fall. The colours in the Puys, Livradois and Dombes regions are especially vibrant at this time of year. Winter brings snow to the high peaks, where it can cover the ground for several months, closing off some of the mountain passes to traffic. The wind in the region of the volcanoes of Auvergne can be intense. But south of Valence and in the southern part of the Cantal region, the climate is much milder, and the winter skies are usually clear thanks to winds blowing up from the Mediterranean. The city of Lyon seems to have a climate all its own: summers are hot and sticky, with thick morning mists, and in the winter a sort of fog seems to hang overhead all day. Spring and autumn are the best times to visit the city, as the weather is usually clearer then.

WEATHER FORECAST

Météo-France offers recorded information at national, regional and local level. This information is updated three times a day and is valid for five days.

National forecast: ☎ 08 92 68 00 00.

Regional forecast: ☎ 08 92 68 01 01.

Local forecast: ☎ 08 92 68 02 followed by the number of the *département* (Ain: 01; Allier: 03; Ardèche: 04; Cantal: 15; Drôme: 26; Haute-Loire: 43; Isère: 38; Loire: 42; Puy-de-Dôme: 63; Rhône: 69).

Mountain weather forecast: ☎ 08 92 68 04 04; for information about snow cover and avalanche risk, ☎ 08 92 68 10 20.

Weather forecast for microlights and light aircraft: ☎ 08 92 68 10 14. Information is also available on www.meteo.fr.

WHAT TO PACK

As little as possible! Cleaning and laundry services are available everywhere. Most personal items can be replaced at reasonable cost. Try to pack everything into one suitcase and a tote bag. Porter help may be in short supply, and new purchases will add to the original weight. Be sure luggage is clearly labelled and old travel tags removed. Do not pack medication in checked luggage, but keep it with you.

KNOW BEFORE YOU GO

Useful Web Addresses

www.ambafrance-us.org
The French Embassy in the USA has a website providing basic information (geography, demographics, history), a news digest and business-related information. It offers special pages for children, and pages devoted to culture, language study and travel, and you can reach other selected French sites (regions, cities, ministries) with a hypertext link.

www.franceguide.com
The French Government Tourist Office / Maison de la France in London site is packed with practical information and tips for those travelling to France. The home page has a number of links to more specific guidance, for American or Canadian travellers for example, or to the FGTO's London pages.

www.FranceKeys.com
This site has plenty of practical information for visiting France. It covers all the regions, with links to tourist offices and related sites. Very useful for planning the details of your tour in France!

www.franceway.com is an on-line magazine which focuses on culture and heritage. For each region, there are also suggestions for activities and practical information on where to stay and how to get there.

www.fr-holidaystore.co.uk
The French Travel Centre in London has gone on-line with this service, providing information on all of the regions of France, including updated special travel offers and details on available accommodation.

www.visiteurope.com
The European Travel Commission provides useful information on travelling to and around 27 European countries, and includes links to some commercial booking services (ie vehicle hire), rail schedules, weather reports and more.

Tourist Offices

For information and assistance in planning a trip to France travellers should apply to the official French Tourist Office in their own country:

Australia – New Zealand
Sydney – BNP Building, 12 Castlereagh Street, Sydney, New South Wales 2000, ☎ (02) 9231 5244 – Fax: (02) 9221 8682.

Canada
Montreal – 1981 Avenue McGill College, Suite 490, Montreal PQ H3A 2W9, ☎ (514) 288-4264 – Fax: (514) 845 4868.
Toronto – 30 St Patrick's Street, Suite 700, Toronto, Ontario, ☎ (416) 979 7587.

Eire
Dublin – 10 Suffolk Street, Dublin 2, ☎ (01) 679 0813 – Fax: (01) 679 0814.

South Africa
P.O. Box 41022, Craig Hall 2024, ☎ (011) 880 8062.

United Kingdom
London – Maison de la France – 178 Piccadilly, London W1J 9AL, ☎ 090 6824 4123 – Fax: 020 7493 6594; info.uk@franceguide.com.

United States
East Coast – New York – 444 Madison Avenue, 16th Floor, NY 10022-6903, ☎ (212) 838-7800 – Fax: (212) 838-7855.
Mid West – Chicago – 676 North Michigan Avenue, Suite 3360, Chicago, IL 60611-2819, ☎ (312) 751-7800 – Fax: (312) 337-6339.
West Coast – Los Angeles – 9454 Wilshire Boulevard, Suite 715, Bev-

erly Hills, CA 90212-2967, ☎ (310) 271-6665 – Fax: (310) 276-2835.

Information can also be requested from **France on Call,** ☎ (202) 659-7779.

LOCAL TOURIST OFFICES

Visitors may also contact local tourist offices for more precise information, to receive brochures and maps. The addresses and telephone numbers of tourist offices in the larger towns are listed after the symbol 🄸, in the introduction to each sight. Below, the addresses are given for local tourist offices of the *départements* and régions covered in this guide. The index lists the *département* after each town.

Départements – Address inquiries to the **Comité Départemental du Tourisme (CDT):**

Ain – 34 rue du Général-Delestraint, BP 78, 01002 Bourg-en-Bresse Cedex, ☎ 04 74 32 31 30. www.ain-tourisme.com

Allier – Pavillon des Marronniers, Parc de Bellevue, BP 65, 03402 Yzeure Cedex, ☎ 04 70 46 81 50. www.allier-tourisme.com

Ardèche – 4 cours du Palais, BP 221, 07002 Privas Cedex, ☎ 04 75 64 04 66. www.ardeche-tourisme.com

Cantal – 36, rue de Sistrières, 15000 Aurillac, ☎ 04 71 63 85 00. www.cantal-tourisme.fr

Drôme – 8 rue Baudin, 26005 Valence, ☎ 04 75 82 19 26. www.drometourisme.com

Haute-Loire – 12 boulevard Philippe-Jourde, BP 332, 43012 Le Puy-en-Velay Cedex, ☎ 04 71 07 41 54. www.mididelauvergne.com

Isère – 14 rue de la République, BP227, 38019 Grenoble Cedex, ☎ 04 76 54 34 36. www.isere-tourisme.com

Loire – 5 place Jean-Jaurès, 42021 St-Étienne Cedex 1, ☎ 04 77 43 59 14. www.cg42.fr

Puy-de-Dôme – Place de la Bourse, 63038 Clermont-Ferrand Cedex 1, ☎ 04 73 42 22 50. www.planetepuydedome.com

Rhône – 35 rue St-Jean, BP 5009, 69245 Cedex 05, ☎ 04 72 61 78 90. www.rhonetourisme.com

Regions
Comité Régional de Développement Touristique d'Auvergne
Parc Technologique Clermont-Ferrand La Pardieu, 7 allée Pierre de Fermat - 63178 AUBIÈRE ☎ 0 810 827 828. www.auvergne-tourisme.info

Comité Régional du Tourisme de la Vallée du Rhône – 104 route de Paris, 69260 Charbonnières-les-Bains, ☎ 04 72 59 21 59. www.crt-rhonealpes.fr

Fourteen towns and areas, labelled **Villes et Pays d'Art et d'Histoire** by the Ministry of Culture, are mentioned in this guide (Clermont-Ferrand, the Dauphiné d'Auvergne, the Forez, the Haut-Allier, Lyon, Montluçon, Moulins, Paladru-Les-Trois-Vals Lake, Le Puy-

Re-enactment of the first flight in a hot-air balloon

J. Sierpinski/SCOPE

en-Velay, Riom, Saint-Étienne, Valence and Vienne). They are particularly active in promoting their architectural and cultural heritage and offer guided tours by highly qualified guides as well as activities for 6 to 12-year-olds. More information is available from local tourist offices and from www.vpah.culture.fr.

International Visitors

EMBASSIES AND CONSULATES

Australia
Embassy – 4 rue Jean-Rey, 75015 Paris ☎ 01 40 59 33 00 – Fax: 01 40 59 33 10.

Canada
Embassy – 35 avenue Montaigne, 75008 Paris ☎ 01 44 43 29 00 – Fax: 01 44 43 29 99.

Eire
Embassy – 4 rue Rude, 75016 Paris ☎ 01 44 17 67 00 – Fax: 01 44 17 67 60.

New Zealand
Embassy – 7 ter rue Léonard-de-Vinci, 75016 Paris ☎ 01 45 01 43 43 – Fax: 01 45 01 43 44.

South Africa
Embassy – 59 quai d'Orsay, 75007 Paris ☎ 01 53 59 23 23 – Fax: 01 53 59 23 33.

UK
Embassy – 35 rue du Faubourg St-Honoré, 75008 Paris ☎ 01 44 51 31 00 – Fax: 01 44 51 31 27.
Consulate – 16 rue d'Anjou, 75008 Paris ☎ 01 44 51 31 01 (visas).

USA
Embassy – 2 avenue Gabriel, 75008 Paris ☎ 01 43 12 22 22 – Fax: 01 42 66 97 83.
Consulate – 2 rue St-Florentin, 75001 Paris ☎ 01 42 96 14 88.

DOCUMENTS

Passport – Nationals of countries within the European Union entering France need only a national identity card (although most airlines require passports). Nationals of other countries must be in possession of a valid national **passport**. In case of loss or theft, report to your embassy or consulate and the local police.

Visa – No **entry visa** is required for Canadian, US or Australian citizens travelling as tourists and staying less than 90 days, except for students planning to study in France. If you think you may need a visa, apply to your local French Consulate.
US citizens should obtain the booklet *Safe Trip Abroad* (US$1), which provides useful information on visa requirements, customs regulations, medical care etc for international travellers. Published by the Government Printing Office, it can be ordered by phone – ☎ (202) 512-1800 – or consulted on-line (www.access.gpo.gov). General passport information is available by phone toll-free from the Federal Information Center (item 5 on the automated menu), ☎ 800-688-9889. US passport application forms can be downloaded from http://travel.state.gov.

CUSTOMS

Apply to the Customs Office (UK) for a leaflet on customs regulations and the full range of duty-free allowances; available from HM Customs and Excise, Thomas Paine House, Angel Square, Torrens Street, London EC1V 1TA, ☎ 08450 109 000. The US Customs Service offers a publication *Know Before You Go* for US citizens: for the office nearest you, consult the phone book, Federal Government, US Treasury (www.customs.ustreas.gov). There are no customs formalities for holidaymakers bringing their caravans into France for a stay of less than six months. No customs document is necessary for pleasure boats and outboard motors for a stay of less than

Spirits (whisky, gin, vodka etc)	10 litres
Fortified wines (vermouth, port etc)	10 litres
Wine (not more than 60 sparkling)	90 litres
Beer	110 litres
Cigarettes	800
Cigarillos	400
Cigars	200
Smoking tobacco	1 kg

six months, but the registration certificate should be kept on board. Americans can take home, tax-free, up to US$400 worth of goods (limited quantities of alcohol and tobacco products); Canadians up to CND$300; Australians up to AUS$400 and New Zealanders up to NZ$700.

Residents from a member state of the European Union are not restricted with regard to purchasing goods for private use, but the recommended allowances for alcoholic beverages and tobacco are as follows:

HEALTH

It is advisable to take out comprehensive insurance coverage as patients receiving medical treatment in French hospitals or clinics must pay the bill. **Nationals of non-EU countries** should check with their insurance companies about policy limitations. Reimbursement can then be negotiated with the insurance company according to the policy held.

British and Irish citizens should apply to the Department of Health and Social Security **before travelling** for a European Health Insurance Card, which entitles the holder to urgent treatment for accident or unexpected illness in EU countries. See www.nhs. uk. A refund of part of the costs of treatment can be obtained on application in person or by post to the local Social Security Offices.

Americans concerned about travel and health can contact the International Association for Medical Assistance to Travelers, which can also provide details of English-speaking doctors in different parts of France: ☎ (716) 754-4883.

First aid, medical advice and chemists' night service rotas are available from chemists/drugstores *(pharmacie)* identified by the green cross sign. All prescription drugs should be clearly labelled; it is recommended that you carry a copy of the prescription.

Useful Numbers

The American Hospital of Paris is open 24hr for emergencies as well as consultations, with English-speaking staff, at 63 boulevard Victor-Hugo, 92200 Neuilly-sur-Seine, ☎ 01 46 41 25 25. Accredited by major insurance companies.

The British Hospital is just outside Paris in Levallois-Perret, 3 rue Barbès, ☎ 01 46 39 22 22.

Accessibility

The sights described in this guide which are easily accessible to people of reduced mobility are indicated in the *Admission times and charges* section by the symbol &.

On TGV and Corail trains operated by the national railway (SNCF), there are special wheelchair slots in 1st class carriages available to holders of 2nd-class tickets. On Eurostar and Thalys, special rates are available for accompanying adults. All airports are equipped to receive physically disabled passengers.

Web-surfers can find information for slow walkers, mature travellers and others with special needs at www. access-able.com. For information on museum access for the disabled contact La Direction, *Les Musées de France*, Service Accueil des Publics Spécifiques, 6 rue des Pyramides, 75041 Paris Cedex 1, ☎ 01 40 15 80 72.

The **Michelin Guide France** and the **Michelin Camping France** indicate hotels and camp sites with facilities suitable for physically handicapped people.

GETTING THERE

By Air

It is very easy to arrange air travel to one of Paris' two airports (Roissy-Charles-de-Gaulle to the north, and Orly to the south). There are also regular flights from the UK and the US to **Lyon-Saint-Exupéry** airport, which is linked to the city centre by a regular shuttle service. Contact airline companies and travel agents for details of package tour flights with a rail link-up or Fly-Drive schemes.

Visitors arriving in **Paris** who wish to reach the city centre or a train station may use public transportation or reserve space on the **Airport Shuttle** (for Roissy-Charles-de-Gaulle ☎ 01 45 38 55 72, for Orly ☎ 01 43 21 06 78). Air France operates a coach service into town with frequent departures (☎ 01 41 56 89 00). The cost and duration of a taxi ride from the airport to the city centre varies with traffic conditions. From Charles-de-Gaulle: about 1hr, 40€; from Orly about 30min, 30€. There is an extra charge (posted in the taxi) for baggage; the extra charge for airport pick-up is on the meter; drivers are usually given a tip of 10-15% of the fare.

By Sea

There are numerous **cross-Channel services** (passenger and car ferries, hovercraft) from the United Kingdom and Ireland, as well as the rail Shuttle through the Channel Tunnel (**Le Shuttle-Eurotunnel,** ☎ 08705 35 35 35. www.eurotunnel.co.uk). To choose the most suitable route between your port of arrival and your destination use the Michelin Tourist and Motoring Atlas France, Michelin map 726 (which gives travel times and mileages) or Michelin maps from the 1:200 000 series (with the orange cover). For details apply to travel agencies or to:

P & O Ferries

Channel House, Channel View Road, Dover CT17 9JT, ☎ 08705 202020 (UK dialling), or +44 1304 864003 (international dialling). www.pogroup.com

Norfolk Line

Norfolk House, Eastern Docks, Dover, Kent CT16 1JA. ☎ 0870 870 10 20. www.hoverspeed.co.uk

Brittany Ferries

Millbay Docks; Plymouth, Devon. PL1 3EW. ☎ 08703 665 333, www.brittany-ferries.com

Portsmouth Commercial Port (and ferry information)

George Byng Way, Portsmouth, Hampshire PO2 8SP. ☎ 01705 297391, Fax 01705 861165, www.portsmouth-port.co.uk

Seafrance

Eastern Docks, Dover, Kent, CT16 1JA, ☎ 0870 443 1653, www.seafrance.fr

By Rail

Eurostar runs via the Channel Tunnel between **London** (Waterloo Station) and **Paris** (Gare du Nord) in less than 3hr (bookings and information ☎ 08705 186 186 in the UK; ☎ +44 1233 617 575, outside UK). In Paris it links to the high-speed rail network (TGV) which covers most of France. There is a TGV service from **Paris** (Gare de Lyon) to Lyon (2hr). Both the Part-Dieu and Perrache stations are connected to the city centre by the metro. Three times a week the **Eurostar Ski Train** takes you directly to winter sports resorts such as Val d'Isère, Tignes and Méribel, leaving from either London or Ashford.

Eurailpass, Flexipass, Eurailpass Youth, EurailDrive Pass and **Saverpass** are travel passes which may be

Gare de Lyon-Perrache

There are numerous **discounts** available when you purchase your tickets in France, from 25-50% below the regular rate. These include discounts for using senior cards and youth cards (the nominative cards with a photograph must be purchased – 44 and 41€, respectively), and lower rates for 2-9 people travelling together (no card required, advance purchase necessary). There are a limited number of discount seats available during peak travel times, and the best discounts are available for travel during off-peak periods.

Tickets must be validated *(composter)* by using the orange automatic date-stamping machines at the platform entrance (failure to do so may result in a fine).

The French railway company SNCF operates a telephone information, reservation and prepayment service in English from 7am to 10pm (French time). In France call ☎ 08 36 35 35 39 (when calling from outside France, drop the initial 0).

purchased by residents of countries outside the European Union. In the US, contact your travel agent or **Rail Europe** 2100 Central Ave. Boulder, CO, 80301 ☎ 1-800-4-EURAIL or **Europrail International** ☎ 1 888 667 9731. If you are a European resident, you can buy an individual country pass, if you are not a resident of the country where you plan to use it. All rail services throughout France can be arranged through **RailEurope** in the UK: Rail Europe House, 34 Tower View, Kings Hill, West Malling, Kent ME19 4ED. Telephone 08705 848 848; www.raileurope.co.uk. Personal callers are welcome to visit the French Travel Centre at 178 Piccadilly, London W1J 9AL. Information on French schedules can be obtained on www.sncf.fr. Here you can book ahead, pay with a credit card, and receive your ticket at home through the mail.

By Coach/Bus

Eurolines (UK), 4 Cardiff Road, Luton, Bedfordshire, LU1 1PP, ☎ 08705 143219, Fax 01582 400694.

Eurolines (Paris), 22 rue Malmaison, 93177 Bagnolet, ☎ 01 49 72 57 80, Fax 01 49 72 57 99.

www.eurolines.com is the international website with information about travelling all over Europe by coach (bus).

GETTING AROUND

Driving in France

The area covered in this guide is easily reached by main motorways and national routes. **Michelin map 726** indicates the main itineraries as well as alternate routes for avoiding heavy traffic during busy holiday periods, and gives estimated travel times. **Michelin map 723** is a detailed atlas of French motorways, indicating tolls, rest areas and services along the route; it includes a table for calculating distances and times. The latest Michelin route-planning service is available on Internet, **www.Via Michelin.com.** Travellers can calculate a precise route using such options as shortest route, route avoiding toll roads, Michelin-recommended route and gain access to tourist information (hotels, restaurants, attractions). The service is available on a pay-per-route basis or by subscription.

The roads are very busy during holiday periods (particularly weekends in July and August) and, to avoid traffic congestion it is advisable to follow the recommended secondary routes (signposted as *Bison Futé – itinéraires bis*). The motorway network includes rest areas *(aires de repos)* and petrol stations *(stations-service)*, usually with restaurant and shopping complexes attached, about every 40km/25mi, so that long-distance drivers have no excuse not to stop for a rest every now and then.

DOCUMENTS

Driving licence – Travellers from other European Union countries and North America can drive in France with a valid national or home-state driving licence. An **international driving licence** is useful because the information on it appears in nine languages (bear in mind that traffic officers are empowered to fine motorists). A permit is available (US$10) from the **National Automobile Club,** 1151 East Hillsdale Boulevard, Foster City, CA 94404 ☎ 650-294-7000 or **national-autoclub.com;** or contact your local branch of the **American Automobile Association.**

Registration papers

For the vehicle, it is necessary to have the registration papers (logbook) and a nationality plate of the approved size.

Insurance

Certain motoring organisations (AAA, AA, RAC) offer accident insurance and breakdown service schemes for members. Check with your current insurance company in regard to coverage while abroad. Because French autoroutes are privately owned, your European Breakdown Cover service does not extend to breakdowns on the autoroute - you must use the emergency telephones, or drive off the autoroute before calling your breakdown service.

HIGHWAY CODE

In France the minimum driving age is 18. Traffic drives on the right. All passengers must wear **seat belts.** Children under the age of 10 must ride in the back seat. Headlights must be switched on in poor visibility and at night; side-lights may be used only when the vehicle is stationary.

In the case of a **breakdown,** a red warning triangle or hazard warning lights are obligatory. In the absence of stop signs at intersections, cars must **give way to the right.** Traffic on main roads outside built-up areas (priority indicated by a yellow diamond sign) and on roundabouts has right of way. Vehicles must stop when the lights turn red at road junctions and may filter to the right only when indicated by an amber arrow.

The regulations on **drinking and driving** (limited to 0.50g/l) and **speeding** are strictly enforced – usually by an on-the-spot fine and/or confiscation of the vehicle.

Speed limits
Although liable to modification, these are as follows:
- toll motorways (autoroutes) 130kph/80mph (110kph/68mph when raining);
- dual carriageways and motorways without tolls 110kph/68mph (100kph/62mph when raining);
- other roads 90kph/56mph (80kph/50mph when raining) and in towns 50kph/31mph;
- outside lane on motorways during daylight, on level ground and with good visibility – minimum speed limit of 80kph/50mph.

Parking regulations
In built-up areas there are zones where parking is either restricted or subject to a fee; tickets should be obtained from the ticket machines (horodateurs – small change necessary) and displayed inside the windscreen on the driver's side; failure to display may result in a fine, or towing away and impoundment. Other parking areas in town may require you to take a ticket when passing through a barrier. To exit, you must pay the parking fee (usually there is a machine located by the exit – sortie) and insert the paid-up card in another machine which will lift the exit gate.

Tolls
In France, most motorway sections are subject to a toll (péage). You can pay in cash or with a credit card (Visa, Mastercard).

Petrol (US: gas)
French service stations dispense: sans plomb 98 (super unleaded 98), sans plomb 95 (super unleaded 95), diesel/gazole (diesel) and GPL (LPG). Prices are listed on signboards on the motorways; it is usually cheaper to fill up after leaving the motorway at the large hypermarkets on the outskirts of towns.

CAR RENTAL

There are car rental agencies at airports, railway stations and in all large towns throughout France. European cars have manual transmission; automatic cars are available only if an advance reservation is made. Drivers must be over 21; between ages 21-25, drivers are required to pay an extra daily fee; some companies allow drivers under 23 only if the reservation has been made through a travel agent. It is relatively expensive to hire a car in France; Americans in particular will notice the difference and should make arrangements before leaving, **take advantage of fly-drive offers when you buy your ticket,** or seek advice from a travel agent, specifying requirements. There are many on-line services that will look for the best prices on car rental around the globe. **Nova** can be contacted at www.renta-car-worldwide.com or ☎ 0800 018 6682 (freephone UK) or ☎ 44 28 4272 8189 (calling from outside the UK). All of the firms listed below have Internet sites for reservations and information. In France, you can call the following numbers:

Avis: ☎ 08 20 05 05 05
Europcar: ☎ 08 25 82 54 57
Budget France: ☎ 08 25 00 35 64
Hertz France: ☎ 01 47 03 49 12
SIXT-Eurorent: ☎ 08 20 00 74 98
National-CITER: ☎ 01 45 22 77 91

A Baron's Limousine ☎ 01 45 30 21 21 provides cars and drivers (English-speaking drivers available).
Worldwide Motorhome Rentals offers fully equipped campervans for rent: mhrww.com or call (US toll-free) US ☎ 888- 519-8969; outside the US ☎ 530-389-8316 or Fax 530-389-8316.
Overseas Motorhome Tours Inc. organises escorted tours and individual rental of recreational vehicles: in the US ☎ 800-322-2127; outside the US ☎ 1-310-543-2590; www.omtinc.com.

WHERE TO STAY AND EAT

Where to Stay

Hotels and Restaurants are described in the Address Books within the *Discovering the Sights* section.

FINDING A HOTEL

Turn to the Address Books throughout Discovering the Sights for descriptions and prices of typical places to stay and eat with local flair. The Legend on the cover flap explains the symbols and abbreviations used in these sections. We have reported the prices and conditions as we observed them, but obviously changes in management and other factors may mean that you will find discrepancies. Please feel free to keep us informed of any major differences you encounter.

Use the **Map of Places to Stay** below to identify recommended places for overnight stops. For an even greater selection, use the red-cover **Michelin Guide France,** with its famously reliable star-rating system and hundreds of establishments all over France. Book ahead to ensure that you get the accommodation you want, not only during the tourist season, but throughout the year, as many towns fill up during trade fairs, arts festivals etc. Some places require an advance deposit or a reconfirmation. Reconfirming is especially important if you plan to arrive after 6pm.

For further assistance, **Loisirs Accueil** is a booking service that has offices in some French *départements* – contact the tourist offices listed above for further information .

A guide to good-value, family-run hotels, **Logis et Auberges de France,** is available from the French tourist office, as are lists of other kinds of accommodation such as hotel-châteaux, bed-and-breakfasts etc.

Relais et Châteaux provides information on booking in luxury hotels with character: 15 rue Galvani, 75017 Paris, ☎ 01 45 72 90 00.

Economy Chain Hotels

If you need a place to stop en route, these can be useful, as they are inexpensive (30-45€ for a double room) and generally located near the main road. While breakfast is available, there may not be a restaurant; rooms are small, with a television and bathroom. Central reservation numbers:

- **Akena** ☎ 01 69 84 85 17
- **B&B** ☎ 0 820 90 29 29 (in France); 33 2 98 33 75 00 (when calling from outside France)
- **Mister Bed** ☎ 01 46 14 38 00
- **Villages Hôtel** ☎ 03 80 60 92 70

The hotels listed below are slightly more expensive (from 45€), and offer a few more amenities and services. Central reservation numbers:

- **Campanile, Climat de France, Kyriad** ☎ 0 825 003 003 (in France); 33 1 64 62 46 46 (when calling from outside France).

Many chains have on-line reservations: www.etaphotel.com; www.ibishotel.com

RENTING A COTTAGE, BED AND BREAKFAST

Rural accommodation

The **Maison des Gîtes de France** is an information service on self-catering accommodation in France. *Gîtes* usually take the form of a cottage or apartment decorated in the local style where visitors can make themselves at home, or bed and breakfast accommodation *(chambres d'hôtes)* which consists of a room and breakfast at a reasonable price.

Contact the Gîtes de France office in Paris: 59 rue St-Lazare, 75439 Paris Cedex 09, ☎ 01 49 70 75 75, or their representative in the UK, **Brittany Ferries,** Millbay Docks; Plymouth, Devonshire. PL1 3EW, ☎ 08703 665 333, **www.brittany-ferries.com.** The Internet site **www.gites-de-france. fr** has a good English version. From the site, you can order catalogues for different regions illustrated with photographs of the properties, as well as specialised catalogues (bed and breakfasts, chalets in skiing areas, farm stays etc). You can also contact the local tourist offices, which may have lists of available properties and local bed and breakfast establishments.

The Fédération Française des Stations Vertes de Vacances, 6 rue Ranfer-de-Bretenières, BP 71698, 21016 Dijon Cedex, ☎ 03 80 54 10 50 – www.stationsvertes.com, is able to provide details of accommodation, leisure facilities and natural attractions in rural locations selected for their tranquillity.

Farm holidays

The guide *Bienvenue à la ferme* is published by and available from the Assemblée Permanente des Chambres d'Agriculture, Service "Agriculture et Tourisme", 9 avenue Georges-V, 75008 Paris, ☎ 01 53 57 11 44 – www.bienvenue-a-la-ferme.com. It includes the addresses of farmers providing guest facilities who have signed a charter drawn up by the Chambers of Agriculture. *Bienvenue à la ferme* farms, vetted for quality and meeting official standards, can be identified by the yellow flower which serves as their logo.

Ramblers

Ramblers can consult the guide entitled *Gîtes d'étape et refuges* by A and S Mouraret (Rando-Éditions, BP 24, 65421 Ibos, ☎ 0 5 62 90 09 90 – www.gites-refuges.com). The guide and the web site are intended mainly for those who enjoy rambling, cycling, climbing, skiing and canoeing-kayaking holidays.

HOSTELS, CAMPING

To obtain an International Youth Hostel Federation card (there is no age requirement, and there is a "senior card" available too), you should contact the IYHF in your own country for information and membership applications (US ☎ 202 783 6161; UK ☎ 01727 855215; Canada ☎ 613-273 7884; Australia ☎ 61-2-9565-1669; UK International Youth Hostel Federation, 2nd Floor, Gate House, Fretherne Road, Welwyn Garden City. Herts AL8 6RD. ☎ +44 (0) 1707 324170). There is a new booking service on the Internet (iyhf.org), which you may use to reserve rooms as early as six months in advance.

The main youth hostel association *(Auberges de Jeunesse)* in France is the **Ligue Française pour les Auberges de la Jeunesse** (67 rue Vergniaud, 75013 Paris, ☎ 01 44 16 78 78; www.auberges-de-jeunesse.com).

There are numerous officially graded **camp sites** with varying standards of facilities throughout the Rhône Valley. The **Michelin Camping France** guide lists a selection of camp sites. The area is very popular with campers in the summer months, so it is wise to reserve in advance.

Where to Eat

Hotels and Restaurants are described in the Address Books within the *Discovering the Sights* section.

Turn to the Address Books throughout Discovering the Sights for descriptions and prices of selected places to eat in the different locations covered in this guide. The Legend on the cover flap explains the symbols and abbreviations used in these sections. Use **The Michelin Guide France,** with its hundreds of establishments all over France, for an even greater choice. If you would like to experience a meal in a highly rated restaurant from the Red Guide, be sure to book ahead! In the countryside, restaurants usually serve lunch between noon and 2pm and dinner between 7.30pm and 10pm. It is not always easy to find something in-between those two meal times, as the "non-stop" restaurant is still a rarity in the provinces. However, a hungry traveller can usually get a sandwich in a café, and ordinary hot dishes may be available in a *brasserie*.

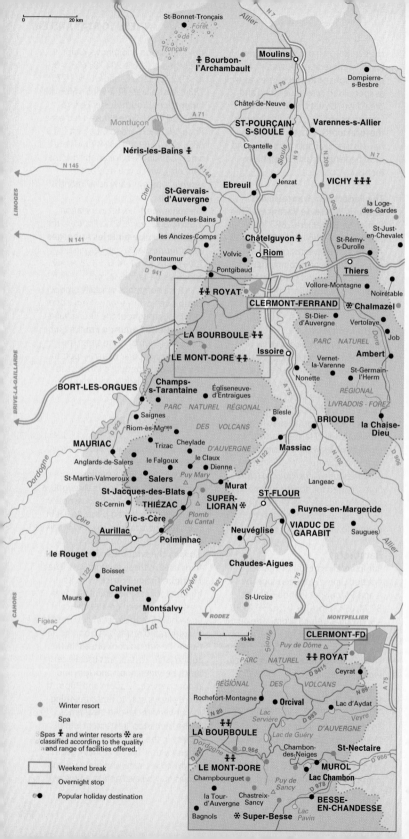

Places to stay

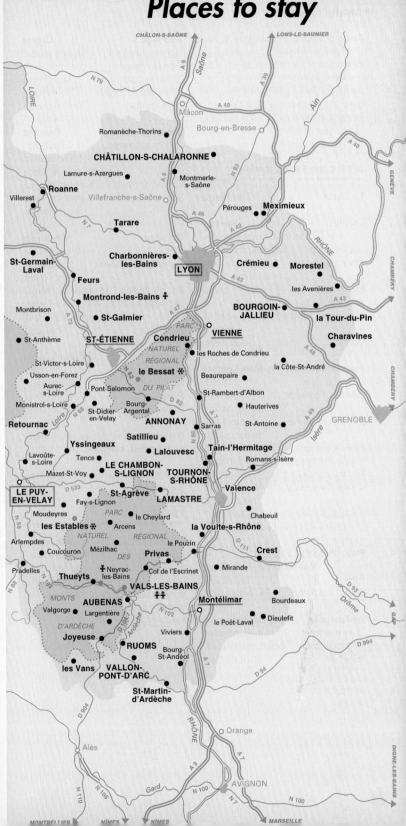

Among places in the Auvergne region that have been awarded the special distinction of *site remarquable du goût* (tempting moments for the palate) are Billom (for its particularly fine pink garlic), St-Nectaire (for its soft cheese made from cow's milk), Salers (for its firm cheese similar to Cantal); www.sitesremarquablesdugout.com.

A TYPICAL FRENCH MENU

La Carte	The Menu

Entrées	**Starters**
Crudités	Platter of raw vegetables
Terrine de lapin	Rabbit terrine (pâté)
Frisée aux lardons	Curly lettuce with diced bacon
Escargots	Snails
Salade au crottin de Chavignol	Goat's cheese on a bed of lettuce
Potage	Soup, broth

Plats (Viandes)	**Main Courses (Meat)**
Bavette à l'échalote	Sirloin with chopped shallots
Faux filet au poivre	Steak in a pepper sauce
Pavé de rumsteck	Thick rump steak
Côtelettes d'agneau	Lamb cutlets
Filet mignon de porc	Pork fillet
Blanquette de veau	Veal stew in a cream sauce
Nos viandes sont garnies	Our meat dishes are served with vegetables

Plats (Poissons, Volaille)	**Main Courses (Fish, Fowl)**
Filets de sole	Sole fillets
Dorade aux herbes	Sea bream with herbs
Saumon grillé	Grilled salmon
Truite meunière	Trout fried in butter
Magret de canard	Breast fillet of duck
Poulet rôti	Roast chicken

Fromage	**Cheese**
Fromage de chèvre	Goat's cheese
Fromage maigre	Low-fat cheese
Fromage à pâte dure	Hard cheese
Fromage à pâte molle	Soft cheese
Fromage râpé	Grated cheese

Desserts	**Desserts**
Tarte aux pommes	Apple tart
Crème caramel	Warm baked custard with caramel sauce
Mousse au chocolat	Chocolate mousse
Sorbet: trois parfums	Sorbet: choose 3 flavours

Boissons	**Beverages**
Bière	Beer
Eau minérale (gazeuse)	(Sparkling) mineral water
Une carafe d'eau	Tap water (no charge)
Vin rouge, vin blanc, rosé	Red wine, white wine, rosé
Jus de fruit	Fruit juice

Menu Enfant	**Children's Menu**
Jambon	Ham
Steak haché	Minced beef
Frites	French fries
Purée	Mashed potatoes

Well-done, medium, rare, raw = **bien cuit, à point, saignant, cru**

For information on local specialities, turn to page 47.

TIPPING

In French restaurants and cafés, a service charge is included. Tipping is not necessary, but French people often leave the small change from their bill on their table, or about 5% for the waiter in a nice restaurant.

WHAT TO DO AND SEE

Outdoor Fun

WATER SPORTS

Natural and artificial lakes offer a wide choice of possibilities for the practice of various water sports: rowing, windsurfing, water skiing, canoeing, kayaking, rafting and canyoning.

Rowing

Club aviron Vichy, 3 avenue de la Croix-St-Martin, 03200 Vichy, ☎ 04 70 32 36 52; leisure activities and competitions.

Canoeing and kayaking

Discover the region from the swirling waters of the Ardèche, the Sornin or the Allier: information on suitable spots for canoeing from the Fédération **Française de Canoë-Kayak, 87** Quai de la Marne, BP 58, 94344 Joinville-le-Pont, ☎ 01 45 11 08 50; www.ffcanoe.asso.fr. Map of French waterways available.

Rafting and canyoning

Rafting is the easiest of these freshwater sports, since it involves going down rivers in inflatable craft steered by an instructor; special equipment is provided.
Canyoning is a technique for bodysurfing down narrow gorges and over falls, as though on a giant water slide. This sport requires protection: wear a wet suit and a helmet.
Information from **AN Rafting Haut-Allier,** Le Bourg, 43580 Monistrol-d'Allier, ☎ 04 71 57 23 90.

FISHING

The abundance of rivers, streams and lakes provides anglers with many opportunities to catch salmon, trout, perch, tench or carp; whatever the site, however, it is necessary to be affiliated to a fishing association and to abide by fishing regulations. Daily fishing permits are available in certain areas.

Contact the local tourist office or apply to the local fishing federations or fishing tackle stores.

Useful Addresses

Conseil supérieur de la pêche, 134 avenue Malakoff, 75016 Paris, ☎ 01 45 02 20 20.

Allier – Fédération de pêche et de protection du milieu aquatique, 8 rue de la Ronde, 03500 St-Pourçain-sur-Sioule, ☎ 04 70 45 42 90.

Cantal – Fédération départementale de pêche et de protection du milieu aquatique, 14 allée du Vialenc, 15000 Aurillac, ☎ 04 71 48 19 25. Association Cantal Pêche, Moulin du Blaud, 15100 Roffiac, ☎ 04 71 60 75 75 or 04 71 46 22 00; www.cdt-cantal.fr. Cantal Pêche publishes a free brochure full of useful advice on fishing and accommodation in this *département.*

Haute-Loire – Fédération de pêche et de protection du milieu aquatique, 32 rue Henri-Chas, Le Val-Vert, 43000 Le Puy-en-Velay, ☎ 04 71 09 09 44.

Loire – Fédération de la Loire pour la Pêche et la Protection du Milieu Aquatique, 14 allée de l'Europe, 42480 La Fouillouse, ☎ 04 77 02 20 00.

Puy-de-Dôme – Fédération de pêche et de protection du milieu aquatique, Site de Marmilhat Sud, 63370 Lempdes, ☎ 04 73 92 56 29. The federation's annual publication, *Le Pêcheur du Puy-de-Dôme,* includes a map of rivers and lakes.

Rhône – Fédération de pêche, Le Norly, 42 chemin Moulin-Carron, 69130 Écully, ☎ 04 72 18 01 80; www.rhonepechenature.org.

Lake/reservoir	Département	Acreage	Swimming	Boating	Fishing
Isle et Bardais (Etang de Pirot)	03	173	🏊	⛵	🎣
Prémilhat (Etang de Sault)	03	50	🏊	⛵	🎣
St-Bonnet-Tronçais (Etang de)	03	109	🏊	⛵	🎣
Vichy (Lac d'Allier)	03	297	🏊	⛵	🎣
Faverolles (Barrage de Granval)	15	2 718	🏊	⛵	🎣
Lanobre (Lac de Val)	15	3 460	🏊	⛵	🎣
Pleaux (Lac d'Enchanet)	15	1 013	🏊	⛵	🎣
St-Gérons (lac de St-Étienne-Cantalès)	15	1 384	🏊	⛵	🎣
Trémouille (Lac de Lastioulles)	15	311	🏊	⛵	🎣
Sarroux-les-Aubazines (Lac de Bort)	19	3 460	🏊	⛵	🎣
Le Bouchet-St-Nicolas (Lac du Bouchet)	43	84	🏊	⛵	🎣
Champagne-le-Vieux (Lac des Sources)	43	17	🏊	–	🎣
Saugues (Lac de)	43	7	🏊	⛵	🎣
Aubusson d'Auvergne (Lac de Courpière)	63	69	🏊	⛵	🎣
Arlanc	63	3.5	–	–	–
Ambert	63	6	–	–	–
Aydat (Lac d')	63	161	🏊	⛵	
Besse-en-Chandesse (Lac des Hermines) (Lac Pavin)	63	109	🏊	⛵	🎣
Chambon-sur-Lac (Lac Chambon)	63	148	🏊	⛵	🎣
Charbonnières-les-Vieilles (Gour de Tazenat)	63	82	🏊	–	–
Châtelguyon (Les Prades)	63	12	–	–	–
Condat-en-Combraille (Corteix)	63	16	–	–	–
Cournon-d'Auvergne	63	15	–	–	–
Cunlhat (La Barge)	63	10	–	–	–
Fades-Besserve	63	988	–	–	–
Guéry (Lac)	63	62	–	–	–
La Peyrouse (Lac des Marins)	63	32	🏊	⛵	🎣
Miremont (Lac des 4 Cantons d'Auvergne)	63	988	🏊	⛵	🎣
Thiers (Iloa)	63	42	–	–	–
Servant (La Prade)	63	20	–	–	–
St-Rémy-sur-Durolle (Lac des Prades)	63	35	🏊	⛵	🎣

HIKING

Exploring the region on foot is an enchanting way of discovering the landscape and the life of the country-side. Many long-distance footpaths *(Sentiers de Grande Randonnée* or "GR") cover the area described in this guide. Short-distance paths *(Sentiers de Petite Randonnée* or "PR") and medium-distance paths offer walks ranging from a few hours to a couple of days.

A collection of *Topo-Guides* showing the routes and the time needed, details of access points, accommodation and places of interest en route for footpaths throughout France is published by the **Fédération Française de la Randonnée Pédestre,** 14 rue Riquet, 75019 Paris, ☎ 01 44 89 93 90; some of the guides have been translated into English and are available in many bookshops in the region. You can also order the catalogue of 170 publications through the Internet at the association's site **www.ffrandonnee.fr** (in French).

Useful Addresses

Comité départemental de randonnée pédestre de l'Allier, Centre Éric Tabarly, 03300 Cusset, ☎ 04 70 96 00 26. The Comité publishes a *Topo-guide* of the Montagne Bourbonnaise area.

Comité départemental de randonnée pédestre du Cantal, Maison des Sports, 15000 Aurillac, ☎ 04 71 63 75 29.

Comité départemental de randonnée pédestre de la Haute-Loire, La Croisée des chemins, 23 rue Boucherie-Basse, 43000 Le Puy-en-Velay, ☎ 04 71 04 15 95 or 06 08 50 84 80; www.lacroiseedeschemins.com.

Comité départemental de randonnée pédestre du Puy-de-Dôme, Résidence des Lycées, 70 avenue des Paulines, 63000 Clermont-Ferrand Cedex, ☎ 04 73 91 94 01.

Chamina, 5 rue Pierre-le-Vénérable, 63057 Clermont-Ferrand Cedex 1, ☎ 04 73 92 81 44; www.chamina.com. This association promotes rambling and mountain biking throughout the Massif Central region and the western slopes of the Rhône Valley.

Play It Safe

Safety first is the rule for everyone when it comes to exploring the mountains as a climber, skier or hiker. The risk associated with avalanches, mud slides, falling rocks, bad weather, fog, glacially cold waters, the dangers of becoming lost or miscalculating distances, should not be underestimated.

Avalanches occur naturally when the upper layer of snow is unstable, in particular after heavy snowfalls, and may be set off by the passage of numerous skiers or hikers over a precise spot. A scale of risk, from 1 to 5, has been developed and is posted daily at resorts and the base of hiking trails. It is important to consult this *Bulletin Neige et Avalanche* (BNA) before setting off on any expeditions cross-country or hors-piste.

Lightning storms are often preceded by sudden gusts of wind, and put climbers and hikers in danger. In the event, avoid high ground, and do not move along a ridge top; do not seek shelter under overhanging rocks, isolated trees in otherwise open areas, at the entrance to caves or other openings in the rocks, or in the proximity of metal fences or gates. An automobile is a good refuge.

ROCK-CLIMBING

There are numerous opportunities to tackle cliff faces, particularly in the Auvergne region. Information can be obtained from the **Club Alpin Français** (section Auvergne), 3 rue Maréchal-Joffre, 63000 Clermont-Ferrand, ☎ 04 73 90 81 62, or the **Comité Départemental de la Fédération Française de la Montagne et de l'Escalade,** 22ter impasse Bonnabaud, 63000 Clermont-Ferrand, ☎ 04 73 29 24 71.

In January and February, some winter sports resorts offer an introduction to scaling frozen waterfalls:

Club alpin français du Haut-Cantal, 3 place du Monument, 15400 Riom-ès-Montagnes, ☎ 04 71 78 14 63.

Le Mont-Dore: contact the Peloton de Gendarmerie de Montagne (mountain squad of the Gendarmerie Nationale), rue des Chasseurs Alpins, 63240 Le Mont-Dore, ☎ 04 73 65 04 06.

SKIING

The Auvergne region is well equipped for the practice of Alpine skiing with three important resorts: Mont-Dore (◐ *see MONT-DORE*), Super-Besse (◐ *see BESSE*) and Super-Lioran (◐ *see Le LIORAN*), where the **Ski Pass Massif Central** can be used. It is also ideal for those who prefer cross-country skiing as there is an extensive network of tracks spread over twelve main ski areas.

The Massif du Pilat and the high plateaux of the Ardèche are also suitable for cross-country skiing and ski touring.

In addition, **summer skiing** and **sledging** are popular summer activities in Le Mont-Dore, Super-Besse and Picherande; information is available from tourist offices.

Useful Addresses

General information – Contact **Ski France,** an association of winter sports resorts, for their annual publications *Guide Pratique Hiver/Été* and *Guide des Tarifs* (both free), 61 boulevard Haussmann, 75008 Paris, ☎ 01 47 42 23 32.

Other useful contacts include:

Montagne Auvergne, Centre Couthon-Delille, 23 place Delille, 63000 Clermont-Ferrand, ☎ 04 73 90 23 14.

Association de gestion du domaine nordique des crêtes du Forez, Mairie, 63480 Vertolaye, ☎ 04 73 95 20 64.

Domaine nordique Lioran-Haute Planèze, Col de Prat de Bouc, 15300 Albepierre-Bredons, ☎ 04 71 73 32 13; www.cantal-nature.com.

École de ski français de Super-Besse, 1 ronde de Vassivière, 63610 Super-Besse, ☎ 04 73 79 61 75.

Snow-cover information – The following provide up-to-date information about snow conditions in the various ski areas.

Domaine nordique des crêtes du Forez: ☎ 04 73 95 20 61.
Super-Besse: ☎ 04 73 79 62 92.
Zone nordique du Mézenc: ☎ 04 71 08 34 33.
Stations du massif du Pilat: ☎ 04 77 20 43 43.
Stations des monts du Forez: ☎ 04 77 24 83 11.

Cyberspace

Net-surfers can log in to **www.crt-auvergne.com;** the regional tourist office site has information on ski resorts and conditions. Another site for information and reservations is **www.skifrance.fr,** including all the latest updates on snow conditions in French resorts (some sites also list available accommodation). www.super-besse.com offers the possibility of visualising the resort's weather conditions in real time via several webcams.

Scaling a frozen waterfall, Sancy

S. Sauvignier/MICHELIN

HANG-GLIDING AND PARAGLIDING

The Auvergne mountains and the Massif du Mézenc in the Ardèche offer exceptional opportunities practising hang-gliding and paragliding.

Ligue Auvergne de vol libre, 4 chemin des Garennes, 63960 Veyre-Monton, ☎ 04 73 69 72 00.

École Ailes Libres Auvergne Limousin, 63730 Les Martres de Veyre, ☎ 04 73 39 72 72 or 06 87 79 42 74. Departures are from the Camping de La Font Bleix.

Archipel Volcans, route de Clermont, 63122 Laschamps, ☎ 04 73 62 15 15; www.archipel-volcans.com; other facilities include hot-air ballooning, rambling, snowshoeing, mountain biking etc.

Quatre Vents, rue de la Tonne à Montrodeix, 63870 Orcines, ☎ 04 73 62 29 30; flight over the Chaîne des Puys or the Sancy mountain.range

Para l'Aile, 13 rue des Alouettes, 63800 Cournon-d'Auvergne, ☎ 04 73 84 45 00 or 06 80 08 25 41.

Vol Can, Centre Espace Volcan, Route du Col de Moreno, Laschamps, 63122 St-Genès-Champanelle, ☎ 04 73 62 26 00; www.espacevolcan.fr.

Mont-Dore Parapente, Club de Parapente du Mont Dore, contact the tourist office.

Delta Auvergne, La Fougedoire, 63600 Ambert, ☎ 04 73 82 91 41 or 06 80 40 07 00; www.delta-auvergne.com.

Barbule, École ardéchoise de parapente, 07140 Les Vans, ☎ 04 75 39 36 67; www.parapente-fr.com/barbule.

Acro d'Aile, Association de parapente; contact M. Jobard, ☎ 06 88 16 82 57.

CYCLING AND MOUNTAIN BIKING

Tourist offices should be able to provide lists of local firms which hire bicycles and mountain bikes *(vélos tout terrain,* or VTT). Some SNCF stations organise bike rentals, and mountain bikes can be hired in season from information points within the Pilat park. A leaflet giving details is available from railway stations. Local tourist offices often have details of suggested cycle and mountain bike routes. Useful information can be obtained from the **Fédération Française de Cyclotourisme,** 12 rue Louis-Bertrand, 94200 Ivry-sur-Seine, ☎ 01 56 20 88 88; www.ffct.org. You can also apply to the **Fédération Française de Cyclisme,** 5 rue de Rome, 93561 Rosny-sous-Bois Cedex, ☎ 01 49 35 69 24; www.ffc.fr. This organisation publishes an official guide listing 45 000km/28 000mi of marked mountain-bike tracks.

RIDING TOURS

For information about riding holidays, contact the **Comité national de tourisme équestre,** 9 boulevard Macdonald 75019 Paris, ☎ 01 53 26 15 50, which publishes the annual handbook *Cheval Nature, l'Officiel du tourisme équestre en France,* giving details of selected riding stables and equestrian establishments throughout France. At regional level, contact:

Association régionale du tourisme équestre d'Auvergne (ARTE), Roland Renaglia, 63420 Apchat, ☎ 04 73 71 84 30.

Comité regional des sports équestres d'Auvergne, 46 boulevard Pasteur, 63000 Clermont-Ferrand, ☎ 04 73 34 86 06.

Association Rhône-Alpes pour le tourisme équestre, Maison du tourisme, 14 rue de la République, BP 227, 38019 Grenoble Cedex, ☎ 04 76 44 56 18.

GOLF

For locations, addresses and telephone numbers of golf courses in France, consult the map *Golfs, Les Parcours Français* published by Éditions Plein-Sud based on Michelin map 989.

Fédération française de golf, 68 rue Anatole-France, 92309 Levallois-Perret Cedex, ☎ 01 41 49 77 00; www.ffgolf.org.

EXPLORING CAVES

Comité départemental de spéléologie, route d'Enval, 63200 St-Genès-l'Enfant, ☎ 04 73 38 71 29.

KARTING

Commission régionale de karting, 15 rue Cheval, 63100 Clermont-Ferrand, ☎ 04 73 23 35 26.

Kartingliss, 11 rue Louis-Blériot, 63800 Cournon-d'Auvergne, ☎ 04 73 84 27 41; www.kartingliss.fr.

Concept Kart Indoor, 98 avenue de Chazeuil, 03150 Varennes-sur-Allier, ☎ 04 70 45 61 61.

Activities for Children Kids

This region of France has a lot to offer children from having fun with water in amusement parks such as the Parc aquatique d'Ambert (☎ 04 73 82 14 23), the Centre aquatique de Chamalières (☎ 04 73 29 78 78) or Iloa in Thiers (☎ 04 73 80 14 90 or 04 73 80 88 80) to visiting zoos, châteaux, museums and sights of special interest. ὀ *See also Tourist trains and Eco-tourism.*
Throughout the *Discovering the Sights* section of the guide, sights of particular interest to children are indicated with a Kids symbol. Some attractions may offer discount fees for children.

Spas

There are many spa resorts in the region: Bourbon-l'Archambault, La Bourboule, Châteauneuf-les-Bains, Châtelguyon, Chaudes-Aigues, Le Mont-Dore, Montrond-les-Bains, Néris-les-Bains, Neyrac-les-Bains, Royat-Chamalières, St-Laurent-les-Bains, St-Nectaire, Vals-les-Bains, Vichy. You can obtain brochures and information by contacting the following:

Chaîne thermale du soleil, 32 avenue de l'Opéra, 75002 Paris, ☎ 01 44 71 37 00; www.sante-eau.com.

Union Nationale des Établissements Thermaux, 1 rue Cels, 75014 Paris, ☎ 01 53 91 05 75; www.france-thermale.org.

Auvergne thermale, 8 avenue Anatole-France, 63130 Royat, ☎ 04 73 34 72 80.

Calendar of Events

JANUARY

Villefranche-sur-Saône
Fête des Conscrits. ☎ 04 74 07 27 40; www.villefranche.net

FEBRUARY

Clermont-Ferrand
International Short-Film Festival. ☎ 04 73 91 65 73
Le Mont Dore - La Bourboule
Festival of Jazz.
☎ 04 73 65 20 21 (Mont Dore)
☎ 04 73 65 57 71 (La Bourboule)
www.sancy-snowjazz.com

MARCH

Clermont-Ferrand
"Vidéoformes": International video and multimedia art festival. ☎ 04 73 17 02 17
Auvergne
"Chamineige": trek across the Cévennes from La Margeride to Mont Aigoual, on cross-country

skis, mountain bikes and on foot.
☎ 04 73 31 20 32.

MARCH

Lyon
International Fair. ☎ 04 72 22 33 37

MAUNDY THURSDAY

Le Puy-en-Velay
Torchlight procession of the White
Penitents in hooded robes in the
streets around the cathedral.
☎ 04 71 09 38 41
Saugues
Procession of the White Penitents
at nightfall.

MAY

Vichy
Une Saison en Eté: theatre, clas-
sical music, opera, variety shows
at the Vichy Opera House from
May to October. ☎ 04 70 30 50 30;
www.ville-vichy.fr
Allanche
Fete de l'Estive ☎ 04 71 20 48 43

EVE OF ASCENSION DAY

Orcival
Pilgrimage in honour of the Virgin
Mary: torchlight procession and
midnight mass.

WHITSUN

Lyon
International French Bowls Tournament (Tournoi Bouliste).
☎ 04 78 37 16 10

SUNDAY FOLLOWING 15 MAY

Clermont-Ferrand
Feast of Our Lady of the Port ending with an afternoon procession
through the old town.

FRENCH MOTHERS' DAY WEEKEND (LAST SUNDAY IN MAY) – ON EVEN YEARS

Villerest
Medieval Festival: procession and
tour of ramparts. ☎ 04 77 69 69 67

JUNE

Clermont-Ferrand
Medieval Festival in Montferrand.
☎ 04 73 23 19 29
Vic-le-Comte
Celtrad: Celtic music festival. ☎ 04
73 69 02 12

FRIDAY NEAREST TO 24 JUNE

Villefranche-sur-Saône
Midsummer Night: bonfires, singers, illuminations. ☎ 04 74 65 04 48

JULY

Forez
Concerts of classical music in
churches and castles of the Forez
region. ☎ 04 73 51 55 67
Auvergne
Thermathlon du Sancy: fun trek
along the Route des Villes d'Eaux
of the Massif Central (moun-
tain biking, hiking, canoeing,
archery…). ☎ 04 73 31 20 32
Montélimar
Festival "Voix et Guitares du
Monde" and international guitar
competition. ☎ 04 75 00 77 55;
www.festivalvoixetguitares.com
Orcines
Open Golf des Volcans: International golf championship (last
week of the month). ☎ 04 73 62 15
51. www.golfdesvolcans.com
Issoire
International Folklore Festival.
☎ 04 73 89 92 85
Ambert
Festival de Folklore ☎ 04 73 82 14
49. www.livradoue-dansaire.com
Royat
Festival VOLCADIVA - song festival,
concerts and recitals ☎ 04 73 29
74 70. www.volcadiva.mp3.ms

Vollore
  Festival des Concerts de Vollore
  - classical music, jazz and 'musique
  tzigane' ☎ 04 73 51 55 67.
  www.letransfo.fr

Le Puy-en-Velay
  Festival de Musiques Vocales
  ☎ 06 72 58 27 67

Gannat
  Cultures du Monde: world folklore
  festival. ☎ 04 70 90 12 67.
  www.gannat.com

JULY-AUGUST

Saint-Agrève (grange de Clavières)
  International Art Festival (music,
  art photography, painting).
  ☎ 04 75 30 22 43

AUGUST

Le Puy-en-Velay
  Marian Festival: procession in honour of Our Lady of Le Puy. ☎ 04 71
  09 38 41. www.ot-lepuyenvelay.fr

La Font-Sainte, Cheylade
  Pilgrimage of young shepherds
  who gather for a procession and
  the "shepherds' meal".

La Chaise-Dieu
  International Music Festival. ☎ 04
  71 09 48 28. www.chaise-dieu.com

Aurillac
  International Street Theatre Festival. ☎ 04 71 45 47 45.
  www.aurillac.net

St-Pourçain-sur-Sioule
  Wine Festival. ☎ 04 70 45 32 73

Mont Brouilly
  Wine-producers' pilgrimage to
  Brouilly Chapel. ☎ 04 74 66 82 19

SEPTEMBER

Ravel
  Pottery market (3rd weekend).
  ☎ 04 73 68 44 74

SEPTEMBER TO DECEMBER

**Beaujolais, Coteaux du Rhône and
  du Forez**
  Grape Harvest and Wine Festivals
  in the wine-growing regions.

Street theatre festival in Aurillac

OCTOBER

Montbrison
  Fourme Cheese Festival; procession of flower-decked floats.
  ☎ 04 77 96 18 18

Clermont-Ferrand
  International Jazz Festival. ☎ 04
  73 93 70 83. www.jazzentete.com

9-11 NOVEMBER

Le Puy-en-Velay
  International Hot-Air Balloon Rally.
  ☎ 04 71 02 73 18

8 DECEMBER

Lyon
  Festival of Light. ☎ 04 72 10 30 30

Shopping

Most of the larger shops are open
Mondays to Saturdays from 9am to
6.30 or 7.30pm. Smaller, individual
shops may close for lunch. Food
shops – grocers, wine merchants and
bakeries – are generally open from
7am to 6.30 or 7.30pm; some open on
Sunday mornings. Many food shops
close between noon and 2pm and on
Mondays. Bakery and pastry shops
sometimes close on Wednesdays.
Hypermarkets usually stay open non-
stop from 9am until 9pm or even later.
People travelling to the USA cannot

import plant products or fresh food, including fruit, cheeses and nuts. It is permitted to carry tinned products or preserves.

FAIRS AND MARKETS

Traditional fairs – These offer visitors an opportunity to witness long-standing local customs; the most colourful ones are listed below.

* **Tournon-sur-Rhône,** 29 August: onion fair
* **St-Sorlin-en-Valloire,** 1st Sat in September: foal fair
* **Claveyson,** 11 November: truffle fair
* **Chénelette,** 11 November: goat and cattle fair
* **Romans-sur-Isère,** from the last Sat in September to the 1st Sun in October: Dauphiné Fair

Markets – The most important fruit and vegetable market in the Rhône Valley takes place in **Pont-de-l'Isère** daily except Sundays from May to September, on Mondays, Wednesdays and Fridays the rest of the year. Other markets in the Rhône Valley:

* **Bourg-de-Péage:** Thu morning
* **Hauterives:** Tue morning
* **Romans-sur-Isère:** Tue, Fri and Sun mornings
* **Ruoms:** Fri morning
* **St-Donat-sur-l'Herbasse:** Mon morning
* **St-Rambert-d'Albon:** Fri morning
* **Tain-l'Hermitage:** Sat
* **Les Vans:** Sat morning; a traditional handicraft market livens up the town's historic centre between 6 and 10pm on Tue in July and August.
* **Villeneuve-de-Berg:** Wed morning; activities are organised on Tue evenings throughout July and during the first fortnight of August.

LOCAL SPECIALITIES

Beaujolais and **Côtes-du-Rhône** wines go well with local cheeses such as **Picodon,** made from goat's milk, or **St-Marcellin,** made from a subtle mixture of goat's and cow's milk.

You may be tempted by a pair of fine **shoes** from Romans-sur-Isère, once the capital of the shoe industry (visit the interesting local museum), or by a hand-painted silk scarf or tie from Lyon, or even by **woollen clothes** from the local manufacture in St-Pierreville (Eyrieux Valley).

If you are looking for ideas, visit the **Marché de la Création** (painting, sculpture, pottery…) which takes place in Lyon along quai Romain Rolland on Sunday mornings or the **Marché de l'Artisanat** (handicraft) which takes place along quai Fulchiron, also on Sunday mornings.

Discounts

Significant discounts are available for senior citizens, students, young people under the age of 25, teachers, and groups for public transportation, museums and monuments and for some leisure activities such as the cinema (at certain times of day). Bring student or senior cards with you, and bring along some extra passport-size photos for discount travel cards.

The **International Student Travel Confederation** (www.isic.org), global administrator of the International Student and Teacher Identity Cards, is an association of student travel organisations around the world. ISTC members collectively negotiate benefits with airlines, governments, and providers of other goods and services for the student and teacher community, both in their own country and around the world. The non-profit association sells international ID cards for students, under 25-year-olds and teachers (who may get discounts on museum entrances, for example). The ISTC is also active in a network of international education and work exchange programmes. The corporate headquarters address is Herengracht 479, 1017 BS Amsterdam, The Netherlands ☏ 31 20 421 28 00; Fax 31 20 421 28 10.

USEFUL WORDS AND PHRASES

Here are some French words you may see on local maps or road signs

SIGHTS

abbaye	abbey
beffroi	belfry
chapelle	chapel
château	castle
cimetière	cemetery
cloître	cloisters
cour	courtyard
couvent	convent
écluse	lock (canal)
église	church
fontaine	fountain
halle	covered market
jardin	garden
mairie	town hall
maison	house
marché	market
monastère	monastery
moulin	windmill
musée	museum
parc	park
place	square
pont	bridge
port	port/harbour
porte	gateway
quai	quay
remparts	ramparts
rue	street
statue	statue
tour	tower

NATURAL SITES

abîme	chasm
aven	swallow-hole
barrage	dam
belvédère	viewpoint
cascade	waterfall
col	pass
corniche	ledge
côte	coast, hillside
forêt	forest
grotte	cave
lac	lake
plage	beach
rivière	river
ruisseau	stream
signal	beacon

source	spring
vallée	valley

Here are a few French translations for things you might need to say

SHOPPING

bank	la banque
baker's	la boulangerie
big	grand
butcher's	la boucherie
chemist's/drugstore	la pharmacie
closed	fermé
cough syrup	du sirop pour la toux
throat lozenges	des pastilles pour la gorge
entrance	l'entrée
exit	la sortie
fishmonger's	la poissonnerie
grocer's	l'épicerie
newsagent, bookshop	la librairie
open	ouvert
post office	la poste
shop	le magasin
small	petit
stamps	des timbres

ON THE ROAD

car park	le parking
driving licence	le permis de conduire
(to the) east	(à l') est
garage (for repairs)	le garage
(to the) left	(à) gauche
motorway/highway	l'autoroute
(to the) north	(au) nord
petrol/gas	l'essence
petrol/gas station	la station essence
(to the) right	(à) droite
(to the) south	(au) sud
straight ahead	tout droit
toll	le péage
traffic lights	le feu tricolore
tyre	le pneu
(to the) west	(à l') ouest

On national and departmental roads, there are often roundabouts (traffic circles) just outside the towns, which serve to slow traffic down. At a French roundabout (**rond point**), you are likely to see signs pointing to **Centre Ville** (city centre) or to other towns (the French use towns as directional indicators, rather than cardinal points). You are also likely to see a sign for **Toutes Directions** (all directions – this is often the bypass road to avoid going through the town) or **Autres Directions** (other directions – in other words, any place that isn't indicated on one of the other signs on the roundabout!).

TIME

today	aujourd'hui
tomorrow	demain
yesterday	hier
winter	hiver
spring	printemps
summer	été
autumn/fall	automne
week	semaine
Monday	lundi
Tuesday	mardi
Wednesday	mercredi
Thursday	jeudi
Friday	vendredi
Saturday	samedi
Sunday	dimanche

NUMBERS

0	zéro
1	un(e)
2	deux
3	trois
4	quatre
5	cinq
6	six
7	sept
8	huit
9	neuf
10	dix
11	onze
12	douze
13	treize
14	quatorze
15	quinze
16	seize
17	dix-sept
18	dix-huit
19	dix-neuf
20	vingt
30	trente
40	quarante
50	cinquante
60	soixante
70	soixante-dix
80	quatre-vingt
90	quatre-vingt-dix
100	cent
1000	mille

A FEW USEFUL PHRASES

Hello/good morning!	**Bonjour!**
Goodbye!	**Au revoir!**
Thank you!	**Merci!**
Excuse me	**Excusez-moi**
Yes/no	**Oui/non**
I am sorry	**Pardon**
Why?	**Pourquoi?**
When?	**Quand?**
Please	**S'il vous plaît**
Do you speak English?	**Parlez-vous anglais?**
I don't understand.	**Je ne comprends pas**
Please talk more slowly	**Parlez plus lentement, s'il vous plaît**
Where is …?	**Où est…?**
When does the … leave?	**À quelle heure part…?**
When does the … arrive?	**À quelle heure arrive…?**
When does the museum open?	**À quelle heure ouvre le musée?**
When does the film/show start?	**À quelle heure commence le film/le spectacle?**
When is breakfast served?	**À quelle heure sert-on le petit-déjeuner?**
How much does it cost?	**Combien est-ce que cela coûte?**
Where can I buy an English paper?	**Où puis-je acheter un journal en anglais?**
Where is the nearest petrol station/gas station?	**Où se trouve la station essence la plus proche?**
Where can I change traveller's cheques?	**Où puis-je échanger des traveller's cheques?**
Where are the toilets?	**Où sont les toilettes?**
Can I pay with a credit card?	**Est-ce que je peux payer avec ma carte bancaire?**

BASIC INFORMATION

Business Hours

Most of the larger shops are open Mondays to Saturdays from 9am to 6.30 or 7.30pm. Smaller, individual shops may close during the lunch hour. Food shops – grocers, wine merchants and bakeries – are generally open from 7am to 6.30 or 7.30pm; some open on Sunday mornings. Many food shops close between noon and 2pm and on Mondays. Bakery and pastry shops sometimes close on Wednesdays.

Although business hours vary from branch to branch, banks are usually open from 9am to noon and 2pm to 5pm and are closed either on Mondays or Saturdays. Banks close early on the day before a bank holiday.

Post offices open Mondays to Fridays, 8am to 7pm, Saturdays, 8am to noon. National museums and art galleries are closed on Tuesdays; municipal museums are generally closed on Mondays.

Electricity

In France the electric current is 220 volts. Circular two-pin plugs are the rule. Adapters and converters (for hairdryers, for example) should be bought before you leave home; they are on sale in most airports. If you have a rechargeable device (video camera, portable computer, battery recharger), read the instructions carefully or contact the manufacturer or retailer. Sometimes these items only require a plug adapter, in other cases you must use a voltage converter as well or risk ruining your device.

Mail

Smaller branch post offices often close at lunchtime between noon and 2pm and in the afternoon at 4pm.
Postage via air mail to

UK: letter (20g) 0.60€
North America: letter (20g) 1.00€
Australia and NZ: letter (20g) 1.00€

Stamps are also available from newsagents and tobacconists.
Stamp collectors should ask for *timbres de collection* in any post office.
Poste Restante (General Delivery) mail should be addressed as follows: Name, Poste Restante, Poste Centrale, post code of the *département* followed by town name, France. The Michelin Guide France gives local post codes.

Medical Emergencies

  See Health in Know Before You Go.

Money

There are no restrictions on the amount of currency visitors can take into France. Visitors carrying a lot of cash are advised to complete a currency declaration form on arrival, because there are restrictions on currency export.

BANKS

Although business hours vary from branch to branch, banks are usually open from 9am to noon and 2pm to 5pm and are closed either on Mondays or Saturdays. Banks close early on the day before a bank holiday. A passport is necessary as identification when cashing travellers cheques in banks. Commission charges vary and hotels usually charge more than banks for cashing cheques.

One of the most economical ways to use your money in France is by using **ATM machines** to get cash directly from your bank account (with a debit card) or to use your credit card to get a cash advance. Be sure to remember your PIN number, you will need it to use cash dispensers and to pay with

Notes and Coins

The euro banknotes were designed by Robert Kalinan, an Austrian artist. His designs were inspired by the theme "Ages and styles of European Architecture". Windows and gateways feature on the front of the banknotes, bridges feature on the reverse, symbolising the European spirit of openness and co-operation. The images are stylised representations of the typical architectural style of each period, rather than specific structures.

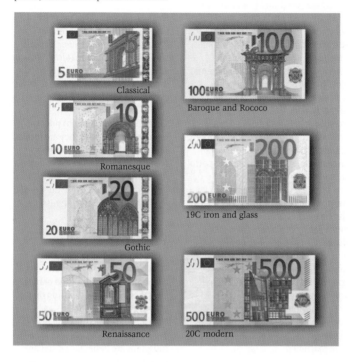

Classical

Baroque and Rococo

Romanesque

19C iron and glass

Gothic

Renaissance   20C modern

Euro coins have one face common to all 12 countries in the European single currency area or "Eurozone" (currently Austria, Belgium, Finland, France, Germany, Greece, Ireland, Italy, Luxembourg, The Netherlands, Portugal and Spain) and a reverse side specific to each country, created by their own national artists.

Euro banknotes look the same throughout the Eurozone. All Euro banknotes and coins can be used anywhere in this area.

your card in shops, restaurants etc. Code pads are numeric; use a telephone pad to translate a letter code into numbers. Pin numbers have 4 digits in France; inquire with the issuing company or bank if the code you usually use is longer. Visa is the most widely accepted credit card, followed by Mastercard; other cards, credit and debit (Diners Club, Plus, Cirrus etc) are also accepted in some cash machines. American Express is more often accepted in premium establishments. Most places post signs indicating which card they accept; if you don't see such a sign and want to pay with a card, ask before ordering or making a selection. Cards are widely accepted in shops, hypermarkets, hotels and restaurants, at tollbooths and in petrol stations.

Before you leave home, check with the bank that issued your card for emergency replacement procedures. Carry your card number and emergency phone numbers separate from your wallet and handbag; leave a copy of this information with someone you can easily reach. If your card is lost or stolen while you are in France, call one of the following 24-hour hotlines: These numbers are also listed at most ATM machines.

American Express ☎ 01 47 77 72 00	
Visa ☎ 0 800 901 179	
MasterCard/Eurocard ☎ 0 800 901 387	
Diners Club ☎ 0 810 314 519	

You must report any loss or theft of credit cards or travellers cheques to the local police who will issue you with a certificate (useful proof to show the issuing company).

PRICES AND TIPS

Since a service charge is automatically included in the prices of meals and accommodation in France, it is not necessary to tip in restaurants and hotels. However, if the service in a restaurant is especially good or if you have enjoyed a fine meal, an extra tip (this is the *pourboire,* rather than the *service)* will be appreciated. Usually 2 to 4€ is enough, but if the bill is big (a large party or a luxury restaurant), it is not uncommon to leave 7 to 8€ or more.

Restaurants usually charge for meals in two ways: a menu that is a fixed-price menu with 2 or 3 courses, sometimes a small jug (*pichet*) of wine, all for a stated price, or à la carte, the more expensive way, with each course ordered separately.

Cafés have very different prices, depending on where they are located. The price of a drink or a coffee is cheaper if you stand at the counter (*comptoir*) than if you sit down (*salle*) and sometimes it is even more expensive if you sit outdoors (*terrasse*).

Public Holidays

Public services, museums and other monuments may be closed or may vary their hours of admission on the following public holidays:
National museums and art galleries are closed on Tuesdays; municipal museums are generally closed on Mondays. In addition to the usual

1 January	New Year's Day (*Jour de l'An*)
	Easter Day and Easter Monday (*Pâques*)
1 May	May Day (*Fête du Travail*)
8 May	VE Day (*Anniversaire 1945*)
Thurs 40 days after Easter	Ascension Day (*Ascension*)
7th Sun-Mon after Easter	Whit Sunday and Monday (*Pentecôte*)
14 July	France's National Day (*Fête Nationale*)
15 August	Assumption (*Assomption*)
1 November	All Saints' Day (*Toussaint*)
11 November	Armistice Day (*Armistice 1918*)
25 December	Christmas Day (*Noël*)

school holidays at Christmas and in the spring and summer, there are long mid-term breaks (10 days to a fortnight) in February and early November.

Taxes

There is a Value Added Tax in France *(TVA)* ranging from 5.5% to 19.6% on almost every purchase. However, non-European visitors who spend more than 175€ (figure subject to change) in any one participating store can get the VAT amount refunded. Usually, you fill out a form at the store, showing your passport. Upon leaving the country, you submit all forms to customs for approval (they may want to see the goods, so if possible don't pack them in checked luggage). The refund is usually paid directly into your bank or credit card account, or it can be sent by mail. Big department stores that cater to tourists provide special services to help you; be sure to mention that you plan to seek a refund before you pay for goods (no refund is possible for tax on services). If you are visiting two or more countries within the European Union, you submit the forms only on departure from the last EU country. The refund is worth while for those visitors who would like to buy fashions, furniture or other fairly expensive items, but remember, the minimum amount must be spent in a single shop (though not necessarily on the same day).

Telephone

Most public phones in France use pre-paid phone cards *(télécartes)*, rather than coins. Some telephone booths accept credit cards (Visa, Mastercard/Eurocard). *Télécartes* (50 or 120 units) can be bought in post offices, branches of France Télécom, *bureaux de tabac* (cafés that sell cigarettes) and newsagents and can be used to make calls in France and abroad. Calls can be received at phone boxes where the blue bell sign is shown; the phone will

Emergency numbers	
Police:	17
SAMU (Paramedics):	15
Fire (Pompiers):	18
European emergency call:	112

not ring, so keep your eye on the little message screen.

NATIONAL CALLS

French telephone numbers have 10 digits. Paris and Paris region numbers begin with 01; 02 in north-west France; 03 in north-east France; 04 in south-east France and Corsica; 05 in south-west France.

INTERNATIONAL CALLS

To call France from abroad, dial the country code (33) + 9-digit number (omit the initial 0). When calling abroad from France dial 00, then dial the country code followed by the area code and number of your correspondent.

International dialling codes (00 + code):

Australia	☎ 61
New Zealand	☎ 64
Canada	☎ 1
United Kingdom	☎ 44
Eire	☎ 353
United States	☎ 1

International Information: 32 12
International operator: 31 23
Local directory assistance: 12
Toll-free numbers in France begin with 0 800.

AT&T	☎ 0-800 99 00 11
Sprint	☎ 0-800 99 00 87
Canada Direct	☎ 0-800 99 00 16

Minitel – France Télécom operates a system offering directory enquiries (free of charge up to 3min), travel and entertainment reservations, and other services (cost per minute varies). These small computer-like terminals can be found in some post offices, hotels and France Télécom agencies and in many French homes. 3614 PAGES E is the code for **directory assistance in English:** turn on the unit, dial 3614, hit the connexion button when you get the tone, type in "PAGES E", and follow the instructions on the screen.

CELLULAR PHONES

In France these have numbers which begin with 06. Two-watt (lighter, shorter reach) and eight-watt models are on the market, using the Orange (France Télécom) or SFR networks. *Mobicartes* are prepaid phone cards that fit into mobile units. Cell phone rentals (delivery or airport pick-up provided):

A.L.T. Rent A Phone	☎ 01 48 00 06 06, E-mail altlocjve.fr
Rent a Cell Express	☎ 01 53 93 78 00, Fax 01 53 93 78 09
Ellinas Phone Rental	☎ 01 47 20 70 00

Time

France is 1hr ahead of Greenwich Mean Time (GMT). France goes on daylight-saving time from the last Sunday in March to the last Sunday in October.

In France "am" and "pm" are not used but the 24-hour clock is widely applied.

Australia and New Zealand are not observing daylight saving time (DST) at the moment.

When it is **noon in France,** it is
3am in Los Angeles
6am in New York
11am in Dublin
11am in London
7pm in Perth (6pm in summer)
9pm in Sydney (8pm in summer
11pm in Auckland (10pm in summer)

Conversion tables

Weights and measures

1 kilogram (kg)	2.2 pounds (lb)	2.2 pounds
1 metric ton (tn)	1.1 tons	1.1 tons

to convert kilograms to pounds, multiply by 2.2

1 litre (l)	2.1 pints (pt)	1.8 pints
1 litre	0.3 gallon (gal)	0.2 gallon

to convert litres to gallons, multiply by 0.26 (US) or 0.22 (UK)

1 hectare (ha)	2.5 acres	2.5 acres
1 square kilometre (km²)	0.4 square miles (sq mi)	0.4 square miles

to convert hectares to acres, multiply by 2.4

1centimetre (cm)	0.4 inches (in)	0.4 inches
1 metre (m)	3.3 feet (ft) - 39.4 inches - 1.1 yards (yd)	
1 kilometre (km)	0.6 miles (mi)	0.6 miles

to convert metres to feet, multiply by 3.28, kilometres to miles, multiply by 0.6

Clothing

Women								Men
	35	4	2½	40	7½	7		
	36	5	3½	41	8½	8		
	37	6	4½	42	9½	9		
Shoes	38	7	5½	43	10½	10	Shoes	
	39	8	6½	44	11½	11		
	40	9	7½	45	12½	12		
	41	10	8½	46	13½	13		
	36	4	8	46	36	36		
	38	6	10	48	38	38		
Dresses &	40	8	12	50	40	40	Suits	
Suits	42	12	14	52	42	42		
	44	14	16	54	44	44		
	46	16	18	56	46	48		
	36	08	30	37	14½	14,5		
	38	10	32	38	15	15		
Blouses &	40	12	14	39	15½	15½	Shirts	
sweaters	42	14	36	40	15¾	15¾		
	44	16	38	41	16	16		
	46	18	40	42	16½	16½		

Sizes often vary depending on the designer. These equivalents are given for guidance only.

Speed

kph	10	30	50	70	80	90	100	110	120	130
mph	6	19	31	43	50	56	62	68	75	81

Temperature

Celsius (°C)	0°	5°	10°	15°	20°	25°	30°	40°	60°	80°	100°
Fahrenheit (°F)	32°	41°	50°	59°	68°	77°	86°	104°	140°	176°	212°

To convert Celsius into Fahrenheit, multiply °C by 9, divide by 5, and add 32.
To convert Fahrenheit into Celsius, subtract 32 from °F, multiply by 5, and divide by 9.

Côte-Rôtie vineyards
J. Damase/MICHELIN

NATURE

The name **Auvergne** conjures up a vision of a superb natural environment of outstanding beauty, a rugged landscape of mountain ranges and volcanoes, and lakes and springs in the heart of France. The area has been less accessible from the rest of the country since time immemorial because of a lack of roads or railways. The local people are proud and austere, and agriculture remains a primary industry.

The **Rhône Valley**, on the other hand, is long and wide. It is an important through route for road and rail, a melting pot of different cultures and an area at the forefront of industrial progress, which seems destined to play an increasingly important role within Europe in the future. The region is dominated by Lyon, the second largest city in France, which has the lively cultural life of any major conurbation, with museums, a new opera house and a long-standing tradition of good food.

Rhône Valley

THE RHÔNE CORRIDOR

La Dombes – This is a clay plateau dotted with lakes which ends in the fairly sheer **"côtières"** of the river Saône to the west and the Rhône to the south. In the north, the plateau runs into Bresse. The waters of the melting glacier in the Rhône Valley dug shallow dips into the surface of the land and left moraines, an accumulation of debris swept along by the glacier, on the edge of the dips. It is on these **poypes** or slight rises that the villages were built. The **Dombes** is now a charming area of tranquil countryside, with lines of trees, countless birds, and calm lakes reflecting the sky above.

Lower Dauphiné

The countryside in Lower Dauphiné is a succession of stony plateaux, plains and hills.
The Île Crémieu is a limestone plateau separated from the Jura to the north by the Rhône and to the west by an unusual cliff. The water that infiltrated the soil created a series of caves, the best-known of which are the Grottes de la Balme.
The **Balmes area** west of Vienne is partly covered in vineyards. It consists of granite and shale hills separated from Mont Pilat by the Rhône. It extends into the **Terres Froides plateau** which is slashed into strips by narrow valleys filled with fields of vegetables.
The **Bonnevaux and Chambaran plateaux** are vast expanses of woodland stretching south from Vienne and almost totally devoid of human habitation.
The wide fertile **Bièvre and Valloire plains** specialise in cereal crops. They indicate the course once followed by the Isère but abandoned after the ice had receded.
The **Isère Valley** itself opens out onto the Valence plateau; its well-cultivated terraces are covered with magnificent walnut groves.

The Valence and Tricastin areas

From Tain to the Donzère gorge, the Rhône Valley widens to the east of the river, forming a patchwork of plains until it reaches the foothills of the Préalpes.
The **Valence plain** consists of a series of alluvial terraces built up in steps. Its irrigated fields and its climate are a foretaste of the south of France and the Mediterranean. It was here that the "Tree of Gold," the mulberry, was first planted in the 17C and provided the local inhabitants with a reasonable living from the cultivation of silkworms. Nowadays, the many orchards have maintained the old-fashioned appearance of the countryside where hedgerows abounded.
The **Montélimar basin,** south of the Cruas gorge, is similar to but narrower than the Valence plain; olive trees grow on the south-facing slopes.

Suspension bridge over the Rhône at Tournon

The **Tricastin area,** crossed by the River Lauzon and River Lez, is a succession of arid hills covered with vineyards and olive trees. Its old villages perched on defensive sites form remarkable look-out posts. That flat irrigated land is divided into small fields protected from the wind by rows of cypress trees.

THE EDGE OF THE MASSIF CENTRAL

The Massif Central ends to the east in a crystalline scarp slope high above the Rhône Valley. It is a formidable precipice consisting of a mountain range that was broken down, raised up then overturned by the after-effects of Alpine folding. Since the Tertiary Era, it has been severely eroded by the rivers that dig deep into it, forming narrow gorges.

The Beaujolais region

To the north, the upper Beaujolais is a mountainous zone of mainly granite soil thrown up during the Primary Era. Tributaries of the Saône run down its steep slopes from west to east.

The Lower Beaujolais, to the south, is formed of sedimentary soils which were broken up during the upheavals of the Secondary Era. These soil types include a limestone which is almost ochre in colour which has earned the area in which it is found the nickname Land of Golden Stone. The landscape is one of gently rolling hills, none of which reaches more than 650m/2 133ft above sea level. Economically, there is a clear demarcation of this region east to west, between the escarpment *(La Côte)* overlooking the Saône Valley in the east, which is the wine-producing region, and the hills *(La Montagne)* or hinterland to the west, in which forests, crop-farming and industry predominate.

The Lyonnais area

Set between the St-Étienne basin and the city of Lyon, the plateau is dotted with high grassy hills, pine forests, beech woods and orchards. The Mont-d'Or is a rugged area (highest peak: Mont Verdun, altitude 625m/2 031ft). The Lyonnais area owes its uniform appearance to the industries that have existed here for centuries. It ends in the Fourvière hill, the superb promontory that stands high above the confluence of the Saône and Rhône and the vast city of Lyon.

Forez and Roannais

In the **Forez mountains,** fields and meadows cover the slopes up to an altitude of 1 000m/3 250ft. Above them are carpets of beech and pine forests, providing the raw material for a large number of sawmills. In summer, animals are taken up for the season to graze on the scrubby mountain tops (on the land called the Hautes Chaumes) rising to the Pierre-sur-Haute moors. At the foot of the mountains is the somewhat waterlogged Forez plain crossed by the River Loire; it was silted up by alluvium in the Tertiary Era. This is dotted with volcanic hillocks where castle and church ruins can be found. The **Roanne basin** is a fertile rural area specialising in animal husbandry and is overlooked, to the west, by the vine-covered slopes of the Madeleine mountain range.

Mont Pilat and the St-Étienne basin

Mont Pilat forms a forest-clad pyramid that has something of a mountainous air about it, rising above the surrounding dales; at the Crêt de la Perdrix, it reaches an altitude of 1 432m/4 654ft. Its peaks are topped with granite boulders known as *chirats* which form superb observation platforms, especially on the east side overlooking the Rhône Valley and Lower Dauphiné some 1 200m/3 900ft below. The St-Étienne basin at the foot of the mountain follows the outline of the almond-shaped coalfield that stretches from the Loire to the Rhône. It corresponds to a concave fold in the carboniferous layers formed at the end of the Primary Era. The basin contains a string of factories, a stark contrast to the pastures on the slopes of Mont Pilat and the Lyonnais mountain range.

The Vivarais area

This forms the largest part of the eastern edge of the Massif Central. Its huge basalt-lava flows running down from the volcanoes in the Velay area, its shale ridges, and the widespread erosion of its limestone make this a landscape full of strange natural features that are a constant source of surprise and amazement.

The **Upper Vivarais** stretches from Mont Pilat and the Velay area to the Rhône Valley. People in the dark, austere countryside in Les Boutières, where the gullies are deep and narrow, earn a living from cattle farming and cutting timber in the pine forests. Further downhill, nearer the banks of the Rhône, there are fruit trees and vineyards. The Annonay plateau to the north is a terrace overlooking the Rhône plain.

The **Vivarais cévenol** (part of the Vivarais lying within the Cévennes range) runs

from the Upper Allier Valley to the Aubenas basin. To the west, the "uplands" are strongly characterised by the volcanoes in the Velay area. They are covered in

pines, beech trees and meadows. To the east, the land consists of shale, forming narrow elongated ridges *(serres)* with steeply sloping sides that separate the

deep valleys in what is a complex landscape.

From Lablachère and Privas to the Rhône Valley, the **Lower Vivarais** is

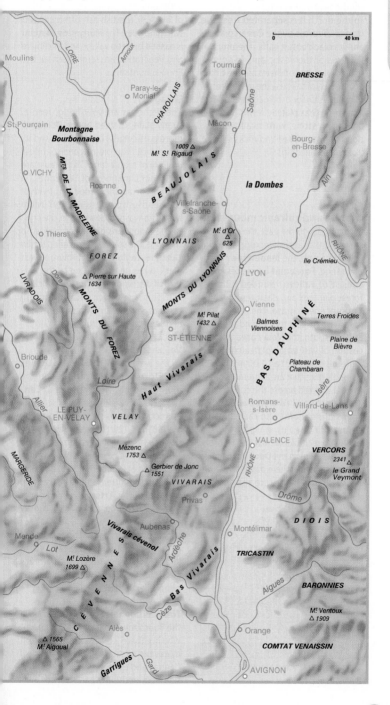

a limestone area with a succession of basins and plateaux in which scrub, olive trees, almond trees, blackberry bushes and vines provide a foretaste of a more southerly environment.

To the north it is separated from the **Upper Vivarais** by the Coiron plateau and its black basalt cliffs. The unusual features of the vast plains *(planèzes)* grazed by flocks of sheep are the **dikes** and **necks** (pinnacles), the most famous of which is the one in Rochemaure. The limestone Gras plateau forms a stretch of whitish stone, with swallowholes, deep narrow gullies and rocks shaped like ruined buildings.

Auvergne

Granite and volcanic mountains

In the region to the east, the climate is hard and the landscape rugged. From north to south, the **Madeleine** mountain range, **Forez and Livradois areas** consist of valleys, rounded hilltops, forest plateaux and pastures on which flocks of sheep graze. The area is covered with forests that provide timber. Further south, the **Velay area** is a succession of vast basalt plateaux lying at altitudes of more than 1 000m/3 250ft beneath skies that are a foretaste of the Riviera. Dotted across the countryside are **outcrops of rock** formed by lava. Crops are generally so rare that the basin around Le Puy, which is irrigated by the Loire, looks almost like an oasis. The mountains in the **Devès area** form one vast plateau where basalt lava flows are covered with pasture and fields of

barley or lentils. Along the watershed between the Loire and Allier basins are deep lakes which fill volcanic craters. The *planèze* (sloping plateau) is dotted with some 150 cinder cones consisting of black or reddish ash often capped with pine trees. The **Margeride plateau** is gashed by deep valleys and its climate and vegetation are reminiscent of the Forez mountains.

Limagnes

The *limagnes* are low-lying, fertile, sunny plains drained by the Dore and, more particularly, by the Allier and its tributaries. The plains consist almost entirely of arable land. To the east are the "poor Limagnes" or "Varennes," a hilly area of marshes, woodland, fields of crops and lush pastures where alluvium has been washed down from the crystalline mountains of the Forez area. To the west, the soil in the so-called fertile Limagnes region is dark brown, almost black. It has been enriched by the mixture of decomposed lava and volcanic ash. This is very rich land, producing tobacco, wheat, sugar beet, vegetable and seed crops and fruit.

Volcanic uplands

To the west of the region, the **Dômes** and **Dore** mountain ranges and the mountains in the **Cézallier** and **Cantal** areas form a striking landscape of extinct volcanoes rising to an altitude of 1 885m/6 126ft at the highest peak, the Puy de Sancy. Around the Puy de Dôme, Puy Mary, Puy de Sancy, La Bourboule and St-Nectaire, forests, woods and pastures alternate with lakes and waterfalls. The **Artense,** which backs onto the Dore mountain range, is a rocky plateau worn away by glaciers; it now provides grazing land for sheep and cattle. The cultivated areas represent land that has been slowly and painfully clawed back from the moors by the few people living there.

The Bourbonnais area – The scenery in the Bourbonnais area is like the people who live there – calm and temperate. It marks the northern edge of the Massif Central, and the gently rolling countryside is covered with a patchwork of small

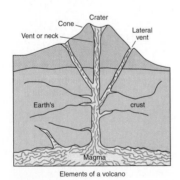

Elements of a volcano

Elements of a volcano

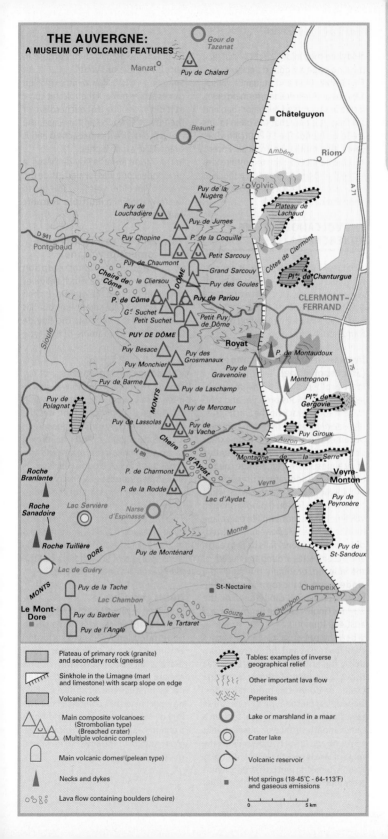

THE AUVERGNE:
A MUSEUM OF VOLCANIC FEATURES

Gour de Tazenat

Manzat

Puy de Chalard

Châtelguyon

Beaunit

Riom

Ambène

Puy de la Nugère

Volvic

Plateau de Lachaud

A 71

Puy de Louchadière

Puy de Jumes

Puy Chopine

P. de la Coquille

Puy de Chaumont

Petit Sarcouy

Côtes de Clermont

le Cliersou

DÔME

Grand Sarcouy

Pl^au de Chanturgue

Cheire de Côme

Puy des Goules

CLERMONT-FERRAND

Pontgibaud

D 941

P. de Côme

Puy de Pariou

G^d Suchet
Petit Suchet

Petit Puy de Dôme

PUY DE DÔME

Royat

P. de Montaudoux

Sioule

Puy Besace

Puy des Grosmanaux

Puy Monchier

Puy de Gravenoire

Montrognon

A 75

Puy de Barme

MONTS

Puy de Laschamp

Pl^au de Gergovie

Puy de Polagnat

Puy de Mercœur

Puy de Lassolas

Puy de la Vache

Puy Giroux

Cheire

Auzon

Montagne de la Serre

Roche Branlante

d'Aydat

P. de Charmont

Veyre

Veyre-Monton

Roche Sanadoire

N 89

P. de la Rodde

Lac d'Aydat

Puy de Peyronère

Roche Tuilière

Lac Servière

Narse d'Espinasse

Monne

Puy de St-Sandoux

DORE

Lac de Guéry

Puy de Monténard

St-Nectaire

Champeix

MONTS

Puy de la Tache

Lac Chambon

Gouze de Chambon

Le Mont-Dore

Puy du Barbier

Puy de l'Angle

le Tartaret

	Plateau of primary rock (granite) and secondary rock (gneiss)			Tables: examples of inverse geographical relief
	Sinkhole in the Limagne (marl and limestone) with scarp slope on edge			Other important lava flow
	Volcanic rock			Peperites
	Main composite volcanoes: (Strombolian type) (Breached crater) (Multiple volcanic complex)			Lake or marshland in a maar
	Main volcanic domes (pelean type)			Crater lake
	Necks and dykes			Volcanic reservoir
	Lava flow containing boulders (cheire)			Hot springs (18-45°C - 64-113°F) and gaseous emissions

0   5 km

fields hemmed in by hedges which give the landscape a wooded appearance. The Besbre, Cher and Aumance valleys are wide and well drained, forming open, fertile areas crossed by major road and rail links. It is here that the main towns are to be found. The St-Pourçain vineyards, the impressive Tronçais Forest, and the conifers on the mountainsides in the Bourbonnais area add a touch of variety to a landscape that is otherwise dominated by grassland.

THE VOLCANOES OF THE AUVERGNE

What makes the Auvergne so unusual is the presence of a large number of volcanoes which, although extinct, are a major feature of the landscape. They vary in appearance depending on their formation, type and age.

Inverse composite volcanoes (Stromboli-type)

In the depths of the earth, magma is subjected to enormous pressure and infiltrates through cracks in the Earth's crust (👆 *see diagram*). When the pressure becomes too great, there is an explosion accompanied by a sudden eruption of incandescent matter. A huge column of gas, smoke and vapour rises into the sky, spreading out like a parasol, while the matter in fusion (spindle-shaped volcanic bombs, gas-swollen pozzolana looking like a very lightweight, dark reddish-coloured stone) falls back to earth and accumulates around the mouth of the volcano, gradually building up a **cinder cone.** At the top is a **crater.** The most typical of all can be seen on the Puy des Goules and the Pariou.
#0304004thmg00

When the pressure inside the Earth's crust decreases and the matter thrown up by the eruption is more fluid, lava flows are created, running from the crater or down the mountainsides. Depending on the type of rock, these **lava flows** *(cheires)* may cool to form a fairly smooth surface or, alternatively, be rough and full of boulders. When the mass of lava is very thick, it contracts as it cools, breaking into prisms or columns (very much like organ pipes, hence their French name *orgues*) such as those in Bort-les-Orgues or Murat.

Sometimes a lava flow or an explosion carries away a piece of the volcanic cone, as it did in the Puy de Louchardière or the Puy de la Vache; in this case, the crater is described as **breached** and is shaped like a half-funnel.

In the Pariou and the Puy de Dôme, a new cinder cone was formed inside the crater of an older volcano. This led to the formation of a **multiple volcanic complex.**

Volcanic domes (Mount Pelée-type composite volcano)

Sometimes, the volcanic eruption throws up a lava paste which solidifies upon contact with the ground. It then forms a dome with steep sides but has no crater at the summit. The Puy de Dôme is a good example of this type of volcano.

Volcanoes with planèzes

When the Cantal volcano was active more than 9 million years ago, it would have been a formidable sight: it had a circumference of 60km/37mi and rose to an altitude of 3 000m/9 750ft. Formed by a succession of layers of lava and ash, it was dissected by erosion which cut its sides into **planèzes** (sloping plateaus) with a tip pointing towards the centre of the volcano.

The Dore mountain range, which is younger than the Cantal volcano (2-3.5 million years), also consists of successions of layers of lava and ash but the *planèzes* are less well-developed.

Necks and dikes

Scattered across the Limagne in total disorder are volcanic systems which penetrated, and were consolidated within, a mass of sedimentary rock that has since been worn away. All that remain are a few spurs of rock called necks or ridges known as dikes, which no longer have their covering of soil. The Puy de Monton near Veyre, and Montrognon near Ceyrat, are typical necks. Montaudoux to the south of Royat is a good example of a dike.

J. Damase/MICHELIN

Lac de Servière

Tables

Ancient lava flows originally spread out across the valleys, protecting the underlying soil from the erosion that cleared the area between rivers and caused an inversion relief. These lava flows now jut out above the surrounding countryside, forming tables such as the Gergovie and Polignac plateaux, the Montagne de la Serre etc.

Lahars and Peperites

Volcanic eruptions are often accompanied by torrential rain and enormous emissions of water vapour. They then cause *lahars* (an Indonesian word) or flows of mud and boulders which progress at astonishing speed, destroying everything in their path. The Pardines plateau near Issoire owes its existence to this type of phenomenon. South of Clermont-Ferrand, some of the small plateaux and hillocks in the Limagne area consist of peperites, rock formations created by underwater volcanic eruptions. Their "peppery" appearance is due to the mixing of lava and sediment from the bed of the lake.

Lakes of volcanic origin

The volcanoes have given the landscape of the Auvergne its very particular relief and the magnificent stretches of water that reflect the surrounding countryside. Many of the lakes in the Auvergne owe their existence to volcanic eruptions. In some places, a lava flow closed off a valley, holding back the waters of a river upstream; examples of this are the Aydat and Guéry lakes (the latter was also formed by the action of glaciers). In other places, a volcano erupted in the middle of a valley, blocking it with its cone, as was the case in Chambon and Montcineyre. Still elsewhere, subsidence caused by underground volcanic activity was filled with run-off water (Lake Chauvet). *Maars* are lakes which were formed in craters (Lake Servière).

The volcanoes of the Auvergne at present

The volcanoes are now more or less well preserved depending on their age and the hardness of their rocks. The **Dômes** mountain range, with its 80 volcanoes that became extinct around 7 000 years ago, has a strikingly fresh-looking relief. The **Dore** mountain range is older and has a more fragmented appearance. The lava flows on Sancy, Aiguiller and Banne d'Ordanche are heaped up to a height of more than 1 000m/3 280ft but water, snow and glaciers have worn away the sides. With its 60km/37mi circumference and altitude of 3 000m/9 750ft, the **Cantal volcano** was even more impressive in its day. The landscapes visible today reveal only a fraction of the original; it is difficult to imagine the initial size of the range.

Mineral spring (iron), Vallée de Chaudefour

Auvergne's Mineral Springs

Whether naturally carbonated or still, water is one of the main sources of wealth in the Auvergne and it has been exploited here since the days of Antiquity. The *département* of Puy-de-Dôme and the Vichy basin alone account for one-third of all French mineral springs.

Origins

Ordinary springs are created by water that seeps into permeable land and eventually meets an impermeable layer down which it runs. When the impermeable layer rises to the surface, the water follows suit. **Mineral springs** are either springs of infiltrated water or springs rising from the depths of the Earth's crust. In this case, substances or gases that have therapeutic properties are added naturally to the water as it flows underground. The adjective **"thermal"** is used more particularly to describe springs with water at a temperature of at least 35°C/95°F when it comes out of the ground; Vichy water, for instance has a temperature of 66°C/150°F and the water in Chaudes-Aigues rises to as much as 82°C/179.6°F.

Resurgent springs

The water in these springs only flows at regular intervals, for example every eight hours. The column of water rising from the depths of the Earth is sub-jected, at some point along its course, to a very high increase in temperature. The steam produced at this point acquires sufficient pressure to project the upper part of the column of water above the surface of the ground. The projection is interrupted for as long as it takes to heat a second column, then the whole process begins again. This type of spring can be found in Bellerive, near Vichy. Thermal springs are located in places where the Earth's crust is weak, for instance in areas of volcanic rock that have been dislocated by fissuring.

Properties of thermal springs

When thermal water rises to the surface, it gives off a very low level of radioactivity which stimulates the human organism. However, the water is very unstable and it deteriorates as soon as it comes out of the ground. This is why, for therapeutic purposes, it is so important to take full advantage of the water where it rises to the surface and why spa towns were built. The composition of the water varies greatly, depending on the type of rocks through which it has passed and the volcanic fissuring that created the spring. People visit Vichy to treat disorders of the digestive system, Royat for heart and arterial disease, Châtelguyon for intestinal problems, Le Mont-Dore for asthma, La Bourboule for respiratory diseases, St-Nectaire for liver complaints, Chaudes-Aigues for rheumatism etc.

Spa towns lost some of their popularity in the aftermath of the Second World War but are now enjoying a revival. The medical aspect of "taking the waters" has been maintained but people also come to keep fit, stay slim, and enjoy a round of golf, a day at the races, or a night at the opera, almost as they did in the 19C.

Mineral water, a boom industry

The French drink more mineral water than any other nationality. This is why the Auvergne is so popular – it has everything they could ask for.

Bottling has required the development of modern techniques, for water is one of the most difficult commodities to package. It is, though, a source of employment for small towns such as Volvic which has become famous not only in France but far beyond its borders.

Flora and Fauna

RHÔNE VALLEY

The Rhône Valley is not only a major road and rail route and intersection of geographical areas, it also combines differing natural environments which have resulted in a huge variety of flora and fauna. Almost 3 000 species of plant, some 60 wild mammals and more than 200 birds have been observed in the forests, plains and lakes. The Pilat Regional Nature Park alone boasts some 90 species of bird.

Flora

In addition to the plants ordinarily found in the centre of France, the area also has mountain plants which have come down from the Alps and the Jura, and Mediterranean plants which have spread up from the south. Because of this, it is possible to find, in the mountains in the Forez area for example, gentians, monkshood, or the superb martagon (or Turk's Cap) lily. This is a very rare plant, a hardy annual growing to a height of 30-80cm/12-30in or even, on occasions, to more than 1.10m/3ft 6in, with clusters of reddish-orange flowers spotted with black growing on a tall stem. Nor is it unusual, on the lower plateaux and hillsides in the Saône and Rhône valleys, to see evergreen oaks, Montpellier aphyllantes, lavender, purple orchids or other varieties of orchid growing in the month of April on dry grasslands.

Fauna

Just like the flora, Mediterranean species of fauna are found in the Rhône Valley as the northernmost habitats are sited in the Rhône basin. Among them is the Provençal field mouse, a tiny rodent, and the mouse-eared bat. Deer are very adaptable creatures and can be seen throughout the region in forested areas. The Rhône Valley is a major point along the migratory routes followed by **birds** flying between Northern Europe and the Mediterranean basin. The banks of the Saône and Rhône are full of larks, buntings, quail, plovers and curlews. It is the **Dombes,** though, that boasts the largest numbers of birds, because of its many lakes. In addition to the numerous web-footed friends, partridges, herons, and song thrushes, birds from all over the world can be seen at the bird sanctuary in Villars-les-Dombes where toucans and parrots rub shoulders with rare species such as the black-tailed godwit, or the corncrake, which is an endangered species.

The wels, the largest freshwater fish

Before it was introduced into France in the second half of the 19C by fish farmers, this species of large catfish was found mainly in the waters of the Caspian Sea and the River Danube. Those living in the Rhône and Saône can grow to a length of 3m/10ft and weigh some 100kg/220lb (14st). It feeds on bream, moorhens, ducks and rats; to kill its prey, it grabs their paws and drags them down to the river-bed until they drown. This little aquatic monster is however short-sighted and dislikes the light, so it waits until nightfall before seeking to catch its food; it is therefore unlikely to be seen, except perhaps on a dinner plate as it is becoming increasingly popular with fishermen.

Beavers of the Île du Beurre

The beaver is a hard-working animal, continuously cutting, felling and nibbling branches of trees in order to build dams and dikes which it cements with mud to create a lodge. These days, though, lodges are no longer built because beavers have changed their habits and they now live in burrows dug into the river banks. They are particularly fond of the banks of the Île du Beurre (in old French, *beurre* meant beaver). This island to the south of Lyon is the last place in France in which beavers live in the wild and, because of this, it has been covered by a preservation order since 1988.

AUVERGNE

The Auvergne has all sorts of landscapes and soils, each with its own particular flora and fauna. Forests, peat bogs and salmon are just some of its many characteristics.

Vegetation at different altitudes

The **forests** in the Auvergne grow in very specific tiers. The hillsides are covered in oak woods with pedunculate oaks on clay soil and sessile oaks on well-drained ground. On the mountains, there are beeches and pines although the conifers predominate only in cold, damp areas (Bois Noirs, Dore mountain range). The beech is the commonest tree in the forests of the Auvergne and can grow to a height of 30-40m/97-130ft after 150 to 300 years. It is easily recognisable for its smooth, grey bark and leaf colouring – red in winter and soft green in spring. Natural pine groves cover the driest hillsides like those in Upper Loire.

The **moors** of the Margeride area often mark the abandonment of pastures or farmland. In fact, moorland precedes the stage at which land is overrun by forest. Ferns, calluna, gorse, myrtle and redcurrants grow here. Gradually, however, the forest takes over, with birches, hazelnut trees and pines being the first trees to appear.

The **mountain pastures** above an altitude of 1 000m/3 280ft provide a natural environment for species which have been observed here for many centuries, such as the three-coloured violet, the scented wild pansy which blooms from April to October, the red-purple saw-wort which is used to produce a yellow dye, and the globe flower, a large, golden flower which seems to be closed in upon itself. The gentian, a delightful yellow flower, is used to make the liqueur that bears its name; other species of gentian produce blue flowers.

The **subalpine stage** of vegetation begins at altitudes of more than 1 400-1 500m/4 600-5 000ft; plant life varies depending on the exposure of the slopes. Calluna and myrtle grow on moorland, and ground-cover plants on grassland, rocks and scree. It is here, from May to July, that the spring anemone blooms, a rare plant with delicately indented leaves and flowers with huge white petals tinged with purple. Mountain arnica, a downy plant with yellow flowers, is used to make creams that prevent bruising. The blue carnation, which is actually a very unusual bluish green in colour, can be seen in tufts only a few inches high on the peaks in the Dore and Cantal mountain ranges.

Peat bogs

Peat bogs are natural environments created by an accumulation of organic matter in damp areas. There are a number of features which lead to the formation

Gentian on the shores of Lac de Guéry

of peat bogs, such as a break in a slope along the course of streams, or cold springs as in the mountains of Cantal. They also tend to form on valley floors, along meanders and streams like the ones in the Upper Forez area, in the bases of volcanic craters that have been rendered impermeable by clay deposits, or overdeepening caused by glacial erosion as was the case in the Margeride, Forez and Artense regions. *Maars* (lakes in the bottom of craters) can also be overrun by vegetation. Examples of this can be seen in the Devès range and the Velay area.

Peat is formed from a range of spongy mosses called sphagnum, which ensure photosynthesis and store water. These mosses can retain up to 30 times their dry weight of water. The bogs are exceptional because some of them have survived for more than 5 000 years and have developed a unique form of plant and animal life.

The herbaceous willow is the smallest tree in the world, the lycopod has remained unchanged for 300 million years, and the dwarf birch is typical of more northerly climes.

There are countless carnivorous plants which have adapted to this environment because they suffer from nitrogen deficiency; they capture small insects by secreting a sticky substance. Two such plants are sundew and drosera which produce droplets that act as multiple mirrors reflecting the light.

The animals are also extraordinary. There are flies and mosquitoes which, because they have had to adapt to cold environments in which they cannot fly, have no wings. Common frogs live on land and only enter the water to spawn. The meadow pipit is a northern bird that is a frequent sight in peat bogs.

The odyssey of the salmon

The life cycle of the salmon is surprising. Born in a river, it stays in the area where it was born for two years (at this stage, it is known as a smelt or parr) before letting the river carry it down to the sea tail-first, during the period known as downstream migration. At this stage its scales turn white.

Certain salmon travel as far as the seas off Greenland. Here, they grow and acquire their more familiar appearance – it is the shrimps on which they feed that give them their "salmon pink" colouring.

Two years later the salmon swims up the Loire to return to its spawning grounds in Allier or Upper Loire, in particular around Brioude which is famous as the "salmon's paradise"; the trip can take several months. It is said that salmon return to the place of their own birth thanks to an olfactory memory and the return is known as **homing.** When the fish arrives, it is exhausted and very thin, because it has had to overcome a number of obstacles, quite apart from the fact that it does not feed in rivers. The female burrows into the gravel on the river bed with her tail and lays the eggs that the male covers with his milt. The salmon then usually die. Sometimes, however, a salmon will make the journey twice.

In the Auvergne, this extraordinary fish is the subject of many a tale or anecdote. One of them recounts how, at the turn of the 19C when the railway line was being built through the Allier gorge, the workmen went on strike because they had nothing to eat – nothing, that is, but salmon!

REGIONAL NATURE PARKS

The Auvergne-Rhône Valley region includes four regional nature parks, described in the Sights section of this guide (see AUBENAS, Monts du FOREZ, Le PILAT and Parc naturel regional des VOLCANS D'AUVERGNE).

HISTORY

Time Line

BC PREHISTORY

7500-
2800 **Neolithic Era: Stone Age.**
The volcanoes in the Puys range cease to erupt. Farmer-stock breeders settle in the Rhône Valley and the Massif Central, leaving some 50 dolmens and 20 or more menhirs.

c 1800-
700 **Bronze Age.** Human settlements become denser and the Rhône Valley is the major amber and tin route.
The Celts settle in Gaul. The Helvians settle on the right bank of the Rhône, the Allobroges on the left and the Arverni in the Auvergne.

Arverni domination of the Auvergne
– The main expansion of the Celtic people occurred during the 5C BC, probably as a result of the push southwards by Germanic tribes fleeing the increasingly rigorous climate of Northern Europe. Little is known about them for they had no written literature and they were divided into several different peoples in accordance with criteria that have remained mysterious. What is known beyond a shadow of a doubt is that the Celts in Gaul, such as the **Allobroges** in Lugdunum (Lyon), were subject to the authority of the **Arverni** in the Massif Central. They traded with their own coinage. In order to ensure the submission of other peoples, their sovereigns acted as demagogues throughout the region, in much the same way as Greek tyrants. King Luern, who reigned in the 2C, was famous for his gifts of gold. Rome, worried by his power, launched a military campaign against his son, Bituit, who died in battle with Roman forces near Bollène in 121 BC. The Roman legions settled in Vienne, the capital of the Allobroges. The Arverni monarchy was

no more. The great Celtic families took power and, thereafter, were forced to share it with the Aedui of Burgundy who were allied to Rome. In 52 BC, however, in one last attempt to revive Arverni

Vercingetorix

J. Damase/MICHELIN

authority, **Vercingetorix**, head of the Gauls' resistance to Caesar, recruited an army and defeated the Romans at **Gergovia**. Later, though, besieged in Alésia, he surrendered in order to save his people. This marked the end of Arverni independence.

43 Lyon founded soon after Caesar's conquest of Gaul by one of his lieutenants, Munatius Plancus. Roman settlers arrive and build houses on the hillsides above the banks of the Saône.

27 Lyon, capital of the Gauls (Aquitaine, Lyon area, Belgium); the Rome and Augustus Altar is built on the hill at La Croix-Rousse.

AD

1C The beginnings of Christianity. Preachers come to spread the gospel in the Auvergne and the Rhône Valley.

177 Marcus Aurelius instigates persecution. Christians are martyred in Lyon.

280 Emperor Probus removes the monopoly on sales of wine in Gaul previously enjoyed by the people of Lyon. This marks the start of Lyon's decline and, during the reign of Diocletian (284-305), the city is nothing more than the capital of the Lyon province.

406 After the invasion of the Vandals, the emperor introduces a federation of barbarian states in Gaul with the Visigoths in the Auvergne and the Burgundians on the left bank of the Rhône.

Sidonius Apollinaris stands up to the Visigoths – Sidonius Apollinaris was born in Lyon in AD 432 to a wealthy family of senators; later, his father-in-law, Avitus, was one of the last emperors of the Western world. Sidonius remained in Rome after the death of Avitus in AD 456 and wrote tributes to the emperors. His poetry pleased them and when he returned to the Auvergne, he was elected Bishop of Clermont. Although initially not a very committed Christian, Sidonius realised that the Church was, in those troubled times, the only solidly based institution in the Roman world. Like other aristocrats, he made it the final bastion of the Roman way of life. Euric, King of the Visigoths, who already owned a large part of Aquitaine, threatened the Auvergne. Sidonius headed the resistance and withstood a siege lasting several years in the walled town of Clermont. Eventually the province was transferred to the barbarians in exchange for Provence and Sidonius was sent into exile. Twenty years later, the province passed into the hands of the Franks after the Battle of Vouillé.

5C-9C Founding of the first abbeys – in Lyon, Vienne, Romans, in the Vivarais, the Lyonnais and the Velay.

761-767 Pepin the Short attempts to gain power over the noblemen of the Auvergne by means of military expeditions.

800 Charlemagne is crowned.

843 Treaty of Verdun. Charlemagne's empire is divided into three kingdoms (West, Central, and East). The Auvergne is ruled by Charles the Bald (West Francia); the Rhône Valley by Lothair I (Lotharingia).

9C-10C Power is actually held by the many castle owners, all of them difficult to control. Safe on their feudal mottes, they war against their neighbours, devastate the countryside, attack churches and pillage monasteries.

951 The first pilgrimage to Santiago de Compostela starts from Le Puy-en-Velay.

999 Gerbert, a former monk from Aurillac, is elected to the papacy as Sylvester II. He is the first French Pope and he occupies the papal throne at the end of the first millennium.

1095 Pope Urban II preaches the First Crusade in Clermont. The wave of popular faith aroused by his call arrives just at the right time to channel the warring energies of the turbulent feudal lords.

The Pope has a chance to gauge the vitality of the Church in the Auvergne. The Gregorian Reform purges the parishes by removing the power of the layman. The influence of a few of the great monasteries begins to spread. The counts of Albon, who come from Vienne, extend their territory; their lands, stretching from the Rhône to the Alps, become known as Dauphiné.

11C-12C Founding of new abbeys in the Vivarais area.

Royal intervention in the Auvergne – Divided between their position as vassals to the King of France and their allegiance to the Duke of Aquitaine, the great lords of the Auvergne failed to come to an agreement that would enable them to set up their own State. These feuding lords of mixed loyalties governed large estates with no clearly defined borders, which eventually enabled the sovereign to annex sections of the region little by little over the 12C and 13C; first Riom and the Limagne, then Montferrand and the area subsequently known as Dauphiné and finally Lower Auvergne.

13C-14C The development of towns leads to the granting of numerous municipal charters. Royal authority gains a foothold and is strengthened in Auvergne and the Rhône Valley:
-1210: Philip Augustus annexes the Auvergne to his kingdom.
-1292: Nomination of a royal "guardian" in Lyon.
-1307: The so-called "Philippine" conventions strengthen Philip the Fair's hold on Lyon.
-1308: The Bishop of Viviers recognises royal sovereignty.
-1349: Dauphiné is annexed to France as the States of Dauphiné.

1229 The Treaty of Paris ends the Albigensian Crusade and the influence of the counts of Toulouse in the Vivarais area.

1241-71 The Auvergne is part of the appanage with which Alphonse of Poitiers, St Louis' brother, is endowed. He dies childless and the region is returned to the royal estate.

1262 Marriage of St Louis' son, Philip, to Isabella of Aragon in Clermont.

1337-
1453 Hundred Years War.

1348 The Black Death ravages France.

1360 The Auvergne becomes a duchy and is given to John the Good's son, Jean, Duc de Berry.

15C The first firearms are made in St-Étienne.

1416-25 The Auvergne and the Bourbonnais region are united for 100 years under the authority of the House of Bourbon.

1419 The first fairs in Lyon, instituted by the heir to the throne, the future Charles VII, make the town one of the largest warehouses in the world.

1450 Charles VII grants Lyon a monopoly on the sale of silk throughout the kingdom.

Auvergne, held in appanage by Jean de Berry – The sovereign's hold on the Auvergne took it out of the sphere of influence of Southern France. It was divided in two with the creation of a bailiwick in the mountainous region corresponding to Upper Auvergne. The Church proceeded to follow suit, setting up the bishopric of St-Flour. While the Bourbons continued to increase their power, with a barony that was raised to a duchy in 1327 (the Bourbonnais area), the Auvergne was granted in appanage to Jean, Duc de Berry in 1360. War and epidemics combined with the heavy fiscal pressures imposed by a spendthrift lord. In order to circumvent the rules on land held in appanage, Jean de Berry transferred the Duchy of Auvergne to his son-in-law, the Duke of Bourbon, an action which the monarchy, by then in a weakened position, was obliged to accept formally in 1425. The Bourbons were then at the head of a huge feudal State which continued to exist until the Constable of Bourbon's treachery in 1527.

1473 The first book is printed in Lyon by Barthélemy Buyer.

1494 The start of the Italian Campaign. Charles VIII brings his court to Lyon. The bank in Lyon enjoys a period of rapid development.

1527 After the Constable of Bourbon's treachery, the Auvergne and the Bourbonnais region are confiscated by François I.

1528 The Reformation is preached in Annonay.

1536 A silk-making factory is opened in Lyon.

1546 The first Reform Church is opened in the Lyon area.

1562	Protestants led by Baron des Adrets ransack the Rhône Valley and Forez area.
1572	After the St Bartholomew's Day Massacre, the Auvergne enters a period of chaos. Bloody battles are won in turn by the Huguenots, the royal army, and members of the Catholic League.
1598	Promulgation of the Edict of Nantes which grants freedom of conscience to the Protestants along with limited rights to hold church services, and gives them political equality.

The Reformation and the Wars of Religion – In 1525, the Reformation spread right across the Cévennes thanks to travelling Bible salesmen and merchants. It also spread along the Rhône Valley, through the Vivarais area and along the Durance Valley. Printers in Lyon produced and distributed the doctrines preached in Basle and Geneva over a very wide area. The Auvergne, perhaps partially because of the mountainous lie of the land, was little concerned by the Reformed Religion, except in Issoire and the papermaking areas of Ambert and Aurillac.

The preachers began their work in Annonay. The local people were attracted to Calvinist ideas which complied with their taste for independence. The concepts were spread by craftsmen in the villages, carders and silk merchants travelling to Montpellier via Le Puy-en-Velay and Alès. The ideas were also spread by shoemakers whose shops, like the tanneries, often served as centres of propaganda. By 1550-60, the Reformed Religion had conquered the locality. The property belonging to the Catholic Church was sold and, by the end of the century, Mass was generally no longer being celebrated.

However, Catholics and Protestants were soon to become locked in conflict. The eight wars fought over a period of almost three decades coincided with a period of political instability. Interspersed with ceasefires and edicts aimed at pacifying both sides, they never totally appeased the people's passion. In 1562 the murder of a group of Protestants in Champagne led to the Huguenot uprising, and Catholic resistance was led by the Parliament of Toulouse. The conflict was particularly bitter in the Dauphiné and Vivarais regions where the warring factions laid waste to entire towns and committed massacres. The Baron des Adrets captured the main towns in Dauphiné, where he was the leader of the Huguenot movement, before moving on to decimate the Rhône Valley with his troops and marching to the Forez area where he took Montbrison. After the tragic St Bartholomew's Day massacre (24th August 1572), the conflict took on a more markedly political character and, paradoxically, it led to forms of cooperation between Huguenots and Catholics (united under the banner of the **Catholic League**, who sought political as much as religious power) in the face of royal

S. Van Pouke / Musée de Tournon

Cardinal François de Tournon

authority and power.
Peace was not re-established until the Edict of Nantes was signed.

1629	Siege and destruction of Privas by the king's troops. Richelieu orders the dismantling of fortresses.
17C	Counter-Reformation: founding of a large number of convents.
1643	Accession of Louis XIV.
1685	Revocation of the Edict of Nantes. The dragoons sweep

1704 First edition of the Trévoux Dictionary by the Jesuits in reaction against the Age of Enlightenment.

1783 First public ascent by the Montgolfier brothers in a hot-air balloon.

Auvergne's finest hours – Although the aristocracy in the Auvergne was careful not to become involved in the Fronde Revolt against the monarchy, the king brought the hand of royal justice to bear on the region in order to ensure its submission for all time.

In September 1665 Louis XIV sent commissioners vested with full judicial authority to the Auvergne, in order to provide an exemplary display of royal authority. The return to law and order included the repression of the often tyrannical behaviour and excessive violence used by the local nobility to stamp out revolt among the country people. In the Auvergne as elsewhere, the rural uprisings had resulted from the constraints imposed by a central authority that had not yet acquired its finality.

The Court heard 1 360 cases and passed 692 sentences, of which 450 were handed down by default for the suspects had fled as soon as the first of the 23 executions was carried out. Thereafter, offenders were sentenced in their absence and effigies were hung in their place. This simulation of justice "without any spilling of blood" **(Esprit Fléchier)** nevertheless allowed for the return of a large amount of property and the destruction of castles that had been spared by Richelieu 40 years earlier. The authority of the State and royal justice could be felt by all throughout France. The magistrates also tried to remedy abuses of the system by drawing up regulations on statute labour, weights and measures. The **Intendants** began to check the titles held by the nobility and laid the foundations for a fiscal reform in order to share the burden of taxation more fairly.

through the Vivarais area, ill-treating and massacring the people.

1789 Start of the French Revolution. 14th July: capture of the Bastille Prison. France is subdivided into *départements*.

1790 The first town council is set up in Lyon.

1793 A Resistance movement is set up in Lyon to fight the Convention: the town is subject to vicious reprisals as a result.

In the Auvergne, **Georges Couthon**, a member of the Committee of Public Salvation, orders the demolition of bell-towers in the Auvergne on grounds of equality. Non-juring priests seek refuge in the mountains.

Early 19C Mining begins in the coalfields around St-Étienne.

1804 The Jacquard loom is invented.

1820 Silk production becomes a boom industry in the Vivarais area.

1825 The Seguin brothers build the first suspension bridge over the Rhône.

1832 The St-Étienne-Lyon railway line is inaugurated.

Barbier and Daubrée open a factory in Clermont and begin working with rubber; this is the embryo of the future Michelin group.

1831-34 The silk workers revolt in Lyon.

1850 Pebrine, a disease that attacks silkworms, causes a crisis in the silk industry. There is a sudden sharp drop in the number of silkworm farms.

1855 The railway is extended as far as Clermont.

1870-71 The Fall of the Second Empire; the Third Republic is founded.

1880 Phylloxera destroys half of the vineyards in Ardèche.

Orchards are planted in the Rhône and Eyrieux valleys.

1889 Phylloxera devastates the vineyards in the Limagne.

Late 19C The chemical industry is set up in Lyon and metalworking

J. Damase/MICHELIN

The Lumière brothers

enjoys a period of expansion.

1895   The cinematograph is invented by the Lumière brothers in Lyon.

The birth of the cinematograph – In 1882 a photographer from Besançon named Antoine Lumière opened a workshop in a shed in Lyon and began to produce dry silver bromine plates to a formula that he had invented himself. Within four years he had sold over one million plates under the brand name *Étiquette bleue*. The former photographer's two sons, Louis and Auguste **Lumière**, worked with their father on a new device; the equipment, invented in 1895 and exhibited in Lyon in June 1896, was to be known as the cinematograph.

The general public, after initial indifference, rushed to see the first 10 films – short farces whose humour has withstood the test of time. The first film, *Workers Leaving the Lumière Factory* was followed by *The Arrival of a Train in the Station, The Gardener* (including the famous scene of the gardener being doused with water from the garden hose) and *Baby Food*. The prodigious adventure of the motion picture had just begun.

1939-45   Second World War.
1940   Vichy becomes the capital of occupied France.

The Vichy government – The armistice signed in Compiègne on 22 June 1940 marked the defeat of France, which was divided into two zones – the North was occupied by Nazi Germany and the South was declared a free zone. Parliament, tolling the death knell of the Third Republic, vested all power in **Maréchal Pétain**, the victor of Verdun in 1916. The choice of a seat for the new government fell on the prosperous spa town of Vichy (⚓ *see VICHY*).

The years 1940-44 were dark days indeed. Two films about this period – *L'œil de Vichy*, directed by Claude Chabrol, and *Pétain*, directed by Jean Marboeuf – were produced in 1993 and, since the summer of 1987, there have been organised tours in Vichy to the places occupied by Pétain's government.

1942-44   Lyon is the centre of the French Resistance Movement.
1944   Battles are fought in the Rhône Valley and in the Cantal (Mont Mouchet) as part of the liberation of France. The Germans blow up the bridges over the Rhône.
1946   Founding of the Fourth Republic.
1957   The Treaty of Rome leads to the setting up of the EEC.
1958   Founding of the Fifth Republic.

1969 Georges Pompidou, who was born in Cantal, is elected President of the Republic.

1972 The Auvergne and Rhône-Alpes regions are created.

1974 Valéry Giscard d'Estaing, Mayor of Chamalières (Puy-de-Dôme), is elected President of the Republic.

1981 The first high-speed train service (TGV) is run between Paris and Lyon (journey time: 2hr 40min).

1986 **Superphénix**, Europe's first fast-breeder reactor to operate on an industrial scale, is brought into service in Creys-et-Pusignieu (Isère).

1989 Completion of the motorway link (A 71) between Clermont-Ferrand and Paris (Orléans).

1993 The EU introduces the Single Market.

1996 Lyon's hosting of the G7 summit confirms the city's international role.

2000 Clermont-Auvergne International Airport is inaugurated.

2002 Opening of **VULCANIA**, located in the heart of the Puy range, Vulcania, the European Volcano Park, plunges you deep into the world of volcanoes and the earth sciences. www.vulcania.com

2006 The La Chaise Dieu International Festival's 40th anniversary. Founded by Georges Cziffra in 1966, the La Chaise Dieu Festival is one of France's leading sacred and classical music festivals. www.chaise-dieu.com

Lyon, a centre of the Resistance Movement – Lyon, a city in the southern zone, found itself near the demarcation line after the signing of the armistice in 1940. Countless Parisians sought refuge here and initially it became the intellectual and patriotic heart of France. The city was one of the major centres for the printing of literature, tracts, posters, and journals, many of them more popular with readers than the press that supported Vichy.

Lyon was also a major centre of intelligence work through "Marco Polo," "Electra" and "Alliance" who had connections at the very core of the Vichy administration. Important Resistance actions were carried out in Lyon but they were badly organised until the arrival of **Jean Moulin**, sent by General de Gaulle; the various groups then joined together in 1943 to form the Mouvements Unis de la Résistance (Unified Resistance Movements). Moulin set up an administrative structure for the Resistance, organising services that were common to all the networks and a secret army operating in the south of France and the Rhône Valley. Georges Bidault, who took over after Moulin's arrest, created the Forces Françaises de l'Intérieur (FFI). This is why, when France was finally liberated, General de Gaulle called Lyon the "Capital of the Resistance Movement."

Famous Local Figures

THE RHÔNE VALLEY – A LAND OF INNOVATORS

Few regions in France have given the country so many scientists and engineers as the Lyonnais, Vivarais and Forez areas – the engineer Marc **Seguin** (steam boiler), the physicist André-Marie **Ampère** (electrodynamics), the physiologist Claude **Bernard**, and cinematographers the **Lumière** brothers, to name but a few.

The Montgolfier brothers and the first flight – In the last few years before the French Revolution, the brothers Joseph and Étienne de Montgolfier, descendants of one of the oldest papermaking families in Europe, became famous by successfully achieving the first flights in a hot-air balloon.

Tirelessly continuing his research into a gas that was lighter than air, Joseph completed his first successful experiment with a taffeta envelope which he filled with hot air by burning a mixture of damp straw and wool. His brother joined him in his research and, after a

*Ciselé velvet
(Lyon, Second Empire)*

*Embroidery
(France, Régence period)*

*Silk and linen brocatelle
(Lyon, 1867)*

*Silk lampas
(France, early 18C)*

*Embroidered satin
(France, late 19C)*

*Corded figured silk
(France, 18C)*

Photos Basset/Remerciements a la Banque d'Images Textiles du Musée des Tissus, Lyon

few successful attempts, one of which was carried out in the gardens of the family estate in Vidalon-les-Annonay, they triumphantly launched their first aerostat on place des Cordeliers in Annonay on 4 June 1783. It was so successful that Louis XVI asked them to repeat it in his presence, and so it was that, on 19 September of that same year, the first "manned" flight took place in Versailles, under the control of Étienne and in the presence of the amazed royal family and Court. Attached beneath the balloon was a latticework cage containing the first passengers – a cockerel, a duck and a sheep. In just a few minutes, the **Réveillon** bearing the king's cipher on a blue background rose into the air and then came to rest in Vaucresson woods.

One month later, at the Château de la Muette in Paris, Marquis d'Arlandes and Pilâtre de Rozier completed the first human flight in a hot-air balloon.

The trials and tribulations of an inventor: Jacquard and the weaving loom – Jacquard was born in Lyon in 1752. His father, a small-time figured material manufacturer, employed his son as a drawboy to work the cords that operate the complicated machinery used to form the pattern in silk. The child was in poor health and he was unable to stand the work; he was placed with a bookbinder then with a type founder. However, in a silk worker's family, leaving the trade was seen as a form of failure.

After his father's death, Jacquard tried to set up a fabric factory but his lack of commercial experience and the experiments he undertook to try and perfect the weaving of the fabric left him financially ruined. In 1793 he enlisted with a military regiment. On returning to Lyon, he worked for a manufacturer. He spent his nights working on the design of a new loom and on a machine to manufacture fishing nets. He registered his first patent in 1801. The officers of the Republic were looking for inventors and so Jacquard was brought to Paris where he earned a salary of 3 000 francs. At the newly created **Conservatoire,** he perfected a machine invented by a man from Grenoble named Vaucanson, who had already installed a new type of mill in Aubenas.

In 1804 Jacquard returned to Lyon to complete the work on the loom with which his name has remained linked ever since. In place of the ropes and pedals that required the work of six people, Jacquard substituted a simple mechanism based on perforated cards laid on the loom to define the pattern. A single worker, in place of five in earlier times, could make the most complicated fabrics as easily as plain cloth. In a town that had 20 000 looms, tens of thousands of workers found themselves under threat of losing their jobs. They immediately protested against the new loom which deprived them of work. Despite this, Jacquard succeeded in convincing them of the utility of his invention. By decreasing the production costs, it would be possible to withstand foreign competition and increase sales. Manufacturers set an example and, in 1812, several Jacquard looms were brought into service in Lyon. The experiment worked so well that the name is still in use today – the Jacquard technique is usually known in Britain as Fair Isle.

Thimonnier, the unfortunate inventor of the sewing machine – Unlike Jacquard, Thimonnier did not have the good fortune to see his invention being used in his native country. His father was a dyer from Lyon who had fled the town and its upheavals during the French Revolution. In 1795 the family settled in Amplepuis where the young Thimonnier was apprenticed to a tailor. In 1822 he left the region to set up in business as a tailor near St-Étienne. Haunted by the idea of sewing clothes mechanically, and taking inspiration from the hooks used by embroiderers in the Lyonnais mountain range, he secretly built a wooden and metal device that would produce chain stitch. This was the first sewing machine.

In order to register a patent, the inventor entered a partnership with Auguste Ferrand, a teacher at the Miners' School in St-Étienne. An application was filed on 13 April 1830 in the names of both partners. Ferrand, for his part, succeeded in interesting a man named Beaunier in the idea, an engineer who had already invented the first animal-drawn railway.

Thimonnier then left St-Étienne for Paris where the first mechanical sewing shop soon saw the light of day. There, 80 sewing machines produced goods six times quicker than manual workers, thereby arousing the hatred of Parisian tailors who feared that their profession was on the point of ruin. On the night of 20 to 21 January 1831, 200 workers employed in the sewing and tailoring business ransacked the Parisian workshop. Thimonnier was ruined and he returned to Amplepuis where, in order to feed his large family, he again began work as a tailor. In 1834 he was back in Paris but nobody was interested in mechanical sewing. Two years later, utterly destitute, he travelled south again on foot, carrying his machine on his back and using it to pay for his board and lodging on the way. In 1848, through a man named Magnin, a company from Manchester expressed an interest in his *couso-brodeur*. Worn out by 30 years of work and struggle, Thimonnier died at the age of 64 – without seeing the extraordinary success enjoyed by the sewing machine.

LEADING LIGHTS FROM THE AUVERGNE

538-594 – Gregory of Tours (born in Clermont-Ferrand), churchman and historian

938-1003 – Gerbert d'Aurillac, theologian and scholar who went on to become Pope Sylvester II

1555-1623 – Henri de La Tour d'Auvergne, Marshal of France under Henri IV and Calvinist leader

1623-1662 – Blaise Pascal (Clermont-Ferrand), academic, writer and philosopher

1652-1719 – Michel Rolle (Ambert), mathematician and author of a treaty of algebra

1757-1834 – Marquis de La Fayette (Chavaniac), general and politician

1851-1914 – Fernand Forest (Clermont-Ferrand), inventor (four-stroke engine)

1853-1929 – André Messager (Montluçon), composer

1853-1931 and 1859-1940 – André and **Édouard Michelin** (Clermont-Ferrand), industrialists (rubber tyres and tourist publications)

1884-1932 – Albert Londres (Vichy), journalist and writer

1911-1974 – Georges Pompidou, politician and President of the French Republic (1969-74)

b 1926 – Valéry Giscard d'Estaing, politician and President of the French Republic (1974-81)

ART AND CULTURE

Architecture and Art

RELIGIOUS ARCHITECTURE

VALENCE – Ground plan of St-Appollinaire Cathedral (12C)

The Romanesque cathedral in Valence has undergone many changes, and was much damaged during the Wars of Religion. Renovation and rebuilding efforts, mainly carried out in the 17C and 19C, generally respected the original plans and appearance of the cathedral.

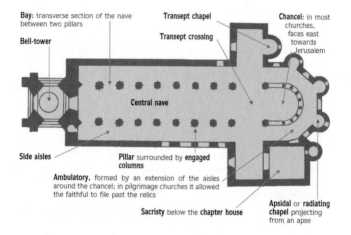

Bay: transverse section of the nave between two pillars

Bell-tower

Transept chapel

Transept crossing

Chancel: in most churches, faces east towards Jerusalem

Central nave

Side aisles

Pillar surrounded by **engaged columns**

Ambulatory, formed by an extension of the aisles around the chancel; in pilgrimage churches it allowed the faithful to file past the relics

Sacristy below the **chapter house**

Apsidal or **radiating chapel** projecting from an apse

LA GARDE-ADHÉMAR – Cross-section of St-Michel Church (12C)

Restored during the 19C, this small Romanesque church illustrates the major developments of Romanesque art in the 12C. It is one of the few churches of the period to have a double apse.

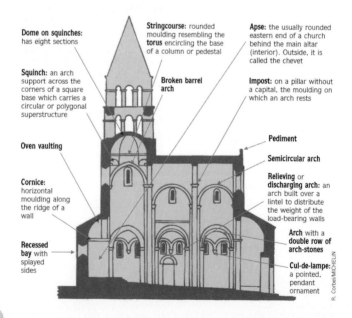

Dome on squinches: has eight sections

Squinch: an arch support across the corners of a square base which carries a circular or polygonal superstructure

Oven vaulting

Cornice: horizontal moulding along the ridge of a wall

Recessed bay with splayed sides

Stringcourse: rounded moulding resembling the **torus** encircling the base of a column or pedestal

Broken barrel arch

Apse: the usually rounded eastern end of a church behind the main altar (interior). Outside, it is called the chevet

Impost: on a pillar without a capital, the moulding on which an arch rests

Pediment

Semicircular arch

Relieving or **discharging arch:** an arch built over a lintel to distribute the weight of the load-bearing walls

Arch with a **double row of arch-stones**

Cul-de-lampe: a pointed, pendant ornament

R. Corbel/MICHELIN

ORCIVAL – Notre-Dame Basilica (12C)

Most of the churches in Auvergne are in the Romanesque style, and belong to a school of design which developed in the 11C and 12C, which has a number of unique characteristics.

Relieving or **discharging arch:** an arch built over a lintel to distribute the weight of the load-bearing walls

Two-storey, **octagonal bell-tower**

Bays: occurring in groups of two, three, four, etc

Geminated bays: occur in pairs

Rounded hip roof covering the chevet

Transept

Gable-wall

Sloping hip roof

Semicircular bay

Apsidal chapel or **radiating chapel**

Modillion: a horizontal bracket or console; here the decorative scrolling recalls wood shavings

Cornice with checkerboard pattern

Buttress: masonry structure bonded to and projecting from the wall, which gives stability

Chevet: the graceful fall of tiered roofs is the most distinctive and attractive feature of churches in Auvergne

R. Corbel/MICHELIN

CLERMONT-FERRAND – Notre-Dame-du-Port Basilica (11C and 12C)

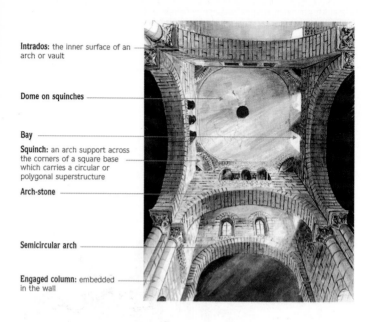

Intrados: the inner surface of an arch or vault

Dome on squinches

Bay

Squinch: an arch support across the corners of a square base which carries a circular or polygonal superstructure

Arch-stone

Semicircular arch

Engaged column: embedded in the wall

ISSOIRE – St-Austremoine Abbey (12C)

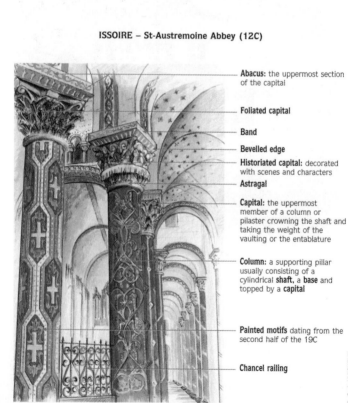

Abacus: the uppermost section of the capital

Foliated capital

Band

Bevelled edge

Historiated capital: decorated with scenes and characters

Astragal

Capital: the uppermost member of a column or pilaster crowning the shaft and taking the weight of the vaulting or the entablature

Column: a supporting pillar usually consisting of a cylindrical **shaft**, a **base** and topped by a **capital**

Painted motifs dating from the second half of the 19C

Chancel railing

R. Corbel/MICHELIN

LE PUY-EN-VELAY – Doorway of St-Michel Chapel (12C)

Seeming to rise out of the rock below it, this chapel has been called the "eighth wonder of the world". Eastern influences are apparent in the polychrome motifs and geometric designs.

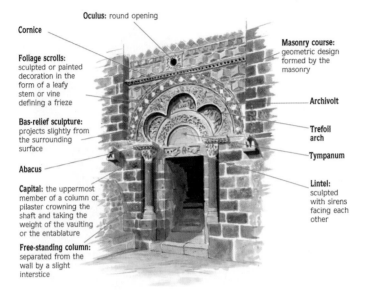

Oculus: round opening

Cornice

Foliage scrolls: sculpted or painted decoration in the form of a leafy stem or vine defining a frieze

Bas-relief sculpture: projects slightly from the surrounding surface

Abacus

Capital: the uppermost member of a column or pilaster crowning the shaft and taking the weight of the vaulting or the entablature

Free-standing column: separated from the wall by a slight interstice

Masonry course: geometric design formed by the masonry

Archivolt

Trefoil arch

Tympanum

Lintel: sculpted with sirens facing each other

CRUAS – Former Abbey (11C to 13C)

This beautiful abbey, typical of the Vivarais region, has managed to withstand the ravages of time. As research continues, new discoveries have brought to light architectural marvels from the Carolingian and Romanesque periods.

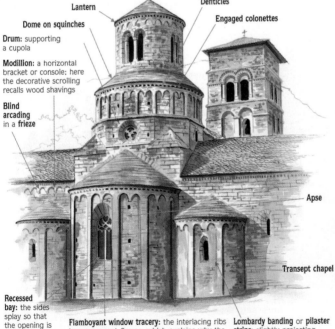

Lantern

Dome on squinches

Drum: supporting a cupola

Modillion: a horizontal bracket or console; here the decorative scrolling recalls wood shavings

Blind arcading in a **frieze**

Denticles

Engaged colonettes

Apse

Transept chapel

Recessed bay: the sides splay so that the opening is wider on one side than on the other

Flamboyant window tracery: the interlacing ribs here represent flames, which explains why the term Flamboyant was applied to Late Gothic architecture

Lombardy banding or **pilaster strips:** slightly projecting vertical bands, linked by a frieze of small arches on top

MILITARY ARCHITECTURE

TOURNEMIRE – Château d'Anjony (15C)

Pepper-pot roof

Crenel: notch between merlons on a battlemented parapet

Merlon: solid part between the indentations (embrasure or crenels) in a battlement

Watch-path

Machicolation: an overhanging, crenellated defensive structure with floor opening for dropping boiling oil, missiles, etc on attackers

Curtain wall: an enclosing wall between two towers

Corner tower

ST-POURÇAIN-SUR-BESBRE
Fortified gate of Thoury Château (15C)

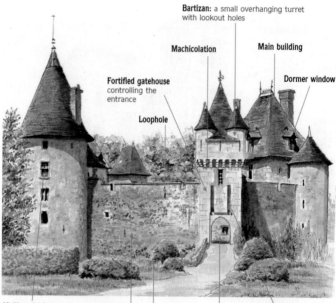

Bartizan: a small overhanging turret with lookout holes

Machicolation

Main building

Fortified gatehouse controlling the entrance

Dormer window

Loophole

Mullioned window: the mullions are the vertical parts of the tracery, separating and supporting the window

Curtain wall

Slots for **swipe beams** (wooden beams to which the chains raising the drawbridge were attached)

Moat: wide ditch filled with water, protecting the curtain wall and towers

Entrance gate

R. Corbel/MICHELIN

CIVIL ARCHITECTURE

MARCY-L'ÉTOILE – Château de Lacroix-Laval (17C – 18C)

Renovated under the guidance of Soufflot in the 18C, this château was ransacked from cellar to attic during the French Revolution. It has since been restored several times, but has kept the classic façade typical of family manor houses in the 18C.

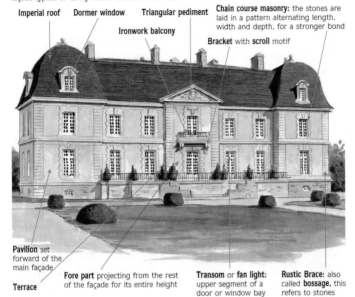

Imperial roof

Dormer window

Triangular pediment

Ironwork balcony

Chain course masonry: the stones are laid in a pattern alternating length, width and depth, for a stronger bond

Bracket with **scroll** motif

Pavilion set forward of the main façade

Terrace

Fore part projecting from the rest of the façade for its entire height

Transom or **fan light:** upper segment of a door or window bay

Rustic Brace: also called **bossage**, this refers to stones which project beyond the mortar joint

INDUSTRIAL ARCHITECTURE

LYON – Halle Tony-Garnier (1914)

The covered market is a display of technical prowess: the 18000m^2/193 750sq ft area stands without interior pillars. Designed by local architect Tony Garnier, it now serves for cultural events and trade fairs, and remains a landmark of contemporary architecture.

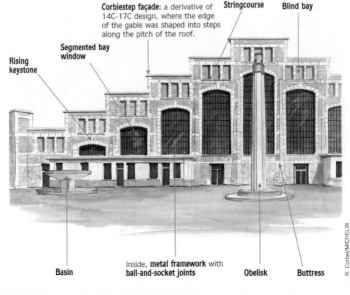

Corbiestep façade: a derivative of 14C-17C design, where the edge of the gable was shaped into steps along the pitch of the roof.

Stringcourse

Blind bay

Segmented bay window

Rising keystone

Basin

Inside, **metal framework** with **ball-and-socket joints**

Obelisk

Buttress

R. Corbel/MICHELIN

SPA-RESORT ARCHITECTURE

LE MONT-DORE – Caesar's spring gallery (1890 and 1935-38)

The design expresses the architectural eclecticism typical of spa towns. The inspiration can be traced to the Roman baths of Antiquity; the high ceilings and ornate decoration lend grandeur. The distinctive Romanesque style of Auvergne creates an atmosphere reminiscent of an opulent temple.

Transverse arch: semicircular, with **arch-stones** in an alternating white (limestone) and grey (andesite) pattern, typical of the Romanesque style in Auvergne

Cabochons in yellow glass

Entablature and **capitals** stucco moulding

Tympanum with **fresco** (Roman baths of Mont-Dore)

Coffered barrel vault

Colonnade of **engaged columns**

Grand arcade with false transom (fan light)

Claustra: a slab of stone or terracotta pierced in a geometric pattern, forming a bay

Floor laid with **tile** and **glass bricks**

Aedicula: a niche in the form of a **tabernacle**, from which Caesar's spring flows

R. Corbel/MICHELIN

ROMAN ARCHITECTURE IN THE RHÔNE VALLEY

By the 1C, the region had become the starting point for the conquest of Germany and Lyon was the capital of Gaul. In the 2C, major road building and town planning work was undertaken in Vienne and Lyon, then at the height of their power. However, the fires, pillaging and devastations by the Barbarians, coupled with the later destruction during the Middle Ages – when the ancient public buildings were used as quarries and the marble statues were used to stoke the limestone kilns – destroyed the remains of the old civilisation.

From 1922 in Vienne and 1933 in Lyon, archaeologists began to uncover a number of outstanding groups of buildings, in particular small theatres adjacent to smaller buildings or odeons. The digs are continuing today. Some of the buildings are still being unearthed and large areas remain to be explored, in particular in St-Romain-en-Gal on the right bank of the Rhône where part of a residential district has been uncovered.

Theatres

These consisted of tiers of seats ending in a colonnade known as the **cavea**, an orchestra pit, a dais used by dignitaries and a raised stage *(scena)*. The actors performed in front of a wall with doors in it through which they made their entrances. Behind the wall at the back of the stage were the richly decorated, actors' dressing rooms and the stores. Beyond that was a portico opening onto gardens where the actors walked before entering the stage. Spectators could stroll there during intervals or take shelter from the rain. The acoustics in Roman theatres are still a source of amazement, even in buildings that have been half destroyed; it is easy to imagine how perfect they must have been 2 000 years ago.

Temples

A closed sanctuary contained the effigy of a god or the emperor, and an open vestibule. They were partially or totally surrounded by a colonnade. The Temple of Augustus and Livia in Vienne is one of the best preserved anywhere.

Roman baths

Roman baths were public and free of charge. They were not only public baths but also fitness centres, meeting places and a place for games and entertainment. Romans had acquired extensive knowledge concerning water supplies and heating. Water was brought to the baths by an aqueduct, stored in tanks then piped through a system of lead and mortar ducts. Waste water was carried away through a sewage system. The water and rooms were heated by a system of hearths and hypocausts in the basement. The hot air obtained by the burning of coal and wood circulated through a conduit built into the walls. The buildings were vast, sumptuous and luxurious. There were columns and capitals decorated with vivid colours, mosaic facing on the walls, coloured marble floor and wall coverings, richly coffered ceilings, and frescoes and statues like those found in the remains of the Roman baths in Ste-Colombe near Vienne.

Amphitheatres

Shows were staged in the arena, usually oval in shape. There were fights between wild beasts or gladiators, and people sentenced to death were executed. Around the arena were tiers of seats for the audience. Lyon, the official centre for the worship of Rome in Gaul, had its own amphitheatre. It was here, in AD 177 during the reign of Marcus Aurelius, that the Christians of Lyon were martyred.

Circus

The circus attracted crowds of people who enjoyed watching chariot racing. In the middle of the track was a long rectangular construction – the **spina** – marked at each end by huge, semicircular stones. The horses and drivers wore the colours of the rival factions organising the competitions. Built partly of timber, the circus was, despite its impressive size (several hundred yards long and over 100yd wide), particularly vulnerable to destruction. Two circuses in France have been the subject of an archaeological dig – one in Arles and one in Vienne where the **pyramid** that marked the centre of the **spina** is still visible.

Aqueducts

On the plateau to the south-west of Lyon stand well-preserved sections of aqueduct (Arches de Chaponost, 🕭 *see LYON: Monts du Lyonnais)*. Aqueducts were one of the essential features of any town. The tall arches built to maintain the level of the pipes were monuments in their own right. Indeed, the aqueduct, more than any other construction, is a striking illustration of the building skills of the Romans who attached very great importance to the quality of the water supplied to their towns and cities.

Decorative arts

The large, delicately coloured mosaics found in Lyon (circus games, Bacchus etc) prove that mosaic makers were particularly active in Lyon. The medallions that decorated the sides of vases were made by potters from Lyon and Vienne who excelled in illustrations of scenes from mythology or everyday life.

RELIGIOUS ARCHITECTURE

The Romanesque period

There is no Romanesque School inherent to the Rhône Valley since the region, situated as it is at the junction of countless roads, was influenced by artists from Italy, Burgundy, Provence – and the Auvergne. In the Auvergne a Romanesque School developed which is considered one of the most unusual in the history of the architecture of the Western world, giving the churches an air of similarity that is immediately apparent. It originated in the 11C. After the great invasions and the establishment of the Capetian kingdom, the Auvergne enjoyed a period of prosperity. The local people undertook land clearance, acquiring new areas of land and instigating new building projects. In the 11C this movement was amplified by the Gregorian Reform and the desire on the part of men of the Church for independence from lay authorities. Gradually, countless churches and chapels were built across the countryside and, even today, they reveal something of the soul of the Auvergne and its people, for they are all built with an economic use of resources and an immense simplicity. This is what gives the architecture its strength.

The churches in Clermont-Ferrand (Notre-Dame-du-Port), Issoire, Orcival, St-Nectaire and St-Saturnin are just some of the finest examples of this Romanesque style in which the beauty is both austere and logical. Yet it is also worth seeking out churches that are almost forgotten because they are less well known or because they are lost in the depths of the countryside. They include treasures such as the coloured spire on St-Julien in Brioude, the frescoes in Ébreuil, the capitals in Mozac, and the domes of Notre-Dame-du-Puy which are redolent of the Orient.

An unusual school

It developed in the 11C and 12C within the large diocese of Clermont. The churches, often small but always beautifully proportioned, give an impression of being much bigger than they actually are. Paul Bourget describes the appearance of these churches, powerful and rugged as those who created them: "Seen from the east end, especially with the tight semicircle of chapels huddled up against the mass of the main building, these churches give a striking impression of aplomb and unity".

Volcanic building materials

In Limagne, arkose, a yellowish metamorphic sandstone, was used until the 13C. Volcanic lava stone was first used for bonding beneath load-bearing arches, in the upper sections of buildings which did not support the weight of the vaulting and to which they added a touch of colour. In the 13C improvements to the quality of tools made it possible to cut the hard blocks of lava stone and developments in stone-cutting techniques made it the commonest building material available.

Great churches in Lower Auvergne

The layout of the churches slowly changed to meet new needs arising out of pilgrimages. The basic layout is the one seen in Clermont Cathedral, which was consecrated in AD 946 and was the first one to have an ambulatory and radiating chapels. Today, all that remains is the crypt. Yet it took a period of trial and error (churches in Ennezat, Glaine-Montaigut) to achieve the perfection of the 12C buildings.

Exterior

West Front – Exposed to the weather and almost devoid of decoration, the west front – which includes a porch – forms a stark contrast to the east end because of its austerity. In some cases, it is topped by a central bell-tower and two side towers.

Bell-towers – Two-storey, traceried, octagonal bell-towers were a source of light, emerging from the mass of the building around the dome. They stood high above the chancel and ambulatory. In Auvergne, there are a large number of bell-cotes *(clocher à peigne)* – gable walls with openings in which the bells are hung in one or two tiers.

Side walls – The windows in the side aisles are built inside enormous load-bearing arches that support the walls. Beneath these arches, the stone often has a decorative role through its colour or layout. Above them is the line of the clerestory in which the windows are linked by arcading. A few portals include the pentagonal lintel that is particular to the Auvergne School.

East end – The magnificent layout of the various levels at the east end makes it the most beautiful and most characteristic part of the Auvergne churches. This masterpiece of austerity counter-balances the thrust from the octagonal bell-tower. It stands like a carefully combined pyramid, giving an impression of harmony and security through the perfection of each of its elements and the regularity of the design.

Nave of Notre-Dame-du-Port, Clermont-Ferrand

J. Damase/MICHELIN

Interior

The nave is often stark; the only decorative features are the capitals and they are not immediately apparent because most of these buildings are very dark. The narthex lies beyond the porch and constitutes the first span of the church. Huge arches support the gallery and the weight of the bell-tower if it has been built above the west front.

Nave and vaulting – The wide naves lined with side aisles providing extra support were designed to cater for large numbers of pilgrims. Heavy Romanesque barrel vaulting replaced roof rafters which were too susceptible to fire and which, between the 5C and 11C, led to the loss of many churches. Above the side aisles with their ribbed vaulting were vaulted galleries that were designed to provide direct support for the nave and to let light into the upper section of the church from the small windows they contained.

Chancel – This part of the church was reserved for the clergy and the celebration of Mass. By raising it up a few steps and lowering the vaulting, perspective made it appear larger than it actually was and drew attention to it. It was here that sculptors gave free rein to their talent and the beautifully designed carved capitals in the chancel are often the finest in the church.

In large churches, the chancel included a straight bay. Behind it was a semicircle around which tall columns, set out in such a way as to avoid blocking the light, extended into small raised arches forming a sort of crown. The capitals here were often the most complex and intricate in the church.

Ambulatory – In large churches, an ambulatory extended beyond the side aisles and skirted the chancel. An even number of radiating chapels formed a crown around the ambulatory so that, on major feast days, several Masses could be celebrated simultaneously. The chapels were separated from each other by windows. In churches dedicated to other saints, a side chapel was dedicated to the Blessed Virgin Mary (the Lady Chapel).

Transept and dome – The construction of the transept posed a difficult problem for architects; they had to design large ribbed vaulting capable of supporting the entire weight of the central bell-tower and which was formed by the interpenetration of the vaulting in the nave and the arms of the transept.

In Issoire and Notre-Dame-du-Port, for example, the vaulting in the arms of the transept has been built at the same height as the vaulting in the nave. Then half-barrel vaulting buttresses the upper sections, forming an initial tier leading onto the second level including the dome and supporting the bell-tower. Squinches were built in order to pass from the square layout of the transept to the dome mounted on an octagonal base.

Crypt – Beneath the chancel in large churches, there is often a crypt laid out like the church above it. The chancel in the crypt, like the one in the upper church, is flanked by an ambulatory decorated with radiating chapels. The crypt never extends westwards beyond the transept. It is used for worship of the Blessed Virgin Mary or the relics of saints.

Decorative features

Capitals – The capitals are magnificently carved with fanciful scenes. Most of them are to be found around the chancel (see above). Many artists did not merely illustrate scenes from the Bible, they introduced an entire portrait gallery of figures that were as numerous as they were varied: figures from Antiquity rub shoulders with eagles, mermaids, centaurs, minotaurs, telamones, snakes, genies, figures from the Orient, griffons and birds drinking out of a chalice. Beside them are the heroes of medieval epics, the founders of the church, knights in armour dating from the period of the First Crusade and local saints. The sculptors included animals and figures, some from a fantasy world, such as monkeys wearing chains, donkeys playing musical instruments, angels and devils. Finally, the Virtues and Vices are depicted, with a certain degree of humour, in caricatures such as the one illustrating Anger or a miser storing his money away in a pot.

Often subjects are grouped in sequences so that the entire building, or part of it, centres on a single theme. There is the sacred character of the church emphasised by an illustration of the Temple or Jerusalem the Celestial City, and there is religious symbolism, with scenes from the Old Testament paving the way for scenes from the New Testament, signs of the Zodiac etc.

Virgin Mary in Majesty, Issoire

J. Damase/MICHELIN

Statues of the Virgin Mary in Majesty and statue-reliquaries – Worship of the Blessed Virgin Mary has always been an important part of religion in the Auvergne for, in Celtic countries, the Christian religion was grafted onto worship of a mother-goddess. These statues@ are striking for their hieratic attitudes, attractive for the honesty of the faces, modelled on those of country women, and admirable for the symbolism of their long, protective hands. The best of these statues can be seen in Mozac, Notre-Dame-du-Port, Orcival and Marsat.

Statue-reliquaries are original creations from the Auvergne and they combined the artistry of the carver with the skill of the enamellers of Limoges. Together, they produced superb pieces in gold and silver ornamented with precious stones. These statues dating from the 12C represent the earliest stages of sculpture in France. The most famous are the bust of St Baudime, the arm-reliquary of St Nectaire in St-Nectaire, and the bust of St Césaire in Maurs.

The Gothic Period

Gothic architecture came from the north and took some time to spread further south. It reached Lyon in the early 13C but the Rhône Valley has none of the great churches of which Northern France is so proud and it continued to be subject to the influence of the south as is evident in the width of the buildings and the horizontal line of the roofs.

The Auvergne, strong in its own Romanesque School, resisted change for a long time. Not until the language of Northern France, *langue d'oïl,* was introduced in place of the Southern French *langue d'oc,* after the province had been conquered by Philip Augustus, did the Rayonnant Gothic style gain a foothold on the rebellious region, to the detriment of the sources of inspiration from further south which had been predominant until that time. This change of style marked the seizure of the province by the Capetians. There were, though, two main currents in the architectural style – Northern French Gothic and Languedoc Gothic.

Northern French Gothic

Clermont Cathedral, dating from the 13C and 14C, is only very vaguely reminiscent of the great buildings of the Paris basin and not until the 19C was Gothic architecture introduced into its west front and spires designed by the architect Viollet-le-Duc. Lava stone from Volvic, a building material that was too hard to be carved but which architects liked for its strength, resistance and permanence, gave the cathedral an austerity that even the sun cannot brighten up. The roofs on the chapels and side aisles consist of stone slabs forming a terrace beneath the flying buttresses, a very unusual design that was totally unknown in the north of France.

The same stylistic movement can be seen in the Ste-Chapelle in Riom, which was designed by the Dammartin brothers who had worked on the Louvre during the reign of Charles V, the Ste-Chapelle in Aigueperse and the chancel in Moulins Cathedral.

Languedoc Gothic

Characterised by a wide nave devoid of side aisles, side chapels inserted between the piers and the absence of flying buttresses, this was the commonest style in the area. The abbey church at La Chaise-Dieu, a masterpiece of monastic architecture, is a fine example, as are other churches commissioned by the mendicant orders such as the Marthuret Church in Riom or Notre-Dame-des-Neiges in Aurillac.

Painting

A vast selection of medieval painting has been preserved within the Auvergne. The frescoes in the church of St-Julien in Brioude, for instance, date from the 12C; there is the 13C representation of the legend of St George in one of the ambulatory chapels in Clermont Cathedral, and the 14C Assumption and Coronation of the Virgin Mary in Billom. From the 15C are the Last Judgement in Issoire, St George Slaying the Dragon in Ébreuil, the Dance of Death in La Chaise-Dieu, and the frescoes in Ennezat. The triptych painted on wood by the Maître de Moulins is considered to be one of the

J. Damase/MICHELIN

Château de Cordès

last masterpieces of Gothic painting in France.

MILITARY AND CIVIL ARCHITECTURE

Defensive castles

During the days of the feudal system, the country was dotted with castles; by building fortresses, lords, viscounts and barons could display their power and authority compared to that of the king. This is why there are so many castles, with outlines that adapt to the shape of the rock beneath them. From the 13C, they were subject to successive attacks by the troops under Philip Augustus, who conquered 120 of them from 1210 onwards, to destruction during the Hundred Years War and, at the end of the conflict, to destruction by villagers who, at enormous cost, succeeded in routing the mercenaries and captains who were using them as a source of building material for their own houses. The castles were again damaged during the Wars of Religion, dismantled on the orders of Richelieu and Louis XIV then, later, further damaged by the French Revolution.

It is not difficult to imagine, despite their often ruined state today, how these great castles once looked.

The gentler architecture of the Renaissance

The influence of the Italian Renaissance travelled to Northern France via the Rhône corridor and in the 15C it slowly penetrated the Auvergne where a certain taste for well-being made itself apparent after the end of the war. The fortresses were turned into charming residences in which ornamentation supplanted systems of defence, even if, in the Auvergne, the austerity of the building in lava stone remained intact. Numerous castles were bought up by gentlemen of the robe or members of the middle classes who had recently acquired wealth through trade. Alterations softened the severity of older buildings; Cordès Castle was endowed with arbours and gardens designed by the famous 17C landscape architect Le Nôtre, for example, and Ravel was extended by three new wings. In the Rhône Valley, the same phenomenon can be seen today in the Maison des Chevaliers in Viviers, some of the houses in the St-Jean and St-Nizier districts of Lyon and in the Château de la Bastie-d'Urfé which is decorated with a superb gallery.

Town planning during the Classical period

In Lyon this manifested itself in a new form of town planning, which can be seen mainly in the 17C Terreaux district around the town hall. In the 18C, a new concept of urban layout was introduced, based on speculation. The Bellecour and Perrache districts were built on the site of former marshes. The main feature of these areas is place Bellecour, laid out during the reign of Louis XIV and flanked by Louis XVI residences.

Soufflot, designer of the Panthéon church in Paris, was one of the architects who, along with A-M Perrache and A Morrand, accelerated the development of urban planning so that it was launched on a bigger and grander scale. In his desire to pay homage to the buildings of Antiquity, and using his position as a leader in the Louis XVI style, he built bridges, houses along quaysides and the majestic hospice (Hôtel-Dieu) with its multifaceted dome.

The 19C and the architecture of the Auvergne spas: a fantasy world

In the spa towns of the 19C, "taking the waters" was not a new idea but it was during this period that it became fashionable. On the pretext of taking the waters and enjoying a rest, members of high society, and those with power or money, flocked to spa towns. Their visits were an opportunity to lead an active social life and it was this that governed the architectural style. In the centre of the town were the pump rooms, a veritable palace to which the architects paid particular attention; around them were the park and springs built to resemble Ancient Greek or Roman temples. The casino and the luxury hotels were decorated with an exuberance that was almost Baroque. In the streets of the town, troubadour-style castles stood next to Venetian palaces, and Henri IV residences rubbed shoulders with Art Nouveau mansions.

The history of this architecture, designed for enjoyment and pleasure, is a history of intermingling. The eclectic mix was the result of ideas by the most fashionable urban architects of the day combined with those of the architects of the Auvergne who were inspired by a long tradition based on Early Romanesque architecture and the volcanic and granite rocks available locally; these ideas were also influenced by the mixture of water and a natural environment with a town of stone, including its culture and its social events. Even the railway stations were not forgotten, since they provided the first impression for visitors who had just arrived. The result was a luxurious style of architecture full of exuberance and voluptuousness in the dream world constituted by the resorts in the heart of the Auvergne.

The new opera house in Lyon, a fine example of 20C architecture

Throughout the 19C and 20C Lyon was considered an ideal place for architectural experiments. In 1825 iron suspension bridges were built over the Rhône, using new techniques. In 1896 the basilica on Fourvière hill was completed in an eclectic Byzantine-cum-medieval style.

In the 1970s, with a view to the launch of the high-speed train service which would bring Lyon to within 2hr of Paris, a major development was begun in the La Part-Dieu district: a new business centre that was to take the city to the forefront of Europe's business world. In 1993 the latest architectural feat was completed; the old opera house designed in 1831 had to be renovated and it was **Jean Nouvel** who took up the gauntlet. All that remains of the old building are the four walls and an old foyer decorated with gold leaf and stucco work; the interior of the building has been gutted. Inside, a vast glass vault, high-tech lighting systems and a suspended auditorium are just some of the innovative features in the building. The outer shell of the opera house was retained, because the 19C architects had designed the ideal size for song and music. The U-shape common to Italian opera houses was also kept.

In the Rhône Valley, the most spectacular architectural project completed during the late 20C is undoubtedly **Lyon-Saint-Exupéry International Airport**, previously known as Lyon-Satolas.

Traditional Rural Housing

Over the centuries, changes in rural housing have kept pace with changes in agricultural work. Housing has also been subject to the influence of neighbouring regions and new building techniques.

AUVERGNE

Roofs

Owing to its geographical situation the Auvergne is in contact with two civilisations, "the Northern French one in which roofs are built with a 45° slope and flat tiles, and that of the Mediterranean basin in which the roofs have a slope of 30° and rounded tiles" (Max Derruau). In the mountains, thatch is replaced by slate or corrugated iron. The most attractive roofs are those made of stone slabs called lauzes that look like gigantic tortoise shells. They can only be mounted on a steeply sloping roof with a very strong set of rafters. On the plains, the old round tiles and rows of guttering once common in the countryside are beginning to lose ground in the face of competition from more stable mass-produced tiles.

Housing in the Limagne

The houses with upper storeys, which belong to wine-growers or farmers specialising in mixed agriculture, are commonplace in the old villages huddling on the hillsides. The ground floor is used for work (stables, cellars) and the upper floor is the house, reached by an outside flight of steps leading to a balcony sheltered by a porch roof.

Freestone, in particular Volvic stone, was used mainly for the houses of the bourgeoisie.

Housing in the mountains

These houses are sturdy buildings, constructed from large blocks of basalt. The heavy roofs extend below the top of the walls. The single building contains both dwelling and byre side by side. They always face south, and are sheltered from bad weather by the haybarn. Doors and windows are narrow and the roof drops down to the ground at the rear of the building. In the Upper Livradois area, the house is raised and is separate from the farm buildings.

Housing in the Velay area

Houses in this area are unusual as their walls are made of ashlar, with a predominance of grey or dark-red lava stone in volcanic areas, light-coloured granite in areas of older soil, and yellow arkose in areas of sedimentary rock. The blocks of stone are cemented together using a mortar that is often mixed with pozzolana, a reddish volcanic gravel. In the villages, a bell turret indicates the village hall (assemblée) or "maison de la béate."

Shepherds' and cowherds' huts

A buron is a squat, stone-roofed temporary dwelling high up in the mountains, used by cowherds during periods of trans-humance. This was where the cheese and butter was made which the cantalès, or master of the buron, then sent down to the valleys from time to time. A small number of these huts are still in use. In the Livradois and Forez areas, and on the slopes of Mont Pilat, there are "jass-eries" or "mountain farms" used during the summer months. Solidly built of stone with thatched roofs, they consist of a living room, a byre and a cheese cellar below.

RHÔNE VALLEY

Housing in the Forez and Lyonnais areas

Houses in the Forez area are farmsteads enclosed by high walls around a central courtyard. The walls are often made of rows of stones set at a slant. In the Dombes area, the farmhouses are elongated and have an upper storey. External pebbledash protects the walls made of terracotta bricks or cob.

Housing in the Rhône Valley

On the **Valence and Montélimar plains,** the walls often have no doors or windows on the north side since this is where the mistral wind blows. Additional protection is often provided by a row of thuyas, cypress and plane trees. Large, isolated farmsteads consist of a group of buildings around a walled

From Beaujolais to Lower Vavarais

House in the Beaujolais region

Farm and dovecote on Dombes plateau

Jasserie: summer farmstead in the Forez mountains

House in Lower Dauphiné

Farm in the Mézenc range

House in Lower Vivarais

R. Corbel/MICHELIN

courtyard, and their external walls, devoid of doors or windows, make them look like fort-resses.

Housing in Lower Dauphiné

Between Bourbe and Isère, pebbles or **"rolled stones"** were often used as a building material because they were commonplace in this area of moraine and alluvial deposits. The stones are assembled end on, on a bed of mortar, and the angle changes from one level to the next.

In some areas (eg Morestel and Creys) there is a style of roofing that has been imported from the Préalpes: **crow-stepped or corbie-stepped gabling.** The flat-tiled roofs are supported by the gables of the side walls on which the rise is set back. The "steps" are roofed with an overhanging stone slab, giving the houses a very special appearance.

Housing in the Upper Vivarais area

On the edges of the Velay area, along the Mézenc range and on the high plateaux above the upper reaches of the River Ardèche and River Eyrieux, the houses are low and squat with stone-slabbed roofs, seeming almost weighed down by this shell designed to withstand bad weather. The houses have granite or basalt walls with few doors or windows and most of the farmers specialise in stock breeding. The first room was the cowshed with an earth or stone-slabbed floor. A wooden partition separated it from the kitchen where hole-in-the-wall beds were built into the thickness of the walls. Above the byre was the hayloft which was equipped with trap doors so that, in winter, the animals could be fed without the farmer having to brave the weather outside..

On the St-Agrève plateau, the granite farmhouses have an upper storey and bedrooms next to the hayloft. Access is via a ramp on the side facing the mountain.

Housing in the Lower Vivarais area

Houses here have an upper storey and are built in a square, like southern French houses. The gently sloping roofs have half-round tiles. At the top of the wall, between wall and roof, there is typically a double or triple row of guttering made with fragments of tiles mounted in mortar. The south-facing wall is often decorated with a trellis.

The **silk wormery** often opened onto the *couradou*. Until 1850, it was an essential part of the house and a vital feature of life in the Vivarois area.

In the middle Ardèche Valley, most of the houses are constructed of limestone.

Traditions in the Auvergne

Because of the isolated nature of much of the Auvergne countryside, many ancient traditions have survived; today, the inhabitants are doing their utmost to preserve the special character of this region and the cultural heritage.

Fêtes and festivals

Many of the old customs are upheld on the most important occasions. Bonfires are still lit on the mountain tops to celebrate the summer solstice (Feast of St John), and local fêtes have kept up the tradition of the music and songs played to young girls by the young men of the village. There has also been a revival of country festivals to celebrate haymaking, cheesemaking, harvesting, grape harvests, etc.

Costume

Today every folk group has its own interpretation of traditional costume. The men wear the *biaude,* a voluminous dark blue smock over a pair of coarse black trousers, with a brightly coloured scarf, a wide-brimmed, black felt hat and the clogs or hob-nailed boots that are so vital when tapping out the dance rhythm. The women are dressed in long, waisted, multicoloured dresses with an embroidered apron and a headdress that varies depending on the region.

The bourrée

This dance dates back a long time but it has been synonymous with the Auvergne since the 18C. The *bourrée* enacts the chasing of a coquettish young girl by an enterprising young

La Bourrée

man, whom she alternately runs away from and then beckons to.

Processions and pilgrimages

Worship of the Virgin Mary is very important in the Auvergne. Countless churches and chapels have been dedicated to her; it is said that St Austremoine dedicated a chapel to her in Clermont in the 3C. Indeed, the statues of the Virgin Mary in the Auvergne are among the oldest in France.

Processions and pilgrimages in honour of the Blessed Virgin remain very much alive and are quite spectacular. The processions to Notre-Dame-du-Port (Clermont-Ferrand) or Orcival, and the pilgrimages to Mauriac and Thiézac in Cantal and to Marsat and Monton in Puy-de-Dôme are the most popular. However, worship of the Virgin is also associated with work in the fields and with farm animals. Notre-Dame-de-Vassivière in the Dore mountain range accompanies the animals during transhumance: at the beginning of the summer the statue is carried from Besse to the chapel further up the mountainside; it is taken down again early in autumn. Though the worship of the saints is a less solemn affair, it too remains important, as can be seen from a study of place names. The saints with healing powers have fallen victim to the progress of medicine but sometimes people pray to them as a last resort.

Literary Life

THE LANGUAGE

Like all the regions in France the Auvergne has its own language, which has undergone continual development since the days of Antiquity, in accordance with historical and political upheaval and, more especially, as a result of local experiences. This means that the borders of the area in which the dialect of the Auvergne is spoken do not correspond to the historical and administrative borders of the province.

Auvergnat, the dialect of the Auvergne, which is considered to be similar to North Occitan, is said to have developed from a so-called Medio-Roman language used in the part of Central France occupied by the Romans and which gradually died out in the face of competition from *oïl*, the language of Northern France and, therefore, the language of power and authority which was usually concentrated on the Paris basin. The dialect spoken in and around Aurillac is closer to the Guyennais dialect spoken in the south-west of France (Aquitaine), which was under English domination for a considerable time, but it has nevertheless been influenced by Auvergnat. Bourbonnais is a Northern French language.

A FEW GREAT WRITERS FROM THE AUVERGNE

Local writers have brought fame to a few of the Auvergne's prelates among them Sidonius Apollinaris, Gerbert (10C) and Massillon who gave Louis XIV's funeral oration in the 18C. The Auvergne also had poets such as Théodore de Banville (1823-91) who founded the Parnassian School of Poetry and philosophers such as Pierre Teilhard de Chardin (1881-1955). In the 20C, Henri Pourrat and the chronicler Alexandre Vialatte have both described their native land, each in his own style. Of all the Auvergne authors, the best-known is Blaise Pascal though Gregory of Tours, the medieval chronicler, is almost equally important.

Gregory of Tours

He was born c 583 in Clermont-Ferrand into a rich family of Senators. He spent most of his life in Tours, to which he was appointed Bishop in 573, yet he never forgot the place of his birth. His *History of the Franks* which retraces the reigns of the Merovingian kings and their ancestors is one of the main sources of historical information about the Auvergne during the Dark Ages and not until the 14C was there any other chronicle about the region.

Gregory of Tours tells, for example, how, when Clovis' son, Thierry, took possession of the region, the people of the Auvergne, who already had a strong regional identity, rebelled against annexation to Austrasia which was situated at the easternmost tip of Gaul.

Yet Gregory of Tours was not only concerned with the Auvergne. His work covers the whole of Gaul and is one of the only sources of information about that time. Indeed, it is the first historical work concerning the kingdom of the Franks that has survived to this day. As a Christian, Gregory of Tours interpreted signs of divine intervention in order to explain changes in the world but he was also a careful observer of the real world. He had a marked visual sense and he enjoyed describing things he saw, while carefully seeking the truth through differing sources of information which he had no hesitation in comparing and contrasting.

Blaise Pascal

It was in 1623 that Pascal, undoubtedly the most famous native of the Auvergne, was born in Clermont-Ferrand. His mother died when he was three years old and it was his father, President of the Court of Aids (forerunner of the Customs & Excise) in Clermont, who brought him up. In 1631 Pascal senior came to Paris to devote all his time to his son who was already showing signs of extraordinary intelligence. Châteaubriand described him as a "terrifying genius." At the age of 11 he wrote a treatise on sound and, at 19, he invented his first mathematical machine to assist him in his calculations. In 1646 Pascal entered Port-Royal, the abbey where he wrote his treatises on Physics and Philosophy. He then left the abbey to lead a life among high society where he discovered that "the heart has its reasons which reason ignores." It was at this time that he wrote his *Discourse on the Passions of Love.* Soon, though, he began to suffer from the "emptiness" of his life. In 1664 he survived a carriage accident and believed that this was a sign from on high. He retired to Port-Royal, which he was never again to leave, and continued his writings. It was because his memory played tricks on him that he began noting his *Thoughts,* with a view to writing an *Apology of the Christian Religion.* This was his most famous work, but was never completed. Pascal died in 1662, at the age of 39.

Blaise Pascal

J. Damase/MICHELIN

THE REGION TODAY

Economy

INDUSTRY

Industry came into being in the 16C with the introduction of silk working around Lyon, paid for by the capital earned from fairs. Later, the coalfields in the area were a major factor leading to the expansion of industry. Once the seams had been worked out, the energy supply was provided by the hydroelectric plants and, since the 1970s and 1980s, by the nuclear power plants along the Rhône Valley. Around Clermont-Ferrand the major industry is tyre making.

Metal working

After the gradual shut-down of the coal mines in the area around St-Étienne, the metalworking sector began to specialise in the production of steels, rare metals, fissile products for use in the nuclear industry, and smelting, a sector that benefits from the high demand for moulded components (boiler-making, pipes). The region along the Rhône ranks second to the Paris basin in the field of mechanical engineering (machine tools, precision engineering, car manufacture). Electrical and electronic engineering are well represented with companies producing high-voltage equipment, communications equipment and domestic appliances. Until the 19C, tin and copper were the two main materials used in the Auvergne.

Textiles

After the silk workers' revolts in 1831 and 1834 in the streets and alleyways of Lyon, the textile industry relocated to villages and manufacturers distributed the jobs (weaving and dyeing) to a rural work force. This was the so-called outworker system which still functions today. The importance of silk has decreased greatly in the face of competition from man-made fibres but the weaving of silky fabrics made of a combination of fibres and threads of all types has remained famous. The new

Sparkling water from Vichy

J. Damase/MICHELIN

products have remained faithful to the innovation and tasteful designs which won Lyon its reputation for silks.
The production and weaving of man-made textiles is carried out in Valence (nylon and polyester) and Roanne (viscose). The industry has many offshoots like dyeing and dressing, and clothing (ready-to-wear, sportswear, lingerie, hosiery, curtains, net curtains, ribbons, elastic, lace).

Chemicals

A major chemical industry developed in Lyon in order to meet the needs of the textile industry. It was here that one of Europe's petrochemical centres was established. In Feyzin, there is a large oil refinery and the Institut Français du Pétrole has set up its largest research centre here. The region currently leads the field in certain areas of the chemical industry, notably fungicides, paint, varnish and, especially, pharmaceuticals.

Additional industries

Other industrial activities in the region include tyre making, food processing (dairy products, pork meat products, health foods), shoemaking, cabinet-making, quarrying (Volvic), and mineral-water bottling (Vichy, Volvic) as well as the production of building materials, glass, wires, cables, leather, paper, jewellery, tobacco and enamelled lava (signposts, viewing tables). Thiers is one of France's major cutlery-making centres. Traditionally, industry in the Auvergne has centred around specialist crafts, production frequently operating on a cottage-industry scale, such as coppersmithing (Cantal), lacemaking (Velay) and papermaking (Livradois).

Administration offices (local authority and government offices etc) and tourism also play an important part in the local economy; traditional industries (eg cheese-making) no longer do any more than "top it up".

Harnessing the Rhône

Important works upstream and downstream of Lyon, completed during the second half of the 20C, have offered this highly industrialised region the possibility of tapping the power resources of the mighty Rhône (16 billion kWh are produced yearly). At the same time, a series of canals provide a total of 330km/205mi of navigable waterways between Lyon and the sea.

AGRICULTURE

The Auvergne is first and foremost a rural area, in marked contrast to the Rhône Valley, where industry predominates. Life on farms experienced profound change during the 20C: the introduction of motor vehicles, and the destruction of hedgerows which ended the subdivision of properties into small fields. In many places, the traditional landscape of fields and narrow lanes lined with walnut trees has given way to one of wide, open fields. Farmers, who are decreasing in number, have also had to comply with the milk quotas imposed on them by the EU; despite these difficulties, animal breeding and crop farming remain an important part of the economy of the region.

Stock breeding

The high plateaux and mountains are popular with cattle breeders and, to a lesser extent, sheep farmers. The pastures on the slopes of the Dômes and tures on the slopes of the Dômes and Dore mountain ranges provide grazing land for the **Salers** breed of cattle (of which it is said that its fiery red coat turns pale if it leaves the basalt areas of Cantal), the French black and white Friesian, and the Montbéliarde. Dairy herds predominate in every part of the region.

Towards the middle of May the animals leave their byres and, for the five months of summer, live on the mountain pastures which are now fenced so that there is no need for a herdsman to be in attendance. In days gone by, cowherds had a squat, low summer hut called a *buron,* built to withstand the wind.

The **fairs** give visitors an opportunity to enjoy the busiest moments of rural life. They are held in most of the centrally situated localities and in other places that lie in the heart of the stock-breeding areas. The largest fairs are held in late summer and in autumn.

Crops – In the Auvergne, wheat, barley and oats have traditionally been grown on the fertile black soil of the Limagnes, and now also sugar beet, tobacco, sunflowers and fodder or maize crops from selected strains of seeds.

At the southern end of the Rhône Valley the dampness and cold of maritime or continental climates gives way to the heat and radiant skies of the south of France – almond and olive trees and a few mulberry bushes can be seen in the countryside.

The natural environment here is both crop- and farmer-friendly. The land is fertile and easy to irrigate; the soil is light and siliceous; well-sheltered corries and dales benefit from the spring sunshine.

Orchards

It was in 1880 that fruit production took over from wine, after the vineyards had been blighted by phylloxera. The long, fruit-producing season, made possible by careful selection of varieties and the differences in exposure or altitude, enable the orchards in the Rhône Valley to produce one-third of all French fruit. Every type of fruit can be found here – raspberries, redcurrants and blackcurrants in Isère, sweet chestnuts in Ardèche, cherries, apricots, apples and pears and, in particular, peaches, the fruit that has made the Eyrieux Valley famous.

In the Auvergne the orchards are declining, but they continue to supply the main ingredients for local factories making candied fruit and fruit-jelly.

Vineyards

The vineyards in the Rhône Valley, which were already popular in Roman times, underwent massive expansion after the crisis in the silkworm-breeding industry in the mid-19C. Today, the vineyards cover more than 150 000ha/579sq mi, one-third of which produces high-quality wines. The best are the **Côtes du Rhône.** Châteauneuf-du-Pape, St-Joseph, Crozes-Hermitage, Hermitage, Côte-Rôtie, Château-Grillet and Condrieu are wines that age well, and have brought the area its reputation for excellence. With an annual output of 3.5 million hectolitres of *appellations contrôlées*, the Rhône Valley vineyards account for 15% of the total French production of fine wines.

The vineyards stretch for 200km/124mi producing a variety of wines thanks to the **types of vines** selected: Marsanne and Viognier for the whites, Syrah and Grenache for the reds. The wines also vary depending on the different types of soil on which the vines are planted – the crumbly granite of the gorges, and the sands, pebbles or marl that predominate in alluvial plains. There are climatic differences in the basins and, finally, the terraces that climb the hillsides between this area and the Alps face in different directions.

Further north, the vineyards of the **Beaujolais** – which are usually grouped with those of neighbouring Burgundy in wine guides – produce wines which go very well indeed with the traditional cuisine of Lyon, where they are to be found in every local brasserie or *bouchon*. The third Thursday in November is a 'red letter' day locally (and further afield, now that the reputation of Beaujolais wines has spread abroad!) as it marks *l'arrivée du beaujolais nouveau*, or the release for sale to the public of the latest Beaujolais vintage *(vin primeur)*. For further details on Beaujolais wines, 🐌 see *BEAUJOLAIS*.

The limestone hillsides to each side of the Limagnes used to be covered with vineyards. Nowadays, some of the wines fall within the all-enveloping name Côtes d'Auvergne, among them Châtaugay, Corent, Boudes and St-Pourçain.

Food and Drink

The Rhône Valley abounds in good food because it is situated at the heart of various regions containing an outstanding wealth of local produce. Bresse is famous for its poultry, the Charolais area produces beef, the Dombes region abounds in game, the lakes of Savoy teem with fish and the Forez and Rhône valleys specialise in fruit.

The Auvergne, a rugged area of countryside, is not the place for complex, sophisticated cuisine; it specialises in family cooking – good food and plenty of it. Here the speciality foods are as diverse as they are appetising.

LYON

In the 19C silk workers ate, like their employers, in small family-run restaurants; there was no snobbery in Lyon when it came to good food. The dishes served were based on cheap cuts of meat and offal, but the food was plentiful and tasty. Diners could eat sausages, potted pork, black sausage, pigs' trotters, knuckle of veal and other stewed meats.

The tradition of good food remains unchanged. Today, local specialities include spicy saveloy sausage with truffles and pistachio nuts, pigs' trotters and tails, cardoons with marrow

Côtes du Rhone wines

J. Damase/MICHELIN

No "fast food" here

J. Damase/MICHELIN

bone jelly, pork brawn in vinaigrette, and gently stewed tripe. Other dishes include braised, stuffed trout, fish in Burgundy wine, poultry – especially chicken cooked in stock with thin slivers of truffle inserted between the skin and the meat, and chicken in cream.

Forez

Hunting, shooting, fishing and stock breeding provide the basic ingredients for a delicate, tasty type of cooking. Among the local dishes are crayfish and trout from the River Lignon, or poultry and meat of outstanding quality. Also on offer may be a local form of pork pie, a dish of duck, a delicious local ham, Feurs sausage or, in the autumn, game pâté, sometimes even woodcock.

Vivarais

Food here is rustic; this is the land of chestnuts and wild mushrooms such as St George's agaric and boletus. Among the filling, tasty specialities are partridge with cabbage, thrush with grapes, chicken cooked in a bladder, chicken with crayfish, goose and turkey with chestnuts, hare with *poivrade* (a highly seasoned sauce), and pork meat products from Ardèche. During the summer, the cherries, apricots, peaches, pears, plums and apples are among the finest such fruits found anywhere in France.

Lower Dauphiné

The Rhône Valley area of Lower Dauphiné marks the transition between the Lyonnais area and Provence. This is the land of *gratin dauphinois* (potatoes sliced and baked in milk), veal with leeks, *pognes* (brioches, a sort of sweet bread) in Romans and Valence, cheese from St-Marcellin, Grignan-style braised beef and the inimitable Montélimar nougat.

AUVERGNE

The food in the Auvergne has traditionally been farm cooking, and as a result it has been accused of lacking any appreciable local specialities; this criticism is, happily, totally unfounded.

The people of the Auvergne have taken great national specialities and adapted them to suit local taste so that, in the Auvergne, food is rich and sometimes heavy but it is always extremely good.

Meat and fish

The *coq au vin* (chicken stew) is delicious, especially when flavoured with a good wine. The *tripoux* from Aurillac, St-Flour and Chaudes-Aigues are wonderful, too: likewise sheep's feet stuffed and folded up in pieces of sheep's stomach. There is ham from Maurs, local sausages, fried gudgeon, trout from mountain streams, eels from the Dore, and salmon from the Allier.

Vegetables

The *truffade* from Aurillac is a smooth blend of fresh Tomme cheese and mashed potatoes; seasoned with garlic in Chaudes-Aigues and Aubrac, it is called *aligot*. Potato paté, a light pastry browned in the oven with a lot of fresh cream and potatoes, is one of the specialities of the Montluçon and Gannat area. Morel mushrooms are cooked with cream and used to fill omelettes and stuff poultry. Peas from the Planèze and green lentils from Le Puy are well-known to gourmets.

Cheeses

This is one of the region's main specialities. The round, flat St-Nectaire is a delight when well matured. There is also

Some cheeses of the Auvergne: (left to right) Cantal, Bleu d'Auvergne, Fourme d'Ambert, St-Nectaire

Fourme d'Ambert and Fourme de Montbrison, a blue cheese with an orange-tinted rind, Bleu d'Auvergne and Cantal. These are the best-known of the local cheeses but there is in addition Murol, a variant of St-Nectaire, or the garlic-flavoured Gaperon, made on the plains and shaped like a rounded cone. Cabecou goat's cheese is made in the Margeride area, around Aurillac and Salers.

Locally, the cheese usually known as Cantal is called Fourme, named after the wooden mould (or form) used to hold it together. This word gave the French language the word *formage* (forming) which later became *fromage* (cheese). It takes the milk of 20 to 30 cows to make a 40kg/88lb Cantal cheese. The milk is collected in a narrow, deep vat called a *gerle*. The rennet is then added before the mixture is heated and allowed to drain. The curd is then known as Tomme. After being left to stand for three days, it is crumbled and salted, then placed in a mould where it is pressed in order to extract the whey. The Fourme placed in the cellar below the mountain hut is periodically turned until it matures. Among the cheeses still made on farms are St-Nectaire and Fourme d'Ambert but these days most of the milk is processed in cooperatives or dairies to make Cantal Laitier (indicated by a square label) or Bleu d'Auvergne, a cow's milk cheese with a fermented curd to which mould is added; it is reminiscent of Roquefort.

Desserts

In Lower Auvergne and the Ambert Plain, two of the specialities are *millards*, tarts made with unstoned cherries or grapes, and *pompes*, large, heavy cakes filled with fruit. Cantal has the *fouasse* which is a type of sweet bread. A *picoussel* is a buckwheat flour flan filled with plums and seasoned with herbs. In Salers, the speciality is the *carré*.

WINES

The Auvergne still boasts a few wines like the famous St-Pourçain, produced on the slopes of the Limagne, which can be left to age for up to four years, or Côtes d'Auvergne wines (Châteaugay and Corent), known since Roman times. But the best wine-growing areas are to be found in the Rhône Valley, where Beaujolais and Côtes du Rhône are produced.

Côtes du Rhône

The vineyards on the Côtes du Rhône are thought to be the oldest in France, founded on vine stock said to have been introduced by the Greeks several centuries BC. They stretch along both banks of the river like a narrow ribbon, producing wines whose quality and balance are guaranteed by a skilful blend of varieties of grape. The reds should be consumed slightly cool, the whites well chilled. Côte-Rôtie wines have a bouquet reminiscent of violets; the wines from the Hermitage exude the scent of raspberries. Château-Condrieu and Château-Grillet are among the greatest of all French white wines. If drunk young, they are a marvellous accompaniment to a crayfish gratin. Cornas was much appreciated by Charlemagne. St-Péray and the fresh, bubbling, musky Clairette de Die are both sparkling wines. Finally, further south where the valley enters Provence, the vineyards produce the warm, friendly Châteauneuf-du-Pape, a powerful wine with a purple robe, Gigondas, the sweet, suave and flavoursome Muscat from Beaumes-de-Venise and, on the other bank of the Rhône, the rosés from Tavel and the reds and rosés from Lirac and Chusclan.

East end of the old abbey in Issoire
S. Sauvignier/MICHELIN

AIGUEPERSE

POPULATION 2 505
MICHELIN MAPS 326: G-6

This charming town at the heart of Limagne country is circled by avenues that have replaced the former ramparts. Treasures inside the Church of Notre-Dame (rebuilt in the 19C in Gothic style), with its 13C east end and transept, include a 15C wooden Deposition, fine family tombs, a 13C fresco and 18C panelling. The Sainte-Chapelle is the 15C chapel from the old castle (disappeared) and has a Flamboyant doorway and a gargoyled and pinnacled west front. The Hôtel de Ville (town hall) is housed in a 17C convent building; note the three jack o' the clocks who chime the hours.

JACQUES VERNET

154 Grande-Rue - ☎ *04 73 63 61 85 - summer: 7am-7pm, winter: Tue-Sun 7am-7pm - closed 2 wks in Feb, 1 wk in Jun.* In 1933 the grandfather took over this pastry and chocolate shop in the village centre; nowadays, the affair is in his grandson's nimble, talented hands. He prepares renowned specialities, including delicious praline creations and melt-in-your-mouth marzipans, not to mention his wickedly tempting chocolate confections. But don't take our word for it – drop in and indulge!

Excursion

Discovering La Limagne
70km/43.5mi – allow 3hr
This itinerary runs across the Limagne, a vast fertile plain extending north of Clermont-Ferrand towards the Bourbonnais region.

▶ *Leave Aigueperse to the N: D 151 leads to the Butte de Montpensier, 4km/2.5mi further on.*

Butte de Montpensier
Montpensier "Hill" (alt 441m/1 447ft) is a typical volcanic neck. From it, there is a fine view over the Limagne plain.

Limagne plain

J. Damase/MICHELIN

A fortress once stood on the hilltop and it was here that King Louis VIII, the father of St Louis, died in 1226 on his return from the Albigensian Crusade. The castle was razed to the ground on the orders of Richelieu in the 17C. The village has a small Romanesque church.

▶ *Continue along D 151 until you reach the crossroads, then take D 93 on the right.*

Château d'Effiat – ♿ *See Château d'EFFIAT.*

▶ *Take D 93 and drive to Bas-et-Lezat, then take D 63.*

Villeneuve-les-Cerfs

A picturesque **dovecote**★ stands in a meadow at the entrance to the village *(at the intersection of D 210 and D 63, on the left coming from Randan).*

Traditional dovecote

A few of the villages in the Limagne still have their **dovecotes**. Some stand alone in the middle of fields; others stand adjacent to, or near, farm buildings. Most of them are square with tiled roofs and central turrets with the niches that enable the pigeons to fly away and come home to roost. They are half-timbered and mounted on posts to protect the young birds from predators. Until the 19C, pigeon droppings were a precious source of fertiliser for the soil.

▶ *Continue along D 63 until you reach the intersection with D 1093 and turn right.*

After 5km/3mi you will notice on your left the **Butte de Montgacon**, offering lovely views of the Limagne and the Puy mountain range in the far distance.

Maringues

This large village of Gallo-Roman origin, a busy agricultural trading centre, stands along the recently canalised Morge. Until the mid 19C, wool and leather working were the traditional local activities: around 1850 there were 60 tanneries operating along the river. The 12C Romanesque **church** *(By appointment. Apply to M. le Curé (parish priest) or M. Hérault.* ☎ *04 73 68 71 33 or 04 73 68 74 02)* has interesting carved capitals and keystones and a 15C Entombment. There are some interesting old houses near the old corn exchange.

▶ *Leave to the SW and take D 224, heading for Riom.*

Église d'Ennezat★

Ennezat, a large farming village on the Limagne plain lies near marshes in a landscape of vast, geometrical fields separated by drainage ditches and rows of aspen trees and willows. Digging reveals black earth which is very fertile, as is obvious from the huge silos at the north-west exit to the village along the road to Clerlande (D 20); they help to maintain the Limagne's reputation as a "grain store." The former collegiate **church**★, sometimes known as the "Cathedral of the Marshes," consists of two very different sections. The nave, side aisles and transept are built of arkose – a pale-coloured stone – in the purest of Auvergne Romanesque styles and date from the 11C; the chancel of lava stone, surrounded by an ambulatory and radiating chapels, was rebuilt in the 13C in Gothic style to a more extensive layout, to replace the old Romanesque chancel. From the outside, the east end is tall and elegant. The nave and chancel have been restored, the narthex and south and west doorways are 19C.

In the second span of the north side aisle in the chancel, note a fresco dating from 1420, with the theme "The Meeting of the Three Living and the Three Dead," and, near the door into the sacristy, a deeply moving and expressive, 17C wooden *Pietà*.

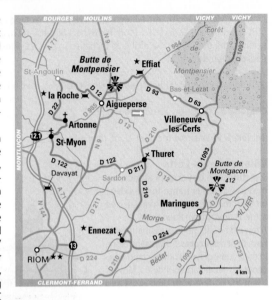

▶ *Leave Ennezat and follow the diverted route to Vichy on D 210.*

Thuret

A 13C keep dominates the village. The **church** is largely 11C: it comprises a handsome ensemble of east end and bell-tower, with a fine south doorway (note the carved pentagonal lintel). Inside, there is a Black Virgin and some interesting carved and painted capitals (Adam and Eve, Eucharistic symbols etc).

▶ *Leave Thuret on D 211 in the direction of Riom and drive to Sardon. Enter Sardon on D 51, then, on leaving the town, turn left onto D 122 until you reach the junction with D 985. Turn right onto D 985 and go to St-Myon.*

Église de St-Myon

There is a charming little Romanesque church here with a fine stone-slabbed roof and a west front overlooking a tiny square with trees.

▶ *Continue along D 223 to the E.*

Artonne

The village retains numerous sections of its medieval town wall. St Martin of Tours came here to pray at the tomb of St Vitaline. The **church** (🕐 all year, daily, 2-5pm. Contact M. Jean-Michel Farges, ☎ 04 73 33 30 91), formerly a collegiate church founded in 1048 and built over a pre-Romanesque building that included Gallo-Roman features, is strangely set in the middle of the village. It is a huge building and has undergone extensive alteration but it still has a 10C and 11C nave with ribbed barrel vaulting and a vast east end. Fine wrought-iron grilles close off the chancel rebuilt in the 12C. The former chapter-house is situated in the north aisle.

🔲 **Coteau du Puy St-Jean**, 500m/547yd. A nature discovery trail leads to a viewpoint overlooking the village.

▶ *Drive NW out of Artonne and turn right onto D 22 towards St-Agoulin then follow D 12.*

Château de la Roche
🕐 *Jul-mid-Sep: daily except Tue 2.30-5.30pm, Sun and public holidays 3-5.30pm. 7€ (children 4€)* ☎ *04 73 63 65 81.*

This medieval manor, slightly altered in the 16C, was the fief of the vassal families of the dukes of Bourbon. It was elevated to a castellany by Charles III, the rebel commander-in-chief of the French armies, for Jean de L'Hospital, his doctor. The illustrious **Michel de L'Hospital** was born at La Roche, which he was given as a dowry in 1537.

A vaulted porch leads to the main courtyard surrounded on three sides by buildings. The fourth side has been closed off since the 16C by a balustrade of Volvic stone decorated with four fawns representing the four seasons.

A staircase tower joined to the keep leads to the first-floor **bedroom of Michel de L'Hospital** containing historical souvenirs and objects belonging to the Chancellor. On the second floor, the **guard room** which led to the rampart walk (cob walls) contains some fine 15C to 17C armour; the walls display the coats of arms of the various owners of the castle. Return to the first floor to admire the 17C **drawing room** decorated with a beamed ceiling and a wooden fireplace; the walls are hung with an Aubusson tapestry depicting Solomon and the Queen of Sheba; there is also a beautiful marquetry cabinet and a 15C carved wedding chest. The only light in the tiny oratory enters via the stained-glass window. The visit ends with an 18C room (collection of monogrammed plates) and the **old kitchen** (14C fireplace, copper pans and a cantou, a sort of bench which also served to store salt).

Championing the Cause of Tolerance

Château de la Roche near Aigueperse was the birthplace of Michel de l'Hospital (1505-73). Chancellor of France under Catherine de' Medici, he became Catherine's chief collaborator in the policy of religious tolerance. He supported the Edict of Romorantin (1560), which deprived the secular courts of jurisdiction in cases involving religion, and he instigated the edicts granting liberty of conscience (1561) and restricted liberty of worship (1562). When the second War of Religion broke out in 1567, he was forced to renounce his duties by Charles and Henri de Guise. After he retired, he developed a taste for Latin poetry.

▶ *Continue along D 12, which takes you back to Aigueperse.*

AMBERT

POPULATION 7 309
MICHELIN MAP 326: J-9

The small, seemingly-isolated town of Ambert lies in the middle of a low, wide plain between the Livradois and Forez mountains. Formerly known for the production of paper and religious artefacts, Ambert is nowadays a centre of more diversified economic activity (including the manufacture of braiding) and the ideal starting point of excursions across the surrounding high pastures.
🗓 *4 pl. de l'Hôtel-de-Ville, 63600 AMBERT,* ☎ *04 73 82 61 90. www.tourisme.fr/office-de-tourisme/ambert.htm.*

A Bit of History

Papermaking and the Wars of Religion – Ambert's origins are obscure but the town began to make a name for itself in the 15C, when the paper industry here came into its own; in the 16C this area boasted more than 300 mills, each jealously protecting its own manufacturing secrets. The main market was Lyon with its many printers. The church of St-Jean, the "cathedral" of the Livradois area, was built during this prosperous period.

However, Ambert was not safe from national political upheavals and became involved in the Wars of Religion. On 15 February 1577 the town was taken by Merle the formidable Huguenot leader, who massacred all prisoners. Catholic armies rushed to the rescue. Lacking the manpower to defend the town, Merle hit upon a brilliant stratagem: statues were taken from the local churches, given helmets and posted on the city walls. Astonished to see the defendants maintain their position under enemy fire and believing them to be invulnerable, the besiegers eventually withdrew. The city subsequently came under the control of members of the Catholic League, who did not surrender until 1596.

The Athens of the Auvergne – Ambert has produced a long line of outstanding personalities: in the 17C the theory of equations took a giant step forward through the work of mathematician **Michel Rolle**; in the 19C the composer **Emmanuel Chabrier** (1841-94) and the erudite poet **Maurice Faucon** showed an unusually high degree of sensitivity in their respective fields.

In the early 20C Ambert became a hotbed of intellectuals who included philosophers, writers and geographers (Pierre de Nolhac, Alexandre Vialatte, Cécile Sauvage, Antoine Sylvère, Claude Dravaine, Lucien Gachon) who all focused their intellect on their native or adoptive Livradois area. Another famous son of the Livradois area was **Henri Pourrat** (1887-1959), who formed a link between the rural and industrial worlds, and who in his novels, short stories and historical works wrote chiefly about country life in the Auvergne, expressing "the poetry of the soil, Man's purposes and the spirit of civilisations" to quote A Vialatte. The municipal and university library at Clermont-Ferrand runs an Henri-Pourrat Centre displaying the author's archives and library.

Town Walk

Visitors will enjoy a pleasant stroll through Ambert's historic centre which has retained some of its timber-framed houses.

▶ *Start from the tourist office.*

Hôtel de Ville

Boulevard Henri IV. The town hall, an unusual circular building, has been immortalised in literature by Jules Romains: the "large rotunda" is the meeting place of heroes in his novel Copains (Chums), who visit Ambert and mystify its inhabitants by playing practical jokes on them.

▶ *Walk down rue de l'Enfer then rue de Goye. Turn right onto rue du Chicot then left onto rue de la Grave.*

J. Damase/MICHELIN

The circular town hall

Église St-Jean★

Place St-Jean. The church of St-Jean, built between 1471 and 1518, is a typical example of Flamboyant Gothic architecture, except for the upper part of the tower and a chapel which both date from the Renaissance. The flights of fancy of the Gothic sculptor were restrained by the hard granite used to build the church. The tower is surrounded by machicolations; the southern façade features a fine portal. Inside, note the irregular size of the arch spans. In the first chapel on the left is a 16C painted wooden *Pietà* known as Our Lady of Layre. The gilded-lead altar in the transept crossing was designed by Philippe Kaeppelin.

Climb to the top of the bell-tower for a panoramic view of the town.

▶ *From the south doorway, follow rue de la République on the left then turn left again along rue du Château (when you reach the inn, you will see a street on the left leading to the Musée de la Fourme et du Fromage, see below) and return to the tourist office along rue de l'Enfer.*

Sights

Maison de la Fourme et du Fromage

Off rue du Château. 🕐 *Jul-Aug: guided tours (1hr) 9am-7pm; Sep: 9am-noon, 2-7pm; Apr-Jun: daily except Mon 9am-noon, 2-7pm; Oct-Nov and Feb-Mar: Tue, Thu, Fri and Sat 9am-noon, 2-7pm. 5€.* ☎ *04 73 82 49 23.*

This museum devoted to cheesemaking is housed in a 15C building. Guided tours describe the manufacture of **fourme d'ambert,** the delicious local blue cheese and the discovery by accident of the process of cheesemaking. In a laboratory the four fundamental stages of production are revealed: curdling the milk, pouring it into a mould, leaving it to drain, drying it. Two upper rooms concentrate on cheesemaking in detail, and explain the precise conditions needed to make Fourme d'Ambert in particular. In the cellar various local cheeses are left to mature, which can take 28 days or more.

Musée de la Machine Agricole et à Vapeur

Rue de l'Industrie, S of Ambert via D 269. ⚒ ⏱ *Mid-Apr to mid-Oct: 2-6pm (Jul and Aug: 10am-12.30pm, 2-6.30pm); open all year for groups by arrangement.* ⏱ *Closed mid-Dec - mid-Jan). 5€.* ☎ *04 73 82 60 42. http://agrivap.free.fr*

This museum installed in a former saw mill boasts a large collection of steam-powered machines from the early 20C.

Pride of place is given to a SACM-Pinguet micro-power plant, designed to power the saw mill. It consists of a steam-powered generator dating from 1906 and a boiler built in 1909 that is heated by wood chips and offcuts. The agricultural implements in the harvesting and threshing section clearly illustrate the evolution from horse-power to engine-power. The tractor hall displays many different models from various countries, including a brand new wooden tractor.

Excursions

Livradois-Forez tourist train★

🔲 *Panoramic or Picasso tourist train. Ambert/Arlanc/La Chaise-Dieu round trip: Jul and Aug: Tue, Thu, Sun, leaves at 2.15pm, returns at 6.30pm (mid-Jul to mid-Aug: additional service Fri). 11€ return. Courpière/Ambert/La Chaise-Dieu round trip in Aug: Wed, leaves at 8.45am, returns at 7.30pm. 17€ return. Ambert/Courpière round trip: mid-Jul to mid-Aug: Mon, leaves at 2.15pm, returns at 5.15pm. 10€ return. Ambert/La Chaise-Dieu round trip: mid-Jul to mid-Aug: Sun leaves at 10am, returns at 12.50pm. Steam train. Ambert/Olliergues round trip: mid-Jul to end Aug: Sat, leaves at 2.15pm, returns at 5.30pm. 10€ return. AGRIVAP "tourist train", La Gare, 63600 Ambert.* ☎ *04 73 82 43 88.*

In the summer, a panoramic tourist train travels along the Dore Valley via Ambert giving visitors an opportunity to see the typical landscapes of the Livradois-Forez Regional Park.

Moulin Richard-de-Bas★

5km/3mi E along D 996, and turn left onto D 57 which runs up the Lagat Valley. Guided tours (1hr, last admission 1hr before closing time) ⏱ *9.30am-12.30pm, 2-6pm (Jul and Aug: 9.30am-7pm).* ⏱ *Closed 1 Jan and 25 Dec. 6€ (children: 4€).* ☎ *04 73 82 03 11. www.richarddebas.com.*

Old houses and paper mills, still surmounted by pine stretchers on which paper or printed sheets were hung to dry, are evidence of the industrial importance of the Lagat Valley which, for several centuries, was one of the main papermaking centres in France. Today, Richard-de-Bas is the only remaining mill in activity.

The mill was put back into operation in 1943 following efforts by **La Feuille Blanche** (The White Sheet), an association of Friends of Paper and Graphic Arts. A Paper Museum is housed within the mill, where visitors may take part in the different stages of papermaking, using materials and techniques that have barely changed over the last 500 years. The museum is also interesting for the insight it provides into the way of life of the Masters and Fellows of Papermaking.

The **main room** served as both kitchen and dining hall; seven or eight people gathered around the table to eat: the governor, his family, his workers and his apprentice;

the women ate standing up. The furniture on view today belonged to the last inhabitant here, who died in 1937. There are also frying pans in which *pandale* – grated potato pancake – was cooked, and a salt-mill shaped like a curled up fox.

The **bedroom** has three built-in beds, one of which is almost entirely enclosed: this was reserved for the apprentice, who began his training at the age of 7 or 8. The lacemaker's frame on the table was illuminated by a *doulie*, a glass ball filled with water which magnified the light from the candle.

The apprentice's bed

The **Tsaï-Loun Room** follows the history of paper since its invention by the Chinese (105 AD), who were inspired by wasps' nests, to the year 1326 when three men from the Auvergne who had been taken prisoner in Damascus returned and introduced the technique to the Ambert region, using the acidic spring waters of the Forez mountains. Other rooms look at the production process. Old fragments of white fabric (linen, cotton) are cut into small pieces; pine mallets with steel teeth are then used to crush the pieces of fabric. The paper paste, rinsed through with water to which glue has been added (to stop the paper from absorbing too much ink) is poured into a vat; at this stage the petals and ferns which are used to make **flower paper** (one of this mill's specialities) are added. After it has been drained through a brass wire strainer (the *forme* or mould on which the watermark of the mill is sewn in relief), the still damp sheet of paper is placed between two sheets of felt; a press then exerts a pressure of 40t down on lots of 100 sheets, which are then hung up in the drying rooms.

The mill produces an average of 400 to 500 sheets daily.

Parc Zoologique du Bouy

8.5km/5 mi S along D 906 and right onto D 56 to Champetières. 🧒 🕐 *Feb-Nov: 10am-6pm (Oct-Nov, Wed, Sat, Sun).* 🕐 *Dec-Jan. 7€ (children: 4€).* ☎ *04 73 82 13 29.*

The zoo covers an area of 50ha/123 acres planted with beautiful Scotch firs, spruce, Douglas firs and sequoias which blend into the surrounding forest. Many species of animal, whose habits and characteristics are explained on information panels, live here in semi-liberty: birds, monkeys, lions, lynx, jackals, hyenas, wolves, kangaroos, camels, bison, white deer, emus etc. A children's playground completes the zoo's attractions.

Le Val Lagat

60km/37mi round tour – allow one day

▶ *Leave Ambert by the E along D 966, heading towards Montbrison.*

Musée de l'école 1900

In Saint-Martin-des-Olmes. 🕐 *Jun-Sep: 9am-noon, 2-7pm; school holidays: 10am-noon, 2-7pm; Sat-Sun: 2-6pm. 5€ (children: 3€).* ☎ *04 73 72 66 80.*

The village school, dating from the 1880s and closed in 1989, houses this interesting school museum which recreates the atmosphere of a classroom at the turn of the 20C, the playground with period toys, the dining hall and the teacher's apartment, not forgetting the garden with its vegetable patch and hen house.

▶ *Turn back and take the first road on the right.*

Moulin Richard-de-Bas★ – ⓒ *See above.*

▶ *Turn around and, at Valeyre, turn right onto D 67.*

A discovery trail, **Le Chemin des Papetiers,** starts from Valeyre and runs along the steep mule track followed by rag-pickers, offering an insight into the history of papermaking from its prosperous beginnings in the 15C to its decline in the 19C. As the road climbs it offers good views over the Ambert plain, La Chaise-Dieu plateau and the Livradois. The winding road then skirts the Valcivières cirque.

Cirque de Valcivières

This attractive cirque shelters several hamlets on its stream-strewn slopes and among the fields.

Turn right onto D 106 which wends its way past fields and meadows, through a beechwood and up to Col des Supeyres, offering a **panoramic view**★ of the cirque, the Livradois and, in the distance, the Dore and Dômes mountain ranges.

Col des Supeyres

Alt 1 366m/4 481ft. This pass on the eastern edge of the Livradois-Forez Nature Park is surrounded by a landscape more reminiscent of steppes: badly-drained mountain pastures, without a soul in sight. The sense of ruggedness and isolation is particularly strong at the bottom of the road leading to Pierre sur Haute (it becomes a dirt track 1km/0.6mi from the start).

Un colporteur et des jasseries

From Col des Supeyres, walk through high pastures along a discovery trail, following in the footsteps of pedlars of bygone days.

On the way down to St-Anthème, the road runs along the Jasseries (mountain farms) du Grand Genévrier; one of them is open to visitors.

Jasserie du Coq-Noir

ⓞ *Mid-Jun to mid-Sep: noon-7pm; May to mid-Jun and mid-Sep to early Nov: Sat-Sun and public holidays noon-7pm; by appointment the rest of the year.* ☎ *04 73 82 96 94.*
This former summer farm offers valuable insight into mountain farming, roof thatching and cheesemaking. A snack of milk rye bread and Fourme (local cheese) is available.

▶ *Return to Col des Supeyres and Valcivières.*

After Valcivières the route follows a rock-strewn ravine to emerge above the Ambert plain and then descends the lower slopes of the Forez mountains.

▶ *D 66, then D 906 will take you back to Ambert.*

From the Livradois to the Dore

100km/62mi round tour – allow all day including hikes
▶ *Leave Ambert by the W along D 996, heading towards St-Amand-Roche-Savine.*

The road between Le Monestier and St-Amand will take you past the **Domaine Noble des Escures** (⚬⇀ *not open to the public*), a small castle with corner turrets and bartizans that Henri Pourrat used as a setting for his novel *Gaspard des Montagnes*.

St-Amand-Roche-Savine

Every summer, this charming hamlet nestling amid the Livradois heights welcomes many visitors, especially during the lively rock festival held in the streets. The 15C-

Monts du Livradois

16C church features a fine doorway and the interior presents details of frescoes and historically listed furniture.

▶ *Drive N and, 1km/0.5mi after leaving St-Amand, turn right onto D 87, then D 65.*

Cunlhat

Pretty trading community formerly specialised in woolmaking, surrounded by lush wooded vegetation perfect for country walks. Note the fine façades and the **Prieurale St-Martin,** a 12C and 16C church commissioned by a lord from Montboissier. A walk (1hr) through the town, entitled *La balade des cinq fontaines,* is detailed in a leaflet available from the tourist office.

▶ *Leave Cunlhat to the S and drive along D 105 to St-Eloy-la-Glacière; turn left after entering the village.*

La ferme des Bois Noirs

🕐 *2-7pm; Easter-end Oct: Sat, Sun and public holidays (daily, mid-Jun - mid-Sep). 5€ (children: 3€).* ☎ *04 73 72 13 47.*

Unaltered since it was built in 1763, this farmhouse illustrates the life and work of a peasant family in the Livradois region, a poor mountainous area where men had to take on seasonal work (tree-felling in the nearby forests) to supplement the meagre income the family derived from farming. The kitchen-cum-living-room is the warmest room in the house; it contains the bread oven, the dairy tools and the stone sink. Next door is the bedroom with its box-beds and wooden chest for storing clothes. Adjacent are the barn and stables with the labourer's room; curing with salt takes place in the attic. A collection of tools is exhibited upstairs and the shed contains various machines; don't miss the garden with its beehive.

▶ *Drive back to St-Eloy and turn left onto D 105 to Fournols.*

Fournols

This small summer resort is clustered around its Gothic church. It still boasts several fine old mansions. The fortified 13C **church** built on the site of a former castle presents an imposing square porch and an alcove containing a 16C *Pietà*. Note the listed 11C *capital* (dismantled), the finely sculpted **stalls** and the gilded wooden statues (18C).

▶ *D 37 will take you to St-Germain-l'Herm.*

St-Germain-l'Herm

Summer holiday resort offering a wide range of activities (literary festival, flea markets, walks). Typical **fortified church** (12C and 16C) and **corbelled houses** in the old village.

▶ *Follow D 999 and turn right onto D 999A; drive through St-Bonnet-le-Chastel, once dominated by a huge fortress. Proceed until you reach Novacelles.*

Novacelles

You will enjoy visiting this small village tucked away in a valley watered by the Dollore. The church features a fine collection of 14C frescoes discovered in the 1960s.

▶ *Take D 105 to St-Sauveur-la-Sagne, then D 38 along the Dore gorges. Turn right onto D 907.*

La Chaise-Dieu –   *See La CHAISE-DIEU.*

▶ *Drive N out of La Chaise-Dieu along D 906 then turn right onto D 202.*

Dore-l'Église

The village, situated at the confluence of the Dore and Dorette, has a 12C church which underwent alterations in the 15C. A wide flight of steps leads up to a fine **porch** with triple coving, the last of which is decorated with imaginary animals. The doors still have their 14C **strap hinges.** To the left of the church is a **Gallo-Roman memorial.**

▶ *Take D 906 N.*

Arlanc

This small market town with its typical old streets occupies a delightful site hemmed in between the Forez and Livradois mountains.

The **church of St-Pierre,** a Romanesque building with particularly fine stonework is definitely worth a visit; note the capital carved with long faces (2nd pillar on the right). The **Musée de la Dentelle** (*Mid-Apr to May and first fortnight in Oct: weekends 3-6pm; Jun and Sep: daily 3-6pm; Jul-Aug: 10am-12.30pm, 3-6.30pm. 3€. ☎ 04 73 95 00 03. www.arlanc.com/musee_dentelle.htm*) is housed in the vaulted cellars of the Mairie (town hall). Throughout the Auvergne the lacemaking tradition dates back to the late 16C, though its heyday in Arlanc was in the late 19C when the Chabrier company launched a type of handmade lace, named "Renaissance," which was an immediate success. The museum owns several pieces: tablecloths, handkerchiefs, veils, a few dresses, together with lacemaking equipment. An audio-visual display *(in French)* explains the techniques used for making bobbin lace. In season, visitors can watch a lacemaker at work.

Jardin pour la Terre

Pleasant access by the many narrow alleys of the old town.   *Daily, May-Sep: 2-7pm (guided tours Jul-Aug only, daily). 6€ (children: 3.50€). ☎ 04 73 95 00 71. www.jardin-pourlaterre.com*

This 6ha/15-acre garden retraces the history of small trees and shrubberies coming from all five continents and their adjustment to European climatic conditions. It also enlightens visitors on the adventures and maritime routes of the world's greatest explorers.

Marsac-en-Livradois

On the square to the south of the church stands the old White Penitents' Chapel. It houses the **Musée des Pénitents Blancs du Livradois** (♿🕐 *Jul-Aug: guided tours (45min) 10am-noon, 3-7pm; low season: apply to the town hall in advance.* ☎ *04 73 95 60 08 www.cc-livradois.fr/marsac/penitent*), a museum bursting with memorabilia relating to this brotherhood. A recorded commentary *(in French)* accompanied by religious music evokes the life and rituals of the old penitent order.

▶ *Go back to Ambert on D 906.*

ANNONAY

POPULATION 17 522
MICHELIN MAP 331: K-2

Annonay is located in a deep cleft of the Vivarais plateau, at the confluence of the River Deûme and River Cance. In the Middle Ages, the exceptional quality of the water here encouraged a leather and wool industry to be established which then flourished.

Being one of the first towns to uphold the principles of the Reformation, Annonay suffered greatly during the Wars of Religion. In the 17C, however, following the establishment in the town of the Johannot and Montgolfier families' paperworks, Annonay began to prosper once again. 🛈 *Pl. des Cordeliers, 07100 ANNONAY.* ☎ *04 75 33 24 51. www.ardeche-verte.com*

Today, traditional industries around the town are complemented by a wide array of other activities including coach building, mechanical engineering, the production of industrial felts, wool, shoes, health food and pharmaceutical products. These modern businesses located in the surrounding uplands form a striking contrast with the façades of historical Annonay.

The native city of the Montgolfier brothers (♿ *see below*), Annonay was also the home of one of their descendants, **Marc Seguin** (1786-1875), the engineer who improved the steam boiler. His model, used in 1830 for Stephenson's Rocket, increased the train's speed from 9kph/5.6mph to a maximum of 60kph/37mph.

An aerostatic experiment – Observing that hot air rises, the **Montgolfier brothers** decided to harness this energy; after several successful experiments, they were ready to test their process in public. On 4 June 1783, in the presence of the States General of the Vivarais area, they launched a balloon of 769m3/27 157cu ft. The strips forming the balloon itself were made of packaging fabric and paper, held together by some 1 800 buttons. Rising in nine and a half minutes to a maximum height of 1 000-2 000m or 3 250-6 500ft (according to different eyewitness accounts) the balloon remained in the air for half an hour and

Reconstitution of the first flight

Fr. Isler/MICHELIN

finally landed more than 2km/1mi from its launch site. The aerostat, the forerunner of the aeroplane, was born.

This feat is commemorated by an obelisk at the roundabout in avenue Marc-Seguin, a plaque on place des Cordeliers, where the experiment was conducted, and an annual reconstruction of the historic first flight *(see Calendar of events)*.

Old Town

The old quarter on the hills overlooking the two rivers is currently benefiting from a major restoration project.

▷ *Start out from place de la Libération.*

On this square stands a statue of the Montgolfier brothers, erected in 1883 to commemorate the first centenary of their aerostatic experiments.

A little lookout point on the left of the post office offers a **view** of the Cance Valley and Mignot Park.

▷ *Turn onto rue Boissy-d'Anglas.*

Chapelle de Trachin

This Gothic chapel is all that remains of a priory founded in 1320 by Guy Trachin, a wealthy resident of Annonay. Having escaped destruction during the Wars of Religion, it served alternately as a brotherhood chapel and a parish church. The tall stone spire dates from the 16C. The north porch bears a bust of the founder, and is topped by a 17C Madonna and Child.

▷ *From the bottom of place de la Liberté turn onto Montée du Château.*

Fortified Gates

Montée du Château forms a steep incline up to the old machicolated gate; a second gate also survives, at the end of rue de Bourgville.

▷ *Rue Montgolfier leads to the bridge of the same name.*

Pont Montgolfier

This bridge spans the Deûme. Upstream, the view is of the humpback **Valgelas bridge** (14C) and the convent of Ste-Marie (16C). Downstream, the Deûme flows into the **Défilé des Fouines,** a dark, narrow rocky gorge overlooked by abandoned taweries, where skins were once prepared as part of the leather-making process.

Place des Cordeliers

The square is named after a Franciscan convent which once occupied the site of the theatre. A plaque on the right of the tourist office commemorates the Montgolfier brothers' first public experiment.

▷ *Walk to Valgelas bridge and follow Voûtes Soubise, a vaulted passageway, to the steps of rue Barville. Turn right onto rue de Deûme and continue to avenue de l'Europe.*

Avenue de l'Europe partly covers the Deûme. From the intersection with rue de la Valette there is a **view** west over the **Tour des Martyrs** (12C-13C), the last remnant of the old ramparts, and the former convent of Ste-Marie.

Place de la Liberté

This square located in the centre of the old town becomes a bustling hub of trade on market days *(Wednesdays and Saturdays)*. The north-western side of the square is graced by a statue of Marc Seguin. The square provides an attractive view of Trachin Chapel.

Rue Franki-Kramer
Annonay's old high street, like the nearby place Grenette and place Mayol, is flanked by picturesque 16C, 17C and 18C houses. A plaque on the left commemorates Marc Seguin's birthplace. The house on the next corner still shows iron cladding designed to protect its walls.

▶ *Walk through place Grenette and return to rue Franki-Kramer.*

The 17C alms church at no 15 is now used as a Protestant church.

▶ *Follow the passage, cross place Mayol, then take rue Ste-Marie to rue des Consuls.*

On the left stands an old mansion with mullioned windows.

Additional Sights

Musée Vivarois César-Filhol
🕐 *Jul-Aug: 2.30-6pm; Sep-Jun: Wed, Sat-Sun 2.30-6pm.* 🕐 *Closed 14 Jul, 15 Aug, public holidays. 2.50€.* ☎ *04 75 67 67 93. www.mairie-annonay.fr.*
This ancient royal bailiwick dating from 1700 contains interesting collections on old Annonay, its famous citizens and the folklore of the Vivarois area. Local works of art include a beautiful 16C wooden Crucifix and a touching 17C wooden *Pietà*. The museum also has a reconstruction of a kitchen from the Ardèche region and a

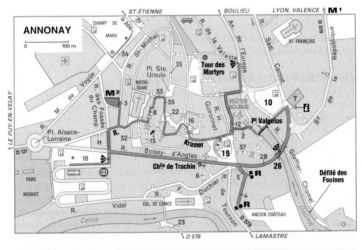

ANNONAY		Cordeliers Pl. des	10	Montgolfier Pont	26
		Deûme R. de	12	Montgolfier R.	28
Barville. R.	2	Épiphanie R.	13	Poterne R. de la	32
Bechetoille R. J.-B.	3	Frachon R. E.	15	Réforme R. de la	33
Boissy-d'Anglas R.		Grenette Pl.	16	St-Étienne R.	34
Bourgville R. de	4	Libération Pl. de la	18	Ste-Marie R.	35
Château Montée du	5	Liberté Pl. de la	19	Valgelas R.	37
Clocher R. du	6	Mayol Pl.	22		
Consuls R. des	8	Meyzonnier R.	23		

Musée des Papeteries Canson et Montgolfier	M¹	Musée vivarois César-Filhol	M²	Portes fortifiées	R

Address Book

EATING OUT

☺☺ **Restaurant La Moustache Gourmande** – & *Le Village - 07430 St-Clair – 3.5km/2mi from Annonay. Take D 206, then D 342 via Bouliu-lès-Annonay -* ☎ *04 75 67 01 81 - closed Feb school holidays, 15 days in Sep and Wed.* This restaurant in a charming village is run by a jovial chef from Charente. It owes its fine reputation to the freshness of the ingredients, the nice selection of sea food dishes, the pastel-toned dining room and the terrace with an exceptional view of the wooded hills beyond.

WHERE TO STAY

☺☺☺ **Hôtel D'Ay** – *Gourdan golf course - 6.5km/4mi N of Annonay via D 519, then N 82 dir. St-Étienne -* ☎ *04 75 67 01 00. www.domainestclair.fr -* 🅿 *- 35 rms:* �}ñ *10€ - restaurant* ☺☺*. Savour the ambient quietude in this modern hotel located on a tree-dotted 18-hole golf course. Well equiped spacious rooms with wicker furnishings, the nicest of which are on the first floor.

☺ **Chambre d'hôte La Désirade** – *07340 St-Désirat - 15km/9mi E of Annonay via D 82 dir. Andance, and secondary road -* ☎ *04 75 34 21 88 - http://ph.meunier.free.fr - closed Christmas and 1 Jan -* ✎ *- reserv. required - 6 rms - meals* ☺☺*.* Set amid grapevines and trees, this entirely renovated 19C bourgeois house certainly does not want for charm. The pleasant, bright rooms give either onto the courtyard with its magnolia, or the park and vineyard. Regional cuisine.

RECREATION

Les Accros-branchés – *Chemin du Grand Murier, 07100 Annonay* ☎ *04 75 67 52 20. www.acrobranche.org.* Treetop rambles are for thrill-seekers and nature lovers. The professional guides assure safety.

---

wide range of documentation on the Montgolfier brothers, Marc Seguin (model of his 1828 locomotive) and on the Seguin brothers, inventors in 1908 of the "Gnome" rotating aircraft engine.

Musée des Papeteries Canson et Montgolfier

2.5km/1.5mi NE. Leave Annonay on Boulevard de la République, following signs to Valence. Turn left just before the Davézieux Industrial Estate; the road goes downhill and is marked "Musée des Papeteries Canson et Montgolfier." Park in the car park in front of the church. ⏱ *Jul-Aug: guided tours (1hr30min) by arrangement one week in advance. 2.15-6pm; Sep-Jun: Wed and Sun 2.30-6pm.* ⏱ *Closed Easter and 25 Dec. 4€.* ☎ *04 75 69 87 19.*

The museum is laid out in the house where the brothers Joseph and Étienne de Montgolfier, the inventors of the hot-air balloon, were born; it retraces the history of the paperworks established on the banks of the Deûme, particularly the Vidalon paperworks, appointed purveyors to the court in 1784 for its quality products. The museum presents a traditional papermaking workshop with a vat, a set of moulds, a stretcher and a wooden press. Many documents, explanatory panels and tools show the development of techniques used in Vidalon from the time of the first papermill, established by the Chelles family from Beaujeu. The display provides a fascinating glimpse of papermaking techniques used in the Far East. The museum also focuses on daily life and customs in the papermaking industry before the French Revolution, and there is a reconstruction of an old laboratory and the office of a paper manufacturer at the turn of the 20C. The vast workshop in the vaulted cellar houses large machines including a cylinder mould papermaking machine, the link between manual and contemporary techniques. Here, visitors can watch traditional manual manufacturing techniques.

Excursions

Safari-Parc de Peaugres★

6km/4mi to the NE by Boulevard de la République. 🧒 ♿🕐 *Jun-Aug: 9.30am-6pm; Mar-May and Sep to late Oct: 10am-4.30pm (Sat-Sun, school and public holidays 9.30am-5pm).* 🕐 *Closed 25 Dec. 17€ (3-12-year-olds: 12.50€).* ☎ *04 75 33 00 32. www.safari-peaugres.com*

Located at the foot of the Pilat massif, laid out on either side of N 82, this nature reserve is home to 400 mammals, 300 birds and around 60 reptiles. If you visit the zoo **by car,** you must comply with the safety regulations. The tarred road winds its way through four enclosed areas, affording close views of monkeys, zebras, bears, dromadaries, buffaloes, yaks, hippopotamuses, elephants and deer. Those who are **on foot** may see aquatic birds, giraffes, ostriches and African antelopes. The manor houses a vivarium that contains lizards, boas, pythons, caimans and dogfish. After the monkey park, the tour ends with lions and large cats (tigers, cheetahs) seen through a glass tunnel. A group of sea-lions and some 20 penguins can be seen in and around a pool.

Boulieu

5km/3mi to the N on avenue de l'Europe. Former fortified village with square ramparts flanking the main street.

Château de Thorrenc

10km/7mi to the NE. After the bus station turn right onto D 370, then left onto D 291. 🔒 *Not open to the public.* This recently restored 11C castle dominates the Thor-rençon precipice.

Barrage du Ternay

10km/7mi to the north on D 206, then N 82 and D 306. This dam erected in 1867 to sup-ply water to Annonay is set against a charming backdrop of cedar trees and a lake.

St-Désirat

13km east. From Davézieux, follow D 82 for about 7km/4.5mi then turn left onto a small road leading to St-Désirat.

Musée de l'Alambic★

🕐 *Sep-Jun: daily, 8am-noon, 2-6.30pm (Sat-Sun and public holidays 10am-noon, 2-6.30pm) (last admission 1hr before closing); Jul-Aug: 8am-7pm, Sat-Sun and pub-lic holidays 10am-7pm.* 🕐 *Closed 1 Jan and 25 Dec. No charge.* ☎ *04 75 34 23 11. www.jeangauthier.com*

Housed inside the Gauthier distillery, this interesting museum recalls the life and work of distillers who used to travel from farm to farm to distil the 10l of brandy to which each farmer was entitled every year. This privilege was abolished in 1960 and travelling distill-ers were replaced by strictly controlled distilleries. The museum includes films and reconstructed scenes illustrating the successive stages of the distilling process. Visitors are then invited to taste the local pear brandy.

J. Damase/MICHELIN

Copper distilling vats

The Ay and Cance valleys

Round tour of 48km/29mi – allow 2hr. Leave Annonay by rue de Tournon to the S heading for Lamastre.

Quintenas-le-Peyron
The village is dominated by the fine 14C belfry of its Romanesque church.

▷ *In Quintenas, on the right, facing the church, follow directions for St-Romain-d'Ay.*

The narrow road meanders through the countryside, affording pretty views of the Haut-Vivarais.

▷ *Leave the church of St-Romain on your left and drive to D 6; turn left. After 90m/100yd, on the right, a steep road leads to Notre-Dame-d'Ay.*

Notre-Dame-d'Ay
This modest sanctuary perched on top of a rocky outcrop is a popular place of pilgrimage.

▷ *Turn back, turn right onto D 6, then take D 221 to Sarras. In Sarras, turn left onto N 86 and after 2km/1mi, before the bridge spanning the River Cance, turn left onto D 270.*

The corniche road follows the steep banks of the Cance Valley, carpeted with oak trees. The **Roche Péréandre**★ looms majestically at a height of 40m/131ft.

▷ *Proceed along D 270, then D 371 until you reach Annonay.*

GORGES DE L'ARDÈCHE★★★

MICHELIN MAPS 331: I-7 TO J-8

The Ardèche gorge, overlooked by an audaciously engineered road, ranks among the most impressive sites of natural beauty in the south of France; a large part of the gorge is now a nature reserve. In 1993, this exceptional stretch of landscape was listed as a major national site (Grand Site d'Intérêt National).

▷ **Orient Yourself:** it is difficult to get a complete overview of the gorges, but the view from the panoramic road is as good as any.
◉ **Don't Miss:** The Pont d'Arc
◷ **Organizing Your Time:** You should allow a whole day to do a complete circuit
▣ **Especially for kids:** If the water is calm, take a canoe trip on the river (*see Canoe hire*).
◔ **Also see:** Bourg-St-Andéol, Vallon-Pont-d'Arc and Les Vans

Spates and droughts – The Ardèche rises in the Mazan massif (alt 1 467m/4 813ft). After a 119km/74mi journey, it flows into the Rhône, just upstream from Pont-St-Esprit. In the upper valley the Ardèche cuts a steep downhill course, but it is in the lower valley that some of the more interesting formations due to erosion are to be seen. Here the river has carved a passage through the limestone strata of the plateau, which had already been undermined from the inside by subterranean streams. The Ardèche's tributaries flowing down from the mountain accentuate its sporadic yet typically Mediterranean flow: autumn spates give way to a shallow stream in winter, then swell into spring torrents, before subsiding to a comparative trickle during the summer. During the autumn spates, when the river's volume can increase dramatically from 2.5m3/s (88cu ft/s) to 7 000m3/s (247 100cu ft/s), there is a tremendous convergence of flood waters at Vallon-Pont-d'Arc. A powerful wall of water can sweep down the valley at 15-20kph/9-12mph an hour! The strength of these erratic flood waters is such that the river pushes the flow of the Rhône eastwards and deposits a pile of alluvial debris in its river bed. In 1890, the force of the Ardèche spate was so strong that it cut right across the course of the Rhône and broke through the Lauzon dike on the opposite bank. The level of the Ardèche drops as suddenly as it rises.

Excursion

1 Route panoramique

38km/24mi starting from Vallon-Pont-d'Arc – allow half a day
The D 290 **panoramic road** overlooks the gorge from the clifftops at the edge of the Gras plateau, giving breathtaking views from the many look-out points (belvédères) along the way.

Vallon-Pont-d'Arc

This town is the departure point for boat trips down the gorge. South-east of the town, on the slope of a hill, stand the ruins of Vieux Vallon Castle, a reminder of the old medieval village here. On the ground floor of the Mairie (town hall housed in a Louis XIII mansion) are seven 17C Aubusson **tapestries** in a remarkable state of preservation, with their colours still extremely fresh.

Exposition Grotte Chauvet-Pont-d'Arc

Stay in a cattle-breeding ranch, visit the estate and observe the different herds…a must for those who wish to have a taste of life on a ranch. ☎ 05 65 42 47 46. www. le-saloon.com
At the end of 1994, a set of cave paintings and engravings of exceptional interest was discovered on the site of the Combe-d'Arc in the Ardèche gorge. Part of a vast

network of underground galleries, the cave (named **Grotte Chauvet** after the man who discovered it) features a large number of black or red paintings and engravings on its walls. These depict some 400 animals, including horses, mammoths, bears, woolly rhinoceroses, cats and aurochs; figures of a hyena and an owl are also portrayed, which is exceptionally rare. Geometrical motifs and outlines of hands – both positive and reversed-out – appear alongside these figures, in which the artists' skill is reflected by the accuracy of their draughtsmanship and the way they have managed to portray movement and relief.

Initial studies of these works of art date them from the Upper Palaeolithic Age, about 30 000 years before our time. The number, quality and originality of these animal paintings place the Vallon-Pont-d'Arc cave on a level with the Cosquer cave discovered in the *calanques* east of Marseille and the Lascaux cave in the Dordogne, in terms of the importance of their contribution to the study of cave paintings worldwide. Furthermore, as the cave has remained untouched since the Palaeolithic Age, it constitutes an enormous potential site of investigation for palaeontologists, who will analyse the bones of bear-like mammals found scattered in the cave, and for archaeologists, who will use the numerous artefacts and other evidence (fireplaces, chipped flints, footprints etc) to be found on the site to learn more about the activities of our ancestors.

For the time being, only specialists are allowed into the cave; but eventually some kind of reproduction is planned (much as at Lascaux) so that the cave's hidden treasures can be admired by all interested parties. In the mean time, there is an exhibition on the wonders to be found in Grotte Chauvet and other caves of the Ardèche Valley in rue Miarou in Vallon-Pont-d'Arc.

▶ *Head S for Pont-d'Arc on D 290.*

The road skirts the foot of the ruins of **Vieux Vallon Castle** and after crossing the Ibie, comes to the Ardèche. On the left is the **Grotte des Tunnels**, a cave through which an underground torrent once ran, and then **Grotte des Huguenots** (🕐 *Mid-Jun to end Aug: 10am-7pm; rest of the year: on request. 4€ (children: 3€). ☎ 04 75 88 06 71)*, which houses an exhibition on speleology, prehistory and the history of the Huguenot population of the southern Vivarais region.

Pont-d'Arc★★
Park in one of the car parks on either side of the viewpoint.

🚶 The river flows under this natural arch (34m/111ft high, 59m/193ft wide at water level). At one time the river skirted this promontory, following the route now taken by the road; the arch would have been just a gulley through which underground

Pont-d'Arc

waters drained. General erosion and the undermining activities of the river must have worn away the land around the arch, and then the river itself, during some particularly large spate, abandoned its old meander to slip through the passage, which it has subsequently made larger *(the arch can be reached along a footpath starting 150m/165yd on the Vallon side of the viewpoint)*.

Beyond Pont-d'Arc the landscape becomes more impressive still. The river follows a series of gentle curves, interspersed with rapids, at the bottom of a deserted gorge 30km/19mi long. The height of the surrounding cliffs – some of them reaching 300m/984ft – together with their rich colouring and dramatic appearance leave a lasting impression.

After Chames the road veers round to the left at the bottom of Tiourre Valley which forms an impressive, rocky **cirque**★ before reaching the edge of the plateau.

Belvédère du Serre de Tourre★★

Poised almost vertically above the Ardèche, which flows 200m/656ft below, this viewpoint offers a superb **view** of the meander known as the **Pas du Mousse**, with the ruins of the 16C Château d'Ebbo$ clearly visible on the rocky promontory.

The broad tourist road follows the tortuous relief of the cliffs on the east bank, running through forests of evergreen oaks, first the Bois Bouchas and then the Bois Malbosc.

Belvédères de Gaud★★

There is a fine view of the upstream sweep of the Gaud meander and the turrets of its small 19C castle.

Belvédères d'Autridge★

To reach the two viewpoints, take the panoramic curve. The needle of rock known as Aiguille de Morsanne soars up from the Ardèche like the prow of a ship.

Some 500m/550yd beyond a majestic coomb (Combe d'Agrimont), there are splendid **vistas**★★ back upstream of the magnificent meander with the Morsanne needle in the foreground.

Belvédères de Gournier★★

These viewpoints are well situated, 200m/656ft above the Ardèche. Below, the Gournier farm lies in ruins in a small meadow beside the river, which finds a way through the Toupine rocks (toupine means cooking pot).

▶ *Continue to the Marzal chasm along the road across the Gras plateau (D 590).*

Aven de Marzal★

Interior temperature 14°C/57°F; 743 steps.

The chasm is a natural well, which leads to a number of caves. These are rich in magnificent stalagmites, stalactites and other limestone formations, ranging from brown-ochre to snow-white in colour. Near the first, the Salle du Tombeau, are the bones of animals which fell into the chasm (bear, deer, bison).

You can also visit the **Musée du Monde Souterrain** (&⊙ *Apr-Sep: 10am-6pm; Mar, Oct and Nov: Sun and public holidays 2-6pm. No charge.* ☎ *04 75 55 14 82),* a museum devoted to the history of speleology in France. The **Zoo Préhistorique** (& *07700 Saint Remèze. Apr-Sep: daily, 10am-6pm; Mar and Oct-Nov: Sun, public and school holidays, 1-5.30pm. 8€ (children: 5.50€); ticket including Aven de Marzal: 14€ (children: 8.50€)* ☎ *04 75 55 14 82)* is laid out along a shaded route displaying life-size reproductions of extinct animals that lived from the Primary to the Quaternary Era.

▶ *D 201 leads to Bidon.*

Bidon

This tiny peaceful village boasts a **Musée de la Vie** (Museum of Life – ♿🕐 *Apr to mid-Nov: 10am-6pm.* 🕐 *Closed the rest of the year. 6€ (6-14-year-olds: 3€).* ☎ *04 75 04 08 79)* illustrating the evolution of the universe from the initial Big Bang to the present time.

▶ *Return to the La Madeleine junction and leave the car in one of the car parks by the Belvédère de la Madeleine.*

This is the **Haute Corniche**★★★, the most outstanding section of the drive, offering breathtaking views of the gorge from a series of viewpoints in quick succession.

Belvédère de la Madeleine★

Access to the parking area via a surfaced road from April onwards, when the gate is open. From here there is an imposing view of the Madeleine "fortress" a rocky outcrop blocking the view of the rest of the gorge downstream. These are the highest cliffs of the entire gorge, towering 300m/984ft above the river valley.

🚶 From the parking area, a steep stony footpath leads through thick vegetation to the Belvédère de la Cathédrale (♿ *see below).*

Grotte de la Madeleine★

🕐 *Saint-Remèze. Jul-Aug: 9am-7pm; Apr-Jun and Sep: 10am-6pm; Oct: 10am-5pm. Last visit 1h before closure. 7€ (children: 4.50€).* ☎ *04 75 04 22 20. www.grottemadeleine. com*

This cave (discovered in 1887) was carved out by an underground river which once drained part of the Gras plateau. Enter through the Grotte Obscure, then follow a tunnel hewn out of the rock (♿ *steep stairway)* which leads to the Salle du Chaos, a vast chamber divided into two by a mass of columns coming down from the cave roof.

Belvédère de la Cathédrale★★

15min on foot there and back. Stay near the crossroads and take the lane on the left level with the fence.

La Haute Corniche

J. Damase/MICHELIN

Address Book

PRACTICAL INFORMATION

A FRAGILE ENVIRONMENT

The Ardèche Nature Reserve is a conservation area, so every effort should be made to protect its ecosystem. In particular, visitors must not light a fire, leave behind rubbish, pick plants or stray from the signposted footpaths. Picnicking is possible all along the way. Camping or bivouacking are prohibited outside authorised camp sites (see overnight stops below).

DOWNRIVER BY BOAT OR CANOE

The whole trip (starting upriver from Pont d'Arc) means covering a distance of 30km/18.6mi; however, it is possible to shorten the distance to 24km/15mi by starting from Chames. If you feel like a boat trip without any physical exertion, contact the Confrérie des Bateliers de l'Ardèche (information and bookings available at the tourist office in Vallon). The river can be explored by canoe year-round, although the best time is in May, June (except weekends) and September (daily); during the cold season (October to April), canoeists should wear a waterproof and isothermal suit. Depending on the season and the water level, it is wise to allow six to nine hours to complete the trip (departures are not allowed after 6pm). There are a few difficult passages (rapids) which require a good canoeing technique; in addition, it is essential to know how to swim. Life jackets must be worn by participants and heavy fines are applied to those who do not comply with regulations; these are available from hiring companies, town halls, tourist offices and gendarmeries (police stations in country areas).

Canoe hire – Some 50 hiring companies, based in Vallon-Pont-d'Arc, Salavas, Ruoms, St-Martin, St-Remèze, propose unaccompanied and guided trips lasting one or two days for an average price of 30€ (one day) or 40€ (two days without accommodation) per person (children under 7 years of age are not allowed on these trips). A list of hiring companies is available from tourist offices in Ruoms (rue Alphonse-Daudet, 07120 Ruoms,

☎ 04 75 93 91 90), Vallon-Pont-d'Arc (Cité administrative, 07150 Vallon-Pont-d'Arc, ☎ 04 75 88 04 01) and St-Martin-d'Ardèche (place de l'Église, 07700 St-Martin-d'Ardèche, ☎ 04 75 98 70 91). For unaccompanied trips, it is necessary to book an overnight stop from central booking offices located in the above-mentioned tourist offices.

Overnight stops – Overnight stops along the gorge are allowed in two places only: Aire Naturelle de Gaud and Aire Naturelle de Gournier; 5€ or 8€ (under a tent). Longer stays are possible at two camp sites: Camping des Templiers (naturism, ☎ 04 75 04 28 58) and Camping des Grottes de St-Marcel (☎ 04 75 04 14 65).

FOLLOWING THE GORGE ON FOOT

Before embarking upon a walk along the gorge, remember to check the weather forecast and signs indicating daily water levels to be sure of being able to cross the fords safely.

Allow two days for the 21km/13mi hike from Chames (starting point just beyond the village in a bend; two information panels, parking area below the road). Start early in the morning, wear adequate walking shoes, take 2l of water (it gets very hot in the middle of the day), some food, a first-aid kit and a pair of sandals for crossing the fords. Apart from the two fords, there are a few difficult passages all equipped with handrails.

A topoguide, Les Gorges de l'Ardèche et leurs plateaux (no 2, Gilbert de Cochet) is published by the Syndicat Intercommunal des Gorges de l'Ardèche et de leur Région Naturelle (SIGARN ☎ 04 75 98 77 31).

J. Damase/MICHELIN

This look-out point gives an unparalleled view of one of the most fascinating natural sights along the gorge: an immense jagged rock known as the "Cathedral," whose rocky spires rise sheer above the river.

Balcon des Templiers
From the "Templars' Balcony" there are striking views of a tight loop in the river, cut deep into the magnificent surrounding rock walls. Down below, a small spur is crowned by the ruins of a leper hospital *(maladrerie)* founded by the Knights Templar.

Belvédère de la Maladrerie
From here there is a good view of the "Cathedral" rock upstream.

Belvédère de la Coutelle
This viewpoint overlooks the Ardèche from a dizzying height of 180m/590ft. To the right is the end of the Garn ramparts; to the left, along the axis of the gorge, are the Castelviel rocks. The Fève and Cadière rapids can also be seen.

Grand Belvédère★
The view from here takes in the exit of the gorge and the final meander of the river.
The information centre of the Grotte St-Marcel stands 200m/219yd downstream from the Grand Belvédère, on the left side of D 290.

Grotte de St-Marcel★
🕐 *guided tours (1h): Jul-Aug: 10am-7pm; mid-Mar to Jun and Sep: 10am-6pm; Oct to Mid-Nov: 10am-5pm. 8€ (Children 4.50€). Last amission 1h before closing.* ☎ *04 75 04 38 07. www.guideweb.com/ardeche/grotte/st-marcel*
A tunnel dug through the rock leads into chambers and passageways lined with stalagmites and stalactites in diverse shapes and colours, tinted by calcite, iron oxide, manganese, etc.
A footpath running round the site enables visitors to discover the interesting local flora (holm-oaks, box trees, rock roses…) as well as two megaliths *(leaflet available on location).*

Belvédère du Colombier★
From here, there is a lovely view over a meander enclosed by walls entirely of rock.
The road follows a loop along a dry valley, skirts the Dona Vierna promontory and makes a long detour along the Louby Valley.

Belvédère du Ranc-Pointu★★
This viewpoint at the mouth of the Louby Valley overlooks the last incised

meander of the Ardèche. Note the various phenomena caused by erosion: striation, potholes and caves.

From here the landscape changes dramatically on the way down to St-Martin: the bare defile gives way to a cultivated valley which opens out as it gets nearer the Rhône. On the opposite bank, the village of **Aiguèze** *(see below)* can be seen clinging to a rocky crest.

St-Martin-d'Ardèche

This is the first settlement since Vallon and a favourite haunt of anglers, ramblers and canoeists.

▶ *Cross the river via the narrow suspension bridge then turn left onto D 901 and immediately right again onto D 180.*

Aiguèze

Leave the car in the parking area at the entrance to the village. This medieval village crowns the last clifftops along the gorge. The 14C fort has a watch-path which offers fine **views** ★ of the mouth of the gorge, with Mont Ventoux in the distance and the suspension bridge linking Aiguèze to St-Martin-d'Ardèche in the foreground.

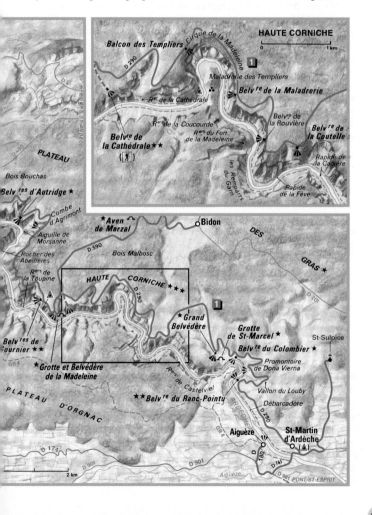

② Plateau d'Orgnac

45km/28mi itinerary starting from Aven d'Orgnac. 🚶 *See Aven d'ORGNAC.*

Following the Ardèche Gorges★★★
Whether you follow the gorge on foot, by boat or canoe, this trip will offer you an unforgettable experience.

By boat or canoe
After a long, calm stretch, the river flows into a bend and enters the gorge. The impressive Rapide du Charlemagne over which towers the enormous rock of the same name, comes just before the natural arch of Pont-d'Arc. To the left is the Cirque d'Estre and the Chauvet cave; further on to the right, the entrance to the Ebbo cave comes into sight, followed by the Pas du Mousse rock, a narrow passage in the cliff leading to the plateau; to the left stands the Aiguille rock. After passing the foot of the tall Saleyron cliffs, the river forms some rapids, such as Dent Noire, before reaching the sweeping Gaud meander and cirque marked by the small castle. Rapids alternate with smooth-flowing stretches beneath impressive cliffs. Note the Morsanne needle to the left and the jagged red and black Rocher des Abeillières to the right. After negotiating the boulders and cauldrons of the Toupine de Gournier (where the river bed is 18m/60ft deep in places) the Rocher de la Cathédrale looms into sight in the distance, after about 4hr on the river. Just before you actually pass this rock, the river takes you past one of the natural openings into La Madeleine cave.

The stretch of river at the foot of the Rochers de la Madeleine, passing beneath towering cliffs, is one of the most beautiful along the river. The river forms straits, rapids and limpid reaches as it passes between bare rock faces which contrast strongly with the evergreen oaks of the surrounding countryside. Downriver from the strange-looking Coucourde rock (Provençal for "crane") and the Castelvieil cliff, the opening of St-Marcel cave appears on the left and, as you round a bend, the Dona Vierna promontory and the Belvédère du Ranc-Pointu can be seen. The cliffs melt away as the valley finally widens out, overlooked by the tower of Aiguèze on the edge of the rocky outcrop to the right.

On foot
🚶 *See Practical Information above.* Two-day hiking tour with an overnight stop at the Gournier bivouac (booking essential). A good pair of binoculars is essential if you want to spot the rare Bonelli's eagle who reigns supreme over the gorge. Local flora is equally rich and varied: juniper, broom, savory, white oaks and holm-oaks.

ARDES-SUR-COUZE

POPULATION 547
MICHELIN 326: F-10

This old fortified town, once capital of the Duchy of Mercœur, has a 15C **church** *Jul and Aug: guided tours 10-11am, 2-5pm. ☎ 04 73 71 80 39.)* in front of which there is a cross dating from the same period with an image of the Virgin and Child on one of its sides. Inside the church, the gilt-wood high altar (17C) features eight remarkable little sculpture groups depicting the Passion. Near the chancel a strange carved wooden bas-relief adorns the shrine of St Hubert. Opposite the pulpit, there is a 16C stone **Pietà**, and the chapel at the back of the church contains a 15C lectern. 🅘 *Pl. de la Fontaine, 63420 ARDES, ☎ 04 73 71 80 39. www.ardes-couze.auvergne.net*

The **Musée des Vieux Métiers** *(Jun to mid-Sep: 10am-noon, 2-7pm. 3€. ☎ 04 73 71 81 41.)* shows exhibits relating to traditional crafts in the area, mainly used during the 19C. At the reception there is a small shop where you can buy locally produced goods.

Kids To round off the visit, spend a few hours at the **Parc Animalier du Cézallier** ⏰ *Apr-Sep: daily 10am-7pm; Oct-Mar, Sun 2pm-dusk (Easter and Christmas, daily 2pm-dusk). 8€ (children: 5€). ☎ 04 73 71 82 86. www.zoo-cezallier.com*, a cross between a traditional zoo and a safari park. A great many animals of all types can be seen in relative freedom. A playing area has been set aside for children.

Excursion

Wild valleys of the Cézallier

55km/34mi – about 3hr
This round tour is linked to that of the Couze de Pavin and Couze de Chambon (see Besse) via the Gorges de Courgoul (11km/6.8mi) between Saurier and Valbeleix.

▶ *Leave Ardes to the W along D 36.*

Vallée de Rentières★
The valley of the Couze d'Ardes, a tiny tributary of the Allier, is known as the Rentières d'Ardes between Ardes and St-Alyre upstream. The river cuts deeply into the Cézallier plateaus, forming a narrow furrow with valley sides carpeted with greenery. Opposite the village of Rentières stand the ruins of **Mercœur Château**.

▶ *Carry on along D 36.*

St-Alyre-ès-Montagne – 🖰 *See Monts du CÉZALLIER.*

▶ *On leaving the village, follow D 36 as far as the junction with D 32.*

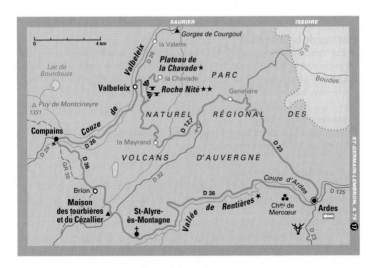

Maison des Tourbières et du Cézallier

🕐 *Jul-Sep: guided tours of the peat bog (1hr), unaccompanied visits of the building 10am-noon, 1.30-7pm. 5€. ☎ 04 73 71 78 98.*

This information centre presents the local area: wetlands, relics of the Ice Age, and local flora.

▶ *Carry on along D 36.*

The road takes you through the village of **Brion,** overlooked by some very striking basalt columns.

▶ *Follow D 36.*

Peat bogs

J. Damase/MICHELIN

Compains

Not far from this village is the spot where the Couze de Valbeleix rises; the river is most probably fed by the waters of Montcineyre Lake.

The **church** has a Romanesque nave and a Gothic chancel surmounted by a tall white steeple.

▶ *Take D 26 E.*

The road crosses the lava flow emitted by the Puy de Montcineyre when it erupted in this valley 6 000 years ago.

Valbeleix

The valley of the Couze de Valbeleix forms an almost perfect U-shaped cross-section. The round-topped hill which rises above the village and closes off the valley is a good example of a glacial threshold.

Further on, tiny hanging glacial cirques on the west bank of the Couze give an idea of the depth of the ice which filled this valley 10 000 years ago.

▶ *Turn right, past the church in Valbeleix, on D 127 for just over a mile, then left on D 641 towards La Chavade.*

Plateau de la Chavade★

To reach this plateau the road climbs up through the heart of a beech grove. Leave the car in the parking area cleared at the foot of a stand of pine trees twisted into strange shapes by their exposure to the elements. Walk to the two viewing tables, one of which can be seen from the car park, about 270m/300yd off to the right.

Belvedere *(1st viewpoint)*

This commands a magnificent **view**★★ of the U-shaped valley of the Couze de Valbeleix and of the Dore mountain range.

La Roche Nité *(2nd viewpoint)*

There is a superb **view**★★ of the volcanic mountain ranges of the Cézallier and Dore mountain range, in which lava flows were truncated 10 000 years ago by gigantic tongues of ice.

▶ *Rejoin D 127 towards Mayrand. Past Genelière, turn right onto D 23 leading to Ardes.*

ARLEMPDES★

POPULATION 142
MICHELIN MAP 331: F-4 – LOCAL MAP SEE GORGES DE LA LOIRE

Arlempdes occupies one of the most striking **sites**★★ in the Velay area. Perched on a spur of volcanic rock, the ruins of a medieval castle overlook the Loire gorge from a height of 80m/260ft.

Visiting Arlempdes

Village
The village huddling below the castle boasts a fortified 11C gate and a charming church. On the small square in front of the church stands a beautiful 15C cross decorated with figures.

Castle
15min on foot there and back. Follow the path to the left of the church, leading under an arch to the entrance gate. ◷ *Jul-Aug: guided tours (30min) 2-5.30pm; Mar-Jun and Sep-Oct: 8am-6pm. 3€.* ☎ *04 71 57 19 47.*
The castle was built by the lords of Montlaur in the 13C and, despite its impregnable position, has been sacked on numerous occasions. At the very top of the rocky outcrop are the remains of a small chapel built of red volcanic rock.

⊜⊜ **Hôtel du Manoir** – ☎ 04 71 57 17 14 - *closed 2 Nov to 8 Mar - 16 rms:* ⊆ 6€ - *restaurant* ⊜⊜. A family-run hotel-restaurant is housed in this massive stone residence at the foot of the château. Its small rooms are clean; some overlook the gorges of the Loire. Go through the bar to reach the rustic dining room. Simple, traditional cuisine.

Arlempdes

Y. Travert/PHOTONONSTOP

From the east end of the chapel there is an impressive **view**★★ over the Loire gorge.

The north wall with its well-preserved merlons and battlements overlooks the magnificent basalt lava flows on the opposite bank. From the foot of the right-hand tower there is a view down into the Loire Valley lying at the foot of a striking basalt needle.

Excursion

Volcanic Plateaux★

Various local villages are built on or of volcanic stone. A half-day tour *(56km/35mi)* of this region would take in **St-Paul-de-Tartas** *(S via D 54 and D 500)* with its Roman-esque church built of purplish volcanic rock; the attractive, once-fortified village of **Pradelles** *(S)*, with a **local museum** in one of the houses with Renaissance windows on the market square, and the **Musée Vivant du Cheval de Trait** (Draught-Horse Museum – ♿🕐 *Apr-Aug: Sat-Sun and school holidays 10am-7pm. 8€ (children: 6€).* ☎ *04 71 00 87 87)* housed in a 19C inn (including reconstructed workshops and a collection of carriages dating from the end of the 19C as well as various breeds of donkeys); the Romanesque church at **Lespéron** *(SW of Pradelles)*, an interesting example of a mountain sanctuary; the **Auberge de Peyrebeille** *(NE, via Lavillatte, on N 102)*, an inn with a gruesome history; and the church with a Romanesque doorway at **Coucouron** *(N of the inn via D 16)*.

▶ *Return to Arlempdes along D 298 then turn right onto D 500 and immediately left onto D 54.*

AUBENAS

POPULATION 11 018

MICHELIN MAP 331: I-6

Aubenas stands in an impressive **setting**★, perched on a spur of rock overlooking the Ardèche. The roads hugging the Coiron cliffs to the east reveal a wonderful **view** of the valley below. Aubenas is known for its *marrons glacés* (**candied chest-nuts) and jam.** 🛈 *4 bd Gambetta, 07200 AUBENAS,* ☎ *04 75 89 02 03. www.aubenas-tourisme.com.* 🕐 *Jul-Aug: guides tours (1h45) of the old town starting from the castle, 4€. For details, contact the cultural dept. at the town hall,* ☎ *04 75 87 81 11.*

A Bit of History

A local peasant revolt – Following the bitter winter of 1669-70 which killed all the local olive trees, rumours of new taxes fuelled deep-seated dissatisfaction. On 30 April 1670 a farm inspector was stoned in Aubenas; the ringleader of the attackers was thrown into prison, but the rioters, led by a country squire from La Chapelle-sous-Aubenas, **Antoine du Roure**, effected his release the very next day. While the governor of Languedoc played for time by holding negotiations, Roure's men captured Aubenas. Towards the end of July, the rebels fought the royal army at Lavilledieu. The peasants were massacred, and Roure was subsequently executed in Montpellier. Aubenas and La Chapelle were condemned to pay heavy fines as a reflection of royal wrath.

Address Book

EATING OUT

Le Fournil – *34 r. du 4-Septembre - ☎ 04 75 93 58 68 - closed Feb, Nov and Christmas school holidays, 22 Jun to 9 Jul, Sun and Mon.* This old house in a minor side street welcomes diners onto its patio when the weather is amenable. There or in the small vaulted dining room, you'll be able to choose between several appetizing fixed-price menus that highlight regional specialities.

WHERE TO STAY

Hôtel Cévenol – *77 bd Gambetta - ☎ 04 75 35 00 10 - 🅿 - 44 rms: 7€.* A modest family hotel built in the 1970s; located downtown and offering medium-sized, neat and tidy rooms with a bath or shower. Try to get one on the street, they're roomier.

Hôtel Ibis – *Rte de Montélimar - ☎ 04 75 35 44 45 - 🅿 - 43 rms: 6€ - restaurant.* On the edge of town going towards Montélimar, this chain hotel holds no surprises: modern, clean rooms, wood veneer furniture, good soundproofing and air-conditioning. Under a wood frame roof, the dining room bay windows look out over the pool.

Camping Le Chamadou – *Mas de Chaussy, 07120 Balazuc - 3.5km/2.1mi E of Balazuc via D 294, then dir. St-Maurice and secondary road - ☎ 04 75 37 00 56 - www.camping-le-chamadou. com - open Apr through 15 Sep - reserv. advised in summer - 86 sites: food service.* This little spot in the countryside will suit vacationers on a nature quest to a tee. Generally very well maintained, the only thing that's missing is a bit of shade. Simple comfort; pool, mini-golf, fishing pond and bungalows at your disposal.

Chambre d'hôte La Gibaudelle – *Lieu-dit Le Juge - 07200 Mercuer - 5km/3mi W of Aubenas via D 235 and dir. Ailhon - ☎ 04 75 93 77 75 - pierra-max. gadin@wanadoo.fr - 3 rms - meals.* Just 5 minutes from Aubenas, this little house on a small road is a haven of calm. Surrounded by pines, the lovely garden melts into the nature around it. The decor in the bedrooms is a bit old-fashioned, but the terrace and pool are sure to please.

Chambre d'hôte Le Mas de Mazan – *07200 Mercuer - 5km/3mi NW of Aubenas via D 104 and D 435 - ☎ 04 75 35 41 88 - http://perso.orange.fr/mas-demazan - 5 rms.* This couple welcomes guests to their farm with warmth and enthusiasm. Delighted to share their passion for the region and open the doors of their typically Cévenole farm to visitors, they'll make sure your stay in the area is a memorable one. Simple decor and congenial ambience.

ON THE TOWN

Boulevard de Vernon - Plenty of bars are to be found along this boulevard. If you're not attracted to the sound of pinball machines and motor scooters, steer clear of the Brasserie du Champ de Mars (where the local kids hang out) and head for the bar of La Coupole, which organizes concerts in the summer, or the very British pub Au Bureau.

RECREATION

Aérodrome de Aubenas-Ardèche-Méridionale – *Rte de l'Aérodrome - D 504 - 07202 Lanas - ☎ 04 75 35 23 80 – daily until nightfall.* This aerodrome, open since 1976. encompasses several activities open to tourists: a ULM club run by Patrice Constantin, Champion of France 1989 (you'll be in good hands), an aero-club offering first flights, a bar and a restaurant.

Les Intra-terrestres – *17 faubourg jean mathon, 07200 Aubenas - ☎ 04 75 93 49 78 - www.ardeche-canyoning.com - 9am-noon, 3pm-7pm in season. Reservations by phone – from 30€ (half day) to 45€ (day).* Although the Intra-terrestres organise speleological excursions into the bowels of underground Ardèche, claustrophobic friends have not been overlooked! There are also plenty of outdoor activities available, such as rappelling down canyons and climbing up rocks, for example. If you have children with you, or if thrill-seeking is not your cup of tea, you might enjoy joining in on one of their splendid rambles.

SHOPPING

La Musette – *4 place de l'Airette - ☎ 04 75 35 21 73 - Tue-Sat 9am-12.30pm, 3.30pm-7pm (Sat, 9am-12.30pm). Closed public holidays.* Open since 1996, this shop run by 11 associates organises 'tasting days' throughout the year featuring products such as goat cheese, foie gras, and snails. They sell a tempting and complete range of regional specialities, including bread, meat, chestnuts and honey.

La Table Gourmande – *16 rue de Bernardy - ☎ 04 75 93 37 22 - all year, Tue-Sat 8am-12.30pm, 2-7.30pm.* Founded in 1901, La Table Gourmande is a veritable Aubenas institution. All of the region's specialities are sold here, from candied chestnuts and sausages to the different eaux-de-vie, chestnut liqueurs and fruity little wines of the Ardèche. Excellent value for your money.

Le Petit Ardéchois – *quartier des Champs - 07200 St-Etienne-de-Fontbellon - ☎ 04 75 89 11 79 - 8am-7pm closed public holidays.* Located 4km/2.4mi from Aubenas, this cottage industry confectionery makes 25 different kinds of nougat in copper tubs and kettles according to traditional candy-making methods. Try the chestnut and blueberry nougats: delicious!

L'Atelier des Douceurs – *R. de Tartary - ☎ 04 75 93 89 66 - www.atelier-des-douceurs.fr - Mon-Sat 9am-noon, 2-7pm - closed public holidays.* Out of work at age 48, Jean-Louis Pascal decided to try something completely different. A native of northern France, he relocated to Ardèche in 1982 and created his confectionery in Aubenas in 1997. Success came his way, and several prizes have acknowledged his happy initiative. His sweetmeats – caramels, marshmallows, lollypops, nougats, etc. – are all made the old-fashioned way.

Marrons glacés Sabaton – *Chemin de la Plaine - via Rte de Montélimar. Enter the factory's front hall to reach the shop. - ☎ 04 75 87 83 87 - all year, Mon-Fri 8am-12.30pm, 1.30-6.30pm and Sat in Dec.* The nec-plus-ultra in candied chestnuts and crystallized fruit, the Sabaton family has been a local forerunner in sweets since 1907.

Maison des Artisans – *Le Village - ☎ 04 75 37 78 08 - Jul-Aug: 10am-noon, 3-7pm; Apr-Jun and Sep: 10am-noon, 3-6pm - closed Oct-Mar.* Don't leave Balazuc without visiting the Maison des Artisans, where an interesting selection of pottery and regional products is presented.

Town Walk

Old houses

The 16C "House of Gargoyles" stands opposite the château; its tall polygonal turret is decorated with magnificent gargoyles and there are attractive, mullioned windows adorning the façade. There is a charming 16C staircase-turret in the courtyard of the "Maison de Castrevieille" on place Parmentier; handsome town houses line rue Jourdan. Delightful little arches span rue Delichères.

Viewing table

Near the tourist office. The view extends over Mont Ste-Marguerite, the Vals gap, Gourdon rock, Col d'Escrinet and the mountain ridges of the Coiron.

Sights

Château

Place de l'Hôtel-de-Ville. 🕐 *Jul-Aug: guided tours (1h30) Jul-Aug: 11am, 2pm, 3pm, 4pm and 5pm; Jun and Sep: daily except Sun and Mon, 10.30am, 2pm; Oct-May: Tue, Thu, Fri and Sat, 2pm.* 🕐 *Closed public holidays except 14 Jul and 15 Aug. 4€. ☎ 04 75 87 81 11. www.aubenas.fr.*

The oldest parts of this fine building date from the 12C. The castle was gradually enlarged and embellished by a succession of illustrious families, among them the Montlaurs, the Ornanos and the Vogüés.

The main **façade**★, flanked by machicolated round towers, became the main entrance in the 18C following the addition of two large pedimented doorways. Decorative glazed tiles (such as those found in Burgundy) brighten up the building, which is crowned by a 12C keep with bartizans. The inner courtyard is adorned with 15C and 16C turrets, encasing spiral staircases, and a beautiful 18C staircase; the **panelled and furnished rooms** exude the charming atmosphere of an 18C mansion. In one room, works by the Symbolist painter Chaurand-Neyrac (1878-1948) are on display.

Dôme St-Benoît

Place de la Grenette, NW of the town centre. ♿ ⏰ *Jul-Aug: guided tours at 5pm leaving from in front of the Tourist Office. Contact the cultural dept at the town hall,* ☎ *04 75 87 81 11.*

This hexagonal building is the former Benedictine chapel of Aubenas (17C-18C). The marshal of Ornano and his wife are buried in the mausoleum inside (dating from 1640).

Église St-Laurent

Rue Delichères, far end from the château. The chancel contains a group of three carved wooden altarpieces in the Jesuit style. The church also boasts a beautifully carved wooden pulpit dating from the 17C.

Excursions

Jastres Panorama★

7.5km/4.5mi SE via N 102. 4km/2.5mi beyond the bridge spanning the Ardèche, turn left on the access road to an industrial estate. After 200m/220yd, turn right onto a tarred road. After 1km/0.6mi turn left on a rocky uphill road. Park at the top. Allow 30min on foot there and back.

🔖 The edge of the plateau was the site of a prehistoric settlement. Where the road ends, the view encompasses the entire Lower Ardèche, the Aubenas Valley, and the Coiron range to the north-east.

Défilés de l'Ardèche★

44km/27mi – about 2hr

▶ *Take D 104 from Aubenas to St-Étienne-de-Fontbellon, then turn left onto D 579.*

The light-filled Ardèche Valley forms a wide dip stretching to the basin of the Lower Chassezac in the west. The river flows through a succession of fertile basins, in which its green waters contrast strikingly with the light-coloured gravel and golden sand of the river banks and steep-sided ravines.

Here the road runs close to the river, in between orchards and vineyards.

J. Damase/MICHELIN

Vogüé

The village of ancient, arch-spanned streets dominated by a castle is built against a cliff overlooking the Ardèche.

Vogüé

The vast 16C **château** (🕐 *Jul to mid-Sep: daily 10.30am-6.30pm; Apr to end Jun: Thu-Sun and public holidays 2-6pm; mid-Sep to end Oct: Sat-Sun and public holidays 2-6pm. 4€ (Children: 2€) ☏ 04 75 37 01 95. www.chateaudevogue.net)*, which still belongs to the Vogüé family, replaced the original medieval fortress and now houses exhibitions on the Vivarais region throughout the ages, as well as cultural events.

▶ *Head back S to D 1, then D 401 on the left to Rochecolombe.*

Rochecolombe★

5.5km/3mi S of Vogüé. The medieval village of Rochecolombe occupies a secluded **site**★ overlooking a small, clear stream rising from the bottom of a limestone corrie. There are in fact two villages of Rochecolombe: the upper one is the first one, reached by road, with houses clustered around a church built in 1858. From the square in the upper village, turn left onto a small tarmacked road down towards a bridge across the stream.

▶ *Park a little further along, just before a bend, and follow the footpath down to the water's edge.*

On the right stands the **medieval village,** at the foot of the ruins of a square tower and the charming bell-tower of a Romanesque chapel. At the bottom of the corrie, which is enclosed by tall limestone cliffs with wild scrub clinging to their ledges, are two **Vauclusian springs.**

▶ *Return towards Vogüé on D 579 and turn left onto D 114 after crossing the Ardèche.*

In Lanas, the road crosses the river over a narrow bridge, offering an attractive view of the point where the Auzon flows into the Ardèche.

▶ *In St-Maurice-d'Ardèche turn right onto D 579, then right onto D 294 just after the station in Balazuc.*

The road climbs uphill, giving a **view**★ of the basin in the shadow of the Coiron.

Balazuc★

This once-fortified limestone village is perched on the clifftop above a secluded gorge. Cross the bridge to the opposite bank *(park by the road to the left)* for a good view of the village, dominated by the belfry of its Romanesque church and the remains of its watchtowers.

▶ *During the summer season, leave the car in the car park before entering the village.*

Like many other villages in the Lower Vivarais area, Balazuc was founded by a Saracen colony in the 8C and 9C. It now makes a pleasant place for a stroll, particularly in the old streets leading up to the castle, which are bright with flowers in season.

🚶 For a pleasant walk downstream along the banks of the Ardèche, take the dirt track to the left of the bridge at the foot of the village. Here the river flows through a narrow passage between walls of rock. On the cliffs on the right bank stand the ruins of Reine Jeanne Tower.

From the road up to the top of the plateau on the west bank there is a **view**★ of the entire gorge. From the arid, rocky plateau, where only boxwood and juniper thrive, the road winds its way down to Uzer in the valley; opposite, the hills around Largentière and one of the towers in the village of Montréal can be seen, against a backdrop of the Cham du Cros and Tanargue ranges to the north-west and the Mont Lozère summit just visible to the south-west.

▶ *Take D 104 to Uzer; on reaching Bellevue, follow D 4 to Ruoms.*

The entrance to the Ligne gorge is marked by a narrow rocky passage. A beautiful **view** unfolds upstream of the Ardèche at the confluence of the two rivers in the shadow of cliffs almost 100m/328ft high. The regularity of the rock strata makes them a particularly striking sight.

The Ligne gorge is followed by the **Défilé de Ruoms**★, alongside which the road passes through picturesque tunnels in the rock. In between, it looks down onto the clear green waters of the river. Just beyond the tunnels, straight ahead further along the valley, the domed outline of the Sampzon rock comes into sight.

▶ *Take the bridge on the left to Ruoms.*

Ruoms
The old walled centre of this town lies within a quadrilateral of ramparts flanked by seven round towers. The Romanesque **church** has an unusual arcaded belfry decorated with inlaid motifs made of volcanic rock.

▶ *Leave Ruoms on D 579, heading towards Vallon. On the right bank of the Ardèche, take a narrow, winding road making its way up the mountain.*

Rocher de Sampzon
🚶 *Leave the car in the car park down from the church of Sampzon and go to the summit (45min on foot there and back) on the tarmacked road, then on the path level with the platform.*

From the top *(television relay station)*, the **panorama**★★ encompasses the Vallon basin, the Orgnac plateau and the meanders of the River Ardèche.

Labeaume
West of Ruoms *(D 245)* lies Labeaume, an attractive village at the edge of a gorge with arcaded streets and galleried houses.

▶ *To the left of the church, take an alley leading to a shaded esplanade skirting the river. For the best view of the village, cross the bridge and walk up the path on the opposite bank.*

Gorges de La Beaume★
The walk along the left bank of the river is most pleasant, offering pretty views of the shimmering waters and the limestone cliffs, which erosion has sculpted into curious shapes.

Montagne and Haute Vallée de l'Ardèche★

▶ *Leave Aubenas N along D 104 and follow the upper Ardèche Valley to Pont-de-Labeaume; turn right onto D 536 towards Montpezat-sous-Bauzon.*

🚶 Parc naturel regional des Monts d'Ardèche
La Prade, BP 3, 07560 Montpezat-sous-Bauzon, ☎ 04 75 94 35 20. www.parc-monts-ardeche.fr.

Founded on the intitiative of local chestnut growers, this regional nature park was inaugurated in 2001. It covers a third of the *département* (180 000ha/444 798 acres) comprising 132 municipalities committed to the protection and development of the natural and cultural heritage of the Monts d'Ardèche, and aims to retain and, if possible, increase the local population and to welcome tourists and ramblers.

Montpezat-sous-Bauzon
The old village has given its name to an amazing electrical complex set up in 1954, consisting of several dams designed to collect the waters coming from the upper Loire Valley and its tributaries. The nearby **Lac d'Issarlès** is used as a reservoir. The building of an **underground factory** 60m/197ft beneath the river bed has enabled engineers to increase the total distance the water falls. The **Pont de Veyrières dam** now regulates the flow of water discharged by the factory.

Éperon de Pourcheyrolles★
Coming from Pont-de-Labeaume, 800m/880yd before reaching Montpezat, turn right onto the short tarmacked lane located 600m/660yd after the entrance to the power station. Leave the car at the end of the road and head upstream towards the concrete ruins (15min on foot there and back). About 100m/110yd below the last iron mast, a promontory offers splendid views of the basalt outcrop bearing the ruins of the medieval castle of Pourcheyrolles.

Église Notre-Dame-de-Prévenchère
After crossing the bridge spanning the Fontaulière, drive along the minor road on the right. The interior of this sober 12C-13C church is characterised by four short naves featuring Romanesque or Gothic vaulting. Note the unusual vaulting in the polygonal side chapels.

Driving back towards Montpezat, you will encounter the **town** with its narrow main street flanked by old granite houses built in the mountain style: curved façades, low porches resting on round arches. One of them, on the right, stands out because of its black volcanic stone front and its pretty sculpted ornamentation (17C).

▶ *Take D 536 towards Suc de Bauzon until you reach D 110. Turn left to go to St-Cirgues-en-Montagne.*

St-Cirgues-en-Montagne
The **church** in St-Cirgues is a Romanesque building with typical belfry and foundations. The cornice in the east end is decorated with animals' heads, acanthus leaves etc.

▶ *Take D 239 S heading towards Mazan-l'Abbaye.*

Mazan-l'Abbaye★
Situated in a clearing of Mazan Forest, this 12C abbey was the first Cistercian sanctuary built in the province of Languedoc. The monks of Mazan subsequently founded the abbeys of Sénanque and Le Thoronet in Provence. Unfortunately only ruins and part of the cloisters remain of the huge abbey, except for the arcading above the side chapel overlooking the Mazan stream.

Nearby, the castle built with stones taken from the abbey ruins is dominated by the bell-tower of its small church.

Forêt de Mazan★
Hiking tour, allow 3hr on foot. Leave Mazan on D 239 heading to Col de la Chavade and after 400m/440yd, after a sharp bend, turn left onto a beaten track (forbidden to cars). You will end up on D 239 near the sawmill (scierie) in Banne. Keep to the right to reach the Maison Forestière in Banne and continue along D 239 to go back to Mazan.

Small waterfalls, moss-covered rocks and wild forest fruits (blueberries, raspberries) will provide a charming backdrop to your walk through the lush undergrowth of pine trees.

▶ *Continue along D 239, which leads to Col de la Chavade and the start of the Ardèche Valley.*

Col de la Chavade

Alt 1 266m/4 150ft. This pass marks the watershed between the Atlantic Ocean and the Mediterranean. A few mountain farms are to be found nearby.

N 102 between Le Puy and Viviers follows the traditional route from the Velay area to the Rhône Valley. The horizontal lines of the sloping plateau *(planèze)* are abruptly broken by the dip down into the Ardèche Valley. Just over a mile beyond the pass, the road crosses the River Ardèche, which cascades down on the left.

Pont de Neyrac

The drive, which is quite hilly, offers beautiful views down the valley, overlooked from the right by the rounded summit of Croix de Bauzon and the jagged outline of Abraham's rock.

The harshness of this mountain valley is softened by a few sunny orchards surrounding the villages, by rambling plants on house fronts and retaining walls, and by humpback bridges used by travellers in the Middle Ages. Adding to the interest of the drive, the road passes the ruins of feudal castles: **Château des Montlaur** upstream from Mayres, the tall round tower of **Château de Chadenac** downstream of Mayres.

Mayres

This village lies in a wooded gorge. About 1km/0.6mi downstream of Mayres, a footbridge over the Ardèche offers an attractive **view**★ of the village and the upper valley.

Thueyts★

This small town surrounded by orchards lies on a thick and impressive basalt flow, the remains of an ancient volcanic eruption. Local trade consists mainly of a fruit market, various workshops, and quarrying building stone. The **viewpoint** on N 102 to the east of town *(car park)* offers a good view of the lava flow and the Pont du Diable ("Devil's Bridge") in the valley below. A **waymarked footpath**★ (⏱ *1hr 30min there and back; follow the red arrows)* leads along the edge of the lava flow. Just upstream from the Pont du Diable, the Ardèche flows through a narrow gorge, making an interesting **scene**★ against the dark backdrop of the basalt cliffs. Two sets of steps – the **Échelle du Roi** *(narrow, steep and can be slippery)* and the **Échelle de la Reine** *(easier, allow an extra 30min there and back)* – lead up to the top of the basalt cliffs, affording pretty views of the river valley.

On leaving Thueyts along N 102, there is a view of the valley and the Montagne Ste-Marguerite towering to the north.

Neyrac-les-Bains♨

This small spa town known to the Romans backs onto the slopes of the

○○ **Hôtel des Marronniers** – Pl. du Champs-de-Mar, Thueyts - ☎ 04 75 36 40 16 - hotel.lesmarronniers@club-internet.fr - closed 20 Dec to 5 Mar and Mon - 🅿 - 17 rms - ⌑ 7€ - restaurant ○○. This hotel-restaurant sits on the village square, where the market or local boules team presides depending on what day it is. In nice weather, pool and terrace beckon behind the building. Small carpeted rooms, classic fare and easy-going ambience.

Soulhiol volcano. In the Middle Ages its bicarbonated hot springs were thought to cure leprosy.

▶ *At the exit of Pont-de-Labeaume turn left following signs to Notre-Dame de Niègles; the road drops into a valley before reaching a plateau. Park the car down on the right.*

Notre-Dame de Niègles

The church stands on a hill overlooking the river. Little remains of the original 10C building owing to subsequent additions and alterations. The building has an 18C doorway and an 11C apse. The church interior is lit through circular windows, or oculi. There is a pretty little graveyard in front of the church.
The road back to Pont-de-Labeaume commands pleasant views of the medieval fortress of Ventadour.

Château de Ventadour

🕐 *Jul-Sep: guided tours (45min) 9am-noon, 2-7pm, Sat-Sun 3-7pm. 3€ (left to the visitor's appreciation).* ☎ *04 75 38 00 92.*
Partly demolished and abandoned, this imposing medieval fortress would have eventually disappeared without the valiant efforts of Pierre Pottier who undertook to restore it. Ever since 1969, he has, with the help of his wife, led successive teams of voluntary workers.

Vals-les-Bains ‡‡ – 🕭 *See VALS-LES-BAINS.*

Labégude

The Ardèche flows right by a glassworks in this village.

▶ *D 104 leads back to Aubenas.*

AURILLAC★

POPULATION 30 551
MICHELIN MAP 330: C-5 – LOCAL MAP SEE MONTS DU CANTAL

Aurillac, the business and tourist capital of Upper Auvergne, is a modern town that has sprung up around an old neighbourhood with narrow, winding streets.
🛈 *Pl. du Square, 15000 AURILLAC,* ☎ *04 71 48 46 58.*

A Bit of History

Gerbert, the first French Pope (10C-11C) – Aurillac's Gallo-Roman origins were brought to light by the discovery of a 1C temple (Rue Jacques-Prévert, reached from avenue Milhaud). In the 9C St Gerald, Count of Auvergne, built an abbey, laying the foundations for the city's future prosperity; this abbey gave Christianity its first French Pope. Gerbert, a shepherd from the Aurillac area, attracted the attention of the monks of St-Géraud, who quickly taught this unusually bright student everything they knew. After completing his studies at the abbey, Gerbert left for Spain where he studied medicine and mathematics at the Moorish universities. According to certain authors, it was Gerbert who introduced the use of Arabic numerals into the Western world. He built the first pendulum clock, invented an astrolabe for sailors and improved the church organ. His extensive knowledge brought him to the attention of Emperor

Otto, who appointed him private tutor to his son. Gerbert, a theologian steeped in classical culture, was the driving force behind the Ottonian renaissance. In AD 999 he became Pope under the name Sylvester II. He was the "Pope of the Millennium," who managed to impose the "Truce of God" – whereby hostilities were suspended on certain days and during certain seasons – on the feudal classes.

Gold-washers – According to Gerbert's contemporaries, his knowledge smacked of witchcraft. The gold flakes found in the River Jordanne were popularly ascribed to his spells.

The gold industry was born, but remained fairly primitive: flakes of gold were collected by holding a fleece in the water to trap them.

In the 14C a new process was invented by a certain **Jean de la Roquetaillade**, who had been brought up as a child by a gold-washer and had then taken Holy Orders at the abbey of St-Géraud: he covered slanted boards with coarse cloth which then caught the gold flakes in its weave.

Brother Jean, besides being an inspired preacher, also possessed powers of prophecy. Four centuries in advance, he forecast the ruin of the clergy and nobility, and the fall of the monarchy. The church authorities did not appreciate predictions of this kind and Brother Jean was jailed by his bishop. After reoffending, the Pope imprisoned him for four years in the dungeons of Avignon.

Baron des Adrets (16C) – The people of Aurillac remained at odds with their lord, the abbot, but eventually managed to obtain administrative autonomy, as the consuls' residence (Maison Consulaire) proves.

The town was flourishing when it became involved in the Wars of Religion. In 1561 the governor ordered the slaughter of the large local Protestant population. They were avenged eight years later by the Baron des Adrets, a Protestant leader notorious for his brutality. His men began by swooping down on the monasteries on the outskirts of the town, burning or flaying the monks alive. On the night of 6 September 1569 the Huguenots blew up the town gate and burst their way in on the slumbering citizens, who were caught entirely unawares and so put up minimal resistance. All the town's main buildings were razed to the ground.

In 1581 the Protestants returned but were repelled, so the story goes, by the miraculous intervention of the Virgin Mary. To commemorate this event, the townspeople built the Chapelle d'Aurinques *(see below)*.

From lace to umbrellas – Aubenas was struggling to recover from these events for many years until Colbert founded a laceworks which doubled as a gold and silver smithy. This entrepreneur also encouraged other industries, such as boiler-making and tanning, which have since declined. Modern Aurillac's economy is based on agriculture and the manufacture of furniture, cheese, plastics and umbrellas.

Over the last two centuries Aurillac has provided several major historical figures: General Delzons, who fought in Napoleon's Russian campaign; De Parieu, a government minister; Émile Duclaux, the biochemist who was Pasteur's assistant; Arsène Vermenouze, an author who wrote in the dialect of Southern France; **Paul Doumer**, the French President assassinated in 1934; and, more recently, the surgeon and writer Professor **Henri Mondor**.

Old Town

Place St-Géraud

The Romanesque façade with arcades and colonettes which stands opposite the church entrance probably belonged to a hospice for pilgrims on their way to Santiago de Compostela in Spain. The colonial house on the left dates from the late 15C. The 12C basin in the middle of the square is made of serpentine, a dark, marbled

Address Book

EATING OUT

A QUICK BITE

⌐ **Le Bouchon Fromager** – *3 pl. du Buis - ☎ 04 71 48 07 80 - Mon-Sat noon-2pm, 7pm-11pm - ⊡*. Both wine bar and cheese restaurant, this inviting, rustic eatery is often packed with patrons enjoying a fine wine served by the glass and the delicious cuisine of the Cantal. When the clock strikes the cocktail hour, try a *pelou*, a local aperitif composed of chestnut creme liqueur and white wine.

A LEISURELY MEAL

⌐ **Poivre et Sel** – *4 r. du 14-Juillet - ☎ 04 71 64 20 20 - poivre.sel@wanadoo.fr - Mon-Sat noon-2.30pm, 7-11pm - closed 2 wks in Feb and 1 wk in Nov - reserv. recommended.* Hesitating between local fare and traditional French cuisine? This small restaurant can satisfy every whim thanks to well-prepared dishes made from fresh ingredients. A simple, pleasant address, despite the rather stark decor.

⌐ **Le Terroir** – *5 r. du Buis - ☎ 04 71 64 31 26 - Tue -Sat noon-2pm, 7-10.30pm - closed 25 Dec, 1 Jan.* Aficionados of cheeses, truffades and other regional specialities, napkins on your laps! Cheese and Auvergnat fare are proffered here – add a glass of wine and you're all set. The convivial atmosphere and affordable prices more than compensate for the plain surroundings.

⌐⌐ **La Reine Margot** – *19 r. G.-de-Veyre - ☎ 04 71 48 26 46 - closed Sat and Sun lunch, Sun and Mon evening.* A restaurant in a small street downtown. The main, 1950s-style dining room is decorated with painted woodwork illustrating the life of Queen Margot. Well-prepared cuisine at reasonable prices.

⌐⌐ **La Belle Époque** – *15130 Sansac-de-Marmiesse - 7km/4.2mi W of Aurillac via N122 and D153 - ☎ 04 71 62 87 87 - daily Apr-Oct.* A restaurant set in an old, secluded house in the countryside. The smart interior design features murals depicting the 1920s, fine furniture and nicely set tables. Add delicious, traditional food and an extremely amiable

welcome and you have a restaurant that is often full to capacity.

WHERE TO STAY

⌐ **Camping Village de Vacances la Gineste** – *15150 Arnac - 5km/3mi NE of Barrage d'Enchanet via D 61 - ☎ 04 71 62 91 90 - www.mairie-arnac.fr - reserv. recommended - 115 sites - food service.* Set in a lovely natural environment, this piece of land at the end of a road enjoys an exceptional location on a peninsula along the Lac d'Enchanet. Water sports of every description and horse riding are on the programme. Terraced camp sites along the lake.

⌐ **Delcher** – *20 r. Carmes - ☎ 04 71 48 01 69 - www.hotel-delcher.com - closed 2 wks in Jul and 23-31 Dec - Ᵽ - 23 rms - ⊡ 7€ - restaurant ⌐⌐ closed Sun evening.* The presence of medieval gold prospectors still makes itself felt in this street running alongside the Jordanne. Simple rooms; garrets on the top floor. In one of the rooms and in the salon, one finds frescoes painted by the Danish artist Gorm Hansen in exchange for rent. Traditional cuisine and contemporary decor.

⌐⌐ **Chambre d'hôte de Barathe** – *Barathe - 15130 Giou-de-Mamou - 7km/4.2mi E of Aurillac via N 122 and D 58 - ☎ 04 71 64 61 72 - barathe@wanadoo.fr - ⊡ - reserv. required - 5 rms.* The windows of this fine old house built in 1777 open onto a superb landscape and the irresistible sound of cowbells tinkling in the distance. The dining room, with its handsome period furnishings and scullery, is grand and the renovated bedrooms are enchanting.

⌐⌐⌐ **Grand Hôtel de Bordeaux** – *2 av. de la République - ☎ 04 71 48 01 84 - bestwestern@hotel-de-bordeaux.fr - 32 rms - ⊡ 10€.* On a corner of place du Square, this elegant, early 20C hotel has a glass awning above the entrance. Most of the cosy rooms are spacious; they are decorated along a Napoleon II or Louis-Philippe theme. Pleasant, intimate English-style bar.

SHOPPING

Distillerie Louis-Couderc – *14 r. Victor-Hugo - ☎ 04 71 48 01 50 - www.*

distillerie-couderc.com - Tue-Sat 9am-noon, 2pm-7pm - closed public holidays. Founded in 1908, the Couderc distillery sells a wide variety of regional products made from gentian root, chestnut cream and berries. The house speciality is the volc'an, a popular Auvergnat aperitif made from 1/3 chestnut cream and 2/3 gentian liquor. This is also an excellent address for collectors of miniature bottles of alcohol.

Les Étains d'Auvergne – *Rte de Toulouse - direction Maurs via N 122 - turn left 100m/110yd after the 'Géant shopping centre' roundabout -* ☎ *04 71 63 66 80 - Mon-Sat 9am-12.30pm, 1.30pm-7.30pm - closed Sun Oct-May*. The craftsman Daniel Vollet is the product of four generations of pewter smiths. His handiwork, created according to the tradition of the pewter smiths of the Haute-Auvergne, includes a broad range of impeccably crafted items, from soup dishes to pitchers.

Parapluies Piganiol – *28 r. des Forgerons -* ☎ *04 71 43 05 51 - Tue-Sat 9am-noon, 2pm-7pm, Mon 2pm-7pm in Aug and Dec - closed public holidays*. Piganiol have been manufacturing umbrellas in Aurillac since 1884. They offer a fine selection of colourful models, including the 'Aurillac', an umbrella typical of the region.

Troupenat – *6 pl. de l'Hôtel-de-Ville -* ☎ *04 71 48 35 10*. This well-known bakery displays an impressive selection of house specialities in a posh setting befitting its celebrated bread, the pain paillasse. Other starring roles are given to the pain des Volcans, a blend of rye and wheat flours, flax and poppy seeds and wheat germ, and delectable pastries such as the tarte aux truffes glacées.

La Poterie du Don – *Le Don - 9km/5.4mi SW of Montsalvy via D 19 and D 119 - 15120 Montsalvy -* ☎ *04 71 49 95 65 - potdon@club-internet.fr - 9am-noon, 2pm-6.30pm except Oct-Mar, closed Sat except holidays*. Nigel and Suzy Atkins, potters who specialise in salt-glazed stoneware, create utilitarian and decorative pieces that are all the rage.

rock. The east end of the church overlooks the old graveyard where some ancient sarcophagi can be seen.

Église St-Géraud

This old abbey church shows traces of a long and complex architectural evolution. It was founded in the late 9C by Count Gerald and became a stopover for pilgrims on their way to Santiago de Compostela. Enlarged in the 10C and again in the 11C, it then underwent extensive alteration from 1530 to 1536. In 1569 it was destroyed by the Protestants, at that time the masters of Aurillac. Charles de Noailles, Bishop of St-Flour, rebuilt it in the first half of the 17C. Its walls were raised and Gothic vaulting was added. The remains of the earlier Romanesque constructions were hidden under a roughcast finish. In 1794 the Romanesque tower over the narthex was demolished. The last two bays in the nave and the steeple were added by 19C architects. The restoration work carried out from 1965 to 1972 revealed some interesting Romanesque remains.

The **nave** has a balanced and unified appearance owing to its size and the perspective created by its pillars, rising straight to the lierne and tierceron vaulting. The stoups are made of two Romanesque capitals. The organ loft contains a large 18C organ. An 18C *Pietà* stands in a niche at the back.

The **Chapel of St-Géraud** contains beautiful stone fragments: two carved Romanesque slabs, one of which is decorated with animals back to back; capitals with palm-leaf and interlaced motifs; a pre-Romanesque sculpture supporting a reliquary is decorated with a scene from the story of Samson. The 18C statue of St Gerald is made of gilded wood.

On the end wall in the **south transept** is a major decorative feature from the 11C building – a triple arch with a pointed arch in the centre. The **chapel of Notre-**

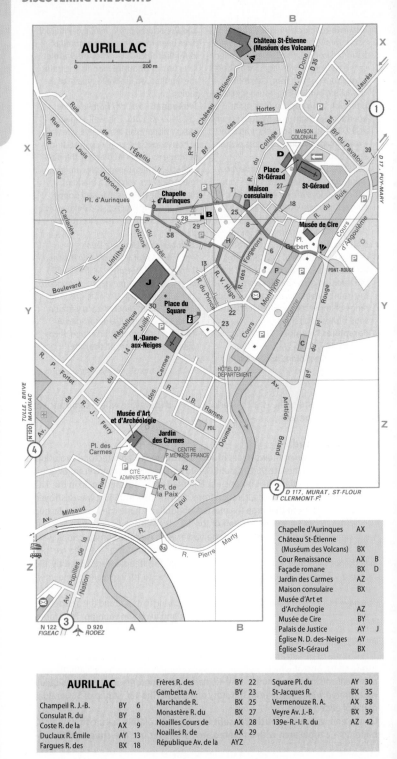

AURILLAC

0   200 m

Château St-Étienne
(Muséum des Volcans)

Place
St-Géraud

Maison
consulaire

St-Géraud

Chapelle
d'Aurinques

MAISON
COLONIALE

Musée de Cire

PONT-ROUGE

Place du
Square

N.-Dame-
aux-Neiges

HÔTEL DU
DÉPARTEMENT

Musée d'Art
et d'Archéologie

Jardin
des Carmes

CENTRE
P.MENDES-FRANCE

CITÉ
ADMINISTRATIVE

Pl. de
la Paix

TULLE · BRIVE
MAURIAC

N 122
FIGEAC

D 920
RODEZ

D 117, MURAT, ST-FLOUR
CLERMONT-Fᵈ

Chapelle d'Aurinques	AX
Château St-Étienne (Muséum des Volcans)	BX
Cour Renaissance	AX B
Façade romane	BX D
Jardin des Carmes	AZ
Maison consulaire	BX
Musée d'Art et d'Archéologie	AZ
Musée de Cire	BY
Palais de Justice	AY J
Église N. D. des-Neiges	AY
Église St-Géraud	BX

AURILLAC

Champeil R. J.-B.	BY 6	Frères R. des	BY 22	Square Pl. du	AY 30
Consulat R. du	BY 8	Gambetta Av.	BY 23	St-Jacques R.	BX 35
Coste R. de la	AX 9	Marchande R.	BX 25	Vermenouze R. A.	AX 38
Duclaux R. Émile	AY 13	Monastère R. du	BX 27	Veyre Av. J.-B.	BX 39
Fargues R. des	BX 18	Noailles Cours de	AX 28	139e-R.-I. R. du	AZ 42
		Noailles R. de	AX 29		
		République Av. de la	AYZ		

Dame-du-Cœur (Our Lady of the Heart) has 15C vaulting and beautiful wooden panelling from the early 20C.
The canopied high altar in the chancel is made of multicoloured marble and dates from 1762.

▶ *Walk down rue du Monastère and rue des Forgerons and turn right onto rue Victor-Hugo.*

On reaching the 19C Hôtel de Ville, follow rue Vermenouze to place d'Aurinques. The **Chapelle d'Aurinques,** built at the end of the 16C in a tower in the city wall, was completed in the 19C by an upper chapel.

▶ *Follow rue de la Coste.*

No 7 in rue de Noailles, on the right, has a **Renaissance courtyard** *(access through cours de Noailles).*

▶ *Return to rue de la Coste.*

No 4 in rue du Consulat has a staircase tower.

Maison Consulaire
This Renaissance building has been restored and turned into an exhibition hall. Note the sculptures adorning the door on rue de la Coste.

▶ *Continue to place Gerbert.*

Musée de Cire
🕐 *Mid-May to mid-Sep: Tue-Sat 3-7pm. 4€.* ☎ *04 71 48 64 38.*
A dozen or so scenes featuring waxwork figures bring to life the events and personalities which left their mark on the history of Aurillac.

View of the Jordanne
The old houses along the River Jordanne can be seen from a spot near Pont Rouge (Red Bridge) and Cours d'Angoulême. The square boasts a statue of Pope Silvester II by David d'Angers.

Understanding Volcanoes

Château St-Étienne
The castle keep dates from the 13C; the rest of the buildings date mostly from the late 19C. The upper terrace offers a magnificent view of the Jordanne Valley and the Cantal mountains, as well as of Aurillac in its valley. A permanent information centre on the environment of Upper Auvergne and a museum have been set up in the château, together with a shop of the "Volcans" Nature Park.

Musée des Volcans★
🧒🕐 *Jan to mid-Jun and mid-Sep to end Dec: Tue-Sat 2-6pm; mid-Jun to mid-Sep: Mon-Sat 10am-6.30pm except Sun 2-6pm.* 🕐 *Closed Easter Mon, 1 May, 14 Jul, 11 Nov, 22 to 25 Dec, 29 Dec to 1 Jan. 4€ (Under-18s: no charge).* ☎ *04 71 48 07 00.*
The Volcano Museum includes four large rooms offering interactive models, multimedia terminals and video films to explain volcanic phenomena.

Une planète agitée... la Terre (The Earth, a Restless Planet): cross-sections illustrate the moving phenomena that occur on the earth's surface.

J. Damase/MICHELIN

Aurillac

Le Cantal sur une terre qui change (The Cantal Region on a Changing Planet): the geological history of the Cantal massif is explained with puzzles and dioramas, one of which shows the aspect of the Cantal volcano eight million years ago.

Des volcans et des hommes (Volcanoes and Man): the negative effects of volcanoes (240 000 victims during the past 400 years) are offset by their positive action (formation of the atmosphere, fertilization of the soil). Visitors are shown a reconstruction of a city destroyed by a volcanic eruption and the techniques used to forecast eruptions and earthquakes are explained.

Le Cantal, volcan aménagé (The Cantal, a Tamed Volcano): visitors are shown how fauna and flora have adjusted to the region's geological specificity from the Ice Age to today.

The Carmes District

Place du Square
South of the old town, the Carmes district, with its large shaded park, is a haven of peace and quiet.

Palais de Justice
🕐 *Daily except Sat-Sun 8.30am-noon, 1.30-5pm.* 🕐 *Closed public holidays. No charge.* ☎ *04 71 45 59 59.*
The Assizes Chamber in the law courts contains three 17C Flemish tapestries.

Église Notre-Dame-des-Neiges or Notre-Dame-des-Cordeliers
🕐 *Daily except Sat-Sun.*
This chapel, once part of a 14C Franciscan monastery, was rebuilt in the 17C. A chapel on the left contains a widely revered **Black Virgin** from the 18C. The sacristy in the Gothic style is in the old **chapter house,** where the pointed vaulting is supported by two columns. This room gives access to an elegant 15C chapel; note the fine Renaissance lectern.

Jardin des Carmes
Once part of a monastery, this pleasant garden gives access to an arts centre.

Musée d'Art et d'Archéologie
Centre Pierre Mendès France, 37 rue des carmes.
♿🕐 *Feb-Oct: daily except Sun and Mon 10am-noon, 2-6pm (Jul and Aug: daily 10am-noon, 2-6pm, Sun 2-6pm).* 🕐 *Closed public holidays, and 25 May. 2.50€.* ☎ *04 71 45 46 10.* The Art and Archaeology Museum is housed in the former Visitandines Convent (17C) which, after the Revolution, was used as a stud farm before being recently turned into an arts centre.

First floor
The museum evokes lifestyles and housing in Cantal from the earliest days of human settlement until the 19C. The visit begins with a reconstruction of the inside of a typical Cantal house, complete with a light and sound display. The museum collections built up from local excavations include a series of Palaeolithic bifaces, and tools from the Mesolithic Ages (from the site at Cuze de Neussargues) and the Neolithic Ages (notably polished bifaced axes and flints from Mur-de-Barrez). There are also objects from burial mounds (painted ceramics and arms from the Iron Age).

The collection from the Gallo-Roman period includes objects found during the excavation of the Aron temple in Aurillac: a 1C **tomb** with a glass urn in perfect condition. The collection from medieval times includes all the furnishings found at Chastel-sur-Murat, a settlement that was occupied continuously from the Neolithic Age until the Renaissance. An information centre contains computer records on the museum collections which can be consulted.

Second floor
This floor is given over to art collections. The paintings feature 17C French, Dutch and Italian Schools, French painters from the second half of the 18C (Nattier, Joseph Vernet, Verhulst), "official" 19C painters (Cabanel, Richard, Couture) and contemporary painters (Boutet de Monvel, Lebourg and Lebasque).

The most striking sculptures include *Napoleon* by Chaudet, *Victor Hugo* by Rodin (plaster), *Rodin* by Camille Claudel (bronze), and *A Peasant from the Abruzzi* by Landowski (bronze).

Two rooms are reserved for rotating exhibitions by well-known international photographers (Callahan, Fontana, Sandek).

Les Écuries
♿🕐 *Daily except Sun 1.30-6.30pm (last admission 6pm). No charge.* ☎ *04 71 45 46 08.*
A museum annexe in the former stables houses contemporary art exhibitions (painting, sculpture and photography).

Excursions

From the Cère to the Maronne

100km/62mi – allow one day

This is an ideal outing for those who are keen on dams, rivers and gorges.

▷ *Leave Aurillac on N 122 heading towards Figeac.*

Sansac-de-Marmiesse
A restored barn on the outskirts of the village houses the town hall and the **Maison du Bâtiy** (🕐 *Daily except Sat-Sun and public holidays: 10am-noon, 2-5pm. No charge.* ☎ *04 71 47 74 75*), a local museum illustrating the 13 different areas which make up the Cantal region with their specific types of rural housing and traditions.

▶ *Continue along N 122 then turn right onto D 64 to Viescamp and on to the dam on the River Cère.*

Barrage de St-Étienne-Cantalès★

An imposing dam resembling a vault contains the waters of the River Cère, forming a reservoir of an estimated capacity of 133 million m3/4 696 million cu ft. The view is enhanced by the charming sight of small islets, peninsulas and jagged coastlines.

▶ *D 207, then D 7 lead to Laroquebrou, a pretty village on the banks of the Cère.*

Laroquebrou

Small municipality located at the entrance to the Cère gorges, dominated by an isolated outcrop bearing a statue of the Virgin Mary and the ruins of the **castle** (🕐 *Mid-Jul to mid-Aug: 10am-noon, 3-7pm.* 🕐 *Closed 1st Sun in Aug. 2€.* ☎ *04 71 46 07 97*), once home to the Lords of Montal. The terrace fronting the castle offers a lovely view of the surrounding landscape.

▶ *Follow D 653 that cuts across N 120 at Pont d'Orgon, then take D 2 for 15km/9mi. Turn right onto D 302 and continue until you reach the Enchanet dam spanning the Maronne, a tributary of the Dordogne.*

Barrage d'Enchanet★

Its elegant silhouette is set against the backdrop of the Maronne gorges. D 61 offers a good overall view of the dam and its peaceful waters.

▶ *D 442 leads to St-Santin-Cantalès. Continue on D 52 and go back to Aurillac via St-Victor.*

Through Chestnut Grove Country

100km/62mi – allow one day

This round tour through "La Châtaigneraie Cantalienne" offers an interesting insight into local chestnut land, with long plateaux, luxuriant valleys and typical architecture.

▶ *South of Aurillac, drive through Arpajon-sur-Cère and onto D 6 (2km/1.2mi).*

Arpajon-sur-Cère, Arboretum

Kids 🕐 *8am-8pm. Free admission.* ☎ *04 71 43 27 72.*

Enjoy a pleasant stroll through gardens of different styles including the Devil's garden, the pond, the maple grove, the oak grove… *Guided tours in summer (including tasting), themed weekends in spring and autumn.*

▶ *Return to Arpajon-sur-Cère, turn right onto D 58, which leads to Conros.*

Château de Conros

🕐 *Jul-Aug: 2-6pm. 6€.* ☎ *04 71 63 50 27. www.chateau-conros.com*

On a spur of rock high above a meander of the River Cère stands the massive medieval keep that once belonged to the Astorgs, lords of Aurillac. Over the centuries it has been transformed into a majestic residence. The square tower topped by a strange lantern-turret dates from the 12C as does the main part of the building, which was extended in the 15C. It is flanked on the north side by a machicolated tower with a pepper-pot roof.

The guard-room on the first floor has an attractive Renaissance fireplace, the upper section of which is decorated with 15C frescoes. Maxims in old French have been carved on the lintel.

J. Damase/MICHELIN

Château de Conros

On the second floor is the surprisingly large Knights' Chamber, (20m/65ft x 8m/26ft). A tour of the attic gives visitors an opportunity to admire the superb oak rafters and the roof of stone slabs, all of them pegged into place. In the north tower, the floor is covered with shingle as protection against fire.

▶ *Continue along D 58 to the intersection with D 17, turn left and drive 12km/7.5mi; D 66 leads to Marcolès (3km/1.9mi).*

Marcolès
In this restored medieval city, characteristic narrow lanes stem from rue Longue closed off by an elegant 15C **porch**.
West of the village, D 64 leads to the **Rochers de Faulat** (1.5km/0.9mi) where several megaliths stand on a mound planted with oak trees.

▶ *Take D 64, then D 17 and follow the banks of the River Rance.*

Entraygues
Small village featuring a château typical of the area with its pretty pepper-pot roofs.

▶ *Go on driving until you reach Maurs.*

Maurs
Maurs is situated to the south-west of the mountains in Cantal on a hill beside the River Rance, and is the main town in the **La Châtaigneraie** area. The granite plateau is almost entirely covered with undulating moorland and gashed by green valleys where most of the local population lives.
In Maurs, which still has the circular layout dating back to the days when it was a fortress, there is a definite air of Southern France; this is the start of the "Cantal Riviera" with its flowers and vineyards, thus explaining why Maurs has been dubbed the "Nice of Cantal." The **Benedictine abbey** in Maurs, founded in the 10C, no doubt gave rise to the development of the village. By the late Middle Ages, Maurs had become one of the six "good towns" in Upper Auvergne and the seat of a provostship. It suffered during the Wars of Religion: captured and recaptured by the Huguenots in 1568 and 1583, it was pillaged and ransacked; in 1643 peasant rebels from the Rouergue sought refuge here and the King's troops were forced to

intervene. The French Revolution brought serious disorder in its wake, in particular the destruction of the monastery.

The **church** (ⓒ *Guided tours available, ask at the tourist office.* ☎ *04 71 46 73 72*), dating from the 14C, is preceded by a carved doorway (15C-16C); inside there is a nave but no side aisles as in most churches in Southern France. The chapel on the right contains one of the most remarkable pieces of gold and silverware in Cantal. It is a **bust-reliquary**★ of St Césaire made of wood but covered with silver and gilded copper (13C); it contains the head of the Archbishop of Arles who is shown wearing his liturgical vestments. The statue is especially striking for the strangeness of the wide-open eyes and the symbolic lengthening of the fingers. In the chancel is a set of fifteen 16C choir stalls topped by eleven 15C wooden **statues**★ surrounding the altar. The statue of St John, to the right of the Cross, is particularly expressive – note the way in which he is gazing towards Christ. To the left of the Cross is St Benedict, holding a crozier in his right hand and the Rule of the Order in his left.

▶ *Follow D 663 towards Decazeville then D 28 to Mourjou.*

Mourjou

Ⓚⓘⓓⓢ The convivial **Maison de la Châtaigne** (♿ⓒ *Jul-Aug: 10.30am-6pm; Jun and Sep: 2-6pm; Apr-May and Oct: Sat-Sun and public holidays 2-6pm. 5€ (Children: 2.50€.* ☎ *04 71 49 98 00. www.mourjou.com)* retraces the use of chestnuts through the ages.

▶ *Follow D 28 to Calvinet, then take D 19 and drive 15km/9mi to Montsalvy.*

Montsalvy

Nestling on the Plateau de la Châtaigneraie, this once fortified town has kept several of its original gates. The church (⊶ *currently closed to the public*) features a Romanesque nave, Gothic vaulting (15C), and a 15C **wooden Christ.** The **east end,** consisting of a central chapel and two side chapels, dates entirely from the Romanesque period. Near the church stand the **ruins** of the former abbey: the cloisters, the chapter-house, and the 14C refectory which has now been restored.

Puy de l'Arbre

Leave Montsalvy to the N on D 920 heading towards Aurillac. After 1km/0.5mi, turn right onto an extremely narrow tarmacked lane leading to the summit (alt 825m/2 707ft). The viewing table offers a fine **panorama**★ over the Cantal massif, the Carladez, the Barrez, the Aubrac, the Causses, the chestnut groves and Aurillac Basin.

▶ *Come back to Aurillac on D 920.*

AUZON★

POPULATION 817

MICHELIN MAP 331: C-1

Auzon's dramatic **setting**★ on a sheer-sided spur of rock overlooking the valley of the river that shares its name is best appreciated when seen from D 5, coming from the Allier Valley. This old fortified town still has many traces of its ramparts and castle and boasts a fine collegiate church. 🛈 *Pl. Barreyre, 43390 AUZON,* ☎ *04 71 76 18 11.*

A Perched Village

Church

30min. ⏱ *Guided tours 9-11.30am, 2pm-6pm. Appy to town hall.* ☎ *04 71 76 11 42.*

The narrow streets and alleys of the old town lead to an open square on which a fortified church stands, built on a rock, on the site of a 5C church from which the stone altar and font have survived.

The building has a beautiful Romanesque east end and a solid porch with sculpted capitals. The gate still has its 12C iron strap hinges and strips of leather. Inside, on the right of the nave, is an interesting white-stone statue of St Peter (late 15C). To the left of the entrance to the chancel is a 12C wooden reliquary of Christ. A small two-storey chapel opposite the entrance, entirely decorated with 14C murals, houses a graceful 15C statue of **Our Lady of the Portal**★★, made of white stone. The church contains many old statues and an unusual 15C organ loft.

B. Kaufmann/MICHELIN

Virgin and child, Notre-Dame-du-Portail

Écomusée du Pays d'Auzon

⏱ *Apr to mid-Sep: guided tours (1hr30) daily except Thu 10am-noon, 2-6pm. 4€.* ☎ *04 71 76 14 80.*

All the items in this regional museum (exhibitions on traditional arts and crafts, minerals etc) have been given or lent by people living in Auzon or in the region.

Excursion

Brassac-les-Mines

6km/4mi NE of Auzon on D 16. Coal mining in Brassac dates back to the 15C. When the Briare Canal was opened in 1664, local tradesmen gained access to the River Seine and this was the start of a flourishing commerce between Paris and the upper Loire region, concentrating mainly on coal, wine and timber. The disused mines now house the fascinating **Musée de la Mine** (⏱ *Mid-Apr to end Sep: guided tours (1hr) daily except Mon 10am-noon, 2-7pm. 5€ (children: 2€).* ☎ *04 73 54 30 88*). Mines, mining techniques and life as a miner are explained, with the help of tools and machinery. A trip down the mine shows the statue of St Barbara (patron saint of miners) and the stables for the pit ponies.

Also in Brassac is the **Musée Peynet** (⏱ *Apr-Sep: daily except Mon 10am-noon, 2-6pm, Sun 10am-12.30pm (Jul-Aug: daily 10am-noon, 2-7pm). 5€ (children: 2€).* ☎ *04 73 54 30 88*), named after the cartoonist Raymond Peynet, whose endearing portrayal of valentine lovers made him an extremely popular figure in post-war France. Peynet was born in Paris in 1908 and first began working as a draughtsman for the advertising business. His first cartoons were published in the English newspaper *The Boulvardier* around the mid-1930s. He soon gained widespread recognition: Princess Anne was given a set of 12 Peynet dolls on her first official visit to France!

LAC D'AYDAT★

MICHELIN MAP 326: E-9

This lake, situated at an altitude of 825m/2 706ft, is a perfect example of a volcanic reservoir; its waters were retained by the Aydat lava flow *(see Introduction: Volcanoes of the Auvergne)*. This tranquil stretch of water, reaching a maximum depth of 15m/49ft, is ideal for boating and angling. It lies in a wooded setting and is a delightful destination for an outing.

Near the north bank is a small island called St-Sidoine in memory of the country house that **Sidonius Apollinaris**, Bishop of Clermont in the 5C, is said to have had built for himself on the shores of the lake. 🛈 *Sauteyras, 63970 Lac d'AYDAT,* ☎ *04 73 79 37 69. www.aydat.com*

Excursion

The Lava Trail

40km/37mi round trip – allow 2hr
This round tour gives you the opportunity to admire Aydat Lake from several different viewpoints and to discover a variety of landscapes.

Aydat
Note the church and its unusual buttresses in the shape of adjacent turrets.

▶ *Leave Aydat on D 90 towards Sauteyras. Turn right towards Rouillas-*

> ⛺ **CAMPING CHADELAS**
>
> **63970 Aydat** - *2km/1.2mi NE of Aydat - take D 90 then road on right (near the lake) -* ☎ *04 73 79 38 09 - www.campingchadelas.com - open 29 Mar-4 Nov - reserv. recommended - 150 sites: - food service.* A pleasant, hilly pine forest is where you will find this camp site by the lake. Shaded sites, children's playground and a variety of activities and pastimes nearby.

J. Damase/MICHELIN

Lac d'Adyat

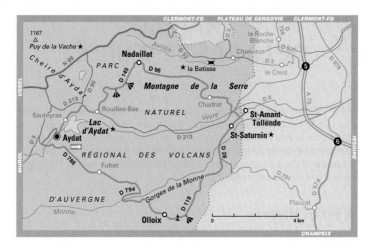

Bas then left onto D 145. There are numerous views of the Serre mountain range (☞ see below).

Nadaillat

A fine example of a village built of black lava stone.

▶ *Leave Nadaillat to the E on D 96.*

Montagne de la Serre

The long backbone of the Serre juts out like a promontory into the Limagne plain. It is a typical example of "inversion relief."

▶ *Continue N to St-Amant on D 96.*

St-Amant-Tallende

This village and its shops form an attractive sight seen from the medieval bridge. Note the fortified house in the old town.

▶ *Continue along D 8.*

St-Saturnin★ – ☞ *See SAINT-SATURNIN.*

▶ *D 28 and D 119 go through an austere landscape of cropped grass dotted with rocks, but they provide some extensive views before reaching Olloix. Stop near the multilobed cross on the roadside to enjoy the panoramic view.*

Olloix

This village consists of a string of old houses stretching out along the road. It was once the seat of a commandery of the Knights of St John of Jerusalem (Order of Malta) and one of its daughter-houses was the Knights Hospitallers' commandery in La Sauvetat. The **church** (🕐 *Open Sun and school holidays 11am-6pm.* ☎ *04 73 39 32 13 (town hall))* contains the tomb and recumbent figure of Odon of Montaigu. The road down into the Monne gorge (D 794) provides a number of delightful views.

▶ *Beyond Fohet, D 788 to the right of the calvary leads back to Aydat.*

CHÂTEAU
DE LA BASTIE-D'URFÉ★

MICHELIN MAP 327: D-5 – 7KM/4.3MI E OF BOËN

In the 15C, the rough lords of Urfé built a manor on the banks of the River Lignon. The family's rise to power was rapid. During the Italian Wars Claude d'Urfé spent several years in Rome as an ambassador, and on his return to France he converted Bastie manor into a Renaissance château. **Honoré d'Urfé** (1567-1625), grandson of the ambassador and author of the first French novel, *L'Astrée*, grew up in these refined surroundings.

A Bit of History

Unhappy in love – After graduating from Tournon College, Honoré d'Urfé returned to Bastie, where he stayed as the guest of his elder brother. The latter's wife, the beautiful Diane de Châteaumorand, a passionate woman disappointed by her husband, aroused burning passion in the young man. After obtaining the annulment of her first marriage, which had never been consummated, Diane wed her former brother-in-law in 1600. The couple moved to her castle in Châteaumorand, northwest of La Pacaudière. This second marriage was no more successful than the first. Honoré d'Urfé fled from Châteaumorand and started writing L'Astrée, for which he had already begun to draft a few ideas on his return from Tournon. Published between 1607 and 1628, this extraordinarily popular saga 5 000 pages long set the fashion in France for the novel and all things pastoral. The interminable love affair of a shepherd, Céladon, and his shepherdess, Astrée, became a bible for the 17C "honest man."

A Renaissance Residence *allow 1hr*

🕐 *Guided tour (45m): Apr-Jun and Sep-Oct: 10am-noon, 2.30-6pm (Jul and Aug: 10am-noon, 1-6pm); Nov-Mar: Wed, Fri, Sat, Sun, 2-5pm.* 🕐 *25 Dec-1 Jan. 5€.* ☎ *04 77 97 54 68.*

The original manor (14C-15C) was enlarged in the 16C by Claude d'Urfé, who brought artists from Italy to help with the decoration.

The main courtyard is flanked on the left by a wing reserved for the guard and on the right by an Italian-style construction consisting of two superimposed galleries linked by a stairway with a crouching sphinx on a pedestal at the bottom. The ground floor of the central building includes the famous **Rockwork Grotto★★**, or Cool Room, richly decorated with pebbles, shells and multicoloured sand which form the background from which figures stand out in relief. The pagan decoration of this room gives way to the biblical scenes adorning the adjacent **chapel** which has a very fine coffered **ceiling★** of gilded stucco. Many

Neptune in the Rockwork Grotto

J. Damase/MICHELIN

elements which once formed the decoration of the chapel are unfortunately scattered in various estates and museums.

The rooms on the first floor have beautifully painted ceilings and most of the rooms still feature their original furnishings and panelling. There are also many fine tapestries in the château.

The gardens have been landscaped once again into a beautiful setting where water and greenery mingle harmoniously.

BEAUJOLAIS★★

MICHELIN MAP 327 : F-2/4/4, G-2/3/4, H-2/3/4

According to an old French saying, Lyon is fed by three rivers, the Rhône, the Saône and... the Beaujolais. It is true that the Beaujolais is renowned both within and beyond French borders largely as a wine-growing region, but although this industry makes a substantial contribution to local economy, it is by no means the region's only source of income.

▶ **Orient Yourself:** The best way of getting your bearings is to take a tour of the vineyards - *dégustation* is optional, but not recommended for the driver - you will be rewarded with some wonderful views of hills and valleys.

⊘ **Don't Miss:** The 15C chateau de Corcelles, built to defend the border with Burgundy.

⊙ **Organizing Your Time:** Get the feel of the region by visiting Villefranche-sur-Saône first, and then plan your driving tour. Allow two days to tour the region.

⌚ **Also see:** la Dombes, Châtillon-sur-Chalaronne, Lyon, Mont d'Or Lyonnais

A Bit of History

The Beaujolais region owes its name to the aristocratic **Beaujeu** family, who were at the height of their power from the 9C to the 11C, founding Villefranche-sur-Saône and Belleville Abbey. In 1400, Édouard de Beaujeu gave his estate to the House of

The "Compagnons du Beaujolais" brotherhood

Bourbon-Montpensier, one of whose members, Pierre de Bourbon, married Louis XI's daughter, thereafter known as Anne de Beaujeu. The Beaujolais passed briefly into the hands of the French Crown under François I, who confiscated it among other territories from the Connétable de Bourbon as punishment for his somewhat negative attitude towards his monarch, but by 1560, the Bourbon-Montpensiers had been reinstated as landlords. Anne-Marie-Louise d'Orléans, Duchesse de Montpensier, who was known as **"La Grande Mademoiselle"** (she was renowned for her love affairs and her active support of the Roman Catholic Fronde movement), bequeathed the Beaujolais to the House of Orléans, who remained its owners until the Revolution.

Geographical Notes

The Beaujolais is a mountain range which stretches between the Loire and Rhône valleys, on the line where the Atlantic and Mediterranean watersheds meet. The region is clearly delimited to the west and east, but less so to the north and south, where it gradually gives way to the Charollais region and the Lyonnais mountain range.

With a maximum altitude of 1 009m/3 310ft at St-Rigaud, the Beaujolais is best qualified as hilly, rather than mountainous. Its distinguishing features are numerous mountain plateaux crisscrossed by narrow sinuous valleys, and an asymmetrical relief from east to west. To the east the land drops sharply down to the river plain of the Saône, whereas to the west it slopes gently away. The cliffs formed by the subsidence of the Saône river bed are home to the vineyards of the "Côte Beaujolaise," whereas the rest of the region forms "La Montagne."

La Montagne – Picturesque hills and valleys, and landscapes which are as varied as they are appealing, make this a region well worth exploring. Vast panoramic views unfold from the crests of ridges or from the many look-out points over the Saône Valley as far as the foothills of the Jura and the snow-capped Alpine peaks on the horizon. The upper slopes of the mountains are carpeted with broom and pines, whereas lower down there are stands of oak separated by wide open clearings. Geographically speaking, the area is strategically located for trade and transport, nestled near Lyon, half way between the Loire and Rhône valleys. A number of industries have blossomed here.

A textile industry has evolved gradually in and around the mountain towns. Labours undertaken a century ago, when the areas around Monsols and the upper valley of the Azergues were planted with conifers, are also bearing fruit, as magnificent plantations of Douglas firs supply a thriving timber industry. Thus the timber and textile industries of La Montagne, together with the vineyards of the lower slopes, constitute a rich source of income for the Beaujolais.

Beaujolais Wine

Beaujolais vineyards and the wine they produce have broadcast the region's reputation far beyond the borders of France.

The vine has been cultivated here since Roman occupation, with varying degrees of success; having flourished during the Middle Ages, it was virtually abandoned during the 17C, but taken up again in the 18C, when Lyon, the "Beaujolais syphon," ceased to be the only market and Beaujolais wines began to be transported to Paris. The market expanded still further as the road and rail networks evolved, and vine-growing became a monoculture in the region.

Nowadays, the vineyards stretch from the mountain slopes near Mâcon in the north to the Azergues Valley towards Lyon in the south, covering the sides of the hills exposed to the sun, overlooking the course of the Saône. A single grape variety – the Gamay – is used to produce the light and fruity red Beaujolais wines with their characters

Address Book

EATING OUT

🍽 **Auberge Vigneronne** – *69430 Régnier-Durette - 5km/3mi S of Beaujeu via D 78 -* ☎ *04 74 04 35 95 - www.beaujeu. com - closed Mon, and Tue evening from Oct-Apr.* Near the church and beyond a handsome stone façade, here's an inn serving classic Beaujolais fare, with a wine cellar downstairs where chosen vintages may be sampled. The second dining room, with a splendid fireplace, is warmer and more enjoyable. Summertime terrace.

🍽 **Le Coq à Juliénas** – *Pl. du Marché - 69840 Juliénas -* ☎ *04 74 04 41 98 - www.coq-julienas.com - closed 22 Dec to 22 Jan and Wed.* The cock is the king of wine country - or at least of this stylish establishment on the Place de Juliénas. Behind its blue shutters, the well-decorated dining room is the showplace for an impressive collection of roosters of all sorts to be admired while savouring the gourmet cuisine.

🍽 **La Terrasse du Beaujolais** – *Rte d'Avenas - 69115 Chiroubles -* ☎ *04 74 69 90 79 - closed 8 Dec-1 Mar (except Sat lunch, Sun lunch) and Mon evening in Jul-Aug.* Above Chiroubles on the road to the Col de Fût d'Avenas, this restaurant offers an exceptional view of the mounts of Beaujolais from the dining room and terrace. Regional cuisine – the bread, terrines and pastries are all homemade - and salon de thé and snacks in the afternoon.

🍽 **Les Platanes de Chénas** – *Aux Deschamps - 69840 Chénas - 2km/1.2mi N of Chénas via D 68 -* ☎ *03 85 36 79 80 - closed Feb, 23-28 Dec, Tue and Wed except Jul-Aug.* Let others do the work – you're on holiday! Have a seat on the shady terrace and enjoy the view of the Chénas vineyards while treating your taste buds to local vintages and hearty cuisine.

🍽 **Christian Mabeau** – *69460 Odenas - 15km/9mi NW of Villefranche via D 43 -* ☎ *04 74 03 41 79 - christian. mabeau@france-beaujolais.com - closed 2-12 Jan, 30 Aug to 12 Sep, Sun evening and Mon except public holidays.* Located in the heart of the village of Odenas, this little family restaurant sets up a few tables on the terrace, right across from the grapevines, as soon as the weather is fine. Pleasant dining room and fixed-price menus to be accompanied with a selection from the extensive regional wine list.

WHERE TO STAY

🛏 **Chambre d'hôte Domaine des Quarante Écus** – *Les Vergers - 69430 Lantignié - 4km/2.4mi E of Beaujeu via D 78 -* ☎ *04 74 04 85 80 -* 🚫 *- 5 rms.* This vineyard owes its name to the *arbre aux quarante écus*, the tree of forty coins – that is, the Ginkgo biloba - planted in front of the house. In an enclosed garden and orchard, surrounded by grape vines, you can enjoy the bucolic calm while sipping a glass of Quarante Écus wine.

🛏 **Chambre d'hôte M. et Mme Bonnot** – *Le bourg - 69430 Les Ardillats - 5km/3mi NW of Beaujeu via D 37 -* ☎ *04 74 04 80 20 - closed Jan -* 🚫 *- 5 rms - meals* 🍽. A most enjoyable stopover thanks to the ambient friendliness, the delicious meals and the attractive wine cellar dedicated to (what else?) Beaujolais wines. Old mangers give the dining room a rustic feel; each guest room has a different fruit theme.

🛏 **Chambre d'hôte Domaine de Romarand** – *69430 Quincié-en-Beaujolais - 9km/5.4mi SE of Beaujeu. Take D 37, D 9, and dir. Château de Varennes -* ☎ *04 74 04 34 49 – closed 25 Dec-1 Jan - reserv. required - 3 rms - meals* 🍽🍽. The U-shaped courtyard of this handsome stone house gives onto rows of grapevines. Overseen by the winemakers themselves, the modern rooms are comfortable and the pool promises delicious moments of repose – after the plentiful breakfast, for example.

🛏 **Hôtel Les Vignes** – *Rte de St-Amour - 69840 Juliénas -* ☎ *04 74 04 43 70 - www.hoteldesvignes.com - closed 7-22 Feb, 21-28 Dec and Sun from Dec to Mar -* 🅿 *- 22 rms -* 🍽 *10€.* On the St-Amour road leading out of Juliénas, this house is set in the heart of the Beaujolais. The building is undeniably sober and the rooms, refurbished one by one, are suitably functional. The luminous breakfast room has a sunny colour scheme.

⊜⊜ **Chambre d'hôte Domaine de La Grosse Pierre** – *69115 Chiroubles* - ☎ *04 74 69 12 17 - www.chiroubles-passot.com - closed Dec and Jan - 5 rms*. The perfect address for a total immersion halt in the heart of the Beaujolais region, this handsome house amid the grapevines offers a few pleasant, albeit rather simply fitted-out, guest rooms. Wine tastings are held in the vaulted cellar.

⊜⊜ **Chambre d'hôte Gérard Lagneau** – *Huire - 69430 Quincié-en-Beaujolais - Take D 37, dir. Beaujeu and road on the left opposite the Avia service station* - ☎ *04 74 69 20 70 - jeacagneau@ wanadoo.fr -* ⊠ *- reserv. required - 4 rms - meals* ⊜⊜. Set in the middle of vineyards, this handsome residence in local stone is a convenient starting point for your visit of the Beaujolais. Understated bedrooms. Your host has his own wine cellar where you can taste and buy.

TAKE A BREAK

La Maison des Vignerons – *Le Bourg - 69115 Chiroubles -* ☎ *04 74 69 14 94 - summer: daily 10am-noon, 2.30pm-6.30pm; rest of the year 10am-noon, 2pm-6pm*. Located in the small village of Chiroubles, The Winemakers' House collects and vinifies grapes from 100 hectares (250 acres) of *appellation contrôlée* vineyards belonging to 80 different owners.

SHOPPING

In wine-growing regions such as the Beaujolais, many wine-producers offer tours of their cellars, enabling visitors to discover an array of different vintages through tastings and knowledgeable explanations. Some of these cellars are famous – those of Château de la Chaize (108m/354ft long!), Clochemerle and Villié-Morgon, for example – but it is also worth the wine lover's while to visit other wineries. It may be necessary to call ahead – contact the 'Pays Beaujolais' Association for information.

A few choices among the many wineries where tastings are held:

Cave Beaujolaise de Quincié – *Le Bourg - 69430 Quincié-en-Beaujolais -* ☎ *04 74 04 34 17 - cavedequincie@terre-net. fr - Mon-Fri 8.30am-noon, 2pm-6.30pm, Sat 9am-noon, 2pm-6pm, Sun 3pm-6pm*. Founded in 1928 at the foot of Mont

Brouilly, this Cave Coopérative du Beaujolais reunites nearly 300 winegrowers. A full range of *appellation contrôlée* wines from the region, including Beaujolais Villages (many prize-winning vintages), is available. Tastings and sales in the cellar.

Cave des Producteurs des Grands Vins de Fleurie – *Le Bourg - 69820 Fleurie -* ☎ *04 74 04 11 70 - www. cavefleurie.com - 9am-noon, 2pm-7pm; Sun, 9am-noon, 2.30-7.30pm - closed Christmas and New Year's*. The grande dame of Beaujolais wine cellars, this co-op opened in 1927. One third of the Fleurie wines are made here, in addition to other wines classified by climate such as La Chapelle des Bois and Les Garants. The *cave's* most illustrious cuvées are 'Cardinal Bienfaiteur' and 'Présidente Marguerite'.

Cave du Château de Chénas – *La Bruyère - 69840 Chénas -* ☎ *04 74 04 48 19 - Mon-Sat 8am-noon, 2pm-6pm, Sun and public holidays 2.30pm-7pm*. Located in the magnificent Château de Chénas, this vintners' association created in 1934 has 275 members. The vaulted cellar and maturing storehouse date from 1670 and are well worth a visit. Moulin-à-vent and Chénas Sélection de la Haute are the star vintages here.

La Cave de Clochemerle – *Le Bourg - 69460 Vaux-en-Beaujolais -* ☎ *04 74 03 26 58 - 10.30am-noon, 3pm-7.30pm - closed 25 Dec and 1 Jan*. The cave, housed in a splendid cellar built in the 17C, was inaugurated in 1956 by Gabriel Chevallier, who wrote the mordant portrait of village life, *'Clochemerle'*. The book's humour is illustrated by the frescoes and sketches adorning the walls, to be scrutinized while area wines are sampled... without moderation: the cave guarantees your safe return via wheelbarrow, if need be!

La Maison des Beaujolais – *441 avenue de l'Europe - 69220 St-Jean-d'Ardières -* ☎ *04 74 66 16 46 - www.lamaisondes-beaujolais.com - daily 11am-9pm, summer 'til 10pm - closed Christmas school holidays*. The sign tells the name of the game: this establishment is dedicated to Beaujolais wines. Through tastings, a shop and a restaurant, visitors can become acquainted with this famous winemaking region and its produce.

Caveau des Beaujolais-villages – *Pl. de l'Hôtel-de-Ville - 69430 Beaujeu - ☎ 04 74 04 81 18 - May-Nov: 10.30am-1pm, 2pm-7.30pm - closed 3 wks in Jan.* The handsome bust of Bacchus points the way to this cellar in the lower floor of the Marius-Audin museum. A broad range of Beaujolais-villages may be tasted here.

Moulin à Huile – *29 rue des Écharmeaux - 69430 Beaujeu - ☎ 04 74 69 28 06 - Mon-Sat 8.30am-noon, 2.30pm-7pm - closed 1-8 Jan and public holidays.* The big old millstone of this 19C oil mill still crushes nuts (walnuts, filberts, pine nuts…) and seeds to make the most flavourful virgin oils imaginable. Visits and tastings.

determined by the soil in which the grapes were grown. Beaujolais vineyards can in fact be divided into two distinct areas of production.

Coteaux de Beaujolais

North of Villefranche, the soil, granitic in origin, is gritty and clay-based – the perfect terrain for the Gamay vine. This is the region of **Beaujolais-Villages** and the 10 officially recognised "vintage" Beaujolais wines, or *crus*: Moulin-à-Vent, Fleurie, Morgon, Chiroubles, Juliénas, Chénas, Côte de Brouilly, Brouilly, St-Amour and Régnié.

Pays des Pierres Dorées

Between Villefranche and the Azergues Valley in the "land of golden stone," the soil is composed more of sedimentary rocks which alter the flavour of the wine produced from grapes grown in this ground. The wines produced here are the more ordinary "Beaujolais" and "Beaujolais Supérieur" labels.

Unlike most other red wines, Beaujolais is best drunk while young, and should be served slightly chilled. It is possible to taste local wines in many places – look out for signs advertising *'Dégustation'* in wine cellars large or small *(caveaux, celliers, châteaux)*. There are several local wine-tasting brotherhoods *(confréries)*, of which the *"Compagnons du Beaujolais,"* the *"Gosiers Secs de Clochemerle"* and the *"Grappilleurs des Pierres Dorées"* are perhaps the most active in promoting the glories of Beaujolais wine.

Beaujolais Vineyards★

① From Villefranche-sur-Saône to St-Amour-Bellevue

98km/61mi – allow 5hr – see local map below
The road winds its way through the vineyards, at first climbing the granite escarpments, then dropping down towards the Saône Valley.

▷ *Leave Villefranche on D 504, take D 19 on the right, then D 44 on the left.*

Montmelas-St-Sorlin

Drive round to the north of the feudal castle (not open to the public), which was restored in the 19C by Dupasquier, a student of Viollet-le-Duc. The castle, complete with high crenellated walls, turrets and a keep, looks most imposing, perched in solitary splendour on a rocky crag.

▷ *Carry on from Montmelas as far as Col de St-Bonnet. From the pass, an unsurfaced track leads off to the right to the St-Bonnet beacon.*

Signal de St-Bonnet
30min on foot there and back.

From the east end of the chapel there is a broad view of Montmelas in the foreground, set against the hills and vineyards of the Beaujolais and beyond them the Saône Valley. To the south-west lie the mountains of the Lyonnais and Tarare regions.

▶ *From the pass, take D 20 on the right.*

Cloisters in Salles

J. Damase/MICHELIN

St-Julien
This pretty little wine-growing village is the birthplace of the doctor **Claude Bernard** (1813-78). He was born the son of a wine-grower and earned part of the money for his studies by working in a chemist's. He became a professor at the Collège de France and a member of the Académie Française. The **Musée Claude-Bernard** (🕐 *daily except Mon and Tue. Apr-Sep: 10am-noon, 2-6pm (Oct to Feb: closing time: 5pm).* 🕐 *Closed Mar, 1 Jan 1 May, 25 Dec. 5€ (children: 3€).* ☎ *04 74 67 51 44)* recalls his work in the field of physiology, in particular on the absorption of fats and sugars by the liver. The museum garden leads to the house where Claude Bernard was born.

▶ *Take D 19 as far as Salles.*

Salles-Arbuissonnas-en-Beaujolais
The monks of Cluny founded a **priory** in Salles as early as the 10C. This was taken over by nuns of the Benedictine Order in the 14C, who ran it until they were replaced by "aristocratic" canonesses in the 18C. The 11C chancel contains the prior's chair (16C) and the choir stalls (18C). The 15C **chapter house** *(reached through the garden and the cloisters to the south of the church – light switch near the door on the left –* 🕐 *daily 8am-dusk)* has been converted into a museum; note its vaulting, supported on a central pillar, and the elegant keystones decorated with the symbols of the four Evangelists. An elegantly arcaded gallery is all that remains of the Romanesque **cloisters** *(reached through the little Flamboyant Gothic doorway to the south of the church's west front).* Around **place du Chapitre,** shaded by plane trees, stand the houses once inhabited by the canonesses. There is a good view of the plain east end of the church and of the Romanesque tower with a pyramidal roof, a very common feature of churches of this period in the Beaujolais region.

▶ *From Salles, take D 35, then D 49E to the right.*

Vaux-en-Beaujolais
This wine-growing village and the ribaldry of its wine-tippling inhabitants in the 1920s inspired **Gabriel Chevallier**(1895-1969) to write his satirical novel Cloche-merle.

▶ *Carry on along D 49E through Le Perréon and then take D 62 to Charentay.*

The unusual shape of the Château d'Arginy comes into sight 1km/0.6mi east of Charentay.

On the map below, the wine-producing area is shown in green – Names of grands crus are underlined in red.

Château d'Arginy

All that remains of the castle is the great red-brick tower known as the Tour d'Alchimie. This is shrouded in mystery: some say it was used by the Knights Templar to hide their treasure, brought here by Guichard de Beaujeu, the nephew of Jacques de Molay, Grand Master of the Order who was burned at the stake in Paris in 1314.

▷ *Follow D 68, turn left onto D 19, then right onto D 37 to Belleville.*

Belleville

This old fortified town situated on the crossroads of the north-south and east-west communications routes is now a centre of wine-production and industry (manufacture of agricultural machinery). The 12C **church** was once part of an abbey run by Augustinian canons, founded by the lords of Beaujeu. The square belfry above

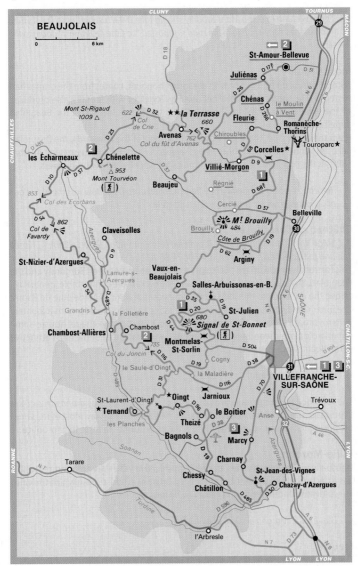

the south transept was added in the 13C. The handsome Romanesque doorway leading into the Gothic body of the church is decorated with geometric motifs on the outer arch. Inside the church, naïve style sculpted decoration on the capitals represents the Seven Deadly Sins.

The **Hôtel-Dieu** (&⊙ *guided tours (1hr): Aug-Sep: daily except Mon and Tue, 10am-4pm; Apr-Jul and Oct-Nov: daily except Sun-Tue, 10am-4pm.* ⊙ *Closed public holidays.* 5€ *(children: 3€).* ☎ *04 74 66 44 67),* built in the 18C to replace the old hospital, was in use for the care of the sick until 1991. The three large rooms are divided into characteristic alcoves with white curtains, and are connected to the chapel through openings with finely wrought iron railings. The dispensary contains a collection of porcelain dating from the 17C and 18C, which is set off by the surrounding walnut fittings.

Beyond Cercié *(carry on along D 37),* the road skirts Mont Brouilly.

▸ *Those wishing to climb Mont Brouilly should take D 43, turn left onto D 43E, then 100m/110yd further on take the road signposted "La Côte de Brouilly" again to the left.*

Mont Brouilly

Côte de Brouilly, a fruity wine with a fragrant bouquet, comes from the grapes harvested on the sunny slopes of Mont Brouilly. Together with Brouilly, also produced by the villages around Mont Brouilly, this is the most southern of the Beaujolais appellations.

From the esplanade, there is a marvellous **view**★ of the vineyards, the Beaujolais hills, the Saône Valley and the Dombes region. A chapel at the summit (alt 484m/1 588ft) is the object of an annual autumn pilgrimage by local wine-growers.

▸ *Return to Cercié. On leaving the village turn left onto D 68E towards the old village of Corcelles, then continue onto D 9 to the left.*

Château de Corcelles★

&⊙*Mar-Nov: 10am-noon, 2.30-6.30pm; Dec-Feb: 10am-noon, 2.30-5.30pm.* ⊙*Closed Sun and public holidays. No charge.* ☎ *04 74 66 00 24.*

This fortress was built in the 15C to protect the border between Burgundy and the Beaujolais. It was converted in the 16C, and took on a more comfortable, genteel air. Above the entrance to the keep is the family coat of arms of Madeleine de Ragny. The inner courtyard is surrounded by Renaissance arcades and contains a fountain with an ornate piece of 15C wrought-iron work on top. The chapel houses some remarkable Gothic woodwork. The huge 17C wine vat is one of the most attractive in the Beaujolais.

▸ *Rejoin D 9 to the right.*

The road goes through vineyards of some of the most famous *grands crus* of the Beaujolais, affording pretty views of the Saône Valley on the way. Most of the wine-producing villages en route offer visitors the opportunity to taste their produce.

Villié-Morgon

Unusually for Beaujolais wines, the wine produced in Villié-Morgon matures well. It has a particularly fruity taste because of the broken up schist soil in which the vines are cultivated. Interesting wine cellars *(wine tasting).*

▸ *Leave Villié-Morgon on D 68 heading N.*

Fleurie

The fine, light Fleurie wines are best drunk young. Fine wine cellars.

Villié-Morgon vineyards

▶ *In Fleurie take D 32 E, then turn left onto D 186.*

Romanèche-Thorins
The famous Moulin-à-Vent wine is produced here and in the neighbouring village of Chénas. There is a wine museum located in the railway station – **Le Hameau en Beaujolais – SA Dubœuf** ★ (🕐 *Apr-Oct 9am-7pm; Nov-Dec and Feb-Mar 10am-6pm* 🕐 *Closed 2 weeks in Jan, 25 Dec. 13-16€ (children up to 15, no charge)* ☎ *03 85 35 22 22. www.hameauduvin.com).* The **Musée du Compagnonnage Guillon** (🕐 *Jan-May and Oct-Dec, 2-6pm; Jun-Sep, 10am-6pm.* 🕐 *Closed 1 May, 15 Dec to 1 Jan. 4€, no charge 1st Sunday in the month.* ☎ *03 85 35 22 02)* displays exhibits from the days of itinerant craftsmen; there are some particularly fine examples of their work.

▶ *At the Maison-Blanche crossroads on N 6, take D 466B, leading to St-Romain-des-Îles.*

Parc Zoologique et d'Attractions Touroparc★
🔥🕐 Kids *9.30am-6pm.* ☎ *03 85 35 51 53. 13€. www.touroparc.com*
In a delightfully verdant setting dotted with ochre buildings, this 10ha/25-acre zoo and breeding centre presents birds and animals from the five continents. Apart from the big cats, most of the beasts are allowed to roam freely on the premises. The zoo also has a leisure park, a picnic area and a small tourist train.

▶ *Rejoin D 266, which goes through the hamlet of Moulin-à-Vent, to D 68.*

Chénas
Home of robust, top quality Moulin-à-Vent and the lighter, no less excellent Chénas.

Juliénas
The strong wines from this locality can still be tasted in the **Cellier de la Vieille Église** (🔥🕐 *all year, daily, 9.45am-noon, 2.30-6.30pm.* 🕐 *1-15 Jan, mid-Feb-Mar. No charge.* ☎ *04 74 04 42 98),* tasting cellars in an old deconsecrated church converted for this purpose. The church walls are covered with pictures of Bacchanalian revels. By the exit to the village, taking D 137, there is a beautiful 16C-17C tithe house (Maison de la Dîme), easily recognised by its arcaded façade.

▶ *Drive on to St-Amour-Bellevue.*

St-Amour-Bellevue

This village at the northerly tip of the Beaujolais produces dark-red wines with plenty of body and high quality white wines.

Mountain Tour★

② From St-Amour-Bellevue to Villefranche sur-Saône

134km/83mi – allow 6hr – see local map above
This pretty drive climbs through vine-clad hills to dark pine forests, then drops down to the Azergues Valley, in which a number of sawmills have been set up.

St-Amour-Bellevue and Juliénas – ⚲ *See above.*

▶ *From Juliénas, take D 26 uphill, going through two passes one after the other (Col de Durbize at 550m/1 804ft and Col du Truges at 445m/1 460ft).*

Beaujeu

The capital of the Beaujolais lies amid vine-covered hillsides.

Les Sources du Beaujolais

&⚲ ⏲ *Jul-Aug: 10am-12.30pm, 2-7pm; Mar-Jun and Sep-Dec: daily except Tue, 10am-12.30pm, 2-6pm. ⏲ Closed 25 Dec, Jan-Feb. 6€ (children: 3€). ☎ 04 74 69 20 56. www.beaujeu.com*
Entrance through the Maison de Pays, opposite the church. This wine centre is a modern and original museum devoted to the historical development of the Beaujolais area through video films, with a presentation of the regional production. Note the remarkable life-size model of a barge. On the first floor, a series of models and a film recreate the atmosphere of rural life in a wine-growing area.

Église St-Nicolas

Same as for "Les Sources du Beaujolais," ☎ 04 74 69 20 56.
The Romanesque church tower is the only remaining original feature of this unusual-looking church built in 1130 from uneven blocks of black rock.

Musée des Traditions Populaires Marius-Audin

⏲ *Jun-Sep: 10am-12.30pm, 2.30-7pm; May: 10am-noon, 2-6pm; Mar-Apr and Oct-Nov: daily except Mon and Tue, 10am-noon, 2-6pm. ⏲ Closed Dec-Feb. 2€. ☎ 04 74 69 22 88. www.beaujeu.com*
Audin (1872-1951) was a printer from Beaujeu who founded this museum of traditional folk art in 1942. The first floor houses a collection of dolls, some dressed in 19C French fashions and others in folk costumes from French and Italian regions. Doll's furniture, toys and knick-knacks surround this miniature society. The section contains the reconstructed interior of a 19C farmer's house, as well as the various tools used by cobblers, tanners, coopers, wine-growers and farmers, and furniture and other objects from the hospital at Beaujeu: bed, enamelware, porcelain night-lights and enema syringes. Above the entrance to the wine cellar, where there is the opportunity of tasting some Beaujolais-Villages wine, a handsome Antique head of the Roman wine god watches over the proceedings.

▶ *Follow D 26 and D 18 to La Terrasse.*

La Terrasse★★

Alt 660m/2 165ft. *Viewing table.* The broad **view** from a bend in D 18 about 800m/0.5mi after Col du Fût d'Avenas takes in the Saône Valley, with behind it the Bresse plateaus, the Jura peaks and (in clear weather) the Alps, with Mont Blanc, as well as the Vanoise and Pelvoux massifs.

J. Damase/MICHELIN

Avenas

The Roman road from Lyon to Autun once passed through this village. The late-12C **church** contains a lovely 12C white-limestone **altar**★, which depicts

Limestone altar in Avenas

Christ seated in Majesty in a mandorla, surrounded by the symbols of the Evangelists and six seated Apostles on either side. The sides show scenes from the life of the Virgin Mary *(left)* and King Louis, the donor *(right)* – this is assumed to be Louis VII, although the inscription does not clarify this.

▶ *Take D 18E, then D 32.*

Shortly before the pass (Col de Crie), there is a beautiful view north down the Grosne Orientale Valley. As the road carries on downhill, it passes Mont St-Rigaud on the right, the highest peak in the region at 1 009m/3 310ft above sea level.

Chénelette

This small village lies in a charming wooded setting. The **Tourvéon** (alt 953m/3 127ft) towers above it. This summit was once the site of the great fortress of Gane-lon. According to the *Chanson de Roland,* Ganelon betrayed Charlemagne's army, bringing about its defeat and the death of Roland at Roncevaux. For this, he was put into a barrel lined with nails and cast off the Tourvéon peak.

His castle *(to visit the ruins, 45min on foot there and back)* was probably destroyed on the orders of Louis the Pious.

Les Écharmeaux

This summer holiday resort is set against a backdrop of pine forests and meadows near the mountain pass of the same name, which is an important junction for several of the main roads through the Beaujolais (alt 720m/2 662ft). From the pass, there is a fine view of the steep slopes of the Haut Beaujolais to the north.

From Les Écharmeaux, follow D 10 towards Ranchal. It crosses the Aillets pass and, after a stretch through forest, the Écorbans pass. Between Ranchal and St-Nizier-d'Azergues, D 54 affords some charming **views**★ of the Azergues Valley. Beyond **Col de Favardy** (alt 862m/2 828ft) there is a look-out point over an impressive **panorama**★ to the north-east: in the foreground lies the Azergues Valley, and in the distance loom the Tourvéon peak and the foothills of the Beaujolais.

St-Nizier-d'Azergues

This small town occupies a pleasant site above the Azergues Valley.
The pretty road carries on to Grandris.

▶ *After Grandris, turn left onto D 504 as far as La Folletière, then left again on D 485 which runs along the upper valley of the Azergues and through Lamure-sur-Azergues. In Le Gravier, turn right onto D 9.*

Claveisolles

This little village perched on a spur is well known for its plantations of coniferous trees. In the 19C, the Comte du Sablon introduced Douglas firs from America. The present forest cover is among the most beautiful in France.

▶ *Drive back to D 485 and turn left to Chambost-Allières.*

Chambost-Allières

This is an amalgamation of two very different villages: Allières in the valley, which is quite a busy place with a lot of passing traffic; and **Chambost,** a charming little rural hamlet above the valley, which is reached via D 116.

The road from Chambost-Allières to Cogny via Le Saule-d'Oingt makes a very **pretty drive★★.** It climbs up to the Joncin pass (alt 735m/2 411ft) and then runs along the ridge, offering a lovely **view★** of the Alps in clear weather.

▶ *In Le Saule-d'Oingt, turn left onto D 31, then left again onto D 19.*

As the road drops down to the valley, the view stretches over the Saône Valley, the Bresse region and the Jura foothills.

▶ *D 504 leads back to Villefranche.*

Le Pays Des Pierres Dorées★★

③ Round tour leaving from Villefranche-sur-Saône

59km/37mi – allow 4hr – see local map above

This trip explores the **Pays des Pierres Dorées** which owes its name to the pretty ochre-coloured local stone used to build farmsteads, castles and whole villages in the region.

▶ *From Villefranche, take D 70 S.*

This pretty **ridge-top road★** *(route de crête)* gives views down into the Saône Valley.

Marcy

Outside this market town *(reached along a small road to the left, signposted Tour Chappe)* stands a **telegraph tower** (🕐 *Mar-Nov: Sun. 2.30-6pm (Nov: closing time: 5pm). No charge.* ☎ *04 74 67 02 21 (town hall)* 🕐 *Dec-Feb. 2€)* built by Claude Chappe in 1799. The original semaphore mechanism, with moveable arms, was used to transmit visual messages until 1850.

From the foot of the tower, there is a sweeping view of the Saône Valley, the Dombes and the mountains of the Lyonnais and Beaujolais regions.

Charnay

This small fortified town at the top of a hill still has the remains of its original citadel in the shape of a 12C feudal castle. In the town square, surrounded by 15C and 16C houses built of golden stone, stands the church, which contains a beautiful Gothic statue of St Christopher in polychrome stone (12C). Higher up, the imposing 17C castle now houses the town hall.

▶ *Take a narrow road heading S from Charnay to St-Jean-des-Vignes.*

St-Jean-des-Vignes

There is a good view of the countryside around Lyon from the small church perched on a hillside amid a riot of flowers in season.

Espace Pierres Folles

🕐 *Mar to Nov: 9am-12.30pm, 2-6pm, Wed, Sat-Sun and public holidays 2.30-6pm. 5€.* ☎ *04 78 43 69 20. www.espace-pierres-folles.asso.fr*

A museum has been founded to reflect the presence of a number of important geological sites in this area. Part of the museum is given over to an exhibition on the history of the planet, as revealed by the composition of the sub-soil. Display cases, tableaux and films illustrate the slow evolution of life on Earth; the aquarium of live nautiluses (cephalopod molluscs) and the hologram of the "flight of the pterosaurs" are particularly interesting. The rest of the museum is devoted to displays on the local countryside, and the ways in which its resources are being tapped by industry and tourism.

The museum also boasts botanical gardens containing about 400 species of herbaceous plants and shrubs indigenous to the local region and typical of dry limestone areas.

Note that the Association Pays Beaujolais coordinates the creation and development throughout the region of many centres devoted to Beaujolais wines, on specific themes: geology in St-Jean-des-Vignes, history in Beaujeu, crafts and techniques in Theizé, wine tasting in St-Jean-d'Ardières.

▶ *Rejoin D 30 to reach Chazay-d'Azergues.*

Chazay-d'Azergues

All that remains of the fortified town overlooking the Azergues is the belfry, a few 15C and 16C houses and a town gateway known as the Porte de Babouin after a juggler who, disguised as a bear, rescued his feudal lord's wife and young daughter from a blazing tower, for which he was rewarded with the daughter's hand in marriage. The 15C castle (⚬━ *not open to the public*) was once the residence of the abbots of Ainay.

▶ *Take D 30 as far as Lozanne, then D 485 to Châtillon.*

Châtillon

A fortress built in the 12C and 13C to protect the mouth of the Azergues Valley towers masterfully over this village. The **Chapelle St-Barthélemy** *(reached via a steep signposted path to the left of the parish church - (*🕐 *Mid-Apr to Oct: Sun and public holidays, 2.30-6pm.* ☎ *04 78 43 92 66)*, originally part of the fortress itself, was extended in the 15C by Geoffroy de Balzac. Inside the chapel there are paintings by Lavergne and Hippolyte Flandrin. The corbelled chevet is a most unusual feature. The Esplanade du Vingtain, running below the church, gives a good view of the village. By the road *(D 76)* out of the village, towards Alix, there is a pretty covered well *(puits sarrasin)*.

▶ *Carry on along D 485.*

Chessy

The Flamboyant Gothic church contains a handsome 16C font and a statue depicting St Martha subduing a dragon.

Near Chessy, a rich seam of copper which belonged to Jacques Cœur was once mined. The ore obtained was known as **chessylite** and was a variety of azurite with a beautiful blue glint to it, highly prized by collectors.

▶ *Take D 19 to Bagnols.*

Bagnols

In this village is a 15C castle which has been restored and converted into a hotel. The church, dating from the same period, features a beautiful pendant keystone. There are some very pretty 15C-16C houses with porches on the village square.

▶ *Go back to D 19 and follow it to the left.*

Le Boitier

As you leave this hamlet, the road takes you past the Clos de la Platière, which belonged to the Rolands, a couple who became famous during the Revolution. **Mme Roland de la Platière** stands out from her contemporaries as an exceptionally cultured, well-educated woman who forged numerous close connections with the politicians of her age. However, she made no secret of her antipathy towards Danton and Robespierre and paid for this in 1793 by being sent to the guillotine. Her husband, who as Home Secretary (since 1791) had tried to save the life of Louis XVI and had been forced to flee Paris when he failed, committed suicide on receiving the news of his wife's death.

Theizé

Parking areas to the right of the road. Follow the street which goes up from the right of the church square. This village, characteristic of the Pierres Dorées area, has two churches and two castles. The main tourist attraction is the **Site de Rochebonne** in the upper part of the village, which includes the former chapel and the château. The 16C **chapel** (◷ *Jul-Aug, daily except Tue, 3-6pm; May-Jun and Sep-Oct: Sat, Sun and public holidays, 3-6pm. 3€. ☎ 04 74 71 16 10. www.theize-en-beaujolais.com)* which has a Flamboyant Gothic chancel with keystone pendentive, hosts exhibitions and concerts. The Classical façade of the château has a triangular pediment and is framed between two round towers. The building has been converted into an Oenology Centre on Beaujolais wine (ground floor). Note the fine staircase.

Oingt★

All that remains of the once mighty fortress here is the Porte de Nizy, the gateway at the entrance to the village. Narrow streets lined with beautiful houses lead to the church, an old castle chapel dating from the 14C. Note on the brackets supporting the arches of the chancel the carved faces of Guichard IV, his wife and their six children. From the top of the **tower** (◷*Jul-Aug: 3-7pm; mid-Apr to end Jun and Sep: Sat, Sun and public holidays, 3-7pm. ◷ Oct to mid-Apr. 2€. ☎ 04 74 71 21 24. www. oingt.com)* there is a marvellous view of the Lyonnais and Beaujolais hills and the Azergues Valley. In the town itself, the two pedestrian streets and the 16C Maison Commune (restored) are interesting.

▶ *Carry on along D 96.*

In **St-Laurent-d'Oingt**, note the church with a porch.

▶ *At the junction with D 485, turn right.*

On the left stands the old fortified town of Ternand.

Ternand★

Once the bastion of the archbishops of Lyon, Ternand retains some of its earlier fortifications, such as the keep and the watch-path, from which there is a good view of the Tarare hills and the Azergues Valley. The most interesting features inside the **church** (*Apply to the town hall for a guided tour. ☎ 04 74 71 33 43)* are the Carolingian capitals in the chancel and the mural paintings dating from the same period in the crypt.

Château de Jarnioux

▶ *Turn back through Les Planches and follow D 31.*

The pass **road**★★ over **Col du Saule-d'Oingt** is extremely pretty. Picturesque farmsteads on the hillside overlook meadows below. From Le Saule-d'Oingt, heading down towards Villefranche, there is a broad view of the Saône Valley.

▶ *At La Maladière turn right towards Jarnioux.*

Jarnioux

The **castle** (🕙 *Early Jul to mid-Jul and mid-Aug to end Sep: guided tours (50min) Mon, Wed, Fri. 2-6pm, Tue and Thu 9am-noon.* 🕙 *Closed rest of year, 14 Jul, and 15 Aug. 4€ (children: 2.50€).* ☎ *04 74 03 80 85)*, built between the 15C and 17C, has six towers and includes a particularly charming Renaissance section. The grand entrance gateway, which still bears traces of a drawbridge, leads into two courtyards, one after the other.

▶ *Take D 116 and D 38 back to Villefranche.*

BESSE-EN-CHANDESSE★

POPULATION 1 672
MICHELIN MAP 326: E-9

With its old houses and fortifications, Besse is a picturesque and charming town, and the beauty of its surroundings makes it a popular place to stay. The town is the setting for a biological research centre specialising in the study of regional flora and fauna, which was set up by the Faculty of Science of Clermont-Ferrand University. 🛈 *Pl. du Dr-Alfred-Pipet, 63610 BESSE-EN-CHANDESSE,* ☎ *04 73 79 52 84.*

Old Town

Houses with picturesque corbelled turrets line the narrow streets of the old town.

Église St-André★

This Romanesque church dates from the late 12C, with side chapels built in the 17C and 18C. The chancel, originally added in 1555, was restored in the 19C.
The interior is dark with narrow aisles. The lightly carved **capitals** are decorated with foliate designs or narrative scenes (The Rich Man's Feast, Crucifixion of St Andrew). Note the 16C **choir stalls** (beautiful misericords) and, behind the high altar, the revered statue of Our Lady of Vassivière.

Rue des Boucheries★

This is a quaint street with black houses made of lava stone. Note the 15C shops and **Queen Margot's House** (15C), on the corner with rue Mercière. According to local legend, Marguerite de Valois lived in this house. Its Gothic doorway, surmounted by a coat of arms, opens onto a beautiful spiral staircase.

Town Gate★

Corner of rue de l'Abbé and Le Petit Mèze. In the 16C this gate, which is protected by a barbican, was adapted to the use of fire arms. The belfry was added at a later date.

Address Book

EATING OUT AND WHERE TO STAY

Le Levant – *20 r. de l'Abbé-Blot, 63610 Besse & St Anastaise -* ☎ *04 73 79 50 17 (closed Wed).* How do you like your trout? With cabbage, wild mushrooms or lentils? Or would you prefer a different regional dish? There's plenty of choice here, served in a decor that seems to be firmly grounded in the 1970s.

Auberge du Lac Pavin – *Au Lac Pavin - 4km/2.4mi W of Besse via D 149 -* ☎ *04 73 79 62 79. www.lac-pavin. com - closed 1 Nov-20 Dec.* The fish – char, among others – served in this restaurant once lived in the alpine lake that you see from the dining room. The owner, who is also the chef, prepares simple dishes from fresh ingredients. A few modest rooms have views of the lake.

Hostellerie du Beffroy – *26 rue Abbé Blot* ☎ *04 73 79 50 08 - closed 4 Nov to 26 Dec, Mon and Tue except in Jul-Aug and Feb, Wed lunch in Jul-Aug - reserv. required Sun –* ⌐*10€ - meals* ⌐. *www.lebeffroy.com.* This handsome 15C building in the village centre used to be the guardhouse. The gourmet fare is served in a charming dining room with white-draped tables and old wooden beams.

Ferme-auberge La Voûte – *8 r. de la Mastre - 63320 Clémensat - 5km/3mi S of Champeix via D 28 -* ☎ *04 73 71 10 82 - open Sun lunch and Sat, evenings Jul-Aug except Sun and Mon -* ⌐ *- reserv. required.* A very popular farm-inn nestling in a small village. The vaulted dining room is often crowded with savvy diners enjoying fare from the farm, local recipes or savoury Auvergnat specialities (to be ordered ahead). Spacious, recently refurbished bedrooms.

Auberge du Point de Vue – *Trossagne - 63610 St-Pierre-Colamine - 7km/4.2mi NW of Besse via D 978 and D 619 -* ☎ *04 73 96 31 45 - closed Jan, Mon, Tue evening and Wed evening except school holidays - reserv. recommended.* The view from the terrace of this aptly named inn is breathtaking. Whether you dine al fresco in the summer or by the fireplace in the winter, local cuisine is the mainstay here, chosen à la carte or from one of the hearty fixed-price menus.

Château du Bailli

These remains of the outer town wall are visible from the road *(north-west)* behind the church.

Additional Sights

Musée du Ski

Rue de la Boucherie. ◷ *School holidays: 9am-noon, 2-7pm. 3€.* ☎ *04 73 79 57 30.*
www.sancy.com
This Skiing Museum is the first of its kind in France. Among the displays are 30 different pairs of skis, a 1925 bobsleigh, ski boots and shoes, and a pair of 1910 skates. Prints and photographs show Besse at the turn of the 20C, when this sport was first introduced here, and Super-Besse in 1958, during the early days of the new ski resort.

Maison de l'Eau et de la Pêche

Rue de la Boucherie, Besse-en-Chandesse. ♿◷ *mid-Jun to mid-Sep, daily except Sat 10am-noon, 2-7pm (last admission 1hr before closing).* ◷ *Closed 1 Jan and 25 Dec. 4€.* ☎ *04 73 79 55 52.*
Located on the banks of the Couze de Pavin, 800m/0.5mi from the town centre, this house belonging to the Parc des Volcans contains an exhibition centre displaying local aquatic species, equipped with various pedagogical tools (videofilms, microscopes, models, computer terminals).
For information about themed rambles, apply to the tourist office or to the Maison de l'Eau et de la Pêche.

Excursions

Super-Besse✶

Super-Besse (alt 1 350m/4 430ft) – a high-altitude outpost of Besse – is first and foremost promoted as a winter sports resort, but it is also popular in summer because of its quiet, peaceful surroundings.
There are a variety of chalets and holiday residences available. The vast, south-facing ski slopes are reached by ski lift; additional facilities include a skating rink and a swimming pool.

Ski area

This recently created resort (1961), developed at the foot of Puy de la Perdrix (alt 1816m/5 958ft), has 40km/25mi of south-facing ski slopes, 17 drag-lifts, three chair-lifts, and a gondola leading to 27 Alpine-ski runs (seven green, six blue, eleven red and three black runs). The ski pass sold on location gives access to the Mont-Dore skiing area (🖝 *see Le MONT-DORE*). Snow-cannon equipment provides adequate snow cover.

Cross-country skiing takes place south of Super-Besse, where a track leads down to Lac Pavin. Cross-country tracks totalling 120km/75mi wind their way between the frozen lakes through this thickly wooded area.
In summer, the nearby lake (14ha/34 acres) can be used for swimming, canoeing and windsurfing. 🚶The area is ideal for rambling – all that is required is a pair of stout hiking boots.

Puy Ferrand

15min by cable-car, then 45min on foot there and back from Super-Besse.

Lac Pavin

🚶 The cable-car for Perdrix leaves from the Biche corrie and ends at the peak of Puy de la Perdrix. Follow the crest to the summit of Puy Ferrand, which offers a **view**★★ of the Dore mountain range, the lakes and Chaudefour Valley.

Lac Pavin★★

4.5km/3mi SW of Besse via D 149, which is a one-way road, joining up with D 978 from Besse to Condat, or via the "Fraux road" S of Besse which connects Besse to Pavin via a pasture-covered mountain. There is no time-limit in the parking area at the intersection of D 978 and the by-road; the lakeside car park is restricted to 1hr.

The Fraux parking area offers a lovely **view**★ of the lake.

This 44ha/109-acre lake (alt 1 197m/3 927ft) surrounded by forests and superb rocks, is one of the most beautiful in the Auvergne.

The glittering waters of Lac Pavin are populated by char and trout which sometimes reach an enormous size. The lake is ideal for boating and fishing. It is almost circular in shape and has a maximum depth of 92m/302ft.

The lake bed was formed by a formidable volcanic explosion which hollowed out a crater on the northern flank of the Puy de Montchal.

In the past, it was said that the old town of Besse was swallowed up by the lake as a divine punishment, and that throwing a stone into it would unleash terrific storms; this is why it is called Pavin, from the Latin *pavens* meaning dreadful.

🚶 A gentle path offers a very pleasant stroll around the lake (about 45min on foot). It is possible to climb to the Puy de Montchal from here.

Puy de Montchal★★

Access: from either the south end of Lake Pavin or the end of the "Fraux road" – 1hr 30min on foot there and back.

🚶 The summit (alt 1 411m/4 629ft) offers a magnificent **panorama**★★ – to the north-west, the Dore mountain range; to the north, the Dômes mountain range, clustered around Puy de Dôme; further to the east, the Couzes and Comté valleys; to the north-east and east, the Livradois and Forez mountains and to the south-east, in the far distance, the Chaise-Dieu plateau and Velay mountains. In the foreground, Anglard falls, Montcineyre Puy and lake, and the Cézallier mountains; to the south-west, the Cantal mountains. To the west, the view is masked by the edge of the crater.

Chapelle de Vassivière

8km/5mi W along D 978 W towards La Tour-d'Auvergne; 3km/1.9mi beyond the crossroads separating Lac Pavin from Super-Besse, turn right onto a small road.

During the summer, this 16C pilgrimage chapel, standing in a beautiful rural setting, houses the statue of Our Lady of Vassivière. On 2 July, the Feast of the Ascent, this Black Madonna, borne aloft by the "Carriers of Our Lady," solemnly leaves the church of St-André in Besse, where it returns on the first Sunday after 21 September, the Feast of the Descent.

Lac de Montcineyre

8km/5mi SW along D 36. Skirt Lac de Bourdouze and, 1km/0.6mi further on, follow a path on the right (1km/0.6mi).

Crescent-shaped Montcineyre Lake owes its existence to the wooded Puy Montcineyre, which dams the valley.

Follow the lakeshore along the foot of the volcano for an attractive view of the Massif du Sancy (see Massif du SANCY).

Exploring the Couze Valleys

65km/40mi – allow one day

Leaving from Besse, take D 633, a charming corniche road offering interesting views of the Couze de Pavin Valley and the Courgoul gorges. It becomes D 619 after crossing Trossagne.

▶ *Turn right onto the narrow road running above the Grottes de Jonas.*

Grottes de Jonas

 Feb-Oct and Christmas school holidays: guided tours (50min). 6€ (under 16, free).
☎ 04 73 88 57 98. www.grottedejonas.com

The most rudimentary of these man-made caves carved out of the volcanic tufa in a cliff were doubtless inhabited in prehistoric times. Over the centuries their descendants also made use of them; in the Middle Ages a chapel – its vaulting still bears traces of **frescoes** dating from 1100 – and a fortress were built in the caves. The tower of the fortress contains a spiral staircase with 80 or so steps carved into

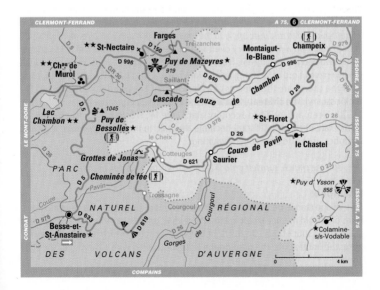

the rock; it leads up to apartments laid out over several floors. On the right, on the way up, note the sink containing a drain for waste water. Note also the missile room with the place reserved for the projectiles, the bakery and the bread oven.

▶ *Return to Le Cheix and turn right onto D 978 then right again onto D 621.*

Cheminée de Fée de Cotteuges

15min on foot there and back. Before reaching the hamlet, turn right onto the Bedeaux track.

Fairy's Chimney

This path leads through a wood to an earth pillar standing among excavations. This interesting geological formation, known as the "Fairy's Chimney" is a clay column topped by a block of hard rock.

Beyond Cotteuges the road crosses one of the *cheires* (lava flows) that are a characteristic feature of this area. Further on, high above to the left of the road, stand a number of superb sheer-sided rocks. The river has carved a course in the granite bedrock, resulting in rugged, rocky valley sides to which pine trees cling precariously.

▶ *Continue along D 621.*

Saurier

This is an old fortified village. Left of the road crossing the River Couze there is an attractive view of the old bridge and its chapel. The valley narrows again and basalt rocks can be seen on the hillsides.

▶ *Take D 26 towards Issoire.*

St-Floret★

First of all, take a look at Chastel plateau, probably the original site of the village. The **Église du Chastel** (🕐 *Mid-Jun to mid-Sep: guided tours daily except Tue and Wed 2-6pm; mid-Sep to mid-Jun: apply to the town hall (Mon and Thu 2-7pm).* ☎ *04 73 71 10 39*) is built on a promontory overlooking the Couze de Pavin. The north chapel contains a delightful early-15C **fresco** depicting St John the Baptist presenting Jean de Bellenaves, Lord of St-Floret, and his family to the Virgin Mary and the Child Jesus. Near the church are the remains of a Merovingian graveyard (tombs dug into the rock, ossuary). The **château**, located in the village of St-Floret itself, was built in the 13C (the keep) and modified a century later. Large 14C **frescoes**★ depicting episodes from a tale of chivalry (Tristan) decorate the walls in the lower chamber; a second chamber, above, features ogival vaulting.

▶ *After the church, turn left onto D 28, which will take you to Champeix.*

Champeix

This village stands between hillsides that were once carpeted with vineyards. The ruins of the old medieval castle, the "Marchidial," stand high above the village on a sheer-sided spur of rock. On the right bank is the church, which has a Romanesque apse; the lintel above the door on the left is decorated with a carving of the Holy Trinity.

Site du Marchidial

Can be reached on foot starting from the bridge; access by car: follow D 28 towards St-Floret; after 1km/0.6mi, turn right towards the college.

🚶 Situated in the upper part of Champeix, this district owes its name to the markets and fairs which used to take place on the plateau during the Middle Ages. A narrow lane running east leads to the ruins of the former medieval fortress offering a fine view. The area being renovated centres round the 12C **Chapelle St-Jean** (🕐 *Jul and Aug: 10.30am-12.30pm, 3-6.30pm. Guided tours by request. No charge.* ☎ *04 73 96 73 39*), which contains ancient frescoes. A spiral staircase leads up to a terrace from which there is a fine panorama of the surrounding area. The presbytery has been turned into an exhibition room.

▶ *Leave Champeix heading W towards St-Nectaire on D 996.*

Montaigut-le-Blanc

The village lies in the shadow of its ruined castle. Its somewhat Mediterranean appearance – houses with flat roofs and rounded tiles, terraced vineyards, and fruit trees at the head of the valley – heralds the Limagne plateau.

▶ *Carry on along D 996 for another mile or so. Turn right onto D 640. Just after Trei-zanches, turn left onto D 150.*

Farges

This hamlet is home to an interesting group of **troglodytic houses** (🕐 *(1hr): May-Sep and school holidays: 10am-noon, 2-6pm (Jul and Aug: 10am-6pm); last admission 1hr before closing;* 🕐 *Oct-Apr. 6€ (children: 4€).* ☎ *04 73 88 52 25*), hollowed out of the white tufa, which date from the Middle Ages. Visitors may also like to discover more about the maturing process of St-Nectaire cheese, in a cellar where this takes place. The traditional method of making St-Nectaire can be viewed at **Ferme Bel-lonte** (♿🕐 *8.30-10.30am, 5.30-7pm (cows milked at 7.45am and 5pm). No charge.* ☎ *04 73 88 52 25*).

A little further on from Farges, a quarry comes into sight to the right of the road. The powdery white rock extracted here is pumice stone, evidence of the tremendous volcanic eruptions that shook this region millions of years ago.

▶ *Carry on along D 150, then turn left.*

Puy de Mazeyres★

Alt 919m/3 015ft. From the hilltop, there is a beautiful **panorama** of the Dore mountain range (viewing table).

▶ *Rejoin D 150.*

St-Nectaire★★ – ♿ *See ST-NECTAIRE.*

▶ *From St-Nectaire-le-Bas, take D 996 towards Champeix, as far as Saillant.*

Cascade de Saillant

In this village the river tumbles over a basalt outcrop, forming a waterfall. There is a pretty view of it from D 622.

▶ *Return to St-Nectaire and take D 996 towards Le Mont-Dore.*

Château de Murol★★ – ♿ *See Château de MUROL.*

▶ *Leave Murol on D 996, then turn left at the junction with D 5.*

The road runs along the slopes of the Tartaret volcano. Note to the left, in a tiny quarry, the volcanic cinders which make up the cone.

Lac Chambon★★ – ♿ See Château de MUROL.

▶ *Return to Murol and turn right onto D 5 towards Besse-en-Chandesse. After 2km/1.2mi turn right onto D 619, then after about 100m/110yd turn left.*

Puy de Bessolles★

Alt 1 045m/3 428ft. This peak is one of the best look-out points in the Couzes region, giving an impressive view of the Dore mountain range and Lake Chambon.
🧗 *Follow the footpath signposted Plateau de Bessolles–Panorama. Allow 45min on foot to get to the viewpoint and back, and 2hr to follow the footpath right round the plateau (signposted in yellow).*

▶ *Go back to Besse-en-Chandesse via D 5.*

BILLOM

POPULATION 4 246
MICHELIN MAP 326: H-8

Billom is situated on the Limagne plain at the foot of the Livradois mountains. It flourished in the Middle Ages and had a university before Clermont-Ferrand. This university, transformed in the 16C, became the first Jesuit college and was well-known throughout the Auvergne. 🛈 *13 r. Carnot, 63160 BILLOM, ☎ 04 73 68 39 85. www.billom.com*

During the Reign of Terror in the wake of the French Revolution, Couthon, a member of the Convention, issued a famous edict ordering the demolition of all belfries in the province on the basis that they were "contrary to equality"; this was how the church of St-Cerneuf lost its elegant little tower.

Modern Billom plies a wide variety of economic activities: sawmills, wood veneering, car body workshops, industrial brush and ironware works. Cultivation of the regional speciality, garlic, is declining, but many companies continue to store and sort fresh garlic for consumption or to process it for pharmaceuticals, powders and garlic paste. A garlic fair takes place during the second weekend in August.

Medieval District

▶ *Start from the Hôtel de Ville.*

Follow quai de la Terraille to place du Creux-du-Marché, surrounded by old houses. Cross Pont du Marché-aux-Grains (Grain Market Bridge): three troughs and gutters hewn out of Volvic stone are visible on the parapet on the right – they were used to measure grain.

Walking up rue de l'Étézon, note the 16C belfry on the right and the 16C **Maison du Bailli** (Bailiff's House) at the top of the street.

▶ *Turn left, and walk past the former trade tribunal to place des Écoles.*

Maison du Chapitre

This 15C mansion, known as the chapter-house, was part of the medieval university and was used as a prison during the Revolution.

Porte de l'Évêché

This gateway into the medieval town marked the first line of fortifications.

Église St-Cerneuf★

This Gothic church was erected over an old Romanesque church from which part of the chancel, the ambulatory and a crypt remain. The doors in the front portal still have their unusual 13C strap hinges.

At the end of the nave, on the left of the entrance, note a 15C Entombment, a beautiful stone statue of an angel and 15C paintings; note also the 15C Pietà on the right.

The chancel is surrounded by a 12C **wrought-iron choir screen**★. A carved capital in the ambulatory tells the story of Zachaeus, a topic rarely illustrated in religious art. The Rosary Chapel to the

EATING OUT

🍴🍴 **Auberge du Ver Luisant** – 63910 Bouzel - 12km/7.2mi NW of Billom via D 229 and D 10 - ☎ 04 73 62 93 83 - closed 1-6 Jan, 15 Aug-9 Sep, Wed evening, Sun evening and Mon - The dining room of this village restaurant set in former stables has handsome wooden beams and a mezzanine. The contemporary cuisine is fresh and well prepared, with several fixed-price menus to choose from.
🍴🍴 **Le Paris** – 6 r. des Lucioles - 63520 St-Dier-d'Auvergne - 16km/9.6mi SE of Billom via D 997 - ☎ 04 73 70 80 67 - hotrestparis@aol.com - closed Jan, Sun evening and Tue except Jul-Aug - reserv. recommended. Locals are quite fond of this simple, inviting village inn with an outdoor terrace used as soon as the weather warms up. The traditional, appetizing dishes served here are just right and the dessert trolley is frankly irresistible.

right of the chancel (formerly the chapel of the Aycelin de Montaigut family, ransacked by Couthon in 1793) is decorated with a series of 14C frescoes in which the colours and the drapery are quite remarkable: they depict the Assumption and the Coronation of the Virgin Mary, angels playing musical instruments, the symbols of the Evangelists and, facing each other, the Church and the Synagogue. In a niche above the tomb of an archbishop stands a naïve 14C **Nativity**. The side chapel, known as the Chapel of the Precious Blood, contains two 17C wooden low-relief sculptures representing the Flagellation and Christ being Crowned with Thorns.

Crypt★

This 11C crypt, austere and extremely beautiful, is one of the oldest in the Auvergne. It follows the outline of the original east end with its ambulatory, opening out onto four radiating chapels. The first one, on the right, is decorated with 13C frescoes illustrating scenes from the life of St Margaret. The groined vaulting is supported by six sturdy columns and, in the centre, four lighter columns. A silver reliquary decorated with instruments of the Passion is said to contain pieces of the Holy Cross.

▶ *Turn right on leaving the church, walk round the building and turn left onto rue Pertuybout.*

Maison de l'Échevin

The entrance to this 16C alderman's house features an attractive staircase tower and a well with its wheel.

Rue des Boucheries

This narrow street paved with pointed stones, with no pavement and a gutter running down the middle, is flanked by medieval houses including the **Maison du Doyen** (Deanery, no 20) which has a beautiful basket-handle arch over its window and a Renaissance staircase, and the 15C **Maison du Boucher** (Butcher's House,

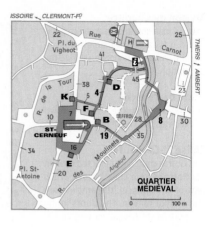

BILLOM

Boucheries R. des	4
Chanoines R. des	5
Coirier Pl. L.	7
Creux du Marché Pl. du	8
Croix de la Mission R.	10
Écoles Pl. des	16
Ététzon R. de l'	19
Évêché R. de l'	20
Gare Av. de la	22
Halle Pl. de la	23
Libération R. de la	25
Marché aux Grains	
Pont du	28
Mioche R. du Col.	30
Mont Mouchet R. du	34
Notre Dame R.	35
Pertuybout R.	38
St-Jacques R.	41
Terraille Quai de la	45

Maison de L'Échevin	K	Maison du Boucher	D	Maison du Doyen	F
Maison du Bailli	B	Maison du Chapitre	E		

no 5) which has stone walls on one side, half-timbered walls on the other and two overhanging upper floors.

Excursions

Discovering the Val d'Allier

50km/31mi – allow 3hr

▶ *Leave Billom along D 997 towards Pont-du-Château and turn left onto D 81.*

Chas
This old fortified village has kept its gateway and turret and its Romanesque church, fronted by a Renaissance porch and a pretty fountain.

Chauriat
Located north of the Comté, this small wine-growing village stands out because of its two churches. The deconsecrated **Église Ste-Marie** was built in Merovingian times and still features some interesting capitals. The **Église St-Julien** is characteristic of the Auvergnat Romanesque style. The exterior is striking for its very unusual marquetry of multicoloured stones, arranged geometrically but not to any set pattern on its **gable**★ and under the arches of the right transept arm, as well as under the relief arches and in the upper parts of the nave. Inside, the large columns of the nave are topped by foliated or narrative capitals (the 3rd on the right shows the Miracle of the Loaves and the Washing of the Feet). The high dome with its octagonal base is supported by powerful Romanesque arches. Note the 12C statue of the Virgin Mary in Majesty.

▶ *Drive to Pont-du-Château along D 4.*

Pont-du-Château
For a long time this strategically important town was fortified: it was the location of the only bridge spanning the River Allier between Moulins and Brioude. The **Église Ste-Martine** (🕐 Jul-Aug: 2–6pm. ☎ 04 73 83 20 27) presents fine capitals, historiated

These hills are known locally as Turlurons

and decorated with leaf motifs, a prettily sculpted wooden pulpit, a reliquary and various altarpieces. During the 19C Pont-du-Château was a busy port loading up goods for Paris; this history is recalled in the **Musée Pierre-Mondanel** (⏱ *Jul-Aug: guided tours (1hr): 10am-noon, 2-6pm, Sat-Sun 2-6pm; Sep-Jun: by appointment. 2.50€ (museum and castle: 3€).* ☎ *04 73 83 73 98)*, housed in the kitchens of an old château (extensive view from the terrace). It uses models of boats among the exhibits to tell of river fishing, life for the mariners etc.

▶ *Leave Pont-du-Château to the S and take D 1 heading towards Vic-le-Comte.*

The road meanders along the banks of the River Allier, offering pretty views of the mountain ranges.

▶ *Turn left onto D 117, which crosses Mirefleurs. Follow a steep slope towards the road to Bosséol.*

Château de Bosséol – ♿ *See VIC-LE-COMTE.*

▶ *Continue along D 117, then D 301 towards St-Julien-de-Coppel.*

Drive up through Notre-Dame-des-Roches, a small chapel perched on a rock, to enjoy the view of Billom country.

▶ *Continue on D 118 to see the ruins of Coppel Tower; just before La Beauté, turn left. D 14 will take you back to Billow through the lush Angaud Valley.*

Châteaux in Livradois Country

45km/28mi – allow 3hr
This route provides lovely views of the first Livradois summits and gives access to the main strongholds in the Pays de St-Dier.

Château de Montmorin
⏱ *1-15 Jun and 15 Jul-31 Aug, daily, 2-6pm (last tour at 5pm). 5€ (6-12-year-olds: 2.50€).* ☎ *04 73 68 30 94.*
This former citadel used to consist of a keep flanked by round towers; it now lies largely in ruins.

Several rooms in the main building have been turned into a museum. The former stables house an interesting collection of tools from old crafts (smith, farrier, clog-maker, cooper etc) and the finds from excavations at the castle site. The guard-room contains Louis XIII furniture and arms from the 15C to the 17C. Upstairs, a room has been set aside for popular arts and crafts, and includes domestic objects and furniture.

The **view** from the battlements overlooks the Livradois region on one side and the Monts range on the other.

▶ *Take D 337, then D 338 towards St-Dier-d'Auvergne, then Fayet-le-Château.*

St-Dier-d'Auvergne

The 12C **church** *(Guided tours (1hr) on request daily except Sun 2-7pm. No charge. ☎ 04 73 70 80 34)* here was fortified in the 15C; it has a buttressed west front with arcading. Three aisles, a large chancel and three radiating chapels make up the inside. Note the interesting carved capitals (figures, foliage, sirens etc).

▶ *Drive 5km/3mi to the S on D 997.*

Les Martinanches

Nestling at the bottom of a valley and surrounded by a moat is a **castle** *(🕐 Easter-Nov, guided tours, 2-6.30pm, except Sat of Jul and Aug (Sun, public holidays, 2-6pm). 5.50€ (Children: over 12 years, 4.50€; under 12 years, 3.50€). ☎ 04 73 70 81 98. www. chateau-des-martinanches.com)*, built originally in the 11C but altered in the 15C and the 19C. Inside there are beamed ceilings, fine porcelain and earthenware, and period furniture.

Château de Mauzun

30min on foot there and back. In the village of Mauzun, follow the path that runs up to the ruins. 🕐 Sat, Sun, Easter to mid-June and October, and daily (except Mon), mid-Jun to end Sep. Walking shoes recommended. Medieval pageant in Aug, 10am-7pm. 6.50€. ☎ 04 73 70 76 14.

The mighty fortress standing on a spur of basalt rock, once the property of the bishops of Clermont-Ferrand, offers a fine panoramic view of the Limagne plain. The famous preacher, Bishop Massillon of Clermont, had the fortress demolished because he did not have enough money for its upkeep. He retained only a few rooms for priests who were being detained for disciplinary reasons. The site was later abandoned and used as a quarry. Although still in ruins, the castle retains its two defensive walls and 20 towers. Visitors walk round the outer wall with its sixteen towers then into the bailey where the local population took refuge in case of attack and which was used for gun practice in peace time. In the guard-room containing a model of the site, a video shows the restoration work in progress. Inside the castle protected by the remaining four towers, visitors can see a network of galleries at various levels.

▶ *Take D 20 to Neuville, then D 152.*

Église de Glaine-Montaigut

This church marks the transition between the Carolingian style and the Auvergnat Romanesque style. The 11C nave has a rounded vault with no transverse arch. The crossing is surmounted by a dome. The narrow side aisles topped by half-barrel vaulting are separated from the nave by heavy columns. The 12C chancel has fine capitals.

▶ *D 152 and D 229 lead back to Billom.*

BORT-LES-ORGUES

POPULATION 3 534
MICHELIN MAP 330: Q-3

Situated in pleasant surroundings in the Dordogne Valley, Bort owes its fame to the celebrated basalt columns which overlook it and to its enormous dam.

The town, straddling the boundary between the former territories of the Arverni and Lemovici tribes, flourished in the Middle Ages. Charles VII granted it the right to build a town wall, of which a few ruins survive.

For many years Bort was known for its tanning works, which are recovering from a difficult period, but the local economy is now sustained by other industries.
🏛 *Pl. Marmontel, 19110 BORT-LES-ORGUES ☎ 05 55 96 02 49.*

Sights

Barrage de Bort★★

The dam's sheer size makes it a showcase of hydroelectric production in the Dordogne. Its reservoir is partly filled by water from the Rhue, a tributary of the Dordogne. The road running along the top of the dam (390m/425yd long) overlooks the reservoir upstream dotted with **cruisers** *(🕐 May-Sep: boat trip (1hr) Château de Val/DordogneValley; Jul to mid-Sep: boat trip (1hr) Bort dam/château de Val 11am and 2-5pm. 6€ return (5-14-year-olds: 4€, 2-4-year-olds: 2€). Speedboats offering panoramic views. ☎ 04 71 40 30 14)*, and the main power plant and spillway downstream. Only 300m/328yd away beside D 979 on the west bank, a viewpoint at Les Aubazines gives a more extensive view over the 1 400ha/3 459 acres of reservoir.

A **tourist itinerary** *(Circuit Visiteurs – Guided tours on request; apply to the Tourist office, ☎ 05 55 96 02 49.)* can be followed, starting from the foot of the dam on the west bank between the hamlet of Les Granges and Bort's tanning and leather works. This

Orgues de Bort

Ecav/PIX

WHERE TO STAY

🛏🛏 **Le Rider** – *Av. de la Gare* - ☎ *05 55 96 00 47 - www.lerider.com - closed 28 Jun-6 Jul and 15 Dec-4 Jan - 24 rms -* 🛏 *5€ - restaurant* 🍴. Repainted façade, reinforced soundproofing – this discreet building located across from the train station is regularly upgraded for improved comfort. Meals are taken in a dining room–veranda with wrought-iron furniture and an original trompe-l'œil fresco depicting a house front and an imaginary country landscape. Traditional cuisine.

🛏 **Camping Municipal de la Siauve** – *15270 Lanobre - 3.5km/2.2mi N of Bort-les-Orgues via D 922 and secondary road -* ☎ *04 71 40 31 85 - open 31 May-14 Sep - reserv. recommended - 220 sites*. Located on the edge of the lake in a particularly fine natural environment, this is the perfect camp site for a stimulating out-of-doors holiday. Choose among beach activities, fishing and sight-seeing on foot or by bicycle. Chalets and cabins for rent.

explains, through a working model and a video, the production of hydroelectricity in the Dordogne basin and its tributaries.

Church

The extremely simple architecture of Bort's church (12C and 15C) highlights a few fine works of art including a 15C statue of St Anne holding the Madonna and Child in her arms, beautiful modern stained-glass windows, and a bronze Crucifix by the sculptor Chavigner.

Outside, there are traces of fortifications near the east end. A 17C priory stands right by the church.

Cascade du Saut de la Saule

2.5km/1.5mi, then 30min on foot there and back. Leave Bort on D 922 towards Mauriac and turn left onto the road running up to the clinic (Institut Médico-Pédagogique). Follow the footpath (signposted) across the Rhue, then turn left and follow the river.

🔹 The path soon reaches the little gorge where churning pebbles caught by the waters have hollowed out the gneiss to form so-called "giant's cauldrons."

Walk on to the outcrop beyond, which overlooks the Saut de la Saule; here the Rhue crosses a threshold of rock 5-6m/16-20ft high.

Excursions

Orgues de Bort★

Round trip of 15km/9mi – allow 2hr

▶ *Leave Bort on D 979 towards Limoges; near the graveyard, turn uphill onto D 127.*

As the road climbs, there is a beautiful view of the Rhue Valley on the left.

▶ *Just after the last houses in Chantery, park and turn right onto some steps leading directly to the foot of the columnar basalt–signposted "Grottes des Orgues."*

These impressive phonolite columns cover a distance of about 2km/1mi and vary in height from 80 to100m/260 to 330ft.

▶ *Return to D 127 and, 2km/1.2mi further on, turn right onto a road (signposted) which leads to a car park near the television transmitter on the basalt plateau, at an altitude of 769m/2 525ft.*

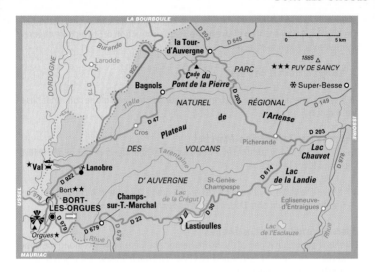

▶ *Park and walk (15min there and back) to a viewing table from which there is a different view of the columnar basalt on the right.*

⬛ The vast **panorama** ★★ extends over the Dordogne Valley, the Artense and Cantal regions and the Dore mountain range. To the south-west lies Lake Madic, relic of an earlier course of the Dordogne. From the spot known as the "Man's Head" *(Tête de l'Homme)*, reached by following the path along the ridge *(care required)*, there is an extensive view of the surrounding countryside with the town of Bort in the foreground.

▶ *Return to the car and follow D 127 for another 500m/0.3mi: here a path on the left leads to a rocky outcrop (15min on foot there and back).*

From here there is a panoramic view over Puy de Sancy, the mountains of Cantal, the Dordogne and its tributaries, the Monédières range and the Millevaches plateau. At the pass on Puy de Bort (alt 859m/2 880ft), there is a delightful view to the left of the vertiginous road. On the way back to Bort, D 979 provides a view of the charming **Château de Pierrefitte** *(right)* and a splendid view of the Bort reservoir and dam.

The Artense

85km/53mi – allow 4hr

The Artense, a granite plateau south-west of the Dore mountain range in the wedge formed by the River Dordogne and River Rhue, is cut across by the Tarentaine, a tributary of the Rhue which rises from Puy de Sancy. Early in the Quaternary Era the plateau was covered with vast glaciers which slid down from the Dore mountain range and from the mountains in Cantal and the Cézallier region. The glaciers left behind marked reminders of their existence, lending this region its highly unusual appearance: a greatly varied relief with peaks separated by small basins that are now lakes, peat bogs or marshy grasslands; and large rocks on which the weight of the slow-moving mass of ice carved deep grooves. In a landscape typical of the Auvergne, the Artense is graced by charming copses, but the region was long known for the poverty of its soil. Local inhabitants continue to cultivate rye, but new methods have enabled them to introduce barley and oats and, more recently, maize. The marshes are gradually being drained, making it possible to breed red Salers cattle, more and more frequently sharing their pastures with black-and-white Friesians. Most of the milk produced by these cattle is used to make Cantal cheese and particularly the local blue cheese, **Bleu d'Auvergne**. Farm production of St-Nectaire cheese is another major source of income.

▶ *Leave Bort to the E on D 979*

As it climbs the hillside, the road provides wonderful views of the columnar basalt around Bort.

Champs-sur-Tarentaine-Marchal
This holiday resort is huddled in a wooded valley near the confluence of the River Rhue and River Tarentaine.

▶ *Leave Champs-sur-Tarentaine-Marchal N along D 49 towards Lanobre and turn immediately right onto D 22, a pretty road winding across the plateau.*

Barrage and Lac de Lastioulles
This huge arch-dam is part of the hydroelectric engineering works along the upper Tarentaine. An outdoor leisure park has been laid out in pleasant surroundings, on the north side of the reservoir.
The road runs alongside the reservoir, passes **La Crégut Lake** on the left and then goes through St-Genès-Champespe.

▶ *Drive though St-Genès-Champespe and follow D 614 towards Issoire. As you come out of the village, take D 30 on the right.*

Lac de la Landie
This lake is surrounded by peaceful meadows and woodlands.

▶ *Rejoin D 614 then take D 203 on the right to Lac Chauvet.*

Lac Chauvet – 🖕 *See Massif du SANCY.*

La Tour-d'Auvergne – 🖕 *See Massif du SANCY.*

▶ *Drive SW out of La Tour-d'Auvergne along D 47.*

The road to Bagnols passes the foot of the tumultuous Pont de la Pierre waterfall on the left.

Bagnols
This village lies in the Tialle Valley, an undulating region of meadows and copses. Beyond Cros, the road winds down into the Tialle Valley.

▶ *Shortly after entering the Cantal département, turn left onto D 922.*

Lanobre
The 12C church here is a good example of the Romanesque style typical of the Upper Auvergne.

Château de Val★
🕐 mid-Jun to mid-Sep: guided tours (45min), daily 10am-noon, 2-6.30pm (last admission 45min before closing); rest of year: daily except Tue 10am-noon, 2-5.30pm; Christmas and All Saints school holidays: 2-5.30pm. 4.50€ (Children: 3€). ☎ 04 71 40 30 20. www.chateau-de-val.com. 🕐 mid-Oct to Feb.

J. Damase/MICHELIN

Château de Val

Since the reservoir and dam at Bort became operational, the settingaa in which Château de Val stands is extremely picturesque. When the reservoir is full, the castle stands fairly and squarely on a rocky island which can be reached only across a narrow dike.

Walk a little way to the left for a charming view of the château, which dates from the 15C. The exterior, with its quaint pepper-pot towers, is evocative of the elegance of the period the château was built.

The interior features some fine staircases and two magnificent Renaissance fireplaces. Every year, exhibitions of contemporary art are organised on the first floor. A watch-path runs beneath the eaves. The chapel of St-Blaise houses an information centre about Val at the beginning of the 20C and about the building of the dam and on the origins of the castle.

At the foot of the castle are a beach *(lifeguards in attendance)*, a watersports centre and an embarkation point for **boat trips** *(Trip through the valleys and gorges of the Dordogne (1hr) Jul-Aug: at 11.15am and 2-5.30pm; May and Sep: 3pm; Apr and Oct: by appointment. 6€ (children: 2€ and 4€). Speedboats offer panoramic views* along the Dordogne Valley: ☎ *04 71 40 30 14).*

▶ *Turn back. At the crossroads take D 922 on the right to get back to Bort.*

BOURBON-L'ARCHAMBAULT⚕

POPULATION 2 564
MICHELIN MAP 326: F-3

The name of this little town, overlooked by the ruins of its feudal castle, serves as a reminder of the Celtic god, Borvo, protector of thermal springs, and, secondly, of the first lords of Bourbon, the Archambaults. The spring water has been appreciated since the days of Roman settlement here; it comes out of the ground at a temperature of 55ºC/131ºF and is recommended for the treatment of rheumatism, paralysis and functional rehabilitation. 🛈 *1 pl. des Thermes, 03160 BOURBON-L'ARCHAMBAULT.* ☎ *04 70 67 09 79.*

Distinguished visitors – The waters at Bourbon, brought back into fashion by Gaston of Orléans, Louis XIII's brother, attracted many famous figures of the 17C, including Madame de Montespan, Louis XIV's favourite mistress who died here in disgrace in 1707.

For 30 years, Charles-Maurice de Talleyrand-Périgord (1754-1838), Prince of Bénévent and France's Minister of Foreign Affairs, visited Bourbon-l'Archambault every August to take the waters, which he considered the best guarantee of good health. His private swimming pool commemorates his visits in its name, "The Prince's Bath." His suite was visited by local personalities whose company he thoroughly enjoyed. He held court, played whist, delighted in the pleasures of conversation, chatted with his barber and played pranks on his Latinist doctor.

He and many other celebrities expressed their gratitude by making improvements and adding embellishments to the town.

The Spa Resort

Nouveau Parc

The thermal establishment, built in 1885, is situated in the middle of the park, together with the casino; Allées de Montespan, commemorating Louis XIV's mistress, run through the park and lead to the new park which commands a **view**★ north-east of the promontory where there was once an awesome stronghold protected by 20 towers. The thermal establishment contains ceramics from the Parvilliers workshops, dating from 1885; they are now on the list of Historic Monuments.

Address Book

EATING OUT

◗ **Les Bourbons** – *6 pl. de l'Hôtel-de-Ville - ☎ 04 70 67 17 99 - closed Mon-Tue in winter.* An appealing restaurant in the town centre housed in a building reportedly dating from the 17C. Exposed stones and beams, parquet flooring and a fireplace lend character to the dining room where a choice of traditional dishes is presented on the blackboard. Friendly welcome and moderate prices.

WHERE TO STAY

◗ **Chambre d'hôte Le Chalet de la Neverdière** – *Les Ferrons - 03160 Ygrande - 10km/6mi SW of Bourbon-l'Archambault on D 953 and D 94 dir. Cosne-d'Allier then another 2km/1.2mi via secondary road - ☎ 04 70 66 31 67 - ▱ - 4 rms - meals ◗.* Here is a curious chalet – dating from the early 20C, it has an ochre-edged façade and a roof up in the clouds. The rooms are large and simply furnished; a generous breakfast is prepared and served by your host.

◗◗ **Grand Hôtel Montespan-Talleyrand** – *Pl. des Thermes - ☎ 04 70 67 00 24 - www.hotel-montespan.com - closed 21 Oct-31 Mar - 45 rms - ▱ 9€ - restaurant ◗◗.* Mme de Montespan, Mme de Sévigné and Talleyrand figure among the famous guests who have sojourned in these three houses attached to the spa. The establishment now features an inviting lounge, a dining room with wooden beams and a pleasant garden with a pool. Most of the well-kept rooms are spacious.

◗◗ **Les Thermes** – *Av. Charles-Louis-Philippe - ☎ 04 70 67 00 15 - http://hotel-des-thermes.com - closed 1 Nov-7 Mar - 22 rms - ▱ 10€ - restaurant ◗◗.* Cross the flower-filled courtyard of this hotel opposite the spa to discover a place brimming with old-fashioned charm. The dining room's velvet and tapestries set the tone for classic cuisine. Spacious bedrooms with period furniture; gracious, traditional service.

Musée Augustin Bernard

🕐 1 Mar-31 Oct, Tue-Fri, guided visits at 2.30pm and 4.30pm, from the Office of Tourism. 3€ (children under 14, free.) ☎ 04 70 67 09 79.

This museum, founded in 1937, is housed in the former pump rooms, also known as the "King's House," built by Gaston of Orléans in the town centre.

The first floor includes a reconstruction of a local home and there are regional head-dresses and costumes on display. Farm implements testify to the region's rural past. The mezzanine contains a 12C Virgin Mary in Majesty and a collection of 17C and 18C Nevers china (faience) chemist's jars.

Église St-Georges

Unaccompanied visits daily; guided tours Mon 2.30-5.30pm. ☎ 04 70 67 03 44.

This church was erected in the 12C, altered and enlarged in the 15C and again in the 19C; it has beautiful capitals, including one of angels playing musical instruments in the corner of the south transept and, above the font, a 16C carving of Mary Magdalene with facial features typical of the Bourbons.

The presbytery, on the left when leaving the church, houses the church treasure including three beautiful reliquaries, one of which contains a thorn from the Crown of Thorns and a fragment of the True Cross.

After visiting the church, walk down to the town centre along rue de la République and admire the view of the fortified old town and of the ruins of its fortress.

Quiquengrogne Tower

This tower in the south-east corner of the old castle wall was erected by Louis II in order to keep watch over the town. It is topped by an 18C belfry.

Château

🕐 Feb to mid-Nov: guided tours (1hr15min, last departure 30min before closing) 2-6pm (mid-Jun to mid-Sep: 10am-7pm). 6€. ☎ 04 70 67 02 30. Rue de la Sainte Chapelle.

🚶 In summer, it is advisable to walk up to the castle. Leave the car near the town hall or the tourist office. Louis II of Bourbon turned Bourbon castle into a princely residence, but the destruction wrought from 1793 onwards, in the wake of the Revolution, left nothing but the three northern towers, each of which has two rooms with superb pointed vaulting. Their surroundings can be viewed from the top of the towers, reached by a spiral staircase. The roof of the left tower (Black Virgin, sundial, jack o' the clock) commands a viewa of the city, the lake with its mill and the Bourbonnais region.

Excursions

Bocage Bourbonnais
Round trip of 45km/28mi – allow 2hr

▶ Leave Bourbon-l'Archambault heading N on D 1 towards Nevers.

The Bocage Bourbonnais is a pleasantly undulating region, crisscrossed by hedges and dotted with forest groves which thrive in the heavy, clayey soil otherwise unsuited for farming.

Église de Franchesse
Note the fine bell-tower in typical local style and the interesting capitals.

▶ Take D 135 towards Ygrande.

Les Vignes

This hamlet is the home of the **Musée Émile-Guillaumin** (🕒 *May, Jun, Sep, and Oct, 3-6pm, Thu, Sat, Sun and public holidays; Jul-Aug, 3-6pm, Wed-Sun and public holidays. 3€. ☎ 04 70 66 37 90. http://musee-emile-guillaumin.planet-allier.com).* This farmer-writer (1873-1951) chronicled the joys and griefs of the tenant farmers of the Bourbonnais area. His books, *La Vie d'un Simple* and *Le Syndicat de Bougignoux,* give a well-documented insight into the rural world of the Allier at the turn of the 20C.

▷ *Drive SW out of Les Vignes along D 953.*

Église d'Ygrande

The 12C church boasts one of the most beautiful stone spires in the region.

▷ *Leave Ygrande SE along D 192. In St-Aubin-le-Monial, turn left on D 492. At the crossroads, turn right onto D 18. Drive through Gipcy and turn right onto D 11. Continue until you reach Meillers.*

Église de Meillers

Note the interesting lintel.

▷ *Leave Meillers to the W on D 18. After the crossroads with D 11, turn right onto D 58.*

Église d'Autry-Issards

The main entrance to the **church** is topped by a signed lintel. Inside, on the right of the chancel, there is a fine Deposition, a late-15C work by the Flemish School.

▷ *Drive NE out of Autry-Issards along D 58 which leads to St-Menoux.*

Église de St-Menoux★

At the heart of a peaceful village lying between Bourbon-l'Archambault and Moulins, stands one of the loveliest places of worship in the Bourbonnais. The present **church** was erected during the second half of the 12C, on the site of a 10C sanctuary built in honour of Menulphus, a Breton bishop, who died in the village in the 7C.

Exterior

The east end is organised elegantly beneath the high silhouette of the belfry, flanked by its staircase tower. A large semicircular portal leads into the 11C **narthex**. It is decorated with primitive capitals, and houses a Lapidary Museum which has a bas-relief depicting, in a mandorla, Christ giving benediction, surrounded by the symbols of the four Evangelists and a Pascal Lamb.

Interior

The 13C nave, altered in the 15C, and the low-relief sculptures display numerous works of art, including a 16C Compassionate Virgin in the right side-aisle and a carved oak **altar** in the left side-aisle.

The **chancel★★**, with its pleasing proportions, is closed by pillars with capitals surmounted by plain arches separated from the upper windows by a Greek key pattern.

In the **ambulatory**, the alternate use of pillars and fluted pilasters shows Bur-

The sarcophagus of St Menoux

J. Damase/MICHELIN

gundian influence. The sarcophagus behind the High Altar houses the remains of St Menoux who, in centuries past, had the reputation of healing the simple-minded. The people to be cured put their heads into a cavity in the side of the sarcophagus, whence comes the name *débredinoire*, given to this odd monument.

▶ *Continue along D 58.*

Église d'Agonges

Pretty church carved in pink sandstone. The friezes on the façade are decorated with animal motifs and the interior features figurative capitals.

▶ *Leave to the NW and drive on D 252 for 4km/2.5mi, heading for Franchesse, then turn left. D 139 will take you back to Bourbon.*

LA BOURBOULE⚜⚜

POPULATION 2 043
MICHELIN MAP 326: D-9

La Bourboule, located at an altitude of 852m/2 800ft in the lush valley of the Upper Dordogne, enjoys a climate with few seasonal variations. This well-known spa and rest resort offers many facilities for children.

The town is situated at the confluence of the Dordogne which, at this point, is no more than a mountain stream 12km/7.5mi from its source, and the Vendeix, a tributary which also takes its source in the Sancy range. The resort's pump rooms, casino, town hall and gardens line the banks of the two rivers, which are crossed by a dozen or so bridges and footbridges. 🛈 *15 pl. de la République, 63150 La BOURBOULE, ☎ 04 73 65 57 71. www.bourboule.com. The tourist office offers guided tours of the town and accompanied treks (with snow shoes, on foot or mountain bike) or coach trips through the surrounding area.*

▶ **Orient Yourself:** La Bourboule isn't especially large and the best way to get a feel for the place is on foot (👢 *see Town Walk*). The more energetic can walk up to La Banne d'Ordanche (1hr return) for a splendid view over the valley and the town.

🅿 **Parking:** Opposite the Parc Fenestre, on Ave Agis Ledru.

WHERE TO STAY

🍴🍴 **L' Aviation** – R. de Metz - ☎ 04 73 81 32 32 - aviation@nat.fr - closed 1 Oct-19 Dec - 41 rms - 🛏 7€ - restaurant 🍴🍴. Parc Fenêstre, a few steps from this 1900s gable-ended dwelling, is a nice place for your morning jog. The hotel's practical rooms can be a bit outmoded but are neat and tidy. Simple cuisine. Indoor pool and fitness room.

RECREATION

In summer, the La-Bourboule-Charlannes complex organises guided mountain-bike excursions (110km/68mi of marked tracks). Those who prefer rambling have a wide choice of itineraries crisscrossing the Massif du Sancy along some 670km/416mi of waymarked paths. In winter the Charlannes plateau becomes a pleasant cross-country skiing area (58km/36mi of tracks); ski tours are organised by the École du Ski Français (ESF).

- ⏱ **Organizing Your Time:** Take a ride in the little tourist train, and then explore the town on foot before wandering off up the valley sides.
- **Kids** **Especially for Kids:** Parc Fenestre, a splendid wooded park with children's play area (👉 *see Parc Fenestre*).

The Spa Resort

La Bourboule's first spa was opened in 1821. At the time, its cabins were closed off with serge curtains, revealing the bathers at the whim of the wind. The bathing water was used by several patients in turn, and water for the showers was pumped manually by an elderly peasant. In 1854 Thénard the chemist discovered arsenic in the waters of La Bourboule: when the news spread, every house-owner in the town promptly began exploring his property in the hope of finding his own spring and each person did his utmost to excavate faster and pump harder than his neighbour. Today, the town's springs are managed by the Société Thermale de La Bourboule and the Compagnie des Eaux Minérales. There are two springs in La Bourboule – a hot spring at Choussy-Perrière (60°C/140°F), and a cold spring at Fenêstre (19°C/66°F). Their waters contain metalloid arsenic and are used to treat respiratory diseases and dermatoses using techniques such as inhalations, sprays and electro-sprays, baths and showers.

Treatment is available in two spa centres: **Choussy** and **Grands Thermes** (⏱ *May-Sep: guided tours (1hr) Tue and Fri at 5.30pm (Jul and Aug: daily except Sun at 5.30pm); Apr: Wed at 5.30pm. Book in the morning at the thermal establishment shop. 1€. ☎ 04 73 81 41 00*).

The resort has all the facilities of a major spa town including tennis courts, stables, a swimming pool, an amusement park etc.

LA BOURBOULE								
Alsace-Lorraine Av.	BY	2	Gambetta Quai	AZ	7	Lacoste Pl. G.	AY	16
Clemenceau Bd G.	ABY		Guéneau-de-Mussy Av.	AY	8	Libération Q. de la	AZ	17
États-Unis Av. des	BY	3	Hôtel de Ville Quai	AY	10	Mangin Av. du Général	AZ	19
Féron Quai	BY		Jeanne-d'Arc Quai	BY	12	République Pl. de la	AZ	21
Foch Av. Mar.	AY	6	Jet-d'eau Square du	AY	13	Souvenir Pl. du	BY	22
			Joffre Sq. du Mar.	BY	15	Victoire Pl. de la	AY	23

Parc Fenestre★

Kids ○ *Access to the park is free: Apr-end Jun, 2-6pm; Jul-Aug, 2-7pm. The Little Train: Jul-Aug: 10am-noon, 2-7pm; Apr-Jun and Sep, 3-7pm.* ○ *Closed Oct to Christmas school holidays.5€ (Children: 3€).* ☎ *04 73 81 14 60. www.parcfenestre.com.*

This splendid wooded park – partly planted with sequoias – is a charming place for outings *(on foot or in a little train)* and relaxation. The children's play area consists of wide expanses of lawn and outdoor games. An additional attraction is the cable-car linking the park with the **Charlannes plateau.**

Town Walk

A pleasant walk round the town will give you an opportunity to admire the Victorian-style architecture of the hotels and to understand how the city developed at the foot of the Roche des Fées. Near the church, a convincing pastiche of Romanesque art, you can see the **Maison Rozier** and its imposing balcony *(Boulevard Georges-Clemenceau)*, the Grands Thermes, the former town hall, now a chocolate factory called the Marquise de Sévigné, and the casino, a listed, entirely renovated building.
All the narrow streets turning off quai de l'Hôtel-de-Ville to the right lead to the Parc Fenestre, a children's paradise.

Parc Fenestre★ – 👣 *See above.*

Roche des Fées
1hr on foot there and back. Take the footpath from place G.-Lacoste.
🚹 This granite "Fairy Rock" rises some 50m/162ft above the spa and provides an attractive view of the town and its surroundings.

Excursions

St-Sauves-d'Auvergne
4km/2.5mi NW along D 996. This village, situated on the north bank of the Dordogne, houses an interesting museum for children of all ages.

Le Monde Merveilleux du Train et de la Miniature
Kids ○ *daily, Easter-Nov: 10am-noon, 2-6.30pm; the rest of the year: 2.30-6pm.* ○ *Closed Dec-Mar. 4.50€ (Children: 3.50€)* ☎ *04 73 81 13 72.*
This museum on three levels contains collections of toys and models (cars and lorries). There is a train diorama on a scale of 1:87 as well as the reconstruction of a typical village from the Auvergne, with miniatures picturing ancient crafts.

Le Mont-Dore‡‡
7km/4.3mi E along D 130. 👣 *See Le MONT-DORE.*

Hiking Tours

① Tales of Toinette

10km/7mi N of La Bourboule. Leave the town on D 88.

Murat-le-Quaire
A rocky spur, once the site of a castle, marks the entrance to this village of houses with stone-tile roofs. There is a look-out point on the spur with a pretty view of the upper section of the Dordogne Valley. Besides its role as a rural holiday destina-

tion, Murat-le-Quaire hosts a Bread Festival every other year (odd numbers) as part of its campaign to preserve local tradition. In summer, regional products are sold inside a barn.

▶ *From the church, take D 609 towards La Banne d'Ordanche, as far as the school.*

Scénomusée La Toinette et Julien★

&♿ ⏲ *Mid-Apr to Sep: guided tours of the Maison de la Toinette (45min) and the Julien barn (30min), Easter to mid-Nov: 10am-noon, 2-7pm; Christmas to Easter: 2-6pm (also 10am-noon during school holidays). ⏲ Closed mid-Nov to late Dec. Toinette: 5€, Julien: 3.50€, combined ticket: 7€ (5-15-year-olds: 2.60€, 2€ and 3.50€). ☎ 04 73 81 12 28. www.toinette.com*

A gateway opens into a large courtyard in which the town hall and the museum are to be found.

The museum contains an account of rural life through the seasons in the Dore mountain range region of the Auvergne during the 19C, interestingly presented through the eyes of a local woman of that period, a certain Toinette Chaumard. Innovative use of technology adds sound and even smells to the four tableaux which make up this fascinating display.

Beyond the belvedere lies the **Grange de Julien**, a barn where Toinette's young son returns from his travels and reflects on the future prospects of rural life in the area.

▶ *Carry on along D 609 past a lake on the left, then follow it uphill round a series of hairpin bends with pleasant views, as far as a car park at the end of the road.*

La Banne d'Ordanche★★

1hr on foot there and back.

🥾 From the car park a steep footpath leads uphill to a viewing table. La Banne d'Ordanche (in the dialect of the Auvergne *banne* means "horn") rises from a grassy hillock. From the top of this basalt outcrop (alt 1 512m/4 961ft) – the remains of the central chimney of an old volcano – there is a magnificent **panoramic view**★★ of the Dordogne Valley and the surrounding mountains, the Puy de Sancy range, Puy de l'Angle, the Dômes mountain range and the Limousin area.

② Tour of Waterfalls

Trip of 3km/2mi – allow 4hr

▶ *Leave La Bourboule on D 130 along the Dordogne towards Le Mont-Dore. 1.5km/0.9mi after the swimming pool a track leads off opposite the Mont-Dore water company building (left of the road). Leave the car.*

🥾 *Take the GR 30 footpath to the right. Go past a farm and uphill into the forest. After 15min walk, take a path to the right which cuts downhill.*

La Banne d'Ordanche

Cascade de la Vernière★

The Vernière waterfall is formed by a large volcanic rock which obstructs the bed of the Cliergue.

▷ *Return to the path and turn onto the track leading to the Plat à Barbe refreshment kiosk. Here it is possible to go down a stepped path (dangerous except in summer) to a platform constructed opposite the Plat à Barbe waterfall.*

Cascade du Plat à Barbe★

🕐 *Mid-Apr to Sep: 8am-7pm. 4€.*

This 17m/50ft-high waterfall owes its name (literally "shaving dish") to the dip worn in the rock by its waters.

③ The Brigand's Den

4km/2.5mi trip – allow 4hr

▷ *Leave La Bourboule to the S on D 88 towards La Tour-d'Auvergne. 3.5km/2.3mi on past Parc Fenêstre, turn right and leave the car at Vendeix-Haut.*

Roche Vendeix★

30min on foot there and back. – Access along a footpath off D 88 by an inn. 30min on foot there and back.

🚶 This rock of prismatic basalt carries the ruins of a castle which was re-fortified in the 14C by **Aimerigot Marcheix**, an infamous local brigand who was eventually caught by the king's men in 1390; he was taken to Paris and subsequently beheaded and quartered. From the summit of the rock (alt 1 131m/3 710ft) there is a fine panorama over the region.

④ From Woodland to Valley

7km/4.5mi trip – allow 1hr

▷ *Leave La Bourboule to the W on D 129 towards La Tour-d'Auvergne via Col de la Sœur. About 500m/0.3mi after crossing the Dordogne, beyond a crossroads, leave the car and take a footpath branching off to the right.*

Lac du Barrage
30min on foot there and back.

🚶 This delightful path runs through Charlet woods to the dam whose reservoir stretches for 1km/0.6mi along the Dordogne Valley.

▷ *Continue along D 129 and, 3km/1.9mi further on, turn left onto D 610.*

Plateau de Charlannes
The Charlannes plateau (alt 1 250m/4 100ft) with its beautiful undergrowth is popular with spa patients for its restful scenery; it offers panoramic views of the Dore and Cantal mountains. In winter, it attracts cross-country skiers.

BRIOUDE ★★

POPULATION 6 820
MICHELIN MAP 331: C-2

Brioude is a small, bustling town situated on a terrace overlooking the lush Allier plain. 🛈 *Pl. Lafayette, 43100 BRIOUDE, ☎ 04 71 74 97 49. www.brioude.com*

A saint, and a bandit from the Alps – Legend has it that a tribune of the Roman Legion named Julian, who was born in the Vienne region and was converted to Christianity, sought refuge in Brioude and was martyred in the year AD 304. Pilgrims flocked to Brioude to pray at St Julian's tomb, particularly during the time of St Gregory of Tours (6C).

From the 9C onwards, the God-fearing town was subject to the authority of the canon-counts of St-Julien and remained so until the French Revolution, which put an end to their aristocratic tyranny.

Folk tales in Brioude still make reference to Mandrin, the notorious smuggler from Dauphiné. On 26 August 1754 he entered the town with a band of armed men, sought out the manager of the warehouse where tobacco was stored and taxed (the Farmers General held a monopoly on the sale of tobacco) and made the unfortunate man purchase a large batch of contraband Nicotine grass at an excessively high price. Mandrin then withdrew, while the people of Brioude turned a blind eye for they were delighted at the trick played on a system which they hated. The victim, however, never recovered from the shock; he died eight days later.

Basilique St-Julien ★★

St Julian's Basilica (74.15m/243ft long) is the largest Romanesque church in the area, a "vast stone-built shrine standing over a famous tomb" (Bernard Craplet). It is typical of the Romanesque style seen in the Auvergne with its tiered east end and varying colours of masonry, though it differs in other respects – the portals are topped with smooth or carved coving or zigzag moulding instead of the traditional string-course of billet moulding. The ornamentation at the east end is also noticeably Burgundian in style.

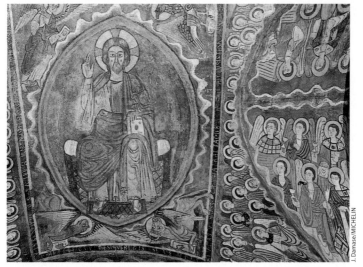

Frescoes in the Basilique St-Julien

Exterior

Building began on the church as it stands today with the narthex in 1060, and was completed in 1180 (chancel and east end). Its nave was raised and given rib vaulting in 1259 but the west front and square bell-tower above it were rebuilt in the 19C, as was the octagonal bell-tower above the transept crossing.

Walk round the basilica (it is particularly impressive from rue du Chapitre and place Grégoire-de-Tours) and take a look at the attractive east end and side porches.

East end★★

The fine concentric layout makes this the most remarkable part of the building. It is one of the last examples of Romanesque architecture in the Auvergne. The tall apsidal nave is decorated with a string-course of wide black and white mosaics; at the base of the nave is the ambulatory opening onto five radiating chapels supported by buttresses. Roofed with tiers of stone slabs, the east end includes cornices with carved modillions depicting monsters, human figures, foliage and slashes, in addition to semicircular arched windows flanked by colonnettes. Moulded arcades rest on the decorated capitals of the colonnettes. Jutting out from behind the east end are the flat walls of a false transept. Its flat machicolated roofs, side walls with loopholes and a vast pointed arch are a reminder that the basilica of St-Julien was once a fortified church.

Porches★

The side porches with their groin vaulting constitute the oldest part of the church. They have an unusual appearance, the result of their use as chapels during the 16C and the inclusion of a gallery over the top. The north porch still contains the remains of a 12C stucco tympanum depicting the Ascension.

The south porch has fine capitals decorated with foliage. The panelled door, once covered in hide, still has its Romanesque strap hinges and bronze door knockers, one in the shape of a lion's head and the other suggesting the head of a monkey.

Interior

The nave is particularly striking for its size and the warm hues of the red sandstone walls and pillars. The narthex, with its three galleries opening onto the nave, and the first four bays of the nave itself are the oldest features of the church (late 11C), as shown by the magnificent huge pillars flanked by engaged columns, and the austere style. It forms a stark contrast to the abundance of architectural features in the remainder of the nave and the chancel, which were built a century later. Their upper sections were altered in the Gothic style in the 13C and 14C.

The delightful polychrome pebble **pavement**★ dating from the 16C in the nave and from the pre-Romanesque era in the fifth bay in the centre, was uncovered, together with the small crypt beneath the chancel (probably on the spot of St Julian's tomb), following restoration and excavation work.

Capitals★★

The church contains a large number of capitals embellished with acanthus leaves, narrative scenes or themes that are commonplace in the Auvergne churches (imaginary or mythological creatures, human figures, masks, scenes from Hell). They are situated high on the columns which divide each pillar into sections.

Furniture, paintings

The basilica contains a number of altarpieces and old statues that are also worthy of note. The walls and pillars in the first bays, the ambulatory and the north gallery above the narthex still contain traces of 12C and 13C paintings, which are surprising for their diversity, "modernism" and spirited representations of human figures.

Turn to the right on entering the basilica to see:

(**1**) – (south aisle) 14C statue of Christ the Leper (Crucifix), carved in polychrome wood with canvas backing, brought here from the former leper hospital in La Bajesse near Brioude.

(**2**) – (south aisle) 14C statue of Virgin Mary in childbirth (recumbent) in polychrome wood.

(**3**) – (south aisle) 14C statue of Madonna with Bird carved in lava stone.

(**4**) – (5th bay, south pillar) capital of Christ in Majesty surrounded by the four Evangelists.

(**5**) – (first pillars of transept) carved corbels of heads of royal figures, facing each other.

(**6**) – (chancel) carved altarpiece (17C) behind the High Altar.

(**7**) – (chancel, north pillar) capital depicting the Holy Women.

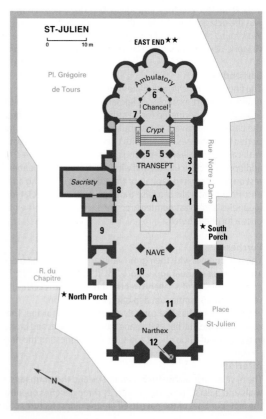

(**8**) – (north aisle) 14C gilt wooden statue of the Madonna with Bird.

(**9**) – (Chapel of the Cross) altarpiece attributed to the 17C sculptor Vaneau.

(**10**) – (3rd bay, north pillar) two capitals of groups of soldiers around a wounded soldier or prisoner; angels and demons carrying off souls.

(**11**) – (south pillar in narthex) capital of the Punishment of the Moneylender; painting of a woman in profile, with an enlarged eye.

(**12**) – (St Michael's Chapel) – in the south gallery of the narthex *(access by a spiral staircase with 30 steps)* – 12C frescoes depicting Christ in Glory, the Punishment of the Fallen Angels, the Triumph of the Virtues over the Vices etc; capital depicting donkeys playing musical instruments.

Town Walk

Hôtel de Ville

This is built on the site of the former castle of the canon-counts of St-Julien. There is a fine view over the Brioude section of the Limagne plain and the Livradois range from the neighbouring terrace.

Old houses

In the district around the basilica, a network of narrow streets contains a number of old buildings with remarkable façades. To the north, on the corner of rue Talairat: 17C mansion with turrets and carved door; rue du 4-Septembre: no 29, Lace Centre *(see below)*; no 25, 16C shop with arcades; no 22, 15C building known as **Mandrin's House** (temporary exhibitions); place St-Julien: 15C half-timbered house; south of the basilica: no 21 rue de la Tour d'Auvergne, 18C mansion; place Eugène-Gilbert, Romanesque house with turret.

Hôtel de la Dentelle

🕐 *Apr-Oct: Mon-Fri, 10am-noon, 2-6pm, Sat, 3-6pm.* 🕐 *Sun and public holidays. 4.50 € (Children: 3.50€)* ☎ *04 71 74 80 02. www.hoteldeladentelle.com*

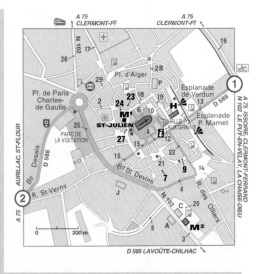

BRIOUDE

Assas R. d'	2
Blum Av. Léon	3
Briand Bd Aristide	4
Chambriard Av. P.	5
Chapitre R. du	6
Chèvrerie R. de la	7
Commerce R. du	8
Gilbert Pl. Eugène	9
Grégoire-de-Tours Pl.	10
La-Fayette Pl.	12
Lamothe Av. de	13
Liberté Pl. de la	14
Maigne R. J.	15
Mendès-France Av. P.	16
Michel-de-l'Hospital R.	17
Pascal R.	18
République R. de la	19
Résistance Pl. de la	20
St-Jean Pl.	21
Sébastopol R.	22
Séguret R.	23
Talairat R.	24
Vercingétorix Bd	25
Victor-Hugo Av.	26
4-Septembre R. du	27
14-Juillet R. du	28
21-Juin-1944 R. du	29

Hôtel de Ville	H	Maison du Saumon	
Hôtel de la Dentelle	M¹	et de la Rivière	M²

The centre, housed in the 15C former residence of the counts of Brioude, contains collections of old and contemporary lacework and lacemaking equipment as well as a workshop where lacemakers can be seen at work.

Maison du Saumon et de la Rivière

&♿ ⏱ *Apr-Sep, Mon-Sat, 10am-noon, 2-6pm (Jul-Aug: 10am-7pm); Feb-Mar and Oct-Dec, 2-6pm. Sun, 2-6pm (Jul-Aug, 10am-7pm).* ⏱ *Jan. 5€ (Children: 3€.* ☎ *04 71 74 91 43.*
The Atlantic salmon or salmo salar, which reaches the spawning grounds of the Upper Allier at the end of its 800km/500mi journey upstream, is part and parcel of Brioude's history.

Before learning about the importance of salmon fishing in the Brioude area in bygone days, visitors can see over 30 local species of river wildlife, including parr (young salmon), grayling, barbel and bream. The main attraction is the "salmon river," a curved length of glass 25m/82ft in circumference, where migratory fish swim in simulated currents and still waters.

Excursions

Churches of the Haut-Allier and Sénouire Valley★★

120km/75mi – allow one day

▶ *Leave Brioude to the E on N 102, heading for Puy-en-Velay.*

Vieille-Brioude

An impressive winepress (6.10m/20ft long) dating from 1873 stands in place de la Croix, testifying to the town's important wine-growing activities in the past. A whole network of cellars and galleries on several levels had been dug through the rocky spur on which Vieille-Brioude is perched.

Musée-jardin de la Vigne

⏱ *Mid-Jun to mid-Sep: 9am-7pm. No charge.* ☎ *04 71 50 90 18. place de l'église*
Located at one end of the town, the Romanesque

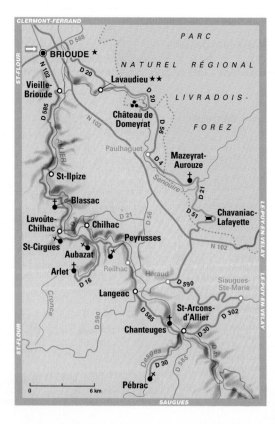

church of St-Vincent stands in the middle of a garden where flowers grow next to herbs and medicinal plants and where visitors can follow a wine-growing trail.

▷ *In Vieille-Brioude, turn right onto D 585, which follows the Upper Valley of the Allier towards Lavoûte-Chilhac.*

St-Ilpize

This medieval town, clinging to a basalt rock and towering 150m/492ft above the River Allier, is crowned by the ruins of a castle. The defensive walls enclose a 14C **chapel** *(Guided tours available, contact the town hall, ☎ 04 71 74 70 73)* with an apse of polychrome tufa and a basalt gable wall containing the church bells.

Address Book

EATING OUT

☞ **Pons** – *7 r. d'Assas -* ☎ *04 71 50 00 03 - closed 16-24 Jun, 10 Nov-10 Dec, Sun evening, Tue evening and Mon - reserv. recommended.* The local population patronizes this restaurant next to the Basilique St-Julien for its friendly atmosphere and regional cooking. Follow their lead and come enjoy a meal in the country-style dining room.

WHERE TO STAY

☞ **Poste et Champanne** – *1 bd du Dr-Devins -* ☎ *04 71 50 14 62 - closed 25 Jan-1 Mar, Sun evening except Jul-Aug and Mon lunch -* 🞠🅿 *- 20 rms -* ⌒ *6.50€ - restaurant* ☞ The main house of this family hotel features a dining room and a few bedrooms, the most basic with showers only. The annexes next door have more recent rooms and studios with kitchenettes. The appetizing regional cuisine is one reason why customers keep coming back.

☞☞ **Ermitage St-Vincent** – *Pl. de l'Église - 43100 Vieille-Brioude -* ☎ *04 71 50 96 47 - closed Dec-Jan -* 🞠 *- 5 rms - meals* ☞☞. Large, comfortable bedrooms, a garden bursting with flowers along the burbling river, an exceptionally attentive welcome: this skilfully restored presbytery has everything to recommend it. Your host is at your service should you need help organising your cultural or sports-oriented holiday.

☞☞ **Sophie Pougheon Chambre d'hôte** – *Le Prieuré - 43100 Lamothe -* ☎ *04 71 76 44 61 -* 🞠 *- 5 rms.* Built on the heights above Brioude, this ancient priory, part of which was built in the 12C, offers a superb panoramic view of the town and surrounding landscape. The smart interior boasts a discerning decoration scheme, stylish furniture and family paintings and memorabilia. One of the guest rooms is located in the old keep. Home-style breakfasts to look forward to.

RECREATION

Canoe rental – *Pont de Lamothe -* ☎ *04 71 50 43 82 - open Jun-mid-Sep.* A club (based at the foot of the Lamothe bridge) rents canoes and kayaks for adventures on the Allier between Brioude and Prades. You can benefit from instruction before setting out, and if you wish, hire a licensed guide to accompany you.

SHOPPING

Cave Saint-Julien – *17 r. du Commerce -* ☎ *04 71 74 90 18.* Wines from all corners of France garnish the shelves of this shop under a vaulted ceiling, along with bottles of champagne, other alcoholic beverages and 50-odd kinds of tea. The irresistible smell of Guatamalan or Mexican coffee beans being roasted wafts into the first part of the shop where Valette foie gras and Velay preserves surround an impressive display of dried mushrooms.

Gilles Guinet – *10 r. du Commerce -* ☎ *04 71 50 12 47.* Vanilla bavaroise, nougatine, caramelised pears (*le Manon*) and la tarte dentellière vie for attention in the pastryshop, unless your tastes lean toward the family speciality, *la bombe au miel* (iced honey bombe) or the chef's invention, *le pavé brivadois* with a pralined ganache base.

▶ *Rejoin D 585 and turn right onto D 144.*

Église de Blassac
Guided tours Jul-Aug: Wed and Sat 3-6pm.
The church is built on a flow of basalt. Its chancel contains a set of 14C frescoes depicting Christ in Glory, St Michael slaying the Dragon and scenes from the life of the Virgin Mary.

▶ *Rejoin D 585.*

Lavoûte-Chilhac
🛈 *Le Bourg, 43380 LAVOÛTE-CHILHAC* ☎ *04 71 77 46 57.*
This village is built on the banks of the Allier, which washes up against the walls of the houses. It has an elegant 11C bridge, restored in the 15C, and a Gothic **church** (🕓 *Open daily 9am-6pm.*) surrounded by the buildings of an 18C Benedictine abbey. The church has a single, wide nave. Note the large 12C Crucifix opposite the pulpit and the beautifully carved wooden door of the original 11C church. The treasury contains a statue of Notre-Dame-Trouvée, who is venerated throughout the region.

Maison des Oiseaux du Haut-Allier
🕓 *Jul-Aug: Sun-Fri, 10am-noon, 2.30-6.30pm; Jun and Sep: Wed and Sun, 2.30-6pm; May: Sun, 2.30-6pm; Easter: Mon-Fri, 2.30-6.30pm.* 🕓 *Sat. 5€ (children: 3€).* ☎ *04 71 77 43 52.*
This information centre of the Ligue pour la Protection des Oiseaux (LPO, Society for the Protection of Birds) presents the bird population of the Gorges de l'Allier and organises nature trails in season.

▶ *Rejoin D 585, which at this point hugs a meander in the Allier, giving a good view of the surrounding countryside.*

Église de St-Cirgues
🕓 *Open daily 9am-6pm.*
To the right of the road stands a church with an unusual tower. Inside, the two bays and the splays of the windows in the chancel are covered with interesting frescoes. Note the springing of the chancel vaulting, which rests on pilasters carved in human forms, themselves supported on consoles shaped like human faces.

▶ *Carry on along D 585.*

Église d'Aubazat
This village in a pleasant setting has a church containing a Pietà and interesting polychrome wooden statues representing an Entombment (15C).

▶ *Rejoin D 585 for a further 500m/550yd, and at the crossroads turn right onto D 41, and then right again onto D 16.*

Église d'Arlet
This tiny hamlet nestling at the bottom of the Cronce Valley has a small Romanesque church containing a remarkable 12C Byzantine Crucifix, an 11C statue of St Peter and a beautiful 15C painted wooden triptych, reminiscent of those produced by the Rhenish School.
From D 585, there is a view of the steep basalt cliffs on the opposite river bank and the village of Chilhac.

Chilhac

Small village built on a terrace of columnar basalt. Its **Musée Paléontologique** (🕐 *daily, Easter to end-Jun and Sep-Oct: 3-7pm; Jul-Aug: 10am-noon, 3-7pm.* 🕐 *Nov-Easter. 4.50€.* ☎ *04 71 77 47 26)* presents artefacts uncovered on local excavation sites since 1960: fossils of animals, particularly large mammals and man-made tools.

Église de Peyrusses

Guided tours Wed 2-6pm. ☎ *04 71 77 17 35.*
This church contains an interesting Virgin Mary in Majesty and splendid – if somewhat faded – frescoes depicting the Dormition of the Virgin.

▶ *Follow D 585 through Reilhac.*

Langeac

This busy little town lies in a wide cultivated "corridor" at the downstream end of the Allier gorge. One or two old houses are still to be seen along its streets.
The Gothic **church** contains choir stalls and a pulpit dating from the 16C. Note the 12C font, in a chapel left of the chancel, and the 15C Entombment in another chapel, in which the wall is decorated with two 15C paintings showing an Annunciation and a Virgin and Child. The church also has a handsome 14C wrought-iron grille.

▶ *Leave Langeac S along D 585.*

Église de Chanteuges

This attractive Romanesque church belonged to a local abbey which used to be the summer residence of the abbots of La Chaise-Dieu. The church is built with warm-coloured volcanic stone. Note the large window in the west front (16C); the pretty sculpted capitals in the nave, especially on the south side; and the finely carved Renaissance choir stalls.
North of the church is the arcade of the old cloisters, from where there is a good view of the Allier Valley. The 16C Abbot's chapel has a delicately carved door frame.

▶ *Turn right, under a railway bridge, onto D 30.*

Pébrac

After running along the pretty little valley of the Desges between pine-covered slopes, the road brings you to this quiet hillside village with red-roofed houses and the ruins of an 11C **abbey.** The abbey church, flanked by a square tower, underwent extensive alteration in the 15C when the height of the nave was raised by adding pointed vaulting. Beautiful carved capitals have survived from the Romanesque era, one of which shows two large heads vomiting serpents.
The **treasury** contains interesting items of church plate, including a chased copper box with sides decorated with scenes from everyday life in the 13C (troubadour, tournament) and the Pébrac Nativity Scene with its skilfully sculpted painted wooden statues.

▶ *Return to the intersection with D 585 and carry straight on along D 30, crossing to the opposite bank of the Allier.*

St-Arcons-d'Allier

The **church** in the upper part of the village has a very classic Romanesque nave with basalt columns. Its arcades are roofed by sturdy relief arches. The **Musée du Fer Blanc** (🕐 *Jul-Aug: daily 3-7pm. 4€.* ☎ *04 71 74 02 04 (town hall))* displays miscellaneous items made of tinplate: religious objects, lamps, moulds etc.

▶ *Cross the River Allier, drive through St-Arcons and take D 302 to Saugues. Turn left onto D 590, heading for Langeac. When you reach the locality called "Héraud," turn right.*

Château de Chavaniac-Lafayette

🕐 *Apr to mid-Nov: daily except Tue 10am-noon, 2-6pm (Jul and Aug: daily 9am-6pm). 5.50€. ☎ 04 71 77 50 32. www.chateau-lafayette.com*

The residence where Marie-Joseph-Gilbert, **Marquis de La Fayette**, was born on 6 September 1757, stands on one of the final outcrops of the Livradois area above the Allier Valley; the history of Franco-American relations is more important here, however, than any archaeological feature.

At the age of 19, La Fayette, aware of events brewing in America, obtained a secondment contract. One month later news arrived in Paris that the American States had proclaimed their independence; La Fayette, stirred by the "rebels'" cause, decided to give it his support and he financed the cost of his expedition out of his own huge personal fortune. He landed in Georgetown in 1777, became friendly with Washington, and fought by the American's side. .

The audio-guided tour leads visitors from room to room: a general biographical exhibition provides an introduction to the visit; next comes the kitchen where La Fayette's childhood is evoked, then the treasure room where personal objects and letters are displayed; this leads to the bedroom where he was born…his marriage is mentioned and the Grande Galerie recalls the ideas of the Age of Enlightenment; this is followed by a film on La Fayette's stay in America.

Other episodes from the general's life should be presented sometime in the future.

The grounds are graced by a pretty rose garden and three small lakes.

▶ *Leave Chavaniac to the W on D 51; at the first crossroads, turn right onto D 21, then take D 4.*

Mazeyrat-Aurouze

This village has a lovely **church** (🕐 *Mon and Thu 2-6pm by appointment. Apply to the town hall, ☎ 04 71 76 82 70)* built in pink stone, decorated with frescoes depicting the daily life of monks and peasants.

▶ *Go back to Brioude via the Sénouire Valley, by taking D 4 to Paulhaguet, then D 56.*

Domeyrat

The **castle** (🕐 *Apr-Oct, daily, 10am-noon, 2-5pm. 5€ (Children: 4€). ☎ 04 71 76 69 12)* ruins dominating the Sénouire and its Romanesque bridge are a fine example of medieval military architecture. Dismantled in 1795, it still towers proudly above the River Sénouire spanned by the five-arches of a Romanesque bridge. There is a reconstruction of daily life in a 13C feudal castle.

▶ *Continue along D 20, then D 203.*

Lavaudieu★★ – 👌 *See LAVAUDIEU.*

▶ *Return to Brioude on D 20.*

MONTS DU CANTAL★★★

MICHELIN MAP 330 : D-3 TO E-5

The mountains of Cantal, formed by the largest extinct volcano in France, embrace scenery that is the most magnificent in the Auvergne. Several of the peaks rise to more than 1 700m/5 580ft. Some, like the Puy Griou, are jagged; others, such as Puy Mary, are pyramid-shaped. The highest summit, Plomb du Cantal, is rounded and soars to a height of 1 855m/6 085ft. From the mountain heartlands, deep, picturesque valleys fan out, providing easy access for visitors.

▶ **Orient Yourself:** This is very much walking country without any clearly defined centres of habitation. As driving tours are not all that easy, probably the best way of familiarising yourself with the terrain is to drive or walk up one of the valleys, just to get a feel for the place.
- **Don't Miss:** The Puy Mary, not the highest, but a superb vantage point.
- **Also See:** Peyrol Pass at the very centre of the massif.

Geographical Notes

The Etna of the Auvergne – In its heyday at the end of the Tertiary Era the volcano in Cantal reached an altitude of 3 000m/9 840ft. It included a number of vents from which flowed the viscous lava that solidified into needles as soon as it was ejected from the crater, or the more fluid lava that spread out all round the volcano over an area some 70km/44mi in diameter. The viscous lava has given us the jagged peaks in the range such as Puy Griou, which more or less marks the centre of the former crater. The fluid lava formed the wide open plateaux called *planèzes* which owe their lush pasturage and fertile farmland to the fertilising elements incorporated into the soil by the lava flows as they gradually decomposed.

Effects of erosion – Glaciers formed in Cantal during the Quaternary Era. Their slow but powerful action, combined with that of the rivers and streams, wore down the summit of the mountain, carving deep into its sides, uncovering the lava plugs that filled the vents, digging out the corries that later became the valleys, and giving the mountain range the appearance it has today. The heart of the range is a slender crest marking the edge of a vast indented dip; this is the site of the old crater.
The most significant, and most characteristic, reminder of the gigantic volcano, which has now been worn away by erosion, is the layout of the valleys, all of which radiate out from the centre of the range.

Dairy industry – The entire range was once covered by forest. In the 13C the woodland was still extensive but, gradually, land was cleared by shepherds and today it has disappeared in all but the entrance to a few valleys (Alagnon, Rhue de Cheylade, Mars). Thanks to the basalt content of the lava, which produces better quality pasture than the trachyte in the Dore mountain range, Cantal has become best-known as a pastoral region. On its vast areas of pasture around the burons or cheesemakers' huts, where excellent mountain cheeses used to be produced, herds of small Salers cattle with mahogany-red coats graze. This is one of France's foremost dairy regions.

Excursions

If you would like to go on a guided hike or mountain-bike excursion, contact the local guides' office: Bureau des accompagnateurs, Le Caylat, 15590 Lascelle, ☎ 04 71 47 97 20.

1 Route du Lioran★★

55km/34mi – about 4hr
This itinerary follows the Cère and Alagnon valleys.

Aurillac★ – 🐾 *See Aurillac.*

▸ *Leave Aurillac E along D 117.*

The villages along the road have picturesque houses with hipped roofs that are typical of this area.
The road then runs into the wide, attractive Cère Valley.

Polminhac
The houses in the village huddle round the foot of a rock topped by Pesteils Castle.

Château de Pesteils – 🐾 *See VIC-SUR-CÈRE.*

Comblat
Gothic manor house with alterations.

Vic-sur-Cère★ – 🐾 *See VIC-SUR-CÈRE.*

Pas de Cère★★
45min on foot there and back. The footpath leads off N 122, 3km/2mi upstream from Vic-sur-Cère.
🚶 The path crosses a small meadow, then runs down through the woods to the Cère. The river flows between high, narrow walls of rock. The bed of the river is strewn with volcanic boulders which have tumbled down from the hillsides and which are now covered with a thick growth of plant life.

Cascade de la Roucolle
3.5km/2.3mi from Vic and 500m/0.3mi from the start of the footpath is another path to the right leading to an observation platform only 2min further on.
From here, there is a wonderful view of the Roucolle waterfall and the Cère gorge.

Thiézac – 🐾 *See VIC-SUR-CÈRE.*

Pas de Compaing★
High above the road on the left are tall cliffs from which, in rainy weather or when the snow melts, drops the superb **Malbec waterfall** (🐾 *it is inadvisable to park immediately below the cliffs because of the risk of a rockfall*).
A short distance further on, the valley narrows and the road runs along the hilltop high above the deep gorge known as Pas de Compaing.
Further on, the road enters the St-Jacques-des-Blats basin and the view extends to the end of the Cère Valley, with the conical outline of Puy Griou to the left.

St-Jacques-des-Blats
This is an ideal centre for hikers.

Col de Cère★
The new road (D 67) skirting the Lioran road tunnel crosses the watershed separating the Dordogne basin into which flows the Cère, and the Loire basin into which flows the Alagnon. From this threshold (alt 1 294m/4 245ft) there are some superb views and evidence of conflicting influences from north and south. Just below the pass, the impressive pyramidal outline of Puy Griou can be seen to the left, in the distance. Beyond the wide, light-filled Cère Valley is the narrow Alagnon Valley made even darker by the pine forests lining it.

Le Lioran and Super-Lioran★ – 👣 *See Le LIORAN.*

Gorges de l'Alagnon★ – 👣 *See MASSIAC.*

Beyond the **Pierre-Taillade bridge** which carries N 122 across a narrow stream fanning out in its course, the hillsides to the left of the road gradually lose their covering of trees. The valley widens but the scenery is more sombre than in the Cère Valley.

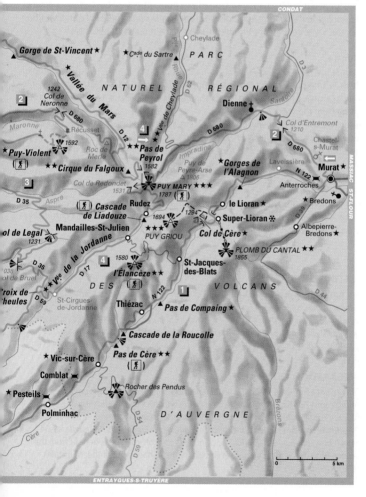

A few miles beyond Laveissière, the road runs along the foot of the handsome **Château d'Anterroches** (15C but restored), then the basalt rocks above Murat come into view. To the right is Bredons with its church; to the left, Bonnevie dominated by a statue of the Virgin Mary.

② Peyrol Pass★★

80km/50mi – about 6hr
This itinerary runs through "Puys" country along the Impradine, Mars and Maronne valleys.
⌖ *D 680 which crosses the Peyrol pass is usually blocked by snow from November to June.*

Murat★ – ♿ *See MURAT.*

▸ *Leave Murat NW on D 680.*

As the road begins to climb, Plomb du Cantal, Puy de Peyre-Arse and Puy Griou come into view, one after the other, to the left. The road then skirts the foot of Chastel rock, topped by a 13C chapel, and runs down from Entremont pass offering views of the Dore mountain range in the distance and Puy Mary on the left. From the bridge over the Santoire there is a wonderful view of the mountains of Cantal.

Dienne

Against the north wall of the 12C Romanesque church is a 13C wooden statue of Christ with a particularly moving expression. There is also a Nativity scene in a carved giltwood frame, dating from the reign of Louis XVI, and a carved stone stoup dating from the 16C.
As the road climbs up towards the Peyrol pass, it clings to the sheer sides of Puy Mary and provides superb **views**★★ over the Impradine and Rhue de Cheylade valleys, the Dore mountain range and the Cézallier area; few other roads in the Auvergne provide such breathtaking views.

Pas de Peyrol★★

Alt 1 582m/5 190ft. This is the highest mountain pass in the Massif Central.
In the foreground, there is a magnificent view of the wooded Falgoux corrie overlooked by the Roc d'Auzière.

EATING OUT
🍽 **Buron de la Brèche de Rolland** – *Col d'Eylac - 15300 Lavigerie - 7km/4.2mi N of Lavigerie via D 680 -* ☎ *04 71 20 81 43 - open May-1 Nov, daily 6.30am-10pm -* 🚫 Positively breathtaking: this small inn, perched 1 460m/4 820ft high, offers a fabulous view of the Vallée de Cheylade, the Brèche de Rolland, the Puy Mary etc. Dishes include local delicatessen, *truffade*, stuffed cabbage, *pounti*... All of Auvergne in a nutshell!

RECREATION
Parapente Puy-Mary – *15400 Le-Claux -* ☎ *04 71 78 95 21 - www.parapente-puy-mary.com – Apr-Oct: from 9am.* Let the professionals in this school introduce you to the joys of paragliding: 5-day courses, weekend specials and first-jump initiation.
Mountain guides – *Bureau des accompagnateurs, le Caylat, 15590 Lascelle,* ☎ *04 71 47 97 20. www.cantal-randonnee.com.* On foot or off-road bike, benefit from the knowledge of the licensed guides who share their knowledge of the mountains, the local flora and fauna.

J. Damase/MICHELIN

The ridge along the top of the Puy Mary

Puy Mary★★★

Viewing table. Steep climb – 1hr on foot there and back from the Peyrol pass – keep to the signposted track at all times.

🚶 The footpath follows the north-west ridge of the mountain. From the summit (alt 1 787m/5 862ft) there is a breathtaking view of Cantal's gigantic extinct volcano and a superb **panoramic view** over the crystalline plateaux that form the base of the volcanic area of the Auvergne. Also visible are the jagged peaks or the gently rolling hills of the Dore mountain range and the Cézallier, Livradois and Forez ranges. In the foreground is a striking view of the gigantic fan formed by the valleys radiating out from the centre of this natural water tower, separated by massive ridges with altitudes that decrease in the distance. To the north of Plomb du Cantal is the Alagnon Valley followed by the Impradine, Santoire and Rhue de Cheylade valleys to the left, then the Falgoux, Maronne and Doire valleys. To the south is the Jordanne Valley and the Cère Valley.

The human features added to this geological landscape are fascinating. Rural life varies with the altitude across this countryside divided by deep corries. In the depths of the valleys near the villages are fields of crops and meadows. In the lesser exposed areas are birch woods (which supply firewood) followed by beeches half way up the slopes (timber for building etc), and recently planted conifers. At higher altitudes are the alpine pastures dotted with burons (the huts once lived in by shepherds during the summer, where they made cheese) surrounded by ash trees.

The drive down from Pas de Peyrol affords splendid views over the Mars Valley.

Cirque du Falgoux★★

The Mars Valley starts here, as the river gouges out a course for itself along the foot of Puy Mary. The corrie is flanked by rocks and forests which provide a wonderful setting.

▶ *Head NW along D 12.*

Vallée du Mars★

The road follows the valley, in which there is a striking contrast between the shaded slopes, covered in woodland but devoid of houses, and the sunny slopes carpeted with meadows and trees, and dotted with houses.

In the **Gorge de St-Vincent**★ the valley narrows and at one of the bends there is only enough room for the road and the river. Note the tall cliffs to the right, with a few examples of columnar basalt.

To the left of the road beyond the gorge is the **Château de Chanterelle,** a fortified residence dating from the 17C with later restoration. It has a parapet walkway and a stone-slabbed roof.

▶ *Return to D 680 (or drive to Salers on D 212 – follow signs to Anglards – and D 22).*

At the pass known as Col de Néronne, the road moves to the other side of the hill and overlooks the wide, glacial Maronne Valley far below.

Puy Violent★

Ramblers will enjoy the walk to the slopes of Puy Violent, leaving from St-Paul-de-Salers.

▶ *Go to Vielmur and turn left. Follow a narrow shepherd's lane which leads beyond the Croix des Vachers.*

🔼 The walk to the top of the mountain (2hr 30min there and back) affords a lovely panorama, namely of the Maronne Valley.

▶ *You can also follow GR400 by going to Col de Nérone and taking D 680 until you reach Récusset, a secluded village overlooking the Maronne Valley. Alternately, follow the Chamina route that passes near Puy Violent and takes you back to Récusset (signposted in green, allow 3hr 45min).*

③ Crest Road★★

60km/38 miles – about 4hr
This itinerary takes over from the previous one and runs along the Aspre and Doire valleys.
☺ *The road up to Col de Legal is usually blocked by snow from December to April.*

Salers★★ – ⓒ See Salers.

▶ *Leave Salers on D 35 E.*

Running along the western slopes of Cantal's ancient volcano, the road crosses a few of the valleys which fan out from the heart of the range. It hairpins down into the Maronne Valley then crosses the river and enters the Aspre Valley.
The traces left by the ancient glaciers that formed these valleys are obvious, even today. On the hillsides, covered with hillocks of moraine, are huge boulders carried there by the ice and now left lying scattered across the meadows. In some places, houses have been built between the rocks.

Fontanges

To the right, at the entrance to the village, is a **monolithic chapel** dug into a mass of volcanic rock; entry is through a wrought-iron door set between colonnettes and archivolts. From the statue of the Virgin Mary set on the rock *(accessible via steps carved out of the rock)*, the view stretches right across the village. The **castle,** which now lies in ruins, once belonged to the family of Mademoiselle de Fontanges, Louis XIV's mistress who died at the age of 20. The 15C **Église St-Vincent** incorporates a Romanesque bell-tower with eight semicircular openings.
From the Aspre Valley, the road enters and crosses the Bertrande Valley then runs into the Doire Valley.

▶ *Continue along D 35 which follows the Aspre.*

Col de Legal

Alt 1 231m/4 039ft. From this pass there is a view in the distance over the plateaux of the Limousin area. The road runs down towards Bruel pass and provides a delightful view over the Doire Valley before skirting a number of valleys.

▶ *At Col de Bruel turn right onto D 60 to Tournemire.*

Tournemire – 🕐 *See TOURNEMIRE.*

Château d'Anjony★ – 🕐 *See TOURNEMIRE.*

▶ *Turn back and take D 35 to the right.*

Beyond the Croix de Cheules, D 35, which is called the **Route des Crêtes**★★ (Crest Road) follows the long ridge that separates the Authre and Jordanne valleys, and the journey provides some very attractive views of them.

▶ *After 6km/4mi, turn right onto D 58 to Marmanhac.*

Château de Sédaiges

🕐 *Early Jun to mid-Sep: guided tours (1hr) 2-6.30pm. 5€. ☎ 04 71 47 30 01. www.chateausedaiges.com*

Sédaiges, rebuilt in the 15C and modified in the 18C and 19C, is neo-Gothic in style. The tour begins in the lower room and the chapel (18C polychrome wood Madonna). On the floor above, a room fitted with light and sound equipment displays five 18C **Flemish tapestries.** The furnishings and decor of the two salons and the dining room reflect the lifestyle of a 19C aristocratic family.

▶ *Return to the Route des Crêtes, D 35.*

As the road slopes down towards Aurillac, the broad plain at the edge of the town can be seen stretching away, whereas to the left there is a magnificent view of the Jordanne Valley. This drive downhill is particularly rewarding at sunset.

Aurillac★ – 🕐 *See AURILLAC.*

4️⃣ Vallée de la Jordanne★★

25km/15mi from Pas de Peyrol to the Croix de Cheules – about 1hr 30min

Pas de Peyrol★★ – 🕐 *See above.*

▶ *Leave the pass on D 17 S.*

The cliffroad overlooks the superb Falgoux corrie where the River Mars rises. Beyond Redondet pass there is a view of Plomb du Cantal and Puy Griou before the road runs down into the Jordanne Valley.

Rudez

Huddled together, the village houses cling to the mountain slopes in order to leave the valley floor free for pasture.

🍴🍴 **Ferme-auberge du Bruel** – *15310 St-Illide - 7km/4.2mi W of St-Cernin via D 43 - ☎ 04 71 49 72 27 - françoise.fleys@wanadoo.fr - closed Feb and Mon-Thu - reserv. required.* Ah, lunch in the garden! And not just any lunch – but a delicious farm-fresh meal featuring plump duck, home-made cheese and the flavours of Auvergne: sensational! Worth going out of one's way for.

Vallée de la Jordanne★★

The slopes that flank this picturesque valley, also known as the upper Jordanne Valley, are lush and green, and carpeted with meadows screened by clumps of trees. Here and there are a few rocky escarpments dotted with caves. The River Jordanne contains gold which used to be sought by gold washers but the low value of the grains of gold-dust found in the river did not pay for the work and so the gold-washing stopped.

Cascade de Liadouze

15min on foot there and back. Beyond Rudez, turn left off D 17 just beyond a bench and follow the path that leads down to the Jordanne (park by the bridge). Do not cross the river. Instead, walk about 100m/109yd along the right bank.

The waterfall drops over a threshold of rock into a narrow gorge.

Mandailles

This village, lying in picturesque surroundings, is the starting point of numerous rambles.

▶ *Turn right onto D59.*

The road crosses the Jordanne then wends its way up the hillside.

Croix de Cheules

The crossroads marks the start of the Crest Road.

Hikes and Mountain-Bike Tours

Several itineraries explore the Plomb du Cantal massif, starting from Murat, Albepierre, Le Lioran, Laveissière and Saint-Jacques-des-Blats. A topoguide is available; for information, apply to Domaine Lioran-Haute Planèze, Col de Prat de Bouc, 15300 Albepierre, ☎ 04 71 73 32 13. www.cantal-nature.com.

L'Élancèze

▶ *From Mandailles, follow D 317 and park the car at the pass.*

About 3hr there and back from Col du Perthus. The stony path (steep in parts, good walking shoes essential), starts on the right and leads towards a beech wood.

During the climb to the summit, you will see three pits in relatively good condition; designed to catch wolves, these 3-4m/10-13ft deep holes were covered over with branches on which bait was placed. The last wolves were caught in this way around 1915.

From the summit, there is a superb **view**★★ of the Jordanne and Cère valleys and, in the distance, Aurillac and the Monts du Cantal (Puy Mary, Plomb du Cantal). With a bit of luck you will spot some chamois or roe deer.

MONTS DU CÉZALLIER ★

MICHELIN MAP 326 : E-10 TO G-11

The Cézallier range is situated between the Dore mountain range and the mountains of Cantal; it consists of a succession of granite plateaux lying at an altitude of more than 1 200m/3 940ft, which were covered with a layer of basalt during the Tertiary Era.

The volcanoes, from which the flows spread out all over the area, have neither cones nor craters. Indeed, they scarcely even jut out from above the surrounding countryside because the lava produced by eruptions was very fluid and therefore did not build up around the vents of the volcano. The highest peak, the Signal du Luguet, reaches an altitude of 1 551m/5 088ft whereas the edges of the plateau descend to altitudes of 1 200m or 1 000m/3 940ft or 3 280ft. On the eastern side in particular the plateaux are gashed by impressive valleys.

The Cézallier range is one vast area of pasture dotted with former shepherd's huts (burons) and a few villages with huge barns and byres, and fountains made out of old drinking troughs. Here, in the summer months, thousands of heads of cattle graze on the plateaux. The Institut National de la Recherche Agronomique (National Institute for Agricultural Research) has an experimental farm in Marcenat where students and staff study stock-rearing at high altitudes.

The local people supplement their income by digging up gentian roots, used in the production of an alcoholic drink.

Despite its lack of hotels and places to stay, the Cézallier area is popular with those who enjoy wide open spaces, solitude and fresh air, and also with winter sports enthusiasts, especially cross-country skiers since the lie of the land is ideal for this sport. Downhill skiing is also catered for, although facilities are, as yet, still limited (resorts include Parrot, Allanche and Marcenat). The area is part of a regional park, the Parc Naturel Régional des Volcans d'Auvergne. Two trips are described below; the first leads through the "mountains" and the second follows the valley which plunges down to the River Alagnon to the east of the range.

Excursions

1 Alpine Pastures

90km/56mi – about 5hr

Condat – ♿ *See CONDAT.*

▶ *Leave Condat S on D 679 towards Allanche.*

The road skirts a stretch of water that is a recent reconstruction of a lake originally built in the 12C by monks.

Abbaye de Féniers

Park in the hamlet of Féniers and walk to the abbey ruins. The Cistercian abbey founded in the late 12C was rebuilt in 1686 and closed down during the French Revolution. The buildings were partially destroyed by fire in 1872; only a few vestiges of the abbey buildings, cloisters and church have survived.

A small oratory chapel backing onto the ruins houses a statue of the Virgin Mary dating from the 15C.

> *Turn right onto D 16.*

The road to St-Bonnet-de-Condat runs down into the Santoire Valley and through a picturesque wooded **gorge.**

> *In St-Bonnet-de-Condat turn left onto D 36.*

High pastures

Marcenat
This is a modest winter sports resort which has also specialised in the production and selling of local cheese. One local curiosity is the **Maison de la Foudre** (Jul-Aug: 10.30am-noon, 2.15-6pm; Jun and Sep: 2.15-5.30pm; mid-Apr to May: Sat-Sun and public holidays 3-5pm. 5€ (children: 3€). ☎ 04 71 78 85 00), presenting an exhibition of photographs of thunder and lightning taken during violent storms by an enthusiastic meteorologist.
Beyond Marcenat there are some superb views to the left of the road, over the Cézallier range.

Les Prades
Columnar basalt. From the summit, there is a delightful view of Landeyrat and the Upper Allanche Valley cutting into the planèze.

> *Turn left off D 679 onto D 39 then D 23. Both of these roads cross the plateau.*

Apcher
A short distance to the west of this village, an attractive waterfall drops down from the edge of the plateau.

> *On leaving Anzat-le-Luguet, leave D 23 and turn left onto D 271.*

Parrot
Small winter sports resort.

Signal du Luguet★
1hr 30min on foot there and back from Parrot. Climb up to the summit across the meadows slightly to the left of the ski lift.
 The wooded summit (alt 1 551m/5 088ft) scarcely stands out above the plateaux. From it there is a vast **panoramic view**★ over the Dore mountain range and the mountains of Cantal.

> *Continue along D 721 to Boutaresse then turn right onto D 724.*

The road twists and turns through picturesque scenery.

St-Alyre-ès-Montagne
On a rise near the small village is the south-facing church overlooking superb countryside nestled in the shadow of Mount Gamet. The church is unusual for the strange, primitive carvings on its tympanum and for the billet-moulding on the east end.

> *Leave St-Alyre W along D 36, then 3km/1.9mi further on, turn left onto D 32.*

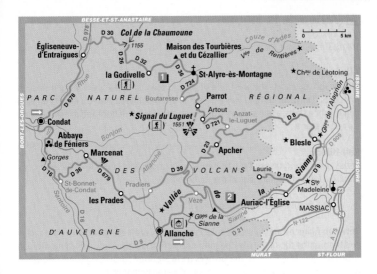

Maison des Tourbières et du Cézallier – ♿ *See ARDES.*

▶ *Continue along D 32.*

La Godivelle

This is a typical Cézallier hamlet with sturdy granite houses and a large, round foun-tain. Its other main feature is its geographical location, between a crater lake, the Lac d'En Haut (Upper Lake), and another, peaty lake, the Lac d'En Bas (Lower Lake), the haunt of countless migratory birds.

Ramble

🚶 *3hr 30min there and back, starting from La Godivelle; follow the yellow markings; keep dogs on a leash.* Walk across the peat bogs and high pastures as far as Jassy and return to La Godivelle via the lakes of Saint-Alyre and En-Bas.

▶ *Drive N out of La Godivelle along D 32, then 3km/1.9mi further on, turn right onto D 26.*

Col de la Chaumoune

Alt 1 155m/3 790ft. Near this mountain pass are recent conifer plantations.

▶ *Turn left onto D 30 and, 6km/3.7mi further on, turn left again onto D 978.*

Égliseneuve-d'Entraigues

This small summer holiday resort (alt 952m/3 123ft) has a Romanesque church dis-playing fine capitals and a sculpted wooden altarpiece. Do not miss the attractive regional Cheese Museum housed inside a barn. The **Maison des Fromages** (⏱ *Mid-Jun to mid-Sep: 2-6pm (Jul and Aug: 10am-12.30pm, 2.30-7pm); Nov, Christmas, Feb and Easter school holidays and all public holidays: on request. 3.50€.* ☎ *04 73 71 92 01 or 04 73 71 93 69)* is of interest to those wishing to find out about the history and production of local cheeses (St-Nectaire, Cantal, Bleu d'Auvergne, Fourme d'Ambert). An audio-visual presentation ends the visit.

▶ *D 678 leads back to Condat along the lovely Rhue Valley.*

2 Vallée de la Sianne

50km/31mi – about 1hr 30min

Allanche
Winter sports resort. The west end of the old town still has a few remnants of its ramparts. The **church** (🕐 *Daily except Sun afternoon 9am-noon, 3-6pm*) contains Renaissance stalls, a painting on wood from the Flemish School and a moving Pietà carved in stone.

Rail-biking
Pedal away along disused tracks between Allanche and Lugarde or Neussargues aboard a kind of pedalo! *(Ask at the tourist office).*

▶ *Head E from Allanche on D 9 towards Chavanon.*

Between Allanche and Vèze, the road crosses the Cézallier's great alpine meadows and then, at the top of the rise, the mountains of Cantal come into view. The cliffroad subsequently runs down to the **Gorges de la Sianne**★, providing some fine views of the ravine on the way. The hillsides are covered with forest.
Beyond several gorges where huge boulders jut out from above both banks of the river, the valley widens out, becoming less sombre, and fruit trees appear.

Auriac-l'Église
This village is attractively situated to the right of the road.
Lovers of Romanesque art will enjoy a detour via Laurie where the church houses a fine polychrome wooden statue of the Virgin Mary.

▶ *Turn right onto D 8.*

Blesle★ – 👶 *See MASSIAC.*

▶ *Return to Allanche via the Bellan Valley, Anzat-le-Luguet, and D 23, which will take you back to Vèze.*

You can also pursue your route towards Massiac and the Alagnon gorges (👶 see MASSIAC).

LA CHAISE-DIEU★★

POPULATION 772
MICHELIN MAP 331: E-2
40KM/25MI NE OF LE PUY-EN-VELAY

Set amid lush green countryside with gently-rolling hills at an altitude of more than 1 000m/3 280ft, the vast buildings and ornate architectural style of the famous abbey of La Chaise-Dieu come as a magnificent surprise. The abbey derives its name from the Latin "Casa Dei," meaning "the House of God." A renowned music festival takes place at the end of August in the abbey church and Cziffra Hall. 🛈 *Pl. de la Mairie, 43160 La CHAISE-DIEU, ☎ 04 71 00 01 16. www.tourisme.fr/lachaisedieu*

▶ **Orient Yourself:** La Chaise-Dieu is all about its abbey, so the best way to orient yourself is to wander the maze of streets and see how the abbey would have dominated the original community here

☞ **Don't Miss:** The old houses in the narrow streets adjacent to the place de l'Eglise

⏱ **Organizing Your Time:** Explore first, and then spend some time in the abbey, especially the cloisters

A Bit of History

Foundation of the abbey – In 1043 Robert de Turlande, a former canon from Brioude, withdrew with a few companions to this desolate plateau. He was soon joined by increasing numbers of followers and founded a monastery under the Benedictine Rule for which, in 1052, he obtained the Pope's protection. Its success continued to grow to the extent that, at Robert's death in 1067, the monastery had 300 monks and 49 priories (including a convent, in Lavaudieu). Increasing numbers of priories continued to be founded as far away as Italy and Spain (250 altogether) and this, taken with the flow of gifts and scope of its spiritual influence, made La Chaise-Dieu the third most important French monastic order in the mid-12C.

The Abbot was all-powerful. He was accountable to nobody but the Pope and, every year, he convened the Chapter General. In the 12C and 13C the abbots maintained the Order's independence and kept alive the spirit in which the abbey had been founded, thereby avoiding the excesses which weakened the great abbey at Cluny.

Papacy of Clement VI – The situation suddenly deteriorated in the early 14C, when the abbot's authority was undermined and several priories broke away from the mother-house. The election, however, in Avignon, of Pope Clement VI – one of the abbey's former novices and monks – brought a halt to this decline. The Pope had the church rebuilt as it is today between 1344 and 1352 to designs by an architect from Southern France named Hugues Morel. The Pope's nephew, Gregory XI, completed the building (last three bays in the nave and the abbey buildings).

In the early years of the 16C, Jacques de St-Nectaire gave the abbey a dazzling set of tapestries.

J. Damase/MICHELIN

Église Abbatiale St-Robert

Contemporary rebirth – After centuries of decline, the abbey finally attracted attention in the early years of the 20C; yet it was not completely restored until after the Second World War. In 1965 the pianist **Georges Cziffra** fell in love with the abbey, and founded a festival of religious music in aid of the restoration project. Repair work on the great organ was begun in 1977 and not finished until 1995. The Festival de la Chaise-Dieu continues to make a name for itself as one of the main festivals of its type in France.

The Abbey

Église Abbatiale St-Robert★★

🕐 May-Oct: daily, 9am-noon, 2-7pm; Nov-Apr: daily except Sun morning, 10am-noon, 2-5pm. 🕐 Jan, Mon in Dec and Feb, 25 Dec and 1 Jan. 5€ ☎ 04 71 00 06 06. www. abbaye-chaise-dieu.com

Solidly built of granite, the church gives an impression of grandeur and austerity which seem to reflect the personality of its founder, Clement VI.

West Front

The architecture of the west front is military in style. It overlooks a sloping square decorated with a 17C fountain and is flanked by two towers, neither of which is very high. The portal, including a pier embellished with a statue of St Robert, was dam-

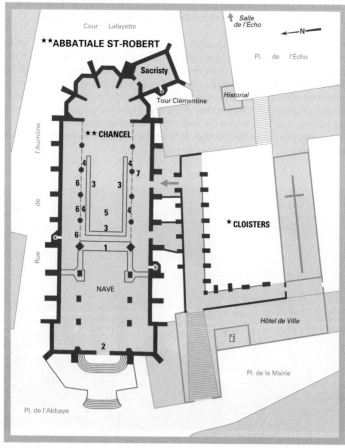

aged by the Huguenots in 1562. The small house concealing the base of the south tower is said to have been used by Cardinal de Rohan.

Nave and side aisles

The interior is an impressive sight. It has a vast nave roofed with flattened vaulting and is flanked by side aisles of the same height. Five radiating chapels open directly off the chancel. A 15C rood screen (**1**) breaks up the perspective and seems to reduce the height of the nave. At the top of it is a fine statue of Christ (1603) with, at the foot of the Cross, two wooden statues representing the Virgin Mary and St John (15C). The superb **organ loft**★ (**2**) facing it dates from the 17C.

Chancel★★

The chancel is surrounded by 144 oak **choir stalls**★★ (**3**) dating from the 15C, decorated with particularly fine carvings depicting a wide range of subjects. Above the enclosure are exquisite **tapestries** ★★★ (**4**) from Arras and Brussels, made of wool, linen and silk, and dating from the early 16C. The subjects are drawn from the Old and New Testaments and illustrate the theme of Salvation copied from the Poor Man's Bible that was so commonplace in the Middle Ages. They are accompanied by legends written in Gothic script.

Coronation of the Virgin tapestry

In the middle of the chancel is Clement VI's tomb (**5**). The Pope had it made during his own lifetime and carved by Pierre Roye, Jean David and Jean de Sanholis. It was originally surrounded by 44 statues representing members of the Pope's family. The Protestants damaged the tomb and all that now remains is the recumbent statue on a black marble slab. The north aisle features the famous fresco of the **Dance of Death**★ (**6**) (2m/6ft 6in high and 26m/85ft long): the three panels juxtapose the great and famous of this world and the dead; the dead are shown inviting the living to dance with them, a reminder of

---

Address Book

EATING OUT

🍴 **Le Lion d'Or** – *Av. de la Gare -* ☎ *04 71 00 01 58 - lion@liondor43.com - closed Jan-Feb.* A restaurant in a traditional Auvergnat dwelling at the end of the town's main street. The generous, carefully prepared fare is served on plates shaped like their contents – quite the original touch! The reasonable prices add to the appeal.

WHERE TO STAY

🛏️🛏️ **Écho et Abbaye** – *Pl. de l'Écho - ☎ 04 71 00 00 45 - closed 12 Nov-26 Mar and Wed except Jul-Aug - 10 rms - ☐ 8€ - restaurant* 🍴🍴. The haunt of numerous luminaries during the music festival, this tranquil hotel behind the abbey has comfortable, well-maintained bedrooms, some with a view of the cloisters. The restaurant serves regional dishes in a pleasant setting.

🛏️ **Chambre d'hôte La Jacquerolle** – *R. Marchédial - ☎ 04 71 00 07 52 - ☐ - 4 rms - ☐ - meals* 🍴 Set in the lower part of the village, this handsome house built of local stone has a dining room furnished in period pieces with a stunning granite fireplace on the first floor. Guest rooms are as welcoming as they are comfortable.

what lies before them. The fresco depicts the powerful to the left, the wealthy in the middle and the craftsmen to the right. This theme was frequently depicted in the 15C, yet never before has it been treated with such realism and such a sense of movement. It was here that the composer **Arthur Honegger** (1892-1955) drew the inspiration, in 1938, for his work The Dance of the Dead, an oratorio with a libretto by Paul Claudel. The north aisle in the chancel contains another two tombs. In the south aisle lies the mutilated tomb of Abbot Renaud de Montclar (**7**) dating from the 14C; it still has its decoration of carved cherubs.

Sacristy
☞ *Not open to the public.* This occupies the ground floor in the Clémentine Tower, a huge military-type construction.

Cloisters★
The cloisters were built at the end of the 14C. Only two galleries have survived to the present day; one of them has an upper storey which was used as a library. Beyond the cloisters is a square: on the left-hand side, the second flight of steps into the hospice leads to the Echo Chamber where two people standing in opposite corners with their backs to each other can speak to each other in whispers and hear each other perfectly. It is said that the layout was designed in the Middle Ages to enable lepers to attend Confession.

Monks' library
This sober, vaulted room follows the line of the north gallery of the cloisters upon which it is built. It contains the abbey **treasury**, in which there are magnificent Brussels tapestries (Crucifixion) on display, as well as a 17C ivory statue of Christ, Clement VI's broken ring and various valuable pieces of church plate.

The Town

Historial de la Chaise-Dieu
🕐 *Jul to mid-Sep: daily 9am-noon, 2-7pm; mid-Apr to end Jun: Sat-Sun 10am-noon, 2-5pm (Jun: daily except Mon); the rest of the year: by appointment. 2.50€. ☎ 04 71 00 06 99. www.abbaye-chaise-dieu.com*
This gallery has been turned into a Waxworks Museum with displays illustrating the abbey's finest hours.

Old houses
In the narrow streets adjacent to place de l'Église are a number of interesting houses with medieval façades. At the bottom of rue de la Côte is La Cloze, a fortified house dating from the 15C.

Musée du Bois et de la Forêt
♿🕐 *May-Oct: 10am-noon, 2.30-6pm.* 🕐 *Nov-Apr. 3€. ☎ 04 71 00 10 35.*
Timber is still the area's main source of income and a local resident has opened a small museum explaining the different stages in the exploitation of nearby forests.

Hikes

Sentier du Serpent d'Or
2hr there and back.
▶ Starting from La Chaise-Dieu *(next to the village hall)*, this Serpent's Lane, named after the golden, meandering waters of the Sénouire, will take you down to the banks of the river, passing through Breuil Forest.

Signal de St-Claude
1km/0.6mi E.

🚶 *Beyond the railway bridge, turn right onto the path that leads to the summit some 600m/660yd further on (alt 1 112m/3 648ft).* Fine panoramic view of Pierre sur Haute, the mountains in the Forez and Lyon areas, Mont Pilat, the Cévennes, the mountains of Cantal and the Dore mountain range.

LE CHAMBON-SUR-LIGNON

POPULATION 2 642
MICHELIN MAP 331: H-3

Le Chambon lies in the Upper Lignon Valley and is a pleasant summer resort with a large number of sporting facilities. The mild climate, pastoral setting and altitude (960m/3 150ft) have made this an ideal location for the numerous children's holiday centres established here. 🛈 *1 rue des Quatre Saisons, 43400 Le CHAMBON-SUR-LIGNON ☎ 04 71 59 71 56.*

Huguenot city – The remote geographical location of Le Chambon enabled its Protestant population to escape religious persecution and remain in the majority. In 1598 the Edict of Nantes granted religious freedom only to Le Chambon and St-Voy in this area; its revocation in 1685 resulted in stubborn, though secret, resistance and a deep attachment to the reformed religion in both towns.

During the Second World War, the village provided many Jews with protection against the enemy.

Today, Le Chambon has a number of Protestant foundations including the **Collège Cévenol,** a major international cultural centre which was opened in 1938.

Excursions

Protestant Plateau★

33km/20mi round trip – about 2hr

▶ *Head S from Le Chambon-sur-Lignon on D 151, then turn onto D 7. In Mazet-St-Voy take the second road on the right to the hamlet of St-Voy. Park on the square in front of the church.*

St-Voy
The tiny Romanesque **church**, dating from the 11C, is dedicated to St Évode, Bishop of Le Puy around AD 374. Its history is closely tied to the arrival of the Reformation in the 16C: from 1560 onwards the population here followed the example set by its

parish priest, Bonnefoy, and converted to the new religion, but the church was used as a Protestant place of worship only for some 15 years.

The building, a granite construction with stone-slabbed roof, has the quaint charm of a country church. The chancel is pure in design and contains windows at different levels, raised from left to right following the rising sun.

▶ *Return to Mazet-St-Voy and follow signposts for the "Foyer de Ski de Fond du Lizieux" (Lizieux Cross-country Skiing Centre). Continue for 1.3km/1mi, turn left onto a dirt track signposted "Pic du Lizieux," then 600m/0.4mi from the chalet there is a footpath off to the left leading to the Pic du Lizieux (park in the lay-by).*

Pic du Lizieux★★

Alt 1 388m/4 554ft. Viewing table. 30min on foot there and back. The most easterly lying volcanic cone in the Velay area overlooks a vast basaltic plain. The hillsides are ideal for cross-country skiing in winter. There is a **panoramic view** over the Yssingeaux region and the Lignon Valley to the north, the Vivarais range to the east, the Boutières chain with its highest peak, Mont Mézenc, to the south and the Meygal range to the west.

▶ *Return to the car and take the narrow road as far as Montbuzat. From there, turn right onto the northbound forest road.*

The road skirts most of Lizieux Forest and provides fine views over the pastures to the west.

▶ *Return to Le Chambon-sur-Lignon via Mazet-St-Voy and D 151.*

Vallée du Lignon

57km/35.5mi round trip. Leave Le Chambon-sur-Lignon on D 103 N.

The River Lignon rises below the north face of Mont Mézenc and crosses the high plateaux of the Velay region before joining the Loire upstream from Monistrol.

As the Lignon flows through the Velay region, it weaves a picturesque course through a succession of wooded gorges and rolling hillsides.

On the outskirts of Tence there are views of the valley from D 103.

Vallée du Lignon

Tence

Located at an altitude of 840m/2 756ft, this hamlet spanning the Lignon and the Sérigoule, both teeming with trout, is an ideal starting-point for excursions. The streets below the church feature houses with characteristic *lauze* roofs and sturdy chimneys built to withstand strong winds. The **church** has a soaring spire, a 17C nave and a 15C Gothic chancel (restored) with the Evangelists' symbols pictured on its transept crossing. The 17C stalls come from the former charter house of Bonnefoy.

Chemin de fer touristique du Velay

This tourist train runs between Tence and Ste-Agrève along the valley and gorge of the River Lignon. There are several return journeys daily from mid-July to the end of August. Contact the tourist office in Tence.

▶ *Leave Tence to the W on D 103, the road to Yssingeaux. After 8km/5mi, turn right onto D 47.*

Barrage de Lavalette

This dam spanning the River Lignon is set against a pretty backdrop of lush countryside.

▶ *Take D 47 N, then turn right onto D 105.*

Montfaucon-en-Velay

The **Chapelle Notre-Dame** lying on the road to Yssingeaux houses altogether 12 paintings (1592) attributed to the Flemish artist **Grimmer** (c1575-1619), representing evangelical symbols. The far end of the church contains a 16C crowned Virgin Mary.

▶ *Continue along D 105 and turn right onto D 233.*

Montregard

A natural belvedere facing the Meygal and Mézenc summits. From the most western mound, enjoy the fine **panorama**★ of the Mézenc massif, Pic du Lizieux, the Yssingeaux basin and the Monts du Velay.

▶ *Return to Tence on D 233 and take D 18 on the right. Continue on D 185 towards Le Chambon-sur-Lignon.*

The cottages in this area are typical of traditional rural architecture, with their granite walls and their two-sided stone-slabbed roofs.

▶ *D 157 will take you back to Le Chambon-sur-Lignon.*

CHARROUX★

POPULATION 330
MICHELIN MAP 326: F-5 – 15KM/9.3MI N OF GANNAT

Charroux is built on a hilltop and was one of the 19 castellanies of the Barony of Bourbon. The old houses, built of dressed stone and ornamented with carved mouldings, have now been restored and make the village particularly attractive.

Walking Tour

Church

This fortified 12C building was once part of the town walls. The advanced post *(right)* is marked by the crenellated tower which formed the bastion. The belfry rises above the transept crossing but its octagonal pyramid-shaped spire has been truncated. Inside, the nave has barrel vaulting and the aisles are roofed with rib vaults. The capitals are decorated with interlacing and foliate designs.

▶ *Leave via the north aisle.*

WHERE TO EAT

⊜⊜ **Ferme St-Sébastien** – *Chemin Bourion -* ☎ *04 70 56 88 83 - closed 7 Jan to 5 Feb, 18-26 Jun, 24 Sep to 2 Oct, Tue except Jul-Aug and Mon - reserv. required.* Native epicureans are justifiably fond of this popular restaurant. The dining room, a blend of contemporary and rustic styles, features works by local artists. Good food and service, lovely atmosphere.

On the square there is a **medieval house** with an overhanging upper storey. On the left stands the belfry, a square tower once used as a watchtower.

Rue de la Poulaillerie

An old stone well stands in the centre of this picturesque street paved with large cobblestones.

Musée de Charroux et de son Canton

Rue de la Poulaillerie. ⏱ *May-Jun, Sat, Sun, 2.30-6.30pm; Jul-Aug, daily except Tue, 2.30-6.30pm. 3.50€ (children: 2€).* ☎ *04 70 56 81 65. www.charroux.com.*

This Regional History Museum is set up in a house with a façade decorated with carvings of animal heads, figures and nailhead moulding; objects and documents provide an insight into the history of the Charroux area. Downstairs there is a display of objects from the Roman era, along with Gothic and Renaissance sculptures, in addition to an exhibition on locally crafted fireplaces. Jambs, mantelpieces and photographs of different designs illustrate the dexterity of the stone cutters in Charroux. A small room contains a reconstruction of the workshop of Jean-Baptiste Cailhe-Decante, a highly reputed 19C maker of stringed instruments and hurdy-gurdies. On the first floor (18C and 19C exhibits), note the three sets of works from the town clock with their intricate cogwheels.

Next to the museum is the Prince of Condé's residence, a former hunting lodge; the first floor has a fine mullioned window.

Porte d'Orient

The **East Gate** was one of the bastions in the town wall. The defensive system is still visible today.

Viewpoint

Viewing table. A circular platform surrounded by a low wall in the shade of an oak tree offers a view over the neighbouring countryside.

Excursions

60km/37mi – allow 2hr 30min

▸ *Leave Charroux to the W and follow D 35 for 2km/1mi, then turn right onto D 68. After crossing the motorway, take D 183 on the left.*

Veauce

As you enter the village, you can admire the east end (12C) of the local **church** (⏱ *Oct-Mar: 9am-6pm; Apr-Sep: 9am-8pm.* ☎ *04 70 58 53 03),* built with fine bronze-coloured masonry. The interior features an unusual chancel and ambulatory with no radiating chapels. Nestling in a large shaded park nearby, the **castle** *(Guided tours (30min) daily except Tue 10.30am-noon, 2.30-6.30pm. 5€.* ☎ *04 70 58 53 27)* is perched on top of a rocky outcrop dominating the River Veauce. Built between the 9C and the 15C, it was partly refurbished during the Renaissance and in the 19C. Legend has it that the old stones are haunted by the ghost of Lucie, a fair maiden who perished

Landscape of the Bourbonnais

here five centuries ago. You can visit the Renaissance Gallery and its stained-glass windows, the Portrait Gallery and the Weapons Gallery. The covered footpath and guards-room have retained their original chestnut framework.

▶ *Leave Veauce to the N on D 118, then D 987. At Croix des Bois, take D 284 on the right.*

Forêt des Colettes

This 2 000ha/4 942-acre forest planted with beech, oak and pine trees is dominated by the Signal de la Bosse (778m/2 553ft) situated near the intersection of D 998 and D 987 *(turn right)*. The nearby kaolin quarries are used in the production of porcelain and faience.

▶ *After crossing Coutansouze, take D 68 on the right.*

Bellenaves

This village has a fine Romanesque church. The interior of the building is decorated with a portrait of Christ with two Angels, the Last Supper and Christ washing his Disciples' feet.

▶ *Leave Bellenaves to the N on D 43.*

Chantelle

On a steep promontory stands a Benedictine abbey, built on the ruins of a former castle and monastery. The nuns who live here produce home-made soaps and eaux de toilette that can be purchased on the premises.

▶ *Take Grand-Rue (D 987) to rue Anne-de-Beaujeu, which leads to the Abbaye St-Vincent.*

The **conventual church** *(Unaccompanied visits of the nave 10.30-11.30am, 2-5pm. ☎ 04 70 56 62 55)* dates from the Romanesque era. Only the nave (attractive capitals) is open to the public. On leaving the convent, go to the nearby terrace to enjoy the view of the Bouble gorges, dominated by the Chantelle rooftops.
It is possible to reach the shaded banks of the river by following the former castle moat.

▶ *Leave Chantelle to the E on D 987. After 6km/4mi, take D 115 on the right.*

Château de Chareil

🕓 Mid-Jun to Mid-Sep: daily except Mon, 10am-noon, 2-6pm. 🕓 mid-Sep to mid-Jun. 3€. ☎ 04 70 56 94 28.

This former stronghold, restored in the 16C, is owned by the State. Part of the exterior has recently been restored: the doorway, the terrace and the 19C well. The interior is notable for its two imposing Renaissance fireplaces and its 16C **mural paintings**★ in varying shades of brown, representing mythological themes (Mars, Venus, Cupid, legend of Adonis).

Types of vines formerly grown throughout the region have been replanted on the slopes of the estate and the outbuildings of the castle now house the cellars.

▶ *Go back to D 987, heading for Chantelle, then take D 115 on the left and proceed to Ussel-d'Allier.*

Ussel-d'Allier

Leave Ussel on D 223 which runs by the church. A dirt track to the left of the road, not far from a statue of the Virgin Mary, leads to a raised viewing table. From there, you can admire a sweeping panorama of the lush Bourbon countryside.

▶ *Return to D 223.*

Église d'Étroussat

The church boasts a series of 14 modern **stained-glass windows**★ attributed to the master glassworker Frédérique Duran. One of the chapels houses a curious 17C **Virgin with Child** in gilded wood – Jesus is portrayed brandishing a spear and slaying a dragon.

▶ *Leave Étroussat to the S on D 35 and drive back to Charroux.*

CHÂTELGUYON

POPULATION 5 241
MICHELIN MAP 326: F-7

Châtelguyon is situated at an altitude of 430m/1 411ft, on the edge of a regional park (Parc Naturel Régional des Volcans d'Auvergne).

The Calvary stands on a hilltop overlooking the centre of town, on the site once occupied by the castle of Count Guy II of Auvergne, after whom the town was named.

From the viewing table admire the mountains, the hillsides in the Forez area, the Limagne plain and the resort in the foreground. 🗓 *Av. de l'Europe, 63140 CHÂTELGUYON, ☎ 04 73 86 01 17. www.ot-chatel-guyon.com*

The Spa Resort

The resort enjoyed a massive boom in the 19C. Pipes bring water from the 12 springs up to the park on the banks of the River Sardon. The main feature of the springs is their magnesium content, the highest in Europe; their temperature varies from

27.5°C to 38°C/81°F to 100°F. The spa itself includes the **Grand Spa** (1st class) and the **Henry Spa** (2nd class) which was completely rebuilt in 1983.

The resort specialises in the treatment of digestive and gynecological disorders. Today, life in the resort centres on the casino-theatre, the park at the foot of Mont Chalusset containing the Grands Thermes, and avenue Baraduc which is lined with cafés and souvenir gift shops.

Entrance to the baths

Sight

Église Ste-Anne

The church is decorated in a very modern style. The stained-glass windows made of Baccarat crystal distil light onto the **Byzantine-style frescoes** painted by the Estonian artist Nicolas Greschny, depicting the Old Testament, the New Testament and visions of the Apocalypse.

Walking Tours

Vallée des Prades★

1hr 30min on foot there and back. From Châtelguyon take D 78 N and turn left onto the wide footpath that follows the right bank of the stream called Les Grosliers, which leads up through the Vallée des Prades (1.5km/1mi).

Scenic woodland walk.

Château de Chazeron – ও *See RIOM: Excursions.*

Vallée de Sans-Souci

45min on foot there and back. From Châtelguyon take D 15 SW, then 200m/219ft further on, after crossing the Sardon, turn right onto the signposted footpath.

Walk along the banks of the Sardon through a pleasantly fresh, wooded valley for about 2km/1.2mi, as far as the ford. The challenging, somewhat rugged path continues from here to some waterfalls (an extra 30min there and back).

WHERE TO STAY AND EAT

⊜ **Beau Site** – *R. Chalusset -* ☎ *04 73 86 00 49 – closed Oct to Apr -* 🅿 *- 30 rms -* ☲ *6€ - restaurant* ⊜ Perched high above the town, overlooking the thermal springs park, this simple little hotel is set in a wild garden colonized by oaks. The restful rooms are modest but well-kept. Budget-friendly restaurant.

⊜ **Paris** – *R. Dr Levadoux -* ☎ *04 73 86 00 12 - 59 rms -* ☲ *6€ - restaurant* ⊜ The bedrooms are to be found in the establishment's main building and in a former chapel in the back. The restaurant offers traditional and regional cuisine amid rustic stone walls and country-style furniture.

CHÂTILLON-SUR-CHALARONNE

POPULATION 3 786

MICHELIN MAP 328: C-4 – LOCAL MAP SEE LA DOMBES

This pretty town, bursting with flowers in season, lying in the shadow of its 11C castle on the border between the Bresse and Dombes areas, spreads along the Chalaronne Valley. Coming into Châtillon from the south-west on the road from Villefranche (D 936), there is a fine **view** over the town's red rooftops, dominated by the impressive bell-tower of the former almshouse.The half-timbered houses with cob or brick walls built in the style typical of the Dombes area (⬤ *see Introduction: Traditional rural housing*) are brightened up in summer with bunches of flowers arranged in wicker baskets called *nids-de-poule* (hens' nests).Every Saturday, a picturesque flower and poultry market is held in the covered market, and the town is also known for making helmets for fire-fighters, soldiers and motorcyclists. ◨ *Pl. du Champ-de-Foire, 01400 CHÂTILLON-SUR-CHALARONNE,* ☎ *04 74 55 02 27.*

Famous sons of Châtillon – Philibert Commerson was born in Châtillon in 1727. As Royal Botanist, he accompanied the Count of Bougainville on his world expedition, bringing back an ornamental shrub from Japan which he called *hortensia* (hydrangea).

Châtillon is proud of the brief visit made by St Vincent de Paul, otherwise known as **Monsieur Vincent.** He was born into a poor peasant family in the south-west of France and decided early on in life to join the priesthood. After becoming tutor to the children of Monsieur de Gondi, General in charge of the Galleys, he asked to be allowed to practise his ministry in a remote parish. He was appointed parish priest

Address Book

EATING OUT

◔ **Restaurant La Gourmandine** – *142 r. Pasteur -* ☎ *04 74 55 15 92 - closed 26 Aug to 1 Sep, Christmas week, Sun evening, Thu evening and Mon except public holidays.* Close by the Place des Halles, this 17C house is easy to spot. The brick and pebble walls add to the dining room's appeal, while the terrace along the river is very pleasant in summer. Regional dishes.

◔ **Auberge de Montessuy** – *Rte de Marlieux - 0.5km/0.3mi via D 7 -* ☎ *04 74 55 05 14 - closed Jan, Mon-Tue - reserv. recommended.* Come satisfy your appetite in this handsome, traditional country inn. A variety of Bressan specialities are served in a dining room where a wrought iron chandelier presenting symbols of the area's different gastronomical orders proudly hangs.

◔◔ **St-Lazare** – *01400 L'Abergement-Clémenciat - 5km/3mi NW of Châtillon via D 7 and D 64C -* ☎ *04 74 24 00 23 - closed Wed, Thu and Sun evenings - reserv. required.* A renowned restaurant in such a small village? Absolutely: the dishes whipped up by the owner and served in this typical regional house with a veranda are well worth the detour. His creative and succulent cuisine is presented in several affordable fixed-price menus.

WHERE TO STAY

◔ **Chambre d'hôte Chez M. et Mme Salmon** – *150 pl. du Champ-de-Foire -* ☎ *04 74 55 06 86 - alsalmon@club-internet.fr - closed Christmas wk -* ⊟ *- 5 rms.* Like us, you'll be enchanted by this seriously charming house with its imposing beams, old furniture and wood staircase. The snug, cosy rooms hint of the gargantuan breakfast to come: not to be missed!

MARKET

There is a colourful covered market on Saturday mornings.

of Châtillon in 1617 but only stayed here for a few months. However, this was long enough for him to begin his charitable work among the poor and destitute. On 23 August he set up the first Brotherhood of Charity (Vincentian Fathers). In 1633 he founded the Society of the Sisters of Charity with St Louise de Marillac; the Order still continues its work today.

Visit

Porte de Villars

All that remains of the ramparts which once protected the town is this 14C quarrystone square tower with limestone masonry courses and corners, which lies to the east. It is a fine example of military architecture, constructed during the days when Châtillon belonged to the House of Savoy (from 1272 until 1601 when the town was annexed to the Kingdom of France).

Place St-Vincent-de-Paul

In the centre of the square stands a bronze statue of St Vincent by Émilien Cabuchet.

Halles

The present **covered market** dates from the 17C and replaced the market built in 1440 which was destroyed by fire. The rafters are supported on 32 pillars, each made from a single trunk of oak. Old houses with open shop fronts, an integral part of the market, can still be seen at one end of the building. Until the 1950s, from late October to mid-November the covered market was used for a "servant-hiring fair."

Bridges and river banks

These are a picturesque sight in summer when the flowers are in bloom, especially around impasse Pietanée and rue Pasteur.

Ramparts of the Vieux Château

These are the remnants of one of the largest strongholds in Bresse. The castle was demolished at the end of the 16C, when the area was invaded by Henri IV's troops.

Sights

Maison St-Vincent

Guided tours. ☎ *04 74 55 26 64.*

St Vincent de Paul was lodged here by a Protestant, M Beynier, for five months while he was the incumbent of Châtillon. He founded the Order of the Sisters of Charity here. The chapel built on the spot where St Vincent's bedroom once stood contains the Foundation Deed of this institution, complete with his signature.

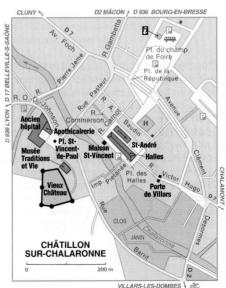

CHÂTILLON
SUR-CHALARONNE

0   200 m

Église St-André

This church was commissioned in the 13C by Philip I of Savoy, and underwent numerous alterations during the 15C. It is a very colourful building with a brick façade and red-tiled roof which is unusually high for the Dombes area. Inside, the nave and side chapels are built of white limestone from the Mâcon region; note the restrained Flamboyant Gothic decoration. The keystone in the apse is finely traceried. The round tower, partly built into the south wall, is all that remains of the original church. At the far end, there is a strikingly realistic statue of St Sebastian carved out of a single piece of walnut wood by a local artist named **Jean Tarrit** (1865-1950).

Musée municipal de Châtillon Traditions et Vie

Same admission times and charges as the Apothecary's dispensary. ☎ *04 74 55 15 70.* Situated along the path leading up to the castle, this museum is devoted to rural life and ancient crafts typical of the Bresse region.

Ancien Hôpital et apothicairerie

♿ 🕐 *Apr-Sep, daily except Mon 10am-noon, 2-6pm (last admission 45min before closing). 3.50€ (combined ticket includes a visit to the Musée municipal Traditions et Vie: 4.50€).* ☎ *04 74 55 15 70.*
The buildings of the old hospital, commissioned by the Count of Châtelard in the 18C, now house the Centre culturel de la Dombes (regional arts centre).
The first room of the pharmacy contains attractive Directoire-style wood panelling and jars made of Meillonnes faience (glazed earthenware). The second room displays a **triptych**★ painted in 1527, which has been completely restored: the centre panel, illustrating the Deposition of Christ, is flanked by panels depicting the Apostles asleep and the Resurrection; in the bottom corners, the donor and his wife are shown kneeling. Note the balanced composition and the rich colours. The nuns' old workroom, its wardrobes decorated with beautiful wood panelling, contains a collection of local costumes.

CHAUDES-AIGUES⚓

POPULATION 986
MICHELIN MAP 330: G-5 – 30KM/18.6MI SW OF ST-FLOUR
LOCAL MAP SEE GORGES DE LA TRUYÈRE

Chaudes-Aigues is ideally situated in the picturesque Remontalou gorge. As its name suggests, there are hot springs here, which have made it not only a spa resort but also a town where hot running water has been piped to houses since ancient times. A number of springs were tapped by the Romans. Today, 32 of the springs are tapped (they are said to be the hottest in Europe), yielding 15 000hl/330 000gal of water each day at temperatures from 45 to 82°C/113 to 179°F. The springs were slow to find widespread popularity, largely because of the difficult access and problems with communications. However, they now seem to be on the verge of a massive boom, firstly due to the opening of the A 75 motorway and secondly thanks to the ongoing renovation work undertaken in order to turn the spa into a modern and functional place for the treatment of rheumatism, arthritis, sciatica, gout etc. Fitness breaks are also available. 🚩 *1 av. Georges-Pompidou, 15110 CHAUDES-AIGUES,* ☎ *04 71 23 52 75. www.chaudesaigues. com*

Source Du Par

This spring alone daily gushes out 5 000hl/132 100gal of water at a temperature that can be as high as 82°C/179°F. It provides the water supply for the spa centre but its waters are also used to heat the school, the swimming pool and, above all, the local houses. It is not uncommon to see local residents filling a bucket at the spring for some immediate practical use. Tourists planning a picnic may like to test the spring's properties for themselves – it can reputedly hard-boil an egg in eight minutes! Three hundred out of the 450 houses in the village benefit from the heat economically supplied by the water, which, in places, still runs through pinewood pipes with a stone slab used as a valve to regulate the flow. This ingenious system, which appears to date back many centuries, makes Chaudes-Aigues the pioneer of central heating.

S. Sauvignier/MICHELIN

Source du Par

Sights

Musée Géothermia
  Apr-Oct and school holidays: daily except Tue 10am-noon, 2-6.30pm (Jul and Aug: daily 10am-6.30pm). Nov-Mar. 5€. ☎ 04 71 23 58 76.
This museum, located behind the Source du Par, unveils some of the secrets of subterranean Chaudes-Aigues. A close, warm atmosphere envelopes visitors as they enter, plunging them straight away into the world of geothermal science. On the ground floor is a description of the course taken by the water and a collection of various exhibits connected with its canalization. The first floor has a display on the fauna to be found in this abyssal zone. Elsewhere in the building there are exhibitions on geothermal science and water cures.

Église St-Martin-et-St-Blaise
This church dates from the Gothic and Renaissance periods. It houses a large altarpiece and the Gonfalon Virgin, taken from the Penitents' Chapel.

Glazed Alcoves
In the streets of the town, there are several glazed alcoves containing old statues of the patron saints of each individual district.

Tour du Couffour
This tower dominates the town on the south side and offers a sweeping panorama of the nearby countryside. It still features its circular medieval keep, where you can discover fragments of painted frescoes.

Excursions

Heading for Aubrac

25km/15.5mi to the S on D 989 and D 13.
Beyond Chaudes-Aigues, the road offers scenic views over the Remontalou Valley, then over the mountains in Cantal. It then climbs up through the Bès Valley in a landscape of granite that, in most places, is harsh and rugged.

La Chaldette

This tiny old spa resort, where the water is warm with a high sulphur content, nestles in the Bès Valley.

St-Urcize

This locality can be found nestling at the foot of a rock crowned by medieval ruins. It is known both as a winter resort and a popular market town.
The **church**, a former priory, is the only sanctuary with an ambulatory in the Haute-Auvergne. The pretty east end is Romanesque (12C), whereas the nave dates from the 13C and the 14C. Inside, the chapel in the north aisle is ornamented by a painting depicting **St Michael Slaying the Dragon**, and the chapel behind the altar contains an **Entombment** scene in tinted stone (15C).

CHAZELLES-SUR-LYON

POPULATION 4 895
MICHELIN MAP 327: F-6 – LOCAL MAP SEE MONTS DU LYONNAIS

Chazelles-sur-Lyon lies in the foothills of the Lyonnais area and owes its fame to the production of high-quality felt hats. The industry enjoyed its heyday in the early 20C when the village boasted some 30 factories. In the 12C, Count Guy II of Forez set up a commandery of the Knights of St John of Jerusalem in Chazelles; all that remains now is one hexagonal tower. Tradition has it that the commanders taught the villagers the art of fulling felt which they themselves had learnt from the Arabs during the Crusades. ▯ *9 pl. J.-B. Galland, 42140 CHA-ZELLES-SUR-LYON,* ☎ *04 77 54 98 86.*

Hats Galore

Musée du Chapeau
🕐 *Guided visits: Sun and public holidays, 2.30-6.30pm; Jul-Aug: 2-6pm; rest of year, daily except Tue.* 🕐 *Closed 1 Jan, 25 Dec. 5€ (children: 2.50€).* ☎ *04 77 94 23 29. www.museeduchapeau.com*
The Hat Museum is housed in a former hat-making factory and comprises 10 reconstructed workshops showing various stages in the manufacture of luxury felt hats: from blowing and basoning the rabbit or hare fur, right through to brushing and napping. The visit is completed by a video made in the last

G. Rose/Musée du Chapeau

Musée du Chapeau – Chéri-Bibi creation

working factory, a diorama, and demonstrations by hat makers on traditional fully operational machines. Every year, part of the exhibition is given over to contemporary hat design, featuring creations by leading fashion labels. The millinery on show includes hats and caps worn by famous personalities from politics and entertainment, namely Grace Kelly, the late French President François Mitterrand and the great chef Paul Bocuse.

CLERMONT-FERRAND★★

POPULATION 137 140
MICHELIN MAP 326: F-8

Clermont-Ferrand is the natural capital of the Auvergne due to its history and industrial development. The city centre is built on a slight rise, all that remains of a volcanic cone. The old houses built of volcanic rock in the "Black Town" huddle in the shade of the cathedral. Over the past 30 years or so, Clermont's urban landscape has undergone major changes. New developments include the **Jaude** district (a vast shopping complex), the **St-Pierre** district (new covered market), the **Fontgiève** district (law courts, residential buildings), and place du 1er-Mai (sculpture by Étienne Martin), all of which combine contemporary architecture with an older urban environment. In October 2006, a new urban tramway was inaugurated, the first phase in a transport revival of the city, and the first tram system in France to use bi-directional pneumatic tyres.

For visitors arriving from the Pontgibaud direction, there is a good general **view**★★ of the town from a **bend** on D 941ᴬ. From left to right, the nearby heights of the Côtes de Clermont and Chanturgue plateau give an indication of the original level of the Limagne plain prior to the major period of erosion. Opposite the platform lies the city itself, dominated by its black cathedral. In the distance, beyond the Allier Valley, are the mountains of the Livradois area. To the right are the Comté volcanoes, Gergovie plateau and Montrognon rock. Avenue Thermale runs along a hilltop north of Royat. From it there are more superb **views**★ over the town of Clermont and the surrounding area. 🛈 *Pl. de la Victoire, 63000 CLERMONT-FERRAND, ☎ 04 73 98 65 00. www.clermont-fd.com. Clermont-Ferrand, which is listed*

Clermont-Ferrand by night

J. Damase/MICHELIN

as a "Town of Art and History", offers discovery tours (2hr) conducted by guide-lecturers approved by the Ministry of Culture and Communication. Jul to mid-Sep: daily except Sun at 3pm; in addition, Tue and Thu at 8.30pm. Montferrand: Tue, Thu and Sat at 3pm. 5.20€. All year round: theme tours (programme varies), museum visits or excursions (Sun at 3pm). Information at the tourist office or on www.vpah.culture.fr

▶ **Orient Yourself:** Join one of the Discovery Tours (*see above*) to get a good overview of what there is to see and do. Most of the bars, brasseries, theatres, pubs and restaurants are downtown, mainly around the place de Jaude, where there is a large shopping centre.

🅿 **Parking:** Parking (charge) is available at a number of locations around the edge of the city centre. It is often better to park on the edge of the *centre ville* and walk in.

😊 **Don't Miss:** The place de Jaude; this is the focal point for everything that's 'happening' in Clermont-Ferrand.

🕐 **Organizing Your Time:** The place de Jaude is a good place to start, to get a feel for the city, before going on to explore more widely.

Kids **Especially for Kids:** Visit the Espace Massif Central, or Vulcania

👆 **Also See:** The cathedral: Notre Dame de l'Assomption

A Bit of History

From Nemessos to Clermont-Ferrand – The Arverni oppidum (settlement) of Nemessos was built on the site of the rise now occupied by the cathedral. Its name, meaning "wooded rise" or "sacred wood," is a reminder that the spot was used by the Druids as a place of worship. Gradually, over the course of the 1C AD, Druidic rites were abandoned.

A new settlement slowly grew up at the junction of several roads below the original town and, in honour of Caesar Augustus, its name was added on to that of the Roman Emperor. Augustonemetum had several major public buildings and a large number of private residences. An aqueduct brought water from the Villars valley to the summit of the rise where it was distributed to the various urban districts from a water tower.

At its height, in the 2C, the town underwent fairly large-scale expansion and its population rose to between 15 000 and 30 000 inhabitants. An ancient description indicates that it was "well-planted with vineyards, full of people, busy with traffic and trade and much given to pomp."

During the early Middle Ages the town sank into decline. It suffered a number of destructive sieges at the hands of the Franks, the Saracens and the Vikings. It was in the 8C that the name "Clermont" was first applied to the fortress destroyed by Pepin the Short in AD 761.

In the 10C the town entered a period of economic revival. Bishop Étienne II had a new cathedral built, the population increased, the town grew beyond the old town walls and there were no less than 34 churches and chapels inside and outside the walls. For centuries the episcopal town of Clermont was rivalled by Montferrand, the count's stronghold, and later by Riom, the seat of the Court of Appeal. Clermont finally won the day and, in 1630, Montferrand merged with its neighbour to form the conurbation known as Clermont-Ferrand.

Blaise Pascal, a man of genius – A few years earlier, the great writer and philosopher **Blaise Pascal** (1623-62) was born in the town. His main works, *Les Provinciales* and *Pensées* (translated into English as *Mr Pascal's Thoughts, Meditations and Prayers*) are considered as masterpieces of French literature. Pascal was not only very gifted in the Arts, but he was also a brilliant scientist with an enormous talent for mathematics and physics. When he was 12, it became obvious that he had outstanding natural ability in geometry. At the age of 16, he amazed the philosopher Descartes with his essay on conic sections entitled *Traité des Sections Coniques*. Two years later, he invented a calculator which is displayed in the Musée du Ranquet *(see below)*. The "wheelbarrow" or "vinaigrette," a two-wheeled sedan chair, was also one of his inventions. It was Pascal, too, who had the idea of the "five *sous* coach service" travelling a fixed route and leaving at regular intervals. The coaches were an immediate success and they paved the way for the Parisian omnibus service. It was Pascal again, with his brother-in-law Périer, who proved the weight of air following an experiment at Le Puy-en-Velay.

Tyre town – It is perhaps surprising that Clermont, situated in the heart of the Auvergne far from the harbours through which rubber and cotton were imported and well away from the major wire-mills, became the leading centre of tyre production in France and, indeed, one of the industry's leading operators worldwide. The story behind this, however, is one of quite humble origins.

In the heyday of Romanticism, c 1830, a former solicitor named Aristide Barbier, who had lost three-quarters of his personal fortune as a result of the difficult financial climate, set up in partnership with his cousin, Edouard Daubrée, a captain in the King's Light Cavalry who had resigned his commission in order to open a small farm machinery factory on the banks of the River Tiretaine. In order to amuse her children, Madame Daubrée, niece of the Scottish chemist **Charles Macintosh** (1766-1843) who had discovered that rubber dissolves in petroleum, made a few rubber balls as she had seen her uncle do. The balls proved so popular that Barbier and Daubrée began mass-producing them. Soon, the factory diversified its output to include other items made of rubber, such as hoses and belts. However, after a period of prosperity, it fell into decline.

In 1886 Barbier's grandsons, the **Michelin brothers** (André and, later, Édouard), took over the works. These two creative geniuses were the first people to apply scientific methods to industrial production. By meeting clients' real needs, carefully observing reality and constantly revising the knowledge and experience they had already acquired, they were able to create the first detachable bicycle tyre (1891). This development was followed by tyres for automobiles in 1895 and the low-pressure "Confort" tyre in 1923. In 1937 the "Métalic" tyre was introduced, with a steel carcass that made lorries a viable proposition as a method of transport, and in 1946 the radial-ply tyre (marketed under the name "X" in 1949) which combined a radial carcass that overcame the problem of overheating and a triangular steel belt to ensure good road-holding. This tyre has been constantly upgraded and improved

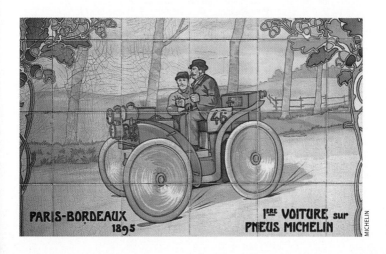

PARIS-BORDEAUX
1895

Iᵉʳᵉ VOITURE sur
PNEUS MICHELIN

MICHELIN

ever since and the technique has most recently been applied to the motorcycle and aviation sectors where it has been put to good use in an expanding market.

In 2006, pneumatic, bi-directional tyes were used, for the first time in France, on the city's new urban tram system.

Old Clermont★★

A leisurely stroll in the old district will take you through the narrow alleys laid out around the cathedral and place de la Victoire, featuring quaint, old-fashioned fountains and houses with lava stone courtyards.

Place de Jaude

The ancient origins of the name of this square remain a subject of controversy. Two Renaissance documents use the name *platea galli* –"rooster square," since in local dialect the word for cockerel is *jô* or *jau*. The square is therefore thought to have been a poultry market.

Another explanation links the origin of the word *jaude* to the name of a suburb of Clermont, known in the Gallic language as *Vasso Galate*. While *wasso* or *vasso* is said to be the name of a Gallic divinity, *galate* is merely a local name which has evolved over the years into *galde* or *gialde* (10C), *jalde* (12C) and, finally, *jaude*.

Place de Jaude is the centre of life in Clermont. It is bordered by paulownias, the only trees that manage to grow on soil infiltrated by petrifying springs and surrounded by department stores, cinemas and, on the south side, by the **Centre Jaude,** a vast modern shopping complex.

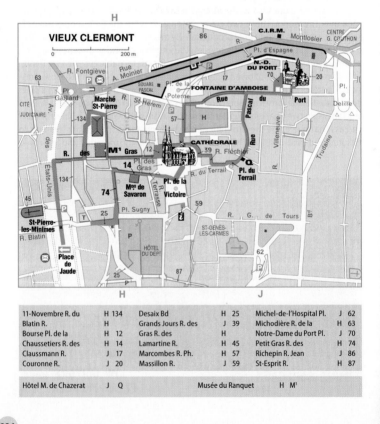

11-Novembre R. du	H	134	Desaix Bd	H	25	Michel-de-l'Hospital Pl.	J 62
Blatin R.	H		Grands Jours R. des	J	39	Michodière R. de la	H 63
Bourse Pl. de la	H	12	Gras R. des	H		Notre-Dame du Port Pl.	J 70
Chaussetiers R. des	H	14	Lamartine R.	H	45	Petit Gras R. des	H 74
Claussmann R.	J	17	Marcombes R. Ph.	H	57	Richepin R. Jean	J 86
Couronne R.	J	20	Massillon R.	J	59	St-Esprit R.	H 87

Hôtel M. de Chazerat	J	Q	Musée du Ranquet	H M¹

Address Book

EATING OUT

BUDGET

⊖ **Le Bougnat** – *29 r. des Chaussetiers - ☎ 04 73 36 36 98 - closed Jul, Mon lunch and Sun .* In the old part of the city near the cathedral, here's a pleasant if basic restaurant with a rural flair. The menu features Auvergnat specialities served in a relaxed atmosphere.

⊖ **Aux Délices de la Treille** – *33 r. de la Treille - ☎ 04 73 91 26 90 - ✗ - reserv. required.* This restaurant nestled in a small street downtown is quite a discovery! Flowery tablecloths, straw chairs and artwork provide a distinctively charming setting for simple, tasty food concocted from fresh ingredients. Colourful terrace in the summer.

MODERATE

⊖⊖ **Le Chardonnay** – *1 pl. Philippe-Marcombes - ☎ 04 73 90 18 28 - closed Sat lunch and Sun - reserv. required evenings.* The appealing slate menu of this popular bar a few steps from the cathedral is a harbinger of the fare to come: regional dishes, delectable and copious. The generous bistro style and the easy-going ambience make for a very enjoyable meal.

⊖⊖ **Brasserie Danielle Bath** – *Pl. du Marché-St-Pierre - ☎ 04 73 31 23 22 - closed Sun-Mon and public holidays.* This attractive bistro is on the ground floor of the new market hall. You can enjoy the brasserie-style cuisine, inventive and flavoursome, in the Belle Époque dining room. Pleasant terrace on the pedestrian plaza in good weather.

WHERE TO STAY

MODERATE

⊖ **Dav'Hôtel Jaude** – *10 r. des Minimes - ☎ 04 73 93 31 49 - 28 rms - ⌧ 6€.* This modern hotel within walking distance of the cathedral is located in a tranquil side street a few steps from the old quarter. Comfortable, functional rooms. Pleasant breakfast room in the colours and patterns of Provence.

⊖⊖ **Hôtel Albert-Élisabeth** – *37 av. Albert-Élisabeth - ☎ 04 73 92 47 41 - 38 rms - ⌧ 6€.* A small hotel near the train station. Somewhat old-fashioned, this family establishment is gradually being renovated. Simple rooms and friendly service.

⊖⊖ **Radio** – *43 av. Pierre-Curie - 63400 Chamalières - ☎ 04 73 30 87 83 - closed 2-25 Jan and 5-14 Nov - ⊞ - 26 rms - ⌧ 9.50€ - restaurant ⊖⊖⊖.* Drawing its inspiration from the very beginnings of the radio era, this hotel's 1930s decoration scheme is repeated throughout the building. Situated in a peaceful residential neighbourhood, the rooms are sober and luminous. Pretty dining room of the art deco genre.

⊖⊖⊖ **Hostellerie St-Martin** – *63170 Pérignat-lès-Sarliève - 8km/5mi S of Clermont via N 9 then D 978 - ☎ 04 73 79 81 00 - ⊞ - 34 rms - ⌧ 8.50€ - restaurant ⊖⊖.* A former Cistercian abbey dating from the 14C, this hotel nestled in a grand park at the foot of the Gergovia plateau is pleasant indeed. Peaceful rooms with a personal touch. A terrace leading into the garden prolongs the inviting dining room. Attractive pool.

ON THE TOWN

Bars, *brasseries*, movie theatres, *crêperies*, pubs, restaurants and tea rooms are where you'll find most of the lively goings-on in neighbourhoods downtown. Many of these are concentrated around the Place de Jaude or near the cathedral, as well as Place Sugny, Rue Fontgiève and Place Gaillard.

L'Aventure – *22 r. des Chaussetiers - ☎ 04 73 31 12 81 - Mon-Sat 6pm-2am.* A friendly atmosphere permeates this little, old-fashioned bistro, the ideal place for discovering and enjoying the charm of Clermont's old quarter. Theme cocktail hours and winter oyster feasts are designed to give patrons a new lease of life. Wine by the glass.

Le Relais de Pascal – *15 r. Pascal - ☎ 04 73 92 21 04 - Tue-Sat from 9am - closed 2 wks in Aug and public holidays.* Care to try some wine from Auvergne? Valuable advice is given here with pleasure to help you choose between the many vintages produced in the area, such as Boudes, Chanturgue or Madargue. A prime address for oenophiles, especially when the wine is bolstered by a bite of Auvergnat ham or cheese.

THEATRE AND ENTERTAINMENT

Contemporary music concerts are held in the Maison des Sports (Place des Bughes). Classical music is generally performed in the Maison des Congrès (blvd Gergovia), where the Orchestre d'Auvergne plays. The auditorium of the Conservatory, the amphitheatre of the Faculty of Law and some churches accommodate chamber music recitals. The 'Rock au Maximum' Festival, early July, is tailor-made to please those who like it LOUD.

Plays are regularly staged at the Opéra Municipal (blvd Desaix) or at the Maison des Congrès. Film buffs gather at "V.O... Le Rio" (rue Sous-les-Vignes) and at the Pathé Capitole to watch foreign films in their original versions rather than dubbed.

La Maison du Tourisme, recently established Place de la Victoire, serves as both tourist office and convention headquarters. It also houses a Massif Central wing and a Romanesque Art exhibit featuring an excellent commented slide show, Le Jeu de la Pierre et de la Foi (The Interplay of Stone and Faith) which gives a fine presentation of this exceptional regional patrimony. English language headsets available.

Le 15ème Avenue – *15 r. des Petits-Gras - ☎ 04 73 37 27 28 - Fri-Sat 10pm-4am - closed mid-Jul to early Sep.* The city's one and only jazz address, this cellar club has unsurprisingly become the rendez-vous of Clermont's swing, hot and free jazz fans. Concerts weekends.

Le Zénith – *Plaine de la Sarilève 63800 Cournon d'Auvergne – reservations on-line at www.fnac.com or contact the Tourist office in Clermont.* The inaugural concert in December 2003 featured Johnny Hallyday, The patriarch of French rock n' roll. The hall seats 8 500 and the first year's schedule includes pop stars and big entertainment spectaculars. In the same complex, a new trade fair area will open in 2004.

SHOPPING

Marché couvert-espace St-Pierre – *Pl. St-Pierre - ☎ 04 73 31 27 88 - Mon-Sat 7am-7:30pm.* This covered food market features a few stands selling regional products (cheese, delicatessen). Chocolate lovers will melt for the pascaline (dark, raspberry flavoured chocolate) and the volcania (truffle), made by hand at the Trianon, 26 rue du 11-Novembre.

La Ruche Trianon – *26 r. du 11-Novembre - ☎ 04 73 37 38 26 - Tue-Fri 10am-7:30pm, Sat 9am-7:30pm.* This fine establishment, nearly a century old, is ever popular among cocoa bean craving clients who come to savour home-made confections like the Volcania, the Pascaline, named after Blaise Pascal, one of Clermont-Ferrand's most illustrious native sons, and fruit jelly candies.

Espace Michelin – *2 place de la Victoire – ☎ 04 73 90 20 50.* Enter Bibendum's world and let him show you the many tourist products he has in his shop!

LEISURE ACTIVITIES

Espace Massif Central – *place de la Victoire – Maison du Tourisme.* This place is the Massif Central's showcase, where the different areas, cultures and traditions are represented in an exhibition and information centre with a rich reference department (topoguides, maps, books CDs of traditional music, CD-Roms and Internet terminals), that is also a lively meeting place for those interested in in nature trails and hikes.

SIT BACK AND RELAX

Gormen's café – *79 av. Édouard-Michelin - ☎ 04 73 90 65 65 - gormens@wanadoo.fr - Tue-Sat 8pm-2am, Sun, Mon for a post-match celebration; exceptional occasions: 3 or 4am - closed mid-Jul to mid-Aug.* Located in what used to be a garage, this hip bar is the rendezvous of students and rugbymen who come to celebrate the famous post-match fiesta 'til they drop. Expect a queue. Theme evenings.

L'Appart – *6 pl. Sugny - ☎ 04 73 91 19 00 - daily from 6pm.* L'Appart, like its namesakes throughout the country, is set up like an apartment, with its assorted rooms decorated accordingly. The mood, with a bent for techno and house, can get pretty wild of an evening...

La Perdrix – *14 r. Terrasse - ☎ 04 73 91 21 35 - Sep-Jun: Mon 5pm-2am, Tue-Sat noon-2am; Jul-Aug: Mon-Sat 6pm-2am.* For nearly thirty years, this bar right in the heart of the historic quarter between cathedral and prefecture has been setting the pace of old city nights. Clermont night owls come in flocks, attracted by the wood and Volvic stone decor, to perch over a beer, whisky or cocktail chosen from the impressive libations menu. Intimate vaulted cellar downstairs.

Le Suffren – **48 pl. de Jaude** - ☎ *04 73 93 40 97 - daily 7:30am-1:30am - closed Christmas, New Year's Day, and 1 May.* Natives in the know frequent this large, chic and cosy café whose terrace is jam-packed whenever the weather is obliging.

Les Goûters de Justine – *11 r. Pascal - ☎ 04 73 92 26 53 - Mon-Fri noon-7pm,*

Sat 2:30pm-7pm. This unique tea room reminds one of a charmingly chaotic antique shop. To be found in a quiet street in Old Clermont, it's the perfect place to relax over a cup of tea or coffee and a pastry or two.

The Mulligan's Irish Pub – *1-3 av. Julien - ☎ 04 73 93 36 70 - Mon-Sat from 8am - closed New Year's Day, 1 May and Christmas.* With atmosphere straight from the Emerald Isle, this pub is one of the top contenders on the Clermont night life scene. Attractive terrace and Irish music.

Église St-Pierre-les-Minimes

🕐 *Daily except Sun.*

This vast domed church building in the Classical style has some fine wood panelling in the chancel.

▶ *Walk down avenue des États-Unis then turn right onto rue des Gras.*

Rue des Gras

A flight of steps used to lead from here right up to the cathedral. The west front of the cathedral is majestically integrated into the line of fine lava stone house fronts. At no 28, note the straight flight of steps, gallery and balcony dating from the 17C. No 22 has two entrances opening onto small inner courtyards. One of them, dating from the 15C, is carved with a man's head; the other is topped by a lintel on which angel musicians are shown surrounding a young woman. At the corner of place des Gras, a Romanesque bas-relief set in the house front represents Christ washing the disciples' feet.

▶ *Take the second street on the left*

Marché St-Pierre

This market is situated at the heart of an old urban district that has been renovated, and stands on the former site of a Romanesque church. It is a bustling centre on which narrow, picturesque shopping streets such as rue de la Boucherie converge.

▶ *Return to rue des Gras then, at place de la Bourse, turn left onto rue Ph.-Marcombes (north of the cathedral) which leads to place de la Poterne.*

Fontaine d'Amboise★

This fountain erected in 1515 by Jacques d'Amboise, Bishop of Clermont, is a very fine piece of Renaissance architecture, carved in lava stone from Volvic. The basin is decorated with charming foliage in the Italian style. The central pyramid is adorned with small, naked figures with water pouring from their mouths, or from the part of the anatomy for which their cousin in Brussels is famous. A hirsute Hercules at the top carries the coat-of-arms of the House of Amboise.

Rue du Port

No 21 *(right)* is a narrow old house with machicolations; on the right, at the corner of Rue Barnier, stands a 16C house with barbican. Note, on the left at no 38, the

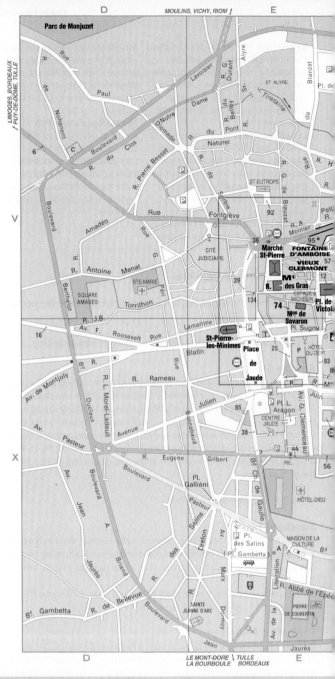

Parc de Monjuzet

MOULINS, VICHY, RIOM ↑

LIMOGES, BORDEAUX / PUY-DE-DÔME, TULLE

ST ALYRE

ST-EUTROPE

FONTGIÈVE

CITÉ JUDICIAIRE

STE-MARIE

SQUARE AMADÉO

Torrilhon

Marché St-Pierre

FONTAINE D'AMBOISE

VIEUX CLERMONT

Mon des Gras

ESPACE MICHELIN

Pl. de Victoi...

Mon de Savaron

Pl. Sugny

St-Pierre-les-Minimes

Place de Jaude

HÔTEL DU DEPT

Pl. L. Aragon

CENTRE JAUDE

Pl. Galliéni

HÔTEL-DIEU

POL.

MAISON DE LA CULTURE

Pl. des Salins

Pl. Gambetta

SAINTE JEANNE D'ARC

PIERRE DE COUBERTIN

LE MONT-DORE \ TULLE
LA BOURBOULE / BORDEAUX

CLERMONT-FERRAND

11-Novembre R. du	EV H 134	
1er-Mai Pl. du	GV	
Abbé-de-l'Épée R.	EX	
Amadéo R.	DV	
Amboise R. d'	FGX	
Anatole-France R.	GX 4	
Aragon Pl. L.	EX	
Ballainvilliers R.	FX 5
Bansac R.	FVX
Barbier-Daubrée Av.	FGV
Baubusse R. H.	EFGV
Bellevue R. de	DX
Belloy R. du	EV
Bergougnan Av. R.	DV 6
Berthelot Bd	DV
Besset R. Pierre	DV
Biauzat R. G.-de	EV
Blanzat R. de	EV
Blatin Bd Cote	FGX
Blatin R.	FGX H
Blum Av. Léon	FGX
Bonnabaud R.	DEX
Bourse Pl. de la	EV H 12
Bughes Pl. des	EFV
Carmes-Déchaux Pl. des	GV
Carnot Av.	FGX
Centre Jaude	EX

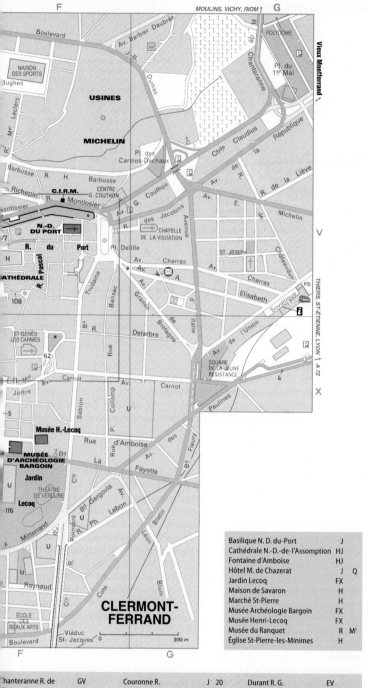

MOULINS, VICHY, RIOM ↑

Vieux Montferrand ↘

V

THIERS, ST-ÉTIENNE, LYON ↓ A 72

X

CLERMONT-FERRAND

300 m

Basilique N. D. du-Port	J
Cathédrale N.-D.-de-l'Assomption	HJ
Fontaine d'Amboise	HJ
Hôtel M. de Chazerat	J Q
Jardin Lecoq	FX
Maison de Savaron	H
Marché St-Pierre	H
Musée Archéologie Bargoin	FX
Musée Henri-Lecoq	FX
Musée du Ranquet	R M¹
Église St-Pierre-les-Minimes	H

Chanteranne R. de	GV	Couronne R.	J 20	Durant R. G.	EV		
Charras Av.	GV	Couthon Av. G.	FGV	Élisabeth Av. A.	GV		
Châteaudun R. de	GV	Delarbre R.	FGX	Espagne Pl. d'	J		
Chaussetiers R. des	H 14	Delille Pl.	FV J	États-Unis Av. des	H EV 29		
Claudius Chaussée	GV	Desaix Bd	EX H 25	La-Fayette Bd	FGX		
Claussat Av. Joseph	DX 16	Diomede R. Paul	DV	Fléchier R.	J		
Haussmann R.	J 17	Dormoy Av. Marx	EX	Fleury Bd	GX		
Clemenceau Av. G.	EX	Drelon R.	EX	Fontgiève R.	DEV H		
Clos Notre-Dame R. du	DEV	Duclaux Bd	DX	Gaillard Pl.	H EV 36		
Collomp R. P.	FX	Dumas Bd J.-B.	FGV	Gallieni Pl.	EX		

241

Gambetta Bd	DX		Lièvre R. de la	GV		Rameau R.	DX	
Gambetta Pl.	EX		Malfreyt Bd L.	EX	56	Raynaud R.	FX	
Gaulle Bd Ch.-de	EX		Marcombes R. Ph.	EV H	57	République Av. de la	GV	
Gergovia Bd	FX		Massillon R.	J	59	Résistance Pl. de la	EX	85
Gilbert R. Eugène	DEX		Menat R. Antoine	DV		Richepin R. Jean	EFV J	86
Gonod R.	EX	38	Michel-de-l'Hospital Pl.	FX J	62	Roosevelt Av. F.	DX	
Grande-Bretagne Av. de	GVX		Michelin Av. É.	GV		Sablon Cours	FX	
Grands Jours R. des	J	39	Michodière R. de la	H	63	St-Alyre R.	EV	
Gras Pl. des	H		Mitterrand Bd F.	EFX		St-Esprit R.	EX H	87
Gras R. des	EV H		Moinier R. A.	EV H		St-Eutrope Pl.	EV	92
Italie Av. d'	GVX		Montjoly Av. de	DX		St-Genes R.	EX	
Jacobins R. des	FGV		Montlosier Petite R.	EFV		St-Hérem R.	H EV	95
Jaude Pl. de	EX H		Montlosier R.	FV J		Salins Pl. des	EX	
Jean-Jaurès Av.	DX		Morel-Ladeuil R. L.	DX		Salins R. des	DEX	
Jean-Jaurès Bd	DEX		Nohanent R. de	DV		Serbie R. de	EV	
Jeune Résistance Square de la	GX		Notre-Dame du Port Pl.	J	70	Sugny Pl.	EX H	
Joffre R. du Mar.	FX		Pascal R.	FV J		Terrail Pl. du	J	
Juin R. Mar.	EX		Pasteur Av.	DX		Terrail R. du	J FV	108
Julien Av.	DEX		Pasteur Bd	DEX		Terrasse R.	H	
Lagarlaye R. de	EX	44	Paulines Av. des	GX		Torrilhon R. J.-B.	DVX	
Lamartine R.	DEX H	45	Péri R. G.	DV		Tours R. G.-de	J	
Lavoisier Bd	DEV		Petit Gras R. des	EV H	74	Trudaine Bd	FVX J	
Lebon R. Ph.	FX		Poincarré Cours R.	FX		Union Soviétique Av. de l'	GVX	
Leclerc R. Mar.	FV		Pont Naturel R. du	EV		Vercingétorix Av.	EFX	116
Libération Av. de la	EX		Port R. du	FV J		Victoire Pl. de la	EV H	
			Poterne Pl. de la	EFV H	77	Villeneuve R.	J	

superb carriage entrance of the residence built in the early 18C for the financier Montlosier.

Basilique Notre-Dame-du-Port★★

Founded in the 6C by Bishop St Avit and burned down by the Vikings, the church was rebuilt with outstanding stylistic unity in the 11C and 12C. The bell-towers and lava, stone roof slabs that replaced the tiles are 19C additions. One section of the narthex belongs to a building that preceded the Romanesque sanctuary. The edifice is now on UNESCO's World Heritage List.

Exterior

The east end, which was restored during the 19C, is a consummate example of Romanesque architecture as used in the Auvergne. Although it is not possible to stand very far back from the building, note the pleasing proportions and the purity of the lines unaffected by the diversity in the decorative features (mosaic of coloured stonework, rose windows, carved modillions, chequerboard cornices).

A Romanesque door is decorated with carvings, but they are in a very poor state of repair. Scenes on the lintel represent the Adoration of the Magi on the left, the Presentation in the Temple in the centre, and Christ's Baptism on the right. On the tympanum, surrounded by an arch projecting beyond the half-circle (a sign of oriental influence), the Lord is shown sitting in Majesty between two seraphim (six-winged angels). The other carvings were added at a later date – Isaiah on the left of the door, and John the Baptist on the right. On the outside of the arch, to the left, is the Annunciation; to the right is a Nativity scene.

Interior

The plain, robust design of Romanesque architecture as developed in the Auvergne is apparent from the entrance. The raised **chancel**★★★, the most attractive part of the building, is strikingly beautiful. It is flanked by an ambulatory with four radiating chapels. There is a profusion of decorative features. Lighting is used to emphasize the details on the **capitals**★, which are among the most famous in the Auvergne. The emotions of the characters are expressed in a lively, energetic manner. One of the capitals shows the struggle between Virtues and Vices. Other capitals illustrate scenes from the life of the Virgin Mary.

Basilique Notre-Dame-du-Port – Detail of the west front

Crypt

This dates from the 11C. Beneath the chancel, the "Underground," dear to the hearts of the local people, has the same layout as the east end. In front of the altar is the carved edge of a well (16C) that existed before the church was built, probably during the days of the Celts and Gauls. On the altar is a small black statue of the Virgin Mary; it is the reproduction of a Byzantine icon, known to exist here since the 13C. Every year, a pilgrimage in honour of the statue attracts huge crowds.

▶ *Leave the church through the narthex and the steps down to place Notre-Dame-du-Port.*

The bare, heavy west front forms a contrast with the remainder of the building; it is preceded by a 16C porch. The austerity and bareness of the old wall are tempered by a row of triple arching beneath the gable, itself consisting of a mosaic of multi-coloured stonework. The square bell-tower above it was added in the 19C. It is built of lava stone from Volvic.

▶ *Follow rue du Port and turn left.*

Rue Pascal

"The streets climb up between careworn façades where gateways open, yawning, onto damp courtyards. In the depths of the iron-coloured shadow is the turret of a spiral staircase, a decorated gallery, a doorway with a lintel shaped like the point of a shield." (Henri Pourrat)

The old house at no 22 has bosses on the ground floor and a wrought-iron balcony.

No 4 is M de Chazerat's residence; he was the last Intendant of the Auvergne and his mansion is a fine late-18C building. The **oval courtyard,** broken up by Ionic pilasters designed in accordance with the principles of the Colossal Order, conveys an impression of majesty. Further down rue de l'Oratoire that runs along the left of the mansion is the Fonds Régional d'Art Contemporain d'Auvergne *(metal doorway on the left)*, a modern arts centre housed in the stables specialising in temporary exhibitions.

▶ *Cross the tiny place du Terrail with its fountain (1664) and go down rue du Terrail. Turn right onto rue Fléchier, leading to rue des Grands-Jours which skirts the east end of the cathedral.*

Place de la Victoire

In the centre is a monument commemorating the Crusades, and a fountain with a statue of Pope Urban II. From this now pedestrian square, there is a general view of the cathedral.

Rue des Chaussetiers

Furniture and carpet shops fill the vaulted ground floors of old houses, and there is an abundance of doors and arches. At no 3, at the corner of rue Terrasse, is the **Maison de Savaron**, a mansion built in 1513. The **courtyard**★ contains a staircase turret linked to the main building by three floors of overhanging landings. The turret includes a superb carved doorway known as the "Door of the Wild Men." At no 10 there is a Gothic doorway and mullioned windows. At the corner of rue des Petits-Gras are Romanesque arches (12C, the oldest examples of this style to be seen in vernacular buildings in Clermont).

Rue des Petits-Gras

At nos 4-6 (windows with grotesque masks), in the second of the two buildings beyond the courtyard, there is a monumental three-storey **staircase**★ supported by corbels and oblique basket-handled arches. The straight flights of steps and landings are a particularly successful example of 18C architecture. Note the wrought-iron balustrade and its lantern with hanging keystone.

Sights

Cathédrale Notre-Dame-de-l'Assomption★★

🕐 *mid-May to mid-Sep: daily 8am to 6pm; rest of year, Mon-Sat, 8am-noon, 2-6pm, Sun, 9.30am-noon, 3-6pm.*

This is a lovely Gothic church with a design based on cathedrals in the Île de France (the Paris region, where Gothic architecture initially developed). Its sombre colour is due to the Volvic lava used in its construction; it is the only major cathedral built of this particular type of stone. The church standing today was begun in 1248, under the direction of Jean Deschamps; a Romanesque church previously stood here, itself replacing one or two earlier churches. Deschamps worked on it until his death c 1295, by which time the east end, transept and first span in the nave had been completed.

Cathédrale Notre-Dame-de-l'Assomption: Virgin and Child in the first south aisle

S. Sauvignier/MICHELIN

The work continued during the first half of the 14C under Pierre de Cébazat, one of the master builders involved in building the monastery of La Chaise-Dieu. From 1866 onwards, Viollet-le-Duc built the narthex, two additional spans in the nave and the fine lava stone spires that can be seen from afar when one approaches Clermont; all the additions were built in the 13C style.

Enter by the north door into the transept, beneath the Bayette Tower. Adjacent to the tower is the Guette Turret, once topped by a look-out post. The impression of ethereal lightness in the nave and, in particular, around the chancel shows the technical skills inherent in the Rayonnant Gothic style. The use of lava stone made it possible to reduce the width of the pillars, the arches of the vaulting, and the various sections of the openings. Note the **stained-glass windows**★★ dating from the 12C to the 20C; the dominant colours are red and blue. The scattering of the French fleur-de-lis motif and the towers of Castile visible on some of the windows would seem to suggest that they date from the days of St Louis; the King may have given them to the cathedral on the occasion of the marriage of his son (the future Philippe III) in the cathedral in 1262. The transept is illuminated by two magnificent rose windows: the one in the south arm is deep red and the one in the north arm is deep violet. The lancets are set within a square.

Set in the gallery of the north transept arm is a clock with a **jack o' the clock** which strikes the hours (**1**) dating from the 16C (the mechanism dates from the 17C and 18C).

Walk round the ambulatory. Note, above the doorway flanked by foliage into the

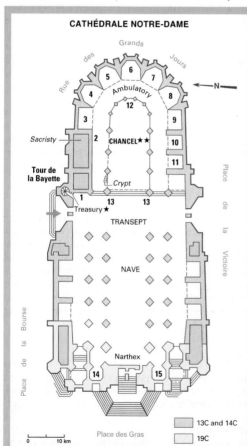

vestry (**2**), three fine votive paintings from the 13C and 15C, each one partly above the other.

(**3**) **Chapelle St-Georges** – Stained-glass window illustrating the life and martyrdom of the saint. Note the 13C fresco also depicting his martyrdom.

(**4**) **Chapelle St-Austremoine** – To the right, Austremoine's arrival in the Auvergne where he was the first bishop. In the centre is an illustration of his martyrdom; to the left, the miracles accomplished after his death. The Baroque altar and Pietà date from the 17C. The painted wooden statues are 19C.

(**5**) **Mary Magdalene windows** – Stained glass illustrating the end of her life. 17C and 18C altar

CATHÉDRALE NOTRE-DAME

Grands Jours
des
Rue
Ambulatory
Sacristy
CHANCEL★★
Tour de la Bayette
Crypt
Treasury ★
TRANSEPT
Place de la Victoire
Place de la Bourse
NAVE
Narthex
Place des Gras
0   10 km

13C and 14C
19C

and Pietà. Statues of the Bishops of Clermont, St Arthème and St Alyre. Painting representing the martyrdom of St Sebastian.

(**6**) **Apsidal chapel** – To the left is the life of John the Baptist; in the centre, the childhood of Christ and to the right the miracle worked by Theophilus. Most remarkable of all is the Romanesque statue of the Blessed Virgin Mary in Majesty. It dates from the same period as the ones in Marsat and Orcival and was probably a copy of the golden Madonna belonging to Étienne II, the prototype statue that was destroyed during the French Revolution (see Introduction, p xxx). Originally the statue was painted but the ebony paint that has covered the face and hands since 1833 led to its being considered, wrongly, as a Black Virgin.

(**7**) **St Bonnet windows** – St Bonnet was Bishop of Clermont in the 7C.

(**8**) **Funeral chapel of the bishops** – In the centre are 12C stained-glass windows from the former cathedral which illustrate the Life of Christ.

(**9**) **Chapelle Ste-Marguerite** – Altarpiece and Adoration of the Shepherds (17C).

(**10**) **St Agatha windows.**

(**11**) **Chapelle St-Arthème** – Endowed with an altarpiece which was rebuilt in 1840 using 17C statues. The **chancel**★★ is closed off by large but light arches. Above the triforium, the long 13C and 14C stained-glass windows (**12**) have a grisaille background and only one large figure per lancet. Recognisable among the illustrations is the Assumption of the Virgin Mary. In the chancel, note the gilded copper High Altar designed by Viollet-le-Duc. Set against the pillars in the transept are two statues of the Virgin Mary and St John (**13**); they were originally part of the rood screen which was demolished during the Revolution. They date from the 15C and were made in an archaic style.

At the west end of the inner north aisle note the 14C statue of Christ of the Last Judgement (**14**), which was once set against the tympanum of the north doorway. At the west end of the inner south aisle is a stained-glass window (1982) by Makaraviez illustrating the Apocalypse of St John (**15**).

Crypt

☛*Closed temporarily during archaeological excavations.*

The crypt was built in the 10C with an ambulatory and radiating chapels, and was altered when the Gothic cathedral was built. It contains a very fine 4C white-marble **sarcophagus**★ decorated with scenes from the Life of Christ. The ambulatory contains 12C-13C murals.

Treasury★

🕐 *Jul to mid-Sep: guided tours (maximum 10 people) daily except Sun and Mon 2.30-5pm; mid-Sep to Jun: by appointment (apply one month in advance). 2€. ☎ 04 73 92 46 61.*

Enter via the Bayette Tower. Situated above the canons' sacristy, on a level with the clock (this is an opportunity to admire from close up Tempus flanked by Mars and Faunus), the treasure includes items dating from the 12C to the 19C. There is gold, silver and enamelware including pyxis, reliquaries, burettes, chalices, ciboria, monstrances and bishops' crosiers, as well as sacerdotal and liturgical vestments. Note the Romanesque sculptures (Virgin Mary in Majesty, large Crucifix and a head of Christ) and the 16C statues (the twelve Apostles).

Tour de la Bayette

250 steps. From the top of the tower there is a fine panoramic view of Clermont and the surrounding countryside. Leave the cathedral by the doorway in the south transept which was designed to be flanked by two towers. The one on the right was demolished during the Revolution; the other one was apparently never completed.

Musée d'Archéologie Bargoin★

🕐 *Daily except Mon 10am-noon, 1-5pm (Sun, 2-7pm).* 🕐 *Closed 1 Jan, 1 May, 1 Nov, 25 Dec. 4€, no charge 1st Sunday in the month. ☎ 04 73 91 37 31.*

This museum, built between 1899 and 1903, houses a sizeable **prehistoric and Gallo-Roman archaeological collection**★ on the ground and basement floors, comprising artefacts discovered locally, particularly during recent excavations in the city of Clermont itself.

The Gallo-Roman period is the best represented, with a marvellous collection of statuettes of animals, men, women and children in white terracotta from Allier, sigillated pottery from Lezoux with fine examples dating from the 2C, vestiges of the great temple of Mercury built on the summit of the Puy-de-Dôme at the

Bronze helmet

Musée Bargoin

beginning of the Imperial era. Note in particular the 3 500 **wooden ex-votos**★ dating from the 1C AD, found around the spring at Les Roches in Chamalières.

The **Carpet Museum** occupies the first and second floors of the Musée Bargoin and includes over 80 carpets from the Middle and Far East: Turkey, the Caucasus, Iran, Afghanistan, Turkestan, Tibet, China etc. These rare pieces, some of which date from the 18C, are the expression of civilizations marked by their nomadic way of life and are at the same time devotional objects rich in spiritual symbolism, invaluable items for everyday domestic use and dazzlingly colourful works of art.

Musée du Ranquet

🕐 *Open in accordance with cultural schedule.* 🕐 *Closed 1 Jan, 25 Dec. 4€, no charge 1st Sunday in the month.*

Under renovation, open for special events. This Renaissance mansion (in the courtyard, note the carved motifs decorating the stair turret) will eventually be devoted to Pascal, science and technique.

Muséum d'histoire naturelle Henri-Lecoq

🕐 *May-Sep, daily except Mon 10am-noon, 2-6pm, (Oct-Apr: closes 5pm).* 🕐 *Closed Sun am, Mon and public holidays. 4.50€.* ☎ *04 73 91 93 78.*

This museum is named after the naturalist Henri Lecoq (1802-71) whose wide-ranging collections of stuffed animals, local rocks and regional flora make this a Natural History Museum very much centred on the Auvergne.

Parks

The attractive **Jardin Lecoq** stretches over an area of 3ha/7 acres right in the town centre. Near the lake is a 14C entrance brought over from the Château de Bien-Assis, built for the Duc de Berry and owned, in the 17C, by Florin Périer, Blaise Pascal's brother-in-law.

Another pleasing patch of greenery is the **Parc Montjuzet,** located to the north of Clermont and offering fine views of the town.

Old Montferrand★★

Montferrand was founded by the counts of Auvergne who built a fortress on a rise that is now the site of place Marcel-Sembat, in order to counter the authority of the bishop, who was also Lord of Clermont. In the early 13C the town was rebuilt on the orders of a powerful woman named Countess Brayère and was turned into a bastide, a fortified hilltop town laid out to a strictly symmetrical geometric pattern. Two main roads cut across each other at right angles; they led to the four gates in the town walls. Narrow alleyways acting as firebreaks were built between the houses. Montferrand was a commercial centre for it lay at the junction of several roads and, in the 15C, the wealthy middle classes began to commission town houses. The narrow plots of land made available by Countess Brayère's town plan, however, forced the architects to design houses that were deep rather than wide: on the street, there was a narrow shop flanked by an entrance porch; beyond, stood an inner courtyard with two or three storeys of galleries and a staircase turret leading to the apartments; on the other side of the courtyard were warehouses for goods. Most of the houses were built with lava stone. Montferrand was so commercially successful that, in the 16C, the king set up law courts – known as the Cour des Aides – to try fiscal and criminal cases. This brought new work for local architects, who had to design

Vieux Montferrand

J. Damase/MICHELIN

mansions for the *noblesse de robe* (new aristocracy whose rank was derived from holding high state office).

The proximity of Clermont caused rivalry and jealousy between the two towns. Montferrand eventually went into decline.

In 1962 work was undertaken to renovate the old town of Montferrand, a project which involved some 80 old town houses. Over the past few years, numerous mansions have retrieved their original façades, decorated with carved heads, balustrades, staircase turrets, cornerstones and lava stone arches contrasting with the honey-coloured "Montferrand roughcast." There are three types of houses, all clearly distinguishable. They range from the modest houses of farmers, wine-growers and vegetable producers (place du Poly) to the half-timbered houses of shopkeepers (rue de la Rodade), in which the stone ground floor includes the arches for the shopfronts, and finally the superb mansions owned by wealthy merchants and officials, built of Volvic stone and decorated with carvings (rue R.J.-Guesde).

▶ *Park in place de la Rodade.*

Place de la Rodade

This square was once known as place de Belregard because of the view over the Puys range. The metal barriers are used during the annual Lava Stone Fair. In the centre stands the Four Seasons fountain made of lava stone from Volvic.

▶ *Enter the old town of Montferrand via rue de la Rodade.*

Hôtel Regin

At no 36. This 15C and 16C town house belonged to a family of magistrates and is typical of the mansions built in Montferrand. In the **courtyard**★ there is a fine statue of St Christopher. To the right, the gallery above is carved with an Annunciation scene. For this reason, the mansion is also known as the Maison de l'Annonciation.

Hôtel Doyac

At no 29. Late-15C mansion built for Jean de Doyac, Royal Bailiff of Montferrand and Minister to Louis XI. Huge, imposing Gothic doorway.

Hôtel du Bailliage

At no 20. Bailiwick House is the former Consuls' Residence. Its gargoyles and vaulted rooms are of particular interest.

After rue de la Rodade widens, a fine set of timbered houses with corbelling comes into view on the left in the renovated district. Their rounded doorways and shop-fronts are set out on high landings that reveal the original level of the roadway. At no 6 there is a fine inner courtyard and a balustered staircase.

▷ *Turn back; at the corner marked by the Maison de l'Échauguette (Watchtower House), turn right onto rue Marmillat.*

Hôtel de la Porte

At no 5. In the courtyard of this mansion, also known as the Architect's House, there is a staircase turret decorated with an interesting Renaissance sculpture dating from 1577.

▷ *Turn right onto rue de la Cerisière.*

Hôtel de la Faye des Forges

At no 2. A glass door protects a delightful inner door with a carved tympanum decorated with lions holding a phylactery. The house opposite has a double timber gallery, an unusual feature in Montferrand.

▷ *Turn left along rue des Cordeliers onto rue Waldeck-Rousseau.*

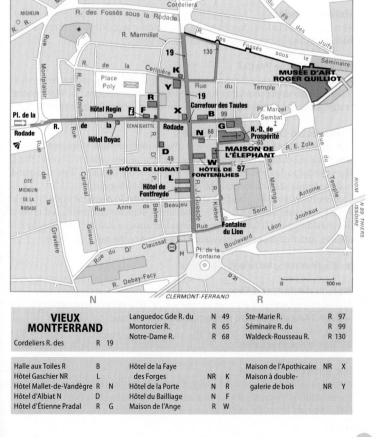

VIEUX MONTFERRAND		Languedoc Gde R. du	N 49	Ste-Marie R.	R 97
		Montorcier R.	R 65	Séminaire R. du	R 99
Cordeliers R. des	R 19	Notre-Dame R.	R 68	Waldeck-Rousseau R.	R 130

Halle aux Toiles R	B	Hôtel de la Faye			Maison de l'Apothicaire	NR X
Hôtel Gaschier NR	L	des Forges	NR K		Maison à double-	
Hôtel Mallet-de-Vandègre R	N	Hôtel de la Porte	N R		galerie de bois	NR Y
Hôtel d'Albiat N	D	Hôtel du Bailliage	N F			
Hôtel d'Étienne Pradal R	G	Maison de l'Ange	R W			

Rue Waldeck-Rousseau runs along the inside of the old ramparts, high above the road laid out along the moat which was once liable to flooding from the River Tiretaine.

▷ *Turn right onto Rue du Temple, back to Rue des Cordeliers.*

Rue des Cordeliers
At no 11, note the Renaissance ground floor flanked by pilasters and the delightful little inner courtyard. No 5 has Renaissance arches on the façade.

Carrefour des Taules
This is the central junction in the old town. Its name is a reminder that this was traditionally where butchers had their stalls. Here the street used to consist of a flight of steps but it was lowered in the 18C to facilitate the passage of carts so that it is now the cellars which are on ground-floor level. Further down, on rue des Cordeliers and rue Jules-Guesde, the former ground floors lie below the level of the road, which was raised by the addition of infill.

Maison de l'Apothicaire
At no 1 rue des Cordeliers. The old Apothecary's House dates from the 15C and has two timbered upper storeys. At the top of the house, the brackets on either side of the gable are decorated with an apothecary carrying his clyster and the patient awaiting his operation.

▷ *Turn left onto rue du Séminaire.*

Halle aux Toiles
At no 3, the old cloth market, there is a long balcony supporting a fine row of four basket-handled arches and corresponding side doors.

Hôtel d'Étienne Pradal
At no 22. The ground floor of this mansion has superb semicircular and basket-handled arches. On the upper storeys are mullioned Renaissance windows. Its "Montferrand roughcast" and cornerstones made of lava stone are typical of the town's architecture.

Église Notre-Dame-de-Prospérité
The west front still has its north tower (the south tower was destroyed in 1793) which was used as a watchtower. It is topped by a lantern called "L'Olivière" (16C). Note the gargoyles protruding from the exterior of the building. Their elongated outlines form a stark contrast to the regular lava stone bonding.
The wide nave (18m/59ft in height and width) is built in the Southern French Gothic style. A fine Flamboyant Gothic rose window lights up the front. Beneath the left bell-tower is the vaulted chapel of St Catherine containing a Romanesque statue of the Virgin Mary in Majesty, part of a tympanum that was destroyed, and on the wall a 16C fresco.

▷ *Continue along rue Kléber.*

Maison d'Adam et d'Eve
At no 4. In the courtyard on a balustrade is a 15C **bas-relief**★ representing Adam and Eve. The staircase turret supports an Italianate loggia.

▷ *Turn left onto rue Kléber.*

Maison de l'Élephant★
At no 12. A 13C Romanesque house. The great arches on the ground floor support the twin bay windows on the first floor. Crowned heads decorate the brackets. On the tympanum above the central bay is a fresco that once depicted an elephant, hence the name given

to the house. Another interpretation has it that "elephant" is a phonetic deformation of "oliphant," the horn used to announce the arrival of an important visitor.

Maison de l'Ange

At no 14. In the courtyard is a small, triangular tympanum above a doorway representing an angel carrying a coat of arms.

In rue Ste-Marie *(left),* at the foot of the passageway that spans the road, there is the old doorway of the Visitation Convent (note the shield flanked by scallop shells).

Fontaine du Lion

The fountain comes from a square to which it had given its name. On the gable is a lion carrying the blazoned coat of arms of Montferrand.

▷ *Turn right twice onto rue R.J.-Guesde.*

Hôtel de Fontfreyde

At no 28. In the courtyard of this mansion, also known as Lucretia's House, there is a delightful Madonna and Child on the Gothic doorway into the staircase turret, carved in the Renaissance style from the same block of lava stone as the tympanum. The balustrade on the gallery bears three fine Italianate medallions depicting Lucretia stabbing herself, torn between her husband and her seducer.

Hôtel Gaschier

At no 20. Three rows of galleries, one above the other, open onto the courtyard (15C-16C). The first floor is supported by superb pillars. There is a tympanum decorated with a coat of arms on the polygonal staircase turret.

Hôtel de Lignat★

At no 18. This, the Lawyer's House, dates from the 16C. Gracious mullioned windows open onto the street. It opens onto Grande-Rue-du-Languedoc through a very elegant door decorated with a garland of roses in the Italian Renaissance style. The courtyard includes an attractive staircase turret rising to three levels of galleries. One of them is decorated with fleurs-de-lis and with the remainder of an Annunciation scene, although it has now worn almost completely away.

Hôtel de Fontenilhes★

At no 13. The house, a fine residence dating from the late 16C, was built of lava stone from Volvic. The courtyard, with its three levels of galleries, has a spiral staircase turret. Note the carvings of lions, griffins, unicorns, and the succession of the three Classical Orders (Doric, Ionic and Corinthian).

▷ *Start walking along rue Notre-Dame.*

Hôtel Mallet-de-Vandègre

At no 2. This building, with its austere courtyard, is said to have been the women's prison.

▷ *Cross carrefour des Taules, walk along rue de la Rodade and turn left onto rue du Dr-Balme.*

At no 5 is a Romanesque house with colonnettes and capitals on the front. At no 11 there is a second **Hôtel d'Albiat** dating from the 16C. In the courtyard, a scene (the legend of the unicorn) is visible on the tympanum above a door but it is in a poor state of repair.

Musée d'Art Roger-Quilliot★★

🚲🕐 *Daily except Mon 10am-6pm.* 🕐 *Closed 1 Jan, 1 May, 1 Nov, 25 Dec. 4.20€, no charge 1st Sunday in the month.* ☎ *04 73 16 11 30.*

A change of use – The history of these premises reflects the history of the two rival towns, Montferrand and Clermont, each in turn the seat of various official bodies. The museum stands on the site of the Palais Vieux above the town walls. It was the seat of the royal bailiwick then of the Cour des Aides of the Auvergne, the Limousin and the Marches; the monumental gateway built in the early 17C in front of the courtyard that precedes the chapel is all that remains of this building. When Montferrand and Clermont were combined, the Cour des Aides moved to Clermont and the Ursuline Order of nuns took over and reconstructed the buildings. The site was turned into a seminary after the Revolution, then into a military hospital from 1914 to 1918, and into barracks for the riot police and *gendarmerie*, before being transformed from 1986 to 1992 into a museum. The buildings and their surroundings are a reflection of Montferrand. They constitute the old "Gateway of the Rising Sun" and open the historic centre of the town to its suburbs.

An exemplary history – The idea of walking around a central open space, as illustrated in the Guggenheim Museum in New York, inspired the architects Adrien Fainsilber (designer of the Cité des Sciences and the Géode at La Villette in Paris) and Claude Gaillard.

The glass roof shaped like a palm-tree, designed by Peter Rice, gives unity to a courtyard with a complex shape. The curves of the concrete staircase, emphasized by metal handrails, elegantly unfold from one floor to the next.

Visitors walk through the various rooms around the courtyard. A sculpture, painting, piece of stairway or section of glass can be seen from a distance, from an unexpected angle, through a framework of Volvic stone. In each room, the light source is concealed, creating an impression of well-being and an atmosphere of meditation.

The collections – These used to be housed in the Bargouin and Le Ranquet museums. The collections are exhibited in chronological order, combining various art forms in the same display, with paintings hung next to sculptures, items of furniture and objets d'art. Highlights of the collections include enamel work from Limousin, Romanesque statues of the Virgin Mary from Auvergne, 17C French, Italian and Flemish paintings and works by Fragonard, Gustave Doré, Théodore Chassériau, Bartholdi.

Peter Rice's "palm-tree" roof

P. Claphm/MICHELIN

The Middle Ages – The *Meeting of bishops* brought here from the church in Enne-zat is a rare example, in France, of a late-13C painting on wood. The rigidity of the Romanesque art work is softened by the expression in the faces and hands, and the use of subtle hues of pinks and beiges. Among 14C and 15C works of art, note **Guil-laume Savaron's travelling chest**, a valuable item made of embossed and gilded leather, representing bathing scenes, hunts, games and dancing. All the figures are dressed in elegant 15C costume.

The first **17C** room contains the **decor**★ from a grand gallery in the Château d'Effiat, unfurled like a screen. The illustrations of nature (lush fertile valleys, streams, dense forests) create a mysterious presence in which the hero Roland is seen as described in the poem by Ariosto, *Orlando Furioso*. There is also a magnificent **Portrait of Vincent Voiture** by Philippe de Champaigne.

The last 17C room includes some interesting Dutch interiors and an extraordinary *Elves Dancing* by David Ryckaert III.

The **18C** begins with the artistry of the portrait-painter. There is a formal portrait notable for the rigidity of the composition *(The Duchess de Maine Picking a Piece of Orange Blossom* from Rigaud's studio), a more intimate and sensual portrait by Christine Van Loo, and a fine study by Duplessis – **Portrait of Antoine Léonard Thomas**★. It shows a refined treatment of ordinary clothing, lends nobility of expression to the facial features of a commoner, and indicates attentive, uncompromising observation of the model.

The **chapel** is used for exhibitions and concerts, and with its black, lava stone bonding it is reminiscent of the austere harmony of Renaissance buildings in Florence.

History, archaeology, tropical landscapes – the Auvergne has inspired artists who shook off the constraints of Classicism and overturned the hierarchy of genres. The great **19C gallery**★ reflects this eclecticism and, through sculptures and paintings, provides an insight into the profusion of artistic creativity during this period. In one of the small rooms is a striking painting by Gustave Doré, *The Tumblers*.

The **20C** is represented by busts (*Madame de Massary* by Camille Claudel) and the paintings from the Maurice Combe Bequest, illustrating modern figurative art of the "Paris School."

Excursions

1 Tour of Volcanoes★★

35km/21mi – allow half a day

▶ *Leave Clermont via place des Carmes-Déchaux and head N on boulevard J.-B. Dumas towards Limoges, then take rue de Blanzat on the right.*

The road rises along the ravine separating the Côtes de Clermont *(to the left)* from the Chanturgue plateau *(to the right)*.

▶ *1.2km/0.8mi after the intersection with boulevard Charcot, turn right and drive on for 300m/330yd until you reach a junction. Park the car and continue on foot.*

A gravel path wends its way up towards the site, running along the edge of the ravine to the left *(allow 1hr there and back)*.

Plateau de Chanturgue★

The Chanturgue plateau (alt 553m/1814ft) constitutes the remains of a vast volcanic table which erosion has worn down into several sections. In the bases of drystone walls, covered with stubble or concealed by the undergrowth, archaeologists have found the remains of what may have been Caesar's lesser encampment.

L'Oppidum des Côtes de Clermont

Proceed along the road for 500m/550yd and leave the car at the start of a lane on the left, in the undergrowth, level with a right-hand turn and walk to the ridge of the Côtes de Clermont plateau (1hr there and back).

🚶 History lovers will enjoy visiting these ruins, the vestiges of a former stronghold.

▶ *Go back down towards Clermont and turn right onto boulevard Charcot, heading for Durtol. Go to avenue du Puy-de-Dôme (D 941A) via avenue de la Paix (D 941), then take côte de la Baraque.*

Puy de Dôme★★★ – 🕓 *See Monts DÔME.*

▶ *In La Font-de-l'Arbre, take D 68.*

Royat – 🕓 *See ROYAT.*

Chamalières

Lying south-west of Clermont, Chamalières is an important residential and business centre and the headquarters for some of the tourist and spa amenities in Royat. The banknotes for the Banque de France used to be printed here.

Église Notre-Dame

🕐 *Daily except Sun afternoon.* ☏ *04 73 37 36 06.*
Of the five churches that once stood in Chamalières, only one is still extant. Its nave consists of the remains of an early building, dating back to a time before the year AD 1000. In the 12C the chancel was extended and rebuilt.

Moulin de la Saigne

Beyond the church take rue de la Coifferie and rue du Languedoc. The swift currents of the River Tiretaine have always favoured the installation of water-wheels: there have been flour mills along the river since the 10C and papermills from the 15C.

▶ *Cross place de Geretsried to no 3 avenue de Fontmaure, within the Carrefour-Europe residential and shopping complex.*

Galerie d'Art Contemporain

♿🕐 *Daily except Sun: 2.30-7pm.* 🕐 *Closed public holidays. No charge.* ☏ *04 73 30 97 22.*
Space is fairly limited in this Modern Art Gallery but the exhibitions are interesting and they attract all the latest names in modern painting and sculpture. The works donated by artists to the gallery form its permanent collections.

▶ *Take avenue de Royat, then rue Blatin to return to the town centre (place de Jaude).*

Parc Bargoin – 🕓 *See ROYAT.*

② The Country South of Clermont★

45km/28mi – allow half a day

▶ *Leave Clermont starting from place de Jaude and take rue Gonod to the S. Then take avenue de la Libération, which leads to N 89.*

Église de Beaumont

The former wine-growing village of Beaumont to the south of Clermont developed round the **Église St-Pierre** (*Sometimes closed Sun afternoons.* ☏ *04 73 44 00 05.*). Founded in the 7C, the church remained attached to a Benedictine convent until

1792 when the religious community was expelled.

St Verny, patron saint of wine-growers from Auvergne stands against the right-hand pillar. Note a Romanesque statue of the Virgin Mary in the south side aisle, a 15C *Pietà* in the north transept and, in the chancel, a late-14C Virgin of the Annunciation.

The church also contains a number of gravestones including that of **Béatrice of Auvergne** (13C, in the chancel).

Ceyrat

At the junction with the road to Boissé-jour, on the left, you will notice the curious remains of a volcano.

▶ *Continue heading S.*

Renaissance fountain

Gorges de Ceyrat

These high granite cliffs have been deeply eroded by the river running through the gorges.

▶ *Go back to N 89 and turn right. After 250m/270yd, turn left onto D 120. Follow the signposting to Château d'Opme.*

Château d'Opme

 ♿⏰ *Easter to end Oct: Sun and public holidays 2.30-7pm.* ⏰ *Nov-Easter. 3.50€.* ☎ *04 73 87 54 85.*

This old fortress (11C) stands high above a mountain pass which was once the route taken by the Roman road from Clermont to Le Puy-en-Velay. It originally belonged to the counts of Auvergne and was converted into an elegant Renaissance château by Antoine de Ribeyre, Treasurer of France under Louis XIII.

The upper terrace is laid out as a formal **French garden** ★ around an ornamental basin with a fountain, the entire area shaded by two avenues of antique lime trees. .

▶ *Return to the intersection of D 3 and D 120 and turn right.*

The road climbs up to the Gergovie plateau, offering pretty views of Clermont, the Puys mountain range with the Monts Dore in the distance.

Plateau de Gergovie★ – ♿ *See Plateau de GERGOVIE.*

▶ *Drive along D 120 to La Roche-Blanche then head for Clermont along D 978. Drive 2km/1.2mi along N 9 and turn left onto D 777 (avenue R.-Maerte); 1.5km/0.9mi further on, turn right onto D 69 (avenue J.-Noellet).*

Aubière

24 bis, Avenue Jean Noëllet. This southern suburb of Clermont has an interesting **Musée de la Vigne et du Vin** (♿⏰ *Easter - Nov: daily, 10am-noon, 2-7pm; Dec-Easter, Sat, Sun, 2-6pm. 5€.* ☎ *04 73 27 60 04*) housed in former cellars. The visit ends with wine-tasting.

▶ *Continue along D 69, then turn left onto boulevard Louis-Loucheur. A little further on, boulevard C.-Bernard will take you back towards place de Jaude.*

CONDAT

POPULATION 1 121
MICHELIN MAP 330: E-2
32KM/20MI SE OF BORT-LES-ORGUES – LOCAL MAP SEE LE CÉZALLIER

This pleasant holiday resort lies in the centre of a fertile basin into which flow the Rhue d'Égliseneuve, Bonjon and Santoire rivers. Its numerous, slate-roofed villas standing on the sunlit slopes of the Rhue Valley were almost all built by local people who went elsewhere to seek their fortune, many of them as linen-drapers. *Le bourg, 15190 CONDAT, ☎ 04 71 78 66 63.*

Excursions

The Alpine Pastures of Le Cézallier★

90km/56mi – about 5hr – local map see Monts du CÉZALLIER

1 From the Rhue Gorge to Gentiane Country

80km/263mi – allow one day

▶ *Leave Condat to the W.*

The D 679 road follows the right bank of the Rhue Valley. The road offers fine views of the gorge and Les Essarts lake-reservoir then enters the lovely Maubert Forest planted with pines and beeches. In the middle of the forest, the Gabacut, having dug numerous cauldrons into the rock, drops down in two successive small waterfalls.

Cascade de Cornillou
30min on foot there and back. 50m/55yd before the exit from the hamlet of Cornillou, park and turn left on a cart track.
Just before reaching a deserted barn, turn right onto an uphill track that soon runs along the shores of a small lake-cum-reservoir. Turn left across a small bridge; 200m/219yd further on, an overgrown path (brambles) leads to the top of the water-fall. A steeply sloping path runs down to its foot.

Gorges de la Rhue★★
Upstream from Embort, the river flows through a magnificent gorge with sides covered in greenery. The ravine widens out at the confluence of the two Rhues, near the Coindre hydroelectric power station.

The Rhues

A number of streams and rivers on the north side of Cantal bear the name Rhue. The largest of them, the Grande Rhue, flows into the Dordogne below Bort-les-Orgues after crossing a bar of rock known as the Saut de la Saule (see BORT-LES-ORGUES), but an underground drainage channel takes some of its water into the Bort reservoir. The Grande Rhue rises in the south of the Dore mountain range near the Biche corrie. Once its waters have been swollen by the Rhue de Cheylade that flows down from the mountains of Cantal, the Grande Rhue flows through very picturesque wooded gorges.

Barrage de Vaussaire

Near Embort. Thanks to the work on the Upper Tarentaine (its waters power the turbines in the plant at Auzurette further upstream, producing 100 million kWh annually), this dam can drain off 757 million m3/613 700 million cu ft of water on average every year, which a 13.5km/8mi tunnel then carries through the wall of the Bort dam.

Between Sarran and Champs, the road follows a wide dry valley where the Rhue once flowed.

Champs-sur-Tarentaine-Marchal – 🕭 *See BORT-LES-ORGUES.*

▶ *Leave Champs E along D 679.*

Bort-les-Orgues – 🕭 *See BORT-LES-ORGUES.*

▶ *Leave Bort on D 922 in the direction of Mauriac and after 5km/3mi turn left onto D 3.*

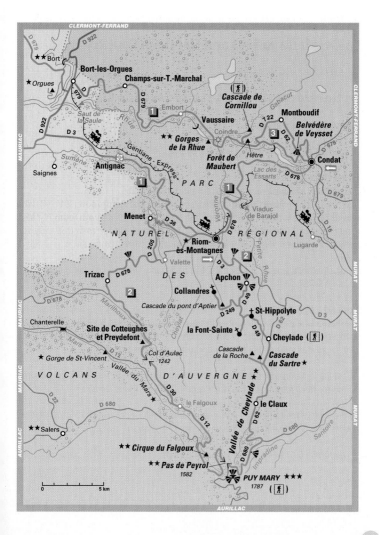

PASTORAL PLEASURES

Ché Marissou – *Le Veysset - 15190 Condat - 3km/1.8mi N of Condat via D 62 - ☎ 04 71 78 55 45 - closed Oct to Mar and open Fri, Sat and Sun except during school holidays - ✉ - reserv. required.* If you're yearning for a real taste of 19C rural Auvergne, this address is for you. Typical Auvergnat decor, with box-bed, bread coffer and period knick-knacks...not to mention the superb fireplace. One meal for all, free of charge for diners under 7 and over 100 years old. This is also the world's smallest hotel: a single room to let!

Véronique Phelut Bed and Breakfast – *Le Veysset - 15190 Condat - 3km/1.8mi N of Condat via D 62 - ☎ 04 71 78 62 96 - veronique.phelut@libertysurf.fr - closed 1 Nov to Easter - ✉ - 4 rms.* A fine address in a gorgeous setting for nature lovers and hikers. The rooms (non-smoking only) are basic but comfortable. Table d'hôte meals except during the summer, when a corner kitchenette is at your service. Peace and quiet guaranteed.

Riom-ès-Montagnes – 🕭 *See RIOM-ÈS-MONTAGNES.*

▷ *D 678 takes you back to Condat, following the opposite side of the Rhue Valley.*

2 Cheylade valleys and Gentiane Country★★

🕭 *See RIOM-ÈS-MONTAGNES.*

3 Belvédère de Veysset and Forêt de Maubert

20km/12.5mi – about 45min

▷ *Leave Condat via the steep, winding D 62 N.*

Belvédère de Veysset

Superb view of Condat and the surrounding countryside.

The road leads to **Montboudif**, birthplace of **Georges Pompidou** (1911-74), who was the President of the French Republic from 1969 to 1974. A **museum** (🕒 *Mid-Jun to mid-Sep: 10am-noon, 2-6pm; Apr to mid-Jun and mid-Sep to Oct: Sat-Sun and holidays 2-6pm. 4€. ☎ 04 71 78 68 68)* is dedicated to his memory.

▷ *Turn left before the church onto D 622 and, a short distance further on, left again onto D 722.*

Forêt de Maubert

The beautiful state-owned Maubert et Gaulis Forest consists of landscaped woodland with a predominance of pines but also beech, lime and a few oaks. The pines and beech grow to remarkable heights and produce prime timber.

▷ *At the junction with D 679 turn right. About 1km/0.6mi further on, turn right onto a very steep forest road. Leave the car and walk on 100m/110yd.*

To the right of the path is the Pierre-et-Paul-Buffault beech tree: it is 44m/144ft tall and its 28m/91ft trunk has a circumference of 2.90m/about 9ft 6in.

▷ *Return to D 679 and turn left towards Condat.*

LA CÔTE-ST-ANDRÉ

POPULATION 4 968
MICHELIN MAP 333: E-5

This small town, a liqueur-producing centre built in a semicircle on a hillside above the Bièvre plain, is the birthplace of *Hector Berlioz* (1803-69). The **Berlioz Festival** is held every year during the second fortnight in August in the covered market and parish church of La Côte-St-André. The Dutch artist **Jongkind** (1819-91), one of the precursors of Impressionism, spent the last years of his life here.

A local lad – Hector Berlioz, the son of a wealthy local doctor, was born in La Côte-St-André in 1803. At the age of 17 he went to Paris to study medicine. He attended lectures but, at the same time, he was a frequent visitor to the opera houses and the library in the Royal Music Academy where, three years later, he began learning composition with Lesueur and Reicha. In 1828 he enjoyed early fame with *Huit Scènes de Faust*. In 1830 he wrote his *Symphonie Fantastique* and won the Grand Prix de Rome.

Thereafter he worked as a music critic in order to earn a living, while at the same time continuing to compose works that brought him success and failure in turn. Among his works were *Requiem, Benvenuto Cellini, Romeo and Juliet, Hungarian March, The Damnation of Faust, The Childhood of Christ* and *The Trojans*.

It was above all in foreign cities that he achieved public recognition – Berlin, Weimar, Vienna, Prague and St Petersburg. He seldom returned to La Côte-St-André. Having failed to win the fame he deserved during his lifetime, Berlioz died in Paris in 1869, but his genius earned him immense posthumous acclaim.

Among European musicians, Berlioz is considered to be the creator of the "symphonic poem", a daring and innovative style of music which, by means of complex orchestration, more flexible rhythmic expression and unexpected combinations of sounds, expressed the aspirations of the Romantic ideal with its enthusiasm for the fantastic and the grandiose. He also left a number of written works, including a *Grand Traité d'Instrumentation et d'Orchestration Moderne*.

Hector Berlioz

J.-L. et M. Bouttier, Musée H.-Berliox, La Côte St-André

Sights

Musée Hector-Berlioz

🕐 *Jun-Sep: daily except Tue 10am-7pm; Oct-May: 10am-6pm.* 🕐 *Closed 1 Jan, 1 May and 25 Dec. Free.* ☎ *04 74 20 24 88. www.musee-hector-berlioz.fr.*
Rue de la République. This museum is housed in the composer's birthplace, a handsome residence built in the late 17C and restored in 1969.

The collection comprises valuable musical scores and early musical instruments, as well as portraits, caricatures, copies of autograph letters and lithographs by Fantin-Latour based on the composer's works. The thematic displays on three floors illustrate the life and works of Berlioz and his place in the history of music. A visit to the kitchen, the dining room, Dr Berlioz' surgery and the room in which Hector was born, introduces the women loved by Berlioz, namely Harriet Smithson, offers a good insight into the Romantic movement and Berlioz's artistic legacy.

Halles

The 13C covered market is striking for its exceptionally large size (29x76m/95x249ft). There are five aisles; note the rafters.

EATING OUT

⊜⊜ **France** – *Pl. de l'Église* - ☎ 04 74 20 25 99. This big pink residence is a bastion of traditional French cooking. Its renowned fare is well appreciated by inhabitants of the region who journey here to savour trout en croûte. A few rooms.

WHERE TO STAY

⊜⊜ **Chambre d'hôte La Ferme des Collines** – *446 r. des Castilles - 38260 Gillonnay* - ☎ *04 74 20 27 93 - mmeyerjulien@aol.fr -* 🚲 *- 5 rms - meals* ⊜⊜. This old farm perched on a hillside facing the vast plain that so inspired Berlioz is the perfect place to come replenish one's batteries. The pleasant rooms are furnished with pieces discovered by the owner, an antique dealer.

▷ *Take the narrow passage des Halles at the far end of the square.*

Note the old houses with timber balconies.

Church

This sanctuary, built between the 11C and 15C, has an interesting belfry of rounded pebbles and brick with white-limestone quoins. Its outline and rich colours often provided the artist Jongkind with inspiration.
Inside, in the Gothic left aisle, note the springers of the fan vaulting on the pillars and, in the chancel, the 18C statue of Christ on the rood screen.

Château Louis XI

Unaccompanied visits of the outside of the chateau all year round.
Built in the 13C for Philip of Savoy on a fine defensive site, this castle was designed as both fortress and residence; it suffered extensive damage during the wars in the 16C but was rebuilt thereafter.
Inside, the Henry Gérard Room (named after the artist Gérard, 1860-1925) boasts a Renaissance fireplace, a set of paintings by the artist and several fine pieces of Provençal furniture.

Le Paradis du chocolat

Kids ⏱ *Guided visits: Sat, Sun, public and school holidays. 6€; unaccompanied visit, please enquire. 3€.*
Chocolate lovers of all ages will enjoy a visit to this temple of chocolate and the delicious creations which they are invited to taste.
The upper terrace offers an extensive **view** of the red roofs of La Côte, the Bièvre plain and the Alps.

Musée des Liqueurs

♿⏱ *Jul to end Sep: daily except Mon and public holidays, 3-6pm. rest of year: Sun and public holidays, 3-6pm.* ⏱ *Closed Jan, Feb, 14 Jul, 15 Aug, 25 Dec. 2.50€.* ☎ *04 74 93 38 10. www.cherryrocher.com.*
The Cherry Rocher company, which was set up in 1705 in a neo-Classical mansion, offers tours of its plant. The museum contains a collection of old machinery (fruit

press, stills, rectifiers, infusers). During the tour of the cellars, note the vast Hungarian oak cask which holds 32 400l/over 7 000gal. Posters and labels advertise liqueurs, brandies and other cordials. At the end of the tour there is a chance to taste one of these liqueurs that have resulted from many years of traditional know-how.

Excursions

Château de Bressieux
8km/3mi S on D 71, then on the narrow road to the left when you leave St-Siméon-de-Bressieux. In the centre of the village, when the road follows a bend, turn left into the small lane (15min on foot there and back). Perched high on a promontory overlooking Bressieux village, the castle ruins make an attractive, picturesque sight.

Marnans
18km/11mi S on D 71, then D 130. Drive through Viriville and take D 156C. This small, unpretentious village on the Chambaran plateau features a fine Romanesque **church.**

Roybon
17km/10.6mi S on D 71. This small town boasts a charming group of buildings with traditional façades characteristic of the area: carved clay and wood decorated with pebbles (note in particular the neo-Romanesque church). This architectural heritage is enhanced by the remains of a medieval rampart. A copy of the Statue of Liberty, which stands at the entrance to New York harbour, offers an unusual contrast.

COURPIÈRE

POPULATION 4 612
MICHELIN MAP 326: I-8 – LOCAL MAP SEE THIERS

The town lies at the entrance to a gorge formed by the River Dore. In addition to its fine church and picturesque houses, Courpière boasts a number of interesting castles in the vicinity and is the ideal starting point of excursions through Livradois country. During the summer season visitors can take the **Livradois-Forez Tourist Train** *(Livradois-Forez tourist railway –*   *See AMBERT)* which runs along the Dore Valley between Courpière and Ambert. The famous designer Coco Chanel spent part of her childhood in Courpière, in the house standing on the corner of rue Desaix and rue Victor-Chamerlat. *Pl. de la Libération, 63120 COURPIÈRE, ☎ 04 73 51 20 27.*

EATING OUT

Les Chênes – *Rte de Piboulet - 63930 Augerolles - 9km/5.4mi SE of Courpière via D 906 and D 42 - ☎ 04 73 53 50 34 - closed early Jul, Christmas school holidays and Sat.* A faithful clientele swears by this restaurant, and rightly so; it offers a convivial welcome, nicely spaced and carefully set tables, and particularly well-prepared traditional fare, cooked by the same family for three generations. Highly recommended!

Old Town

Church★
🕐*Closed Sun.*

This interesting Auvergne-style Romanesque building is topped by a Gothic bell-tower. Walk along the left side of the church to see the east end huddling between old houses. Inside, note the strange capitals on the pillar to the left, at the entrance to the nave; at the transept crossing; and on the stringer of the lower arch at the end of the oven vaulting in the chancel. Other interesting features include a 15C Holy Sepulchre at the end of the right-hand aisle *(the light switch is behind the arch on the right)*, a painting dating from 1585 depicting the Martyrdom of St James the Elder in the north transept and a Romanesque statue of the Virgin Mary made of painted wood in the second chapel in the south aisle.

Near the church, beside the fountain, stands a (restored) Renaissance house.

Excursions

Château d'Aulteribe★
5km/3mi NW along D 223. 🕐*Mid-May to mid-Sep: daily,10am-noon, 2-6.30pm; mid-Sep to mid-May: daily except Mon 10am-noon, 2-5.30pm.* 🕐 *Closed 1 Jan, 1 May, 1 and 11 Nov, 25 Dec. 6.50€.* ☎ *04 73 53 14 55.*

This castle was rebuilt in the 19C in the Romantic style, on the site of an austere medieval construction. Originally the property of the **La Fayette** family, it was purchased in 1775 by Jacques de Pierre. In the 19C, Henriette Onslow and Joseph de Pierre, who were avid collectors of furniture and 17C paintings, bequeathed the estate to the National Historic Monuments Trust.

Inside, note the portrait of Henri IV by Pourbus, the portrait of Richelieu by Philippe de Champaigne and the portrait of **Mademoiselle de Fontanges** painted in the style of Mignard. There are also Louis XV and Louis XVI chairs and items of furniture, and five outstanding Flemish tapestries made to designs by Teniers.

🚶 The **Sentier du Bénitier du Diable** (The Devil's Stoup footpath, *1hr 20min there and back*), starting from the château, offers an insight into the history of the estate.

Château de La Barge
2km/1mi N on D 58 in the direction of Escoutoux. 🕐 *Jul-Aug, Mon-Fri (guided tours: no visit to the interior), 2pm, 3.30pm, 5pm.* 🕐 *May and Sep-Oct. 4€ (children: free)* ☎ *04 73 53 14 51.*

This handsome residence is still circled by its moat. In the 16C the former citadel was converted into a Renaissance château. Two centuries later, it was graced with a terraced garden which its present owners are constantly refurbishing.

Château de Vollore
8km/5mi E along D 7. 🕐 *Jul-Aug: daily, 2-7pm (last admission 45min before closing). 6€ (Children: 4€)* ☎ *04 73 53 71 06.*

This 17C building of pale granite stands on a spur, and is flanked to the south by a large 12C keep and to the north by a 14C tower. Inside, the rooms are sumptuously furnished with paintings, tapestries, furniture and decorative

Vollore

J. Damase/MICHELIN

objects, and mementoes of **General La Fayette** and his involvement in the American War of Independence.

Hikes

Information on the two hikes described below is available from the Parc naturel regional du Livradois-Forez (see Monts du FOREZ).*

Sentier de Saute Ruisseau
7km/4.3mi E of Courpière. Allow 1hr there and back.
This nature trail is a good place to observe **local flora** (yellow iris, meadowsweet) and fauna (crested grebe, woodpecker).

Secret de la Forêt d'Ayguebonne
15km/9.3mi NE of Courpière (Ferme de Naud). Allow 1hr there and back.
This trail invites walkers to discover the **forest vegetation,** natural habitats and silvicultural techniques.

CRÉMIEU

POPULATION 3 169
MICHELIN MAP 333: E-3

Crémieu sits in a narrow valley between fairly rugged hillsides and was once a fortress standing guard over one of the gateways into the Dauphiné region; it was also a busy trading centre. Among the local gastronomic specialities are sabodets (a variety of sausage) and foyesse (a type of cake). *Pl. de la Nation, 38460 CRÉMIEU, ☎ 04 74 90 45 13. www.ville-cremieu.fr*

The Old Quarter

▶ *Start from Porte de la Loi.*

Porte de la Loi
This gateway, once part of the 14C town walls, has a helm roof and machicolations.

▶ *Go through Porte des Augustins.*

IN THE VILLAGE OR ON THE FARM

☞ **Auberge de la Chaite** – *Pl. des Tilleuls* - ☎ *04 74 90 76 63 - closed 22 Apr to 11 May, 20 Dec to 8 Jan, Tue lunch from Oct to Apr, Sun evening and Mon.* Facing the Porte de la Loi, this flowery inn has a big fireplace to warm the dining room in the winter. Beams, country-style furniture and chequered tablecloths round out this standard village stopover.

☞ **Les Basses Portes** – *In Torjonas - 38118 St-Baudille-de-la-Tour -* ☎ *04 74 95 18 23 - www.basses-portes.com -* ☞ *- meals* ☞ This old farm has been extensively remodelled without detracting from its original, pastoral charm. The bedrooms, with their occasionally surprising decor, are a pleasing blend of old and new.

Place de la Nation

The name of this square dates back to the days of the French Revolution. In the north-east corner is a lever-operated well built in 1823.

Hôtel de Ville

&♿🕐 *Daily, 9am-noon, 1.30-5pm (Fri, 4pm, Sat 9am-noon, Sun, 2.30-5.30pm).* 🕐 *Closed public holidays, and Sat, Sun during winter months. No charge.* ☎ *04 74 90 45 13.*

The town hall stands on place de la Nation and is housed in part of what was once an Augustinian friary founded in the 14C. The entrance hall has a coffered ceiling. The doorway on the left leads into the Council Chamber which also has a coffered ceiling; the doorway on the right opens on the Justice of the Peace's Court, once the monks' calefactory. Its pointed vaulting is supported by a central pillar.

Cloisters

The former cloisters *(cloître)* in the Augustinian friary are entered from place de la Nation through a beautiful 18C wrought-iron gate. The gravestones, used as a pavement in the galleries crowned by quadripartite vaulting, were brought here from the church in the late 19C. Some have carvings of craftsmen's tools including the paring knife used by brick-makers or leather tanners. In the south-west corner of the cloisters, on a grid, is the symbol of the Augustinian Order – a heart topped by a flame and pierced by two arrows.

Church

The church was the monastery chapel from 1318 to 1791 and has undergone a number of alterations. The wrought-iron railing from which visitors can see the interior was made by Redersdorff (1982). The furnishings are of particular interest; note the wood panelling on the choir stalls and pulpit, and the wrought-iron railings in the side chapels. Note, too, the geometric form of the pillars, all of them different, and the narrow side aisles with their close quadripartite vaulting.

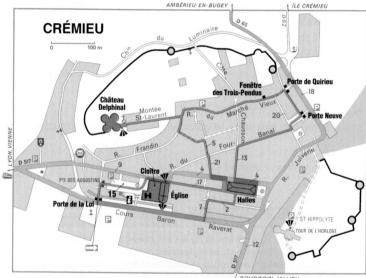

CRÉMIEU					
Adobeurs R. des	2	Loi R. de la	9	Porte Neuve Bd de la	18
Bel R. du Lt-Colonel	4	Moulins Fg des	12	St-Antoine R.	20
Faulchet Côte	5	Mulet R.	13	St-Jean R.	21
Humbert Passage	7	Nation Pl. de la	15		
		Porcherie R.	17		

From the square in front of the church there is a wonderful **view** across to the castle and over the old houses decorated with double or triple eaves.

▶ *Take rue Porcherie to the covered market.*

Halles★
The covered market was built in the 15C. The roof covered in lauzes is supported at each end by a thick wall comprising three arches. Beneath the splendid rafters, note the three aisles, each corresponding to a specific type of trade. At the end on the right are the stone troughs over which the corn measures were once fitted; the grain ran down shoots into sacks.

▶ *Take rue Mulet then turn right onto rue du Four-Banal leading to Porte Neuve.*

Fortified Gateways
Porte Neuve, also known as the François I Gate, was built in the 16C; **Porte de Quirieu,** which has steps and a central gutter, dates from the 14C.

▶ *Head along rue du Marché-Vieux.*

On the right, at no 14, note the 14C Window of the Three Hanged Men (Fenêtre des Trois Pendus).

▶ *Carry on up montée St-Laurent.*

Château Delphinal
⚏ *Not open to the public.* This fortress on St-Laurent hill dates back to the 12C. On the terrace is a chapel dedicated to Notre-Dame-de-la-Salette and from here there is a superb **view** over the stone-slabbed roof of the church and the old monastery. On St-Hippolyte hill to the left are the remains of a 16C fortified Benedictine priory, including the old clock tower *(a footpath on the left leads to a viewing table).*

▶ *Go back down montée St-Laurent; at the bottom turn right and then left onto côte Faulchet.*

At the crossroads with rue du Four-Banal is a 16C house with mullioned windows, the **Maison du Colombier** *(exhibitions).*

▶ *Go down rue St-Jean, rue du Lieutenant-Colonel-Bel and, after skirting the south-west corner of the covered market, rue des Adobeurs.*

This street is lined with tiny low houses that used to contain craft workshops, including those belonging to the town's many tanners.

▶ *Passage Humbert on the left leads to cours Baron-Ravenat.*

As you reach the east end of the church, there is a fine **view** of its hexagonal belfry; the spire rises above one of the old towers in the town walls.

Excursion

If you are tempted by an alternative way of exploring Île Crémieu, apply to Roulottes Dauphiné (Apply directly to this horse-drawn-caravan-hire company, Le Village, 38118 St-Baudille-de-la-Tour, ☎ 04 74 83 86 13). This company hires wagons for the day or horse-drawn caravans for two to seven days.

Île Crémieu: The Land of Stone Roofs

60km/37mi round trip – about 3hr
With its cliffs, lakes, roofs covered in heavy stone slabs known as *lauzes*, fields bordered by standing stones, and country houses, the Île Crémieu region is quite unlike the countryside elsewhere in this area.

▶ *Leave Crémieu on D 52 NE and follow the signs to Optevoz.*

As the road runs up the hill there is a delightful view of Lake Ry and, further up the slope, of the large, modern **Château de St-Julien.**
As the road reaches the plateau there are a number of views of the Bugey area and the Alps.

▶ *Beyond the cool Optevoz basin, follow D 52 as far as Surbaix then turn left on a pleasant little road (D 52⁸) which runs through a valley full of trees and meadows.*

St-Baudille-de-la-Tour

This charming village contains an attractive 15C fortified house, known as the **Maison des Dames,** with a tower covered in lauzes and a porch decorated with a coat of arms; it is the headquarters of Roulottes Dauphiné (see above).

▶ *Drive through Torjonas to D 65 and turn right towards La Balme-les-Grottes.*

La Balme-les-Grottes★

Pleasant village especially known for its grottoes lying at the foot of a cliff marking the edge of the Île Crémieu plateau. The **Grottes de la Balme** *(270 steps –guided visits (1h15)* ◷ *May-Aug: 10am-6pm; Apr and Sep: daily except Mon, 11am, 2-5pm; Feb-Mar and Oct-Dec: Sat, Sun and public holidays, 2-5.30pm.* ◷ *Closed Jan and 25 Dec. 6.50€ (children: 4.50€). ☎ 04 74 90 67 03)* were discovered during the Middle Ages, visited by François I, described as one of the "seven Wonders of Dauphiné", and are said to have been used in the 18C by the infamous brigand Louis Mandrin. A huge porch 40m/131ft high covers two superimposed chapels and leads into a vast chamber, known as the Grande Coupole, filled with rock falls. Several galleries lead from the chamber: the very narrow Mandrin Gallery on the left leads to the balcony of the same name, high above the entrance to the cave; the Lake Gallery skirts a

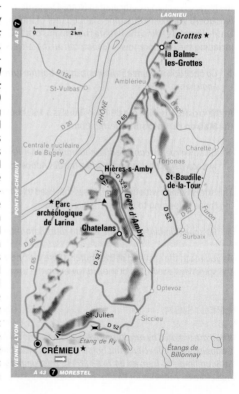

series of small **pools**★★ forming terraces of waterfalls before reaching the underground torrent. A climb up into the area known as the "Upper Cave" where the concretions are particularly numerous brings visitors to the François I Gallery, a veritable labyrinth that leads to a balcony some 30m/98ft above the river bed at the entrance to the cave.

▶ *Turn back along D 65 then take the first on the left, to Hières-sur-Amby.*

Hières-sur-Amby
This tiny village stands at the end of the Amby Valley, at the foot of the Larina plateau. Below the church is the former rectory, dating from the 18C and with a stone-slabbed roof, which is now the **Maison du Patrimoine** (Montée de la Cure – ◷ *Guided visit (2h): Apr-Oct: 2-6pm; Nov-Mar: 2-6pm, but closed Sat-Sun and public holidays. 4€ (12-18, 2€)* ☏ *04 74 95 19 10*). This modern museum houses objects discovered during archaeological digs at Larina *(see below)* including bones, tools, coins and jewellery, and includes a model of a Merovingian farm. Models, videos and a display retrace the origins of the people living in Île Crémieu, and present examples of popular arts, crafts and traditions.
Special effects reconstruct the tomb, found under a tumulus, of a Celtic prince (8C) which was discovered in July 1987 at St-Romain-de-Jalionas. Treasures recovered from the tomb include gold jewellery (torque, bracelet, pin) and the oldest iron knife found in Europe.
If you have time to spare, follow D 65C towards the Château du Cinglé. The drive is pleasant and, on the way, you will see some fine houses roofed with stone slabs *(lauzes)*.

▶ *Drive through Hières-sur-Amby and turn left onto D 52A.*

Gorges d'Amby
The river twists and turns along the foot of rocks covered here and there with scrubby vegetation. There is a view of the 15C Brotel fortified house on the cliff.

▶ *A narrow road off to the right opposite an old cement works crosses the River Amby and runs up a steep hill to Chatelans.*

Chatelans
At the centre of the village is the **Musée de la Lauze** (♿◷ *Daily except Tue 9am-7pm.* ◷ *Closed Jan. No charge.* which explains the traditional techniques in this region for cutting and fitting the stone slabs.
The road to Siccieu provides a number of picturesque views of the Alps.

▶ *In the centre of the village, turn right onto a narrow road that runs for 2.5km/1.5mi to the tip of the plateau, where the Larina archaeological site is located.*

Parc Archéologique de Larina★
Signposted tours and information panels.
The Larina site covers an area of 21ha/52 acres. To the north and west it is bordered by the cliffs overlooking the Rhône plain and Amby Valley; to the south and east by a stone rampart almost 1km/0.6mi long. The existence of human settlements on this site has been evidenced by objects dating from the Neolithic Era (c 3000 BC). From the 5C to the 1C BC, an oppidum (settlement) stood here. Within its walls were huts made of timber or wattle and daub. The discovery of an altar and huge blocks of foundation stone confirmed the existence here in Roman times of a temple dedicated to the god Mercury. Stone quarries were also worked at this period, to provide slabs for roofing. A working face to the north of the main dwelling shows

the structure of the subsoil in Larina, consisting of gritty limestone strata that were easy to cut into flagstones.

At the end of the Roman era and in the early days of the Dark Ages, two large farms existed in succession on this spot. The earlier one (4C and 5C) had a villa at its centre and included a number of farm buildings made of earth and timber over stone foundations that are still clearly visible. From the 6C to 8C a second farm developed around a large stone-built house with a stone-slabbed roof and various outbuildings. On the hillock to the north were two graveyards. In the second one, graves have been uncovered; the dead were buried in coffins made of stone slabs.

From the northernmost tip of the cliff, where there is a statue of the Virgin Mary, there is a superb **view** of the Bugey and Dombes hills, the Beaujolais and Lyonnais mountains, the Feyzin flares and Mont Pilat. In the foreground the view includes the River Rhône and the Bugey nuclear power station.

▶ *Return to Chatelans and follow D 52ⁱ back to Crémieu.*

CREST

POPULATION 7 739
MICHELIN MAP 332: D-5

The town of Crest, situated at the spot where the River Drôme flows into the Valence plain, is particularly proud of its castle keep. The town has grown up around it, with a dual role as market town and a community specialising in food processing. Among the many local gastronomic specialities are *défarde*, a stew made with lamb's feet and tripe, and *picodons*, small goats' cheeses. ⬛ *Pl. du Dr-Maurice-Rozier, 26400 CREST, ☎ 04 75 25 11 38. www.crest-tourisme.com.*

The international **Crest Jazz Festival** takes place every year in August.

A Formidable Keep

Steps up to the keep
Access via steps left of the church of St-Sauveur, up rue du Vieux-Gouvernement and along rue de la Tour. The base of the tower can be reached by car (parking area).

Keep★
184 steps to the upper terrace. ◔ *May to mid-Sep: 10am-7pm; Feb-Apr and mid-Sep to end Oct: 2-6pm; rest of year: Sat-Sun, 2-6pm.* ◔ *Closed January and 25 Dec. 5€ (Children: 2.50€).☎ 04 75 25 32 53.*

The keep in Crest, also known as the "Tower", is all that remains of a fortress which was dismantled in 1633 on the orders of Louis XIII. The keep was erected over Roman foundations on a spur of rock, in various stages between the 11C and the 15C. The north wall, the tallest of the four, reaches a height of almost 52m/169ft; the base of the tower lies at an altitude of 263m/855ft.

The various dungeons and vaulted chambers inside house thematic exhibitions and shows are staged in season. In 1851 the dungeons were used to imprison 600 Republicans who opposed Louis-Napoleon's *coup d'état* (note the graffiti).

The first terrace has a floor of huge stone slabs, all carefully bonded and all sloping down to a central gutter which took rainwater down into the reservoir. The roof, which was added in the 15C, is supported by huge arches and enormous rafters.

From the upper terrace there is a view over the rooftops of Crest and beyond, in a superb **panoramic view**★ to the north-east over Glandasse Mountain and the outcrops of the Vercors, and to the south over the Roche-Courbe range with the Trois-Becs, and Roche Colombe further in the distance. To the west the horizon is broken up by the long narrow ridge of the Vivarais area rising to the Gerbier-de-Jonc and Mézenc, both of which are visible in clear weather.

▶ *At the bottom of rue de la Tour, on walking down to the town from the keep, fork right and follow the hilltop path that runs round the east end of the old Franciscan church (Église des Cordeliers).*

Further down the hill, on the left, are a few steps leading to a vaulted alleyway. This is the five-arched **Portique des Cordeliers** which opens onto the monumental **Escalier des Cordeliers.** With its 124 steps, 80 of which have been carved directly into the rock, this is an impressive sight, especially when seen from below.

Old houses

Along the main thoroughfare and the picturesque neighbouring streets are some of the vast mansions built for the wealthy bourgeoisie in Crest in the 16C and 17C. There are entrances with bossages at no 11 rue des Cuiretteries, in Rue des Boucheries just before the vaulted alleyway leading to rue de l'Hôtel-de-Ville, and at no 2 place du Général-de-Gaulle.

At no 10 rue de la République the rounded entrance includes a keystone carved with foliage; at no 14 the frontage is decorated with three heads in high relief.

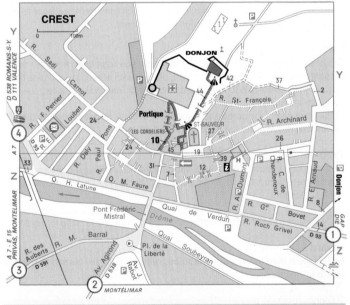

CREST			Dr.-A.-Ricateau Av.	Z	14	Remparts Ch. des	Y	37
			Gaulle Pl. du Gén.-de	YZ	19	République R. de la	YZ	39
			Hôtel-de-Ville R. de	Y	24	Saboury R. de	Y	42
Barbèyère Mtée de la	Y	2	Jourbernon Cours de	Y	26	Tour R. de la	Y	44
Boucheries R. des	Z	7	Julien Pl.	Y	27	Vieux		
Calade R. de la	Z	8	Long R. M.	Z	31	Gouvernement R. du	Y	45
Cordeliers Esc. des	Y	10	Pied Gai Quai	Z	33			
Cuiretteries R. des	Z	12						

Excursions

Jardin des Oiseaux

In Upie, 11km/6.7mi N. Leave Crest on D 538 towards Chabeuil, then take D 142 to the left. Kids ♿ *Jul-Aug: 10am-7pm; Sep-Jun: 10am to dusk. 10€ (children: 6€).* ☎ *04 75 84 45 90. www.jardin-aux-oiseaux.com*

Crest keep

This superb **Bird Sanctuary** is home to over 200 different European and exotic species: humming-birds, crested grebes, flamingoes, pelicans, ostriches, parrots etc. A fascinating **Tropical House** allows these brightly coloured birds to be viewed in a simulation of their natural habitat.

The park contributes, together with other European centres, to the protection and breeding of endangered species. In summer, there are shows involving various species and pony rides for children.

The Hills of Drôme★

Leave Crest to the E on D 93. At Aouste-sur-Sye, cross the Drôme heading for Saoû. After the narrow Lauzens pass, the road climbs to a **cirque**★ *closed off by the* **Trois-Becs** *of Roche-Courbe.*

▶ *At the entrance to the Pertuis gorge through which flows the Vèbre, leave to your left the private road running through the Saoû Forest.*

Forêt de Saoû

This private property is a listed site open to the public, except on certain days during the hunting season. This handsome forest, planted with beech, oak and pine trees, features in its centre a 1930 folly based on the Petit Trianon in Versailles, commissioned by a wealthy Alsatian.

At the other end of the gorge, there is a fine view of the isolated "Rock" to the left; the Rochers des Aiguilles can be seen to the right.

Saoû

This small village is overshadowed by the looming hills marking the entrance to the nearby forest. Saoû is famous for its *picodon* goat's cheese, which has now entered the AOC category.

▶ *In Saoû, take D 538 then soon afterwards D 136 on the left, heading for Soyans.*

Soyans

The village is dominated by the imposing ruins of its castle, burned during the French Revolution.

▶ *Continue on D 136, then take D 6 towards Puy-St-Martin. Take D 107 to Roynac and its old village, then to Col du Devès. Turn left onto D 105, heading for Col de Tartaiguille and Marsanne.*

The drive down offers pretty views of the valley and the outskirts of Marsanne.

Marsanne

This locality was the home town of **Émile Loubet,** President of the French Republic between 1899 and 1906. The vestiges of its medieval past are still visible on their rocky outcrop. Located north of the village, in a clearing of Marsanne Forest, the **Chapelle Notre-Dame-de-Fresneau** has become a popular place of pilgrimage since the 12C.

▶   *Take D 57 to Mirmande.*

Mirmande

Leave the car at the foot of the village. The pretty houses of this former fortified village spread out over the slopes of a hill. Towards 1930, the painter **André Lhote** (1885-1962) came to settle here and many contemporary artists followed in his footsteps, won over by the charm of the area. The climb up to the **Église Ste-Foy** (12C) affords fine views of the Rhône Valley and the Monts du Vivarais.

▶   *Take N 7 to the N until you reach Livron-sur-Drôme. Go towards Allex on D 93A.*

Allex, Aquarium Tropical du Val-de-Drôme

Kids & ○ *Jul to mid-Sep: daily, 10am-7pm; mid-Sep to end Jun, 1.30-6pm.* ○ *Closed 1 Jan and 25 Dec. 6.50€ (4-15-year-olds: 5€).* ☎ *04 75 62 62 11. www.aquarium-des-tropiques.com*
Nature lovers will enjoy visiting this aquarium which presents a variety of freshwater fish usually found in tropical climes (Madagascar and the great lakes in Africa, Central America, Asia and Amazonia).

▶   *Return to Crest on D 93.*

LA DOMBES★

MICHELIN MAP 328: C-4 TO D-5

The Dombes plateau, situated between Lyon and Bourg-en-Bresse and bordered by the River Ain and the River Saône, owes its unusual appearance and its particular charm to the presence of over 1 000 lakes dotted across its entire area. Here and there are low hills, formed by moraine, which were transformed in the Middle Ages into veritable earth fortresses surrounded by moats. Rural housing in the Dombes region is built mainly of cob (*pisé*) whereas the castles and outer walls are built of rough red bricks known as *carrons* (terracotta). The region's history, too, is somewhat out of the ordinary. Dombes was raised to the rank of a principality by François I following the confiscation of the property belonging to the Constable of Bourbon in 1523. A sovereign Parliament sat in Trévoux, its main town, and continued to sit until the mid-18C.

Geographical Notes

The impermeable soil encouraged local people very early on in their history to turn their fields into lakes enclosed by mud dikes. The **Grand Étang de Birieux,** one of the most extensive of the lakes (330ha/815 acres) but now subdivided, dates from the 14C. In the Middle Ages lakes were popular with the nobility because they required little upkeep and, consequently, only a reduced work force. In the 16C Dombes boasted almost 2 000 stretches of water. The excessive number of lakes filled with stagnant water led to an unhealthy climate, however; average life expectancy in Dombes was very low in the days leading up to the French Revolution. In the 19C, thanks to the work instigated by the monks of the abbey of Notre-Dame-des-Dombes, the area of water was decreased by 50%. The land reclaimed in this way was given over to crops.

Nowadays, water still covers an area of approximately 10 000ha/24 711 acres. Most of the lakes are intermittent, one being emptied to fill another: they are filled with water and stocked with fish for a period of six or seven years; they are then drained – using a system of posts to facilitate the operation – and for one year turned over to agriculture. Fishing produces some 2 000t of fish per year (pike, tench, and roach), making this one of the most important lake fishing centres in France: it is well worth an angling trip here in autumn.

The Dombes region is a major producer of milk and beef; the breeding of cross-bred horses is a traditional activity here and it is not unusual to see horses up to their withers in the water of the lakes grazing on brouille, a sort of marsh clover of which they are particularly fond. Stock breeding is complemented by the cultivation of cereal crops (wheat, oats, maize) and oil-producing crops (oilseed rape). Dombes, which lies between the Bresse, Lyon and Beaujolais areas, has gained a solid reputation for good food. Waterfowl is to be found here in abundance.

Excursion

Tour of the Lakes★

Round trip of 99km/61mi from Villars-les-Dombes – allow one day

▶ *Leave Villars on D 2 heading W.*

Bouligneux
In a setting typical of this area stands a 14C brick-built **castle** that looks rather more like a fortress.

Sandrans
This village is known for its medieval earth fortress on which a large house was built in the 19C. Today a hillock remains, clearly visible, surrounded by a moat and crowned

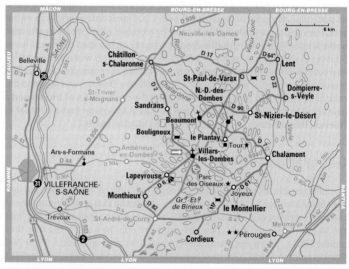

Address Book

EATING OUT

🍴🍴🍴 **Auberge des Bichonnières** – *Rte d'Ars - 01330 Ambérieux-en-Dombes - 11km/6.6mi W of Villars-les-Dombes via D 904 -* ☎ *04 74 00 82 07 - www.aubergedesbichonnieres.com - closed 15 Dec to 15 Jan, Mon and Tue lunch - reserv. required.* An old smallholding characteristic of the farms of the Vallée de la Dombes offers regional specialities presented in fixed-price menus for your pleasure. Seating on the terrace in fine weather.

WHERE TO STAY

🏠🏠 **Chambre d'hôte de Bosseron** *– 325 rte de Genève - 01160 Neuville-sur-Ain - 8km/4.8mi NE of Pont-d'Ain on N 84 -* ☎ *04 74 37 77 06 - arivoire.free.fr - closed Nov-Feb -* 🚫 *- 4 rms.* A lovely setting along the Ain for this property with a personality of its own: hushed atmosphere, carefully chosen furnishings and harmonious colours throughout. Practical, suitably comfortable bedrooms and bathrooms with all the fixtures.

with a round tower built of brick. Albeit plain, the part-Romanesque **church** is one of the most characteristic sanctuaries in the Dombes area. It has a single nave and an apse decorated with Romanesque blind arcading in which the strange shuttle-shaped pilasters bear elongated human figures. There is a rood beam at the entrance to the chancel. Note the statuary and the Gothic font.

Châtillon-sur-Chalaronne – 👌 *See CHÂTILLON-SUR-CHALARONNE.*

▶ *Leave Châtillon E on D 17 towards St-Paul-de-Varax.*

St-Paul-de-Varax
The Romanesque **church** dates back to the 12C. Its west front has fine stonework and blind arcades. The tympanum above the central door shows Christ in Majesty between two angels. A frieze running above the arcading shows the life of the Apostle St Paul and the Last Judgement. The transept crossing is topped by a dome. St-Paul-de-Varax also boasts one of the prettiest manor houses in the Dombes region (🔒 *not open to the public*).

▶ *Drive N along N 83 then turn right onto D64ᴬ.*

Lent
The village still boasts fine 16C monuments: the church belfry (restored in the 18C) and some timber houses. The origins of the Romanesque church here date back to the 9C though its current architecture dates from the 16C.

Dompierre-sur-Veyle
This village grouped around a Romanesque church is near the largest lake in the area (100ha/247 acres): **Le Grand Marais.**

▶ *The D 70 road heading west to St-Nizier passes to the right of various stretches of water which are extensions of Le Grand Marais.*

St-Nizier-le-Désert
This pleasant village offers facilities for fishing and gentle rambles.

▶ *Follow D 90 which crosses N 83 and leads to Marlieux. Drive through the village and join D 7. Just after a bend, take a small road towards Beaumont.*

Le Plantay Tower

Beaumont

The **Chapelle Notre-Dame de Beaumont** (🕐 *guided tours possible, by appointment. 10am-noon, 2-6pm* ☎ *04 74 42 86 35)* stands on the lovely village square. This chapel was once a popular centre of pilgrimage but subsequently fell into a state of disrepair. Recent restoration work has revealed the presence of splendid 15C **frescoes**★ which have been very well preserved.

▶ *Turn back along the small road on which you arrived to the first intersection. The road branching off to the right goes through the hamlet of Villardières, crosses N 83 and leads to Le Plantay.*

Le Plantay

The village is surrounded by the waters of the Grand Châtel. The **tower**★ here (⊶ *not open to the public)*, of large red bricks and decorated with white stone around the machicolations, is a symbol for the region.

Abbaye Notre-Dame-des-Dombes

Monks from this abbey, founded by Cistercians in the 19C, helped to drain the area and cultivated those sections of land which are fertile. The abbey was awarded the Legion of Honour for its heroic contribution to the Resistance movement during the Second World War. In 2001, monks from the Chemin Neuf order took over from the Cistercians.

Chalamont

Alt 334m/1 095ft. This is the highest point in La Dombes. Rue des Halles is lined with a few old houses (15C but restored) with overhanging upper storeys, and a former wash-house.

▶ *Take D 61 to Joyeux.*

There is an attractive 19C house in Joyeux.

▶ *The castle at Le Montellier comes into view on the right.*

Le Montellier

The brick-built **castle** (o⊷ *not open to the public*), the most impressive in La Dombes, is flanked at one end by a keep rising on its earth mound. The village church, of Gothic origin, contains a fine 18C carved altarpiece.

Cordieux

A handsome red-brick manor house stands here.

▶ *Rejoin D 4 and turn left (W) to St-André-de-Corcy; take D 82 to Monthieux.*

Monthieux

The attractive red-brick Romanesque church contains the tombs of the local seigneurs. Breuil manor house (16C), just north of the village, has an interesting Saracen well.

▶ *Head towards Ambérieux-en-Dombes and turn right onto D 6.*

Lapeyrouse

From the war memorial there is a delightful view of the Alps and, in the foreground, the Grand Glareins lakes and the 15C Château de Glareins *(private)*.

▶ *Take D 904 back to Villars.*

MONTS DÔME★★★

MICHELIN MAP 326: D-8 TO E-9

The range of volcanic cones known as the *Chaine des Puys* or *Dôme mountain range* rises to the west of Clermont-Ferrand and stands high above the Limagne plain. Some 80 extinct volcanoes, which look almost as they did when they were active, stretch in a line over a distance of some 40km/25mi *(see Introduction: Volcanoes of the Auvergne).*

From the summit of the Puy de Dôme, the highest of the "cones" with an altitude of 1 465m/4 806ft, the view extends right across the range, over this extraordinary and magnificent landscape.

▶ **Orient Yourself:** The most splendid way of getting an idea of the landscape is to take the shuttle service from Clermont-Ferrand railway station to the Puy de Dôme (⦿ *see Address Book*), or you can simply drive the toll road to the summit.

🅿 **Parking:** Near the summit

🄺🄸🄳🅂 **Especially for Kids:** Vulcania theme park (⦿ *see Parc Européen du Volcanisme VULCANIA*)

⦿ **Also See:** Puy de Pariou - two volcanoes for the price of one!

Geological formation – The Dôme mountain range has the youngest volcanoes in the Auvergne. They came into being in the Quaternary Era and the earliest human settlers may have witnessed their eruptions. The cones, which rise up from the plain in a long string, stand on a plateau of crystalline rocks 900-1 000m/2 950-3 280ft high. Most of the volcanoes rise by only 200-300m/655-985ft above this plateau, with the exception of the Puy de Dôme which rises to 500m/1 640ft above it. These extinct volcanoes are not all the same shape. Several of them, such as the Puy de Dôme, are shaped like bells or domes; others contain a single or double crater, whereas a few have a breached crater. Some of the hillsides are covered only with short grass or moorland but many are wooded. Areas of forest grew naturally but much of it has been planted since the Count of Montlosier set the first example in the early 19C, showing that forests could be grown on land thought of as barren – he was initially taken for a fool. Long black lava flows known as cheires form heaps of rocks dotted with juniper and pines; they are scattered all across the plateau. One of these flows, created by the Puy de Lassolas and the Puy de la Vache, closed off the Veyre Valley and created Lake Aydat.

The Land Of Volcanoes

1 Le Puy de Dôme★★★

11km/7mi from Royat – ♿ *see ROYAT. 1hr on foot there and back.*

The ascent of the Puy de Dôme and the extraordinary panorama visible from the summit, best seen at sunset, are quite unforgettable.

This former volcano is the oldest, the highest (alt 1 465m/4 806ft) and the most famous of the Dôme mountain range, of which it is the centre.

Although more than 1 000m/3 280ft above Clermont, it is barely 500m/1 640ft above the plateau on which it stands. It was only in 1751 that the volcanic origin of these mountains was recognised; until then, it was believed that they were part of gigantic fortifications built by the Romans.

Atmospheric phenomena – During the cold season, a "temperature inversion" often occurs: while the weather in Clermont might be bitterly cold, it might be almost mild on the Dôme. On the 26 December 1879, at 6am, a temperature of -16°C/+3°F was recorded at Clermont and +4°C/+39°F at the top of the Puy de Dôme. This phenomenon, which only occurs during calm weather, is caused by the heavier layers of cold air gradually sinking down into the depression below.

It is for a similar reason that a magnificent "sea of clouds" can sometimes be seen from the Puy de Dôme. While the Limagne plain disappears under a thick carpet of fog, the surrounding mountains emerge like sparkling islands in the sun. This phenomenon mainly occurs in autumn (particularly in November).

Chaine des Puys, Puy de Dôme in the background

J. Damase/MICHELIN

Address Book

SHUTTLE SERVICE

There is a shuttle service between Clermont-Ferrand railway station and the Puy de Dôme or Vulcania (Parc européen du volcanisme): *5€ (5-16 year-olds: 2.50€).* Another shuttle runs between the Puy de Dôme and Vulcania: *1.50€.* ☎ *0 800 500 524 (toll free). Timetable available from the Tourist office in Clermont (☎ see CLERMONT-FERRAND).*

GUIDED TOURS

Free guided tours *(daily from 15 Jun to 15 Sep.* ☎ *04 73 62 21 45)* and free guided rambles *(Jul and Aug; to put your name down:* ☎ *04 73 65 64 00)* are organised by the Information Centre of the Volcans d'Auvergne nature park *(see Parc naturel regional des VOLCANS D'AUVERGNE).*

EATING OUT

☺ **La Fourniale** – *63210 Riom - 3km/1.8mi NW of Randanne via N 89 -* ☎ *04 73 87 16 63 - closed Mon-Tue Sep-Jun, 3 wks in Sep and 15 days early Jan - reserv. required off-season.* Aficionados of authentic Auvergnat cuisine frequent this inn housed in an ex-sheepfold. The setting is as rustic as can be, with wood tables and a stone trough protruding from the wall. Fresh produce and one house speciality, la truffade, a local potato and melted cheese dish.

☺ **Le Village Auvergnat** – *La Font-de-l'Arbre - at the base of the Puy de Dôme - 63870 Orcines -* ☎ *04 73 62 25 34 - closed Mon-Thu evenings off-season - reserv. required.* Located at the foot of the Puy de Dôme among a small hamlet's modern residences, this restaurant serves regional specialities.

☺☺ **Auberge de la Moreno** – *Col de la Moreno - 63122 St-Genès-Champanelle - intersection of D 941 and D 52, on the peak -* ☎ *04 73 87 16 46 - aubergemoreno@wanadoo.fr - closed first 2 wks of Jan and last 2 wks of Nov.* This small inn appeals to diners in search of authenticity, offering satisfying '100% regional' dishes such as truffade, tripoux cantalous (tripe), locally cured ham, stuffed pigs' trotters, Puy lentils, and mountain char (omble chevalier). Spacious, recently appointed rooms.

☺☺ **Le Mont Fraternité** – *Atop the Puy de Dôme - 63870 Orcines -* ☎ *04 73 62 23 00 - closed Nov-Mar - 21.50/35€.* For a meal with an incomparable view, try this fine establishment atop the much-visited Puy de Dôme, the 'Roof of Auvergne'. Daytime diners can board the shuttle to the peak and take their time admiring the splendid panorama, however, in the evenings, you'll need to find other means of transportation. Prices are lower with the fixed brasserie menu, available until 2:30pm.

WHERE TO STAY

☺ **Chambre d'hôte Chez Mme Gauthier Jocelyne** – *Recoleine - 63210 Riom - 3km/1.8mi NW of Randanne via N 89 -* ☎ *04 73 87 10 34 - gauthier.jocelyne@free.fr - closed from 15 Nov to 1 Feb -* ⌿ *- reserv. required off-season - 3 rms.* A warm reception awaits you in this former barn neighbouring the Puy de Dôme mountain range and set in a tranquil and natural environment. The pleasant rooms are comfortable and well-kept, making for a very agreeable sojourn.

☺ **Chambre d'hôte Chez M. Bony** – *Bravant - 63210 Olby - 2km/1.2mi N of Les Quatre-Routes dir. Ussel and secondary road -* ☎ *04 73 87 12 28 - closed 15 Nov-15 Feb -* ⌿ *- 5 rms.* This tastefully renovated farm is located in the heart of a charming village. The comfortable bedrooms (two with mezzanines), kitchen and spacious living-cum-dining room with a fireplace make it an excellent starting point for discovering the puys. Maps and advice on request.

RECREATION

Air-passion-Parapente – *4 pl. St-Jean - 63210 Riom -* ☎ *06 70 00 42 39 - closed Oct-Mar.* Come jump off the Puy de Dôme and soar like a bird above the splendid landscapes of the Parc des Volcans d'Auvergne. Paragliding classes for beginners and seasoned jumpers in a magnificent setting with a 500m/1650ft drop. First flights with two-person parachutes available.

The Michelin Grand Prix

In 1908, when Henri Farman was making the first circular flight (1km/0.6mi) in the world, the Michelin brothers offered a Grand Prix of 100 000 francs to any aviator who could fly from Paris, with a 75kg/165lb passenger on board, to the top of the Puy de Dôme in less than 6hr, skirting the cathedral of Clermont by 1 500m/4 921ft on their right. Only three years later, on 7 March 1911, despite predictions that this feat could not possibly be achieved within less than a half a century, the aviator **Eugène Renaux**, with his passenger Senouque, successfully met the prescribed conditions in just 5hr 11min.

Sacred Mountain – From the earliest times the solitude of this Puy, which is so difficult to get to, has been awe-inspiring. The Gauls made it a sanctuary for their god Lug. The Romans replaced it with the cult of "Mercury of the Dome". They built a magnificent temple to him, the foundations of which were discovered in 1872 during construction of the first observatory. This temple and all its treasures were destroyed by the Barbarian invasions. A Christian sanctuary replaced it.

In the 12C a small chapel, a site of pilgrimage, was dedicated to St Barnabas, one of St Paul's companions. It was very popular for many centuries, then fervour began to wane and the chapel disappeared in the 18C.

According to popular superstition, all the sorcerers of the Auvergne meet on the deserted mountain top for blood-curdling midnight revels.

The weight of air – It is on the Puy de Dôme that **Blaise Pascal** carried out the experiment in 1648 which proved the theory about the weight of air. It had already been noted that mercury rises to about 76cm/30in in a tube in which a vacuum has been created. To explain this phenomenon, it was said that "nature hates vacuums". This axiom however did not satisfy Torricelli; he put forward the hypothesis that it is the weight of the air that pushes the mercury up.

Captivated by this idea, Pascal thought that, if this were the case, the weight of the air should be less at the top of a mountain. As Pascal was in Paris, he asked his brother-in-law to help. The latter chose a fine day, left a mercury barometer in Clermont and went with the Minimes Fathers to the top of the Puy de Dôme. He was overjoyed to see that the mercury rose 8.4cm/3.40in less than it did in Clermont. The theory about the weight of the air had been proven.

Puy-de-Dôme rather than Mont-Dore – In 1790, following the Revolution, administrative *départements* replaced the former provinces in France. There was talk of giving the name Mont-d'Or (Golden Mountain) – as Mont-Dore was then spelled – to the Lower Auvergne constituency, but the deputy for Clermont, Gaultier de Beauzat, was alarmed that such a wealthy sounding name would give the wrong impression to outsiders. He asked for the less compromising name of Puy-de-Dôme, and it was accepted.

Grotte du Puy de Dôme

♿ ⏱ *Mid-Apr to Sep: guided tours (30min) 10am-7pm. 5€ (children: 3.50€).* ☏ 04 73 62 17 41.

A subterranean gallery in a lava flow from the Petit Puy de Dôme has been opened up for visitors. Glass cases attractively present a rock collection from the Auvergne as well as throughout the world. A working stonecutter's workshop completes the visit.

Ascent via the toll road

⏱ *Open to traffic (depending on weather conditions): 7am-9.30pm (mid-Jun to end Aug, 7am-10pm). 5€ (cars), 3€ (motorcycles). May-Sep: road reserved for cyclists Wed and*

Le Puy de Dôme

Sun morning from 7-8.30am (including the descent). Access is prohibited to pedestrians and two-wheeled vehicles with an engine capacity of less than 125cc. ☎ *04 73 62 12 18 (toll) - 04 73 62 21 46 (reception centre Apr-Oct).*
May-Jun and Sep: shuttle service Sat-Sun and public holidays 12.30-6pm, Jul-Aug: shuttle service daily 10am-6pm. Return, 3.50€ (children: 1.40€).

In 1926 this road replaced the tracks used by the miniature steam train which had operated for about 20 years. The road, which is well designed, has a constant slope of 12% for about 4km/2.5mi. As it spirals around the Dôme it offers a wonderful variety of views, becoming more extensive higher up. As the road comes out of the woods on the lower part of the mountain it cuts through domite, a white porous volcanic rock, which can be seen wherever the surface layer has been weathered away.

The first ascent on bicycle took place in 1891 in 28min; in 1913 a high-powered car reached the summit for the first time, in just 11min.

Ascent on foot via the Roman road
Allow 2hr there and back.

Park at Ceyssat pass (alt 1 078m/3 536ft) in a forest of fir trees. It was up this winding path (35-40% slopes) that chariots pulled by five to eight tandem-driven horses transported the materials needed to build the Roman temple and subsequently, in the 19C, the observatory.

The Summit

Reception and Information Centre
🕐 *Apr-Jun and Sep: 10am-6pm, Sat-Sun and public holidays 10am-7pm; Jul-Aug: 9am-7pm; Oct: 10am-6pm. No charge.* ☎ *04 73 62 21 46.*
This houses a display on volcanoes and exhibitions specifically on the Puy de Dôme and on various other sites of interest to be explored in the locality.

A footpath leads around the television transmitter to two viewing tables.

Note the stone commemorating Pascal's experiment set into the main façade of the television building.

Panorama★★★

To the north and south, over a distance of about 30km/19mi, can be seen the 100 or so extinct volcanoes forming the Dôme mountain range, a marvellous museum of volcanic shapes, a lunar landscape unique in France and perhaps in the world.

To the north can be clearly distinguished volcanoes of the same origin as the Puy de Dôme which resemble enormous craterless molehills: Petit Suchet, Clierzou and Sarcouy. The others are all cones of debris topped with craters: Petit Puy de Dôme or Nid de la Poule ("Hen's Nest"), Grand Suchet, Puy de Côme, Pariou, Louchadière.

All the volcanoes to the south have craters: Monchier, Barme, Laschamp, Mercœur etc. On the horizon rises the Dore mountain range. The east overlooks the Limagne with its myriad of towns, villages, fields, hillsides and isolated peaks. In the distance, the heights of Livradois and Forez border the plain. To the west lie the soft contours of the hills of the Limousin plateau.

The view extends over 11 *départements*, one eighth of the total surface area of France. Visibility varies almost from one minute to the next, depending on the clouds and fog. The puys may be covered with grass or heath, with fir-groves or hazel copses. The chain itself is uninhabited as any rain which falls soaks into the volcanic rocks. In summer, flocks from the plateau graze on the Puys but since there is no water, they all return to the stable at night.

It is at sunset that the view is most spectacular. Fiery trails weave through the volcanic cones. The mountain throws its shadow to the east, covering first the Orcines plateau then suddenly reaching Clermont before gradually invading the plain: the extreme tip of its shadow goes right to Thiers.

Temple of Mercury

☞ *No access at present.* This beautiful Temple to the God Mercury (now a ruin) was built by the Romans. Originally it was twice the size of the famous Maison Carrée (1C AD) in Nîmes; 50 sorts of marble were used to decorate it. The television transmitter stands on the original site of a monumental bronze statue of Mercury by the Greek sculptor Zenodorus. It was, according to Pliny the Elder, one of the marvels of the ancient world. On the upper terrace of the ruins can be seen the square base of the sanctuary or *cella*.

The path winds around the ruins and passes in front of the monument recalling Renaux's exploit. It is just below this monument that daring adepts of hang-gliding and paragliding sometimes hurl themselves into empty space.

Excursion

② The Puys Mountain Range★★★

120km/75mi round trip – allow one day

Royat★★ – ♿ *See ROYAT.*

▶ *Leave Royat on D 941C SE then turn right onto D 5.*

The road climbs above the plain until it reaches the granite base from which the volcanic cones rise.

Puy de Gravenoire

There are pozzolana quarries here. This old volcano, now clothed in pine forests, juts out from above the great Limagne fault. Its lava flowed down through the fault towards Royat and Beaumont, then the cone was formed from the materials thrown up during the eruption: ash, scoria and volcanic bombs.

At the top of the rise is the village of **Charade** at the foot of its own extinct volcano, the **Puy de Charade** (👝 *see ROYAT*).

The road then runs along the southern section of the **Clermont-Ferrand-Charade Racing Circuit.** Follow the road through Thèdes and St-Genès-Champanelle and, in Theix, take N 89 which crosses the lava flow at Aydat.

Cheire d'Aydat

This is a lava flow 6km/4mi long and 1 200m/3 937ft wide. It was thrown up by the Lassolas and La Vache volcanoes, and cooled to form a heap of blackened scoria. The desolation of this volcanic landscape is softened to some extent by juniper bushes, broom, birch trees and, on the shores of Lake Aydat for which the lava flow forms a dam, a forest of pines and spruces planted in the second half of the 19C.

▷ *Just beyond Col de la Ventouse, turn right onto D 5 towards Murol and right again along D 788. At the junction turn right towards Randanne.*

On the way to Randanne the road skirts the Puy de Combegrasse where the first gliding competition to be staged in France was held in 1922.

▷ *From Randanne, D 5 leads to the Puy de la Vache.*

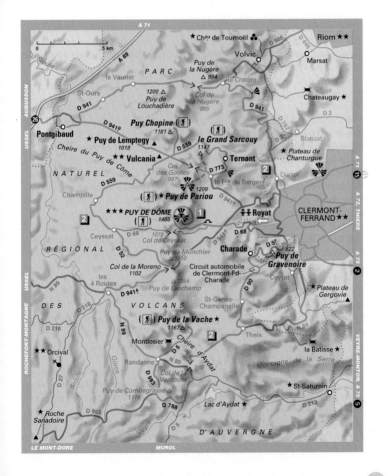

Puy de la Vache
1hr on foot there and back.

This well-shaped volcano (alt 1 167m/3 828ft) offers, along with its neighbour, Puy de Lassolas, one of the most characteristic views of the Dôme chain.

Access – *3km/1.9mi from Randanne (situated along N 89 between Clermont-Ferrand and Le Mont-Dore) on D 5.*

Montlosier Castle
The **Comte de Montlosier,** a returned émigré in the early 19C, wanted to demonstrate that it was possible to make a forest grow in places which had previously been considered barren; the experiment was carried out on his property. Initially considered to be a madman, he eventually gained recognition when the results of his efforts became tangible. His work was taken up and extended by the Forestry Department.

The castle now houses the offices of the Parc Naturel Regional des Volcans d'Auvergne and organises exhibitions devoted to the region.

The path leading to the breached crater of the Puy de la Vache (1hr on foot there and back) runs to the left off D 5. It follows the Cheire d'Aydat, a mass of solidified lava with a rough surface.

The volcano
The crater first spewed ash and slag, which formed the cone, then the lava mounted, filling the crater. Under such enormous pressure the southern flank of the crater gave way, the volcano opened up and a real torrent of molten material poured out over the plateau, forming the present Cheire d'Aydat, 6km/3.7mi long which, by blocking off the Veyre Valley, formed Lake Aydat.

▶ *Return to Randanne and turn right on N 89.*

Near the village of Recoleine, the road crosses a landscape dotted with volcanic rocks (basalt and labradorite) just breaking the surface of the ground. At the crossroads of Les Quatre-Routes, D 941A on the right runs up towards the Puys until it reaches Col de la Moreno (alt 1 102m/3 615ft) between the Puy de Laschamp (south) and the Puy de Monchier (north), both of which are covered in forest. From Col de la Moreno the route runs along D 52 northwards to Ceyssat and Champille, providing interesting views of the numerous volcanic cones above the road. The narrow D 559 (right) crosses the lava flow from the Puy de Côme, swathed in beeches and conifers, then meets D 941B; turn right towards Col des Goules and La Fontaine du Berger.

This area is the site for the theme park **Vulcania**★★, which is devoted to volcanic activity in Auvergne (👋 *see Parc Européen du Volcanisme VULCANIA*).

Le Grand Sarcouy
1hr 30min on foot there and back along a well-marked footpath leading off D 941B just after Col des Goules.

The Grand Sarcouy (alt 1 147m/3 763ft) is still known as a "cauldron" because of its shape. In the south side of this gigantic mass of domite is a vast cavern.

Puy de Pariou★
The Puy de Pariou is located in what was once the security perimeter of a firing range. Since this perimeter was deactivated in Jan 1998, access is possible at all times. However, it is forbidden to enter the actual firing range, especially were the marksmen are placed, in the target trenches or near the projectile receptacles. It is also forbidden to pick up any projectiles, parts of shells or any other suspect items.

Puy de Pariou is one of the most beautiful crater volcanoes in the Puys chain. It consists of two volcanoes one inside the other.

⚡ **Access** – *Take D 941ᴮ W of Clermont; beyond Orcines, 500m/550yd after the Shepherd's Fountain (Fontaine du Berger), park beside the road. Take a path off to the left (1hr 30min on foot there and back). Visitors should know that the Puy de Pariou was used for military training until 1 January 1998. Therefore it is forbidden to walk across the firing range and along the trenches. Likewise, tourists are requested not to pick up any projectile or suspect device lying on the ground.*

The volcano

Step over the side wall of the first crater which produced the still visible lava stretching across the road near Orcines. From here it is possible to climb to the second, far more impressive crater, a regular funnel with a circumference of 950m/3 116ft and a depth of 96m/315ft. From the edge of this crater (alt 1 209m/3 966ft) there are outstanding views of the Dôme mountain range, in particular, to the west, beyond the Clierzou and the Puy de Côme with its two craters that fit perfectly inside one another; to the north, over the Puy Chopine, the Puy de Chaumont and, behind the Puy des Goules, the Sarcouy; to the south, over the Puy de Dôme.

Ternant

Just before reaching Ternant, when on a level with the great cross in the village, the road *(D 773)* provides superb views over Clermont and the Limagne plain.

▶ *Take the path on the right, 300m/330yd before the junction with D 941ᴮ.*

Puy Chopine

2hr on foot there and back.

⚡ In dry weather the path provides access to the summit (alt 1 181m/3 875ft) of the volcanic cone.

▶ *Carry on along D 559 to the junction with D 941B and turn right towards Pontgibaud.*

Puy de Lemptégy★

🕐 *Jul-Aug: guided tours (2hr30) daily 9.30am-6pm; Apr-Jun and Sep-Oct: 10am-5pm; mid-Feb to end Mar, Oct-Nov: 10am-4pm; Christmas period (except 25 Dec and 1 Jan), 2-6pm. Guided tours: 8€ (children: 6€); unaccompanied tours: 7€ (children: 5.50€).* ☎ *04 73 62 23 25. www.auvergne-volcan.com*

This **open-topped volcano** (alt 1 018m/3 340ft) is an old pozzolana quarry hollowed out of a volcanic cone. The site is particularly impressive, as visitors can go down into the very centre of the volcano and see evidence of three successive phases of volcanic activity from 60 000 years ago. A footpath *(2km/1.2mi)* has been laid out, along with a **botanical trail,** to give the best possible overview of the many and varied volcanic features which pepper this landscape and the different kinds of volcanic material which accumulated during its active period: ash, lapilli (cinders), remarkable volcanic bombs and lava. A small train takes visitors to the very heart of the volcano.

At the end of the trail, an exhibition centre and a video complete this volcanic tour.

Night show

Sound and light effects contribute to recreate a volcanic eruption.

Puy de Lemptégy

J. Damase/MICHELIN

▶ *Carry on along D 941ᴮ.*

Pontgibaud

This large peaceful village on the river was known in Gallo-Roman times for its silver-bearing lead mines. **Château Dauphin** (◷ *Easter-Oct: guided tours (1hr) Sun and public holidays 2-6pm (Jul and Aug: daily except Mon 2-7pm). 6.50€ (children: 4€).* ☎ *04 73 88 73 39. www.chateaudauphin.com)* is a lava stone fort which was built in the 12C; six towers of the walls remain in good condition. The main building – a large rectangle with machicolations and crenellations – incorporates a round keep. Inside, there are 18C paintings and miniatures, and 16C-18C furniture. In season, a weekly tour is organised in the evening, when the castle is illuminated, which includes a visit to a magnificent **chapel**★.

The 15C church has interesting furnishings including the font, the marble altar (18C) and some fine paintings.

Gorges and Site de Montfermy★

12km/7.5mi. Allow 1hr. Leave Pontgibaud to the N on D 418 running alongside the Sioule gorges. In Montfermy, leave the car next to the bridge spanning the Sioule.

⬛ Take the path skirting the left bank of the River Sioule, leading to a waterfall and the ruins of an old mill. The peaceful setting here is a popular haunt among anglers, amateur painters and Sunday visitors. The recently restored **frescoes** in the church portray Apostles and Angels, and describe an episode in the history of the former priory.

On leaving Pontgibaud, D 941 begins to climb the west side of the mountain range. Beyond St-Ours and Le Vauriat the road provides stunning views of the **Puy de Louchadière,** one of the main extinct volcanoes in the range, which reaches an altitude of 1 200m/3 937ft and has a breached crater 150m/492ft deep. Further on, to the left, is the easily recognisable outline of the **La Nugère** (alt 994m/3 261ft).

Beyond Col de La Nugère and Le Cratère the road winds down to the Limagne plain. There are several magnificent views from the road as it runs through Durtol to Royat.

Near Durtol is the **Château de Sarcenat,** birthplace in 1881 of **Pierre Teilhard de Chardin,** a Jesuit who became known as a scientist and a philosopher.

CHÂTEAU D'EFFIAT★

MICHELIN MAP 326: G-6

6KM/3.7MI NE OF AIGUEPERSE

On the Vichy-Aigueperse road, which runs through Montpensier Forest, stands the Château d'Effiat, a fine Louis XIII building of considerable historic and architectural interest.

Visit

♿ *Guided tours (1hr30min, last tour leaves 1hr before closing) Jul-Aug: daily except Mon, 2-7pm. 5€ (children: 3€).* ☎ *04 73 63 64 01.*

At the end of a wide avenue of lime trees rises a majestic gateway built of lava stone from the Volvic area. The gateway's pediment is decorated with the emblem and Marquis' crown of the Marshal of Effiat, who owned the château, and surmounted by a helmet between battle standards. Beyond lies a courtyard, bordered by the

Château d'Effiat – The gateway

main building flanked by two pavilions. The façade of the château is decorated with twinned Doric pilasters of lava stone which add an air of great nobility.

Apartments

The mainly 17C furniture, works of art and historical memorabilia have been collected by the Moroges family who bought the château in 1856, at a time when it seemed doomed to be demolished. In the Louis XV boudoir, note the stained glass (from the Sèvres factory) illustrating scenes from the life of **Cinq-Mars** (Henri Coiffier de Ruzé, Marquis de Cinq-Mars (1620-42), favourite of Louis XIII who conspired against Richelieu and was consequently executed; his father was a Marshal of France), the Marshal's seal, and the manuscript relating the trial and execution of Cinq-Mars and his great friend De Thou. In the next room are some of the young Marquis' writings, and edicts promulgated by Louis XIII and his brother, Gaston of Orléans. The guard-room contains a 17C fireplace with a mantelpiece depicting the port of La Rochelle on the west coast of France. It also has Louis XIII furniture which belonged to the Marshal of Effiat, and a number of 18C paintings. The main drawing room has a beamed ceiling which was painted by Italian artists in 1627. Note, too, the wood panelling and the monumental fireplace bearing a mythological scene on the mantelpiece, *Vulcan's Forge*, attributed to the painter Louis Le Nain. The house also contains reminders of the Effiat Royal Military Academy.

Gardens

The gardens, laid out by André Mollet (godfather of the celebrated landscape architect Le Nôtre), are typical of the 17C with vast lakes supplied from underground springs, antique oak trees, a terrace and a grotto.

VALLÉE DE L'EYRIEUX★

MICHELIN MAP 331: J-4 TO K-4/5

The River Eyrieux rises to the north of St-Agrève at an altitude of 1 120m/3 775ft then tumbles down from the high plateaux of the Vivarais area and flows into the Rhône after covering a distance of 70km/44mi. The upper valley has a mountainous appearance, with steep slopes covered with chestnuts and spruce; this is the area known as **Les Boutières.** Downstream from Le Cheylard the torrent flows into gorges, then less rugged basins and rocky narrows alternate until the waters reach the final plain, where they enter the Rhône Valley.

Fearsome spates – The Eyrieux flows swiftly, like a torrent. Because of the sloping ground on its upper course, autumn storms can suddenly swell the main river and its tributaries. From 0.8m3/s in July and August, the rate of flow can increase to a phenomenal 3 600m3/s in just a few hours. During the spate of September 1857, the waters in the Pontpierre narrow near St-Fortunat reached a height of 17.25m/56ft.

Sectors of activity – Old, isolated hamlets cling to the hillsides marked into strips by the low walls surrounding the terraced fields. Larger villages and small towns grew up in the small inner basins in the valley, or at the mouth of tributaries. Some of them have a degree of industrial activity; at Le Cheylard, for instance, there is leatherworking, weaving, dying, plastics manufacturing and jewellery-making. The predominant character of the valley, though, derives from the farming of peaches.

A Peach-Tree Valley

In the spring the peach trees turn this rugged valley into a carpet of pink-petalled blossom. Over the seasons, fields of green vegetables and strawberries complete the agricultural scene.

A model orchard
The widespread cultivation of orchards in the Eyrieux Valley is due to particularly favourable natural conditions: light, warm soil which is easily drained; the valley's

Peach trees in blossom

J.-J. Arcis/RAPHO

Address Book

EATING OUT

📧 **Montagut** – *Pl. de l'Église - 07190 St-Sauveur-de-Montagut -* ☎ *04 75 65 40 31 - closed 1-15 Jan, Mon and Tue except Jul-Aug.* In a small village of the Ardèche dominated by castle ruins, here's a provincial inn with a cheerfully decorated dining room and a vast terrace where classic cuisine is served. Simpler meals are available in the bar patronized by a local clientele.

📧📧 **Auberge de Duzon** – *07440 Alboussière -* ☎ *04 75 58 29 40 - reception@auberge-duzon.fr - closed Sun evening, Mon-Tue.* Set in the heart of the village, this highly charming former post house has been entirely renovated. The rooms resemble those presented in interior decoration magazines; they feature carefully chosen details and a blend of different styles. Appealing restaurant, small bistro (theme evenings regularly organised) and wine cellar.

WHERE TO STAY

📧 **Camping L'Ardéchois** – *07190 St-Sauveur-de-Montagut - 8.5km/5mi W of St-Sauveur via D 102 dir. Albon -* ☎ *04 75 66 61 87 - ardechois.camping@ wanadoo.fr - open 18 Apr-Oct - reserv. recommended - 107 sites – food service.* Nature is splendid in Ardèche, and this family campground is a good home base to discover it from. The small, clear river and shaded sites promise peaceful holidays ahead. Swimming pool and children's club.

---

sheltered site from the Mistral and the winds from the south; spring frosts which are rare; and summers which begin early – all these factors help the fruit to ripen quickly.

The success story of the orchards is also largely due to the determination of the local people. The first trees were planted in 1880, on an experimental basis, at **St-Laurent-du-Pape** which has remained a pilot community ever since. Production methods, carefully improved since that time, have been copied by farmers in neighbouring regions. Gradually the orchards spread over more land in the valley although, since the introduction of mechanisation, the cultivation of peach trees up the hillsides has fallen into sharp decline.

Production

Each orchard covers an average area of no more than 1.5ha/3.5 acres. This division of the land can be explained by the demands of a type of farming which remains, for the most part, a family business. When it reaches maturity, a tree produces 25-40kg/55-88lb of fruit. A 1ha/2.5-acre field commonly produces 10-16t of peaches. Eyrieux peaches have gained a reputation for quality both nationally and on the export market. A large cooperative in Beauchastel now undertakes most of the marketing of the fruit. The valley as a whole produces some 10 000t of peaches every year.

Excursions

Tour of orchards

In the spring, at the end of March, D 120 is the best route to follow in order to admire the fairytale sight of the peach trees in blossom. The season lasts for some time, beginning with the orchards in the lower valley, and creates an extraordinary symphony of colours ranging from pale pink to carmine red and through to purple.

Beauchastel

This listed village is nestled at the foot of its castle in ruins. A pleasant stroll through narrow alleys and covered streets will take you to the **Maison du Patrimoine** and the terrace offering a pretty view of St-Laurent-du-Pape and the nearby valley.

▶ *Rejoin D 21 and head towards St-Laurent-du-Pape.*

St-Laurent-du-Pape

Attractive town at the entrance to the valley, enhanced by its bridge spanning the Eyrieux.

▶ *Keep driving along the valley in the direction of Cheylard.*

St-Sauveur-de-Montagut

Dominated by the ruins of Montagut Château *(access by D 244 and a forest lane)*, the village stands at the confluence of the River Eyrieux and River Gluyère.

▶ *Just before the bridge take D 105 for St-Pierreville.*

The roads runs along the Gluyère Valley, where a beach has been laid out, hugging the river banks almost up to St-Pierreville, offering fine views of the stark, wild countryside. You need to cross the river to get to St-Pierreville.

St-Pierreville

You are now entering the land of chestnut trees! The **Maison du Châtaignier** (🕐 *Apr-Jun and Sep-Nov: Wed, Sun and school holidays, 2-6pm; Jul-Aug: daily, 11am-12.30pm, 2.30-6pm).* 🕐 *Dec-Mar. 3.50€ (children: 2€)* ☎ *04 75 66 64 33. www.chataignier.fr)* presents an instructive exhibition on the local production of chestnuts and the struggle to prevent disease.

Musée Vivant de la Laine et du Mouton

Kids 🕐 *Guided tours (1h30) Jul-Aug: 11am-5pm; Feb-Jun and Sep-Dec: daily, 2-5pm.* 🕐 *Closed Jan. 5.60€ (children: 4€).* ☎ *04 75 66 63 08. www.ardelaine.fr.*
Chestnut picking is not the only activity for which St-Pierreville has made a name for itself. The plateaux flanking the River Eyrieux are perfect for raising sheep. This

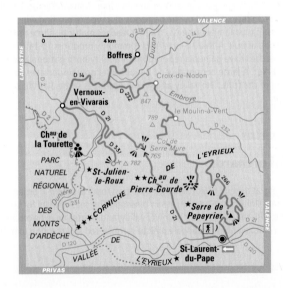

Sheep and Wool Museum presents the different breeds and the types of wool they produce (merino is considered to be the best). Detailed explanations are given about the processing of wool and the tour ends with a visit to the shop, where garments and material for interior decorating can be purchased.

Corniche de l'Eyrieux★★★

70km/43.5mi round trip – allow 2hr 30min

▶ *Leave St-Laurent-du-Pape on D 120 and soon turn right onto D 21 for Vernoux.*

As it winds up to Serre Mure pass (alt 765m/2 509ft), this spectacular crest road offers views of the Vivarois ridges, the upper basin of the Eyrieux and the Boutières region, as well as a fine view of the western slopes of Pierre-Gourde peak. As the road approaches Vernoux, during a rapid descent towards the Dunière gorge, the Château de la Tourette comes into view.

▶ *Turn left onto D 231, then onto D 331.*

St-Julien-le-Roux
From the cemetery around the church, mountains can be seen right along the **horizon**★, above the ruins of Château de la Tourette.

▶ *D 331, D 231 and D 21 lead back to Vernoux.*

Vernoux-en-Vivarais
Vernoux stands on the Vivarais plateau, between the River Eyrieux and the River Doux, in the centre of a large hollow. The pleasant scene of this large village clustered around the tall steeple of its church (19C) can be seen from some way off.

Château de la Tourette
3km/2mi. Park in the car park at Pailler farm and continue on foot: 30min there and back. Direct access to the castle by car is possible by taking a small tarmacked road from Vernoux, following the signs to "La Tourette."
The ruins of this stronghold, which once marked the gateway to the States of Languedoc, lie in an unspoilt **setting**★ and are among the most evocative in the Vivarais. The main building was an enormous keep which still has some of its machicolations and corbelling. The ruins command a plunging view of the Dunière ravine which consists of a series of deeply encased meanders.

▶ *Drive to Boffres situated 8.5km/5mi NE on D 14 and D 219.*

Boffres
The village of Boffres is built on a projection in a semicircle at the foot of its simple pink granite church and the remains of the old fortified castle, and overlooks a peaceful rural setting surrounded by cool chestnut groves.
Just outside the village, a bronze bust by the Ardèche sculptor Gimond has been erected at the edge of the road to the memory of **Vincent d'Indy,** the famous French composer and teacher (1851-1931), born in Paris but descended from a family in the region.
It was at **Château des Faugs,** west of Boffres, that d'Indy came to seek inspiration for his musical works, noting themes which came to him during his walks. He composed his third melody without words from a shepherd's song heard near Les Estables, and his opera Fervaal one misty morning on the peaks of Mont Mézenc.

▶ *Drive to the junction with D 14 and turn left onto D 232.*

The road runs along the hillside, offering fine views of Vernoux-en-Vivarais in the centre of the basin. Beyond Croix-de-Nodon, there are generous glimpses of the Rhône Valley in the distance and clear views of the deep wooded Embroye Valley in the foreground.

▶ *At Le Moulin-à-Vent turn right onto D 266.*

After a long wooded section, the road runs along a spectacular stretch of ledge, opposite Pierre-Gourde peak, in front of the mountain ridges enclosing the Eyrieux Valley.

▶ *A track, off D 286 to the right, leads to the Château de Pierre-Gourde. Park at a pass, in sight of the ruins.*

Panorama from the Château de Pierre-Gourde★★

This medieval castle, now in ruins, occupies a magnificent **site**★. At the foot of the peak on which the keep was built lie the ruins of the main building, parts of the fortified curtain wall and the feudal village.

▶ *Walk left around the ruins to reach a rocky terrace.*

The **panorama** encompasses the Rhône (seen through the Bas-Eyrieux gap) and Trois-Becs (along a straight axis), between the Vercors bar, the Baronnies and Mont Ventoux. Opposite, the jagged backbone of Croix de Bauzon overlooks the Haut-Eyrieux gap; on the horizon, the summit of Mont Mézenc marks the boundary of the complicated network of long, narrow Vivarois ridges.

During the descent, two panoramic bends offer a spectacular view first of the Eyrieux Valley, with its clearly delineated ridges, endlessly repeated, and then of the Rhône Valley, on the left.

▶ *About 5km/3mi from Pierre-Gourde, a sign on the right indicates the Serre de Pepeyrier ridge. Park about 250m/280yd along the road towards the television relay station, and climb up to the edge of the ridge.*

View from Serre de Pepeyrier★

15min on foot there and back.

There is a beautiful **view** from the ridge of the mouth of the Eyrieux Valley with its vast peach orchards, the town of Beauchastel and the Rhône plain; in the background, Mont Ventoux stands out clearly.

Les Boutières★★

64km/40mi round trip leaving from St-Agrève – 🕐 *see SAINT-AGRÈVE.*

FEURS

POPULATION 7 669
MICHELIN MAP 327: E-5

Owing to its strategic location in the Loire Valley, this town was a thriving commercial centre back in the days of the Gauls. Trade remains an important activity today, as illustrated by the lively street markets. In fact, the name of the town is believed to be derived from the Latin word *forum*, symbolising a privileged place for communication and exchange. *Pl. du Forum, 42110 FEURS, ☎ 04 77 26 05 27. www.officedutourismedefeurs.org*

Sights

Musée de Feurs
3 rue Victor-de-Laprade. ◐ *Daily except Sat and public holidays, 2-6pm.* ◐ *Closed 1 Jan, 1 May, 25 Dec and public holidays. 3€.* ☎ *04 77 26 24 48. www.feurs.org*
The museum is devoted to Gaulish and Gallo-Roman archaeology as well as popular arts and crafts. The park is a delightful setting for the reconstructed **villa** displaying marble and stone exhibits, along with a pretty **mosaic** discovered in Feurs.

Église Notre-Dame
Flamboyant Gothic church with three naves. The heavily ornate bell-tower bearing a 15C clock was remodelled in the 19C. Part of the 12C chancel is still standing. On the right, there is a **Virgin with Child** by J-M Bonnassieux. The wainscoting and stalls (18C) were taken from the priory in Pommiers.

Excursions

Plaine du Forez

As soon as you stray from the main roads and explore the more remote spots of the countryside, the Forez basin will delight you by its charming sights. The volcanic spurs dotted around the landscape are often the site of religious sanctuaries, namely St-Romain-le-Puy and Montverdun. Down below, in the plain, *bocage* meadows alternate with ponds and old farmhouses.

Pouilly-lès-Feurs
7km/4.3mi N of Feurs on N 82 and D 58. Former fortified village where the unusual Romanesque church was once attached to a **Cluniac priory** *(Guided tours available*

EATING OUT AND WHERE TO STAY

◌ **Assiette Saltoise** – *42110 Salt-en-Donzy* - ☎ *04 77 26 04 29 - closed Tue evening and Wed.* A country inn beside the small Romanesque church in the heart of a small rural village. The setting – an old house with a shaded terrace and linden trees in front – is plain and simple but the food served herein, typical of the region, is plentiful and well prepared.

◌ **La Bussinière** – *Rte de Lyon* - ☎ *04 77 27 06 36 - la-bussiniere@wanadoo.fr -* ⌂ - *3 rms.* Stylishly decorated, the interior of this establishment on a major road is a successful blend of old and new where imposing wooden beams give guest rooms plenty of character. Impeccable soundproofing for a good night's sleep.

by request at the town hall. ☎ 04 77 26 05 84). Note the sober façade and the harmonious interior, typical of 12C architecture.

West of Pouilly, a small Renaissance pavilion has kept its sculpted pediment and an upstairs loggia.

La Valette

7km/4.3mi NE of Feurs on D 113. 2km/1.2mi E of Salvizinet, after the bridge spanning the Charpassonne, turn right onto the tarmacked lane that starts by the inn. This modest country church nestled on a slope of the Charpassonne Vallon is a small Romanesque building with a single nave and a raised chancel. The somewhat crude furniture is peculiar to the Forez region.

Chambéon

Not far from St-Étienne airport and the River Loire, the **Écopole du Forez** *(6km/3.7mi S of Feurs via N 89 and D 107; signposted from Chambéon and Magneux-Haute-Rive – ☐☐ Guided tours (1h30): 2-6pm (End-Mar to End-Oct: Sun and public holidays, 2-7pm). ☐ Closed 1 Jan and 25 Dec. 4€. ☎ 04 77 27 86 40)* is a preserved park that has become an important centre for studying migratory birds and aquatic fauna. Nature trails totalling 12km/7.5mi run along the banks of the Loire, enlightening visitors on the area's natural resources and riverside vegetation.

MONTS DU FOREZ★★

MICHELIN MAPS 327: B-5/6, C-5/6, D-5/6

The granite mountains in the Forez area form a range some 45km/28mi long. Along the edge are parallel offshoots separating the picturesque valleys, some of which run down to the Dore whereas others head for the Loire. The eastern slopes stand high above the Forez plain; the slopes to the west, the only part of the range in the Auvergne, drop sharply down to the Dore basin and include some attractive beauty spots and magnificent views.

▸ **Orient Yourself:** The Monts du Forez are part of the Parc Naturel Régional Livradois-Forez, so a good place to start is at the Maison du Parc in St-Gervais-sous-Meymont.

▣ **Parking:** At the Maison du Parc.

⊘ **Don't miss:** The panorama from the col du Bréal and from the balcon du Forez.

◐ **Organizing your time:** Allow at least a day-and-a-half to explore the region fully.

◖ **Also see:** Chateau de la Bastie-d'Irfé, Chazelles-sur-Lyon, Feurs, Montbrison and Montverdun.

Up to altitudes of 800-1 000m/2 625-3 280ft, the mountainsides are covered with fields (rye, potatoes) and meadows – this is the zone in which villages have been built. The pure, abundant water supply that rushes down all the slopes of the Forez mountains is used to irrigate meadows where it is cool even in the height of the summer, and to turn the waterwheels in the mills, sawmills, and the last papermill in the Lagat Valley; it also supplies the cutlery works in Thiers. Above are the pine and beech forests covering the hillsides.

At altitudes above 1 200-1 300m/3 937-4 265ft lie the summer pastures which are called the "Hautes-Chaumes" (alpine pastures) of the Forez. On the bare mountain

Address Book

EATING OUT

🍴 **Ferme-auberge du Mazet** – *42990 St-Georges-en-Couzan -* ☎ *04 77 24 80 95 - closed Dec, Jan and Sun evening.* If you've a taste for homemade delicatessen, you're bound to enjoy this farm-inn on the village heights. A convivial atmosphere reigns in the vast dining room where appetizing farm-raised ham and pork dishes are served.

🍴 **Ferme-auberge des Granges** – *Les Granges - 42920 Chalmazel - 5km/3mi SW of Chalmazel dir. Le Col du Béal -* ☎ *04 77 24 80 62 - closed Nov -* 🍴 *- reserv. recommended evenings.* At just 100m/330ft from the slopes, this long chalet is a very convenient place to take it easy and re-energize after a hard day's skiing. The generous meals give healthful farm produce pride of place.

🍴🍴 **Gaudon** – *63880 Le Brugeron - 6km/3.6mi S of La Chambonie via D 101 and D 37 -* ☎ *04 73 72 60 46 - closed Jan, Sun evening, Mon evening and Tue from 15 Sep to 1 Jun.* In the bosom of the Monts du Forez, at the entrance of the village of Brugeron, this traditional house built in 1929 is a handy stopover. The decor is unquestionably out-dated but the small dining rooms are bright. Four menus and a set meal are offered in the restaurant.

WHERE TO STAY

🛏 **Les Genets** – *63880 Le Brugeron -* ☎ *04 73 72 60 36 - closed end Nov to mid-Feb -* 🅿 *- 10 rms -* 🍽 *6€.* Guests can unwind in a pretty park hidden behind this stone house in the heart of the village. The spotless bedrooms sport modern furnishings. Dining room where simplicity is the rule and traditional fare is served.

---

peaks a few spurs of rock jut out from above the middle of scree slopes; Pierre sur Haute is the highest of them all (alt 1 634m/5 360ft).

Parc Naturel Régional Livradois-Forez

The Forez mountains are part of the **Parc Naturel Régional Livradois-Forez** which was set up in 1984 and covers an area of almost 300 000ha/over 740 000 acres. Its aims are to revitalise a declining rural environment and to present and promote local heritage, especially crafts and industry. The park also seeks to encourage rural holidays which do not disturb the environment.

The park's cultural programme includes the music festivals of La Chaise-Dieu and Thiers. The residents of the areas encompassed by the park are proud of their history and the craftsmanship they have practised over the centuries, reflected in various local museums: cutlery-making (Thiers); lacemaking (Arlanc); papermaking (Richard-de-Bas); agriculture and cheesemaking (Ambert).

There are a number of waymarked paths which cover the park, enabling visitors to explore it to the full. Those fond of sports will appreciate the facilities for water sports, riding and paragliding.

The **Maison du Parc** (🕐 *May-Sep: 9am-12.30pm, 1.30-7pm (Sat, Sun, 3-7pm); rst of year: daily except Sat, Sun, 9am-12.30pm, 1.30-5.30pm (Fri, 1.30-4.30pm).* 🕐 *Closed 1 Jan, 1 and 11 Nov, 25 Dec. No charge.* ☎ *04 73 95 57 57. www.parc-livradois-forez.org),* which is the park's information centre, is located in St-Gervais-sous-Meymont.

Excursions

1 Via Col de Béal★

Allow one day

Boën

Boën (pronounced "Bowen"), situated high above the left bank of the Lignon, specialises in metalworking and small-scale mechanical engineering. Boën was the birthplace of Father Terray (1715-78), Comptroller-General of Finances at the end of Louis XV's reign. The unpopular measures he was forced to take in order to re-establish a balanced budget following the excessive spending of the royal court brought him the nickname "Emptier of Purses."

Musée de la vigne★

🕐 *Jul-Aug, daily except Mon, 10am-noon, 2-6.30pm (Sun, 2-6.30pm); rest of year: daily except Mon, 2.30-6.30pm.* 🕐 *Closed Dec-Jan and 1 May. 4€ (children: 2€).* ☎ *04 77 24 08 12. www.boen.fr.*

The elegant 18C Chateau Chabert houses a Winemaking Museum established with a real concern for authenticity, both in its reconstructions of traditional interiors and in its technical presentations of wine-growing. The tour begins on the second floor and takes visitors through a chronological display of furniture, tools, stills and tales of bygone days, which recreate the authentic atmosphere of the wine-growers' life.

▶ *Leave Boën on N 89 NW, 2.5km/1.5mi on from Boën, turn left onto D 6 to Sail-sous-Couzan.*

Sail-sous-Couzan

This peaceful village was suddenly thrown into the limelight on 12 July 1998, when the World Cup final that took place in Paris between France and Brazil saw the victory of the host country. Indeed, Sail is the hometown of the French coach **Aimé Jacquet**, thanks to whom the "blue team" owe their resounding victory.

▶ *Turn right off D 6 onto a very steep tarmacked road leading to the castle ruins.*

Summer Pastures

The Monts du Forez feature a wide range of scenery, much of it covered by dark pine forests. Once above the tree line, the mountain summits, often shrouded in mist or cloud, are vast bleak stretches of moorland – the **Hautes-Chaumes.** This somewhat eery landscape can look more like a moonscape in certain lights. The vast bare wastes are broken only by granite rocks, deep peat bogs or clumps of broom. Nonetheless, man – or rather, woman – has attempted to scratch a living from this unwelcoming environment. A matriarchal society evolved in the mountain farmsteads *(jasseries)* during the summer months; while the menfolk were down in the valley dealing with the harvesting, the women and children would be in charge of looking after the livestock in the summer pastures up in the mountains, where they would also make the famous local Fourme cheese and gather medicinal plants.

This harsh way of life gradually died out, and there are now no more working jasseries. However, some of them have been converted into open-air museums which inform visitors about the daily work and traditions of these "Amazons of the Mountains."

Château de Couzan★

Park at the foot of the ruins; 15min on foot there and back. The ruins of this 11C fortress, one of the most important in the region, stand on a rocky promontory squeezed between the narrow valleys of the River Lignon and River Chagon. What remains of the curtain walls and towers still suggests the strength of the seigneurs of Couzan, the oldest barons of the Forez. There is a good view of the castle walls from a rocky promontory behind the fort, and panoramic **views**★ over the countryside from the ruins which are being restored.

▷ *Return to Sail-sous-Couzan and turn left onto D 97 towards St-Just-en-Bas.*

The road runs along the crest of the hill up above the Upper Lignon Valley overshadowed by Pierre sur Haute before reaching Jeansagnière. Continue on to the pass, **Col de la Loge,** where a curtain of pine trees opens onto a clearing carpeted with grass. Before La Chamba, the forest gives way to more pastoral scenery and the route, skirting a succession of corries filled with fine pastures, provides several outstanding views of the Dore basin and the Livradois area.

▷ *Continue 2km/1.2mi beyond La Chamba and turn left towards Le Brugeron.*

La Chambonie

A village nestling in a pastoral corrie.

▷ *Immediately beyond a sawmill turn right onto D 37.*

After a long climb up through the forest, there is a magnificent view over the Dômes mountain range. Beyond another stretch of road through the forest lie alpine pastures dotted with farmsteads *(jasseries).*

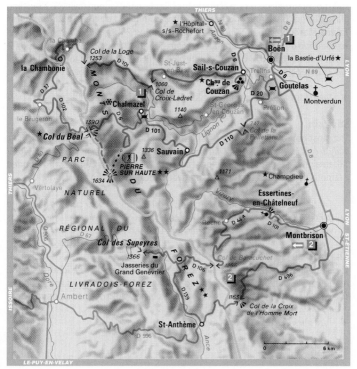

Col du Béal★

From this pass there is a wide **panoramic view** over the mountains of the Auvergne and the Lyonnais area. The pass forms a threshold between the two sides of the Forez mountains.

Pierre sur Haute★★

2hr 30min on foot there and back, recommended in clear weather. Climb directly up to the summit across the alpine pastures and along the crest of the mountain or take the chair-lift. ⏱ Jul to mid-Sep: 2-6pm. 6€. ☎ 04 77 24 85 09.

🚶 Pierre-sur-Haute, the highest peak in the Forez range (alt 1 634m/5 360ft) is a dome-shaped granite mountain topped by military radar installations. The wind-swept moorland that carpets its slopes is gashed here and there by huge rockfalls. Small farmsteads dot the hillsides.

From the summit (beacon and Cross) to the right of the military installations, the **panorama** stretches right across the Forez, the mountains in the Lyonnais area and Beaujolais, the Limagne, the Dômes and Dore mountain ranges, Cantal and the mountains in the Velay and Vivarais areas.

Three types of scenery succeed each other during the rapid trip down from Col du Béal to Chalmazel – alpine pastures, then a superb pine forest and, finally, an area of pine trees and meadows.

▷ *About 7km/4mi from Col du Béal, a road cuts off to the right; it leads to the ski slopes and the Pierre-sur-Haute cable-car.*

On the outskirts of Chalmazel there is an attractive view of the castle down below.

Chalmazel✳

This mountain village, which clings to the hillside in the Lignon ravine, is a bustling place during the winter sports season. It is dominated by the old **Château des Talaru-Marcilly** (13C – ⏱ *Guided visit (45m): Jul-Aug: 2-7pm; Mid-May to end Jun and Sep: Sat, Sun and public holidays, 10am-6pm. 5€ (children: 3.50€). ☎ 04 77 24 88 09. www.chateaudechalmazel.com*), a huge bastion flanked by corner towers which still has its parapet walkway. The chapel is decorated with 16C frescoes.

▷ *Take D 101 to Sauvain.*

Sauvain

The most notable feature of this village is the **Maison Sauvagnarde** (⏱ *Jul-Aug: daily except Mon 2.30-6.30pm; Jun and Sep-Oct: Sun 2.30-6.30pm. 3€. ☎ 04 77 76 82 18)*, an old 17C farmhouse that belonged to the inventor **Louis Lépine**, who founded a famous competition for the most innovative device or technique.

▷ *Continue along D 101 in the direction of Montbrison. Soon after crossing the Lignon at Pont-de-Pierre, turn left onto D 110, heading for Col de la Pelletière. Drive to Trelins via La Bruyère and Prélion (D 20) and take D 20A on the right.*

Château de Goutelas

The château stands on a terrace high above the Forez plain; it is a delightful late-16C residence which has been restored and is now used to host courses and seminars. The courtyard is open to visitors and it is possible to walk round the exterior.

▷ *Turn back and take D 8 back to Boën.*

② Via Col des Supeyres★

70km/44mi – allow half a day

Montbrison – 🚻 *See MONTBRISON.*

▶ *Leave Montbrison to the W along D 101 which climbs up the bare, rocky Vizery ravine. A short detour leads to the village of Essertines.*

Essertines-en-Châtelneuf
From the village, with its small Gothic church with Flamboyant Gothic decoration, there is a view over the Forez plain from which emerges the rocky pinnacle of St-Romain-le-Puy.

▶ *Rejoin D 101 and continue up the valley before turning left on D 44[A]. In Roche turn left onto D 44 and continue via D 113 to Col de Baracuchet.*

From the road there are several glimpses of the Forez plain. The road continues to climb through valleys filled with farms and fields and dominated by wooded peaks. Near the pass, the trees become gnarled and twisted until eventually they give way to a vast clearing from which there is a view of the Ance Valley *(left)* and, opposite the road, the crest of the Forez mountains.
The road *(D 106)* climbs up to Col des Supeyres through alpine pastures, carpeted with heather and dotted with farmsteads, and past the Grand Génevrier farmsteads *(left)*.

Col des Supeyres
Alt 1 366m/4 481ft. This pass on the eastern edge of the Livradois-Forez Nature Park is surrounded by a landscape more reminiscent of steppes: poorly drained mountain pastures, without a soul in sight. The sense of ruggedness and isolation is particularly strong at the bottom of the road leading to Pierre-sur-Haute *(it becomes a dirt track 1km/0.6mi from the start)*. A viewing table on "La Montagne des Allebasses" and a themed footpath *(2hr 30min)* shed light on the way of life in this region (farmsteads, summer pasturing etc).
The route down from the pass towards St-Anthème passes the group of farmsteads known as **Les Jasseries du Grand Genévrier,** one of which is open to the public.

Jasserie du Coq Noir
A visit to this old farmstead (Black Cock Farm) used during the seasonal moving of livestock provides an insight into life in the mountains, into the art of thatching roofs and into the production of Fourme cheeses. A snack of milk, rye bread and Fourme de St-Anthème is available.

▶ *As the road runs down to St-Anthème there are views of the volcanic cones in the Velay area – Meygal, Lizieux, Mézenc and Gerbier-de-Jonc.*

St-Anthème
The red-roofed village nestles in the depths of the Ance Valley.

▶ *Follow D 496 from St-Anthème to return to Montbrison.*

Beyond Col de la Croix de l'Homme Mort, the road provides some very attractive views of the Forez plain, the Monts du Lyonnais area, and Mont Pilat.

GANNAT

POPULATION 5 838
MICHELIN MAP 326: G-6 – 20KM/12.4MI W OF VICHY

This small, ancient town lies on the edge of the Limagne plain and the granite base below the mountains of the Auvergne, on the threshold of the "Gateway to Occitania" which stretches from Broût-Vernet on the plain to the Champs hills, the point of contact between two old forms of French language – *langue d'oc* and *langue d'oïl*. The area is very important archaeologically, and ongoing digs have recently uncovered three well-preserved rhinoceros skeletons thought to be at least 23 million years old, together with the remains of crocodiles and fossilised birds. ⓘ *Pl. des Anciens-de-l'AFN, 03800 GANNAT, ☎ 04 70 90 17 78. www.gannat.auvergne.net*

World Culture Festival – Every summer Gannat is filled with the sounds of traditional folk dancers, musicians and singers who come here from all five continents to take part in an international cultural event which resounds with colour and excitement (see *Calendar of events*).

Sights

Église Ste-Croix

Traces of the original Romanesque church are still visible, especially the north part of the apse where, outside, there is a strange capital depicting the Nativity. The church was rebuilt in the Gothic period and underwent minor alterations on several occasions until the 17C when the east end, ambulatory and belfry were rebuilt.

Castle

The 12C fortress, dismantled in 1566, was used as a prison from 1833 to 1967. The castle has tall 14C walls flanked by corner towers.

Musée Municipal

🕐 *May to end Oct: daily except Tue 2-6pm (Jul and Aug: 10am-noon, 2-6pm). 5€. ☎ 04 70 90 00 50.*

The old warders' apartments and the prison cells now house the museum. Among the items on display (14C-18C parchments from the town's archives, 12C wrought-iron grilles, restored statues, votive images) is a beautiful **Gospel Book**★ with elegant illuminations on vellum. The binding dates from the 10C but was given additional decoration in the 12C. It is covered with silver-gilt and adorned with an antique cameo surrounded by cabochons and *cloisonné* enamelwork. On the other side is an ivory plaque depicting the Crucifixion and the Holy Women at the tomb; it is carved in the Byzantine style (10C).

A typical Bourbonnais kitchen, clogmaker's workshop, saddlery and farm implements are also on display.

Gospel book

J. Damase/MICHELIN

The section called the **Musée de la Résistance** displays photographs, press cuttings and medals which recall the period of French Resistance in the history of the Gannat area. The **Tack Room,** originally from Veauce Castle, contains a wide range of saddles, harnesses, bridles, stirrups, boots and whips.

At the far end of the courtyard is an exhibition of horsedrawn vehicles (brougham, shooting brake, mail coach), also from Veauce Castle.

Several more rooms are given over to an exhibition on palaeontology – one houses the mounted skeleton of a prehistoric rhinoceros.

Excursions

Jenzat

8km/5mi N along N 9 towards Moulins, then left onto D 42. The late-11C **church** here is decorated with 15C paintings in tempera (right side aisle) which are known as "Frescoes by the Masters of Jenzat." These realistic, naïve works depict the Passion of Christ and the Martyrdom of St Catherine. The **Maison du Luthier** (&⏱ *Jun-Sep: Sun-Mon, 2.30-6.30pm (Jul-Aug: daily, Mon-Thu). Guided tours available. 4€. ☎ 04 70 56 81 78)* contains a museum on the craft of making musical instruments, in particular hurdy-gurdies – Jenzat was said to be the European capital in this respect in the 19C (the village still has two resident craftsmen).

Maison Boudet – *3 rte des Claudis - 03800 Jenzat - ☎ 04 70 56 84 01 - 8am-noon, 2pm-6pm.* This workshop exports hurdy-gurdies throughout Europe as well as to the USA! It has been run for two decades by J-C Boudet, who succeeded Pajot, the former hurdy-gurdy man of Jenzat.

Église de Biozat

7km/4.3mi SE along D 119. The beautiful, Romanesque **church** is typical of the Limagne area with its barrel-vaulted nave, half-barrel vaulting in the side aisles, dome over squinches and a number of interesting capitals. Note the naïve style of the 15C frescoes depicting the *Mater Dolorosa*.

▶ *From here you can drive 4km/2.5mi to Effiat and join up with the Limagne discovery trail (⏱ see AIGUEPERSE).*

PLATEAU DE GERGOVIE★

MICHELIN MAP 326: F-8

The Gergovie plateau stands almost 400m/1 300ft above the Allier Valley and the current level of the Limagne plain. It is 1 500m/4 920ft long and 500m/1 640ft wide and its sides form scarp slopes. The basalt table above it, which is 20-30m/65-98ft thick, was formed by a lava flow. The table rises to an altitude of 745m/2 447ft and protects the lower levels of marl and limestone from erosion, thereby producing "inversion relief." The archaeological remains found here are displayed in an exhibition centre which recounts the famous battle.

The Battle of Gergovia – The site of this historic battle is said by some to be Chanturgue plateau, by others to be Gergovie plateau.

In the year 52 BC Caesar was carrying out his seventh military campaign in Gaul; he had just defeated the Gallic army in Bourges and the Gauls had retreated to the mountains of the Massif Central, pursued by six Roman legions. **Vercingétorix**, the leader of the Gallic coalition, had retreated to the Arverni's hillfort in Gergovia, which was defended by a dry stone wall 6m/almost 20ft high. From the ramparts of the Arverni hillfort in **Nemessos**, which might be the "Gergovia" mentioned by Caesar where Vercingétorix came to seek refuge, the Gauls had an extensive view down over the main Roman encampment in Montferrand. One night, Caesar captured the Roche-Blanche hill, by surprise, and set up a lesser encampment there, linking it to the main camp by a ditch along which he could move his troops.

Caesar then ordered his troops to implement a diversionary movement by night, along the Bédat Valley that skirted the Arverni's hillfort, to give Vercingétorix the idea that his army might be attacked from the rear. The next day, three Roman legions moved from the main camp up to the lesser camp and, shortly after mid-day, launched an attack. Vercingétorix, however, was a good strategist and had concealed troops behind the Puy de la Mouchette who put up fierce resistance against the Romans. Furthermore, the Gauls on the plateau – alerted by the shouts of the womenfolk – ran quickly back to the scene of the real battle and routed the Roman legions. At the same time the Aedui, allies of the Romans, arrived from the plain but the Roman soldiers thought they were coming to the aid of the Gauls and Caesar ordered the retreat.Some 46 centurions and 700 legionaries were killed beneath the walls of Gergovia.

Vercingétorix wisely brought his troops to a halt on the plain. The Gauls' success was short-lived, however: their chieftain was besieged in Alésia and finally surrendered to Caesar at the end of the summer.

A Tribute to the Past

Panoramic view★★

A memorial erected in 1900 stands at the end of the road; it consists of a group of rustic columns topped by a winged helmet. From the terrace in front of the Maison de Gergovie 200m/220yd away, there is a wonderful view of the Limagne around Clermont, closed off on the horizon by the mountains in the Forez and Livradois areas, and of the Allier Valley with the extinct volcanoes of the Comté in the distance.

Maison de Gergovie

Access from the terrace or down the hill. &.◯ *May-Oct 10am-12.30pm, 2-6.30pm (Jul and Aug: 10am-7pm); Mar-Apr and Nov: Sat-Sun and public holidays 2-6pm.* ◯ *Closed mid Dec-end Jan. 4€.* ☎ *04 73 79 42 98.*

The Information Centre on the plateau has a **threefold exhibition** – one on geology and local flora illustrated by photographs and models, one on archaeology (grave containing the skeleton of a young woman, day-to-day life of the Gauls in the hillfort) and a third on the history of this important site, Napoleon III's visit and the archaeological digs that have been carried out here. A diorama retraces the various stages in the battle between the Romans and the Gauls. The last room gives visitors information on the controversy between scholars who favour Chanturgue as the site of the battlefield and those who believe that the battle was fought here on Gergovie plateau.

Excursion

12km/7.5mi – allow 2 hr. Leave the plateau de Gergovie and head for Opme, then drive towards Chanonat. At the entrance to the village, turn right for La Batisse.

Château de la Batisse★

◯ *mid-Jun to end Aug, daily except Sat, 2-7pm; Apr to mid-Jun, Sep, Oct, Sun and public holidays, 2.30-6pm. 6 (children: 7-14, 4€, 14-18, 5€) (park only: 4€).*

This château built of pale stone exudes an atmosphere of tranquillity and gracious living which forms a stark contrast to the feudal fortresses of Auvergne. It is flanked by a pepper-pot tower and two corner towers crowned with red-tiled domes and lantern turrets, all that remain of the original 15C castle.

The interior *(enter through the east tower and the former kitchens)* contains a number of interesting items of Louis XIII and Louis XVI furniture, tapestries, weapons and a 16C Pietà.

The **gardens,** laid out by Le Nôtre in the 17C, are being returned to their design with the help of an 18C watercolour which is displayed in the map room. A delightful avenue runs alongside the labyrinth of greenery at the end of the park, leading to the **waterfalls** on the Auzon.

▶ *Return to Chanonat and turn right onto D 3 for Le Crest.*

Le Crest

This wine-growers' village built at the very tip of the Serre mountain range has a 13C church with 14C and 15C alterations.

There is a superb **panoramic view**★ from the old tower – northwards over the Gergovie and Limagne plateaux around Clermont, eastwards over the Allier Valley and the mountains in the Livradois area, southwards and to the south-west over the Dore and Sancy mountain ranges, and to the west and north-west over the Dôme mountain range.

▶ *Go back down towards D 213 and A 75, pass beneath them, and then take the small narrow road that climbs up around the Butte de Monton.*

Monton

This village has its houses spread out over the southern slopes of the mound, crowned by an imposing statue of the Virgin (14m/46ft) carved in white stone and based on the Notre-Dame-du-Puy figure. Our Lady of Monton has become a popular place of pilgrimage in August *(3rd Sunday)*.

Not far from Monton are a series of **troglodyte caves,** affording lovely views of the surrounding countryside.

▶ *Go back to Gergovie via La Roche-Blanche.*

HAUTERIVES

POPULATION 1 333

MICHELIN MAP 332: D-2

The village of Hauterives, situated at the foot of a hillock bearing the ruins of the medieval castle which once belonged to the lords of Clermont, has an unusual tourist attraction – the "Ideal Palace." ▯ *R. du Palais-Idéal, 26390 HAUTERIVES,* ☎ *04 75 68 86 82.*

A visionary postman – In the late 19C the postman in Hauterives, **Ferdinand Cheval**, began bringing home strangely shaped stones every day which he had picked up during his round. In the evenings he would add them to an unusual construction he was building in his garden, based on books he had read and dreams he had had, and possibly also inspired by the remains of petrified springs that were commonplace in this area of the Drôme. When he retired, Cheval continued his work despite the mockery of the local people, tirelessly bringing sand and stones back to

J. Damase/MICHELIN

The Postman's Ideal Palace

his home in a wheelbarrow. After 33 years of relentless labour, he finished his weird and wonderful "Palace." Cheval then spent the last 10 years of his life building his own grave in the cemetery, in the same style. He died in 1924.

Sights

Palais Idéal★

&♿ ◷ *Jul and Aug: 9am-12.30pm, 1.30-7.30pm; Apr-Jun and Sep: 9am-12.30pm, 1.30-6.30pm; Feb-Mar and Oct-Nov: 9.30am-12.30pm, 1.30-5.30pm; Jan and Dec: 9.30am-12.30pm, 1.30-4.30pm.* ◷ *Closed 25 Dec, 1 Jan and mid to end Jan. 5.50€ (children: 4€).* ☎ *04 75 68 81 19. www.facteurcheval.com*

Postman Cheval's Ideal Palace (300m2/358sq yd and some 10m/33ft high) stands in the middle of his garden. It is his dream building, bristling with strange ornamentation and combining every conceivable architectural style.

The east side, the strangest and most intricate of all, is decorated with huge female idols made of reddish pebbles; the entrance to the palace is on the other side. Imitation plants stand side by side with reminders of oriental or medieval palaces.

Address Book

EATING OUT

◉◉🍽 **Yves Leydier** – *26330 Châteauneuf-de-Galaure - 6km/3.6mi SW of Hauterives via D 51* - ☎ *04 75 68 68 02 - closed 17 Feb to 12 Mar, 1-10 Jul, 28-31 Aug, Sun evening except Jul-Aug, Tue evening and Wed.* Located on the village square, this pretty house built of round stones from the Galaure opens out back onto a large garden where children like to play in summer. Adults can also enjoy the surroundings while dining on the shady terrace.

WHERE TO STAY

◉ **Hôtel Le Relais** – ☎ *04 75 68 81 12 - closed mid-Jan to end Feb, Sun evening except Jul-Aug and Mon - 17 rms -* ⌑ *6€ - restaurant* ◉ This village hotel is set in a big old house with an exposed stone façade and white shutters. Recently renovated, it is quite attractive and offers rooms that are simple, yet clean and inviting. A dependable address for travellers on limited budgets.

L'Art en marche
Rue Centrale. ⏰ *Apr-Sep: 10am-12.15pm, 1.30-6pm; Oct-Mar: 10am-12.15pm, 1.30-5.30pm.* ⏰ *Closed Mid-Jan to end-Jan, 1 Jan and 25 Dec. 5€ (6-16-year-olds: 4€).* ☎ *04 75 68 95 40. www.art-en-marche.com*
This museum of "Art Brut" and "Neuve Invention" carries on in the spirit of Cheval's naïve innovations by presenting a large number of international works which cannot be classified.

Les Labyrinthes
3.5km/2.2mi. Follow D 51 towards Le Grand-Serre and turn left in St-Germain. ⏰ *May to Aug: 11am-7pm; Sep: Sat, Sun, 11am-7pm).* ⏰ *Closed Oct-Apr. 5€ (6-16-year-olds: 4€).* ☎ *04 75 68 96 27.*
Kids ♿ Four large mazes, occupying the top of a hill, combine their network of paths and hedges to offer young visitors a thrilling treasure hunt. The Maison des Enfants, located in a shaded position, organises amusing activities involving mosaics.

HÉRISSON

POPULATION 709
MICHELIN MAP 326: D-3 – 23KM/14.3MI N OF MONTLUÇON

The artist **Henri-Joseph Harpignies** (1819-1916) often stayed in Hérisson and this region provided him with the inspiration for some of his finest landscapes, strongly influenced by the Barbizon School. Two 15C fortified gateways and old houses including the "Mousse House" (15C-18C) are to be seen in the village.
🛈 *Mairie, 2 av. Marcellin-Simonnet, 03190 HÉRISSON,* ☎ *04 70 06 82 23.*

Walking Tour

The town has kept several old houses (15C-18C) and two fortified gateways from the 15C, Porte de la Rivière and Porte de la Varenne. The 22 turrets running along the ramparts are no longer standing.

Musée du Terroir
⏰*Jul-Aug: daily except Tue 2.30-6.30pm. 3€.* ☎ *04 70 06 89 40.*
The museum presents an exhibition of farming tools and various artefacts uncovered on excavation sites.

Castle
The impressive mass of beautiful russet-coloured ruins stands high above the village. The castle was built in the 13C, with fortifications added to it under Louis de Bourbon in the 14C *(restoration work in progress)*.

View★
South bank of the River Aumance; access via rue du Calvaire. From the Calvary chapel on the hillside, the **view** extends over the entire village with its porch-belfry, all that remains of the former collegiate church of St-Sauveur (12C-17C), the castle and the Aumance Valley.

Excursion

Vallée de l'Aumance

Round tour of 35km/22mi – allow 1hr

This pretty valley is drained by a gently flowing river which rises near Le Montet, eventually meeting up with the Cher not far from Tronçais Forest.

▶ *Leave Hérisson on D 157 NW.*

Église de Châteloy

The 12C church stands firmly and proudly on the rocks above the valley. Frescoes dating from the 13C to 17C (with later restoration) decorate the chancel and nave. A music festival is held here in season. The graveyard provides a **view**★ of the elegant bell-tower and over the Aumance Valley.

▶ *Continue along D 157.*

Meaulne

This town is situated at the confluence of the River Aumance and River Cher. **Alain-Fournier** (1886-1914) gave its name to the hero in his great novel *Le Grand Meaulnes*, which was set in and around Épineuil-le-Fleuriel (the fictional Ste-Agathe), on the opposite bank of the Cher *(5.5km/3.5mi SW on D 4; see The Green Guide Dordogne-Berry-Limousin).*

▶ *Leave Meaulne S on N 144 towards Montluçon.*

Vallon-en-Sully

This village on the banks of the Berry canal is home to some charming buildings in the local pink sandstone, such as the 12C church. **Vallon Arts et Traditions** (♿ 🕐 *Apr-Jun, Sep, Oct: Sat-Sun and public holidays 3-6pm; Jul and Aug: daily except Tue 3-7pm. 3€. ☎ 04 70 06 51 00)* houses animated tableaux illustrating scenes of daily life and labour in the region in bygone times.

▶ *Take D 11 back to Hérisson.*

LAC D'ISSARLÈS ★

MICHELIN MAP 331:G-4 OR 239 FOLD 47
LOCAL MAP SEE GORGES DE LA LOIRE

The waters of this round and intensely blue-looking lake (alt 1 000m/3 281ft) are used to run the hydroelectric power plant at Montpezat, which can therefore affect the water level, though between 15 June and 15 September the lake is kept full to provide an attractive place for bathing.

Tour of the Lake

The lake occupies an old volcanic crater 138m/452ft deep with a surface area of some 90ha/222 acres. It is possible to walk all the way round (5km/3mi), mostly through

A. de Valroger/MICHELIN

Lake Issarlès

woodland, but it is advisable to enquire before starting out as the woods are some-times flooded owing to the activity of the hydroelectric power plant nearby.

Viewpoint

🚶 *15min there and back. From the south end of the village of Issarlès, follow the path climbing to the left of the beach. It runs through pine woods to the remains of a troglo-dytic dwelling hollowed out of the rock.*
A short way further on, a second rock forms an excellent viewpoint overlooking the lake and its wooded surroundings.

Excursion

Discovering Lauze Country

Allow one day

▶ *Leave Lake Issarlès on D 16 heading for Béage and follow directions for Ste-Eulalie.*

Ste-Eulalie

This village belongs to the municipality of Gerbier-de-Jonc and lies at the source of the River Loire. On the way to the Mont Gerbier de Jonc, another traditional broom-covered farmhouse, **Ferme Philip** *(Visits organised for groups by appointment. 2€ per person.* ☎ *04 75 38 80 00.)*, can be visited.

▶ *Continue along D 122, heading towards Lachamp-Raphaël until you reach the intersection with D 378.*

Ferme de Bourlatier★

🕐*Guided visit (1h): Jun-Aug: 11am-6pm; end May-Jun and Sep: Sat, Sun and public holidays.* 🕐 *rest of year. 2.50€.* ☎ *04 75 38 84 90.*
A fine example of regional rural architecture with its lauze roof tiling, this stately farm-house has been extensively restored in local tradition. Its most salient feature is probably its superb framework, shaped like an inverted hull, able to support the 150t roofwork!

Address Book

WHERE TO STAY

⊜ **Chambre d'hôte L'Herminette** – Bigorre, les Maziaux - 43550 St-Front - 5km/3mi NW of St-Front via D 39 and road on right - ☎ 04 71 59 57 58 - www. auberge-lherminette.com - reserv. required - 6 rms - meals ⊜ A country B&B topped with a traditional lauze stone roof. After a meal inspired by local gastronomy and a revitalizing night's sleep, step next door and visit the ecomuseum dedicated to local history and architecture.

⊜⊜ **Hôtel du Nord** – 07510 Ste-Eulalie - 16km/10mi E of the Lac d'Issarlès via D 16 and D 122 - ☎ 04 75 38 80 09 - closed mid-Nov to mid-Feb, Tue evening and Wed except Jul-Aug - 🅿 - 15 rms - �byꞇ

7.50€ - restaurant ⊜⊜. On the road to Gerbier-de-Jonc, this country inn in a small village is a convenient stopover. Run by the children of the original owners, it is being progressively redecorated and the rooms are very well maintained. Unaffected family fare at attractive prices.

SHOPPING

Auberge des Fermiers du Mézenc – Le Bourg - 43150 Les Estables - ☎ 04 71 08 34 20. For a taste of authentic regional produce, make a small detour and visit this inn where all sorts of Ardeche specialities are sold, including honey, locally-made cheeses, preserves and chestnut pies.

▶ *At the crossroads take D 378, heading for Les Estables and Gerbier-de-Jonc.*

Gerbier-de-Jonc★★

The Gerbier-de-Jonc, rising at an altitude of 1 551m/5 088ft on the crest of the range separating the Loire and Rhône basins, looks like a giant haystack or a huge heap of sheaves when seen from a distance.

The word "Gerbier" is a Latinisation of the Indo-European root *gar* meaning "rock." Similar names are found in other regions of France, in particular in the Pyrenees (Pic du Gar, Pic du Ger, Pic du Jer). The word *jonc* is derived from the Latin jugum meaning "mountain." Gerbier de Jonc therefore literally means "rocky mountain." The Gerbier de Jonc, which is part of the Mézenc range, consists of phonolithic rocks that have a tendency to flake, forming unstable scree slopes and clothing the mountainside in a scaly shell. At the foot of the south-western slope are several small streams; they constitute the sources of the Loire.

Access – Striking views of the Gerbier-de-Jonc can be had from the St-Martial *(to the NE)* or Ste-Eulalie *(to the S)* roads.

The climb

🏃 It is a hard climb to the summit *(45min on foot there and back)*. From the top, though, there is an impressive **panoramic view**★★. On the north-east side the view extends over the dip formed by the Eysse, a tributary of the River Eyrieux. Mont Alambre, the Mézenc and the volcanic Sara close off the horizon to the north; Montfol obstructs the view to the west; the conical La Barre, easily recognisable by its tabular outline, lies in the foreground on the south side. A stretch of the Alps can also be seen in clear weather.

▶ *Proceed towards Les Estables on D 378.*

Ancienne Chartreuse de Bonnefoy

1km/0.6mi from D 378. Nestling in a luxuriant setting, this former charter house founded in the 12C, rebuilt after the Wars of Religion, currently consists of a square tower and the main façade dating from the 18C.

▶ *D 378A, then D 36, will lead to Les Estables.*

Les Estables✳

Alt. 1 367m/4 484ft. This small mountain village lying at the foothills of the Mézenc massif is a popular winter resort offering a wide choice of pistes for both Alpine and cross-country skiing.

▷ *Cross the village heading N and turn right for Mont Mézenc via the Peccata Cross.*

Mont Mézenc★★★

The volcanic Mézenc range (the final "c" is not pronounced) forms a natural barrier that divides the rivers flowing to the Atlantic from those flowing to the Mediterranean. It rises to an altitude of 1 753m/5 751ft at Mont Mézenc, which gave its name to the range as a whole.

Extending northwards into the Meygal, south-eastwards into the Coiron, the Mézenc massif forms the centre of a volcanic trail that cuts across the axis of the Cévennes. It is flanked to the west by the granite mountains at La Margeride and to the east by the crystalline plateaux of the Upper Vivarais. A vast tract of land called the **Zone Nordique du Mézenc** is popular in the winter months for the cross-country skiing it offers; more than 100km/62mi of pistes are maintained around the towns and villages of Fay-sur-Lignon, Chaudeyrolles, Freycenet-la-Cuche, Les Estables and St-Front.

All types of volcanoes – During the Tertiary Era, alpine folding broke up the old central plateau in places, causing a series of volcanic eruptions. Where the Mézenc massif lies today, there were the first craters, though they are no longer recognisable. Later, further eruptions led to the formation of great *planèzes* on the eastern slopes of the Mézenc massif, followed by huge phonolithic cones. The Quaternary Era brought with it the extension of the glaciers, then the last eruptions which filled the valleys with thick flows of basalt.

Despite the erosion, almost every possible type of volcano: Hawaiian where the lava flows were very fluid (*planèzes* on the slopes overlooking the Velay area, and Ray-Pic); Strombolian where the scoria is rough and rugged (Coupe d'Aizac, Bauzon); Vulcanian where the lava has been pulverised into ash and fine scoria (Gravenne de Montpezat); Pelean with thick domes and lava peaks (phonolithic cones such as the Gerbier-de-Jonc).

Hillsides with contrasting appeal – On the Velay side of the Mézenc massif the range looks like a vast, bare plateau. In the summer months it resembles a windswept steppe dotted with low farmhouses crowned with thatched or stone-slabbed roofs. The Vivarais side of the range is rugged terrain, suddenly sweeping down towards the Rhône. The streams have worn the ground down to the granite rocks underneath. Splendid basalt flows – On the hillsides flanking the valleys, erosion has revealed extensive basalt lava flows that are particularly impressive in the upper reaches of the River Ardèche and its tributaries (the Volane, Bourges, Fontaulière and Lignon). These flows, which now take the form of prismatic columnar basalt, have created famous beauty spots such as the Ray-Pic waterfall, the Thueyts causeway, Pourcheyrolles rock, Jaujac and Antraigues.

A majestic procession – The phonolithic cones that appeared at the end of the Tertiary Era form a majestic procession on each side of Mont Mézenc. To the north is Mont Signon (1 454m/4 770ft), to the east Roche Borée and Touron (1 380m/4 528ft), to the south-east Sara (1 520m/4 986ft), Gerbier-de-Jonc (1 551m/5 080ft), the cones of Montivernoux (1 441m/4 727ft) and Areilladou (1 448m/4 750ft), to the south the dome-shaped Pal and Bauzon, to the south-west Montfol (1 601m/5 252ft), and to the west Rocher-Tourte (1 535m/5 036ft) and Mont d'Alambre (1 691m/5 548ft).

Flora in the peaks – The upper Mézenc massif has flora which will delight botanists, including a variety of groundsel which, in all the Massif Central, can only be found at the summit of the Mézenc massif: the famous "Mézenc grass" with silvery leaves and beautiful bright yellow flower-heads. The great mountain violet, Alpine anemone, all sorts of gentians, globe flowers, arnica, willow-herb and saxifrages are the commonest of the plants but it is when the narcissi flower in June that the mountain acquires its finest appearance. A traditional market of medicinal herbs, known as the "Violet Fair," is held in Ste-Eulalie every year.

Access via the Boutières Cross

2.5km/almost 2mi from Les Estables via D 631 E. Park at the Boutières Cross (alt 1 508m/4 948ft).
From the rock above the pass at the Boutières Cross, to the right, there is a superb **view★★** over Sara, Roche Borée and Les Boutières.

▶ *Follow the footpath numbered GR7 (1hr 15min there and back) which climbs up to the left towards the summit.*

Head for the south summit (1753m/5 751ft) via the flat ground in between the two peaks.

Access via the Peccata Cross

3km/2mi NE from Les Estables. Park at the Peccata Cross (alt 1 570m/5 151ft) then follow the path on the right (1hr on foot there and back).
This route climbs up through the woods then twists and turns amid the heather and juniper bushes.

▶ *Bear left towards the north summit (1 749m/5 738t) topped by a cross.*

Panoramic view★★★

From the summit there is a sweeping **panorama**. To the north are the Meygal and Forez mountains; to the west, the Puy basin, the Velay area and the mountains of the Auvergne; to the south lie Lake Issarlès and a string of volcanic cones; and to the east the Saliouse and Eysse gorges, both of which cut into the Boutières area towards the Upper Eyrieux, where deep ravines are interspersed with ridges and peaks. Beyond it are the Alps, the highest peaks of which can be seen in clear weather.

▶ *Rejoin D 274 to the N via the Peccata Cross. At the crossroads with D 39, turn right and follow directions to Fay-sur-Lignon.*

Fay-sur-Lignon

This mountain village (pronounced fa-yee), clinging to the slopes of a phonolithic cone, offers cross-country skiing facilities in winter.

▶ *Take D 39 to St-Front.*

St-Front

The ancient village lying at the foot of a mound offers excellent **views★** of the northeast slopes of the Mézenc massif. Note the 11C church on the village square.

▶ *Take D 263 on the right and drive to St-Front Lake. Rejoin D 39 via Chaudeyrac Forest and continue straight ahead, heading for Le Monastier on D 500. A few miles after the plateau where cattle is left to graze in summer, take D 36 on the right, then D 361 towards Moudeyres.*

Moudeyres

The village still has several typical cottages, namely the **Ferme des Frères Perrel** (◷*Jul to mid-Sep: 10am-noon, 3-7pm. 3€.* ☎ *04 71 05 12 13)*. Apart from its basalt walls, its lauze tiles over the living quarters and its thatched roof crowning the outbuildings, it has kept its original furniture and farming tools.

▶ *Turn back and rejoin D 500. Turn right towards Le Monastier-sur-Gazeille.*

Le Monastier-sur-Gazeille – 🖒 *See Le MONASTIER-SUR-GAZEILLE.*

▶ *Take D 38 on the left to Issarlès. Return to Lake Issarlès.*

ISSOIRE★★

POPULATION 14 470
MICHELIN MAP 326: G-9

Issoire is located on the Couze River, near its junction with the Allier, south of Clermont-Ferrand and on the fertile plain of Limagne. The town is said to have been founded by the Arverni, a powerful Gallic tribe that inhabited the present-day region of Lyon. They gave their name to this region – Auvergne. During the 17th-century religious wars of the Reformation, Issoire suffered severely, and most of the old town was destroyed. Architecturally, pride of place goes to the ornate 12th-century Abbatiale Saint-Austremoine, formerly the church of a Benedictine abbey, and one of the largest Romanesque churches in the Auvergne. But there is an agreeable, provincial ambiance about the place that rewards even the shortest break. Today, surrounded by boulevards, the town is bright, refreshing, and a delight to explore, not least its remarkable Renaissance clock tower, formerly the town belfry, from the top of which there is a fine panoramic view over the town, the Limagne landscape and the Monts Dore and Livradois mountain ranges. ▯ *Pl. du Gén.-de-Gaulle, 63500 ISSOIRE, ☎ 04 73 89 15 90. www.issoire.fr*

▶ **Orient Yourself:** Take a trip up the clocktower for a superb view of the town and surrounding countryside. Then start your tour of the town. Most shops, restaurants and bars cluster around the tower, and along the main street.

🅿 **Parking:** Ample car parking in the centre of town

🅐 **Don't Miss:** The Abbatiale Saint-Austremoine

🕐 **Organizing Your Time:** The town is amazingly compact, with many narrow streets; begin with the clock tower, which also houses a display of local life throughout the turbulent Renaissance period.

High flyers – The **gliding club** at Issoire-le-Broc aerodrome to the south-east of the town attracts numerous French and foreign glider pilots who come to enjoy the strong thermal currents in the locality. These currents can lift gliders released at 800m/2 625ft up to an altitude of more than 10 000m/32 808ft.

Little Geneva – In 1540 a former Dominican monk arrived in Issoire from Germany and converted the Consuls to the Lutheran faith. He was burnt alive on the bailiff's orders but his death led, in fact, to numerous additional conversions. Issoire became a "Little Geneva," washed in the blood of the many martyrs to the new faith.

Walking Tour

The early-19C **corn-exchange,** situated next to the tourist office, has been turned into an entertainment centre. Follow rue Ponteil which starts opposite and leads to the **Tour de l'Horloge** (clock tower, *see Sights below*). On reaching place de la République (the former Grande Place), where a busy market takes place on Saturday mornings, note the 15C **Maison Charrier** with its Gothic doorway and the **fountain** adorning the centre of the square, designed in 1823 by the architect Ledru. Beyond, to the left, is the **Maison aux Arcades;** turn left onto rue des Fours and admire the 15C-17C **Hôtel Bohier** which houses a fine Renaissance staircase. Turn left at the end of the street to reach the **Centre Pomel** *(see Sights below).* Opposite, on the corner of square Cassin, the Maison de la Bascule (weights and measures building) houses the **Musée de la Pierre Philosophale** containing a collection of 1 000 minerals. Walk round the cathedral and back to place de la République. Turn right onto rue de la Berbiziale; on the corner, note the 15C **Maison du Chancelier Duprat** with its rectangular corbelled tower. Continue to place St-Avit; the 18C **Maison Bartin** on the left, has fine wrought-iron balconies.

Abbatiale St-Austremoine★★

St-Austremoine, once the church of a Benedictine abbey, was built in the 12C and dedicated to Austremoine, the first bishop of the Arverni people, martyred in the 3C; it is now the parish church, replacing the neighbouring Église St-Paul, which was destroyed shortly after the French Revolution. The belfry, west front and many of the capitals, were altered in the 19C.

Exterior
The **east end**★★ stands on a wide esplanade. This is the most perfect section of the building, a consummate example of Romanesque architecture as it developed in the Auvergne. No other church boasts such harmonious proportions, such purity of line and such restraint in its decoration. Its powerful, well-balanced design consists of various different elements; note the mosaics and sculptures representing the signs of the Zodiac.

Interior
The two-storey **nave** is especially striking for its magnificent proportions; the painted decoration was added in the mid-19C. Walk up the nave as far as the pulpit to see the ensemble including the transept supported by four huge quadripartite arches lightened by bays, the dome rising to a height of 23m/75ft, and the chancel flanked by its ambulatory. In the right arm of the transept are two outstanding capitals, one illustrating lust and the other the Annunciation.
At the southern entrance to the ambulatory there is one of the finest, and most complete, views of the building as a whole. Walk round the chancel; it is particularly interesting for its superb narrative **capitals**★ depicting the Last Supper and the Visit of the Holy Women to the Tomb. From the back of the Lady Chapel there is a good view down the nave. In the northern arm of the transept are another two capitals: one depicting a man carrying a sheep illustrates the parable of the Good Shepherd; on the other is a demon dragging away two condemned souls.

Crypt
This is one of the finest crypts in the Auvergne. The stocky columns supporting the vaulted roof give an impression of strength that is further emphasized by the total lack of decoration. In the centre is a graceful statue of the Virgin Mary.

The Last Judgement★
Left on leaving the church. This 15C fresco depicts in a very lively manner a theme that was dear to many artists of the day. Here it is treated with character and great verve.

Address Book

EATING OUT

Le Boudes La Vigne – *63340 Boudes - 15km/9mi S of Issoire via D 909 and D 48 -* ☎ *04 73 96 55 66 - closed 2-22 Jan and 24 Aug-5 Sep.* Set in the heart of a quaint wine-making village, this basic hotel has small rooms that are modest but well-kept, and the restaurant, part of which is in the cellar, has its regular patrons.

La Bergerie – *63490 Sarpoil - 10km/6mi E of Issoire via D 999 -* ☎ *04 73 71 02 54 - closed Jan, Mon evening, Tue-Wed Sep-Jun - reserv. required.* A coaching inn and sheepfold in the olden days, this restaurant, featuring old stone walls in the vaulted dining room, has retained its old-fashioned charm. Classic cuisine.

La Cour Carrée – *63500 Perrier - 5km/3mi W of Issoire via D 996 -* ☎ *04 73 55 15 55 - closed Feb and Christmas holidays, Sun evening, Wed evening, Sat lunch Sep-Jun and Mon - reserv. recommended.* This former winemaker's abode is entered via the small square courtyard. In summertime, a terrace is set up here under the big horse chestnut, whereas in winter, you will be seated in the vaulted dining room. Traditional fare.

WHERE TO STAY

Chambre d'hôte Paul Gebrillat et Mireille de Saint Aubain – *Chemin de Siorac - 63500 Perrier - 3km/1.8mi W of Issoire via D 996 -* ☎ *04 73 89 15 02 - www.maison-gebrillat.com - closed 1 Dec-31 Jan - 3 rms.* In a village right near the volcanoes, this pretty 18C house is inviting indeed. Breakfast is served under a trellis in the delightful courtyard planted with flowers. Charming rooms and reliable advice for adventuresome tourists.

Château de Grange Fort – *63500 Les Pradeaux - 7km/4.2mi SE of Issoire - take A 75, exit 13, dir. Parentignat and D 34, rte d'Auzat-sur-Allier -* ☎ *04 73 71 02 43 - chateau@grangefort.com - closed Dec-Mar - 5 rms: 47/70€- 10€ - meals* ☺☺. A 17C château with superb crenellated towers set in the bosom of a park encircled by mountains. The rooms, all unique, may feature a canopy bed, a sculpted door, a parquet floor or original mouldings. Splendid vaulted dining room.

Chambre d'hôte Les Baudarts – *63500 Varennes-sur-Usson - 6km/3.6mi E of Issoire via D 996 and D 123 -* ☎ *04 73 89 05 51 - closed 1 Oct-1 May - 3 rms.* Lost in the middle of the countryside, this Provencal-style house with pink walls and a Romanesque tiled roof is all elegance and sophistication. The spacious bedrooms are tastefully decorated and the living room is superb; the swimming pool and small park are lovely. Not to be missed!

SHOPPING

Maison Chazal – *4 r. Gambetta -* ☎ *04 73 89 20 11.* A handsome establishment with products divided into different sections. The 'roasting room' offers coffee beans from such illustrious provenances as the Galapagos Islands and a wide range of teas; the grocer's shelves are laden with preserves, foie gras, honey and the like; the vaulted wine cellar boasts about 350 different vintages, including 20 from outside of France, and 50-odd brands of whisky.

Pascale et Patrick Védrine – *8 r. du Ponteil -* ☎ *04 73 55 28 18 - vpa@wanadoo.fr.* The unique decor and warm atmosphere set this baker's shop apart. Special breads are made according to traditional recipes and cooked in a wood-burning oven; pastries are also very popular, especially the Ponteil and the Sancy. We suggest you take the time to taste these treats on site – the decor is truly worth discovering.

Sights

Centre Pomel

This houses the **Centre d'Art Roman Georges-Duby** (&⏱ *May-Sep: daily except Mon morning 10am-noon, 2-6pm. No charge. ☏ 04 73 89 56 04. www.terres-romanes-auvergne.com*), which displays the vestiges of the Monastère St-Austremoine.

Tour de l'Horloge

&⏱ *Jun-Sep: daily except Mon 10am-1pm, 2-7pm, (last admission 45min before closing); Oct-May: daily except Mon 2-6pm (Sat 7pm). ⏱ Closed 1 Jan, 1 May, 25 Dec. 5.50€ (children: 3.50€). ☏ 04 73 89 07 70. www.issoire.fr*

The chimes of the Renaissance belfry (15C) can still be heard throughout town. A lively '**Scenovision**' presentation enlightens visitors on the rich and colourful past of Issoire and eight short documentary films retrace the impact of the Renaissance (printing and other great discoveries). Temporary exhibitions are also organised. From the top of the tower there is a panoramic view of the town and the surrounding countryside.

Excursions

Approaching the Livradois

45km/28mi round trip – allow 2hr

▸ *Leave Issoire on D 996 to the SE.*

Château de Parentignat★

4km/2.5mi SE on D 996. ⏱ Mid-May to end Sep: Sat-Sun and public holidays 2.30-6pm (Jul and Aug: daily). 7€ (under-12s: 3.50€). ☏ 04 73 89 51 10. www.parentignat.com

The château was built towards the end of Louis XIV's reign (early 18C) and has remained in the same family since. The main courtyard has formal grass parterres, contrasting with the English-style landscape gardens bordered by orange trees and roses. The ancestral treasures include furniture as well as paintings by Nicolas de Largillière, Mme Vigée-Lebrun, Rigaud and Van Loo. The library contains valuable first editions.

▸ *Continue along D 996 towards Sauxillanges. After 6km/3.7mi, take D 709 on the right.*

Butte d'Usson

The basaltic rock of Usson was once the site of a formidable castle, of which nothing remains but the memory of Marguerite de Valois. "Usson is a town situated on a plain where there is a rock, and three towns one on top of the other in the shape of a Pope's mitre," says an ancient text. The castle was built by the Duc de Berry, and believed to be impregnable. On the door was written "Mind the traitor and the tooth!" meaning that only treason or famine could get the better of it.

View

From a viewing table off D 709 to the north of the town there is a beautiful view of the Limagne d'Issoire in the foreground and the Puys chain in the background. The Puy de la Vache and Puy de Dôme with its television tower can be seen on the extreme right.

Queen Margot (16C-17C)

This princess, popularised by the author Alexandre Dumas, was the sister of Charles IX who gave her in marriage to the King of Navarre (the future Henri IV), saying that, in doing so, he "had given her to all the Huguenots in the Kingdom"– a somewhat indiscreet allusion to the young queen's many love affairs. Her conduct was such that she was forced to seek asylum in Carlat, where her favourite was the young Lord of Aubiac. Fleeing Carlat when the king ordered her arrest, Marguerite took refuge in Ybois Castle, near Orbeil (north-east of Issoire). Henri III sent the Marquis of Canillac to lay siege to the fortress. Canillac seized the queen and Aubiac; instructed by the court, he had her favourite executed. Marguerite was locked up in Usson under the guard of the marquis.

For 20 years Queen Margot led a life of passion, study and devotion. Her husband the king wanted her to agree to having the marriage dissolved. She would only agree, however, after the death of Gabrielle d'Estrées, the king's mistress, not wanting to be replaced (so she wrote to Sully), by "such an ill-esteemed piece of trash." After that, she was able to return to Paris.

Puy d'Usson

A gentle path leads to the summit on which a chapel has been built with a colossal statue of the Virgin Mary; it provides a good **panorama**★ of the region. During the climb, a beautiful set of basalt columns can be seen in an old quarry.

▶ *Return to D 996.*

Sauxillanges

The 11C **church** with 15C alterations contains a mural depicting the Deposition and a 15C statue of Our Lady of the Woods. The Prior's Chapel, now a heritage centre, **Maison du Patrimoine** (⏱*Jul to mid-Sep: guided tours available (1hr30min) 2.30-6.30pm. 3€. ☏ 04 73 96 37 63)*, is part of the remains of a priory founded in 927 and attached to the Cluniac Order. The Gothic vaulting is decorated with interesting hanging keystones bearing the coats of arms of the various priors.

You can take the direct route (D 214) or choose to go the long way to St-Étienne-d'Usson on D 144, enjoying the drive down towards Sarpoil.

▶ *In Bansat, turn right onto D 24, then turn left in St-Martin-des-Plains, heading for Mailhat.*

Église de Mailhat

The delightful little Romanesque church has a square belfry with double openings, and a five-sided apse decorated with blind arcading and modillions. There are interesting carved capitals: on the doorway is a representation of Lust (a woman breast-feeding two serpents) and Avarice (a long-armed man clutching his purse to his chest). In the chancel, the capitals are decorated with figures and foliage.

▶ *D 123 leads to Orsonnette, then to Nonette.*

Nonette★

The village is built on a promontory overlooking the Allier. The half-Romanesque, half-Gothic **church** (⏱*Sat-Sun 10am-6pm. ☏ 04 73 71 65 41)*, once part of a priory, has a carved Romanesque doorway and, inside, a superb late-14C bust of Christ (north chapel).

O The ruins of the 14C **castle** *(45min on foot there and back via a steep path)* stand on a height offering a splendid **panorama**★ over the valley and the mountains.

Dauphiné d'Auvergne★

60km/37mi – allow half a day

At the end of the 12C, the region to the south-west of Issoire between the Cézallier and the Allier Valley, comprising rugged countryside scored by the various Couzes *(see Vallées des COUZES)* flowing between hilly outcrops and basalt plateaux, formed the Dauphiné d'Auvergne, a sort of local, royal fief whose lords and their entourage set up a glittering court in Champeix, Vodable and Mercœur successively. For some years now, an association of local *communes* has been making efforts to rekindle interest in this forgotten little fief, which sank into obscurity before the end of the Middle Ages. Its efforts were rewarded in 1992, when the Dauphiné d'Auvergne was officially declared a "Pays d'Art et d'Histoire" (Region of Historic and Artistic Interest).

▶ *Leave Issoire to the W on D 996, towards Champeix.*

Grottes artificielles de Perrier

The village of Perrier is overlooked by a plateau bristling with bizarrely shaped rocks, evidence of the violent eruptions which took place thousands of years ago in the Dore mountain region, which unleashed gigantic flows of mud mixed with boulders, or **lahars** *(see Introduction: Volcanoes of the Auvergne)*. Erosion subsequently sculpted the fantastic rock formations known as "fairies' chimneys."

Artificial Caves

🚶 *1hr walk there and back. From the church in Perrier, take the footpath to the caves ("Chemin des Grottes").* These caves were hollowed out of the volcanic rock and used as troglodytic dwellings.

▶ *From the caves, follow the route indicated as "vue panoramique."*

From the plateau there is a remarkable **view**★ of the surrounding rocks, the feudal keep, the village and the Couze de Pavin. A footpath runs along the plateau's edge, amid myriad and abundant plant life.

▶ *On leaving Perrier, take D 26 left for 2km/1.2mi, then turn left again onto D 23.*

Tourzel

Small wine-growers' houses in this village bear witness to a viti-cultural past, specifically during the 18C and 19C when Tourzel's main source of income was wine. One of these lava-walled houses is home to a small museum on the pork butcher's trade. Further down, the **Maison de Pays** (🕐*May to mid-Sep: 10am-7pm. No charge. ☎ 04 73 71 40 09),* another house typical of the region, contains

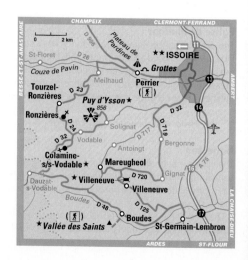

a display evoking scenes from local history, as well as a wide variety of local farm produce.

▶ *Follow D 23 for another 1km/0.6mi, then turn left onto D 124.*

Ronzières

At the entrance to the village, a narrow track (⛔ *closed to traffic*) climbs up to a basalt plateau on which a pre-Romanesque church stands. This building was modified in the late 12C, and features a 15C doorway. Inside, the chapel on the left houses a beautiful Romanesque statue of the Virgin Mary in Majesty, made of polychrome wood and protected behind an imposing 19C set of railings. The capitals supporting the arches of the cupola are Carolingian, from the previous building.

In the church graveyard, on the edge of the plateau, two viewing tables give information on the view of the surrounding countryside, which stretches over the Puy d'Ysson, the Couze de Pavin, Perrier plateau and Lembron plain. Examples of the two volcanic features so characteristic of the Dauphiné d'Auvergne region are easy to pick out.

▶ *Take D 124 as far as Vodable and turn left onto D 32 to Solignat.*

Puy d'Ysson★

Alt 856m/2 808ft. This cone is formed by the chimney of a volcano which emerged during the Tertiary Era; the plug of lava was laid bare by erosion. From the summit, there is a fine **panorama** of the Dore mountain range, the extinct volcanoes of the Comté region, the Limagne around Issoire, the Livradois mountains and the Cézallier.

From here, the villages through which you have already travelled can also clearly be seen: Vodable at the foot of its basalt needle, to the right Ronzières with its church perched up high, and Perrier in the shadow of its plateau.

▶ *Drive back down to Solignat and take D 32 back to Vodable.*

Église de Colamine-sous-Vodable

🕐 *Mid-Jul to early Sep: Sun 3-6.30pm.* ☎ *04 73 71 43 26.*

The church still stands surrounded by its graveyard, on the side of a coomb. It boasts a pretty Romanesque chancel (11C, but restored) and a fine group of polychrome wooden statues, among them a remarkable 12C **Virgin Mary in Majesty**★. The statues were discovered in 1979 during restoration work; they had been walled up since the mid-18C behind the carved 17C altarpiece.

▶ *Rejoin D 32 and travel for 4km/3mi towards Dauzat-sur-Vodable, then turn left onto D 48.*

Boudes

Neatly sheltered by a range of hills to the north and by the Avoiron pinnacle to the west, this village was the only one in the entire region to escape the ravages of phylloxera. Thanks to the good soil here (a combination of clay, limestone and basalt pebbles), local vines produce fine quality wine, including a particularly well regarded white wine. The layout of the vineyards, on a single slope, well-exposed to the sun, and the brightly coloured houses form a striking sight. Note the fine dovecots.

▶ *Leave Boudes to the S, crossing the Couzilloux, and take the track to the right which runs along the side of the graveyard.*

Vallée des Saints★

1hr walk there and back. Leave the car at the start of the track.

⚔ A waymarked path enables visitors to explore this area to the full, admiring the giant red and ochre pyramids with which it is populated, some 10-30m/30-100ft high and strangely sculpted by erosion. Their outlandish silhouettes, like gigantic statues, have earned the valley its name.

The red, iron-oxide bearing clay, from which these features are made, was formed by the transformation of gneiss in the hot and humid tropical climate that prevailed at the beginning of the Tertiary Era.

▶ *Return to Boudes and turn right at the church to rejoin D 48.*

St-Germain-Lembron

This small, once fortified village in the midst of an agricultural region still boasts some 18C houses with double-gabled roofs.

▶ *Take D 48 towards Boudes once again, then turn off to the right after 1km/0.6mi onto D 125.*

The road climbs towards Châlus, from where there are beautiful views of the volcanic necks and tables rising above the Limagne.

Villeneuve-Lembron

Narrow streets lined with old houses and wash-houses surround a 15C church.

Château de Villeneuve★

🕐 *Mid-May to mid-Sep: daily,10am-noon, 2-6.30pm; mid-Sep to mid-May: daily except Mon 10am-noon, 2-5.30pm* 🕐 *Closed 1 Jan, 1 May, 1 and 11 Nov, 25 Dec. 5€ (under 18, free).* ☎ *04 73 96 41 64.*

This seigneurial castle was built for the Aureille family, one of whose members was the diplomat Rigault, who served under Louis XI, Charles VIII, Louis XII and François I and fought alongside Charles VIII in the Italian campaigns. It was Rigault who initiated the restoration and refurbishing of the family château at the end of the 15C.

The castle has a square ground plan with a round tower at each corner and is surrounded by dry moats, for ornamental purposes only. The main building stands around a central courtyard with a covered gallery.

A tour of the interior reveals many treasures, such as handsome ceilings with rafters, interesting woodwork and valuable pieces of furniture. The courtyard **gallery** houses some marvellous 15C paintings (restored) on subjects that reflect Rigault's unfortunate marriage. On leaving the castle, take a look at the stables, in which the vast barrel roof vault is decorated with late-16C frescoes.

▶ *Carry on along D 125 and turn left onto D 720.*

Mareugheol

This is a typical example of a fortified village built during the Middle Ages in order to protect the inhabitants from the marauding bands of robbers which plagued the region. Old stone houses stand along narrow streets within a rectangular fortified wall of which only a few stretches of wall and a stump of corner tower remain. At the bottom of the village there is a tiny village square adorned with a fountain.

▶ *Take D 720 as far as Gignat, then turn left onto D 719, which leads back to Issoire.*

LALOUVESC

POPULATION 494
MICHELIN MAP 331: J-3 OR 246 FOLD 19

This village is entirely dedicated to Saint François-Régis, who died tragically in 1640. A popular place of pilgrimage, Lalouvesc is also a pleasant resort enjoying a privileged site, lush vegetation and invigorating mountain air. *R. St-Régis, 07520 LALOUVESC, ☎ 04 75 67 84 20.*

A Stunning Basilica

Built in the 19C by the architect Bossan, the basilica stands proudly on St François-Régis' former grave. Inside, a reliquary contains the saint's remains. Nearby stands the chapel that pays homage to St François-Régis: personal mementoes, small museum with diorama, work by Serraz. The viewing table fronting the basilica offers a delightful **panorama**★ of the Rhône Valley and the Alps dominating the Ay depression.

Driving Tour

The Haut-Vivarais Plateaux★

Round tour of 62km/38.5mi – allow 2hr 30min

▶ *Leave Lalouvesc on D 532, heading for Tournon, then turn right onto the road to Lamastre.*

The road skirts Besset mountain. The pleasantly shaded route offers charming views of the Mézenc and the two hill villages of Molières and Lafarre.

Col du Buisson

Alt 920m/3 018ft. *Park in the car park.* On a clear day there are far-reaching views to the north-east beyond Pailharès, over to Mont Blanc, Les Grandes Rousses and La Meije. South lies the Doux basin and to the west the peaks of Mont Mézenc and Gerbier-de-Jonc. At the intersection of D 273 and D 236 is the **Village Ardéchois en Miniature** a model of a typical village made from local granite. ◷ *May-Oct: 10am-8pm.* ◷ *rest of year. 2€ (under-8s: no charge). ☎ 04 75 23 14 77.*

▶ *Turn left onto D 273.*

As the road descends, the red roofs of Pailharès come into view.

Pailharès

The village, which stands out from the surrounding countryside on a platform, still has the rectangular layout dating from the days when its old town walls were built.

St-Félicien

The **church** is interesting for its Romanesque sections – the arcading in the

---

COUNTRY INN

⊜⊜ **Fort du Pré** – *43290 St-Bonnet-le-Froid - 11km/6.6mi NW of Lalouvesc via D 532 - ☎ 04 71 59 91 83 - www.le-fort-du-pre.fr - closed 31 Aug to 4 Sep, 1 Dec to 31 Jan, Sun evening and Mon except Jul-Aug -* 🅿 *- 34 rms - ⊡ 9€ - restaurant ⊜⊜. Lost in the countryside, here is a pretty restored farm offering recreational activities (a covered pool and fitness room) and colourful bedrooms. The cheerful dining room gives onto a verdant terrace. Local produce and recipes.*

north aisle where the pilasters are topped by engaged columns. Every June the town hosts an important competition, attended by thousands of sportsmen, consisting of several cycling events.

▶ *In St-Félicien turn left onto D 115.*

The corniche road commands lovely **views**★ of the Rhône Valley.

▶ *In Sattilieu, take D 480 towards St-Symphorien-de-Mahun, then turn left.*

Veyrine
The Romanesque church, characterised by its remarkable simplicity, features a hollow porch ornamented with moulding.

▶ *Return to Lalouvesc on D 578^A, which runs along the slopes of the Chaix mountain.*

LAMASTRE

POPULATION 2 567
MICHELIN MAP 331: J-4

Lamastre, situated at an altitude of 373m/1 224ft on the banks of the River Doux which once powered several mills, relies essentially on tourism and the success of its rock festival. ⓘ *Pl. Mongolfier, 07270 LAMASTRE, ☎ 04 75 06 48 99. www.lamastre.fr.*

Church – The church is situated at the top end of the town, in the old Marcheville district, and is built of attractive pink stone in the Romanesque style. Only the apse, which is decorated on the outside with a multi-lobed opening, dates from the 12C; the remainder is modern. From the terrace in front of the church there is a view down over the town, which lies in the shadow of the remains of its medieval castle.

Address Book

Excursions

View from Rochebloine★★

9km/5.6mi. Leave Lamastre to the W on D 236. At the start of the rise there is a view over the ruins of Retourtour Castle. As far as Nozières, the road runs along the crest of the rise, providing extensive **views**★ over the hills between the River Doux and River Eyrieux then, to the right, over the mound on which stands Boucieu-le-Roi. 2.5km/1.5mi beyond Nozières, a track branches off from the left of the road; the path beyond it leads to the ruins of Rochebloine.

Off a sharp right-hand bend, there is a track leading to the tip of the promontory *(15min on foot there and back)* where there are still a few remains of an ancient fortress. There is a striking **view** of the Upper Doux basin.

Désaignes★

7km/4.3mi W along D 533. The existence of this former Gallo-Roman settlement is evidenced by a great many ruins, including a Roman road. It was to become the most densely populated city in the Vivarais. Of its past glory there remain large sections of the ramparts, a 14C **castle** (⏱ *Jul-Sep: daily except Mon, 2-6pm; Easter to end Oct: Sat-Sun, 2-6pm.* ⏱ *Nov-Easter. 3€.* ☎ *04 75 06 61 19)* housing the **Musée de la Vie Rurale**, and numerous Gothic houses. The nearby lake is popular with both locals and holidaymakers.

Between the Doux and the Eyrieux★

Round trip of 64km/40mi – about 3hr

▶ *Leave Lamastre on D 2 S and turn right onto D 283 to Cluac.*

From the road there are delightful views (right) of the Sumène Valley and the Upper Doux basin.

▶ *In Cluac, turn right onto D 21.*

The descent to Nonières provides a view over a landscape bristling with volcanic domes; then, as D 241 rises to St-Julien-Labrousse, there is an extensive **view**★ over the cones in the Mézenc range from a bend in the road.

Chalencon

This old village, once a fortified town, was the seat of a major barony. From the esplanade bearing the war memorial, in the oldest part of the village, there is a view down over the Eyrieux gorge.

Vernoux-en-Vivarais – ⓑ *See Index.*

Château de la Tourette – ⓑ *Access and description see index.*

▶ *Leave Vernoux on D 14 NE and return to Lamastre on D 105 (left) and D 2 (Col de Montreynaud).*

The route in the shade of the chestnut trees provides a pleasant drive. Note the low cottages on the Châteauneuf-de-Vernoux plateau. From the pass there is a view of the Lamastre basin and the Upper Doux Valley, dominated to the north by the Lalouvesc mountains.

LAPALISSE

POPULATION 3 332
MICHELIN MAP 326: I-5 – 23KM.14.3MI NE OF VICHY

Lapalisse lies on the banks of the River Besbre and is dominated by the outline of its castle. ⓘ *3 r. du Prés.-Roosevelt, 03120 LAPALISSE, ☏ 04 70 99 08 39.*

Château de La Palice★★

Kids ◐ *Apr-Oct: guided tours (1hr), daily, 9am-noon, 2pm-6pm. 5.50€ (children: 2.50€). ☏ 04 70 99 37 58.*

Little remains of the original medieval castle; the building standing today dates from 1527 and was designed by Florentines and is, as a result, an example of early Renaissance architecture.

The somewhat austere façade overlooking the courtyard is relieved by the diamond shapes and chequerboard pattern in multicoloured bricks. Sandstone detailing emphasizes the ridges of the towers and the window surrounds, in accordance with the fashion of the day. There are also ogee lintels, mullioned windows, medallions on the doorway to the central tower, scrolls of foliage, pilasters and Corinthian capitals.

The hall, which contains an early Flemish painting, leads to the dining room furnished in the Italian Renaissance style.

The drawing room once had walls covered with leather from Cordoba; it contains the Chabannes family portraits.

In the **library** hangs a large painting from the Veronese School, *The Republic of Venice Receiving Gifts from the Four Provinces*.

The **Golden Salon**★★ is decorated with a magnificent gilded coffered ceiling and two tapestries of knights, representing Godefroi de Bouillon and Hector. The tapestries, of 15C Flemish manufacture, come from a series of hangings 3.80m/12ft high and 4m/13ft wide, with a 30cm/12in border.

The chapel was rebuilt in the mid-15C but was pillaged during the Revolution. Its crypt contains the Chabannes family vaults. In the outbuildings (fine timber ceiling) there is a collection of standards and flags gathered by a priest from Doyet.

Château de Lapalisse

J. Damase/MICHELIN

Monsieur de La Palice (15C-16C)

Jacques II de Chabannes, Lord of La Palice, Marshal of France, won renown for his valour during the campaign to capture the Milan region. He was killed at the Battle of Pavia in 1525.

The French expression *une verité de La Palice* – meaning something that is so obviously true that it hardly bears pointing out – has its sources in a poem his officers wrote in his honour.

M. de La Palice est mort,
Mort devant Pavie.
Un quart d'heure avant sa mort
Il était encore en vie.

Although they meant to express that he had fought bravely up to the last instant, the words "A quarter hour before his death, he was still alive," have lost their meaning of courage in the face of battle and come to imply naïvety bordering on dim-wittedness.

Musée de l'Art en marche

🕐 *all year, daily, 10am-noon, 2-6pm (Sun, 2-6pm). 5€ (children over 10: 3.50€).* ☎ *04 70 99 21 78. 9, avenue du 8 mai 1945. At the entrance to the village via N 7, parking area nearby.*
Occupying a former industrial site, this museum is devoted to "Art brut," i.e. work of artists who have escaped all forms of conditioning, either cultural or social. The exhibition consists of some 350 works by more than 100 international artists, including J Braunstein, J Monchâtre and M Chichorro.

Excursions

Neuilly-en-Donjon

27km/17mi NE along D 994 then right onto D 989. This small village is mostly known for the delightful **porch**★ of its Romanesque church, characterised by painstaking detail and remarkable craftsmanship. The tympanum portrays the Blessed Virgin and Jesus, the Three Wise Men and a group of Angels. The **capitals** too are worthy of note.

Along the Besbre Valley★

60km/37mi – allow 4hr

▸ *Leave Lapalisse to the NW on D 480, running along the left bank of the Besbre.*

The Besbre Valley contains a surprising variety and number of castles. Only a few are open to visitors, but they are all worth a close look. This quiet little river, which rises in the Bois Noirs (Black Woods) at the foot of the Puy de Montoncel, flows into the Loire south of Bourbon-Lancy. There are many places where anglers can fish for tench, carp, pike and roach. Trout can be found in three of its tributaries, the Têche, the Charnay and the Graveron.

Chavroches

As it climbs towards the castle, the road gives a glimpse of the 15C main building. The gate and outer walls date from the 12C and 13C. The 12C church has an interesting belfry-wall.

Address Book

EATING OUT

⊖⊜ **Auberge de l'Olive** – *Av. de la Gare - 03290 Dompierre-sur-Besbre - ☎ 04 70 34 51 87 - www.auberge-olive.fr - closed 20-29 Sep, Sun evening 1 Dec-15 Apr and Fri except Jul-Aug*. This inn on a busy road is full of surprises. The light and airy veranda is a very inviting setting for a meal, as is the more rustic dining room with fine wooden beams and a lively blue theme. The renovated hotel section is well appointed.

⊖⊜ **Auberge de Boucé** – *Le Bourg - 03150 Boucé - 14km/8.5mi W of Lapalisse via D 480 and D 32 - ☎ 04 70 43 70 59 - closed Feb school holidays, 11-31 Aug, Wed evening Oct-Mar, Sun evening, Tue evening and Mon*. Here is an authentic little family-run village inn replete with café and regular customers. There's something of a bistro ambience in the sparkling clean dining room where abundant, straightforward fare that doesn't strain the budget is served.

WHERE TO STAY

⊖⊜ **Chambre d'hôte Les Vieux Chênes** – *Laprugne - 03120 Servilly - 6km/3.6mi W of Lapalisse via D 480 and D 32 - ☎ 04 70 99 07 53 - closed 1 Nov-15 Mar - ⚑ - 5 rms - meals ⊖⊜*. In this impeccably run country home, the very spacious rooms are downright basic, but we like it anyway. It is surrounded by nature, the reception is charming, and information about the region is readily available.

RECREATION

Cavok Sarl - *Espace Européen de chute libre – Aérodrome de Périgny - ☎ 04 70 99 18 03 - www.lapalisse-aero.com - 18 Apr-30 Sep: daily by appointment, call or send an e-mail*. Parachute jumping for beginners and experienced free-fallers. Tandem jumping with a pro and instruction. Snack bar, swimming pool and camping facilities.

▶ *Drive along the one-way street then turn right and follow D 163 then D 205.*

Jaligny-sur-Besbre

This little town is well known in France for being the adopted home of poet, journalist and novelist **René Fallet**. There is an **exhibition** (◷ *Mon, Thu, Fri 2-6pm, Wed 9am-noon. No charge;* ☎ *04 70 34 69 91*) about him in the old town hall, and a literary prize is awarded annually in his honour. Jaligny is also an agricultural centre famed for its fair; a cattle market and competition are held here every spring and a turkey market in mid-December.

The **Château**★ (⚷ *not open to the public*), visible from afar, across a vast meadow, consists of two sturdy towers with Renaissance windows on either side of a main building with a steep roof.

▶ *Leave Jaligny heading NE along D 21.*

Châtelperron

Small, secluded village dominated by the rounded turrets of its imposing **château** (⚷ *not open to the public*). The **church** organises musical concerts in season. Recent digs (1996-97) have been carried out near Châtelperron, testifying to the existence of a Cro-Magnon settlement in the area.

Préhistorama

Kids ◷ *Apr-Sep: daily except Tue 10am-noon, 2-6pm; Oct-Mar: daily except Mon and Tue 2-5pm. 4€.* ☎ *04 70 34 84 51.*

This museum is housed in the former railway station, next to a pleasant café-cum-restaurant. It retraces the daily life of Neanderthal Man: video presentations show how flint was shaped to make tools and there is a full-size reconstructed dwelling as well as a useful information centre.

▶ *Continue to St-Léon then turn left.*

Puy St-Ambroise
Viewing table. The **view**★ stretches over the entire Besbre Valley and, to the north and west, over the Sologne Bourbonnaise, a flat region studded with copses.

▶ *Return to St-Léon; follow D 53 to Vaumas to rejoin the Besbre Valley.*

Château de Beauvoir★
🕐 *May-Oct: unaccompanied tour of the gardens 9am-7pm; Nov-Apr: 10am-5pm. Guided tours of the castle by appointment (8 days in advance). Apply to Château de Beauvoir, 03290 St-Pourçain-sur-Besbre. No charge.* ☎ *04 70 42 00 44.*

This ancient 13C stronghold shows traces of the 15C renovations carried out by the La Fin family. It differs from the other castles in the region because of its layout: the buildings are set at right-angles to each other. The old watchtower is a typical example of Bourbonnais architecture.

Walk up the central avenue and turn left onto the path alongside the old moat to the gardens.

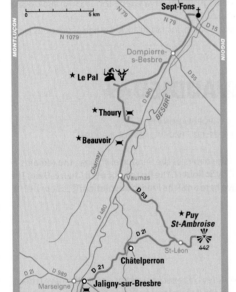

▶ *Continue along D 480, then turn left onto D 296.*

Château de Thoury★
♿ 🕐 *Apr-Oct: guided tours (1hr) 10am-noon, 2-6pm. 4€.* ☎ *04 70 42 00 41.*

This is an attractive 11C, 12C and 15C stronghold, surrounded by a park. High curtain walls link the two main buildings and the machicolated entrance gate which has two turrets with pepper-pot roofs; it is reached via a drawbridge over a moat.

The **tour** takes in the inner courtyard (16C gallery), the guard-room (display on hunting), the dining room, the salon (fine Etruscan vase dating from 450 BC), the watchtower (family mementoes) and the vaulted 11C cellar.

▶ *On leaving the château, turn right.*

Parc Le Pal★
🧒 ♿ 🕐 *Apr, daily except Mon and Fri, 10am-6pm;*

May, daily except Thu and Fri, 10am-6pm; June, daily except Mon and Fri, 10am-6pm (Sun, 10am-7pm); Jul-Aug, daily, 10am-7pm; Sep, Sat Sun, Wed, 10am-6pm. 19€ (3-10-year-olds: 16€; children under 3: no charge). ☎04 70 42 03 60. www.lepal.com.

This 25ha/62-acre park in a forest setting is divided into two sections: an amusement park and a zoo.

The **amusement park** is laid out around place de la Gaîté, a copy of a Parisian square in the middle of the countryside. A dozen or so different attractions include a monorail, rafting, a water train, a caterpillar, a rollercoaster etc. The **zoo** is home to more than 500 species of animals – including elephants, giraffes, big cats, monkeys, deer, waterfowl, parrots and birds of prey – which roam at semi-liberty in an environment reproducing their natural habitat.

▶ *From the park, turn left onto the road back up to D 480. Drive through Dompierre-sur-Besbre, then turn N onto D 55.*

Abbaye de Sept-Fons

This abbey is housed in 18C buildings; the church was rebuilt in 1955. An audio-visual presentation describes monastic life.

The monks make excellent organic food, including a wide range of delicious jams.

LAVAUDIEU★★

POPULATION 225
MICHELIN MAP 331: C-2 – 10KM/6.2MI SE OF BRIOUDE

This hamlet, established on the banks of the Sénouire, still has the remains of an abbey founded in the 11C by St Robert, the first abbot of La Chaise-Dieu. The Benedictines continued to live here until the French Revolution. ▯ *Le Bourg, 43100 LAVAUDIEU, ☎ 04 71 76 46 00.*

Sights

Abbey church

The octagonal belfry has two storeys of semicircular bays. Inside, the nave is decorated with fine 14C **frescoes**★ in the Italianate style: they represent scenes from the Passion and such calamities as the Black Death. In the north transept an early-16C fresco, which has been taken off the wall, illustrates the Martyrdom of St Ursula.

Cloisters★★

🕐 *Mid-Jun to mid-Sep: 10am-noon, 2-6.45pm (last admission 30min before closing); mid-Sep to Oct: daily except Tue 10am-noon, 2-5pm.* 🕐 *Closed 1 Jan, 1 Nov, 25 Dec. 4€ (children: 2€) - tickets include the Maison des Arts et Traditions Populaires. ☎ 04 71 76 08 90.*

Little remains of the abbey buildings but there are particularly fine cloisters (restored), the only ones in the Auvergne to have escaped destruction. They include charming single or double colonnettes, some of them twisted, some cylindrical or polygonal, with capitals decorated with carvings of foliage and

THE ABBEY INN

🍽🍽 **Auberge de l'Abbaye** – ☎ 04 71 76 44 44 - closed 3-9 Feb, Sun evening except summer and Mon. A pleasant rustic atmosphere reigns in this village inn housed in an old stone residence. The tasty regional fare is served in a dining room with exposed beams and a hearth.

Lavaudieu

animals. The projecting upper storey is supported by oak posts. In the refectory is a 12C **mural** (restored) which covers the entire end wall; it shows the Virgin Mary sitting in Majesty flanked by two Angels and the Apostles. Above is an image of Christ surrounded by the symbols of the four Evangelists.

Maison des Arts et Traditions Populaires
🕐 *Mid-Jun to mid-Sep: 10am-noon, 2-6.45pm (last admission 30min before closing); mid-Sep to Oct: daily except Tue 10am-noon, 2-5pm.* 🕐 *Closed 1 Jan, 1 Nov, 25 Dec. 4€ (children: 2€) - tickets include the Cloisters.* ☎ *04 71 76 08 90.*
This Traditional Arts and Crafts Museum is housed in an old peasant baker's house dating from the late 19C. The oven, well, bread trough and counter are still visible. On the ground floor, the living room contains a collection of everyday domestic items. The byre houses tools from old crafts (clogmaking, carpentry). Beside it is the *veillade*, the room where people gathered in the evening to chat, sing and tell stories. The cupboard contains an interesting collection of headdresses and nightcaps. On the first floor are three bedrooms. The so-called Lacemaker's Room contains superb samples of pillow, crochet and bobbin lace and several lengths of trimmings.

Carrefour du Vitrail★
♿🕐 *May-Oct: 9.30am-noon, 2-6.30pm; Nov-Apr: Mon-Fri (Sat-Sun, only by arrangement) 9.30am-noon, 2-6.30pm. 5€.* ☎ *04 71 76 46 11.*
Housed in an elegant farmhouse, this exhibition area devoted to stained glass has been set up by an enthusiastic glass-blower who provides visitors with an insight into the thousand-year-old technique of stained-glass making. **Exhibition rooms** with suitable lighting present a history of this ancient craft through reproductions of famous stained-glass windows (rose-window of La Chaise-Dieu abbey) and house a display of contemporary stained glass.

Excursions

Frugières-le-Pin
3.5km/2.2mi E along D 20. A museum devoted to the French Resistance and the deportation of many of its members was set up here as a tribute to Joseph Lhomenède, who was mayor of the municipality and who died in Buchenwald in 1944.

Musée de la Résistance, de la Déportation et de la Seconde Guerre Mondiale

🕐 *Jun to Oct: 10am-noon, 2-7pm; Nov-May: by appointment. 5€.* ☎ *04 71 76 42 15.*
Located near the former station, the Second World War Museum contains numerous documents, posters, weapons and uniforms as well as moving photographs showing the sacrifices made by underground activists.

Vallée de la Sénouire – 🕐 *See BRIOUDE.*

LEZOUX

POPULATION 4 957
MICHELIN MAP 326: H-8 – 15KM/9.3MI W OF THIERS

In the 2C Lezoux was a major centre of the ceramics industry, which was fuelled by the plastic clay quarried in the Limagne. Within a radius of 3km/2mi, the remains of more than 200 potters' kilns have been uncovered, and pottery made in Lezoux has been found as far away as England and Prussia. The town, in which there is now a large oil-making plant, still has a 15C belfry topped by a tower. It stands adjacent to one of the old town gates. 🔲 *Mairie, le Bourg, 63190 LEZOUX,* ☎ *04 73 73 01 00.*

Musée de la Céramique

🔑 (temporarily closed) The Ceramics Museum contains collections of sigillated pottery (marked with a seal) dating from the 1C to the 4C AD – vases, cups, dishes, goblets, bowls etc – brick-red in colour, with rough but varied decorations in relief (animals, figures, floral motifs). Stamps indicate the names of the potters. The museum also contains moulds and various items used in the building trade, as well as funereal objects and coins. Some of the fragments dating from the 4C carry the influence of Christian iconography.

Excursions

Moissat

5km/3mi S along D 229. The Romanesque **church** at **Moissat-Bas** has retained its very early dome on squinches, its modest triumphal arch, its paintings and old gilt-wood statues. The restoration work undertaken in the chancel has revealed Romanesque arcading with columns and capitals, and paintings dating from the 14C and 15C.

Ravel

6km/3.7mi SE along D 223. This village, set among the pasture and woodland of the Limagne, is easily identified by the château which overlooks its houses and its church.

Château★

Access is either from Ravel by a street, with several very steep sections, which leads off a small square opposite the church, or by a road running through the undergrowth, which branches off D 223 SE of Lezoux. 🕐 *May-Jun: guided tours (1hr) 2-6pm (Sun, 10am-noon, 2-6pm); Jul-Sep: 10am-noon, 2-6pm. 6€.* ☎ *04 73 68 44 63. www.chateauderavel.com*
In 1294, the castle was given by Philip the Fair to his chancellor Pierre Flotte and passed by inheritance and marriage to the D'Estaing family, who had it renovated

Château de Ravel

in the 17C. The most beautiful and best preserved part of its decoration dates from the 18C.

The terrace designed by the landscape architect **Le Nôtre** (17C) looks over a beautiful **panorama**★ of the Limagne countryside and the Puys mountain range.

The walls and towers of the eastern façade of this vast construction date back to feudal times, the main courtyard was built in the 17C and the western wing in the 18C.

The interior still features some of the original furniture. A tour of the wings leads to the Genealogy Room (family portraits), the Coats of Arms Room with its terracotta paved floor (**emblems** from the former States of the Auvergne), the Great Gallery (mementoes of Admiral d'Estaing including a scale model of his ship, paintings depicting naval battles, nautical instruments), the Music Chamber (panelling decorated with musical instruments) and the richly decorated Gold Room (beamed ceiling, four-poster bed, Aubusson tapestries).

Church

The building, in very pure Gothic style, has two 14C stained-glass windows in the nave and another (late 13C) in the sacristy. A strange Romanesque capital acts as a support for a 12C stone stoup. A 14C carved wooden staircase-door is protected by a second door.

LE LIORAN★

MICHELIN MAP 330: E-4 – LOCAL MAP SEE MONTS DU CANTAL

The winter and summer holiday resort of Le Lioran (alt 1 153m/3 782ft) is encircled by the magnificent pine forests that cover the slopes of the Alagnon Valley above meadows dotted with old shepherds' huts (*burons*, used for cheesemaking). ▯ *Super-Lioran, 15300 Le LIORAN, ☎ 04 71 49 50 08. www.lelioran.com*

The tunnels – The **road tunnel** (alt 1 172m/3 845ft) dug in 1839 to avoid the mountain pass which was blocked by snow in the winter months was, for many years, the longest in France (1 412m/4 632ft). A new road *(D 67)* leads across Col de Cère (⟨ *see Monts du CANTAL*) in the summer. The **railway tunnel** up the line from the picturesque station in Le Lioran is 1 960m/6 370ft long. It was dug in 1868 at a depth of 30m/97ft below the road tunnel.

Super-Lioran ✲

Super-Lioran is accessible all year round via Le Lioran (north side of the tunnel); access via D 67 (south side of the tunnel) is only possible when Col de Cère is open.
Situated opposite the high grassy Font-d'Alagnon corrie and closed off by pine woods, this modern **winter sports resort** stands in highly attractive surroundings.
The resort is comprised of three separate sites: Font d'Alagnon, Font de Cère and Prairie des Sagnes.

Skiing area

Most of the ski runs are on the north and east-facing slopes of Plomb du Cantal (alt 1 885m/6 184ft). **Alpine skiing** – there is a cable-car (for a maximum of 80 passengers), 6 chair-lifts and 17 drag-lifts taking skiers to the top of some 40 runs.
People travelling by train can reach Super-Lioran by ski lift from Le Lioran station and return down a green run!

Cross-country skiing takes place in the western part of the resort (Font d'Alagnon and Font de Cère areas) where there are 21km/13mi of marked tracks. There is a vaster Nordic ski area (100km/62mi of tracks) east of the Plomb du Cantal.

Excursions

Maison du Buronnier

2.5km/1.5mi NE of Le Lioran. Drive 500m/550yd along N 122 towards Murat, turn right before the Rau de la Croix bridge then follow a minor road which skirts the railway line (on the right) and the Alagnon gorge (on the left). ⏱ *Mid-Jun to end-Jun, and 1-15 Sep: 2-6pm; Jul and Aug: 10am-12.30pm, 2.30-7pm. 4€ (children: 2€).* ☎ *04 71 20 19 00.*
This Maison du Parc naturel regional des Volcans d'Auvergne is a former cheese-making hut. The exhibits have been laid out to give some insight into the everyday life of the cowherd, the bottler and the herdsman who used to produce the real mountain Cantal cheese.

Gorges de l'Alagnon★

3.5km/2.3mi NE towards Murat, then turn right (signpost) and follow a path 500m/550yd long down to the upper reaches of the river. When the water level is low, it is possible to follow the river bed to the left over a distance of almost 200m/220yd. At the head of this very attractive ravine are piles of huge boulders.

Walks to the Peaks

Plomb du Cantal★★

45min there and back by cable-car and on foot from Super-Lioran. Viewing table.
🔼 At 1 855m/6 085ft. This is the highest peak in the Cantal range. From the summit there is a vast **panoramic view**★★. To the west, beyond the Cère Valley, extend Cantal's great volcanic cones – Griou, Peyre-Arse, Mary, Violent and Chavaroche; to the north the Dore mountain range sloping down to the right towards the undulating countryside of the Cézallier; to the east and south-east the *planèze* with the Margeride range looming above it; to the south

Le Puy Griou

J. Damase/MICHELIN

and south-west the Carladez plateau, the Châtaigneraie and, in the distance, the Rouergue. A number of footpaths lead from the summit to the **Puy Gros** (view of the Cère Valley at Thiézac) or to the Prat de Bouc via the Tombe du Père pass.

Puy Griou★★★

4hr on foot there and back from Super-Lioran. Head for the pastures in La Font d'Alagnon then turn left through the woods to the buildings of a children's holiday camp; there, bear right.

The path rises towards the alpine pastures of Col de Rombière (superb **view**★ over the Jordanne Valley and the great volcanic cones in Cantal) then turns left. A short distance further on, the clear, sharp outline of the Griou comes into view. To get to the summit, there is a strenuous climb over the andesite and phonolithic basalt rocks. From the top, at an altitude of 1 694m/5 557ft, there is an exceptional **panoramic view**★★★ of the Puy Mary, the Puy de Peyre-Arse, and Plomb du Cantal barring the horizon to the north. To the south, to each side of the Élancèze ridge are the Cère and Jordanne (also known as Mandailles) valleys.

GORGES DE LA LOIRE★

MICHELIN MAP 327: C-8/9, D-8, E-7 OR 331: F-2/3, G-2/5, H-1/4

From the Gerbier-de-Jonc to Roanne, the Loire Valley develops from a high, pastoral vale to a series of narrow channels and gorges, and wide basins; the result of a lively geological history. The course of the River Loire follows an ancient marine ditch which felt the effects of the alpine uplift at the end of the Tertiary Era. The Puy, Forez and Roanne basins – veritable rift valleys – forced the river to carve a route for itself through the plateaux separating these basins. In the Velay region the river had to battle against the volcanic outpourings at the end of the Tertiary Era and at the beginning of the Quaternary: at Arlempdes the river managed to find a way through the basalt flows; in the Puy basin, however, the course of the river was forced to shift eastwards. In Forez the Loire gorges, carved through the crystalline base, present a particularly wild appearance at Grangent Lake and around the meanders of St-Victor-sur-Loire.

Artificial lakes – In addition to the spectacular works of nature, there are also attractive man-made landscapes: dams have flooded the former valley to produce La Palisse, Grangent and Villerest lakes; another dam is planned upriver from Le Puy-en-Velay.

Ancient castles and sanctuaries – Overlooking the river stand some fine ruined fortresses and a few old châteaux, perched on rocky spurs or on the side of the wider banks: Arlempdes, Bouzols, Lavoûte-Polignac, Rochebaron...
Romanesque churches, originally often linked to a priory, dot the route along the gorges; the most impressive of these is at Chamalières-sur-Loire.

The Upper Velay Valley★

1 From Gerbier-de-Jonc to Le Puy-en-Velay

115km/71mi – allow a day

Gerbier-de-Jonc★★ – 🕭 *See index.*

The route descends along the pastoral valley; houses with thatched roofs may still be seen at Ste-Eulalie and near Usclades-et-Rieutord. The road then runs beside Lake La Palisse and, a little further, beside an attractive basalt flow (left). The narrow, banked up valley of the Gage is crossed.

Lac d'Issarlès★ – 🕭 *See Lac d'ISSARLÈS.*

Arlempdes★ – 🕭 *See ARLEMPDES.*

Goudet
This small hamlet is dominated by the ruins of Beaufort Château.

St-Martin-de-Fugères
From D 49 above the village there is a fine panoramic **view**★.

Le Puy-en-Velay★★★ – 🕭 *See Le PUY-EN-VELAY.*

② From Le Puy-en-Velay to Retournac

58km/36mi – allow a day

▶ *Leave Le Puy-en-Velay to the N on D 103.*

Leaving the Puy basin the River Loire enters into a wild granite channel: Peyredeyre gorge.

▶ *At Peyredeyre turn right onto D 71.*

Chaspinhac
The small Romanesque **church**, attractively built of red volcanic stone, contains interesting carved capitals. Beside the church, there are extensive views of the Velay countryside.

Château de Lavoûte-Polignac
🕐 *Jun-Sep: guided tours (45min) 10am-1pm, 2-7pm; Apr-May and Oct: 2-6pm.* 🕐 *Closed from 1 Nov to Easter. Price information not provided.* ☎ *04 71 08 50 02.*

Address Book

EATING OUT

🍴 **Ferme-auberge Les Granges** – 43140 La Séauve-sur-Semène - 12km/7.2mi E of Monistrol. Take N 88 dir. St-Étienne, then D 12 and follow signs - ☎ 04 71 61 00 82 - closed Jan-Feb, Sun evening and Mon - 🍴 - reserv. required. Located in a hamlet in the middle of the country, this farm receives guests for a meal of home-style cookery featuring poultry, pork and suckling veal. Evenings, the casse-croûte menu with its rapée (grated potato pancakes) is a bargain.

WHERE TO STAY

🏠 **Chambre d'hôte Les Revers** – 43130 Retournac - 8km/4.8mi SE of Retournac. Take D 103, and follow signs to 'Les Revers' - ☎ 04 71 59 42 81 - closed Oct-Mar - 🏠 - 4 rms. Their love of nature prompted these natives of St. Etienne to retreat to this extraordinarily isolated site between forest and fields. Your host loves and raises horses and organises outings with his guests. Understated rooms and relaxed atmosphere.

The fortress was owned by the Polignac family as early as the 13C, but was later transformed into a comfortable manor house as the castle at Polignac itself remained a powerful stronghold.

Lavoûte-sur-Loire
Above the High Altar in the small Romanesque **church** (🕐 May-Sep: 9am-7pm) stands a remarkable 13C wooden **statue of Christ**★.

Chamalières-sur-Loire
The village stands at the foot of Mont Gerbizon (1 064m/3 490ft high); it is noted for its Romanesque **church**★, which once belonged to a Benedictine priory. This early-12C sanctuary has attractive blind arcading along the exterior (south side and around the apse). Inside, the oven-vaulted apse is quite spectacular; note the three rows of small orifices which each correspond to an acoustic vessel buried in the stonework; blind arcading in the apse links the four apsidal chapels. Note the monolithic carved pier from the old cloisters which was later used as a font: the four figures represent David, Solomon, Isaiah and Jeremiah. A door leads from the north aisle of the church to the ruins of the Romanesque **cloisters** which used to overlook the Loire.

▶ *Shortly after leaving Chamalières, turn left onto D 35 which crosses the Loire and leads to Roche-en-Régnier.*

Roche-en-Régnier
This ancient village hanging above the west bank of the river is overlooked by a volcanic stump crowned by an old defensive tower. From the foot of this tower there is a fine **panorama**★ over the mountains of Velay and Forez, and the volcanic cones of Yssingeaux.

▶ *Follow D 29 to the right to St-André-de-Chalencon. In St-André, turn onto a minor road starting behind the east end of the church then continue along another road running below the cemetery, on the left; 1.8km/1.1mi further on, leave the car in the parking area near the ruins (15min on foot there and back).*

The Loire near Chamalières

B. Kaufmann/MICHELIN

Château de Chalençon

The castle ruins stand proudly on a rocky outcrop, half-way between Le Puy-en-Velay and the Monts Forez.

Promenade de l'Ance

Retrace your steps and take the steep right-hand lane leading to a second stone bridge located upstream. This secluded **site**★ is the ideal backdrop for a pleasant stroll.

▶ *Go back to D 9 and drive on to Retournac.*

Retournac

The part-Romanesque church is of handsome ochre stone and has a sturdy belfry and a stone-slabbed roof. Inside, note the dome on squinches, the elegant chancel, a 16C Italian Madonna and Child, the modern altar and stained-glass windows.

Musée des manufactures de Dentelles

♿ 🕐 *Apr-Sep: 2.30-6pm (Jul-Aug, 2.30-7pm).* 🕐 *rest of year. 4€.* ☎ *04 71 59 41 63. www.ville-retournac.fr.*
This lacemaking museum, housed inside a former manufacture dating from 1913, recreates the atmosphere of a lace-making workshop. During the 19C and 20C, the Haute-Loire region was internationally famous for its lacemaking expertise.

Between Forez and Vivarais★

③ From Retournac to Aurec

35km/22mi – about 2hr

▶ *N of Retournac take D 46 which runs along the plateau W of the Loire.*

Beauzac – *See index.*

Château de Rochebaron – *See index.*

Monistrol-sur-Loire – *See MONISTROL-SUR-LOIRE.*

Aurec-sur-Loire

This small town, nestling inside a meander of the Loire, has retained a harmonious ensemble of medieval buildings recently restored: from the **church**, built on foundations dating back to before 1000 AD, walk through the **castle grounds** (Guillaume de la Roue Tower, 1466) and along the ramparts overlooking the river, then through the Porte David (next to the Maison du Bailli). The **Château du Moine-Sacristain** and its 16C Burgundians' **Tower** house the **Musée de la Vigne et de l'ancien vin des Côtes d'Aurec** which has temporary exhibitions (🕐 *May-Sep and Dec, daily, 2.30-6pm.* 🕐 *rest of the year. 3€.* ☎ *04 77 35 26 55).*

④ From Aurec to St-Just-St-Rambert

30km/19mi – about 3hr

Aurec-sur-Loire stands at the beginning of the dammed **Lac de Grangent**★★. The **route**★★ (D 108 and D 32) from Semène to Grangent dam follows a steep ledge offering lovely views over the wild, sometimes submerged meanders of the river.

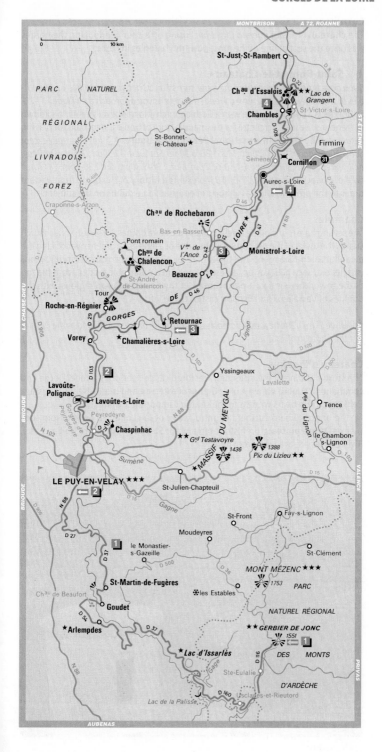

Cornillon

The **château** (⊶ *not open to the public*) rising on a spur overlooking the gorges was once the seat of one of the most powerful baronies in Forez.

▶▶ Saint-Bonnet-le-Château★

If you have time for a detour from the route, turn W on D3 between Cornillion and Chambles to travel here; you will have a wonderful view as you approach the village.

St-Bonnet is a charming place with a Gothic church and medieval streets. It is known in France as the leading centre for the manufacture of boules, steel balls for playing *pétanque*. The **Musée international Pétanque et Boules** (◷ *Jun-Sep: daily except Sun 8.30am-noon, 1.30-6.30pm, Mon 1.30-6.30pm, Sat 10am-12.30pm, 2-6pm; Oct-May: daily except Sun 8.30am-noon, 1.30-6.30pm, Mon 1.30-5.30pm, Sat 1.30-5pm. ◷ Closed public holidays. 4€. ☏ 04 77 50 15 33)* presents a history of the game from ancient times to the present, and has all sorts of entertaining exhibits on the subject.

Chambles

The setting here is one of the loveliest along the Loire gorges – beside a squat church stands the tower of the old castle, on the edge of a high escarpment overlooking the meanders of the Grangent. This tower is a typical example of medieval fortifications with its entrance half way up, accessible only up a collapsible ladder. From the top of the tower there is a vast **panorama**★ of the Forez and Lyon regions, with the outlines of Vassalieux and Essalois castles to the left.

▶ *Drive 2km/1.2mi beyond Chambles and turn right onto a small road to the ruins of the Château d'Essalois.*

Château d'Essalois

The sturdy outline of this splendidly restored castle overlooks a sheer gorge and commands a superb **view**★★ over Grangent reservoir and island. Near the castle a Celtic oppidum bears witness to the strategic importance of this site.

On the opposite bank further delightful views of the Loire can be had from sites such as **Danse plateau** (prehistoric remains) or **St-Victor-sur-Loire** (sailing base). River cruises are available from here.

Château d'Essalois

J. Damase/MICHELIN

Île de Grangent

This island was created when the man-made lake isolated the tongue of a rocky spine on which sit the ruins of Grangent Castle (12C tower) and a small chapel with a red-tiled roof.

St-Just-St-Rambert

This town was once a Gallo-Roman village clinging to the flank of a mound. The **Église St-André**★ *(To visit, ask at the tourist office. ☎ 04 77 52 05 14.)* is a sturdy 11C and 12C building crowned by an 11C fortified bell-tower (west front) and the 12C main **bell-tower**★: it consists of a square lower level decorated with blind arcading and an upper level with twinned openings topped by mitre shapes, between which are small arched openings.

To the north of the church stands the 11C **Chapelle St-Jean** *(Visit combined with the Église St-André by request at the tourist office.)*, once used as the baptistery. To the south of the church is a local museum, the **Musée des Civilisations Le Prieuré** *(⊙ Daily except Tue 2-6pm. ⊙ Closed 1 Jan, 1 May, 25 Dec. 5€. ☎ 04 77 52 03 11.)*, containing a variety of objets d'art linked with the town's past, and also more internationally flavoured collections including works of art from the South Pacific and Africa, most notably some fine **bronzes**★ from Benin.

South of St-Rambert, at the mouth of the Forez basin, the volume of the Loire is increased by the waters of the Furan at the level of Andrézieux, and the river spreads out to flow across the plain between low-lying banks.

LYON

CONURBATION 1 348 832

MICHELIN MAP 327: H/I-5 – LOCAL MAP SEE MONTS DU LYONNAIS

**Twenty centuries of history and a superb geographical situation at the conflu-
ence of the River Saône and the River Rhône give Lyon an appearance quite
unlike any other city and justify its inclusion on UNESCO's World Heritage List.**
🖪 *Pl. Bellecour, 69002 LYON, ☎ 04 72 77 69 69. www.lyon-france.com*

▶ **Orient Yourself:** A pedestrian tour of La Presqu'île, sandwiched between the
Rhône and the Saône, is the best way to get a feel for this massive, but hugely
appealing, city; this is where you'll find most of the shops and restaurants; equally
enlightening is the spectacular view from the Fourvière Basilica.

🅿 **Parking:** Massive underground car park beneath place Bellecour, but be sure to
make a note of exactly where you left the car - getting back to it can be confusing.
Underground parking also at les Célestins, les Terreaux and la République.

⊗ **Don't Miss:** The Fourvière district, but allow most of a day for a worthwhile
exploration.

🕒 **Organizing Your Time:** Begin from place Bellecour, and wander the streets; this
is no place to be methodical! Tours covering one, two or three days are detailed
below, but a longer stay is preferable to gain the most from this magnificent city
(⚑ *see Touring the Town*).

🄺🄸🄳🅂 **Especially for Kids:** Take a boat trip in a Bateau-Mouche, or visit the Musée de
l'Automobile Henri-Malartre. A session with Guignol is popular; likewise visit
the parc de la Tête d'Or

⚑ **Also See:** Vieux Lyon, the 'Old Town', the Monts du Lyonnais, the Mont d'Or
Lyonnais, la Dombes and Vienne.

The River Rhône and River Saône provide the magnificent sight of their very differing courses as they flow past the foot of the two famous hills, Fourvière and La
Croix-Rousse, facing the low plain of Dauphiné. Flowing down from the north, the
Saône skirts the small Mont-d'Or range and enters the Pierre-Scize gorge gouged
out between Fourvière and La Croix-Rousse. The Rhône arrives from the Alps, a
wide river that washes the lower slopes of La Croix-Rousse. During Roman times, the
confluence lay at the foot of the hill. The alluvium built up by the Rhône gradually
pushed the confluence further south and the resulting peninsula became the main
centre of the city. The Fourvière and La Croix-Rousse hills have numerous terraces
from which to admire the town; the views from some of these are famous, including
the Fourvière Basilica viewing table, place Rouville and rue des Fantasques in La
Croix-Rousse. Further away but no less outstanding are the panoramic views from
the Esplanade de Ste-Foy and Mont Thou.

Lyon's current prosperity serves as a reminder of the fact that the city's finest hours,
during the Roman Empire and the Renaissance, were times when trade was of major
importance and the city succeeded in taking full advantage of its outstanding geographical situation. It is, after all, on the road to Italy, between Central and Eastern
France, and midway between Northern France and the southern provinces.

Lyon is not only an industrial city specialising in metalworking, chemistry and building trades, and famous for its silk and synthetic fabrics; it is also a university town
and a world-famous centre in the field of medicine. It has a Court of Appeal and an
archbishopric (the Archbishop of Lyon bears the title "Primate of the Gauls"). The
city is a popular tourist venue, famous for its cuisine: it is one of the best-known
gastronomic centres in France.

Twenty Centuries of History

Capital of the Gauls – According to a Celtic legend two princes, Momoros and Atepomaros, stopped here one day at the confluence of the rivers and decided to build a town. While they were digging the foundations, a flock of crows flew down around them. Recognising the event as evidence of divine intervention, they decided to call their city **Lugdunum** (Crows' Hill).

Julius Caesar set up his base camp here during his relentless campaign to conquer Gaul. After his death, one of his lieutenants, Munatius Plancus, brought Roman settlers here (43 BC). Shortly afterwards Agrippa, who had been ordered by Caesar Augustus to organise Gaul, chose Lugdunum as his capital. The network of imperial roads began in Lyon and five major routes radiated out from the city towards Aquitaine, the Ocean, the Rhine, Arles and Italy. Caesar Augustus stayed in the town; Emperor Claudius was born here. In the 2C, aqueducts brought water to Fourvière from the surrounding mountains.

The city, governed by its council, held a monopoly in the trade of wine throughout Gaul. The mariners in its harbour were powerful shipowners; its potters were veritable industrialists. The wealthiest of the city's traders lived in a separate district, on the Île des Canabae, around where St-Martin-d'Ainay stands today. On the slopes of La Croix-Rousse was the Gallic town, Condate. The Amphitheatre of the Three Gauls (the votive inscription was uncovered in 1958) and the Temple of Rome and Caesar Augustus were the setting for the noisy Assembly of Gauls once a year.

Christianity in Lyon – Lyon became the meeting-place for businessmen from all over the country. Soldiers, merchants and missionaries arrived from Asia Minor and began spreading the new gospel. Soon, a small Christian community developed in the town.

In AD 177 a popular revolt broke out and led to the famous martyrdom of St Pothin, St Blandine and their companions. Twenty years later when **Septimus Severus**, having defeated his competitor Albin (who enjoyed popular support from the locals), decided to set fire to the town, he found that there were still 18 000 Christians in Lyon. He had them massacred; among them featured St Irénée, St Pothin's successor.

This faith has continued through the ages. On 8 December each year, the **Feast of the Immaculate Conception** is celebrated in Lyon with a great deal of pomp and enthusiasm. In the evening, thousands of multicoloured lanterns can be seen in the windows of the city. The origins of this **"Festival of Lights"** date from the occasion of the consecration of the gilded Madonna of Fourvière in 1852. Floods had delayed the work of sculptor Fabish, who was not able to deliver the statue by the deadline of 8 September. Accordingly the ceremony was postponed until 8 December, the Feast of the Immaculate Conception. On the day itself, heavy rainfall resulted in cancellation of the evening festival. However, contrary to all expectations, the rain stopped at precisely the time the festivities had been scheduled to start.

GALLO-ROMAIN LYON

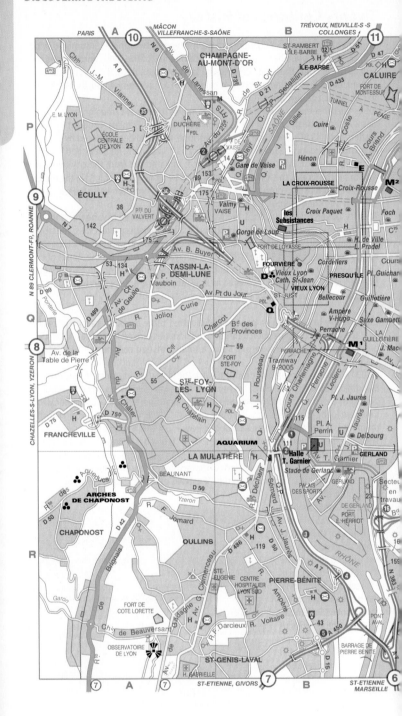

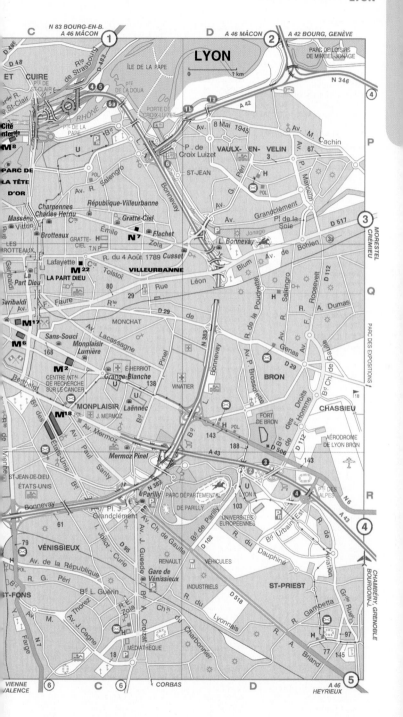

LYON

N 83 BOURG-EN-B.
A 46 MÂCON

A 46 MÂCON

A 42 BOURG, GENÈVE

PARC DE LOISIRS
DE MIRIBEL-JONAGE

N 346

ÎLE DE LA PAPE

0   1 km

D 48

Rte de Strasbourg

ET CUIRE
PTE DE
ST-CLAIR

PTE
DE LA DOUA

PORTE DE
CROIX-LUIZET

A 42

Av. 8 Mai 1945

Av. M. Cachin

Cité nterale

PTE DE LA
PAPE

P. de
Croix Luizet

VAULX- EN- VELIN

Av. 67

M 8

ST-JEAN

H

POL

PARC DE
LA TÊTE
D'OR

Av. R. Salengro

République-Villeurbanne

Av.   Grandclément

Pl. de la
Sole

D 517

Charpennes
Charles Hernu

Gratte-Ciel

Massèna
Vitton

Émile

N 7

Flachet

L. Bonnevay

Av. de Bohlen

D 112

Brotteaux

GRATTE-
CIEL

H
T.N.P

Zola

Cussel

LES
BROTTEAUX

R. du 4 Août 1789

Blum

R. Salengro

Lafayette

M 22

Tolstoï

VILLEURBANNE

Léon

Rue

Av. de

La
Part Dieu

LA PART DIEU

80

29

R te

D 29

de

R. de la Poudrette

R. A. Dumas

D 112

Garibaldi
Av.

F.
Faure

MONCHAT

Av. Lacassagne

N 383

R.   F.   Genas

D 29

M 17

Sans-Souci
Monplaisir
Lumière

168

Pinel

Av. P. Brossolette

BRON

M 6

Berthelot

M 2

CENTRE INTAL.
DE RECHERCHE
SUR LE CANCER

É HERRIOT

Grange-Blanche

U

138

VINATIER

Bd. Ch. de Gaulle

CHASSIEU

MONPLAISIR

Laënnec

J. Mermoz

POL

FORT
DE BRON

H
POL

des   Droits

de   l'Homme

AÉRODROME
DE LYON BRON

M 18

Av. Mermoz

Av. Paul Santy

Mermoz Pinel

143

Bd.

188

A 43

D 506

D 112

143

ST-JEAN-DE-DIEU
ÉTATS-UNIS

N 383

LYON

PTE DES
ALPES

N 6

Bonnevay

Parilly

PARC DÉPARTEMENTAL
DE PARILLY

Bd. Urbain Est

A 43

Pl. J.
Grandclément

103

UNIVERSITÉS
EUROPÉENNES

Av. Ch. de Gaulle

Bd. de Parilly

R. du   Dauphiné

de

79

VÉNISSIEUX

D 95

RENAULT

VÉHICULES

D 102

Av. de

61

H

Av. de la République

J. Joliot - Curie

J. Guesde

Gare de
Vénissieux

INDUSTRIELS

D 518

ST-PRIEST

R. du

Av. de l'Aviation

POL

R. G. Péri

Bd. L. Guérin

Zola

R. E.

R. Gambetta

Gde Rue

ST-FONS

Av. J. Cagne

Thorez

M.

Croizat

Ch in

Lyonnais

du

Charbonnier

R. A. Briand

H

97

Farge

N 7

18

MÉDIATHÈQUE

77

145

VIENNE
VALENCE

CORBAS

A 46
HEYRIEUX

MORESTEL
CRÉMIEU

PARC DES EXPOSITIONS

CHAMBÉRY, GRENOBLE
BOURGOIN-J.

LYON

BRON

8 Mai 1945 R. du	DQ	188
Bonnevay Bd L.	DQ	
Brossolette Av. P.	DQ	
Droits de l'Homme Bd des	DQ	
Genas Rte de	CDQ	
Mendès-France Av. P.	DR	103
Pinel Bd	CQ	
Roosevelt Av. F.	DQR	143

CALUIRE ET CUIRE

Strasbourg Rte de	CP

CHAMPAGNE

Lanessan Av. de	AP

CHAPONOST

Aqueducs Rte des	AR
Brignais Rte de	AR

CHASSIEU

Gaulle Bd Ch.-de	DQ

ECULLY

Champagne Rte de	AP	25
Dr-Terver Av. du	AP	38
Marietton R.	AP	99
Roosevelt Av. F.	AP	142
Vianney Ch. J.-M.	AP	

FRANCHEVILLE

Châter Av. du	AQ
Table de Pierre Av.	AQ

LA MULATIÈRE

Déchant R. S.	BR	
J.-J. Rousseau Quai	BQ	
Mulatière Pont de la	BQ	111
Sémard Quai P.	BR	

LYON

25e Régt de Tirailleurs Sénégalais Av. du	ABP	
Abbé Couturier Passerelle	EFY	
Algérie R. d'	FX	
Annonciade R. de l'	FV	
Antiquaille R. de l'	EY	
Audran R.	FV	
Baleine R. de la	FX	
Barodet R.	EV	
Barre R. de la	FY	
Bât-d'Argent R. du	FX	
Belfort R. de	FV	
Bellecour Pl.	FY	
Bellevue Pl.	FV	
Bertone Pl. M.	FV	
Bodin R.	FV	
Bœuf R. du	EFX	
Bombarde R. de la	FX	
Bon Pasteur R. du	FV	
Bonaparte Pt	FY	
Bondy Q. de	FX	
Bourgogne R. de	BP	14
Brest R. de	FX	
Burdeau R.	FV	
Buyer Av. B.	AQ	
Calas R.	FV	
Canuts Bd des	FV	
Capucins R. des	FV	
Cardinal Decourtray Mtée	EXH	
Carmélites Mtée des	FV	
Carmes Déchaussés Mtée des	EX	
Carnot Pl.	FY	
Célestins Pl. des	FY	

Célestins Q. des	FY	
Célu R.	FV	
Chambaud-de-la-Bruyère Bd	BR	23
Chambonnet R. Col.	FV	
Change Mtée du	EFX	
Change Pl. du	FX	
Charcot R. Cdt	ABQ	
Chardonnet Pl.	FV	
Charité R. de la	FY	
Chartreux Imp. des	EV	
Chartreux R. des	EV	
Chazeaux Mtée des	EX	
Chazette Pl. L.	FV	
Chemin Neuf Mtée du	EXY	
Chenavard R. Paul	FX	
Chevreul R.	FY	
Childebert R.	FY	27
Claude-Bernard Q.	FY	
Claudia R.	FX	
Cléberg R.	EY	
Colbert Pl.	FV	
Comédie Pl. de la	FX	
Comte R. A.	FY	
Condé R. de	EFY	
Constantine R. de	FX	
Courmont Q. J.	FXY	
Couturier R. V.	EFV	
Crimée R. de	FV	
Croix Rousse Bd de la	EFV	
Croix-Rousse Gde-R. de la	FV	
Croix Rousse Pl. de la	FV	
Cuire R. de	FV	
Delorme R. Philibert	FV	
Denfert-Rochereau R.	EV	
Désirée R.	FX	
Diderot R.	FV	
Dr-Gailleton Q. du	FY	
Duhamel R.	FY	
Dumont-d'Urville R.	FV	
Dupont R. P.	EX	
Épies Mtée des	EY	
États-Unis Bd des	CQR	
Fantasques R. des	FV	
Farges R. des	EY	
La-Fayette Pont	FX	88
Feuillants Petite R. des	FV	
Feuillée Pt de la	FX	
Forez Pl. du	FV	
Fourvière °Pl. de	EX	
Franklin R.	FY	
Fulchiron Q.	EFY	
Gadagne R. de	FX	63
Gallieni Pt	FYZ	
Garillan Montée du	EFX	
Garnier Av. T.	BR	
Genas Rte de	CDQ	
Gerson Pl.	FX	
Giraud Cours du Gén.	EV	
Godart R. J.	FV	
Gonin Passage	EVX	
Gorjus R. Henri	EV	
Gourguillon Mtée du	EY	
Gourju Pl. A.	FY	
Gouvernement Pl. du	FX	
Grande Côte Mtée de la	FV	
Grenette R.	FX	
Griffon Pl. du	FV	
Griffon R. du	FV	
Grognard R.	FV	
Guillotière Pt de la	FY	
Imbert-Colomès R.	FV	

Ivry R. d'	FV	
Jacobins Pl. des	FX	
Jacquard R.	EV	
Jayr Q.	BP	
Joffre Q. du Mar.	EY	
Joliot-Curie R.	AQ	
Juin Pont Alphonse	FX	84
Juiverie R.	FX	
Kitchener Marchand Pt	EY	
Lacassagne Av.	CQ	
Lainerie R.	FX	91
Lassagne Quai A.	FV	
Lassalle R. Ph. de	EV	
Lattre-de-Tassigny Pt de	FV	94
Leynaud R. René	FV	
Mail R. du	FV	
Marseille R. de	FYZ	
Martinière R. de la	FX	
Max Av. Adolphe	FY	
Mercière R.	FX	
Mermoz Av. J.	CQ	
Millaud Pl. Éd.	EV	
Montauban R. de	EX	
Morand Pont FX		107
Moulin Quai J.	FX	
Mulatière Pont de la	BQ	111
Neuve-Saint-Jean Pl.	FX	113
Nicolas-de-Lange Mtée	EX	
Ornano R.	EV	
Pasteur Pt	BQ	115
Pasteur R.	FYZ	
Pêcherie Q. de la	FX	
Pelletier R.	FV	
Perron Mtée du	FV	
Pierres Plantées R. des	FV	
Pinel Bd	CQ	
Plat R. du	FY	
Platière R. de la	FX	121
Point du Jour Av. du	ABQ	
Poncet Pl. A.	FY	
Pouteau R.	FV	
Pradel Pl. L.	FX	
Prés.-Édouard-Herriot R. du	FX	
Punaise Ruelle	FX	129
Radisson R. Roger	EXY	
République Pl. de la	FXY	
République R. de la	FXY	
Rockefeller Av.	CQ	138
Rolland Quai Romain	FXY	
Romarin R.	FVX	
Roussy R. Ph.	EV	
Rouville Pl.	EV	
St-Antoine Q.	FX	
St-Barthélémy Montée	EXY	
St-Georges R.	EY	
St-Jean Pl.	EY	
St-Jean R.	FX	
St-Paul Pl.	FX	
St-Paul R.	EX	
St-Polycarpe R.	FVX	151
St-Sébastien Mtée	FV	
St-Simon R.	ABP	153
St-Vincent Passerelle	FX	
St-Vincent Quai	EFX	
Ste-Catherine R.	FX	155
Ste-Hélène R.	FY	
Sala R.	FY	
Santy Av. Paul	CQR	
Sathonay Pl.	FV	
Scize Quai R.	EX	
Tabareau Pl.	EV	
Tables Claudiennes R. des	FV	

Terme R.	FVX		**ST-GENIS-LAVAL**			Marcellin Av. P.	DP	
Terraille R.	FX		Beauvisart Ch. de	AR		Péri Av. G.	DP	
Terreaux Pl. des	FX		Clemenceau Av. Georges	AR		Roosevelt Av. F.	DQ	
Thiaffait Passage	FV		Darcieux R. François	ABR		Salengro Av. R.	DQ	
Thomas Crs A.	CQ	168	Gadagne Av. de	AR		Soie Pont de la	DP	
Tilsitt Q.	FY		**ST-PRIEST**			**VENISSIEUX**		
Tobie-Robatel Pl.	FX		Aviation R. de l'	DR		Bonnevay Bd L.	CR	
Tolozan Pl.	FVX		Briand R. A.	DR		Cachin Av. M.	CR	18
Tourette R. de la	EV		Dauphiné R. du	DR		Cagne Av. J.	CR	
Tramassac R.	FX		Gambetta R.	DR		Charbonnier Ch. du	CDR	
Trinité Pl. de la	EFY		Grande-Rue	DR		Croizat Bd A.	CR	
Trois Maries R. des	FX		Herriot Bd E.	DR	77	Farge Bd Y.	CR	
Turquet Imp.	EY		Lyonnais R. du	DR		Frères L. et É.		
Université Pont de l'	FY		Maréchal R. H.	DR	97	Bertrand R. des	CR	61
Vaubecour R.	EFY		Parilly Bd de	DR		Gaulle Av. Ch.-de	CR	
Vernay R. François	FX		Rostand R. E.	DR	145	Gérin Bd L.	CR	
Viaduc Chemin du	EX		Urbain Est Bd	DR		Grandclément Pl. J.	CR	
Victor-Hugo R.	FY		**STE-FOY**			Guesde Av. J.	CR	
Villeneuve R.	FV		Charcot R. du Cdt	ABQ		Joliot Curie Bd I.	CR	
Vollon Pl. A.	FY		Châtelain R.	AQ		Péri R. G.	CR	
Voraces Cour des	FV		Fonts Ch. des	AQ	55	République Av. de la	CR	
Wilson Pont	FY		Franche-Comté R. de	BQ	59	Thorez Av. M.	CR	
OULLINS			Provinces Bd des	BQ		Vienne Rte de	CQR	
Jean-Jaurès Av.	BR		**TASSIN**			**VILLEURBANNE**		
Jomard R. F.	AR		Foch Av. du Mar.	AQ	53	4 Août 1789 R. du	CQ	
Perron R. du	BR	119	Gaulle Av. Ch.-de	AQ		Blum R. L.	CDQ	
PIERRE-BENITE			République Av. de la	AQ	134	Bonnevay Bd L.	CP	
Ampère R.	BR		Vauboin Pl. P.	AQ		Chirat R. F.	CQ	29
Europe Bd de l'	BR	43	Victor Hugo Av.	APQ	175	Croix Luizet Pont de	CDP	
Voltaire R.	BR		**VAUX-EN-VELIN**			Genas Rte de	CDQ	
ST-DIDIER-AU-MONT-D'OR			8 Mai 1945 Av. du	DP		Jean-Jaurès R.	CQ	80
St-Cyr R. de	BP		Allende Av. S.	DP	3	Poudrette R. de la	DQ	
ST-FONS			Bohlen Av. de	DQ		Salengro Av. R.	CP	
Farge Bd Y.	CR		Cachin Av. M.	DP		Tonkin R. du	CQ	
Jean-Jaurès Av.	CR	79	Dumas R. A.	DQ		Zola Cours Émile	CP	
Semard Bd P.	BR	159	Gaulle Av. Ch.-de	DP	67			
Sembat R. M.	BR	161	Grandclément Av.	DP				

" Condition publique des Soies "	FV	F	La cour des Voraces	FV		Musée de la Civilisation gallo-romaine	EY M[10]
Amphithéâtre des Trois-Gaules	FV		Le Guignol de Lyon Compagnie des Zonzons	FX	T	Musée des Arts décoratifs	FY
Ancienne chapelle de la Vierge	EX	B	Loge du Change	EFX		Musée des Beaux-Arts	FX
Aquarium du Grand Lyon	BR		Maison Baronat	FX	N[3]	Musée des Hospices civils	FY M[14]
Aqueducs romains	BQ	D	Maison Brunet	EV		Musée des Moulages d'Art antique	CQ M[17]
Ateliers de Soierie Vivante	BP	E	Maison Dugas	FX	N[6]	Musée des Tissus	FY
Basilique St-Martin d'Ainay	FY		Maison Thomassin	FX	N[10]	Musée urbain Tony-Garnier	CQ M[18]
Cathédrale ou " Primatiale " St-Jean	FXY		Maison d'Antoine Groslier de Servières	FX	N[1]	Muséum d'histoire naturelle	BP M[20]
Centre d'histoire de la Résistance et de la Déportation	BQ	M[1]	Maison de Claude de Bourg	FX	N[4]	Notre-Dame de Fourvière	EX
			Maison de Paris	FX	N[9]	Nouveau Musée (Institut d'Art Contemporain)	CQ M[22]
Château Lumière	CQ	M[2]	Maison de l'Outarde d'Or	FX	N8	Odéon	EY
Cité internationale	CP		Maison des Avocats	FX	N[2]	Opéra de Lyon	FX
Clocher	FY		Maison des Canuts	FV		Palais St-Pierre	FX
Fresque des Lyonnais	FX		Maison du Crible	FX	N[5]	Parc archéologique de Fourvière	EY
Grand théâtre	EY		Maison du Livre, de l'Image et du Son	CP	N[7]	Parc de la Tête d'Or	CP
Gros Caillou	FV		Maison du Soleil	EFY		Statue de J.-M. Jacquard	FV V
Halle Tony-Garnier	BQR		Manécanterie	EFY		Thermes	EX
Hôtel "La Cour des Loges"	FX	Z	Mausolées de Choulans	BQ	Q	Tour métallique	EX
Hôtel Bullioud	FX	G	Mur des Canuts	FV		les Subsistances	BP
Hôtel Laurencin	FX	K	Musée "La Renaissance des Automates"	EY		Église St-Bonaventure	FX
Hôtel Paterin	FX		Musée Gadagne (Musée historique de Lyon et Musée international de la Marionnette)	FX	M[4]	Église St-Bruno	EV
Hôtel de la Chamarerie	FX	S				Église St-Nizier	FX
Hôtel de ville	FX	H				Église St-Paul	EFX
Hôtel du Gouvernement	FX	X	Musée africain	CQ	M[6]	Église St-Polycarpe	FV
Hôtel-Dieu	FY		Musée d'Art contemporain	CP	M[8]	Arches de Chaponost	AR
Jardin archéologique	FXY		Musée de Fourvière	EX	M[12]		
			Musée de l'Imprimerie	FX	M[16]		

Address Book

OUT AND ABOUT IN LYON

GETTING AROUND

Maps – In addition to the maps included in this guide, Michelin town plans 30 and 31 and Michelin map 110 (the surroundings of Lyon) will be useful.

Access – By road via motorways A 6, A 7, A 42, A 43. The city also boasts a regular 2hr link with Paris by TGV. Perrache and La Part-Dieu stations are close to the town centre by metro. There are flights to and from most major cities via Lyon-St-Exupéry airport, linked to the town centre by a shuttle service.

Parking – There are several underground car parks strategically placed for easy access to the town centre. Some of these are architectural gems, the most spectacular being the *Parc Célestins* by Buren, whose columns adorn the Jardins du Palais-Royal in central Paris.

Public transport – The underground train/subway *(Métro)* is the most convenient mode of public transport, and is especially well-adapted to the needs of tourists. The best-value ticket to buy is the **ticket-liberté**, valid for a day for unlimited travel on the Lyon urban transport network (métro, bus, funicular railway, trolley-bus). Details from TCL (Transports en Commun Lyonnais) kiosks or call ☎ 04 78 71 70 00.

TOURING THE TOWN

Planning your visit – If you have only **one day** to spend in Lyon, then you must devote the morning to Old Lyon (on foot), to the Fourvière terrace and the Roman theatres (use the funicular), but you will not have time to visit the museums; the afternoon should be spent touring the Presqu'île with its Fabric Museum and, either visiting the Fine Arts Museum or an enjoyable walk around the Gros Caillou, on the slopes of the Croix-Rousse.

Two days will enable you to get better acquainted with Fourvière and the various museums and to stroll along the River Saône on the first day. The second

PUBLIC TRANSPORT

day should be devoted to touring the Presqu'île on foot and to visiting its museums (fabrics, printing and hospice museums); you should even have time to take a stroll in the Croix-Rousse district.

During the course of a **third day,** you could explore the Resistance Museum and either the Motor-car Museum in Rochetaillée or the Château de la Poupée in the Lacroix-Laval park *(see Excursions).*

Organised tours – Lyon, which is listed as a "Town of Art and history," offers discovery tours conducted by guide-lecturers approved by the Ministry of Culture and Communication. Information at the tourist office or on www.vpah.culture.fr. The Lyon tourist office offers tours of the city on foot, or by bus, boat, taxi or even helicopter.

Lecture tours are available around Old Lyon, the Croix-Rousse district and the Tony Garnier district.

Unusual – Visit the high parts of Fourvière Basilica (the galleries, the attics where the bells are located) and enjoy an unforgettable view of the historic site of Lyon.

Bateaux-mouches river trips – *13 bis quai Rambaud –* ☎ *04 78 42 96 81 - www.naviginter.fr - departure from quai des Célestins.* These enable visitors to discover a different face of Lyon, seen from its four river banks: one trip explores the confluence of the Saône and Rhône; the other follows the Saône up to and round the Île-Barbe.

EATING OUT

☞ **Le Café 203** – *9 r. du Garet -* ☎ *04 78 28 66 65 - closed 24 Dec to 3 Jan.* Some customers come here for the fresh fare, slate menu and bistro setting. Others yearn for spiritual sustenance: book exhibitions, readings of young authors' works and listenings to recorded creations. There's always a good reason to spend time at Le Café 203.

☞ **100 Tabac** – *23 r. de l'Arbre-Sec -* ☎ *04 78 27 29 14 - closed 24 Dec to 2 Jan.* Non-smokers, heads up: Le Café 203's little sister is smoke-free. The decor features the same elements: light wood, pewter and red shades, whereas the menu lists market-fresh dishes, pasta and waffles at friendly prices.

☞ **Le Casse-Museau** – *2 r. Chavanne -* ☎ *04 72 00 20 52 - closed Tue and Wed evenings, Sun, Mon and public holidays - reserv. required.* Aunt Paulette's 'no chichi bistro' has been going strong since 1947. Her famous garlic chicken has given way to fresh pasta, mixed salads and other more modern fare, but the wine flows freely as ever and the ambience is still convivial. Inexpensive and popular with the natives.

☞ **Chez les Gones** – *102 cours Lafayette, (Halle de Lyon) -* ☎ *04 78 60 91 61 - www.chezlesgones.com - closed Mon.* This tavern set in the bosom of the marketplace does not lack for customers, who come to enjoy the typical Lyon fare, smiling service and ambient good cheer. Small terrace upstairs in fine weather.

☞ **Comptoir du Mail** – *14 r. du Mail, (Croix-Rousse) -* ☎ *04 78 27 71 40 - comptoir.mail@wanadoo.fr - closed 2-25 Aug.* The local population wasted no time in adopting this restaurant serving dishes straight from the marketplace. Hospitable welcome and bistro decor with oilcloth tablecloths and daily specials presented on wall mirrors.

☞ **Le Petit Gadin** – *17 r. Austerlitz -* ☎ *04 78 28 62 33 - closed Aug, Mon lunch, Tue lunch, Sat lunch, Thu and Fri.* One must cross the threshold of this banal-looking establishment across from the Caillou de la Croix-Rousse to understand why we fancy it. The ambience, inviting and gracious, the frescoes and the garden, very sought after in the summer, have won us over – what about you?

☞ **Le Vieux Lyon** – *44 r. St-Jean -* ☎ *04 78 42 48 89.* Local epicureans are all familiar with this tavern, in operation since 1947, where good humour and hospitality reign. The long dining room is hung with photos of Brassens, Brel and Herriot. Homemade Lyonnais cooking.

☞ **Le Petit Carron** – *48 av. Félix-Faure -* ☎ *04 78 60 00 57 - closed 3 wks in Aug, Sat lunch and Sun - reserv. recommended.* The little puppet who inhabits the window of this attractive tavern beckons you into a muted dining room featuring a slate *menu du jour,* composed according to market availability.

Le Jura – *25 r. Tupin -* ☎ *04 78 42 20 57 - closed 28 Jul to 28 Aug, Mon from Sep to Apr, Sat from May to Sep, and Sun - reserv. requested.* Not far from the Rue de la République, this eatery seems to have been here forever! With its 1920s decor and aproned matron overseeing the stoves, it's as genuine as they come.

La Brasserie Georges – *30 cours de Verdun -* ☎ *04 72 56 54 54.* Open since 1836, this brasserie near the Perrache train station is still a favourite Lyon haunt. The enormous central room (listed as a historic property), with its red wall seats, Art Deco chandeliers and old frescoes, is worth a visit in itself. "Good beer, good food" is this eatery's motto.

Le St-Florent – *106 cours Gambetta -* ☎ *04 78 72 32 68 - closed 3 wks in Aug, 1 wk at Christmas, Sat lunch, Mon lunch and Sun - reserv. recommended.* Pluck and cluck: the interior design of this restaurant - egg-yolk yellow, chair backs that look like feathers, etc – give diners a good hint of what to expect from the menu, essentially devoted to the poultry of Bresse.

L'Est – *14 pl. Jules-Ferry, Les Brotteaux station -* ☎ *04 37 24 25 26.* The last of Bocuse's bastions in Lyon: the Brotteaux train station. The decor is that of a big, old-fashioned brasserie where electric trains circumnavigate the dining room. As for the cuisine, the young team serves dishes from the world over at very affordable prices – a highly successful concept!

Brunet – *23 r. Claudia -* ☎ *04 78 37 44 31 - chezbrunet@wanadoo.fr - closed Sun-Mon - reserv. recommended.* An authentic Lyon bouchon (tavern), Brunet has a wood façade, elbow-to-elbow tables, Guignol-marked tableware, tasty little dishes enhanced by an enticing selection of wines by the carafe and black-aproned waiters.

Restaurant des Deux Places – *5 pl. Fernand-Rey -* ☎ *04 78 28 95 10 - closed 15 Jul to 15 Aug, Sat-Mon.* A few steps from the Place Sathonay, this traditional little restaurant boasts a convivial atmosphere, a decor full of rural knick-knacks and time-honoured cuisine featuring a few house specialities, like warm lambs' tongues. A handful of tables are set on the terrace in summer.

Le Mercière – *56 r. Mercière -* ☎ *04 78 37 67 35 - www.le-merciere.com - reserv. recommended.* Located in a passageway giving onto one of the most sought-after restaurant streets in town, here is a picturesque old house where authentic, traditional fare is served in a classic Lyonnais setting.

Lolo Quoi – *42 r. Mercière -* ☎ *04 72 77 60 90.* In this pedestrian street where taverns and chain restaurants abound, those in the know go to Lolo. Minimalist furnishings and thoughtful lighting, modern Italian cuisine and innovative pasta – the Lyon crowd approves wholeheartedly.

Le Caro de Lyon – *25 r. du Bât-d'Argent -* ☎ *04 78 39 58 58 - closed Sun.* This restaurant behind the Opera, designed to resemble a library, welcomes diners into an intimate atmosphere comprised of blond wood, Murano chandeliers, antique knick-knacks and coloured chairs. Savvy Lyonnais come here to enjoy a relaxed meal inspired by the spirits of the south and east.

La Table d'Hippolyte – *22 r. Hippolyte-Flandrin -* ☎ *04 78 27 75 59 - closed Aug, 25 Dec, 1 Jan, Sat lunch, Sun-Mon.* Located in a small street near the Halles de la Martinière, here is a cosy address where curios, old mirrors, dried flowers and hefty objects coexist peacefully. It's the ideal setting for a candlelight supper. Traditional, fine quality cuisine.

WHERE TO STAY

Bon week-end à Lyon – The city of Lyon is an active participant in this weekend package deal practiced throughout France. In addition to a second night in a hotel free of charge, visitors receive gifts and discount coupons for seeing the city and its museums. Enquire at the Office de Tourisme for a list of hotels and conditions.

St-Pierre-des-Terreaux – *8 r. €aul-Chenavard -* ☎ *04 78 28 24 61 - closed 15 days in Aug, and Christmas period - 16 rms -* ⌧ *8€.* A very practical and affordable hotel in the city, opposite the St-Pierre museum and a few steps from the Opera. Pleasant welcome and practical, well-maintained rooms that benefit from efficient soundproofing.

⊜ **Villages Hôtel** – *93 cours Gambetta - ☎ 04 78 62 77 72 - www.villages-hotel. com -* 🅿 *- 114 rms -* ⊡ *4€.* This chain hotel has a lot going for it, such as the central location, proximity to the train station and metro, and comfortable, spacious rooms with king-sized beds. A good address for travellers on limited budgets.

⊜⊜ **Élysée Hôtel** – *92 r. du €rés.- Edouard-Herriot - ☎ 04 78 42 03 15 - elysee-hotel@wanadoo.fr - 29 rms -* ⊡ *9€.* A small family-run hotel where one can enjoy the vitality of the Presqu'île at affordable prices. The petite red and yellow rooms are modest but cheerful and well kept up; those giving onto the back are quieter.

⊜⊜⊜ **Bellecordière** – *18 r. Bellecordière - ☎ 04 78 42 27 78 - www. hotel-bellecordiere.com - 45 rms.* Near the Rhône quayside and the Bellecour metro station, this hotel offers rooms that are smallish but quite suitable for a short stay. They are decorated in the colours of Provence, as is the breakfast room.

⊜⊜⊜ **Hôtel La Résidence** – *18 r. Victor-Hugo - ☎ 04 78 42 63 28 - hotel-la-residence@wanadoo.fr - 67 rms -* ⊡ *7€.* Managed by the same family since 1954, this hotel borders on a pedestrian street quite near the Place Bellecour. Ask for a recently renovated room – the others, with their 1970s furnishings, are definitely from another era; all are neat and clean.

⊜⊜⊜ **Savoies** – *80 r. de la Charité - ☎ 04 78 37 66 94 - hotel.des.savoies@ wanadoo.fr - 46 rms -* ⊡ *5€.* Look for a façade decorated with the Savoie coat of arms in the Perrache train station quarter. The cleanliness of the standard rooms, with their simple furniture and pastel carpets, the convenient garage and reasonable prices make this a popular address with travellers.

⊜⊜⊜ **Hôtel Ariana** – *163 cours Émile-Zola - 69100 Villeurbanne - ☎ 04 78 85 32 33 - www.ariana-hotel.fr -* 🅿 *- 102 rms -* ⊡ *9€.* This is a practical address for those who wish to stay amid the 1930s high-rises of Villeurbanne. Modern, it has air-conditioned, soundproofed rooms with a sober interior design

of grey-tinted furniture. Leave your automobile in the garage and take the metro to downtown Lyon.

⊜⊜⊜ **La Villa du Rhône** – *Chemin de la Lune - 01700 Miribel - 12km/7.2mi NE of Lyon. Take the A 42 dir. Genève, exit €arc de Miribel-Jonage, then dir. le Mas Rillier and la Madone Campanile - ☎ 04 78 55 54 16 - www.lavilladurhone.com -* ⊡⊐ *- 3 rms -* ⊡ *7€ - meals* ⊜⊜*.* Located just outside of Lyon, this is a peaceful residential home overlooking the Vallée du Rhône. The two guest rooms facing the swimming pool give onto the garden; their private terraces have a spectacular view of the River Rhône.

⊜⊜⊜ **Hôtel Bleu Marine** – *4 r. du Mortier - ☎ 04 78 60 03 09 - hotelbleu-marine-lyon@wanadoo.fr - 126 rms -* ⊡ *10€.* This modern, glass-walled hotel on a small street in the Guillotière quarter, a five minute walk from the Place Bellecour, is worth mentioning. The identical rooms, smoking or non-smoking, are bright, practical and well fitted-out.

SHOPPING

Two things stand out about shopping in Lyon - food and fashion. This is a gourmet's paradise, and the shopaholic will find numerous top designer stores and superb markets.

Markets *(Marchés)* – The Marché de la Création, Quai Romain-Rolland and the Marché de l'Artisanat, Quai Fulchiron are held Sunday mornings. These are no run-of-the-mill craft markets, as the workmanship is outstanding. Used book sellers line the Quai de la Pêcherie every afternoon. There are regional products and small taverns at the Halles de Lyon, 102 Cours Lafayette.

For food, head for the Quai Saint-Antoine, where food markets with producers from all over the region set up stall and sell their produce *(Tue-Sun, 7am-12.30pm)*. There is also a Farmers' Market twice a week in the Place Carnot *(Wed, 4-7pm; Sun, 5am-1.30pm)*, in front of the Gare Perrache.

Bonnard – *36 rue Grenette - ☎ 04 78 42 19 63 - 8.30am-1.30pm, 3pm-7.30pm - closed Aug and public holidays.* Come to this delicatessen founded in 1850 and stock up on Lyonnais specialities such as the celebrated *cervelas truffé* (truffled savaloy) and *quenelles de brochet* (pike dumplings). Note the Art Deco decor and glass-paned roof crowned by a splendid lion's head made of copper.

L'Atelier de Soierie – *33 r. Romarin - ☎ 04 72 07 97 83 - Mon-Sat 9am-noon, 2pm-7pm - closed public holidays*. Lyon became the silk capital of France in the 16C. Today, l'Atelier de Soierie continues this tradition of expertise, combining time-honoured methods with hand-painted decorations. Among other specialities, *la panne de velours*, made only in Lyon, is a silk and velvet hand-decorated muslin that is simply gorgeous.

Reynon – *13 rue des Archers - ☎ 04 78 37 39 08 - www.reynon.com - Tue-Sat 8.30am-1.30pm, 3pm-7.30pm - closed end Jul to mid-Aug, public holidays except Christmas and New Year's*. The Reynon family has run this delicatessen since its creation in 1937. They specialise in carefully prepared sausages, rosettes, jésus and various ready-to-enjoy dishes. Francophones with a taste for homespun recipes and anecdotes will enjoy *Le fils du charcutier,* penned by Auguste Reynon.

Les Quenelles Giraudet – *2 r. du Col.-Chambonnet - ☎ 04 72 77 98 58 - www.giraudet.fr - daily except Sun, 9am-7pm (Mon, 11am-7pm) - closed 1-15 Aug*. Giraudet has been making their famous *quenelles* (dumplings) in the purest traditional manner since 1910. The shop also offers over 20 different quenelle-enhancing sauces concocted without artificial flavours or preservatives.

Pignol – *8 pl. Bellecour - ☎ 04 78 37 39 61 - www.pignol.fr - Mon-Sat 8am-7.30pm; Aug: Tue-Sat*. This celebrated caterer has been delighting palates since 1954. Beginning with a back-kitchen debut that was an instant success, the Pignol family has added many feathers to their toques; today they own seven restaurants and two food-production units. For the Davis Cup finals and the Albertville Olympic Games, Pignol was entrusted with organising the meals.

Voisin – *28 r. de la République - ☎ 04 78 42 46 24 - Mon 2pm-7pm ; Tue-Sat 9am-7.30pm*. This confectioner concocts 50-odd kinds of chocolate, fruit jelly candies, candied fruit and other delicious Lyonnais specialities. It also sup-plies its 19 shops in the metropolitan area with freshly roasted coffees and gourmet teas. A must!

Chez Disagn'Cardelli - Petit musée fantastique du Guignol – *6 r. St-Jean - ☎ 04 78 37 01 67 - patrice-cardelli@free.fr - Mon 2.30-7pm, Tue-Sat 11am-1pm, 2.30pm-7pm, Sun 11am-1pm, 3pm-6pm - closed Christmas and New Year's*. Marionettes, music boxes and masks. Downstairs, Guignol's Little Fantastic Museum reveals the fascinating world of the marionettes, robots and music boxes of Lyon. The self-guided tour, available in English (among other languages), lights up as you go.

ON THE TOWN

Rue Ste-Catherine – A very lively street featuring many establishments open 'til the far reaches of the night. *The Albion Public House* is the most British pub in town, *The Shamrock* the most Celtic. Rum fans convene at *La Taverne du Perroquet Bourré* (The Tavern of the Plastered Parrot), while *L'Abreuvoir* is highly recommended for those who fancy good French music. Kebab snack bars abound, ever ready to appease the peckish night owl.

BC Blues – *25 pl. Carnot - ☎ 04 78 37 11 24 - Tue-Sat from noon and 10pm. Discotheque: Wed-Sat from 10.30pm*. Located on Place Carnot, a minute from the Perrache train station, this establishment operates on two different schedules. The pub opens at noon, then at around 10:30pm the club, rather more exclusive, gets going. Jazz concerts with professional musicians are organised several times a month here.

Café Léone – *8 r. de la Monnaie - ☎ 04 78 92 93 70 - May-Oct: noon-2pm, 7pm-1am; Nov-Apr: Mon-Sat noon-2pm, 7pm-1am - closed 31 Dec*. With its tapas served at the bar, just like in Barcelona, San Miguel beer and bullfights on TV, this café is a bona fide Iberian watering hole, lively and noisy as is befitting. Whole rooms may be reserved for evening events.

Hot Club de Lyon – *26 r. Lanterne - ☎ 04 78 39 54 74 - www.hotclubjazz.com - Tue-Thu 9.30pm-1am, Fri 10pm-1am, Sat 4pm-1am - closed end Jul to mid-Sep*. All jazz fans worth their salt frequent Lyon's Hot Club. Located in a cellar, just like its famous predecessors in Paris' Saint-Germain-des-Prés, every kind of jazz, from New Orleans to bossa nova and from Duke Ellington to fusion, is generously represented here. Saturday afternoons are free and drinks are quite affordable.

La Cave des Voyageurs – *7 pl. St-€aul - ☎ 04 78 28 92 28 - www.lacavedes-voyageurs.fr - Tue-Sat 2pm-midnight - closed most of Aug.* An appealing little wine bar with a deliciously 'retro' decor. Burgundies, Mâconnais vintages and Beaujolais may be enjoyed with a plate of delicatessen or cheese at friendly prices.

Casino Le Lyon Vert – *200 av. du Casino - 69890 La Tour-de-Salvagny - ☎ 04 78 87 02 70 - www.lyonvert.com - 10am-4am.* Tempted by the demon of gambling? Feel like spicing up your evening by trying your luck? Attracted to settings like those in the Scorsese film, Casino? Properly attired and over 18? If so, this is your address, with 400 slot machines, video poker, roulette and black jack, plus a restaurant and bar.

Bar de La Tour Rose – *22 r. du Bœuf - ☎ 04 78 37 25 90 - www.tour-rose. com - 5pm-2am.* Molière himself gave a performance on the very site – formerly a Jeu de Paume court – where this bar belonging to a ritzy hotel is now located. Known for its well-stocked cigar humidor, the establishment organises jazz concerts every Friday and Saturday. The drinks menu includes no fewer than 60 cocktails, of which 40 are house creations.

Eden Rock Café – *68 r. Mercière - ☎ 04 78 38 28 18 - www.edenrockcafe.com - Tue noon-1am, Wed-Thu noon-2am, Fri-Sat noon-3am - closed 3 wks in Aug.* In the heart of a pedestrian street that becomes very lively of an evening, this bar is located in a building classified as an historical monument. The decor is magnificent and the menu is worth perusing – if you've never tasted ostrich fillet, this is your chance! Blues, rock and funk concerts weekends.

Le Bartholdi – *6 pl. des Terreaux - ☎ 04 72 10 66 00 - 8am-1am.* This is indubitably one of the biggest and loveliest terraces in Lyon, just across from the Fontaine Bartholdi, named after the very famous sculptor of the Statue of

Liberty. The brasserie is open non-stop. Monthly debates on architecture, the sciences, Italy, international relations, politics and philosophy - public participation welcome - are held here. The second floor salons are reserved for meetings, seminars, cocktail parties and concert soirees.

Le Cintra – *43 r. de la Bourse - ☎ 04 78 42 54 08 - www.cintra-lyon.fr - Mon-Sat 7.30am-5am.* Located next to the Chambre de Commerce, this is the chic rendezvous in Lyon. Businessmen and women meet here to unwind and enjoy the piano bar (nightly from 10pm) after having sealed their latest mega-deals. Note the handsome decor of Lebanese wood, designed in 1921.

Ninkasi Ale House – *267 r. Marcel-Mérieux - ☎ 04 72 76 89 00 - www. ninkasi.fr - Mon-Thu 10am-1am, Fri-Sat 'til 3am.* Microbrewery, vast café, summer terrace, small restaurant and hall where concerts, DJ evenings and other events are held: this former factory near the Gerland stadium is all the rage.
Theatre and entertainment
Pick up one of the local periodicals, such as Lyon Poche: www.lyonpoche. com.

Théâtre National Populaire – *8 pl. Lazare-Gougeon - 69627 Villeurbanne - ☎ 04 78 03 30 00 - presse@tnp-villeurbanne.com - tickets: on site Mon-Fri 11am-6pm; by phone Mon-Fri 10am-6pm.* Villeurbanne banks on its myriad cultural resources, including the Théâtre National Populaire (aka le TNP), one of the city's great successes. Contemporary productions are staged here year round.

Au Pied dans l'Plat – *18 r. Lainerie - ☎ 04 78 27 13 26 - www.aupieddanslplat.fr - Mon-Sat from 8.30pm - closed 26 Jul to 26 Aug.* Lyonnais are very fond of this cabaret located in a handsome arched 15C cellar. Loosely translating as Foot in Mouth, the Pied dans l'Plat puts on dinner shows with a satirical bent in an unbridled, Rabelaisian ambience. Unvaryingly popular for the past 20 years.

Le Guignol de Lyon - *Compagnie des Zonzons – 2 r. Louis-Carrand - ☎ 04 78 28 92 57 - www.guignol-lyon.com – Wed and Sat: 3pm and 4.30pm, Sun 3pm; daily during school holidays.* La Compagnie

des Zonzons stages children's performances that marry burlesque and fantasy,
something like in Tex Avery cartoons,
and give the rather conventional Guignol a second childhood. The shows for
adults, inspired by aspects and events
of life in Lyon, are more malicious.
**Auditorium-Orchestre national de
Lyon** – 149 r. Garibaldi - ☎ 04 78 95 95
95 - www.auditoriumlyon.com - tickets:
Mon-Fri 11am-6pm, concert Saturdays
2pm-6pm - closed most of Aug. The
Auditorium Maurice Ravel regularly
hosts l'Orchestre National de Lyon
which, under the wand of conductor
Emmanuel Krivine, has celebrated
its 30th anniversary. In 1998-99,
the baroque music programme was
honoured by the presence of Philippe
Herrewegue and Fabio Biondi. World
music aficionados have enjoyed discovering music from Bali and the chants of
the Aka Pygmies. Musical films are also
shown.
Maison de la Danse – 8 av. Jean-
Mermoz - ☎ 04 72 78 18 18 - www.
maisondeladanse.com - tickets: Mon-Fri
11.45am-6.45pm - closed mid-Jul to mid-
Aug. From flamenco and tap dancing
to ballet and the traditional dances of
East and West, welcome to the citadel

of the art. The greatest artists perform
here: Maurice Béjart, Carolyn Carlson,
Découflé, the Spanish dancer Cristina
Hoyos, the Ballet National de Cuba and
Grupo Corpo, to name but a few.
Opéra national de Lyon – 1 pl. de
la Comédie - ☎ 0826 305 325 - www.
opera-lyon.org - tickets: Mon-Sat 11am-
7pm - closed late Jul to end Aug. In a
perfect setting, this is one of the city's
most beautiful monuments, thanks to
the immense and splendid glass roof
designed by Jean Nouvel. With a capacity of 1 100 seats, The Opéra includes
an orchestra (60 musicians), a ballet (30
dancers), a choir (26 singers), a troupe
and a solid expertise. With Ivan Fischer
holding the baton, l'Opéra National de
Lyon is an international class company.
A 200-seat amphitheatre is the stage
for a more varied programme, including
classical, jazz and world musics.
Halle Tony-Garnier – 20 pl. Antonin-
Perrin - ☎ 04 72 76 85 85 – www.
halle-tony-garnier.com - visits following
schedule – phone ahead. Since its restoration in 2000, this huge metallic structure presents a remarkable diversity of
events from the Moscow State Circus to
Lionel Richie and Johnny Halliday.

All over the city, thousands of balconies were lit up by tiny lights placed there in a
spontaneous gesture by Lyon residents. This religious custom has become a traditional festival during which the city councillors and store owners inaugurate their
Christmas displays.

Lyon in the Middle Ages – After Charlemagne's reign, Lyon passed from one fam-
ily to another through legacies and dowries. Finally, the city was placed under the
temporal authority of its archbishops.
During this period a large number of major building projects were completed.
Churches and abbeys sprang up in Lyon and the surrounding area. The Pont du
Change (Exchange Bridge) was built over the River Saône; the Pont de la Guillotière,
designed by the Pontiff Brothers, provided access to the other bank of the Rhône.
In the early 14C Lyon was directly annexed to royal authority and it obtained the
right to elect 12 consuls. A municipal charter was proclaimed at Île Barbe in 1312.
The consuls, all of them members of the rich *bourgeoisie*, raised taxes and ensured
that there was law and order. The people of the working classes, who were quick to
rebel and who had not hesitated in besieging the archbishop in his palace, discovered to their cost that the consuls were even more heavy-handed than the clergy
had been.

A cultural centre – At the end of the 15C the setting up of fairs and the development
of banking attracted traders from all over Europe. Social, intellectual and artistic life

blossomed, stimulated by a visit from François I and his sister, Marguerite, who held the most dazzling court.

Famous "booksellers" took the fame of Lyon's printers far and wide. There were 100 printer's workshops in the town in 1515, and more than 400 by 1548.

Painters, sculptors and potters, all of them steeped in Italian culture, prepared the way for the French Renaissance.

Lyon boasted brilliant poets and storytellers such as **François Rabelais** (1494-1553). He was a doctor at the local hospital and, for the fairs in 1532 and 1534, published his works *Gargantua* and *Pantagruel*.

It was, though, a woman, **Louise Labé**, who embodied the spirit of the day, not only for her grace and beauty but also for her skill in poetry. At the age of 20, Louise had developed comprehensive linguistic (Greek, Latin, Spanish and Italian) and musical talents. After a stint at the siege of Perpignan (not for the faint-hearted!), she eventually married a gentleman-ropemaker (*cordier* in French) from Lyon and opened a salon for poets, artists and men of learning, just as Madame de Sévigné was to do a century later. **"La Belle Cordière,"** as she was known, penned some pleasing verse herself, as well as encouraging others.

Scientific advances – Literature and the arts reigned in the Lyon of the 16C. Science became all the rage in the 18C, with the **Jussieu brothers**, famous botanists, and Bourgelat, who founded the first veterinary school in Europe in Lyon in 1762. In 1783 **Jouffroy** tested steam navigation on the Saône with his "Pyroscaphe," the first really viable steamboat; however, it brought him nothing but the ironic nickname of "Jouffroy the Pump."

In 1784 **Joseph Montgolfier** and **Pilâtre de Rozier** succeeded, at Les Brotteaux, in rising into the air on board a hot-air balloon. This was one of the first flights. A few years later, **André-Marie Ampère**, the great physicist, and **Joseph-Marie Jacquard**, who invented a weaving loom, showed their own form of inventive genius.

"Lyon is no more" – During the French Revolution, the residents of Lyon resisted the Convention. Retribution was harsh: on 12 October 1793 the Committee of Public Safety declared that "Lyon waged war on liberty. Lyon is no more." Houses were destroyed, countless local people died, and Lyon was renamed a "Free Commune."

Lyon, City of Light

With the famous **Festival of Lights** held here on 8 December, when the city twinkles with the light of thousands of candles, Lyon was already predisposed to investing generously in street-lighting, and it has done just that in the shape of a project called "Plan Lumière" which places the emphasis on public safety and the highlighting of the city's architectural heritage. Over 100 monuments and locations have been selected for inclusion in a comprehensive and homogenous system of illumination which gives them a whole new dimension. Fourvière Basilica stands out like a lighthouse on the top of its hill; the opera house takes on a futuristic appearance with its huge glass superstructure glowing red; squares such as place des Terreaux or place de la Bourse and the banks of the Saône and the Rhône are lit up by subtle lighting in a variety of colours in warm or cold tones depending on the location. The Part-Dieu district with the distinctive Crédit Lyonnais tower soaring up from it, the Port St-Jean, the Hôtel-Dieu and many more of the city's famous monuments feature in this huge light show which weaves an atmosphere of fairy tale and magic. Along with the various events put on in the evenings, this invitation to explore "Lyon by night" proves irresistible.

A guide to the "Plan Lumière" is available from the tourist office. www.lyon.fr

Lyon's "Mr Punch" – Guignol, the popular wooden puppet who is well-known throughout France, his wife Madelon and his usual sparring partner, Gnafron, whose fine bass voice has coarsened somewhat through excessive consumption of Beaujolais, all embody the popular spirit of the local people in a way that provokes laughter without giving offence. **Laurent Mourguet** (1769-1844), who created Guignol, was a local weaver. The few neighbours for whom he first performed his comedy shows were enthusiastic. Soon, as his success grew, so did his public: he staged performances all over Lyon, in the Petit Tivoli, and in the main avenue in Les Brotteaux where, on Sundays, three rows of chairs were set out. After Mourguet's death his 16 children, all of whom had been trained by him, perpetuated his art form. Nowadays, comedies based on current affairs are played out on the stage of the Guignol de Lyon theatre.

The silk industry – It was silk which, in the 16C, made Lyon a major industrial city; until then most of the silk fabrics in France had been imported from Italy. Two main figures dominate the history of this new industry. In 1536 **Étienne Turquet**, a man from Piedmont in Italy, offered to bring to Lyon silk and velvet weavers from Genoa and set up a factory in Lyon. François I, who was anxious to stem the flow of money out of the country as a result of purchases of foreign silks, accepted his offer. In 1804 **Joseph-Marie Jacquard** invented a loom which, by using a system of punched cards, enabled a single worker to do the work of six. The Croix-Rousse district was filled with its characteristic house-workshops – the upper storeys contained the looms on which the workers wove the silk provided by the manufacturer.

In 1875 a revolution occurred in the silk industry; the introduction of mechanical looms and the change in fashion away from figured fabrics and brocades quickly reduced the silk-workers to abject poverty. Only a few looms continued to exist in Lyon, capable of producing special fabrics at exorbitant prices. Ordinary silks were made by workers in rural areas where labour was less expensive.

Today natural silk imported from Italy or Japan now represents only a minute proportion of the quantities of fabric processed here. It is subject to extremely meticulous care and attention in the silk-workers centre (Maison des Canuts, *see below*).

The so-called "silk-style" weaving, though, using all sorts of fibres (glass, carbon, borum, and aramide) remains one of Lyon's specialities. The traditional know-how of the silk weavers has found direct applications in the production of highly sophisticated parts for the aeronautics, space and electronics industries. These activities are closely linked to chemistry (in research and the combining of new molecules).

Lyon Fair – In the Middle Ages, Lyon was "one of the keys to the kingdom," situated as it was on the frontiers of Savoy, Dauphiné, Italy and Germany on one side, and Beaujolais, Burgundy, Languedoc, Forez and the Auvergne on the other. In 1419 the heir to the French throne, the future Charles VII, having realised the value of this geographical situation in commercial terms, ordered two fairs to be held here every year; he made Lyon one of the largest warehouses in the world. Traders and merchants flocked here from every direction.

From 1463 onwards, thanks to Louis XI, the fairs were held four times a year.

Re-established in 1916 after a long break, the **Lyon International Fair** maintains the city's tradition as a major centre of international business. Running concurrently with the main fair are a number of specialist exhibitions.

A European crossroads – Lyon lies at the centre of a motorway network that links the city to Northern and Southern Europe in the north-south direction and to the Massif Central, Switzerland and Italy in the east-west direction, via St-Étienne, Clermont-Ferrand, Geneva, Annecy, Chambéry and Grenoble.

Since 1981, in addition to the many fast rail links with the rest of France, Lyon has enjoyed even more rapid communications due to the high-speed train (TGV) service. There is a busy international airport, **Lyon-St-Exupéry,** to the east of the town and

La Presqu'île

the Édouard-Herriot harbour to the south of the Gerland district is full of heavy barges waiting to sail up to Auxonne on the Saône *(32km/20mi SE of Dijon)*. A direct river-sea route with no need to offload cargo nor make intermediate stops was opened with Piraeus in 1984, with Algiers in 1986 and with Haïfa in 1991.

Lyon puts on a new face – There has been much development in Lyon since the "daring" tower blocks of the 1930s – including both new projects and restoration schemes in the old parts of the city.

In order to ensure its success in the future, Lyon is developing a number of science and technology parks, which bring together scientific research, higher education and industry. The **Cité Internationale,** between the Rhône and the Tête d'Or park, is the site of an International Conference Centre (capacity 2 000), the head offices of Interpol (the International Criminal Investigation Organisation), a hotel complex and a Museum of Contemporary Art, all housed in a boldly innovative building. To the east, around the university campus, there are major technical research offices and, further out of town, the St-Exupéry TGV station, designed by Spanish architect Calatrava to resemble a bird taking flight, which provides a TGV link to the local airport.

The **Gerland** district, which houses the town's main stadium (renovated and extended for the 1998 World Football Cup), is undergoing continued major development.

The Heart of the City

La Presqu'île and its Squares

Allow one day; museums are dealt with in Sights below

Lyon's main city centre districts lie around place Bellecour. "La Presqu'île" – the Peninsula – has long been the setting of the Lyon trading centre, and until the 19C commerce centred on rue Mercière. Two main pedestrian precincts run across it linking place des Terreaux to Perrache railway station. They are rue de la République to the north and rue Victor-Hugo to the south.

La Presqu'île is the modern face of Lyon. The Rue de la République is bustling with department stores, shops, cinemas and bistros, and the street is lined with buildings typical of 19C Lyon. Their façades incorporate tall windows and lintels decorated with cut sheet-metal signs. Two other shopping streets run from north to south,

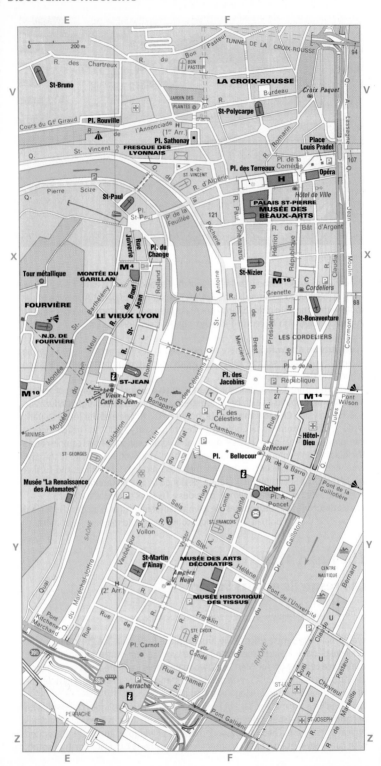

LA PRESQU'ÎLE		Juin Pont Alphonse	FX	84	Morand Pont	FX	107
		La-Fayette Pont	FX	88	Platière R. de la	FX	121
Childebert R.	FY 27	Lattre-de-Tassigny Pt de	FV	94			

Hôtel de ville FX	H	international de la			Musée de la Civilisation gallo-		
Musée Gadagne (Musée		Marionnette)	FX	M⁴	romaine	EY	M¹⁰
historique de Lyon et Musée		Musée de l'Imprimerie	FX	M¹⁶	Musée des Hospices civils FY	M¹⁴	

rue du Président-Herriot and rue Paul-Chenavard. The districts to the south of place Bellecour skirt the former Île des Canabae district, the site of Ainay Abbey.

Place Bellecour

This famous Lyon square, overlooked by the distinctive outline of Fourvière Basilica on its hill to the west, is one of the largest in France (310x200m/1 017x656ft). The huge symmetrical Louis XVI façades lining the west and east sides of the square date from 1800.

The equestrian statue of Louis XIV is known to the locals as the "Bronze Horse." The pedestal is decorated with two bronzes by the Coustou brothers (17C-18C) representing the Rhône and the Saône, each facing in the direction of its respective river. On either side of the pedestal is the inscription: "Masterpiece by Lemot, Sculptor from Lyon." An earlier equestrian statue of the great King by Desjardins (1691) was erected on this spot in 1713. The symbol of royalty was overturned, smashed and melted down during the French Revolution. The present statue (1828) was itself threatened in 1848: it was about to be pulled down when the Commissary Extraordinary of the Republic saved it by suggesting that, if the pompous inscription in honour of Ludovicus Magnus were replaced by a homage to the talent of Lemot, this would constitute just as much of an attack on royalty.

To the south-east of the square, the bell-tower of the 17C former almshouse, the **Hôpital de la Charité**, stands on its own in front of the main post office.

To the north-east of the square, the Banque Nationale de Paris stands on the site of the cinema where the first films by the cinematographer **Lumière** were shown.

Place Louis-Pradel – The square is decorated with a fountain and sculptures by Ipoustéguy, and is an aesthetic combination of old and modern forms.

The Opera house

Opéra de Lyon

On the south side of the square, opposite the Hôtel de Ville, stands the new Lyon opera house, the result of a successful modernisation scheme. The façade of the old building has been preserved and the eight muses of the pediment appear to hold up the enormous glass semicylindrical roof, the design of the architect **Jean Nouvel**. Inside, beyond the original Rococo foyer is the concert hall itself, an Italianate chamber with a seating capacity of 1 300, and a restaurant under the glass roof. The building takes on a particularly impressive appearance during the evening illuminations, which floodlight it in predominantly red tones, throwing its architectural contours into sharp relief.

The successful restoration of the building was rewarded by Lyon Opera being promoted to the rank of a national opera company.

Place des Jacobins

The main feature of the square is the majestic Dominicans' fountain, erected in 1886 in memory of four local artists, Philibert Delorme (architect), Hippolyte Flandrin (painter), Guillaume Coustou (sculptor) and Gérard Audran (engraver), each dressed in the costume of their day.

Place des Terreaux

For the best view, stand on the north side by the pavement cafés. This square, enlivened by flocks of pigeons, is the hub of city life in Lyon. It derives its name from the filling in of a former bed of the Rhône by soil or leaf mould. The confluence of the rivers was situated nearby in Roman times. In 1642 the **Marquis of Cinq-Mars** was beheaded here before a crowd of female spectators who had gathered to see his handsome head roll.

The famous monumental lead **fountain**★ was made by the sculptor Bartholdi. Its four quivering horses symbolise the Rivers running towards the Ocean. The south side of the square is bordered by the 17C façade of the Palais St-Pierre. In 1994, D Buren was entrusted with the restoration of the square. He added an area of granite paving slabs in a harmonious pattern, 14 pillars and 69 water jets, and the whole installation is illuminated to great effect at night.

Hôtel de Ville

This remarkable city hall, which is part Louis XIII in style, was designed by Simon Maupin. It consists of a large rectangle of buildings flanked by pavilions. Inside is the main courtyard, an unusual construction on two levels separated by a semi-circular porch.

▶ *Walk along rue Joseph-Serlin.*

The original façade of the Hôtel de Ville facing place des Terreaux was destroyed by fire in 1674. Jules Hardouin-Mansart and Robert de Cotte were commissioned to refurbish the building and they radically transformed the façade. The side pavilions and belfry were topped by a dome. In the centre, a large rounded tympanum supported by telamones is adorned with an equestrian statue of Henry IV beneath the city's coat of arms.

Vieux Lyon★★★

Lyon old town, which stretches for over 1km/0.6mi between Fourvière and the Saône, includes the **St-Jean district** in the centre, the **St-Paul district** to the north and the **St-Georges district** to the south. This was once the town centre and the seat of all the corporations, in particular those representing silk workers. There were 18 000 looms here at the end of the reign of François I (mid-16C). Traders, bankers, clerks and royal dignitaries lived here, in magnificent town houses.

Almost 300 of these mansions still stand, forming quite an exceptional example of Renaissance housing. In this area, which is covered by a conservation order and has undergone extensive restoration, it is worth noting the variety of decorative features on the houses, the craftsmanship involved in the construction of the mansions, and their substantial height as a result of a lack of space. Many of these 400-year-old houses originally had four floors; additional storeys were added very early on, in order to provide more light for the looms.

Hôtel Bullioud, galerie Delorme

One of the main features of the old town is the numerous passages or alleyways known as **traboules** (from the Latin *trans ambulare* meaning "walking through") especially between rue St-Jean, rue des Trois-Maries and quai Romain-Rolland, rue St-Georges and quai Fulchiron. Since there was not enough space to build an extensive network of streets, these passageways, all perpendicular to the Saône, were built to link the buildings together. They consist of corridors with vaulted or coffered ceilings leading to inner courtyards with Renaissance galleries.

The houses reflect their period of construction (15C-17C) and there are several architectural styles.

The **Late Gothic houses** are distinguishable by the elegant decoration on the Flamboyant façades – multifoiled or ogee arches, flowerets, carved gables decorated with crockets. The windows are often set asymmetrically into the walls. A vaulted corridor leads to an inner courtyard where a corner turret contains a spiral staircase.

Most of the old houses, among them the most beautiful of all the mansions, are built in the **Renaissance style.** The basic structure remains unchanged but the buildings are bigger and include new decorative features of Italian inspiration. The polygonal staircase turrets are beautifully designed and built; each courtyard has its succession of galleries, one above the other, each with surbased arches.

The **French Renaissance houses** are fewer in number. There is a noticeable return to Antiquity with the inclusion of architectural orders. The famous architect **Philibert Delorme** (1515-70), a native of Lyon, launched the new fashion with the gallery on squinches at no 8 rue Juiverie (🚶 *see below*). The main staircase, which was often rectangular, was set in the centre of the façade.

The **late-16C and pre-Classical houses** are distinguished by severe architectural lines. The decoration on the façade appears above the ground floor and includes triangular pediments with a central arch stone in relief, and rusticated bonding. The galleries overlooking the courtyard show Florentine influence with rounded arches supported by round columns.

While walking around the courtyards and passages, besides appreciating the *traboules* themselves, keep an eye open for statues of the Virgin Mary in courtyards or corner niches, attractive carved shop signs, wrought-iron imposts and railings, old wells, and amusing corbels supporting the spring ends of the diagonal ribs of the vaulted passageways.

ST-JEAN AND ST-PAUL DISTRICTS

▶ *Tour starting from place St-Jean.*

Exploring the Traboules

The traboules are private property and some are therefore kept closed by their owners. However, many of the most interesting are nonetheless open to visitors, under the terms of an agreement drawn up between the city of Lyon, the owners and the urban community. They can be accessed by pressing the entry button usually to be found above the interphone or entry code number pads by each main street door. Other traboules, not usually open to the public, can be visited as part of a guided tour organised by the Lyon tourist office. Before beginning a visit, it is advisable to ask at the tourist office for the list of passages that are open to visitors. The best time to explore many of the interior courtyards described in this section is in the morning.

Place St-Jean

In the centre of the square is a fountain with four basins topped by a small openwork pavilion containing a sculpture of the Baptism of Christ. To the east of the square is the cathedral of St-Jean and the choir school.

Manécanterie

To the right of the west front on place St-Jean is the 12C choir school. The front of the building, which lost 0.80m/2ft7ins of its overall height when the ground level was raised, is decorated with a blind storey topped by red-brick incrustations, colonnettes and niches containing statues of human figures. Despite alterations, it has retained its Romanesque appearance.

Primatiale St-Jean★

Dating originally from the 12C, St-Jean Cathedral is a Gothic building erected to complete a Romanesque apse. On the exterior the most notable features are the four towers, two on the west front and two over the arms of the transept. They are only slightly higher than the nave.

In 1245 and 1274 the cathedral was the setting for the two Councils of Lyon. In the following century it was chosen for the consecration of Pope John XXII. In 1600 Henri IV married Marie de' Medici here. More recently, in 1943, the Sixth Grand Pardon was celebrated here. The event is celebrated approximately once every century, when Corpus Christi coincides, on 24 June, with the Feast Day of St John the Baptist, to whom the church is dedicated.

West front

Its horizontal lines are emphasized by the pointed gables on the doorways and the point of the central gable topped by a statue of the Eternal Father. The west front was built in the 15C and constituted the final stage of the building project.

The three portals, with their gables and quatrefoils, were originally decorated with statues but the ornamentation was destroyed during the Wars of Religion by the troops of Baron des Adrets.

The jambs, however, have retained their remarkable early-14C **decoration**★. More than 300 medallions form a sequence of narrative scenes.

On the central portal are illustrations of the labours of the months, the signs of the Zodiac, the story of John the Baptist and the story of the Creation. Those on the left-hand portal depict the stories of Samson, St Peter and the Apocalypse. The portal to the right includes a depiction of the legend of St Theophilus.

Interior

Note the absence of an ambulatory, a characteristic feature of churches in Lyon. The nave, in which the sexpartite arches are supported by slender engaged columns, is a splendid example of Gothic architecture.

The **chancel**★★ is the oldest part of the church, with the apse; the foundations date from the 12C. The decoration in the apse is typical of Romanesque architecture as seen in the Rhône Valley. Round the apse is a series of fluted pilasters supporting a blind storey topped by a frieze of palmettes with russet-red cement incrustations.

Another two similar friezes run above and below the triforium which, with its pilasters and semicircular arcading, contrasts with the Gothic arcading in the nave. The Bishop's Throne is set against

13C stained-glass window (detail)

the wall of the apse. Above the simple pillar that forms the back of the throne, note the tiny Romanesque capital representing Christ. The lower windows in the chancel have early-13C **stained glass**. The most outstanding sections are the medallions in the central window, depicting the Redemption. The stained glass in the clerestory (13C) has undergone extensive restoration; the windows are decorated with figures of the Prophets.

The rose windows in the transept and the great rose window in the west front have Gothic stained glass. In the north transept is an **astronomical clock**★ *(Figures in action at noon, 2pm, 3pm and 4pm ☎ 04 72 48 28 25)* dating from the 14C. It has a strange chime called the Hymn to St John and includes the sound of a cock crowing, and a set of automata representing the Annunciation. The late-15C **Bourbons' Chapel**★ features remarkably elegant Flamboyant Gothic decoration.

Treasury★

Access from the western end of the south aisle. The cathedral treasure, housed on the first floor of the choir school, includes pieces of church plate including a beautiful processional cross decorated with Limoges enamelwork and a cover from a Rhenish psalter, both dating from the 13C. There is also a bishop's crozier (late 16C) made of silver inlaid with niello, objects and liturgical ornaments that belonged to Cardinal Fesch, and 17C Flemish and Aubusson tapestries. Note the beautiful Byzantine ivory casket (9C) decorated with scenes from circus games.

9C casket

▶ *Skirt the cathedral to the right on rue St-Étienne and go to the archaeological gardens.*

Jardin Archéologique

In this archaeological park visitors can see the remains of several buildings that have occupied the former site of the church of St-Étienne to the north of the present cathedral, since the 4C. They include Gallo-Roman baths, a Palaeo-Christian baptistery, and an arch from the 15C church of Ste-Croix.

▶ *The narrow rue Ste-Croix leads to rue St-Jean.*

Rue St-Jean★★

This was the main street in the old town of Lyon and, as such, royal corteges and religious processions passed along it. No 7 has a Flamboyant Gothic façade.

The old **Hôtel de la Chamarerie** at no 37 was built in the 16C for the cleric responsible for overseeing the cathedral cloisters, who was known as the chamarier. The façade, which was modified in the 19C, is in the Flamboyant Gothic style.

The arcading in the galleries of the **Maison des Avocats**★ (Barristers' House) is supported on massive columns and the outbuildings have pink roughcast. Seen from rue de la Bombarde, the house presents a fine example of 16C architecture in the Italian style.

N° **58** has an unusual feature in the shape of a well with a tripartite roof so that it is accessible from the courtyard, the staircase and the workshop.

At no **54**, the **longest traboule** in old Lyon crosses five courtyards before reaching no 27 rue du Bœuf.

Walk past the Palais de Justice to no **52**: the house of printer Guillaume Leroy (late 15C) has a spiral staircase in a round tower. The bays are supported on arches.

No 50 is a fine example of a renovated courtyard enhanced by galleries and a spiral staircase.

The same features can be admired at no 42, which has retained its corbelled passageway resting on sculpted consoles.

At no **36**, a house dating from the late 15C, there is a polygonal tower containing a spiral staircase. The keystones in the galleries are decorated with coats of arms on the first two floors and the well is protected by a shell-shaped canopy embellished with pearls. The niche at the corner of rue St-Jean and place Neuve-St-Jean contains a statue of John the Baptist.

▶ *Take rue du Palais-de-Justice and turn left onto rue des Trois-Maries.*

Rue des Trois-Maries

The "Street of the Three Marys" derives its name from the niche on the pediment of no **7** containing a statue of the Virgin Mary flanked by two Holy Women. On the same side of the street, numerous traboules lead off downhill to the Saône; that from no **9**, for example, gives a view of no 17 quai Romain-Rolland.

Next door, at no **5**, there is another shell-shaped niche containing a statue of the Madonna and Child.

At no **3** a handsome example of French Renaissance has a staircase surmounted by a tower in the centre of its façade; this feature is repeated in the house at no 5 place du Gouvernement.

The façade of no **4** is adorned with a regular arrangement of fluted pilasters and, in the courtyard, a tower in which the spiral staircase is clearly visible through the openwork.

▶ *Retrace your steps to no 6, and cross the traboule leading across two restored courtyards to no 27 rue St-Jean.*

The façade at no **27** has mullioned windows framed by fluted pilasters.

No **28** conceals a magnificent **courtyard**★★ with an imposing tower with a spiral staircase inside it. Note the ceiling of one of the galleries which is decorated with an unusual pattern of ribs.

The **Hôtel Laurencin** at no **24** has a crenellated octagonal tower containing spiral staircase. The loggias on the superimposed galleries feature ribbed vaults.

▶ *Cross place de la Baleine and go to place du Gouvernement.*

Place du Gouvernement

The façade of no **5**, its doorways topped by wrought-iron imposts and a stone balcony, dates from the early 17C.

Hôtel du Gouvernement (16C) stands at no **2**. The upper courtyard lies at the end of a long passageway roofed with ribbed vaulting. All that remains of the well to the right is the shell-shaped top (note the traboule at no 10 quai Romain-Rolland).

▶ *Rejoin rue St-Jean and walk on until you reach place du Change.*

Place du Change

This square, originally called place de la Draperie, was frequented by moneylenders in the 15C and 16C. The **Loge du Change** was designed mainly by Soufflot, the architect who altered the original design between 1747 and 1750. On the upper storey are engaged columns topped by Ionic capitals and carved entablatures. Since 1803 the building has been used as a Protestant church.

Opposite, at no **2**, is the **Maison Thomassin** which has a 15C façade built in the 14C style. On the second floor the mullioned ogee bays rising to trefoiled arches are set into Gothic arches decorated with coats of arms.

▶ *Continue along rue Lainerie.*

Rue Lainerie

Note the vaulted corridor of no **18**. The **Maison de Claude de Bourg** at no **14** has a 15C flower-decked façade which is typical of Lyon, with ornately carved accolades. On the second floor is a shell-shaped corner niche containing a statue of the Virgin Mary.

▶ *To the right is rue Louis-Garrand and the Guignol puppet theatre.*

Rue Lainerie opens onto place St-Paul, where you can glimpse the train station and, further back, the **church**.

J. Damase/MICHELIN

▶ *Turn left onto rue Juiverie.*

Rue Juiverie★

The Jews were expelled from this street in the late 14C and the Italian bankers who replaced them had luxurious mansions built.

Guignol and Gnafron

Le Guignol de Lyon - Compagnie des Zonzons

Guignol, the satirical puppet, is characterised by his black cap under which he has a short plait which he calls his *sarsifis*. His naïvety and waggish banter make him a perfect example of the "urchins" of Lyon. His wife, Madelon, with whom he has frequent arguments, is a model wife, if somewhat prone to grumbling. His inseparable friend is Gnafron whose most notable features are his tall stature and his ruddy nose, an indication of his marked liking for Beaujolais. If anybody asks him what he does for a living, he answers, "Educated people call us cobblers or botchers; the uneducated call us gowks" (*"gnafres"*).

Shows at this Guignol theatre are now a blend of tradition and modern innovation, influenced by contemporary authors and even films.

The **Hôtel Paterin,** also known as "Henri IV's House," at no **4** is an outstanding example of Renaissance architecture. The **staircase** in the courtyard, with its three tiers of arches, one above the other, supported on massive columns, is particularly impressive. To the right is a niche containing a statue of Henri IV.

At no **8**, the second courtyard in the **Hôtel Bullioud** contains the famous **gallery**★★ designed by **Philibert Delorme,** a gem of French Renaissance architecture in Lyon. Delorme built it in 1536 on his return from Rome. Note the squinches supporting the corner pavilions decorated in the Antique style; Doric frieze with an entablature on the lower level including metopes and triglyphs and pilasters with Ionic volutes on the upper level.

The Renaissance façade on the **Maison Antoine Groslier de Servières** (no **10**) has five arches on the ground floor topped by triangular or broken pediments of black marble. In the courtyard is a round tower with mullioned windows containing a spiral staircase. The corbels on the balcony on the first floor are carved with human figures.

The house at no **21** has ogee windows with rounded frontons. There is a Gallo-Roman cellar in its basement. Between nos **16** and **18** rises the picturesque, steep **ruelle Punaise**, which leads onto montée St-Barthélémy. In the Middle Ages it served as an open sewer.

The mansion at no **20** was built by a wealthy 15C gentleman, E Grolier. The façade is decorated with mullioned windows flanked by colonnettes. Note in the courtyard a tower with a spiral staircase inside and the rib-vaulted galleries.

At no **22** is the **Maison Baronat**, which has a corbelled corner turret overlooking montée du Change.

At no **23**, at the corner of rue de la Loge, is the **Maison Dugas** whose long façade is decorated with bosses and lions' heads.

▶ *Turn left onto rue de la Loge, then right into rue de Gadagne.*

Musée Gadagne★

This mansion stretches from no 10 to no 14 rue de Gadagne and is the largest Renaissance building in the old town. In 1545 it was purchased by the **Gadagne Brothers,** bankers of Italian origin who had amassed a colossal fortune. Indeed, the expression "as rich as Gadagne" became a local figure of speech. On the façade set slightly back from the street, note the cant-walled tower and, to the left, the wrought-iron grid of the cellar window, a masterpiece of ironwork. In the inner courtyard, the two main buildings with large mullioned windows are linked by three storeys of galleries. The well, which is topped by a dome covered with scales, was brought here from the Maison du Chamarier (no 37 rue St-Jean); it is said to have been designed by Philibert Delorme. The residence now houses the Local History Museum and the International Museum of Puppetry. *www.museegadagne.com.*

Musée Historique de Lyon★

In the Local History Museum the rooms on the ground floor have been laid out with **religious sculpture**★, including bas-relief sculptures from old churches or abbeys in Lyon, in particular from Ainay, St-Pierre and Île Barbe (Annunciation bas-relief, a mantelpiece known as "Charlemagne's Crown"). The other three floors are partly concerned with the history of Lyon, from the Renaissance period to the 19C. There are collections of glazed earthenware, pewter, local furniture, and an outstanding collection of Nevers faience dating from the 17C and 18C. Numerous documents relating to Lyon in the days of the French Revolution and Napoleonic mementoes (18C town keys) are also on display. The top floor relates the history of journeymen and includes some of their masterpieces.

Musée International de la Marionnette★

Temporarily housed on the second floor of the Musée Historique, the exhibits of this museum include not only Guignol and a number of glove puppets but also an outstanding collection of string and rod puppets and shadow figures from France, England, Belgium, Holland, Venice, Turkey, Russia and the Far East. South of the Hôtel de Gadagne is montée du Garillan.

▷ *Walk across place du Petit-Collège and along rue du Bœuf.*

Rue du Bœuf

This street owes its name to the statue of an ox (or more precisely a bull) at the corner of place Neuve-St-Jean, a work attributed to M Hendricy. The street contains some lovely examples of Renaissance architecture, some of which are occupied by luxury hotels.

At no **6**, "La Cour des Loges" Hotel occupies a fine set of four restored houses. It is possible, with discretion or perhaps stopping for refreshment, to have a look at the beautiful courtyard with its U-shaped galleries on three floors.

No **14** leads into a pretty courtyard with a polygonal tower and galleries supported on arches surmounted by a frieze of Greek motifs.

The **Maison du Crible**★ at no **16** dates from the 17C. It has an ornate doorway with bosses and ringed columns topped by a pediment decorated with a small carving of the Adoration of the Magi said to have been the work of Giambologna. An alleyway with ogival vaulting supported on carved corbels leads to an inner courtyard in which the elegant round tower, with staggered openings, owes its name, **Tour Rose** (Pink Tower), to the colour of its famous roughcast. ⓖ *Do not go up to the terraced gardens.*

J. Damase/MICHELIN

La Tour Rose

"Tour Rose" is also the name of the famous hotel complex which has moved to no **22**. It is possible, with permission from the hotel, to have a look at its two terraced courtyards. A drink in the hotel bar will enable to you see one of the two remaining real tennis courts in old Lyon.

Place Neuve-St-Jean

This old street was transformed into a square under the Consulat. At one end is the sign signalling the beginning of rue du Boeuf, and at the other a niche housing a statue of John the Baptist. At no **4** is a vast building set slightly back from the others which features a superb staircase over arches corresponding to galleries with surbased arches.

▷ *Return to rue du Bœuf.*

The **Maison de l'Outarde d'Or** (House of the Golden Bustard) stands out at no **19** because of its carved stone sign. The courtyard is particularly interesting for its two turrets. One of them is round and built over a squinch; the other, corbelled turret is a rectangle built on an upturned pyramid. Another building of interest can be seen at no **27** (the longest *traboule* in Lyon, leading to no 54 rue St-Jean) with an elegant 16C spiral staircase preceding a succession of three courtyards.

No **36** opens onto a pretty courtyard decorated with restored galleries. It is interesting to compare these *(turn round)* with those of no **38**, which are largely sealed up by additional structures. Most of the galleries were closed off when the district's fortunes sank to make more space and to keep in some heat.

▷ *No 31 opens onto rue de la Bombarde (on the right). Almost opposite, take rue des Antonins, which leads back to place St-Jean.*

From St-Jean metro station it is possible to take the funicular railway up to the top of Fourvière hill and come back down the same way after visiting the Basilica, Gallo-Roman Museum, and Roman theatres.

ST-GEORGES DISTRICT

▷ *Go to rue Mourguet and walk on until you reach place de la Trinité.*

Place de la Trinité

The **Maison du Soleil** (Sun House), which became famous after inspiring the backcloth for the Guignol puppet theatre, lends an old-fashioned touch to the square. The corner recesses in the façade contain statues – St Peter on the right and the Virgin Mary on the left. The sun emblem is set above a mullioned window on the first floor.

The courtyard within *(access via no 2 rue St-Georges)* has elliptical balconies.

Montée du Gourguillon

Set on the hillside in the Fourvière district, this was the usual route taken by carriages heading for the Auvergne in the Middle Ages. It is difficult to imagine the heavy loads climbing such a steep slope. It was also the direct route between the cloisters of St-Jean belonging to the Canon-Counts, and St-Just, the fortified town of the Canon-Barons. At no **2** stands a Renaissance house. Slightly further up the hill is the **Impasse Turquet**, a picturesque passageway with old timber galleries.

Life in Lyon

As the "Gateway to the south of France," where the better qualities of the north of France can be found in a more Mediterranean context embodied not least by the red pantile roofs, Lyon enjoys not only the reputation of being a hard-working, major city, but also of having an outstanding standard of living in which good food plays a leading role. Life in Lyon is characterised above all by its lack of stress or complication. The Lyonnais are creatures of habit, and some of their favourite pastimes can be appreciated by visitors to the city as well, such as watching (perhaps even playing!) the odd game of boules, especially during the boules tournament at Whitsun, taking a quiet stroll along the banks of the Saône or Rhône, or a gentle wander around the sloping streets of La Croix-Rousse, or indulging in a little shopping spree on the peninsula or in the Part-Dieu district. Then there is the pleasure of drinking in the sumptuous Renaissance architecture in the old town, or the peacefulness of the Tête d'Or park early in the morning, not forgetting the rose garden which is an absolute must in June; lengthy conversations over a bottle of Beaujolais in one of Lyon's cafés, the somewhat noisier delights of local festivals, convivial lunches in a crowded Lyon bistro, or bouchon, surrounded by the delicious rich smell of Lyonnais cuisine; and finally, for those who are young at heart, a Sunday afternoon spent watching the antics of the Guignol puppets.

Rue St-Georges

The ground floor of no **3** has basket-handled arches and the springer of the door is decorated with two rampant wrought-iron lions. At no **3 bis** the springer is decorated with a phoenix rising from the flames. At no **6**, the 16C house has a fine interior courtyard (art gallery). The spiral staircase is set in a round tower with sloping windows.

▶ *Continue to no 100 if you want to visit the Automata Museum.*

Musée "La Renaissance des Automates"

Kids *100 rue St-Georges.* &.◯ *Guided visit (1hr): all year, daily, 2.30-6pm.* ◯ *Closed 25 Dec. 7€ (children: 5€).* ☎ *04 72 77 75 20. www.museeautomates.com*
Seven rooms house some 250 automata in perfect working order, displayed according to cultural, traditional and regional themes.

▶ *Turn right when you reach the Église St-Georges and come back via quai Fulchi-ron.*

At no **7** note the house of Moorish design attributed to the architect Bossan.

Fourvière Hill

Allow one day

The Fourvière district of Lyon stands on a hill of the same name; the term **Fourvière** is said to come from the Latin *forum vetus*, relating to the forum situated in the heart of the Roman colony established in 43 BC; its theatre, odeon and aqueducts have survived to this day. The forum, which stood on the site now occupied by the esplanade in front of the basilica, is said to have collapsed in AD 840.

In the 3C people moved from the side of the hill and the stones were reused to rebuild the town at the bottom of the slope. In the Middle Ages the hill was

Fourvière hill

largely given over to farming (in particular vineyards). In the 17C numerous religious orders set up monasteries and convents here, which inspired the historian, Michelet, to make his famous comment about Fourvière, "the hill that prays," opposite La Croix-Rousse, "the hill that works."
Nowadays Fourvière, with its basilica, Roman monuments and museum is, with the old town some 100m/328ft below, one of the most popular tourist venues in Lyon.

THE MONTÉES

The *montées,* or rises, consist of winding flights of steps or steeply sloping streets that climb the Fourvière hill, providing superb views down over the old town. Each of them has its own particular charm.

Montée des Carmes-Déchaussés and Montée Nicolas-de-Lange

The former derives its name (Rise of the Barefoot Carmelites) from the monastery founded in the early 17C which now houses the Regional Archives; it has 238 steps.

VIEUX LYON-FOURVIÈRE

Gadagne R. de	FX 63
Juin Pont Alphonse	FX 84
Lainerie R.	FX 91
Neuve-St-Jean Pl.	FX 113
Punaise Ruelle	FX 129

Ancienne chapelle de la Vierge	EX B
Hôtel "La Cour des Loges"	FX Z
Hôtel Bullioud	FX G
Hôtel Laurencin	FX K
Hôtel Paterin	FX L
Hôtel de la Chamarerie	FX S
Hôtel du Gouvernement	FX X
Le Guignol de Lyon Compagnie des Zonzons	FX T
Maison Baronat	FX N³
Maison Dugas	FX N⁶
Maison Thomassin	FX N¹⁰
Maison d'Antoine Groslier de Servières	FX N¹
Maison de Claude de Bourg	FX N⁴
Maison de Paris	FX N⁹
Maison de l'Outarde d'Or	FX N⁸
Maison des Avocats	FX N²
Maison du Crible	FX N⁵
Musée Gadagne (Musée historique de Lyon et Musée international de la Marionnette)	FX M⁴
Musée de Fourvière	EX M¹²
Musée de la Civilisation gallo-romaine	EY M¹⁰

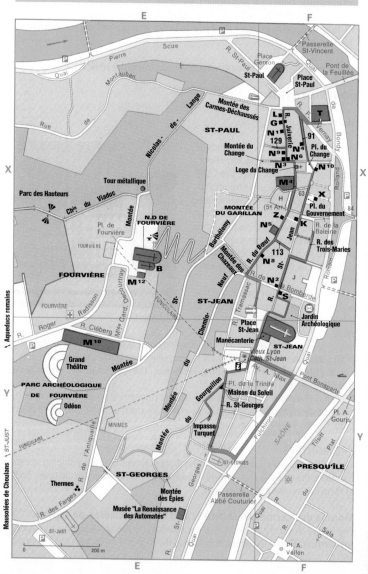

The second has 560 steps which means that there is a total of 798 steps down to place St-Paul from the metal tower *(Tour Métallique)* on Fourvière.

Montée du Change
This links rue de la Loge to montée St-Barthélémy. On the way down, there are interesting views of the spires on the church of St-Nizier which rises from the buildings on the banks of the Saône.

Montée du Garillan★
This is a remarkable series of zigzag flights of steps (224 steps).

Montée des Chazeaux
With its 228 very steep steps, it leads onto montée St-Barthélémy.

Montée du Chemin-Neuf and Montée St-Barthélémy
From these steps there is an extensive view over the rooftops of the old town and St-Jean Cathedral.

Montée du Gourguillon – 🕭 *See St-Georges district above.*

Montée des Épies
This rise climbs up above the St-Georges district, high above the church dedicated to St George, a Neo-Gothic building designed by Bossan, the architect also responsible for Fourvière Basilica.

FOURVIERE SANCTUARY
The history of the religious buildings erected in honour of the Virgin Mary on the site of the Roman forum spans almost eight centuries. The massive basilica standing today at the top of Fourvière hill is an integral part of the Lyon landscape.

Basilique Notre-Dame★
The basilica is a famous place of pilgrimage built to designs by an architect named Bossan after the Franco-Prussian War (1870) in fulfilment of a vow taken by Monsignor de Genouilhac, the Archbishop of Lyon, who undertook to build a church if the enemy did not approach the city. Crenellated walls with machicolations, flanked by octagonal towers, form an odd blend of Byzantine and medieval features. The

Basilique Notre-Dame

J. Damase/MICHELIN

abundance of decoration inside (nave and crypt) is no less unusual. The triple-domed nave has mosaics telling the story of the Virgin Mary and her place in the history of France on the right; on the left is a representation of her place in the history of the Church. By the doorway of the west front is a commemorative stone slab embedded in the pavement recalling the visit of Pope John Paul II in 1986.

Ancienne Chapelle de la Vierge
To the right of the basilica stands the real pilgrimage chapel dating from the 18C: the former Lady Chapel containing a miraculous statue of the Virgin Mary (16C).

Musée de Fourvière
Apr to Jan: 10am-12.30pm, 2-5.30pm. 5€ (children: 3€). ☎ *04 78 25 13 01. www. lyon-fourviere.com*
This museum, housed in the chapel and buildings once belonging to the Jesuit Order, contains a collection of polychrome wooden statues (12C-19C), various projects designed for the basilica in the 19C, and numerous votive offerings.

Viewpoints
From the **esplanade** left of the basilica there is a famous **view**★ over the Peninsula and the west bank of the Rhône overlooked by the tower of the Crédit Lyonnais bank. In the distance, to the east, the mountains silhouetted against the skyline are Bugey, Grandris, the Alps, Chartreuse and Vercors.
For a 360° **panoramic view**★★, climb to the foot of the basilica's observatory (*Basilica – Apr-Oct: daily, 10am-noon, 2.30-4pm. ☎ 04 78 25 13 01*); from there the hillsides of the Lyonnais area, Mont Pilat and Mont-d'Or are visible and, in good weather, also the Alps and Mont Blanc to the west and the Puy de Dôme to the east.

Parc des Hauteurs
Follow a path to the left, just before the Tour Métallique. This ambitious project was set up to enhance visitors' appreciation of Fourvière hill by laying out panoramic walks. The most original construction is that of the "Chemin du Viaduc," a 72m/236ft-long footbridge which gives a breathtaking **view**★ down onto Lyon and La Croix-Rousse.

Tour Métallique
This metal tower was built in 1893 to the same design as the Eiffel Tower but on a smaller scale (85m/279ft high); it is now used as a television transmitter.

Parc Archéologique de Fourvière★
daily 7am-7pm. Closed 1 Jan, 1 May, 1 Nov, 25 Dec. 4€ (under-18s: no charge). ☎ 04 72 38 49 30.
Fourvière archaeological site was opened in 1933 and has brought to light ancient and medieval public buildings in the district: Gallo-Roman baths in rue des Farges, remains of early basilicas in rue des Macchabées and quai Fulchiron (montée de Choulans).

Musée de la Civilisation Gallo-Romaine★★
17 rue Cléberg daily except Mon 10am-6pm (last admission 30min before closing). Closed 1 Jan, 1 May, 1 Nov, 25 Dec. 6€ (children: 4€). No charge, Thu. ☎ 04 72 38 49 30. www.musees-gallo-romains.com.
This museum stands on the hill at Fourvière, at the heart of the district that was once the plateau of the ancient town of Lugdunum. The building designed by the architect Zehrfuss is an unusual spiral concrete structure sunk into the hillside. The museum displays thematic exhibitions of its mainly Gallo-Roman collections. There is a particularly rich stock of epigraphs.

The prehistory section displays a processional chariot from La Côte St-André, dating from the Hallstatt period (8C BC). Following sections illustrate the founding of Lugdunum, its town planning, municipal and provincial authorities, the army, religions, theatre and circus shows, economic and domestic life, worship of the dead and the early days of Christianity in Gaul. There are a number of outstanding items including a **Claudian tablet**★★★, a fine inscription on bronze of the speech made by Emperor Claudius to the Roman Senate in AD 48 in favour of the Gauls, and a **Gallic calendar** from Coligny, also engraved in bronze during the Roman era. Other items worthy of note are the dedicatory inscription of the Three Gauls amphitheatre, a bust of Emperor Caracalla, a silver goblet decorated with Gallic gods, some larvae or funeral masks, and a mosaic depicting circus games (wrestling, lion-taming).

The work of potters, glassmakers, ironmongers and goldsmiths is represented in the collection of ceramics, vases, tools and jewellery. A gold-plate treasure uncovered in the Vaise district in 1992 has been added to the museum's collection.

The room displaying scale models of the Roman theatres contains a large window from where visitors can admire the actual remains.

Théâtres Romains

The group of buildings uncovered near rue de l'Antiquaille includes a theatre built during the reign of Caesar Augustus (1C BC) and extended during the reign of Hadrian (2C AD) and an odeum.

Grand Théâtre

This is the oldest theatre in France. It is similar in size to those in Arles and Orange (108m/354ft in diameter) but smaller than the one in Vienne.

The initial construction dates from the pre-Christian era. The number of tiers of seats was later increased by building on top of the promenades. The paving in the orchestra pit has been reconstructed. The outer circular wall of the theatre shows substructures in which archaeologists have noted the particular attention paid by the builders to exits via underground corridors and to ground drainage through a system of pipes and sewers.

The stage curtain machinery, housed in the orchestra pit, is some of the best preserved of its kind in the Roman world. A model of how it worked is on display in the museum.

▶ *Climb the staircase leading to the top of the tiers of seats.*

From here, the full size of the theatre can be appreciated. It is possible to walk round the upper section by following the Roman road of large granite slabs.

▶ *Walk down the Roman road to the odeum.*

Odeum

Odeums were an elegant venue reserved for music and conferences, and were frequented by the elite. The layout is identical to the theatre but the building was on a much smaller scale.

The thickness of the outer wall suggests that the tiers of seats were protected from the elements by a large overhanging roof. Note the delightful geometrical decor of the pavement in the orchestra pit, which has been reconstructed using fragments found on site, including pink breccia, grey granite and green cipolin.

Behind the odeum, excavations have uncovered traces of a portico running alongside a row of shops.

Area overlooking the theatre

Beyond the paved road behind the theatre, recent excavations have revealed the existence of an impressive residence and not, as was thought at one time, a temple dedicated to Cybele. From the late 1C BC there stood on this huge rectangular esplanade a vast and magnificent house, bordered on one side by shops sheltered by a portico. Early in the 1C AD it was replaced by a large public building. To the east, above the theatre, lie the powerful foundations of an extended platform. At an indeterminate date an enormous cistern was installed here which was no doubt linked to Gier aqueduct.

Aqueducs Romains

On either side of the start of rue Roger-Radisson (once the road west to Aquitaine) are the interesting remains of one of the four aqueducts which provided the town's water supply.

Mausolées de Choulans

In the centre of place Wernert are three mausoleums that serve as reminders of the Gallo-Roman burial ground situated outside the town walls. The one in the centre, the oldest of the three (1C BC), bears an inscription on one of the sides indicating that the monument was built by emancipated slaves once belonging to Calvius Turpion.

La Croix-Rousse

La Croix-Rousse (literally "The Russet Cross") owes its name to a coloured stone Cross which stood at one of the district's crossroads in the days before the French Revolution. The district still has all the character and flavour of a small village community and today remains the last bastion of true Lyon traditionalism. The most fiercely proud inhabitants of La Croix-Rousse are deeply attached to the "Plateau" and look down from a distance on the hustle and bustle below. They might even spend months on end without going down the hill. Each autumn, the air is filled with the smell of roasted chestnuts and the local crêpes *(matefaim)* as the bustling boulevard de La Croix-Rousse plays host to the "Vogue" funfair, an annual event since 1865.

The invention of new looms by **Joseph-Marie Jacquard** (1752-1834) led the "canuts" or silk workers to abandon the low cottages in the St-Jean district and move to larger austere buildings with wide windows that let in the light. In the 19C the streets echoed with the rattle of the hand looms operated by some 30 000 silk workers.

The *traboules* in La Croix-Rousse follow the lie of the land and include a large number of steps. They were used to move bolts of silk about the district without any risk of damage from inclement weather. In 1831, and again in 1834, they were the scene of bloody uprisings when the silk workers waved black flags symbolising poverty and bearing the famous motto: "Life through work or death through conflict."

THE HISTORIC TEXTILE WORKERS DISTRICT

▶ *Round tour starting from place des Terreaux. Go to no 6 (near the fountain), which communicates with rue Ste-Catherine. Turn right and walk down rue Romarin until you reach rue St-Polycarpe. Keep on walking towards the church.*

The **"Condition Publique des Soies"** (Public Silk Packing Works) at no 7 has a porch in which the upper arch is decorated with a majestic lion's head and mulberry leaves (the food of the silkworm). The building now houses a cultural and social centre but it was on these premises during the 19C that the hygrometric packing of silk cloth was monitored since, due to the fact that silk can absorb up to 15% of its weight in water, checks had to be made to ensure that the weight of the fabric actually complied with the official norms.

▶ *Walk up rue de l'Abbé-Rozier.*

At the end stands the church of **St-Polycarpe** dating from the 17C and 18C. From no 19 rue Leynaud (opposite no 14), the passage Thiaffait (derelict) leads up a double flight of steps to rue Burdeau. Opposite no 36 montée du Perron climbs up to **place Chardonnet,** on which stands the monument erected in memory of Count Hilaire de Chardonnet (1839-1924), the inventor of artificial silk.

▶ *Turn right onto rue des Tables-Claudiennes (steps).*

Rue des Tables-Claudiennes (street of the Claudian Tablets) owes its name to the inscriptions on bronze discovered by the draper Gribaud in his vineyard (👍 *see Musée de la Civilisation Gallo-Romaine).*
No 55 is linked to no 20 rue Imbert-Colomès.

▶ *Take no 29 opposite, which communicates with cour des Voraces (steps and lane on the right, then turn left level with a street lamp).*

Cour des Voraces with its imposing flight of steps is an impressive sight. In the 19C it was the meeting place of a silk workers' guild known as the Voraces or Dévorants ("The Ravenous").

▶ *Take rue Bodin to place Bellevue.*

True to its name, this square commands a fine panorama of the surrounding town.

▶ *Follow the steps rising above the square and continue straight on along a steep path that crosses a garden. It will take you to the Gros Caillou.*

The **Gros Caillou** is an erratic boulder left by the glaciers of the Quaternary Era which shaped the landscape on which Lyon stands today. It marks the end of boulevard de la Croix-Rousse where it is possible to make a pause in a shaded spot.

▶ *Take the first street on the right, walk along rue de Belfort and turn left onto rue d'Ivry.*

Maison des Canuts
10 r. d'Ivry. ♿ 🕐 *daily except Mon, Sun and public holidays, 10am-6.30pm. Guided tours (1hr): 11am and 3.30pm.* 🕐 *1st week in Jan and 2nd week in Aug.* 5€ *(children: 3€).* ☎ *04 78 28 62 04. www.maisondescanuts.com.*
At no 10 and no 12, craftsmen and women from the home workers cooperative (Cooptiss) perpetuate the traditions of the Lyon silk workers' and promote the high-quality fabrics they produce. During the guided tour visitors are shown how a draw loom and a velvet loom work. An exhibition of old fabrics (lampas, damasks, brocades, cut-pile velvets) and pictures and portraits woven on silk give an insight into the history of Lyon's silk industry.

▶ *Walk back along rue d'Ivry to rue Dumont-d'Urville, turn left and follow it up to rue Richan (fifth on the right).*

Ateliers de Soierie Vivante★
21 rue Richan. Guided tours (30m) daily except Sun and Mon 9am-noon, 2-6.30pm

Mur des Canuts

At the junction of boulevard des Canuts, rue Denfert-Rochereau and rue Pelletier stands a tall wall adorned with a *trompe-l'œil* mural covering an area of 1 200m2/12 840sq ft. Painted in December 1987 and updated in 1997, it serves as a picturesque reminder of life in one of the districts in La Croix-Rousse. Note, in the windows, the puppet-theatre characters of Guignol, his wife Madelon and the Bailiff.

(Tue 2-6.30pm). ◑ *Closed Aug and public holidays. 3€ (children: 2€).* ☎ *04 78 27 17 13. www.soierie-vivante.asso.fr.*

This association was founded in 1993 to protect and promote the heritage of the Croix-Rousse silk working industry. It organises a number of tours of authentic family-run silk workshops, leaving from the Atelier Municipal de Passementerie, the municipal furniture trimmings workshop (where techniques involved in the manufacture of braid and other trimmings are explained at the start of the tour). Other workshops included in the tour are hand-loom weaving (with some very rare extra wide draw looms exhibited upstairs), machine-loom weaving, velvet weaving, making silk-wrapped thread and trimmings (gimping) and hand painting on silk.

▶ *Return to rue d'Ivry and walk past the Maison des Canuts to rue du Mail which leads to place de la Croix-Rousse.*

On place de la Croix-Rousse is a statue of Jacquard.
The second part of this itinerary is easier since one is often going downhill.

▶ *Walk across the square and along rue des Pierres-Plantées to the junction with rue du Bon-Pasteur.*

From the square there is a fine view of the town and Fourvière hill.

▶ *Walk down the steps (montée de la Grande-Côte lower down,) to rue des Tables-Claudiennes. Turn right towards the Amphithéâtre des Trois-Gaules.*

Amphithéâtre des Trois Gaules

According to the dedication discovered at the bottom of a well in 1958, this venerable spot was built in 19 BC by Rufus as a meeting place for delegates from the 60 Gallic tribes. Extended during the reign of Emperor Hadrian, it became sadly notorious during the days of Marcus Aurelius as the place where followers of the new Christian faith were tortured. Among them was St Blandine who perished here in 177 (a post in the arena marks the site of her martyrdom).
Only the north part of the amphitheatre has been uncovered; when complete, it would have included an arena surrounded by a gully and a podium supporting tiers of seats.

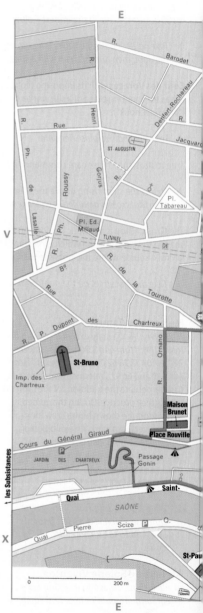

▶ *Via montée des Carmélites, place Morel and rue des Chartreux, walk to rue Ornano. It is possible to reach Église St-Bruno (Baroque church) by continuing along rue des Chartreux, turning left onto rue Dupont then left again.*

▶ *Rue Ornano leads to place Rouville.*

LA CROIX-ROUSSE

Lattre-de-Tassigny Pt de	FV	94
St-Polycarpe R.	FVX	151
Ste-Catherine R.	FX	155

" Condition publique des Soies "	FV	F
Hôtel de ville	FX	H
Statue de J.-M. Jacquard	FV	V

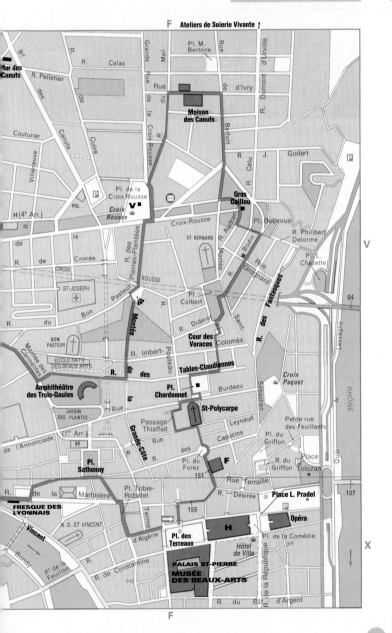

The rooftops of Lyon

J.-L. Barde/SCOPE

Place Rouville

From the square there is a fine **view**★ over Lyon. Jutting out from above the seemingly endless sea of red rooftops on the peninsula is the belfry of the Hôtel de Ville and the Part-Dieu district overlooked by the tower of the Crédit Lyonnais bank on the left, and on the right, the spires of the church of St-Nizier. The final meander of the Saône flows past the hill at Fourvière; the belfry of the church of St-Paul can be seen at the foot of the hill. On the north side of the square, nos 5 and 6 house the **Maison Brunet** with its 365 windows, a typical silk worker's dwelling.

▶ *Head down toward the quaysides of the Saône via passage Gonin.*

To the west, the shaded terraces of the Chartreux gardens overlook the river. Note the games areas reserved for playing boules.

Quai St-Vincent

From the quay there are views over the meander in the Saône overlooked by a row of buildings with Art Nouveau façades (caryatids, floral patterns).
Upriver is a vast architectural complex, known as **Les Subsistances**, consisting of an early-17C cloister, later turned into an army supply-storage space and extended by the addition of a large square building with two mills in the centre. The restored complex is now occupied by artists *(visits: information available at the mill)*.

▶ *Turn back and walk along quai St-Vincent as far as rue de la Martinière.*

At the beginning of the street, on the right, there is a fine painted wall known as the **Fresque des Lyonnais;** it is the work of the Cité de la Création.

▶ *Take rue du Sergent to place Sathonay.*

Place Sathonay

On the north side of the square are the monumental steps of montée de l'Amphithéâtre, flanked by two lion-shaped fountains.

▶ *Rue Vittet leads to place Tobie-Robatel.*

The **École La Martinière des Jeunes Filles** (finishing school for young ladies), built at the turn of the 20C, is a fine example of the architecture of this period, with its polychrome mosaics and wrought-iron entrance.

▶ *Rue Terme and rue d'Algérie lead back to place des Terreaux.*

Sights

La Presqu'île

Église St-Bonaventure

St Bonaventura's Church, which the people of Lyon cherish, has retained its original Franciscan layout.

The generously sized nave was required for the purposes of preaching. The bareness and simplicity of the architecture, on the other hand, are a reminder of the Franciscans' respect for all forms of poverty. St Bonaventura, one of the most famous of all Franciscans, died during the second Council of Lyon in 1274.

Église St-Nizier

Tradition has it that the present church of St-Nizier, much of which dates from the 15C, was built on the site of Lyon's very first church. On the outside, the nave is supported by double flying buttresses which can be seen clearly from rue de la Fromagerie.

The spires on the bell-towers of the church of St-Nizier are one of the outstanding features of Lyon's urban landscape. The Gothic north spire, built of warm-coloured brick, contrasts with the traceried spire on the south bell-tower (19C).

The Renaissance portal is set between four Doric columns and surmounted by a coffered oven vault; it is topped by a neo-Gothic gable.

The main characteristic of the interior (restored) is its 15C Flamboyant Gothic decoration: the ribbed vaulting includes keystones embellished with coats of arms; an intricately carved triforium runs round the entire church.

Note the charming **Madonna and Child**★ by Coysevox in a chapel in the south transept.

Musée de l'Imprimerie ★★

13 rue de la Poulaillerie (metro Cordeliers). ⊙ *Daily except Mon and Tue 9.30am-noon, 2-6pm.* ⊙ *Closed public holidays. 4€ (under-18s: no charge).* ☎ *04 78 37 65 98. www.bm-lyon.fr/musee/imprimerie.htm*

The splendid late-15C Hôtel de la Couronne, once the property of a rich merchant, houses this printing museum.

The collections retrace the glorious history of printing, from the invention of the printing press in the 15C. Rare incunabula (printed before 1500), old printing presses, notices and a large number of old and valuable editions provide an insight into the aesthetics of print and books, the development of printing techniques, cutting procedures (prints, carved woodblocks, engraved copperplates, etchings) and pay homage to Lyon's great book publishers, humanists, illustrators and engravers.

Musée des Hospices civils

1 place de l'Hôpital (Bellecour metro station). ♿⊙ *Jul-Sep: daily except Sat-Sun, 10am-noon, 1.30-5.30pm (Mon, 105.30pm) rest of year: 1st and 3rd Sun in each month, 1.30-5.30pm.* ⊙ *Closed public holidays. 4€ (children under 10, free).* ☎ *04 72 41 30 42.*

This museum is housed in the 17C building of the Hôtel-Dieu extended by Soufflot in the 18C. It contains an important collection of old ceramics used in pharmacies, a considerable amount of furniture including fine chests of drawers, objects made of pewter, objets d'art, in particular a bust by Coustou and a Virgin Mary by Coysevox. Three rooms display wood panelling from the Hôpital de la Charité which no longer exists; the most remarkable are those of the pharmacy (Louis XIII period) with carved motifs and of the archives room (18C). Also on display are instrument cases once used by dentists, surgeons and doctors.

Palais St-Pierre★

Pl. des Terreaux. This 17C and 18C building was formerly the abbey of the Ladies of St Peter, one of the oldest Benedictine abbeys in Lyon, whose nuns were recruited among the highest ranks of French aristocracy. Inside, the buildings have retained part of their original Italianate decor, particularly in the refectory and main staircase. The building fell into disuse during the Revolution and was turned into a museum in the 19C. In 1884 the artist Puvis de Chavannes painted the "Sacred Wood" in the staircase at the entrance to the Fine Arts Gallery.

Ancienne Église St-Pierre

Next to no 23 rue Paul-Chenavard. Note the narrow 12C façade of the former church of St-Pierre and the austere Romanesque doorway flanking superb 18C wooden doors. The church now contains the collection of sculptures belonging to the fine arts gallery.

Musée des Beaux-Arts★★★

20 pl. des Terreaux (Métro Hotel-de-Ville-L.-Pradel) ♿ ⏰ *Daily except Tue, 10am-6pm (Fri, 10.30am-8pm).* ⏰ *Closed public holidays. 6€ (children: free).* ☎ *04 72 10 17 40.* From place des Terreaux, enter the gardens in the former cloisters, where the galleries are surmounted by terraces. Tall loggias crown the corner pavilions on the south side. The statues here include *The Shadow* by Rodin and *Carpeaux at Work* by Bourdelle. After undergoing refurbishment work for eight years, the Musée des Beaux-Arts has now been completely renovated and ranks among the finest museums in France. Its splendid collections, carefully displayed, have been further enriched by the donation of 35 famous Impressionist and modern paintings of Jacqueline Delubac's private collection.

The Fine Arts Gallery presents an exceptional overview of art through the centuries, throughout the world. Its collections are organised into five separate departments: painting, sculpture, antiquities, objets d'art and medals.

Paintings

The rooms contain a selection of works from the great periods in European painting. Canvases from the Italian Renaissance include The Ascension of Christ★ by Perugino, a gift from Pope Pius VII to the city of Lyon, a tender *Nativity* by Lorenzo Costa and a set of Venetian paintings including *Bathsheba* by Veronese, *Danaë* by Tintoretto and two battle scenes by Bassano. There are also works from the Bolognese, Neapolitan, Florentine and Roman Schools. Spanish works include *The Sharing of the Tunic* by El Greco and a striking *St Francis* by Zurbarán. Among the German paintings feature *Christ Carrying the Cross* from the Cologne School and a portrait of a woman by Cranach the Elder. The Flemish and Dutch Schools are represented by Gerard David, Metsys, and Rubens.

The section on French painting has a large collection of works by 17C masters, including Simon Vouet *(Crucifixion)*, Jacques Blanchard *(Danaë)*, Philippe de Champaigne *(Adoration of the Shepherds)* and Charles Le Brun *(Resurrection of Christ)*. The 18C is represented by J-B Greuze *(The Lady of Charity)* and Boucher *(Light of the World)*. The "Salon des Fleurs" heralds the 19C with a graceful statue of Juliette Récamier by J Chinard, a delightful bust of a young girl by Houdon, colourful floral compositions by Antoine Berjon. A large section is devoted to the native artists of Lyon from the 19C including J-M Grobon, Fleury Richard and Pierre Révoil. Other 19C artists from Lyon with work on display here include Bonnefond Flandrin and, above all, Janmot *(Poem of the Soul* – a series of 18 mystic paintings).

Other 19C French masters are also represented: David, Delacroix, Géricault, Corot. Striking works by the Impressionists – Degas, Monet, Sisley, Renoir – as well as Gauguin and members of the Nabi movement, Bonnard and Vuillard lead into a general overview of 20C painting beginning with compositions by Dufy, Villon, Gleizes, Braque *(The Violin)*, Jawlensky, Chagall *(The Cock)*, Severini and Foujita *(Self-portrait)*. Contemporary artists include names such as Masson, Atlan, Max Ernst, Dubuffet and De Staël *(The Cathedral)*.

Ascension of Christ by Perugino

Basset, Cailliure/Musée des Beaux-Arts, Lyon

Sculpture

There are works from the Romanesque to the Gothic and Renaissance periods. Among the 17C to early-20C works, the most outstanding are busts by Coysevox and Lemoyne, *The Three Graces* by Canova, a series of small busts by Daumier, and marble and bronze statues by Etex, Pradier, Bourdelle, Maillol and Rodin.

Antiquities

This department consists of three sections organised by theme. The **Egyptian section** contains the most extensive collections covering art from all the Ancient Egyptian periods. The theme of "life after death" is well illustrated by some magnificent sarcophagi in polychrome wood, amulets and ushabtis (funerary figurines). The Ptolemaic period is represented by the monumental temple doors from Mehamoud. As well as religious practices, everyday life is evoked through steles and funerary masks, instruments and common objects such as a harp, sandals and jewellery. Models in painted wood reproduce scenes showing the main occupations of the Ancient Egyptians. In the **Near and Middle East section,** note the "priest's head" from Assyria, heads of statues from Cyprus and lead sarcophagi from Roman Syria (3C-6C). The final section covers art from **Ancient Greece and Rome,** and includes an exceptional Korah (statue of a young girl) from the Acropolis illustrating the degree of skill attained by the sculptors of Ancient Greece. The famous black-figure ceramic ware, rivalling the later red-figure style in beauty and technique, makes up part of a vast collection of amphorae, kraters, hydria and other vases.

Objets d'art

This section of the museum comprises a huge variety of exhibits from all ages and all continents. From the Middle Ages there are intricate ivories such as the triptych attributed to the Master of the Soissons Diptych; this outstanding degree of workmanship is also evident in the Romanesque and Gothic enamels, many of which are from Limoges, or in the gold- and silverware (late 15C reliquary arm section). Islamic art is well represented with ceramic and bronze ware, and a Persian basin

The Painted Walls of Lyon

The group of artists who painted the Silkworkers' Wall has painted other surprising murals showing aspects of life in Lyon. The majority of these paintings make up the **Musée Urbain Tony-Garnier**.

Other interesting murals include:

- ◆ "Journey through Time in Lyon" at no 98 avenue Lacassagne
- ◆ "Lyon, Health, Life" at no 115 avenue Lacassagne
- ◆ "Introducing Famous Lyon Faces" at no 49 quai St-Vincent
- ◆ "La Cour des Loges" at no 3 place Fousseret

from 1347, with particularly finely worked decoration (silver and gold). There is a set of armour for a horse from the French Renaissance with painstakingly precise ornamentation. This period also encompasses the development of Hispano-Moorish faience, Italian majolica, some of which is decorated with narrative scenes (1533 plate depicting *Hercules and Cacus,* Urbino) and painted enamels such as the altarpiece with 27 plaques attributed to Jean Ier Limousin (late 16C). Subsequent periods are also featured, with 18C French faience, the "La Norenchal" drawing room with its characteristically neo-Classical *trompe-l'œil* decor and Art Nouveau furniture by Hector Guimard.

Note also the Raphaël Collin collection which includes numerous ceramics from China, Korea and Japan (6C-19C).

Medals

The collection of over 40 000 medals, dating from Ancient Greek times to the present, is housed in a room with a splendid coffered ceiling.

Basilique St-Martin-d'Ainay

This church consecrated by Pope Pascal II in 1107 has undergone major alterations. The porch-belfry is topped by a pyramid roof, surrounded by unusual corner acroteria which give it its characteristic outline. Note the animal frieze beneath the cornice between the second and third levels, and the decoration of inlaid bricks.

Inside, the nave is separated from the side aisles by large columns dating from Roman times which support semicircular arches. To the right of the chancel, the Romanesque **capitals**★ depict Adam and Eve with the serpent, the Annunciation, Christ Enthroned, and to the left, Cain killing Abel, Cain and Abel's offering, St Michael slaying the Dragon and John the Baptist showing Christ to his followers.

The south arm of the transept contains **St Blandine's Chapel,** which was originally separate from the main building. Its short crypt is believed to have contained the remains of the martyrs of the year AD 177.

From the corner of rue Bourgelat and rue Adélaïde-Perrin there is a good view of the church including the bell-tower on the west front and the square transept tower.

Musée des Tissus★★★

34 rue de la Charité (metro Ampère–Victor-Hugo). ◷ *Daily except Mon: 10am-5.30pm: 5€ (ticket also valid for Musée des Arts Décoratifs).* ◷ *Closed public holidays.* ☎ *04 78 38 42 00. www.musee-des-tissus.com*

The Textile Museum, founded by the Lyon Chamber of Commerce over a century ago and housed in the Hôtel de Villeroy (1730), former residence of the governor of the province, is the pride of the Lyon people, and a veritable "repository" of decorative fabrics. The prestigious collections come from the most influential Western and Eastern countries as regards fabric design and production.

The first room introduces visitors to the various techniques used in the working of silk, to make satin, silk serge, taffeta, velvet etc. After a video on silk working, the exhibition presents examples of **French textiles** with magnificent material manufactured mainly in Lyon since the beginning of the 17C, the period when the Lyon "factory" was renowned for its excellence. The 18C saw the innovative creations of **Philippe de Lassalle** and **Jean Pillement**: embroidered portraits and "chinoiseries." Note also the **Meuble Gaudin**★, a famous hanging made for Empress Josephine's bedchamber at Fontainebleau. At the beginning of the 19C, textile artists turned to Classical Antiquity for inspiration, as seen in the "Pompeian motif" panel modelled on the dancers of the Herculanum. In the room decorated with *grisailles* of Psyche, small **portraits on velvet**★ illustrate the high degree of precision it was possible to achieve using Gaspard Grégoire's technique (painting on silk thread). The 19C was also marked by the production

Lampas silk

Basset, Caillure/Musée des Tissus, Lyon

of printed textiles on a large scale and the fad for "Indian shawls."

The section devoted to the **Far East** exhibits items dating from the 16C to the 19C: embroidered and painted panels, kimonos from Japan, Imperial robes in K'o-ssu (cut silk tapestry) from China.

The museum possesses a large collection of **liturgical ornaments**★ and robes spanning European production from the 12C to the 18C. From Italy there are some extremely rare fabrics from Palermo and Venice, sumptuous Genoese and Florentine velvets from the Renaissance period with a stylised thistle and pomegranate motif. There are textiles from north-west Europe, besides priceless examples of the art of embroidery, also typical examples of 15C Franco-Flemish art. Spain is represented by Hispano-Moorish fabrics with motifs strongly influenced by Arabian art and by some remarkable 16C silk velvets. Civil costumes are also on display, with the outstanding 14C **doublet**★, made of 32 sections, belonging to Charles de Blois.

The museum also houses, in its **Oriental section,** numerous items typically produced by Ancient Eastern civilisations: woollen and linen Coptic tapestries found during archaeological digs at Antinoöpolis; Sassanian fabrics decorated with hunting scenes or animals fighting; delicate embroideries from the Egypt of the Fatimid Dynasty; Byzantine fabrics. The visit ends with a magnificent collection of **carpets**★ – Persian, Turkish, Chinese and Spanish – from the 15C to the 18C.

Musée des Arts Décoratifs★★

30-34 rue de la Charité. 🕐 *Daily except Mon, 10am-noon, 2-5.30pm.* 🕐 *Closed public holidays. 5€ (ticket also valid for the Musée des Tissus).* ☎ *04 78 38 42 00. www.musee-des-tissus.com*

This museum is housed in a mansion built in 1739 and is mainly devoted to 18C furnishings. The collection includes pieces of furniture, most of them bearing the stamp of great cabinet makers (Hache, Oeben, Riesener), objets d'art, musical instruments (magnificent harpsichord dating from 1716), tapestries (Gobelins, Beauvais, Flanders, Aubusson), porcelain (St-Cloud, Sèvres, Meissen) and faience (glazed earthenwares from Lyon, Moustiers and Marseille). Do not miss, on the second floor, the exceptionally beautiful decoration of the dining room: 18C carved and gilded wood panelling from the Hôtel Régny in Lyon.

Among the sections devoted to Medieval and Renaissance art, the gallery containing over 200 examples of 15C and 16C Italian majolica is of special interest.

Left bank

Musée d'Art Contemporain★

81 Cité Internationale - Quai Charles-de-Gaulle. &.☼ *daily except Mon and Tue noon-7pm. 5€.* ☼ *1 May, 25 Dec.* ☏ *04 72 69 17 17. www.moca-lyon.org.*
This new cultural focus in the Cité Internationale complex is built around the atrium of the old market hall. Its modern structure allows for great flexibility of display and for works of art to be exhibited to their best advantage. The museum collection is presented as a standing exhibition presented alongside "display areas" designed for temporary shows. The collection is very varied, as since its first acquisition (*Ambiente Spaziale* by Fontana) the museum has been a "production centre" with works by Baldessari, Brecht, Filliou, Kosuth, Yvonnet and numerous other artists.

Muséum d'Histoire Naturelle★★

Entrance on boulevard des Belges. &.☼ *Daily except Mon 10am-6pm.* ☼ *Closed 1 Jan, 1 May, 1 Nov and 25 Dec. 4€.* ☏ *04 72 69 05 00. www.museum-lyon.org*
This Natural History Museum, founded in 1879 by the industrialist and scientist **Émile Guimet** (founder of another museum, of the same name, in Paris), is being entirely renovated; while the work is in progress, interesting temporary exhibitions devoted to the peoples of the world are organised.

Centre d'Histoire de la Résistance et de la Déportation★

14 avenue Berthelot (metro Jean-Macé). ☼ *Daily except Mon and Tue. 9am-5.30pm (Sat, Sun, 9.30am-6pm).* ☼ *Closed Christmas school holidays and public holidays except 8 May. 4€ (under-18s: no charge).* ☏ *04 78 72 23 11. www.lyon.fr.*
The museum is set up in part of the buildings which from 1882 to the early 1970s were the Military Medical School and which, from 1942 to 1944, housed the headquarters of the Gestapo in this region. The aim of the museum is to keep alive the memory of the events relating to the Resistance, the Deportation of its members and of the Jews, in France and in Lyon in particular and the Liberation.
An audio-guided tour begins on the first floor with documents, posters, film clips and recorded discussions with major figures of the time. It shows the important part Lyon played in the formation and development of the Resistance Movement. The events of July 1941, the arrest of the Resistance hero **Jean Moulin** in June 1943, and the large-scale public executions held here in August 1944 are all recounted.
Another section looks at the Deportation of the Jews and a chronology of their geno-cide. The importance of propaganda and information in times of war is reaffirmed in the mock-up of a small square pasted with contemporary propaganda posters. An interior has a radio replaying the "personal messages" broadcast from London.
The visit ends with a diorama linking the events that happened in Lyon and In France to contemporary world events.
The cellars of the building, used as prison cells during the Occupation, are now devoted to temporary exhibitions.

Musée des Moulages

3 rue Rachais (metro Garibaldi). ☼ *mid-Sep to end Jun: Tue, Thu 2-6pm.* ☼ *Closed school and public holidays. 2€.* ☏ *04 72 84 81 12.*
This fascinating museum, housed in a recently renovated ready-made clothes work-shop, is devoted to the history of sculpture from archaic Greece to the 19C.

Musée Africain

150 cours Gambetta (metro Garibaldi). ☼ *Daily except Mon and Tue. 2-6pm (last admission 1hr before closing).* ☼ *Closed Aug, 1 Jan, Easter, 1 May, 24, 25 and 31 Dec. 5€.* ☏ *04 78 61 60 98. www.musee-africain-lyon.org*
This museum belongs to the African Missionary Society and has three floors exhibiting over 2 500 objects from West Africa, particularly Benin and Côte d'Ivoire.

Among the collections illustrating everyday life and the social and religious aspects of these countries, note *(first floor)*, the bronze statuettes from Benin, Touareg weaponry and braiding and above all *(second floor)* a set of geometric and figurative weights (Ashanti from Ghana and Baule from the Côte d'Ivoire) used for weighing gold dust. The third floor presents examples of statuettes, masks and other ritual objects from an art steeped in symbolism.

Musée Lumière

25 rue du Premier-Film, Lyon-Monplaisir (metro Monplaisir-Lumière). ☾ *Daily except Mon 11am-6.30pm.* ☾ *Closed 1 Jan, 1 May, 25 Dec. 6€ (children: 5€).* ☎ *04 78 78 18 95. www.institut-lumiere.org*

Antoine Lumière, the father of Auguste and Louis who invented the cinema and the autochrome plate had this residence built between 1889 and 1901 in the majestic style favoured by the wealthy bourgeoisie during the transitional period between the Second Empire and Art Nouveau. The interior is strikingly decorated with lavish wood panelling, sophisticated chandeliers, marquetry floors and floral designs. It houses the **Institut Lumière** and hosts events based on still and moving pictures.

An exhibition retraces the life of the Lumière family and explains the early stages of the cinema. There are public viewings inside the barn and outdoor performances in summer *(apply for details)*.

Musée urbain Tony-Garnier

On both sides of boulevard des États-Unis, between rue Paul-Cazeneuve and rue Jean-Sarrazin; public entrance: 4 rue des Serpollières. ♿ ☾ *Apr-Oct: daily except Mon, 2-6pm (Sat, 11am-7pm); guided visits (1h30), Sat, 2.30pm and 4.30pm; Nov-Mar: daily except Mon, 2-6pm; guided visits (1h30), Sat, 2.30pm.* ☾ *Closed public holidays and school holidays in Dec). 6€ (children: 4€).* ☎ *04 78 75 16 75. www.museeurbaintonygarnier.com*

This group of buildings was built in the 1930s by the urban architect **Tony Garnier**, a native of Lyon whose most famous landmark in Lyon is the great covered market. Since 1991 many of the blind walls of these large buildings have been decorated with murals painted by a group of artists calling themselves **"The City of Creation."**

Having chosen to make an open-air museum, this group produced a series of enormous wall paintings on the theme of Garnier's works: Gerland stadium, the clock tower, the covered market among others. It is possible to visit a show-flat decorated in 1930s style.

Walking Tours

From Cité Internationale to La Part-Dieu

Cité Internationale

This vast complex, comprising an imposing Conference Centre (Palais des Congrès) of 15 000m²/160 500sq ft, cinemas (14 screens), hotels and a Museum of Contemporary Art, was installed between the Tête d'Or Park and the Rhône. A new park is planned to bridge the gap between the Tête d'Or and the banks of the river.

Parc de la Tête d'Or★

♿☾ *Mid-Apr to mid-Oct: 6.30am-10.30pm; mid-Oct to mid-Apr: 6.30am-8.30pm. No charge.* ☎ *04 72 10 30 30. www.lyon.fr.*

The English-style gardens surrounding the Conference Centre cover an area of 105ha/259 acres. The park's name derives from local folklore, which claims that a golden head of Christ is buried here. The entrance is marked by huge wrought-iron gates. The park is an ideal place for city dwellers to go walking and cycling and there is also a narrow-gauge railway. A subway leads to the **Île du Souvenir,** a small island rising from the lake.

Serres★ and Jardin Botanique

🕐 *Gardens: Oct-Mar: 8am-5pm; Apr-Sep: 8am-6pm; Alpine garden: Mar-Oct: 8-11.30am; Serres: Oct-Mar: 9am-4.30pm; Apr-Sep: 9am-5.30pm, except the garden of Madagascar, which is closed 11.30am-1.30pm. No charge.* ☏ *04 72 82 35 02. www.jardin-botanique-lyon.com.*

The **botanical gardens** are laid out to the south-east end of the park and consist of 6ha/15 acres of outdoor plants, great glasshouses containing 7000m2/74 900sq ft of lush tropical vegetation including numerous palm trees, and an Alpine garden where visitors are taken on a miniature tour of the world's mountainous areas and their plant life.

Jardin Zoologique

🕐 *Zoo: 9am-5pm (8pm in summer); Cat and Reptile Houses: 1-5pm (Sat-Sun 2-5pm). No charge.*

The **zoological park** located north of the botanical gardens is one of the oldest in Europe (1858). It has 1 100 animals including numerous wild animals from outside Europe.

West of the zoo lies the deer park. Between the two, on **place** de Guignol, children's activities (merry-go-round, games) and Guignol shows are organised by the **Véritable Guignol du Vieux Lyon** team *(Shows at 3pm, 4pm, 5pm and 6pm (Nov-Mar: no show at 6pm). 4€ (children: 3€)* ☏ *04 78 28 60 41. www.theatre-guignol.com).*

Grande Roseraie★

🕐 *Mid-Apr to mid-Oct: 6am-11pm; mid-Oct to mid-Apr: 6am-9pm. No charge.* ☏ *04 72 69 47 60.*

The **great rose gardens** are laid out between the lake and quai Achille-Lignon, and boast some 70 000 plants representing 350 varieties which are a stunning sight between June and October.

La Part-Dieu district

The name of the district ("God's Area"), would suggest that it was once placed under divine protection by a landowner during the Middle Ages. A vast complex spread out over 22ha/54 acres of what was once Army land, it is built around a pedestrian precinct (raised 6m/20ft above ground level) and consists of a large number of buildings and towers, including government offices, a hotel, the shopping centre (three floors of shopping arcades covering 110 000m2/1 177 000sq ft), the radio studios and the library. To the north-east stands the striking **Maurice Ravel Auditorium,** built in the shape of a shell and with a vault spanning 70m/230ft.

The **Crédit Lyonnais Tower,** affectionately known as "The Pencil" by locals, rises to a height of 140m/460ft above the town below. It has now become the second most famous landmark in the city after the Fourvière Towers, and its brick-red colour blends in well with the rooftops of the old urban districts.

To the east is the new **La Part-Dieu** station built to accommodate the TGV high-speed train. Hotel facilities and residential apartments complete this new development. Modern sculptures and gardens enhance the esplanades.

Level 0 corresponds to the city road network and is reserved for traffic only.

Quaysides along the Rhône

Quai Augagneur, by the Hôtel-Dieu, is lined with imposing bourgeois houses built in the late 19C. This wonderful esplanade beneath the plane trees is enhanced by the lively atmosphere of an open-air market *(except Mondays)*, and is particularly attractive in misty weather, when the river is turbulent and fast-flowing. The district of Les Brotteaux, with its geometrically laid out streets, stretches to the east; it lies on the site of sandbanks *("brotteaux")* once deposited by the Rhône, hence its name. From Wilson bridge the **view**★ extends to the heights of La Croix-Rousse on the other bank, where the tall houses of the former silk workers rise one above the other.

The Credit Lyonnais' "Pencil" tower

To the south of Wilson bridge is La Guillotière bridge, built in 1958 to replace the one built in the 13C by the Pontiffs. It offers a fine **view** over Fourvière hill.

Gerland district

This district sits opposite the confluence of the Rhône and the Saône and has Tony Garnier's great covered meat market at its centre. The area is one large "Science and Technology Park" and incorporates a high-level technical college, the Institut Pasteur, the Institut Mérieux and a sports centre. The International School, built to designs by the architects Jourda and Perraudin, is a glass construction overlooking the Parc Gerland.

Halle Tony-Garnier
Garnier created this huge meat market or abattoir in 1914. Its restored gigantic metal framework rises to a height of 24m/78ft and is now the setting for various cultural and commercial events. Its original architectural style is well set off by nocturnal illuminations.

Excursion

La Mulatière

Grand aquarium de Lyon ★
7 rue S.-Déchant (Bastéro bus stop). Take bus 63 from Perrache towards Oullins. 🅿 *Large car park.* 🕒 *Wed-Sun, 11am-7pm. During school holidays, daily, 11am-7pm. (last admission 1hr before closing)* 🕒 *Closed 1 Jan, 1 May, 24 and 25 Dec. 12€ (4-15-year-olds: 8€).* ☎ *04 72 66 65 66. www.aquariumlyon.fr*
Kids This new, rather unobtrusive building on the banks of the Saône offers visitors a journey to the different rivers and oceans of the world: impressive sheatfish reign supreme in rivers of temperate climates; nearby, sharks swim round a wreck inside a huge pool on two levels; a myriad of small brightly coloured fish of all shapes feel quite at home in tropical waters. After the video film, the tour ends with the room of the five senses and the hands-on basin. There is a snack bar and a shop.

Silk

Silk, the fibre from cocoons produced by the caterpillars of the Bombyx moth, otherwise known as silkworms, was discovered in China, and was brought to France by Louis XI in 1466. The French silk industry did not really begin to evolve until the 16C; at this time Lyon was chosen as the central silk depot, and cultivation of the mulberry bushes on which silkworms feed was begun on a large scale. The industry's expansion continued under Louis XIV, with notable innovators such as Philippe de Lassalle playing a major role in its development, but was brought to an abrupt end by the outbreak of the French Revolution. It received a new lease of life under Napoleon's Empire, finally reaching its apogee in c 1850, shortly after which a devastating silkworm plague broke out, decimating French silkworm breeding centres. This was a blow from which the French silk industry never fully recovered. It also subsequently had to contend with strong foreign competition, the discovery of artificial fibres and mass industrialisation. Nonetheless, Lyon silk production has remained a standard of quality for the fashion world and among French luxury materials.

Sericulture, or the production of silk, involves raising silkworms in special silkworm farms (in French, magnaneries) from the egg to cocoon stage. The silkworm chrysalides are suffocated in steam so that the cocoon can be unraveled as a single long filament of silk. The raw silk obtained at this stage is not strong enough to be woven and so undergoes a preparatory process – reeling, in which the silk fibres from several cocoons are wound together to form a single strand. Bobbins of this thread are arranged on a special frame, then unreeled in batches onto a warp frame. Next the warp is stretched on a draw loom to form parallel threads, across which the weft threads are drawn by a shuttle. To allow the shuttle to pass along with the weft, various mechanical systems for lifting the appropriate warp threads were developed, one of the most famous of which was Jacquard's (using punched cards). Various types of plain weave are possible using silk, to produce taffeta, silk serge and satin, for example. The manufacture of fancier, figured fabrics (with decorative motifs in coloured threads) requires a more complex system, however, using cords known – funnily enough – as simples. As for woven pile fabrics such as velvet, it is necessary to have a second set of warp threads which form the pile. Such fancy fabrics can be smooth (damask, lampas) or textured (brocade, brocatelle).

Silk can also be processed after it has been woven, for example in silkscreen printing, or the manufacture of figured or watered silks.

Villeurbanne

Adjacent to the Part-Dieu district, the municipality of Villeurbanne owes its name to the Villa Urbana, an important agricultural complex established by the Romans on the Cusset hill. The development of the town is relatively recent and it is interesting to note how it has always made a point of being independent from Lyon. After the first wave of silk manufacturers at the end of the 19C, the expansion of the town increased during the 20C and in the 1930s Villeurbanne asserted its specificity by building the spectacular skyscraper district. Today, the town is continuing to develop, concentrating its efforts on culture: a popular national theatre (TNP), an ultra-modern reference library, a museum of contemporary art, the antique-dealers' hall (boulevard de Stalingrad) where no fewer than 150 antique shops can be found.

Skyscrapers
Metro Gratte-Ciel. Around 1930, at the height of the economic crisis, the housing facilities in Villeurbanne were totally inadequate in view of the town's fast-growing population. The mayor, Lazare Goujon, launched his city into a daring development

programme: the town centre, which was the first project to be completed, was soon nicknamed **"Skyscraper City"** as its unique architectural style was more reminiscent of North-American buildings than of French suburbia. The entrance to the district is marked by two 19-storey high towers followed by an alignment of large white buildings. The six residential blocks comprise 1 500 dwellings spread over nine to eleven storeys. Avenue Barbusse ends with the imposing and austere **town hall** designed by R Giroud: a 60m/197ft-high belfry towers over the façade decorated with fluted columns. On the other side, place Docteur-Lazare-Goujon is closed off by the TNP theatre, originally the Labour Hall.

▶ *Walk down cours de la République towards cours Tolstoï and cross over.*

Nouveau Musée (Institut d'Art Contemporain)
11 rue du Docteur-Dolard (metro République). ⟐ ⟐ *Jun-Sep: daily except Mon and Tue 1-7pm (Thu, 1-8pm): Oct-May: daily except Mon and Tue, 1-6pm (Thu, 1-8pm).* ⟐ *Closed 1 Jan, 1 May, 25 Dec.* *4€ (children: no charge).* ☎ *04 78 03 47 00.* www.i-art-c.org
Created in 1978, the Association Nouveau Musée moved into this space a few years ago; there is an information section and a special area presenting themed exhibitions on contemporary art.

Maison du Livre, de l'Image et du Son
247 cours Émile-Zola (metro Flachet). ⟐ ⟐ *Daily except Sun, 11am-7pm (Sat 10am-6pm).* ⟐ *Closed public holidays.* ☎ *04 78 68 04 04.* www.bm.villeurbanne.fr.
This reference library, designed in 1988 by the famous architect Mario Botta, is spread over five storeys round a central light shaft. It includes lending libraries, a video library, a record library and an art library.

West of Lyon

Île Barbe
From the mass of greenery on Île Barbe peeks the tip of a Romanesque bell-tower. The island was once the site of one of the region's most influential abbeys, founded in the 5C, but is now a quiet residential area.

▶ *Leave Lyon to the NW (towards Mâcon), then follow D 7 towards Charbonnières.*

The vast **Lacroix-Laval Park** (119ha/294 acres) (⟐ *May-Sep, 6am-10pm; Oct-Apr, 7am-8pm*) in Marcy-l'Étoile is one of the "lungs" of Lyon. A small tourist train, **Le Furet** takes visitors on a tour of the château and park.

Château de la Poupée★
Kids ⟐ ⟐ *Daily except Mon, 10am-5pm.* ⟐ *Closed 1 Jan, 1 May, 1 Nov, 25 Dec. 4€.* ☎ *04 78 87 87 00.*
At the eastern end of Lacroix-Laval Park stands an elegant 18C château which houses an exceptional private collection of dolls dating from the 18C to the present day. The upper level looks at the manufacture and decoration of dolls, and on the lower level there is a display on the history of dolls as art objects; in each room there are explanatory videos. Set against mock stage props, the old-fashioned ways of making dolls are shown, especially the making of their heads: made of papier maché until the early 19C, they were later made of wax, porcelain and finally biscuit ware. Both porcelain and biscuit are kaolin-based but porcelain turns white during firing whereas biscuit retains its coloured appearance and is therefore nearer to the human complexion, allowing a more realistic look on a doll. Biscuit heads are entirely painted. Other rooms display beautiful dolls' houses and clothes from the 19C. A reconstruction of a contemporary doll-moulding workshop shows the complex techniques involved in making a doll; note the machine for attaching hair to the dolls' heads.

Charbonnières-les-Bains

10km/6mi to the NW, heading towards Mâcon, then N 7. Set in woodland formerly worked by the charcoal burners, the Vale of Charbonnières is a traditional holiday resort popular with the people of Lyon.

The ferruginous spring here was officially discovered by a priest in 1778. Pump rooms and a casino were soon opened. In 1900, people flocked to the spa, which quickly gained a reputation for excellence. The baths were closed down and demolished a few years ago. The Lyon-Charbonnières car rally is famous for its tricky mountain stretches.

Banks of the Saône★

38km/24mi round tour – allow 3hr

▶ *Leave Lyon to the N, in the direction of Trévoux. On the left stands the imposing, lush Île Barbe (see above). The pleasant D 433 follows the east bank of the river, bordered by thick vegetation, as far La Rochetaillée.*

The river banks are a favourite weekend destination with Lyon residents, who come to stroll along the towpath, or to indulge in a light lunch of fried fish washed down with a bottle of Beaujolais in one of the many riverside restaurants.

Musée de l'Automobile Henri-Malartre★★

At the entrance to Rochetaillée-sur-Saône; 2km/1mi after Fontaines-sur-Saône, follow signposts to the right. ◑ *Daily except Mon 9am-6pm (last admission 1hr before closing; Jul and Aug: daily except Mon 10am-7pm).* ◑ *Closed last week in Jan, 1 Jan and 25 Dec. 6€ (children: no charge).* ☎ *04 78 22 18 80. www.musee-malartre.com*

This restored 15C castle purchased by Lyon City Council, and its terraced grounds overlooking the Saône, contain some remarkable collections of motor cars (1890-1986), cycles (1818-1960), motorcycles (1904-64) and public transport vehicles (1886-1935), all in full working order.

In 1929 Henri Malartre was the manager of a breaker's yard. He began his collection in 1931 with a 1898 Rochet-Schneider (in working order), then two years later bought a unique Gobron-Brillié double phaeton, also from 1898.

Of the 150 **cars** on show, 50 date from before 1914 and 18 were built in Lyon, which serves as a reminder of the fact that there were over 100 manufacturers in the region in the adventurous early days of the motor car.

D'après photo du musée de l'Automobile H. Malartre

Lorraine-Dietrich (1925), Musée Henri-Malartre

Some of the exhibits are unique, such as the Rochet-Schneider (1895), the Gobron-Brillié (1898), the Luc Court (1901) and the Thieulin (1908).

Worth noting also are a De Dion Bouton coupé-docteur (1900); a Marne taxi; a set of three Sizaire cars (1908, 1924, 1927); a Bugatti convertible (1930), Hitler's armoured Mercedes (1942), the Hispano-Suiza (1936) used by General de Gaulle after the Liberation of Paris, and the "Pope-Mobile," a Renault Espace used by Pope John Paul II during his visit to Lyon in 1986.

The Gordini Hall displays a collection of **racing cars,** driven by some of the great champions. They include a Rolland Pilain (1923), Talbot Lago (1949) and Gordini (1952).

The collection of cycles ranges from the hobby horse to Anquetil's bicycle, not forgetting the amazing "Penny Farthings."

Over 50 **motorcycles** are on show, including a Herdtlé-Bruneau (1904), the Koehler-Escoffier (1935) ridden by Georges Monneret, side-cars and a Zundapp (1937) used by the German Army in Africa and Russia.

There is also a hall devoted to **public transport.** Exhibits include a double-decker two-way open-top horse-drawn tram (1880; the two horses could be harnessed at both the front or the rear in order to avoid having to turn the vehicle round).

▶ *Drive on towards D 433 and turn right.*

Neuville-sur-Saône

The town lies in a picturesque setting on a bend of the Saône. The church, topped by twin bell-towers dating from the 17C, contains a set of wood panelling by Perrache, a well-known sculptor from Lyon (18C).

Trévoux – *See TRÉVOUX.*

▶ *Take D 933 and turn left onto D 504 towards Villefranche.*

Villefranche-sur-Saône – *See VILLEFRANCHE-SUR-SAÔNE.*

▶ *Return to Lyon on N 6.*

MONTS DU LYONNAIS★

MICHELIN MAP 327: F-6, G-5/6, H-5

The attractive mountainous region lying to the south-west of Lyon has a pastoral appearance with chestnut groves and oakwoods. Land in low-lying valleys is given over to market gardening, vineyards and orchards whereas pastures extend over higher ground. This is essentially a cattle-breeding area where traditional rural housing is still very prominent and industrial activity is confined to the most important towns: Chazelles-sur-Lyon, St-Galmier and Ste-Foy-l'Argentière.

The Hills Around Lyon

Roman Aqueducts

Arches de Chaponost★
At the bottom of the Yzeron Valley in **Beaunant,** stand the impressive remains – about 40 arches – of one of four Gallo-Roman aqueducts which together daily brought 75 000m³/2 648 550cu ft of water to Lyon: **Mont-d'Or, Brévenne, Yzeron** and **Gier**. The sophisticated engineering of this syphon-bridge incorporated an overflow reservoir downstream, where the openings for the pipes are still visible. Further ruins can be seen in **Brignais, Soucieu-en-Jarrest, Craponne** and **Mornant**. In the city of Lyon, there are the remains of an aqueduct leading to the former road to Aquitaine, currently called rue Roger-Radisson.

Excursions

1 From Lyon to St-Étienne

128km/80mi – allow one day

▶ *Leave Lyon to the W on A 6. On leaving Tassin-la-Demi-Lune, follow N 7 for 1km/0.5mi, then turn left onto D 7. At La Rivoire, take D 70 on the left. At Pollionay, the road on*

Chaponost Arches

Pratta/ICONOS

the right climbing through the forest will take you to Croix-du-Banc, which offers lovely views of the Arbresle basin (on the right).

▶ *Beyond Chevinay, take D 24 on the left.*

Col de la Luère★

Pleasant forest pass. Half way between Col de la Luère and Col de Malval, close to St-Bonnet-le-Froid Château, the road affords a nice **view**★ of the Brévenne Valley.

▶ *At Col de Malval, turn right twice, first onto D 50, then onto a forest lane.*

Parc Animalier de Courzieu

Kids ⏰ *Mar-Oct: 10am-7pm. Falconry displays: 2.30pm and 4.30pm. 11€ (children: 8.50€). ☎ 04 74 70 96 10. www.parc-de-courzieu.fr*

The paths of this 20ha/50-acre park running through the undergrowth will introduce visitors to several European species of predators (wolf, lynx, wildcat). The grounds feature an information centre, a playing area for children and a botanical garden.

After Col de Malval, D 113 offers views of the Rhône Valley to the left and the Brévenne Valley to the right. Approximately 800m/0.5mi south of the pass, you can admire a sweeping **panorama**★ of the Rhône plain, the Mont-d'Or (on the left), the Mont Pilat (on the right) and the foothills of the Alps in the distance.

Yzeron

The church affords a lovely **view**★ of the Rhône Valley.

▶ *In St-Martin-en-Haut, take D 113.*

Signal de St-André★★

45min on foot there and back.

🚶 A path off D 113 leads up to this beacon (alt 934m/3 064ft) from which there is a pleasant **panoramic view** over to the Alps *(SE)* and the attractive hill villages *(NW)*.

Riverie

Old medieval hamlet perched on a rocky outcrop. The former covered footpath commands a nice view of the surrounding landscape *(SE)*.

▶ *Leave Riverie to the W on D 2, then in Ste-Catherine, take D 77 until you reach the entrance to St-Martin-la-Plaine. Turn right onto D 37.*

Parc Zoologique de St-Martin-la-Plaine

Kids ⏰ *Apr-Sep: 9am-6pm; Oct, Nov, Feb, Mar: 10am-5pm. ⏰ Dec-Jan. 12€ (3-10-year-olds: 8€). ☎ 04 77 75 18 68. www.espace-zoologique.com*

Near the Gier Valley, this zoo is devoted to the reproduction of endangered species throughout the world. Many animals, some of which are extremely rare, have been lent by other zoos and placed in their natural habitat: gorillas, Siberian tigers and Argentinian wolves.

▶ *Continue along D 37, D 6 and D 54.*

The road to St-Héand affords pretty views of the Monts du Lyonnais and, further along, the Gier Valley and the Loire basin. In St-Héand, the road (D 102) dips into the Furan Valley.

▶ *Take N 82 to St-Étienne.*

2 From St-Étienne to Lyon

108km/67mi – allow one day

▶ *Leave St-Étienne to the N on N 82, which runs along the Furan Valley.*

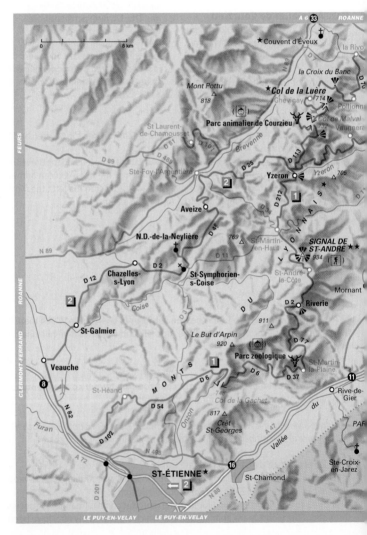

Veauche

Nestled on the edge of a plateau overlooking the Loire, Veauche is popular among archaeologists and art lovers. The **church**, originally a small priory given to Savigny Abbey in 970, was extensively restored in the 15C and 16C. The town also manufactures bottles for St-Galmier mineral water.

St-Galmier

Although the spring coming from this town was known to the Romans, it was only in the early 19C that it was marketed on a large scale, thanks to the enterprising spirit of **Augustin Saturnin Badoit**, who decided to bottle this naturally sparkling water. Backed by an aggressive promotional campaign both in France and abroad, sales of Badoit rapidly reached record figures. The water, which features a high content of bicarbonate, magnesium and potassium, is captured at a depth of 78m/256ft and processed at the nearby **factory** (🕐 *Guided visit by appointment* ☎ *04 77 54 06 08 (tourist office))*.

St-Galmier also has a Flamboyant church with three naves. Note the fine 16C **Virgin**★ attributed to a disciple of Michel Colombe. Resting against the second pillar in the nave, on the right, is a 15C **triptych**★ from the Flemish School. The **hospital** is housed in a former Ursuline convent. The chapel, on the right as you enter, contains a pretty 17C altarpiece in gilded wood.

To visit the **old quarter,** turn right when you leave the hospital, then turn left onto rue Félix-Commarmond. This street lined with old houses leads to place des Roches.

Chazelles-sur-Lyon – 👍 See CHAZELLES-SUR-LYON.

St-Symphorien-sur-Coise

Former fortified village dominated by its Gothic church. The main activity today is the production of salami.

Notre-Dame de la Neylière

Besides the chapel, you can also visit the **Musée d'Océanie** and the **Musée Jean-Claude Colin** (*Apart from the chapel, it is possible to visit the Oceania and Jean-Claude Colin museums by making an appointment at the Neylière, 69590 Pomeys.* ☎ *04 78 48 40 33).* Peaceful sanctuary that offers hospitality to the Marist brothers. The sober chapel, which presents modern frescoes and stained-glass windows, houses the mortal remains of Father **Jean-Claude Colin** (1790-1875), who founded the "Société de Marie" Order.

Aveize

On leaving the village to the north, D 4 commands enchanting views of Ste-Foy-l'Argentière, nestled in the luxuriant Brévenne basin.
Take D 25, the narrow, winding road climbing up towards Montromant. On a bend, as you approach Col de la Croix-de-Part, you can admire splendid vistas of the Brévenne Valley.

▷ *Return to Lyon via Yzeron, Les Arches de Chaponost and D 50.*

MASSIAC

POPULATION 1 857
MICHELIN MAPS 331: H-3 OR 239 FOLD 32

This old village, in an excellent setting by the River Alagnon, is enlivened by a traditional weekly market (Tuesday mornings) and two picturesque annual fairs (June and October). *24 r. du Dr.-Mallet, 15500 MASSIAC, ☎ 04 71 23 07 76.*

A Stroll Through Massiac

The town's glorious past is evidenced by the **old château** (which currently houses the town hall), a fine 17C **wooden house** or a round **stone tower** belonging to the former ramparts.

Église St-André

The church contains a series of polychrome wood statues portraying the Virgin Mary.

Musée Municipal Élise-Rieuf

&♿ *Jul-Sep: daily except Mon 2.30-7pm.* ⊙ *Closed Oct-Apr. 4€.* ☎ *04 71 23 03 95.*
The museum displays portraits of people from the Auvergne and China, Provençal and Scandinavian landscapes and views of Italian towns painted by **Élise Rieuf**, a native of Massiac (1897-1990).

Excursions

Gorges de l'Alagnon★

70km/43.5mi round tour – allow half a day

The road alongside the lower reaches of the River Alagnon, as it cuts its way through gneiss between Le Babory-de-Blesle and Lempdes-sur-Allagnon, makes a most appealing drive *(note that, in the Haute-Loire region, the river is spelt with two "l"s)*.

▷ *Drive N out of Massiac towards Clermont-Ferrand; at the roundabout,*

Ste-Madeleine on its spur

S. Sauvignier/MICHELIN

take the small road which skirts the motorway slip road then passes under the motorway.

Site de la Chapelle Ste-Madeleine★

Park the car near the pylon.

The small 11C chapel stands on top of a spur of basalt rock, at the south-eastern extremity of the Chalet plateau. From this point (alt 708m/2 323ft), there is a fine bird's-eye view of Massiac and the Alagnon Valley.

On the opposite bank of the river, another spur of basalt rock (alt 735m/2 411ft), the Plateau de St-Victor, occupied by prehistoric man, later served as a look-out to keep watch over the Alagnon Valley and the ford across the river.

▷ *Return to the roundabout and follow D 909 N. In Le Babory, turn left onto D 8 which crosses the Alagnon.*

Blesle★

This ancient village on the west bank of the Voireuze was founded around a once-powerful Benedictine abbey. **Église St-Pierre★** (11C-12C – *Guided tours daily 10am-noon, 2.30-6.30pm, Sun 2.30-6.30pm. 3€. ☎ 04 71 76 26 90*), which lost its belfry during the Revolution, has some interesting furniture and statues in the treasury. Other monuments of note include a great square **keep**, a 14C **bell-tower**, all that remains of the church of St-Martin (destroyed in the Revolution), 15C and 16C houses, and the turret and doorway (17C) of the old hospice. Do not fail to visit the **Musée de la Coiffe** (🕐 *May to mid-Sep: daily 9.30am-12.30pm, 3-6.30pm, Sun: 3-6pm. 4€. ☎ 04 71 76 26 90*), set up in a former 16C hospital and presenting over 400 typical headdresses from the Auvergne and Velay areas.

In the **Atelier-exposition "Les Papiers du Silence"** (🕐 *Apr-Oct: Wed-Sun, 2.30-6pm (Jul-Aug: 10am-noon, 2.30-6.30pm). 2€. ☎ 04 71 76 26 90*) waste paper is recycled then used to make pictures and decorative objects. There are demonstrations of paper-shaping and visitors are invited to try their hand at it. The workshop also stages exhibitions.

▷ *Return to the right bank of the Alagnon by taking D 8 in the opposite direction and turn left onto D 909.*

Further north, the ruins of Léotoing Castle can be seen on a high ground to the right *(see below)*. The valley becomes narrower and wilder.

▷ *In Lempdes head N on D 909, in the direction of St-Germain-Lembron. After 3km/2mi take D 35 on the left, then D 141 on the right.*

St-Gervazy

The **castle** is the setting of visits presented by members of the association "La Vie de château," which have been in charge of restoration work for the past 10 years.

The Romanesque **church** houses, in its right chapel, a replica of the 12C Virgin

Enthroned that was stolen a few years ago. Note the fine capitals with leaf motifs adorning the nave.

▶ *Return to Lempdes; follow D 653 S over a distance of 4km/2.5mi then turn right onto D 655.*

Léotoing★

The chapel located at the entrance to the village houses a model of the site and several panels providing information on local history, architecture and traditions. The fine view (viewing table) encompasses the Alagnon gorge, the Cézallier, the Brioude plain, the Livradois, the Plateau de la Chaise-Dieu and the Monts du Velay.

Castle

The tour of the ruins is undertaken at the visitor's own risk; it is not advisable for children or anyone suffering from vertigo; good walking shoes are recommended. Substantial remains of this 14C fortress overlooking the River Alagnon are still visible. To reach them, walk through the fortified gate.

The Romanesque **church** (🕐 *High season.* ☎ *04 71 76 50 68*), remodelled in the 15C, contains traces of a fresco depicting the Deposition and carved capitals.

A minor road runs down to the hamlet of Lanau in a series of hairpin bends, offering interesting glimpses of the Alagnon Valley, Torsiac Castle and Léotoing Castle.

▶ *At the foot of the hill, take D 909 on the left. On leaving Lanau, turn left onto D 19 which later meets up with D 653. Return to Massiac via Grenier-Montgon.*

MAURIAC★

POPULATION 4 019

MICHELIN MAP 330: B-3 – 19KM/11.8MI NW OF SALERS

Situated between the River Dordogne and Puy Mary, this small town, which is an important agricultural trading centre, consists of black, lava stone houses on the edge of a vast basalt plateau. 🛈 *1 r. Chappe-d'Auteroche, 15200 MAURIAC, ☎ 04 71 67 30 26.*

Basilique Notre-Dame-Des-Miracles★

This is the most important Romanesque building in Upper Auvergne, erected between the 12C and the 14C.

Exterior

The elegant east end, the first part of the church to come into view, has three apsidal chapels. To the right of the door, on the right side of the building, is a 13C Lantern of the Dead which once stood in the graveyard. The vast main doorway at the west front is the best piece of Romanesque carving in the area; the tympanum depicts the Ascension of Christ and the signs of the Zodiac decorate the archivolt.

Interior

The interior is plain and simple, and the nave is dimly lit from the clerestory directly above the great arches (note the absence of a gallery). There are some interesting furnishings, including the choir stalls and, at the back of the chancel, the statue of

Our Lady of Miracles carved from walnut wood *(pilgrimage in early May)*. To the right in the transept is a 16C statue of the Virgin Mary with a bird.

In the south aisle stands the superb multicoloured Romanesque **font**★ carved out of trachyte (a volcanic rock). It is decorated with 14 arches, each featuring a different motif. The artist even depicted himself beside the tools of his trade. Nearby, on the wall, are the famous "Saracen's irons" that are steeped in legend: in the 11C two men from the Auvergne, who had just been taken prisoner by the Arabs, prayed to the Virgin Mary of Miracles with such fervour that, the next morning, they were found asleep, with their legs still in irons, in front of the church in Mauriac which stood on the site of the basilica standing today.

Around place Georges-Pompidou are a few old houses including one with double Romanesque bays.

Additional Sights

Note the old houses with twinned Romanesque openings surrounding place Georges-Pompidou;

Monastère St-Pierre

 Daily, 10am-noon, 2-6pm . *Closed Tue during Oct-Mar, I and 8 May. 3€.* *04 71 68 07 24.*

This monastery was once a daughter-house of Église St-Pierre-le-Vif in Sens. It is possible to see a few Gallo-Roman remains, some of the foundations of the Carolingian church (early 9C), the 11C **chapter house** (columns made with local marble) and part of the **cloisters** (14C-15C) separated from the chapter-house by an arch with double columns.

▶ *Follow rue du Collège.*

Hôtel d'Orcet

Currently the Sous-Préfecture. This 16C-18C building incorporates the 12C tympanum that decorated the doorway into the monastery refectory: the carving depicts Samson slaying the lion. On the other side of the street stands the monumental gateway to the former Jesuit college.

▶ *Continue along rue du Dr-E.-Chavialle; the first street on the left leads to the museum.*

Musée des arts et traditions populaires

 Same admission times and charges as the Monastère St-Pierre. *04 71 68 07 24.*

Housed in a former prison, this museum has a range of collections: Gallo-Roman ceramics, religious artefacts etc. There are temporary exhibitions of regional arts and crafts (leather-working, cheesemaking etc).

Excursions

Puy St-Mary

30min on foot there and back starting from Vaysses. Follow the road that branches off D 678 on the NW outskirts of the town and park the car in the hamlet of Les Vaysses.

 Climb up to the chapel at the top of the grassy hill known as Puy St-Mary. From here there is a panoramic view of Mauriac and the mountains of Cantal on one side and the plateaux bordering the Auvergne and the Limousin on the other.

Château de la Vigne

10km/6.2mi S along D 681. ◷ *Mid-Jun to mid-Sep: 2-7pm; rest of year: on demand. Chateau only: 5€ (children: 2.50€); miniature car museum only: 5€ (children: 2.50€); combined ticket: 6€ (children: 3€).* ☎ *04 71 69 00 20.*

This 15C castle is flanked by two round towers topped by pepper-pot roofs, and a square tower that served as a keep and to which, in the 18C, a second building was attached; a watch-path runs around the top. Inside, there are 16C **frescoes** on the walls and ceiling of the Salle de Justice; other rooms are also tastefully appointed (fine panelling; canopied bed with barley-twist columns; coffered ceiling).

J. Damase/MICHELIN

The 18C **dining room** has lovely tapestries, items of Delftware and a huge sideboard. The **chapel**, supported by ribbed vaulting, displays murals that represent Angels carrying the instruments of Passion. The grounds command pretty views of the Cantal mountains.

This is known as the "Troubadour's room"

Salon de l'Automobile Miniature

Kids ◷ *see Chateau de la Vigne above.*

This collection of model vehicles (Dinky Toys, Solido etc) includes examples of touring cars, utility vehicles, racing cars, heavy goods trucks and public service vehicles.

You can go to **Brageac** (5km/3mi on D 137) to see the impressive site of a small Romanesque church perched above the Auze Valley.

Église de Jaleyrac

N of Mauriac along D 138. The church houses some remarkable 13C frescoes depicting notably St George and the Dragon, St Martin and the Poor Man.

Churches of the northern plateaux

Round trip of 70km/44mi – allow one day

▶ *Head NE from Mauriac on D 922 and turn right onto D 678.*

Église du Vigean

In the small church with its unusual belfry there is a delightful **reliquary**★ made of 13C Limousin enamelwork. On the back there is an illustration of the murder of **Thomas Becket**, Archbishop of Canterbury.

▶ *Follow D 678. Note the fine fountain in the village of Conrut. About 2km/1mi before reaching Moussages, take D 12 on the right.*

Chapelle de Jailhac

Take a stroll on the village square (you may ask for the key at the house with *lauze* tiling).

🚶 Walk across the meadow and take the steep path leading to the chapel *(15min on foot there and back).* Fine panorama of the Mars Valley.

▶ *Rejoin D 678.*

Château d'Auzers

Moussages

Overlooking a square decorated with an old fountain and surrounded by old houses is the **church** whose Romanesque east end includes carved modillions. Inside is a Romanesque statue of the **Virgin Mary**★ in Majesty and a carved wooden figure of Christ.

▶ *Leave Moussages N along D 22 then turn right.*

Château d'Auzers★

🕐 *Easter to Oct: guided tours (1hr) 2-6.30pm; rest of year: by arrangement. 5€. ☎ 04 71 78 62 59. www.auzers.com*

This 14C and 16C castle comprises a central building flanked by two high turrets crowned by pepper-pot roofs. Inside, on the ground floor, you will notice the attractive walls alternating white stonework with blue basalt, the stately **fireplace** in the drawing room and the restored 17C **frescoes** adorning the former oratory in the western tower. The first floor houses painstakingly executed **French-style ceilings.** Fine Renaissance and 18C furniture.

The terrace running along the southern façade offers a sweeping **view** of the vast meadows extending to the steep Marilhoux Valley and the Cantal summits in the distance.

▶ *2km/1mi after leaving Auzers, turn right onto D 22, heading towards Saignes.*

Sauvat

The apse of the partly Romanesque **Église St-Martin** is decorated with a series of 15C frescoes.

Saignes

This small but appealing summer resort perched above the Sumène Valley has a Romanesque church built in typical Auvergnat tradition and several quaint 15C **houses**. The rocky promontory still carries vestiges of the former castle and the tiny Chapelle Notre-Dame. Enjoy the view across the valley and Bort-les-Orgues.

▶ *Turn right towards Le Monteil then left onto D 36.*

Chastel-Merlhac

Its circular shape makes this heavily eroded lava flow look like a basalt fortress. Explanations are provided by a panel located near the viewing table; the splendid panorama includes the Puy de Sancy. In the village, the Romanesque **church** (*Contact the town hall, ☎ 04 71 40 64 02*), which was partly rebuilt in Gothic style, houses an interesting carved font.

▶ *Return to Saignes and turn NE onto D 236 towards Riom; turn right onto D 15 then right again onto D 3.*

Antignac

The **Jardins ethnobotaniques** (*daily except Sat at 3pm. ⏱ Closed 1 Jan and 25 Dec. 5€, no charge 1 May. ☎ 04 71 40 23 76*) grow plants of medieval origin found on archaeological sites. The Avena Centre organises medieval meals.

▶ *Leave Antignac along D 3 towards Bort-les-Orgues and turn left onto D 15.*

Verbret

Note the unusual pyramid-shaped bell-tower of the Romanesque church. The interior has a wooden ceiling.

▶ *Continue along D 15 then D 315.*

Ydes-Bourg

Small village set up along the banks of the River Sumène, in an area dotted with basalt peaks. The 12C Romanesque **church** (*⏱ Low season: by appointment, ☎ 04 71 40 62 19*) is dedicated to St George; the south porch depicts the saint slaying the Dragon and the **west porch** is dominated by a curious bell-tower with sculptures portraying the signs of the Zodiac, the Annunciation, Daniel in the Lions' Den and an Angel grabbing a Prophet by his hair. The exhibition called **Insectes du Monde** (*entrance behind the town hall. Kids ♿ ⏱ Jul-Aug: 2-7pm. 3€. ☎ 04 71 40 82 51*) is mainly devoted to butterflies and moths, many of which come from Hungary, Mexico and Pakistan.

▶ *Rejoin D 922 and turn right to Bassignac.*

Bassignac

Kids The **Jardin botanique textile** (*⏱ Mid-Jun to mid-Sep: 10am-noon, 2-7pm. 4€ (children: 2.50€). ☎ 04 71 67 32 50*) is devoted to textiles and weaving. The garden grows more than 150 species of textile plants as well as plants used in dyeing. There are workshops with demonstrations and activities for children. Even the hedges surrounding the garden are made of plaited osier.

▶ *Rejoin D 922 to return to Mauriac.*

Between forest and valley

▶ *Leave Mauriac NW along D 678 towards Égletons, Lapleau.*

Chalvignac

Boat trips (*Boat trips along the River Dordogne. 7€ (children: 4€) ☎ 05 55 28 86 45. www.adndordogne.org*) along the Dordogne in traditional boats, known as gabares, are organised here.
Four waymarked rambles (*5-15km/3-9mi, see panel*), each on a different theme, start from place de l'Église.

▷ *Continue along D 105 which runs close to the 92m/302ft-high Aigle dam. Just before La Ferrière, turn left onto D 678 to the Miers forest lodge.*

Maison forestière de Miers★

At the end of a forest track, just beyond the bridge spanning the Auze. 🕐 *Jul-Aug: 1.30-7pm (last admission 1hr before closing). 4€.* ☎ *04 71 68 22 29 (Jul-Aug) or 04 71 68 27 40.*

Kids Two exhibitions present the forest and its past and present inhabitants. On the ground floor, the stables house a display of traditional crafts connected with forestry such as charcoal-burner and on the first floor there is an interactive exhibition about trees and animals found in forests.

▷ *Return to Mauriac along D 678 on the right.*

LE MONASTIER-SUR-GAZEILLE

POPULATION 1 734
MICHELIN MAP 331: G-4

This large village in Haute-Loire derives its name from the largest Benedictine monastery in the Velay area, founded in the late 7C. St Calmin, Count of Auvergne, founded the monastery and became its first abbot. In AD 728 St Théofrède, his successor, was murdered during a Saracen raid. The monastery was raised from the ruins and for several centuries enjoyed an extraordinarily wide-ranging influence. In the late 12C the abbey boasted 235 daughter-houses or priories. The monastery went into rapid decline in the 16C when commendatory abbots replaced the regular abbots. The abbey buildings standing today, which house the town hall, were built in the 18C. 🛈 *mairie, 43150 le MONASTIER-SUR-GAZEILLE,* ☎ *04 71 08 37 76.*

Stevenson's travels – In front of the post office is a memorial commemorating the travels undertaken across the Cévennes, in the autumn of 1878, by the Scottish writer **Robert Louis Stevenson**, author of *Treasure Island*. As much to satisfy his wish to travel as to try and retrace the spirit that once fired the *Camisards,* or Protestant rebels, Stevenson, then aged 28, decided to cross the Cévennes on foot from Le Monastier to Alès, accompanied only by a somewhat capricious donkey. Sleeping outdoors or in any inns he happened to come across (with one menu for all, and all visitors sleeping in the one room), he took 12 days to reach Alès, via Goudet, Pradelles, Langogne, La Bastide, Le Bleymard, Pont-de-Montvert, Florac and St-Jean-du-Gard. His travel notebook is a mine of humorous and penetrating observations on the wonderful countryside he discovered and the many different people he met on his way. In the heart of the Cévennes, the nobility of spirit in the local people left a deep impression on him.

His travels were full of comic incidents, which he recounts with glee. To carry the strange sleeping bag that he had had made for himself, Stevenson acquired the donkey which he immediately chris-tened Modestine. The conflict between the obsti-nacy of the Scottish novelist and the strong will of the donkey from the Velay lasted for the entire trip: "Modestine's pace is quite beyond description. It was something much slower than a stroll, when a stroll is much slower than a walk. She held back each hoof for an incredibly long time…" Finally, a wily peasant supplied Stevenson with a goad, which did wonders for Modestine's enthusiasm.

Sights

Abbey Church
The Romanesque church built in the 11C underwent extensive alterations in the 15C.

West front★

The façade was built in the 11C. Its volcanic stones of different colours illustrate the decorative technique of Romanesque architects working in the Velay area. The play of colours is most noticeable on the upper storey above the hollow porch, especially around the main window, the corner colonnettes with red twisted bases, and the alternating dark and light keystones topped by mosaic stonework. The cornice along the main triangular pediment is decorated with a frieze of animals, grotesque figures and foliage.

J. Damase/MICHELIN

Nave of the abbey church

Interior
The mighty grey granite pillars in the nave form a stark contrast to the Flamboyant chancel of light-coloured arkose. The transept and side aisles have retained their Romanesque vaulting.

The 15C chancel is surrounded by a small ambulatory opening into five radiating chapels. The second on the right, the last one to be built, is an example of Renaissance style at its purest with its coffered ceiling decorated with coats of arms and medallions. In the north aisle is a fine **organ**★ dating from 1518 (restored) with delicately painted decoration and fine tracery adorning the loft. In the upper section are the arms of the abbot, Gaspard de Tournon, in a shield.

Treasury
🕐 *Mid-Jun to mid-Sep: Tue and Fri 10am-noon (school holidays: Tue 11am-noon, Wed 2-4pm). 3€. ☏ 04 71 08 37 76.*
In the sacristy off the north aisle. The abbey's treasures include a multicoloured stone Pietà dating from the 15C, two lengths of Byzantine silk that were used to shroud the bodies of the founding saints, and a painted wooden statue of the Virgin Mary dating from the 17C. The main exhibit is St Théofrède's **bust-reliquary**★ made of oak covered with silver sheets studded with precious stones.

Musée Municipal
♿🕐 *Jul-Aug: daily except Tue 10.30am-noon, 2-6pm; Sep: daily except Mon, 10.30am-noon, 2.30-5pm; Jun and Oct: daily except Mon, 2.30-5pm.* 🕐 *Nov-May. 2€. ☏ 04 71 03 80 01.*
The local museum is housed in the beautiful vaulted chambers of the **abbey castle** (basement and ground floor). The building which stands today, flanked by four large round towers, was built in 1525 over the foundations of a 14C castle by Charles de Sennecterre (or St-Nectaire) whose family provided ecclesiastical dignitaries for the

Velay area for more than a century and a half (coat of arms with five tapers topped by a crozier).

The collections illustrate the history of regional life (lace, traditional costumes), and the prehistoric period in the Upper Loire Valley. One of the rooms deals solely with **Robert Louis Stevenson**; another has an archaeological collection (remains of the abbey). On the first floor in the south tower is the abbot's chapel where there are traces of 17C frescoes.

Église St-Jean

At the southernmost end of the village stands the old parish church of St-Jean, built in the 9C and altered in the 15C; in spite of extensive restoration work, it has retained a certain austere elegance.

Excursions

La Recoumène Viaduct

2km/1mi. Leave Le Monastier on D 500 E towards Fay, and turn right onto D 535 towards Aubenas. This fine piece of engineering spanning the Gazeille rises to a height of almost 66m/215ft. It was built between 1921 and 1925. Its eight basalt arches were designed to provide a link on the Le Puy-Niègles (Ardèche) railway line but the line was never brought into service. It is the only authorised bungee-jumping site in the Velay region.

Château de Vachères

7.5km/5mi SE of Le Monastier on D 38. ⚷ *Not open to the public.* A massive keep flanked by towers with pepper-pot roofs gives this 13C castle with its blocks of black basalt outlined in white mortar a typically Velay-style appearance.

Freycenet-la-Tour

7km/4.3mi E of Le Monastier on D 500. The tower that gave its name to the village has disappeared but the Romanesque church and the charming shores of Lake Barthes in the heart of a stately forest make this an ideal place for an outing.

MONISTROL-SUR-LOIRE

POPULATION 7 451

MICHELIN MAP 331: H-2

The town has a surprisingly Mediterranean feel about it, both in its appearance and its climate. 🛈 *4 bis r. du Château, 43120 MONISTROL-SUR-LOIRE,* ☎ *04 71 66 03 14.*

The Old Quarter

Château des Evêques

🕐 *Jul-Aug: 9am-noon, 2.30-6pm (Mon, 9am-noon); rest of year: 9am-noon, 2-5.30pm (Mon, 9am-noon)* 🕐 *Closed public holidays except 14 Jul.* ☎ *04 71 66 03 14.*

An avenue of lime trees leads to the large round towers of the old **Bishop's Palace** (14C-18C), which now houses the tourist office and hosts temporary exhibitions. Note the statue of Christ in the Garden of Olives (16C) and the 18C wrought-iron railing.

▶ *Walk round the château on the path to the right.*

Church

🕐 *Daily except Sun afternoon, 8.30am-6.30pm. ☎ 04 71 66 50 62.*

The central nave with its two piers (unique in the Velay region) and the dome over the chancel alone escaped destruction during the Revolution; the 17C bell-tower has regained its original dome.

From the church, take rue du Commerce then the first street on the right.

Take a stroll along the network of narrow **alleyways** and travel back in time, from the Middle Ages to the 17C (Classical façades of the Couvent des Ursulines and Couvent des Capucins).

Excursions

St-Didier-en-Velay

11km/6.8mi E along D 12. This small town, lying in the heart of the Semène Valley, has retained its old quarter, including its Romanesque church and 19C corn exchange which houses a museum of traditional arts and crafts. Note that most houses have unusually wide windows: this is explained by the fact that, in the past, craftsmen making haberdashery in their own home needed as much light as possible.

The Left Bank of the Loire

30km/18.6mi – allow 2hr

▶ *Leave Le Monistrol on D 12 for Bas-en-Basset.*

Château de Rochebaron

330m/330yd above place des Marronniers, take the path running to the left of an old rampart (45min on foot there and back).

🚶 The ruins of this medieval castle (11C-13C), perched on a spur overlooking the Loire, are preceded by three rows of protective walls. Only one round tower, with vaulted rooms linked by a spiral staircase, remains intact. From the end of the spur, there is a good **view**★ of the Loire Valley.

▶ *Turn right onto D 12, then left onto D 125. In Valprivas, go to the top of the village, beyond the church.*

Château de Valprivas

🕐 *Apr-Sep: guided tours (45min) daily except Mon 10.30am-noon, 3.30-6pm; Oct-Mar: by appointment. 4€. ☎ 04 71 66 71 33. www.valprivas.com*

In the court of honour, the round tower features an unusual spiral staircase entirely sculpted in oak and a porch framed by caryatids and crowned by a coat of arms. The chapel is ornamented with **mural paintings**★ executed in the late 16C by disciples of P-P Rubens. The **Centre Culturel de Valprivas** organises concerts on a regular basis.

▶ *Return to Le Monistrol along the narrow road that leads back down to the Ance Valley, crossing Coutenson hamlet.*

Vallée de L'Ance

46km/29mi – allow half a day

▶ *Leave Le Monistrol on D 12, heading for Bas-en-Basset. At the bridge, turn left onto D 42, then take D 44 to Tiranges.*

The road follows the charming Ance Valley and, after crossing Vert, develops into a **cornichea**. There are lovely views of the Loire basin, the Andrable Valley and the Monts du Velay.

▶ *In Tiranges, turn left onto D 24.*

As you are descending towards the River Ance, the Tour de Chalencon looms into sight, perched on its promontory.

▶ *Continue along D 24 until you reach the junction with D 9. Drive up D 9, then take D 29 on the right. Drive through St-André-de-Chalencon and take the road running along the cemetery.*

🚶 *After 2km/1mi, park the car and continue on foot (15min there and back).*

Château de Chalencon – *See Gorges de la LOIRE.*

▶ *Rejoin D 46 towards Beauzac.*

Beauzac

The small 12C-17C **church** here has a Flamboyant portal and an elegant three-storey belfry; a Romanesque crypt lies under the apse. A few houses in the village, built within the old ramparts pierced by two gates, have unusual wooden galleries under the roof which rest on huge corbels.

▶ *Return to Monistrol via Pont de Lignon on D 461 and then N 88.*

MONTBRISON

POPULATION 14 589
MICHELIN MAP 327: D-6

The town is built around a volcanic mound and dominated by the 18C dome of the old Convent of the Visitation (today the law courts), and by the imposing belfry of its Gothic **church**, Notre-Dame-d'Espérance, which was founded in 1226 (restored 1970). It has a 15C Flamboyant porch with a 14C Virgin and Child on the tympanum. The **interior**★ has a long nave, triple lancet windows and a Radiant Gothic chancel. Opposite the church stands **La Diana** *(Guided tours (1hr) Tue 2-5pm, Wed and Sat 9am-noon, 2-5pm.* ○ *Closed public holidays. 5€.* ☎ *04 77 96 01 10. www.ladiana.com)*, **built in 1296; its 14C interior has a coffered and painted wooden ceiling. The Musée d'Allard** *(○ Daily except Tue 2-6pm; guided tours (1h30) on request.* ○ *Closed 1 Jan and 25 Dec. 3€ (children: 2€).* ☎ *04 77 96 39 15. http://musees.loire.fr/allard.htm)* **contains a fine collection of minerals and stuffed birds; upstairs is a doll museum (600 exhibits). The town features several splendid** *hôtels particuliers*, **notably on rue St-Pierre** *(nos 1, 7, 10, 11, 13 and 17)* **and rue Puy-de-la-Bâtie** *(nos 5, 9, 11, 14, 18, 19 and 20)*. **After a visit to the Chapelle des Pénitents, converted into an arts centre, have a rest in the charming Jardin d'Allard, a peaceful park whose trees offer welcome shade in summer.** ⌑ *Cloître des Cordeliers, 42600 MONTBRISON,* ☎ *04 77 96 08 69.*

Excursions

Moingt
3km/1.8mi. Leave Montbrison to the S on D 8. This former Roman city has retained its medieval appearance and narrow winding streets. Note **Église St-Julien** *(○Open during services.)* and its 11C capitals with interlacing ornamentation.

Église de Champdieu★
4.5km/2.8mi N on D 8. Champdieu lies on the edge of the Forez plain and hills. It has a remarkable Romanesque **church** which was built for a Benedictine priory. In the 14C the church and priory buildings were heavily fortified.

The most surprising feature of this church is the extent of its system of defence. High arcading forms machicolations on the south side and the south arm of the transept. A similar system of arcading runs along the walls of the priory built on four sides of a quadrangle, with the church forming the south side. The church has two bell-towers, the more outstanding being the one over the transept, which dates from the Romanesque period and has fine semicircular openings. The second bell-tower, by the west front, dates from the 15C; its base forms the narthex. Note, to the left of the west front's portal, the capital depicting a mermaid with two tails.

Interior
The austerity and marked influence of the Auvergne Romanesque style create a striking impression (Champdieu Priory was a daughter-house of Manglieu Abbey

La Diana

in the Auvergne). Architectural features typical of the Auvergne include the barrel-vaulted nave, and vaulted side aisles with ovolo moulding and projecting arms. The ends of the arms are decorated with arcading surrounding a pointed arch, which is characteristic of this style. Blind arcading with colonnettes and carved capitals decorates the main apse. Underneath the chancel is a late-11C crypt comprising a central section divided into three aisles by colonnettes with carved capitals.

Refectory

Access via a door to the left of the church. The former monks' refectory, on the ground floor of the western part of the priory, has retained its 15C decoration including the painted coffered ceiling and, above the fireplace, a fine mural of the Last Supper.

St-Romain-le-Puy

7km/4.3mi S of Montbrison. The church of the former priory of St-Romain-le-Puy which, at the end of the 10C, belonged to the abbey of St-Martin-d'Ainay in Lyon rises on a volcanic peak emerging from the Forez plain, dominating a St-Gobain glassworks at the foot of the peak. Water is bottled from a mineral spring (Source Parot) north-east of the village near D 8.

Église du Prieuré★

Access by car from place Michalon to a car park half way up the slope. (◕ *Apr-Oct: daily except Tue, 2.30-5pm (Sun, 10.30am-7pm. 2€.* ☎ *04 77 76 92 10)*

From the plateau in front of the church, the panorama encompasses a vast circle of mountains: those of Forez to the west, the Monts d'Uzore to the north, the Tarare mountains and those of the Lyonnais from the north-east to the south-east.

The combination of the church's location, its age, its unusual construction and its carved decoration all make it a very curious building. Traces of several successive construction periods can be seen. The oldest remains are pre-10C (the part near the door and, on the right-hand side, two walled-up doors with bands of brickwork). The walls are made of pink and grey granite quarry stone, mixed with blocks of basalt. The east end is the most interesting part of the church, with its semicircular arch, its partially reticulated masonry work and, in particular, the unusual carved frieze recessed into the underside of the arch, consisting of square and rectangular slabs and decorated with very sober relief motifs.

Interior

The archaic appearance and the asymmetry of the ground plan are particularly striking. The floor of the apse and chancel is higher than the level of the earlier nave. The capitals have floral and geometric decoration.

Remains of **murals** (restored) painted in several stages from the 12C to the 15C are visible in various places. The capitals on the crypt columns depict for the most part animals fighting.

Chalain-d'Uzore

7.5km/4.8mi N of Montbrison. The 14C-16C **château** (◔ *Mid-Jul to end Aug: guided tours (40min) at 2.30pm, 3.30pm and 4.30pm. 4€.* ☎ *04 77 97 13 12)* is notable for its former courtroom, converted into a village hall during the Renaissance (imposing fireplace) and for its gallery with sculpted doors. The terrace commands a lovely vista of the Monts du Forez.

Montrond-les-Bains✝

11km/6.8mi. Leave Montbrison to the E on D 496. This spa resort, recommended for obesity and diabetes, has kept its **château** (◔ *Apr-Jun, daily except Tue, 2-6pm; Jul-Sep: daily except Tue, 2-8pm; Oct: Sat, Sun, 2-6pm.* ◔ *Nov-Easter. 4€.* ☎ *04 77 94 50 31. www.montrond-les-bains.com)*, whose ruins stand proudly on top of a hill near the River Loire.

Kids Although the castle was damaged by fire in the 18C, the outer walls have survived. Beyond the vast porch, decorated with fluted pilasters and capitals, stand the remains of the 14C and 15C building where the lord of the castle lived with his family. Note the fine mullioned windows and the remains of monumental fireplaces. From the towers, the view extends to the nearby plain, Monts du Forez to the west and Mont Pilat to the south-east. The round tower houses an unusual **Musée de la Poste** (Postal Services Museum)

Sury-le-Comtal

10km/6.2mi S. Leave the car on place de l'Église and walk towards the château entrance, to the right of the church. This 17C **château** *(By appointment; apply to the Tourist office.* ☎ *04 77 52 05 14)* features lavish **ornamentation**★ consisting of sculpted ceilings and intricate wainscoting. There are also several fine fireplaces with carved panels. The **church** is Gothic and characterised by diagonal ribbing. Note the fine keystone in the chancel, depicting the Holy Father surrounded by the four Evangelists, and the first chapel in the left side aisle, dating from the Renaissance.

LE MONT-DORE ⚒⚒

POPULATION 1 682
MICHELIN MAP 326: D-9 – 45KM/28MI SW OF CLERMONT-FERRAND

Le Mont-Dore stretches out along the banks of the upper reaches of the River Dordogne in a magnificent corrie in the shadow of the Puy de Sancy; it is a spa town (the season lasts from mid-May to early October) and a remarkably well-equipped winter sports resort. The ski area *(see below)* **covers the north face of the Puy de Sancy and the slopes of Le Capucin. Paths that are waymarked in winter provide an opportunity to discover the unexpected beauty of the volcanic landscape under snow. In summer the resort offers a wide range of leisure facilities and is an ideal base for ramblers or those touring by car.** 🛈 *Av. de la Libération, 63240 Le MONT-DORE, ☎ 04 73 65 20 21. www.mont-dore.com*

The Spa Town

The waters were used by the Gauls in swimming pools, the remains of which have been discovered beneath the Roman baths. The latter were a splendid sight and much larger than the present establishment where it is possible to see the surviving sections. It was not until Louis XIV's reign that the "Mont d'Or," as Mme de Sévigné wrote, regained its clientele – in spite of the fact that there was no road to the resort. The road was not built until the 18C, and the fashion for "taking the waters" emerged in the 19C thanks to the works of Dr Michel Bertrand and the visit here by the turbulent Duchesse de Berry in 1821.

The water has the highest silica content in France and is heavily charged with carbon dioxide. It flows out from lava seams inside the pump rooms at temperatures of 38-44°C/100-111°F. The best-known springs are Madeleine, César, Les Chanteurs and Ramond. The water is used in drinks, inhalations, sprays, baths and showers, to treat asthma, respiratory disorders and rheumatism (in this latter case, thermal gases are also injected subcutaneously).

Inside the spa – Salle des Gaz Thermaux

S. Sauvignier/MICHELIN

Établissement Thermal

🕐 *May to mid-Oct: guided tours (45min) daily except Sun at 2pm, 3pm, 4pm and 5pm; mid-Oct to Apr: daily except Sat-Sun at 3pm.* 🕐 *Closed 1 Jan, 1 May, 25 Dec. 3€.* ☎ *04 73 65 05 10.*

The pump rooms were built between 1817 and 1823 and later extended and modernised. The interior decoration is impressively ornate, drawing on Byzantine, Roman and Auvergne Romanesque art for inspiration. The most remarkable rooms are the **Hall des Sources** and the **Salle des Gaz Thermaux** on the ground floor, and the **Galerie César**★ and the main foyer (**Salle des Pas Perdus**★), with rib-vaulted ceilings painted with frescoes, on the first floor.

Note the lofty rooms, designed to let the "bracing mountain air" infiltrate as much as possible, and the shallow steps, a concession to sufferers of asthma.

The Winter Sports Resort

Le Mont-Dore (alt 1 325m/4 347ft) was one of the first winter resorts in France, going back to 1907. Situated 4km/2.5mi south of the spa town, it takes advantage of the elaborate equipment and activities designed for visitors taking the waters (accommodation, skating rink, swimming pool, entertainment). During the winter season, activities such as alpine skiing (including monoskiing and snowboarding), cross-country skiing, snowshoeing and climbing up frozen waterfalls are available.

Ski area

The **Alpine skiing** runs are located on the north slopes of the Sancy (alt 1 885m/6 184ft) that enjoy long-lasting and adequate snow cover. During the winter season, a free shuttle service provides a link between the town and the slopes, which extend over 42km/26mi. In 1936, Le Mont-Dore was one of the first resorts to acquire a **cable-car**; today, two cars take skiers up to an overhang situated at an altitude of 1 780m/5 840ft, just beneath the summit of the Puy de Sancy. In addition, 17 drag-lifts and a chair-lift give access to 31 runs (15 green, 9 blue, 6 red and 1 black). The **ski pass,** which can be bought in Le Mont-Dore, entitles holders to ski on the Super-Besse skiing area *(see BESSE-EN-CHANDESSE).* The resort is able to use snow-cannon equipment to compensate for inadequate snow cover.

Address Book

EATING OUT

➤ **Mon Clocher** – *5 r. Sauvagnat -* ☎ *04 73 65 05 41.* Mon Clocher is ideally located in the heart of Mont Dore's pedestrian and shopping zone between the church, the casino and the spa. The dining room's decor is unabashedly countrified: old farming implements, shining copper pots hanging from the walls etc. The perfect setting for enjoying the Auvergnat specialities that have ensured this restaurant's good name.

➤ **Le Bougnat** – *23 r. Georges-Clemenceau -* ☎ *04 73 65 28 19 - closed 10 Nov-15 Dec - reserv. required.* The furnishings chosen to decorate this old restored buron are faithful to tradition. You'll be greeted in the former stables before being shown up to the old living quarters, featuring an old box bed and a scullery. Authentic cuisine of Auvergne served and savoured here, *naturellement.*

WHERE TO STAY

➤➤ **Chambre d'hôte La Closerie de Manou** – *Au Genestoux - 3km/1.8mi W of Mont-Dore via D 996, towards Murat-le-Quaire -* ☎ *04 73 65 26 81 - lacloseriedemanou@club-internet.fr - closed 1 Nov-1 Mar -* 🚭 *- 5 rms.* Nestling in verdure, this 18C Auvergnat house is simply enchanting! Its (non-smoking) comfortable bedrooms are harmoniously and tastefully decorated, the reception is delightful and breakfast is succulent.

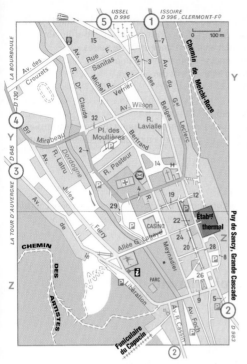

LE MONT-DORE		
Apollinaire R. S.	Y	2
Banc R. Jean	Y	3
Chazotte R. Capitaine	Y	4
Clemenceau Av.	Z	5
Clermont Av. de	Y	7
Déportés R. des	Z	8
Duchâtel R.	Z	9
Favart R.	Y	12
Gaulle Pl. Ch.-de	Y	14
Guyot-Dessaigne Av.	Y	15
Montlosier R.	Y	19
Moulin R. Jean	Z	20
Panthéon Pl. du	Z	22
Ramond R.	Z	24
République Pl. de la	Z	26
Rigny R.	Z	28
Sand Allée G.	YZ	29
19-Mars-1962 R. du	Y	32

For **cross-country skiing,** there are 30km/18.6mi of marked tracks starting 4km/2.5mi west of Le Mont-Dore (below Le Capucin). A 9km/5.6mi stretch provides the link with the Sancy Ouest tracks totalling 284km/177mi.

Hikes

These paths were created to keep the population busy during the long winter months and to offer tourists who came to take the waters new ground to explore. Musicians helped to finance the projects by giving concerts.

Chemin de Melchi-Roze
About 1hr on foot.
This flat path overlooking the town is a delightful place for a stroll in the late afternoon or in cool weather.

Chemin des Artistes★
About 1hr on foot along the path running down to the tennis courts.
This walk leads through the woods and offers attractive views of the resort. It is also possible to reach this path by taking the funicular to Le Capucin *(see below)*; from the upper station, there are two possibilities along picturesque paths: the Chemin des Mille Gouttes (north) and the Chemin des Médecins (south).

Funiculaire du Capucin★
🕐 *May-Oct: 10am-noon, 2-6pm (Jul and Aug: 9.30am-6.45pm). 5€.* ☎ *04 73 65 01 25.*
This elegant 100-year-old funicular recently regained its Belle Epoque look. Inaugurated in 1898, it was electrically powered from the start, whereas the resort itself was not yet enjoying the benefits of this new type of energy. The picturesque funicular

consists of two beautifully kept wooden carriages, which provide a shuttle service up a steep 600m/1 969ft to the Salon du Capucin at a steady speed of 1m/about 1yd per second. The journey is punctuated by strange creaking noises.
The upper station houses the engine room where an impressive tangled mass of boxwood gears, cogwheels and leather belts can be seen.

Salon du Capucin
10min by funicular then 8min on foot.
This pleasant clearing, a highly popular destination during the peak season, lies at an altitude of 1 286m/4 220ft. It is reached by a picturesque funicular railway dating from the Edwardian era.

Pic du Capucin★
1hr walk from Salon du Capucin.
The path runs for some distance through the woods. From the summit of Le Capucin (alt 1 465m/4 806ft) there is a particularly fine view of the Massif du Sancy.

Excursions

Towards Col de la Croix-Morand

Fontaine Pétrifiante
3km/2mi NW along D 996.

Waterfalls
3km/2mi NE via Le Queureuilh and Prends-toi-Garde hamlets. About 3hr on foot.
The most outstanding of the three cascades (Saut du Loup, Queureuilh and Rossignolet) is the **Queureuilh★** which drops down a basalt cliff (30m/97ft) in a very attractive natural setting.

Puy de la Tache
5km/3mi E then 1hr 30min on foot there and back.
The road rises in a series of hairpin bends up to **Col de la Croix-Morand** (alt 1 401m/4 596ft) where the landscape becomes increasingly rugged and bare.
From here it is possible to walk up to the summit of the Puy de la Tache (alt 1 627m/5 338ft) by following the route of the old ski lift. At the top there is a vast **panorama★★** over the ridge dominated by the Puy de Sancy to the south, and over the Puy de Dôme to the north, easily recognisable for its television transmitter.

Towards Le Capucin and Le Sancy

Grande Cascade★
3.5km SE along D 36. About 1hr 30min on foot. Beware the access path can be slippery.

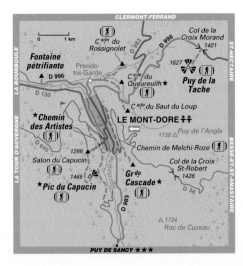

🏃 This wonderful waterfall drops down a height of 30m/98ft. At the foot of the waterfall, a footbridge leads to steps which climb up to the Plateau de Durbise (also accessible via a steep path which runs down from D 36, shortly before Col de la Croix St-Robert).

Pic du Capucin★
🏃 *3km SW along D 213 and then a forest road. About 1hr on foot from the Salon du Capucin (see above).*

Puy de Sancy★★★
🏃 *Sancy station situated 4km/2.5mi along D 983. Cable-car ride (3min) then 20min on foot to the summit (👝 see Massif du SANCY).*

LE MONT-D'OR LYONNAIS★

MICHELIN MAP 327: H-4

High above the Saône upstream from Lyon is the small Mont-d'Or range, an area bursting with rustic charm. From the peaks there are a number of attractive views.

An island of limestone – From the north, the Mont-d'Or looks like a reef emerging from the ample Saône Valley, because of its modest proportions (6km/4mi long and 12km/7.5mi wide) and its high peaks (Verdun 625m/2 050ft, Thou 609m/1 998ft, Cindre 469m/1 538ft). The limestone outcrops bring a rich yellow-ochre tinge to the landscape. The quarries were first worked in the 15C.

Vegetation and housing – The south-facing slopes are fairly arid and are dotted with wild box and shrubs; whereas the north-facing slopes are more wooded. Orchards, vineyards, blooming gardens, meadows and small fields of crops make up the delightful landscape of the inner valleys.

Excursion

Tour of the Peaks

55km/34mi – about 2hr 30min

▶ *Leave Lyon on N 6 NW, and turn right onto D 42 to Limonest. In the centre of the village turn right onto D 73 then, at the exit to the village, left onto D 92 towards Col du Mont Verdun.*

The road skirts **Château de la Barollière** (18C), flanked by square towers, and provides a number of engaging **views**★ of the mountains in the Lyon area.
At the pass, **Col du Mont Verdun,** stands a fort built in 1875 *(access forbidden).*

▶ *At the pass, turn left.*

During the descent there are attractive views of the Saône Valley.

▶ *Beyond the first few houses in Poleymieux, turn left then right and drive along a dirt track for 200m/220yd. Walk up to Croix-Rampau (the path climbs up to the left).*

Croix-Rampau★

Viewing table. In good weather the **panoramic view** extends from the Puy de Dôme to Mont Blanc.

▶ *Return to Poleymieux, head for the church, then drive up the valley to Ampère's house.*

Maison d'Ampère

🕐 *Daily except Tue 10am-noon, 2-6pm.* 🕐 *Closed 1 Jan. 4€ (children: 2€).* ☎ *04 78 91 90 77.*

The scientist **André-Marie Ampère** (1775-1836) from Lyon spent his childhood and early manhood here. His discoveries in mathematics, physics and chemistry placed him among the foremost pioneers in the scientific field in the 19C, though his absent-mindedness is also legendary. The **Musée de l'Électricité**★ displays a range of equipment used to conduct basic experiments on electrical currents, and magnets.

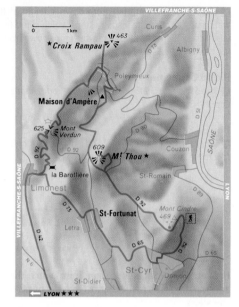

▶ *Follow the signs to St-Didier then, at the first junction, bear left towards Mont Thou.*

View from Mont Thou★

About 50m/164ft from the summit *(army property, access forbidden)* there is an esplanade commanding a view of the Saône Valley, Mont Cindre and the Greater Lyon district.

▶ *On the way down from Mont Thou, head for Mont Cindre. Pass to the right of the transmitter and turn onto D 92 to St-Cyr. The first large bend marks the start of a nature trail: "Sentier des rapaces" (birds of prey trail).*

🚶 This discovery trail follows a rural footpath over a distance of 1.9km/12mi through an area where birds of prey can be seen in large numbers.

▶ *In St-Cyr, dominated by its old keep, turn right onto D 65 towards Limonest then right again onto the road leading to St-Fortunat.*

St-Fortunat

The village stretches along its narrow main street on top of a steep rocky ridge. Half way up the hill is a chapel with a Flamboyant Gothic doorway.

▶ *At the top end of St-Fortunat turn left and drive back down towards St-Didier, then immediately turn right onto D 73.*

There are views of the Monts du Lyonnais beyond Fourvière hill.

▶ *Return to Lyon on N 6.s*

MONTÉLIMAR

POPULATION 31 344
MICHELIN MAP 332: B-6

The name Montélimar derives from a feudal fortress, "Mont-Adhémar," built in the 12C by the powerful Adhémar family. The last member of the family was the Comte de Grignan who lived in the 17C and was the son-in-law of **Madame de Sévigné**, the lady of letters. Of the nine gates that were once part of the town walls, only the **Porte St-Martin** to the north of the town, still stands. The diversion of the Rhône towards Montélimar feeds the **Châteauneuf Power Plant.** *Allées Provençales, 26200 MONTÉLIMAR, ☎ 04 75 01 00 20. www.montelimar.net.*

Nougat – The nougat industry is fairly recent; originally the sweetmeat was made by artisans. In the 16C almond trees were brought to France from Asia; Olivier de Serres had some planted in his estate at Le Pradel (west of Montélimar). The popularity of almond-growing across the Gras plateau, and the ready supply of honey from Provence and the Alps, were behind the growth of the nougat industry in Montélimar.

Old Town

In the centre, around the 15C **Collégiale Ste-Croix**, rebuilt after the Wars of Religion, most of the streets have overhanging eaves. **Place du Marché,** lined with

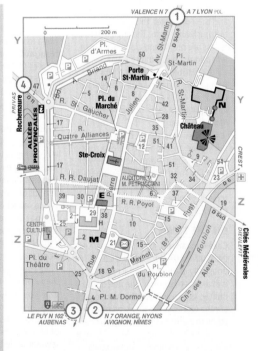

MONTÉLIMAR

Adhémar R.	Z	2
Aygu Av.	Z	4
Baudina R.	Y	5
Blanc Pl. L.	Z	6
Bourgneuf R.	Y	8
Carmes Pl. des	Y	9
Chemin Neuf R. du	Z	10
Clercs Pl. des	Y	12
Corneroche R.	Y	14
Cuiraterie R.	Z	15
Desmarais Bd Marre	Y	17
Dormoy Pl. M.	Z	18
Espoulette Av. d'	Z	19
Europe Pl. de l'	Z	21
Fust Pl. du	Y	23
Gaulle Bd Gén.-de	Z	25
Juiverie R.	Y	28
Julien R. Pierre	YZ	
Loubet Pl. Émile	Z	29
Loubet R. Émile	Z	30
Meyer R. M.	Y	32
Monnaie-Vieille R.	Y	34
Montant-au-Château R.	Y	35
Planel Pl. A.	Z	37
Poitiers R. Diane de	Z	38
Porte Neuve R.	Z	39
Prado Pl. du	Y	41
Puits Neuf R. du	Y	42
Rochemaure Av. de	Y	47
St-Martin Montée	Y	50
St-Pierre R.	Y	51
Villeneuve Av. de	Y	54

Maison de Diane de Poitiers	Z	E	Musée de la Miniature	Z M	
			Tour de Narbonne	Y	N

Address Book

EATING OUT

🍽 **Le Grillon** – *40 r. Cuiraterie - ☎ 04 75 01 79 02 - closed 12 Jul to 2 Aug, Thu, Sun evening and Mon.* Located on a little street in the old town, this restaurant has an inconspicuous façade that leads to a big dining room at the end of a corridor. The chef has an inventive streak and there are some very reasonably priced fixed menus.

🍽 **Francis 'Les Senteurs de Provence'** – *202 Rte de Mareille - 2.5km/1.5mi S of Montélimar via N 7 - ☎ 04 75 01 43 82 - closed Sun evening and Wed except public holidays.* This establishment is popular with the townsfolk. Just outside the city limits, it sports a bright new façade and modern furnishings. Always busy, Francis serves delicious menus at prices that please. *Bon appétit!*

WHERE TO STAY

🍽 **Provence** – *118 av. Jean-Jaurès - ☎ 04 75 01 11 67 - closed 15 Jan to 15 Feb and Sat from Nov to Feb - ▣ - 16 rms - ⬛ 7€.* Managed by a couple from Alsace and their daughter, this hotel is modest but spick-and-span. The small, identical rooms are bright and clean. A convenient address without pretence.

🍽🍽🍽 **Hôtel Les Hospitaliers** – *26160 Poët-Laval - 5km/3mi W of Dieulefit via D 540 - ☎ 04 75 46 22 32 - www.hotel-les-hospitaliers.com - closed 10 Nov to 14 Mar - ▣ - 22 rms - ⬛ 10€ - restaurant 🍽🍽🍽.* Enjoying a select location in the village, this hotel occupies a cluster of stone houses with a superb view of the valleys and mountains. Rooms with period furnishings; pool and panoramic terrace. Cuisine with a modern flair and tempting wine list.

ON THE TOWN

Café Cantante – *18 r. Roger-Poyol - ☎ 04 75 00 01 30 - Mon-Sat 6pm-2am.* This unusually alluring, original nightspot is in a class of its own. The fine house, built in 1906, is worth discovering, as are the works of the many painters who come to exhibit their works of art here year-round. Libations include regional wines served by the glass, cocktails and whiskies. Jazz and salsa concerts Thursday evenings.

THEATRE

Théâtre Municipal – *1 pl. du Théâtre - ☎ 04 75 00 79 01 - regie.spectacle.montelimar@wanadoo.fr - tickets: Tue-Fri 10am-12.30pm, 3.30pm-6.30pm - closed Jul-Aug and public holidays.* Built in 1885 in the pure neo-Classical style popular during the Third Republic (staid Doric columns neighbouring frolicking naked nymphs), the municipal theatre is a symbol of Montélimar's 'Golden Age', when native son Émile Loubet was elected President of the Republic. The season's programme generally includes popular theatre, dance performances and classical music concerts, making this one of the Drôme's cultural hotspots.

HOW SWEET IT IS

Nougat factories – Try to visit one of the small-scale or industrial confectioners during the manufacturing process; some places make nougat all day, others in the morning only. The Office de Tourisme has a complete list of factories open to visitors.

Nougat Chabert and Guillot – *9 rue Charles-Chabert - ☎ 04 75 00 82 00 - Mon-Sat 8am-12.30pm, 2pm-7pm; Tue-Fri 8am-7.15pm - closed public holidays.* For nougat aficionados, pros and amateurs alike, this establishment founded in 1913 makes the quintessential Montélimar nougat. Countless employees have trained here before founding their own businesses in the footsteps of their ancestor. The most famous of these is the Rucher de Provence, launched in 1938.

Nougat Diane de Poytiers – *99 avenue Jean-Jaurès (on the N7 north of the city) - ☎ 04 75 01 67 02 - www.diane-de-poytiers.fr - confectionery: winter: Mon-Fri 9am-noon, 2pm-6pm; summer: Tue-Sat 9am-noon, 2pm-6pm; shop: 9am-12.30pm, 2pm-7pm. Guided tours from early Jun to mid-Sep - closed 25 Dec and 1 Jan.* This confectionery is Montélimar's oldest, and the recipe elaborated when it was founded nearly a century ago is still used today. Visitors are taken on an

informative guided tour of the plant, where they can watch nougat being made in period kettles and taste the delectably chewy result.
Au Rucher de Provence – *35 bd Desmarais -* ☎ *04 75 52 01 59 - rucher. de.provence@wanadoo.fr - shop: daily 8am-7.30pm; confectionery: tours Mon-Fri 8am-11.30am, by appointment weekends.* The Bonnieu family makes high-quality nougat under two brand names: Stoupany, the oldest brand name in Montélimar (since 1787), and Le Rucher de Provence, launched in 1938. Here the sweets are made in the traditional manner, and, as the owner will tell you, they may *only* be purchased in select shops in Montélimar.

Escobar Patissier-Confiseur-Chocolatier-Glacier – *2 pl. Léopold-Blanc -* ☎ *04 75 01 25 53 - www.nougats-escobar. com - Mon 9.30am-12.30pm, 2pm-7pm; Tue-Sat 8am-12.30pm, 2pm-7.30pm; Sun and public holidays 8am-1pm, 3pm-6.30pm - closed Sun and public holidays Jun through Aug.* Elected 'Best in France' in 1982, this pastry and chocolate chef belongs to the elite set of genuine Montélimar artisans. His *gâteau aux trois chocolats* is a must; his nougat recipe is, of course, a house secret. Try the *rocher du parc,* a chocolate-coated praline made with almonds from Provence with a touch of lavender honey.

arcades surmounted by colourful façades and wrought-iron balconies, has a typically southern feel about it.
Place Émile-Loubet boasts **Diane de Poitiers' house** on the north side; it has a beautiful façade with mullioned windows.

Sights

Château
🕐 *Jul-Aug: 9.30-11.30am, 2-6pm; rest of year: 9.30-11.30am, 2-5.30pm.* 🕐 *Closed Tue from Nov-Mar, 1 Jan, 25 Dec). 4€ (under-11s: no charge).* ☎ *04 75 00 62 30.*
The original fortress (12C) to the east of the town was extended in the 14C by order of the Pope. Only the seigneur's lodgings (main apartments) and the watch-path are open to the public.
On the north side is the massive **Narbonne Tower.** From the ground floor in the keep, a spiral staircase leads up to the parapet walkway from which there is a vast **panoramic view** westwards over the town and eastwards over the Préalpes in Drôme.
The west front of the main apartments has nine beautiful **Romanesque windows** on the first floor. Exhibitions of contemporary art are regularly staged.

Allées provençales★
These wide half-pedestrianised avenues, made up of several boulevards over a distance of more than 1km/0.6mi have recently been relaid. Their shaded pavement cafés are the hub of the town's activity and their numerous boutiques offer a wide choice of regional products.

Musée de la Miniature
🕐 *Jul-Aug: 10am-6pm; Sep-Jun: daily except Mon and Tue. 2-6pm.* 🕐 *Closed Jan, 1 Nov, 25 Dec. 5€ (children: 3.50€).* ☎ *04 75 53 79 24. www.ville-montelimar.com.*
The success of the International Miniature Festival led to the rotating exhibition housed inside the chapel of the former Hôtel-Dieu (19C hospital). The miniatures have to meet certain criteria such as the use of the original material and a scale of 1:12.

Excursions

Château de Rochemaure★

7km/4.5mi via D 11 NW – allow 45min. Near Rochemaure Church (follow signs to: Château) take the minor road to the right of the Mairie. ⓘ *Mid-Jul to mid-Aug: daily except Tue, 10am-noon, 3-7pm.* ⓘ *Closed rest of year. 3€.* ☎ *04 75 49 08 07.*

The ruins of Rochemaure Castle stand on an impressive **site**★★ on the southern edge of the Coiron plateau, where basalt rocks (rochemaure means "black rocks") contrast with the limestone escarpment along the Rhône. The castle (12C-14C) was besieged by the Huguenots in the 16C and 17C and abandoned in the 18C.

Members of the many noble families that have owned the castle – Adhémar, Anduze, Levis-Vendatour, Rohan-Soubise – are buried in the 13C Gothic **Chapelle Notre-Dame-des-Anges** *(on the right of the road leading up to the castle).*

▶ *Turn left as you reach the plateau and leave the car below the castle walls. A surfaced road veering to the left leads to the ruins.*

The imposing 12C square **keep** is surmounted by a pentagonal tower which enabled the archers to vary their angle of fire.

The **view**★ embraces *(below)* the 19C pseudo-medieval Rhône suspension bridge, *(north)* the cooling towers of the Cruas-Meysse power station and the Rochemaure dam, *(east)* the Montélimar plain and *(south)* the Donzère gorge.

The old village

On your way back from the castle, take rue du Faubourg in front of the town hall (Mairie), then take rue de la Violle. The streets are lined with houses presenting medieval façades; The south end of the village is guarded by the Porte des Tournelles.

Pic de Chenavari★★

4.5km/2.8mi N of Rochemaure Castle. At the foot of the Chapelle St-Laurent, take the road on the right, heading for Les Videaux. Then turn left onto Chemin des Freydières and keep on climbing. Ignore the right-hand lane leading to a farmhouse and take the dirt track to the plateau with electric pylons. From here you can easily reach the summit (45min on foot there and back).

From the top (507m/1 663ft) there is a **view** of Rochemaure Castle and the Rhône, *(east)* of the Vercors and the Barronies and *(south)* of the Lower Ardèche.

Le Teil

6km/4mi W on N 102. This industrial town located on the right bank of the Rhône, dominated by its 13C castle ruins, owes its prosperity to its chalk cliffs. In the early 19C, small local businesses had already begun working the open-air quarries to produce cement and lime.

Église de Mélas

Leave the car on the square overlooking the church. Access is by the door on the right. The 10C **baptistery**, built on the site of a former necropolis, stands out on account of its honeycomb design.

Notre-Dame-d'Aiguebelle

20km/12.5mi S of Montélimar on D 56. The abbey was founded in 1137 at the instigation of St Bernard, Abbot of Clairvaux. Today the lives of the monks are governed by strict rules and they devote themselves to prayer, manual work and intellectual pursuits, as well as making a famous liquor. The **abbey church,** the only section open to the public, is designed in pure Cistercian tradition.

Small Medieval Towns★

Round tour of 78km/48.5mi. Allow 3hr 30min. Leave Montélimar on D 540. After 2km/1mi, on the right, stands a former factory where you can park the car.

Montboucher-sur-Jabron

Set up in a former mill, the **Musée de la Soie** evokes the silk industry that was once the main source of income for the area.

Inside the silk museum

▶ *Just after the underpass beneath the motorway, turn right towards Puygiron.*

Puygiron

Dominated by its ancient castle (13C-16C), this village is remarkable for its attractive **site**★, offering lovely views of Les Trois-Becs, Marsanne and the Coiron plateau.

▶ *Rejoin D 540 and turn right.*

La Bégude-de-Mazenc★

Turn left on D 9 in the modern village and take the small road to the fortified gateway.
This attractive medieval hanging village, partly-ruined, is a particularly good example of the pretty old villages of this type in the area around Montélimar.

▶ *D 540 follows the Jabron Valley upstream, in the direction of Dieulefit.*

Le Poët-Laval

The village occupies a steep, rocky **site**★ and has kept some of its medieval vestiges: the church's belfry and Romanesque apse, a 12C keep and sections of the old ramparts. The old temple, set up in a 15C knight's residence during the 17C, houses the public library (texts on the area's history) and the **Musée du Protestantisme Dauphinois** (🕐 Apr-Sep: 11am-noon, 3-6.30pm (Fri and Sun 3-6.30pm). 4€. ☎ 04 75 46 46 33. www.museeduprotestantismedauphinois.org), devoted to Protestant religion in the Dauphiné region.

Dieulefit

Cosily nestled in a wide stretch of the Jabron Valley, this small town of Protestant tradition is an important centre for tourism.
D 538 follows the Lez Valley downstream, amid the medieval ruins of Béconne and the 14C Blacon keep.

▶ *Turn right onto D 14, heading towards Taulignan.*

Taulignan – 👣 *See The Green Guide Provence.*

Grignan★ – 👣 *See The Green Guide Provence.*

▶ *Return to Montélimar on D 4.*

There are lovely **views** of the Vercors foothills and the Roubion basin. As you drive down towards Fraysse, you will catch a glimpse of the impressive ruins of the **Château de Rochefort-en-Valdaine,** overlooking the wooded valley of La Citelles.

MONTLUÇON

POPULATION 41 362
MICHELIN MAP 326: C-4

The economic capital of the Bourbonnais area, facing the first outcrops of the Combraille hills, mostly huddles round the castle that once belonged to the dukes of Bourbon but its industrial suburbs stretch over a long distance northwards, up the Cher Valley. ⓘ *5 pl. Piquand, 03100 MONTLUÇON, ☎ 04 70 05 11 44. www. montlucontourisme.com. Montluçon, which is listed as a "Town of Art and history," offers discovery tours conducted by guide-lecturers approved by the Ministry of Culture and Communication. Information at the tourist office.*

Successful rebirth – The completion of the Berry Canal in 1841 linked the iron seams of Berry and the coalfields of Commentry. Because of this, throughout the Second Empire when the steel industry began to develop, Montluçon enjoyed rapid expansion. It became the centre of a major railway network and its functions as a trading and administrative centre spilled over into the surrounding countryside.

By the turn of the 20C, the iron seams and coal faces had been exhausted and the death knell sounded for the smelting works. A serious crisis, with vast social repercussions, hit the town and its surrounding area.

The current industrial activity is fairly diverse and includes electro-mechanics, tyre making, mechanical engineering, chemistry, furniture etc.

Musical Son – André Messager (1853-1929), the composer, first became known as a conductor in Covent Garden in London, then in the opera house in Paris. However, he quickly gained a reputation as a brilliant composer of operettas containing a large number of popular and elegant airs, refrains and ballets. One of his most famous performances was in 1902 when he directed and conducted Claude Debussy's opera *Pelléas and Mélisande*.

Old Town★

▶ *Start from avenue Marx-Dormoy and head for the castle.*

Château des Ducs de Bourbon
The castle was built during the Hundred Years War (14C-15C) by Louis II de Bourbon and his successors, Jean I and Charles I.
Banks of flowers climb the old walls, and the castle itself consists of a vast rectangular building flanked, on the town side, by a turret and a large rectangular tower with crenellations.

▶ *Turn right onto rue des Serruriers and continue along Grand-Rue.*

This old street is lined with 15C houses (nos 42, 39 and 27).
Continue to place Notre-Dame with its 18C buildings. Stroll through **passage du Doyenné** which leads to place de la Comédie. On Saturday mornings this part of the old town is filled with colour and bustle thanks to its flower market.

Église Notre-Dame
The church, never completed, was built on the orders of Louis II de Bourbon in the 15C; it stands on the site of a Romanesque sanctuary of which one apsidal chapel still remains. The south aisle is very plain and it is topped by an attractive traceried balustrade. Inside, only the nave and south aisle were rebuilt. On the north side,

the Romanesque wall has pointed arches opening onto three side chapels. The church contains a number of works of art: a stone statue of Christ awaiting His torturers (late 15C) at the end of the nave, a 15C *Pietà*, a statue of John the Baptist in the first chapel on the left, and a statue of Our Lady of Montluçon (17C) to the right of the chancel.

▶ *Turn left along rue du Château.*

Castle esplanade

This is a pleasant spot for a stroll. From here there is a **view**★ over the entire town, the industrial estates beyond and, in the distance, the first outcrops of the Massif Central, the peaceful Cher Valley and the Berry region. On this side, the castle stands in the shadow of the clock tower and its first floor is decorated with a timbered gallery including red and black surbedded brick hoardings.

▶ *Return to place Notre-Dame and turn left onto rue de la Fontaine.*

Rue Pierre-Petit leads to the **Président-Wilson Gardens**; rue des Cinq-Piliers on the left leads to the picturesque place St-Pierre.

MONTLUÇON						
		Forges R. Porte	CZ 17	Piquand R. E.	BZ	32
		Jean-Jaurès Pl.	CZ 18	République Av.	BY	
Barathon R.	CZ 2	Menut R. L.	CY 22	St-Pierre Pl.	BCZ	35
Château R. du	CZ 6	Notre-Dame Pl.	CZ 25	St-Pierre R. Fg	BY	36
Courtais Bd de	BCZ	Notre-Dame R.	CZ 26	St-Roch R.	BCZ	38
Favières Quai	BY 15	Petit R. P.	CY 30	Serruriers R.	BCZ	42
Fontaine R. de la	CZ 16	Picasso R. P.	CY 31	5 Piliers R. des	CZ	52

Église St-Pierre

The church of St-Pierre, built in the 12C and 13C, is hidden by houses, some of which date from the 15C. The impressive cylindrical pillars at the transept crossing give the **interior**★ a simplicity and nobility that are totally unexpected.

Narrow passages known as *berrichons* lead from the nave to the transept crossings. There are several notable works of art including the font and a 15C statue of Christ (left of the nave), a 16C Pietà in a chapel to the right, a 16C stone cross (behind the High Altar) and, in the apsidal chapels, another *Pietà* and a magnificent statue of

Address Book

EATING OUT

A QUICK BITE

L'Eau à la Bouche – *26 r. Grande - ☎ 04 70 03 82 92.* Very popular when the lunch hour strikes, this establishment serves meals centered around sandwiches, fondues, grilled titbits and *tartiflettes*, made from high quality local ingredients. Countrified decor with exposed beams, enjoyable atmosphere and friendly welcome.

A LEISURELY MEAL

La Vie en Rose – *7 r. de la Fontaine - ☎ 04 70 03 88 79 - closed Sun lunch.* Outside, a pretty pink façade; inside, orange-toned walls, old photos and advertising posters round out this restaurant's bistro-style decor. The menu offers Bourbon specialities, featuring famous Charolais beef, served with soft jazz in the background.

Le Grenier à Sel – *Pl. des Toiles - ☎ 04 70 05 53 79 - contact@ le grenierasel.fr - restaurant closed Feb school holidays, 27 Oct-2 Nov, Sat lunch in winter, Mon lunch in Jul-Aug, Sun evening and Mon rest of year.* This attractive, ivy-covered manor in the old quarter of Montluçon is surrounded by a walled garden. The contemporary fare is flavoursome and the spacious, pleasantly furnished rooms are conducive to a good night's sleep.

WHERE TO STAY

Château St-Jean – *Near the Hippodrome - ☎ 04 70 02 71 71 - www. chateaustjean.net - ⊡ - 20 rms - ⌂ 10€ - restaurant ⊜⊜⊜.* The stone walls of this lovely 15C manor by a park contribute to its timeless appeal. The pretty, spacious rooms are soothingly quiet. Medieval ambience in the dining room under the vaulted ceiling of a 12C chapel. Covered pool.

ON THE TOWN

Le Perceval – *3 pl. Ste-Anne - ☎ 04 70 28 38 28 - Mon-Thu 2pm-2am, Fri-Sat 2pm-3am.* Repose and well-being define this luxurious, yet relaxed, bar. Curled up in a leather booth or taking it easy on a comfy chair, you'll enjoy sipping champagnes, whiskies or exotic cocktails in the velvety atmosphere.

SHOWTIME

Le Guingois – *3 r. Ernest-Montusès - ☎ 04 70 05 88 18 - le.guingois@wanadoo. fr - tickets from 8.30pm - closed Jul-Aug.* Dedicated to contemporary music of all genres, Le Guingois gives new talents space to perform and be heard. Musics of the world, modern jazz and French compositions are in the spotlight weekly in this dynamic and original nightclub-café.

SHOPPING

Baujard – *73 bd de Courtais - ☎ 04 70 05 05 86.* Having manned the ovens for the past 30 years, this pastry-chef is a pastmaster in the confection of chocolate delicacies, traditional pastries and iced desserts that delight the refined sweet tooth. The fresh, elegant decor – pastel shades, crown moulding and high ceiling – invite lingering and it's just as well, given that Baujard is also a tearoom.

La Ferme St-Pierre – *3 Pl. de la Poterie - ☎ 04 70 28 89 00.* Three farmers joined forces to create this shop selling produce straight from the farm. The result is a very nice choice of poultry and related products, such as foie gras, magret and confits, plus milk and goat cheese. Also available are preserved pork, delicatessen, jam, honey and mustard from Charroux.

Mary Magdalene★★ dating from the late 15C, "a very young girl with a slender waist, almost still a child" (Émile Mâle).

▶ Rue St-Roch and rue des Serruriers lead back to the foot of the castle opposite the statue of Marx Dormoy, former Mayor of Montluçon.

Sights

Musée des Musiques Populaires

🕐 Daily except Tue 2-7pm (Oct-Mar: 2-6pm). 🕐 Closed 1 Jan, 1 and 8 May, 14 Jul, 1 and 11 Nov, 25 Dec. 4€. ☎ 04 70 02 56 57.

This museum housed in the former **château des ducs de Bourbon** has recently undergone extensive renovation. Today there are 711 instruments in the collections and six workshops making and repairing stringed instruments as well as hurdy-gurdies, bagpipes and brasses. There is a good library of documents relating to instruments of all the families, including electric instruments and percussion.

Château de la Louvière

Leave Montluçon to the E on N 145 towards Montmarault. 500m/547yd past the hospital, turn right onto avenue du Cimetière de l'Est. 🕐 Jul to mid-Sep: daily except Tue 2-7pm; mid-Sep to Jun: daily except Tue 2-6pm. 🕐 Closed 1 Jan, 1 May, 8 May, 14 Jul, 25/12. 3€. ☎ 04 70 05 04 91. Gardens open all year.

In 1926, **François Joseph Troubat-le-Houx**, an art enthusiast, had this château built, based on the design of the façades of the Petit Trianon in Versailles. The interior features furniture, tapestries and objets d'art from the 17C, 18C and 19C. The castle grounds combine French and English style gardens.

Excursions

Discovering the Canal de Berry

65km/40.5mi – allow 3hr

This round trip, running west and north of Montluçon, offers an interesting insight into the area's cultural heritage.

▶ Leave Montluçon to the NW on D 916, heading for Boussac.

Domérat

The Romanesque **church** (🕐 Weekdays 2-6.30pm. Apply to the town hall to visit ☎ 04 70 64 20 01) has kept its east end and its chancel. Note the unusual **11C crypt** and the **frescoes** in the chancel and radiating chapels. In one of the castle's outbuildings, the **Musée de la Vigne** (♿ Apr-Sep: Sat-Sun and public holidays 3-6pm. No charge. ☎ 04 70 64 20 01) illustrates the techniques of wine-growing and winemaking in the Allier département.

Huriel

12km/7mi NW on D 916. 12C **keep** (🕐 Jul and Aug: daily except Mon (open Mon when exhibition is on) 10am-noon, 2.30-6.30pm; Jun and Sep-Dec: daily except Sat-Sun by request; apply to the town hall during office hours (8.30am-noon, 2-6pm). No Charge; museum: 3€. Town hall: ☎ 04 70 28 60 08) and church.

▶ Leave Huriel to the N and take D 40 to La Chapelaude, then take D 943 on the left for 11km/6.8mi. At the locality called Goëlat, turn right.

Église de St-Désiré★

This remarkable Romanesque construction was once an 11C priory. The **interior** stands out on account of its stark, sober design. The nave and side aisles feature barrel vaulting and the transept crossing is crowned by a cupola with pendentives. On the lower level, two staircases flanking the chancel lead to the **crypt**, the oldest part of the church.

▶ *Take D 479 N of St-Désiré, then follow D 30.*

Scuplture, St-Désiré church: anyone you know?

J. Damase/MICHELIN

Vallon-en-Sully – 🕭 *See HÉRISSON.*

▶ *Return towards Montluçon on D 301, running along the River Cher and the Berry Canal. We recommend that you stop at Magnette; from there cross the canal.*

Musée du Canal de Berry

🕐 *Jul-Sep: guided tours (1hr30min) 2.30pm-8pm (last admission 1hr before closing). 3€ (children: 1€).* ☎ *04 70 06 70 92.* The museum will enlighten visitors on the history of the canal and the successive stages of its construction.

🏃 The tow path along the canal offers good opportunities for jogging and mountain biking.

Former Mining Country

50km/31mi – allow 3hr

▶ *Leave Montluçon to the SE on N 144 in the direction of Clermont-Ferrand.*

Néris-les-Bains✝

🛈 *Av. Max-Dormoy, 03310 NÉRIS-LES-BAINS,* ☎ *04 70 03 11 03.*

This peaceful health resort was once a thriving Gallo-Roman city. You can visit the church, the Merovingian necropolis and its sarcophagi, the amphitheatre, the ancient baths and the **Maison du Patrimoine** (🕐 *Apr-Oct: guided tours (1hr) daily except Mon and Tue 3-6pm.* 🕐 *Closed 1 May. 4€.* ☎ *04 70 03 42 11),* which displays Gallo-Roman artefacts discovered in Néris: ceramic pieces, coins, jewellery, and sculptures in bronze and other materials.

🏃 Rambling can be enjoyed along the old railroad between Néris and Montluçon. Information available from the tourist office.

▶ *Leave Néris to the E on D 998.*

Commentry

Until the end of the First World War, Commentry was at the heart of an area devoted almost entirely to mining. Today this activity has been replaced by chemical, mechanical and siderurgical industries.

▶ *Leave Commentry to the SE and continue along D 998.*

Église de Colombier

Crowned by an elegant 12C belfry, the church and its nearby priory, defended by a citadel, form a harmonious architectural ensemble. The 6C apostle **St Patrocle** died in this monastery which became a popular place of pilgrimage.

▶ *Leave Colombier to the N on D 200.*

Malicorne

Besides the **church** (🕐 *Weekdays. Apply to the town hall.* ☎ *04 70 64 90 06.*), the most interesting sight to visit in Malicorne is the **Jardin-Verger** (🕐 *Jun-Sep: 10am-noon, 3-6pm. 5€ (children: 3€).* ☎ *04 70 64 87 39),* a dazzling garden-orchard bursting with colour: the rose garden alone boasts several hundred varieties blossoming between June and September.

▶ *Leave Malicorne to the N on D 69. In Doyet, turn right onto N 145, heading for Moulins. After 2km/1mi, turn left onto D 438.*

Donjon de la Souche

👁‍🗨 *Not open to the public.* This superbly restored square 13C and 14C keep is surrounded by multifoil machicolations.

▶ *Continue along D 438 towards D 38. Turn right. Cross the railway tracks, then the motorway and turn left onto D 157. At Deneuille-les-Mines take D 33 on the left. After St-Angel, skirt the roundabout and continue along D 33, which will soon take you back to Montluçon via N 145.*

MORESTEL

POPULATION 3 097
MICHELIN MAP 333: F-3

The lovely setting and exceptional luminosity here have attracted countless artists since the mid-19C, namely Corot, Daubigny and Turner; this has earned Morestel the nickname of "Painters' Town." **Auguste Ravier** (1814-95), who was a friend of Corot's, spent the latter part of his life in Morestel. This gifted artist came to specialise in sunsets and their subtle palette of gray, bluish tinges. The D 517 road from Crémieu gives a delightful **view** of the village of Morestel, dominated by its Gothic church and the remains of a 12C square tower. 🛈 *100 pl. des Halles, 38150 MORESTEL,* ☎ *04 74 80 19 59.*

A Painter's Paradise

Maison Ravier

🕐 *Mar to Nov: daily except Tue 2.30-6.30pm.* 🕐 *Closed first fortnight in May. 4€ (under-18s: 2€).* ☎ *04 74 80 06 80. www.maisonravier.com*
Painters often have good taste, as is clearly evidenced by this handsome residence that was home to Auguste Ravier between 1867 and 1895. The house has been bought by the municipality and is presently used to host quality art exhibitions.

Tour Médiévale

Jul-Aug: daily except Mon, 10am-noon, 2.30-7pm; mid-Mar to end Jun and Sep-Nov: daily except Mon, 2.30-6.30pm; Sun and public holidays, 10am-noon, 2.30-7pm. *Jan to mid-Mar. No charge.* ☎ *04 74 33 04 51.*

This former keep is what remains of the 11C citadel overlooking the town. It offers lovely views of the surrounding region and will soon be converted into a cultural centre.

Excursions

Château de Mérieu

8km/5mi N along D 16. The mainly 17C château lies in a magnificent **setting**★ on the west bank of the River Rhône, amid meadows and woodlands that stand out on the slopes of the southern end of the Bugey area.

Brangues

6km/4mi E on D 60A. This village in the Bas-Dauphiné is outstanding on account of its handsome houses, their white chalk walls and their wide flat roofs.

Paul Claudel's Tomb

Access on D 60 E of Brangues. The French author **Paul Claudel** (1868-1955) had grown fond of Brangues Château, a large 18C mansion located north-west of the village. Every year he would organise a huge family gathering there to celebrate the New Year. It was his will to be buried in the castle grounds, beside his beloved wife.

Centrale Nucléaire de Creys-Malville

11km/6.8mi N. This complex was originally inaugurated as a commercial prototype, whose objective was to produce electricity and plutonium. However, **Superphenix**, the fast neutron reactor of industrial size, was closed down in 1998. From the observation platform at the end of the car park there is a view right across the site.

Parc d'Attractions Walibi Rhône-Alpes★

Kids *15km/9.5mi S. Leave Morestel on N 75 S towards Grenoble and in Veyrins turn left towards Les Avenières; D 40 on the right leads to the park (signposted).* *It is recommended to check opening times. 30€ (3-11-year-olds: 20€).* ☎ *04 74 33 71 80. www. walibi.com.*

This is one of the eight Walibi parks in Europe. Created in Belgium, France and the Netherlands from 1975 onwards, these parks are named after the Australian kangaroo. The Avenières Park covers an area of 35ha/86 acres and is surrounded by lakes; with its countless attractions and two shows, it has much to offer those who enjoy thrills and spills. In an atmosphere styled on the Wild West, visitors can ride the spine-chilling **Boomerang**★ with its three loops, take a cruise on the **Pirates' ship,** get caught up in the terrible tentacles of the **Giant Octopus** or try rafting

---

STAYING NEAR WALIBI

⊜ **Hôtel Servhotel** – *Rte de Grenoble -* ☎ *04 74 80 06 22 - closed 25-30 Dec -* 🅿 *- 21 rms -* ⌑ *7€.* The Walibi Rhône-Alpes amusement park being only 10km//6mi away, this is above all a practical address. Simple, modern rooms and cordial reception.

⊜⊜ **Vieille Maison** – *38490 Aoste - 7km/4.2mi SE of Walibi via D 40 -* ☎ *04 76 31 60 15 - closed 9 Sep to 7 Oct and 23 Dec to 3 Jan -* 🅿 *- 17 rms -* ⌑ *7€ – restaurant* ⊜⊜*.* An old stagecoach inn nestled in a verdant garden offering bedrooms with a rustic accent. The restaurant, with its fireplace, beams, straw chairs and copper vessels, has a provincial charm. Courtyard terrace graced with handsome horse chestnuts; covered pool.

down the **Canadian River**. Small merry-go-rounds, clowns and a ranch with ponies will amuse younger visitors. The **Tamtamtour** will take you on an exotic boat ride through the tropical jungle. The park can also be visited in a miniature train and the lake crossed by paddle steamer.

Among the shows providing regular entertainment, do not miss the **Legend of Prince Thibaud**★, an equestrian show set against a medieval background.

However, in summer, the most popular part of the park is its aqualand known as **Aqualibi**★ where the water is maintained at a steady 25°C/77°F.

There are numerous possibilities for having a meal or a snack.

MOULINS★

POPULATION 21 892
MICHELIN MAP 326: H-3

Moulins lies on the banks of the River Allier and is the quietly charming main town of the Bourbonnais area. It boasts a range of economic and industrial activities linked to the rich farmland of the Moulins region, with food industries, shoe factories and machine tool production. The wide avenues and streets of the old town are an ideal place for a stroll. *11 r. François-Péron, 03000 MOULINS, ☎ 04 70 44 14 14. www.ville-moulins.fr . Moulins, which is listed as a "Town of Art and history", offers discovery tours conducted by heritage guides approved by the Ministry of Culture and Communication. 5€. Information available at the Maison du Patrimoine et du Tourisme, ☎ 04 70 48 51 18.*

A Bit of History

The Duchy of Bourbonnais – Bourbon lands first appeared in history books in the early 10C but it took more than three centuries for the lords and, later, the counts of Bourbon to create a State capable of rivalling its powerful neighbours, Berry and Burgundy. The Bourbons achieved their aim by taking advantage of their geographical location between the kingdom of France and the duchies of Auvergne and Aquitaine,

Triptych by the Master of Moulins

Address Book

EATING OUT

Restaurant des Cours – *36 cours Jean-Jaurès* - ☎ *04 70 44 25 66* - *http://restaurant-des-cours.com* - *closed 9-18 Feb, 14-31 Jul and Wed*. This fetching bourgeois house in the heart of the city is embellished by a lacework of Virginia creeper. The knick-knacks, handsome furniture and floral bouquets all contribute to its refined appeal. Surprisingly affordable traditional cuisine, thanks to the fixed-price menus.

Logis Henri IV – *03340 Neuilly-le-Réal - 16km/9.6mi SE of Moulins via N 7 and D 989* - ☎ *04 70 43 87 64* - *closed 17 Feb-7 Mar, 2-5 Sep, Sun evening and Mon*. The logis was a hunting lodge back in the 16C. You'll enter the half-timbered dining room with its pretty tiled floor via the perron. They offer a good choice of fixed-price menus featuring classic fare.

WHERE TO STAY

Parc – *31 av. du Gén.-Leclerc* - ☎ *04 70 44 12 25* - *www.hotel-moulins.com* - *closed 11-26 Jul, 26 Sep-4 Oct and 23 Dec-4 Jan* - P - *28 rms* - ⌸ *7€* - *restaurant*. A few steps from a verdant park and the train station, this establishment is run by a family who will do everything in its power to make your stay a pleasant one. Modest, well-kept bedrooms and two dining rooms, rustic and contemporary, with colourful bamboo chairs.

ON THE TOWN

La Bodega – *12 r. du Four* - ☎ *04 70 20 59 55* - *Tue-Thu 10am-1am, Fri-Sat 11am-2am, Sun 2pm-1am - closed 3 wks in Aug*. Definitively the most appealing venue in Moulins. Laughter rings out at all hours among the faded walls covered with unexpected decorations: a painted tortoise shell and a shark bell, among others, whereas further on an old jukebox is peacefully sighing its last to a rumba beat. Overflowing with anachronistic charm.

Le Grand Café – *49 pl. d'Allier* - ☎ *04 70 44 00 05* - *summer: daily 8am-1am; rest of the year: closed Sun, Tue, 1 Jan and 25 Dec*. Built in 1899, this café is classified as an historic monument. An imposing fresco honouring Gambrinus, the god of ale, surrounds customers whereas enormous mirrors copy their images ad infinitum. Emphatically worth discovering.

Le Vieux Moulins – *2 r. de l'Ancien-Palais* - ☎ *04 70 20 67 81* - *summer: Mon-Sat noon-4pm, 7.30pm-11.30pm, Sun 7pm-11.30pm; rest of the year: closed Sun - closed 2 wks in Nov, lunch and public holidays*. Contrary to what some locals used to believe, this eminently agreeable establishment has always been a *crêperie*. Moreover, the bar now has a terrace on the pedestrian street, the pavement of which is used by the owner to organize her concerts and other original goings-on.

RECREATION

Poneys et nature en Bourbonnais – *La Solée - 5km/3mi E of Moulins via D12 dir. Aérodrome Dompierre and road on left - 03400 Yzeure* - ☎ *04 70 34 68 94* - *9.30am-7.30pm*. As an introduction to outdoor riding, the 'Poney et Nature' association offers excursions on horseback with a guide schooled in equestrian tourism.

SHOPPING

Fossey – *10 r. François-Péron* - ☎ *04 70 44 08 70*. Frédérick Fossey got his pastry-chef wings studying under some of France's best sweets craftsmen. He now creates his own mouth-watering confections, the most sought-after of which are chocolate-based. The tearoom also offers the *Moulinois*, a luscious pastry starring hazelnuts and praline, sans chocolate.

Les Palets d'Or – *11 r. de Paris* - ☎ *04 70 44 02 71* - *Tue-Sat 9.30am-12.15pm, 2pm-7.15pm, Sun and public holidays 9.30am-12.30pm*. Palets d'or (gold disks), are cream and coffee-filled chocolates that were originally created in this very shop in…1898! The current owner, who studied at the ever-famous Lenôtre, continues the palet tradition and adds sweetmeats of his own invention: *le Pêché du diable* (Devil's Sin), the Yucata or the *Folies de l'écureuil* (Squirrel's Follies), among others.

placing their troops at the service of the crown. In the name of Philip Augustus, Guy de Dampierre led the conquest of the Auvergne and was then entrusted with its protection. Archambaud VIII was a leading figure in the Albigensian Crusade, and Archambaud IX accompanied St Louis to the Holy Land.

This alliance with royal authority, combined with a skilful policy of marriage (Béatrice de Bourbon married Robert, Count of Clermont, St Louis' sixth child, in 1265), facilitated the building of a vast State and led to eight Bourbons becoming King of France. In 1327 the Barony of Bourbon became a duchy and, in the following year, it was raised to the peerage by Philip VI.

Arts at the Court of Moulins – The duchy enjoyed its golden age during the 15C and, at the same time, the court in Moulins entered a period of splendour and brilliance, with artists summoned here by Charles I, Jean II, Pierre II and Anne of France. Pierre de Nesson recounted the misfortunes of Jean I; the Flemish musician Jean Ockeghem sang for Charles I before moving on to the king's chapel. Sculpture flourished under Jean II, firstly with Jacques Morel, then with Michel Colombe and his followers, Jean de Rouen and Jean de Chartres. It is, however, the painters who produced the finest works, with Jean Perréal, Jean Richer and above all the **Master of Moulins** who created the famous "Triptych." The court also attracted poets such as Jean Lemaire de Belges and Jean Marot.

Cathédrale Notre-Dame

A good overall view of the cathedral may be had from the old covered market, a 17C arcaded building. The towers and the nave (both 19C) are an extension of the former collegiate church built in Flamboyant Gothic style between 1474 and 1507, which includes the chancel and ambulatory with flat east end.

The cathedral is particularly interesting for its works of art and **stained-glass windows**★★, which depict famous figures from the Bourbons' Court.

1) **St Catherine's or the Dukes' Window** – Late 15C. The window shows the Cardinal of Bourbon on the right and Pierre II and Anne of France on the left, worshipping St Catherine; at the top is an illustration of the life of St Catherine of Alexandria.

2) **Crucifixion Window** – Late 15C. The blood of Christ is being collected by angels. The bottom of the window shows **The Entombment of Christ**★ (16C).

3) **Window of the Virgin Mary Enthroned** – Late 15C.

4) **Tree of Jesse Window** – 16C.

5) **Elegant spiral staircase.**

6) **Window of the Suffering and Triumphant Church** – Early 16C.

7) **Window of the Church Militant** – 16C. The Crown of Thorns is handed over to the King.

8) **Chapel of the Black Virgin** – The Black Virgin, a replica of the one in Le Puy-en-Velay, serves as a reminder that Moulins was one of the stopovers used by pilgrims on their way to Le Puy-en-Velay and Santiago de Compostela. A wooden polychrome low-relief sculpture depicts the death of the Virgin Mary.

9) **Chapter Chapel** – The centre of the stained-glass window depicts the martyrdom of St Barbara.

10) **Classical Painting** – Two Carthusian monks.

11) **The Annunciation** – 18C painting on each side of the doorway.

12) **Window depicting the life of the Virgin Mary.**

13) **St Mary Magdalene Window** – 16C.

14) **Window of Christ on the Cross** – Late 15C.

15) **St Elizabeth of Hungary's Window** – Early 16C.

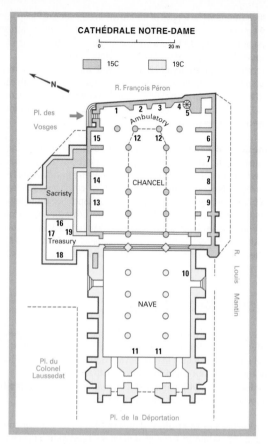

CATHÉDRALE NOTRE-DAME

0 ————— 20 m

15C   19C

R. François Péron

Pl. des
Vosges

Ambulatory

CHANCEL

Sacristy

Treasury

NAVE

Pl. du
Colonel
Laussedat

R. Louis Mantin

Pl. de la Déportation

16) Triptych by the Master of Moulins★★★ – ⊙ *Apr-Sep: guided tours (20min)*
9.30am-noon, 2-6pm; Oct-Mar: daily except Tue 10-noon, 2-5pm (last admission
30min before closing). ⊙ *Closed Sun morning, 1 Jan, 25 Dec. Free admission.* ☏ *04*
70 20 89 65.

This splendid painting on wood, probably completed in 1498, is considered to
be one of the last masterpieces of Gothic painting in France. There is still some
doubt as to the identity of the artist, the names of Jean Bourdichon, Jean Perréal and Jean Prévost have been mooted in the past but the current opinion of
art critics tends to favour Jean Hey. There are affinities with the Flemish School
in the attitudes of the figures, whereas the drawing of the faces and foreheads
suggests the Florentine School. The vivid colours and graceful attitudes of the
figures lend the work wonderful freshness. The triptych was commissioned by
Pierre II, Duke of Bourbon, and his wife Anne of France (Anne de Beaujeu, 1462-
1522) who are depicted on the inner panels.

The outer panels are decorated with a painting of the Annunciation in *grisaille*.

On the inside, the Virgin Mary, her eyes lowered towards the Infant Jesus, stands
out against a background filled with the sun and a rainbow, which gives great
perspective to the picture as a whole. The light emanating from Christ and His
mother brings a luminous quality to the entire composition.

The room also contains a 17C ivory crucifix reliquary (**17**) mounted on an ebony stand,
the Aubery Triptych (**18**) and the Bethlehem Triptych (**19**) attributed to the 16C Flemish painter Joos van Cleve; the subject matter is taken from the Life of Christ.

Walking Tour

Cathedral District

▶ *Leave the cathedral by the north door, walk round the east end of the church and go down rue Grenier, then rue des Orfèvres.*

Jacquemart★

The belfry, topped by a timber-framed roof and a campanile housing the bells and automata, was once the symbol of the town's privileges as a borough. Today, the Jacquemart family announce the time of day for those working in, or visiting, the city. The clock tower was burnt down in 1655 and was once again ravaged by fire in 1946. The following year it was rebuilt by public subscription.

Father Jacquemart, in his grenadier's uniform, and his wife Jacquette sound the hours, while their children Jacquelin and Jacqueline strike the half and quarter hours.

Musée Bourbonnais – *See Sights below.*

Donjon de la Mal Coiffée

All that remains of the old castle is a massive keep restored in the 15C and named the "Dishevelled" because of its roof; this was originally the angle tower in the north-west corner of the old ducal palace (see Sights below).

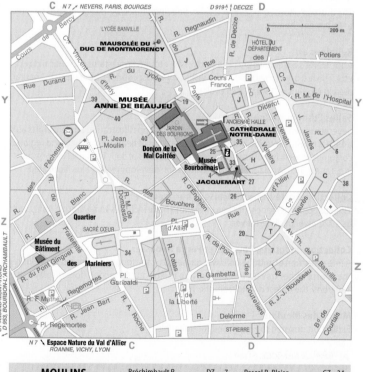

MOULINS			Bréchimbault R.	DZ	7	Pascal R. Blaise-	CZ	34
			Fausses Braies R. des	DY	19	Péron R. F.	DY	35
Allier Pl. d'	CDZ		Flèche R. de la	DZ	20	Tanneries R. des	DY	38
Allier R. d'	CDZ		Grenier R.	DY	25	Tinland R. M.	CY	39
Ancien Palais R.	DY	4	Horloge R. de l'	DZ	26	Vert Galand R. du	CDY	40
Bourgogne R. de	DY	6	Hôtel de Ville Pl. de l'	DY	27	4 Septembre R.	DZ	42
			Orfèvres R. des	DY	33			

Pavillon dit d' Anne de Beaujeu

The so-called Anne de Beaujeu Pavilion is the only remaining part of the extension to the ducal palace commissioned by the princess around 1495.

This elegant construction is one of the earliest examples of Renaissance architecture in France and was used in later years by King Charles VIII.

A porch tower stands in front of the Italianate façade, which presents six arcades decorated with the initials of Peter and Anne of Beaujeu and the emblems of the Bourbons, the belt of hope, thistle and stag beetle. The pavilion houses the Musée d'Art et d'Archéologie (*see Musée Anne de Beaujeu in Sights below*).

Quartier des Mariniers

While you are visiting the historical heart of Moulins, you can explore the neigh-bourhood formerly occupied by the town's community of bargemen, starting from the Église du Sacré-Cœur *(rue Mathé, rue Jean-Bart, rue des Rivages and rue du Pont-Guinguet).*

Sights

Musée Bourbonnais

Apr-Sep: Mon, Tue, 9.30-11.30am, 3-6.30pm, Wed-Sun, 3-6.30pm; Oct-Mar: Mon, Tue, 9.30-11.30am, 2-5.30pm, Wed-Sun, 2-5.30pm. *Closed 1 Jan, 1 May, 25 Dec. 5€.* *04 70 44 39 03.*

The museum, housed in several 15C-17C buildings linked by 17C galleries, is devoted to four main themes:

Religious art

Abbé Déret's collections are displayed on the ground floor (statues, liturgical objects etc). The history of the Order of the Visitation whose founder, St Jeanne de Chantal, died in Moulins in 1641, is also evoked.

Salles Ethnographiques

Several rooms contain reconstructions of workshops illustrating ancient crafts and a 19C farmhouse interior. Note the fine collections of headdresses, hats and regional costumes as well as musical instruments and objects of daily life. Local history (print-ing, tanning, town planning and architectural development) is also illustrated.

Collection d'orfèvrerie française et européenne

This collection of French and European gold plate includes some unique items such as a 17C ewer in gilded silver.

Collection de Jouets, Poupées et Fers à Repasser

A fine collection of antique dolls was gathered by the founder of the museum during the course of her travels. In addition, two rooms on the second floor display some 160 irons, the oldest dating from the 16C.

Musée des Moulins

Exhibition devoted to French and foreign mills.

▷ *Take rue de l'Ancien-Palais.*

Donjon de la Mal Coiffée

Closed for restoration.

This recently restored keep will soon become one of the area's most attractive sights. It was used as a prison until 1986 and its walls still bear the inscriptions of those who were incarcerated there.

Musée Anne de Beaujeu★★

⏰ Daily except Tue: 10am-noon, 2-6pm (Jul-Aug: daily except Tue 10am-6pm). ⏰ Closed 1 Jan, 1 May, 25 Dec. 5€ (children: 2.50€). ☎ 04 70 20 48 47. http://musee-anne-de-beaujeu.cg03.fr

This museum occupies the so-called Anne de Beaujeu Pavilion, the only remaining part of the extension to the ducal palace.

The ground floor is devoted to **archaeology, sculpture** and **medieval painting.** Exhibits include a comprehensive collection of prehistoric and protohistoric artefacts, numerous items from the Gallo-Roman civilisation, **medieval statues** from the 12C to 16C and some superb altarpiece panels from the Austrian School and the Flemish School, in addition to a Madonna with Child known as the "Beautiful Madonna," a work by an early-15C artist from Salzburg.

Room 5 has rare 12C Meuse enamel. Room 6 has a fine collection of 16C-18C **faience** (French and Italian).

Among the canvases, note the preparatory study of a painting by JP Laurens entitled *Les Hommes du Saint-Office* which can be compared with the final work.

Musée du Bâtiment

18 rue du Pont-Guinguet. ⏰ Daily except Mon and Tue 2-6pm. ⏰ Closed 1 Jan, 1 May, 1 Nov, 25 Dec. 4€ (under-12s: no charge). ☎ 04 70 34 23 69. http://musee-batiment.pays-allier.com

Tools, building materials, techniques but also fixtures and fittings of bygone days are displayed in this unusual and interesting museum housed in a fine 18C building.

Mausolée du Duc de Montmorency★

Chapelle de la Visitation, rue de Paris. ⏰ Jul-Aug: guided tours (45min) Sat 3-5pm. 3€. ☎ 04 70 48 51 18.

The mausoleum, completed in 1653, is the work of Parisian artists, the Anguier Brothers, and was commissioned by the wife of Henri II of Montmorency after she was widowed by Richelieu in 1632 and sent to the Convent of the Visitation in Moulins (now the high school). It was transported in pieces by road from Paris to Montargis and then by waterway.

The Duke, dressed in a finely worked suit of armour, and the Duchess, surrounded by Strength, Generosity, Bravery in Battle, and Faith, lie on a heavy marble sarcophagus. The pediment is decorated with the collars of the Orders of St Michael and the Holy Ghost flanking the Montmorency coat of arms.

Espace Nature du Val d'Allier

6 boulevard de Nomazy. ♿⏰ Apr-Oct: daily except Mon and Tue. 2-6pm (Jul and Aug: daily). 5€ (children: 2.50€) ☎ 04 70 44 46 29.

This information centre enlightens visitors on the rich variety of the fauna to be found in the Allier département.

The **Val d'Allier nature reserve** extends over an area of 1 450ha/3 583 acres on both banks of the River Allier, between Moulins and St-Pourçain-sur-Sioule. Visitors must comply with the reserve's strict regulations; information about guided nature rambles organised by the Ligue pour la Protection des Oiseaux (LPO, society for the protection of birds) is available from the Espace Nature.

Excursion

Châteaux in the Bourbonnais Area

100km/62mi – allow one day

▶ Leave Moulins to the NE heading towards N 7, then turn right onto D 12.

Yzeure

The village of Yzeure is older than Moulins, and was the seat of the parish until the Hundred Years War. At the back of a vast square stands the 12C-15C **Église St-Pierre** (⏲ *Daily except Sat-Sun: 9.30am-11.30am, 2-4.30pm. Apply to the tourism dept of the town hall, place Jules-Ferry.* ☎ *04 70 48 53 36),* which is dedicated to St Peter and is unusual for

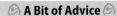

🍃 A Bit of Advice 🍃

Nature Rides: Poneys et nature en Bourbonnais – 03400 Yzeure - ☎ 04 70 34 68 94 - 9.30am-7.30pm. The "Poney et Nature" association organises riding tours led by a qualified guide/instructor.

its 18C square tower topped by a balustrade. Note the Burgundy style capitals on the main doorway and in the nave. The 11C crypt is particularly interesting.

Château de Seganges

⚷ *Not open to the public.* Small château built at the same time as the Anne de Beaujeu Pavilion.

▶ *Continue along D 29D, then turn right onto D 29.*

The road wends its way through Munet Forest, offering pretty glimpses of both coniferous and broad-leaved trees.

▶ *Leaving the forest, take D 133 on the left. At the entrance to Auroüer, continue along D 133 on the left.*

Château du Riau

⏲ *Apr-Sep: guided tours (1hr) daily except Tue 2.30-6.30pm (last admission 30min before closing). 5€.* ☎ *04 70 43 34 47.*

The Riau estate comprises several buildings dating from the 15C to the 18C which lie in a lovely green setting on the border of the Allier and Nièvre regions. The most remarkable building is the **tithe barn**★ erected in 1584, with its stables on the lower ground floor and grain storage on the three upper floors; the top floor, with its beautiful timber roof, provides an attractive view of the castle, moat, **fortified gatehouse** and dovecote.

The fortified gatehouse contains the chapel (prayer stool inlaid with mother-of-pearl) and the guard-room. In the square tower, a 15C staircase with a wooden balustrade leads to **bedrooms** decorated in Louis XV, Louis XVI and Empire styles. The outbuildings date from the 16C and 17C.

▶ *Continue along D 133 until you reach Villeneuve-sur-Allier. On leaving the village, turn right onto D 433.*

Arboretum de Balaine★

♿⏲ *Mar-Nov: 9am-noon, 2-7pm (last admission 1hr before closing). 8€ (under-8s: no charge; 8-12-year-olds: 5€).* ☎ *04 70 43 30 07.*

This 20ha/50-acre botanical garden founded in 1804 is landscaped in the English style and includes numerous species: various types of fir (Caucasian, Spanish, Douglas), giant sequoias, oaks, Cedar of Lebanon and locally grown varieties. The trees are pleasantly set amid beautiful shrubs of rhododendron, azalea, bamboo and dogwood.

▶ *Return to Villeneuve-sur-Allier and take D 133 to Bourbon-l'Archambault on the right. After leaving Bagneux, D 133, then D 13 cut across the forest of Les Prieurés Bagnolet. Leave D 13 at the end of a straight section and turn right onto D 54. Soon afterwards, proceed straight ahead on C 3.*

St-Menoux★ – 👁 *See BOURBON-L'ARCHAMBAULT.*

▶ *Leave St-Menoux to the S on D 253.*

Souvigny★★ – 👁 *See SOUVIGNY.*

▶ *Leave Souvigny to the E on D 945,
heading for Moulins. On leaving the
village, turn right onto D 34, which
crosses the railway line.*

Besson

This village has an interesting Romanesque church with a single nave. Note
the Château de Rochefort, whose ruins
overlook the Guèze Valley.

Sequoia

J. Damase/MICHELIN

▶ *Leave Besson to the SW on D 34.*

Château du Vieux Bostz

🕐 *May-Sep: 2.30-6.30pm.* ☎ *04 70 42 80 84.*
This castle, dating from the 15C and 16C, is curious because of its many square and
round turrets crowned by delicate belfries. The château is currently undergoing
restoration *(18C quarters and roof)*. During the summer season, the place is used as
a venue for art exhibitions, as well as concerts and theatrical performances.

▶ *Continue along D 34. At the crossroads, turn left onto D 291, then take D 292 on the
right.*

Château de Fourchaud

Huge, imposing castle featuring two massive towers with pepper-pot roofs and
a sturdy-looking keep. Originally erected in the 14C, the stronghold was heavily
restored during the following century.

▶ *Continue along D 292. In Bresnay, take D 34 for 4km/2.5mi, then turn left onto D
33.*

Châtel-de-Neuvre

Pretty village with a Romanesque church built on a promontory dominating the Allier
Valley. Enjoy the **view**★ extending over the nearby river and landscape.

▶ *Leave Châtel-de-Neuvre to the E on D 32, crossing the Allier, then turn left onto D
300.*

Toulon-sur-Allier

This hamlet used to be an important centre for the production of pottery back in
Gallo-Roman times.

▶ *Leave Toulon-sur-Allier to the S on N 7, then take N 79 on the right. After crossing
the Allier, take N 9 to Moulins on the right.*

Bressolles

Small village situated north-east of the charming **Prieurés Moladier Forest**.

▶ *Rejoin N 9, leading back to Moulins.*

MURAT★

POPULATION 2 153
MICHELIN MAP 330: F-4
25KM/15.5MI NW OF ST-FLOUR – LOCAL MAP SEE MONTS DU CANTAL

Murat lies in the pleasant Alagnon Valley, in a scenic **setting★★**. Its grey houses with stone-slabbed roofs rise picturesquely on terraces up the slopes of the basaltic Bonnevie hill. Two other steep peaks overlook the small town: Chastel rock to the north-west and Bredons rock to the south-east topped by an interesting Romanesque church. Murat is an ideal centre from which to tour the volcanoes of Cantal and enjoy rambling in the surrounding State-owned forest. In August there is a large influx of music lovers who come to enjoy the International Festival of World Music and Dance. *R. du fg-Notre-Dame, 15300 MURAT,* ☎ *04 71 20 09 47. www.murat.com*

Diatom processing – At the bottom of the valley, powerful chimneys expel water vapour in an often spectacular way. They belong to the factories of the Celite company which treats 200t of diatomite every day. Diatom is a silica-rich earth extracted from a seam at Foufouilloux (4km/3mi away), containing thousands of fossilised microscopic algae. It is known for its isolating properties and is used in the filtering of foodstuffs and in certain industrial situations but is indispensable to the chemical and pharmaceutical industries. Crushing and drying processes (the earth contains 60% humidity) precedes the final calcination. Over half of the 60t produced goes to the beer-producing regions in Northern Europe.

Nothing is impregnable to the French – The **Count of Anterroches,** who was born near Murat, is remembered for his reply to the proposal by the English, at Fontenoy, to fire first: "Gentlemen, we never fire first. Fire yourselves." This was not simply a gesture of courtesy but rather an application of the tactic by which troops would come under fire first and then march on the enemy while the latter were reloading their muskets. Anterroches is also credited with another famous saying: as he stood before Maastricht, someone declared that the town was impregnable; "Nothing", replied Anterroches, "is impregnable to the French."

Murat

Town Walk

There are explanatory panels throughout the medieval town; a brochure is available from the tourist office.

Église Notre-Dame-des-Oliviers

The church dates from the late Gothic period but has a modern west front. The central chapel in the north aisle contains a picture by the Spanish School depicting an episode from the life of St Dominic: his pilgrimage to Santiago de Compostela. Another chapel situated in the north aisle has a Black Virgin (a copy of the original stolen in 1983) which is the subject of an annual ceremony.

Halle

This covered market is a fine example of 19C ironwork architecture.

Former Bailiff's Court

The building dates from the 16C and opens onto rue de l'Argenterie through a doorway decorated with moulding.

Maison Rodier

This elegant Renaissance style building has some attractive bonding in trachyte (a type of volcanic rock) and a corbelled watchtower.

Consul's Residence

Faubourg Notre-Dame. The late-15C stone façade has two storeys with narrow windows topped by an ornament. Note the two carved angels above the door, part of which consists of linenfold panels.

Rocher de Bonnevie

The sides of this hill feature strange basalt columns which are remarkable for the uniformity and length of their prisms. A castle once stood on the hill but it was razed to the ground on the orders of Richelieu; it did, however, take six months and six hundredweight of gunpowder to complete the task.

A statue of Our Lady of Upper Auvergne, clad in white, now stands on the site of the former castle. There is a fine view over Murat, the Alagnon Valley, the mountains of Cantal and the Chevade Valley.

Additional Sight

Maison de la Faune

🕒 *School holidays: 10am-noon, 2-6pm; outside school holidays: 10am-noon, 2-5pm, Sun 2-5pm (Jul and Aug: 10am-noon, 3-7pm); guided tours available (1hr30min).* 🕒 *Closed mid-Nov to late Dec, Christmas and New Year's Day 5€ (children 3€).* ☎ *04 71 20 00 52.*

This former mansion has retained a late-15C turret. Inside, a large collection of beetles and butterflies, stuffed birds and animals are displayed in reconstructions of their natural environment.

Excursions

Église de Bredons★

SE along D 926. Apply to the town hall. ☎ *04 71 20 02 80.*

The small fortified 11C church is all that remains of the Benedictine priory. The doorway on the south side has billet moulding. Inside, note the monumental giltwood altarpiece completed in 1710 for the High Altar; the intricate detail and abundance of gold and polychrome make this a grandiose piece of decoration. The Resurrection is depicted in the centre. Other giltwood altar screens decorate the chapels.

Albepierre-Bredons★

5km/3mi SW on D 39. This tiny village built on a volcanic hill overlooks the Alagnon Valley. Underground houses were once built into the caves in the rock. From the top of the village, there is an interesting view of Murat below and of the Rocher de Bonnevie in the distance.

AL FRESCO

◷◷ **Le Jarrousset** – *3km/1.8mi E of Murat via N 122 dir. Clermont-Ferrand - ☎ 04 71 20 10 69 - www.restaurant-le-jarrousset.com - closed 12 Nov-15 Jan, Tue except Jul-Aug and Mon.* This rural restaurant in a pavilion set back a bit from the road has a contemporary-style dining room with a veranda giving onto the garden and a terrace in summer. Their fixed-price lunch menus will allow you to enjoy refined fare without having to break open the piggy bank.

CHÂTEAU DE MUROL★★

MICHELIN MAP 326: E-9 – 5KM/3MI W OF ST-NECTAIRE
LOCAL MAP SEE BESSE-EN-CHANDESSE

The 13C castle stands on top of a picturesque hill covered with a thick layer of basalt, close to the pleasant Lac Chambon. *R. Jassaguet, 63790 MUROL, ☎ 04 73 88 62 62. www.grandevallee.com*

A Bit of History

It was a descendant of the lords of Murol, Guillaume de Sam, an erudite baron and patron of the arts, who completed the original, inner fortress by building the keep, the second chapel and the eastern buildings. The castle, after passing into the hands of the powerful D'Estaing family in the 15C, was lavishly ornamented and, at the beginning of the following century, encircled by a huge curtain wall flanked with towers.

Murol emerged victorious from a siege during the time of the Catholic League. Peril having been averted, Jean d'Estaing foresook his vast abode and built the charming pavilion at the foot of the inner castle. Abandoned some time afterwards, Murol was spared by Richelieu because of the D'Estaing family's influence at court. After being used as a prison for some time, it became a robbers' hideout during the Revolution. During the 19C it fell into ruin and the inhabitants of the region came here looking for building stone. Its classification as a historical monument put an end to the pillaging.

A Proud Fortress★★

◷ *Apr-Jun and Sep-Oct: daily, 10am-12.30pm, 1.30-6.30pm; Jul-Aug: Wed-Sat, 10am-7pm; Nov-Mar: Sat, Sun, public and school holidays, 2-5pm.* ◷*Closed 14 Jul. 8€ (children: 5€). ☎ 04 73 88 67 11. www.chateaudemurol.com*

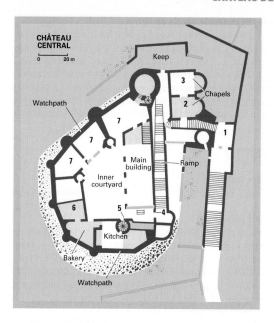

In recent years, extensive alterations have been made to the castle. Guided tours and colourful evening shows are organized by the *Compagnons de Gabriel* to provide an authentic medieval atmosphere. Visitors pass through the outer curtain wall through a fortified gatehouse on the southside, passing the Murol tower on the right. The Renaissance Pavilion (**1**) stands in the outer courtyard (the windows provide an attractive view of the Capitaine tower).

To the north is the inner castle (Château Central), its 10m/33ft walls rising above a 15m/49ft-thick basalt base. Next to the keep, connected to a tower of smaller dimensions by a curtain wall, are the chapels. The first (**2**) was built in the 13C; the second (**3**) in the 15C, and though of greater proportions is less graceful. A stepped ramp leads up to an elegant door (**4**) decorated with the Murol and Gaspard d'Estaing coats of arms. In the inner courtyard, note the gallery once surmounted by the Knights' Hall followed by the guard-room.

Take the spiral stairway of the Chautignat tower up to the terrace from which there is a very beautiful **panorama**★ of Murol, the Couze Valley, Lake Chambon, the Dore mountain range and Tartaret volcano. The watch-path leads to the Châtelaine tower (note the 16C door **5**). Next come the kitchen, the bakery and its outbuildings (**6**). The adjacent rooms (**7**) were living quarters.

▶ *On leaving the castle, walk down to the village via a footpath running alongside a small zoo(800m/875yd). Cross the road and walk through the gate leading into the Parc Municipal.*

Parc municipal du Prélong

Once part of a private estate (the house now contains the Musée des Peintres de l'école de Murols), the park boasts a beautiful collection of azaleas, rhododendrons and camellias. The French-style garden has alleyways lined with box trees leading to the rose-garden, offering a striking contrast with the English-style park. An interesting botanical trail runs across a 3ha/7.40-acre area. At the entrance stands the **Chaumière** (🕐 *Daily 3-6pm*) which houses a small archaeological collection (Gallo-Roman finds excavated locally).

Musée des Peintres de l'école de Murols

🕐 *Jun-Oct: daily 10am-noon, 2-6pm; Nov-May: Sat-Sun and school holidays except Tue, 2-6pm.* 🕐 *Closed 1 Jan, 1 May, 25 Dec. 4€. ☏ 04 73 88 60 06. www.musee-murol.net* At the turn of the 20C, some 50 landscape painters found inspiration in and around the village. Gathered round Abbé Boudal, who was the initiator of this artistic movement, and V Charenton who was its leader, this group of artists was close to two contemporary trends, Impressionism and Fauvism. The permanent collection is displayed in five rooms and another room is reserved for temporary exhibitions.

Excursions

Puy de Bessolles★

2km/1mi S on D 5. 🚶 *See BESSE-EN-CHANDESSE: Exploring the Couze Valleys.*

Lac Chambon★★

1.5km/0.9mi W along D 996. The lake was formed by the Tartaret volcano, one of the youngest in the Auvergne, which erupted in the middle of the Couze Valley and stemmed the flow of water. It is a vast (60ha/148 acres) but fairly shallow lake (12m/39ft deep) lying in a very attractive setting at an altitude of 877m/2 880ft. It is dotted with tiny islands and has an extremely jagged shoreline, except on the north side where it is skirted by D 996 and to the south-east where there is a large beach.

Saut de la Pucelle

To the north of the lake is a slender rocky peak known as the Saut de la Pucelle (Maiden's Leap) which rises to a height of almost 100m/328ft; it is all that remains of the ancient **Dent du Marais** volcano (🚶 *1hr 30min on foot there and back*). It is said that a young shepherdess who was being assiduously

> 🍽️ **Le Pavillon Bleu** – *Le Lac Chambon - 63790 Chambon-sur-Lac -* ☏ *04 73 85 89 52. http://perso.orange. fr/pavillonbleumartin -* 🍴 *- 3 rms.* Right on the lake, this house offers three wood-panelled bedrooms (two with a balcony giving onto the water), each with a different decoration scheme. Hearty breakfasts are served in a verdant sitting room embellished by aquariums.

Lac Chambon

J. Damase/MICHELIN

courted by a nobleman against her wishes threw herself off the top of the cliff but miraculously reached the bottom without injury. She was unwise enough to tell her disbelieving companions about the exploit and, in an effort to convince them of the truth of her tale, jumped off the cliff again; this time, she crashed to the ground and was killed.

Chambon-sur-Lac

The village lies at the end of the Couze de Chaudefour, in a mountainous area to the west of the lake, and consists of a group of houses huddling round the church.

Church

This 12C building, which was partly engulfed by floodwater from the Couze, has a lintel over the main doorway decorated with a carving of the martyrdom of St Stephen. On the square is a haloed cross dating from the 15C.

In the graveyard at the end of the path forking off to the left of the Murol road (some 200m/220yd from Chambon) stands a funeral chapel decorated on the outside with coloured motifs. Inside are a number of curious capitals.

Chambon-des-Neiges ❄

The tiny skiing resort of Chambon-des-Neiges (Chambon 1200 and Chambon 1400) lies high above the Chaudefour Valley (see Massif du SANCY). The resort is equipped with snow-making facilities; it has a number of pistes designed for both Alpine skiing and cross-country skiing.

ORCIVAL ★★

POPULATION 244

MICHELIN MAP 326: E-8 – 27KM/16.8MI SW OF CLERMONT-FERRAND

Orcival, a small town in a cool valley watered by the River Sioulet, has a superb Romanesque church founded by monks from La Chaise-Dieu. 🚹 *Le Bourg, 63210 ORCIVAL,* ☎ *04 73 65 89 77. www.terresdomes-sancy.com*

Basilique Notre-Dame ★★

Guided tours available starting at 3pm, contact the parish priest, ☎ *04 73 65 81 49 or 04 73 65 91 00.*

This grey mass of volcanic andesite was probably erected during the first half of the 12C and, judging by its remarkable stylistic unity, was the result of uninterrupted construction.

Exterior

The many tiers of the rear part of the building rise attractively up to the spire (truncated during the Revolution) of the octagonal two-storey bell tower with its twin openings. The very beautiful, although sparsely decorated, east end has four radiating apsidal chapels; one

Notre-Dame

J. Damase/MICHELIN

of these, on the south side, encompasses the crypt level.

The panels of the three doors still have their Romanesque hinges and ironwork; the most elaborate, with ornamental foliage and human heads, are on the south door (known as St John's door). In thanksgiving for released prisoners, chains have been hung from the blind arcades in the southern part of the transept, next to the entrance. A high gable wall forms the west façade.

> ⊜ **Chambre d'hôte Château de Voissieux** – 63210 St-Bonnet-près-Orcival - 4km/2.4mi NE of Orcival via D 27 and D 556 - ☎ 04 73 65 81 02 - closed Nov-Jan - 🍽 - 3 rms. Nestling in a park in the heart of the Auvergne countryside, a B&B in a 13C château built of volcanic stone. A fine staircase leads to very peaceful, cosy guestrooms that are furnished without excess. The kitchen features a splendid fireplace.

Interior

The most striking features are the slender pillars and the way the light disperses through the church, through an increasing number of windows from the nave to the transept, culminating in the chancel where most of the light is concentrated. Capitals of particular interest are to be found in the ambulatory (carved with fabulous animals, birds, fish and demons) and in the nave where most have foliate designs. Only one is historiated, that decorating the first pillar to the south, surmounted by the words "Fol Dives" and depicting the **Chastisement of the Miser.** The granite high altar rests on a serpentine marble base. Behind it, on a column, is a famous **Virgin Enthroned**★ with silver and gilt ornamentation. This venerated statue attracts numerous pilgrims, particularly on Ascension Thursday.

Under the chancel a vast, well-lit **crypt** reproduces the same plan. Note the gilt-lead altar (a modern work by the sculptor Kaeppelin) and a charming wooden 14C Virgin with Child.

Excursion

Château de Cordès

2.5km/1.5mi N along D 27. 🕐 Guided tours (30min) 10am-noon, 2-6pm. Unaccompanied tours of the gardens. 5€. ☎ 04 73 65 81 34.

An avenue lined with hedgerows enclosing two beautiful formal flowerbeds designed by André Le Nôtre (17C) leads up to this charming 13C-15C manor house, restored in the 17C. Inside, the tour includes the drawing room with its plasterwork decoration, the dining room, and the basement rooms including a guard-room with an old well which still has its winch and wheel. The chapel contains the magnificent tombstone of Yves II of Allègre, who died in Ravenna in 1512, and a beautiful Carrara marble altarpiece.

AVEN D'ORGNAC★★★

MICHELIN MAP 331: I-8 – LOCAL MAP SEE GORGES DE L'ARDÈCHE

Until 19 August 1935 the people of Orgnac-l'Aven had paid little attention to the swallow-hole known to them as "Le Bertras." **Robert de Joly** (1887-1968), President of the Speleology Society of France, who explored it at that time, then described its wealth of interesting features to them. He was an engineer with the College of Electricity in Paris and an enthusiastic potholer. He was also a daring explorer of this area of the Cévennes, where he lived, and he played a vital role in the development of equipment and techniques used in underground explorations. The huge chambers in the swallow-hole were formed by the action of underground water from infiltrations in the cracked limestone rocks. The first concretions, some of which were 10m/33ft in diameter, were broken by an earthquake at the end of the Tertiary Era. These truncated or overturned columns then became the base for more recent stalagmites.

A Fantastic Underground Maze

Temperature below earth 13°C/55°F. 🕐 *Guided tours (1hr) Jul-Aug: 9.30am-8pm; Apr-Jun and Sep: 9.30am-5.30pm; Oct to mid-Nov: 9.30am-noon, 2-5.15pm; Feb-Mar and Christmas holidays: 10.30am-noon, 2-4.45pm.* 🕐 *Mid-Nov to end Jan. Cave and museum: 10€ (children: 6€).* ☎ *04 75 38 65 10. www.orgnac.com*

The **Upper Chamber** (Salle Supérieure) is amazing for its sheer size (height : 17-40m/56-131ft; length: 250m/ 820ft; width: 125m/410ft) and the views in and around it. The dim light from the natural mouth of the swallow-hole gives it a bluish tinge that appears somewhat unreal. It contains a number of magnificent stalagmites, in an incredible variety of shapes. The largest (in the centre) have the appearance of pine cones. For the most part, the height of the gallery roof has prevented stalagmites from joining up with the stalactites overhead to form columns; instead they have thickened at their base until some reach quite impressive dimensions. Other, more slender stalagmites look like piles of plates, as a result of the slow oozing of water through the high, thin roof. Beneath the lower sections of cave roof are slim candle-like formations, with straight or tapering sides.

In the niche of a huge formation of draperies and stalagmites like organ pipes is an urn containing the heart of Robert de Joly.

In the **Rockfall Chamber** (Salle du Chaos), filled with concretions from the Upper Chamber, there are magnificent

S. Van Poucke/AVEN D'ORGNAC

Upper Chamber, Aven d'Orgnac

"drapes" of various colours – white, red and brown – hanging from a crack in the cave roof.

The **Red Chamber** (Salle Rouge) has a fantastic decor centred around colossal pillars of calcite. It owes its name to the layer of clay, the residue of the dissolving calcite, which covers floor, walls and concretions alike.

The climax of the tour is the **Grand Theatre** viewpoint overlooking a huge chamber which, at first, is in total darkness; however, music gradually fills the cave and, combined with light effects underlining details round the rock walls, creates a spellbinding atmosphere.

Rando' souterraine

🕐 *July and Aug: by appointment. Groups of 4 to 8 persons over 10 years of age. From 40€. ☎ 04 75 38 65 10. www.orgnac.com*

Cave enthusiasts may like to take part in this 3-hour underground ramble, available to groups of restricted size only, through the red chambers, a magnificent part of the cavern which has been left as it was when discovered apart from the installation of electric lighting. This walk is an ideal compromise between standard guided tours of caves and full-blown potholing "in the raw," and is not unduly problematic or physically taxing.

Odysséee souterraine

🕐 *all year: by appointment. Individuals, or groups of 4 to 8 persons over 14 years of age. Individuals, 60€; groups from 55€. ☎ 04 75 38 65 10. www.orgnac.com*

This 8-hour potholing adventure is only suitable for visitors in good physical condition: one day spent exploring parts of this vast underground network left in their natural state, under the supervision of a fully qualified guide.

Musée de Préhistoire

♿🕐*Same admission times and charges as the cave (see above). ☎ 04 75 38 65 10. www.orgnac.com*

The rooms, laid out around a patio, contain the finds from archaeological digs in Ardèche and the north of Gard. They date from the Lower Palaeolithic to the Iron Age (from 350 000 to 600 years BC). Reconstructions, including an Acheulian hut from Orgnac 3, a flint workshop and a cave decorated with a Lion's Head provide an insight into the everyday life of prehistoric man.

Excursions

1 Gorges de l'Ardèche, Route panoramique★★★

38km/24mi itinerary, 👣 see Gorges de l'ARDÈCHE.

2 Plateau d'Orgnac

45km/28mi itinerary starting from Aven d'Orgnac; local map 👣 see Gorges de l'ARDÈCHE.

Barjac

The narrow streets of the upper town, lined with fine 18C houses surround the castle now a cultural centre (cinema and multimedia library). From the esplanade overlooking the valley, there is a fine view of the Cévennes mountains. Twice a year (Easter weekend and around 15 August), Barjac holds an antique fair which attracts enthusiasts and specialists from all over the region.

▶ *Follow D 979 N; in Vagnas, turn right onto D 355.*

Labastide-de-Virac

This fortified village on the boundary between the Languedoc and Vivarais regions is an ideal departure point for outings to the Aveyron gorge or the Orgnac plateau. Just north of the village stands a 15C castle, the **Château des Roure** (🕐 *Mid-Apr to Jun and Sep: daily except Wed. 2-6pm (Jul and Aug: daily 10am-7pm). 6€ (ticket including Musée de la Soie: 8€). ☎ 04 75 38 61 13. www.chateaudesroure.com)*, which guarded the passage through the gorge at the Pont-d'Arc. The two round towers were pulled down in 1629 during the Wars of Religion. Since 1825, the castle has belonged to the family of sculptor James Pradier (1795-1825) whose forebears were tenant farmers to the counts of Roure; he carved the statues representing Lille and Strasbourg on place de la Concorde in Paris. The tour takes in the Florentine courtyard, a spiral staircase and the great hall with its fine chimney-piece. The castle watch-path overlooks the Ardèche and Gras plateaux, and in fine weather Mont Lozère and Mont Mézenc can be seen to the north. The tour ends with an exhibition of handmade silk goods. A working silkworm farm illustrates traditional methods of silkworm breeding.

▸ *Beyond Labastide, turn left off D 217.*

The road runs through **Les Crottes**, a ruined village *(partly restored)* destroyed during the Second World War. A stele commemorates the inhabitants who were shot by the Nazis on 3 March 1944. Continue to the **Belvédère du Méandre de Gaud**. This promontory commands an excellent **view**★★ of the Ardèche and the Gaud cirque.

▸ *Drive back to D 217 and turn left; a minor road on the right leads to Aven de la Forestière.*

Aven de la Forestière★

🕐 *Apr-Sep: guided tours (1hr) 10am-7pm. 6€ (children: 4€). ☎ 04 75 38 63 08. www. laforestiere.net*
This cavern, first explored by A Sonzogni in 1966, was opened to tourists in 1968. It is not far below ground and is easily accessible. The cleverly lit chambers contain a wealth of fine concretions in interesting shapes and subtle colours. A small underground zoo is home to a variety of fish, shellfish, frogs, toads and insects.

LAC DE PALADRU ★

MICHELIN MAP 333: G-5

Lake Paladru (390ha/964 acres) lies at the bottom of a depression originally formed by a glacier, surrounded by the green hills of Lower Dauphiné. The lake, mainly supplied by rain and snow, has a tributary at its southern end, the Fure, which flows down to the River Isère. Its beautiful emerald waters form a lovely stretch 6km/4mi long which, during summer months, attracts many watersports enthusiasts and ramblers from Lyon and the Dauphiné region. Anglers will find a wide variety of fish to test their skill, including char and freshwater crayfish.

The hillside farms overlooking the lake and Upper Bourbre Valley will appeal to those interested in traditional rural architecture: these houses are remarkable for their imposing eaves, sometimes reaching over the barn almost right down to the ground. The walls are made of mud, sometimes combined with shingle.

EATING OUT

Hôtel Les Bains – *345 r. Principale - 38850 Charavines - 1km/0.6mi S of Lac de Pal-adru via D 50 -* ☎ *04 76 06 60 20 - hotel.desbains@wanadoo.fr - closed 1 Jan to 14 Feb.* Don't be misled by the name – it's not a bath that awaits you here, but a meal. This restaurant's appealing, old-fashioned decor – parquet, bistro furnishings, flowered plates – is most enjoyable. Traditional cuisine with one speciality: *la friture,* tiny fish fried whole.

WHERE TO STAY

Chambre d'hôte Mme Ferrard – *145 chemin de Béluran, lieu-dit Vers-Ars - 38730 Le Pin - 1km/0.6mi SW of the Lac de Paladru via D 50 -* ☎ *04 76 06 68 82 - - 5 rms - meals* This old farm, being restored progressively, looks out over the Lac de Paladru on one side, and fields and forests on the other. Nearly all of the comfy, cosy bedrooms enjoy a view of the emerald-coloured waters; three come equipped with a kitchenette.

Wood Civilisation

The southern part of Lake Paladru harbours two extremely interesting submerged archaeological sites. Far from reinforcing the existence of lake dwelling communities (houses built on stilts), the discovery of a large number of piles and planks emerging at low water level proves the existence of houses built directly on lacustrian chalk shoals which were affected on several occasions by variations in the level of the lake.

The variety and abundance of the remains discovered as well as an analysis of pollen contained in the sediment have helped define the nature of the surrounding forest mantle and the daily activities of the inhabitants, who were mostly woodlanders. Wood, which was abundant in the region, was used for numerous purposes, including building and domestic items.

Summer resort of "Les Baigneurs"

This is a Neolithic farming village that underwent two successive phases of occupation around the year 2700 BC, both connected with the Saône-Rhône civilization. The presence of axe handles, wooden spoons, flint stones, spindle-whorls and charred debris indicate the practice of several different crafts as well as burn-beating after deforestation–fertilisation of the soil by burning felled trees – in preparation for cropping (wheat, poppies, flax).

Village of Colletière

This site to the south, currently under 6m/20ft of water, reveals a fortified village set up towards the end of the 10C, following a considerable drop in the level of the lake as a result of the climate warming up. The inhabitants were forced to abandon their belongings and flee the village in early 1000, however, after a sudden rise in the water level. Colletière is of great archaeological interest because the total immersion of the site has protected it from pillage or decay.

The inhabitants were farmers, stock-breeders and fishermen. The discovery of riding equipment, lances and heavier weapons would indicate that there were knights with regular military duties whose task was to protect the community. The peas-ant-fisherfolk of Colletière were thus also warriors. This pre-feudal society was governed by egalitarian laws concerning work and seems to have been more than able to provide for all its needs. The good condition of the dwellings has enabled specialists to reconstruct the original dwellings with a good degree of accuracy, using a model to represent the three buildings identified. Archaeologists believe that the village accommodated around 100 people. The lakeside environment has preserved numerous everyday objects, usually too fragile to survive to modern times: such as intact leather shoes, textiles, rare wooden musical instruments (tambourine, oboe, mouthpiece of some bagpipes), games (a complete chess set) and even toy weapons (crossbow). The study of the remains of food and of other debris suggests that tasks were equally shared by members of the community and that there was little or no hierarchy.

Towards 1040, and the abandonment of the lakeside villages, the colonisation of the lake shores continued with earth castles *(mottes castrales)* being built on the neighbouring hills or slopes. Many were replaced by stone constructions in the 12C and became the strongholds of the great Dauphiné families – the Tour de Clermont (& *see below*), Les Trois Croix (in Paladru), Château de Virieu, La Louvatière and Château de Montclar.

Around The Lake

Musée du Lac de Paladru

🕐 *Jul-Aug: daily except Mon, 3-7pm; May: Sat, Sun and public holidays, 2-6pm; Jun and Sep: daily except Mon, 2-6pm. 3€ (12-18s, 2€).* ☎ *04 76 55 77 47. www.museelacde-paladru.com*

This museum displays the finds of underwater archaeological excavations of the drowned Neolithic and medieval villages. Superb models and audio-visual presentations help to evoke the way of life for local people during these two periods of transition in the lake's history.

Tour of lake★

Leaving from Charavines, a number of easy walks are possible, giving good views of the lake and surrounding countryside. It is possible to walk all round the lake *(for details ask at the tourist office in Paladru)*. The Maison du Pays d'Art et d'Histoire de Paladru organises **heritage trails (visites-découvertes du patrimoine** – *The Pays du lac de Paladru-Les Trois Vals, which is listed as a "Town of Art and History," offers discovery tours (2hr) conducted by guide-lecturers approved by the Ministry of Culture and Communication. 5€. Information at the Musée du lac de Paladru in Charavines).* Two scenic roads – D 50 and D 50^D *(which becomes D 90)* – encircle the lake (15km/9.5mi). They connect the lively resort of **Charavines** on the southern point of the lake to the more peaceful village of Paladru at the other end. Along the walk, it is possible to see swans and other forms of birdlife making their home among the reeds on the lake shore.

Taking the A 48 motorway towards Chambéry *(signposted route)*, note the purity of line of the 16C **Silve Bénite** (Tithe Barn) which houses temporary exhibitions in season.

F. da Costa

Paladru Lake archaeological site

Excursions

Tour de Clermont

🚶 *45min. From Charavines, take the footpath along the Fure as far as the D 50 bridge, then take the trail waymarked in yellow off to the left which goes uphill through fields. After going through the hamlet of La Grangière, take the path on the left up to the Tour de Clermont.*

This proud 13C pentagonal keep with three storeys is all that remains of the powerful stronghold of Clermont, destroyed at the beginning of the 17C. The top of the tower has disappeared, and the doorway was knocked out after the original date of construction (before this, a footbridge was lowered from the first floor). This was the residence of one of the oldest families of the Dauphiné, which would marry into Burgundy to give rise to the Clermont-Tonnerre branch of the family.

La Croix des Cochettes

🚶 *45min. This is a steeper walk than the one described above, but it is better signposted. From the car park in Colletière, take the footpath uphill, waymarked in orange, towards Louisias. Where the land levels out, turn E along the hillside to join a footpath waymarked in blue which leads to the Cochettes Cross.*

Admire the panoramic view of the lake.

Château de Virieu★

7.5km/5mi NW on D 17. ♿🕐 *Mid-Apr to Oct: guided tours (45m) Sat-Sun and public holidays 2-6pm (Jul-Aug: daily except Mon). 6€ (children: 3€).* ☎ *04 74 88 27 32. www.chateau-de-virieu.com*

The castle overlooking the Upper Bourbre Valley dates from the 11C to 18C, and was restored at the beginning of the 20C; it still looks like a fortress.

Note, in particular, the ancient 15C kitchen with its huge flattened arch, and a plaque bearing the original coat of arms of the Carthusian Order, the Great Hall, and the bedroom where Louis XIII slept in 1622 on his way back from Montpellier after signing the peace treaty. During his stay in Virieu he donated several cannon which have been preserved, together with their fleur-de-lis mounts, under the arcades of the inner courtyard.

PÉROUGES★★

POPULATION 1 103

MICHELIN MAP 328: E-5 – LOCAL MAP SEE LA DOMBES

Pérouges is perched on a hilltop and surrounded by ramparts; it remains a model of medieval architecture, with narrow winding streets and ancient houses, making it very popular with visitors.

Pérouges has such an authentic historical flavour that it is often used as the setting for period films by French directors. 🖪 *Entrée de la Cité, 01800 PÉROUGES,* ☎ *04 74 61 01 14.*

▶ **Orient yourself:** Pérouges is not very large, so a good place to start is at the very heart, in the beautiful market square.
☺ **Don't miss:** place de la Halle.
🅿 **Parking:** There is limited parking, but you will find a car park near the church.
🕐 **Organising you time:** allow 2h to explore the town
♿ **Also see:** Crémieu, la Dombes, Mont-d'Or Lyonnais, Morestel

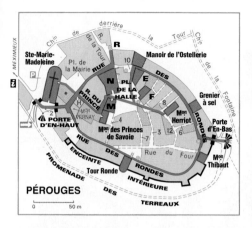

PÉROUGES

Boulevard	2
Brune R. de la	3
Contreforts R. des	4
Filaterie R. de la	6
Halle-au-Four R.	7
Herriot R. É.	8
Place R. de la	10
Tambour R. du	12

Maison Cazin	E
Maison du Vieux-St-Georges	F
Musée du Vieux-Pérouges	M
Ostellerie	N
Puits de la Tour	R

Grandeur and decadence – During the Middle Ages and up to the French annexation (1601) the town was disputed many times by the sovereigns of Dauphiné and Savoy; the siege of 1468 remains famous as one such episode. Claude Fabre de Vaugelas (1585-1650), the famous Academician and arbiter of French grammar, was one of the barons of Pérouges.

In the rich and active town centre, hundreds of craftsmen wove fabric from hemp grown in the surrounding fields.

In the 19C the town's prosperity waned considerably: Pérouges was too far from the railway line and local craftsmen could no longer compete with industry. From the 1 500 people who lived here during its days of glory, the population fell to 90.

In 1909-10 the town nearly disappeared altogether: many of the owners turned to mass destruction and entire blocks of old houses were pulled down. Fortunately, an historical society from Lyon and a few artists from Pérouges stepped in, helped by the School of Arts. The most interesting houses were bought, sensitively restored, and classified as historical monuments. Thus the main part of the town was saved. This effort to safeguard the town's history continues under the auspices of the Historical Pérouges Committee and the inhabitants.

Old streets, old houses – Most of the houses in Pérouges, rebuilt after the 1468 siege, mark the transition between the Gothic and Renaissance styles. Many feature basket-handle arches and rectangular windows with stone latticework, often joined in twos or threes. The houses of the gentry and richer townsfolk can be recognised by their large dimensions and luxurious interiors: spacious rooms with high ceilings, carved beams, monumental fireplaces, frescoes both inside and out. The houses of the artisans and merchants were more modest, with semicircular openings to light the workshop or serve as counters to display their goods. The oldest houses are half-timbered, with projecting upper storeys. The streets have barely changed since the Middle Ages. Narrow and winding, they had double-sloping paving with a drainage channel in the middle. The roofs, with their large eaves, protected the inner side of the pavement, reserved for people enjoying prestige; the commoners had to give way to them and walk in the middle of the street.

Walking Tour★★

Park outside the town wall to the left of the church or in the car park downhill.

Place de la Halle

Corrieras/CONOS, Lyon

Porte d'En-Haut★

This Upper Gateway, the main entrance to Pérouges, was also the most exposed, due to the gentle slope of the land. Its defence was reinforced by the fortress-church and a barbican. A house, Maison Vernay, can be seen through the Gothic doorway. From the forecourt, there is an attractive view of the countryside on the other side of the moat.

Rue du Prince★

This was once the main road. Butchers, basket-makers, drapers, the armourer and apothecary held shop here. The stone tables of the street stalls can still be seen. At one end stands the **Maison des Princes de Savoie** (Combined visit with the musée du Vieux-Pérouges), which presently houses a museum (& see below).

Place de la Halle★★★

This market square is one of the prettiest in France. It derives its name from the covered markets or **Halles** which stood here and were burnt to the ground in 1839. The splendid lime tree in the middle is a Liberty Tree planted in 1792 in commemoration of the French Revolution. The houses lining the square are quite charming.

Ostellerie

This inn has a sign bearing the town's coat of arms. The half-timbered east façade is 13C whereas the south front is Renaissance. The main room on the ground floor has a 15C monumental fireplace as well as furniture and ceramics from Bresse.

Musée du Vieux-Pérouges

🕐 Guided visit (45m): Apr-Sep: 10am-noon, 2-6pm. 4€. ☏ 04 74 61 00 88.

This museum is housed partly in the Maison des Princes de Savoie and in the Maison Heer which opens onto place de la Halle through an arcade with Gothic pillars. The museum collections illustrate the history and archaeology of Dombes and Bresse and include engravings, utensils, furniture and fine pottery; a weaver's workshop with a loom has been recreated on the ground floor.

From the watchtower there is a **panoramic view** of the town's red roofs and chimneys, with the Bugey mountains in the distance and, below, the hortulus (medieval garden) of the Maison des Princes de Savoie.

Maison du Vieux-St-Georges

A shell-shaped niche on the façade houses an unusual wooden 15C statue of St George, patron saint of Pérouges, mounted on a horse.

▶ *Take the narrow street which goes downhill from the corner of the square.*

Maison Herriot

This is a very sumptuous-looking house with large windows (semicircular on the ground floor, mullioned on the first floor).

▶ *Return to the square and take rue de la Place, to the N.*

Maison Cazin

This, one of the loveliest houses in Pérouges, has projecting upper floors and half-timbering. The semicircular windows on the ground floor are latticed.

▶ *Turn right onto rue des Rondes.*

Opposite Maison Cazin, with its back to the northern ramparts, stands the **Manoir de l'Ostellerie,** once known as Maison Messimy.

Rue des Rondes★

This street still has most of its ancient paving and central drainage channel. The old houses on either side, including the **Grenier à Sel** (Salt Store) and **Maison Thibaut,** are protected by wide eaves.

Porte d'En-Bas

The Lower Gateway is older than the Upper Gateway, and of semicircular design. On the outside there is an inscription referring to the 1468 siege, in rather approximate Latin, which can be translated as follows: "Pérouges of the Pérougians! Impregnable town! Those rascally Dauphinois wanted to take it but they could not. So they went off with the doors, the hinges and the locks instead. May the devil take them!" The gateway commands an attractive **view**★ of the surrounding countryside, the Bugey mountains and, in fine weather, the Alps.

▶ *Rue des Rondes leads round to place de l'Église.*

Église Ste-Marie-Madeleine

This 15C church looks like a fortress with its north-western wall incorporating crenellations, arrow slits and very high, narrow openings. The belfry, destroyed during the Revolution, was rebuilt under the Empire and given the four-webbed vault typical of the Franche-Comté. The watch-path, which went right round the curtain wall, continues through the church above the side vaults and along the galleries on the façade. Inside, note the set of emblazoned keystones; the central vault, in particular, has the blazon of the House of Savoy and the symbols of the four Evangelists. On the right of the chancel stands a 17C polychrome wooden statue of St George.

Address Book

EATING OUT

☞ **Auberge du Coq** – *R. des Rondes -* ☎ *04 74 61 05 47 - closed Feb, Sun evening, Tue lunch from Apr to Nov and Sun evening, Mon, Tue from Dec to Apr.* Located in an alley paved with river stones, this restaurant reminds you of eateries of the past. The owner, an Italian from Pérouges, whips up some special dishes, including *soufflé de quenelles*, farm-raised chicken and frogs.

☞☞ **Auberge de Campagne du Mollard** – *01320 Châtillon-la-Palud – 13.6km/8mi NE of Pérouges via D 984 and D 904, dir. Chalamont, and road on left -* ☎ *04 74 35 66 09 -* ✄ *- reserv. required.* This farm settled amid the fields invites guests to stay over in its rooms furnished with attractive sculpted wood pieces. Enjoy an authentic farm meal served in the rustic dining room with a mezzanine.

WHERE TO STAY

☞ **Chambre d'hôte M. et Mme Debeney-Truchon** – *'L'Hôpital' - 01150 Chazey-sur-Ain - 9km/5.4mi E of Pérouges. Take N 84, then D 40 and secondary road -* ☎ *04 74 61 95 87 -* ✄ *- 6 rms.* Come to this village farm and be won over by the hearty reception and simplicity of the setting. Monsieur will be honoured to show you how he makes his bread.

☞☞☞☞ **Ostellerie du Vieux Pérouges** – ☎ *04 74 61 00 88 - thibaut@ostellerie.com -* 🅿 *- 15 rms -* 🛏 *12€ - restaurant* ☞☞☞. The fame of this magnificent manor in the heart of the village has spread beyond national borders since Bill Clinton dined here in 1997. There's no question that the Ostellerie, with its typically Bressan decor, is a fine place to stop. Two classes of rooms with prices to match.

▶ *Rejoin rue des Rondes which leads to rue de la Tour.*

Puits de la Tour

For a long time this well supplied water to the entire town. The tower built by the Romans was destroyed in 1749 (the presbytery occupies part of the site). A lantern in the upper part of the tower was used to send light signals to similar towers forming a relay right to Lyon.

The two curtain walls

The path uphill from the Upper Gateway leads to **Promenade des Terreaux**★ in the moat of the outer curtain wall of which there are now only vestigial remains; the inner curtain wall *(enceinte intérieure)* is almost complete, it serves as a foundation for the houses along rue des Rondes. The **Round Tower,** against which the house of the Sergeant of Justice is built, was formerly used as a prison.

Excursions

Montuel

9.5km/6mi. Leave Pérouges along N 84 towards Lyon. Montuel has retained several interesting buildings worth admiring. Take a stroll through the flower-decked town starting from the collegiate church of Notre-Dame-du-Marais (16C-17C) past the chapel of the former Visitation Convent (note the fine façade), then the 12C St-Stephen's porch, note the mullioned windows along Grande-Rue and do not miss the carved wood decoration of the **apothecary's shop** (🕐 *May-Oct: Wed and Sat 3-6pm; Nov-Apr: Sat 3-6pm.* 🕐 *Closed public holidays. 3€. Guided tours (45m).* ☎ *04 78 06 06 23).*

St-Maurice-de-Gourdans
12km/6.6mi S on D 65B. This village lies on the edge of a plateau dominating the confluence of the River Ain and the River Rhône. The 12C **church** has been cleverly restored to reveal its original masonry: limestone and stone chippings taken from the bed of the Rhône, with alternating layers of small bricks and flat pebbles. The **interior**★ is striking because of its old-fashioned appearance: the single nave is a long, low cradle resting on a series of blind arcades.

Centre Nucléaire de Production d'Electricité du Bugey
11km/6.8mi. Leave St-Maurice-de-Gourdans E along D 84; turn right onto D 65 towards Loyettes then left onto D 20 shortly before Loyettes.
Overlooked by the Île Crémieu, this nuclear power plant is located in **St-Vulbas,** on the right bank of the Rhône. The visit consists in a technical presentation of the plant, followed by a tour of some of its installations: cooling tower, turbine and condenser hall. The visit ends with an explanation of the control room simulator. The information centre provides documents on the production and consumption of energy, on nuclear technology and on the different types of power plants.

LE PILAT★★

MICHELIN MAP 327: F-7 TO G-8

The Massif du Pilat lies to the east of St-Étienne, between the Loire basin and the Rhône Valley. The influence of the Mediterranean to the east and the Atlantic to the west makes it something of a watershed, particularly at Chaubouret Pass (alt 1 363m/4 471ft); it also acts as a water tower for the St-Étienne region. The coolness of its fir plantations, swift streams and high pastures contrasts with the industrial aspect of the Ondaine, Janon and Gier valleys. Formation of the massif goes back to the Hercynian fold: it was then a high mountain with its folds lying in a south-west-north-east direction. During the Secondary Era, erosion reduced it to a plateau, sloping down towards the present-day Rhône Valley; the plateau was then covered with water leaving several layers of sediment. During the Tertiary Era, the water withdrew. The Alpine fold then caused subsidence of the Rhône Valley and tilting of the massif. Le Pilat, having been "rejuvenated," rose to an altitude of 1 500m/4 921ft while the rivers – the Gier in the north and the Limony in the south – slid to the foot of the faults. During the Quaternary Era, erosion took its toll once again.

The grass-covered summits – Crêt de la Perdrix culminating at 1 432m/4 698ft and Crêt de l'Œillon at 1 370m/4 495ft – bristle with strange piles of granite blocks called **chirats**, resulting from complete erosion of the summits.
Many rivers rise near the summits and flow rapidly down towards the Gier, the Rhône or the Loire along steep-sided valleys. The Gier itself, close to its source, crosses a *chirat* at the **Saut du Gier** falls.

A Tribute To Nature

Parc Naturel Régional du Pilat
Created in 1974, the park covers 65 000ha/160 610 acres and contains about 50 towns and villages in the Rhône and Loire *départements*. The countryside is extremely diverse: forests of beech and fir at high altitude, pastureland on the plateaux, orchards

Address Book

EATING OUT

Auberge Vernollon – *42220 Colombier-sous-Pilat - 8km/4.8mi E of Le Bessat. Take D 8, then D 63 towards Le Col de l'Œillon -* ☎ *04 77 51 56 58 - odilegrange@aol.com - closed 1 Dec to 28 Feb, Mon in summer and Mon-Fri lunch off-season - reserv. required.* While travelling on the road towards the summit of the Œillon, stop in at this old, tastefully restored farm. The patronne's able cuisine is delectable – to be enjoyed under the magnificent wood frame ceiling in the barn or on the terrace with a panoramic view. Dinner shows are organised in the spring. Three no-frills guest rooms.

Chanterelle – *Sagnemorte - 42520 Roisey -* ☎ *04 74 87 47 27 - granet. daniel@wanadoo.fr - closed Jan-Feb, Sun evening and Mon - reserv. required.* Located in a wooded, well-landscaped park, this stylish chalet looks out over a superb panorama of the Rhône Valley and the peaks of the Pilat. Classic cuisine with a special touch served in a contemporary setting.

WHERE TO STAY

Chambre d'hôte Le Moulin du Bost – *42131 La Valla-en-Gier - 13km/8mi N of Le Bessat. Take D 2, then D 76 after La Valla-en-Gier dir. Doizieux -* ☎ *04 77 20 06 62 - moulinbost@aol.com - closed 1 Nov to Easter -* 🛏 *- 3 rms - meals* 🍴🍽️. An impassioned trekker and member of the 'relais randonneurs' (lodgings for hikers), the owner of this house located in the Parc Naturel Régional du Pilat can recommend rambles adapted to your capacity and desires. Simple rooms and generous fare. An address for communing with nature.

Chambre d'hôte La Rivoire – *42220 St-Julien-Molin-Molette - 5km/3mi E of Bourg-Argental via N 82 -* ☎ *04 77 39 65 44 - info@larivoire.net -* 🛏 *- reserv. required in winter - 5 rms - meals* 🍴🍽️. What a charming house, with its round tower and generous vegetable garden! It dominates the Vallée de la Déôme - an ideal vantage point with a splendid view that can be admired from all the bedrooms and the terrace. A restful sojourn guaranteed.

Castel-Guéret – *42220 St-Julien-Molin-Molette - 1km/0.6mi N of St-Julien via D 8, dir. Le Bessat -* ☎ *04 77 51 56 04 -* 🛏 *- reserv. required - 5 rms - meals* 🍴🍽️. A noble 19C manor framed by a vast park. Carefully restored in the spirit of the era, the interior still has its original parquet floor. Bedrooms are furnished in Louis XV and Louis XVI styles; bathrooms have been allowed to join the present day.

and vineyards along the banks of the Rhône. Committed to preserving nature and the environment, Pilat Park promotes rural, craft, tourist and cultural activities.

Maison du Parc

Moulin de Virieu in Pélussin. 🕐 *Easter to mid-Nov: 9.30am-12.30pm, 2-6pm (Sat-Sun and public holidays 9.30am-12.30pm, 2-6.30pm); mid-Nov to Easter: daily except Sun 10am-12.30pm, 2-6pm (Fri 5pm, Tue 2-6pm). Reserve centre and tourist office, Moulin de Virieu 42410 Pélussin.* ☎ *04 74 87 52 00. www.parc-naturel-pilat.fr. Accompanied treks, discovery excursions, activities. Programme on request.*

The park's main information centre also organises exhibitions, special activities and hikes.

To facilitate an introduction to flora and fauna within the regional park there are 500km/310mi of marked footpaths (brown and white stripes), including sections of GR7 and GR42 (Grande Randonnée long-distance footpaths, marked with red and white stripes), three nature trails (each forming a 3-4km/1.9-2.5mi round trips, inquire at Maison du Parc) and eight special themed trails each identified by a number.

The **Jean-Jacques Rousseau trail,** from Condrieu to La Jasserie ① is a reminder that the philosopher and writer came to

The rolling landscape of the Pilat hills

Mont Pilat in 1769 for botanical reasons; the **flora trail** ⑨ takes the rambler quickly (22km/14mi) from the almost Mediterranean vegetation of the Malleval region to the subalpine formation of Perdrix ridge, from prickly pear to mountain tobacco. The **ornithological trail,** between St-Pierre-de-Bœuf and St-Sabin Chapel features up to 90 registered species of birds (particularly from mid-May to mid-June), including mallard on St-Pierre Lake, diving cingle near the torrents, crossbill in the fir forests and rock bunting on the gorse heath.

To promote traditional activities and revive near-forgotten crafts, the park has opened the **Maison des Arts et Traditions Populaires La Béate** (🕓 *Jul-Sep: Sun and public holidays, 2.30-6.30pm. No charge.* ☎ *04 77 51 24 70)* in Marlhes, the **Maison de la Passementerie** (trimmings – 🕓 *Early May to mid-Oct: Sat-Sun 2.30-6.30pm; other days by appointment. 2€.* ☎ *04 77 39 93 38)* in Jonzieux and the **Maison des Tresses et Lacets** (braids and ribbons – ♿🕓 *Jul-Aug: daily except Tue 2.30-6pm; Feb-Jun and Sep-Dec: daily except Tue and Sat 2.30-6pm. 4€ (children: 2.50€).* ☎ *04 77 20 91 06)* in La Terrasse-sur-Dorlay.

Tourist and sporting facilities include the St-Pierre-de-Bœuf Leisure Park which has an artificial river for canoeing and kayaking; the canoe base at Terrasse-sur-Dorlay; downhill skiing resorts at La Jasserie and Graix, and cross-country ski clubs at Le Bessat, Burdignes, St-Régis-du-Coin and St-Genest-Malifaux. Other sites are suitable for climbing, hang-gliding, cycling and orienteering. Mountain-biking facilities are being developed, with numerous waymarked tracks categorised by degree of difficulty.

Festivals such as Apple Day on 11 November at Pélussin (the headquarters of the park), the Farm Produce Fair in Bourg-Argental in June, the Wine Fair in Chavanay (second weekend in December) and the Cheese and Wine Fair in Condrieu (1 May) provide an introduction to local produce.

Excursion

From St-Étienne to Condrieu

89km/56mi – about 6hr, not including St-Étienne

▸ *Leave St-Étienne on D 8 SE.*

During the climb, the strategic site of Rochetaillée can be seen.

Rochetaillée

This is a small village perched on a narrow rocky channel between two ravines, below the ruins of a feudal castle.

Gouffre d'Enfer★★

1hr on foot there and back.

To the right of the inn, Auberge de la Cascade, a path follows the bed of the old torrent to the foot of the dam. The site is impressive: the heavily gouged walls of rock come together to form a dark, narrow gully, dramatically named **"Chasm of Hell."** The dam was built in 1866 to supply water to St-Étienne; steps lead up to the top of it. The reservoir laps the edges of fir-covered slopes. Some 50m/55yd on the left, steps lead to the **viewpoint** opposite Rochetaillée.

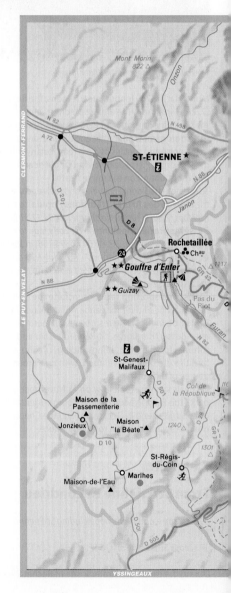

▶ *To get back to the car, turn left and follow the path on the right running past the Maison des Ponts et Chaussées.*

Beyond Rochetaillée, there are attractive views (right) over the dams of Gouffre d'Enfer and Pas-du-Riot.

Le Bessat ✳

Small summer and winter resort.

▶ *Beyond Le Bessat, take D 63 towards La Croix-de-Chaubouret.*

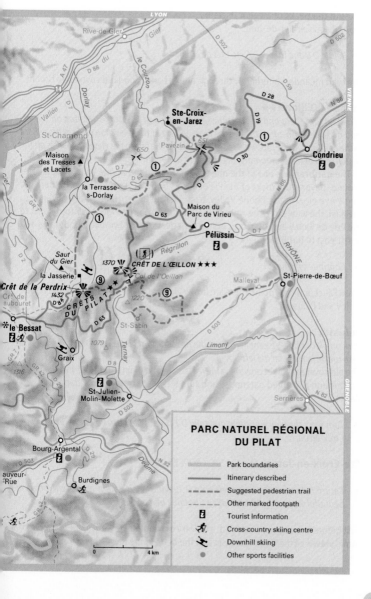

PARC NATUREL RÉGIONAL DU PILAT

Park boundaries
Itinerary described
Suggested pedestrian trail
Other marked footpath
🛈 Tourist Information
Cross-country skiing centre
Downhill skiing
Other sports facilities

Crêt de la Perdrix★

Just after La Croix-de-Chaubouret turn left onto D 8^A towards La Jasserie.
The road winds past spruce, mountain pastures and heathland.

▶ *After about 5km/3mi, at the top of the climb, park near the path leading to Perdrix ridge (15min on foot there and back) which is crowned with a chirat (granite rock).*

The **panorama** from the viewing table takes in the peaks of Mézenc, Lizieux, Meygal and Gerbier-de-Jonc.

> ### ☺ A Bit of Advice ☺
>
> Regional parks are different from national parks in their concept and purpose. They are inhabited areas selected for development of the local economy through specific activities (the creation of cooperatives, promotion of crafts), the preservation of the natural and cultural heritage (museums, architecture) and the appreciation of the distinctive character of the region.

▶ *Rejoin D 8 and follow D 63 to Crêt de l'Œillon.*

The road meanders alternately through fir trees and moorland covered in broom.

Crêt de l'Œillon★★★

15min on foot there and back. At the Croix de l'Œillon pass, take the road on the left leading to the turn-off to the private road ending at the television relay station. Park in the car park. At the top, walk to the left around the fence; the viewing table is on the eastern end of the promontory, at the foot of a monumental cross.

🚶 The **panorama** is one of the most spectacular in the Rhône Valley. In the foreground, beyond the rocks of the Pic des Trois Dents (Three Teeth Peak), there is a bird's-eye view of the Rhône Valley, from Vienne to Serrières. In the distance to the east, the view stretches right to the Alps; south-east to Mont Ventoux; west to the Puy de Sancy and the Forez mountains; north to the Lyonnais mountains and north-east to the Jura.

▶ *Continue to Pélussin.*

From Faucharat viewpoint, there are lovely views of the Régrillon Valley, the Rhône Valley and Pélussin.

Pélussin

Park on place Abbé-Vincent in front of the hospital. Walk down rue Dr-Soubeyran and take rue de la Halle on the left.
The old covered market provides a view of the Rhône plain and the town of Pélussin. Go through a fortified gatehouse and turn left. Note the ancient chapel and castle.

▶ *Turn back the way you came and take D 7 right to Pavezin Pass. Continue to Ste-Croix-en-Jarez.*

Ste-Croix-en-Jarez – 🕭 *See STE-CROIX-EN-JAREZ.*

▶ *Return to Pavezin Pass, turn left onto D 30 which, as it begins its descent, offers a beautiful view of the Rhône Valley. Continue along D 19 and D 28 to Condrieu.*

Just before arriving, in a bend with a Calvary overlooking the town, there is a panoramic **view**★ of the Condrieu basin and the bend in the Rhône below.

Condrieu

One of the largest markets in the region is held here, specialising in fruit and early vegetables. The town is also famed for its excellent white wine, made from the cepage *viognier*. The **church** has a Gothic doorway with a tympanum bearing fragments of a Romanesque bas-relief. Next to it stands **Maison de la Gabelle,** a house with an attractive 16C façade. The port – the town was once renowned for its sailors – is a pleasant place for a stroll, with its slightly Mediterranean feel.

Excursion

Bourg-Argental

This small busy town lying at the foot of the Pilat massif has specialised in local craft and industrial activities. The church, rebuilt in the Romanesque style in the 19C, presents a sculpted **doorway** (12C). Note the tympanum: the lower level is illustrated with scenes taken from the life of the Virgin Mary, showing a hint of Cluniac influence.

PRIVAS

POPULATION 9 170
MICHELIN MAP 331: J-5

Privas occupies an unusual **site★** in the Ouvèze basin, at the foot of Mont Toulon; a good example of relief inversion, the lava flow on which it stands was once at the bottom of the valley and is now in relief since the ancient unprotected calcareous heights have been eroded. Business in the town concentrates on small industry (milling, sprung bed bases) and the manufacture of *marrons glacés* (candied sweet chestnuts), of which it is the capital. ￭ *Pl. du Gén.-de-Gaulle, 07000 PRIVAS, ☎ 04 75 64 33 35.*

Siege of Privas

The "Boulevard of the Reformation" – Privas played a key role in the Wars of Religion which earned it the title of "Boulevard de la Réforme." A priest from Privas, Jacques Valery (or Vallier), first introduced the Reformation to Privas in 1534.
Right in the throes of religious dissent, the town was one of the strongholds conceded to the Protestants by Henri IV under the Edict of Nantes in 1598.

The taking of Privas – Richelieu's unification policy and the undying hatred of the people revived the religious conflict which was fanned in the Vivarais by a question of marriage: Paule de Chambaud, widow of the Huguenot leader, Jacques de Chambaud, heir to the barony of Privas, had the choice of two suitors, one Roman Catholic and the other Protestant. She chose the youngest, Claude de Hautefort-Lestrange, a Roman Catholic, to the outrage of the people of Privas, most of whom were Protestants and opposed to having a follower of the Pope as their lord.
Fighting resumed. In 1629 the Royal Army, under the command of Schomberg and Biron, set up camp near Privas. Cardinal Richelieu took up lodgings in Entrevaux Castle while Louis XIII was housed south of the town, in a dwelling now known as the Logis du Roi (King's Residence).

Address Book

EATING OUT

◷◷ **Le Corentin** – *2 pl. de la République - ☎ 04 75 64 75 75 - closed 1-15 May, 15-30 Sep, 22 Dec to 6 Jan, Wed evening and Sun.* On a small, calm and shady square, this crêperie also serves well-prepared bistro fare and a regional menu called 'Goûter l'Ardèche' (Taste the Ardèche), perfect for discovering the flavours of the area: quail, jellied pork jowls and *criques* (potatoes), picodon goats' cheese and homemade ice creams.

WHERE TO STAY

◷◷ **Hôtel Chaumette** – *Av. Vanel - ☎ 04 75 64 30 66 - www.hotelchaumette. fr - ℗ - 36 rms - ⧖ 12€ - restaurant ◷◷.* One must go beyond the door of this hotel to discover the inviting interior featuring Provençal and African colours and decorative touches. Ask if one of the pretty, renovated rooms is available. Pleasant dining room with contemporary furniture and a wood parquet. Summer terrace and pool.

◷◷◷ **Chambre d'hôte Château de Fontblachère** – *07210 St-Lager-Bressac - 15km/9mi SE of Privas. Take D 22, then D 2 and left onto D 322 opposite the village of St-Lager-Bressac, and follow signs - ☎*

04 75 65 15 02 - www.chateau-fontblach-ere.com - closed Nov-Feb; open weekends off-season - 5 rms: 90/120€ - meals 25€. Nestling in the hills of the Ardèche, this gorgeous home promises a peaceful stopover in a simple, elegant setting. Stylish bedrooms painted with natural pigments. Pool, tennis and jacuzzi hidden in a splendid park. Two self-catering cottages for longer halts.

SHOPPING

Clément Faugier – *Chemin du Logis-du-Roy - ☎ 04 75 64 07 11 - www. clement-faugier.fr - Mon-Thu 8.15am-11.30am, 1.45pm-5.30pm (Fri 4.30pm) - closed 25 Jul to 24 Aug.* Since 1882, this factory has been making chestnut delicacies, including chestnut crème, candied chestnuts, chestnuts in cognac, in syrup, etc. Products are sold individually or in pretty gift baskets. A small museum and a video share the secrets of chestnut confection.

RECREATION

Plan d'eau de la Neuve – *2km/1mi N on D 2, then turn left on D 260.* In the Mézayon valley, near an abandoned mill, the swimming beach is supervised by lifeguards in the summer.

The townspeople, who counted only 1 600 defenders, were no match for the 20 000 strong Royal Army. After 16 days of siege, the town was taken by storm, pillaged and burnt, and the inhabitants were massacred. The booty was declared "very rich," the Protestants of Boutières having brought their most precious possessions into the town square for safety.

Some of the defenders took refuge on Mont Toulon; one of the leaders, preferring to "be burned rather than hung," set fire to the gunpowder. His companions, panic-stricken, ran outside where they were killed by the king's soldiers.

Privas takes revenge – The inhabitants who managed to escape later obtained the right to return although they were pursued from court to court by their lord, the Viscount of Lestrange, who claimed the price of his destroyed castle – at least until 1632. He was implicated in one of Gaston d'Orléans' plots against the king, was taken prisoner and whipped publicly in Privas, then executed in Pont-St-Esprit. Shortly afterwards, the construction of a bridge over the Ouvèze sealed the reconciliation between royal power and the people of Privas, who gradually rebuilt the ruins of their city.

Pont Louis XIII (15C)

J. Damase/MICHELIN

Sights

Mont-Toulon
1hr there and back – park near the museum and walk up boulevard du Montoulon.
🚶 A signpost marks the path to the right that goes to the hilltop, where there is a monumental **calvary** (three crosses) and a good **view**★ over the town, the Ouvèze Valley, the Rhône and the Alps.

Pont Louis-XIII
South of the town centre. The bridge spanning the River Ouvèze has preserved its coping of rough stone corbels and offers a good view of Privas.

Excursions

Le Bouschet de Pranles
15km/9.3mi N along D 2 and D 344. A small **Protestant Museum** (🕐 *Jul-Aug: 10am-noon, 2-6pm; May-Jun: Sat, Sun and public holidays, 2-6pm; Sep: 2-6pm.* 🕐*Closed Oct-Apr, and Mondays. 4€.* ☎ *04 75 64 22 74)* has been set up in the birthplace of Pierre Durand, one of the Desert Fathers in the 18C, and his sister Marie Durand. This 18C Huguenot heroine was locked up in the tower of Constance d'Aigues-Mortes for 38 years (1730-68). Pranles has become the Mecca of Protestantism in the Vivarais region; a Protestant gathering is held here on Whit Monday every year.

Plateau du Coiron★★

77km/48mi from Privas – allow half a day

▶ *Head S from Privas along D 7, following signs to Villeneuve-de-Berg.*

The deeply-eroded volcanic bar that forms the Coiron plateau marks, to the north, the limit of the Lower Vivarais area. Its black basalt rocks cut across the line of hills from the Escrinet pass to the River Rhône, creating the starkly contrasting Rochemaure dikes. The upper part of the Coiron plateau takes the form of a vast, bare *planèze* with an average altitude of 800m/2 652ft rising from the banks of the Rhône in a north-westerly direction.

The road crosses the Ouvèze basin then enters the sun-baked Bayonne gorge. As the road climbs the hillside, there is a succession of superb views of Privas and the surrounding area. Suddenly, though, where the basalt has covered the base of the mountain, the scenery becomes darker and gloomier.

▸ *At the junction with the road to Freyssenet, turn left towards Taverne.*

The **planèze** stretches away as undulating moorland dotted with juniper bushes, box and broom, a landscape bereft of human habitation were it not for the hamlet of Taverne.

▸ *In Taverne, take D 213.*

Between the Fontenelle Pass (Col de Fontenelle) and the hamlet of Les Molières, a broad gap in the hills provides a view of the River Rhône in the distance. In the foreground are basalt columns down which runs a thin stream of water. On one of the hillsides to the right, erosion has worn the rock down to the underlying limestone layer. The road then runs steeply down to Les Molières along the side of the ravine where the various strata in the rock are clearly visible.

Before arriving in St-Martin-le-Supérieur, the road gives a delightful view of the charming little Romanesque church with its belfry-wall.

▸ *Beyond St-Martin-l'Inférieur turn right along the Lower Lavézon Valley. The river bed is covered with large, rounded, black and white boulders.*

Meysse

15min on foot there and back. The old village can be discerned behind its façade of more modern housing. Around the old Romanesque church, now deconsecrated and in a poor state of repair, is a network of narrow streets and vaulted passages.

▸ *Leave Meysse on N 86 S.*

To the right of the road on the outskirts of the village stands a pinnacle of basalt rock. Beyond it are the ruins of Rochemaure Castle.

Château de Rochemaure★ – 👣 *See MONTÉLIMAR.*

Pic de Chenavari★★ – 👣 *See MONTÉLIMAR.*

▸ *Return to Meysse and follow D 2 up the Lower Lavézon Valley; turn right towards St-Vincent-de-Barrès.*

The road runs through the vast **Barrès** basin with its fertile farmland. It then follows a tributary valley of the River Rhône which separates the limestone uplands of Cruas to the east from the volcanic Coiron plateau to the west.

St-Vincent-de-Barrès

This is a lovely village perched on a basalt neck jutting out from above the Barrès plain. It is dwarfed by the basalt towers of its old fortress. From the esplanade in front of the church there is a view over the Barrès area.

▸ *Return to Privas via Chomérac.*

LE PUY-EN-VELAY★★★

POPULATION 20 490
MICHELIN MAP 331: F-3

The **site**★★★ of Le Puy-en-Velay, one of the most extraordinary in France, is unforgettable. Out of a rich plain set in a depression rise enormous peaks of volcanic origin: the steepest, the St-Michel rock (or Mont d'Aiguilhe) is surmounted by a Romanesque chapel making it even higher; the largest, Corneille rock (or Mont d'Anis) is crowned by a monumental statue of the Virgin Mary. This strange and splendid vision is complemented by a visit to the church of Notre-Dame du Puy, no less strange, almost oriental, which houses the Black Virgin still venerated by numerous pilgrims. On Saturday, market day, the town is a striking sight: place du Breuil and the old streets between the square and the market become incredibly busy. In autumn, the **Festival of the Bird King** (Fêtes du roi de l'Oiseau) is held, in commemoration of an age-old local custom: it is a competition to determine the town's best archer, celebrated in a Renaissance atmosphere which pervades the upper end of the town during these festivities.

A **tourist train** (The train runs past the main sights of the town. May-Sep: guided trip (45min), departures every hour 10-11am and 2-5pm (also 6pm in Jul-Aug). 6€ (children: 3€). ☎ 04 71 02 70 70) takes visitors round the town from May to September.

🛈 Pl. du Breuil, 43000 Le PUY-EN-VELAY, ☎ 04 71 09 38 41. Le Puy-en-Velay, which is listed as a "Town of Art and history," offers discovery tours (2hr) conducted by guide-lecturers approved by the Ministry of Culture and Communication. Jul and Aug: information at the tourist office or on www.vpah.culture.fr

▸ **Orient Yourself:** Take the tourist train (see above) to get an idea of the layout and what there is to see and do. Then take a walk around the Old Town around Corneille rock.

🅿 **Parking:** There are plenty of car parks around the southern ring road, but precious few within the town itself.

⊘ **Don't Miss:** St Michel-d'Aiguilhe.

🕓 **Organizing Your Time:** Head for the cathedral area first, and then wander the streets, or follow one of the Town Walks (👣 see above). Allow a full day to explore.

👣 **Also See:** Cathédrale Notre-Dame, Arlempdes, gorges de la Loire.

The Puy basin – It owes its initial formation to the collapse of the Vellave plateau, an after-effect of the Alpine folding which occurred during the Tertiary period. Sediment stripped from the surrounding hills then partly filled the basin in which a gorge was cut by the River Loire. At the end of the Tertiary Era a series of volcanic eruptions convulsed the region; the bed of the Loire was shifted east.

During the Quaternary Era the erosion began again, forming spurs from the most resistant of the volcanic reefs, of various origins; these include basalt tables, the remains of lava flows (Polignac rock), volcanic chimneys (St-Michel rock, Espaly and Arbousset peaks) and parts of eruptive cones (Corneille and Ceyssac rocks, Denise volcano). As the lava flow cooled, combinations of prismatic columns were formed, such as those at Espaly. It is to these volcanic phenomena that the basin owes its highly original physiognomy.

A Bit of History

City of the Virgin Mary – The Velay capital of the Roman era, Ruessium, has been identified at St-Paulien nearby, to the north-west.

The site of Le Puy seems to have been an ancient place of pagan worship (remains of a 1C sanctuary among the cathedral foundations), evangelised in the 3C. Apparitions of the Virgin Mary and miraculous cures near a dolmen capstone (since known as the "Fever Stone") encouraged the first bishops to come and settle here, probably at the end of the 5C. A basilica was erected, then a cathedral, around which a town soon developed, the old Ruessium having been deposed.

In the Middle Ages, pilgrimages to Le Puy were particularly popular since it was also a point of departure for the pilgrimage to Santiago de Compostela in Spain. Along with Chartres, Le Puy is the oldest site of Marian worship in France. Kings, princes and crowds of humble origin flocked here to invoke the mother of God.

In the 12C the havoc wrought by a group of privateers, known as **Les Cotereaux**, posed a serious threat to the pilgrimages and all they contributed to the town in terms of prosperity and renown. The Virgin, in an apparition to a carpenter named Durand, ordered a holy war against the Cotereaux.

The **Black Virgin** brought even greater fame to Le Puy. The present statue, dating from 1856 replaces the original one mutilated and burnt during the French Revolution.

Le Puy-en-Velay has remained the city of the Virgin Mary; the tall statue of Notre-Dame de France, at the top of Corneille rock, evokes both a past and a destiny.

City of lace – In Le Puy and the Velay, as well as in the region of Arlanc, hand-made lace was once an important part of the local economy. It most probably originated in the 17C and soon began to develop so that a special organisation was established. In all the villages, women worked at home for merchants in the neighbouring towns. "Collectors" who provided the lacemakers with thread and cartoons (patterns), served as intermediaries. This extra income was vital to the poor peasants in the region.

Originally reserved for the gentry, lace became so popular that, in 1640, the

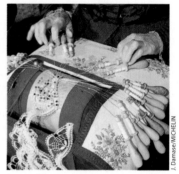

Lacemaking

Toulouse Parliament outlawed its use as clothing. A Jesuit father, Jean-François Régis (1597-1640), moved by the distress of the lacemakers who suddenly found themselves out of work, managed to have the ban lifted. Moreover, he invited his fellow missionaries to make Le Puy lace known throughout the world. This benefactor from Le Puy later became the patron saint of lacemakers. The chapel of the Jesuit college, where he spent five years of his ministry, is now the church of St-Georges-St-Régis. The lace trade retained its religious overtones for a long time: the art was passed on not only from mother to daughter but also by religious women known as "the beatified" who also taught catechism and cared for the sick.

In the summer, a small tourist train takes visitors round the town's main sights.

Address Book

EATING OUT

◔◕🖫 **Lapierre** – *6 r. des Capucins - ☏ 04 71 09 08 44 - closed Dec to Jan, weekends and public holidays.* A little family restaurant off the beaten path serving flavoursome traditional fare (including famous Puy lentils) enhanced by organic produce here and there. Two dining rooms, one of which is decorated in a winter garden scheme.

◔◕ **La Renouée** – *In Cheyrac - 43800 St-Vincent - 16km/10mi N of Le Puy via D 103 and secondary road - ☏ 04 71 08 55 94 - closed Jan, Feb, Tue, Wed and Thu evenings from 12 Nov to 31 Dec.* Cross the little garden to discover a house that feels like home. Country-style dining room with a stone fireplace featuring tasty regional cuisine that won't break the bank.

WHERE TO STAY

◔ **Dyke Hôtel** – *37 bd du Mar.-Fayolle - ☏ 04 71 09 05 30 - closed Christmas week, 1 Jan - 15 rms - ⊿ 6€.* This family hotel downtown could be a convenient stopover if you're passing through Le Puy. The contemporary rooms are small but tidy. Breakfast is served in the bar-room, in the company of local regulars.

◔◕ **Chambre d'hôte La Paravent** – *43700 Chaspinhac - 10km/6mi NE of Le Puy via D 103 dir. Retournac, then D 71 - ☏ 04 71 03 54 75 - michel-jourde@ wanadoo.fr - ✉ - 5 rms - meals ◔◕.* You'll be pleasantly pampered in this attractive country house just a few kilometres from Le Puy. The decor is authentic and the cosy bedrooms are very welcoming; some even have a small sitting room attached. A stopover overseen by a likeable couple who are happy to share their passion for lace and lace making.

SHOPPING

Market – *Pl. du Plot – Sat morning.* On this splendid public square with a lovely water fountain, the country comes to pay its opulent respects to the city in the form of baskets overflowing with the finest farm produce; berries and mushrooms in season.

Marché aux puces (Flea market) – *Pl. du Clauzel – Sat and fair days.* Bargain hunters, second-hand buffs and bric-a-brac enthusiasts take note: terrific flea markets are regularly organised on the Place du Clauzel.

Rue des Tables. While strolling along this highly charming pedestrian street, you'll notice that a good number of the shops sell lace. One can often admire lace makers at work here.

Centre d'enseignement de la dentelle (lace making centre) – *38/40 r. Raphaël - ☏ 04 71 02 01 68 - www. ladentelledupuy.com - mid-Jun to mid-Sep: Mon-Fri 9-11.30am, 1.30-5pm, Sat 9.30am-5pm; rest of year: Mon-Fri 9.30-11.30am, 1.30-5pm - closed public holidays. 2€.* We can thank St. François-Régis, patron saint of lace workers, for inspiring the creation of this establishment allowing us to discover lace in an original manner! An entertaining video tells the tale of how lace making was developed in Le Puy as early as the 15C. Exhibitions round out the presentation. And for those who prefer practice to theory, introductory spindling classes are organised in the learning centre (by the hour).

Chocolaterie du Velay – *70 r. Pannessac - ☏ 04 71 09 34 82 - Tue-Sat 8am-7.30pm, Sun 8am-1pm. Closed 15-30 Jun and 1-15 Sep.* This chocolate confectioner contributes to the trade's good name thanks to excellent creations such as his homemade fruit jelly candies (including an organic *pâte de verveine*), chocolates and organic verbena jelly.

Maison de la Lentille verte du Puy – *R. des Tables - ☏ 04 71 02 60 44 - www. lalentilleverteddupuy.com - from Jul to mid-Sep: 10am-12.30pm, 2pm-7pm.* Emblem of the region, the Le Puy green lentil was the first vegetable in France to receive an AOC (Appellation d'Origine Controllée) label. This 15C site, entirely dedicated to these famous iron-rich pulses, has videos, informative brochures and a boutique selling a surprisingly broad range of products made from the tiny convex disks.

Distillerie de la Verveine du Velay-Pagès – *ZI de Blavozy - Approx. 6km/3.6mi E of Le Puy via N 88, exit ZI de Blavozy, dir. St-Étienne - 43700 St-Germain-Laprade - ☏ 04 71 03 04*

11 - pages-verveine@verveine.com - ◐ all year: Mar-Dec: Tue-Sat 10am-noon, 1.30-6.30pm (Jul-Aug: daily); Jan-Feb: Tue-Sat, 1.30-4.30pm - closed public holidays – 6€ (children: 3€). The Pagès distillery takes visitors on a discovery tour of the production of Verveine du Velay liqueur. The recipe, invented in 1859 by J. Rumillet-Charretier and still used today, requires no fewer than 32 plants. Products may be sampled in an exhibition hall.

Pisciculture des eaux de Vourzac – Rte de Lourdes, moulin de Gauthier - 43320 Sanssac-l'Église - ☎ 04 71 09 43 84 - Mon-Fri 9am-5pm. At 700m/2300ft high, this fish farm is the bastion of the noble trout. Raised in spring water ponds, it is subsequently sold in the shop in the form of oak smoke-cured fillets, carpaccio, terrines and more.

Sabarot – Z.A. Lacombe - 43320 Chaspuzac - ☎ 04 71 08 09 10 - www.sabarot-wassner.fr - Mon-Thu 9am-noon, 2pm-5pm, Fri 9am-noon, 2pm-4pm; closed Wed and Fri afternoons in summer. Founded in 1819, Sabarot was originally a flourmill. A century later, the company branched out into the Le Puy lentil, followed by other pulses and mushrooms. Everything it makes or processes may be purchased in the factory store.

ON THE TOWN

Le Michelet – 5 bis pl. Michelet - ☎ 04 71 09 02 74 - Mon-Wed 7.30am-1am, Thu 7.30am-2am, Fri-Sat 9am-4am. 1960s America and its symbols (a petrol pump, licence plates, photos of actors and movie posters) seem to attract the hippest young inhabitants of Le Puy, who gather here to have a drink and take advantage of the weekend theme evenings. Rum bar upstairs.

Le Bistrot – 7 pl. de la Halle - ☎ 04 71 02 27 08 - Tue-Fri 5pm-1am; Sat 10am-12.30pm, 5pm-2am - closed Sun-Mon and last 2 wks of Aug. All one has to do is delicately place an elbow near one's tipple on the bar to find oneself transported to an atmosphere of bistros of yore. The terrace is calm despite its proximity to the old town and its myriad visitors. Musical ambience with an accent on jazz and French music.

The King's Head English Pub – Pl. du Marché-couvert - ☎ 04 71 02 50 35 – Mon-Fri 5pm-1am, Sat 10am-1am – closed 1st week of Jul. The decor is rustic, the choice of beers and whiskies inspired and the atmosphere as English as can be in this pub offering a respectable choice of ales and whiskies. Light meals include the Le Puy version of fish and chips. A traditional music concert is held the first Wednesday of each month.

La distillerie – 29 pl. du Breuil - ☎ 04 71 04 91 12 - Mon-Sat 8am-1am, Sun 8am-7pm. Here, the interior design invites you to linger(wood benches and shelves, a copper still, old tools) and the terrace, set in an inner courtyard amid barrels, is delightful. Products from the Verveine du Velay distillery may be purchased here.

A Perched Chapel

St-Michel-d'Aiguilhe★★

◐ May-Sep: 9am-6.30pm (mid-Jul to end Aug, 6.45pm); mid-Mar to end Apr and Oct to mid-Nov: 9.30am-noon, 2-5.30pm; Feb to mid-Mar and Christmas period: 2-5pm. ◐ Closed 1 Jan and 25 Dec. 3€. ☎ 04 71 09 50 03.

St-Michel Chapel crowns St-Michel rock, a gigantic needle of lava which rises up in a single shaft to a height of 80m/262ft above ground level. Its slender belfry, in the form of a minaret, looks like a pointed finger of rock.

▸ Walk up montée de Gouteyron linking the Aiguilhe rock and the upper town. Alternatively, you can reach the foot of the rock by car and park nearby.

This chapel probably replaced a temple dedicated to Mercury. The building standing today, which dates from the 10C-12C, shows Oriental inspiration in its trefoil portal, its decoration of arabesques and its black, white, grey and red stone **mosaics.** Inside,

St-Michel-d'Aiguilhe

the highly irregular ground plan follows the contours of the rock. The complexity of the vaulting testifies to the architects' ability to make the most of the site. The small columns, which form a sort of ambulatory around a short nave, are surmounted by carved capitals.

The vaulting above the small apse is decorated with 10C **paintings.** On the right, objets d'art found under the altar in 1955 are on display; note in particular a small 11C wooden reliquary Christ and a 13C Byzantine ivory cask.

A covered watch-path goes around the chapel, overlooking **Vieux Pont,** the old cusp bridge that spans the River Borne.

Walking Tours

1 The Treasure Trail★★★

The cathedral dominates the upper part of the town, which is one large conservation area (35ha/86 acres).

Start from place des Tables with its graceful Chorister Fountain (15C) and walk up to the cathedral via the picturesque **rue des Tables** lined with stone steps bordered by several old houses.

Cathédrale Notre-Dame★★★

🕐 *Ask at the tourist office for times of guided tours.* ☎ *04 71 05 45 52.*

This marvellous Romanesque building, now on UNESCO's World Heritage List, owes its unusual appearance to the influence of the Orient; Byzantine influence, a result of the crusades, can also be seen in the octagonal domes over the nave.

The original church corresponds to the present east end. When work was begun to extend it in the 12C, shortage of space quickly became a problem. The last bays of the nave (built two by two, in two stages), together with the west porch, were built virtually above a sheer drop, with the tall arcades serving as open piling. At the end of the 12C, the For Porch and St-Jean Porch were added. Extensive restoration was carried out on the cathedral in the 19C.

A wide staircase leads to the unusual west front with its polychrome floor slabs and mosaics where Hispano-Moorish influence is evident.

Route under the cathedral

Steps lead to the main door under the four bays built in the 12C. At the level of the second bay, two 12C **panelled doors**★ close off two side chapels; their faint decoration in relief recounts the life of Christ. In the following bay, two restored **frescoes** can be seen: the Virgin Mother (13C) on the left and the Transfiguration of Our Lord on the right. Go through the main door, framed by two red porphyry columns. Straight ahead, the main staircase leads right into the cathedral, opposite the High Altar, which led to the saying that "One enters Notre-Dame du Puy through the navel and leaves through the ears."

▶ *Take the central staircase or, if it is closed, the right-hand one which leads to a door in the side aisle.*

Interior

The most unusual feature of the church is the series of domes which cover the nave (that over the transept crossing is modern). Note the pulpit (**1**) and the beautiful high altar (**2**), which supports the wooden statue replacing the original Black Virgin burnt during the Revolution.

The Baroque organ, recently restored, is located at the west end of the nave. Bishop Jean de Bourbon's 15C fleur-de-lis tapestry hangs at the end of the chancel.

In the north aisle hangs a large painting by Jean Solvain known as the "Vow of the Plague" (1630) (**3**) illustrating a thanksgiving procession held in place du For.

In the north arm of the transept are beautiful Romanesque frescoes: the Holy Women at the tomb (**4**) and the Martyrdom of St Catherine of Alexandria (**5**).

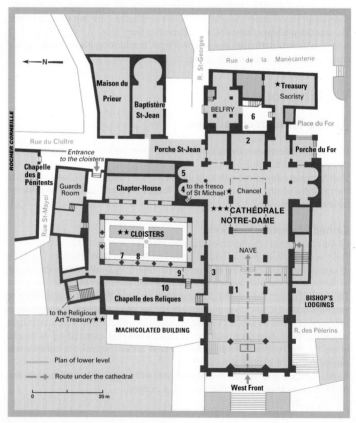

A gallery on the left contains a **fresco of St Michael**★ (late 11C–early 12C), the largest known painting in France depicting the Archangel Michael.

The famous stone known as the **"Pierre des fièvres"** (**12**) is in the chapel next to St-Jean Porch.

The finest pieces of the **treasury**★ displayed in the sacristy are, from the 15C, a Pietà oil on panel of the Burgundian School, a gold-plated copper head of Christ; from the 17C, an ivory Christ, a Rhône boat crew's cross and walnut panelling.

For Porch

This porch with highly elaborate capitals dates back to the late 12C. The smallest door is known as the "Papal Door" because of the inscription above it. In the inside corner, the ribs rest on a pilaster which supports an open hand coming out of the wall.

From the small place du For there is an attractive overall view of the site and a particularly good view of the belfry, a pyramid-shaped construction with seven levels standing out slightly from the highly restored east end.

▷ *Walk around the east end via rue de la Manécanterie.*

St-Jean Porch

This porch preceded by a large flattened arcade was designed for sovereigns to pass through; it connects the cathedral to the 10C and 11C baptistery, whose entrance is flanked by two stone lions. The leather-covered doors have beautiful 12C strap hinges (wrought-iron brackets).

▷ *Pass under the belfry to the small courtyard adjoining the east end of the cathedral.*

On the way, note the tombs of abbots and canons, and in the courtyard (**6**), behind the Romanesque well, the Gallo-Roman low-relief sculptures incorporated into the base of the east end and the frieze above: they depict hunting scenes.

Cloisters★★

The beautiful cloisters abut the north face of the cathedral; each gallery is from a different period; the oldest, to the south, is Romanesque. The **historiated** capitals in the west gallery include one (**7**) depicting a dispute about an abbot's crook, and another (**8**) showing a centaur.

J. Damase/MICHELIN

Cloisters of Notre-Dame Cathedral

A remarkable **Romanesque railing**★ (**9**) closes the west gallery. From the south-west corner of the cloisters, a Romanesque chimney can be seen rising above the altar boys' house.

Around the cloisters, above the arcades, is a delicately decorated **cornice** illustrating a medieval bestiary. The polychrome arch stones and the quoins with their black, white, red and ochre lozenges form a decor reminiscent of Islamic art.

A door in the east gallery leads to the **chapter house,** which in the 14C was a funeral chapel, with its entrance framed by ribbed pilasters with double fluting.

The south wall is decorated with a 13C fresco depicting the Crucifixion *(light switch by the entrance)*.

Machicolated Building

This massive structure sheltering behind the chapel is the old Velay State Room. The building was part of the fortifications of the cathedral and bishop's palace in the 13C.

It comprises two floors that are accessible to the public: the lower level houses the Chapel of Relics, access to which is via the north aisle of the cathedral, and the upper level contains the Religious Art Treasury which is part of the Cloisters Museum.

Chapel of Relics

The Chapel of Relics or Winter Chapel (it opens off the north aisle of the cathedral) derives its name from the beautiful gold altarpiece which, until the Revolution, housed relics brought to Notre-Dame du Puy. The room, the former library of St-Mayol University, was decorated on its eastern wall in the 15C with the now famous painting depicting the **Liberal Arts**★ (**10**), a rare French primitive work. Each of the liberal arts (Grammar, Logic, Rhetoric, Music) is represented by a seated woman and an allegorical character. The detail of the fabrics and jewellery provides a good insight into the tastes of the period.

Religious Art Treasury★★

The Treasury, displayed in the former **Velay State Room** above the Chapel of Relics, contains a large number of works of art, including an 11C silk cope, a 13C engraved enamel reliquary, a polychrome-stone 15C nursing Virgin, a magnificent 16C embroidered cloak for the Black Virgin, and a remarkable piece of 15C **parchment** showing the Genesis of the World to the Resurrection.

The paintings include the **Adoration of the Shepherds** by Parier (1598) and **The Holy Family** attributed to Jean Van Eyck (15C). The art of the Montpellier sculptor, **Pierre Vaneau** (1653-94), who worked extensively for the Bishop of Le Puy, is represented by panels illustrating mythological subjects and by two statues of slaves carved in walnut.

Penitents' Chapel

○ *Jul-Aug: 2-6pm.* ☎ *04 71 09 38 41.*

The entrance is through a panelled wooden door carved in the Renaissance style and flanked by two groups of wreathed columns.

Inside, the paintings decorating the gallery, the panelled walls of the nave and, in particular, the beautiful coffered ceiling, recount the Life of the Virgin Mary. They were produced in the 17C and 18C.

The instruments of the Passion and the numerous staffs of the Brotherhood of the White Penitents, founded in 1584, are still carried during processions, in particular on Maundy Thursday.

St-Jean Baptistery

This building, dating back to the 10C and 11C, and connected to the cathedral by the porch of the same name, served as a baptistery for all the parishes in the town during the Revolution. The southern entrance is flanked with eroded stone lions. Inside is a pyramid-shaped font.

Prior's Lodgings

🕐 *Jul to mid-Sep: 10am-noon, 2-6pm. 1€.* ☎ *04 71 05 62 75.*

Adjoining St-Jean Baptistery, the vaulted rooms of the former residence of the administrator of baptisms house an historical exhibition on Velay, and a remarkable collection of rural and craftsmen's tools.

Rocher Corneille

🕐 *May-Sep: 9am-7pm (Jul and Aug: 7.30pm); mid-Mar to end Apr: 9am-6pm; Oct to mid-Mar and Christmas school holidays: 10am-5pm; Dec-Jan Sun 2-5pm. 3€.* ☎ *04 71 04 11 33.*

This is the remainder of a cone, no doubt belonging to the volcano of which St-Michel rock is the chimney.

From the platform there is a panoramic **view**★ of the town's red rooftops and Le Puy basin, as well as St-Michel rock (north-west), behind which can be seen Polignac Castle.

The rock is surmounted by a monumental **statue of Notre-Dame-de-France** erected in 1860 by national subscription. This cast iron statue is 16m/52ft high and weighs 110t. An outstanding 213 cannon from among the trophies from the capture of Sebastopol given to contractors by Napoleon III were melted down to cast it. It is possible to go up inside the statue to neck level.

▶ *Return to place des Tables.*

② **The Old Quarter**★

The tall, red-roofed houses of the old town cluster around Corneille rock, while the circular boulevards mark the beginning of the lower, more modern town.

From place des Tables in front of the cathedral, there is an interesting view over the city.

▶ *Turn left onto Rue Raphaël.*

Prominent citizens and members of the middle class once lived in this street. At no 38 is the Lace Centre; no 56 is a handsome 16C building on five levels, known as the **Logis des Alix Selliers.**

▶ *At the end of this street turn left onto rue Saulnerie then left again onto rue Roche-Taillade.*

On the corner with rue Cardinal de Polignac is the 15C **Hôtel du Lac de Fugères** and, further to the right at no 8, the **Hôtel de Polignac,** the Polignac family mansion with its 15C polygonal tower.

Back beyond rue Roche-Taillade, at no 3 rue Vaneau, rises the **Hôtel des Laval d'Arlempdes.**

▶ *Walk back down rue Roche-Taillade which runs onto rue Chênebouterie.*

Note, at no 8, the courtyard with a 15C turret, and opposite at no 9, the birthplace (16C) of Marshal Payolle. The road leads to **place du Plot** which, at the end of the week, bustles with a colourful market around **La Bidoire fountain,** dated 1246. Nearby, at no 8 **rue Courrerie** there remains an interesting 16C façade next to the Hôtel de Marminhac with arched windows bearing keystones carved with masks.

Continue to place du Martouret – the site of many executions during the Revolution – where the Hôtel de Ville stands.

▶ *Return to place du Plot and follow rue Pannessac.*

This part-pedestrianised street is bordered by elegant 16C and 17C Renaissance houses with overhanging fronts, sometimes flanked by a tower or watch-turret (nos 16, 18, 23). To the right, some of the alleys – **rue Philibert, rue du Chamarlenc** – retain a medieval character. The façade of no 16 rue Chamarlenc, known as the Demeure des Cornards (the Cornards were companions whose prerogative it was to poke fun at the town's burghers) is adorned with two horned heads, one laughing, the other sticking out its tongue, surmounted by satirical inscriptions.

At no 42 Rue Pannessac, the **Logis des André,** and at no 46 the 17C **Logis des Frères Michel** decorated on the ground floor with masks and carved quoins, and on the upper storeys with masks, garlands and scrolls, both reveal the opulence of the wealthy merchant who lived in this district. At the end of the street, the 14C **Pannessac Tower** retains a level of trefoiled machicolations. It is the last remaining trace of the original 18 fortified gateways, with twinned towers which allowed access through the town walls.

The writer Jules Vallès, a native of Le Puy, described the tough childhood he had endured in the old town in the first volume of his trilogy *L'Enfant, Le Bachelier* and *L'Insurgé.*

Sights

Musée Crozatier

🕐 *May-Sep: daily except Tue 10am-noon, 2-6pm (mid-Jun to mid-Sep: daily); Oct-Nov and Mar-Apr: daily except Tue 10am-noon, 2-4pm, Sun 2-4pm.* 🕐 *Closed Dec-Jan, 1 May and 1 and 11 Nov. 4€, no charge Sun from Oct to Apr.* ☎ *04 71 06 62 40.*

The museum collections are housed in an imposing building (1865) erected at the bottom of the Henri Vinay garden, which includes, among other monuments, the beautiful portal from Vorey Priory.

On the ground floor, on either side of the space devoted to temporary exhibitions, is a **lapidary collection**★ (Gallo- Roman, Romanesque and Gothic art) containing historiated capitals and sculptures from the cathedral. On the same floor, three rooms illustrate various inventions and technical developments with the help of panels and models: **praxinoscope,** an ancestor of the cine projector, invented in 1877 by Émile Reynaud; a prototype of a sewing machine by Pierre Clair (1828). The basement houses a beautiful 18C **French berline coach.**

The first floor is devoted to local arts and crafts; note in particular a rich collection of handmade **lace**★ from the 16C to the present day, including magnificent bobbin and needlepoint work.

The second floor, reached by a 17C revolving door brought from the Convent of the Visitation, is given over to

A French berline, for travelling in style

A. de Valroger/MICHELIN

Atelier du peintre Chaleyé	BY	B	Hôtel des Laval			Rocher Corneille	BY
Cathédrale Notre-Dame	BY		d'Arlempdes	AY	K	St-Michel-d'Aiguilhe	AY
Chapelle des Pénitents	BY	D	Hôtel du Lac de Fugères	AY	F	Statue N.-D. de France	BY
Cloître	BY		Jardin Vinay	AZ		Tour Pannessac	AY	V
Fontaine de la Bidoire	AZ	E	Musée Crozatier	AZ		Vieux pont	BY
Hôtel de Polignac	BY	L	Portail du Prieuré de Vorey	BZ	S	Église St-Laurent	AY

LE-PUY-EN-VELAY

Aiguières R. Porte	AZ	2	Dentelle Av. de la	BZ	Pierret R.	BZ	37
Aiguilhe Av. d'	AY		Dr-Chantemesse Bd	AY	24	Plot Pl. du	AZ	38
Aiguilhe Rte d'	BY		Dupuy Av. Ch.	BZ		Pourrat Av. Henri	BY
Becdelièvre R.	AY	3	Farges R. des	AY		Raphaël R.	AY	39
Bonneville Av. de	BY		Farigoule R.	BZ		République Bd de la	BY	40
Bouillon R. du	BY	5	La-Fayette R. Gén.	BYZ		Roche-Taillade R.	AY	42
Breuil Pl. du	AZ		Fayolle Bd Mar.	BZ		Saint-François-Régis R.	BY	43
Cadelade Pl.	BZ		Foch Av. Mar.	BZ		Saint-Georges R.	BY	45
Card.-de-Polignac R.	BY	8	For Pl. du	BY	27	Saint-Gilles R.	AZ
Carnot Bd	AY		Gambetta Bd	AY	29	Saint-Jean R. du Fg	BY	46
Cathédrale Av. de la	AY		Gaulle Av. Gén.-de	ABZ	30	Saint-Louis Bd	AZ
Chamarlenc R. du	AY	10	Gouteyron R.	AY	31	Saint-Maurice Pl.	AY	47
Charbonnier Av. C.	AZ	12	Grangevieille R.	AY	32	Séguret R.	AY	48
Chaussade R.	BZ		Jourde Bd Philippe	BZ		Tables Pl. des	AY	49
Chênebouterie R.	AY	13	La-Fayette R. Gén.	BYZ		Tables R. des	AY	52
Clair Bd A.	AZ	14	Martin R. A.	AZ		Tanneries R. des	BZ
Clemenceau Av. G.	BZ		Martouret Pl. du	ABZ	34	Vallès R. J.	BY	54
Collège R. du	BZ	17	Michelet Pl.	BZ		Vaneau R.	AY	55
Consulat R. du	AY	19	Monseigneur-de-Galard Pl.	AY		Verdun R.	BY	58
Courrerie R.	AZ	20	Monteil R. A.-de	AY	35	Vibert R.	AZ
Crozatier R.	BZ	23	Montferrand Bd	AY		Victor-Hugo Cours	BZ
			Moulins R. des	BZ		Vieux Pont	BY
			Pannessac R.	AY			
			Philibert R.	AY	36		

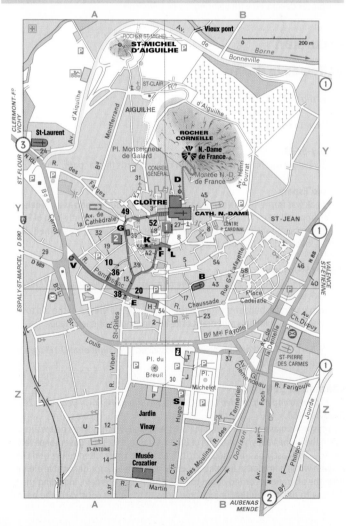

the Fine Arts. The top floor houses the natural history section with an ornithological collection containing nearly 400 species.

Église St-Laurent

The church of St-Laurent is a rare example of Gothic art in Velay; it dates from the 14C and was part of a Dominican convent. The doorway of the west front was built in the Flamboyant style.

Inside, the nave, shouldered by two side aisles and covered with ribbed vaulting, is surprisingly large. In the chancel, on the right, lies the tomb of **Bertrand du Guesclin** which contains the entrails of the Commander in Chief of the French armies, a national hero who died in 1380 during a siege. Work carried out in the chancel led to the discovery of the tomb of Bishop Bernard de Montaigu (13C).

On the left of the church a former 14C chapel, known as the chapter house, has been uncovered.

Église du Collège

At the beginning of the 17C, a Jesuit priest named Martellange built a building in the new Italian Baroque style for the order's newly founded college. It contains gilt altarpieces decorated with paintings by Guy François.

Excursion

Vallée de la Borne

Round trip of 60km/37mi – allow half a day

▷ *Leave Le Puy SW on D 590 to Espaly-St-Marcel.*

Espaly-St-Marcel

Shortly before reaching the railway, turn right towards the car park.

Piton d'Espaly

This peak was formerly crowned with a castle which, after serving as a residence for the bishops of Le Puy (Charles VII, while dauphin then subsequently king of France, was given hospitality here during his frequent pilgrimages), was ruined during battles involving the Catholic League *(private)*.

Rocher St-Joseph

🕐 *Sanctuary: Apr-Oct: 8am-7pm.* 🕐 *Nov-Mar: closed Mon. Pilgrimage: 19 Mar and 1 May. 3€.* ☎ *04 71 09 16 71.*

The upper terrace, built at the foot of the statue, offers a **view**★ of the old town of Le Puy-en-Velay, with its cathedral, Corneille rock and St-Michel Chapel.

▷ *Rejoin D 590 and continue towards Chaspuzac. Turn right onto D 113 then right again onto D 112.*

Château de St-Vidal

🕐 *mid-Jul to end Aug: guided tours (30min) 2-6.30pm. 4€ (6-14-year-olds: 2€).* ☎ *04 71 08 03 68.*

This castle, its massive towers dominating the village which clusters below around a rise in the Borne Valley, was the fief of Baron Antoine de la Tour, governor of Velay in the 16C. The castle has retained from its feudal days the vaulted cellars and Gothic kitchen with its immense fireplaces. Gothic and Renaissance decorative elements from the alterations carried out in the 15C and 16C still remain, including the galleries with ribbed vaulting lining three sides of the inner courtyard, the beamed

The Oracle of Apollo

The rock has been famous since Roman times when it was the site of a temple dedicated to Apollo famous for its oracles. Emperor Claudius visited it in AD 47. The oracles were pronounced by an enormous mask of Apollo. The pilgrim, arriving at the foot of the rock, placed his offerings in a room where he said his wishes out loud. He was unaware that his words could be clearly heard in the temple through a funnel-shaped well hollowed out in the rock. While he laboured up the hillside, the priests prepared their answer; using a megaphone, they made the words come out of the god's stone mouth, before the admiring yet terrified pilgrim.

ceiling and carved stone doorway of the State Room, and the southern façade. A spiral staircase leads to the top floor of the church tower (14C-16C) which was reserved for the artillery.

▶ *Return to D 113, turn right towards Clazelle then left onto N 102 and right again onto D 25. When the castle appears in the distance, turn left.*

Château de Rochelambert

🕐 *Apr-Sep: daily except Thu 10am-noon, 2-6pm (last admission 30min before closing); Oct-Mar: by appointment.* 🕐 *Closed 1 Jan, 25 Dec. 4€.* ☎ *04 71 00 48 99.*
Built on the banks of the River Borne, this 15C-16C castle set in pastoral surroundings was the setting of one of George Sand's novels, Jean de la Roche. It contains fine furniture and works of art.

▶ *Continue along the minor road for 2km/1.2mi then turn left onto D 131.*

Allègre

This village nestles round the ruins of a feudal castle built on the southern edge of the Boury volcano. Once through the Porte de Monsieur, you will see the Chapelle de Notre-Dame de l'Oratoire standing in the centre of the square. Walk up to the "gallows" to admire the panoramic view of the Velay region to the south and of Mont Bar to the east.

Tourbière du Mont Bar

This Stromboli-type volcano is the only one of its kind in France for its crater is filled with a peat bog. A marked footpath leads to the bog and enables visitors to walk all the way round. (🚶 *2hr there and back).* The climb is rather steep (good shoes are essential as the ground is slippery) but shaded by fir trees. There are explanatory panels along the way.

▶ *Leave Allègre S along D 13.*

St-Paulien

Once the capital of the Velay region, this village was a bishopric until the 6C.
The church is a fine example of Romanesque style from Auvergne. The interior was remodelled in the 17C: the three original naves were joined together to form one single nave and the chancel and ambulatory were brought together under a single vault. This created an impression of spaciousness and simplicity. Note the fine Romanesque capitals in the apsidal chapels.

▶ *Leave St-Paulien S along D 906 then follow N 102.*

Polignac

Polignac★

Rising proudly on its basalt hillock, the fortress of Polignac still has imposing remains of its powerful martial past from both Antiquity and the Middle Ages. The view of the site, from N 102, is superb.

Church

This is a beautiful Romanesque building with a Gothic porch. Note the 12C Romanesque-Byzantine dome; there are 15C frescoes in both the chancel and the chapel on the right of the chancel. Above the door of the southern side aisle is a modern stained-glass window representing three of the most famous members of the Polignac family: on the right, Viscount Heracles who died in the battle of Antioch; in the centre, Cardinal Melchior de Polignac; on the left, Prince Jules de Polignac.

Château

☞ *Closed for restoration.*

The building, which could house 800 soldiers as well as the family and servants, is perched on an enormous basalt platform, the remaining fragment of a lava flow; the platform sits on a softer strata of rock which has been protected from erosion as a consequence. It has sheer sides, which dispensed with the need to build high curtain walls.

▶ *Return to N 102 which leads back to Le Puy.*

RIOM★★

POPULATION 18 548

MICHELIN MAP 326: F-7 – 15KM/9.5MI N OF CLERMONT-FERRAND

The old town of Riom perched on a small hill on the western edge of the Limagne region still reflects the splendour of bygone days within the ring of boulevards laid out on its now demolished walls.  *16 r. du Commerce, 63200 RIOM, ☎ 04 73 38 59 45. www.riom.auvergne.com. Riom, which is listed as a "Town of Art and history," offers discovery tours conducted by guide-lecturers approved by the Ministry of Culture and Communication. Information at the service Animation du patrimoine (heritage dept.), at the Tourist office or on www.vpah.culture.fr*

A Bit of History

Le Puy-en-Velay capital city – At the beginning of the 13C Philippe Auguste's campaign was instrumental in making Riom's fortune as the monarchy decided to base the officers of its administration here.

In 1360 Duc **Jean de Berry**, the son of Jean le Bon (the Good), was given the Land of Auvergne, elevated to a duchy, as an apanage. The Duke, ostentatious and extravagant, was surrounded by a brilliant court of artists and chose Riom as one of his favourite places of residence. He ordered extensive work to be carried out on the old castle which he had converted by the architect Gui de Dammartin.

After the Duke's death, Riom and the Duchy of Auvergne passed to the Bourbon family. The town remained very much attached to the king; when **Joan of Arc** needed powder and arrows for the siege of La Charité-sur-Loire, she appealed to the people of Riom, who were reputed for their wealth. They pledged 60 gold écus but were slow to send them. In 1430 the townspeople received a letter of reminder; the

RIOM			
Bade Fg de la	2	Cour de l'Hôtel Guimoneau	B
Chabrol R.	3	Fontaine Desaix	E
Châtelguyon Av. de	4	Fontaine d'Adam et Éve	D
Commerce R. du		Hôtel Arnoux-de-	
Croisier R.	6	Maison-Rouge	G
Daurat R.	7	Hôtel de Ville	H
Delille R.	8	Maison des Consuls	K
Fédération Pl. de la	9	Musée Mandet	M¹
Hellénie R.	10	Musée régional d'Auvergne	M²
Horloge R. de l'		Sainte-Chapelle	N
Hôtel des Monnaies R. de l'	12	Tour de l'Horloge	R
Hôtel de Ville R. de l'	13		
Laurent Pl. J.-B.	14		
Layat Fg	15		
Libération Av. de la	16		
Madeline Av. du Cdt	17		
Marthuret R. du	18		
Martyrs de la Résistance Pl. des	19		
Menut Pl. Marinette	20		
Pré Madame Promenade du	21		
République Bd de la	22		
Reynouard Av. J.	23		
Romme R. G.	26		
St-Amable R.	27		
St-Louis R.	29		
Soanen Pl. Jean	32		
Soubrany R.	34		
Taules Coin des	36		

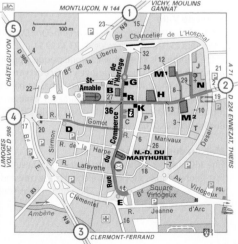

Address Book

EATING OUT

🍽🍽 **Le Flamboyant** – *21 bis r. de l'Horloge - ☎ 04 73 63 07 97 - restaurant. leflamboyant@wanadoo.fr - closed 15-28 Sep, Tue lunch and Mon.* Located in an historical edifice of the old town that used to be a girls' school, this restaurant welcomes diners in three small rooms decorated with watercolours and flowery curtains. Several fixed-price menus.

WHERE TO STAY

🍽🍽 **Chambre d'hôte Mme Beaujeard** – *8 r. de la Limagne, lieu-dit Chaptes - 63460 Beauregard-Vendon - 9km/5.4mi N of Riom via N 144 and D 122 - ☎ 04 73 63 35 62 - closed 1 Nov-1 Mar except by advance booking - ⌷ - 3 rms.* This bucolic, bourgeois home is encircled by a pretty garden that comes into its own in the summer. Hearty breakfasts are served in the cosy living room.

🍽🍽 **Honnorat Nicole et Stéphan** – *25 r. de l'Église - 63200 Davayat - 7km/4.2mi N of Riom via N 144 - ☎ 04 73 63 58 20 - ⌷ - 4 rms.* A handsome bourgeois residence (c 1810) designed along the lines of Italian neo-Classicism. Guests stay in the orangerie, an elegant outbuilding surrounded by a superb garden; each smart, well-kept room has its own decoration scheme. Delicious preserves made with fruit from the orchard on the breakfast table.

priceless letter has been preserved at the town hall, though the saint's hair, caught in the wax seal on the letter, has now disappeared.

Walking Tour

▶ *Start from place des Martyrs-de-la-Résistance.*

Sainte-Chapelle★

In the Palais de Justice. 🕐 *Jul-Aug: guided tours (30min) daily except Sat-Sun 10am-noon, 2.30-5.30pm (last admission 30min before closing); Jun and Sep: daily except Sat-Sun 3-5pm; Apr-May: Wed 3-5pm.* 🕐 *Closed 1 Jan, 1and 8 May, 14 Jul, 15 Aug, 25 Dec. 2€. ☎ 04 73 38 99 94.*

The chapel (14C), the only remainder of the Duke of Berry's castle, has some remarkable late-15C **stained-glass windows★** in the chancel.

Walk along rue de l'Hôtel-de-Ville to the town hall.

Hôtel de Ville

♿🕐 *Tours of the courtyard, Apr-Sep: 8am-7pm; Oct-Mar: 8am-5pm.* 🕐 *Closed 1 Jan, 1 May and 25 Dec. No charge. ☎ 04 73 38 99 94.*

In the vestibule is an enamelled stone plaque reproducing the letter from Joan of Arc to the people of Riom. The lovely 16C **courtyard★** is enclosed by two buildings decorated with vaulted arcades; note the basket-handled arches and a staircase turret with a carved door. Beneath the arcades stand two bronze sculptures by Rodin, including *Gallia Victrix* (modelled on Camille Claudel) and a marble sculpture by Rivoire *(the Kiss of Glory)*.

Maison des Consuls★

Fine 16C residence. The ground floor of the Consuls' House has five archways. The first-floor windows support an elegant frieze crowned by two busts of women and two busts of Roman emperors. The wooden house opposite dates from the 15C.

Carrefour des Taules

Near this crossroads *(taule is an old word for stall)* which forms the intersection of the main streets of old Riom stand some of the town's most interesting old houses. There are façades with carved windows at the corner of rue de l'Hôtel-de-Ville and rue de l'Horloge.

Rue de l'Horloge

The street is lined with old mansions with remarkable courtyards *(see below)* and beautiful windows such as those of no 4 and above all no 12. The town's belfry, with its gilt clock face, stands at the beginning of the street.

Tour de l'Horloge★

🕐 *Apr-Sep: 10am-noon, 2-6pm; Oct-Mar: 10am-noon, 2-5pm.* 🕐 *Closed 1 Jan, 25 Dec and days when the fair is held.* ☎ *04 73 38 99 94.*

Surmounted by a 17C dome, this octagonal Renaissance tower rests on a square medieval base. It houses an exhibition retracing the history of the town *(Riom, Ville d'Art et d'Histoire d'Hier à Aujourd'hui)*. One hundred and thirty steps lead to the terrace which offers a splendid **panorama** of the town and the surrounding area: enamelled-lava viewing tables face the four cardinal points.

Hôtel Arnoux-de-Maison-Rouge

7 rue de l'Horloge. The corridor, lit with oval windows, leads to a delightful early-17C courtyard *(guided tour only)*.

Cour de l'Hôtel Guimoneau★

12 rue de l'Horloge. 16C door. Go through the corridor into the attractive courtyard. The staircase is decorated with delicate carvings including an Annunciation. On the left, the gallery incorporates four statuettes representing, from left to right, Fortitude, Justice, Prudence and Temperance.

Note the medallions on the courtyard walls; two of them, at the back, depict the master and mistress of the house peering through small windows.

▷ *Return to carrefour des Taules and turn right onto rue St-Amable.*

Basilique St-Amable

Only the nave and part of the transept remain from the original 12C church. The chancel, from the early 13C, is a combination of Romanesque and Gothic (capitals with full-face figures and large crockets). The northern side chapels, with their fine ribbing on carved figure bases, date from the 15C; the southern side chapels and the west front are 18C. The sacristy features fine wood panelling (1687) around the chapter's chancel, and an interesting collection of silks.

▷ *Follow rue du Commerce, turn right onto rue Hyppolyte-Gomot and walk to the intersection with rue Sirmon.*

The numerous **fountains** that were erected in Riom in the 17C and 18C make strolling through the town very pleasant. One of the most famous is the 17C **Adam and Eve Fountain,** decorated with caryatids, by the Riom sculptor Languille; opposite stands a Renaissance house with arcades.

▷ *Return to the crossroads and take rue du Commerce.*

Rue du Commerce

The modern sculptures of lava stone contrast with older works of the same material, at no 36, note the caryatids of the Hôtel Valette de Rochevert.

Église Notre-Dame-du-Marthuret★

This church was built in the Languedoc style; it dates from the 14C and 15C. The west front was extensively damaged during the French Revolution; a copy of the Virgin with a Bird stands against the pier.

The interior was altered in the 17C and 19C by the addition of chapels (chancel and south side) and false side aisles. There are several interesting 15C and 16C stained-glass windows, and, in particular, in the first chapel on the right, the splendid **Virgin with a Bird**★★★. This famous 14C work came from the sculpture studios established by Jean de Berry; their reputation rivalled those of the court of the dukes of Dijon. It was saved during the Revolution by the butchers' corporation, who hid it in a cellar.

On place J.-B.-Laurent, the fountain recalls the Hero of the Battle of Marengo, **General Desaix** (1768-1800), who was born in Ayat-sur-Sioule.

Additional Sights

Musée Régional d'Auvergne★

🕐 *Jun-Sep: daily except Tue 10am-noon, 2.30-6pm; Oct-May: 10am-noon, 2-5.30pm.* 🕐 *Closed on some public holidays. 5€, no charge Wed.* ☎ *04 73 38 17 31.*

This Regional Museum of Arts, Crafts and Traditions, laid out on three floors, houses a remarkable collection of farming implements, rural and craft tools, furniture, games, domestic items and costumes which, with the reconstruction of typical Auvergne interiors, reflect the physiognomy of the province prior to the Industrial Revolution. The collection of headdresses and the room of religious statuary (13C-18C) are particularly interesting.

Musée Mandet★

🕐 *Jun-Sep: daily except Tue 10am-noon, 2.30-6pm; Oct-May: daily except Tue 10am-noon, 2-5.30pm.* 🕐 *Closed on certain public holidays. 5€, no charge Wed.* ☎ *04 73 38 18 53.*

This museum is arranged into two private mansions: one, Hôtel Dufraisse (built 1740), houses the painting collections; the other, Hôtel Desaix, houses the Richard Bequest. The first rooms display the **painting collection.** On the first floor, rooms decorated with delicate woodwork present a series of paintings from the 17C Flemish and Dutch Schools and the 17C and 18C French Schools. The second floor is given over to 19C painting, particularly the works of Alphonse Cornet, an artist from Riom.

The **Richard Bequest** includes interesting collections of ornamental objets d'art.

Excursion

Discovering Les Combrailles

Round trip of 75km/46.6mi – allow half a day

▶ *Leave Riom W on D 986 towards Pontgibaud.*

Mozac★★

This town lies at the gateway to Riom and is famous for the capitals and treasure in its church. An abbey was founded here by St Calmin in the 7C.

Church★

It is still possible to see sections of the pre-Romanesque building: the lower storeys of the belfry-porch and the crypt with reused Gallo-Roman masonry. The church was built in the 12C to a design inspired by the great churches of the Auvergne, but underwent major reconstruction in the 15C following an earthquake. During the French Revolution the cloisters and part of the abbey buildings were demolished. Remains from the Romanesque period include a series of fine **capitals**★★ in the nave and north side aisle which are renowned for their importance in the history of Romanesque sculpture. At the end of the nave are two of these very beautiful 12C capitals; they were originally part of the ambulatory, which no longer exists. One depicts four kneeling telamones and the second, the more famous of the two, depicts the female saints around Christ's tomb, holding jars of perfume in their hands. On another side of the capital is a carving of three soldiers asleep in front of Christ's tomb.

On the approach to the chancel there is a rich Romanesque bestiary visible, with griffins, men astride goats, dragons, a corded monkey (third pillar on the left), centaurs, birds of paradise, masks etc.

On the floor of the chancel is a third capital depicting four angels closing the mouths of four other characters; this is an illustration of a passage from St John's Book of Revelations. The chancel also contains 15C stalls. A 15C wood carving of the Madonna with a Bird stands near the baptistery.

The right aisle leads off to the former cloisters where the old tympanum (12C) may be seen.

Treasury★★

The most priceless object is the enamel **reliquary of St Calmin**★★, said to date back to 1168. It is displayed in a glass case in the right arm of the transept. The chapel protected by railings in the right aisle contains the reliquary of St Austremoine (17C), one of the few painted reliquaries in France.

▷ *Rejoin D 986 and follow it towards Pontgibaud.*

Volvic – 🕭 *See VOLVIC.*

▷ *N of Volvic, before the D 15-D 83 junction, turn left.*

Château de Tournoël★★ – 🕭 *See Château de TOURNOËL.*

▷ *Return to Volvic and take D 15 left alongside the graveyard. At the D 15 exit to Enval, leave the car just before the bridge spanning the Ambène.*

Gorges d'Enval★

30min on foot there and back.

🚶 Having crossed the bridge, take a path uphill to the left along the shaded banks of the river. After a few minutes of occasionally strenuous walking, cross the ford over the mountain stream, which forms a waterfall here that drops down into a picturesque gorge.

▷ *Continue to Charbonnières-les-Varennes then turn left onto D 16 towards Paugnat.*

Manoir de Veygoux

🕭🕐 *Jul-Aug: 10am-noon, 2-7pm (last admission 1hr before closing); May-Jun: daily except Thu 10am-noon, 2-6pm; Feb-Apr and Sep to mid-Nov: daily except Mon 2-6pm. 7€ (under-15s: 3.50€).* ☎ *04 73 33 83 00.*

The manor, where General Desaix spent his childhood, is partly concealed by a building recently added. Walk round the building to see the restored façade. Inside, there is a modern illustration of the life of this general who won fame during the Revolution and later in Bonaparte's army. The Egyptian campaign is illustrated in the outbuilding where sheep used to be kept. In addition, there is an exhibition devoted to the Combrailles area and its picturesque landscapes.

Return to Charbonnières-les-Varennes then drive to Châtelguyon.

Châtelguyon✝ – 🔊 *See CHÂTELGUYON.*

▶ *Leave Châtelguyon on D 415 towards Manzat.*

Château de Chazeron
🕐 *May-Jun, and Sep: 3-6pm. Jul-Aug, 2.30-6.30pm. 7€ (children: 4€).* ☎ *04 73 86 59 46.*

To the east of this castle is a rest area in a pleasant setting with a good view of Châtelguyon.

This medieval castle was altered in the 17C by the architect Mansart. A staircase was built on the site of the former east tower, three of the outer walls were also demolished and the moat filled in, then two wings were built, one of them containing the servants' kitchen (south wing).

The tour, arranged in chronological order, provides a lively insight into the history of the castle from its origin to the 20C (12C guard-room, 17C kitchens). From the top of the 25m/82ft-high west tower there is a good view of the Allier, the Limagne and the Sardon Valley.

The château is now a cultural centre, with exhibitions of drawings and avant-garde furniture.

▶ *Follow D 415 to the junction with D 227. Turn right at Pont de la Ganne on D 19 towards Combronde.*

Gour de Tazenat★
Allow 1hr on foot there and back. It is also possible to reach the viewpoint over the lake by car along a small track 200m/220yd on from the start of the footpath.

🚶 A footpath leads around the lake: leave from the refreshment stand in an anticlockwise direction. The first part of the footpath is flat but becomes steep in places along the second part. The green waters of Lake Tazenat lie in a volcanic crater, or maar. The lake has an area of 32ha/79 acres and a maximum depth of 70m/230ft, and marks the northern boundary of the Puys range.

Gour de Tazenat

The lakesides are over 50m/164ft high and are wooded, except for the north and north-east sides which are carpeted with stubbly grass.

▶ *In Charbonnières-les-Vieilles, take D 408 NE to Montcel then turn left to St-Hilaire-la-Croix.*

Église St-Hilaire-la-Croix
This attractive building stands on the shores of the "Red Lake," whose waters once mingled with the blood of martyrs, or so says local tradition. The lofty late-12C church shows strong Limousin influence (capitals decorated with palmettes and foliage motifs). Note the late-15C **statue of St Madeleine,** which became listed in 1913 and whose graceful lines are reminiscent of statuary from the Île de France. The **priory ruins** nearby house a vast upstairs gallery shaped like a **hull** that hosts temporary art exhibitions.

▶ *Take N 144 to Combronde, then S of the village take D 412.*

Sources Pétrifiantes de Gimeaux

&. ○ *all year except Jan, daily: guided tours (45min) 9.30am-noon, 2-6.30pm.* ○ *Christmas period and Jan 3€ (children: 2€).* ☎ *04 73 63 57 59.*

These natural thermal mineral springs are a geological phenomenon known locally as the "volcano." The industry of encrusting objects with lime dates back to the early 19C and uses tried and trusted techniques.

▶ *Carry on along D 17 on the banks of the Danade.*

Château de Davayat

&. ○ *Mid-Jul to end Aug: guided tours (45min) daily except Sat 2.30-6pm. 5€.* ☎ *04 73 63 30 27.*

A fine avenue of chestnut trees leads to this Louis XIII manor house built by Blaise Roze, a wealthy merchant from Riom. The ambitious plans for the house and formal gardens were curtailed at Roze's death.

Inside, the rooms contain paintings, fine furniture and decorative items. In the dining room, covered with an unusual ceiling which helps to reflect light around the room, there is a collection of Greek **terracotta figurines** dating from the 4C BC. A collection of **fans** is on display in the games room, and various costumes (18C ball gown, gentlemen's outfits, court robes) and miscellaneous objects of interest in the billiard room. The main courtyard offers a good view of the façade and its two sundials, one showing the hours, the other the seasons.

▶ *Return to Riom via St-Bonnet along N 144.*

RIOM-ÈS-MONTAGNES★

POPULATION 3 000
MICHELIN MAP 330: E-2 – LOCAL MAP SEE CONDAT

Situated in the western part of the Parc Régional des Volcans, Riom-ès-Montagnes is a small town linking the Rhue Valley to the Cantal mountain range and a thriving commercial centre with an important cheese industry. The production of an aperitif based on the gentian plant contributes to the prosperity of the town which is the ideal starting point of excursions through gentian country, its high pastures and Romanesque churches. ⓘ *place Charles de Gaulle, 15400 Riom-ès-Montagnes,* ☎ *04 71 78 07 37.*

Sights

Église St-Georges★

The only remaining parts of the original 11C are the chancel, the apse, the dome and the transept. The nave is 12C, the belfry Gothic. Inside, the capitals in the chancel are interesting: on the left is a scene from local history showing the battle between the knights of the Auvergne and the Saracens (carrying round shields); opposite, the judgement of Solomon.

Espace Avèze

&. ○ *Mid-Jun to mid-Sep: 10am-12.30pm, 3-7pm; the rest of the year: by appointment. No charge.* ☎ *04 71 78 03 04.*

Address Book

EATING OUT AND WHERE TO STAY

☞ **St-Georges** – *5 av. du Capitaine-Chevalier - 15400 Riom-ès-Montagnes - 17km/10mi SW of Condat via D 678 - ☎ 04 71 78 00 15 - www.hotel-saint-georges.com – closed 3-30 Nov and Sun evening - 14 rms -* 6€ *- restaurant* ☞☞. You'll be surprised to find such a modern hotel in this small mountain village. Behind its 19C façade, the practical rooms are agreeably spacious. Information about what to visit in the region for the asking.

☞☞ **Le Peyre Arse** – *Les Côts du Claux - 15400 Riom-ès-Montagnes - ☎ 04 71 78 93 32 - www.hotel-peyre-arse.com - closed Nov -* 🅿 *- 29 rms -* 7€ *- restaurant* ☞☞. The building at the edge of the village dates from the 1980s. The rooms are serviceable and clean and the restuarant (serving local dishes) is decorated in an intimate bistrot style. There is a nice covered pool and a terrace with a great view of the Cantal range.

☞☞☞ **Le Couvent** – *Le bourg - 15400 Trizac - ☎ 04 71 78 67 51 - www.lecouvent.fr - open Easter to Sept -* 🛏 *- 4 rms.* This unusual building used to be a convent, then a Catholic boarding school for young ladies. A large stairway leads to the rooms set up in the former classrooms; each is tastefully decorated in a unique style.

FLY-FISHING

The Lac du Roussillou (5ha/12 acres) is the paradise of fly-fishing enthusiasts: a 2km/1.2mi stretch along its shores has been specially adapted for trout fishing in the lake's pure waters. *Mid-Feb to early Dec, from 8.30am - ☎ 04 71 78 22 94. www.pechetruite.com/Lacs_reservoirs/roussiloue.htm*

This firm, founded in 1929, produces an aperitif based on the gentian plant picked in the surrounding mountains. An exhibition space, offering a view of the bottling hall, is devoted to the gentian and its use in the production of the aperitive. Avèze is the only gentian-based drink extracted by soaking the plant for nine months in a mixture of water and alcohol.

Gentiane Express

Runs daily in Jul-Aug, Sun and public holidays mid-Apr to end of Sep; allow 3 to 6 hours return. Booking essential. ☎ 05 55 96 88 59. See www.gentiane-express-cfha.com for seasonal charges.

This tourist train takes passengers across high pastures where the famous Salers cattle graze in summer. The itinerary links Bort-les-Orgues and Lugarde via Riom-ès-Montagnes and the Barajol viaduct.

Brasserie de l'Ecir

🕐 *11am-11pm. ☎ 04 71 78 06 98.*
This brewery produces the *Pastourela*, made with the pure water of the Cantal area. The quality of the water is such that there is no need to filter or pasteurise the beer brewed here. The visit ends with beer tasting…naturally.

Mountain Gentiane

J. Damase/MICHELIN

Excursions

St-Étienne-de-Choimeil
14km/8.7mi NW along D 3 then D 205. Turn right before the Romanesque church.

Botanical trail
🚶 *3.5km/2.2mi round tour; allow 1hr.* This pleasant ramble through woodland offers the opportunity of discovering the local flora in its natural environment.

② Cheylade valleys and Gentiane Country★★

90km/56mi – about one day – local map 👌 *see CONDAT*

▶ *If leaving from Condat, drive W along D 678.*

After crossing the dry Sapchat Valley, once the bed of the Rhue, and the Rhue de Cheylade Valley, the road overlooks the wooded Véronne Valley and runs along its hillside. Riom-ès-Montagne appears in the midst of a fresh pastoral setting.

Riom-ès-Montagnes★ – 👌 *See above.*

▶ *Head S from Riom along D 3.*

Soon *(4km/3mi from Riom)*, a superb **panoramic view** unfolds to the left over the Dore mountain range and the upper plateaux of the Cézallier area. Beyond lie the ruins of the Château d'Apchon and the mountains of Cantal.

Apchon
This is a typical Cantal village with its sturdy houses in volcanic stone. On the village square stands a **church** with a belfry-porch and a huge 17C giltwood altarpiece inside. A footpath leads off from rue de la Porte-du-Barre to a viewing table and the **castle ruins** *(30min on foot there and back; access to the ruins could be dangerous for children)*. There is a good **view**★ of the surrounding countryside from the top of the rocky pinnacle where the ruins stand.

▶ *Leave Apchon S (D 249) then turn right onto D 63.*

Collandres
The Romanesque church of this tiny village stands on the site of a former look-out post which kept watch over the Véronne Valley. The massive-looking building is typical of the local architectural style. Walk through the belfry-porch to admire the altarpiece from the Apchon School.
The road, which goes past the church, runs across high pastures where cattle graze in summer. In the Cantal region, these pastures extend over an area of some 80 000ha/197 688 acres. Turn left at the first junction towards La Chatonnière. The road runs through woodland and pastureland dotted with burons (shepherds' huts) and farms. Besides cattle grazing in the fields, you are likely to see birds of prey and herons.

▶ *Return to Collandres and leave the village S along D 263.*

Cascade du pont d'Aptier
This waterfall in its unspoilt setting is the ideal place for a picnic.

▶ *Beyond the bridge, turn left onto D 249.*

Chapelle de la Font-Sainte

🕐 *Mid-Jun to mid-Sep: 9am-7pm.* ☎ *04 71 78 93 62.*

This 19C chapel, a popular place of pilgrimage, can be seen in the middle of the fields. The small statue of the Virgin Mary, the patron saint of shepherds, spends the summer in the high pastures and goes down again at the end of the season to spend the autumn and winter in the church of Cheylade. Note the stone cross on the right of the church and walk to the fountain where the clear water is said to have miraculous powers.

The road *(D 49)* runs through St-Hippolyte and down to the Rhue de Cheylade. After crossing the river, the Puy Mary is visible to the right of a long ridge starting at the Puy de Peyre-Arse.

Cheylade

This resort above the Rhue is popular with anglers and is a good starting point for rambles *(several itineraries)*. The interior of its **church** has undergone alteration on several occasions; the chancel, which still has a few carved capitals (mermaids, acanthus leaves, interlacing), and the apse are the oldest parts of the church. The nave and side aisles were roofed in the 17C with a remarkable **coffered ceiling**★ made of oak and painted with angels, flowers and animals in a naïve style. Behind the High Altar there is a 14C wooden Crucifix and, to the left of the chancel at the entrance to the Sacred Heart Chapel, a shield bearing the arms of the D'Estaing family, one of whose members found glory on the battlefield at Bouvines in 1214. There is also a wooden statue of St Leger (15C).

▷ *2.5km/1.5mi S of Cheylade, turn right on D 262. Park near a bridge and walk a further 100m/110yd to the right.*

Cascade du Sartre★

The waterfall is formed by the Rhue which flows down a drop of 30m/98ft.

Continue along D 262 and, beyond another bridge, turn right on a path offering an attractive view of the **Cascade de la Roche**, a waterfall formed by a tributary of the Rhue which drops down over the rocks in a series of mini-cascades.

▷ *Turn back and continue along D 62.*

Le Claux

This small resort is ideal for the practice of a variety of outdoor activities: cross-country skiing and snowshoeing in winter (**Maison de Montagne** – ☎ *04 71 78 93 88*), paragliding, climbing, riding and rambling in summer.

Beyond Le Claux, the view of the Puy Mary and the Cheylade Valley with its forested floor becomes increasingly impressive. The road rises in a series of hairpin bends and continues through woods until it reaches the alpine pastures. It then crosses Col de Serres and arrives at the Impradine Valley, hollowed into a bowl shape by ancient glaciers. During the final climb up to Pas de Peyrol, the road crosses the Eylac pass, clings to the sheer sides of the Puy Mary and provides a number of splendid **views**★ over the Impradine and Rhue de Cheylade valleys, the Dore mountain range, and the Cézallier area.

Pas de Peyrol★★ – 🕐 *See Monts du CANTAL.*

▷ *Go back 3km/1.9mi along D 62, then turn right onto D 23, heading for Dienne.*

The road hugs the steep Impradine and Santoire valleys.

Puy Mary★★★ – 👣 *See Monts du CANTAL.*

▶ *Leave Puy Mary along D 680 then turn right onto D 12 towards Le Falgoux. Beyond Col d'Aulac, turn left as you enter the Marihou woods.*

Site de Cotteughes et Preydefont
The remains of drystone huts abandoned during the Middle Ages testify to the area's long-standing cattle breeding tradition.

Trizac
This large village is renowned for its cattle markets. The Romanesque church has a 13C belfry-porch. Inside, note the capitals decorating the chancel, the 12C-13C Virgin Mary in a sitting position and several Baroque altarpieces. The stained-glass windows in the transept and the chancel were reconstructed from the remains of 15C windows recently discovered.
The road *(D 678)* running through pastures dotted with broom offers a fine view of the Artense plateau.

▶ *Turn right onto D 205.*

Menet
As the road runs down towards the village, it affords views of its harmonious white buildings, including the 12C church which has beautifully carved capitals. The nearby lake offers relaxing activities (angling, pedalo, etc.).

▶ *Leave Menet E; D 36 runs through woodland back to Riom.*

ROANNE

CONURBATION 80 272
MICHELIN MAP 327: D-3

Rodumna, as the town was called in ancient times, dates back to more than a century before the birth of Christ. In the 11C the lords of Roanne built a fortress. The Seignieury of Roanne belonged in turn to the counts of Forez, Jacques Cœur, the dukes of Bourbon and the dukes of Roanne. The inauguration of the Roanne-Digoin canal in 1838 brought intense activity to the port of Roanne, thereby determining the town's industrial vocation. 🛈 *1 cours de la République, 42300 ROANNE, ☎ 04 77 71 51 77. www.leroannais.com*

Home weavers

The textile industry took off around Roanne in 1880, when 6 000 factory workers were employed. By the end of the 19C its impact stretched from the Madeleine mountain range in the west to the hills of Beaujolais in the east. From the 16C, cloth-making, a cottage industry without any specific framework, began to be organised by merchants from Lyon who provided the raw materials and established conditions for the manufacturing system.

Home weavers worked in a separate building or annexe to their home and continued to work the land to increase their income.

Modern Roanne – Roanne is one of the best-known French textile centres for ready-made garments, hosiery and knitted goods (second in France) and towelling. Its other economic activities are highly diversified: food processing, metallurgy, armoured tanks, tools, boiler making, tanning, dyes, paper mills, plastics and tyres. A Michelin tyre production unit has been operating in the north-east of the town since 1974.

The local gastronomy has earned a well-deserved reputation for excellence and the town boasts several fine restaurants, including one of the most famous establishments in France.

Revolutionary faience (Nevers 1793)

Sights

Musée des Beaux-Arts et d'archéologie Joseph-Déchelette

🕐 *Daily except Tue 10am-noon, 2-6pm (Sat 10am-6pm, Sun 2-6pm).* 🕐 *Closed public holidays. 4€, no charge Wed afternoon.* ☎ *04 77 23 68 77.*

This eclectic museum, housed in an early-18C mansion, was founded by the archaeologist **Joseph Déchelette** (1862-1914), a native of the town. He gathered the rich **archaeological collections** which include many Gallo-Roman artefacts found during the course of excavations in the region. An important stock, shown in rotation, illustrates the prehistoric and Egyptian periods.

The museum is also known for its fine collections of faience including items of 16C and 17C Italian **majolica**, as well as earthenware from the famous 18C French manufactures such as Nevers, Rouen, Moustiers or Marseille. An impressive amount of space is devoted to a themed display of faience decorated with **motifs on the theme of the Revolution**★ (300 items) which includes some highly original works (bottles shaped like books and decorated with historical scenes). More recent creations illustrate the trends of contemporary ceramics.

The other rooms contain paintings and sculptures from the 15C to the 20C.

Place de-Lattre-de-Tassigny

The site of the old castle (part of its keep still stands) is flanked by the church of **St-Étienne** with its 15C stained-glass window depicting the martyrdom of St Sebastian (on the right, 2nd bay in the nave).

Gallo-Roman potters' kilns (2C AD) are visible beyond the chancel. North of the church is the **Caveau de Roanne,** a small half-timbered house.

Cabanes and Saint-Rambertes

Until the end of the 17C, traffic on the River Loire was only possible downstream of Roanne. Oak boats called *cabanes* (cabins), because of the shelter they offered, carried passengers and goods between Roanne and Paris, on the Briare canal (opened in 1538), or between Roanne and Nantes.

In the 18C work was carried out on the Loire to make it navigable upstream of Roanne. New boats, built of St-Rambert pine – from which they derived their name, *saint-rambertes* – transported coal and wine from St-Étienne to Roanne and Nantes. On arriving at their destination, they were either sold or dismantled because they could not sail upstream. Every year, the bargemen would visit their corporation's chapel, St-Nicolas-du-Port, near the wharf.

Address Book

EATING OUT

Le Central – *20 cours de la République (opposite the train station) -* ☎ *04 77 67 72 72 - closed 2 wks in Aug, 24 Dec to 5 Jan, Sun-Mon - reserv. requested.* Right next to the Troisgros brothers' restaurant (see entry below), this bistro-grocery also belongs to the famous family. Simple, contemporary cuisine is served here. The jars of preserves that serve as decor are for sale, so you can take the memories home.

Le Relais de la Vieille Tour *- 42155 St-Maurice-sur-Loire -* ☎ *04 77 63 16 83 - closed Mon-Tue from Mar to May, Mon-Thu from Dec to Feb.* This family address is quite agreeable: bourgeois furniture and flowers in the restaurant downstairs, a summer terrace with a view upstairs. Traditional fare.

Ma Chaumière *- 3 r. St-Marc - 42120 Le Coteau - right bank of the Loire -* ☎ *04 77 67 25 93 - closed 29 Jul to 22 Aug, Sun evening and Mon.* A warm reception awaits you in this restaurant with its stylish green façade. Located between downtown and the quay, it's managed by people who love their work and pamper their clients. The traditional cuisine is prepared from fresh ingredients.

Le Marcassin – *Rte de St-Alban-les-Eaux - 42153 Riorges - 3km/1.8mi W of Roanne via D 31 -* ☎ *04 77 71 30 18 - closed Feb school holidays, 2 wks in Aug, Sun evening, Fri evening and Sat.* After visiting the Maille museum in Riorges, you might try this family offering modern fare in fixed-price menus and à la carte. Pleasant contemporary dining room and terrace used when the sun shines. Very basic rooms.

Troisgros *- Pl. de la Gare -* ☎ *04 77 71 66 97 - www.troisgros. fr - closed Feb school holidays, 2 wks in Aug, Tue-Wed - reserv. essential.* With three Michelin stars, this is a veritable institution that sets the standard for French gastronomy. The Troisgros family receives its guests in a setting where modernism, quality, luxury and sobriety intermingle in perfect elegance.

WHERE TO STAY

Chambre d'hôte M et Mme Pras – *Magnerot - 42370 St-Haon-le-Vieux - 4km/2.4mi N of Renaison via D 8 and D 81 -* ☎ *04 77 64 45 56 - closed 15 Nov to 15 Mar and during grape harvest - ⌷ - 3 rms.* A small house with pale green shutters on the way to the village featuring a friendly, straightforward interior decoration scheme and entirely refurbished guest rooms. Your hosts, wine makers by trade, enjoy explaining the different facettes of the Roanne vineyard.

Grand Hôtel – *18 cours de la République, opposite the train station -* ☎ *04 77 71 48 82 - closed 2-25 Aug and 20 Dec to 5 Jan -* 🅿 *- 31 rms - ⌷ 9€.* Just across from the Roanne train station, this well-maintained hotel dating from the early 20C has undergone recent renovations under the impetus of a new management team. Rooms of different sizes. A convenient address.

Chambre d'hôte L'Échauguette – *Ruelle Guy-de-la-Mure - 42155 St-Jean St-Maurice-sur-Loire - 12km/7.2mi SW of Roanne via D 53 and D 203 -* ☎ *04 77 63 15 89 - www.echauguette-alex.com - ⌷ - 4 rms - meals ⌷.* Located on the edge of town, L'Échauguette dominates a hill-circled lake. Each room is different; breakfast is served in the kitchen or, if the weather is fine, on the summer terrace where you can enjoy the panoramic view... to the last drop.

Chambre d'hôte Domaine de Champfleury – *Le Bourg - 42155 Lentigny - 8km/4.8mi SW of Roanne via D 53 -* ☎ *04 77 63 31 43 - closed 15 Nov to 15 Mar - ⌷ - reserv. recommended in winter - 3 rms.* This attractive 19C bourgeois house surrounded by century-old trees in a handsome park is owned by a charming lady whose guests are treated as friends. Needless to say, you'll be shamelessly spoiled here. Perfect for a thorough rest. Tennis court for the asking.

SHOPPING

Pralus – *8 rue Charles-de-Gaulle -* ☎ *04 77 71 24 10.* Pralulines, butter brioches studded with praline, almonds and hazelnuts, are responsible for this establishment's renown. Available in 300g/10oz and 600g/20oz sizes.

Robert Sérol et Fils – *Les Estinaudes - 42370 Renaison -* ☎ *04 77 64 44 04 - www.domaine-serol.com - Mon-Sat 8.30am-12.30pm, 1.30pm-7pm, Sun by appointment.* For the past 15 years, this 20ha/50 acre vineyard has been supplying the Troisgros establishments with red and rosé Côte Roannaise wines. Magnificent view of grapevines and plain. The cellar where winery products may be sampled and purchased is pleasant.

Terre Paysanne – *174 route de Villemontais - 42300 Villerest -* ☎ *04 77 72 26 13.* Housed in a wonderfully restored old barn, this shop offers a broad range of products - including wine, fruit juice, oil, mustard, preserves, delicatessen, poultry and beer - made or raised by farmers and artisans of the Loire region.

A popular marina

Traffic on the canal from Roanne to Digoin and in the port of Roanne, which was important until 1945, declined rapidly from 1970 onwards and came to a halt in 1992. This has been offset by an increase in pleasure boating with the opening of locks on Sundays during the summer months. **Barge trips** *(Several types of trip are proposed (1/2 day, 1 day or more) from or to Roanne aboard the barge "L'Infatigable". Groups take priority. Marins d'Eau Douce, Port de plaisance de Briennon.* ☎ *04 77 69 92 92)* are also organised on the canal.

Parc des Canaux

In Briennon. Kids ⏱ *Jul-Aug: guided tours (45min) 10am-noon, 2-7pm; Easter to May and Sep-early Nov: 2-6pm. 6€ (3-12-year-olds: 3€).* ☎ *04 77 60 75 79 or 04 77 69 92 92.*
This park, located along the canal between Roanne and Digoin, has a lot to offer children interested in inland navigation: a real barge turned into a museum and a hands-on system of miniatures locks and barge.

Chapelle St-Nicolas-du-Port

The small chapel can be seen near the wharfs of the port. The date on the pediment – 1630 – marks the year the bargemen made a vow to erect a chapel to their patron saint if they were spared the death throes of the plague.

Excursions

Montagny

14km/8.7mi E along D 504. On leaving Montagny, follow the signpost indicating "La Roseraie."

Roseraie Dorieux

⏱ *Jul-Sep: free access to the rose garden; rest of the year, please enquire for opening hours.* ☎ *04 77 66 11 46.*
This colourful and fragrant rose garden and nursery is freely accessible from July to September.

Plateau de la Verrerie

▸ *Leave Roanne W along D 9 to Renaison then follow D 47 to La Grand'Borne and turn right onto D 478 which leads to La Tourbière. To get back, follow D 39 from Col de la Rivière then D 9 to Roanne or D 4 if you fancy a detour via Briennon.*

🏃 The solitary road climbs through the forest before reaching the Plateau de la Verrerie which offers a pleasant ramble and a panoramic view of the Roanne plain.

Le Crozet

25km/15.5km NW on N 7. The flower-decked houses of this small medieval town are spread out along the foothills of the Madeleine mountains.

▶ *Leave the car at the entrance to Le Crozet.*

You enter the old main square by the **Grand-Porte,** flanked by two round towers that are truncated and partly concealed by houses.

Maison du Connétable

Note the fine front with its pretty wooden panels. The adjoining house with walled-in arcades used to be a cobbler's workshop (15C).

Maison Dauphin

A former meat market, this heavily restored late-15C house has kept its charming Renaissance windows.

Maison Papon★

Enter the courtyard to fully appreciate the handsome Renaissance façade made with enamelled ceramics and embellished with mullioned windows.

Tour de guet

The 12C keep standing near the 19C church has lost its machicolated crown. From the top the view embraces the Monts de la Madeleine to the south and the Monts du Charolais to the east *(viewing table).*

Maison des Amis du Vieux Crozet

🕐 *Jun-Sep: daily except Mon and Tue 3-7pm; rest of the year by appointment, 2€.* ☎ *04 77 64 11 06 (tourist office).*
A peasant's interior has been carefully reconstructed in this 15C residence, alongside an old-fashioned smithy and a clog-maker's workshop.

Côte Roannaise★

A line of vineyard-covered slopes running north-south, known as the "Côte," dominates the Roanne basin to the west. Beyond the Côte and separated from it by the Rouchin and Tache valleys, rise the granite hills of the **Madeleine** mountain range culminating in the **Pierre du Jour** (1 165m/3 822ft), and forming an extension of the Forez mountain range and Bois Noirs (Black Woods).
Contrasting with the harshness of the Madeleine mountains, the Côte is gentle and colourful, with rectangular houses, often roughcast with green shutters and red-tiled double pitched roofs, reddish soil, and vineyards that produce reputed AOC *(Appellation d'Origine Contrôlée)* red wines, as well as rosés and whites.

▶ *Leave Roanne on D 9 W and turn left onto D 51 to St-André-d'Apchon.*

There is an pretty view of the hills up ahead.

St-André-d'Apchon

At the centre of the town, in a secluded setting, stands a 16C château built for the Marshal of St-André which has preserved its original façade decorated with Renaissance medallions.

▶ *From the War Memorial, walk up the street with the Lion d'Or Hotel on the corner, then along the covered passageway 30m/33yd on the right, next to a butcher's shop.*

The **church** in Flamboyant Gothic style, is decorated with 16C stained-glass windows. Note the Renaissance portal to the right of the bell-tower: on the tympanum is a beautiful stone statue of St Andrew (16C), surmounted by a small effigy of the Eternal Father. Note also the glazed tile roof.

▶ *Continue along D 51 to Arcon.*

The road twisting uphill above St-André offers a series of vistas of the Roanne plain.

▶ *Leave Arcon to the N, to Les Grands-Murcins and its arboretum.*

Les Grands-Murcins
15min on foot there and back.
🔼 The arboretum, created in 1936-37 at the heart of a 150ha/370-acre national forest (average altitude 770m/2 526ft) is particularly rich in coniferous trees, including Himalayan weeping pines, *Abies alba* fir trees, Tsuga canadensis with their curtain-like branches and Douglas firs that thrive locally at an altitude of less than 900m/2 952ft. From the viewing table, there is a good **view** of the Roanne plain and Lyonnais hills.

▶ *Return to Arcon and head S to La Croix-Trévingt. Turn right onto D 51 towards St-Priest.*

Rocher de Rochefort★
The Rochefort Rock is equipped with a viewing table: **views** of the Roanne plain, the Beaujolais and Lyonnais hills.

▶ *Return to La Croix-Trévingt. Turn left onto D 51 and left again onto D 41 along the Rouchain Valley to the dam.*

Barrage du Rouchain
Duplicating the Tache dam to supply Roanne with drinking water, this dam (1977), made of rockfill, is 230m/754ft long, 55m/180ft high, 9m/30ft wide at the crown and 190m/623ft at the base. Equipped with a spillway on the River Rouchain, the barrage has a capacity of 6 500 000m3/230 million cu ft and occupies three valleys.

Barrage de la Tache
This dam (221m/725ft long and 51m/167ft high) was built between 1888 and 1892. Its width, which is only 4m/13ft at the top, increases to 47.5m/156ft at the base. It is a gravity dam, that is, the sheer mass of the dam resists the pressure of the water. It has a capacity of 3 326 000m3/117 408 000cu ft.

Renaison
This is the economic heart of the Côte Roannaise. Its neo-Gothic church houses a Romantic organ by organ-builder John Abbey.

▶ *Turn back then follow D 9 to La Croix-du-Sud.*

On the way, a **look-out rock**★ on the left offers an attractive view of the Tache reservoir. The road up to the pass looks out over the Madeleine mountain range.

La Croix-du-Sud
This pass is a major intersection on the rise separating the Madeleine mountain range from the Côte, and the valley of the Teyssonne from that of the Tache.
During the **descent**★ along D 39 (sharp right), notice the different bands of vegetation depending on the altitude: on the crest, heathland or woodland; below,

pastureland and small crops; further down there are vineyards and, in the distance, the plain with its meadows and vast estates.

St-Haon-le-Châtel★

Park on the square at the top of the village and go through a fortified gateway with studded wooden doors to the left of a butcher's shop. The **fortified village**★ has preserved its medieval appearance and some of its ramparts. The restored **church** (12C-17C) is a modest building, with typical furniture from the Forez region.

▶ *Take D 8 N to Ambierle.*

Ambierle★

This pretty town, exposed to the morning sun, is set amid vineyards that yield a pleasant rosé wine. There is an old Cluniac priory in the upper part of the village. The late-15C **church**★ is in the Flamboyant Gothic style. Inside, the nave is narrow and elegant; magnificent 15C **stained-glass windows**★ fill the five 13m/42ft-high windows of the chancel, and the windows of the side chapels and north aisle. On the High Altar stands a 15C **Flemish altarpiece**★ with painted panels attributed to Rogier van der Weyden. The **Musée Alice-Taverne** (🕐 Feb-Nov: 10am-noon, 2-6pm. 4€ (children: 2€). ☎ 04 77 65 60 99) focuses on traditional home life in the region – the fascinating games, costumes, superstitions of local life – and has recreations of various interiors (workshop, inn etc).

Painted panel in Ambierle church

▶ *Take D 8 and D 9 back to Roanne.*

On the left is an attractive view of the large round tower of **Château de Boisy** (⚷ *not open to the public*). This castle (14C-16C) belonged successively to the Couzan family, Jacques Cœur, and the Gouffier family, and occupies an important position in the history of Roanne: it was for Arthur Gouffier, his old tutor, that François I elevated the estate of Boisy to the rank of duchy of Roanne.

Gorges Roannaises de la Loire★

Round trip of 139km/87mi – allow half a day

▶ *Leave Roanne to the S along avenue de la Libération. Turn right by the station onto D 43 and then right again onto D 56 to Commelle-Vernay viewpoint (signposted).*

Construction of the Villerest dam upstream of Roanne created a new "Loire Lake," 33km/20.5mi long, which attracts numerous sailing enthusiasts in the summer.

Belvédère de Commelle-Vernay★

The **view** encompasses Roanne and its outskirts and the Vernay bridge to the north, the town and dam of Villerest and the modern installations of the Villerest paper mills to the west with, in the background, the Madeleine mountain range.

A small **tourist train** (🚃🕐 *Reservations required: Mar-Oct: 9.30am, 11am, 3pm, 4.30pm and 6pm. 6€ (children: 5€). ☎ 04 77 68 58 12. www.le-petit-train-touristique.net) offers a 7km/4.3mi ride along the shores of Lake Villerest.

Barrage de Villerest

Designed to combat low water levels and floods on the Loire, this is a solid concrete arch gravity dam with a crown length of 469m/1 538ft. Its curved shape reinforces its stability. The variable-level reservoir is 30km/19mi long and has an average width of 250m/820ft.

▶ *Cross over the dam to Villerest.*

Villerest

The old **medieval town**★ is a pleasant place to visit; there are many houses with corbelled construction or timber-framed walls, and the remains of ramparts. The 13C **Porte de Bise** is the starting point for a tour on foot; points of particular interest are highlighted on information boards. During the summer, crafts are sold from the traditional street stalls.

Musée de l'Heure et du Feu

🕐 *Apr-Jun and Sep-Oct: Sat-Sun and public holidays 2.30-6.30pm (Jul-Sep: daily). 4€. ☎ 04 77 69 71 97.*
This unusual museum is divided into two parts, the **Section on Fire**★ traces the history of the creation and the upkeep of domestic fire since Antiquity and across different countries. The other section houses an eclectic mix of **unusual watches and clocks** from the 18C to the 20C, more lighters, amusing caricatures, and numerous items fashioned from bits of munitions by soldiers in the trenches.

▶ *Leave to the W and head for St-Jean-St-Maurice-sur-Loire.*

St-Maurice-sur-Loire★

This town occupies a picturesque **site**★ overlooking the river. The old houses cling to a spur crowned by the ruins of a medieval castle. **La Mure-Chantois Manor** has an ornate doorway featuring statues of Adam and Eve, and a staircase tower with a fine sculpted fronton. The **church** has a Romanesque apse decorated with 13C

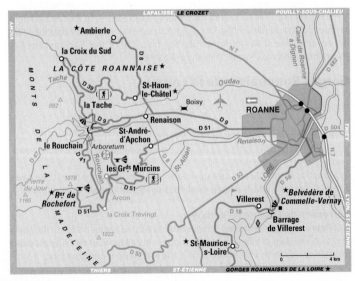

Romanesque murals in the church at St-Maurice-sur-Loire

murals depicting the Annunciation, the Visitation, the Nativity and the Flight into Egypt (left), the Massacre of the Innocents and the Garden of Eden (right).

▶ *Drive towards Bully, down the hill towards the Loire and over the bridge at Presle. Turn right onto D 56 and continue along the east bank of the river.*

The route goes through an attractive rocky passage past Château de la Roche.

Château de la Roche
🕐 *Jul-Aug: 10.30am-noon, 2-7pm; Apr-Jun: daily except Wed 2-7pm; Nov-Mar: Thu-Sun, 2-6pm; Sep-Oct: daily except Wed, 2-6 (Sat, Sun, 7pm). 4€. ☎ 04 77 64 97 68. www. lechateaudelaroche.com.*
This medieval manor presents the history of the Gorges de la Loire area and a model of the gorge in a refined 17C decor (painted panels on the walls and ceilings).

▶ *Shortly after the Chessieux viaduct the road meets N 82 near Balbigny; turn left towards Neulise. After 6km/4mi turn right onto D 5.*

St-Marcel-de-Félines
This peaceful village facing the Forez mountains has a 12C fortified house which was altered in the 16C into a **château** (🕐 *Easter to Oct: Sun and public holidays 2-6pm. 5€. ☎ 04 77 63 54 98).* A bridge over the old moat leads to an inner courtyard of Italian inspiration. Inside, the decoration of the reception rooms is unified by the 17C wall and ceiling **paintings**★.

▶ *Rejoin N 82 and continue to Neulise; turn right onto D 38. At Croizet turn right, cross the River Gand and take the path to the right.*

Château de l'Aubépin
🕐 *Daily except Tue and Wed 10am-noon, 2-5pm.* 🕐 *Closed 15 Aug. No charge.*
This lovely old château (16C-18C), flanked by corner pavilions is topped with a watch-turret set back from an avant-corps decorated with masks.

▶ *Return to Roanne on N 82.*

The road offers views of the Roanne vineyards and the Loire Valley downstream.

ROMANS-SUR-ISÈRE

POPULATION 32 667
MICHELIN MAP 332: D-3

The town is built on a hillside opposite Bourg-de-Péage, whose name is a reminder of the toll once collected by the Chapter of St Barnard to cross the bridge linking the two towns. Romans, a flourishing trade centre in the Middle Ages, was once the capital of footwear. Lovers of good food will appreciate the local *pogne,* which is a type of *brioche* or sweet bread flavoured with orange blossom, *saint-genis* (praline *pogne*) and goats' cheese, *Tomme* (which is also used to make the local dish *ravioles*). *Pl. Jean-Jaurès, 26100 ROMANS-SUR-ISÈRE,* ☎ *04 75 02 28 72.* ⏰ *Apr-Oct: 9am-7pm, Sat, 9am-6pm. Sun and public holidays, 9.30am-12.30pm; rest of year: 9am-6pm, Sun and public holidays, 9am-12.30pm.* ⏰ *1 Jan, 1 May and 25 Dec.*

Dauphiné joins France – From the 11C on, the counts of Albon, natives of Vienne, gradually took over the region – stretching from the Rhône Valley to the Alps – which was eventually to form Dauphiné. The origin of the name "Dau-phin," given to members of the dynasty which then reigned over Dauphiné, remains uncertain.

The last of the Vienne dauphins, Humbert II, lived mostly at Beauvoir Castle, opposite St-Marcellin *(25km/15.5mi NE).* After the death of his son, which left him without an heir, he sold Dauphiné to the French crown. It was in St-Barnard Collegiate Church that the treaty unifying the Dauphiné region, formerly part of the Holy Roman Empire, to France, was solemnly signed on 30 March 1349.

This province was to become the attribute of the oldest sons of the kings of France, who subsequently bore the title of Dauphin.

Old Town

▶ *Start from place du Pont.*

A maze of picturesque streets surrounds St-Barnard Collegiate Church and, half way down the hill from the church, place de la Presle and place Jacquemart.

Collégiale St-Barnard

Quai U.-Chevalier. ♿⏰ *Mid-Jun to mid-Sep: guided tours (1hr), daily, 10am-noon, 2.30-6pm, Sun and public holidays 2.30-6pm; rst of year by arrangement. 3€. Apply in advance:* ☎ *04 75 72 43 58.*

In the 9C St Barnard, archbishop of Vienne, founded a monastery here. It was destroyed in the 12C and replaced by a Romanesque church of which the western porch, the northern portal and lower parts of the nave still remain. Towards the middle of the 13C the chancel and transept were rebuilt in Gothic style. Largely destroyed by the Protestants in the 16C, the church was completely restored in the 18C.

Exterior

Seen from the bridge (Pont Vieux), the massive silhouette of the church is reflected in the Isère. To the west, on the piers of the Romanesque portal, are statues of apostles, grouped in pairs and resting on lions, one of which is devouring a human and the other a sheep. Although damaged, they are nevertheless very interesting.

Interior

The interior is unusual for its Romanesque arcade reinforcing the walls of the nave; the arches rest on columns with capitals decorated with foliate designs or narrative

Address Book

EATING OUT

☞ **Le Chevet de St-Barnard** – *1 pl. aux Herbes - ☎ 04 75 05 04 78 - closed 14 Jul to 4 Aug, Sun evening, Tue evening and Wed*. At the foot of the St-Barnard church, this attractive 14C residence, formerly a bishop's palace, is partly used as a restaurant. Managed by a young couple, it is popular with the locals who appreciate the affordable, appetizing fixed-price menus.

WHERE TO STAY

☞ **Chambre d'hôte Chez M. et Mme Imbert** – *'Les Marais', Hameau de St-Didier - 26300 St-Didier-de-Charpey - 9km/5.4mi S of Romans. Take D 538 to Alixan, then left onto road to St-Didier - ☎ 04 75 47 03 50 - http://perso.wanadoo.fr/les-marais - 3 rms*. The former stables belonging to this family farm now contain pleasant, simple bedrooms decorated with old country furniture and flowered wallpaper. Meals, with an accent on regional cookery, are served with the family. A small agricultural museum for your inspection.

LOCAL SPECIALITIES

Shopping – Gourmets are fond of *pognes*, brioches with orange flower blossoms, so-named because Roman housewives traditionally would take a pougne, or fistful, of the household bread dough to make this sweet treat. Also popular are *Saint-Genis* (pralined pognes), goat cheese *ravioles* and *tomme de chèvre*, a local goat cheese.

Ravioles Mère Maury – *38 rue Félix-Faure - ☎ 04 75 05 99 17 - Mon-Fri 8am-12.30pm, 2pm-7pm, Sat 8am-7pm and Sun morning - closed 1 Jan and 1 May*. A century-old shop selling the famous *ravioles* – mini-raviolis by the sheet – sold in packages of 9, 18 or 30 sheets. Mère Maury also sells other local products such as honey, jam, lemonade, sweets and regional wines.

Chizat Jean-Louis et Christine – *Pont de l'Herbasse - 26600 Granges-les-Beaumont - ☎ 04 75 71 61 48 – May-Aug: Mon-Sat 9am-noon, 4pm-7pm, Sep: 3pm-7pm - closed afternoons Nov-Apr and public holidays*. A family farm where customers gather their own fruit and vegetables. All the necessary tools (spades, wheelbarrows, knives) are available at the entrance; once your harvest is ready, you need only weigh and pay.

scenes. Above is a Gothic triforium comprising 160 arches which go right round the building. In the chancel there are 14C murals.

On the right of the nave, the **Chapel of the Holy Sacrament** contains a 16C **hanging**★★ consisting of nine panels and believed to be of Flemish inspiration. These remarkable pieces embroidered in wool and highlighted with silk thread depict scenes from the Passion, from the Garden of Gethsemane on the Mount of Olives to the Resurrection. The figures, in reddish-brown tones, form compact groups against a dark blue background; notice, on the altar side, the Crucifixion, Golgotha and Entombment. On the central vault, a 15C fresco retraces two episodes evoking the life of the three martyrs from Vienne whose relics were venerated in the church.

▶ *Take rue Pêcherie, opposite the west end of the church.*

Escalier Josaphat

These **steps** go down from rue Pêcherie towards the houses with their wooden balconies on place de la Presle.

The stairway is part of the "Great Journey" or Way of the Cross which attracts a large crowd of people on Good Friday.

▶ *Rue du Fuseau runs straight onto rue de l'Armillerie.*

At no 15 rue du Mouton, off to the right, the Gothic windows on the first floor are now mullioned windows; above, the outline of a sheep's head carved in a projecting stone can just be made out.

At no 17, the semicircular door features nail-head ornamentation.

▶ *Continue towards place Fontaine-Couverte.*

Place Fontaine-Couverte

This square in the heart of the old town is decorated with a modern fountain representing a flautist.

Côte Jacquemart

The hill is lined with 13C and 14C houses.

Le Jacquemart

This is an old square tower from the outer curtain wall of Romans, converted into a belfry in the 15C and given a Jack-o'-the-clock, which since 1830 has proudly sported the costume of a 1792 volunteer.

▶ *Facing towards the river, turn left to côte des Cordeliers which runs along part of the moat of the inner curtain wall; walk down to rue Fontaine-des-Cordeliers and rue St-Nicolas.*

Hôtel Thomé

This fine town house presents a Renaissance façade with beautiful mullioned windows on the upper floors. On the right, a Virgin and Child stands in a niche.

▶ *Continue towards the river via rue Sabaton and turn right onto rue des Clercs.*

Rue des Clercs

The street is very picturesque with rounded cobblestones. Notice, opposite the town's archives, the portal decorated with fine chiselling.

Rue des Trois-Carreaux

This is an extension of rue des Clercs. At its intersection with **place aux Herbes** there is a monumental door, surmounted by an unusual corbelled construction with machicolations.

Place Maurice-Faure

Beside St-Barnard, to the right of the St-Jean door on the north side of the church, is a beautiful house with a corner tower.

On the north-west corner of the square is **rue de l'Écosserie,** in which the first houses are joined by an arch.

Sights

Musée International de la Chaussure

🕐 *Jul-Aug: daily, 10am-6pm; Sun and public holidays 2.30-6pm; May-Jun and Sep: daily except Mon 10am-6pm, Sun and public holidays 2.30-6pm; Jan-Apr and Oct-Dec: daily except Sun, 10am-5pm, Sun and public holidays 2.30-6pm.* 🕐 *Closed 1 Jan, 1 May, 1 Nov, 25 Dec. 4.50€ (children: 2.50€).* ☎ *04 75 05 51 81. www.ville-romans.com*

The Shoe Museum is located to the east of town in a vast building – the old Visitation Convent – which was constructed between the 17C and 19C. The museum entrance is reached through the gateway in rue Bistour, across terraced gardens in front of the building which is adorned with an elegant colonnade.

Shoe Collection★

The museum aims to present the technical, ethnographic and aesthetic aspects
of footwear. Numerous documents and
other material trace the evolution of the
shoemaker's craft and associated activities in the town of Romans (dressing and
tanning leather etc).

In the old nuns' cells, the collections of
footwear are displayed in chronological
and thematic order from Antiquity to
1900. Some of them are extremely com-

Lady's shoes (17C)

prehensive, such as that of Paris designer Victor Guillen. The Jacquemart collection
and Harms' original collection of buckles are also interesting. There is a great variety
of exhibits from the five continents including mummified feet of ancient Egypt as
well as original designs by André Pérugia (20C). These sumptuous, amusing and
enigmatic shoes reveal the ingenuity of their creators and evoke the customs of
their country of origin and fashion throughout the ages: Roman sandals, cracowes
whose length varied with social rank, pattens inlaid with tortoiseshell and pearl
from Mauritania, Indian moccasins from North America, shoes from Ardèche used
to open chestnuts and ankle boots from the Belle Epoque. The collections, which
are constantly being enriched by numerous donations, are displayed in rotation
in temporary exhibitions. The 18C and 19C paintings on the theme of shoes and
shoemaking add another angle of interest to the museum visit.

Musée de la Résistance et de la Déportation

Three rooms in the right wing retrace the secret life of the members of the Resistance
in the Drôme *département* during the Second Word War, with the aid of documents
and an audio-visual projection (20min).

Excursions

Mours-St-Eusèbe

4km/2.5mi N. Leave Romans on D 538 then turn right onto D 608. The village church
has kept only its bell-tower, at the west end, and the south wall of the nave from the
11C. It houses an interesting **Musée Diocésain d'Art Sacré★** *(⊙ May-Oct: guided
tours (1hr30min) daily except Sat 2.30-6.30pm. 4€. ☎ 04 75 02 36 16. www.musee-
art-sacre.com)* with rich collections of sacred art (15C-20C) arranged according to a
new theme each year. Among the liturgical objects used in various Drôme churches
there are a beautiful set of vestments (copes, embroidered and woven chasubles,
often highlighted with gold or silver thread), altar cloths in fine lace from Le Puy,
Bruges and Chantilly, poignant polychrome wooden statues representing St Roc,
St John and the Virgin Mary as well as a magnificent monstrance designed by Viollet-le-Duc and crafted by Armand Calliat, a goldsmith from Lyon. Popular piety is
represented by procession banners, Isère boatmen's crosses, *gonfalons* (standards
used by ecclesiastics and corporations) and small objects made from paper rolls.
At the back of the church, the old sacristy houses a collection of religious plate of
Dauphiné origin.

Hostun

*14km/8.7mi E. Leave Romans E towards St-Nazaire-en-Royans. Shortly beyond L'Écancière,
turn right onto D 125C to Hostun.*

Kids No wonder a strange atmosphere pervades this small village close to the Vercors
massif! An old farm (at Les Guerbys) has been turned into **Le Monde Merveilleux
des Lutins** (the wonderful world of elves – ⊙ *Jun-Aug: 10am-6.30pm; Apr, May*

and school holidays: 2-6pm; Sep: Sun, 2-6pm; Dec: Wed, Sat, Sun, 2-6pm. ○ *Closed Jan-Mar, Sep and Oct. 7€ (children: 5.50€).* ☎ *04 75 48 89 79. www.mondedeslutins. com),* a fantasy realm where children can meet all kinds of mysterious characters from enchanted lands: trolls, gnomes, sprites, gremlins and other goblins at last united in a lively magic dance.

Les Collines

51km/31.7mi round tour. Allow 2hr. Leave Romans to the NW by D 53 (towards the swimming-pool).

St-Donat-sur-l'Herbasse
This old Drôme village is a popular haunt among music lovers. The 12C-16C **collegiate church** houses modern organs designed after plans made by the famous Silbermann Brothers (3 keyboards, 3 sets of pipes). Every year the church hosts a prestigious **John Sebastian Bach Festival.** ☎ 04 75 45 10 29

▸ *Leave St-Donat on D 584 and head N for Bathernay.*

Bathernay
This pretty village enjoys a charming setting in the midst of the lush countryside. West of Bathernay a narrow road leads to the octagonal tower of **Ratières.**

▸ *Take D 207 to the S, then D 53 for 1.3km/0.9mi; A path to the right will take you to the Chapelle St-Andéol.*

Chapelle St-Andéol
The small chapel commands a superb **panorama** over the Isère Valley, the Galaure Basin and Mont Pilat.

▸ *A small, picturesque road to the S rejoins D 112. Turn left in Bren and return to St-Donat, where D 53 leads back to Romans.*

ROYAT

POPULATION 4 658

MICHELIN MAP 326: F-8 – 3KM/1.9MI W OF CLERMONT-FERRAND

Royat, on the heights overlooking Clermont-Ferrand from the west, is a large, elegant thermal spa terraced on the slopes of the cool Tiretaine Valley. It lies on the western fault of the Limagne and it is to this location that it owes its springs. The Tiretaine flows down from the granite plateau at the base of the Dômes mountain range; until it leaves Royat, it is a torrent. The bottom of its bed was filled with a lava flow from the Petit Puy de Dôme, the waters then cut gorges in it; as a result, many sills are crossed by waterfalls, making the spa very picturesque.
🚶 *1 av. Auguste-Rouzaud, 63130 ROYAT,* ☎ *04 73 29 74 70. www.ot-royat.com*

The waters – The waters of Royat were known to the Arverni, whose capital Gergovie was close by, and were subsequently exploited by the Romans who built magnificent public baths here. Although the baths met with mixed success until the mid-19C, they have enjoyed relentless popularity and fame ever since. A hydropathic establishment was built and the visit here by Empress Eugénie in 1862 launched Royat as a spa. Until 1914 it was the stopping place of kings and princes.

The resort – Five springs are used. The most abundant is the Eugénie spring whose Gallo-Roman water catchment was rediscovered. It has a flow rate of 1 000l/220gal per minute at a temperature of 31.5˚C/88.7˚F and releases a large amount of radioactive thermal gas at the same time. The temperature of the other springs goes down to 14˚C/57˚F. St-Mart, which has a Celtic water catchment, bears the name of the saint who, in the 6C, founded a monastery on the site of the present spa gardens. St Victor's spring was tapped by the Romans. The other springs are César, with a Gallo-Roman water catchment, and Velleda. The waters are used for drinking, carbo-gas baths and thermal gas injections, for the treatment of heart and artery complaints, cellulitis and osteo-arthritis. A new spring, the Auraline spring, captured and put into service in 1989, ensures that most of the needs for thermal water are met.

Royat also offers the usual distractions of a watering place: parks, casino, concerts, theatre, cinema, tennis, 9-hole golf course in Charade *(6km/3.7mi)*.

The Spa

Parc thermal
This spa garden, completed by the new English-style park through which flows the River Tiretaine, contains the hydropathic establishment and the casino. The remains of the **Gallo-Roman public baths,** which included several pools, can be seen. One of the pools, uncovered and restored, had mosaic-covered arches and marble-covered walls. Terracotta pipes brought the water which then flowed into the pool in small, semicircular cascades.

▶ *At the end of the park.*

Grotte des Laveuses
The "Washerwomen's Cave" is on the banks of the Tiretaine. Several springs gush forth from the volcanic walls and gather in a pool before flowing into the Tiretaine.

▶ *Walk back or take the lift.*

Église St-Léger★
This fascinating fortified building, which departs from the classical type of Auvergne Romanesque church, resembles the churches of Provence. It was built at the end of the 11C on the site of a former sanctuary and belonged to Mozac Abbey which enlarged it by rebuilding the chancel, and fortified it at the beginning of the 13C to withstand the assaults of the Count of Auvergne. The belfry is 19C. The old priory, joined to the left arm of the transept, was also fortified. There are two beautiful Gothic rose windows, one in the wall of the south transept, the other at the east end. It is possible to visit the crypt where 10C capitals have been reused.

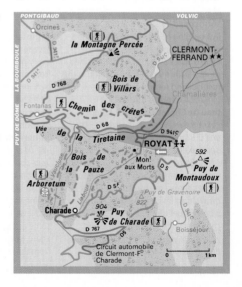

Nearby, on place Cohendy, stands a **calvary,** sculpted in lava stone, dated 1486.

Maison du Passé
🕐 *Daily except Sun and holidays 3-6pm. 3€.* ☎ *04 73 29 98 18.*
This museum offers visitors a journey through the town's history with lively reconstructions and characters in period costume.

▶ *Walk to boulevard de la Taillerie.*

Address Book

EATING OUT
🍽🍽 **L'Hostalet** – *Bd Barrieu -* ☎ *04 73 35 82 67 - closed 5 Jan-5 Mar, Sun except public holidays and Mon.* It's true that this family-run restaurant sandwiched between a garage and another house is rather old hat, but perhaps that's what gives it its quirky charm. Warm reception, traditional cuisine and fine old wines.

🍽🍽 **La Pépinière** – *11 av. Pasteur -* ☎ *04 73 35 81 19 - www.hotel-la-pepiniere. com.* This venerable old building with a veranda attached houses a rustic dining room adorned with modern paintings. The chef proposes toothsome contemporary cuisine in addition to a more traditional menu. Remodelled bedrooms in a verdant setting.

WHERE TO STAY
🛏 **Le Chalet Camille** – *21 bd Barrieu -* ☎ *04 73 35 80 87 - chalet.camille@ wanadoo.fr - closed Sun evening Nov-Mar -* 🅿 *- 21 rms -* 🍴 *6€ - restaurant* 🍽 Surrounded by a little garden, this family boarding house in a 1920s pavilion blends right in with the spirit of the nearby spa. Basic but well-maintained rooms. Daily menu to be sampled in the rustic dining room.

🛏🛏🛏 **Chambre d'hôte Château de Charade** – *63130 Charade - 6km/3.6mi SW of Royat - take D 941 C and D 5 towards the race track ('circuit automobile') -* ☎ *04 73 35 91 67 - closed 1 Nov-Easter -* 🔲 *- 5 rms -* 🍴 *7€.* Take a vast park planted with trees of all sorts, add a château guarded by two towers, throw in an inviting decor featuring wood embellishments and carefully chosen second-hand furniture and what have you got? This thoroughly delightful B&B near Royat!

ON THE TOWN
Casino de Royat – *Allée du Pariou -* ☎ *04 73 29 52 52 - croyat@wanadoo. fr - Mon-Fri 10am-3am, weekends 4am.* This gamblers' paradise boasts 120 slot machines plus traditional games such as *boule,* roulette and black jack. Dancing devotees can cut up the floor weekends at the Pariou as well as during thé-dansants Thursday afternoons. A bar, the Jack'pot Café, and a restaurant, Le Lucullus, round out the leisure complex.

Le Cintra – *2 av. Abbé-Védrine -* ☎ *04 73 35 95 50 - Mar-Oct: Tue-Sun 11am-1am; Nov-Feb: Wed-Sun - closed 1st half of Nov and 2nd half of Feb.* A short walk from the spa park, this chic, plush pub is a favourite among spa-goers who come here to forget about their diets over a glass or two. Pleasant terrace, most popular late mornings and evenings.

SHOPPING
Chocolaterie du Vieux-Royat – *15 bis r. Nationale -* ☎ *04 73 35 87 18.* Whiffs of the tantalizing scent of chocolate escape this roomy boutique. Each and every piece of their chocolate, made from pure cocoa butter, is prepared by hand. Pralines, marzipan, gianduja, *ganache,* orangettes, *palets d'or.* Sample these heavenly treats in the small tearoom.

Taillerie de Royat – *1 bd de la Taillerie -* ☎ *04 73 35 81 25 - Tue-Sat 9am-noon, 2pm-6pm - closed Jan, Sun-Mon and public holidays.* Early-20C furnishings and design lend panache to this shop selling sophisticated decorative objects and jewellery embellished with handsome gemstones (amethyst, fluorine, agate, jasper...), some of which come from the region.

Taillerie de Pierres Fines
Leave town to the W. Inside this workshop semi-precious stones – rock crystal, agate, tourmaline, amethyst etc – are cut and made into jewellery.

Parc Bargoin
From Église St-Léger, follow avenue Jean-Jaurès then avenue Anatole-France.
This is a well laid out 8ha/20-acre park on hilly land, and a botanical garden. It is home to some magnificent trees, including the largest maple in France (250 years old, diameter of 7.5m/25ft). From the top of a little tower there is a lovely view of Clermont-Ferrand.

Walking Tours

A map of the area on place Allard indicates a number of signposted trails for hikers, leaving from Royat.

Bois de Villars
1hr. These woods contain superb undergrowth and offer lovely views of the Limagne and the Livradois mountains. Well-preserved remains of the Roman way between Clermont-Ferrand and Limoges may be seen.

Puy de Montaudoux
Leave Royat on D 941c to the S. At the junction with D 5, take the track on the left which leads up to the Puy.
1hr. From the summit (alt 592m/1 942ft) there is a charming view of the Limagne.

Arboretum de Royat and Bois de la Pauze
Leave Royat to the W on D 68.
Allow 2hr. In the Tiretaine Valley, 140m/150yd after the bridge (Pont des Soupirs), take the path on the left running along the Vaucluse stream and leading to the park. *From the car park, rejoin Royat by the Pauze pine wood.*

Puy de Charade
3hr. Rue de la Pause leads to a path climbing to the village of **Charade** at the foot of its own extinct volcano, the Puy de Charade. This basalt cone has a lava flow trailing as far as Puy de Gravenoire. Take the minor road on the left which leads to the Gravenoire Telecom relay. From the summit (alt 904m/2 966ft), there is a **view** of the Dômes mountain range, the Limagne, and the mountains of Forez and Dore.

▶ *From Charade, several paths lead back to Royat via Bois de la Pauze.*

Vallée de la Tiretaine and Chemin des Crêtes
Leave Royat to the W.
Allow 2hr. The road wends its way up the luxuriant valley of the River Tiretaine. In Fontanas, cross the Tiretaine, then turn right onto the Chemin des Crêtes which leads back to Royat via Le Paradis.

Excursions

Clermont-Ferrand-Charade Racing Circuit
18km/11.2mi to the S. This outing can be combined with a tour of Charade and Puy de Gravenoire. This high-mountain racing circuit, the only one in France, has hosted four Formula 1 Grand Prix events (1965, 1969, 1970, 1972). After being redesigned, it

is now 4km/2.5mi long. Every year it becomes the backdrop to the popular "Trophées d'Auvergne" race.

La Montagne Percée

7km/4.3mi to the N. Leave the car at the intersection of D 941A and take the path immediately on the right, level with the milestone. After 300m/330yd, you will reach the Montagne Percée rock.

🏃 *15min there and back.* The promontory commands a lovely vista of Clermont-Ferrand and its outskirts.

RUYNES-EN-MARGERIDE

POPULATION 648

MICHELIN MAP 330: H-4

La Margeride is a granite range lying parallel to the volcanic mountains of Velay. It stretches from the River Allier in the east to the high volcanic plateaux of the Aubrac area in the west. The highest section, known as **"La Montagne,"** lies at an average altitude of 1 400m/4 590ft. It consists of rounded plateaux covered with vast, monotonous pastures interspersed with forests of pines, fir and birches. North of Mende, the Palais du Roi and Boulaine plateaux bristle with granite boulders, which have been worn down by erosion and now resemble colonnades or obelisks, and rounded blocks teetering one on top of the other. Below the Montagne lie **"Les Plaines,"** undulating stretches of land broken up by numerous spurs of rock. The population is denser here, living in large, isolated farmhouses or grouped together in small hamlets. The main resources of this area are timber and cattle as well as uranium. The Music Festival at Saugues is a major event. Since 1975 the **Écomusée de Margeride** has specialised in a study of rural society in this region. The open-air museum helps to preserve the natural and cultural heritage and gives visitors an insight into traditional lifestyles through the restoration of typical buildings, exhibitions, walks and regional discovery

Pierre Allègre farmstead, Loubarasse

holidays. To the west of the range is the **Gévaudan,** a lower-lying plateau (alt 1 000-1 200m/3 280-3 940ft) that forms a sort of corridor dominated by the Aubrac which has the same physical features as La Margeride. ▯ *Le Bourg, 15320 RUYNES-EN-MARGERIDE, ☏ 04 71 23 43 32. www.margeride-truyere.com*

Open-Air Regional Nature Museum

Écomusée de la Margeride★

This local information centre has its headquarters at Ruynes-en-Margeride (east of the Garabit viaduct), and is divided into four main sites:

Tour de Ruynes
🕐 *Jul-Aug: 10am-1pm, 3-7pm; Jun and Sep: 2-6pm; also open during all school holidays (last admission 45min before closing). 4€. ☏ 04 71 23 42 96.*
In the building adjoining this medieval tower, an exhibition entitled "Voyage en Margeride, une Aventure de Pierre Plantade" presents the region in an instructive and entertaining manner: soil structure, flora, aspects of rural life, landscapes.
Outside, a botanical garden – **Jardin de St-Martin** – surrounding the tower contains various plants found in the natural environment of La Margeride, mainly heath and peat bog. The inner courtyard evokes the culture of yesteryear by hosting various events in the local tradition.

Ferme de Pierre Allègre★
17km/11mi S of Ruynes, via D 4, D 48 and N 9. Guided tours (1hr) Jul-Aug: 10am-1pm, 3-7pm; Jun and Sep: 2-6pm; also open during all school holidays (last admission 45min before closing). 4€. ☏ 04 71 23 42 96.
This country farmstead, situated in the centre of **Loubaresse** village, evokes the way of life of a typical Margeride peasant family in the late 19C.
On the ground floor is the living room which was also used as a kitchen, dining room and bedroom (box beds); the chimney-stove *(tchantou)* made this a cosy place to spend winter evenings with family and friends. At the back of the room is the scullery for work that involved using water. On the first floor are the communal bedroom

Écomusée de la Margeride, Ruynes-en-Margeride

and a tiny bedroom destined for the eldest son and his wife. Adjoining the main buildings are the byre (ground floor) and the barn (upper floor).

The tour then takes in the rest of the complex, enclosed by hedges of elder and hawthorn, including the woodshed, the bread oven and the beehives (in front of the house), the pigsty and the shed (in front of the byre) and the vegetable patch and orchard (to the east). Take a peek at the hut mounted on a cart (in the shed) used by the shepherd during the summer up in the mountain pastures.

École de Clémence Fontille

5km/3mi SW of Ruynes on D 13, or 9km/6mi NW of Loubaresse on N 9 and D 13. Guided tours (30min) Jul and Aug: 10am-1pm, 3-7pm; Jun and Sep: 2-6pm (last admission 45min before closing) 4€. ☎ 04 71 23 42 96.

This old classroom illustrates what rural primary school education was like at the beginning of the 20C: school benches and desks with inkwells, slates, teacher's desk on a dais, and blackboard.

Excursions

Viaduc de Garabit★★

7km/4.3mi SW of Ruynes on D 13. ♿ *See Gorges de la TRUYÈRE.*

Gorges de l'Allier –* ♿ *See SAUGUES.*

Le Mont Mouchet

50km/31mi – allow 3hr

Mont Mouchet (alt 1 495m/4 904ft) is one of the peaks in the Margeride range and, in May 1944, it became one of the main centres of the Resistance in the Massif Central. On 2 June, 3 000 men from the French Maquis pushed enemy forces back beyond Paulhac. On 10 June, after occupying Ruynes-en-Margeride, where 27 civilians were massacred, a large German detachment pillaged and set fire to Clavières, but were halted by the Resistance Movement and had to withdraw to St-Flour. The following day the Germans again attacked Clavières, but the Maquis had had time to organise its defences.

A national monument to the French Resistance Movement was erected, in memory of these battles, and faces the Mont Mouchet Forestry Commission Centre that had been used by the Resistance in the Auvergne as its headquarters. A **museum** (♿🕐 *May to mid-Sep: 9.30am-noon, 2-7pm; mid-Sep to mid-Oct: Sat-Sun, 10am-noon, 2-6pm. 5€. ☎ 04 71 74 11 91*) contains documents and photographs from the war describing the Resistance Movement in the Auvergne.

As it leaves the clearing, the road wends its way through **Auvers Forest,** known locally for its mushrooms and blueberries. A lane on the left leads to a viewing table (2km/1mi).

▶ *Go back to D 113, turn left, then 2km/1mi further on, turn left again onto D 41.*

Auvers

Near the church, a granite base supports a monumental bronze statue depicting **"La Bête du Gévaudan,"** a wild animal that devoured cattle and terrorised local farmers in the area; it was eventually hunted down and shot near Auvers by Jean Chastel on 19 June 1767.

▶ *Continue along D 41, which skirts the east slope of the Mont Mouchet. After 5km/3mi, turn left onto D 412. D 4 will take you back to Ruynes.*

SAINT-AGRÈVE

POPULATION 2 762
MICHELIN MAP 331: I-3

This is a pleasant resort on the slopes of Mont Chiniac, a pine-covered mountain offering extensive views over the Mézenc range. ▮ *Hôtel de Ville, 07320 ST-AGRÈVE,* ☏ *04 75 30 15 06.*

Excursions

Mont Chiniac★★
Alt 1 120m/3 675ft. Viewing table. *From place de la République, follow montée des Sports then turn left at a crossroads (access on foot: follow rue de l'Église).*
The road leads to the summit of Mont Chiniac crowned with fir trees.
Leave the car on a platform to the left, 150m/164yd before the viewing table.
The view encompasses the Massif du Mézenc to the south-west, the Massif du Meygal to the west and the Monts de Lalouvesc to the north-east.

Le Velay tourist train
Allow one day. ♿ *See Le CHAMBON-SUR-LIGNON.* This small railway overlooks the Lignon gorges, then meanders through the wooded valleys and green hills of the Haut-Vivarais and Le Velay.

Lac de Devesset
8km/5mi N on D 9. This 48ha/119-acre leisure centre provides facilities for many water sports (swimming, sailing etc).

Les Boutières★★

64km/40mi round trip leaving from St-Agrève – allow 2hr 30min

▶   *Leave St-Agrève to the S on D 120, heading towards Le Cheylard.*

During the drive down, you will enjoy pretty views of the Mézenc, then the road enters the Eyrieux defile.

Lac de Devesset

TREAT YOURSELF

⊜⊜⊜ **Domaine de Rilhac** – *2km/1.2mi SE of St-Agrève via D 120, D 21, then secondary road -* ☎ *04 75 30 20 20 - closed Jan-Feb, Tue evening, Thu lunch and Wed.* Take the time to stop here for a meal – you'll be glad you did. The house, a renovated Ardèche farm, is suberb; the food is prepared with brio by the young owner who makes a point of preparing appetizing fare at affordable prices. A few rooms for those yearning for a night (or more) of peace and quiet.

▶ *Take D 120 south. At the exit to St-Julien-Boutières, turn right onto D 101.*

Fay-sur-Lignon

This mountain-village (pronounced fa-yee) offers cross-country skiing facilities in winter. There is a good **view**★ of the surrounding mountains from the graveyard next to the church.

▶ *Take D 262 S and turn left to St-Clément.*

St-Clément

From here there are attractive **views**★★ of the Gerbier de Jonc, Suc de Sara and Mont Mézenc mountains, in line with the valley of the River Saliouse.

▶ *Rejoin D 262; turn left onto D 410. Continue to Lachapelle-sous-Chanéac and, beyond, to Armanas.*

This is a winding and attractive route with lovely views over the basin of the upper Eyrieux and of the confluence of the River Eysse and River Eyrieux.

▶ *In Armanas turn left and then right onto D 478 to Le Bourget and Rochebonne.*

Ruins of Rochebonne★

Park by the side of the road.

🚶 The magnificent **site**★★ is the setting for the fissured, granitic ruins of the medieval castle, overlooked to the west by Mont Mézenc.

Walk down to the ruins *(30min there and back)*. A path leads past other rocks framing a ravine, dotted with pine trees, where a torrent falls in small cascades.

▶ *Continue along D 478 towards Beauvert and down to D 21 which leads back to St-Agrève.*

ST-ANTOINE-L'ABBAYE★

POPULATION 910
MICHELIN MAP 333: E-2

Nestling in an undulation of the Chambaran plateau north of the River Isère is the old village of St-Antoine-l'Abbaye, which is dominated by an imposing Gothic abbey church. 🛈 *Pl. Ferdinand-Gilibert, 38160 ST-ANTOINE-L'ABBAYE,* ☎ *04 76 36 44 46. www.sainteantoineabbeye.fr.*

St Anthony's fire – In the 11C a nobleman from Vienne, Jocelyn de Châteauneuf, made a pilgrimage to the Holy Land. On his return he brought back from Constantinople the bones of Anthony the Great, the original "desert father," who lived in the Upper Nile Valley. In the Middle Ages this saint owed his popularity as much to the pig who was the daily companion of his hermitic life as to his battles with the devil.

The relics in the church of La Motte-St-Didier, which took the name of St-Antoine, were entrusted by the Bishop of Vienne to Benedictines from Montmajour Abbey. A first monastery was built. Not long after, in 1089, a dreadful epidemic broke out in Dauphiné – erysipelas, or St Anthony's fire. It was a sort of gangrene which burnt away the limbs. The saint's relics drew a large crowd of sick and poor people; to help and care for them, a group of young nobles created the Brotherhood of Charity.

A powerful order – In the 13C the brothers managed to supplant the Benedictines. In 1297 the brotherhood became the Hospital Brothers of St Anthony; the Antonine monks founded hospices all over Europe.

The great abbey church of St-Antoine, which took from the 13C to the 15C to build, was visited by popes, emperors from Germany, and kings of France who came to kneel before the relics.

Abbey Church★ *1hr*

▶ *Leave the car in the car park situated 100m/110yd behind the tourist office.*

The entrance to the abbey church is at the top of the village, through the 17C **main entrance gate** (Entrée d'Honneur), now the town hall (Hôtel de Ville), with its glazed mosaic tiles. Three portals with broken pediments decorate the façade. The frame around the central portal, which has retained its wooden doors, features two Ionic columns. The side portals present nail-head ornamentation.

▶ *Walk through the portal which leads to an esplanade surrounded by the old hospital buildings now occupied by craftsmen, artists and antique dealers. Continue up to the church.*

The square fronting the church provides an attractive view of the façade and the two monumental doors. One of the doors leads to the old gardens and the other overlooks a set of steps going down to the village.

Façade

Flamboyant Gothic portals are extended on each side by the low windows of the first side chapels, and an immense Flamboyant opening punctuates the middle of the façade. The **centre portal**★, decorated with arching adorned with statuettes, is the

B. Kaufmann/MICHELIN

work of Antoine le Moiturier, who stayed at St-Antoine from 1461 to 1464 before going to Dijon to execute the tomb of the Duke of Burgundy, John the Fearless. In the centre of the portal is the Eternal Father surrounded by cherubs. The lower row depicts Moses, seated, with the Tablets of the Law, on the right, and above, the Sibyl.

Interior

♿🕐 *guided visits (1h): mid-Jun to Mid-Sep: daily except Tue, 3-6pm, Sun and public holidays, 2-5pm; Mar to mid-Jun, and mid-Sep-Oct, Wed, Fri and Sat, 3-6pm, Sun and public holidays, 2-7pm.* 🕐 *Nov-Mar.* 4€. ☎ 04 76 36 44 46.

The interior is quite large: 62m/203ft long, 22m/72ft high and 36m/118ft wide. The nave has seven bays and a false transept marked with galleries at mid-height. Chapels lead off the side aisles; the 2nd and 6th chapels on the left and the 2nd, 4th and 7th on the right have restored 15C and 16C frescoes.

The three bays of the chancel end in a polygonal apse with a circular base (13C) which is the oldest part of the building. The triforium reveals the progression of the construction: in the apse there are twinned pointed arches, in the nave, later trefoil arches.

No fewer than 97 stalls by the master carpenter François Hanard furnish the chancel. Ten **Aubusson tapestries** (17C) depicting the story of Joseph decorate the chancel, the transept and chapels along the right side aisle; they bear the coat of arms of the Antonine monks, recognisable from the T or *tau* representing the Cross of St Anthony.

The High Altar, designed as a marble mausoleum embellished with chiselled bronzes, houses the shrine of St Anthony, covered with embossed silver plate (17C). The organ case is 17C (restored); concerts are regularly held.

Treasury★

It houses a 16C ivory **Crucifix**★ famous for its expression of agony, various reliquaries and reliquary busts, and surgical instruments donated by the last patient to be cared for by the Antonines and recalling the hospital vocation of the Order; in the second room hangs a painting by Ribera, *St Mary the Egyptian* (17C); the third room is decorated with delightful woodwork in Rococo style – it contains a cope chest.

Musée Départemental

♿🕐 *Jul-Aug, daily except Tue, 11am-12.30pm, 1.30-6pm; Mar-Jun and Sep-Oct, daily except Tue, 2-6pm.* 🕐 *Closed 1 May.* ☎ 04 76 36 40 68. www.musee-saint-antoine.fr
This museum, located in the monastery's old novitiate, contains works by Jean Vinay (1907-78), a landscape artist from Dauphiné, and thematic exhibitions by his friends from the Paris School, and exhibitions on the Middle Ages or the Antonine Order.

Excursions

St-Marcellin

10km/6.2mi to the E on D 27, then D 20 on the right. This town, where the last Viennese dauphin Humbert II set up his Parliament in the 14C, was badly hit by the Wars of Religion: besieged twice by the Baron des Adrets, it was subsequently recovered by the Catholics in 1568.

The colourful Saturday market and annual fairs attract a great many locals from Bas-Grésivaudan; the area is known for *Saint-Marcellin*, a small, round cheese made with cow's milk that has a soft and moulded rind. The **Promenade de Joud** affords pretty views of the Isère Valley and the Royans, overlooked by the Vercors ramparts.

Chatte

8km/5mi to the SE on D 27. The most interesting sight in this small village is its **Jardin Ferroviaire** (Kids ⊙ ⅙ *Apr-Aug: 10am-7pm (Jul-Aug: 8pm); Mar and Sep-Oct: Sat, Sun, public and school holidays, 10am-7pm. 7€ (children: 5€). ⊙ Nov-Feb. ☎ 04 76 38 54 55. www.jardin-ferroviaire.com)* a miniature park complete with paths and 200 plant varieties, cut across by 1km/0.6mi of tiny tracks served by 30 trains. A charming outing for children and parents alike.

La Sône

6km/3.7mi to the S on D 20, then on D 71. This village stands in a lush, peaceful setting along the banks of the Isère. Do not miss the **Jardin des Fontaines Pétrifiantes** (⊙ *Jun-Aug: 10am-6.30pm (last entry, 5.45pm); May and Sep-Oct: daily except Mon, 10am-6pm (last entry, 5.15pm). 6€ (children: 4€). ☎ 04 76 64 43 42. www.jardin-des-fontaines. com)*, set up in a niche where petrified water concretions have coated the surrounding relief and objects with glittering crystals. The leafy grounds, featuring around 15 000 plant species, are enhanced by a series of basins and small waterfalls.

The most picturesque way to visit the region is to go on a **boat ride** (Kids ⅙ ⊙ *Jul-Aug: cruise with commentaries (1hr30) daily at 10.30am, 2pm and 4pm from St Nazaire en Royans, and 11.30am, 3pm from La Sône; Apr-Jun and Sep to mid-Oct: inquire about departure times. 9€ (children: 6€). ☎ 04 76 64 43 42)* on board the Royans-Vercors paddle-boat, which will enlighten you on the local fauna and flora lying at the foot of the Vercors *(commentary).*

SAINT-CERNIN

POPULATION 1 128
MICHELIN MAP 330: C-4

This small town is a pleasant base from which to explore the western Cantal mountain range. One of the most striking features of the surrounding country-side is the castle of Anjony. Strategically located on the tip of the Tournemire promontory, it dominates the lush landscape of the Doire Valley with its four tall towers.

St-Louis Church

The 12C **Église St-Louis**, dominated by its bell-tower, was altered in the 15C and boasts some fine **woodwork**★ (note in particular the misericords on the 14 choir stalls, from the chapter-house at St-Chamant), a handsome Louis XIV lectern near the pulpit and lovely **corbels** carved into the basalt of the church's east end.

Gorges de la Maronne★

55km/34.2mi round tour – allow 2hr

▶ *Leave St-Cernin to the N towards D 922; head for Mauriac and turn onto the first road on the right.*

Château du Cambon

🕐 *Jul-Aug: guided tours (45min) 2.30-6.30pm. Unaccompanied tour of the grounds. 4€ (children: 1,50€). 18C show: 6€. By appointment.* ☎ *04 71 47 60 48.*

This fine 18C castle, built of dark basalt stone, has been whitewashed. The owner takes visitors on a guided tour, from the chapel and the first-floor bedrooms to the ground-floor reception rooms. Rich 18C furniture and video presentation of festivities during the Age of Enlightenment.

▶ *Rejoin D 922 towards Mauriac.*

St-Chamant

The **church** (🕐 *Jul-Aug: noon-7pm.* ☎ *04 71 69 22 20 (town hall).*) here contains eight choir stalls decorated with painted panelsa. The **château** (🕐 *Jul-Aug: guided tours (45min) 2.30-6.30pm; by appointment the rest of the year. 5€.* ☎ *04 71 69 26 85)* is 17C with a 15C square machicolated keep; inside are wonderful **tapestries**★, in very good condition, decorated with themes including spring, mythological events and the crusades. The castle chapel houses a lovely gilded wooden altarpiece (18C) depicting the Holy Family.

▶ *Leave St-Chamant to the W on D 42. Rejoin D 922.*

St-Martin-Valmeroux

A small glove-making centre with a Gothic church, an old fountain and the ruins of a castle, Château de Crèvecœur.

▶ *Leave St-Martin to the W on D 37.*

The winding road to Loupiac dominates the Maronne Valley, flanked by luxuriant slopes. Beyond Loupiac stands the ruins of Branzac Castle.

Château de Branzac

This massive keep with corner towers representative of Cantal fortified architecture is now just a picturesque ruin on the end of a promontory.

▶ *Return to D 37.*

🚶 Opposite the last house in St-Christophe-les-Gorges, on the road to St-Martin-Cantalès, take the path *(45min on foot there and back)*, cross the railway tracks and go to the chapel Notre-Dame-du-Château.

Notre-Dame-du-Château

The chapel is an attractive building roofed with lauzes, sitting in a lovely **setting**★ overlooking a double meander of the river.

▶ *Leave St-Christophe-les-Gorges to the south on D 6.*

Gorges de la Maronne★

The valley narrows and enters a charming canyon bordered by lush vegetation.

▶ *Continue along D 6, entering the Gorges de la Bertrande.*

Église de St-Illide

This Romanesque church (👁‍🗨 *closed to the public)* was enlarged in the 15C; it features interesting choir stalls (from St-Chamant) and a fine lectern.

▶ *Leave St-Illide E and follow D 43 back to St-Cernin.*

ST-ÉTIENNE★

CONURBATION 291 960
MICHELIN MAP 327: F-7 – LOCAL MAP SEE LE PILAT

St-Étienne lies at the bottom of the Furan depression, close to the green Massif du Pilat, Grangent Lake and the Forez plain. The town is located at the centre of a coal basin which supplied over 500 million tonnes of coal until the mines were closed in the 1980s. Since then St-Étienne has adopted a new image: the façades of its buildings have been cleaned, its gardens and parks renovated in the city centre. The busiest area lies along a north-south axis: place Jean-Jaurès, place de l'Hôtel-de-Ville. The 15C and 16C main church of St-Étienne, popularly known as the "**Grand'Église**," remains dear to the hearts of the native *gagas,* the nickname still used by the inhabitants of St-Étienne when speaking of themselves. The home town of the composer **Jules Émile Frédéric Massenet** (1842-1912), has an intellectual and artistic life which extends over the whole of Forez. 🛈 *16 av. de la Libération, 42000 ST-ÉTIENNE,* ☎ *04 77 49 39 00/39 03. www.tourisme-st-etienne.com*

A Bit of History

In the 12C St-Étienne was nothing more than a village on the banks of the Furan, by-passed by the major communication routes. Owing to the presence of coal, however, and the enterprising spirit of the inhabitants, it was later to undergo extraordinary development, the population of the town shooting up from 3 700 in 1515 to 45 000 in 1826, and to 146 000 in 1901, while the industrial estate spread to the west, the east and the north.

Armeville – In 1296 the people of St-Étienne started working coal quarries for domestic needs, then to feed the forges which produced the first knives, followed by cutting and thrusting weapons, crossbows and finally, firearms – St-Étienne was quick to make this change in direction in the manufacture of arms.
In 1570 the Arms Manufacturers' Lodge consisted of 40 trades. Mass production was already being practised. In 1746 the Royal Arms Factory was founded. During the Revolution this activity was to earn the town the name of Armeville.

From St-Étienne to Andrézieux – In May 1827 the first French railway, built to plans by Beaunier, was inaugurated: it ran between St-Étienne and Andrézieux over a distance of 21km/13mi and was used to transport coal; the wagons were pulled by horses. This ancestor of modern means of transport, perfected in 1829 thanks to the tube boiler developed by Marc Seguin, led to a revolution in transport and a prodigious boom in industry.

The town that made everything – To the ribbon industry, imported from Italy, was added shirred fabric at the end of the 19C.

To escape the Depression, the region of St-Étienne had already specialised in quality steels, tools, hunting guns, bicycles and automobile parts.

Industrial redeployment – The mines, which were the basis of industrial development in the past, saw their coal production decrease regularly between 1960 and 1980.

Tramway

This gradual closing was planned, allowing the metallurgical and textile industries time to restructure themselves; they now operate in conjunction with diversified activities such as precision mechanics, electronics, food processing, plastics and cardboard manufacturing.

Musée D'Art Moderne★★ *2hr*

&⏱ *Daily except Tue 10am-6pm (last entry 5.45pm).* ⏱ *Closed 1 Jan, 1 May, 14 Jul, 15 Aug, 1 Nov, 25 Dec. 5€. No charge 2nd Sun in the month.* ☎ *04 77 79 52 52. www. agglo-st-etienne.fr*

▶ *4.5km/3mi from the city centre. Leave St-Étienne N via rue Bergson towards La Terrasse and follow signs to the Musée d'Art Moderne.*

This vast art gallery located in the town of St-Priest-en-Jarez was designed by the architect D Guichard; it is devoted to 20C art, of which it provides an interesting retrospective owing to its policy of continual acquisition. The sober, functional building looks like an industrial structure from the outside. Its walls, covered with black ceramic panels, are a reminder of the important role played by coal in this region in the past. The exhibition area, laid out to encourage contemplation, covers nearly 4 000m2/43 000sq ft.

The museum is a lively meeting place with a specialised library, conference rooms, a children's workshop, a museum shop and a restaurant.

Modern Art (1900-45)

The small and medium-sized works which form a collection showing clearly the development of abstract art are exhibited in the rooms to the left of the main entrance: **Monet** *(Water Lilies)*, Kupka *(The Blue Ribbon)*, Chabaud *(Red Nude,* its pure colours characteristic of Fauvism), Magnelli, the **Dada** movement with derisive,

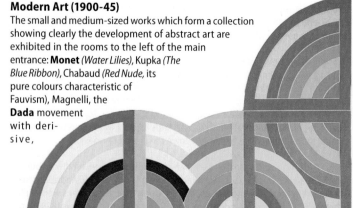

Agbatana II by Frank Stella

even absurd works (*The Fiancé* by Picabia, *Assemblage* by Schwitters) then **Cubism** defined by Braque and Picasso, Robert Delaunay (*Portrait of Madame Heim*) and Léger (*Composition with three women*).

Following in their wake, the **Surrealists,** with Brauner, Ernst, Miró and Masson, sought to introduce the dream world into their works. During the 1930s, **abstract art** developed another vision of the world with Hélion, Freundlich and M Cahn.

Contemporary art since 1945

The paintings, generally large, are displayed in the central part of the museum, just behind "Espace Zéro," a vast composition in white-ceramic tiles by Jean-Pierre Raynaud contrasts with the exterior of the building.

The 1950s saw an abundance of new types of **abstract art:** the Geometric Abstraction incarnated by Sonia Delaunay, Hélion, Herbin, or Bram van Velde and Atlan contrasted with the Lyrical Abstraction leaning towards Graphism of Hartung and Soulages.

The 1960s marked the peak in consumer consumption; the **New Realists** rediscovered everyday objects. They are assembled by Arman, compressed by César, torn by Hains. Space itself is materialised by Klein (*monochrome*). Adepts of Narrative Figuration, such as Monory, Rancillac, and Adami, used photographic or advertising media, sometimes even comic strips.

It was the era of **Pop Art** with Dine, Warhol (Self-Portrait) and Lichtenstein. **Minimal Art** was initiated by Stella who produced modular geometric structures such as *Agbatana II* (1968). **Arte Povera** (Merz, Zorio and Penone), seeing Art as an active force, sought to portray the energy of the simplest objects.

The **Supports/Surfaces** group is well-represented here with Viallat (paint on tarpaulin), Dezeuze (strips of wood stapled together and stained), Grand and Saytour. There are works by the German artist **Baselitz** (*Elke VI*) and the French painter **Dubuffet**, the initiator of l'**Art brut** ("raw art"), is well represented with a dozen or so works including *Le Site Illusoire, Le Déchiffreur* and works executed after 1980.

Old Town★

Start out from **place du Peuple,** which used to be the market square in the Middle Ages. On the corner of rue Mercière a 16C tower rises above an arcade; a timber-framed house stands opposite.

Cross the avenue used by the trams to reach rue Denis-Escoffier, which marks the entrance to the old Outre-Furan district. At the junction of rue des Martyrs-de-Vingré is an unusual mid-18C house, adorned with a statue, which is typical, with its eaves with four rows of tiles and its large, visible beams, of the urban architecture to be found in Forez. On the left at no 3 rue Georges-Dupré a massive façade includes imposing lintels in one piece. Turn back and follow rue des Martyrs-de-Vingré; nos 19 and 30 are examples of 18C houses incorporating weaving lofts or workshops. Note also the arcades with bosses on the second floor.

▷ *After reaching place Neuve, turn right onto rue Nautin, which leads to rue Michelet.*

Rue Michelet

This artery, pierced along the north-south axis parallel to rue Gambetta, contains some examples of innovative architecture from the 1930s (nos 34, 36, 42 and in particular no 44, an imposing building in reinforced concrete).

▷ *Continue along rue Nautin and rejoin rue Gambetta, which you need to cross to get to place W.-Rousseau. Skirt the square dominated by the former castle, which now houses the Fine Arts Academy (École des Beaux-Arts). Rue du Théâtre leads to place Boivin (note the corbelled houses on the left).*

Address Book

TRAMWAY

The tramway is the best way to get around town. You can buy a one-day pass and rent an audio tape to serve as a guide to help you discover St-Étienne. Information at the Office de tourisme, ☎ 04 77 49 39 00.

EATING OUT

🍽 **L'Escargot d'Or** – *5 cours Victor-Hugo* - ☎ *04 77 41 24 04 - closed 1-10 Mar, 29 Jul to 26 Aug, Sun evening and Mon.* A restaurant above a bar near the *Musée d'Art et d'Industrie*. The dining room is decorated in a 'garden' spirit, with houseplants and wicker chairs. Nicely presented traditional cuisine.

🍽🍽 **Corne d'Aurochs** – *18 r. Michel-Servet* - ☎ *04 77 32 27 27 - closed 1-4 May, 27 Jul to 25 Aug, Mon lunch, Sat lunch and Sun.* Just a short walk from the *hôtel de ville*, here's a bistro after our own hearts. In a funky decor comprised of a collection of bric-a-brac, antiques and etchings, a joyful atmosphere is maintained by the very convivial chieftain of the Corne. Cuisine of the Lyon tavern genre.

🍽🍽🍽 **La Nouvelle** – *30 r. St-Jean* - ☎ *04 77 32 32 60 - closed 2-12 Jan, 10-25 Aug, Sun and Mon.* This restaurant in a pedestrian street, with its modern decor featuring upholstered chairs, Japanese paper lamps and a superb painting by Jouy, is most elegant. The refined setting is in perfect harmony with the inventive cuisine concocted by the young owner-chef.

WHERE TO STAY

Bon week-end en ville – St-Etienne is an active participant in this weekend package deal practiced throughout France. In addition to your second night in a hotel free of charge, you will receive gifts and discount coupons for visiting the city and its museums. Enquire at the Office de Tourisme for a list of hotels and conditions.

🛏 **Hôtel Carnot** – *11 bd Jules-Janin* - ☎ *04 77 74 27 16 - closed 2- 24 Aug - 24 rms -* ☐ *8€.* This hotel near the Carnot train station has a steady flow of regular customers who appreciate the warm reception and reasonable prices. The comfort is fairly modest but rooms are well maintained.

🛏🛏 **Hôtel Ténor** – *12 r. Blanqui* - ☎ *04 77 33 79 88 - www.hoteltenor.com - 64 rms -* ☐ *8€.* A hotel in a modern residential building a minute's walk from the Place de l'Hôtel-de-Ville, Ténor has its entry hall on the 3rd floor. The small, practical rooms are equipped with wood veneer furniture. A simple, practical address run by a friendly team.

SIT BACK AND RELAX

Le Helder – *4 pl. Dorian* - ☎ *04 77 32 36 43 – 7.30am-8pm.* Brasserie, salon de thé, pastry shop, ice cream parlour and chocolate shop: Le Helder is a multi-talented destination. Open since 1950, a recent facelift has rejuvenated the establishment; its irresistible menu will delight gourmands - especially the ice-cream fanciers among them.

ON THE TOWN

Place Jean-Jaurès – Opposite the St-Charles church, not far from the heart of the city, this big square is where natives of St-Étienne rendezvous. Partly shaded (which gives it additional summer appeal), la Place Jean-Jaurès is bordered by numerous cafés that like to show off their large terraces.

Square du Temps Passé – This square is a reminder that St-Étienne is a green city boasting many parks. On one side, la Rue Richelandière is currently a hot spot of Stéphanois nightlife. Here you will find many restaurants (like the Central Park, very hip), and two discotheques (Le V.I.P. and Le Duplex).

Le Midi-Minuit – *14 pl. Jean-Jaurès* - ☎ *04 77 32 41 64 - Mon-Fri 7am-2am, Sat 1pm-2am, Sun 1.30pm-2am.* The woodwork, piano and plush seats attract something of a yuppie clientele. The idea: two rooms, two bars, two moods (the second room is reserved for private soirées or business dinners). Whisky fans can have their pick of some hundred different brands. Plenty of cocktails and many kinds of beer. A limited food menu at all hours.

Le Piccadilly – *3 pl. Neuve - ☎ 04 77 32 28 75 - Mon-Sat 10am-1.30am*. Located in the heart of the historic quarter, this establishment prides itself on possessing one of the city's most handsome terraces. The decor, heterogeneous and multi-coloured, is attractive, and the ambience, ever excellent, attracts a young, faithful crowd. Prices are reasonable enough; the lunch menus are worth a try. Concerts weekends.

THEATRE AND ENTERTAINMENT

Comédie de St-Étienne, Centre Dramatique National – *7 av. du Prés.-Émile-Loubet - ☎ 04 77 25 01 24 - www.comédie-de-saint-etienne. fr - tickets: Mon-Fri 2-7pm - closed end Jul to end Aug and public holidays*. This centre was founded in 1947 in order to initiate and promote drama outside of the capital. Today it orchestrates a permanent troupe of actors, a stage set workshop and a costumes atelier, as well as four different performance halls: Théâtre Jean Dasté, Théâtre René Lesage, l'Usine and Le Théâtre du Park in Andrézieux-Bouthéon. While the theatre's essential role is to stage new productions, it also hosts performances by guest companies.

L'Esplanade - Opéra Théâtre de St-Étienne – *Allée Shakespeare, Jardin des Plantes, BP 237 - ☎ 04 77 47 83 47 - www.saint-etienne.fr - tickets: Mon-Fri 2pm-7pm - closed mid-Jul to Aug*. Until it was damaged by fire (presumably arson) in September, 1998, this theatre was the focal point of cultural animation in St-Etienne. The reopening of the Esplanade in early 2001 brought new gratification to the city's theatre, ballet and operetta enthusiasts.

Le Triomphe - *4 sq. Violette - ☎ 04 77 32 22 16 - tickets: Tue-Sat, 2-8pm - closed Jul-Aug*. This café-theatre in a converted cinema cultivates in its shows the spirit, the culture, the accents, and the language of the region. A wide range of music evenings - jazz, French song - feature also.

Le Tamora – *15 r. Dormoy - ☎ 04 77 32 36 97 - Wed, 10pm-3am, Thu 7pm-3am, Fri-Sat 7pm-4am - closed 2 wks in Aug*. Known in St-Étienne for its karaoke evenings, this club has hosted the popular French songsters Gilbert Montagné, Zouk Machine, and Larusso, who used their visits to promote newcomers on the music scene. The rum-based cocktails are delectable and the exotic decor is very comfortable.

Nouvel Espace Culturel – *9 r. Claudius-Cottier - 42270 St-Priest-en-Jarez - ☎ 04 77 74 41 81 - nec.spj@wanadoo.fr - tickets: Mon-Fri, 8.30am-4.30pm - closed Aug and weekends*. The Nouvel Espace Culturel was created in 1991 in a suburb close to Saint-Étienne. Many professional and amateur theatre troupes from all over France appear here performing new works or repertory pieces. Each year, the NEC organises a dance festival called 'Les mais de la danse'. Concerts, songs and children's shows are featured in the effervescent programmes.

SHOPPING

Manufrance MF – *6 r. de Lodi - ☎ 04 77 21 29 92 - manufrance@wanadoo.fr - Mon-Sat 10am-6.45pm - closed public holidays*. Many of the French nostalgically remember spending hours thumbing through the pages of the enormous catalogue printed by La Manufacture des Armes et Cycles de St-Étienne, the legendary company originally founded in 1893 by Étienne Mimard. Today, the store sells a multitude of DIY, gardening, household, leisure, decoration, hunting and fishing items.

Chocolate Weiss – *8 rue du Gén.-Foy - ☎ 04 77 49 41 48 - www.weiss.fr - Mon 2pm-7pm, Tue-Sat 9am-7pm - closed Easter, Ascension Day, 14 Jul, 15 Aug and New Year's*. Marrying a long history of savoir-faire and the finest cocoa available, Weiss has been St-Étienne's chocolate citadel since 1882. The most famous names in French and foreign cuisine do their shopping here. Their *napolitains, nougamandines* and *nougatelles*, to name but a few, are well worth a try.

Place Boivin

This marks the site of the former 15C north rampart. Walk down rue Émile-Loubet; there is a fine façade adorned with five caryatids at no 12, the 16C **Maison de "Marcellin-Allard."** Return to the square, one corner of which is occupied by the church known as the Grand'Église. To the right of the church, at the beginning of rue de la Ville, note the two handsome façades (15C and 16C): no 5, known as the **Maison François I** is decorated with five Renaissance medallions. One side of the square is occupied by the Église St-Étienne, known as the Grand'Église.

Grand'Église

The church of St-Étienne is the only remaining example of Gothic architecture in St-Étienne, and its parish is the oldest in the city. The church was built in local Forez sandstone in the 15C; the bell-tower was added in the 17C. In the first chapel on the left there is a fine 16C polychrome entombment. The chancel in Flamboyant Gothic style dates from the mid-15C and the stained-glass windows date from the 19C.

▶ *On leaving the church, turn right and rejoin rue Ste-Catherine, leading down to rue du Général-Foy. Turn left towards place Jean-Jaurès.*

Place de l'Hôtel-de-Ville, the main town square, and place Jean-Jaurès form the hub of city life in St-Étienne.

Place Jean-Jaurès

In the summer season this recently renovated square is a delight with its pretty bandstand and its plane trees offering a welcome patch of shade. At one end stands St-Charles Cathedral.

▶ *Rue Gérentet leads to place Dorian, then rue Alsace-Lorraine will take you back to place du Peuple.*

Sights

View

From the paths of the botanical gardens, and in particular from the terrace in front of the **Maison de la Culture** (1969), there are typical **views** of the town which lies in the hollow of the Furan basin and is dominated, on the opposite slope, by Ste-Barbe hill and, further away, by two bings, gradually being covered with vegetation.

J. Damase/MICHELIN

The planetarium

Musée du Vieux St-Étienne

Entrance in the second courtyard on the left. 🕐 *Daily except Sun, Mon and public hols, 2.30-6pm. 3€ (children: no charge).* ☏ *04 77 25 74 32. www.vieux-saint-etienne.com*
An 18C toll marker, from the old Outre-Furan district, signals the entrance to the Hôtel de Villeneuve (18C). The City Museum inside is arranged on the first floor, in a series of rooms with fine moulded and coffered ceilings. The first charter mentioning St-Étienne (1258) is on display, together with various maps and engravings illustrating the expansion of the city.

Musée d'Art et d'Industrie

🕐 *Daily except Tue 10am-6pm, Mon 10am-12.30pm and 1.30-6pm (last admission 30min before closing).* 🕐 *Closed 1 Jan, 1 May, 14 Jul, 15 Aug, 1 Nov and 25 Dec. 4.50€.* ☏ *04 77 49 73 00.*
This Art and Industry Museum located in the former Palais des Arts is a real repository of local and regional know-how relating to toolmaking and the evolution of equipment and machinery from the 16C up to the present day.

Site of the old Manufacture des Armes et Cycles de St-Étienne

Cours Fauriel. Laid out under the Second Empire to be, together with Avenue de la Libération, one of the showcases of the industrial expansion in St-Étienne, cours Fauriel was occupied by the buildings of the Arms Factory which were built by Léon Lamaizière in 1893, and which were in use until 1985. One part of the site has been restored and converted into a conference centre, with offices, shops and a planetarium.

Planetarium

Espace Fauriel, 28 rue P.-et-D.-Ponchardier. Kids 🕐 *Apr-Aug: shows (1hr30min) Wed at 3.30pm, Sat-Sun at 3.30pm and 4.45pm; Sep-Mar: additional show at 2.15pm; Feb and Easter school holidays: daily at 2.15pm, 3.30pm and, 4.45pm. By appointment.* 🕐 *Closed Sep, 1 Jan, 1 May, 25 Dec. 6€ (children: 5€).* ☏ *04 77 33 43 01. www.astronef.fr*
Crowned by a hemispherical dome, this planetarium is fitted with highly sophisticated equipment which enhances the appeal of its shows about the universe. Most impressive is the astronomical simulator, able to calculate and project onto the screen the movements of the planets and of some 3 000 stars.

Puits Couriot, Musée de la Mine★

Guided tours (1hr30min) daily except Tue at 10.30am and 3.30pm, Sat-Sun at 2.15pm. Audio-guided tours daily except Tue 3.45-5.30pm (departure every 10min), Sat-Sun 2.45-5.30pm. 🕐 *Closed 1 Jan, 1 May, 14 Jul, 15 Aug, 1 Nov, 25 Dec. Guided tour: 6€ (children: 4.50€), audio-guided tour: 5€ (children: 4€). No charge 1st Sunday in the month.* ☏ *04 77 43 83 26.*
Puits Couriot was exploited from 1913 to 1973 by the Houillères du Bassin de la Loire (Loire Basin Coal-Mining Company). During its peak the seam here produced 3 000t of coal per day and employed 1 500 miners.
The visit begins in the **Salle des Pendus★**, a vast locker room where, as space was limited, their clothes were hung from the ceiling to dry. The adjoining shower is evidence of the collective

Puits Couriot

Musée de la Mine, St-Étienne

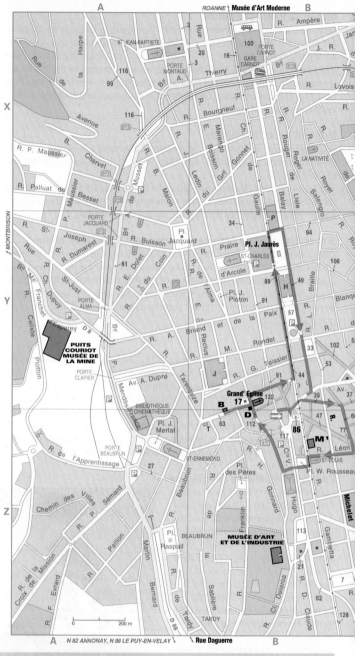

ROANNE \ **Musée d'Art Moderne**

N 82 ANNONAY, N 88 LE PUY-EN-VELAY \ **Rue Daguerre**

ST-ÉTIENNE			Apprentissage R. de l'	AZ		Bergson R.		BX	16
			Arago R.	CZ		Bernard Bd M.		AZ	
			Arcole R. d'	ABY		Blanc R. Ph.		CY	
11-Novembre R. du	BZ	128	Badouillère R. de la	CZ	9	Blanqui R.		BY	
Albert-1er Bd	ABX	3	Balay R.	BXY		Boisson R. E.		BX	
Alliés R. des	CY		Barbusse R. H.	CZ	12	Boivin Pl.		BY	17
Alma R. de	BY		Beaubrun R.	AZ		Bourgneuf R.		ABX	
Ampère R.	BX		Bérard R. P.	BCY	14	Braille R. L.		BY	
Anatole-France Pl.	BZ	7							

Dolet R. E.	AY	
Dorian Pl.	BY	33
Dormoy R. M.	BXY	34
Drs-H.-et-B.-Muller R. des	CX	
Dumarest R.	AY	
Dupont R. Pierre	CX	
Dupré Av. A.	AY	
Dupré R. G.	BY	37
Dupuy R. Ch.	AY	
Durafour R. A.	CZ	38
Escoffier R. D.	BY	39
Éternité R. de l'	BXY	
Evrard R. F.	AZ	
Fauriel Cours	CZ	
Ferdinand R.	CXY	
Fougerolle R.	CZ	41
Fourneyron Pl.	CY	42
Foy R. Gén.	BY	44
Franchet d'Esperey Bd Mar.	AY	
Francs-Maçons R. des	BCZ	
Franklin R.	BZ	
Frappa R. J.	BZ	47
Gambetta R.	BZ	
Gaulle R. Ch.-de	BXY	
Gérentet R.	BY	49
Gervais R. E.	CY	50
Gillet R. F.	BY	52
Gonnard R. H.	BZ	
Gonnet R. du Gd	BX	
Grand Moulin R. du	BY	53
Guesde Pl. J.	BY	56
Harpe R. de la	AX	
Hôtel-de-Ville Pl. de l'	BY	57
Jacob R.	CX	58
Jacquard Pl.	AY	
Janin Bd J.	BCX	
Jean-Jaurès Pl.	BY	
Krumnow Bd F.	AY	61
Lassaigne R.	CZ	
Lavoisier R.	BCX	
Leclerc R. du Gén.	BZ	62
Ledin R. J.	ABX	
Libération Av. de la	BCY	
Loubet Av. du Président E.	BZ	63
Malon R. B.	AX	
Marengo R.	BX	
Martyrs-de-Vingré R. des	BYZ	66
Maussier R. P.	AXY	
Mendès-France Bd Pierre	AYZ	
Merlat Pl. J.	AZ	
Michelet R.	BYZ	
Mimard R. Étienne	CYZ	
Moine Pl. Antonin	CYZ	68
Montat R. de la	CY	
Moulin Pl. J.	CY	72
Mulatière R. de la	CZ	75
Musset Bd A. de	AXY	
Nadaud Cours G.	CYZ	
Nautin R. L.	BCZ	
Neuve Pl.	BZ	77
Neyron R.	CXY	
Paillon R.	AZ	
Painlevé Pl. P.	CY	
Palluat de Besset R.	AX	
Pères Pl. des	BZ	
Peuple Pl. du	BZ	86
Ploton Pl. J.	BY	
Plotton R. C.	AYZ	
Pointe-Cadet R.	BCZ	87
Praire R.	BY	
Président-Wilson R.	BY	89
Raspail Pl.	AZ	

Briand et de la Paix R. A.	ABY		Comte Pl. Louis	BZ	21
Buisson R.	AY		Croix de Mission R. de la	AZ	
Chantegrillet Allée	CYZ		Cugnot R.	XY	
Charvet Av. B.	AX		Delaroa R. Cl.	BZ	
Chavanelle Pl.	CZ	18	Denfert-Rochereau Av.	CY	26
Claude R. D.	BZ		Descours R.	AZ	27
Clovis-Hugues R.	BX	20	Desjoyaux R.	BCX	
Coin R. du	AY		Dr-G.-Dujol Sq.	CX	

Reclus R. E.	ABY	St-Jean R.	BY 102	Thierry Bd A.	ABX	
République R. de la	BCY	St-Joseph R.	AY	Thomas Pl. A.	BZ	113
Résistance R. de la	BY 91	St-Just R.	AY	Tiblier Verne R.	CX	
Richelaudière R. de la	CY	Salengro R. Roger	BXY	Tilleuls R. des	AX	116
Rivière R. du Sergent	CX 93	Sauzéa Cours H.	CY 103	Tissot R. J.-C	CZ	
Robert R.	BY 94	Sémard R. P.	AZ	Treyve R. du	BCX	
Rondet R. M.	ABY	Servet R. M.	BY 106	Ursules Pl. des	BZ	117
Rouget-de-Lisle R.	BXY	Soulié R. L.	CX	Valbenoite Bd	CZ	119
Rousseau Pl. W.	BZ	Stalingrad Square de	CY 109	Victor-Hugo Cours	BZ	
Royet R.	BXY	Tardy R. de	AZ	Ville R. de la	BY	122
Rozier R. du	CZ	Tarentaize R.	ABY	Villeboeuf Pl.	CZ	123
Ruel R. A.	AX 99	Tavernier R. P.	CXY	Villes Chemin des	AZ	
Sablière R. de la	BZ	Teissier R. G.	BY			
Sadi-Carnot Pl.	BX 100	Théâtre R. du	BYZ 112			

Grand'Église	BY	Maison de la Culture	CZ	St-Étienne	BZ M¹
Maison Francois-1er	BYZ D	Musée d'Art Moderne	BX	Planétarium	CZ
Maison de Marcellin-		Musée d'Art et d'Industrie	BZ	Puits Couriot, musée	
Allard	BYZ B	Musée du Vieux		de la Mine	AY

life they led. Visitors are taken down to the lower galleries in the cages used to take miners down at the start of their shift and then to bring up the coal during the rest of the day, and sometimes for bringing up the wounded. The visit continues with the **extracting-machine room** and the **power room.**

Before returning to the surface, a representation of St Barbara, the patron saint of miners, may be seen in a niche, bringing to mind the religious and lay festivals in which all mining towns participate on 4 December each year.

Excursions

Firminy
11km/6.8mi. Leave St-Étienne to the S on D 88. Firminy lies in the Ondaine Valley, half way between the mountains and the St-Étienne plain. The town is known for its urban appearance stamped by the famous architect **Le Corbusier** – housing complex, arts centre, stadium and St-Peter's Church (unfinished) – making it the second **"Le Corbusier site"**★ in the world after Chandigarh in India.

Château des Bruneaux
Château: daily except Mon, 2-6pm. Mine: guided tours Sun and public holidays 2.30-5pm. ⏱ *Closed 1 Jan, 1 Nov, 25 Dec. Château only: 3.50€ (children: 2€); château and mine: 5€ (children: 3.50€).* ☎ *04 77 89 38 46. www.multitex.fr/bruneaux*
The castle features a nailer's workshop and a collection of toys. The outbuildings house a reconstructed mine showing the different types of support structures used.

Le Pertuiset
15km/9.3mi. Leave St-Étienne to the SW on D 25. This hanging bridge marking the transition between the industrial city and the wild Loire gorges provides access to the driving tours.

St-Didier-en-Velay – ♿ *See MONISTROL-SUR-LOIRE.*

Vallée du Gier
The Gier Valley running from Terrenoire to Givors forms a steep canyon flanked by verdant slopes.

St-Chamond
7km/4.3mi to the W on N 88. This is the industrial cradle of the area, bringing together a wide variety of factories (iron, steel, plastics, dyes, mechanics, synthetics etc). It is

also the birthplace of former racing driver **Alain Prost**, affectionately nicknamed "Professor of the Track," who became famous by winning the Formula One World Champion title four times (1985, 1986, 1989, 1993).

Rive-de-Gier
20km/12.5mi to the W on N 88, then on D 88. An industrial town, dating back to the early 18C.

Givors
30km/18.6mi to the W on N 88, then A 47. The vestiges of Château St-Gérald *(access by the housing estate "Les Étoiles" built on the hillside)* command a view of the town hall, the two churches in Givors and the River Rhône.

The Belvederes

▶ *Leave St-Étienne to the S along Cours Fauriel (D 8). N 82 makes its way along the Furet ravine, dotted with schist outcrops.*

Col du Grand-Bois
Charming forest site.

▶ *Turn around and drive to Planfoy. There, turn left and rejoin Guizay.*

View from Guizay★★
From the foot of the Sacré-Cœur statue there is a fine extensive view over the town. The village of **Rochetaillée** can be seen, to the far right, perched on its crest. To the left unfolds the Ondaine corridor: Le Chambon-Feugerolles, Firminy and the hills of Forez.

▶ *D 88 takes you back to St-Étienne.*

Grangent Dam

▶ *Leave St-Étienne on D 8 and drive to Roche-la-Molière. There, take D 3A towards St-Victor. In Le Berlan, turn left onto D 25. After 1km/0.6mi turn right onto the road to Quéret. Drive past Trémas village (on the right) and after 400m/400yd, turn right. On leaving Quéret, on the square, take the steep road going downhill.*

Plateau de la Danse
45min on foot there and back. Leave the car in the car park and follow the path signposted "Point de Vue" that disappears into the woods.
🚶 This region, steeped in local history and legends, has a rocky belvedere commanding a lovely **view**★ of Grangent Dam and Island, St-Victor promontory, Essalois Château, and the church and medieval tower in Chambles.

▶ *Return to the car and drive to St-Victor.*

St-Victor-sur-Loire
This pretty village adorned with roses occupies a charming **site**★ overlooking the artificial lake formed by the Loire upstream of Grangent. The **sailing base** is a popular meeting-place in summer and there are facilities for many other sports and leisure activities.
The Romanesque church remodelled in the 16C and 17C features a fine organ case and interesting modern stained-glass windows. The open-air theatre and the **castle** (🕐 9am-noon, 2.30-5.30pm, Sat-Sun 2.30-5.30pm. 🕐 Closed Aug, 1 Jan, 25 Dec. No charge. ☎ 04 77 90 49 29. www.chateau-saint-victor.fr) sporting its 11C towers are perched on top of the hill.

ST-FLOUR★★

POPULATION 6 625
MICHELIN MAP 330: G-4

St-Flour is perched on the end of the *planèze* which bears its name, at an altitude of 881m/2 890ft on a basaltic table 100m/330ft above the River Ander. The beauty of its site★★ can be best appreciated from an eastern approach which reveals a line of houses dominated by the massive towers of the cathedral, looming above rocky escarpments. The town developed around the tomb of St Flour, one of the Evangelists preaching in the Auvergne in the 4C. During the Middle Ages, under the administration of three elected consuls, it had a population of 7 000 people. In 1317 the Pope made it a cathedral town. *Cours Spy-des-Ternes, 15100 ST-FLOUR, ☎ 04 71 60 22 50. www.saint-flour.com*

▶ **Orient Yourself:** There are two towns, one, a modern, busy place on the plain, the other, perched imperiously on a huge rocky upthrust overlooking the Ander and Lescure valleys, a network of old streets and cranky buildings, wherein lies all the interest.

P Parking: There are ample parking areas in both the upper and lower town; beware the *priorité à droite* in some of the upper town streets

Address Book

EATING OUT

☺ **Chez Geneviève** – *25 r. des Lacs, ville haute* - ☎ 04 71 60 17 97 - closed 1 wk in Feb, 1 wk in Jun, 15 Oct-5 Nov, Mon evening, Tue evening and Sun except 2 Jul-8 Sep. On a pedestrian street in the city centre, this small, no-frills restaurant is very convivial. Seated between beams and wainscot, diners come savour local specialities, such as the *tripoux de St-Flour,* made fresh. Quite affordable.

WHERE TO STAY

☺ **Grand Hôtel de l'Étape** – *18 av. de la République, ville basse* - ☎ 04 71 60 13 03 - info@hotel-etape.com - closed Sun evening Sep-Jun - 🖭 8€ - restaurant 🖭. The whole family teams up to run this traditional hotel of the lower town, built in the 1970s and offering modern bedrooms. The tasty cuisine is made from regional recipes; most of the vegetables come straight from the garden.

☺ **Chambre d'hôte et ferme-auberge Ruisselet** – *15100 Roffiac - 3km/1.8mi W of St-Flour via D 926* - ☎ 04 71 60 11 33 - 5 rms - 🖭. Stop at this hospitable farm-inn and sample local dishes made with ingredients from their cattle farm. Pretty, comfortable and spacious bedrooms for a half-board holiday. Good tips for discovering the region given with pleasure.

☺ **La Pagnoune** – *Valadour - 15320 Loubaresse* - ☎ 04 71 73 74 69 - auberge-lapagnoune.com - closed Feb, 1-15 Oct and Mon - 🖭 - 7 rms - 🖭 5.50€. Built in 1877, this farm is a halt with a personality of its own. The rustic bedrooms are decorated with flair and the dining room is well worth a glimpse: exposed stones, two granite fireplaces, rustic furniture, an alcoved bed and farm tools contribute to its unabashedly pastoral flavour. Local produce on the dinner plate.

SHOPPING

Le Manoir des Saveurs – *54 av. du Lioran* - ☎ 04 71 60 47 24. Make sure you visit this grand shop housing a grocer's and a bakery. The former's shelves are laden with cheeses (including raw milk Cantal from Chez Charrade, *Ecir d'Aubrac* and *Gaperon*) tripoux, pounti, Valette foie gras and sweets. The latter offers a selection of 25 dif-ferent kinds of baked bread. Enjoy it all here or take your purchases on a picnic!

- 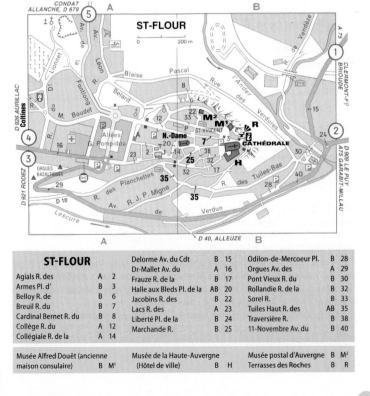**Don't Miss:** The view from the town walls, or the museum in the Hotel de Ville
- **Organizing Your Time:** You will need half a day to explore the upper town; the lower town holds less appeal
- **Also See:** The Gothic cathedral, built of sombre local stone

Revolt of the Tuchins – During the Hundred Years War St-Flour was close to the battlefield. The Treaty of Brétigny (1360) made St-Flour a frontier town, "France's key to Guienne" (Aquitaine). Fear of the English grew but it was the mercenaries, more than the English, who controlled the country from the fortresses of Saillant and Alleuze. The town was often attacked, its outlying districts burnt and pillaged. The consuls made pacts with the enemy who, in return for a fee, agreed to leave the people of St-Flour in peace. However, the truce was endangered by some of the inhabitants, nicknamed the *Tuchins*, who saw it as tantamount to capitulation, and who were seen as patriots by the lower classes. Formed secretly into a band, they waged implacable guerilla warfare on the occupant. After 1384 the *Tuchins* also attacked the rich and privileged orders, and became outright robbers. Having become dangerous to local authorities, they were overcome by the troops of the Duc de Berry.

Cathedral★

Built in late-Gothic style, it stands on the vast place des Armes and is a reminder of the town's vocation as a stronghold. Its construction, begun after the collapse in 1396 of the Romanesque basilica which preceded it, was not completed until the late 15C. The architect had previously worked for the Duc de Berry, which explains why the construction is not in the usual style of the region. On the west front, the

ST-FLOUR			Delorme Av. du Cdt	B	15	Odilon-de-Mercoeur Pl.	B	28
			Dr-Mallet Av. du	A	16	Orgues Av. des	A	29
Agials R. des	A	2	Frauze R. de la	B	17	Pont Vieux R. du	B	30
Armes Pl. d'	B	3	Halle aux Bleds Pl. de la	AB	20	Rollandie R. de la	B	32
Belloy R. de	B	6	Jacobins R. des	B	22	Sorel R.	B	33
Breuil R. du	B	7	Lacs R. des	A	23	Tuiles Haut R. des	AB	35
Cardinal Bernet R. du	B	8	Liberté Pl. de la	B	24	Traversière R.	B	38
Collège R. du	A	12	Marchande R.	B	25	11-Novembre Av. du	B	40
Collégiale R. de la	A	14						

Musée Alfred Douët (ancienne maison consulaire)	B	M¹	Musée de la Haute-Auvergne (Hôtel de ville)	B	H	Musée postal d'Auvergne	B	M²
						Terrasses des Roches	B	R

right-hand tower is pierced with square mullioned windows letting daylight into two rooms once used as a prison.

Inside, the lines of the five aisles are strikingly sober. Under the organ loft, a 15C mural depicts **Purgatory and Hell.** Note, against the left pillar at the entrance to the chancel, the large wooden **Crucifix**★ (13C or 15C) known as the "Beautiful Black God"; the 15C *Pietà* in the chapel of the Holy Sacrament and, in the Tomb Chapel, a gilded bronze shrine containing the relics of St Flour.

Town Walk

Old streets

From place d'Armes, lined with arcades and old façades (particularly at the corner of rue de Belloy), walk to rue Sorel and the church of St-Vincent, a former Dominican convent.

Follow rue des Jacobins on the left, then rue de la Collégiale named after a disused 14C church: **Notre-Dame collegiate church** whose apse has Flamboyant windows. **rue Marchande** has a few interesting old houses, including no 31, the governor's house, a 15C mansion whose façade and courtyard can be seen, and at no 15, Hôtel Brisson with a 16C courtyard, its original windows separated by columns with rope moulding.

Other interesting streets include **rue du Breuil** (15C house at no 8), and **rue des Tuiles-Haut** (old houses).

Ancienne Maison Consulaire

The façade of this former consul's residence dates from the 16C. The courtyard (enter through no 17 bis), from which can be seen three houses successively bought by consuls in the 14C and 15C to serve as their consular establishment, has an old well, a 15C staircase turret and various painted inscriptions. It houses the Musée d'Art et d'Histoire Alfred-Douët (& see Museums below).

Terrasse des Roches

Behind the east end of the cathedral. From this square on the old ramparts there is a lovely view of the lower part of the town, the Ander Valley and the Margeride mountains.

Museums

St-Flour prides itself on its rich cultural heritage and its many museums, which will enlighten you on local art and history. A nice way to round off this tour would be to visit the four museums in Ruynes-en-Margeride (& see RUYNES-EN-MARGERIDE).

Musée de la Haute-Auvergne

Place d'Armes. 🕐 *Mid-Apr to mid-Oct: 10am-noon, 2-6pm; mid-Oct to mid-Apr: daily except Sun and public holidays, 10am-noon, 2-6pm.* 🕐 *Closed 1 Jan, Easter, 1 May, 1 and 11 Nov, 25 Dec. 4€.* ☎ *04 71 60 22 32.*

This museum is located in the former bishop's palace rebuilt in the 17C. Displays in the low 15C vaulted rooms explain how blue-veined Fourme cheese is made (including Cantal and Salers varieties) and the different facets of pastoral life, particularly the shepherd's huts or *burons* where the cheese is made.

On the ground floor, in the former chapel, note a 12C polychrome wooden statue of St Peter from the church at Albepierre-Bredons, a 14C statue of St Flour, nine 16C carved wooden panels and a lovely set of Marian statues from the 12C to the 18C. The next room leads to the chapter-house, the only vestige of the Cluniac priory, where the treasure of the cathedral of St-Pierre and portraits of bishops are displayed.

View of St-Flour

The exhibits on the first floor concentrate on Auvergne folklore: popular music and its traditional instruments, hats and headdresses, a collection of regional carved-wood pieces, Cantal furniture (chests, cupboards, dressers, wooden bed panelling).

The contents of the archaeological section mainly come from the digs at Mons and also from Laurie, near Massiac. A beautiful bronze **brassard**★ consisting of six rings attached with a bar, and bracelets and swords are the main items displayed.

Musée d'Art et d'Histoire Alfred-Douët

 Mid-Apr to mid-Oct: guided tours (45min), Mon-Fri, 9am-noon, 2-6pm, Sat-Sun and public holidays 10am-noon, 2-6pm; mid-Oct to mid-Apr: Mon-Fri, 9am-noon, 2-6pm, Sat, 10am-noon, 2-6pm. Closed 1 May. 3.40€. ☎ 04 71 60 44 99. www. musee-douet.com

Beyond the entrance hall with its collection of ancient weapons is the library which boasts Diderot's Encyclopaedia; the guard-room with its monumental fireplace, and the Consul Room where fine tapestries hang, contain Renaissance furniture; the Louis XVI bedroom with painted wood panelling displays 18C furniture and the gallery is exclusively decorated with 17C paintings and furniture. In addition, you will see fine Limousin enamels, glassware as well as a collection of pewter and copper.

In a small oratory, note a *Pietà* and a 15C Christ with His hands bound.

Musée Postal d'Auvergne

 Juln-Oct: 10am-noon, 2-7pm. 3.50€ (children: 1.50€). ☎ 04 71 60 38 03.

This Postal Museum, occupying an old monastery, contains a collection of 6 000 items retracing the history of postal services since the 17C. The local postal service is given special emphasis, with the reconstruction of Ytrac post office (1900), and a horse-drawn sledge used until 1950 to enable mail to be delivered in the Margeride mountain region even when it was under a thick covering of snow.

Excursions

Roffiac

2km/1.2mi W along D 40.

An old restored mill, **Moulin du Blaud** (hours variable, ring tourist office for information, or ☎ 04 71 60 75 75), houses a trout information centre: all you want to know about this freshwater fish which you can catch (no licence required; fishing tackle hiring facilities) in the lake. The museum, which illustrates fishing in the past, includes an observation laboratory, aquariums and a model of a dam. A nature-discovery trail runs round the lake.

Coltines
12km/7.5mi W. Leave St-Flour along D 926 towards Murat then turn right onto D 14 to Coltines.

Musée de l'Agriculture
Kids &🕘 *Jul-Aug: 10am-noon, 2-6.30pm; Feb-Jun and Sep-Nov: 10am-noon, 2-5.30pm, Sun 2-5.30pm; Dec-Jan: 2-5pm, Sat by appointment.* 🕘 *Closed 1 Jan, 25 Dec. 4€. No charge on 8 May.* ☎ *04 71 73 27 30. www.coltines.com*
Located in a 17C house, this interactive museum is devoted to agriculture in the Auvergne region from the beginning of the 20C to the 1950s.

Vallée de l'Ander
40km/25mi – allow 4hr

▶ *Leave St-Flour E onto D 990. After crossing the River Ander, turn right onto D 250.*

Gorges de l'Ander
Continue along the edge of the river which runs between both rocky and wooded slopes. The path ends in a very picturesque meander, at the hamlet of Le Bout du Monde ("World's End").

▶ *Turn around and at the crossroads take D 250 on the left, then left again onto a small road leading to Grizols. After the village, turn left onto D 40.*

Site du Château d'Alleuze★★ – 🕭 *See Gorges de la TRUYÈRE.*

▶ *Leave Alleuze to the N on D 116.*

Villedieu
The **church,** half-Romanesque, half-Gothic, has an attractive door with a wrought-iron knocker. In the chancel, notice the beautiful High Altar, the staffs and finely carved lectern.

▶ *Continue along D 116. At the intersection turn right onto D 921, then onto D 926, heading for Murat.*

Église de Roffiac
The church is a little Romanesque building from the beginning of the 12C; it belonged to the castle (14C) now gone except for a tower.

▶ *Leave Roffiac to the N on D 104. Park in the hamlet of Le Sailhant.*

Cascade du Sailhant
15min on foot there and back.
🚶 The path to Le Sailhant (or Le Babory) waterfall weaves among the houses bordering the beautiful volcanic rocks on which Château du Sailhant is built.
The tiny cascade falls into a semicircle of tall cliffs; in the hollow lies a small lake. It is also possible to park at the entrance to the château and walk the short distance to the edge of the cliff, which offers a bird's-eye view of the cascade and the lake in its rocky surrounds.

▶ *Leave Le Sailhant S along D 40. Further on, D 979 leads back to St-Flour.*

ST-GERMAIN-LAVAL

POPULATION 1 488
MICHELIN MAP 327: D-5

This pretty mountain village is watered by the River Aix. The surrounding hills form a delightful natural setting, where the vegetation switches from golden brown to deep green, depending on the season. The 18C **Église de la Madeleine**, crowned by a saucer dome, is used to host temporary art exhibitions in summer. The **parish church** at the far end of the village houses a stone statue of Moses (1065), on the right as you enter, and a small polychrome wooden Pietà in an al-cove above the font. On place de la Mairie, the **museum** *(Guided tours (15min) daily except Sat-Sun 8.30am-noon, 2-5pm. No charge.* ☎ *04 77 65 41 30)* **installed in** the former château displays tapestries, furniture and miniature objects from France and Oriental countries. Note the two splendid Aubusson tapestries in the village hall. Place de la Mairie is lined with old houses, one of which has wooden panels: it is the birthplace of the explorer **Greysolon du Luth**. ▯ *28 r. R.-Lugnier, 42260 ST-GERMAIN-LAVAL,* ☎ *04 77 65 48 75.*

Excursions

Chapelle Notre-Dame-de-Laval
1.3km/0.9mi W of St-Germain on D 38. This Gothic chapel rises majestically on the banks of the Aix. The gabled façade features two basket-arch doorways and the interior houses a statue of the Black Virgin. Our Lady of Laval was a popular place of pilgrimage during the Middle Ages and in the 17C.

Commanderie de Verrières
2.5km/1.5mi. Leave St-Germain on D 1, heading for Balbigny. Take D 21, then turn left onto a narrow lane leading to the commandery. Adjoining the buildings of a former commandery, the 12C **chapel** is a sober construction made with light-coloured granite. The interior has a nave covered with barrel vaulting. On the esplanade stands a fine 15C cross.

Automusée du Forez
4km/2.5mi. Leave St-Germain on D 8, heading for Roanne. Just before the underpass, turn left onto a lane leading to the car park of the museum. ⚅ ⏱ *10am-noon, 2-6pm (Nov-Mar: daily except Mon 10am-noon, 2-5pm).* ⏱ *last 2 wks in Dec. 6€ (children: 4€).* ☎ *04 77 65 53 47. www.automusee.fr*
This Automobile Museum displays around 100 cars belonging to private collectors *(some are for sale)*, manufactured by prestigious names such as Voisin, Talbot, Delahaye, Ferrari and Panhard.

Pommiers★
3km/1.9mi E of St-Germain on D 21. The view is far prettier when the town is approached by the S on D 94. You will succumb to the charm of this quaint perched village lying on the borders of the Forez and Roannais regions. The site was already occupied in Roman times but the locality prospered around a Benedictine monastery in the 9C. During the 14C, Pommiers, like many other local towns, enhanced its defensive capacities by building ramparts to protect its citizens. The striking 11C and 12C church presents a series of 16C **frescoes** and a fine wooden **bust of Christ** from the 13C. The 16C conventual buildings were rebuilt in the 17C and 18C and an imposing set of cloisters now gives onto the old Romanesque church.

An interesting exhibition on local art in prehistoric, Gallo-Roman and medieval days is shown at the **Musée du Vieux Pommiers**. The former abbey church is presently used as the parish church and the priory has been turned into a **cultural centre** *(Ask for information, ☎ 04 77 65 44 88)* which regularly organises concerts and conferences.

Vallée de l'Onzon and Vallée de l'Aix

90km/56mi – allow half a day

▶ *Leave St-Germain to the S on D 8. In Boën (see Monts du FOREZ), take N 89 on the right to L'Hôpital-sous-Rochefort.*

L'Hôpital-sous-Rochefort
This village was fortified in the 15C and has retained two of its doorways. The 12C church has a narrow nave housing a superb **Virgin with Child**★★ in polychrome wood dating from the late 15C. This life-size statue is a paragon of vivacity and grace.

▶ *Leave L'Hôpital-sous-Rochefort to the W on D 21, heading for St-Didier-sous-Rochefort. This road gives onto the lane leading to Rochefort (old hill village). Rejoin D 21 and follow directions for St-Didier-sous-Rochefort.*

St-Laurent
Note the fine 15C cross next to the church.

▶ *Take D 21 to St-Didier-sous-Rochefort.*

Between St-Didier-sous-Rochefort and St-Julien-la-Vêtre, a huge megalith, **La Pierre Branlante,** stands on the edge of the road *(D 73)*.

▶ *N 89 leads to Noirétable.*

Noirétable
This pleasant mountain resort has retained its traditional economic activities (timber industry, cutlery). The 15C Flamboyant Gothic church has a remarkable porch, which used to be larger and served as a covered market. All the 17C statues carved out of black Volvic stone were brought here from the Hermitage monastery during the Revolution.

▶ *Take N 89 towards Thiers and, after leaving the village, turn right onto D 24.*

Cervières
Park the car on the esplanade at the entrance to the village. The squat **Gothic church** has diagonal ribs resting on sculpted brackets depicting masks. Note the Pietà in the naïve tradition. Also note the fine Renaissance house opposite the church. Walk through the vaulted passageway beneath the house and skirt the former fortifications on the left to a new granite arch; a steep street leads back to the church. The market ground beyond the town hall commands a lovely view of the surrounding countryside.

La Maison des Grenadières
🕐 *Apr-Oct: daily except Tue 2.30-6pm; Nov and Mar: Sta-Sun 2.30-6pm.* 🕐 *Closed Dec-Feb. 5€ (under-12s: no charge, 12-18: 4€). ☎ 04 77 24 98 71. www.grenadieres.com*

Housed in a picturesque Renaissance residence, this museum is devoted to gold-thread embroidery and the skilful workers who decorate civil and military ceremonial clothes (tools, drawings, costumes).

▸ *Go to Champoly on D 53. Leaving Champoly (E), take the narrow signposted road leading to the site of Château d'Urfé.*

Château d'Urfé
45min on foot there and back.

This 12C-15C stronghold was once home to the Urfé family, before they moved to Bastie-d'Urfé (& *see Château de la BASTIE-d'URFÉ*). The castle is currently undergoing restoration. The **viewing table** installed at the top of the keep affords a superb vista of the Monts du Lyonnais and the foothills of the Monts d'Auvergne.

A. de Valroger/MICHELIN

Château d'Urfé

▸ *Drive back towards Champoly. Leave D 24 on the right and take D 53, a charming road leading to St-Just-en-Chevalet. Follow D 1 to the SE.*

Grézolles
Village dominated by the slate bell-tower of its 16C chapel.

▸ *Go to St-Martin-la-Sauveté and, S of the village, turn left onto D 20, a path leading to the belvedere.*

Belvédère de la Sauveté★
Viewing table. 15min on foot there and back.

The path takes you to the foot of the water tower and a statue of the Virgin Mary, offering a sweeping **panorama** of the area.

▸ *Return to St-Martin and take D 38 on the right, heading for St-Germain-Laval.*

ST-NECTAIRE★

POPULATION 675
MICHELIN MAP 326: E-9
25KM/15.5MI W OF ISSOIRE

Two villages are grouped together under this name: the thermal spa of St-Nectaire-le-Bas (Lower St-Nectaire), which spreads out over 2km/1mi in a green valley, and the old village of St-Nectaire-le-Haut (Upper St-Nectaire) dominated by its magnificent **church**. Mont Cornadore, on which St-Nectaire is built and which means "water reservoir," was inhabited in Celtic times. The Romans built public baths here. In the Middle Ages a Benedictine priory was established as an offshoot of La Chaise-Dieu Abbey; a castle, no trace of which remains, was also built on the hill. It was inhabited by the glorious St-Nectaire family whose most famous member was **Madeleine de St-Nectaire** – young, beautiful and virtuous, widowed early, always followed by 60 men on horseback; she sided with the Protestants in the Wars of Religion, defeated the king's lieutenant in Upper Auvergne and ended up killing him by her own hand. The name "St-Nectaire" is also given to a well-known cheese, made with pasteurized or unpasteurized milk (& see Introduction: Food and drink) which has been produced for centuries in a well-defined area within the Cantal and Puy-de-Dôme départements. 🛈 Les Grands Thermes, 63710 ST-NECTAIRE, ☎ 04 73 88 50 86.

St-Nectaire-Le-Haut

Église St-Nectaire★★

This church constructed around 1160 is typical of Romanesque architecture in the Auvergne; it occupies a very beautiful site near the Dore mountain range. It was built in honour of St Nectaire, the companion of St Austremoine and monks from La Chaise-Dieu were the first priests in charge of it. The damage which occurred during the Revolution required extensive renovation work in 1875 (belfry, towers, west front).

A good **view** of the church is possible from Chemin de la Parre, east of the church, beyond the tributary.

Exterior

The west front, crude, almost sparse, has a simple rounded doorway. The east end, on the other hand, with its magnificent ground plan, is crowned with a belfry rebuilt in the 19C. The restrained decoration of the east end includes a delicate mosaic frieze incorporating rose windows, blind arcades with fine colonnettes and small gable walls supporting the chapel roofs.

Interior

The inside is remarkable for the unity of its style. A narthex, with a robust three-bay arcade decorating its upper storey, precedes the nave, which is barrel-vaulted without transverse ribbing and flanked by narrow side aisles with groined vaulting surmounted by galleries. The attractive chancel, not as high as the nave, has six elegant columns topped by interesting capitals, and an ambulatory opening onto three radiating chapels.

St-Nectaire

B. Kaufmann/MICHELIN

Some 103 magnificent **capitals**★★, carved by an artist with a lively imagination and a strong sense of composition, decorate the nave and chancel. Although the figures are somewhat heavy, the verve with which they have been treated lends them remarkable vitality. The Life of Christ, the Old and New Testaments, scenes from Revelations and the miracles of St Nectaire provide the main themes, together with those of the bestiary (Donkey playing a Lyre, Monkey Trainer etc).

Despite having been pillaged during the Revolution, the **Treasury**★★ still contains some beautiful works: the gilded copper bust of **St Baudime**★★ (12C); the polychrome Virgin of Mount Cornadore (12C); a 15C embossed silver reliquary arm of St Nectaire; two gold binding plates decorated with Limoges enamelwork (12C).

Grottes du Mont Cornadore

🕐 *Feb-Oct and Christmas school holidays: guided tours (35min).* 🕐 *Closed the rest of the year. 6€ (6-12-year-olds: 4.50€).* ☎ *04 73 88 57 97.*

Address Book

EATING OUT

🍽 **Auberge de l'Âne** – *Les Arnats - 8km/4.8mi N of St-Nectaire via D 150 and D 643 -* ☎ *04 73 88 50 39 - closed Oct and Mon-Tue except Jul-Aug - reserv. required.* Lying in a tiny hamlet on the hilltops above St-Nectaire, this country inn has been serving typical Auvergnat fare for 40 years. Plain and simple dining room, oilcloth table cloths and paper napkins.

WHERE TO STAY

🛏 **Chambre d'hôte Guilhot Élisabeth et Marc** – *Sailles - 2km/1.2mi N of St-Nectaire-le-Haut via D 150 and D 643 -* ☎ *04 73 88 50 69 - ⚐ - 3 rms.* A quiet, simple home located in a hamlet offering a magnificent view of the St-Nectaire church and Sancy mountains. Rooms (one of which is designed for a whole family) are located in a building connected to the owners' house. Vaulted breakfast room with a pretty fireplace.

🛏🛏 **Régina** – *St-Nectaire-le-Bas-Est -* ☎ *04 73 88 54 55 - regina.st-nectaire@wanadoo.fr - closed Nov-Jan -* 🅿 *- 17 rms -* 🍴 *6€ - restaurant 🍽🍽.* You can't miss the little tower that marks a corner of this hotel built in 1904. The rooms are smallish, but bright and clean. The dining room has retained its Art Deco period decor. Heated pool in summer.

🛏🛏🛏 **Chambre d'hôte Le Chastel Montaigu** – *63320 Montaigut-le-Blanc - 10km/6mi E of St-Nectaire via D 996 -* ☎ *04 73 96 28 49 - www.le-chastel-montaigu.com - closed 20 Dec-1 Mar - 5 rms.* What a splendid spot! Go ahead and splurge on a stopover (minimum two nights in summer) in this fortified castle dating from the Middle Ages. You'll sleep in the turret, in one of the delightful, beautifully furnished rooms. Ask for the 'Gothic' room and bask in the evening sun on the terrace.

REGIONAL SPECIALITIES

La Musette – *Rte de Champeix -* ☎ *04 73 88 53 96 - lamusette@wanadoo.fr - 8am-8pm, 'til 10pm in season.* This shop proposes a wide range of regional specialities, such as jams, salt ham, liqueurs and cheeses from Auvergne, all confected by local craftspeople chosen for their remarkable savoir-faire. A slide show explains the process of cheese making while highlighting the enchanting landscapes of the Saint-Nectaire region.

Ferme Bellonte – *Farges - in St-Nectaire-le-Haut take RD150, dir. Olloix -* ☎ *04 73 88 52 25 - Les Mystères de Farges: school holidays: daily 10am-noon, 2pm-7pm; Farm: daily 7.45am (milking), 8.30am-10.30am (cheesemaking), 5pm (milking), 5pm-7pm (cheesemaking).* The Bellonte family will take you under their expert wing and show you the highlights of their farm, from the milking of their cows to the confection of their farm-made Saint-Nectaire cheese, the creamy, hazelnut-flavoured marvel that became famous at the table of King Louis XIV. 'Les Mystères de Farges,' a small museum and sound and light show, gives visitors a glimpse of the traditional way of life.

The Romans built public baths in these caves, where today visitors can discover the source of the spa water, its medical uses and petrifying properties.

Maison du Saint-Nectaire
🕐 *May-Sep, daily, 10am-noon, 2-6pm (Jul-Aug, 10am-7pm).* 🕐 *Closed the rest of the year. 5€.* ☎ *04 73 88 57 96.*
A video show *(in French)* explains the origin of farmhouse St-Nectaire cheese, how it is made and matured. There is a demonstration cellar and a sampling at the end of the visit.

The Spa Resort ⚕

The thermal spa, with smart shops lining D 996, has more than 40 springs. Their waters gush forth at temperatures ranging from 8-56°C/46-133°F. Its treatment installations are grouped together in the modern Gravières spa establishment; the waters are used to treat kidney and metabolic complaints.

Fontaines Pétrifiantes
🕐 *Jun-Sep: guided tours (45min) 9am-noon, 2-7pm; rest of year: daily except Mon 9am-noon, 2-5.30pm.* 🕐 *Closed 1 Jan, 25 Dec. 3€.* ☎ *04 73 88 50 80. www.fontaines-petrifiantes.fr*
The water gushes forth at more than 50°C/122°F from volcanic faults. Since 1821, seven generations of the same family have developed the technique of petrification (👣 *see CLERMONT-FERRAND)*, turning it into a real art form.

Dolmen
Located in the upper part of the park, east of the river, it consists of a fine granite slab resting on four standing stones.

Hiking Tours

Puy de Châteauneuf
30min on foot there and back. Fairly steep climb. Follow the street climbing up from the north-east end of the church, then take a rocky path on the left.
🚶 The path leads to the top of the Puy (alt 934m/3 064ft) from where there is an attractive view of the Dore mountain range. The side of the mountain is hollowed out by nine caves which, like the Jonas caves (👣 *see BESSE: Exploring the Couze Valleys),* were probably inhabited in prehistoric times, then used again in the Middle Ages.

Puy d'Éraigne
30min on foot there and back. Follow a rocky and very difficult path branching off to the left from the road to Sapchat, D 150.
🚶 From the summit (alt 895m/2 936ft) there is a stunning vista of the Dore mountain range.

Cascade de Saillant
2km/1.2mi E of St-Nectaire-le-Bas. 👣 *See BESSE-EN-CHANDESSE, Exploring the Couze valleys.*

ST-POURÇAIN-SUR-SIOULE★

POPULATION 5 266
MICHELIN MAP 326: G-5 – 30KM/18.6MI S OF MOULINS

This small market town, which is an important crossroads on the River Sioule, is popular with trout fishermen and hiking enthusiasts. It owes its name to St Pourçain (died c 532), a former slave, turned monk, who defended the Auvergne from the ravages of Thierry, son of Clovis, the king of the Franks. ▯ *13 pl. du Mar.-Foch, 03500 St-Pourçain-sur-Sioule, ☎ 04 70 45 32 73. www.tourismesaintpourcinois.com*

One of the oldest vineyards in France – Tradition has it that grapevine first appeared on the sunny hillsides of the Bouble and the Sioule valleys a little before the Christian era. The stony ground of this region is particularly suitable to vine growing, which developed rapidly during Roman times, and later at the demand of the monasteries and local squires. At the end of the 18C, 8 000ha/19 760 acres were under cultivation. Destroyed by phylloxera in 1892, the vineyards were later replanted and now cover 600ha/1 483 acres.

A wine fair takes place on the last weekend in February and the wine festival is celebrated during the last weekend in August.

Walking Tour

A touring map of the town is available from the tourist office.

From place Maréchal-Foch, with its attractive fountain dominated by the **belfry** of the ancient monastery, walk through the covered passageway to the carefully restored courtyard, cours des Bénédictins, which offers a beautiful view of the bell-tower and imposing roof of the church of Ste-Croix.

▸ *Enter the church, flanked by houses on each side, through the door leading into cours des Bénédictins.*

Église Ste-Croix★

Guided tours available; apply to the Tourist office, ☎ 04 70 45 32 73.

This vast, former abbey church was constructed in several stages from the 11C to the 15C. The chancel, built fairly late, is not in the axis of the nave, which has Gothic arches surmounted by a false triforium. Whimsical, humorous carvings decorate the misericords of the 15C stalls. The north arm of the transept houses a 16C **Ecce Homo:** this polychrome sculpture cut from a single block of stone depicts Christ at the hands of Pontius Pilate. In the apse, the two northern semicircular chapels with arched windows are Romanesque.

The sacristy, in the five remaining bays of the cloisters, has carved capitals and a 15C stone *Pietà* (damaged).

▸ *For a good view of the east end, leave by the main portal and turn right towards place Clemenceau.*

Musée de la Vigne et du Terroir★

1 cours des Bénédictins. ◷ Mar-Dec, daily except Mon, 2-6pm (Jul-Sep, daily, 10am-noon, 2.30-6.30pm). ◷ Closed mid-Nov to end Mar. 4€. ☎ 04 70 45 32 73 or 04 70 45 62 07.

Great care has been taken in presenting the history of the region's main agricultural activity. A spiral staircase in the clock tower (15C) leads to rooms with attractive beams and stonework. Here a large number of items show the different aspects of

Address Book

EATING OUT

🍴🍴 **Auberge de l'Aubrelle** – 32 r. des Béthères - ☎ 04 70 45 41 65 - closed mid-Oct to mid-Nov and Mon-Tue - reserv. required. Right near the centre of St-Pourçain, this restaurant in a park is as quaint as an old-time music café, with its terrace on the banks of the Sioule, fish-rich menu and singing owner who livens up the evenings. Wintertime, take shelter in the attractive dining room with fireplace and parquet floor.

WHERE TO STAY

🏠🏠 **Chambre d'hôte Demeure d'Hauterive** – 03340 La Ferté-Hauterive - 12km/7.2mi N of St-Pourçain-sur-Sioule via N 9 and D 32 - ☎ 04 70 43 04 85 - ⬚ - 5 rms - meals 🍴🍴. This stately home built in 1850 is an enjoyable place to stay. Its bedrooms, especially the ones downstairs, are roomy and prettily decorated. There's also a self-catering cottage available.

🏠🏠🏠🏠 **Château de Theillat** – 03150 Varennes-sur-Allier - 18km/11mi SE of St-Pourçain-sur-Sioule - take D 46, N 7, N 209 and D 214 - ☎ 04 70 99 86 70 - closed 16 Oct-14 Mar - 🅿 - 18 rms - 🍽 11€ - restaurant 🍴🍴🍴. Reveries abound as one strolls along the paths of the delightful park belonging to this 19C castle. Climb the majestic staircase up to your quarters, then come back down to dine in the plush dining room with purple draperies and crystal chandeliers. Pool and tennis court.

vine-growing and winemaking: cooper's tools, weights and measures, a showcase on phylloxera, winemaking instruments etc. The museum's two most important exhibits are: a four-chambered horse-drawn still dating back to 1889 and a huge 17C press with a vertical wheel which, turned by three or four men, could press up to 300kg/660lb of grapes. The museum also presents the region's rural architecture as well as the history of the local vineyards and of the town of St-Pourçain, including an account of feasts and rituals concerning vineyards and wine (brotherhood's banner, costumes etc).

Palais de la Miniature

Gare de St-Pourçain. 🚼 ♿🕐 *mid-Apr to mid-Nov, daily except Tue, 3-7pm; mid-Jun-Aug, 10am-noon, 3-7pm. 5€ (children: 3€).* ☎ 04 70 45 99 01.
A railway network comprising trains and carriages on a scale of 1:87 runs through Bourbonnais landscapes. Light and sound effects bring life to a panoramic setting representing the imaginary village of Venezy and the surrounding area, which has the main geographical and industrial characteristics of the region.

Excursion

Exploring the Limagne Bourbonnaise

75km/46.6mi round tour – allow 3hr

▷ *Leave St-Pourçain to the W on D 46, heading for Montmarault. Just before Venteuil village, turn right onto D 1.*

Église de Saulcet

This church crowned by an octagonal belfry features lovely 12C, 13C and 14C **frescoes**.

▷ *Leave Saulcet N on D 415.*

Frescoes in the church in Saulcet

Verneuil-en-Bourbonnais

Ancient medieval village of the Bourbonnais area. The former church **Notre-Dame-sur-l'Eau** (& *Mid-Jul to end Aug: 3-7.30pm. 1€.* ☎ *04 70 45 48 80*) overlooks the River Douzenan and hosts temporary exhibitions in summer. The **Musée du Lavage et du Repassage** (& ⏲ *Jun-Aug: 3-7pm; Sep-May: by appointment.* ⏲ *Closed 1 Jan and 25 Dec. 2.50€ (under-12s: no charge).* ☎ *04 70 45 91 53)* presents an interesting collection of irons for domestic use, ranging from the early Chinese saucepans to the first electrically-powered device marketed by Calor in 1917.

▶ *Leave Verneuil to the NE towards D 18. At the crossroads turn right. After 2.5km/1.5mi, turn right onto RN 9, then 90m/100yd further on, take D 532 on the left to Chazeuil. Take N 7 until you reach Varennes-sur-Allier. On leaving the town, turn left onto D 21, heading for Jaligny.*

Hospice de Gayette

Impressive sight in which a 15C keep has been incorporated into a set of classical buildings.

▶ *Leave the hospice to the S and follow D 521, then turn right onto D 268. Take D 23 on the left, then D 268 on the right. In Rongères, take D 172 and head E.*

Château du Méage

Elegant 15C and 18C manor house, flanked by round turrets and a square tower and circled by a moat.

▶ *Continue along D 172, then turn left to join D 32.*

Château de Montaigu-le-Blin

⚷ *Not open to the public.* This 13C citadel was commissioned by Philippe Auguste with a view to extending his influence towards the south.

▶ *Take D 172 to the S and drive to St-Gérand-le-Puy. Cross N 7. Skirt the church, then turn right onto D 906 then D 52.*

Seuillet

Note the beautiful Romanesque church.

▶ *Continue along D 52, then take N 209 on the right.*

Billy

Backed by hills in the north and overlooking the Allier Valley to the south, this village is the ideal starting point of hikes through the surrounding area (a map of the three marked itineraries is available from the tourist office); in addition, the lake will appeal to anglers and the river to canoeists.

Château

🕐 *May-Jun and Sep: guided tours (1hr) daily except Mon 10am-noon, 2-6pm (Jul-Aug: daily 10am-noon, 2-7pm); Apr and Oct: Sat-Sun and public holidays 10am-noon, 2-5.30pm. 4€. ☏ 04 70 43 51 51.*

This 12C fortress still bears the marks of the attack it suffered in 1576. Extensive restoration has reinforced the ruins, in particular the keep which is now accessible to the public. The keep houses the squire's lodgings with outside latrine above the guardroom where visitors can see a model of the castle.

After a visit to the castle, take a walk along the old ramparts for a fine **view**★ of the village and the surrounding area.

Church

It stands on the site of a former priory; this explains why it is not at the heart of the village which huddled round the castle for protection. Note the Romanesque crypt and the 16C chapel.

▶ *Leave Billy to the W on D 130.*

This delightful drive takes you through the beautiful oak forest of Marcenat.

▶ *2km/1.2mi before Loriges, take a narrow road on the left.*

Abbaye de St-Gilbert★

⚠ *Closed for renovation work.*

This former 12C abbey features a chapter-house with pretty vaulting and a curious warming room with an imposing fireplace.

▶ *Follow D 6 for 500m/0.3mi, then turn right onto D 277, which leads back to St-Pourçain via Ambon.*

ST-SATURNIN★

POPULATION 964

MICHELIN MAP 326: F-9 – 18KM/11.2MI S OF CLERMONT-FERRAND

This village in the Monne Valley was the home of the barons of La Tour d'Auvergne who later became the counts of Auvergne. This is the family which produced Catherine de' Medici – daughter of Lorenzo de' Medici and Madeleine de La Tour d'Auvergne – who became Queen of France after marrying Henri II. St-Saturnin attracted a colony of painters and several writers, including novelist and critic **Paul Bourget** (1852-1935). The location of St-Saturnin near the Monts Dômes and the Couzes and Comté valleys, its picturesque streets, its castle and its little square with a charming 16C fountain, make this an attractive tourist destination.

Sights

Parking recommended on place du 8-Mai (shaded square beside D 8).

Church★★
Guided tours available; contact Mme Hortefeux between 9am and 7pm, ☎ 04 73 39 30 13.

The medieval village

The church was built in the 12C and is very simple. Despite the lack of apsidal chapels, the **east end** is nonetheless quite attractive. The radiating transept chapels, the wide ambulatory around the semicircular chancel, and the powerful mass of the transept, which has the best-preserved octagonal bell tower in the Auvergne, form a remarkable architectural whole. The external decoration is elaborate, with its strings of billet-moulding, its modillions and its set of arches, some of them remarkable just for the alternate colouring of their basalt and arkose archstones. In contrast to this lavish decoration, the side buttresses and simple end-wall of the west front are striking in their lack of ornamentation.

Inside, note the high barrel-vault of the nave, the galleries above the side aisles with their groined vaulting, the elevation of the transept crossing with its supporting diaphragm arches and the crypt resting on powerful pillars.

In the chancel is a gilt-wood High Altar from the castle chapel, bearing the monogram of Henri IV and Marguerite de Valois, Queen Margot (👉 *see ISSOIRE*), the lady of St-Saturnin.

Next to the church is the small 11C **Ste-Madeleine Chapel** *(Contact Mme van Graagh at the town hall, ☎ 04 73 39 30 77)*, fortified in the 14C.

Château
🕐 *Mid-Jun to mid-Sep: guided tours (45min) 10am-noon, 2-6.30pm; Mid-Apr to mid-Jun and mid-Sep to end Oct: Sun and public holidays 2-6pm. 4€ (children: 2.50€). ☎ 04 73 39 39 64. www.chateaudesaintsaturnin.com*

This imposing fortress, which has undergone extensive restoration, is typical of the military architecture of the Middle Ages: triple curtain wall, ramparts, towers with machicolations and crenellations. The main part of the building, with a massive, late-15C roof, is flanked by two wings (14C and 15C). The keep, the watch-path (views of the village and its surroundings) and formal gardens are open to visitors.

Excursion

Abbaye Notre-Dame-de-Randol
2km/1mi SW on D 28 and D 28^A. The road to Randol provides an attractive view of this modern church overlooking the **Monne Valley**.

WINE

Cave St-Verny – *2 rte d'Issoire - at the intersection of D 978 and D 8 - take A 75 exit no 6 - 63960 Veyre-Monton - ☎ 04 73 69 60 11 - www.saint-verny.com - Tue-Sat 9am-noon, 2pm-6.30pm - book ahead for visits of the storehouses - closed public holidays.* Located in the heart of a vineyard region that used to be the third most productive in France (before phylloxera came and wreaked its deadly havoc), now in full renaissance, the Cave Saint-Verny takes visitors through its winery before inviting them to taste a few different Côtes d'Auvergne vintages (white, red or rosé).

The church is noteworthy for its pleasing proportions and the height of its nave. Inside, the most striking element is the soaring aspect of the **chancel**★ brought on by the slope of the nave and the height of the slender pillars, which rise right up to the vault. The oval chancel, flooded with light diffused through modern *grisaille* windows, is extremely elegant.

The south chapel is devoted to St Benedict. In the north chapel, dedicated to the Holy Family, note the stained-glass windows depicting the Mysteries of the Rosary.

STE-CROIX-EN-JAREZ

POPULATION 351
MICHELIN MAP 327: G-7 – LOCAL MAP SEE LE PILAT

The Carthusian monastery of Ste-Croix (Holy Cross) was founded in 1280 by Béatrix de Roussillon. During the Revolution the Carthusian fathers, who spent their time praying, studying and performing manual tasks, were forced to leave Ste-Croix; the monastery was then split up, the cloisters demolished in 1840 and, in 1888, Ste-Croix became a municipality.

The village which occupies the buildings of the former Carthusian monastery, in the Upper Couzon Valley, is therefore somewhat unusual. *Point d'accueil, 42800 STE-CROIX-EN-JAREZ, ☎ 04 77 20 20 81.*

Former Carthusian Monastery

May-Sep: daily except Wed, 10am-noon, 2-6pm; Mar-Apr and Oct-Nov: daily except Mon and Wed, 10am-noon, 2-6pm; Nov-Feb: daily except Mon, Wed and Fri 10am-noon, 2-5pm. 4€. ☎ 04 77 20 20 81.

Façade

On the façade of the former convent buildings, a **monumental granite doorway** was opened up in the 17C, flanked by round towers made of schist quarry stone. In the centre are the armorial bearings of the Carthusian monks: a globe bearing a cross, surrounded by seven stars symbolising St Bruno, founder of the order, and his six companions.

On each side of the main portal can be seen the ancient curtain wall, incorporated into houses and defended, at each end, by two angle towers.

▶ *Go through the doorway into the first courtyard.*

Cour des Frères

This vast rectangular courtyard is bordered by buildings which, in the past, housed the activities of the lay and oblate brothers (linked to the order not by vows but by civil contracts) who were needed to maintain the material life of the community: presses, cellars, bakery, workshops, forges, stables etc. The church bell-tower, visible from the courtyard, dates from the 19C. On the left, a vaulted **passageway** (**1**) leads to the entrance of the vegetable garden, which runs along the River Couzon; notice the beautiful 17C **wrought-iron transom** (**2**) above the old wooden door.

The end of the courtyard, on the left, gives onto a cobbled street, which, in the past, was completely covered – the **"corridor"** leading to the common rooms (refectory for Sunday meals and certain feast days, library etc).

▶ *Walk along the corridor.*

Church

The portal is marked by two stone holy-water stoups on each side. The 17C building has 16C and 17C woodwork and 14C stalls, with misericords and armrests decorated with carvings: grimacing mask, local peasant woman's headdress, animals etc. The back wall, above the portal, is decorated with three paintings depicting the Martyrdom of St Sebastian (a copy of a painting by Mantegna) in the centre; St Charles Borromeo, kneeling, on the left; and St Bruno, refusing the episcopate, dressed in the white scapular of the Carthusian habit, on the right.

The chancel leads to the remains of the original church: the **former chapter house** (**3**) and **former sacristy** (**4**) from the 13C, containing restored 14C **frescoes**★ which illustrate, with striking realism, the Coronation of the Virgin Mary, the Crucifixion (inspired by Giotto) and the funeral of Thibaud de Vassalieu who, in 1312, negotiated with Philip the Fair to attach the Lyonnais region to the French crown.

Above the Crucifixion can be seen a group of Carthusian monks from Ste-Croix.

▶ *On leaving the church, the old vaulted kitchen with its monumental fireplace is visible opposite (exhibitions). At the end of the corridor there is a second courtyard. To the left of the entrance is the reception, in the old monastery bakery.*

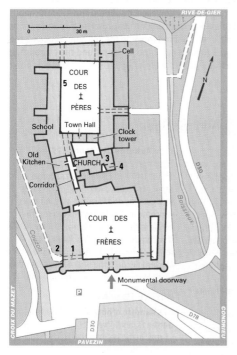

Cour des Pères

This courtyard used to have cloisters around it, leading into the monks' cells. The cloisters no longer exist and the cells have been turned into flats, the town hall, a school etc. Each cell had an oratory, a bedroom, a terrace and promenade at courtyard level; on the lower level was the woodhouse, the workshop and garden; on weekdays, the monks received their food through a hatch next to their cell door.

Over one of the cells, on the western side of the courtyard, is a **low-relief sculpture** (**5**) depicting St Bruno meditating on death.

In the south-east corner is the legendary **clock tower**, which lost its dial during the French Revolution.

SALERS★★

POPULATION 359
MICHELIN MAP 330: C-4
20KM/12.4MI SE OF MAURIAC – LOCAL MAP SEE MONTS DU CANTAL

Salers is one of the prettiest little towns in Upper Auvergne and has a very distinctive character. It stands at an altitude of 951m/3 120ft on its planèze and has retained, from its military and judicial past, a rare set of ramparts and old houses, grouped together on a pinnacle giving a magnificent view of the confluence of the River Aspre and River Maronne. Just outside Salers, on the road to Pas de Peyrol, stands the chapel of Notre-Dame-de-Lorette.

Salers is also a tasty farmhouse cheese made from unpasteurized full-cream milk.
🛈 Pl. Tyssandier-d'Escous, 15140 SALERS, ☎ 04 71 40 70 68. www.pays-de-salers.com

A Bit of History

Arms and the gown (15C-16C) – The twofold character of the buildings in Salers can be explained by the town's history. Initially unwalled, it suffered cruelly at the hands of the English and the mercenaries "free companions" who roamed the highways; as a result the ramparts were built, and still stand today. In the 16C Salers became the seat of the bailiwick of the Upper Mountains of the Auvergne and the established *bourgeois* families, from which the judges were selected, started building their impressive turreted houses.

Address Book

EATING OUT

🍽🍽 **La Diligence** – *R. du Beffroi* - ☎ 04 71 40 75 39 - closed 12 Nov-1 Apr. Don't be fooled by the modern look of this establishment – the dishes served here are traditional local fare. If the crêpes won't satisfy your appetite, the *truffade, tripoux, pounti*, or *potée auvergnate* will, especially when washed down with a native wine. Convivial atmosphere around big farm tables.

🍽🍽 **Les Sorbiers** – *Le Bourg* - 15380 Anglars-de-Salers - 9km/5.4mi N of Salers via D 22 - ☎ 04 71 40 02 87 - open evenings Apr-end Sep, Sat lunch and Sun lunch Jul-Sep - 🚭 - reserv. required. Stuffed cabbage, truffade, delicatessen - everything on the menu is homemade from farm fresh products. Once you've settled into the dining room with exposed stone walls and wood tables, take the time to savour the plentiful family cuisine served within. Six B&B guestrooms.

🍽🍽 **Auberge de l'Aspre** – *15140 Fontanges - 6km/3.6mi S of Salers via D 35* - ☎ 04 71 40 75 76 - www.auberge-aspre.com - closed Dec-Jan, Sun evening, Wed evening and Mon Oct-May. A hearty welcome awaits you in this old country house with a pleasant garden. A lawn chair on the grass or a cocktail on the terrace: what more could one desire? Modern decor in the bedrooms; fireplace in the dining room and veranda.

WHERE TO STAY

🍽 **Chambre d'hôte M. et Mme Prudent** – *R. des Nobles* - ☎ 04 71 40 75 36 - 6 rms. In the heart of Salers, this stunning 17C house has a charm all its own. The simple rooms are comfortable, the pretty garden looks out towards the volcanoes, and breakfast is served either outdoors or in a handsome room typical of the region, unless you'd rather be served in bed.

Religious excess (18C) – The main feast day in Salers was traditionally the anniversary of the birth of the Virgin Mary. On one occasion, the coveted title of King of the Festival was auctioned off, and the recipient, a vainglorious burgher, had the idea of running wine through the public fountains – a much appreciated act of generosity which then became customary. During the ensuing pilgrimages, however, the free-flowing wine led to countless brawls and beatings, leaving people wounded or even dead. In the end, such excesses had to be forbidden, the taverns closed and the brawlers fined; subsequently, the number of pilgrims decreased considerably.

Walking Tour

Eglise St-Mathieu★
If closed, the keys are available at the home of Mme Andzieu, ☎ 04 71 40 72 15.
12C porch still remains from the Romanesque church which predated the present church, begun in the 15C. The bell tower, which was struck by lightning, was rebuilt in the 19C.
Note, on the portal, the billet-moulding and sculptures on the upper covings. Inside, on the right, is an **Entombment**★ given to the church in 1495: it is made of polychrome stone and was inspired by Burgundian art. On each side of the chancel are paintings attributed to Ribera (17C). In the chancel there is a lectern from the end of Louis XIII's reign (mid-17C); above hang four 17C Aubusson tapestries. At the back of the church, a fifth tapestry depicts the Descent from the Cross.

▷ *On leaving the church, pass a fountain on the left and follow rue du Beffroi uphill.*

Go under the Tour de l'Horloge (clock tower also known as Belfry Gate), flanked by a round tower with machicolations. Just beyond the gate, on the right, is the house of Pierre Lizet with its Gothic window and Renaissance portal.

Place Tyssandier-d'Escous
The old houses of dark lavastone with their clean, sober lines, flanked by corbelled round or polygonal turrets, and their pepperpot or many-sided roofs, look like a stage-set; the scene is completed by a fountain in the centre.
On the main square a monument has been raised to Tyssandier d'Escous who improved the region's breed of cattle in the 19C and made it famous under the name of the "Salers breed."

At home in Salers

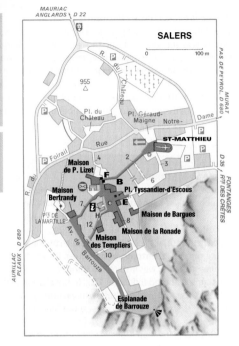

SALERS

Beffroi R. du	2
Courbière R.	3
Coustil R. du	4
Couvent R. du	6
Martille R. de la	7
Nobles R. des	8
Ste-Barbe R.	10
Templiers R. des	12

Maison d'un Bailli dite ancien Bailliage	B
Maison de Flojeac	E
Tour de l'Horloge	F

Ancien Baillage

Guided tours (30min) 11-11.30am, 2.30-5.30pm (closed Sun morning). 3€. ☎ 04 71 40 70 59.

This Renaissance building, the former Bailiff's Court, stands at the corner of rue du Beffroi. It is a vast residence of fine architectural design, flanked by two corner towers. Inside are several rooms open to view, one of which has a beautiful Renaissance fireplace.

In the inner court, adjoining the main building, rises a massive octagonal tower with a watchtower.

Maison de Flojeac

Opposite the tourist office. The house has a turret with canted corners.

Maison de la Ronade

Guided tours (40min). 3€. ☎ 04 71 40 76 18. The owner is a local guide and organises guided tours of the town by day (1hr), 9.30am-noon, 2-6pm. 2€, or by night, May-Sep (2hr) 5€.

This building has a tower rising five storeys high. It has been converted into a guesthouse and tearoom.

▶ *At the entrance to rue du Couvent, on the right, a wooden door leads to a large courtyard.*

Maison des Templiers - Musée de Salers

Rue des Templiers, on the left of the tourist office. ◷ Apr to mid-Nov: daily except Tue 10.30am-noon, 2.30-5.30pm (Jul-Aug: daily 10.30am-noon, 2.30-6.30pm). 3€. ☎ 04 71 40 75 97.

The 15C building houses an exhibition on the town's folklore and past: reconstruction of Auvergne interiors, cheesemaking, chemist's shop dating from 1890, religious objects and garments.

> *Turn left onto avenue de Barrouze.*

Esplanade de Barrouze
The small, shaded park here offers an impressive **view**★ of the Maronne, Rat and Aspre valleys and the Puy Violent massif.

> *Retrace your steps and turn right onto rue de la Martille.*

Maison Bertrandy
The house has a round tower and an attractive door.

> *Return to Grande-Place, then take rue du Beffroi back to the church.*

Excursions

Chapelle Notre-Dame-de-Lorette
The chapel stands at the entrance to Salers, on the road to Peyrol. Since the 14C it has been used to hold services intended to keep diseases and poor harvests at bay.

Maison du Fromage, de la Vache Salers et de la gentiane
4km/2.5mi from Salers on the road to Puy Mary. ○ *Early Apr to Oct: 10am-7pm (last admission 1hr before closing). 4€ (8-12-year-olds: 2.50€).* ☎ *04 71 40 70 71.*
Appropriately located in a restored buron (shepherd's hut), this "cheese house" retraces the history of the Salers breed of cattle and of the local cheesemaking tradition; fine collection of tools. Another *buron* presents the history of the "Salers," a liqueur made from the gentian plant. Note the first still used in 1885 when the Labounoux family started making the liqueur. Visitors are invited to taste the cheese and the liqueur at the end of the tour.

Anglards-de-Salers
10km/6.2mi N on D 22. The Auvergne-style church with its octagonal belfry is built in a fairly pure style. It has a ribbed barrel vault and a dome over pendentives. Below it stands the **Château de la Trémolière** (15C – ○ *Jun-Sep: 2-7pm (Jul-Aug, 10.30am-12.30pm, 2-7pm).* ○ *Closed Mon morning. 4€ (under-12s: no charge).* ☎ *04 71 40 00 02*) which houses a collection of 16C Aubusson **tapestries**.

> *You can continue this excursion by pressing on towards Mauriac (see MAURIAC).*

MASSIF DU SANCY★★★

MICHELIN MAP 326: D-9

The Massif du Sancy, which forms part of the Dore mountain range, consists of a set of extinct volcanoes. It is one of the most picturesque areas in the Auvergne thanks to the dramatic power of some of the peaks, the depth of its valleys, its waterfalls and its lakes. The highest peak in the range, Puy de Sancy, rises to an altitude of 1 885m/6 184ft and is the highest summit in central France.

> **Orient Yourself:** Just 30 miles SW of Clermont Ferrand, within the Parc Naturel Régional Volcans d'Auvergne
> **Don't Miss:** The panorama from the Puy de Sancy, the highest peak in central France (*see Excursions*)

🕐 **Organizing Your Time:** Allow a full day for a driving tour of the area, and much longer to explore on foot

🖐 **Also See:** Le Mont Dore (🖐 *see LE MONT DORE*)

Fire and Ice

Three huge volcanoes – The mighty system of volcanoes, of which the last remains form the Dore mountain range, evolved at the end of the Tertiary era. At its zenith, it covered an area three times larger than that of Vesuvius and consisted of three large cones in juxtaposition (Sancy, Banne d'Ordanche and Aiguiller) whose craters opened at an altitude of almost 2 500m/8 202ft. The Sancy cone consists of a plug of trachyte where the exterior has been worn away by erosion. Volcanic lakes add a touch of beauty to the landscape which, at altitudes of 1 100-1 400m/3 600-4 600ft, is covered with forests of pine, spruce and beech. Lower down the slopes are valleys with meadows and hedgerows.

Rhinoceros in the Auvergne – Between the periods when the volcanoes were active, life returned to the Dore area.

Footprints and bones found among the volcanic ash prove that laurel, bamboo and other plants which are now found only in hotter climes once grew on the slopes of the volcanoes, whereas rhinoceros, elephants and fierce carnivorous creatures such as sabre-toothed tigers roamed the countryside.

Former glaciers –The great period of glaciation which spread across Europe at the beginning of the Quaternary Era covered the Dore mountain range with an ice cap more than 100m/328ft thick. This considerable mass dug out corries and deep

Sancy mountain massif

J. Damase/MICHELIN

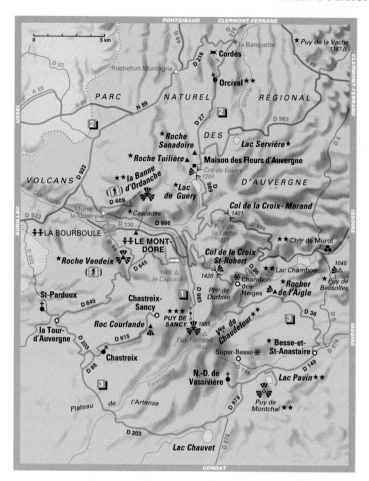

valleys, created the scarp slopes down which the waterfalls cascade, and threw into relief the most resistant sections of mountain, the peaks and enormous rocks that add to the picturesque beauty of the Dore mountain range.

Final throes – Decapitated and dismantled by the glaciers and by the surging melt waters that accompanied the fusion of the ice flows, the central area of the range looked very much as it does today when the first human settlers arrived. It was then that a new volcanic upthrust occurred along the edges: secondary volcanoes erupted, closing off valleys with their cones and lava flows, gouging out craters and creating a number of lakes. These were the final throes of volcanic activity in the Dore mountain range.

Excursions

① Puy de Sancy★★★

*From Le Mont-Dore (see Le MONT-DORE), drive to the upper part of the winter resort (4km/2.5mi) in order to reach the **cable-car station**. After a 3min ride, allow 45min on foot to the summit.*

Panorama★★★

Viewing table. Rising to an altitude of 1 885m/6 184ft, Puy de Sancy in the Dore mountain range is the highest peak in central France.

When the weather is exceptionally clear the **panoramic view** stretches as far as the Dauphiné Alps. Nearer are the Dômes mountain range to the north-east, the Cantal range to the south and, in the foreground, the Dore mountain range.

2 The Northern Slopes★★★

A round trip of 85km/53mi – allow half a day

It is also possible to start this trip from La BOURBOULE.

Le Mont-Dore ♯♯ – 🕭 *See Le MONT-DORE.*

▶ *Leave Le Mont-Dore N along D 983; 3km/1.9mi further on, turn right onto D 996.*

Col de la Croix-Morand

Alt 1 404m/4 606ft. This pass is also known as **Col de Diane,** although the real pass of this name is set away from the road. It used to have a bad reputation, for according to a local saying, "The Col de la Croix-Morand claims one man every year."

▶ *Return to D 983 and turn right (beware: in winter, this road is sometimes blocked by snow).*

After driving through the forest then through a valley with hillsides covered with basalt rock falls, the road reaches Lake Guéry (**view** of the Sancy massif).

Lac de Guéry★

The lake (alt 1 244m/4 081ft) covers an area of 25ha/62 acres and reaches a maximum depth of 16m/52ft. It was formed by a basalt flow which arrived from a south-easterly direction, closing off the end of the valley.

The pastures are studded with black rocks and the surrounding pine forests create a rather austere environment lightened in the springtime by great expanses of snow.

To the south are the outlines of the peaks in the Sancy range. The road runs high above the wooded Cirque du Chausse.

Lac de Guéry

Maison des Fleurs d'Auvergne

🕐 Mid-Jun to mid-Sep: 10am-7pm; May to mid-Jun: Sat-Sun and public holidays 10am-6pm. 4€. ☎ 04 73 65 20 09. http://maisondesfleurs.free.fr/

Located at Col de Guéry (alt 1 268m/4 160ft), this centre belonging to the Parc Naturel Régional des Volcans d'Auvergne, proposes an introduction to the local flora. Built round an ecological garden where it is possible to stroll at leisure, the centre offers its visitors the possibility of taking part in various workshops in order to make it easier for them to understand this fragile element of the ecosystem. In summer, the Maison de la Flore d'Auvergne organises themed hikes.

Roches Tuilière et Sanadoire★

From Col de Guéry there is a superb **view**★★ over the deep, wooded Chausse corrie from which the rocks of Tuilière and Sanadoire stand out.

To the left is **Tuilière rock**★ consisting of prismatic columnar trachyte in sheaves, once the chimney of a ruined volcano. **Sanadoire rock**★ to the right is all that remains of a volcanic cone. Until the 15C it was topped by an almost impregnable castle which was used as a refuge during the Hundred Years War by the mercenaries who terrorised the area. The large valley between the rocks was dug out by a glacier.

Near the junction of D 27 and D 983, a path off D 983 leads to a rocky promontory; from here, if facing Sanadoire rock, a surprising echo created by the phonolite can be heard.

▶ *Continue along D 983.*

Lac Servière★

This lake is a former crater with gently sloping sides, except to the south where it cuts into the Puy de Combe-Perret. It covers an area of 15ha/37 acres and has a depth of 26m/85ft. A round lake as unruffled as a mirror, its shores are lined with pines and firs, and meadows.

▶ *Turn back and follow D 27 on the right.*

Orcival★★ – 🐾 *See ORCIVAL.*

▶ *Leave Orcival N along D 27.*

Château de Cordès – 🐾 *See ORCIVAL.*

▶ *In La Baraquette turn left towards Rochefort-Montagne and Murat-le-Quaire. Turn left onto D 609.*

La Banne d'Ordanche★★ – 🐾 *See La BOURBOULE.*

▶ *Beyond Murat-le-Quaire, return either to La Bourboule on D 609 or to Le Mont-Dore on D 996.*

As well as the long-distance footpaths (Grande Randonnée), marked with red and white stripes, and the local paths (Pays Balisé), marked in red and yellow, there are many other interesting footpaths. Information available from local tourist offices.

③ Tour of the Sancy Range★★

85km/53mi round trip – allow one day – 🐾 see local map above

Some of the roads may be blocked by snow from November to April. The trip can also start from La BOURBOULE.

Le Mont-Dore⚕⚕ – ⛪ *See Le MONT-DORE.*

▶ *Leave Le Mont-Dore E on D 983 and turn left onto D 36.*

Col de la Croix-St-Robert

Alt 1 426m/4 678ft. From the pass there is a superb **panoramic view**★★ to the west over the Millevaches plateau, to the east over Lake Chambon, Murol plateau and castle and, in the distance, the mountains in the Forez and Livradois areas.

The road runs down beyond the pass towards Besse-en-Chandesse across the **Durbise plateau** with its vast expanse of pasture where the winter sports resort of **Chambon-des-Neiges** has been built.

▶ *Continue along D 36 and leave the car in the parking area at the entrance of the site.*

Vallée de Chaudefour★★

This interesting valley was gouged out of the granite and lava by the glaciers of the Quaternary Era, which covered the slopes of the Dore mountain range, and by the River Couze which flowed through the area after the glaciers had melted.

The valley floor and lower slopes boast abundant plant life. Some of the upper slopes and peaks are gashed by ravines, others bristle with rocks which have been laid bare and carved into strange shapes by erosion.

Geology enthusiasts will discover interesting examples of volcanic rock, and there are many good climbs for those with a keen interest in mountaineering.

Vallée de Chaudefour

Viewpoint

From a small bridge spanning the Couze, a ferruginous spring can be seen and there is a picturesque view over the valley floor forming a majestic amphitheatre. When facing Puy Ferrand, with the Roc de la Perdrix to the left and, opposite, the sharp pointed pyramid of the Aiguille standing out against its slopes.

To the right of Puy Ferrand stand some interesting rock formations, the Crête de Coq and the Dent de la Rancune. Further right still stands the Rocher des Dents; at its foot is a natural archway known as The Gateway or The Pierced Rock.

▶ *Return to the car park and continue along D 36.*

Rocher de l'Aigle★

From "Eagle's Rock" there is a striking view of the Chaudefour Valley and the Dore mountain range.

▶ *Keep driving along D 36.*

Besse-en-Chandesse★ – ⛪ *See BESSE-EN-CHANDESSE.*

▶ *Leave Besse SW along D 149.*

FAMILY STYLE

🍴 **Central Hôtel** – 63113 Picherande - 5km/3mi W of Lac Chauvet via D 203 - ☎ 04 73 22 30 79 - closed 30 Sep-1 Dec and lunch - restaurant for hotel guests only - 16 rms - ⌂ 6€. Set right in the village, this family home built in 1930 has a rather out-dated decor but it is impeccably run. Simple, inexpensive meals. Bathrooms are shared, but at these prices a little inconvenience is to be expected. Family atmosphere.

Lac Pavin★★ – 👶 *See BESSE-EN-CHANDESSE.*

▶ *Return to D 978 and turn left.*

Chapelle de Vassivière – 👶 *See BESSE-EN-CHANDESSE.*

▶ *Turn round and then turn right onto D 978 towards La Tour-d'Auvergne.*

Lac Chauvet

Lake Chauvet is surrounded by woods and pastures, and was formed by a series of volcanic eruptions which caused soil subsidence.

▶ *Return to D 203 and turn left; 12km/7.5mi further on, turn right onto D 88.*

Chastreix

Winter sports in Chastreix-Sancy. The **church** is a fine building with a nave but no side aisles. Note the 14C porch and, to the left of the nave, the 18C altarpiece.

▶ *Leave Chastreix N on D 615.*

Roc de Courlande

The road leads to the winter sports resort of **Chastreix-Sancy** (ideal for cross-country skiing) then to Courlande rock on the west side of the Puy de Sancy. From the car park to the right of the road there is an extensive **view**★ of the Artense plateau in the foreground, overshadowed by the Cantal mountains. The Dordogne Valley lies to the right.

▶ *Turn back to rejoin D 203 and turn right.*

La Tour-d'Auvergne

This is a small town in a delightful, rustic setting crisscrossed by streams forming waterfalls. It lies at an altitude of 990m/3 218ft on a basalt plateau ending in prismatic columnar basalt rock that can be seen near the church. The market place laid out on the top of these prisms seems to be made of gigantic cobblestones.

▶ *Continue NW along D 203.*

Église de St-Pardoux

Interesting Gothic **church** which still has 13C strap hinges on its doors and a fine gilt-wood altarpiece.

▶ *Return to La Tour-d'Auvergne and drive NE on D 645.*

Roche Vendeix★ – 👶 *See La BOURBOULE.*

▶ *Return either to La Bourboule by continuing along D 88 beyond Vendeix rock, or to Le Mont-Dore by turning right onto D 645.*

SAUGUES

POPULATION 2 013

MICHELIN MAP 330: D-4 – 44KM/27MI SW OF LE PUY-EN-VELAY

This small town favoured by anglers is the site of a number of large markets. It is dominated by an ancient keep known as the "Englishmen's Tower." On Maundy Thursday, at nightfall, a longstanding traditional Procession of the Penitents is held; among the White Penitents with their lanterns and the staff of their brotherhood are other penitents, dressed in red, barefoot, with a cowl over their heads, carrying the Cross and Instruments of the Passion (crown of thorns, nails, spear etc). Between the Margeride and the Allier, which cuts an almost uniformly narrow valley forming magnificent gorges, lies Saugues country with its stone walls, mountain streams and harsh climate. ▯ *Cours St-Gervais, 43170 SAUGUES, ☎ 04 71 77 71 38.*

Sights

Musée Fantastique de la Bête du Gévaudan

◐ *Mid to end-Jun and 1st to mid-Sep: 2.30-6.30pm; Jul-Aug, 10am-noon, 2.30-6.30pm. 4€ (children: 2.50€). ☎ 04 71 77 64 22. http://site.voila.fr/macbet*

This new museum is dedicated to the notorious creature that slayed and devoured countless sheep, goats and shepherds in the 18C, locally known as "La Bête du Gévaudan." Its predatory acts were confined to the territory lying between Saugues, Ruynes-en-Margeride, St-Flour and Langogne. The museum exhibits include life-size plaster casts of historical characters that recount the area's history.

Tour des Anglais

◐ *Jul-Aug: 10am-noon, 2.30-6.30pm. 2.50€. ☎ 04 71 77 64 22.*

The name of this tower dates back to the Hundred Years War. The Treaty of Brétigny (8 May 1360) put an end to the contracts of the "mercenaries" enlisted in the English army. They became **free companions**, dubbed "The Englishmen," living on pillage and robbery, and soon took over the town. The royal troops did not succeed in ousting them and it was only once they had been paid off in gold that they finally left.

The square tower, with its machicolations and arrow slits, is an example of 12C military architecture. A panorama of the region can be enjoyed from the top of the tower.

Church

The church, surmounted by an octagonal bell-tower, houses a 12C Auvergne Virgin and a 15C *Pietà* as well as the shrine of St Bénilde. Three beautiful gold processional crosses are displayed in the treasury chapel.

WHERE TO STAY

➰➰ **Chambre d'hôte des Gabales** – *Rte du Puy-en-Velay - ☎ 04 71 77 86 92 - www.lesgabales.com - closed Dec-Jan except during Christmas school holidays - ⬚ - reserv. required - 5 rms.* Skilful renovations have given this bourgeois house built in the 1930s a new appeal. Improvements include parquet floors in the sitting and dining rooms, period wainscotting, and pleasant, personalised bedrooms of the Renaissance or Louis XVI genre.

RECREATION

Sportival – *43380 Villeneuve-d'Allier - ☎ 04 71 74 70 42 - csvasportival@wanadoo.fr - open weekends May-Jun, daily Jul to mid-Sep - office open Mon-Fri 8.30am-noon. Reservations taken until 15 Oct.* This centre offers lots of outdoor activites: climbing, canoeing, kayaking, adventure trails, hiking, off-road biking and more. The site is magnificent, in the heart of the Allier gorge. Qualified staff at your service.

Diorama sur St Bénilde

Mid-Apr to end Sep: 2-5pm. No charge. ☎ *04 71 77 82 53.*
Thirteen set-pieces retrace the life of **Pierre Romançon** (1805-62), Brother Bénilde of the Christian Schools, the first state primary school teacher in Saugues, who was canonised in 1967. The exhibition is held in the actual school where he taught and was the principal.

Excursions

Tour de la Clauze
10km/6.2mi SW of Saugues on D 33. This impressive-looking tower was originally built to keep watch over La Margeride. What remains of the formidable citadel is the donjon, once surrounded by fortified walls. The stronghold played an important role during the Wars of Religion but subsequently slipped into neglect.

From the Allier Gorges to the Devès

Round tour of 105km/65.2mi – allow 4hr

▶ *Leave Saugues to the N on D 585.*

St-Arcons-d'Allier – ⚬ *See BRIOUDE.*

▶ *Take D 48 which runs along the east bank of the Allier.*

Chapelle Ste-Marie-des-Chazes
This isolated chapel on the east bank of the Allier stands on a peaceful spot at the foot of a striking basalt rock. A monumental flight of 30 steps leads to a porch-belfry (rebuilt in the 19C) crowned by a conical lantern.

▶ *Cross the Allier once more before going through St-Julien-des-Chazes and carrying on along D 48.*

Ste-Marie-des-Chazes

B. Kaufmann/MICHELIN

Prades
This small village is situated in a splendid **setting**★ hemmed in by the valley sides. The sinuous D 301, half cut into the valley slopes, commands some beautiful views. After dropping downhill a little, it runs along the foot of the ruins of the **Château de Rochegude.**

Monistrol-d'Allier
This village lies in a very impressive **setting**★ in the Allier valley.

▶ *Leave Monistrol E on D 589, and turn right in St-Privat-d'Allier onto D 40.*

St-Didier-d'Allier
This small village occupies a precarious site on a steep-sided rock.

▶ *Take D 40 as far as Le Pont-d'Alleyras, then turn left onto D 33.*

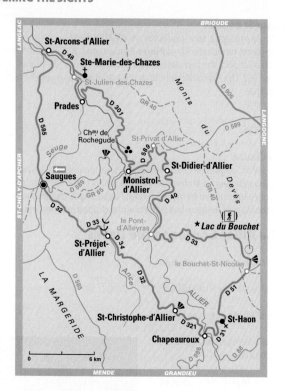

Lac du Bouchet★

A woodland footpath leads round the lake; allow 45min.

This lake lies 1 205m/3 953ft above sea level. It is 28m/92ft deep and covers an area of 43ha/106 acres at the bottom of an old crater which is responsible for its almost circular shape. The surrounding lake shore is covered with a forest of pine, spruce and fir trees which were planted between 1860 and 1900. In 1982, a violent storm devastated 100ha/247 acres of the forest, much of which was subsequently replanted. No river or stream is known to feed the lake, nor any overflow channel, yet the clarity and freshness of the lake's waters show that they are being constantly renewed.

On the road leaving the lakeside heading towards Le Bouchet-St-Nicolas, at the edge of the forest, there is a beautiful view of the volcanic Velay countryside and more particularly the Meygal and Mézenc mountain ranges.

St-Haon

The village built on the edge of the plateau has a church with a remarkable late-12C apse.

▶ *Follow D 31.*

Chapeauroux

This hamlet is built on the confluence of the Allier and the Chapeauroux in an attractive valley crossed by a sweeping railway viaduct with 28 arches.

▶ *On leaving Chapeauroux, turn right onto D 321.*

St-Christophe-d'Allier
From the road leading up the steep slope to this village there is a broad view of the Allier gorge.

▶ *Follow D 32 and just before it crosses the Ance, turn right onto D 34.*

St-Préjet-d'Allier
This village on the eastern flank of the Margeride has two dams spanning the Ance: La Valette and Pouzas.

▶ *Take D 33 alongside the graveyard. It leads back to Saugues.*

Picturesque alternative
The scenic road D 589, which runs from Saugues to Monistrol, affords incredible views of the gorge carved out of the granite by the Allier and from time to time also of the enormous basalt boulders on the river's banks.

SERRIÈRES

POPULATION 1 078

MICHELIN MAP 331: K-2 – 32KM/20MI S OF VIENNE

This old bargemen's town on the banks of the Rhône features an interesting museum, housed in St-Sornin Chapel (12C-14C) in the southern part of the town, recalling the old way of life along the river.

Sight

Musée des Mariniers du Rhône
  Closed for restoration work. Town hall. ☎ *04 75 34 00 46.*
Under the church's wooden roof are displayed the humble souvenirs of bargemen, known as *culs-de-piau* ("leather bottoms" because of their leather-lined trousers):

From Boatmen to Self-Propelled Barges

The Greeks who settled in Marseille around 600 BC used the Rhône to bring back tin from Cornwall in Britain. During Roman times, commercial boating became even more important: the river was the main artery for the wine trade. The Rhône boatmen formed the most powerful of all the corporations in the Roman towns.

Under the Ancien Régime (before the French Revolution) passenger barges connected the riverside towns, which all had their own port, leading to an intensely active life on the river. This beautiful waterway is, however, very dangerous when in spate or when the mistral blows. Madame de Sévigné suffered hours of anguish knowing that her daughter was travelling along "that devil of a Rhône."

In 1829 steam boats appeared on the Rhône and traffic became even more dense. The advent of the railway nearly ruined river transport, but the discovery and exploitation of water's potential as a source of energy, and engineering work on the river rejuvenated the Rhône. After work carried out by the Compagnie Nationale du Rhône, the tugboats of the past were replaced by 1 500t self-propelled barges and push tows of 5 000t and more. The traffic includes hydrocarbons, metallurgical and agricultural products and building materials.

megaphones, rudder bars used to fix the towing horses' chains, a crew's table from a riverside inn, journeymen's staffs, embroidered ceremonial waistcoats, horsehair rings decorated with glass beads, several specimens of **crew's crosses**. The crosses, fixed to the prow of the boat, were to protect the crew from the ever-present perils of the river. They were decorated with emblems of the Passion, naïvely carved and painted: nails and studs, Judas purses, legionnaires' dice, whips, droplets of Christ's blood, the hand of Justice etc. At the top was a cock, symbol of virility and, in particular, of the captain's constant vigilance.

Excursions

Malleval

10km/6mi on N 86 N and D 503 left just after St-Pierre-de-Bœuf. The road climbs the deep Malleval gorge with its sinister sounding name ("Valley of Evil"). Just after the pretty Saut de Laurette waterfall on the right, turn right onto a narrow road which leads up to Malleval.

The 16C houses of the village, once fortified, are built on a rocky spur crowned by the church and the ruins of the old castle. Malleval is the departure point for the flora trail through the Parc Naturel Régional du Pilat.

▶ *There is a lovely view of Malleval and the gorge from the road towards Pélussin; pull over and park shortly after a very sharp left-hand bend.*

Champagne

6km/3.7mi S via N 86. The **church** *(Guided tours available by appointment. ☎ 04 75 34 19 20)* here is largely 12C and is the only one in the Rhône Valley to have a nave vaulted with a series of domes on squinches: three domes cover the nave and a fourth hangs over the transept crossing. The vaulted aisles are surmounted by a gallery which opens onto the nave by twinned, trefoil-arched openings. There are beautiful 15C choir stalls and, on the tympanum above the central door, scenes of the Last Supper and the Passion.

At the entrance to Andance, at the foot of some granite needles, it is possible to see, in the distance on the east bank, the silhouette of the tall Albon Tower.

Andance

10km/6.2mi S via N 86. The church here houses a remarkable **crew's cross**★ in the right chapel; there are also fine Romanesque pilasters.

▶ *Cross the Rhône via the suspension bridge (1827) and take D 122A, which runs under the motorway, to Albon Tower.*

Tour d'Albon and Château de Mantaille

The ruined Albon Tower commands a sweeping panorama extending into the far distance. It was the counts of Albon who, by increasing their territories, from the 11C onwards, created the Dauphiné region. The graffiti adorning the tower include one commemorating the centenary of the Storming of the Bastille. From the foot of the tower the vast **panorama**★ takes in the Rhône Valley, from St-Vallier gorge to St-Rambert plain, the mouth of the Valloire, and the Cévennes to the west.

Some 4km/2.5mi east stand the ruins of Mantaille Castle; it was here that Boson was crowned king of Burgundy in the year 879.

GORGES DE LA SIOULE★★

MICHELIN MAP 326: C-5 TO E-7 – 30KM/18.6MI NW OF RIOM

The upper course of the River Sioule has a winding, undulating character as it flows down the Dômes mountain range, contrasting with the lower course which is flat with numerous islands in the Limagne basin. As erosion brought down the level of this calcareous basin, the Sioule, flowing at an increasing speed, cut into the granitic plateau upstream, thereby hollowing out a gorge between the outlying areas of Ébreuil and Châteauneuf-les-Bains. An intricate network of footpaths and bridlepaths enable visitors to discover the attractions of the area, which is also ideal for fishing and canoeing.

Excursions

1 Gorges and Castles

40km/25mi – about 3hr

Ébreuil

The small town lies on the banks of the River Sioule which, having crossed the famous gorge of the same name, flows through a wide, fertile valley. The **Église St-Léger**★, built in the 10C and 13C, was part of a Benedictine abbey whose buildings were replaced in the 18C by the present hospice (to the right of the west front) and by an abbot's palace (behind the east end) that is now a retirement home.

The timber-roofed nave and transept were built in the Romanesque style; the chancel and its radiating chapels are Early Gothic.

The belfry-porch, remarkable for the purity of its architectural design, was added to the 11C west front around 1125. Above the portal is a tympanum decorated with three Romanesque high-relief sculptures – a figure of Christ giving Blessing flanked by two of the Apostles. The strap hinges and door knockers date from the 12C.

The interior includes superb **frescoes**★ dating from the 12C and 15C. The 12C paintings decorating the gallery depict St Austremoine, first Bishop of Clermont, the martyrdom of St Valery and St Pancras, and the three archangels, Michael, Gabriel and Raphael. The 15C fresco on a pillar to the right of the nave shows St George slaying the Dragon. Behind the High Altar on a stone column is the superb **reliquary of St Léger**★ (16C) made of wood covered with silver-gilt. In one of the apsidal chapels is a 16C statue of the Virgin Mary seated.

▶ *Leave Ébreuil to the W on D 915.*

The corniche road, 4km/2.5mi after Ébreuil, overlooks the Sioule. On the steeper and more rugged slope on the right, bare granite alternates with heather. Beyond Péraclos, the road descends down to the river's edge.

J. Damase/MICHELIN

Detail of a fresco in the church of St-Léger

Château de Chouvigny

🕐 *May-Sep: Sat-Sun and public holidays 2.30-5.30pm (Jul and Aug: daily 10am-noon, 2.30-6.30pm). 5€. ☎ 04 70 90 44 95.*

This Bourbonnais-style fortress is built on a spur of rock in a delighful **setting**★ in a valley, its impressive crenellated silhouette towering high above the gorge of the River Sioule flowing below. This fine example of medieval architecture has been tastefully restored.

The Great Hall or main drawing room was once used as a court room, and the two seats from which justice was dispensed may still be seen. The coats of arms of the castle's various owners are displayed above the fireplace.

Cross the small Hunting Gallery to the terrace, from which there is a wonderful **view** over the gorge, barred on the right by the Roc Armand. Beyond this is the watchtower, with two loopholes set at an angle to each other (allowing the bowman to protect himself) and an iron cramp (making it possible to see as far down as the foot of the castle), followed by the Treasure Tower equipped with a safe embedded into the wall; it dates from the days of King Louis IX, better-known as St Louis (13C).

Gorges de Chouvigny★★

At the entrance to the gorge the road cuts through a rocky headland, the left part of which, detached from the rest, is called **Roc Armand.** The summit can be reached by a staircase cut out of the rock. Upstream, there is a beautiful view of the gorge – wooded slopes spiked with granite tips – whereas downstream, Chouvigny Castle can be seen. Beyond Armand rock, the gorge becomes very picturesque. At the entrance to a tunnel there is a **viewpoint** on the left, over a bend in the Sioule dominated by high cliffs. Upstream, the Sioule flows silently and smoothly down. Below the viewpoint, however, it flows quickly and noisily through a mass of pebbles; it is gradually wearing down a shelf which interrupts the natural slope. The picturesque valley unfolds a succession of wild-looking gorges and green narrow stretches.

Menat

This small village was once home to a Benedictine monastery founded in the 6C. Today there remain the 12C abbey church, vestiges of the 15C cloisters, along with the buildings housing the town hall and the Museum of Paleontology.

Musée de Paléontologie: "Le Gîte à Fossiles"

🕐 *Jun-Sep: daily except Tue 10.30am-noon, 2-6.30pm; Apr-May: Sat-Sun and public holidays 10am-noon, 2-6.30pm. 3.50€. ☎ 04 73 85 54 22.*

The museum is chiefly devoted to the small geological basin of Menat, dating from the end of the Secondary Era. The exhibition "La Marche vers l'Homme" illustrates the evolution of life on earth from the first cell up to modern Man.

Pont-de-Menat

This is an ideal point of departure for canoeing and kayaking. Crossing the river, there is an attractive view *(right)* of the old humpback bridge. Soon, on the edge of a cliff ahead, the romantic ruins of **Château-Rocher** (13C) loom into sight. Immediately below the ruins is an attractive view of a bend in the Sioule, a typical example of an incised meander: the concave bank *(this side)*, excavated by the direct attack of the current, is steep; the convex bank *(opposite)*, which receives the alluvial deposits, is low and cultivated.

The road then rises, providing greater views of the river; it reaches its culmination just before the intersection with D 99 from St-Rémy-de-Blot. Forming a ledge above a small, still-active mill, it offers a remarkable view of the entire valley.

Lisseuil

Here the road reaches the bottom of the valley. The village church has a beautiful Romanesque Virgin (13C) in its restored chancel.

Address Book

EATING OUT

🍽️🍽️ **Restaurant Vindrié** – *Gorges de la Sioule - 63560 Servant -* ☎ *04 73 85 51 48 - vindrie@toques-auvergne.com -* 🚭. This family restaurant is set right in the heart of the Gorges de la Sioule area, just next to the river. Tasty food with a nice choice of fish dishes and a very impressive wine list with over 45,000 bottles waiting patiently in the cellar! Pleasant summer terrace under an ivy cover.

WHERE TO STAY

🛏️ **Montarlet** – *63390 St. Gervais d'Auvergne - 3km/1.8mi W of St-Gervais-d'Auvergne via D 532, dir. Espinasse then turn left -* ☎ *04 73 85 87 10 - montarlet@ libertysurf.fr - 3 rms.* Located in a lovely, natural environment, this old farm is a most pleasant stopover. The restored bedrooms are delightful, with their sponge-painted walls, antiques and carefully chosen fabrics. Park with a view of the hills of Auvergne.

🛏️🛏️ **Castel Hôtel 1904** – *63390 St-Gervais-d'Auvergne -* ☎ *04 73 85 70 42 - closed 12 Nov-14 Mar -* 🅿️ *- 17 rms-* 🛏️ *9€ - restaurant* 🍽️🍽️🍽️. This handsome, flowery 17C manor became a hotel in 1904. The inviting interior is a reminder of centuries past with its period furniture, waxed parquets, grandfather clocks and statuettes. You'll discover appetizing, innovative cuisine in the more formal restaurant, whereas meals at the bistro, Le Comtoir à Moustaches, are of good value.

RECREATION

Sioule Loisirs – *Pont de Menat - 63560 Menat -* ☎ *04 73 85 52 87 - www.val-de-sioule.com/loisire.html - May-Sep: from 9am, reservations required.* Canoe and kayak rentals for trips down the Sioule. All-day and half-day itineraries possible.

Ayat-sur-Sioule

An attractive road leads to this village, once the home of General Desaix (1768-1800), one of Napoleon's officers.

Châteauneuf-les-Bains

This thermal spa (alt 390m/1 279ft) actually consists of several hamlets. Twenty-two springs are tapped here, providing cold water for bottling and hot water (ranging from 28-36°C/82-96°F) for the baths treating rheumatism and nervous disorders. Nearby, **Pic Alibert** and **Presqu'île de St-Cyr** offer fine views of the surrounding area.

2️⃣ Queuille Meander

60km/38mi – about 3hr 30min

Châteauneuf-les-Bains – ⛄ *See above.*

▶ *Take D 227 W.*

St-Gervais-d'Auvergne

The village is built on a knoll. Its Gothic church still has some Romanesque features: a portal in the transept and, on the left side, a watchtower with a curious gargoyle. Beautiful lime trees shade the terrace by the church. The **Maison des Combrailles** *(Place R-Gauvin, BP 25, 63390 St-Gervais d'Auvergne. Information:* ☎ *04 73 85 82 08)* provides information on the area.

South of St-Gervais the road winds through the middle of a wood, offering some lovely views of the Sioule before crossing the river at the foot of Les Garachons hydroelectric power station. It then runs along the east bank which follows numerous meanders and circumvents the seams of porphyry which lie in its path.

Viaduc des Fades★

This structure, built by the engineer Vidard at the beginning of the 20C, has a total length of more than 440m/1 440ft and is one of the highest rail viaducts in Europe. Its metal deck is supported by two granite piers 144m/472ft apart and 92m/302ft high. It stands 133m/436ft above the Sioule.

Barrage de Besserve

The **dam,** located upstream of the viaduct, is a gravity dam – its strength is provided by its sheer mass. It is 8m/26ft wide at the top, 68m/223ft high and its crown is 235m/771ft long.

Méandre de Queuille★★

Park by the church of Queuille. Walk behind the east end of the church (past the superb lime trees) and continue through the undergrowth to a viewpoint at the end of the promontory overlooking the Queuille meander, formed by the Sioule after it was widened by a dam. This side, the concave bank of the loop, is high and spiked with rocks; opposite, on the convex side, the river forms a tight circle around the Murat "peninsula," a long wooded headland.

Barrage de Queuille

Downstream from the meander is another gravity **dam** (⟳ *see above),* with a length of 116m/380ft at the top where it is 5m/16ft wide compared with 24.30m/80ft at the base, which incorporates a power plant.

▶ *Return to Les Ancizes-Comps and turn left on D 61.*

The road provides a magnificent descent through the Sioule Valley.

Méandre de Queuille

Chartreuse de Port-Ste-Marie
Visits by appointment. ☎ *04 73 26 68 44.*
At the bottom of the valley, perched on the edge of a rock, are the ruins of a **Carthusian monastery** founded in the 13C. Destroyed during the Revolution, it is gradually being restored.
The road climbs back up to the plateau, offering pretty views of the River Sioulet.

Miremont
The Romanesque church here with its massive square bell-tower rises up on a peak dominating a loop in the River Sioulet.

SOUVIGNY

POPULATION 1 952
MICHELIN MAP 326: G-3 – 13KM/8MI W OF MOULINS

Souvigny, which lies in the middle of a rich farming area, retains the most beautiful sanctuary in the Bourbonnais region, a reminder of the town's past splendour.
🛈 *Pl. Aristide-Briand, 03210 SOUVIGNY,* ☎ *04 70 43 99 75.*

Resting place of the Dukes of Bourbon – In 916 Aymard, lieutenant of the Duke of Aquitaine, sold his land at Souvigny to the monks of Cluny; in doing so he bestowed an uncommon destiny upon the former Carolingian villa here.
Two famous abbots from the powerful Burgundian abbey died in the monastery founded here: St Mayeul in 994 and St Odilon in 1049. The saintliness of the two men, soon united in the same tomb, drew numerous pilgrims to Souvigny, and the oldest of the Cluny priories, showered with gifts, developed dramatically.
The lords of Bourbon, descendants of Aymard, created a state around Souvigny which was to become the Duchy of the Bourbonnais. In the 14C and 15C the monastery underwent further alterations when Duke Louis II and Duke Charles I decided to make the sanctuary their necropolis.

Abbey

Église Prieurale St-Pierre-et-St-Paul★★

Unaccompanied visits of the nave. Guided tours of the funerary chapels, the cloister and the sacristy (1hr) daily except Tue 9am-noon, 2-6pm (7pm in Jul-Aug). Apply to the Musée de Souvigny. 4€ (ticket including the museum: 7€). ☎ 04 70 43 99 75.

The **west front** of the original Romanesque edifice, of which only the left door remains, was preceded in the 15C by an avant-corps with a portal and a wide Flamboyant opening. Two Romanesque bell-towers, connected since the 15C by a gable with a rose window, dominate the priory. The three Romanesque bays in the centre of the façade belonged to the original building consecrated in 1064. The north side shows the church's different stages of construction: the towers, the second aisle and the ambulatory are 12C whereas the upper part of the nave and the transept are 15C.

Nave and aisles

The interior has surprisingly large dimensions: 87m/285ft by 28m/92ft. The double side aisles flanking the nave, and the double transept are evidence of Cluniac influence.

The inner aisles, built in the 11C, are very narrow with barrel vaulting whereas the outer aisles, which are later, have groined or pointed vaulting.

- Finely carved tomb of St Mayeul
- Capital depicting monks minting money, a reminder of the priory's ancient privilege.
- Fragment of a 13C bishop's tomb.
- Bas-relief of the Immaculate Conception.
- Stone **reliquary-cupboard**★ (15C), with four wooden shutters painted with scenes from the lives of St Mayeul and St Odilon.

Chapelle Vieille★

The old chapel has a beautiful stone screen in Flamboyant Gothic style.

- Tomb of **Louis II of Bourbon,** known as Louis the Good, and his wife, Anne of Auvergne. The two marble recumbent figures are still extremely realistic, despite the defacements.
- 15C **Entombment**.

Chapelle Neuve★★

The new chapel is larger than the old chapel and has a very fine enclosure.

- Tomb of Charles I and his wife, Agnes of Burgundy by Jacques Morel. The recumbent figures, clothed in flowing cloaks, rest on a black marble slab.
- A graceful Mary Magdalene from the late 15C.
- The Virgin, Child and St John (16C).
- Small 15C *Pietà*.

The left apsidal chapel, off the ambulatory, houses a 13C polychrome statue of Our Lady of Joy. The sacristy, built in the 18C, has some fine wood panelling and an ivory Christ.

Cloisters

Access via the south aisle of the church or via the monastery buildings erected in the 17C, to the right of the church.

Only one side of these 15C cloisters remains, with groined vaulting because of the arrangement of the pillars. French-style gardens have been laid out on the site of the former priory buildings.

Sights

Église St-Marc
This church, now disused, stands opposite the northern side of the priory church and is built in the Burgundian Romanesque style. The interior has been converted into an auditorium.

Musée de Souvigny
🕐 *Daily except Tue 9am-noon, 2-6pm (7pm in Jul-Aug). 4€ (children: 1€; ticket including the Église prieurale: 7€).* ☎ *04 70 43 99 75.*

This museum to the right of the priory church houses lapidary and local history collections, as well as a glassworking exhibition. Next to the sarcophagi, recumbent figures and capitals stands a 12C **calendar**★★, the most striking piece in the collection. This 1.80m/5ft 9in octagonal pillar, weighing 840kg/1 848lb (over 0.75t), is carved on two sides with scenes showing the labours of the months and the corresponding signs of the Zodiac; symbols of strange peoples and fabulous animals adorn the other faces. Other exhibits include a collection of silver coins minted by the Souvigny monks during the Middle Ages.

Detail from a 12C calendar

Local history is recalled in the Souvigny glassworks founded in 1755: the master glassmakers' tools and examples of glassware (carafe stoppers, pharmacy bottles, champagne glasses) on show are reminiscent of this ancient craft.

A 3t canoe, hollowed out of a tree trunk, which was discovered in the River Allier in 1980 is also on display; it dates from around the year 1000.

Excursion

Discovering the Combraille Bourbonnaise

65km/40.5mi round tour - allow 4hr

This lush *bocage* countryside with its pretty churches will charm all visitors.

▶ *Leave Souvigny to the SW on D 945, heading for Le Montet.*

Noyant-d'Allier
The most striking feature of this former miners' town is its **pagoda**, surrounded by Buddha statues.

▶ *Continue N on D 18.*

Église de Meillers
The church is crowned by an unusual belfry. The chapel to the left of the chancel houses a late-12C Virgin.

▶ *Leave Meillers to the S on D 18, then turn right onto D 106.*

The **Côtes-Matras** command an enjoyable vista of the Allier plain.

Le Montet

The 12C Église St-Gervais-et-St-Protais was fortified in the 14C but today only the nave and the side aisles have survived the ravages of time.

▶ *Leave Le Montet to the W on D 22, heading towards Cosne-d'Allier. After 9km/5.6mi, turn right onto D 68.*

Buxières-les-Mines

This locality features the very last open-air coal mine in the area *(recently closed down)* and a church built in local sandstone.

Église St-Maurice

This church has a curious two-tier bell tower and a blind nave crowned by barrel vaulting. The pillars are embellished with capitals featuring leaf motifs.

▶ *Return to Souvigny via D 289, then D 11, driving along the Gros-Bois and Messarges oak forests.*

MASSIF DU TANARGUE★★

MICHELIN MAP 331: G/H-6

At the southern end of the high volcanic lands of the Velay and Vivarais rises the Tanargue, a crystalline range made up of granite, gneiss and micaschist. Its shredded appearance is due to the upheavals of the Tertiary and Quaternary Eras. This is one of the wildest regions in the Vivarais.

The storms in Tanargue are famous, especially for their violence in autumn. Sudden spates, given added power by the steepness of the terrain, transform local mountain rivers into raging torrents, which nonetheless subside as quickly as they swell.

▶ **Orient Yourself:** To the south of the Ardèche, the massif du Tanargue is easily accessible from the N102, although the minor roads are rather tortuous

😊 **Don't Miss:** The view from the cols de Meyrans and the Croix-de-Bauzon

🕐 **Organizing Your Time:** Allow three hours or more for a tour of the massif by car, and much longer for exploration on foot, of course

👣 **Also See:** Aubenas, Largentière, Ruoms, Thueyts, Vals-les-Bains and Les Vans

Excursion

From Vals-les-Bains to Valgorge

80km/50mi – about 3hr

Vals-les-Bains♨♨ – 👣 *See VALS-LES-BAINS.*

▶ *Leave Vals-les-Bains on N 102 S towards Le Puy-en-Velay. At Pont-de-Labeaume take D 5 to Jaujac.*

The route passes the basalt flows of the Lignon Valley; 2km/1mi beyond Pont-de-Labeaume, at a signpost, park and walk up to the edge of the volcanic platform on which the road runs; here and there the **basalt flow**★ takes on a striking appearance of perfectly vertical tube-like sections, some of a blue-grey colour.

J. Damase/MICHELIN

Basalt flow in Jaujac

Jaujac

This village has attractive 15C and 16C houses, especially in the Chastelas district on the west bank, and the ruins of its old fortified castle. To the southeast rises the "Jaujac dish," an ancient volcano from which the flows of the Lignon emerged, and where mineral springs emanate.

Leaving Jaujac, the small 15C **Château de Bruget** comes into sight on the right.

From La Souche the road becomes more mountainous; the tip of Abraham's Rock stands ahead to the right, dark slopes covered in pines lie to the left;

Col de la Croix de Bauzon★

From this pass (alt 1 308m/4 291ft) the view extends over the valleys of the Borne and the Masméjean to the mountains of the Margeride; to the east, the Lignon basin continues into the Aubenas depression. A small ski resort has been created at the foot of the Tanargue slopes, between La Souche and St-Étienne-de-Ludgarès *(information available from the tourist office in St-Étienne-de-Ludgarès)*.

▷ *Follow D 19 towards St-Étienne-de-Lugdarès and turn left on D 301 (narrow road).*

Gorges de la Borne★

Beyond a stretch of route across broom-covered moorland, the descent to Borne offers plunging views over the gorge. To the west is the profile of Le Goulet mountain. **Borne**★ itself is a village in a secluded site, on a ledge above the deeply embanked torrent. Within a rocky corrie on a spur lie the ruins of a castle, overlooking the waters. A small road leads to the tiny hamlet of **Mas-de-Truc**, seemingly lost in the mountains.

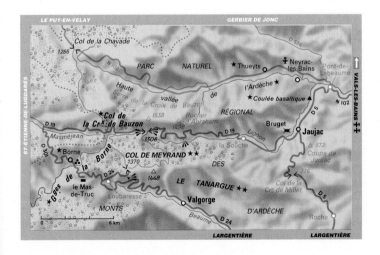

▶ *Continue to Col de Meyrand, via Loubaresse. As far as the village the road is narrow and sometimes impassable due to rockfalls.*

Col de Meyrand★★

Alt 1 371m/4 499ft. From this pass a splendid ledge is suddenly revealed; there is a viewing table below the pass, to the left on an isolated rock. An extensive panorama is visible, from left to right, over the summit of the Tanargue, the Valgorge Valley, the Ardèche depression overlooked by the Dent de Rez, the Valgorge ridge opposite and, to the right, the back of Mont Lozère.

▶ *Turn back.*

Beyond Loubaresse there are views along the channel down to Valgorge, then of stretches shaded by chestnut trees. The road drops downhill, twisting along the upper valley of the Beaume.

Valgorge

This small village is situated within a lush setting of vineyards and orchards.

▶ *Continue on D 24 until you reach Roche and take D 5 on the left.*

The road follows the Ligne Valley up to Col de la Croix-de-Millet (alt 776m/2 546ft).

▶ *D 5 leads back to Jaujac and Pont-de-Labeaume. There, take N 102 on the right, heading for Vals.*

TAUVES

POPULATION 863
MICHELIN MAP 326: C-9 – 13KM/8.1MI W OF LA BOURBOULE

Tauves, a pretty village with houses crowned by slate roofs, is built along the River Mortagne, a tributary of the Dordogne. ▮ *Pl. de la Mairie, 63680 La TOUR-D'AUVERGNE, ☎ 04 73 21 79 78. www.sancy-artense.com*

Sights

Église

The 14C Romanesque church is a squat building with massive buttresses and a belfry-porch with machicolations. The exterior is decorated with carved corbels. Inside, the first four bays of the nave are spanned by ribbed barrel vaults, the fifth bay and the chancel by diagonal vaults. There are some interesting capitals, both foliated and narrative, several Baroque altarpieces and a 17C Pietà. Note also a 16C bell.

Maison de l'Artisanat Rural

🕓 *Apr-Sep: 10am-noon, 2.30-7pm; Oct-Mar: school holidays only: 10am-noon, 3-6pm. No charge.* ☎ *04 73 21 16 18.*
This is both an exhibition centre and shop displaying examples of local crafts: carved wood, silk fabric, pottery, puppets etc. On Thursday afternoons in July and August, you can see artisans at work during a demonstration. For children there is a Friday workshop that explains the art of puppetry.

Excursions

Menhir de la Pierre des Quatre-Curés

Off D 922 on leaving Tauves, heading for La Bourboule, near Les Croûtes village. Tauves features numerous megalithic ruins but the most impressive monument is undoubtedly this towering basaltic menhir that can be spotted from afar.

Discovering the Gorges d'Avèze★

60km/38mi round tour – allow 3hr

▶ *Drive W out of Tauves along D 29.*

Singles

This former miners' village has a pleasantly located church that overlooks the Burande and the Dordogne gorges.

▶ *Return to "La Guinguette" (the paradise of anglers) and continue on D 73 until you reach Messeix.*

Messeix

This little town was once famous for its coal mines. The Romanesque church here was altered in the Gothic period but has retained its attractive 13C entrance.

▶ *Follow D 987 towards Tauves.*

Gorges d'Avèze★

This rocky gorge, situated on the border of the Puy-de-Dôme and of the Corrèze regions, offers breathtaking views of the upper section of the River Dordogne which takes its source at the Puy de Sancy, some 30km/18.5mi east of the gorge.

Avèze

The church presents interesting furnishings (altarpieces, statues of St Roch and St Blaise). Nice panorama of the nearby gorges.

▶ *Return to Tauves on D 987. You can make a detour via St-Sauves to admire its superb setting, a result of the glacial period ( see La BOURBOULE).*

THIERS★★

POPULATION 13 338

MICHELIN MAP 326: I-7 – 37KM/23MI E OF CLERMONT-FERRAND

The site★★ on which the town is built – on the side of a ravine through which the River Durolle flows – the magnificent view it offers over the Limagne and the Dômes mountain range, and the town's historical district make Thiers an attractive destination for tourists. It is the waters of the Durolle which made Thiers' fortune: paper and knives have been made here since the 15C and although papermaking has nearly disappeared, cutlery-making continues to contribute to the town's renown. The town was first founded on the south bank of the Durolle, around the original church of Le Moutier. Thiers was pillaged and razed to the ground by the Franks in 532 but rose from its ruins when the Bishop of Clermont, Avitus, built a sanctuary on the opposite bank, around the tomb of the martyr St Genès. Later, a fortified castle was built near the new church and the town started to develop on the north bank. Thiers subsequently became the seat of a barony. 🈳 *Château du Pirou, 63300 THIERS, ☎ 04 73 80 65 65. www. auvergne-centrefrance.com. Mid-Jun to mid-Sep: guided tours of the medieval district (1hr30min) Thu at 4pm. Apply to the Tourist office.*

▶ **Orient Yourself:** Thiers lies within the Parc Naturel Régional du Livradois-Forez, just 40km/25ml east of Clermont-Ferrand
🅿 **Parking:** Beside the Eglise St Genès, and at the northern end of town
👁 **Don't Miss:** The view from the Terrasse du Rempart; Maison des Couteliers (👌 see below)
🕐 **Organizing Your Time:** Allow half a day to explore this lovely town
👌 **Also See:** Chateau et Jardins de la Chassaigne

The Thiers cutlery trade – For many centuries Thiers has been the largest French cutlery manufacturing centre.

The origin of the town's specialisation dates back to the Middle Ages: legend has it that Auvergne knights from the first crusade (1096-99) brought back the secret of cutlery manufacture; in fact, the Thiers metallurgical industry dates back to the 14C. By the 16C the town's cutlery trade had developed sufficiently for it to start exporting its products to Spain, The Netherlands and Lombardy. Blades of all types were sharpened on grinding wheels powered by the waters of the Durolle. Cutlery production has subsequently been modernised, leaving the traditional figure of the knife-grinder lying face down over his grinding-wheel with his dog lying on his legs to keep him warm as but an image of the past. Developments in technology and electricity have led to enormous factories. Today Thiers still has nearly 300 manufacturers or craftsmen.

The Festival du Couteau d'Art (artistic cutlery festival) takes place during the third weekend in April.

Thiers cutlery

The Cradle of French Cutlery

Maison des Couteliers
21 and 23 rue de la Coutellerie. 🕐 *Jul-Aug: 10am-6.30pm (last admission 45min before closing); the rest of the year: daily except Mon 10am-noon, 2-6pm. Guided tours of the workshops (20min).* 🕐 *Closed Jan, 1 May, 1 Nov, 25 Dec. 5€. ☎ 04 73 80 58 86. www.musee-coutellerie-thiers.com. Guided tours of the Vallée des Rouets (30min) on request. 4€.*

Five rooms are devoted to the history of the cutlery industry in Thiers: history and origins, crafts and techniques, working conditions, leisure, commercialisation and advertising etc. Exhibits include documents, photos, tools and machinery, huge knifes and miniature ones, and various hallmarks from 1591 to 1857. Part of the exhibition space is devoted to sharpeners (model of a workshop).

A passage leads to no 21 where visitors can see a sharpener at work, lying down with his dog on his legs.

Musée de la Coutellerie

58 rue de la Coutellerie. 🕐 *Jul-Aug: 10am-6.30pm (last admission 45min before closing); the rest of the year: daily except Mon 10am-noon, 2-6pm. Guided tours of the workshops (20min).* 🕐 *Closed Jan, 1 May, 1 Nov, 25 Dec. 5€.* ☎ *04 73 80 58 86. www.musee-coutellerie-thiers.com. Guided tours of the Vallée des Rouets (30min) on request. 4€.*

Here, craftsmen may be watched working on the different phases of the manufacture of a knife. Workshops on the ground floor specialise in the polishing, shaping, mounting and carving of top-quality knives in limited numbers. In the basement *a son et lumière* show evokes the deafening world of the forge (power-hammer, furnace etc). The first floor presents folding knives and various knives made in Thiers during the 19C and 20C. Note, in particular, the collection donated by Frédéric-Albert Peter, a cutler-goldsmith from Paris, which includes some beautiful items: knives, pocket knives, cigar-cutters, quill-cutters etc. The second floor is devoted to straight knives, from the Middle-Ages to the 1920s. A room is devoted to contemporary creations.

Walking Tours

1 The Old City★

A number of 15C, 16C and 17C half-timbered houses have been restored in the centre of the old town (Vieux Thiers). These picturesque houses line narrow, winding streets known as peddes, many of them reserved for pedestrians.

▷ *Start from place de la Mutualité and walk down rue Prosper-Marilhat leading onto rue Terrasse.*

Terrasse du Rempart★

The terrace offers a beautiful **panorama**★ of the Limagne, the Dore mountain range and the Dômes mountain range. The view of the sunset can be magnificent from here. The viewing table is made of enamelled lava stone.

▷ *50m/55yd further on, turn right onto rue du Bourg.*

Rue du Bourg

At nos 10 and 14 note the 15C Volvic-stone doorways; no 20 is a 16C house.

Place du Pirou

This square is dominated by the early-15C **Maison du Pirou**★. The house, with its pointed gables and timbered façade, is a handsome example of civil architecture of the Middle Ages. It houses the tourist office.

Rue Grenette

No 8 is a 16C and 17C house (Maison dite de Lauzun).

Rue de la Coutellerie

Note the unusual houses at no 12 and 14, the latter with wooden corbels carved in a somewhat free and vigorous style. No 21, the **Maison de l'Homme des Bois** (15C), is decorated with an enigmatic ape-like figure. This house and the ancient alderman's house at no 58 contain the Cutlers' Centre and the Cutlery Museum.

▷ *Follow rue Chabot on the left and take the first street on the left leading to the steps; turn left then first right onto impasse Jean-Brugière.*

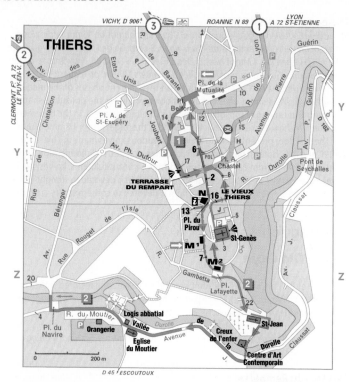

THIERS

VICHY, D 906 ③ ROANNE N 89 ① LYON A 72 ST-ETIENNE

THIERS			Coutellerie R. de la	Z	7	Marilhat R. Prosper	Y	14
Bourg R. du	Y	2	Dumas R. Alexandre	Y	8	Mitterrand R. F.	Y	15
Brugière Imp. Jean	Z	3	Dr-Dumas R. des	Y	9	Pirou R. du	Y	16
Clermont R. de	Z	4	Duchasseint Pl.	Y	10	Terrasse R.	Y	17
Chabot R. M.	Z	5	Grammonts R. des	Y	12	Voltaire Av.	Z	20
Conchette R.	Y	6	Grenette R.	Z	13	4-Septembre R. du	Z	22

Maison des Couteliers	Z	M¹	Maison du Pirou	Y	N	Musée de la Coutellerie	Z	M²

Église St-Genès

This Romanesque church has undergone many alterations. The west front and the
bell-tower have been rebuilt but the south transept retains the interesting polychrome decoration on its gable and its graceful windows.

▶ *Walk through the public gardens surrounding the east end of the church of St-Genès.*

The north door, which gives onto place du Palais, is preceded by an 18C porch, in the
wall of which an elegantly carved 14C recess has been incorporated.
Inside, the dome crowning the transept crossing is the largest in the Auvergne.

▶ *Turn right onto rue du Palais and leave place du Pirou to the right.*

Rue du Pirou

At no 11 stands the Maison des Sept Péchés Capitaux, named after the decoration
(Seven Deadly Sins) on the seven beams supporting the first floor; at no 9, note a
corbelled construction.
Further along is the "Coin des Hasards," an intersection dominated by the tower of
Maître Raymond (15C), one of the ancient towers from the Thiers feudal castle.

▷ *Continue along rue Alexandre-Dumas and place Antonin-Chastel. Take a few steps to the left and follow rue Conchette.*

Rue Conchette

In the courtyard at no 4 there is a 16C staircase; at no 10, a beautiful inner façade on pillars. At no 18, in the small courtyard with its turret, two 16C medallions. This was the wealthy district of the town.

▷ *Return to place de la Mutualité.*

② The Old Manufacturing Valley

This is a walking tour, starting from the Maison des Couteliers. The return journey is by local bus (TUT).

▷ *Walk down rue du Quatre-Septembre, heading towards the Creux de l'Enfer (sign-posted itinerary). You will reach place St-Jean and its church.*

Église St-Jean

This church (15C but restored) occupies a picturesque site overlooking the Durolle. From the neighbouring cemetery there is a lovely view of the plain and the Auvergne mountains.

▷ *A path to the right as you leave the church runs round the church and leads to Creux de l'Enfer.*

Creux de l'Enfer, Centre d'Art Contemporain

& ⏱ *Daily 2-7pm.* ⏱ *Closed 1 Jan and 25 Dec. No charge.* ☎ *04 73 80 26 56. www.creuxdelenfer.net*

This contemporary arts centre is set up on the premises of a former factory facing the impressive Durolle waterfall. Exhibitions focus on unusual aspects of modern art that draw inspiration from the nearby landscape. The site is also used as a workshop where painters and sculptors can engage in experimental projects.

▷ *Walk along avenue Joseph-Claussat.*

Creux de l'Enfer

Vallée de la Durolle

The route follows the Durolle. The river's many waterfalls once operated numerous cutlery works. There were at least 140 falls over a distance of 3km/2mi. The most picturesque are those known as the **Creux de l'Enfer** ("Hell-Hole") falls, just before St-Jean bridge, and the **Creux du Salien** falls, just after Seychalles bridge (15C).

Legend has it that St Genès, tracked by soldiers, made his mule jump across the valley near the Creux de l'Enfer falls. The spot where the saint came down with his mule is called **Saut du Moine** ("Monk's Jump"). The route is lined with many old, disused factories.

Église du Moutier

☞ *Closed for restoration.* The church was part of the powerful Benedictine abbey founded in the 7C. In 1882 it was reduced in height and badly disfigured. Inside, note the capitals in the narthex and the bas-relief sculptures in the east end wall.

At the corner of avenue Joseph-Claussat stands the fortified **Logis abbatial du Moutier** (🕐 *Jul-Aug: daily except Mon and Tue 2.30-6.30pm.* ☎ *04 73 80 59 08*), the last remains of the abbey, which has been restored.

Orangerie

🕐 *all year: Tue-Fri, 9am-noon, 2-5.30pm, Sat-Sun 2-5.30pm.* 🕐 *Closed 1 Jan, 1 May, 1 and 11 Nov, 25 Dec. No charge.* ☎ *04 73 80 53 53.*

Located in Moutier park, the orangery has been turned into an information centre on the environment. The large hothouse is landscaped: pool, walls made of plants and exotic species contrast with a desert environment.

▸ *Continue along rue du Moutier to place du Navire (note the Pont du Navire, listed as a historic monument) then travel back to the town centre by public transport (from the church of Moutier).*

Excursions

Château et Jardins de la Chassaigne

2.5km/1.5mi from the town centre. Leave Thiers N towards Vichy. Beyond the tunnel, turn left onto D 94C, and follow signposts to the castle. Visitors enter through the gardens. 🕐 *Jun-Aug: daily except Tue 2.30-6pm. 5€.* ☎ *04 73 80 59 08.*

The 15C manor, which had already suffered during the Revolution was dismantled at the beginning of the 20C, its trees were felled with the exception of the lime tree in the main courtyard. Although the castle was still inhabited, its upkeep was totally neglected until it acquired new owners in 1986. Guided tours take visitors past a fine doorway, up a spiral staircase to the Gothic chapel decorated with 17C murals (fruit and flowers). Three rooms contain exhibitions about events and life in the past *(these change every year)*. The visit ends with a stroll through the English-style gardens.

ILOA "Les Rives de Thiers"

12km/7.5mi. At the large roundabout at the entrance to Thiers, head for Vichy. Take the fork at the toll-check and at the next roundabout turn left. Follow signs to ILOA. This large 70ha/173-acre leisure park offers facilities for a great many sports: rambling, cycling, riding, swimming, tennis and golf.

St-Rémy-sur-Durolle

9km/6mi N on N 89 and a small road on the left.

The scenic road winds through woodland before reaching St-Rémy. This cutlery-making centre is built on the southern flank of "Thiers mountain," an extension of the Bois Noirs massif.

▸ *In St-Rémy, take a road uphill on the left to the wayside cross. Leave the car near the sports ground and walk to the top of the cliff (🚶 15min there and back).*

From the wayside cross, the **panorama**★ *(viewing table)* includes the Forez mountains, the Margerides, the Plomb du Cantal and the Dômes mountain range. North-east of St-Rémy, on the right of D 201, a large lake offers various watersports, swimming, sailing, rowing.

Driving Tours

Les Margerides★

Round tour of 15km-9.5mi – about 45min

▶ *Leave Thiers NE along N 89 towards Lyon.*

From the look-out point by the turn-off to St-Rémy, there is an attractive view over to the right of the Durolle gorge, Thiers and the Limagne. The opposite bank is dominated by the Margerides rocks.

▶ *In Château-Gaillard, take the first turning to the right. Park the car at the entrance.*

Vallée des Rouets

Walking shoes are necessary. Tickets bought at the Maison des Couteliers in Thiers (valid until end Sep) include the cost of a guided tour of the Rouet Lyonnet. Otherwise, buy you ticket at the entrance to the site: 4€ (children: 2€). Access to the two itineraries is free. Jun-Sep: daily except Mon noon-6pm (last tour begins at 5pm); Jul-Aug noon-6.30pm. ☎ 04 73 80 58 86.

The various paths formerly used by craftsmen have been restored and are now clearly signposted, offering interesting views of both architectural features and natural sites *(two itineraries: 1km/0.6mi and 2.5km/1.5mi).*

There used to be 27 cutlery workshops in the valley; the last one in operation was the Rouet Lyonnet (1816) which closed down in 1976. The owner worked in it for 30 years, before adapting it so that he could go on practising his craft for his own pleasure (you can see his energy-saving machines). In 1900 there were 7 or 8 sharpeners working on water-wheel-powered machines and as many polishers (they were often the sharpeners' wives and children).

▶ *Beyond Château-Gaillard and Bellevue turn right on D 320.*

The road crosses the river and winds through green and fertile countryside.

▶ *On leaving Vernières there is a beautiful view of the Durolle Valley, the village of St-Rémy set on the mountainside and, in the background, the Bois Noirs massif; D 102 descends towards Thiers and makes a sharp right-hand bend, just near Borbes rock (on the left).*

Rocher de Borbes

From the rock there is an extensive **view**★ of the Limagne, the Dômes and the Dore mountain ranges, the Livradois and, in clear weather, the Cantal mountains.
From the viewpoint 2km/1.2mi further on, there is a superb view of Thiers and the Durolle Valley.

▶ *Continue on D 102 to return to Thiers.*

From La Dore to Monts Forez★★

130km/81mi itinerary – allow one day

Despite having identical names, the Dore mountain torrent – which, flowing into the Dogne, creates the River Dordogne in the Dore mountain range at the foot of the Puy de Sancy – and this River Dore, which flows through a narrow gorge separating the Livradois and Forez ranges, should not be confused. This Dore is a tributary on the right bank of the Allier, rising in the mountains of the Livradois area. It flows down in a south-easterly direction into deep, granite gorges then turns northwards to cross, at a leisurely pace, the Ambert plateau, a small gully lined by the mountains of Forez.
Downstream from Ambert, the Dore crosses the granite bedrock on which Olliergues stands through picturesque gorges with moderately steep, wooded sides before entering the Limagne area, its waters now swollen by the Couzon and Durolle, and going on to flow into the River Allier south of Vichy at the bridge in Ris, after covering a distance of 140km/87mi.

▶ *Leave Thiers to the W and drive up to Pont-de-Dore. Follow D 906, Then D 44 on the right.*

Château d'Aulteribe★ – ♿ *See COURPIÈRE: Excursions.*

▶ *Take D 223 then turn right onto D 906.*

Courpière – ♿ *See COURPIÈRE.*

▶ *Soon after leaving Courpière, continue towards Ambert on D 906. Turn right onto D 315.*

Sauviat

This village, attractively situated on a spur of rock, stands high above a meander of the River Dore as it flows through a narrow valley. From the observation platform behind the old town hall, the view extends over the dam and the hydroelectric power station it supplies. The 14C granite church has a single aisle and a massive square belfry.

▶ *Drive down on D 316 and rejoin D 906 on the right.*

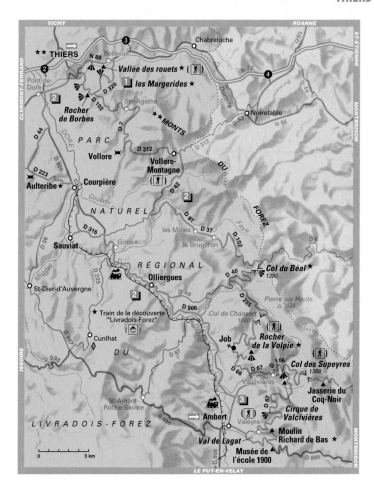

Olliergues

Pleasantly situated on the north bank of the River Dore, over which there is a pretty 15C bridge to the south of town, Olliergues has terraces of houses rising up the hillside and features a castle (restored) which once belonged to Marshal Turenne's family. Opposite the church's pretty bell-tower stands the square castle keep, which houses a museum devoted to traditional crafts and trades, the **Musée des Métiers et des Traditions** (*Apr-Sep: guided tours (1hr) 10am-noon, 2-6pm (7pm in Jul-Aug); Jan-Mar and Oct-Nov: daily except Sun and Mon 10am-noon, 2-6pm. 4€. 04 73 95 54 90).* The small medieval bridge at the south entrance to the village dates from the 15C. It commands a lovely view of Olliergues and the impetuous River Dore.

▶ *Continue driving towards Ambert and 3km/2mi before reaching Ambert, turn right onto D 66 and right again onto a narrow road leading to Volpie rock.*

Rocher de la Volpie★
Park beside a group of houses and follow the footpath waymarked in red, which climbs through woodland to the left of a farm building.
1hr there and back. From the rocky Volpie peak the **view**★ stretches over the Livradois mountains with the Ambert plain in the foreground.

Summer pastures in the Forez

Those reluctant to tackle the climb can take a path to the right beyond the farm, which leads across the meadows to the foot of the rock *(20min there and back)*.

▶ *Rejoin D 66 and turn right.*

Église de Job
Superb 15C **church** topped by a large square belfry.

▶ *D 255 to the right then D 40 lead to Col du Béal.*

Col du Béal★
From this pass (alt 1 390m/4 560ft) there is a wide **panoramic view** over the mountains of the Auvergne and the Lyonnais area.

▶ *Leave Col du Béal on D 102.*

The road crosses vast expanses of pasture and soon provides a superb view of the mountains of the Livradois area, the Dore and Dômes mountain ranges and the Limagne around Clermont.

▶ *In Brugeron, take D 37 towards Olliergues and, when you reach the hamlet of Les Mines, turn right onto D 97.*

The road follows the picturesque Faye Valley.

▶ *Shortly after crossing the River Faye, turn right onto D 42.*

Vollore-Montagne
This mountain village is an ideal centre for walkers.
The forests, the charming landscapes of woodland and meadow, and the attractive local beauty spots make this part of the journey extremely enjoyable.

▶ *Drive W out of Vollore-Montagne along D 312.*

Château de Vollore – See COURPIÈRE.

▶ *Drive N along D 7; 7km/4mi beyond Ste-Agathe, the road begins its descent towards Thiers via the Margerides route.*

TOURNEMIRE★

POPULATION 145
MICHELIN MAPS 330: C-4 – LOCAL MAP SEE MONTS DU CANTAL

This lovely village in the heart of the Cantal mountains has been recognised as one of the most beautiful villages in France. The lava-stone houses are covered with slate roofs. The small, Romanesque **church** (🕐 *Jul-Aug: guided tours by appointment 3-6pm.* ☎ *04 71 47 61 34.)* here is built of coloured volcanic tufa. It contains a valuable reliquary containing a thorn allegedly from the Crown of Christ.

Château d'Anjony★

🕐 *Mid-Feb to mid-Nov: guided tours (45min) daily, 2-6.30pm (Jul-Aug: 11 and 11.30, 2-6.30pm, daily except Sun). 7€ (children: 4€).*

This castle of reddish basalt is one of the most remarkable castles in Upper Auvergne. Strategically located on the tip of the Tournemire promontory, it dominates the lush landscape of the Doire Valley with its four tall towers (height 40m/130ft). The castle was built in the 15C by Louis II of Anjony, the companion of Dunois and Joan of Arc, near the towers of Tournemire which had been held in joint fief by his family and the Tournemires since 1351. This dual ownership led to three centuries of bloody rivalry between the families, one of old feudal stock, the other having prospered through business and service to the royal family. The feud ended around 1650.

The main hall on the first floor boasts a coffered ceiling with three tiers of beams, and throughout the castle there are some fine furnishings and furniture: a vast fireplace, tapestries from Aubusson and Flanders, a tester bed, a reclining seat. The chapel in the south-eastern tower is decorated with 16C **frescoes** showing scenes from the Life of Christ. An alcove contains the statue of Our Lady of Anjony, a Black Virgin and Child of painted and gilded wood. The Knights' Hall on the second floor has **frescoes**★ of Michel of Anjony and his wife Germaine of Foix in late-16C dress, and scenes illustrating the legend of the Nine Valiant Knights from a medieval poem. The third-floor audience chamber with diagonal vaulting has walls hung with two large tapestries, including a Flemish verdure (hunting scene).

The Knights' Hall in the château d'Anjony

TOURNON-SUR-RHÔNE★

POPULATION 9 946
MICHELIN MAP 331: L-3

This busy town on the Rhône overlooks **Tain-l'Hermitage** on the opposite bank, which is famed for its fine wines. 🚉 *Hôtel de la Tourette BP 108, 07300 TOURNON-SUR-RHÔNE, ☎ 04 75 08 10 23/41 28. www.ville-tournon.com.*

The Town

Tournon-sur-Rhône boasts a 15C-16C **château** (🕐 *Jul-Aug: 10am-noon, 2-6pm; mid-Mar to May and Sep-Oct, daily except Wed, 2-6pm; Jun, 2-6pm. 4€.* 🕐 *Nov to mid-Mar and 1 May.* ☎ *04 75 08 10 30)*, containing a museum about bargemen working on the Rhône, set in a charming **terraced garden**★, and the 14C **St-Julien Collegiate Church** with some fine murals and paintings beneath a coffered ceiling. The **Lycée Gabriel-Fauré** has an attractive Renaissance doorway, a collection of busts and tapestries inside, and a chapel with a handsome 18C façade and a Jesuit-style interior with interesting 17C decor.

Excursions

Pierre-Aiguille Belvedere★
5km/3mi N. Leave Tain in the direction of Larnage, then follow directions. This belvedere dominating the Rhône rises to a height of 344m/1 129ft. The far-reaching views from

---

Address Book

EATING OUT

😋😋 **Le Chaudron** – *7 r. St-Antoine - ☎ 04 75 08 17 90 - closed 5-25 Aug, 24 Dec to 3 Jan, Thu evening and Sun.* In a partly pedestrian zone between the docks and the hospital, this restaurant has an inviting decor marrying leather wall seats, bistro chairs and blond wood. The delectable, contemporary cuisine is served on the terrace in the summer. Quite a success!

WHERE TO STAY

😋😋 **Hôtel Les Amandiers** – *13 av. de Nîmes - b 04 75 07 24 10 - www.hotel-amandiers.com -* 🅿 *- 25 rms -* 🍽 *7€.* This recent hotel located outside of the centre of town is the perfect home base for discovering the region and scrambling up and down the famous vineyard-covered hills surrounding the city. Spacious rooms, practical and sober, with modern furnishings.

SHOPPING

The Tain-l'Hermitage vineyards – Stretched along the left bank of the river, Tain is famous for its wine, one of the most celebrated Côtes-du-Rhônes. Hermitage rouge is a delicate, full-bodied wine of a deep ruby hue, while Hermitage blanc is golden and dry. Syrah grapes are used for the red, Roussanne and Maranne for the white. Approximately 3,500 hectolitres are produced per annum.

Domaine Courbis – *Rte de St-Romain - 07130 Châteaubourg - ☎ 04 75 81 81 60 - domaine-courbis@wanadoo.fr - Mon-Fri 9am-noon, 2pm-6pm, Sat by appointment.* This vineyard has been handed down from father to son since the 16C. Different much sought-after vintages are produced here, such as the Cornas 'La Sabarotte' and red and white Saint-Josephs. Once there, make sure you visit the fabulous 'Les Royes' site, a pleasure to behold.

Tournon on the banks of the Rhone

here encompass Tain-l'Hermitage and its famous vineyard; the town of Tournon across the river; the foothills of Vercors with the Alps in the background to the east; the Doux Valley, the Mézenc and the Gerbier-de-Jonc peaks to the west.

Chantemerle-les-Blés

11km/7mi. Leave Tain heading for Romans and turn left onto D 109, which goes under the motorway. Leave the car on the square behind the post office. Then take the path to the right of the memorial, at the foot of a chapel. This hamlet has kept its humble and sober church, enhanced by a number of ornamental features. The surrounding setting and luxuriant slopes are indeed a stunning sight (15min on foot there and back).

Chemin de Fer du Vivarais

Kids *Return trips between Tournon and Lamastre(2hr aboard a steam train or a railcar) Jul-Aug: departure at 10am (return during the afternoon); June-Aug: daily 10am; May and Sept: Sat, Sun, 10am. 20€ return (children: 15€).* ☎ *04 78 28 83 34.*
This is a day-long excursion aboard an old train powered by a 19C steam locomotive. From the platform, you can enjoy the view as the train puffs along the Doux Valley, past orchards and vineyards, then climbs upwards through heather, pines and chestnut trees. After Colombier-le-Vieux, it emerges from the gorges to reach Boucieu-le-Roi and Lamastre.

Panoramic Route★★★

▶ *Leave Tournon-sur-Rhône to the S via rue du Dr-Cadet and rue Greffieux towards St-Romain-de-Lerps.*

From Tournon to Valence the **panoramic road**★★★ along the hillside offers magnificent views. The road out of town climbs steeply in a series of hairpin bends, giving breathtaking views.

▶ *In Plats turn left by the War Memorial onto GR 42.*

View from St-Romain-de-Lerps★★★

On a platform bearing a television transmitter, near a small chapel not far from the tower, are two viewpoints. The **panorama** from here is immense, covering 13 *départements*. This is one of the most impressive views to be had along the Rhône: to the east, above the Valence plain, rises the Vercors bar, dominated by the Moucherolle needle and the dome of the Grand Veymont; beyond sparkle the distant, snow-capped peaks of the Alps and the mass of Mont Blanc. To the north, along the axis of the Rhône and slightly to the left, stands Mont Pilat; to the south looms Mont Ventoux. Westwards lie the plateaux and the greenhouses of the Vivarais. The summit of Mont Mézenc overlooks this jumble of ridges from a distance.

▶ *From St-Romain-de-Lerps take D 287 down to St-Péray; the road offers wonderful views over the Valence basin. Return to Tournon-sur-Rhône on N 86.*

Gorges du Doux via the Corniche Road★

50km/31mi – allow 2hr

▶ *Leave Tournon-sur-Rhône on the road to Lamastre.*

The road runs along the pretty orchards of the Doux basin. The **corniche road**★ dominates the Doux gorges, planted with oak, broom, ferns, boxwood and pine trees.

▶ *Take D 209 on the right, heading for Boucieu-le-Roi.*

Boucieu-le-Roi
This village was once the seat of the old royal bailiwick in the Upper Vivarais area. The church (13C-16C) has an attractive silhouette.

▶ *Return to Tournon-sur-Rhône via Colombier-le-Vieux and D 234, running on the opposite side of the gorges, through a stretch of wild vegetation.*

Défilé de St-Vallier★

▶ *Leave Tournon-sur-Rhône to the N on N 86.*

Vion
The **church** (*Tours by appointment with M. Campana, r. du Midi, 07610 Vion, ☎ 04 75 08 25 87*), partly Romanesque, has a transept crossing with capitals illustrating the life of Christ and the Virgin.

▶ *In Vion, take the narrow road that leads to D 532. At Croix de Fraysse, head for St-Jeure-d'Ay, then turn right onto D 6. About 7km/4.3mi further on, take D 506 on the right, leading down to Ozon.*

The steep descent to Ozon offers spectacular **views**★★ from two sharp bends over **St-Vallier Gorges**★, and over the orchards and vineyards occupying the terraces along the river.

▶ *Return to Sarras and St-Vallier, then take N 7 to Tain-l'Hermitage along the east bank of the Rhône.*

This section of the valley, which narrows into a corridor again, is the most evocative of the Rhône in medieval times: ruins of feudal strongholds and old defensive towers and watchtowers line the escarpments. The entrance to **Serves-sur-Rhône** is preceded by a superb **view,** ahead, of the impressive remains of its castle. On the west bank stands the rival tower of **Arras-sur-Rhône**.
Beyond the turning to Crozes-Hermitage a wild-looking hill known as Pierre-Aiguille, into which the railway line disappears, forces the road back towards the river. Note the small, table-shaped rock with a sign on it; when the river is in spate, it disappears beneath the water level. To the left, the hillsides fall back, revealing the Hermitage slopes adorned with the characteristic stripes of its vineyard.

TRÉVOUX

POPULATION 6 392
MICHELIN MAP 328: B-5 – LOCAL MAP SEE LA DOMBES

This town is built on different levels along the steep bank of the Saône, its colourful façades and flower-filled gardens all facing southwards. Trévoux stands at the intersection of three Roman roads; it was once the capital of the Principality of Dombes, the seat of a sovereign Parliament, and was independent until 1762. After the Duke of Maine decreed that the town's magistrates and members of Parliament must also be residents, a number of mansions were built in the 18C, along the alleyways of the old districts. In the 17C and 18C the town was one of the most brilliant intellectual centres in France. Its printing house, founded in 1603, was famous. In 1704 the Jesuits published the first edition of the famous Trévoux Dictionary; under their supervision, the Trévoux Journal fought a relentless campaign against Voltaire and the "Encyclopædic" philosophers for 30 years. *Pl. du Pont BP 108, 01600 TRÉVOUX, ☎ 04 74 00 36 32. www.tourisme.fr/trevoux*

Old Town

Park in boulevard des Combattants. Walk to place de la Terrasse which overlooks the Saône (viewing table). The Palais du Parlement is on the other side of rue du Palais.

Palais du Parlement

🕐 *May-Sep: (guided tours, 45m), Sat, Sun and public holidays. Ask at tourist office for the hours.* 🕐 *Closed Sat-Sun (Oct-Apr), 1 Jan and 25 Dec. 2€ Sat-Sun (under-12s: no charge).* ☎ *04 74 00 36 32.*

Parliament House was built at the end of the 17C; the Dombes Parliament sat from 1697 to 1771.

The hall leads into the courtroom with its beautiful beamed ceiling with painted decoration; note, on the extreme right of the second beam from the back, the pompous initials SPQD: *Senatus Populusque Dumborum* (meaning the Senate and people of Dombes, a parody of the Roman initials SPQR). At the back of the room is a portrait of the Duke of Maine by Rigaud.

Rue du Gouvernement

On either side of the street, just below the church, the Trévoux Dictionary and Journal were written and printed. The Jesuits who lived on the right, in the tall, spacious Maison des Pères – main entrance is at nos 3 and 9 Grande-Rue – had only to cross the street to take their manuscripts to the printers opposite.

Further down are a number of old houses: the house of the Governor of Dombes, that of the Grande Mademoiselle and the Mint, their austere façades concealing terraces overlooking the Saône. The intersection with rue Casse-Cou (Break-Neck Street), so named because of its steep slope, offers an interesting view.

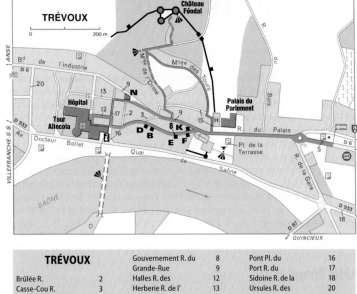

TRÉVOUX		Gouvernement R. du	8	Pont Pl. du	16
		Grande-Rue	9	Port R. du	17
Brûlée R.	2	Halles R. des	12	Sidoine R. de la	18
Casse-Cou R.	3	Herberie R. de l'	13	Ursules R. des	20
Combattants Bd des	5	Montsec R.	15		

Hôtel de la Grande		Hôtel du Gouverneur de		Maison des Pères	K
Mademoiselle	B	Dombes	E	Tour de l'Arsenal	N
Hôtel de la Monnaie	D	Imprimerie	F		

▶ *Take Rue des Halles to the hospital.*

Hôpital

🕙 *May-Sep: guided tours (30min) of the Apothecary's dispensary: from the tourist office at 3pm and 4.30pm. 2€. ☎ 04 74 00 36 32.*
The hospital was founded in 1686 by La Grande Mademoiselle; it still has the original wood-panelled pharmacy and a beautiful collection of pottery from Gien and Nevers. Alincola tower (13C-17C), surmounted by a lantern dome, can be seen on the embankment.

▶ *Return to rue des Halles and turn left onto rue du Port. Turn right onto rue de l'Herberie.*

This street was once reserved for Jews. The intersection of rue de l'Herberie and Grande-Rue forms a triangle dominated by the square-shaped Arsenal tower of 1405 which was later converted into a belfry.

▶ *Walk up montée de l'Orme to the castle.*

Château Féodal

🕙 *Jul-Aug: daily except Thu; May-Jun and Sep: Sat, Sun and public holidays; Mar-Apr and from Oct to mid-Nov: Sun and public holidays: enquire at tourist office for times. 2€ (under-12s: no charge). ☎ 04 74 00 36 32.*
Remains of the medieval castle (14C); from the top of the octagonal tower there is a view of the Saône.

▶ *Walk down montée des Tours, then return along rue du Palais back to boulevard des Combattants.*

LE TRICASTIN★

MICHELIN MAP 332: B-8

The Tricastin plain, with **Pierrelatte** at the centre, is encircled by three moun-tainous ranges, in which veins of iron and lignite have been found, which were first mined as long ago as the 4C BC by the Celts. The area marks the transition between the north and the south of France, with a climate and vegetation not unlike Provence. There is major industry here, most of it linked to the production of nuclear energy, though a zone has been set aside for agricultural use.

Excursions

A String of Charming Villages

St-Paul-Trois-Châteaux
The old town is surrounded by the remains of ramparts but has never had the three castles that its name – St-Paul-Three-Castles – would suggest. It was appointed capital of the region during Roman times, under the name "Augusta Tricastinorum." During the second half of the 4C, the first part of its Roman name was replaced by the name Paul, commemorating one of the town's first bishops. The name of the old capital of "Tricastini" may possibly have been Frenchified by a clerk in the 16C to "Trois Châteaux," though there is no evidence for this theory. The town was a bishopric until the Revolution.
Modern St-Paul sits at the heart of the main truffle region of France.

Cathedral★
This imposing building, begun in the 11C and completed in the 12C, is a remarkable example of Provençal Romanesque architecture.

Exterior
Most striking is the exceptional height of the transept walls and the powerful aspect of the nave. A few decorative details contrast with the austerity of the walls, particularly the portal on the west front – finely carved arching frames the 17C wooden doors.

Interior
Enter through the south door. The nave with its three bays, barrel-vaulted on transverse arches and supported by side-aisles, has a magnificent elevation (24m/79ft). The bay preceding the transept has a blind triforium on the first floor; the alcoves, framed by pilasters and colonettes, surmount a frieze of finely carved drapery. A dome on pendentives covers the transept crossing. The apse, with its oven vault, has flat rib-bing; access to the crossing is via a triumphal arch with a double offset.
Other features of interest include the organ case built in 1704 by the Avignon sculptor Boisselin; the bas-relief on the second pillar on the left, depicting the Last Judge-ment; the 14C and 15C frescoes; and a 12C mosaic behind the High Altar. The 17C giltwood former High Altar stands in the north side aisle.

Maison de la Truffe et du Tricastin
🕐 *Jun-Sep: 9am-noon, 3-7pm (Sun, 10am-noon, 3-7pm; Mon, 3-7pm); Mar-May and Oct-Nov: daily except Sun 9am-noon, 2-6pm (Mon, 2-6pm); Dec-Feb: daily except Mon, 9am-noon, 2-6pm, Sun 10am-noon, 2-6pm.* 🕐 *Closed public holidays. 3.50€.* ☎ *04 75 96 61 29.*
The Truffle Centre, located inside the tourist centre (eastern end of the cathedral), houses an exhibition with posters, showcases and a video projection on the cultiva-

tion and marketing of what is known as the "black diamond" of the Tricastin region, and an ingredient in many tasty local dishes.

In the vaulted cellars below, wines from the Tricastin hills are on display, together with several old winemaking implements.

St-Restitut

The village **church**★ in Provençal Romanesque style has wonderful **carved decoration**★ (polygonal east end with finely carved cornice; south door; elegant cornice around the nave; arcading in the apse). The **Funerary Tower** to the side of the church is said to be built over the tomb of St Restitut. It has an 11C base with a frieze and a carved cornice; the frieze consists of a chequered border around carved panels depicting biblical themes, a medieval bestiary or contemporary trades. The upper part was restored when the church was built.

The **Chapelle du St-Sépulcre** (400m/437yd from the village; 🚶 15min there and back) is a small hexagonal chapel built in 1504 by a bishop on his return from a pilgrimage to the Holy Land.

Route des Carrières

Leaving St-Restitut along D 59A, turn right onto a twisting road running across the limestone plateau. Quarries were worked here between the 18C and the early 20C.

La Garde-Adhémar

This old village is signalled from some distance away by its church, perched on a rise. It is an ideal spot for a stroll, with its picturesque limestone houses, its vaulted alleyways and its narrow, winding streets with their arches. In the Middle Ages this village was a major fortress belonging to the Adhémar family. In the 16C a Renaissance château was built for **Antoine Escalin**, Baron de la Garde, who started life as a mere shepherd then became a soldier; he ended his career as one of François I's ambas-

J. Damase/MICHELIN

Old press

sadors and as General in charge of the French galleys. Old town walls can be seen on the north side; to the south of the village is a fortified gate and a few ruins, not far from the huge Cross erected on a Roman base.

Church★

This Romanesque building is remarkable for its two apses and the attractive outline of its two-storey octagonal belfry topped by a stocky pyramid. Thanks to the writer **Prosper Mérimée** (1830-70), at the time Inspector of Historic Monuments, it underwent major restoration in the mid-19C. A finely carved frieze runs round the western apse and the apsidal chapels. The very plain interior has a high, short nave flanked by narrow side aisles. Note a lovely 12C Romanesque statue of the Virgin Mary in the north chapel. On 24 December, a Provençal Midnight Mass is celebrated here, which includes a Nativity play with real animals.

Chapelle des Pénitents

🕐 *For entry ask at Club Unesco. No charge.* ☎ *04 75 04 41 58.*
This chapel has 12C twinned windows on the west side; they can be seen from the church square. From the 17C to the 19C the chapel was the meeting place of the members of a brotherhood of White Penitents, as shown on the fresco decorating the south wall; today it houses an exhibition about La Garde-Adhémar and an audio-visual presentation, "Le Tricastin en Images," which gives a historical view of the region.

View★

From the terrace there is a panoramic view of the Pierrelatte plain below the outcrops of the Vivarais area, with the Dent de Rez jutting out from above the rocks. Immediately below the terrace is a garden filled with aromatic and medicinal herbs and plants.

Chapelle du Val-des-Nymphes

2km/1.2mi E on D 472. In a valley kept cool by many little waterfalls and which, as its name suggests, was once a place of pagan worship, stand the ruins of a 12C chapel. For a long while a ruin, this Romanesque chapel was restored from 1991 and an elegant timber ceiling now covers the nave. The fine semicircular apse still has its two rows of arcading. The upper section of the west front is decorated with three blind arches topped by a pediment.

Clansayes★

Park the car and head for the far end of the promontory, with its monumental statue of the Virgin. From here there is an extensive **view**★★ over the Tricastin area and its peaks carved by erosion.

Barry★

Backing onto a cliff into which several of its houses are carved, this troglodytic village has been inhabited from prehistoric times to the Second World War; though now abandoned, it is undergoing restoration. The chapel (17C) and various houses may be discerned. Fine **views**★★ over the valley.

Rhône-harnessing works at Donzère-Mondragon

As it came out of the very picturesque Donzère-Mondragon canyon, the Rhône used to spread out into several arms across the Pierrelatte plain. From the 17C onwards, various attempts were made to harness the river and its course was somewhat modified. However, the harnessing works that gave the landscape its present aspect were undertaken by the Compagnie Nationale du Rhône between 1948 and 1952; as a result the plain became a vast island linked to the neighbouring land by two railway bridges and eight road bridges.

Crocodile farm

Agricultural land was drained and irrigation greatly improved by water pumped from the canal.

Canal

Measuring 28km/17.4mi long, 145m/476ft wide and 10m/33ft deep, the canal links the municipalities of Donzère and Mondragon 31km/19.3mi apart via the river. There is a 17km/10.6mi-long feeder canal to supply the power station and an 11km/6.8mi tail-race.

Upstream of **Bollène** is the **hydroelectric power station** and **lock** complex which forms a 340m/1 115ft-long dam. Using a maximum drop of 23m/75ft, the power station produces over 2 000 million kWh per year.

These harnessing works have greatly improved navigation on the Rhône over a distance of 40km/24mi.

Slightly further upstream of the power station is the vast **Tricastin Nuclear Power Plant.**

La Ferme aux Crocodiles

Kids &. ⓞ Mar-Sep: 9.30am-7pm; Oct-Mar: 9.30am-5pm. 9€ (children: 6€). ☎ 04 75 04 33 73. www.lafermeauxcrocodiles.com.

This crocodile farm is stocked with a great many species from countries all over the world (Cuba, America, Egypt), installed in large basins. Further on, visitors can discover a vast hothouse containing tropical vegetation and superb exotic birds. From the many footbridges, visitors can watch some 300 crocodiles from the Nile region basking in the sun or swimming in dark waters.

FORÊT DE TRONÇAIS★★★

MICHELIN MAP 326: D-3 – 30KM/18.6MI N OF MONTLUÇON

Tronçais Forest is located at the junction of the Berry and Bourbonnais regions; it has a total surface area of over 10 000ha/24 711 acres and contains a remarkable plantation of trees. Its many pools and beauty spots make it a popular recreational area. ⓘ Pl. du Champ-de-Foire, C3350 CÉRILLY, ☎ 04 70 67 55 89. www.onf.fr/foret/dossier/troncais/

Trials and tribulations – Tronçais Forest, after being administered by the dukes of Bourbon, was confiscated in 1527 together with the other lands owned by the High Constable. Poorly managed and neglected in the 16C and 17C, it slowly deteriorated. The devastation wrought by livestock, the improper use of certain parts of the forest by neighbouring parishes or lords, and the uncontrolled felling of trees meant that by 1670 nearly three quarters of the forest had been ruined.

A majestic alley

To meet the country's requirements for ship timber, Colbert undertook to protect and replant the royal forest. The new plantations were not to be used until the trees were 200 years old. In 1788 the opening of the Tronçais Iron Foundry led to fresh destruction of the forest with two-thirds of its surface area reduced to coppice with standards in order to produce the charcoal needed for the manufacture of cast iron. In 1832 conservation measures were fortunately taken and the forest was replanted on the basis of a cutting cycle of 160 years. This was extended to 180, then to 225 years in 1928.

Cultivating the forest – Tronçais Forest is divided into series, which in turn are divided into blocks. Oak trees account for 70% of its plantations, with beech and Scotch fir the second most densely planted species.

The main aim of the forest remains the production of high quality timber. The most sought-after trees are therefore of exceptional dimensions, their trunks sometimes more than 20m/65ft high and 1m/3ft in diameter at a man's standing height.

To achieve this, the area around the most promising oaks must be surrounded by other trees during the oaks' growth period, then gradually cleared by successive felling.

Logs with a diameter of 50cm/20in and more are sliced in specialised industrial yards far from the forest. Some are exported to other EU countries (particularly Germany). The veneers produced supply the cabinetmaking industries and are eventually sent abroad – to Sweden, the USA, Belgium. Oaks that are 40-50cm/16-20in in diameter provide wood for cooperage (split or made into staves to make barrels); Tronçais oak is particularly prized for the maturing of cognac and claret. Oak trees of small diameter or lesser quality are converted into building timber or firewood.

The equilibrium of the forest requires selective felling so that mature trees can be replaced by entire blocks.

"Discovering the forest" – The forest offers walkers additional attractions besides the contemplation of its oak trees. Mushroom pickers will find *boletus, hydnum, russula* and *chanterelles*. There is also quite a large population of red deer, roe deer and wild boar. Great crested grebes can often be glimpsed on Pirot Lake. In season, **guided tours** *(For one or two months in summer, departure from the rond de Tronçais. Contact the forestry commission office. ☎ 04 70 46 82 00. For information on tourist activities, contact the Association du Pays de Tronçais in Cérilly. ☎ 04 70 67 55 89)* of the forest are organised.

Excursions

Ainay-le-Château

3km/1.9mi N of the forest on D 953. Formerly part of Berry and old Aquitaine, Ainay became a Bourbonnais stronghold in the late 12C. Although the castle has not survived, there remain vestiges of the ramparts (towers, sections of wall). The 12C Porte de l'Horloge in the main street was once used as a guard-room and prison. The **Église St-Étienne** was built in the 16C on the site of a former Romanesque church. The west doorway, giving onto a small square overlooking the Sologne, is adorned with a fine Virgin with Child from the 17C. Note the 16C paintings decorating the nave and the unusual font in the baptistery.

1 **Eastern Sologne Region★★★**

20km/12.5mi – about 2hr

Cérilly

This was the home of the writer **Charles-Louis Philippe** (1874-1909), the author of semi-autobiographical novels based on his memories. His **birthplace** (☉ *May-Oct: Sat-Sun and public holidays 3-6pm* ☉ *Nov-Apr. 3€.* ☎ *04 70 67 52 00)*, at no 5 in the street which bears his name, is open to the public.

▷ *Leave Cérilly to the N on D 111 which leads through the eastern part of the forest. Cross over Rond de Brot roundabout and D 978A, then take the first tarmacked road on the left, Ligne de Cros-Chaud.*

Étang de Pirot★

Rond des Pêcheurs offers a lovely overall **view** of the vast Lake Pirot.

▷ *Take Ligne des Pêcheurs, then turn right on D 978A.*

Fontaine Viljot

On the right-hand side of the road (170m/557ft). Park on the left verge. Oaks and conifers form a charming decor around the crystal clear water of this spring. Legend has it that, if a maiden wishes to marry, she must throw a pin into the spring; if the pin pricks the bottom, the maiden has "pricked a heart." Nowadays, small change appears to have replaced pins...

South of the Rond Viljot, walk to the Square Oak *(Chêne Carré)*. This 300-year-old tree has a total height of 26m/85ft and, at a height of 1.30m/4ft 3in from the ground, a circumference of 5.96m/19ft 6in.

Émile-Guillaumin and Charles-Louis-Philippe Oak Trees

These two trees close to the roadside to the north commemorate two novelists from the region.

▷ *At Rond Gardien, turn sharp right onto the Planche-gross forest road (one-way) up to the car park.*

Rond de la Cave

30min on foot there and back.

⬛ This large, sheltered picnic area lies at the very heart of the forest.

FORÊT DE TRONÇAIS

0 2 km

Return to **Rond Gardien** *(viewing table)* and continue to Tronçais. The factory here was built on the edge of Lake Tronçais.

▶ *Take D 250 on the right.*

Étang de St-Bonnet★

The lake, to the left of the road, sits in a very attractive setting. The bathing area and path around it are popular destinations for a walk.

Futaie Colbert★

30min on foot.

There is a marked trail which begins and ends at Rond du Vieux-Morat. Beautiful plantation of 300-year-old oaks in a cool, undulating setting (protected area).

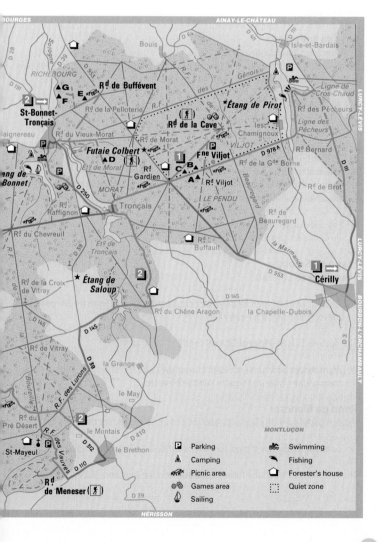

WHERE TO STAY AND EATING OUT

🍴 **Le Tronçais** – 03360 Tronçais - ☎ 04 70 06 11 95 - closed 16 Nov-14 Mar, Sun evening, Mon and Tue off-season - 🅿 - 12 rms - 🛏 8€ - restaurant 🍴🍴. Feel like going fishing? Grab a rod and cast off in the pond of the pretty, shady park surrounding this agreeable abode. Calm, spacious bedrooms. Bright dining room with bay windows opening out onto the countryside.

🍴🍴 **Chambre d'hôte l'Ombre de Goziniere** – 03350 Theneuille - ☎ 04 70 67 59 17 - pamelaline@wanadoo.fr - closed Oct-Easter - 🚫 - reserv. required - 3 rms - meals 🍴🍴. Formerly an outbuilding belonging to the neighbouring manor house, this attractive 17C edifice has been very nicely renovated. Gorgeous garret bedrooms where chequered fabrics, solid beams and rustic furniture create a very pleasant country atmosphere. Round swimming pool in the garden.

Stebbing Oak
1.5km/0.9mi from Rond du Vieux-Morat. Isolated in the middle of a plantation of young trees is a typical 300-year-old oak (37m/121ft high and 3.95m/13ft in circumference).

Rond de Buffévent
2km/1mi from Rond du Vieux-Morat.
🚶 Short walks south-west along the forest road lead to magnificent 300-year-old oaks: **Jacques-Chevalier, Jumeaux** (the Twins) and **Sentinelle** (the Sentry).

② Western Sologne Region★

30km/19mi – about 1hr

St-Bonnet-Tronçais
A pleasant place to stay on the edge of the forest. Guided tours of the surrounding area are organised by the **Centre permanent d'initiatives pour l'environnement** (CPIE – Avenue Nicolas-Rambourg, Tronçais, 03360 St-Bonnet-Tronçais, ☎ 04 70 06 14 69).

▶ From St-Bonnet-Tronçais take D 250 S; beyond Tronçais factory turn right; at Rond du Chêne Aragon turn right on D 145.

Étang de Saloup★
The road bisects the lake.

▶ Turn left on D 39, then follow route Forestière des Lurons. From the car park, take the footpath (past a no-entry sign).

The path ends at **St-Mayeul Chapel** overlooking a ravine.

▶ From the car park turn right onto the narrow route Forestière des Vauves winding through the ravine and right to Rond de Meneser.

Rond de Meneser
Various paths provide pleasant walks (minimum 30min on foot there and back).

▶ Continue on the forest road; turn left on D 110; in Le Breton turn left on D 312.

The road runs through the forest to **Meaulne** in the Aumance Valley.

GORGES DE LA TRUYÈRE★★

The River Truyère has carved narrow, deep and sinuous gorges, often wooded and rugged-looking, through the granite plateaus of Upper Auvergne. These are among the most attractive natural sites in central France. Dams, built to serve the needs of hydroelectric power stations, have transformed them into one long lake without affecting their picturesque aspect, except when the waters are low. There is no road which closely follows the river for very far, though many cross it, offering lovely views. ▮ Laval, 15320 CHALIERS, ☎ 04 71 73 72 21.

▶ **Orient Yourself:** The gorges lie a short distance to the south of St Flour
⊗ **Don't Miss:** The Viaduc de Garabit
⊙ **Organizing Your Time:** A visit to the gorges can be combined with a tour of St Flour (↪ see St FLOUR): allow a day to visit both, but ideally more
♨ **Also See:** Chateau d'Alleuze

Excursions

① Along the Grandval Reservoir★★

60km/37mi – about 2hr

▶ *From the 165m/541ft-long Garabit bridge there is a view of the viaduct.*

Viaduc de Garabit★★

The Garabit viaduct is an elegant, and very bold, construction designed by an engineer named Léon Boyer and built (1882-84) by **Gustave Eiffel**. It has an overall length of 564m/1 850ft and stretches across the River Truyère at a height of 123m/403ft. Its 448m/1 470ft superstructure is supported by a bold metal arch.

Since the Grandval dam was built, the water below the viaduct has risen to the level of the supporting piles of the bridge, which still stands 95m/311ft above the maximum level of the dam's waters. It was the experience gained in Garabit that enabled Eiffel to design and build his famous 300m/984ft tower in Paris for the 1889 World Fair.

The slopes of the deeply incised valley are alternately covered with woodland or dotted with jagged boulders.

▶ *At the southern end of the bridge turn right to Faverolles.*

The route crosses the rocky Arcomie ravine and the Arling stream and con-

EATING OUT

⊜⊜ **Auberge du Pont de Lanau** – 15260 Lanau - 11.5km/8mi N of Chaudes-Aigues via D 921 - ☎ 04 71 23 57 76 - www.auberge-du-pont-de-lanau.com - closed 20 Dec-1 Feb and Mon lunch. If you're visiting in winter, come warm yourself by the wood fire crackling in the big stone fireplace of the cosy, attractive dining room. Traditional cuisine with a regional touch. A few pleasant rooms.

WHERE TO STAY

⊜ **Le Beau Site** – 15320 Garabit - ☎ 04 71 23 41 46 - www.beau-site-hotel.com - closed 4 Nov-9 Apr - ᴘ - 17 rms - ⊑ 7€ - restaurant ⊜⊜. This hotel's name suits it to a tee. 'The Beautiful Site' boasts a view of the viaduct and lake, a garden with a pool and a tennis court. The rooms, with stuccoed walls, are modern. One of the two dining rooms looks out over the splendid view. Generous full-board cuisine.

tinues to Faverolles where the Cantal, Margeride and Aubrac mountains come successively into view.

Château du Chassan

🕐 *End Jun to early Sep: guided tours (30min) 2-6.30pm.* 🕐 *Nov-Easter. 4€.* ☎ *04 71 23 42 20 or 04 71 23 43 91.*

In a region where medieval fortresses abound, this château provides a more peaceful addition to the landscape. In the 18C Jean-François de Ponsonnaille demolished the feudal castle of Faverolles in order to build the present house, which has remained in the family ever since.

The main building, with its austere façade, is embellished by a carved balcony and flanked by two wings, one of which is still lived in, whereas the other has been turned into an exhibition hall.

The hallway has a stone staircase topped with a basket-handled arch. A 15C horse-blanket on the wall bears the Ponsonnaille family coat of arms: three bells or cowbells flanked by two lions and topped with the count's coronet. In the dining room, the oak dresser still occupies the place for which it was made; its well-proportioned design distracts from any inherent heaviness. On the walls of the drawing room and antechamber hang fine Felletin tapestries (famous 15C Creuse manufacturer) depicting biblical themes. The tapestries in the drawing room have been cut to size to fit into sections of wall.

Belvédère de Mallet★★

Park after a sharp left-hand bend and walk to the promontory (🚶 10min there and back). From here, there is a splendid view over Grandval reservoir. From D 13 turn right on D 40 through Fridefont, and down along a twisting route to the ridge of the dam itself.

Barrage de Grandval★

This "multiple-arch," concrete dam is 376m/1 233ft long, 78.8m/259ft high and has six 50m/164ft arches supported by thick buttresses. The central arch of the dam houses a circular power station beneath a metal dome which produces 144 million kWh per year. The lake formed upstream of the dam is 28km/17mi long and has a surface area of 1 100ha/2 718 acres. **Boat trips** (🕐 *May-Oct: Lunch cruise (3hr15min) on the Grandval reservoir starting from 30€ (cruise and meal). Boat trips: Gorges de la Truyère, Viaduc, Motorway flyover: 45min (7€), 2hr (9.50€), Château d'Alleuze + gorges de la Truyère).* ☎ *04 71 23 49 40)* are organised on the lake during the spring and summer seasons.

After a very sharp left-hand bend the road drops into a wooded valley, offering splendid views of the ruins of Alleuze Castle.

Château d'Alleuze★★

The castle ruins may be reached by car along D 48. Park the car near the grave-yard and follow the steep path for 5min.

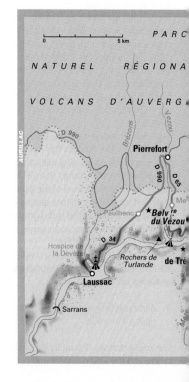

The fortress was built in the 13C by the Constables of the Auvergne but belonged to the Bishops of Clermont when, during the Hundred Years War, **Bernard de Garlan** – an adventurer who sided with the English – took it by storm and set up camp. For seven years he terrorised the region, pillaging a wide area and holding it to ransom. In order to ensure that Garlan was not the first of many, the inhabitants of St-Flour burnt the castle down in 1405.

Near the hill topped by the castle is a modern Calvary which stands next to the old church (12C-15C) of Alleuze and the graveyard.

Views of the castle★★

The D 48 scenic road, west of Barry, skirts the narrow Alleuze Valley, providing some breathtaking views of the castle and its ruins, a vast keep flanked by four round towers standing on a spur of barren rock, almost 30m/98ft above Grandval reservoir.

An even better view of the site may be had from the village of **La Barge**. Park beside the war memorial and turn left towards the church and the Calvary. From here it is possible to follow a path marking the Stations of the Cross laid out along the ridge of a rocky promontory (15min on foot there and back).

▷ In Alleuze turn back and take D 48 towards Lavastrie, then D 921 left to Chaudes-Aigues.

② **The Planèze★**

40km/25mi – about 2hr

At the foot of the Plomb du Cantal, the St-Flour *planèze* unfolds to the east and south-east at an average of 1 000m/3 280ft above sea level; a vast plateau on which few trees thrive, but where fields of crops stretch as far as the eye can see, earning the region its reputation as the agricultural heart of Upper Auvergne.

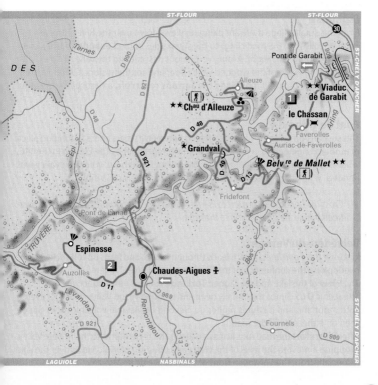

Château d'Alleuze

Chaudes-Aigues✝ – ♿ *See CHAUDES-AIGUES.*

The route briefly follows the west bank of the Remontalou Valley then turns right onto the *planèze* which offers extensive views of St-Flour plateau, and the Cantal and Margeride mountain ranges.

Espinasse
From this small village there are plunging views down over the River Truyère. From Auzolles on, the road clings to the steep sides of the **Lévandes Valley,** overlooking it from a fair height. A long, vertiginous descent into the valley follows, with breathtaking views of the wooded valley floor and southern slopes. After crossing the Lévandes, the road runs along the **Sarrans reservoir,** a particularly beautiful lake when water levels are high.

Pont de Tréboul★
This suspension bridge is 159m/5 21ft long between its piers and is a stunning piece of modern engineering. It replaced a Gothic bridge, built by the English in the 14C, which was submerged, together with the village of Tréboul, when the valley was flooded. When the water levels are low, the old bridge is still visible.

▶ *Cross the bridge and turn left to Pierrefort. Park the car 600m/660yd after the overhead bridge, beyond a bend to the right.*

Belvédère du Vézou★
🚶 *15min there and back.* A path leads through broom and ferns up to a rocky height overlooking the confluence of the River Vézou and River Truyère.
The **view** of the lake and the jagged **Turlande rocks** is very attractive.
The scenic D 65 climbs the initially deep and wooded Vézou Valley which is covered with moorland and pastures higher up. Beyond Le Meynial volcanic rocks can be seen on either side of the road.
After **Pierrefort** the road runs across a plateau and then returns to the Truyère Valley, dropping almost to the level of the water and offering splendid views over the lake (especially from the Calvary in front of the Hospice de la Devèze).

Pont de Tréboul

Laussac

The village is built on a promontory that the flooding of the valley has turned into a peninsula.

The northern part of the gorge is described in this guide, whereas the south-western section is described in the Languedoc-Roussillon-Tarn Gorges guide (♿ see ENTRAYGUES-SUR-TRUYÈRE).

VALENCE★

CONURBATION 117 448
MICHELIN MAP 332: C-4

This ancient Gaulish city, named Colonia Julia Valentia by the Romans at the beginning of the 2C BC, owes its development to its location on the Rhône, near the meeting of the tributary valleys of the Doux, Eyrieux, Isère and Drôme which mark out a vast internal basin and where the flora and fauna of Mediterranean France begin. The city, dominated by St-Apollinaire Cathedral, is built on a series of terraces going down to the river. Old Valence, surrounded by boulevards built in the 19C on the site of the old ramparts, has a network of shopping streets and picturesque sloping lanes, animated in season by the "Summer Festivals" *(see Calendar of events).* 🚉 *Parvis de la Gare, 26000 VALENCE, ☎ 0892 707 099. www.tourisme-valence.com.*

Valence, which is listed as a "Town of Art and History", offers discovery tours (2hr) conducted by guide-lecturers approved by the Ministry of Culture and Communication. 4€. Information at the offices of Valence Ville d'Art et d'Histoire, ☎ 04 75 79 20 86

A centre of attraction – The city, which is served by a large network of communications (A 7 motorway, N 7 national highway, River Rhône, airport), is the true centre of the Middle Rhône Valley and a focal point for entertainment and other attractions within the Drôme and Ardèche *départements.*

The population of Greater Valence, including the outlying suburbs spread out on either side of the Rhône – Bourg-lès-Valence, St-Péray, Portes-lès-Valence, Granges – has today reached more than 100 000 inhabitants, including numerous students enrolled at the Law Faculty and engineering schools.

A Bit of History

Rabelaisian studies – In 1452 the dauphin Louis, who was to begin his reign a few years later under the name of Louis XI and who, at the time, was preparing for his kingly role in his princedom of Dauphiné, founded a university in Valence consisting of five faculties, including an Arts Faculty. Among the students was **François Rabelais**. He was to recall his student days here in his tales of the adventures of his hero Pantagruel.

Courses were given by reputed masters, including the lawyer Cujas. Besides studying under this strict academic taskmaster, Rabelais is said to have had a love affair with his daughter.

Bonaparte in Valence – In 1785 Napoleon Bonaparte, a 16-year-old military cadet, arrived in Valence to improve his knowledge of warfare at the School of Artillery. Every morning, he went to the Polygon to direct his bombardiers' tactical exercises.

He lived almost directly opposite the Maison des Têtes (see below) which was occupied by a bookseller named Marc Aurel. Bonaparte soon befriended him, and in less than a year had read his entire stock. The future emperor had already embarked on a voyage of self-discovery. In a letter to a friend, he used a striking image to describe himself: "the southern blood which runs through my veins flows with the rapidity of the Rhône...."

Aurel's son was to publish the famous Souper de Beaucaire, in which Bonaparte set forth his ideas about the Revolution, a few years later in Avignon.

Old Town

▷ *Leave from Peynet kiosk.*

Kiosque Peynet

This structure, built in 1880, owes its name to the artist **Raymond Peynet** (1908-99) who once drew a sketch of a pair of lovers seated beside it.

Champ-de-Mars

This vast esplanade, built on a hillside opposite the Rhône, overlooks Jouvet Park. From the belvedere there is a beautiful **view**★ of Crussol mountains. The sunsets visible from here, which throw the mountain range into relief, are famous, although it is at sunrise that the view of Crussol is the most striking.

▷ *Take the staircase below the belvedere and cross avenue Gambetta. The narrow rue des Repenties and côte St-Estève lead round the cathedral and onto place du Pendentif.*

Pendentif

This small funerary monument was built in 1548, in the Antique style. The structure is completely open with a semicircular arch on each side, and has lovely proportions. It draws its name from the shape of its vault, reminiscent of the pendentives of a dome; note the curious lance-shaped pattern above the interior corner pillars.

Cathédrale St-Apollinaire

This vast Romanesque construction was largely rebuilt during the 17C in the primitive style.

The neo-Romanesque belfry (19C) has a white Crussol limestone base; the two upper floors are made of yellow sandstone from Châteauneuf-d'Isère.

▷ *Enter the cathedral through the north door.*

Under the porch, on the left, notice the lintel from the original portal; its carved compartments represent the Annunciation, the Nativity, the Adoration of the Magi and the Magi before Herod.

VALENCE

Alsace Bd d'	CY	Dragonne Pl. de la	CY 26	Pérollerie R.	BY 59	
Arménie R. d'	CY 4	Farre R. du Gén.	CZ 29	Petit Paradis R.	BY 60	
Augier R. Emile	CYZ	Félix-Faure Av.	CZ	Pierre Pl. de la	BY 62	
Balais R. des	BCY 5	Gaulle Bd du Gén.-de	CZ 32	Repenties R. des	BZ 65	
Bancel Bd	CY 6	Huguenel Pl. Ch.	CY 36	Sabaterie R.	BY 68	
Belle Image R.	CY 9	Jacquet R. V.	BZ 37	République Pl. de la	CZ	
Bonaparte R. du Lieutenant	BCY 12	Jeu-de-Paume R. du	CYZ 39	St-Didier R.	BCZ 71	
Chambaud R. Mirabel	BZ 15	Lecardonnel Pl. L.	CY 42	St-Estève Côte	BY 72	
Championnet Pl.	BCZ 16	Leclerc Pl. Gén.	CY 43	St-Martin Côte et R.	BY 77	
Chapeliers Côte des	BY 17	Liberté Pl. de la	CY 45	St-Nicolas Q.	BY 78	
Clerc Bd M.	CYZ 22	Madier-de-Montjau R.	CY 47	Saunière R.	CZ 80	
Clercs Pl. des	BCZ 23	Mistral Pont Frédéric	BZ 50	Sylvante Côte	BY 84	
Docteur-Schweitzer R. du	BY 25	Montalivet Pl. de	CY 51	Temple R. du	BCY 85	
		Ormeaux Pl. des	BZ 55	Université Pl. de l'	CZ 88	
		Palais Pl. du	CZ 56	Vernoux R.	CY 90	
		Paré R. Ambroise	BY 57	Victor-Hugo Av.	CZ	

Cathédrale St-Apollinaire	BZ	Maison Dupré-Latour	BY K	Pendentif	BZ N
Champ de Mars	BZ	Maison des Têtes	CY	Église St-Jean	CY
Kiosque Peynet	BZ	Musée des Beaux-Arts	BZ M		

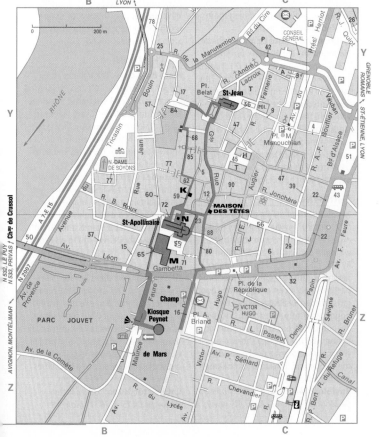

Address Book

EATING OUT

🍴🍷🛏 **L'Auberge du Pin** – *285 bis av. Victor-Hugo* - ☎ *04 75 44 53 86* - *pic@ relaischateaux.com* - *closed Wed from Oct to May.* What a delightful Provençal bistro! The atmosphere is warm, the colours are southern, vivacious and cheerful, the tables are of wrought iron, the chairs are of straw and regional products are displayed in the window. Inside or under the shade of the century-old trees on the summer terrace, treat yourself to a slice of the good life!

WHERE TO STAY

🛏🛏 **Hôtel St-Jacques** – *9 fg St-Jacques* - ☎ *04 75 78 26 16* - *hotel-stjacques-valence@wanadoo.fr* - 🅿 - *29 rms* - ⊡ *6€.* Not too far from the centre of town, this is a practical, modern hotel. Its refurbished rooms are somewhat basic but well soundproofed. Several menus are served in the restaurant's inviting dining room divided into three sections.

🛏 **Chambre d'hôte La Mare** – *Rte de Montmeyran - 26800 Étoile-sur-Rhône - 15km/9mi SE of Valence via D 111 and D 111B* - ☎ *04 75 59 33 79* - 🍴 - *4 rms.* This family farm is the right place to become acquainted with the local savoir-vivre and the charm of the Drômois landscape. Charming bedrooms with homemade furnishings. Delectable breakfasts feature house preserves, fresh from the garden, and pastries made by your hostess herself.

SHOPPING

Nivon – *17 avenue Pierre-Semard - b 04 75 44 03 37 - www.nivon.com - daily except Mon, 6am-7.30pm - closed last wk in Jan and 3 wks in Jul.* Established in 1852 and managed by the Maurin family for three generations, the Nivon pastryshop does an exceptionally good job with two local specialities: the pogne, a buttery sourdough brioche flavoured with orange flower, rum or lemon; and the *Suisse*, a shortbread with candied orange peel packed into the dough and flavoured in the same manner as the pogne.

Ravioles Mère Maury – *76 r. Madier-de-Montjau* - ☎ *04 75 42 57 41 - www. raviolesmaury.com - Tue-Sat 9am-noon, 2pm-7pm.* If you've never tasted ravioles - succulent little cheese-filled pasta squares - hurry to Mère Maury and stock up. In Paris, original ravioles (prepared in Romans-sur-Isère) are so outrageously expensive that one often settles for the industrial kind, whereas this little shop sells hand-made ravioles, including delicate basil-flavoured ones, at surprisingly affordable prices.

A Swiss in Valence – *Le Suisse* is a sweet, orange-flavoured brioche shaped like a little person. Traditionally eaten on Palm Sunday, it is said to owe its name to Pope Pie VI who was arrested by Général Berthier and transported to Valence where he died, imprisoned, in 1799. There are two versions explaining the term: either the pastries were made to resemble the uniforms of the Swiss guards, or *Le Suisse* was, in fact, none other than Napoléon I himself. Whichever is true, those with a sweet tooth will be happy to learn that they are now sold year-round!

ON THE TOWN

Place de la Gare. The Valence train station, serving the TGV and frequented by scores of tourists in transit, may well be the hub of the city. Every weekend, young Valence natives studying in Lyon, Grenoble or Marseilles return in droves and make merry in the cafés and pubs clustered around the square.

Place des Clercs. This elegant square in the city centre is lined with bars and restaurants. Saturdays - market days - it is overwhelmed with highly colourful fruit and vegetable stands and vendors selling just about everything else you can imagine.

Le Djam – *11 Grand-Rue* - ☎ *04 75 43 32 32 - Jul-Aug: 6pm-2am; Sep-Jun: Mon-Thu 6pm-1am, Fri-Sat 6pm-2am.* An original decoration scheme reigns in this small neighbourhood bar reminiscent of Alice in Wonderland. Sink into a chair shaped like a spade, heart, diamond or club before ordering an excellent glass of punch while listening to jazz, blues or ballads. Terrace on the street.

Café Victor-Hugo – *30 av. Victor-Hugo* - ☎ *04 75 40 18 11 - Mon-Sat*

7am-2am. Valence's chic literary café - chic but vivacious! Lunchtime, it is a noisy brasserie, and then in the afternoon ladies come gossip over their hot cocoas while students play billiards upstairs. Gérard Rousset, former member of the national rugby team, has orchestrated this successful symphony of generations and social classes – bravo!

Le Malvern – *27 r. Denis-Papin - ☎ 04 75 44 10 07 - Jul-Aug: 9.30am-2am; Sep-Jun: Sun-Thu 7am-1am, Fri-Sat 'til 2am - closed 1 wk Aug and Christmas*. With its 100 beers (16 on tap), 80 whiskies and rather rustic decor of the Irish pub ilk, this convivial, trendy bar is a favourite. You can try your aim at the weekly (boozy) darts contests or attend concerts alternating rock, blues and Celtic music.

Le Blue Note – *Quartier des Fontaines - 26120 Chabeuil - ☎ 04 75 85 24 77 - www.lebluenote.com - Thu-Sat and public holiday eves from 10.30pm*. Without a doubt, this techno stronghold is the area's top discotheque. Lost in the middle of the countryside, Le Blue Note is actually two discos in one: the first, devoted to the latest sounds, hops to an eardrum-threatening beat, while the second, jazzier and smoother, leads to an enormous bar. One can navigate between the two as desired.

THEATRE

Comédie de Valence – *1 pl. Charles-Huguerel - ☎ 04 75 78 41 70 - comedie. de.valence@wanadoo.fr - tickets: Tue-Fri 1pm-7pm, Sat from 1pm on performance days - closed Aug*. The Centre Dramatique National de Valence has one theatre, La Fabrique, located at 78 av. Maurice-Faure. Most shows and concerts, however, are staged at the Théâtre Le Bel Image, located Place Charles-Huguenel. This handsome 873-seat theatre has a nice bar that is open for drinks before the show and during intermissions.

RECREATION

Marina – *Chemin de l'Épervière - ☎ 04 75 81 18 93 - port.plaisance@drome.cci. fr - Apr-Oct: daily 9am-noon, 2pm-8pm; Nov-Mar: Mon-Sat 8am-noon, 2pm-6pm – closed public holidays*. The Port de l'Épervière, with its 32.000 m2 basin, is the Rhône river's number one harbour. Several clubs organise sports activities here, including wind-surfing, water-skiing, para-skiing. There are also a bowling lane, a tennis facility, a pool, a campground, a hotel and several restaurants.

Interior★

The influence of Auvergne Romanesque architecture is evident; the nave, with its barrel vaulting and transverse arches, is lit by the aisle windows. An arcade separates the chancel from the ambulatory. Note the depth of the transept arms, unusual in Rhône buildings. Behind the chancel stalls is a cenotaph-bust of Pope Pius VI, who died in Valence in 1799.

▶ *Leave through the south door.*

Under the porch *(left)*, on the carved tympanum of the original portal, is Christ giving benediction, and on the lintel Christ multiplying the loaves.

▶ *Walk around the east end.*

Note the elegant billet-moulding above the arcades of the apse and the transept arms.

Musée des Beaux-Arts

The Fine Arts Museum is set up in the former bishop's palace (♿ see below).

▶ *Take rue du Lieutenant-Bonaparte, then rue Pérollerie to reach the Maison Dupré-Latour.*

Maison Dupré-Latour

Visit only as part of tour of the town (2h). 4€. ☏ 04 75 79 20 86.
The interior courtyard of no 7 has a Renaissance staircase turret with a door surrounded by a remarkable carved frame.

▶ *From place de la Pierre, take rue St-James on the left then follow rue Sabaterie and rue Malizard.*

On the left stands the former St-Ruf temple. As you reach the public gardens, you will get a good view of Crussol in the distance.

▶ *Head for place St-Jean via côte des Chapeliers.*

Église St-Jean

This church was rebuilt in the 19C. The porch features some interesting original Romanesque capitals.

▶ *Walk along Grande-Rue.*

Maison des Têtes★

The "House of Heads" at no 57 is recognisable by the abundance and originality of the sculptures on its façade. Note two standing figures (Eve is on the left) and, under the roof, the four enormous haut-relief heads symbolising the winds, after which this Renaissance house (1532) was named.

▶ *Grand-Rue, then rue Saunière, lead back to place du Champ-de-Mars.*

Additional Sight

Musée des Beaux-Arts

🕐 *Mid-Jun to Sep: daily except Mon 10am-noon, 2-6.45pm, Sun 2-6.45pm; Oct to mid-Jun: daily except Mon 2-5.45pm.* 🕐 *Closed public holidays. 5€ (under-16s: no charge), no charge 1st Sunday in the month. ☏ 04 75 79 20 80. www.musee-valence.org*

B. Kaufmann/MICHELIN

Maison des Têtes – Detail of the façade

The Fine Arts Museum is located in the former bishop's palace and its main feature is a collection of 97 **red-chalk sketches**★★, drawings and paintings by the landscape artist **Hubert Robert** (1733-1808). Most are views of Rome and the Roman countryside.

After starting his career in Paris in the sculpture studio of Michel-Ange Slodtz, who was responsible for the archbishops' mausoleum in Vienne, Hubert Robert lived in Rome from 1754 to 1765, following in the wake of the painters Claude Lorrain and Joseph Vernet.

Ruins were a very fashionable subject at that time, and during his 11 years in Rome Robert filled his books with sketches and drawings in which the architecture of ancient and papal Rome served as a backdrop for scenes from everyday life.

When he returned to Paris, the painter used his sketch books as raw material for his paintings and new drawings, which show an astonishing grasp of perspective combined with an extremely light touch. The museum also has works by **Fragonard** and Ango, two of Robert's companions in Rome as well as extensive works from the French, Flemish, Dutch and Italian Schools of the 16C to the 19C, with a fine collection of naturalistic landscapes from the Barbizon School and other pre-Impressionists.

The contemporary art section, with works by the painters Bram van Velde, Michaux, Hantaï and Bryen and the sculptors B Pagès, M Gérard and Toni Grand, illustrates the abstract movement during the second half of the 20C.

The museum has in addition an archaeological collection (prehistoric, Gallo-Roman and medieval) which includes two Gallo-Roman mosaics depicting the Labours of Hercules and Orpheus charming the animals. The lapidary collection contains a Renaissance garden door from the Maison des Têtes (*see opposite*).

Excursions

Crussol★★

5km/3mi W along N 532, via St-Péray. On the top of Crussol Mountain (200m/656ft above the plain) stands the ruined **Château de Crussol**, one of the most grandiose **beauty spots**★★★ in the Rhône Valley. The smooth grain of the white Crussol stone makes it ideal for building.

A hilltop fortress

In the 12C, Bastet de Crussol chose this site for his fortress. The ambition of the "insignificant lords of Crussol" took them to the highest-ranking offices in the kingdom. One of the Crussols was Chamberlain to Louis XI, another became heir to the County of Uzès through marriage. His son, Seneschal of Beaucaire and Nîmes, took part in the Italian Campaigns with Charles VIII and Louis XII. Their official duties took the Crussols away from the uncomfortable ancestral home and it was partially demolished in

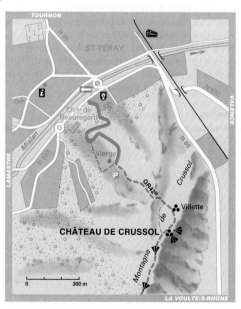

the 17C. Bonaparte is supposed to have scaled the cliff at Crussol in a particularly death-defying feat of bravado with one of his brothers in 1785 while garrisoned in Valence.

▶ *In St-Péray take the road past the Château de Beauregard (⚷ not open to the public). There is a car park at the end of the road behind the statue of the Virgin Mary. Then take the path to the ruins (1hr on foot there and back). It is highly recommended to take particular care in case of rain, when the stones become slippery.*

🚶 After passing the fortified north gateway in the old castle walls, follow the path on the left. It climbs up through the remains of the **"villette,"** where the people who lived on the plain sought refuge in times of danger.

Take the path on the left which runs inside the walls then head for the squire's living quarters. Perched on a rocky promontory, the castle towers 230m/755ft above the Rhône. Inside the keep, a belvedere offers a view of the Valence plain, the Bourg-lès-Valence dam, and the confluence of the River Rhône and River Isère. The peaks of Vercors, Roche Colombe and Trois-Becs form a magnificent backdrop.

The scarp slope on the south side *(add about 30min extra)* provides a **view**★★ of the ruins jutting out from amid the rock and over the last outcrops of the Massif Central.

Soyons

3.5km/2.2mi S on N 86. This village is situated on the west bank of the Rhône, on the site of important prehistoric and medieval settlements. It derives its name from "Soïo," a local god revered by the Gauls in the 7C BC. Excavations carried out in the surrounding hills are gradually revealing a wealth of information spanning 150 000 years. The **Musée Archéologique** (&🕐 *Jul-Aug: 10am-7pm (last admission 1hr before closing); Apr-Jun and Sep-Oct: Wed-Sun, 2-6pm.* 🕐 *Closed Nov-Jan. 4€.* ☎ *04 75 60 88 86)* displays a collection of Gallo-Roman finds (ground floor) whereas the first floor is devoted to prehistoric man and his environment.

Grottoes★

Soon after leaving Soyons S along N 86, turn right towards a parking area. A botanical trail runs up the side of the hill and leads to the grottoes. 🕐 *Jul-Aug: guided tours (1hr) 10am-7pm (last admission 1hr before closing); Apr-Jun and Sep-Oct: 2-6pm. 7€ (under-7s: no charge).* ☎ *04 75 60 88 86.*

These caves are important for the study of Neanderthal man. The network of underground galleries starts from the **Trou du Renard.** The grottoes were occupied at an early date by men and cave animals. Over the centuries, bones from bears, wolves and lions have been uncovered here.

Fouilles de la Brégoule

These archaeological digs, opened in 1980, have revealed artefacts spanning around 10 000 years.

VALS-LES-BAINS♨♨

POPULATION 3 536
MICHELIN MAP 331: I-6 – LOCAL MAP SEE MASSIF DU TANARGUE

This spa resort lies in a surprising setting at the bottom of the deeply-encased Volane Valley. The town has developed along the valley, resulting in a narrow urban corridor of about 2km/1mi long but on average only 300m/330yd wide. About 145 springs rise here and many of these have been exploited since 1600 though the town only became popular as a spa resort in the mid-19C. The waters here are cold (13oC/55oF) and rich in sodium bicarbonate; the difference between the springs lies in their degree of mineralisation. The waters, which are mainly used for drinking (several million bottles are exported from Vals each year) have a settling effect on the stomach and at the same time a stimulating effect on the liver. They are recommended for treating diabetes and nutrient deficiencies, in which case the waters may be taken in showers, baths and massages as well as taken orally. ▯ *116 bis r. Jean-Jaurès, 07600 VALS-LES-BAINS, ☎ 04 75 37 49 27 or 04 75 94 68 26. www.vals-les-bains.com*

Intermittent Spring
East bank. This spring (discovered in 1865) gushes forth from the middle of the park at the southern end of town. It rises to a height of 8m/26ft every six hours (11.30am and 5.30pm in summer, 10.30am and 4.30pm in winter).

Rocher des Combes
2km/1.2mi E via a road alongside the hospital – 15min on foot there and back. This is one of many excursions starting from Vals.
▯ From the viewing table (alt 480m/1 574ft) there is a good view over the surrounding mountains.

Excursions

Vallée de la Volane and Vallée de la Bourges★★
Round trip of 69km/43mi – about 4hr

▷   *Leave Vals on D 578 N to Mézilhac.*

The Volane Valley is lined with terraced hamlets, dotted with boulders and darkened by ancient basalt flows. The site of Antraigues, perched on its rocky promontory, marks the end of the lava flows.

Antraigues-sur-Volane
This delightful hill village is clustered around a shaded square lined with attractive terraces and patronised by enthusiastic *boules* players in high season.

Mézilhac
The village stands on the sill between the Eyrieux and Ardèche valleys. From a basalt peak crowned by a cross there is a splendid **view**★ north-west to the

Relaxing at the spa

J. Damase/MICHELIN

599

Gerbier de Jonc peak and the Mézenc range, north-east to the Boutières cirque and south down the Volane Valley.

▶ *Take D 122 along the crest to Lachamp-Raphaël then take D 215 down to Burzet.*

Cascade du Ray-Pic★★

45min on foot there and back. Park in the car park to the right of the road.

🏃 A path leads to the foot of these impressive falls, where the river gushes between two overhanging walls of basalt in an austere landscape at the bottom of a ravine.

Burzet

This village is renowned for its annual procession, commemorating Christ's Passion, up to a calvary overlooking the village and the River Bourges flowing beside it. Note the imposing west front of the Flamboyant Gothic church.

▶ *Return to Vals via St-Pierre-de-Colombier, Juvinas and D 243, a pretty little road through the Bézorges Valley. Alternatively, it is possible to drive to Montpezat along D 26, then follow D 536 and join up with the tour described under AUBENAS.*

Col de l'Escrinet★

85km/53mi – allow 3hr

▶ *Leave Vals on D 578B.*

Ucel

Ancient village built in a circle on a hilltop overlooking the River Ardèche.

▶ *In St-Privat, turn left onto D 259, running along the Luol and Boulogne valleys.*

You will enjoy driving through the pretty landscape of orchards and vineyards, alternating with pine and chestnut groves.

Village of Ucel

J. Damase/MICHELIN

St-Julien-du-Serre

The village has an interesting 12C Romanesque **church** (🕐 *Jul-Aug: Sat, 3-6pm. Rest of the year, contact the town hall.* ☎ *04 75 37 95 28)* with an unusual silhouette, its apse supported by hefty flying buttresses.

▶ *Drive through St-Michel-de-Boulogne to the ruins of the Château de Boulogne.*

Château de Boulogne★

This was originally a fortress, built by the Poitiers family on a spur between two ravines. The castle was transformed over the centuries into a sumptuous residence which escaped the ravages of the Revolution, but was partly demolished in 1820. The magnificent **gateway**★★, which René de Hautefort had built in the late 16C, incorporates twisted columns drawing on Renaissance tradition.

▶ *Turn round and take D 256 on the right. Drive through Gourdon, then turn right onto D 122, skirting Roc de Gourdon. After 2km/1.2mi, turn left onto a charming narrow lane that leads to Pourchères.*

Pourchères

The 12C church built on the nearby slopes features a single nave and a semicircular apse. Note the 12C font and 17C wooden Christ.

▷ *Turn round and take D 122 on the left, then N 104, heading for Col de l'Escrinet.*

Col de l'Escrinet

Alt 787m/2 582ft. This pretty pass provides access to both the south of Ardèche and the Plateau du Coiron. It offers a fine **panorama** encompassing the Plateau du Coiron, Privas Valley, Tanargue massif and Mont Lozère.

▷ *Before driving down towards Aubenas, turn left onto D 224, heading for Freyssenet.*

Crête de Blandine

Alt 1 017m/3 336ft. Park the car on the flat area and head for the television transmitter. This crest is the highest summit of the plateau. The view extends over Privas to the east and Mirabel and Aubenas to the south.

▷ *Return to Col de l'Escrinet, then drive back to Vals via St-Privat and Ucel.*

The Massif du Tanargue round tour (see Massif du TANARGUE) from Vals-les-Bains to Valgorge is another possibility offered to you in this area.

Address Book

WHERE TO STAY

Chambre d'hôte Bourlenc – *Rte de St-Andéol - 07200 St-Julien-du-Serre - 3.5km/2mi from St-Julien-du-Serre via D 218 dir. St-Andéol-de-Vals -* ☎ *04 75 37 69 95 -- - reserv. required - 5 rms - meals* . Remodelled by the owners, the bedrooms have a splendid view of the Col de Lescrinet. Meals feature organic garden vegetables and meat from the farm, plus, in spring, wild plants from the vicinity.

Grand Hôtel des Bains – ☎ *04 75 37 42 13 - grand.hotel.des.bains@ wanadoo.fr - closed 1 Nov to 28 Mar -* - *64 rms -* *10€ - restaurant* . The imposing façade, harmonious volumes and succession of dining rooms and lounges are a tribute to the ritzy origins of this hotel located behind the spa. Sheltered pool.

ON THE TOWN

Casino – *Av. Claude-Expilly-* ☎ *04 75 88 77 77 - www.casinodevals.fr - noon-3am.* Located in a scenic, rather old-fashioned park also housing a theatre and a cinema, this casino is comprised of 60 enticing slot machines, a bar, a discotheque and a restaurant. Summertime, you can enjoy the orchestra and dinner dances organised on the terrace (Thursday to Sunday).

Aux Chandelles – *4 av. Chabalier – A few miles from Aubenas near the casino -* ☎ *04 75 37 46 83 - pierreaubert@msn. com – open daily (except Tue in Aug) from 6.30pm.* This Mexican bar looks like a gangster hideout straight out of a Sergio Leone western. The ambience is warm and lively; in addition to the inevitable Corona beer, the drinks menu features an imaginative list.

SHOPPING

Brasserie Bourganel – *7 avenue Claude-Expilly -* ☎ *04 75 94 03 16 - www. bieres-bourganel.com - Apr-May, Oct: daily except Sun, 10am-noon, 2.45pm-7.15pm (Sat, 4-7.15pm)- closed Oct-Mar and 1 May.* Set on the banks of the Volane, this brewery, inaugurated in 2000, organizes informative hour-long visits followed by tastings of its pilsners. Unusual ales sharing the spotlight include blueberry beer and chestnut beer.

LES VANS

POPULATION 2 664
MICHELIN MAP 331: G-7

In the heart of the Lower Vivarais, in the middle of a fertile basin watered by the River Chassezac and dominated to the west by the jagged spire of the Barre ridge lies the town of Les Vans (pronounce the 's' on Vans). The setting, for those arriving from the Cévennes, is a magnificent Mediterranean scene, with an austere landscape of schist ridges to the north giving way to the dazzling white limestone of the south. Like many other parts of France, Les Vans was caught up in the religious strife which accompanied the Reformation and Counter-Reformation.
🛈 Pl. Léopold-Ollier, 07140 Les VANS, ☎ 04 75 37 24 48. www.les-vans.com

Visit

Renowned for its lively market (Saturday mornings) and its colony of artists, the town offers a pleasant stroll through the old district, a place brightened up by fountains and fine old houses.

Église

Built in Jesuit style during the 17C, the church has been extensively restored. The two **altarpieces**★ it contains were designed in 1682 by Jean Enguelbert, an artist from Antwerp. The 18C **stalls** come from the Abbaye des Chambons.

Temple

Situated slightly away from the town centre, the Protestant church, built in 1826, replaced an earlier building.

Bois de Païolive★

Planted with sessile oaks and dotted with white-grey limestone rocks sculpted by erosion, this forest is a curious sight indeed, spreading on either side of Le Chassezac, south-east of Le Vans.

▶ D 252 cuts across the wood from W to E.

Clairière★

🚶 Pleasant, shaded clearing on a small mound which provides the perfect spot for a picnic. Follow the signposted path to discover the nearby rocks.

Corniche du Chassezac★★

Leave the car on the large parking area to the left of the road leading to Mazet-Plage – 30min on foot there and back.
🚶 Follow the signs indicating "Corniche" to discover the breathtaking Chassezac ravine, flanked by high cliffs pitted with holes.

▶ *Retrace your steps.*

Mazet-Plage

Starting from D 252, a path leads to a camp site near the river after 300m/330yd.
The site of Mazet is situated at the mouth of the Chassezac gorges and provides facilities for a host of sporting and leisure activities (swimming, sunbathing, canoeing, climbing, rambling). To gain access to the more remote spots, cross the river and head for **Casteljau**. There are specially laid-out parking areas.

Address Book

EATING OUT

◎◎◎ **Chez Vincent et Michèle 'Le Lagon'** – *07460 Berrias-et-Casteljau - 10km/6mi E of Les Vans. Take D 901, D 252 and follow signs to V.V.F. - ☎ 04 75 39 35 33 - closed Oct-Apr, Mon and Tue from Mar to Jun - reserv. recommended.* Summertime, amid the rocky gorges, you can savour Le Lagon's fine cuisine by the waterfall pool, or, more simply, have a pizza on the terrace next door. Off-season, take a seat at La Bastide, located in a splendid 15C farmhouse.

WHERE TO STAY

◎ **Camping La Source** – *07460 Berrias-et-Casteljau - 12km/7.2mi SE of Les Vans via D 901 and D 202 - ☎ 04 75 39 39 13 - camping.la.source@wanadoo.fr - open Apr-Sep - ✂ - reserv. recommended - 81 sites - food service.* This fairly new campground has been well planned: the clearly defined sites are already protected from the sun. The bar, pizzeria and grocery, located in the same building, provide on-site sustenance. Enticing pool.

◎ **Chambre d'hôte La Passiflore** – *07460 St-Paul-le-Jeune - 13km/8mi S of Les Vans via D 901, then D 104 dir. Alès - ☎ 04 75 39 80 74 - closed mid-Dec to mid-Jan - ✂ - 3 rms.* Yes, the road is close by, but not to worry: the well-insulated house is truly pleasant and the Flemish owners enjoy making a fuss over their guests. Start your day with a delightful breakfast under the garden bower next to the aviary.

◎◎◎ **Chambre d'hôte L'Ensolleiade** – *07460 Casteljau - 10km/6mi SE of Les Vans via D 901 and D 252 - ☎ 04 75 39 01 14 - www.ensolleiade.com - closed 10 Nov to 1 Apr - ✂ - 5 rms.* The bedrooms of this peaceful low house in the middle of the countryside are simple, sunny and spacious. You will appreciate the beauty of walks in nature and the freshness of a dip in the pool, unless you would rather catch forty winks under the cherry trees.

◎◎◎ **La Santoline** – *07430 Beaulieu - 13km/8mi SE of Les Vans via D 901, D 202 and D 252 - ☎ 04 75 39 01 91 - www.lasantoline.com - closed Oct-Apr - 8 rms - ☕ 10€.* Isolated in the middle of the garrigue, this 16C edifice will delight those who yearn for peace and quiet. Colourful elegance prevails in the differently decorated rooms. Supper, for residents only, is served in a pretty, arched dining room. Pool and garden for your pleasure.

SHOPPING

Notre-Dame des Neiges – *07590 St-Laurent-les-Bains - ☎ 04 66 46 00 02 - caves.ndneiges@wanadoo.fr.* Since 1890, this Cistercian abbey has been selling wine grown in the Gard and matured in its cellars. In addition to bottles of white, red, rosé and sparkling wines and liqueurs, you can also stock up on regional and 'monastic' goods such as honey, preserves, biscuits and syrups.

Excursions

Naves

On leaving Vans, head for Villefort, then turn left onto D 408. This is an attractive medieval village, which draws many an artist to capture its charms on canvas. You can enjoy a stroll along the River Chassezac, where willows grow along the rocky banks.

Banne

6km/4mi from the intersection between D 901 and D 252. Leave the car on the square. Climb up the ramp behind the wayside cross.

🚶 You will reach a flat area planted with grass, overlooking the Jalès basin. The rocks offer a fine **panorama**★ over the distant Gard and Lower Ardèche. The long vaulted gallery was once used as stables for Banne Château, which no longer stands.

Musée de l'Œuf décoré et de l'Icône
 ♿🕐 *Mid-Mar to end-Jun and Sep: daily except Tue and Wed 3-6pm (Jul-Aug: daily 10.30am-12.30pm, 3-6.30pm). 5€ (children: 3€).* ☎ *04 75 39 85 11.*
This museum houses a collection of Russian icons from the 18C to the 20C and an amazing collection of Easter eggs (real ones and porcelain ones) decorated by different methods.

Cévennes Vivarais Corniche Road

49km/30mi from La Bastide-Puylaurent to Joyeuse – allow 2hr
This scenic crest road cuts a breathtaking course through the mountains of the Cévennes Vivarais, giving spectacular views of the surrounding countryside as it passes from one mountain ridge to the next. The beautiful natural scenery through which it travels modulates gradually during the trip, from the arid ridges running from the River Drobie up to the Tanargue massif, to the softer hills of Lower Ardèche.

La Bastide-Puylaurent
This village was founded in the 19C during construction of the railway line from Paris to Nîmes. It is a pleasant place to spend some time in summer; its charms include the clear fresh air of its site in the Upper Allier Valley and the soothing beauty of the surrounding hillsides covered in woodland and meadows.

▶ *Leave La Bastide E on D 906, then turn left onto D 4.*

Trappe de Notre-Dame-des-Neiges
This Cistercian abbey, founded in 1850, is tucked miles from anywhere amid pine trees and beech woods, surrounded by a ring of mountains which protect it from the winds sweeping across the mountain plateaux of the Vivarais. The present buildings were built in the wake of a fire which devastated the original abbey on its hilltop site in 1912.
In 1878, on his *Travels with a Donkey in the Cévennes,* the Scottish writer **Robert Louis Stevenson** spent a couple of days at the abbey, during which – as a Protestant – he had to endure the zealous efforts of two monks determined to convert him and save his soul by engaging him in lengthy religious debate. Other famous inmates of the abbey include French explorer-and-soldier-turned-monk **Charles de Foucauld** (1858-1916), who did his novitiate here in the first half of 1890.
As the road drops down to St-Laurent-les-Bains, a left bend gives a stunning **view**★★ of the mouth of Borne gap.

St-Laurent-les-Bains
Tucked in the hollow of a narrow valley, this small spa town specialises in the treatment of various forms of rheumatism. The main street, where there is a hot spring (53°C/127°F), gives a good view of a ridge crowned by the ruins of an old tower.
The road continues downhill and crosses the Borne, before climbing steeply once more and passing through a beautiful pine forest. This eventually gives way to a rather bleak landscape of tall rocky crests.
Note, to the right, a tiny hamlet called **Petit Paris** perched in solitary splendour above granite boulders.
On a ledge shortly before Peyre, there is another good view to the right, this time of the pretty village of **Thines**★★ in its charming setting on a rocky outcrop overlooking a ravine (👁 *see Vallée du Chassezac below*).

▶ *Carry on along D 4 through Peyre.*

Beyond Peyre, the appearance of vines in the surrounding landscape heralds that of other Mediterranean plant species.

▶ *Follow D 4 through Planzolles and Lablachère to Joyeuse.*

The brightness of the limestone lowlands with their white rocks, vineyards and fragrant Mediterranean scrub *(garrigue)* is a world away from the rugged schist ridges encountered at the start of the trip.

Joyeuse
The town, with a number of interesting old houses, spreads out on terraces opposite the Tanargue massif.

Villages of the Cévennes Vivarais★
Round tour of 34km/21mi – about 2hr 30min

▶ *Leave Les Vans on D 10 N; turn right on D 250.*

Chambonas
This is a village with a part-Romanesque church (carved frieze at the east end) and an old château (12C-17C) with towers covered in glazed tiles, and formal gardens said to have been laid out by Le Nôtre.

▶ *Follow D 250.*

The road runs alongside the Chassezac, crosses the Sûre and climbs a sandstone slope between vineyards and stands of evergreens.

Payzac
There is a charming rural church (12C-15C) here.

▶ *Take D 207 towards St-Jean-de-Pourcharesse.*

The sandstone landscape modulates from grey to red tones. After the village of Brès, with its red-stone houses, the surrounding rock becomes schist and the road twists its way among chestnut groves.

St-Jean-de-Pourcharesse
A typical local church, built of schist with a roof covered in stone slabs *(lauzes)* stands in this village.

▶ *Take the road to Lauriol village.*

From here, the road passes more chestnut groves in a landscape slashed by ravines, to the edges of which cling tiny hamlets. Note the interesting stone-slabbed roofs.

St-Pierre-le-Déchausselat
This village is built on terraces. From the vineyards of the farm below the church there is an attractive view over the surrounding countryside.

▶ *Return to Les Vans via Chambonas.*

Vallée du Chassezac★

Round trip of 77km/48 mi – about 3hr

▶ *Leave Les Vans on D 901 towards Villefort and take D 113 right.*

Gorges de Chassezac

Gravières

The **church** here (12C-15C – 🕐 *Visits by appointment with Mme Pradeilles.* ☏ *04 75 37 31 07*) has a sturdy belfry. Inside, in the wall of the chancel (left), there is a 14C Tree of Jesse of carved stone (damaged). The gilded altarpiece and Gothic chapels are also interesting.

🚶 *Allow 3hr.* 👧 A 6km/3.7mi round tour starting from **La Virade du Batistou** runs right round the village inviting children to discover rural life at the beginning of the 20C *(information and brochure available from the tourist office in Les Vans).*

▶ *Continue along D 113 and, beyond the bridge on the River Chassezac, turn right on D 413.*

Les Salelles

This village overlooks a meander in the Chassezac. The **church of St-Sauveur** *(Guided tours Thu. Times posted on the door.)* is a Gothic edifice built of warm red sandstone. The fortified belfry, destroyed by lightning, was rebuilt in the early 20C.

▶ *Follow the valley along D 113 (note the number of hydroelectric dams and power plants along the river) and turn right on D 513 to Thines.*

Thines★★

This small village sits on a spectacular **site**★★ perched above the Thines torrent and its ravine. It boasts old houses clinging to the rock, narrow alleyways and a fine Romanesque **church:** the doorway has four statue-columns and a lintel bearing a frieze of small figures. The **east end**★ is particularly attractive, with a cornice adorned with fanciful motifs below which is a blind arcade resting on carved consoles and engaged columns. The alternating colour of the stonework – pink sandstone, grey granite and white limestone – adds to the charm of the building.

▶ *Continue up Chassezac Valley, past another dam and the hydroelectric power station at Pied-de-Borne. Cross the River Borne. At Les Beaumes turn right onto a small road which drops back into the valley and crosses the Borne.*

The road climbs again, twisting up to Montselgues plateau (average alt 1 000m /3 280ft).

Montselgues

This tiny village in the middle of a vast undulating plateau, dotted with wild narcissi and broom in June, has a sturdy church with a lovely Romanesque doorway. The village is a cross-country skiing centre.

▶ *Head NE out of the village on D 304. Turn right on D 4 to return to Les Vans.*

Shortly before Peyre, there is a good **view**★ to the right of Thines down below. Return to Le Vans via Pont de Chambonas

VICHY

POPULATION 26 528
MICHELIN MAP 326: H-6

Vichy, a world famous spa resort and holiday town, attracts numerous visitors because of its high quality shopping facilities and the very wide range of entertainment it has to offer: casino-theatre, cabarets, festivals, concerts, exhibitions, lectures, horse races. The parks along the banks of the River Allier add to the pleasure of staying here. The multi-purpose sports centre (Centre Omnisports), which is situated north of the town, is one of the best designed sports complexes in Europe. Lake Allier (nearly 100ha/250 acres), which was created after the construction of a dam bridge on the river downstream from the town, is used for international competitions (rowing, regattas, water-skiing etc). The Sporting Club completes the complex with its 18-hole golf course, tennis courts and swimming pool. *19 r. du Parc, 03200 VICHY, ☎ 04 70 98 71 94. www.ville-vichy.fr*

▶ **Orient Yourself:** North-east of Clermont-Ferrand, set on the River Allier
📖 **Parking:** There is ample parking in the town centre
👁 **Don't Miss:** The Spa district (👣 *see Town Walks*)
🕐 **Organizing Your Time:** You can comfortably explore the town in half a day, but a longer period will give you time to experience its spa facilities
👣 **Also See:** Old Vichy, and Chateau de Busset

The Vichy Government

From early July 1940 until 20 August 1944, Vichy was the capital of the French State during Nazi German occupation of the north of France. Vichy, with a direct railway line to Paris (the "Thermal-Express"), relatively modern telephone links, and many hotels which could be requisitioned for government offices, was chosen in preference to cities such as Clermont-Ferrand, Marseille or Toulouse. It had the added advantage of being quite close to the line of demarcation (level with Moulins) between occupied and unoccupied France. Maréchal Pétain, hero of Verdun during the First World War, was granted full executive powers by the French parliament. He and his Cabinet had their headquarters in the Pavillon Sévigné, while most of the other government members and senior administrators were housed at the Hôtel du Parc, the War Ministry at the Thermal (now the Aletti Palace), and foreign diplomats at – appropriately enough – the Ambassadeurs.

The disproportionate centralisation of government power in this city (the only government department installed elsewhere was the commission for youth projects at Châtelguyon) was accompanied by a strictly monitored exercise of power and the laying aside of the fundamental principles of democracy. During the dark days of the Vichy regime, the city was subject to a permanent police presence, with the oppressive atmosphere further heightened by furtive and unexplained comings and goings, cowed public apathy and an overriding austerity totally at odds with the city's previous role as a health and leisure resort. On 20 August 1944, the representatives of the toppled regime who had remained in place were taken back to Germany by the Nazis as they retreated. Six days later the Free French Forces entered the city.

The Spa Resort

The healing properties of Vichy water were appreciated by the Romans, who built a small spa town here – Vicus Calidus. After a long period of relative obscurity, Vichy's vocation as a spa was resurrected in the 17C.

A day in the life of a 17C bather – This is an account by Madame de Sévigné, who came here to cure her rheumatism:

"I took the waters this morning, my dear. Oh! How awful they are! At 6am we go to the spring; everyone is there; we drink and pull the most awful faces – just imagine, the water is boiling hot, with a most unpleasant taste of saltpetre. We walk back and forth, we come and go, we stroll about. Finally, we have luncheon. After eating, we go visiting. At 5pm we go walking in the most delightful places. At 7pm we have a light supper. We go to bed at 10pm. Today, I began taking showers. What an excellent preparation for purgatory! Then we get into a warm bed – and that is what makes you better."

Water, water everywhere

S. Sauvignier/MICHELIN

Famous bathers – During the 18C the daughters of Louis XV, Mesdames Adelaide and Victoire, came to spend the season here. One of the springs now bears their name (Source Mesdames). In 1799 Maria-Letizia Bonaparte, Napoleon's mother, came here. In 1810 the Emperor himself created the Parc des Sources. In 1821 the Duchess of Angoulême laid the first stone of the thermal establishment. Napoleon III came on several occasions to take the waters at Vichy and the spa became extremely fashionable. A series of chalets was built alongside the new Allier park, with their façades all facing the gardens, at the Emperor's request, in order to avoid the obsessive ovations. Since the Second Empire, countless celebrities have come to spend a pleasant holiday here while tending their health. The local facilities are remarkable and the town is constantly improving them.

The Vichy springs

Vichy's mineral and thermal springs contain mainly bicarbonate of soda and carbonic acid. The main springs (see below) belong to the State and are operated by a contracting company founded in 1853. The waters here are used to treat conditions of the liver, gall-bladder and stomach, diabetes, migraines, nutritional and digestive disorders, and also rheumatological complaints.

Waters from the Grande Grille, Hôpital and, in particular, Célestins springs, are bottled and exported the world over.

Hot springs – These are the basis of the Vichy drinking cures. The **Grande Grille** is named after the grille which used to protect it from thirsty animals. The bubbling water (temperature 40˚C/104˚F) comes up from a depth of 1 000-1 200m/3 280-4 028ft. The **Chomel** (temperature 41˚C/106˚F) is named after the doctor who captured the spring in 1750 and managed the waters. A third hot spring, the **Hôpital** (temperature 33˚C/91.4˚F), rises in a rotunda-shaped pavilion behind the Casino.

Cold springs – Part of the regimen includes drinking the water. The **Parc** (temperature 24˚C/75˚F) gushes forth in the Parc des Sources. The **Lucas** (temperature 24˚C/75˚F) is named after the doctor and inspector who bought the spring at the

VICHY

Belgique R. de	BZ	3	Glénard Pl. Frantz	BY	9	Parc R. du	BZ	22
Briand Av. A.	BZ	4	Gramont Av. de	CY	10	Colombier R. Hubert	BZ	23
Casino R. du	BZ	5	Hôtel des Postes R.	CY	14	Prés.-Eisenhower Av. du	BY	25
Clemenceau R. G.	BZ	6	Alquié R.	BY	15	Prés.-Wilson R.	BZ	26
Coulon Av. P.	BY	7	Lattre-de-T. Bd Mar.-de	BY	17	Prunelle R.	BZ	27
Foch R. Mar.	CZ	8	Lucas R.	BY	18	Porte-Verrier R. de la	BZ	31
			Besse R.	CZ	20	Tour R. de la	BZ	32

Castel Franc	BZ	F	Musée de l'Opéra			Médiathèque Valéry		
Castel flamand	BZ	K	de Vichy	BZ	M¹	Larbaud	CZ	B
Kiosque à musique	BZ	D	Musée des Arts d'Afrique			Source des Célestins	CZ	S
Maison de Madame			et d'Asie	BY	M²			
de Sévigné	BZE							

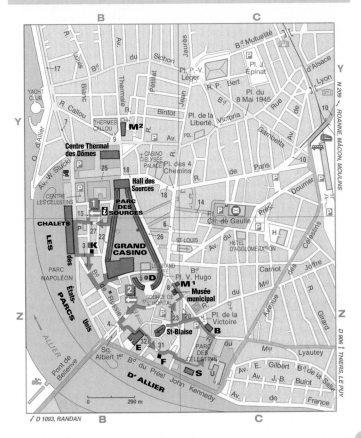

Address Book

EATING OUT

🍴🍴 **Brasserie du Casino** – *4 r. du Casino -* ☎ *04 70 98 23 06 - closed 16 Feb-3 Mar, 20 Oct-13 Nov, Tue-Wed.* Come experience an authentic brasserie from the 1930s! It's all here: the old-fashioned atmosphere, the ambient gaiety, and tables so close to one another that you can eavesdrop on your neighbour. Menu featuring fish and traditional brasserie fare.

🍴🍴 **La Colombière** – *03200 Abrest - 5km/3mi SE of Vichy via D 906 -* ☎ *04 70 98 69 15 - lacolombiere@wanadoo. fr - closed mid-Jan to mid-Feb, 6-21 Oct, Sun evening and Mon.* This 1950s villa with a dovecote by the side of the road is rather imposing. Ask for a table near the bay windows overlooking the terraced garden and the Allier Valley. Bountiful cuisine with a good choice of fixed-price menus.

🍴🍴 **La Fontaine** – *03300 Vichy-Rhue -* ☎ *04 70 31 37 45 - fontaine-vichy@ wanadoo.fr - closed 15-30 Oct, 17 Dec-7 Jan, Mon evening, Tue evening and Wed.* 'The Fountain' is a wellspring of well-being in all seasons. Wintertime, the central fireplace shares its warmth with diners, whereas summertime a peaceful brook melodiously babbles by the shady terrace. Traditional and regional cuisine.

🍴🍴 **Chez Mémère** – *R. Claude-Decloitre - 03700 Bellerive-sur-Allier -* ☎ *04 70 59 89 00 - closed Feb school holidays, 15 days in Oct-Nov and Christmas wk - reserv. recommended weekends.* The façade is nothing special, but customers line up to dine at Chez Mémère. The highly enthusiastic, self-taught chef whips up tasty, well-prepared dishes that are served on the bucolic shaded terrace along the Allier, or indoors in the pleasant wood-panelled dining room.

WHERE TO STAY

🛏 **Atlanta** – *23 r. Pasteur -* ☎ *04 70 98 42 95 - closed 13 Dec-13 Jan - 13 rms -* ⬛ *6€.* Here's a small, inexpensive hotel near the train station. The simple rooms are spic-and-span and well-soundproofed. Summertime you can have your breakfast on the flower-decked patio.

🛏 **Arverna Hôtel** – *12 r. Desbrest -* ☎ *04 70 31 31 19 - closed 17-26 Oct, 17 Dec-5 Jan and Sun Dec-Feb - 26 rms -* ⬛ *6€.* A family hotel in a shady street between the train station and the spas. Bedrooms are small, functional and clean; those on the top floor have sloping ceilings. The breakfast room opens onto a pocket garden.

🛏🛏 **Aletti Palace Hôtel** – *3 pl. Joseph-Aletti -* ☎ *04 70 30 20 20 - aletti. palace.best.western@wanadoo.fr - 126 rms -* ⬛ *12€.* Belle Epoque architecture and ambience in this palatial former spa near the Parcs d'Allier. The rooms, of varying sizes, are furnished in the Art Deco style. Elegant dining room and traditional cuisine in the La Véranda restaurant. Heated pool.

🛏🛏🛏 **Sofitel Les Célestins** – *111 bd des États-Unis -* ☎ *04 70 30 82 00 - H3241@accor-hotels.com - closed 7-25 Dec - 131 rms -* ⬛ *16€.* A big, modern and very chic hotel on the banks of the Lac d'Allier, with a complete fitness centre geared towards pampering your body and mind. Bright, sizeable rooms. Two restaurants: the traditional Bistro des Célestins or the versatile Jardins de l'Empereur, serving gastronomic or dietetic meals.

ON THE TOWN

L'Ascot Bar – *3 pl. Joseph-Aletti -* ☎ *04 70 30 20 20 - from 11am.* With its Art Deco and posh interior, this Vichy bar is a classic. Come have a drink here in a fine musical setting.

Le Blue Note – *111 bd des États-Unis -* ☎ *04 70 30 82 00 - noon-midnight - closed 8-25 Dec.* An inviting piano-bar frequented by spa-goers and celebrities visiting Vichy. Remarkable cocktails menu. Live music from 7pm onwards Fri, Sat and Sun. When the weather allows it, the musicians go out and play on the terrace facing the Parc d'Allier.

Le Grand Café – *7 r. du Casino -* ☎ *04 70 97 16 45 - grand-cafe@wanadoo.fr - 10am-3am.* Its location right in the middle of the thermal park and the high quality of its bar, snack and traditional restaurants, casino, discotheque and dance hall, make this the most popular of the spa establishments. Always packed, the terrace under the protective horse chestnuts is the best vantage point for enjoying the goings-on in the music kiosk. Ballroom dance enthusiasts can step out at the Dancing La Belle Époque, whereas more sedentary spa-goers can try their luck at the slot machines and at *boule*.

Le Samoa – 13 sq. de la Source-de-l'Hôpital - ☎ 04 70 59 94 46 - opens at 8.30am - closed Sun morning in winter. Under the shady arcades lining the square, this Vichy institution is jam-packed whenever there's an event on at the music kiosk. At other moments, tourists and spa-goers can take their time and enjoy home-made ice cream on the peaceful terrace.

Casino de Vichy 'Élysée Palace' – *Passage de la Comédie - ☎ 04 70 97 93 37 - casinos.de.vichy@wanadoo.fr - Mon-Fri 10am-3am, weekends until 4am; disco: Thu-Sat; roulette, black-jack: Wed-Sun.* Slot machines and traditional games *(boule,* blackjack, French and English roulette) vie for the favours of enthusiasts. The Élysée Club discotheque and a theatre round out the casino complex.

SHOWTIME

Palais des Congrès - *Opéra de Vichy – 5 r. du Casino, BP 2805 - ☎ 04 70 30 50 30/04 70 30 50 56 - billetterie.opera@ville-vichy.fr - tickets: Tue-Sat 1.30pm-6.30pm; phone reservations: Tue-Fri 10am-12.30pm - closed Sun-Mon except performance days.* A citadel of Vichy culture, this handsome Art Nouveau-style opera house has opted for an exacting programme alternating opera, theatre, dance and even pop music. Habitants of Vichy and spa-goers alike line up to reserve their seats for these popular events.

SHOPPING

Aux Marocains – *32 r. Georges-Clemenceau - ☎ 04 70 98 30 33.* Red marble from Italy, a gigantic bronze chandelier, woodwork decorated with gold leaf: this is one very chic confectioner's! The laboratory in the basement guards the secret of the *Marocain,* a hard caramel with a soft caramel centre, created in the 1920s. Other tempting specialities include candied fruit and barley sugar.

Calondre – *Passage de l'Amirauté - ☎ 04 70 98 40 57.* Although it has been restored, this pastry shop founded in 1880 has kept its wonderfully old-fashioned character. The Napoleon III decor – painted ceiling, cream-coloured walls – sets the scene for a display of appetizing pastries such as the *Tranche de Vienne*.

Pastillerie de Vichy – *94 allée des Ailes - ☎ 04 70 30 94 70 - Mon-Thu 9am-noon, 2pm-6pm, Fri 9am-11am - closed 29 Jul-18 Aug, Sat-Sun and public holidays.* After having visited the packaging workshop and seen the slide show, you'll know everything there is to know about the production of the legendary *Pastille de Vichy.*

Vichy Prunelle – *38 r. Montaret - ☎ 04 70 98 20 02 - vichy-prunelle@wanadoo.fr - 9am-noon, 2pm-7pm, Sun and public holidays 10am-noon, 2.30pm-7pm - closed Mon off-season.* This big, old-fashioned confectionary sells house specialities, such as the *Perles de la Marquise* (grilled hazelnuts in vanilla or chocolate-flavoured sugar), marshmallows, Auvergne fruit jellies, the famous pastilles and the Vichy barley-sugar that the Marquise de Sévigné would undoubtedly have fancied.

beginning of the 19C on behalf of the State. The **Célestins** has a temperature of 21.5°C/71°F.

Thermal establishments – The Centre Thermal des Dômes can provide up to 2 500 people with thermal and related treatment each morning. The Callou pump room, like that of the Célestins, boasts the latest technical innovations.

Walking Tours

1 The Spa District★

The "spa resort" architecture of the late 19C and early 20C, the period when Vichy, the "Queen of Spa Towns," was at its most popular, is well worth a closer look. The buildings of the Vichy spa complex have been carefully restored and listed as protected for some years now, and make up a rich and unique part of France's architectural heritage.

Vichy architects were spurred on in their quest for originality and the unexpected by the resort's air of worldliness and sophistication; this was a place where monotony was not permitted and where extravagant gestures ruled the day. The various artistic influences at work here include Byzantine, Auvergne Romanesque and Florentine Quattrocento, with the style of English cottages and Alpine chalets also being emulated. The result is a delightfully anarchic "Baroque eclecticism" in which architecture of every style and every period can be seen.

Parc des Sources★

This beautiful park planted with chestnut and plane trees was laid out on the orders of Napoleon I and links a number of springs. The spa district effectively grew up around it, and it has remained the centre of the town's spa industry and leisure facilities.

In the morning the district is permeated with the peculiar atmosphere of the spa, punctuated by the comings and goings of people taking the waters, gathering in clusters around the springs as they await their "glass of water."

In the afternoon and on gala evenings, fashionable society comes to life, going for an evening stroll, having a drink on the terrace of the Grand Café or attending some glittering function.

Hall des Sources

Fed by the waters of Vichy's six thermal springs, the **Pump Room** is built of glass and metal, and its very transparency and the fluidity of its design bring to mind the element which is dispensed within.

Centre Thermal des Dômes

The luxury assembly rooms in a neo-Moorish style were designed by Charles Lecoeur, architect of the Grand Casino, and inaugurated in 1903. The central dome and corner

The Source des Celestins in Vichy

S. Sauvignier/MICHELIN

cupolas are covered in gold enamelled roof tiles. Frescoes *(The Bath, The Spring)* by the Symbolist painter Alphonse Osbert adorn the hall inside.

Grand Casino★

The Grand Casino, which opened in 1865, represents the important influence of general good spirits on people's health. The first of its kind in France, it housed various assembly rooms and gaming halls beneath a single roof. From 1900 to 1903, it was renovated and extended with the addition of an opera house under the direction of architect Charles Lecoeur. Inside, the superb Art Nouveau decor is the work of wrought-iron worker Émile Robert and master glass-artist François Chigot. The main façade, in Belle Epoque (early 20C) style, overlooks the park, to which it is linked by a beautiful flight of steps.

A comprehensive renovation project combined with the conversion of the gaming hall into a conference centre has restored this building to its former splendour.

Covered arcades

These are beautifully delicate Art Nouveau creations in wrought iron, crafted by Émile Robert for the 1889 World Exhibition in Paris and transferred to Vichy in 1900.
The balustrade of the **bandstand,** also the work of Robert, forms a garland of musical motifs *(several concerts a week are given here in season).*

Hotels, chalets and villas

Despite the demolition of the prestigious Queen's Hotel, most of the grand hotels on which Vichy's reputation is based have survived intact. The Hôtel du Parc (21-23 rue du Parc), to the left of the tourist office, is among the most impressive neo-Baroque buildings in town. Walk along rue du Parc and turn onto rue Prunelle *(first on the right)* where the mansion at no 8 is a pastiche of an English cottage. Take a glimpse along rue Alquié *(on the right)* which looks like an English street. The row of **chalets**★ lining avenue des États-Unis (nos 101 to 109bis) was built from 1862 to house Napoleon III and his entourage, who used to come regularly to take the waters at Vichy. Turn onto rue de Belgique *(second on the left)* to admire the Venitian-style villa with St Mark's lions at no 7 and the **Castel Flamand**★ at nos 2-2bis. Retrace your steps and turn left onto rue Alquié leading to boulevard de Russie. The Palais des Parcs (the old Ruhl) at no 15 is another neo-Baroque hotel. It was after the fall of the Empire that architects unleashed the full power of their imagination to create truly eccentric buildings. There are some remarkable examples of florid design along boulevard de Russie (neo-Classical at nos 17, 19 and **21**★, Art Deco at no 29). On your way to rue du Casino, note in rue du Parc (on the left) the neo-Louis XIII style façade of the Hôtel des Ambassadeurs.

2 Old Vichy

▶ *Start from the Source de l'Hôpital. Follow avenue A.-Briand to reach square Albert-1ᵉʳ (signposting).*

Note the Ermitage du Pont-Neuf Hotel, which exemplifies Art Deco style. The **Maison de Madame de Sévigné,** constructed during the time of Louis XIII, has been extensively restored and converted into a hotel (Pavillon Sévigny). The Marquise of Sévigné would stay here when she came to spend the season at Vichy.

▶ *Continue along rue de la Tour (on the right) then rue Verrier (on the right) and walk past the 16C Castel Franc, remodelled in the 19C when it became the town hall.*

Source des Célestins

The water from this spring now flows as far as the Pump Room, but it is worth taking the short walk to have a look at the elegant Louis XV pavillion which houses the spring itself.

The Célestins Park contains some magnificent evergreen trees, as well as traces of the old convent after which the spring and the park are named.

▶ *Head for rue du Mar.-Lyautey.*

Médiathèque Valéry-Larbaud★

🚹🕐 *Guided tours (1hr) Sat at 11am and 3pm. No charge.* ☎ *04 70 58 42 50.*

The local multimedia library presents a fascinating exhibition on the author **Valéry Larbaud,** who was born in Vichy in 1881. Around 14 000 books, 180 manuscripts, 8 800 letters and many other documents are displayed on antique furniture.

▶ *From place de la Victoire, turn left onto rue d'Allier. Look to your right along rue Besse; no 2 was the birthplace of the famous reporter Albert Londres (1884-1932).*

Église St-Blaise

The old church, altered many times over, has a highly venerated Black Virgin, known as Our Lady of the Sick and Suffering; only the statue's head is original (12C).

The new church has some beautiful modern stained-glass windows and mosaics. There is a lovely view from the belfry.

▶ *On leaving the church, follow rue Hubert-Colombier lined with villas illustrating a variety of styles. Turn left onto rue du Mar.-Foch.*

Musée Municipal

🕐 *Daily except Mon 2-6pm, Sat 2-5pm.*🕐 *Closed Sun and public holidays (Oct-Apr) and during Christmas holidays. No charge.* ☎ *04 70 32 12 97.*

Set up in the Centre Culturel Valéry-Larbaud, this small museum is devoted to local archaeology, contemporary painting, as well as coins and medals from Vichy. There is a collection of modern painting and sculpture with works by Gustave Moreau and Picasso. One room is devoted to Louis Neillot (1898-1973), a local landscape painter, who had a strong admiration for Cézanne.

▶ *The Opera Museum is opposite.*

Musée de l'Opéra de Vichy

🕐 *Daily except Mon 3-6pm. 3€ (children: 2€).* ☎ *04 70 58 48 20. http://opera.vichy. musee.free.fr/*

This museum presents in rotation the archives of the Grand Casino Theatre which were faithfully kept until the 1960s: costumes, accessories, posters, stage documents, programmes of all the operas performed from 1901 onwards...and some 10 000 photographs of artists, of famous people who visited the town, illustrating life in the spa resort.

Additional Sights

Musée des Arts d'Afrique et d'Asie

16 avenue Thermale (opposite Thermes Callou). 🕐 *Apr-Oct: daily except Mon 2-6pm. 3€.* ☎ *04 70 97 76 40. www.musee-aaa.com*

The former Musée du Missionnaire was completely reorganised in 2000-02. Exhibits collected by missionaries and private donations (4 000 items all together) were entered in a catalogue for the first time since the foundation of the museum in 1923.

A quarter of the collection is now displayed in eight rooms, inside a house dating from 1881 and it is planned to renew the exhibition regularly. A room on the ground floor retraces the history of the museum, another room is devoted to musical instruments from around the world. Asian art is also represented on this floor: furniture, coins from 720 BC to today, cloisonné enamels from Canton, statues of Buddha.

African art is displayed upstairs: objects of daily life (furniture, pottery) religious objects (small statues, amulets), objects used in performing rites (masks).

Parcs d'Allier★

These beautiful landscape gardens created at the request of Emperor Napoleon III are built on land reclaimed from the river. They are graced with trees of various species, lakes with swans and ducks, rock gardens, rose gardens and flowerbeds, and are ideal for long, peaceful strolls.

The Parc du Soleil provides all sorts of attractions for children.

Excursion

Around Vichy

75km/46.6mi – allow 2hr 30min.

▶ *Leave Vichy to the SE on D 906. Before entering Abrest turn left onto D 126, heading for Cusset, then right onto D 270 to Vernet. At the entrance to the village, on the right, a narrow road leads to a platform especially laid out as a site.*

Site des Hurlements

Viewing table. The view extends over the Vichy basin, the Allier Valley, the Limagne, the Monts Dôme and Bois Noirs.

▶ *Rejoin D 906 and continue until you reach the entrance to St-Yorre.*

St-Yorre

This small town famed for its numerous springs of mineral water has become an important centre for glassmaking and bottling.

▶ *Leave St-Yorre to the E on D 121.*

Château de Busset

🕐 *Jun-Sep: guided tours (45min) daily except Wed 2.30-6.30pm; Apr-May and Oct: Sat-Sun and public holidays 2-6pm. 5€. (children 3€). ☎ 04 70 59 13 97. www.busset.com*

Erected on a granite promontory over-looking the Allier Valley, this elegant castle has belonged to the same family for 14 generations. Although considerably remodelled since it was built in the 13C, the edifice has retained a drawbridge and four defensive towers including the fine **Tour d'Orion** topped by an octagonal roof.

Several galleries are open to the public; one of them contains beautiful 16C **frescoes**★ illustrating the maxims of a local poet; there are also 15C **murals** in the oratory situated in the prison tower. The only original pieces of furniture are

Busset

S. Sauvignier/MICHELIN

a 16C bed where King Henri IV slept when he visited his cousin César de Bourbon, the then Lord of Busset. and a heavy carved-oak chest offered by Caesar Borgia to his daughter Louise when she married Philippe de Bourbon in 1530.

From the terrace there is a magnificent **view** of the French and Italian-style gardens and, beyond, of the Limagne plain and Puys mountain range.

▶ *On leaving Busset, turn left onto D 121 running by the cemetery, then take D 995 on the left. D 995 crosses the River Sichon, offering pleasant views of the lower valley.*

Cusset

This town on the outskirts of Vichy is circled by wide avenues lined with century-old trees. **Place Victor-Hugo** has several gabled houses, notably the Taverne Louis XI. The door and window of the **Maison Barathon** are embellished with fine late-16C sculptures. Set up in Tour Prisonnière, the only vestiges of the 15C curtain wall, the **Musée Municipal** (🕐 *Jun-Oct: daily except Mon 2-7pm (guided tours of the underground passages). 4€. ☎ 04 70 96 29 17)* presents an exhibition on local history through an extensive collection of documents, weapons, costumes and headdresses, drawings, paintings, old implements and street plaques. The heavy wooden doors studded with iron locks remind visitors that this was once used as a prison.

▶ *Leave Cusset to the NE on D 906B.*

St-Étienne-de-Vicq

This hamlet has a Romanesque church with unusual architectural features. Note the historiated capitals at the entrance to the chancel.

▶ *Rejoin D 906ᴮ. In Bost, turn right onto D 190.*
At the church crossroads, take D 558, then turn right onto D 907. In Les Gadons, take D 174 on the right.

Pastillerie Vichy

🕐 *Daily except Sat-Sun 9am-noon, 2-6pm, Fri 2-6pm. Slide show (15min). 🕐 Closed public holidays, end Jul to mid-Aug. No charge. ☎ 04 70 30 94 70.*

A gangway overlooking the workshop will introduce visitors to the art of making and packaging **Pastilles de Vichy,** a type of boiled sweet made with Vichy water that became popular in the days of Empress Eugénie.

▶ *Bear right towards St-Germain-des-Fossés, then turn left onto D 27. In Vendat, take D 279 running along the railway tracks.*

Cognat

300m/330yd beyond the village, turn left onto a lane leading to the church. This unusual 12C building stands on a knoll commanding a pretty **view** of the Limagne and Monts Dôme.

▶ *Return to Cognat and turn right onto D 117.*

The road cuts across Montpensier Forest *(see AIGUEPERSE).*

Brugheas

🏃 Lying on the banks of the Sarmon, half way between the forests of Boucharde (to the east) and Montpensier (to the west), this village is an ideal starting-point for country walks and bicycles rides.

▷ *Leave Brugheas to the SE on D 221, heading for Hauterive. Before reaching the locality known as "La Tour," turn left onto the narrow stony lane bordered with meadows and small ponds.*

Source du Dôme

This bubbling spring, the hottest in the Vichy basin, yields algae that are used in the preparation of mineral mud baths. Opposite is the Source du Lys.

▷ *The path runs on for 700m/766yd through a small wood then across pastoral countryside. On reaching the surfaced road, turn left onto D 131 which leads back to Vichy via Bellerive bridge.*

VIC-LE-COMTE★

POPULATION 4 404

MICHELIN MAP 326: G-9 – 16KM/10MI N OF ISSOIRE

Vic-le-Comte lies in the middle of **Comté**, a region made up of a series of volcanoes which appeared in the Limagne at the end of the Tertiary Era, forming a transition between the plain and the Livradois mountains. The highest reaches an altitude of 807m/2 647ft, rising 400m/1 312ft above the Limagne. Most of the volcanoes have been eroded and only their chimneys remain, sometimes combined with outliers of lava flow. They are often crowned with ruined fortresses. There are more than 50 eruptive pinnacles, now covered in woodland; in the past, grape vines grew on the more exposed slopes. In the 8C a priory was established in the village (vicus in Latin) – which was probably of Gallo-Roman origin – by the Benedictine monks of Manglieu.

At the beginning of the 13C the Count of Auvergne, Gui II, after being defeated by King Philippe Auguste, saw his estate reduced to the Vic-le-Comte region, which was well protected by a ring of fortresses (Buron, Busséol etc). During the same period, the Cistercian abbey of Le Bouchet, near Yronde, became the necropolis of the regional lords. Through his marriage to an Auvergne heiress, a descendant of the kings of Scotland, John Stuart, Count of La Marche, took possession of the earldom and embellished the castle built by his predecessors at Vic-le-Comte. All that remains now is a doorway and the Sainte-Chapelle. From 1651 up to the time of the French Revolution, the earldom of Auvergne belonged to the dukes of Bouillon. Today, Vic-le-Comte has a papermill owned by the Bank of France which makes the watermarked paper used for bank notes printed in Chamalières. *Les Pradets, 63114 MONTPEYROUX, ☎ 04 73 96 68 80. www.vic-le-comte.fr*

Walking Tour

Sainte-Chapelle★

This, the Holy Chapel, is a beautiful Gothic building heralding the Renaissance. The cornice is decorated with sculptures of mythical beasts, crockets, thistles and human figures.

In the chancel, the statues of the Apostles, sheltered by canopies along the springing line of the vault ribs, date from the Renaissance; several have been restored. Catherine de' Medici, who owned Vic-le-Comte at one time, had the gallery and balustrade added.

The richly coloured **stained-glass windows**★, depicting scenes from the Old and New Testaments, have been restored. The very fine stone **altarpiece**★ (1520) is the work of the Florentine artists who made the balustrade: at the bottom, the three Cardinal Virtues and a wooden statue of St Anthony; at the top, the Three Theological Virtues. Note the 17C wrought-iron lectern and the interesting 15C painted-wood polyptych, illustrating the Passion and Entombment.

Window in the Sainte-Chapelle

Église St-Jean

This Romanesque church near the river was refurbished during the Gothic period. Note the fine 14C door. Inside, on either side of the chancel, are 13C and 14C frescoes depicting the lives of John the Baptist and St Blaise; in the nave, on the left, is a beautiful 15C wooden Crucifixion; the left-hand chapel contains a 16C statue of Our Lady of Compassion.

Old houses

Rue Porte-Robin (north-east of the Sainte-Chapelle) has several buildings with 15C and 16C façades. From the north-western end of the chapel go round to the right as far as the old town gate, **Porte Robin,** the only remains of the fortified curtain wall. Place du Vieux-Marché has a 16C fountain.

Continue straight ahead towards rue du Palais, at the entrance to which are two corbelled houses.

▶ *Take the covered passage on the right, rue des Farges, then rue de Coulogne beyond; turn back.*

Excursions

Manglieu

11km/6.8mi E on D 225. The village, once the site of a Benedictine abbey, lies in the Ailloux Valley, at a short distance from D 225 between Vic-le-Comte and Cunlhat. The **abbey church**★, which has undergone extensive external restoration, is particularly interesting for its interior. Enter the church by the attractive Romanesque doorway. Beneath the porch topped by a gallery is a sarcophagus to the left and two gravestones, the one on the left dating from the Carolingian period and the other

---

TWO COSY PROPOSALS

☻☻ **Chambre d'hôte Chris et Marcel Astruc** – *R. du Donjon - 63114 Montpeyroux - 8km/4.8mi SW of Vic-le-Comte - take A 75, exit 7 -* ☎ *04 73 96 69 42 - marcelastruc@ wanadoo.fr -* 🖻 *- 5 rms.* Built at the foot of the 13C donjon, this very attractive house offers personalized, tastefully decorated guestrooms on two levels, one of which has a fireplace. Stone is present throughout, giving the house a genuine charm.

☻☻ **Chambre d'hôte Les Pradets** – *Les Pradets - 63114 Montpeyroux -* ☎ *04 73 96 63 40 -* 🖻. Go to the end of an alleyway in the picturesque fortified village of Montpeyroux to discover this pretty residence. The cosy sitting room invites repose; guest rooms owe their charm to the parquet floors, carpets, rustic furniture and paintings by area artists. Garden in the inner courtyard.

Merovingian in origin. The nave was rebuilt in the 16C. The narrow 10C chancel is spoilt by distemper and a modern ceiling; it opens out from a triumphal arch supported on two ancient columns that were reused for this purpose.

Castles and Wine-Growing Villages

45km/28mi – allow half a day.

▶ *Drive S out of town along D 49. In Yronde, take D 136.*

Yronde
This is where Le Bouchet Abbey once stood. Note the lovely small church.

Buron
The road runs round the village, overlooked by the ruins of a castle perched on a peak of basalt rock.

▶ *Cross the River Allier and take D 229 on the left.*

Coudes
This ancient wine-growing village situated at the confluence of the Allier and Couze de Chambon once thrived on an important river traffic of wine bound for Paris.

▶ *Continue along D 229, across the A 75 motorway, then turn right on D 797.*

Montpeyroux★
Leave the car in the parking area at the exit of the motorway and explore the village on foot. This fortified hillside village overlooks the River Allier to the east and the A 75 motorway to the west. A medieval gateway gives access to narrow twisting lanes leading to the three-storey 13C **keep** (🕐 *May to mid-Oct: 10am-noon, 2-6pm; Mar-Apr: Sat 2-5pm, Sun and public holidays 2-6pm; Oct-Feb: during school holidays only. 2€ (under-12s: no charge). ☎ 04 73 96 62 68)*; from the top *(beware, access can be tricky)*, there is a fine panoramic view. Some of the old houses in the village have been carefully restored and their cellars are a reminder of the wine-growing past of the village which now welcomes a colony of artists and craftsmen.

View of Montpeyroux

▷ *Continue along D 797. In Authezat, turn left on D 96.*

La Sauvetat

This once fortified village has retained part of an ancient commander's residence belonging to the order of St John at Jerusalem and some old houses (12C-14C) in typical local style. The doorway of the **keep** (13C and 14C) is surmounted by the emblem of the order of St John and of Odon of Montaigu, head of the order in Auvergne. In the north transept of the **church** *(Visits can only be made by request at the town hall.* ☎ *04 73 39 52 55)*, inside a recess closed off by a railing, stands an interesting 14C Virgin and Child; the gilt and enamelled-copper statue was made in the region's workshops.

▷ *Leave La Sauvetat NE along D 630, cross the A 75 motorway and rejoin D 96.*

Corent

This village overlooking the River Allier clings to the north-eastern slopes of the Puy de Corent; it is known for its high-quality wine, one of the five vintages making up the Côtes d'Auvergne *appellation*.

▷ *Continue along D 786 then follow D 751 and cross the River Allier.*

The road follows the east bank of the river, jotted with wine-growing villages such as Mirefleurs *(D 1)*, La Roche-Noire and St-Georges-sur-Allier *(D 118)*.

▷ *On leaving St-Georges-sur-Allier, turn right on D 759.*

Château de Busséol★

🕐 *Mid-Jun to mid-Sep: guided tours (45min) 10am-noon, 2.30-6.30pm; rest of year: Sat-Sun and public holidays 2.30-5.30pm. 6€.* ☎ *04 73 69 00 84.*

The main façade collapsed in 1963 but has since been rebuilt with Romanesque-style windows.

Inside, note a **fireplace**★ which is still used today, with a rounded Romanesque mantelpiece, the circular room with domed roof in the main tower and the antique furniture. An interesting hanging garden adjoins the building. The view from the parapet stretches over part of the Dore and Dôme mountain ranges and the Limagne plain: "I am Busséol, near Billom," it says on an old manuscript, "I can see far and wide."

The small road branching off D 118 between St-Georges-sur-Allier and Lignat offers the best view of the castle.

▷ *Leave Busséol S and follow D 4 then continue on D 229. In the hamlet of Benaud, turn right on D 116 then take D 81. Park the car in St-Maurice and continue on foot.*

Puy de St-Romain★

45min on foot there and back.

🚶 The setting of the puy is striking; the summit, an ancient place of worship nearly 450m/1 476ft above the River Allier (alt 779m/2 560ft), offers a breathtaking **panorama**★ encompassing the Comté *Puys,* the Forez mountains, the Livradois mountains, the Vic-le-Comte basin, the Allier Valley, the Cézallier and Cantal mountains, the Dore and Dôme mountain ranges, Clermont-Ferrand and the Limagne.

▷ *Go to Longues on D 758 then follow D 1 and D 225 back to Vic-le-Comte.*

VIC-SUR-CÈRE★

POPULATION 1 890
MICHELIN MAP 330: D-5
20KM/12.4MI NE OF AURILLAC – LOCAL MAP SEE MONTS DU CANTAL

The old town of Vic in the Cère Valley, with its picturesque houses clustered around the church, is a spa town at an altitude of 681m/2 234ft with a mineral spring (pump room). *Av. André-Mercier, 15800 VIC-SUR-CÈRE, ☎ 04 71 47 50 68.*

A Bit of History

The "mad monk" – In the 12C Pierre de Vic, the youngest son of one of the local families, who had been forced to enter the church despite not having a religious vocation, was put in charge of a rich priory when he was still very young; he turned it into a pleasure-dome, composing drinking songs and love ballads there.
He gradually wearied of his sedentary life, however, and began to travel and sing his ballads at the courts of Philippe Auguste, Richard the Lionheart and the King of Aragon. The "mad monk," as he called himself, carried off first prize at the Courts of Love Literary Tournament and won the Golden Hawk at a contest at Le Puy.

Winning barrels (16C) – During the Wars of Religion an episode occurred near Vic which exemplifies the cunning of **Captain Merle.** He was escorting a convoy of supplies for the Huguenots when the Roman Catholics ambushed him in a gorge. Merle ordered the men to cut the mules' traces and flee. After they had gone some distance, he stopped the stampeding men, having calculated that the Catholics would fall upon the casks of wine instead of pursuing Merle's men. He proved to be right; after rallying his men, he counter-attacked, wiping out his drunken adversaries.
It was about this time that the bailiff's court was set up in Vic and the magistrates began to build their stately homes in the old part of the town.

Mademoiselle de Fontanges (17C) – Marie-Angélique d'Escorailles, a favourite of Louis XIV, was born at Cropières Castle (south-east of Vic). Her royal favour, however, was short-lived: she was said to be "as pretty as a picture, and as thick as a brick." She was awarded the title Duchess of Fontanges on giving birth in 1681 to a son, but she died of complications shortly afterwards, aged barely 20 years – "killed in the line of duty," as the Marquise of Sévigné somewhat cattily put it. It can hardly be said that the king missed her – Madame de Maintenon arrived just in time to console him.

Old Town

Turreted houses still grace the town centre, testifying to the city's former prosperity.

▶ *For a tour of the old city, allow 20-30min. Leave from place de l'Hôtel-de-Ville. Turn left towards place de Monaco.*

Note the elegant turreted house at no 4 passage du Chevalier-des-Huttes.

▶ *Turn left towards place de Monaco.*

WHERE TO STAY AND EATING OUT

⊜⊜ **Auberge des Montagnes** – *15800 Pailherols - 13km/8mi SE of Vic-sur-Cère via D 54 -* ☎ *04 71 47 57 01 - www.auberge-des-montagnes.com - closed 10 Oct-20 Dec -* 🅿 *- 22 rms -* ⊑ *7€.* If you'd like to benefit from the area's splendid natural environment, this characteristic house nestled in the heart of a little village is the place to stay. Hiking, cross-country skiing, mountain biking or swimming in one of the hotel's two pools – anything is possible. Simple rooms and tasty Auvergnat cuisine.

⊜⊜ **Family Hôtel** – *Av. Émile-Duclaux -* ☎ *04 71 47 50 49 - www.family-hotel.fr - closed 1-17 Dec -* 🅿 *- 39 rms -* ⊑ *7€ - restaurant* ⊜⊜. The name is well chosen: this hotel-club is just the thing for a family stay. Summer pool, covered pool, tennis court, ping-pong, a park, outings and events – they've got it all. Unpretentious cuisine; sober, functional rooms and studios.

Maison des Princes de Monaco

South of the church, off rue Coffinhal. This 15C house *(no 4)* served as a residence on several occasions for the princes of Monaco, to whom Louis XIII had given the Carladez region in 1642, the capital of which was Vic, and which remained in their possession until the Revolution.

The house has a turret with a mullioned window and a door surmounted by a badly damaged bas-relief depicting the Annunciation.

▶ *Continue on rue Coffinhal.*

Maison Dejou

At no 5, there is a small *hôtel particulier* from the late 17C with a semicircular pediment.

Retrace your steps. On the left, note the tower adjoining the façade of the École St-Antoine on rue du Moine-de-Montaudon.

▶ *Walk down to place de l'Église, pass behind the east end and follow the path to the waterfall.*

Lou Cap Del Liou

Pretty old mill spanning the Iraliot.

▶ *Walk up to the church.*

Église St-Pierre

This partly Romanesque building has undergone many alterations. Note the graceful apse and the curious modillions on the south façade. The interior has several features of *interest*: 13C and 15C keystones, 17C gilt-wood statues (St Roch and St Agnes), Pietà (in a north transept recess).

Opposite the church, the former bailiwick is now private property. Walk up to the calvary along rue du Dr-Civiale. From the chapel there is a fine panoramic view of the town.

Hiking Tours

Cascade du Trou de la Conche and Rocher de Maisonne

Behind the church, take the street leading to a footbridge over the Iraliot. On the other side of the torrent, walk up a very steep path. 🚶 *1hr 45min there and back.*

At the top of the rise the road divides: *(left)* to Trou de la Conche cascade, a very pretty setting; *(right)* to the top of Maisonne rock, surmounted by a Cross and giving a fine view of Vic and the valley below.

Grotte des Anglais

Leave Vic on N 122 towards Murat and immediately turn onto the road to La Prade. Park on the platform. 🚶 *1hr there and back.*

A small knoll commands a nice view of the spa, with Curebourse plateau and wood in the background.

▶ *Go to Fournol village (vestiges of a Roman bridge down below). Bear left to rejoin and cross RN 122.*

Opposite, slightly to the right, a signposted trail leads to the **Grotte des Anglais,** a cave that gave shelter to bandits and highway robbers during the Hundred Years War.

Excursions

Thiézac

9km.5.6mi NE along N 122. This is a sunny summer resort with a Gothic church (Église St-Martin) which houses a painted 15C statue of Christ seated at the Calvary, a 17C giltwood altarpiece and a fragment of a lace altar-covering given by Anne of Austria; and a chapel **(Chapelle Notre-Dame-de-Consolation)** which overlooks the village – it was after undertaking a pilgrimage here that Anne of Austria conceived, after 22 childless years of marriage, the future Louis XIV. The ceiling inside is adorned with 45 decorative paintings and roundels.

Cascade de Faillitoux

5km/3.1mi to the W. Leave Thiézac on the road to Vic and, soon after the graveyard, turn right onto D 59. Around 3km/2.1mi further on, the road goes through Lasmolineries village, offering views of the Faillitoux waterfall flowing from its basalt ledge.

Upper Goul Valley and Carladès

80km/50mi – allow one day

▶ *Leave Vic to the SE on D 54, heading for Raulhac and Mur-de-Barrez.*

Rocher des Pendus

Leave the car near Col de Curebourse (997m/3 271ft) and take the path on the right, opposite Auberge des Monts. 🚶 *45min there and back.* From this rock there is an extensive **panorama**★★ over the Cère Valley, the Cantal mountain range, Carladès rock, the Châtaigneraie and the Aurillac basin.

▶ *Continue along D 54.*

Église de Jou-sous-Monjou

Interesting Romanesque church with a fine belfry and a porch resting on a slender column.

▶ *Take D 59, then D 600 until you reach Raulhac.*

On the way, note the Château de Cropières (⊶ *not open to the public, but visible from the road*), a typical manor house from the Cantal region.

▶ *Continue along D 600 towards Mur-de-Barrez.*

Château de Messilhac

🕐 *Mid-Jun to end Aug: guided tours (50min) 2.30-6.30pm. 4€. ☎ 04 71 49 55 55.*

At the end of a beaten track, this former fortress stands proudly in a delightful bucolic setting. It was heavily remodelled in the 16C. The Renaissance façade, flanked by two square towers crowned by pointed roofs, is pierced with mullioned windows. The imposing **staircase** presents diagonal ribs and sculpted ornamentation depicting the Angels of Good and Evil.

▶ *On leaving Mur-de-Barrez, D 990 and D 459, on the right, lead to Ronesque rock.*

Rocher de Ronesque★★

This basalt rock forms a plateau 280m/918ft long and 180m/590ft wide, dominating the entire countryside. It was formed in the same way as Carlat rock on an old plain first covered by volcano activity then deeply gashed by large valleys.

The picturesque **hamlet** at the foot of the rock is typical of the Cantal where the houses often have roofs of stone slabs called lauzes. There used to be a fortified castle in Ronesque, given by Hugues, Count of Rodez, to Alphonse II, King of Aragon, in 1167. Alphonse wanted to establish a kingdom from Catalonia to Aquitaine for which Ronesque and Carlat would have been the outlying posts. Subsequently, the castle became the property of the Rastinhac de Messillac family.

Ascent of the rock

The little chapel can be reached by car. Viewing table (on the north side, opposite the chapel). From here the immense plateau and a magnificent **panorama**★★ can be seen: Carlat rock lies to the north-west *(move slightly to the left)*, the Cantal mountains to the north and the Aubrac mountains to the south. To the north, below, stands Messilhac Castle in the Goul Valley.

Rocher de Carlat★

The scenery here is typical of the Carlat area. The region was covered with basalt by lava flows from the volcanoes of Cantal; erosion fragmented the coating of rock, isolating a few flows which now stand, sheer-sided, at the top of steep hillsides. With its delightful valleys and its houses with steeply sloping hipped roofs of stone slabs surrounded by gardens and orchards, the Carlat region is a pleasant place to stay or travel around.

Carlat rock itself was once topped by a castle which protected the Upper Auvergne against invasion from Aquitaine and Spain.

▶ *Cross the breach and skirt, to the left, the north side of the rock.*

Rocher de Carlat

The Viscounts of Carlat

In the 12C the turbulent viscounts of Carlat became counts of Rodez. During the reign of Louis XI (15C), the Lord of Carlat, **Jacques d'Armagnac,** rebelled on several occasions. He was twice pardoned by the sovereign but was finally captured in Carlat after a siege lasting 18 months, taken to the Bastille where he was imprisoned in one of the iron cages that Louis XI was so fond of, and sentenced by a committee which had him tortured in order to make him speak "clearly." He was beheaded in the covered market in Paris.

The breach which cuts the rock in two was said to have been man-made, to isolate the western section on which the castle stood.

Climb the Escalier de la Reine (Queen's Staircase) carved out of the rock to reach the northern edge of the plateau; there is a wonderful **view**★ of the mountains of Cantal. Then climb Murgat rock, topped by a statue of the Virgin Mary: the view stretches southwards beyond the village, to the Carlat region. In the distance, to the left, is the rock and chapel at Ronesque.

▶ *Continue on D 990 until you reach Vézac. D 208 on the right leads to Polminhac.*

Château de Pesteils★

🕐 *Apr-Sep, 2-6.30pm (Jul and Aug: 10am-7pm). 6.550€. ☎ 04 71 47 44 36. www. chateau-pesteils-cantal.com.*

This beautiful medieval castle, built on a rocky promontory on the north bank of the River Cère overlooking the town of Polminhac, east of Aurillac, was one of the strongholds designed to defend the valley; it took the name Pesteils in the 16C. Some of the scenes in Jean Cocteau's film *Love Eternal* (1943) were filmed here.

The imposing 13C square keep, 35m/115ft high, is crowned with a machicolated watch-path. It overlooks terraces which closely follow the line of the old ramparts.

The tour begins with the guard-room followed by the main drawing room, lavishly decorated with tapestries, paintings and fine furniture. Two bedrooms on the first floor have ceilings which were painted in the 17C.

One of the rooms in the keep, which is connected to the second floor of the main building by a small stone bridge, has two 15C frescoes, one depicting a master and his pupil, and the other four heroes from antiquity.

On a clear day, the summit of the Plomb du Cantal can be seen from the watch-path.

Grand Salon

Château de Pesteils

▶ *Visits by candlelight are organised in summer.*

VIENNE★★

POPULATION 29 975
MICHELIN MAP 333: C-4

Vienne, "perched like an altar on the buttresses of the noble Dauphiné," to quote a local poet, is a town of exceptional interest. In a delightful **setting**★ basking in sunlight reflected from the Rhône, a Gothic cathedral stands next to a Roman temple, whereas Romanesque cloisters and several ancient churches rub shoulders with an Antique theatre. The charm of "Vienne the Beautiful" of Roman times is enhanced by the charm of "Vienne the Holy," the Christian city. The flower-filled pedestrian precinct, along cours Brillier and around the Hôtel de Ville, is a popular place for a leisurely stroll. A large market is held in the town centre every Saturday morning. Two bridges connect Vienne to the west bank of the Rhône. The old suspension bridge is now used as a footbridge; the modern bridge (1949) has a remarkable central arch with a span of 108m/354ft. A 15C humpbacked bridge spans the Gère. ▯ *Cours Brillier, 38200 VIENNE, ☎ 04 74 53 80 30. www.vienne-tourisme.com.*

▸ **Orient Yourself:** Situated 38km/24ml to the south of Lyon, and 52km/32ml east of St Etienne

▯ **Parking:** There are ample parking areas to the south of the town

☺ **Don't Miss:** The important Gallo-Roman city of St-Romain-en-Gal; the cathedral of St Maurice, and the Temple of Augustus ad Livia

◷ **Organizing Your Time:** Allow half a day to explore Vienne; maybe an hour to visit St Romain

☝ **Also See:** Lyon; the Chateau de Septème; les Monts du Lyonnais

A Bit of History

Vienne the Beautiful – More than 50 years before Julius Caesar conquered Gaul, the stamping ground of the Allobroges tribe – of which Vienne became the capital in the 1C BC – was subjugated by the Roman legions. In the absence of a more open site, the town was chosen for its geographical location which was easier to manage than that of Lyon as there was only one river to cross.

Public monuments were erected at the foot of Mont Pipet, with private residences and trade and craft establishments on both banks. Vienne soon extended its suburbs beyond the Rhône to the present-day villages of Ste-Colombe and St-Romain-en-Gal (see below). Drapers, leather workers and potters had flourishing businesses and the poet Martial described the town as "Vienne the Beautiful."

Joys and sorrows of "Greater Burgundy" – After the Western Roman Empire was dissolved in 476 and despite political confusion, Vienne remained a centre of artistic achievement: the construction of the church and necropolis of St-Pierre was continued; the foundations were laid for the abbey of St-André-le-Bas. The incessant in-fighting between the Carolingians for Charlemagne's heritage enabled Boson, Count of Vienne, Arles and Provence to proclaim himself "King of Burgundy" at Mantaille Castle in 879. His palace was in Vienne.

Vienne, the Holy City – As the distant Holy Roman Emperor only exercised nominal suzerainty, the temporal authority of the bishops, who were also the counts of Viennois, held sway over the city and over an area of land on the east bank of the Rhône. Around the abbey of St-André-le-Bas, which was at the height of its power, a large Jewish community plied a thriving trade. Two famous prelates sat on the

Address Book

EATING OUT

La Chamade – *24 r. Juiverie -* ☎ *04 74 85 30 34 - closed mid-Aug.* Exhausted after having climbed the steep alleys of the Medieval city centre? Gather your strength in this discreet little restaurant. The decor of white walls, yellow tablecloths and indirect lighting is simple, the service efficient and the prices quite affordable.

L'Estancot – *4 r. de la Table-Ronde -* ☎ *04 74 85 12 09 - closed 1-15 Sep, Christmas to mid-Jan, Sun-Mon and public holidays.* Interested in trying some *criques*, the delicious, Ardéchois potato pancake dish? Then come take a seat in this restaurant behind the St-André-le-Bas church. Featured for dinner daily, they can be ordered with vegetables, foie gras or prawns.

La Medina - *71 r. de Bourgogne -* ☎ *04 74 53 51 35 - closed mid-Jul to Aug.* Here, amid the cuisine and colours of Morocco, is a popular meeting place, a splendid setting in which to appreciate couscous and tagines.

WHERE TO STAY

Camping Bontemps – *38150 Vernioz - 19km/12mi S of Vienne via N 7, D 131 and D 37 -* ☎ *04 74 57 83 52 - info@ campinglebontemps.com - open Apr-Sep -* ⚑ *- reserv. recommended - 100 sites - food service.* Tourism and sports are on this campground's programme. Set off hiking or sight-seeing to discover the region – unless you'd rather stay put and take advantage of the on-site sports facilities to go horseback riding, mountain biking or swimming in the pool. Bungalows available.

Hôtel Central - *7 r. de l'Archevêché -* ☎ *04 74 85 18 38 - www. hotel-central-vienne.com - closed 9-14 Aug and 6 Dec to 18 Jan - 25 rms -* ☲ *7€.* In the heart of the city, as its name implies, this simple hotel's best feature is its central location. The impeccably kept rooms are spacious enough and have been fitted with wood veneer furniture.

La Margotine – *Chemin de Pré-Margot - 38370 St-Prim - 3km/1.8mi from Les Roches de Condrieu -* ☎ *04 74 56 44 27 - www.lamargotine.com - 6 rms.* A villa built in the 1970s whose principal attribute is its position overlooking the Vallée du Rhône and its vineyards. Personalized bedrooms, some a bit compact; three benefit from the fine view. Breakfast on the panoramic veranda.

ON THE TOWN

Canicule – *5 r. Cornemuse -* ☎ *04 74 85 40 22 - Tue-Thu, Sun 8pm-1am, Fri-Sat 'til 3am..* 'La canicule' means 'the dog days' - will this new cocktail bar succeed in turning up the heat in the rather complacent city of Vienne? In a pretty, exotic setting, you can order sizeable cocktails spiked with varying (generally generous) quantities of alcohol. A small dance floor attracts more energetic patrons. Warning: the prices are fairly high.

Bar du Temple – *5 pl. du Gén.-de-Gaulle -* ☎ *04 74 31 94 19 - summer: 7am-midnight; rest of the year: Mon-Sat - closed public holidays.* This is THE café that everyone who's anyone in Vienne knows about. Its best feature is the superb terrace at the foot of the Temple d'Auguste and de Livie. In spite of the influx of tourists, it has retained its convivial ambience and regular clientele.

O'Donoghue's Pub – *45 r. Francisque-Bonnier -* ☎ *04 74 53 67 08 - 4pm-3am.* All year round, this Little Brittany in Vienne holds Celtic music concerts attended by a cluster of Breton 'ex-pats'. Composed of two small rooms with a nautical decor, the pub is run under the expert hand of a lively, fervent Bretonne. If you've never tasted a Coreff, typical Breton beer, this is your chance.

The Celtic House - *5 r. Allmer -* ☎ *04 74 53 43 40 - 5pm-3am.* The House is managed by an ex-rugbyman, epicurean to boot. If you'd care to have a bite between two beers or while watching a rugby match with a specialist, there's no doubt that this address is for you.

SHOPPING

Markets – On Saturday mornings, the streets of centre city, from the banks of the Rhône to the Jardin de Cybèle, overflow with enticing market displays.

This is the perfect time to shop for a few bottles of Côte-Rôtie, a delicious Côte-du-Rhône wine made in the region.

Ets Patissier Jean-Guy – *16 place de Miremont* - ☎ *04 74 85 08 77* - *Tue-Sun 8am-7.30pm* - *closed last wk of Jan and Jun.* Founded in the 1970s and remodelled in 2000, this pastry shop-cum-tearoom's fine reputation has spread throughout the province. Its chocolate, made with the finest cocoa beans, pastries made with grade AA butter, ice cream and cakes are devilishly delicious. The varied clientele is not limited to powdered ladies sipping Earl Grey and nibbling babas au rhum – the young set also comes here to indulge in the finer things of life.

Maison J. Colombier – *Rte de Marennes* - *15km/9mi N of Vienne via N 7 and D 36 - 38200 Villette-de-Vienne* - ☎ *04 74 57 98 05* - *www.poire-colombier.com* - *Mon-Sat 9am-noon, 2pm-7pm, holidays by appointment.* Joannès Colombier invented Poire William's in the 1930s; today his daughter and son-in-law oversee the production of this heady, aromatic pear brandy. Try to visit in September-October, when the still simmers and exquisite wafts of eau-de-vie perfume the atmosphere.

THEATRE

Théâtre de Vienne – *4 r. Chantelouve* - ☎ *04 74 85 00 05* - *mid-Sep to Jul: Mon-Fri 10am-noon, 2pm-6.30pm, Sat 3pm-6pm performance days.* Built in the early 18C, when Marivaux, Goldoni and Beaumarchais prevailed, this theatre, whose façade was renovated in 1930, exudes history and charm. Events of all genres are staged here, including drama, classical and pop music, dance, opera and children's shows.

throne of the "primate of the primates of the Gauls – **Gui de Bourgogne** (1088-1119), crowned Pope in his own cathedral under the name of Calixtus II, and **Jean de Bernin** (1218-66), who directed the extensions to the cathedral of St-Maurice based on Gothic principles, ordered restoration of the Roman bridge over the Rhône, and built a hospital and the Château de la Bâtie.

Numerous ecclesiastical councils were held in the town, notably that which suppressed the Order of the Templars in 1312.

An unequal combat – The presence of Church land within the confines of the Kingdom and Empire did not leave the French monarchy indifferent. In 1335 Philippe de Valois annexed Ste-Colombe and had a tower built to mark the takeover. In 1349 the eldest sons of the House of France were endowed with the Dauphiné region as an apanage; they were to vie with the archbishop for temporal jurisdiction of the town itself. The Dauphin Louis, the future Louis XI, had himself appointed joint sovereign lord of the city, concurrently with the archbishop. French annexation was completed in the 15C, when Dauphiné was finally united with France.

Modern times – During the centuries of the Renaissance and the absolute monarchy, Vienne's decline offers a painful contrast with the prosperity of Lyon – commercial activity collapsed and the population dropped by one-fifth between 1650 and the beginning of the 18C. Even the bridge over the Rhône, swept away by flooding in 1651, was not rebuilt until the 19C. A certain industrial rebirth occurred once the Revolution had swept away the Ancien Régime, however, with the establishment of clothing manufacturers along the Gère. Leather work, the fruit trade and numerous processing industries have reactivated local business today.

Walking Tour

Roman and Christian Vienne★★

▶ *Leave from place St-Maurice.*

Cathédrale St-Maurice★★

Built from the 12C to 16C, the cathedral combines both Romanesque and Gothic elements. The patronage of St Maurice is a reminder of the veneration given to martyrs of the Theban Legion in the Burgundian kingdoms.

B. Kaufmann/MICHELIN

Doorways

The west front with its three doorways is adorned with fine Flamboyant ornamentation. Although the Wars of Religion deprived it of the statues decorating the niches of the engaged piers and tympana, the delightful decoration of the covings has fortunately remained intact.

Cathédrale St-Maurice

The late-14C **south doorway** *(right)* has two covings: the inner row depicts the prophets seated under canopies; the outer row has pairs of musician angels. The gestures and attitudes of the figures make for a very lively group.

The **central doorway,** with its cut-off gable, dates from the late 15C. It has three covings with sculptures which are to be read horizontally. They depict related episodes from the Old and New Testament.

In the tympanum of the portal, above the twisted columns, there are two statues personifying the Church on the left and the Synagogue on the right.

The **north doorway** *(left),* from the second half of the 15C, is devoted to the Virgin. At the top of the central niche two angels with folded wings are carrying the Virgin's crown. The inside coving depicts six-winged cherubim; on the outside coving, musician angels are involved in various liturgical functions.

Interior

The vast (97m/318ft long), luminous tripartite nave, with no transept, reflects a surprising harmony despite its construction over a period of four centuries.

The far seven bays enclosing the Gothic nave are Romanesque. Reminiscent of Roman times, the piers are flanked with antique-style pilasters and fluted half-columns; this stage of construction, from the early 12C, is contemporary with or slightly later than the pontificate of Gui de Bourgogne.

The four bays of the nave nearest the west front were built in the 15C in pure Gothic style, their engaged columns rising in an unbroken line to the base of the ribbing.

A marble bench runs around the circumference of the apse; the bishop's throne (cathedra) sits in the axis of the nave. Above the bench, small columns support a cornice above a marble frieze inlaid with brown cement; a second frieze, in the same style, runs above the triforium.

This decorative technique is of oriental inspiration – the first example is to be found in the church of Hagia Sophia in Istanbul (Constantinople) – and reached the Rhône Valley via Italy (San Marco in Venice); it is characteristic of Viennois-Lyonnais art: the apse of St-Jean Cathedral in Lyon is a typical example. The **Romanesque capitals** form a decorative whole, closely inspired by Antiquity. They feature narrative scenes (right aisle) or whimsical subjects; some are in a transitional style, with the figures concealed by foliate designs.

In the apse, on the right of the High Altar, stands the **mausoleum** of archbishops Arnaud de Montmorin and Henri-Oswald de La Tour d'Auvergne (1747), by **Michel-Ange Slodtz;** it is one of the finest 18C works in Dauphiné.

Around the chancel 16C **Flemish tapestries** depict scenes from the life of St Maurice.

A splendid Renaissance stained-glass window, the **Adoration of the Magi,** throws light from the east into the chancel from the right aisle. The stained-glass clerestory windows in the chancel date from the 16C; the central window depicts St Maurice, in armour, with St Peter.

The north aisle has interesting sculptures: between the sixth and seventh chapel a large 13C bas-relief depicting the meeting of Herod and the Magi is striking for the very noble poses; an amusing detail is the two grotesque heads on either side of Herod, symbolizing his two-facedness – one, turned towards the kings, appears to listen to them attentively while the other, unseen by them, is laughing maliciously.

A covered passageway (north aisle) once connected the cathedral to the ancient cloisters, which no longer exist. Notice, by the entrance, the capitals with their very fine foliate decorations. Above the arch is a white-marble frieze reproducing the signs of the Zodiac; in the 16C these were changed around to correspond to the new order of the year fixed by the Edict of Roussillon (with 1 January as the start of the year, instead of the previous regional variations), which explains why the monogram of Christ with the alpha and omega which was originally in the centre of the frieze is now out of place.

In the passageway, a Gothic arcade frames three Romanesque statues in the archaic manner; on the left, St Peter; on the right, St John the Evangelist and St Paul. The long flowing drapery and the feet inclined on an oblique support evoke Languedoc art – note the ascetic head of St Paul, looking meditatively from under heavy eyelids.

▶ *Leave the cathedral along the covered passageway (north aisle).*

Outside, the decoration on the door of the north wall combines Romanesque and Gothic elements with Roman fragments. Beneath the pointed arch, delicate griffons and leaves decorate the lintel.

Place St-Paul was once the site of the cloisters.

▶ *Walk to place du Palais.*

You will be taken aback by the beauty of the Roman temple standing in the centre of the square, pleasantly contrasting with the 18C façades of the houses framing place du Palais.

Temple of Augustus and Livia★★

This is a rectangular building of agreeable proportions. Its dimensions (24m/79ft long, 14.5m/47ft wide and 17m/56ft high) are approximately the same as those of the Maison Carrée, the well-known Roman temple in Nîmes. A row of six Corinthian columns supports the entablature on the façade and the sides; the carved ornamentation is better preserved on the north side. The rear part, which is the oldest, probably dates from the end of the 1C BC.

The façade, facing east, overlooked the forum. It was rebuilt under the reign of Augustus, perhaps after a fire. Its triangular pediment bore a bronze inscription to the glory of Augustus and Livia, his wife. Inside was the statue of the deified emperor.

The temple has undergone numerous alterations. During the Middle Ages it was turned into a church and all the columns were linked together by a wall. The seat of the Jacobite Club during the Revolution, it was used to celebrate the cult of the goddess Reason; it was subsequently used as a court, a museum and a

Roman temple

J. Damase/MICHELIN

library and it was not until the mid-19C that the walls were removed from the columns and the building restored.

▶ *Rue des Clercs leads to the church of St-André-le-Bas.*

Église and Cloître St-André-le-Bas★ – 👤 *See below.*

▶ *Take rue de la Table-Ronde to rue Marchande.*

At no 32, there is a beautiful portal with coving and a carved arch stone.

▶ *Continue to rue des Orfèvres.*

No 11 has a 15C-16C inner courtyard whereas no 9 has a beautiful Renaissance façade.

▶ *Turn around and take rue du Collège on the right.*

Église St-André-le-Haut
This church was once a Jesuit College chapel but was consecrated to St Louis in 1725; it has a beautiful Classical façade.

Théâtre Romain★ – *See below.*

▶ *Take rue des Célestes, then walk down montée St-Marcel to rue Victor-Hugo and the archaeological gardens.*

Jardin Archéologique
A white-stone double archway is the only remaining part of a **portico,** thought in the past to be part of some Roman baths; note the fine decorative frieze on the inside. On the right of the portico is a wall which formed the northern side of a **theatre** said to have been reserved for performances of the Mysteries of Cybele. The set-backs in the wall correspond to passageways providing access to the tiered seats.

▶ *Take rue Chantelouve, then rue Ponsard to the Musée des Beaux-Arts.*

Musée des Beaux-Arts et d'Archéologie – *See below.*

▶ *Cours Romestang, then boulevard de la République, lead to place St-Pierre.*

Additional Sights

Église St-André-le-Bas★
Same admission times as for the cloister (see below). ☎ *04 74 85 50 42.*
Apart from the lower parts of the east end, the apse (except the central bay), a large part of the southern wall and a few later additions, the church is mainly 12C. The large freestone gable wall provides an unusual decorative effect. The whole of the decoration is remarkable: piers and colonnettes on the twin openings, small festooned arches ending in consoles bearing expressive masks.
The Salle du Patrimoine (Heritage Gallery) hosts a **standing exhibition** on the theme "The Many Faces of Vienne."

▶ *Walk into the southern courtyard flanked by the base of the bell-tower.*

The first mask to be seen is poking out an enormous tongue.

VIENNE

11-Novembre R. du	AZ	43
Allmer R.	BZ	2
Allobroges Pl. des	AZ	
Anatole-France Quai	BCY	
Aqueducs Ch. des	CY	
Asiaticus Bd	AZ	
Beaumur Montée	BCZ	
Boson R.	AZ	
Bourgogne R. de	BY	
Brenier R. J.	BY	
Briand Pl. A.	BY	3
Brillier Cours	ABZ	
Capucins Pl. des	BCY	
Célestes R. des	CY	4
Chantelouve R.	BY	5
Charité R. de la	BCY	6
Cirque R. du	CY	7

Clémentine R.	BY	8
Clercs R. des	BY	9
Collège R. du	BY	10
Coupe-Jarret Montée	BZ	
Éperon R. de l'	BY	12
Gère R. de	CY	
Jacquier R. H.		
Jean-Jaurès Q.	AYZ	
Jeu-de-Paume Pl. du	BY	15
Jouffray Pl. C.	AZ	
Juiverie R. de la	BZ	16
Lattre-de-Tassigny		
Pont de	ABY	
Laurent R. Florentin	AZ	
Marchande R.	BY	
Miremont Pl. de	BY	18
Mitterrand Pl. F.	BY	19
Orfèvres R. des	BY	20
Pajot Quai	BY	22
Palais Pl. du	BY	23

Peyron R.	BZ	24
Pilori Pl. du	BY	25
Pipet R.	CY	
Pompidou Bd Georges	AZ	
Ponsard R.	BY	28
République Bd et Pl.	ABZ	29
Riondet Quai	AZ	
Rivoire Pl. A.	CY	
Romanet R. E.	ABZ	
Romestang Cours	BZ	
St-André-le-Haut R.	CY	34
St-Louis Pl.	BY	
St-Marcel Montée	CYZ	
St-Maurice Pl.	AY	
St-Paul Pl.	BY	
St-Pierre Pl.	AZ	
Schneider R.	CY	37
Sémard Pl. P.	BZ	
Table-Ronde R. de la	BY	38
Thomas R. A.	CY	

Tupinières Montée des	CZ	
Ursulines R. des	CY	39
Verdun Cours de	AZ	
Victor-Hugo R.	BCYZ	

STE-COLOMBE
(Rhône)

Briand Pl. A.	AY
Cochard R.	AY
Égalité Pl. de l'	AY
Garon R.	AY
Herbouville Q. d'	AY
Joubert Av.	AY
Nationale R.	AY
Petits Jardins R. des	AY

Ancienne Église		
St-Pierre	AZ	
Cathédrale St-Maurice	BY	
Cité gallo-romaine de		
St-Romain-en-Gal		
(Musée)	AY	
Jardin archéologique		
(Portique)	BY	
Mont Pipet	CY	
Musée de la Draperie	AZ	
Musée des Beaux-Arts et		
d'Archéologie	BY	M¹
Palais du Miroir	AY	
Pont Suspendu	AY	
Pont de Lattre-de-		
Tassigny	AY	
Porte de l'Ambulance	CY	N
Pyramide	AZ	
Temple d'Auguste		
et de Livie	BY	R
Théâtre romain	CY	
Tour-Philippe-de-Valois	AY	
Église St-André-le-Haut	CY	
Église St-Martin	CY	
Église de Ste-Colombe	AY	
Église et cloître		
St-André-le-Bas	BY	

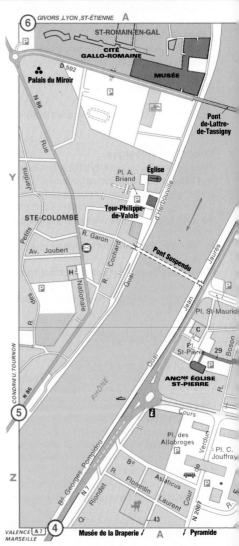

The nave was originally covered with timber framing; the restoration in 1152 consisted of raising and vaulting it, which required the construction of outside flying buttresses and reinforcement of the walls by arches and piers.

The decoration of the fluted pilasters is attributed to Guillaume Martin who signed and dated his work (1152) on the base of the second pier from the right; the most beautiful capitals depict Samson overwhelming the Lion (second pier from the left). The two superb Corinthian capitals at the entrance to the apse are from a Roman monument. An exhibition area situated below the church presents a large wooden statue of St Andrew (17C) with a magnificent face; the painted wood panel depicting the Adoration of the Magi (1543) is displayed in the Museum of Fine Arts.

▶ *Leave the church through the north door.*

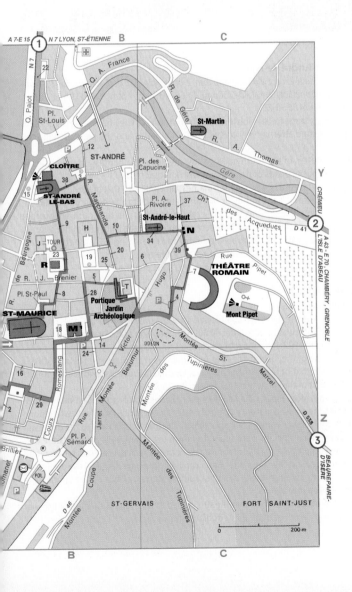

St-André-le-Bas cloisters

Cloître St-André-le-Bas★

🕐 *Apr-Oct: daily except Mon 9.30am-1pm, 2-6pm; Nov-Mar: daily except Mon 9.30am-12.30pm, 2-5pm (Sat, Sun, 1.30-5.30pm).* 🕐 *Closed 1 Jan, 1 May, 1 and 11 Nov, 25 Dec. 2.50€.* ☎ *04 74 85 50 42.*

These small, trapezoidal cloisters date from the 12C. They have a series of blind arcades, resting alternatively on twinned colonnettes and the piers marking the bays.

The colonnettes in the south gallery show an element of fantasy: spiral or zigzag fluting, strings of beads or palm leaves with knotted stems.

The cloisters house a large collection of Christian epitaphs – that of Fœdula, a townswoman of Vienne baptised by St Martin, dates back to the beginning of the 5C – and medieval inscriptions from funerary monuments. In the south-east corner are fragments of the chancel (stone screen separating the clergy from the faithful) decorated with strapwork, rope-moulding and interlacing (9C), together with a white-marble altar (11C) from the church of St-Pierre.

The terrace provides a view of the Rhône and Ste-Colombe.

Théâtre Romain★

As for the cloister.

The Roman theatre had been abandoned since the time of Emperor Constantine, in the early 4C, and was buried under 80 000m³/2.8 million sq ft of earth when excavations began in 1922; it has now been completely uncovered.

This was one of the largest theatres in Roman Gaul; its diameter (131m/430ft) is greater than that of the Roman theatre at Orange in Provence and is only 1m/3ft less than that of the great theatre of Marcellus in Rome.

Backing onto Mont Pipet, it had 46 tiers over a series of well-preserved vaulted passageways; the dressed masonry stone of the tiers was entirely faced with white stone slabs. It could seat nearly 13 500 spectators. The four tiers closest to the orchestra pit, reserved for officials, were separated from the others by a green-marble balustrade. Some of the marble slabs on the floor of the stalls can still be seen and the front panel on the stage floor has a copy of a fine animal frieze, the original of which, made of white marble, is in the Lapidary Museum. Unusually, a temple rose above the top row of tiers.

Every year in summer, the main theatre is used as a venue for the highly popular international **Jazz Festival** (🕯 *see Calendar of events*).

Musée des Beaux-Arts et d'Archéologie

As for the cloister.

The Fine Arts and Archaeology Museum is housed in a 19C covered market and comprises several collections: prehistoric and Gallo-Roman antiquities; 18C French earthenware (Moustiers, Lyon, Roanne, Marseille, Rouen, Nevers); paintings from the 17C and 18C European Schools and the Lyon, Vienne and Dauphiné Schools; works by the Vienne sculptor, J Bernard (1866-1931).

Note in particular the 3C Roman silverware (goblets, platter finely engraved with pastoral and hunting scenes), discovered by accident on the current site of place C.-Jouffray in 1984.

Ancienne Église St-Pierre★

The church of St-Pierre, now converted into a Lapidary Museum, is the oldest building of Christian Vienne, dating back to the 5C. The church, mainly used as a funerary basilica, was the burial place of the bishops of Vienne. St-Pierre, built "outside the walls," was to suffer from the devastations of the Saracens in about 725, followed by those of the Carolingian princes in 882.

In the 12C the abbey of St-Pierre was at the height of its prosperity. It was at that time that the beautiful Romanesque bell-tower, forming a porch at ground level, was built to a rectangular plan. The openings at the intermediate level are surmounted by trefoil arches, reminiscent of Velay art. It was at this time that the nave was divided into three by a number of large archways (restored in the 19C).

Juno

The **south door** (12C) used to lead to the abbey cloisters. Two small octagonal columns are topped by capitals symbolising Humility and Pride on the left and Charity on the right. The inscription on the tympanum frames a magnificent statue of St Peter which could be compared with the statues on the north porch of the church of St-Maurice, particularly with regard to the technique of the garments, with their long, almost concentric folds.

Musée Lapidaire

As for the cloister.

On the left and opposite the entrance of the Lapidary Museum are two Roman works: a monumental head of Juno and a beautiful marble statue, the "Tutela" or protective goddess of the town.

In the apse, on the left, lies the beautiful marble **sarcophagus** of St Léonien, a 6C Vienne monk, with a symbolic decor of peacocks pecking grapes.

Note, in the chapel to the right of the apse, a **crouching Venus,** a collection of amphorae, busts of emperors and a marble low-relief sculpture depicting a sacrificial ceremony.

Nearby, the **church of St-Martin** (🕐 *Mon and Thu, 9.30-11am, Wed, 9.30-11am, 3-6.30pm),* decorated with frescoes by the painter Maurice Denis (1870-1943), who belonged to the Nabis movement, has a very fine, ancient carved-wood crucifix.

St-Romain-en-Gal and Ste-Colombe *allow 3hr*

St-Romain-en-Gal and Ste-Colombe, on the west bank of the Rhône, are located in the Rhône administrative *département* whereas Vienne, opposite, is in the Isère *département*. In Ancient times, these three towns formed a single urban centre.

Gallo-Roman City of St-Romain-en-Gal★★

Excavations of the site since 1967 have unearthed an urban district including not only sumptuous villas but also businesses, workshops and thermae (hot baths). The most outstanding finds are displayed in the museum.

Museum★

&⊙ all year, daily except Mon 10am-6pm. ⊙ Closed 1 Jan, 1 May, 1 Nov, 25 Dec. 4€; no charge on Thu. ☎ 04 74 38 49 32. www.musees-gallo-romains.com.

This on-site museum was designed as a showcase which presents the archaeological site on the one hand and the Rhône and Vienne of today on the other hand. It is housed in a structure resting on piles, fixed in the walls of the **Maison au Lion** (Lion House) due to be excavated at the beginning of the 21C.

A staircase, situated just before the entrance, leads to a terrace offering a panoramic view of the town, the river and the excavations. The site includes a wealth of workshops and sumptuous residences, the most splendid of all being the **Maison des Dieux Océan** (House of the Ocean Gods).

The **Dieux Océan mosaic★**, now the emblem of the site, welcomes visitors and entices them to discover the marvellous works of art of the Gallo-Roman period. Vienne was a thriving city under Roman occupation; the River Rhône, which played a key role in the town's prosperity, separated the city itself from the more residential district of St-Romain-en-Gal which, even so, was quite lively according to some recent finds: **Thermes des Lutteurs** (Wrestlers' baths) and a huge open space covering 80 000m2/95 680sq yd.

Local craft was thriving: pottery (note the splendid oven and the huge *dolia* which contained up to 1 000l/220gal of wine), bone-carving and fabric-making. The piles found in the Rhône and the reconstruction of a merchant ship (from a model found in Toulon) emphasize the economic importance of the river. Two models illustrate

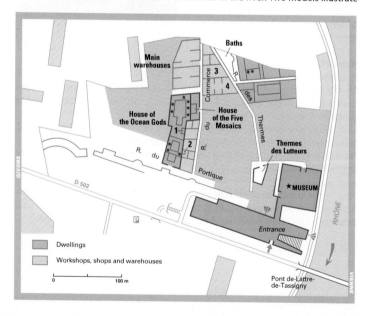

the activity of Vienne's and St-Romain-en-Gal's warehouses which covered an area of 60 000m²/71 760sq yd.

However, the main asset of the site are the magnificent floor mosaics which are as beautiful as the *opus sectile* pavings, made with much larger marble slabs. Motifs were often inspired by mythological subjects. Walls were usually tastefully painted with great refinement as the **Échassiers**★ and the **Lutteurs** paintings testify.

A large section of the museum is devoted to the vast houses of the nobility which often covered more than 1 000m²/1

Duck mosaic

196sq yd, the main areas being the entrance *(atrium)*, the garden *(vividarium)*, the dining room *(triclinium)* and the bedroom *(cubiculum)*. Several footbridges enable visitors to get an overall view of these reconstructed areas. The visit ends with the splendid mosaic representing the **Châtiment de Lycurgue**★★ (Lycurgus' Punishment).

Information terminals and an audio-visual room *(showing five films)* are invaluable for those who wish to learn more about the period and about the latest excavating and restoration techniques.

Archaeological site★

The remains found in the area of over 3ha/7.4 acres which has been excavated so far indicate occupation from the end of the 1C BC to the 3C AD, though the structure of the area does not correspond to the grid layout usually adopted by the Romans; three roads and two streets mark out five irregular plots, which have not been completely cleared. A portico runs along the side of **rue du Portique,** from east to west. **Rue du Commerce** and **rue des Thermes,** which run approximately north-south, converge in the northern part of the site.

The roads are made of large smooth granite slabs above sewers designed to collect wastewater and discharge it into the Rhône.

Dwellings

At the entrance to the site is a vast residence, the **House of the Ocean Gods,** running north-south and forming a rectangle 110m/360ft long and 24m/79ft wide; its southern entrance is its only connection with the outside. The vestibule had a mosaic floor depicting ocean gods with bearded heads and long flowing hair, and marine motifs. Next is a small garden with a peristyle enclosing two pools – one U-shaped and the other rectangular. The large garden to the north, with its portico, occupying one third of the surface area, is slightly off-centre with regard to the other rooms. To the west can be seen a restored **hypocaust** heating system (**1**).

To the north of the House of the Ocean Gods is the **House of the Five Mosaics,** named after the different mosaic floors discovered mainly in the peristyle, the *triclinium* and the reception room.

North-east of the site, on the other side of rue des Thermes, is another residential area with **houses,** and **baths** that follow a typically Roman arrangement: hypocaust, *caldarium* (hot room), *tepidarium* (warm room) and *frigidarium* (cold room). Near the entrance, other baths have been excavated and the beautiful murals of the **Thermes des Lutteurs** have been added to the museum's collections but a faithful copy helps to preserve the beauty of the place.

Workshops, shops and warehouses

These are spread out unevenly over the site. Between the House of the Ocean Gods and rue des Thermes are several rooms, one of which (**2**) shows an ingenious device to preserve perishable foods: carefully arranged amphorae are fixed in the earth by their necks, thus creating an underfloor space.

Along rue du Commerce, to the north-west, stand **large warehouses** or "horrea," covering more than 3 000m2/32 100sq ft. The eastern façade has a single entrance, large enough for carts to pass through. Around the central courtyard are compartments with a floor drained by a system of upturned amphorae (*see above*).

The triangular block formed by rue du Commerce and rue des Thermes is a craftsmen's district, bordered to the east and the west by porticoes. The rooms in the northern building contain a network of pipes; this area is followed, to the south, by a workshop consisting of nine rooms arranged around a central courtyard. The presence of basins in some of the rooms suggests that they were used by fullers or dyers (**3**). The base of the triangle, known as "the market" (**4**), was occupied by workshops and shops.

The discovery of colouring products, at the corner of rue du Portique and rue du Commerce, indicates the existence of a small dyer's workshop.

Sainte-Colombe

During Roman times this suburb was filled with luxurious residences decorated with works of art and immense mosaics. The most important discoveries were made in the **Palais du Miroir.** Vast thermae were given this name in the 17C because one of the pools was thought to be an ornamental lake; its remains are visible at the boundary between Ste-Colombe and St-Romain-en-Gal.

Tour Philippe-de-Valois

The tower was built next to the Rhône by Philippe de Valois in 1343, after Ste-Colombe became part of the royal domain.

Church

This ancient chapel contains a remarkable 14C **sculpture group**★ in white marble of St Anne instructing the Virgin Mary *(left of the entrance)*.

Excursions

La Pyramide

Leave Vienne S on cours de Verdun and turn right onto boulevard F-Point. The monument (about 20m/65ft high) rests on a small square portico and used to adorn the central forecourt of the vast Vienne amphitheatre in the 4C.

During the Middle Ages it was thought to be the tomb of Pontius Pilate; according to legend, after leaving Jerusalem for Vienne, the Roman procurator, struck with remorse, threw himself into the Rhône. Pilat mountain range is said to be named after this event (there is a similar legend attached to Mount Pilate near Lucerne in Switzerland).

Trips by bateaux-mouches are available in both directions between Vienne and Lyon during the tourist season.

Ternay

13km/8mi N. Leave Vienne N on N 7 and turn left onto D 150^E. The 12C **church,** perched on the edge of a hillock overlooking the Rhône, is an interesting example of the Rhône Romanesque School. It belonged to a Cluniac priory and was formerly dedicated to St Mayol. The upper part of the west front, the south front and the apsidal chapels consist of alternate rows of brick and tufa.

J. Damase/MICHELIN

Venus turns her face to Septème Castle

Inside, the most attractive part is the main apse, with its oven vault and blind arcade with pilasters carved with interesting capitals. South of the church can be seen the remains of the cloisters.

Beauvoir-de-Marc

19km/12mi E. Leave Vienne on D 502 and, at La Détourbe, turn left onto D 53^B. The small 11C-14C **church** with its painted, coffered ceiling consisting of 70 caissons stands on a hillside. A path leads to the top of the hillock – notice the layers of rounded pebbles in the subsoil along the slope. At the foot of the statue of the Virgin Mary *(viewing table)* there is a **panorama**⋆ of the Viennois hills, dominated by the sombre mass of Mont Pilat to the west.

St-Mamert

13km/8mi S. Leave Vienne on N 7 S and turn left onto D 131^A. The **chapel of St-Mamert,** with its 11C belfry-wall and 17C restored interior, is built on a terrace of pebbles which offers an extensive view of the Pilat mountain range.

Château de Septème

12km/7.5mi E on D 502 and D 75. 🕐 *Apr-Oct: guided tours (45min) Sat-Sun and public holidays 2-6pm. 6€ (under-10s: free; 11-18-year-olds: 4€).* ☏ *04 74 58 26 05.*
Not far from Septème village, this picturesque castle was built in the 14C and 15C and remodelled in the 16C; overlooking the inner courtyard are Renaissance loggias on two storeys and a colonnaded gallery. Note the monumental, 60m/197ft-deep well.
The castle is surrounded by curtain walls dating from an earlier age: extending over almost 1km/0.6mi, they have kept many of their loopholes and part of the watch-path.

VILLARS-LES-DOMBES

POPULATION 4 190
MICHELIN MAP 327: J-3/4 OR 328: D-4 – LOCAL MAP SEE LA DOMBES

The flower-decked town of Villars-les-Dombes lies on the east bank of the River Chalaronne, at the heart of the Dombes region famous for the diversity of its bird population.

A Bird's Paradise

Parc des oiseaux★
1km/0.6mi S of Villars on N 83. ♿🕐 *May-Sep: 9.30am-7.30pm (Jul-Aug, 9.30am-9.30pm); Oct-Apr: 9.30am-5.30pm. From 7€ (children: From 6€).* ☎ *04 74 98 05 54. www.parc-des-oiseaux.com*

Kids This bird sanctuary, located close to the Dombes Nature Reserve, along one of the main migration routes in Europe, has a surface area of 23ha/57 acres, 10ha/25 acres of which are occupied by ponds. Over 2 000 birds from the five continents live in the park, from the African ostrich to the South American fly-bird to the Australian penguin.

At the entrance, the **"Birds' House"** provides a warm, humid atmosphere for a wonderful selection of brightly coloured exotic birds – hornbills from South-East Asia, gouras from New Guinea, toucans etc. Enjoy a walk round the park along the footpaths running round the lakes (it is possible to take the small tourist train) which are the breeding ground of large birds such as common herons and night herons as well as rarer species living in giant aviaries. Besides the spectacular **Vallée des rapaces** (Birds of prey), the **Volière du Pantanal** (tropical aviary) and the **Cité des perroquets** (parrots) are also fascinating. The park is engaged in several conservation programmes aimed at endangered species. These are explained to children through various activities in the **Maison des enfants.**

Church
This Gothic building with its panelled nave is decorated in the Flamboyant style. At the back of the apse *(right)* note the interesting 18C **Virgin and Child★**.

Spoon-bill

J. Damase/MICHELIN

VILLEFRANCHE-SUR-SAÔNE

POPULATION 59 261
MICHELIN MAP 327: H-4 – LOCAL MAPS SEE BEAUJOLAIS AND LA DOMBES

This busy industrial and commercial city is the capital of the **Beaujolais** region. It was founded in 1140 by the lords of Beaujeu, to match the Anse fortress belonging to the Archbishops of Lyon. The settlement sprang up quickly, and in 1260 Guichard IV de Beaujeu granted the town a charter, which earned it the name of *Ville Franche*, **meaning free town.** 🛈 *96 r. de la Sous-Préfecture, 69400 VILLEFRANCHE-SUR-SAÔNE,* ☎ *04 74 07 27 40. www.villefranche.net.*

La Vague – Every year, on the last Sunday in January, local conscripts celebrate the **Fête des Conscrits.** Those eligible to take part are men between the ages of 20 and 80. Dress code for the occasion is a black suit and top hat, decorated with a coloured ribbon (different colour for each decade: 20s, 30s etc). At 11am the participants form up into a procession, in which they link arms and, clutching colourful bouquets of mimosa and carnations, make their way along rue Nationale close on each others' heels, in what is known as the Friendship Wave *(La Vague de l'Amitié).*

"La Vague"

J. Damase/MICHELIN

Modern Villefranche – In addition to its historical role as a wine trading centre, Villefranche now earns its living from the manufacture of sports and work wear (Joannès Sabot founded an overalls factory here in 1887), shirts and hosiery. The metallurgy, mechanical and food-processing industries are also represented here.

The numbering of houses in Villefranche is based on a metric system, calculating the distance of each house from the beginning of the street. Street numbers run from rue Nationale east and west, and south from the north of town.

Visit

Old houses
Guided tour of the town: mid-Jun to mid-Sep: Sat, 9.30am and 3pm. 7€. ☎ *04 74 07 27 40. www.villefranche.net*
Most of the town's oldest houses built between the 15C and 18C are to be found along **rue Nationale.** They have relatively narrow façades, because of a tax imposed on the width of house façades in 1260, to make up for the exemption from taxes and the other privileges which had been granted to the town in its charter.

Odd-numbered side of the road
Note nos 375 (vaulted passageway), 401 (16C openwork spiral staircase in the courtyard) and, at no 17 rue Grenette the turret staircase with skylights. In the courtyard of no 507 the well is surmounted by a shell-shaped canopy in the courtyard. At no 523, the **Hôtel de Mignot de Bussy** is a lovely Renaissance building with a spiral staircase, mullion windows and shell-shaped niche containing an elegant statue. Behind the splendid 1760 façade of no 561, a vaulted passageway with sculpted

supports leads to a 16C courtyard surrounded by pink-walled buildings. The **Maison Eymin** at no 761 has an 18C façade with four levels of arches in the courtyard, hammer-wrought coats of arms (damaged) and an elegant turret housing a spiral staircase. No 793, once the residence of the Roland de la Platière family, is indicated by a medallion and a commemorative plaque and features a monumental staircase with a beautiful wrought-iron bannister.

Even-numbered side of the road

From no 400, there is a good view of the polygonal tower and sculpted stone balustrade of the Italian Renaissance house at no 407 opposite. A 15C half-timbered house stands on the corner of rue du Faucon and rue Nationale (no 476). At no 486, at the back of the alley on the right, a Renaissance bas-relief depicts two cherubs with chubby cheeks holding coats of arms with the date 1537.

The **Auberge de la Coupe d'Or** at no 528 was the oldest inn in Villefranche (late 14C) before it was transformed in the 17C. On the corner of rue Paul-Bert, the façade on the right (no 596) with crocket gables dates from the late 15C, and that on the left with moulded mullioned windows and medallions is Renaissance. Note the Gothic corner niche at no 706. A passage at no 810 leads to a restored courtyard (well, arcade, turret).

The old **town hall** at no 816 was completed in 1660. The façade is built of beautiful warm golden Jarnioux stone and has a solid oak door decorated with cast-iron nails. The house at no 834 was built in the late 15C and has a charming courtyard with a staircase turret. The coat of arms is that of Pierre II de Bourbon and Anne de Beaujeu.

VILLEFRANCHE-SUR-SAÔNE							
Nationale R.			Ancien hôtel de ville	BZ	B		
République R. de la	AZ	41	Auberge de la Coupe d'Or	BY	D		
Carnot Pl.	BZ	9	Savigny R. J.-M.	AZ	47	Hôtel Mignot de Bussy	BY	E
Faucon R. du	BY	19	Sous-Préfecture Pl.	AZ	49	Maison Eymin	BZ	F
Fayettes R. des	BZ	20	Sous-Préfecture R.	AZ	50	Niche du Pélican	AZ	K
Grange-Blazet R.	BZ	23	Stalingrad R. de	BZ	52			

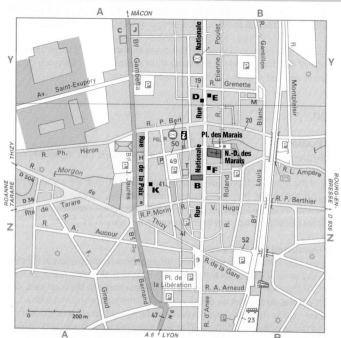

Address Book

EATING OUT

🍴 **Ferme-auberge La Bicheronne**
– *Le Bicheron - 01480 Fareins - 10km/6mi
NE of Villefranche. Take D 44, then at
Beauregard take dir. Château de Fléchères
via D 933 and 2nd road on right towards
'Le Bicheron' -* ☎ *04 74 67 81 01 - closed
Jan, Mon and Thu – reserv. recommended.* Wielding her saucepans and whisks,
the owner of this farm has been delighting well-fed guests for over twenty
years. Her farm chickens and guinea
fowl, generally accompanied by a *gratin
dauphinois*, are popular with the natives
who appreciate her culinary talents.

WHERE TO STAY

🛏🛏 **Emile Job** – *01190 Montmerle-sur-
Saône - 13km/8mi N of Villefranche. Take
N 6 to St-Georges-de-Reneins, then D 20
-* ☎ *04 74 69 33 92 - www.hoteldurivage.*
*com - closed 1-15 Mar, 22 Oct to 14 Nov,
Sun evening from Oct to May, Tue lunch
from Jun to Sep and Mon - 22 rms -* 🖾
8€ – restaurant 🍴🍴. Located just
before the bridge crossing the Saône,
here is a hotel-restaurant with a lovely
terrace surrounded by linden trees.
The rooms are bourgeois and clean,
the renovated dining room is rather
elegant, the menus are varied and the
reception is hospitable: most enjoyable.

🛏🛏🛏 **Hôtel Plaisance** – *96 av. de
la Libération -* ☎ *04 74 65 33 52 - www.
beaujolais-hotel.com - closed 24 Dec to 1
Jan -* 🅿 *- 68 rms -* 🖾 *9€.* An impeccably managed family hotel across from
l'Esplanade de la Libération. True, the
decor in the lounge is somewhat dated,
but the recently renovated rooms, each
with its own style, are clean and nicely
furnished.

Rue de la Paix

The façade of the building to the south of the post office features a "pelican niche,"
a Gothic sculpture decorated with finials and pinnacles. Next to it, set slightly further
back, is a pretty Renaissance well.

Place des Marais

This pretty square to the north-east of the church contains a fountain and is enclosed
by modern houses with arcades, painted in shades of pink and ochre. On the corner
with rue Nationale, a ceramic plaque depicts Pierre II de Bourbon and Anne de Beaujeu in the same pose as that on the famous triptych by the Master of Moulins.

Notre-Dame-des-Marais

In the 13C a chapel was built in honour of a statue of the Virgin Mary which had been
found in a nearby marsh (marais); all that now remains of it is the small Romanesque
tower above the chancel. The magnificent Late Gothic (16C) façade of the church
was donated by Pierre de Bourbon and Anne de Beaujeu.
Inside, the nave is surprisingly high and has pretty vaulting decorated with sculpture
and pendant keystones. The organ was made by J Callinet in 1835. Note the gargoyles
on the north façade; one of them represents lust.

Excursions

Ars-sur-Formans

6km/3.7mi E along D 904. This tiny Dombes village was once the spiritual charge of
the priest **Jean-Marie Vianney** (1786-1859), who was canonised in 1925. The "priest
of Ars" subsequently became the patron saint of parish priests and the village has
therefore become a popular place of pilgrimage.

Pilgrimage

The small village church is now abutted by a basilica built in 1862 to plans by Pierre Bossan. Inside, the saint's body reposes in a magnificent shrine. The bare concrete crypt, built half underground and 55m/179ft long, is the work of one of the architects of the basilica dedicated to St Pius X in Lourdes.

The old presbytery has been kept as it was when the priest of Ars died. Visitors can see the kitchen, the priest's bedroom and the "relics room," containing mementoes of the priest. An audio-visual show in a room by the presbytery gives an insight into the saint's personality. The **Chapelle du Coeur** (🕐 *Possibility of guided visits. No charge.* ☎ *04 74 08 17 17. www.arsnet.org)* houses a repository which contains the priest's heart, and a marble statue by the sculptor Émilien Cabuchet (1819-1902) showing the priest at prayer.

The largest annual pilgrimage takes place on 4 August, the anniversary of the priest's death.

L'Historial

Walk down the high street. ♿🕐 *Mar-Aug: 10am-noon, 2-6pm, Mon 2-6pm; Sep-Feb: Sat-Sun, public and school holidays, 2-5pm. 5€ (under 7s, free; 7-15, 3€).* ☎ *04 74 00 70 22. www.musee-ars.org.*

Thirty-five waxworks figures, made by the workshops of the Musée Grévin (Paris' answer to Madame Tussaud's), are displayed in a series of 17 tableaux illustrating scenes from the life of the saintly priest.

Château de Fléchères★

6km/3.7mi NE along D 933. The early-17C château stands in a shaded 30ha/74-acre park offering pleasant strolls. Built by a wealthy Protestant from Lyon, the edifice included a *temple* (Protestant church) on the third floor of the central building. The huge hall beneath the church was used for gatherings of the local Protestant community. The owner's living quarters were confined to the wings, which were lower than the central building. The interior is decorated with superb Italian frescoes (1632) believed to be the work of Pietro Ricchi.

VIVIERS

POPULATION 3 413
MICHELIN MAP 331: K-7

It was this episcopal town, created in the 5C, which gave its name to the province of Vivarais. Its location, boxed in between Jouannade hill and the rocky peak on which the upper town is built, meant that it remained almost untouched by the Industrial Revolution. Only the quarries, originally opened in about 1750 by the Pavin brothers in the hamlet of Lafarge north of the town to produce cement, are witness to the conversion of a small Ardèche business into a firm of international rank. The ecclesiastical town, built at the foot of the cathedral, commands a view of the Rhône as it enters Donzère gorge. The contrast between the cliffs on either side of the river, the isolated peaks in the middle of the gap and the stately flowing river upstream of Châteauneuf power plant form a picturesque sight. 🛈 *5 Pl. Riquet, 07220 VIVIERS,* ☎ *04 75 52 77 00.*

The bishops of Viviers – After Alba-la-Romaine, the Roman capital of the Helvia people, fell into ruins, Bishop Ausonne went to live in Vivarium, at the confluence of the Escoutay and the Rhône where the city had its port, at the foot of a rock on which a Roman *castrum* was established. The first cathedral was built on the rock.

In the 5C the upper town was fortified. In 1119 Pope Calixtus III inaugurated a new Romanesque cathedral. A college of canons settled into Château-Vieux, which, enclosed by still-visible ramparts, became an ecclesiastical quarter.

Numerous donations and skilful politics gradually turned the Viviers bishops into the overlords of an immense domain east of the Rhône – the Vivarais. They fiercely defended its independence against the covetousness of the counts of Toulouse, sharing ownership with them of the Largentière mines and minting their own coins. In 1248, St Louis, leaving for the seventh crusade, was their guest at Château-Vieux.

At the end of the 13C the French monarchy wanted to expand its territory into the Rhône Valley. The Bishop of Viviers finally recognised the suzerainty of the King of France in 1308; a large part of the Vivarais became "Crown" land, whereas the west bank of the Rhône remained "Empire" land, under the distant control of the Holy Roman Emperor.

At the foot of the rock, inside a second set of ramparts, a medieval city began to develop. All that remains of the defence towers and the main doors is a clock tower, the **Tour de l'Horloge,** which was extensively refurbished in the 19C. In 1498 Claude de Tournon, once the chaplain of Anne of Brittany, became Bishop of Viviers; he had the Romanesque cathedral destroyed and a Flamboyant Gothic chancel built.

Noël Albert, a nouveau-riche entrepreneur who had made his fortune in the salt trade and tax collection, had the Renaissance façade of the Maison des Chevaliers built. After becoming head of the Protestants, he captured the ecclesiastical city. As a result, the cathedral was partly ruined and the cloisters and canon's buildings destroyed. Albert was arrested and beheaded, but the bishop had already fled Viviers and did not return until 1731. That year, François Reynaud de Villeneuve began construction of the current bishop's palace according to the drawings of the Avignon architect J-B Franque.

On Boxing Day (26 December) Viviers, like all the towns in the south of France in the Middle Ages, organised a "Fête des Fous," or "Madmen's Festival," a highly irreverent parody of ecclesiastical customs, with actors playing members of the clergy and a "mad bishop" who "governed" the city for three days.

The general merrymaking and drinking bouts led to such excesses that the bishops eventually banned the festivities, which were later resumed with a lesser degree of licentiousness until finally they came to an end in the 18C.

Old Town★

The ecclesiastical town is distinct from the lower town, built to the west on the less steep slope of the rock. They communicated via two gates, **Porte de la Gâche** to the west and **Porte de l'Abri** to the south. The houses in the lower town, in a tight cluster, are roofed with Roman tiles; sometimes the walls are made of calcareous quarry stone mixed with basalt. They generally consist of two upper storeys and a ground floor housing a high cellar or a shop. Most of them have kept their medieval appearance despite the many alterations which have been carried out over the centuries. The houses in the ecclesiastical town hide their gardens and courtyards behind bare walls with semicircular openings, sometimes surmounted by a coat of arms.

▸ *Park on place de la Roubine. Follow rue J.-B.-Serre and Grande-Rue as far as place de la République.*

From the eastern corner of the square there is a view of the ruins of Châteauvieux Tower.

Maison des Chevaliers

The "Knights' House," also called the house of Noël Albert, was built in 1546. On the beautiful Renaissance façade observe the four high-relief figures on the lower

Maison des Chevaliers

part, separated by corbels decorated with acanthus leaf designs, and coats of arms surmounted by a helmet. The ornate window-frames on the first floor consist of columns and fluted pilasters with Ionic capitals; rams' heads and garlands of leaves have been carved on the lintels, between the modillions. Above are two bas-reliefs: on the left, a cavalcade of knights on horseback and on the right, a jousting tournament.

Over to the right, across rue de la République, an archway with small Gothic openings is decorated with several carved heads.

Grande-Rue

This street is lined with meticulously dressed façades, some of which have ornate portals surmounted by wrought-iron balconies such as **Hôtel de Tourville** and **Hôtel de Beaulieu** (18C). Occasionally the houses are enhanced by picturesque details, such as the beautiful Romanesque twinned windows coupled together by a column topped by a capital.

Grande-Rue leads to a series of little cross-streets, narrow, stepped and often spanned by arches.

Beyond the site of the former Porte Latrau lies a square planted with plane trees.

Place Prosper-Allignol

The square is flanked by two buildings erected between 1732 and 1738 by Franque. Their Classical symmetry and neat stonework makes them beautiful examples of 18C Viviers architecture: the former bishop's palace, preceded by a garden, houses the **Hôtel de Ville,** whereas **Hôtel de Roqueplane** is the seat of the current Catholic diocese.

▶ *Walk up the steep montée de l'Abri, which passes under Porte de l'Abri and leads to place de l'Ormeau.*

The street offers a fine view over the chapel of Notre-Dame du Rhône, rebuilt by Franque, and the mouth of the Donzère gorge.

Place de l'Ormeau

The square, lined with old canons' houses (17C) owes its name to a centuries-old elm tree *(ormeau)* which perished in 1976; a new tree has been planted. From the square, the rich Flamboyant decoration of the cathedral's east end can be admired.

▶ *Take the parapet walk (Chemin de Ronde) around the cathedral; from place de la Plaine, a passageway north leads to a vast terrace.*

Belvédère de Châteauvieux

This belvedere, built on a natural acropolis at one time washed by the Rhône during floods, stands 40m/131ft above place de la Roubine. The **view** from west to east embraces the old roofs of the city, the clock tower, the enormous cutting formed by the Lafarge quarries, the cooling towers of Cruas power station and the factory at Châteauneuf.

In fine weather, the view extends *(north-east)* to Trois-Becs and Chaudière pass, the first foothills of the Vercors massif.

The ruins of a medieval tower can be seen in the south-west corner of the terrace.

▸ *Turn round and go downhill via rue de Châteauvieux (on the right) to Porte de la Gâche.*

With its smooth cobblestones, covered passageways and arches, rue de Châteauvieux has a picturesque medieval air.

▸ *Climb the steps to the tower.*

Tower

In the 12C this tower formed the entrance to the upper town. Only the square part of the building existed at the time, with a Romanesque chapel dedicated to St Michael on the first floor. The octagonal 14C top floor is covered with a paved platform surmounted by a watch-turret: the *Bramardière,* from which the brameur would sound the alarm in case of danger.

The tower, since turned into the cathedral belfry, is connected to it by a quadrangular portico with Gothic openings.

Cathédrale St-Vincent

The only remains of the 12C Romanesque building are the porch, the west front and the lower part of the nave walls.

The chancel, built at the end of the 15C by Bishop Claude de Tournon, is remarkable for its Flamboyant **ribbed vaulting** ★ and the fenestration of its stained-glass

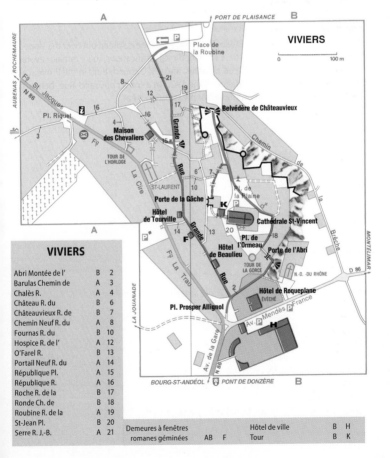

VIVIERS

Abri Montée de l'	B	2
Barulas Chemin de	A	3
Chalès R.	A	4
Château R. du	B	6
Châteauvieux R. de	B	7
Chemin Neuf R. du	A	8
Fournas R. du	B	10
Hospice R. de l'	A	12
O'Farel R.	B	13
Portail Neuf R. du	A	14
République Pl.	A	15
République R.	A	16
Roche R. de la	B	17
Ronde Ch. de	B	18
Roubine R. de la	A	19
St-Jean Pl.	B	20
Serre R. J.-B.	A	21

Demeures à fenêtres romanes géminées	AB	F	Hôtel de ville	B	H
			Tour	B	K

windows. The nave (rebuilt in the 18C) has a meticulously dressed flat stone vault by Franque.

On the left of the organ (19C) is an **Annunciation** attributed to Mignard.

Excursions

Viewing point from the Chapelle Notre-Dame-de-Montcham★

The belvedere to the right of the chapel commands a lovely panorama of Mont Ventoux.

Défilé de Donzère★★

14km/9mi S on D 73 and D 144 to Donzère and then D 486 to the river. This is a very picturesque canyon through which the River Rhône flows. The vertical wall of the west bank contrasts with the isolated peaks lining the east bank. The sharpest of these is crowned by a statue of St Michael, the guardian of this passage which was once feared by boatmen. This point is traditionally considered to be the gateway into Provence. The bridges upstream and downstream of the canyon offer attractive views of it.

▶ *Do not stop on the bridges. Park the car after crossing the first bridge, within sight of Viviers, and walk down to the Rhône along the path leading to the camp site (15min on foot there and back).*

Donzère

About 5km/3mi S on N 86 and D 486. The terraced village is spread out over the slopes of a hill, at the foot of a 15C castle. Of the medieval fortifications, there remain several vaulted streets, ramparts pierced by gates, and a 12C church built in the Provençal Romanesque style and remodelled in the 19C. On a corner of Grand-Rue, beneath a porch, note the stone instruments for measuring wheat.

PARC NATUREL RÉGIONAL DES VOLCANS D'AUVERGNE

MICHELIN MAPS 326: E-6 TO F-9 AND 330: E-1 TO F-5

This park is the largest of all France's regional nature parks, covering more than 395 000ha/976 045 acres along a north-south axis of about 120km/75mi. It encompasses 153 localities in the *départements* of Puy-de-Dôme and Cantal and has a resident population of 91 000. Five main natural regions make up the park: the **Dôme** mountain range of volcanic hills *(puys)*; the **Dore** massif, the vast grass-covered basalt plains of **Cézallier**; the **Artense** with its granite hills, moorland and valleys dotted with lakes and peat bogs; and the **Cantal** mountains.

The main aim of the park, founded in 1977, is to protect the region's exceptional natural and architectural heritage, which it does by running nature reserves and making good any sites which have fallen into disrepair. It is also involved in boosting the local rural economy – based largely on agriculture and handicrafts – and developing tourism in the region (information centres, overnight lodging for ramblers, marked footpaths and itineraries, cross-country skiing).

Maisons du Parc

The following centres inform visitors about activities within the park and present the local flora and fauna as well as typical local products.

- Maison des Fromages, Égliseneuve d'Entraigues
- Maison du Buronnier, Belles-Aigues near Laveissière
- Maison de la Pierre, Volvic
- Maison de l'Eau et de la Pêche, Besse-en-Chandesse
- Maison de la Faune, Murat
- Maison des Fleurs d'Auvergne, Lac de Guéry
- Maison des Tourbières, St-Alyre-ès-Montagne
- La Chaumière de Granier, Thiézac

Fauna and flora

The region's extremely varied flora includes some 2 000 different species; among these are gentians, Alpine anemones, bilberries, valerians…as well as plants which grow in bogs. The local fauna is just as varied. Mountainous areas are the natural habitat of moufflons, chamois and marmots. Wild boars, roe-deer, foxes, martens and genets (rarer) live in forests. There are numerous birds of prey including eagle owls and other owls, short-toed eagles, kites, and goshawks.

STAYING IN THE PARK

🍽🍽 **Les Voyageurs** – *15380 Le Falgoux -* ☎ *04 71 69 51 59 - closed 5 Nov-20 Jan and Wed evening except May-Sep - 14 rms -* 🛏 *6€ - restaurant* 🍽🍽. A cantou (large hearth lined with benches) has pride of place in the bar belonging to this traditional Auvergne inn. The rooms, recently rejuvenated, have retained their rustic character. Spacious country-style dining room peeking out at the mountains.

🍽🍽 **Eterlou** – *15380 Le Falgoux -* ☎ *04 71 69 51 14 - closed 12 Nov to 30 Mar - 10 rms -* 🛏 *7€*. A small village hotel-restaurant with a view of the mountains. Of a contemporary, streamlined style, the studio bedrooms are located in an old house behind the church. A rustic dining room and veranda are the setting for a meal with regional overtones.

VOLVIC

POPULATION 4 202

MICHELIN MAP 326: F-7 – 14KM/8.7MI N OF CLERMONT-FERRAND

Volvic is built on the edge of the solidified lava flow from Nugère volcano. The village is not only famous for the extremely pure water of its spring, filtered through thick layers of volcanic rock and now exported throughout the world, but also for the quarrying and processing of its lava. ☐ Pl. de l'Église, 63530 VOLVIC, ☎ 04 73 33 58 73. www.volvic-tourisme.com

Volvic lava – Andesite, extracted from open quarries, is both solid and light; this pale-grey rock has been used as building stone since the 13C and the fact that many buildings in the Auvergne are black is due to atmospheric pollution and not to the stone's original colour. Volvic cemetery is full of extraordinary monuments cut from this stone.

The hardness of the lava and the fact that it can be enamelled at high temperatures have made it popular, for more than a century, for the manufacture of signs and plaques which have to stand up to the weather: clock faces, street signs, level gauges etc. As a result of its exceptional qualities, this rock was chosen by Michelin's road sign department to make enamelled lava corner-posts, signposts, wall plaques etc from 1920 to 1970. Andesite is also used to make apparatus used in the chemical industry, because of its excellent resistance to acids.

Sights

Church

This was part of the old priory of Mozat; its nave and façade were rebuilt during the 19C. The vast 12C chancel is surrounded by an ambulatory opening onto three radiating chapels; a beautiful wrought-iron grille, from the Romanesque period, closes the axial chapel. There are interesting historiated capitals. At the entrance to the chancel, on the left, note the 14C Virgin with a Bird.

Musée Municipal Marcel-Sahut

⚅⚄⚅ Mid-Feb to mid-Jun and Mid-Sep-Nov: daily except Mon and Tue, 2-5pm; mid-Jun to mid-Sep: daily except Mon, 2-6pm. ⚅ Closed Dec-Jan, 1 May. 3€, no charge on Wed. ☎ 04 73 33 57 33.

The museum displays many works by Sahut, who was a native of this region, including charcoal sketches, watercolours and paintings (View of Nantes, The Tumbler).

The first rooms in this museum contain Far Eastern and African art, though the majority of the exhibitions concentrate on 19C and 20C drawings, engravings and paintings.

Drawings★ by Daumier and Grévin show the art of the caricaturist under the Second Empire.

The last room has an unusual **collection of half-coconut shells**★ which are decorated with scenes engraved by prisoners in the French penal colonies of Cayenne and New Caledonia in the 18C and 19C.

Maison de la Pierre de Volvic

⚅ Mar to mid-Nov: guided tours (1hr) 10am-noon, 2-6pm. Wear warm clothing in all seasons (temperature between 5°C/41°F and 14°C/57°F). ⚅ Closed 1 May. 5€. ☎ 04 73 33 56 92.

A former underground quarry has been used to create the House of Stone, a centre focusing on lava and lava quarrying. Visitors travel to the heart of a **lava flow**★ from the Puy de la Nugère, while a soundtrack reproduces the noises during different phases of a volcanic eruption.

The result of quarrying can be seen in the uneven ceiling, supported by three enormous piers cut directly from the lava, one of which is in the form of a crescent. An audio-visual presentation retracing the origins of volcanism in the Auvergne, quarry work and the use of Volvic stone complete the visit.

Volvic Springs
🕐 *Apr-Oct: Mon-Fri, 9am-noon, 2-6pm.* 🕐 *Closed 1 May. No charge.* ☎ *04 73 64 51 24.*

In the **Information Centre** there is a presentation of the hydrologic characteristics of the Volvic area and of the bottling of its mineral water; there are also audio-visual shows about the Auvergne and its volcanoes.

🚶 A network of footpaths on the site provides visitors with opportunities for walks *(from 15min to 1hr 45min).*

Statue of Notre-Dame-de-la-Garde
Access: from the spring (continue along the road then turn right) or from Volvic (via rue de la Bannière and rue du Calvaire, then park near the water tower).

🚶 A path *(15min there and back)* leads to the monumental statue of the Virgin, from which there is a beautiful panorama.

Excursion

Exploring the Monts Dôme

25km/15.5mi – allow half a day

▶ *Leave Volvic to the N on D 15, heading for Châtelguyon. Turn left before the graveyard.*

Château de Tournoël★
🕐 *Apr-Jun and Sep: daily except Mon, 2-6pm; Jul-Aug: 10am-12.30pm, 2-7pm. 6€ (children: 3€).* ☎ *04 73 33 53 06. www.tournoel.com*

Château de Tournoël

Two Eccentric Owners

Around 1500, Tournoël Castle was owned by a 21-year-old widow, Françoise de Talaru, who used all her charms to attract the high society of Riom to the castle, with a never-ending succession of hunts, feasts, games and balls. However, a covetous rival in the shape of her brother-in-law, joint-guardian of her daughter, on whom he also appeared to have designs, gave her some cause for concern. She managed to drive him from the castle but the judge of Montferrand, to whom the matter was referred, severely reprimanded the widow calling her "Circe, Melusine, magician and witch" and stripped her of her guardianship. The artful Françoise, however, promised her seven-year-old daughter to the judge's son in marriage and even managed to bewitch the old judge himself, who married her and died soon afterwards.

Charles de Montvallet was one of the members of the Auvergne nobility to be condemned in 1665 in the wake of the Fronde uprising against the French monarchy. In his time, he had fathered so many illegitimate children, that he had them brought up at Tournoël Castle so that he could employ them as domestic help. One was even given the job title "Chef des Bâtards."

Tournoël Castle, rising on the crest of a rocky spur overlooking the whole of the Limagne, is one of the most interesting castles in the Auvergne. The castle was owned by the counts of Auvergne when Philippe Auguste, king of France, captured and almost entirely destroyed it in 1213. In the 14C, however, it was rebuilt by Hugues de la Roche, who widened the bases of the towers.

The ruined castle changed hands in 2000 and the new owner has declared his intention to be able to live in it within five years. Visits will continue during the restoration of the castle.

Near the entrance to the castle is a viewing table from which there is a beautiful view of the Limagne plain, the Forez mountains and the Livradois.

Pass the 16C **Tour des Miches** (Loaf Tower), which used to defend the entrance, on the right. Its name derives from the lumps in its walls of lava, which looked like large loaves of bread. The castle consists of three sections: a massive square keep protected by a double curtain wall, a high circular keep enclosed within a triangular curtain wall, and, between the two, the main buildings built around a courtyard.

Ground floor

A steep climb leads up to the entrance to the first courtyard. It contains a square keep with foundations that date back to the 12C. Enter into the main courtyard (**1**); to the right of a highly ornate turret (15C) is the "Vat Room" (**2**) with its winepress and, standing behind a large pillar, an enormous stone tun which could contain 13 000l/2 860gal of wine. On the left of the turret are the kitchen, with its impressive fireplace, and the offices and outhouses. Opposite are some of the apartments.

The Great Hall, which is now roofless, contains a beautiful fireplace. In front of the window is a stone (**3**) with two unequal cavities which was used to collect one tenth of the grain harvested on the estate, by way of taxes. To the right are the owner's apartments, where Lucrèce de Gadagne died in 1615. The adjoining courtyard, known as the Fountain Courtyard, leads to an imposing 14C keep, (32m/105ft high) encircled, half way up, by a series of machicolations added in the 15C.

First floor

Climb the staircase inside the turret in the main courtyard. On the first floor, above the offices, is a bedroom which was once painted (exhibition about the castle). A ceilingless room in the square keep gives a view of the upper room and two beautiful fireplaces, one above the other. The gallery opening onto the courtyard is that of the chapel: an Annunciation has been carved on the back of the entrance door.

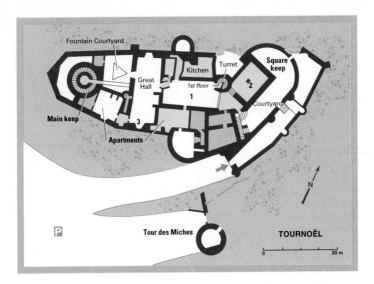

Main keep

On the right, in the gallery, a staircase leads to the watch-path. A footbridge gives access to the entrance of the circular keep; its three floors are linked by a staircase hewn from the 4m/13ft-thick wall. The **panorama**★ from the platform encompasses the Limagne, Forez, Comté and Livradois regions. The three basaltic plateaux which form long promontories projecting from the Dômes plateau can be seen clearly: the closest is that of Châteaugay, the next is Côte de Clermont and the furthest away is the Gergovie plateau.

▶ *Rejoin D 15 and continue towards Enval.*

Châtelguyon ⚑ – ♿ *See CHÂTELGUYON.*

▶ *Leave Châtelguyon to the SW on D 227.*

Mozac★★ – ♿ *See RIOM.*

Riom★★ – ♿ *See RIOM.*

▶ *Leave Riom to the SW on D 83.*

Église de Marsat

Built in the 11C and 12C, the church consists of two, heavily restored adjoining naves. An alcove houses a collection of precious objects, notably a splendid reliquary cross in gilded silver and rock crystal, thought to date back to the days of Louis XIII. In the chancel of the left-hand chapel, an outstanding 12C **Black Virgin**★★ in painted wood is fervently worshipped by parishioners. Note the curious wheel hanging from the vaulted ceiling, around which a wax thread has been wound in accordance with local tradition.

▶ *Leave Marsat on D 446, heading for Riom. It joins up with N 9 at the entrance to the town. Drive for 3km/1.9mi towards Clermont-Ferrand, then turn right onto D 402.*

Châteaugay

The town lies on the edge of a basaltic plateau and is overlooked by the squat outline of its castle. From the town, there are wide views over the Limagne plain and the surrounding mountains. The neighbouring hillsides produce a famous wine; its full-bodied flavour, reminiscent of Beaujolais, was once appreciated by Charles VI and Henri IV. Châteaugay was built in the 14C by Pierre de Giac, Chancellor of France, and its history is a tragic one. It was in the keep that the grandson of the Chancellor poisoned his wife, Jeanne de Giac, who had won over the heart of John the Fearless, Duke of Burgundy, before becoming one of his murderers' accomplices. After being appointed minister to Charles VII, Giac himself was arrested, tortured, sewn into a sack and drowned.

Later, the beautiful Madeleine de Châteaugay fell madly in love with Charles of Valois, Charles XI's illegitimate son, and remained faithful to him even though, having been discovered to be a conspirator, he was imprisoned in the Bastille for many years. After he had abandoned her, she was stabbed to death by her vassals during a hunt.

In the years leading up to the French Revolution, **La Fayette** often came to Châteaugay to prepare "the reforms" with his friend the Marquis of Châteaugay, who appeared to be a supporter of revolutionary ideas; despite this, the marquis became one of the leaders of the Army of Émigrés in Coblenz in 1792.

WHERE TO STAY

⊜⊜ **La Rose des Vents** – 63530 Luzet - 4km/2.4mi W of Volvic via D 986 rte de Pontgibaud - ☎ 04 73 33 50 77 - www.hotel-volvic.com - closed Christmas-Easter - 🅿 - 26 rms - 🛏 8€ - restaurant ⊜⊜. Enjoy an undisturbed night's rest in this rather lofty hotel with a view of the Puy de Dôme. Smallish but well-equipped rooms. A pool and tennis court for energetic guests.

GO FISH

Pisciculture du Château de St-Genest-l'Enfant – 63200 Malauzat - ☎ 04 73 64 14 54. Set in a basin of the Volvic fault, this establishment benefits from the proximity of a spring whose water is irreproachably pure, at a constant temperature of 9°C/48°F year-round. Anglers can try for trout, char and salmon, whereas fish fanciers with less time to spare can fill their baskets with ready-made rillettes, house-smoked fillets, tartare, carpaccio, paupiettes etc.

Castle

Enter the inner courtyard where four out of the five wells (now blocked up) which were used as reservoirs in times of siege are still to be seen. A fine Renaissance door is decorated with the coat of arms of the Laqueuille family who made alterations to the castle during the 16C.

Keep★

🕐 Jul to mid-Sep: guided tours (45min) 2-6pm; 2€. Apply to the town hall. ☎ 04 73 87 24 35. www.chateaugay.net

The square keep built in lava stone is the most interesting part of the castle; it is almost the only one in the Auvergne to have remained intact. Richelieu did not include it in his demolition orders, and during the French Revolution, Couthon, a member of the National Convention, was unable to raze it to the ground. It has four floors with access via a spiral staircase. Three rooms contain a collection of works by the artist Paul Trilloux based on the theme of "The Quest for the Holy Grail."

From the platform there is a fine **panoramic view**★ over the Puys range, the hills of the Livradois and Forez areas and the Limagne plain.

PARC EUROPÉEN DU VOLCANISME VULCANIA★★

MICHELIN MAP 326: E-7 – 15KM/9.3MI NW OF CLERMONT-FERRAND

This gigantic theme park is devoted to the history of Auvergne and more specifi-cally to its geological formation. Designed after plans by the architects **Hans Hollein** and **Philippe Tixier**, the park aims to spread knowledge about volcanoes and other earth sciences, while contributing towards the protection of natural sites in Auvergne.

The Regional Council of Auvergne launched the project by organising an interna-tional competition to choose the most suitable plans. The result is truly impres-sive: a total area of 57ha/140 acres comprising a great number of demonstrations and reconstructions relating to volcanic activity. 🛈 *Conseil régional d'Auvergne, Vulcania, BP 60, 63402 CHAMALIÈRES,* ☎ *04 73 31 85 65.*

Tour of Vulcania

15km/9.3mi W of Clermont-Ferrand along D 941B. 🕐 Kids *Mid-Mar to 7 Oct: daily except Mon, Tue, 9.30am-5.30pm; Apr-Aug: 9.30am-5.30pm (Jul-Aug: 7pm).* 🕐 *Closed 1 Apr. 19.50€ (5-16-year-olds: 12€). Allow one day.* ☎ *0820 827 828. www.vulcania.com.*

The **Allée de la Grande Coulée,** an imposing 165m/542ft-long wall, leads to the **Caldera,** a circular area where the **Great Cone** is situated. The glowing crater marks the start of a fascinating journey to the centre of the Earth. You are invited to walk through a succession of wide spaces and galleries showing more or less spectacular aspects of volcanic activity, such as the **Rumbling Gallery,** which re-creates the conditions of an erupting volcano, complete with incandescent projections and formidable sound effects! You can either follow the suggested itinerary or travel as you please in a highly interactive way **"From the Cosmos to the Centre of the Earth"** then **"In the heart of a vol-cano"**; you can learn about the mean-ing of volcanoes in different cultures in **"Of volcanoes and men"** and end your visit with the **Volcanic Garden,** a huge, brightly lit greenhouse where a wide variety of plant species thrive on volcanic soil, or in the **Showroom,** where a giant screen projects impressive images of volcanic eruptions in coun-tries all over the world.

> ⊝⊜ **Les Genêts fleuris** - *Lieu-dit Bonnabaud - 63230 St-Pierre-le-Chas-tel -* ☎ *04 73 88 75 81 - 5 rms - meals* ⊝⊜. The Puy mountain ranges, the Château de Bonnabaud, the St-Pierre-le-Chastel church: all are on view when you stay at this old, lov-ingly restored farm. Simple, comfort-able and well-tended bedrooms, plus a small library-cum-sitting room. The table d'hôte features specialities from the Auvergne.

Katia and Maurice Kraft

The **Kraft area** pays tribute to these great volcanologists who travelled all over the world, witnessed more than 150 volcanic eruptions and brought back more than 300 hours of film and some 350 000 slides before disappearing in 1991 dur-ing the eruption of the Unzen volcano in Japan.

YSSINGEAUX

POPULATION 6 118
MICHELIN MAP 331: G-3

Yssingeaux, one of France's largest municipalities, nestles at the heart of a region whose landscape pleasantly combines lush hillsides with stark stretches of volcanic rock. The area is an ideal starting-point for rambles and other types of excursion and it also has delicious local specialities.

Sights

Hôtel de Ville
The town hall is set up in the 15C château, formerly the summer residence of the bishops of Le Puy.

Musée St-Roch - Apothicairerie
&. ⏱ *Jul-Aug: daily except Mon and Tue 2.30-6.30pm; rest of year by arrangement. 4€ (children: 2€).* ☎ *04 71 65 77 00.*
This collection of faience crockery, displayed in the hospital's old chapel, is one of the most important in France.

Excursion

Massif du Meygal and Pays des Sucs★

57km/35.4mi – allow 2hr

▶ *Leave Yssingeaux to the S on D 7, then after 3km/2mi turn right onto D 42.*

Forêt du Meygal
This forest covering around 1 200ha/3 000 acres was planted between 1865 and 1880. Comprised mainly of coniferous species (fir, spruce, Scots pine), the forest is cut across from north to south by two roads.

▶ *After the Araules crossroads, turn right onto D 18, heading for Queyrières, then turn left onto the first forest lane, signposted in red and blue, that disappears into the undergrowth. At the next intersection, take the left-hand lane running along the east slope of the Grand Testavoyre. Leave the car at the leisure centre in the middle of a clearing.*

Grand Testavoyre★★
Follow the forest road on the east side and leave the car in the parking area located 300m/330yd from the forest lodge.
🚶 A path through ferns and bilberry bushes leads to the summit from which there are splendid **panoramic views** over the volcanic landscape.

▶ *Continue through the forest.*

The west road goes past the **Maison des Copains** which became famous after it was mentioned in a novel by the French writer **Jules Romains**.

▶ *The left-hand forest lane leads to D 15.*

The route skirts the Meygal massif to the south. Making your way towards St-Julien-Chapteuil through a mountainous landscape, you will cross **Boussoulet** village, where the groups of houses are roofed with locally made *lauze* tiles of phonolithic rock.

St-Julien-Chapteuil

The village occupies an unusual **site**★ in the middle of a leafy basin watered by the Sumène, bristling with volcanic peaks. The Romanesque **church** on its rocky shelf has undergone extensive renovation: the façade and bell-tower are modern. The **Musée Jules-Romains** (🕑 *Jul-Aug: 10-noon, 3-6pm (Sun, 10am-12.30pm); rest of year: daily except Sat and Sun, 10am-noon, 3-6pm (Tue and Thu, 3-6pm). 2€. ☎ 04 71 08 77 70. www.auvergne-paysdumeygal.com)* is devoted to the life and literary achievements of the author **Jules Romains** (1885-1972).

▷ *Leave St-Julien to the N and take D 26 towards St-Pierre-Eynac.*

St-Pierre-Eynac

Pretty country **church** with a Romanesque doorway underneath a Renaissance porch. During the drive to Aupinhac, note the **view** of Le Puy and the basin to the left: you can see the cathedral, the Corneille rock and St-Michel-d'Aiguilhe.

▷ *Continue towards St-Étienne village on D 26 after crossing N 88. Take D 71 N towards Malrevers. After Rosières, turn right onto D 7.*

On the left you will drive past the Suc de Jalore, and the Suc d'Émeral in the distance.

▷ *Take the first road on the right after the cemetery on the road to Mortesagne.*

The route is dominated by the Suc d'Eyme, which you can spot on the left. There is a 16C fortified house in Mortesagne. The narrow tarmacked road on the right leads to the foot of the Suc de Glavenas. During the drive down towards **Glavenas,** enjoy the **view**★ of the church perched above a curious landscape.

▷ *Return to Yssingeaux on D 431 and N 88.*

J. Damase/MICHELIN

A

Abbatiale St-Austremoine 310
Abbaye de Féniers 213
Abbaye de Sept-Fons 324
Abbaye de St-Gilbert 534
Abbaye Notre-Dame-de-Randol 535
Abbaye Notre-Dame-des-Dombes 274
Activities for Children 44
Agriculture 100
Aigueperse 106
Aiguèze 129
Ainay-le-Château 583
Alain-Fournier 304
Albepierre-Bredons 434
Albert, Noël 645
Allanche 216
Allègre 471
Allobroges 70
Ambert 109
Ambierle 489
Ampère, André-Marie 76, 349, 410
Ancienne Chartreuse de Bonnefoy 306
Andance 552
Anglards-de-Salers 541
Annonay 117
Antignac 396
Antraigues-sur-Volane 599
Apcher 214
Apchon 481
Apollinaris, Sidonius 71, 154
Arboretum 150
Arboretum de Balaine 430
Arc, Joan of 473
Arches de Chaponost 386
Ardes-sur-Couze 130
Arlanc 116
Arlempdes 133
Arpajon-sur-Cère 150
Arras-sur-Rhône 576
Ars-sur-Formans 643
Artonne 108
Aubenas 134
Aubière 255
Aurec-sur-Loire 332
Auriac-l'Église 216
Aurillac 142
Automusée du Forez 525
Auvers 502
Auzon 152
Aveize 390
Avenas 167
Aven d'Orgnac 438
Aven de la Forestière 441
Aven de Marzal 125
Avèze 563
Ayat-sur-Sioule 555
Aydat 154

B

Badoit, Augustin Saturnin 389
Bagnols 170, 186
Baigneurs, Les 442
Balazuc 138
Balcon des Templiers 128
Balme-les-Grottes, La 266
Banks 50
Banne 603
Barjac 440
Barrage and Lac de Lastioulles 186
Barrage d'Enchanet 150
Barrage de
  Besserve 556
  Bort 183
  Grandval 588
  la Tache 488
  Lavalette 223
  Queuille 556
  St-Étienne-Cantalès 150
  Vaussaire 257
  Villerest 490

Barrage du Rouchain 488
Barrage du Ternay 121
Barry 581
Basic information 50
Basilique Notre-Dame-Des-Miracles 392
Basilique St-Julien 196
Bassignac 396
Bastide-Puylaurent, La 604
Bathernay 496
Béatrice of Auvergne 255
Beauchastel 288
Beaujeu 166
Beaujolais 157
Beaujolais-Villages 161
Beaujolais wine 158
Beaumont 274
Beaunant 386
Beauvoir-de-Marc 639
Beauzac 401
Becket, Thomas 394
Bed and Breakfast 34
Bellenaves 225
Belleville 163
Belvédère de
  Commelle-Vernay 489
  la Cathédrale 126
  la Coutelle 128
  la Madeleine 126
  la Maladrerie 128
  la Sauveté 527
  Mallet 588
  Veysset 258

Belvédère du
  Colombier 128
  Ranc-Pointu 128
  Serre de Tourre 125
  Vézou 590

Belvederes, The 519
Belvédères d'Autridge 125
Belvédères de Gaud 125
Belvédères de Gournier 125
Berlioz, Hector 259
Bernard, Claude 162
Bernin, Jean de 628
Berry, Jean de 72, 473
Besbre Valley 321
Bessat, Le 453
Besse-en-Chandesse 171
Besson 431
Bidon 126
Billom 178
Billy 534
Blesle 391
Bocage Bourbonnais 189
Boën 294
Boffres 289
Bois de Païolive 602
Bort-les-Orgues 183
Boucieu-le-Roi 576
Boudes 315
Boulieu 121
Bouligneux 272
Bourbon-L'Archambault 187
Bourboule, La 191
Bourg-Argental 455
Bourget, Paul 534
Bourgogne, Gui de 628
Bourlatier, Ferme de 305
Boussoulet 657
Boutières, Les 503
Brangues 422
Brassac-les-Mines 153
Bressolles 431
Brigand's Den 195
Brioude 196
Brugheas 616
Buron 619
Burzet 600
Butte d'Usson 312
Butte de Montgacon 107
Butte de Montpensier 106
Buxières-les-Mines 560

C

Caesar 70
Calendar of events 44
Camping 35
Carladès 623
Car Rental 33
Cascade de
  Cornillou 256
  Faillitoux 623
  la Roucolle 206
  la Vernière 195
  Liadouze 212
  Saillant 177, 530

Cascade du
  Plat à Barbe 195
  pont d'Aptier 481
  Ray-Pic 600
  Sailhant 524
  Sartre 482
  Saut de la Saule 184
  Trou de la Conche and
    Rocher de Maisonne 622

Catholic League 73
Centrale Nucléaire de Creys-Malville 422
Centre d'Art Contemporain 567
Centre d'Art Roman Georges-Duby 312
Centre Nucléaire de Production d'Electricité
  du Bugey 449
Centre permanent d'initiatives pour
  l'environnement 586
Cérilly 584
Cervières 526
Cévennes Vivarais 605
Ceyrat 255
Chabrier, Emmanuel 110
Chaise-Dieu, La 216
Chalain-d'Uzore 404
Chalamont 274
Chaldette, La 232
Chalencon 319
Chalmazel 296
Chalvignac 396
Chamalières 254
Chamalières-sur-Loire 331
Chambéon 292
Chambles 334
Chambon-des-Neiges 437
Chambon-sur-Lac 437
Chambon-Sur-Lignon, Le 221
Chambonas 605
Chambonie, La 295
Chambost-Allières 168
Champagne 552
Champeix 176
Champs-sur-Tarentaine-Marchal 186
Chantelle 225
Chantemerle-les-Blés 575
Chapeauroux 550
Chapelle de
  Jailhac 394
  la Font-Sainte 482
  Trachin 118
  Vassivière 175

Chapelle du Val-des-Nymphes 581
Chapelle Notre-Dame-de-Fresneau 271
Chapelle Notre-Dame-de-Laval 525
Chapelle St-Andéol 496
Chapelle St-Barthélemy 169
Chapelle St-Jean 177, 335
Chapelle Ste-Marie-des-Chazes 549
Charbonnières-les-Bains 384

Charnay 168
Charroux 223
Chartreuse de Port-Ste-Marie 557
Chas 180
Chaspinhac 330
Chastel-Merlhac 396
Chastreix 547
Château
  d'Alleuze 588
  d'Anjony 573
  d'Auzers 395
  d'Effiat 284
  d'Essalois 334
  d'Opme 255
  d'Urfé 527
  d'Arginy 163
  d'Aulteribe 262
  de Beauvoir 323
  de Boisy 489
  de Boulogne 600
  de Branzac 508
  de Bressieux 261
  de Busséol 620
  de Busset 615
  de Chalençon 332
  de Chareil 226
  de Chavaniac-Lafayette 204
  de Chazeron 478
  de Chouvigny 554
  de Conros 150
  de Corcelles 164
  de Cordès 438
  de Couzan 295
  de Davayat 479
  de Fléchères 644
  de Fourchaud 431
  de Goutelas 296
  de l'Aubépin 491
  de La Barge 262
  de la Bastie-d'Urfé 156
  de la Batisse 300
  de La Palice 320
  de la Roche 109, 491
  de la Tourette 289
  de la Trémolière 541
  de la Vigne 394
  de Lavoûte-Polignac 330
  de Mantaille 552
  de Mérieu 422
  de Messilhac 623
  de Montaigu-le-Blin 533
  de Montmorin 181
  de Murol 434
  de Parentignat 312
  de Pesteils 625
  de Rochebaron 400
  de Rochelambert 471
  de Rochemaure 414
  des Bruneaux 518
  de Sédaiges 211
  de Seganges 430
  de Septème 639
  des Roure 441
  de St-Vidal 470
  de Thorrenc 121
  de Thour 323
  de Tournoël 651
  de Vachères 399
  de Val 186
  de Valprivas 400
  de Ventadour 142
  de Villeneuve 316
  de Virieu 444
  de Vollore 262
  du Bailli 173
  du Cambon 508
  du Chassan 588
  du Méage 533
  du Riau 430
  du Vieux Bostz 431
Château et jardins de la Chassaigne 568
Châteaugay 654
Châteauneuf-les-Bains 555
Château St-Étienne 147
Châteaux in Livradois Country 181
Châtel-de-Neuvre 431
Chatelans 267
Châtelguyon 226
Châtelperron 322
Châtillon 169
Châtillon-sur-Chalaronne 228
Chatte 507
Chaudes-Aigues 230
Chaumière 435
Chauriat 180
Chauvet, Grotte 124
Chavroches 321
Chazay-d'Azergues 169
Chazelles-sur-Lyon 232
Cheire d'Aydat 281
Chemicals 99
Chemin de Fer du Vivarais 575
Chemin de fer touristique du Velay 222
Cheminée de Fée de Cotteuges 176
Chénas 165
Chénelette 167
Chessy 169
Cheval, Ferdinand 301
Chevallier, Gabriel 162
Cheylade 482
Cheylade valleys 481
Chilhac 203
Cinematograph 75
Cinq-Mars 285
Cirque de Valcivières 114
Cirque du Falgoux 209
Clairière 602
Clansayes 581
Classical period 92
Claude Bernard 76
Claudel, Paul 422
Claux, Le 482

INDEX

Claveisolles 168
Clermont-Ferrand 233
Clermont-Ferrand-
    Charade Racing Circuit 499
Clermont Cathedral 91
Cochettes, La Croix des 444
Cognat 616
Col de
    Cère 207
    Favardy 167
    l'Escrinet 600, 601
    la Chaumoune 215
    la Chavade 141
    la Croix-Morand 544
    la Croix-St-Robert 546
    la Croix de Bauzon 561
    la Luère 387
    Legal 211
    Meyrand 562

Col des Supeyres 114, 297
Col du Béal 296, 572
Col du Buisson 317
Col du Grand-Bois 519
Colin, Jean-Claude 389
Collandres 481
Colletière 442
Colombier 421
Coltines 524
Comblat 206
Combrailles, Les 476
Commanderie de Verrières 525
Commentry 420
Compains 132
Condat 256
Condrieu 455
Cordieux 275
Corent 620
Corniche de l'Eyrieux 289
Corniche du Chassezac 602
Cornillon 334
Côte Roannaise 487
Côte-St-André 259
Coteaux de Beaujolais 161
Coudes 619
Courpière 261
Couthon, Georges 74
Crémieu 263
Crest 268
Crest, Le 301
Crêt de l'Œillon 454
Crêt de la Perdrix 454
Crête de Blandine 601
Crocodiles, La Ferme aux 582
Croix-Rampau 410
Crops 100
Crozet, Le 487
Crussol 597
Cunlhat 115

Cusset 616
Customs 28
Cycling 43
Cziffra, Georges 218

D

d'Indy, Vincent 289
d'Aurillac, Gerbert 79
d'Auvergne, Henri de La Tour 79
d'Estaing, Valéry Giscard 79
d'Ordanche, La Banne 194
Dauphiné d'Auvergne 314
Déchelette, Joseph 484
Défilé de Donzère 648
Défilé de Ruoms 139
Défilé de St-Vallier 576
Défilés de l'Ardèche 137
Delorme, Philibert 355
Déportation et de la Seconde Guerre
    Mondiale, Museum 326
Désaignes 319
Desaix, General 476
Dienne 208
Dieulefit 415
Discounts 47
Dombes, La 271
Dôme, Le Puy de 276
Domérat 419
Dôme St-Benoît 137
Domeyrat 204
Dompierre-sur-Veyle 273
Donjon de la Souche 421
Dore-l'Église 116
Dorées, Le Pays Des Pierres 168
Doumer, Paul 143
Driving Tours 16
Drôme, Hills of 270

E

Ébreuil 553
École de Clémence Fontille 502
Écomusée du Pays d'Auzon 153
Economy 99
Écopole du Forez 292
Église Abbatiale St-Robert 218
Église d'
    Agonges 191
    Arlet 202
    Aubazat 202
    Autry-Issards 190
    Ygrande 190

Église d'Étroussat 226
Église d'Ennezat 107
Église de
    Biozat 299
    Blassac 202
    Bredons 433
    Champdieu 402

Église de
  Chanteuges 203
  Châteloy 304
  Colamine-sous-Vodable 315
  Colombier 421
  Franchesse 189
  Jaleyrac 394
  Job 572
  Jou-sous-Monjou 623
  Mailhat 313
  Marsat 653
  Meillers 190, 559
  Peyrusses 203
  Roffiac 524
  Saulcet 532
  St-Cirgues 202
  St-Illide 509
  St-Menoux 190
  St-Myon 108
  St-Pardoux 547

Église du Chastel 176
Église du Prieuré 403
Église du Vigean 394
Égliseneuve-d'Entraigues 215
Église Notre-Dame-de-Prévenchère 140
Église Notre-Dame-des-Neiges 148
Église St-André 172
Église St-Géraud 145
Église St-Hilaire-la-Croix 478
Église St-Jean 111
Église St-Laurent 137
Église St-Maurice 560
Église St-Pierre 391
Église Ste-Martine 180
Eiffel, Gustave 587
Embassies and consulates 28
Émile-Guillaumin and Charles-Louis-
   Philippe Oak Trees 584
Entraygues 151
Éperon de Pourcheyrolles 140
Escalin, Antoine 580
Espaly-St-Marcel 470
Espinasse 590
Essertines-en-Châtelneuf 297
Estables, Les 307
Étang de Pirot 584
Étang de Saloup 586
Étang de St-Bonnet 585
Exposition Grotte
   Chauvet-Pont-d'Arc 123

F
Fallet, René 322
Famous local figures 76
Farges 177
Faucon, Maurice 110
Fay-sur-Lignon 308, 504
Ferme de Bourlatier 305
Ferme de Pierre Allègre 501

Ferme Philip 305
Feurs 291
Firminy 518
Fishing 39
Fleurie 164
Flora and Fauna 67
Fontaine Pétrifiante 408
Fontaine Viljot 584
Fontanges 210
Forest, Fernand 79
Forêt de Maubert 258
Forêt de Mazan 140
Forêt de Saoû 270
Forêt de Tronçais 582
Forêt des Colettes 225
Forêt du Meygal 656
Fouilles de la Brégoule 598
Fournols 115
Fourvière Hill 363
Freycenet-la-Tour 399
Frugières-le-Pin 325
Furet, Le 383
Futaie Colbert 585

G
Gannat 298
Garde-Adhémar, La 580
Garlan, Bernard de 589
Gentiane Country 481
Gentiane Express 480
Gerbier-de-Jonc 306
Gergovia 70
Gergovie Plateau 299
Getting around 32
Givors 519
Glavenas 657
Godivelle, La 215
Golf 44
Gorges and Site de Montfermy 284
Gorges d'Amby 267
Gorges d'Avèze 563
Gorges d'Enval 477
Gorges de
  Ceyrat 255
  Chouvigny 554
  l'Alagnon 328, 390
  l'Ander 524
  l'Ardèche 122
  La Beaume 139
  la Borne 561
  la Loire 329
  la Maronne 508, 509
  la Rhue 256
  la Sioule 553
  la Truyère 587
Gorges du Doux 576
Gorges Roannaises de la Loire 489
Gothic period 91
Goudet 330

Gouffre d'Enfer 452
Goul Valley 623
Gour de Tazenat 478
Grand Belvédère 128
Grande Cascade 408
Grands-Murcins, Les 488
Grand Testavoyre 656
Grandval Reservoir 587
Grangent Dam 519
Gravières 606
Gregory of Tours 98
Grézolles 527
Grimmer 223
Grotte de la Madeleine 126
Grotte des Anglais 623
Grotte de St-Marcel 128
Grotte du Puy de Dôme 278
Grottes artificielles de Perrier 314
Grottes de Jonas 175
Grottes de la Balme 266
Guesclin, Bertrand du 470
Guignol de Lyon 359
Guimet, Émile 378
Guizay 519

H

Hang-gliding 43
Harpignies, Henri-Joseph 303
Haut-Vivarais Plateaux 317
Haute Corniche 126
Hauterives 301
Health 29
Henri-Malartre
    Automobile Museum 384
Hérisson 303
Heritage Trails 443
Hières-sur-Amby 267
Hiking 41
Historial de la Chaise-Dieu 220
History 70
Hollein, Hans 655
Honegger, Arthur 220
Honoré d'Urfé 156
Hospice de Gayette 533
Hostels 35
Hostun 495
Huriel 419

I, J

Île Barbe 383
Île de Grangent 335
Intendants 74
International Visitors 28
Issoire 309
Jacquard 78
Jacquard, Joseph-Marie 349, 350, 368
Jacquet, Aimé 294
Jailhac 394

Jaligny-sur-Besbre 322
Jardin des Carmes 148
Jardin des Fontaines Pétrifiantes 507
Jardin des Oiseaux 270
Jardin Ferroviaire 507
Jardin pour la Terre 116
Jarnioux 171
Jasserie du Coq-Noir 114
Jasserie du Coq Noir 297
Jasseries, Un colporteur et des 114
Jastres Panorama 137
Jaujac 561
Jenzat 299
Joly, Robert de 438
Jongkind 259
Joyeuse 605
Juliénas 165, 166
Jussieu brothers 349

K, L

Karting 44
Kraft, Maurice and Katia 655
L'Hôpital-sous-Rochefort 526
L'Oppidum des Côtes de Clermont 254
L'Élancèze 212
Labastide-de-Virac 441
Labé, Louise 349
Labeaume 139
La Bégude-de-Mazenc 415
Labyrinthes, Les 303
Lac Chambon 178, 436
Lac Chauvet 547
Lac d'Issarlès 304
Lac d'Aydat 154
Lac de
    Devesset 503
    Guéry 544
    la Landie 186
    Montcineyre 175
    Paladru 441

Lac du Barrage 196
Lac du Bouchet 550
La Côte-St-André 259
Lac Pavin 174
La Croix-du-Sud 488
Lac Servière 545
Lagat, Le Val 113
Lalouvesc 317
Lamastre 318
Langeac 203
Languedoc Gothic 91
Lanobre 186
Lapalisse 320
Lapeyrouse 275
Lassalle, Philippe de 377
Laussac 591
Lavaudieu 324
Lavoûte-Chilhac 202

Lavoûte-sur-Loire 331
Le Boitier 170
Le Hameau en Beaujolais –
    SA Duboeuf 165
Le Monastier-sur-Gazeille 397
Le mont-d'Or Lyonnais 409
Lent 273
Léotoing 392
Lépine, Louis 296
Les Écharmeaux 167
Les Prades 214
Les Rives de Thiers 568
Les Vans 602
Lezoux 326
Lfier 120
Lhote, André 271
Limagne, La 106
Lioran, Le 327
Lisseuil 554
Literary life 97
Livradois 312
Livradois-Forez Park 293
Livradois-Forez tourist train 112
Local tourist offices 27
Londres, Albert 79
Loubet, Émile 271
Lumière, Auguste 75
Lyon 336

M

Macintosh, Charles 235
Madeleine mountains 487
Mademoiselle de Fontanges 262
Mail 50
Mailhat, Eglise de 313
Maison Consulaire 147
Maison d'Ampère 410
Maison de
    la Faune 433
    la Flore d'Auvergne 545
    la Foudre 214
    la Fourme et du Fromage 111
    la Truffe et du Tricastin 579
    Montagne 482
    Pays 314

Maison des
    Combrailles 555
    Fromages 215
    Grenadières 526
    Oiseaux du Haut-Allier 202
    Tourbières et du Cézallier 132

Maison du
    Bâtiy 149
    Buronnier 328
    Châtaignier 288
    Fromage 541
    Parc 450
    Patrimoine 313, 420

Maison forestière de Miers 397
Maison Rozier 193
Maisons du Parc 649
Malicorne 421
Malleval 552
Mandailles 212
Manglieu 618
Manoir de Veygoux 477
Marcenat 214
Marcheix, Aimerigot 195
Marcolès 151
Marcy 168
Mareugheol 316
Margerides, Les 569
Margot, Queen 313
Maringues 107
Marnans 261
Marquis de La Fayette 79, 204, 263
Marsac-en-Livradois 117
Marsanne 271
Martinanches, Les 182
Massiac 390
Massif du Meygal 656
Massif du Sancy 541
Massif du Tanargue 560
Maubert Forest 258
Mauriac 392
Maurs 151
Mauzun 182
Mayres 141
Mazan-l'Abbaye 140
Mazet-Plage 602
Mazeyrat-Aurouze 204
Méandre de Queuille 556
Meaulne 304
Menat 554
Menet 483
Menhir de la Pierre des
    Quatre-Curés 563
Mérimée, Prosper 581
Messager, André 79
Messeix 563
Metal working 99
Meysse 458
Mézilhac 599
Michel de L'Hospital 109
Michelin, Édouard 79
Michelin brothers 235
Miremont 557
Mirmande 271
Moingt 402
Moissat 326
Mondor, Henri 143
Money 50
Monistrol-d'Allier 549
Monistrol-sur-Loire 399
Mont-Dore, Le 405
Montagne de la Serre 155

INDEX

Montagny 486
Montaigut-le-Blanc 177
Montboucher-sur-Jabron 415
Montbrison 401
Mont Brouilly 164
Mont Chiniac 503
Montées, Lyon 363
Montélimar 411
Montellier, Le 275
Montet, Le 560
Montfaucon-en-Velay 223
Montferrand 247
Montgolfier, Joseph 349
Montgolfier brothers 76, 117
Monthieux 275
Montlosier Castle 282
Montmelas-St-Sorlin 161
Mont Mézenc 307
Mont Mouchet 502
Monton 301
Montpeyroux 619
Montpezat-sous-Bauzon 140
Montregard 223
Montrond-les-Bains 404
Montsalvy 152
Monts Dôme 275
Monts du
    Cantal 205
    Cézallier 213
    Forez 292
    Lyonnais 386
Montselgues 607
Mont Thou 410
Montuel 448
Morestel 421
Moudeyres 308
Moulin, Jean 76, 378
Moulin du Blaud 523
Moulin Richard-de-Bas 112
Moulins 423
Mountain Biking 43
Mourguet, Laurent 350
Mourjou 152
Mours-St-Eusèbe 495
Moussages 395
Mousse, Pas du 125
Mozac 476
Mulatière, La 381
Murat 432
Murat-le-Quaire 193
Murol, Chateau 434
Musée Alice-Taverne 489
Musée Archéologique 598
Musée Claude-Bernard 162
Musée d'Art Roger-Quilliot 252
Musée d'Art et d'Archéologie 149
Musée de
    Charroux et de son Canton 224

Musée de
    Cire 147
    l'Automobile Henri-Malartre 384
    l'Alambic 121
    l'école 1900 113
    la Coiffe 391
    la Machine Agricole et à Vapeur 112
    la Résistance 326
    la Vigne 419
    Paléontologie: 'Le Gîte à Fossiles' 554

Musée des
    Beaux-Arts, Lyon 374
    Mariniers du Rhône 551
    Métiers et des Traditions 571
    Papeteries Canson et Montgolfier 120
    Vieux Métiers 131
    Volcans 147

Musée Diocésain d'Art Sacré 495
Musée du
    Bois et de la Forêt 220
    Compagnonnage Guillon 165
    Fer Blanc 203
    Lac de Paladru 443
    Lavage et du Repassage 533

Musée Émile-Guillaumin 190
Musée international
    Pétanque et Boules 334
Musée Mandet 476
Musée Paléontologique 203
Musée Pierre-Mondanel 181
Musée Régional d'Auvergne 476
Musée Vivant de la Laine
    et du Mouton 288
Musée Vivarois César-Filhol 119

N

Nadaillat 155
Nature 58
Nature parks and reserves 23
Naves 603
Néris-les-Bains 420
Neuilly-en-Donjon 321
Neylière, Notre-Dame de la 389
Neyrac-les-Bains 141
Noirétable 526
Noirs, La ferme des Bois 115
Nonette 313
Northern French Gothic 91
Notre-Dame
    d'Aiguebelle 414
    d'Ay 122
    du-Château 508
    sur-l'Eau 533
    de la Neylière 389
    de Niègles 142

Nouvel, Jean 93, 354
Novacelles 116
Noyant-d'Allier 559

O, P

Oingt 170
Olliergues 571
Olloix 155
Orchards 100
Orcival 437
Orgues de Bort 184
Outdoor Fun 39
Pailharès 317
Paragliding 43
Parc Animalier de Courzieu 387
Parc Animalier du Cézallier 131
Parc Archéologique de Larina 267
Parc d'Attractions Walibi
    Rhône-Alpe 422
Parc Européen du
    Volcanisme Vulcania 655
Parc Fenestre 193
Parc Le Pal 323
Parc naturel regional
    des Monts d'Ardèche 139
Parc naturel régional
    des Volcans d'Auvergne 649
Parc naturel Régional
    Livradois-Forez 293
Parc Zoologique de
    St-Martin-la-Plaine 387
Parc Zoologique du Bouy 113
Parc Zoologique et
    d'Attractions Touroparc 165
Parrot 214
Pascal, Blaise 79, 98, 234, 278
Pas de Cère 206
Pas de Compaing 206
Pas de Peyrol 208
Pastillerie Vichy 616
Paul Claudel's Tomb 422
Pays des Sucs 656
Payzac 605
Pébrac 203
Pélussin 454
Percée, La Montagne 500
Pérouges 444
Pertuiset, Le 518
Pétain, Maréchal 75
Peynet, Raymond 592
Peyrol Pass 208
Philippe, Charles-Louis 584
Pic de Chenavari 414
Pic du Capucin 409
Pic du Lizieux 222
Pierre-Aiguille Belvedere 574
Pierre du Jour 487
Pierre sur Haute 296
Pilat, Le 449
Pillement, Jean 377
Piton d'Espaly 470
Place de la Liberté 118

Place des Cordeliers 118
Place St-Géraud 143
Planèze, The 589
Plantay, Le 274
Plateau d'Orgnac 130
Plateau de
    Chanturgue 253
    Charlannes 196
    Gergovie 299
    la Chavade 132
    la Danse 519
    la Verrerie 486

Plateau du Coiron 457
Platière, Mme Roland de la 170
Plomb du Cantal 328
Poët-Laval, Le 415
Polignac 472
Polminhac 206
Pommiers 525
Pompidou, Georges 79, 258
Pont-d'Arc 124
Pont-de-Menat 554
Pont-du-Château 180
Pont de Tréboul 590
Pontgibaud 284
Pont Montgolfier 118
Porte d'Orient 224
Pouilly-lès-Feurs 291
Poupées et Fers à Repasser 428
Pourchères 601
Pourrat, Henri 110
Prades 549
Pranles, Le Bouschet de 457
Préhistorama 322
Presqu'île, La 351
Privas 455
Prost, Alain 519
Protestant Plateau 221
Public Holidays 52
Puy-en-Velay, Le 459
Puy Chopine 283
Puy d'Usson 313
Puy d'Ysson 315
Puy d'Éraigne 530
Puy de
    Bessolles 178, 436
    Châteauneuf 530
    Gravenoire 280
    l'Arbre 152
    la Tache 408
    la Vache 282
    Lemptégy 283
    Mazeyres 177
    Montchal 174
    Pariou 282
    Sancy 409, 543
    St-Romain 620
Puy Ferrand 173
Puygiron 415

Puy Griou 329
Puy Mary 209
Puy St-Ambroise 323
Puy St-Mary 393
Puy Violent 210
Pyramide, La 638

Q, R

Queuille Meander 555
Quintenas-le-Peyron 122
Rabelais, François 349, 592
Ravel 326
Ravier, Auguste 421
Renaison 488
Renaux, Eugène 278
Renting a cottage 34
Resistance Movement 76
Retournac 332
Rhues 256
Riding Tours 43
Rieuf, Élise 390
Riom 473
Riom-ès-Montagnes 479
Rive-de-Gier 519
River and canal cruising 23
Riverie 387
Roanne 483
Robert, Hubert 597
Roc de Courlande 547
Roche-en-Régnier 331
Rochebloine 319
Rochecolombe 138
Roche des Fées 193
Roche Péréandre 122
Rocher de
  Borbes 570
  Carlat 624
  l'Aigle 546
  la Volpie 571
  Rochefort 488
  Ronesque 624
  Sampzon 139

Rocher des Combes 599
Rocher des Pendus 623
Rocher St-Joseph 470
Roches Tuilière et Sanadoire 545
Rochetaillée 452
Roche Vendeix 195
Rock-Climbing 41
Roffiac 523
Rolle, Michel 79, 110
Romains, Jules 656, 657
Romançon, Pierre 549
Romanèche-Thorins 165
Romanesque period 88
Romans-sur-Isère 492
Rond de Buffévent 586
Rond de la Cave 584

Rond de Meneser 586
Ronzières 315
Roquetaillade, Jean de la 143
Roseraie Dorieux 486
Roure, Antoine du 134
Route des Carrières 580
Royat 496
Roybon 261
Rozier, Pilâtre de 349
Rudez 211
Rue de la Poulaillerie 224
Rue des Boucheries 172
Ruins of Rochebonne 504
Ruoms 139
Ruynes-en-Margeride 500

S

Safari-Parc de Peaugres 121
Saignes 395
Sail-sous-Couzan 294
Saint-Agrève 503
Saint-Bonnet-le-Château 334
Saint-Cernin 507
Salelles, Les 606
Salers 538
Salles-Arbuissonnas-en-Beaujolais 162
Sancy Range 545
Sandrans 272
Sansac-de-Marmiesse 149
Saoû 270
Sarcouy, Le Grand 282
Sauges 548
Saurier 176
Saut de la Pucelle 436
Sauvain 296
Sauvat 395
Sauvetat, La 620
Sauviat 570
Sauxillanges 313
Scénomusée La Toinette et Julien 194
Secret de la Forêt d'Ayguebonne 263
Seguin, Marc 76, 117
Sentier de Saute Ruisseau 263
Sentier du Bénitier du Diable 262
Sentier du Serpent d'Or 220
Serrières 551
Serves-sur-Rhône 576
Seuillet 533
Severus, Septimus 337
Sévigné, Madame de 613
Shopping 46
Signal de St-André 387
Signal de St-Bonnet 162
Signal de St-Claude 221
Signal du Luguet 214
Silk 382
Singles 563
Site de Cotteughes et Preydefont 483

Site de la Chapelle Ste-Madeleine 391
Site de Rochebonne 170
Site du Marchidial 177
Skiing 42
Slodtz, Michel-Ange 629
Sologne Region 584, 586
Sône, La 507
Source du Dôme 617
Source Du Par 231
Sources Pétrifiantes de Gimeaux 479
Soyans 270
Soyons 598
Spas 44
St-Alyre-ès-Montagne 214
St-Amand-Roche-Savine 114
St-Amant-Tallende 155
St-Amour-Bellevue 166
St-André-d'Apchon 487
St-Anthème 297
St-Antoine-L'Abbaye 504
St-Arcons-d'Allier 203
St-Austremoine 310
St-Baudille-de-la-Tour 266
St-Bonnet-Tronçais 586
St-Chamant 508
St-Chamond 518
St-Christophe-d'Allier 551
St-Cirgues-en-Montagne 140
St-Clément 504
St-Désirat 121
St-Didier-d'Allier 549
St-Didier-en-Velay 400
St-Dier-d'Auvergne 182
St-Donat-sur-l'Herbasse 496
St-Étienne 509
St-Étienne-de-Choimeil 481
St-Étienne-de-Vicq 616
St-Félicien 317
St-Floret 176
St-Flour 520
St-Fortunat 410
St-Front 308
St-Galmier 389
St-Germain-l'Herm 116
St-Germain-Laval 525
St-Germain-Lembron 316
St-Gervais-d'Auvergne 555
St-Gervazy 391
St-Haon 550
St-Haon-le-Châtel 489
St-Ilpize 201
St-Jacques-des-Blats 207
St-Jean-de-Pourcharesse 605
St-Jean-des-Vignes 169
St-Julien 162
St-Julien-Chapteuil 657
St-Julien-du-Serre 600
St-Julien-le-Roux 289

St-Just-St-Rambert 335
St-Laurent 526
St-Laurent-d'Oingt 170
St-Laurent-du-Pape 288
St-Laurent-les-Bains 604
St-Mamert 639
St-Marcel-de-Félines 491
St-Marcellin 507
St-Martin-d'Ardèche 129
St-Martin-de-Fugères 330
St-Martin-Valmeroux 508
St-Maurice-de-Gourdans 449
St-Maurice-sur-Loire 490
St-Nectaire 527
St-Nectaire-Le-Haut 528
St-Nizier-d'Azergues 167
St-Nizier-le-Désert 273
St-Paul-de-Varax 273
St-Paul-Trois-Châteaux 579
St-Paulien 471
St-Pierre-Eynac 657
St-Pierre-le-Déchausselat 605
St-Pierreville 288
St-Pourçain-Sur-Sioule 531
St-Préjet-d'Allier 551
St-Rémy-sur-Durolle 568
St-Restitut 580
St-Romain-de-Lerps 575
St-Romain-en-Gal 636
St-Romain-le-Puy 403
St-Saturnin 534
St-Sauves-d'Auvergne 193
St-Sauveur-de-Montagut 288
St-Sauveur Church 606
St-Symphorien-sur-Coise 389
St-Urcize 232
St-Vallier Gorges 576
St-Victor-sur-Loire 519
St-Vincent-de-Barrès 458
St-Voy 221
St-Yorre 615
Ste-Colombe 636
Ste-Croix-en-Jarez 536
Ste-Eulalie 305
Ste-Madeleine Chapel 535
Stebbing Oak 586
Stevenson, Robert Louis 397, 399, 604
Stock breeding 100
Super-Besse 173
Super-Lioran 328
Sury-le-Comtal 404

T, U, V
Tarrit, Jean 230
Tauves 562
Taxes 53
Teil, Le 414
Telephone 53

INDEX

Tence 222
Ternand 170
Ternay 638
Terrasse, La 167
Textiles 99
Theizé 170
Themed Tours 19
The Rhône Corridor 58
Thiers 563
Thiézac 623
Thimonnier 78
Thines 606
This 491
Thueyts 141
Thuret 108
Tixier, Philippe 655
Toulon-sur-Allier 431
Tour-d'Auvergne, La 547
Tourbière du mont Bar 471
Tour d'Albon 552
Tour de la Clauze 549
Tourist Offices 26
Tourist trains 21
Tournemire 573
Tournon-sur-Rhône 574
Tourzel 314
Traboules 356
Trappe de Notre-Dame-des-Neiges 604
Trévoux 577
Tricastin, Le 579
Trizac 483
Troubat-le-Houx, François Joseph 419
20C architecture 93
Ucel 600
Ussel-d'Allier 226
de la Vache Salers et de la gentiane 541
Valbeleix 132
Val d'Allier 180
Valence 591
Valette, La 292
Valgorge 562
Vallée de
    Chaudefour 546
    L'Ance 401
    l'Eyrieux 286
    la Bourges 599
    la Durolle 568
    la Jordanne 212
    la Volane 599
    Rentières 131
    Sans-Souci 227

Vallée des Prades 227
Vallée des Rouets 569
Vallée des Saints 315
Vallée du Gier 518
Vallée du Lignon 222
Vallée du Mars 209
Vallon-en-Sully 304

Vallon-Pont-d'Arc 123
Vallon Arts et Traditions 304
Vals-les-Bains 142, 599
Vaneau, Pierre 466
Vaux-en-Beaujolais 162
Veauce 224
Veauche 389
Velay Valley, Upper 329
Verbret 396
Vercingétorix 70, 299
Verneuil-en-Bourbonnais 533
Vernoux-en-Vivarais 289
Veyrine 318
Viaduc de Garabit 502, 587
Viaduc des Fades 556
Viaduct, La Recoumène 399
Vic-Le-Comte 617
Vic-Sur-Cère 621
Vichy 607
Vichy government 75, 607
Vieille-Brioude 200
Vignes, Les 190
Village Ardéchois en Miniature 317
Villars-Les-Dombes 640
Villedieu 524
Villefranche-sur-Saône 641
Villeneuve-Lembron 316
Villeneuve-les-Cerfs 107
Villerest 490
Villeurbanne 382
Villié-Morgon 164
Vineyards 101
Vion 576
Visigoths 71
Viviers 644
Vogüé 137
Volcanic Plateaux 134
Volcanoes of the Auvergne 64
Vollore-Montagne 572
Volvic 650
Vorey 331

W, Y

Wars of Religion 73
Water Sports 39
Where to Eat 35
Where to Stay 34
Wine-tasting 20
Wine 103
Ydes-Bourg 396
Yronde 619
Yssingeaux 656
Yzeron 387
Yzeure 430

ACCOMMODATIONS

Ambert
Ma Cachette 111
Annonay
Hôtel D'Ay 120
La Désirade 120
Arlempdes
Hôtel du Manoir 133
Aubenas
Camping Le Chamadou 135
Hôtel Cévenol 135
Hôtel Ibis 135
La Gibaudelle 135
Le Mas de Mazan 135
Aurillac
Camping Village de
Vacances la Gineste 144
Chambre d'hôte de Barathe 144
Delcher 144
Grand Hôtel de Bordeaux 144
Aven d'Orgnac
Domain de la Sérénité 439
Aydat
Camping Chadelas 154
Beaujolais Region
Domaine de La Grosse Pierre 160
Domaine de Romarand 159
Domaine des Quarante Écus 159
Gérard Lagneau 160
Hôtel Les Vignes 159
M. et Mme Bonnot 159
Besse-en-Chandesse
Ferme-auberge La Voûte 172
Hostellerie du Beffroy 172
Bort-Les-Orgues
Camping Municipal de la Siauve 184
Le Rider 184
Bourbon-L'Archambault
Grand Hôtel Montespan-Talleyrand 188
Le Chalet de la Neverdière 188
Les Bourbons 188
Les Thermes 188
Brioude
Ermitage St-Vincent 201
Poste et Champanne 201
Sophie Pougheon Chambre d'hôte 201
Brullioles
La Maison de Noémi 387
Châtelguyon
Beau Site 227
Paris 227
Châtillon-sur-Chalaronne
Chez M. et Mme Salmon 228
Chaudes-Aigues
Beauséjour 231
Clermont-Ferrand
Dav'Hôtel Jaude 237
Hostellerie St-Martin 237
Hôtel Albert-Élisabeth 237
Radio 237
Crémieu
Auberge de la Chaite 263
Les Basses Portes 263

Feurs
La Bussinière 291
Garabit
Le Beau Site 587
Hauterives
Le Relais 302
Issoire
Château de Grange Fort 311
Les Baudarts 311
Paul Gebrillat et
Mireille de Saint Aubain 311
La Bourboule
L'Aviation 191
Lac Chauvet
Central Hôtel 547
La Chaise-Dieu
Écho et Abbaye 219
La Jacquerolle 219
La Côte-St-André
La Ferme des Collines 260
Lac Pavin
Auberge du Lac Pavin 172
Lalouvesc
Fort du Pré 317
Lapalisse
Les Vieux Chênes 322
Lavaudieu
Auberge de l'Abbaye 324
Le Brugeron
Les Genets 293
Le Chambon-sur-Lignon
Hôtel L'Escuelle 221
Le Falgoux
Eterlou 649
Les Voyageurs 649
Lemastre
Hôtel du Midi 318
Le Mont-Dore
La Closerie de Manou 406
Le Pilat
Castel-Guéret 450
La Rivoire 450
Le Moulin du Bost 450
Le Pin
Mme Ferrard 442
Le Puy-en-Velay
Dyke Hôtel 461
La Paravent 461
Les Vans
Camping La Source 603
L'Ensolleiade 603
La Passiflore 603
La Santoline 603
Le Tricastin
Domaine de Magne 580
Tricastin 580
Le Veysset
Ché Marissou 258
Véronique Phelut Bed and Breakfast 258
Lyon
Bellecordière 345
Élysée Hôtel 345
Hôtel Ariana 345
Hôtel Bleu Marine 345

INDEX

Hôtel La Résidence 345
La Villa du Rhône 345
Savoies 345
St-Pierre-des-Terreaux 344
Villages Hôtel 345
Massiac
Auberge de Margaridou 391
La Bougnate 391
Montbrison
Camping Le Bigi 403
Marytel 403
Montélimar
Hôtel Les Hospitaliers 412
Provence 412
Montluçon
Château St-Jean 418
Moulins
Parc 424
Neuville-sur-Ain
Bosseron 273
Olby
Chez M. Bony 277
Orcival
Château de Voissieux 438
Pérouges
M. et Mme Debeney-Truchon 448
Ostellerie du Vieux Pérouges 448
Privas
Château de Fontblachère 456
Hôtel Chaumette 456
Retournac
Les Revers 330
Riom
Chez Mme Gauthier Jocelyne 277
Honnorat Nicole et Stéphan 474
Mme Beaujeard 474
Riom-ès-Montagnes
Le Couvent 480
Le Peyre Arse 480
St-Georges 480
Roanne
Domaine de Champfleury 485
Grand Hôtel 485
L'Échauguette 485
M et Mme Pras 485
Romans-sur-Isère
M. et Mme Imbert 493
Royat
Château de Charade 498
Le Chalet Camille 498
Salers
M. et Mme Prudent 538
Saugues
des Gabales 548
St-Antoine-L'Abbaye
Les Voureys 506
St-Étienne
Hôtel Carnot 512
Hôtel Ténor 512
St-Flour
Auberge Ruisselet 520
Grand Hôtel de l'Étape 520
La Pagnoune 520

St-Front
L'Herminette 306
St-Nectaire
Guilhot Élisabeth et Marc 529
Le Chastel Montaigu 529
Régina 529
St-Pierre-le-Chastel
Les Genêts Fleuris 655
St-Pourçain-Sur-Sioule
Château de Theillat 532
Demeure d'Hauterive 532
St-Sauveur-de-Montagut
Camping L'Ardéchois 287
St. Gervais d'Auvergne
Castel Hôtel 1904 555
Montarlet 555
Ste-Eulalie
Hôtel du Nord 306
Theneuille
L'Ombre de Goziniere 586
Thiers
Éliotel 569
Thueyts
Hôtel des Marronniers 141
Tournon-sur-Rhône
Hôtel Les Amandiers 574
Trévoux
Auberge de campagne Petit Veyssieux 577
Tronçais
Le Tronçais 586
Valence
Hôtel St-Jacques 594
La Mare 594
Vallon-Pont-d'Arc
Camping Le Provençal 123
Le Clos des Bruyères 123
Vals-les-Bains
Bourlenc 601
Grand Hôtel des Bains 601
Vic-Le-Comte
Chris et Marcel Astruc 618
Les Pradets 618
Vic-sur-Cère
Auberge des Montagnes 622
Family Hôtel 622
Vichy
Aletti Palace Hôtel 610
Arverna Hôtel 610
Atlanta 610
Sofitel Les Célestins 610
Vienne
Camping Bontemps 627
Hôtel Central 627
La Margotine 627
Villars-Les-Dombes
Ribotel 640
Villefranche-sur-Saône
Emile Job 643
Hôtel Plaisance 643
Volvic
La Rose des Vents 654
Walibi
Hôtel Servhotel 422
Vieille Maison 422

RESTAURANTS

Aiguèze
L'Auberge Sarrasine 123

Alboussière
Auberge de Duzon 287

Ambérieux-en-Dombes
Auberge des Bichonnières 273

Ambert
Les Copains 111

Annonay
La Moustache Gourmande 120
Ardes-Sur-Couze
Le Beffroi 131

Aubenas
Le Fournil 135

Aurillac
La Belle Époque 144
La Reine Margot 144
Le Bouchon Fromager 144
Le Terroir 144
Poivre et Sel 144

Aven d'Orgnac
L'Esplanade 439
Les Stalagmites 439

Beaujolais Region
Auberge Vigneronne 159
Christian Mabeau 159
La Terrasse du Beaujolais 159
Le Coq à Juliénas 159
Les Platanes de Chénas 159

Besse-en-Chandesse
Auberge du Point de Vue 172
Ferme-auberge La Voûte 172
Hostellerie du Beffroy 172
Le Levant 172

Billom
Auberge du Ver Luisant 179
Le Paris 179

Bransac
Table du Barret 400

Brioude
Pons 201

Chalmazel
Ferme-auberge des Granges 293

Chambon-sur-Lac
Le Pavillon Bleu 436

Charavines
Hôtel Les Bains 442

Charroux
Ferme St-Sébastien 224

Châtelguyon
Paris 227

Châtillon-sur-Chalaronne
Auberge de Montessuy 228
Restaurant La Gourmandine 228
St-Lazare 228

Clermont-Ferrand
Aux Délices de la Treille 237
Brasserie Danielle Bath 237
Le Bougnat 237
Le Chardonnay 237

Col d'Eylac
Buron de la Brèche de Rolland 208

Confolent
L'Air du Temps 400

Courpière
Les Chênes 261

Feurs
Assiette Saltoise 291

Hauterives
Yves Leydier 302

Issoire
La Bergerie 311
La Cour Carrée 311
Le Boudes La Vigne 311

La Chaise-Dieu
Le Lion d'Or 219

La Côte-St-André
France 260

Lac Pavin
Auberge du Lac Pavin 172

Lanau
Auberge du Pont de Lanau 587

Lapalisse
Auberge de Boucé 322
Auberge de l'Olive 322

La Séauve-sur-Semène
Ferme-auberge Les Granges 330

Le Brugeron
Gaudon 293

Le Mont-Dore
Le Bougnat 406
Mon Clocher 406

Le Pilat
Auberge Vernollon 450
Chanterelle 450

Le Puy-en-Velay
Lapierre 461
La Renouée 461

Les Vans
Chez Vincent et Michèle 'Le Lagon' 603

Le Tricastin
Logis de l'Escalin 580

Lyon
100 Tabac 343
Brunet 344
Chez les Gones 343
Comptoir du Mail 343
L'Est 344
La Brasserie Georges 344
La Table d'Hippolyte 344
Le Café 203 343
Le Caro de Lyon 344
Le Casse-Museau 343
Le Mercière 344
Le Petit Carron 343
Le Petit Gadin 343
Le St-Florent 344
Le Vieux Lyon 343
Lolo Quoi 344
Restaurant des Deux Places 344

Massiac
Auberge de Margaridou 391

Montbrison
Le Vieux Logis 403

Montélimar
Francis 'Les Senteurs de Provence' 412

INDEX

Le Grillon 412
Montluçon
L'Eau à la Bouche 418
La Vie en Rose 418
Le Grenier à Sel 418
Moulins
Logis Henri IV 424
Restaurant des Cours 424
Murat
Le Jarrousset 434
Orcines
La Font-de-l'Arbre 277
Le Mont Fraternité 277
Pérouges
Auberge de Campagne du Mollard 448
Auberge du Coq 448
Privas
Le Corentin 456
Riom
La Fourniale 277
Le Flamboyant 474
Riverie
Auberge de campagne La Picoraille 387
Roanne
Le Central 485
Le Marcassin 485
Le Relais de la Vieille Tour 485
Ma Chaumière 485
Troisgros 485
Romans-sur-Isère
Le Chevet de St-Barnard 493
Royat
L'Hostalet 498
La Pépinière 498
Saint-Agrève
Domaine de Rilhac 504
Salers
Auberge de l'Aspre 538
La Diligence 538
Les Sorbiers 538
Servant
Restaurant Vindrié 555

St-Étienne
Corne d'Aurochs 512
L'Escargot d'Or 512
La Nouvelle 512
St-Flour
Chez Geneviève 520
St-Genès-Champanelle
Auberge de la Moreno 277
St-Georges-en-Couzan
Ferme-auberge du Mazet 293
St-Illide
Ferme-auberge du Bruel 211
St-Marcellin
Le Restaurant des Remparts 506
St-Nectaire
Auberge de l'Âne 529
St-Pourçain-Sur-Sioule
Auberge de l'Aubrelle 532
St-Sauveur-de-Montagut
Montagut 287
Thiers
Moulin Bleu 569
Tournon-sur-Rhône
Le Chaudron 574
Valence
L'Auberge du Pin 594
Vichy
Brasserie du Casino 610
Chez Mémère 610
La Colombière 610
La Fontaine 610
Vienne
L'Estancot 627
La Chamade 627
La Medina 627
Villars-Les-Dombes
Le Col Vert 640
Villefranche-sur-Saône
Ferme-auberge La Bicheronne 643

LIST OF MAPS

THEMATIC MAPS

Principal sights. 8
Driving tours. 11
Places to stay. 36
Landscapes. 60
Volcanoes of Auvergne 63
Gallo-Roman Lyon. 337

MONUMENTS, MUSEUMS AND SITES

Basilique St-Julien, Brioude 198
Abbatiale St-Robert, La Chaise-Dieu. .218
Notre-Dame de l'Assomption,
    Clermont-Ferrand 245
Notre-Dame Cathédrale, Moulins . . . 426
Château de Murol 435
Notre-Dame Cathédrale,
    Le Puy-en-Velay 464
Former Carthusian monastery,
    Ste-Croix-en-Jarez. 537
Gallo-Roman city
    of St-Romain-en-Gal. 637
Château de Tournoël 653

LOCAL MAPS FOR TOURING

La Limagne
    Around Aigueperse 109
Gorges de l'Ardèche 128
Around Ardes 131
Parc régional des volcans
    Around Lac d'Aydat 155
Le Beaujolais. 163
The Couze Valleys
    Around Besse-en-Chandesse 176
Parc régional des Volcans
    Around Bort 185
Around La Bourboul 194
Churches in the Haut-Allier
    Around Brioude 200
Les Monts du Cantal 206
Les Monts du Cézallier. 215
Around Condat. 257
Around Crémieu 266
La Dombes. 272
Monts Dôme 281
Vallée de l'Eyrieux 288
Monts du Forez 295
Dauphiné d'Auvergne
    Around Issoire 314
Vallée de la Besbre 323
Gorges de la Loire 333
Monts du Lyonnais 388
Around Le Mont-Dore 408
Le Mont-d'Or Lyonnais. 410
Pilat Regional Nature Park 452

Around Roanne 490
Walks around Royat 497
Massif du Sancy 543
Around Saugues: Gorges de l'Allier . . 550
Gorges de la Sioule 556
Massif du Tanargue. 561
Around Thiers: Monts du Forez. 571
Forêt de Tronçais 584
Gorges de la Truyère. 588
Walk to Château de Crussol 597

TOWN PLANS

Annonay. 119
Aurillac 146
Billom 180
La Bourboule 192
Brioude. 199
Châtillon-sur-Chalaronne 229
Vieux Clermont 236
Clermont Ferrand 240
Vieux Montferrand 249
Crémieu 264
Crest. 269
Lyon 338
    Public transport map. 342
    La Presqu'île 352
    Old town-Fourvière 364
    La Croix-Rousse 370

Le Mont-Dore 407
Montélimar 412
Montluçon. 417
Moulins. 427
Pérouges 445
Le Puy-en-Velay 469
Riom 473
St-Étienne 516
St-Flour 521
Salers. 540
Thiers. 566
Trévoux. 578
Valence 593
Vichy 609
Vienne. 632
Villefranche-sur-Saône 642
Viviers 647

MAPS AND PLANS

COMPANION PUBLICATIONS

Motorists who plan ahead will always have the appropriate maps at hand. Michelin products are complementary: for each of the sites listed in The Green Guide, map references are indicated which help you find your location on our range of maps. The image below shows the maps to use for each geographic area covered in this guide.

- The regional maps at a scale of 1:200 000 nos 519, 522, 523 and 526, which cover the main roads and secondary roads, include useful indications for finding tourist attractions. In addition to identifying the nature of the road ways, the maps show castles, churches and other religious edifices, scenic view points, megalithic monuments, swimming beaches on lakes and rivers, swimming pools, golf courses, race-courses, air fields, and more.

- The Local Maps maps at a scale of 1:150 000 and 1:175 000 are the latest maps in our collection. They include useful symbols for identifying tourist attractions, town plans and an index. The map diagram below indicates which maps you need to travel in Auvergne and the Rhône Valley.

- And remember to travel with the latest edition of the map of France no 721 (1:1 000 000), which gives an overall view of the region, and the main access roads which connect it to the rest of France. Convenient Atlas formats (spiral, hard cover and "mini") are also available.

Michelin is pleased to offer travellers a route-planning service on the internet: www.ViaMichelin.com. Choose the shortest route, a route without tolls, or the Michelin recommended route to your destination; you can also access information about hotels and restaurants from the *Michelin Guide France*.

Bon voyage!

Selected monuments and sights

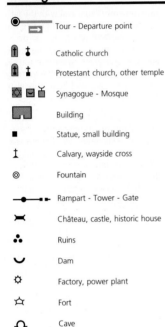

◉ ➡	Tour - Departure point
⌂ ‡	Catholic church
⌂ ‡	Protestant church, other temple
✡ ☩ ⌂	Synagogue - Mosque
▭	Building
■	Statue, small building
‡	Calvary, wayside cross
◎	Fountain
━●━■━	Rampart - Tower - Gate
✕	Château, castle, historic house
⁘	Ruins
◡	Dam
✿	Factory, power plant
✩	Fort
∩	Cave
▱	Troglodyte dwelling
⊤	Prehistoric site
⊤	Viewing table
Ⅶ	Viewpoint
▲	Other place of interest

Sports and recreation

🏇	Racecourse
⛸	Skating rink
⌇ ⌇	Outdoor, indoor swimming pool
🎥	Multiplex Cinema
⛵	Marina, sailing centre
⌂	Trail refuge hut
□-■-■-□	Cable cars, gondolas
□-+++++-□	Funicular, rack railway
🚂	Tourist train
◆	Recreation area, park
🎭	Theme, amusement park
Ⅶ	Wildlife park, zoo
✿	Gardens, park, arboretum
◎	Bird sanctuary, aviary
🚶	Walking tour, footpath
😊	Of special interest to children

Abbreviations

A	Agricultural office (Chambre d'agriculture)
C	Chamber of Commerce (Chambre de commerce)
H	Town hall (Hôtel de ville)
J	Law courts (Palais de justice)
M	Museum (Musée)
P	Local authority offices (Préfecture, sous-préfecture)
POL.	Police station (Police)
🛡	Police station (Gendarmerie)
T	Theatre (Théâtre)
U	University (Université)

676

LEGEND

	Sight	Seaside resort	Winter sports resort	Spa
Highly recommended	★★★	⚲⚲⚲	✸✸✸	‡‡‡
Recommended	★★	⚲⚲	✸✸	‡‡
Interesting	★	⚲	✸	‡

Additional symbols

🛈	Tourist information
═══ ═══	Motorway or other primary route
❶ ❶	Junction: complete, limited
⇥⇤ ══	Pedestrian street
ɪ═════ɪ	Unsuitable for traffic, street subject to restrictions
▭▭▭▭ ----	Steps – Footpath
🚂 🚊	Train station – Auto-train station
🚌 S.N.C.F	Coach (bus) station
●─┼─●	Tram
⌂	Metro, underground
P R	Park-and-Ride
♿	Access for the disabled
✉	Post office
☎	Telephone
▱	Covered market
⋅✗⋅	Barracks
△	Drawbridge
∪	Quarry
✗	Mine
B F	Car ferry (river or lake)
🚢	Ferry service: cars and passengers
⛴	Foot passengers only
③	Access route number common to Michelin maps and town plans
Bert (R.)...	Main shopping street
AZ **B**	Map co-ordinates

Hotels and restaurants

Hotels- price categories:

	Provinces	Large cities
⊝	<40 €	<60 €
⊝⊝	40 to 65 €	60 to 90 €
⊝⊝⊝	65 to 100 €	90 to 130 €
⊝⊝⊝⊝	>100 €	>130 €

Restaurants- price categories:

	Provinces	Large cities
⊝	<14 €	<16 €
⊝⊝	14 to 25 €	16 to 30 €
⊝⊝⊝	25 to 40 €	30 to 50 €
⊝⊝⊝⊝	>40 €	>50 €

20 rooms :	Number of rooms
⊐ *6.85 €*	Price of breakfast; when not given, it is included in the price of the room (i.e., for bed-and-breakfast)
120 sites :	Number of camp sites
rest.	Lodging where meals are served
reserv	Reservation recommended
⬠̸	No credit cards accepted
P	Reserved parking for hotel patrons
🏊	Swimming Pool
▤	Air conditioning
🚭	Hotel: non-smoking rooms Restaurant: non-smoking section
♿	Rooms accessible to persons of reduced mobility

The prices correspond to the higher rates of the tourist season

Michelin North America
One Parkway South – Greenville, SC 29615 USA
☎ 800-423-0485
www.MichelinTravel.com
michelin.guides@us.michelin.com

Manufacture française des pneumatiques Michelin

Société en commandite par actions au capital de 304 000 000 EUR
Place des Carmes-Déchaux – 63000 Clermont-Ferrand (France)
R.C.S. Clermont-Fd B 855 200 507